Fodor's New SEVENTH EDITION

Scandinavia

The complete guide, thoroughly up-to-date

Packed with details that will make your trip

The must-see sights, off and on the beaten path

What to see, what to skip

Mix-and-match vacation itineraries

City strolls, countryside adventures

Smart lodging and dining options

Essential local do's and taboos

Transportation tips, distances and directions

Key contacts, savvy travel tips

When to go, what to pack

Clear, accurate, easy-to-use maps

Books to read, videos to watch

Fodor's Travel Publications, Inc.
New York • Toronto • London • Sydney • Auckland
www.fodors.com/

Fodor's Scandinavia

EDITORS: Caragh Rockwood, Rebecca Miller

Editorial Contributors: Steven K. Amsterdam, Robert Andrews, Tim Bird, Robert Blake, David Brown, Daniel Cooper, Michael Kissane, Christina Knight, Marius Meland, Shelley Pannill, Jennifer Paull, Karina Porcelli, Heidi Sarna, Helayne Schiff, M. T. Schwartzman (Gold Guide editor), Eric Sjogren, Dinah A. Spritzer

Editorial Production: Tom Holton

Maps: David Lindroth, *cartographer*; Steven K. Amsterdam, *map editor*

Design: Fabrizio La Rocca, *creative director*; Guido Caroti, *associate art director*; Jolie Novak, *photo editor*

Production/Manufacturing: Mike Costa

Cover Photograph: Blaine Harrington III

Copyright

Seventh Edition

ISBN 0–679–03531–1

Special Sales

PRINTED IN THE UNITED STATES OF AMERICA

10 9 8 7 6 5 4 3 2 1

CONTENTS

ON THE ROAD WITH FODOR'S

WE'RE ALWAYS THRILLED to get letters from readers, especially ones like this:

It took us an hour to decide what book to buy and we now know we picked the best one. Your book was wonderful, easy to follow, very accurate, and good on pointing out eating places, informal as well as formal. When we saw other people using your book, we would look at each other and smile.

Our editors and writers are deeply committed to making every Fodor's guide "the best one"—not only accurate but always charming, brimming with sound recommendations and solid ideas, right on the mark in describing restaurants and hotels, and full of fascinating facts that make you view what you've traveled to see in a rich new light.

About Our Writers

Our success in achieving our goals—and in helping to make your trip the best of all possible vacations—is a credit to the hard work of our extraordinary writers and editors.

While working as a journalist in Oslo, native Texan **Shelley Pannill** interviewed scores of Norwegians, including Liv Ullmann, and covered topics ranging from whaling to travel to the Nobel Peace Prize. A graduate of the Columbia University Graduate School of Journalism, Shelley has written news and features for United Press International, *The European* (London), and *The Star-Ledger* (NJ).

Freelance writer **Karina Porcelli** divides her time between Copenhagen and Washington, D.C.

Journalist and translator **Michael J. Kissane** has been living in Iceland for over 14 years. He has written for *Barron's*, the Associated Press, and for Icelandic publishers. He is occasionally distracted by fly fishing and nature photography.

British journalist **Tim Bird** has lived in Helsinki for 15 years, contributing articles and photographs to many magazines and books about Finland and her neighbors, and developing a special interest in the profound changes taking place in the Baltic Sea region.

Since leaving SAS, where he was information manager at the company's technical division, Stockholm-based writer **Daniel Cooper** has specialized in travel journalism.

A huge fan of Scandinavian culture, editor **Rebecca Miller** lived in Norway for several years. While there, she tried everything from *lutefisk* to glacier skiing. She now resides in New York City.

New This Year

We're proud to announce that the American Society of Travel Agents has endorsed Fodor's as its guidebook of choice. ASTA is the world's largest and most influential travel trade association, operating in more than 170 countries, with 27,000 members pledged to adhere to a strict code of ethics reflecting the Society's motto, "Integrity in Travel." ASTA shares Fodor's devotion to providing smart, honest travel information and advice to travelers, and we've long recommended that our readers consult ASTA member agents for the experience and professionalism they bring to the table.

On the Web, check out Fodor's site (www.fodors.com/) for information on major destinations around the world and travel-savvy interactive features. The Web site also lists the 85-plus radio stations nationwide that carry *Fodor's Travel Show*, a live call-in program that airs every weekend. Tune in to hear guests discuss their wonderful adventures—or call in to get answers for your most pressing travel questions.

How to Use This Book

Organization

Up front is the **Gold Guide,** an easy-to-use section divided alphabetically by topic. Under each listing you'll find tips and information that will help you accomplish what you need to in Scandinavia. You'll also find addresses and telephone numbers of organizations and companies that offer destination-related services and detailed information and publications.

The first chapter in the guide, Destination: Scandinavia helps get you in the mood for your trip. New and Noteworthy cues you in on trends and happenings, What's Where gets you oriented, Great itineraries suggests some stellar tours, Fodor's Choice showcases our top picks, and Festivals and Seasonal Events alerts you to special events you'll want to seek out.

Chapters in *Fodor's Scandinavia* are arranged alphabetically by country. Each chapter begins with a synopsis of the country's pleasures and pastimes, followed by an exploring section with recommended itineraries and tips on when to visit. Chapters are then broken into major regions and cities, with recommended walking or driving tours. Within each city, sights are covered alphabetically. Within each region, towns are covered in logical geographical order, and attractive stretches of road and minor points of interest between them are indicated by the designation *En Route*. In city and regional sections, Off the Beaten Path sights appear after the places from which they are most easily accessible. Within town sections, all restaurants and lodgings are grouped together. The A-to-Z section at the end of each region or city covers getting there, getting around, and helpful contacts and resources. A countrywide A-to-Z—an expanded version of the regional A-to-Z sections—appears at the end of each chapter.

At the end of the book you'll find Portraits, with a chronology of the history of Scandinavia, followed by suggestions for any pretrip research you want to do, from recommended reading to movies on tape with Scandinavia as a backdrop.

Icons and Symbols

★   Our special recommendations
✕   Restaurant
🏠   Lodging establishment
✕🏠   Lodging establishment whose restaurant warrants a special trip
⚠   Campgrounds
☺   Good for kids (rubber duckie)
☞   Sends you to another section of the guide for more information
✉   Address
☎   Telephone number
☉   Opening and closing times

🖼   Admission prices (those we give apply to adults; substantially reduced fees are almost always available for children, students, and senior citizens)

Numbers in white and black circles that appear on the maps, in the margins, and within the tours correspond to one another.

Dining and Lodging

The restaurants and lodgings we list are the cream of the crop in each price range. Price charts appear in the Pleasures and Pastimes section that follows each chapter introduction.

Hotel Facilities

We always list the facilities that are available—but we don't specify whether they cost extra: When pricing accommodations, always ask what's included. Assume that all rooms have private baths unless otherwise noted. Breakfast is almost always included in the price of Scandinavian hotels.

Restaurant Reservations and Dress Codes

Reservations are always a good idea; we note only when they're essential or when they are not accepted. Book as far ahead as you can, and reconfirm when you get to town. Unless otherwise noted, the restaurants listed are open daily for lunch and dinner. We mention dress only when men are required to wear a jacket or a jacket and tie.

Credit Cards

The following abbreviations are used: **AE,** American Express; **D,** Discover; **DC,** Diners Club; **MC,** MasterCard; and **V,** Visa.

Don't Forget to Write

You can use this book in the confidence that all prices and opening times are based on information supplied to us at press time. Time inevitably brings changes, however, so always confirm information when it matters—especially if you're making a detour to visit a specific place. Fodor's cannot accept responsibility for any errors. In addition, when making reservations be sure to mention if you have a disability or are traveling with children, if you prefer a private bath or a certain type of bed, or if you have specific dietary needs or other concerns.

Were the restaurants we recommended as described? Did our hotel picks exceed your expectations? Did you find a museum we recommended a waste of time? If you have complaints, we'll look into them and revise our entries when the facts warrant it. If you've discovered a special place that we haven't included, we'll pass the information along to our correspondents and have them check it out. So send us your feedback, positive *and* negative: E-mail us at editors@fodors.com (specifying the name of the book on the subject line) or write the Scandinavia editor at Fodor's, 201 East 50th Street, New York, New York 10022. Have a wonderful trip!

Karen Cure
Editorial Director

Scandinavia

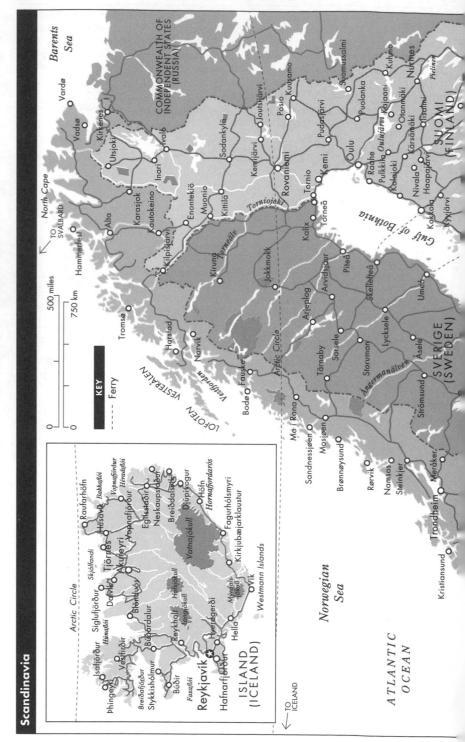

Barents Sea

North Cape

Vardø

Vadsø

Kirkenes

Hammerfest

TO SVALBARD

Utsjoki

Ivalo

Inari

Alta

Karasjok

Kautokeino

Kilpisjärvi

Enontekiö

Muonio

Kittilä

Sodankylä

Kemijärvi

Joutsijärvi

Posio

Kuusamo

Suomussalmi

Kuhmo

Nurmes

Pielinen

SUOMI (FINLAND)

Puolanka

Oulankajärvi

Kajaani

Otanmäki

Kärsämäki

Iisalmi

Pudasjärvi

Oulu

Raahe

Pulkkila

Kalajoki

Nivala

Haapajärvi

Kokkola

Kyrjärvi

Rovaniemi

Kemi

Tornio

Torneå

KEY

Ferry

500 miles

750 km

Tromsø

Harstad

Narvik

LOFOTEN

VESTERÅLEN

Vestfjorden

Bodø

Fauske

Mo i Rana

Sandnessjøen

Mosjøen

Brønnøysund

Rørvik

Namsos

Steinkjer

Trondheim

Kristiansund

Kiruna

Jokkmokk

Arctic Circle

Torniojoki

Torneälv

Kalix

Arjeplog

Arvidsjaur

Piteå

Skellefteå

Umeå

Tärnaby

Sorsele

Storuman

Lycksele

Åsele

SVERIGE (SWEDEN)

Ångermanälven

Strömsund

Meråker

COMMONWEALTH OF INDEPENDENT STATES (RUSSIA)

Gulf of Bothnia

Arctic Circle

Norwegian Sea

ATLANTIC OCEAN

Raufarhöfn

Bakkafjöri

Vopnafjörður

Þórshöfn

Húsavík

Héraðsflói

Vopnafjörður

Skjálfandi

Egilsstaðir

Siglufjörður

Neskaupstaður

Akureyri

Dalvík

Breiðdalsvík

Djúpivogur

Höfn

Hornafjarðarós

Vatnajökull

Fagurhólsmyri

Kirkjubæjarklaustur

Brjánslækur

Blönduós

Hofsjökull

Langjökull

Mýrdalsjökull

Ísafjörður

Vík

Hnnaflói

Westmann Islands

Breiðafjörður

Stykkishólmur

Búðir

Búðardalur

Reykholt

Vestfirðir

Hella

Hveragerði

Hafnarfjörður

★ Reykjavík

ISLAND (ICELAND)

Faxaflói

Þingeyri

Arctic Circle

TO ICELAND

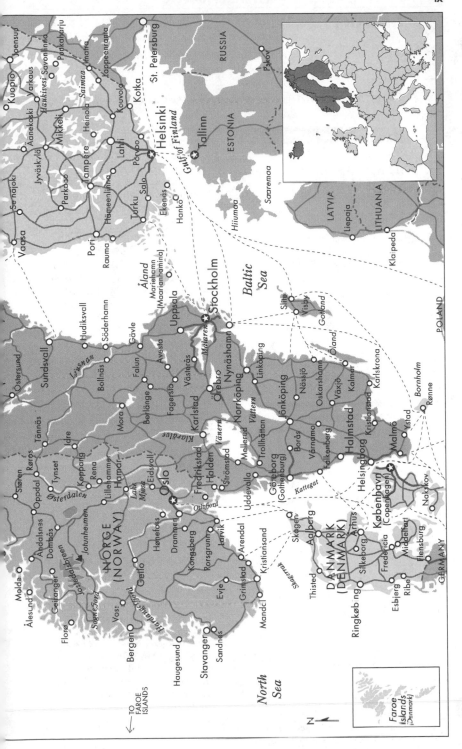

SMART TRAVEL TIPS A TO Z

*Basic Information on Traveling in Scandinavia,
Savvy Tips to Make Your Trip a Breeze, and
Companies and Organizations to Contact*

A

AIR TRAVEL

MAJOR AIRLINE OR LOW-COST CARRIER?

Most people choose a flight based on price. Yet there are other issues to consider. Major airlines offer the greatest number of departures; smaller airlines—including regional, low-cost, and no-frill airlines—usually have a more limited number of flights daily. Major airlines have frequent-flyer partners, which allow you to credit mileage earned on one airline to your account with another. Low-cost airlines offer a definite price advantage and fewer restrictions, such as advance-purchase requirements. Safety-wise, low-cost carriers as a group have a good history, but **check the safety record before booking** any low-cost carrier; call the Federal Aviation Administration's Consumer Hotline (☞ Airline Complaints, *below*).

➤ MAJOR AIRLINES: **American** (☎ 800/433–7300) to Stockholm. **Delta** (☎ 800/221–1212) to Copenhagen. **Finnair** (☎ 800/950–5000) to Stockholm, Copenhagen, Reykjavík, Oslo. **Icelandair** (☎ 800/223–5500) to Reykjavík. **Scandinavian Airlines (SAS)** (☎ 800/221–2350) to Stockholm, Copenhagen, Reykjavík, Oslo.

GET THE LOWEST FARE

The least-expensive airfares to Scandinavia are priced for round-trip travel. Major airlines usually require that you **book far in advance and stay at least seven days** and no more than 30 to get the lowest fares. Ask about "ultrasaver" fares, which are the cheapest; they must be booked 90 days in advance and are nonrefundable. A little more expensive are "supersaver" fares, which require only a 30-day advance purchase. Remember that penalties for refunds or scheduling changes are stiffer for international tickets, usually about $150. International flights are also sensitive to the season: **plan to fly in the off season** for the cheapest fares. If your destination or home city has more than one gateway, **compare prices to and from different airports.** Also price flights scheduled for off-peak hours, which may be significantly less expensive.

To save money on flights from the United Kingdom and back, **look into an APEX or Super-PEX ticket.** APEX tickets must be booked in advance and have certain restrictions. Super-PEX tickets can be purchased at the airport on the day of departure—subject to availability.

DON'T STOP UNLESS YOU MUST

When you book, **look for nonstop flights** and **remember that "direct" flights stop at least once.** International flights on a country's flag carrier are almost always nonstop; U.S. airlines often fly direct. Try to **avoid connecting flights,** which require a change of plane. Two airlines may jointly operate a connecting flight, so ask if your airline operates every segment—you may find that your preferred carrier flies you only part of the way.

USE AN AGENT

Travel agents, especially those who specialize in finding the lowest fares (☞ Discounts & Deals, *below*), can be especially helpful when booking a plane ticket. When you're quoted a price, **ask your agent if the price is likely to get any lower.** Good agents know the seasonal fluctuations of airfares and can usually anticipate a sale or fare war. However, waiting can be risky: The fare could go *up* as seats become scarce, and you may wait so long that your preferred flight sells out. A wait-and-see strategy works best if your plans are flexible, but if you must arrive and depart on certain dates, don't delay.

CHECK WITH CONSOLIDATORS

Consolidators buy tickets for scheduled flights at reduced rates from the airlines then sell them at prices that beat the best fare available directly from the airlines, usually without advance restrictions. Sometimes you can even get your money back if you need to return the ticket. Carefully read the fine print detailing penalties for changes and cancellations, and **confirm your consolidator reservation with the airline.**

➤ CONSOLIDATORS: **United States Air Consolidators Association** (✉ 925 L St., Suite 220, Sacramento, CA 95814, ☎ 916/441–4166, FAX 916/441–3520).

CONSIDER A CHARTER

Charters usually have the lowest fares but are not dependable. Departures are infrequent and seldom on time, flights can be delayed for up to 48 hours or can be canceled for any reason up to 10 days before you're scheduled to leave. Itineraries and prices can change after you've booked your flight, so you must **be very careful to choose a legitimate charter carrier.** Don't commit to a charter operator that doesn't follow proper booking procedures. Be especially careful when buying a charter ticket. Read the fine print in regard to refund policies. If you can't pay with a credit card, **make your check payable to a charter carrier's escrow account** (unless you're dealing with a travel agent, in which case his or her check should be made payable to the escrow account). The name of the bank should be in the charter contract.

Airlines routinely overbook planes, knowing that not everyone with a ticket will show up, but sometimes everyone does. When that happens, airlines ask for volunteers to give up their seats. In return these volunteers usually get a certificate for a free flight and are rebooked on the next flight out. If there are not enough volunteers the airline must choose who will be denied boarding. The first to get bumped are passengers who checked in late and those flying on discounted tickets, **so get to the gate and check in as early as possible,** especially during peak periods.

Always **bring a photo ID to the airport.** You may be asked to show it before you are allowed to check in.

ENJOY THE FLIGHT

For more legroom, **request an emergency-aisle seat;** don't however, sit in the row in front of the emergency aisle or in front of a bulkhead, where seats may not recline.

If you don't like airline food, **ask for special meals when booking.** These can be vegetarian, low cholesterol, or kosher, for example.

To avoid jet lag try to maintain a normal routine while traveling. At night **get some sleep.** By day **eat light meals, drink water (avoid alcohol), and move about the cabin** to stretch your legs.

Some carriers have prohibited smoking throughout their systems; others allow smoking only on certain routes or even certain departures from that route, so **contact your carrier in regard to its smoking policy.**

COMPLAIN IF NECESSARY

If your baggage goes astray or your flight goes awry, complain right away. Most carriers require that you file a claim immediately.

➤ AIRLINE COMPLAINTS: **U.S. Department of Transportation Aviation Consumer Protection Division** (✉ C-75, Room 4107, Washington, DC 20590, ☎ 202/366–2220). **Federal Aviation Administration (FAA) Consumer Hotline** (☎ 800/322–7873).

WITHIN SCANDINAVIA

Scandinavia is larger than it looks on a map, and many native travelers choose to fly between the capital cities, using trains and buses for domestic travel.

If you are traveling from south to north in Norway, Sweden, or Finland, flying is a necessity: Stavanger in southern Norway is as close to Rome, Italy, as it is to the northern tip of Norway.

For international travelers, one or two stopovers can often be purchased more cheaply along with an international ticket. With SAS, the least expensive tickets (Jackpot) are round-trip, must include a Saturday night,

THE GOLD GUIDE / SMART TRAVEL TIPS

and can be bought only within Scandinavia from seven to 14 days ahead. Ask about low rates for hotels and car rental in connection with Jackpot tickets. Weekend Jackpot tickets can be bought right up to flight time. SAS also gives couples who travel together a discount off some tickets and significant discounts on SAS hotels and car rentals. Low-priced round-trip weekend excursions from one Scandinavian capital to another (minimum three-day stay) can be bought one day in advance from SAS.

AIRPORTS

MAJOR AIRPORTS

Major gateways to Scandinavia include Iceland's **Keflavík International Airport**, 50 km (31 mi) southwest of Reykjavík. Denmark's **Kastrup International Airport** 10 km (6 mi) southeast of Copenhagen. Sweden's **Arlanda International Airport** 41 km (26 mi) north of Stockholm. Norway's **Fornebu Airport**, about 15 km (9 mi) southwest of Oslo. Finland's **Helsinki-Vantaa International Airport**, 20 km (14 mi) north of Helsinki.

➤ AIRPORT INFORMATION: Iceland **Keflavík International Airport** (☎ 011–354–425–1/0200). Denmark **Kastrup International Airport** (☎ 011–45–31/54–17–01). Sweden **Arlanda International Airport** (☎ 011–46–8/767–6100). Norway **Fornebu Airport** (☎ 011–47–224/97598). Finland **Helsinki-Vantaa International Airport** (☎ 011–358–060/08100).

FLYING TIME

Flying time from New York to Reykjavík is 5½ hours; to Copenhagen, 7¾ hours; to Stockholm, 8 hours; to Oslo, 7½ hours; to Helsinki, 8 hours. From Los Angeles to Copenhagen, flying time is 9¾ hours; to Helsinki, 11¼ hours.

B

BOAT TRAVEL

Taking a ferry isn't only fun, it's often necessary in Scandinavia. Many companies arrange package trips, some offering a rental car and hotel accommodations as part of the deal.

Ferry crossings often last overnight. The trip between Copenhagen and Oslo, for example, takes approximately 16 hours, most lines leaving at about 5 PM and arriving about 9 the next morning. The direct cruise between Stockholm and Helsinki takes 12 hours, usually leaving at about 6 PM and arriving the next morning at 9. The shortest ferry route runs between Helsingør, Denmark, and Helsingborg, Sweden; it takes only 25 minutes.

➤ MAJOR OPERATORS: **Color Line** (✉ Box 30, DK–9850 Hirsthals, Denmark, ☎ 45/99–56–19–66, ℻ 45/98–94–50–92; Hjortneskaia, Box 1422 Vika, N–0115 Oslo, Norway, ☎ 47/22–94–44–00, ℻ 47/22–83–07–71; c/o Bergen Line, Inc., 505 5th Ave., New York, NY 10017, ☎ 800/323–7436, ℻ 212/983–1275; Tyne Commission Quay, North Shields NE29 6EA, Newcastle, England, ☎ 0191/296–1313, ℻ 091/296–1540). **ScandLines** (✉ Box 1, DK–3000 Helsingør, Denmark, ☎ 45/49–26–26–83, ℻ 45/49–26–11–24; Knutpunkten 44, S–252 78 Helsingborg, Sweden, ☎ 46/42–18–61–00, ℻ 46/42–18–74–10).

FERRIES FROM ENGLAND

The chief operator between England and many points within Scandinavia is DFDS/Scandinavian Seaways, with ships connecting Harwich and Newcastle to Göteborg and Amsterdam.

➤ MAJOR OPERATOR: **DFDS/Scandinavian Seaways** (✉ Sankt Annae Plads 30, DK–1295 Copenhagen, Denmark, ☎ 45/33–42–30–00, ℻ 45/33–42–30–69; DFDS Travel Centre, 15 Hanover St., London W1R 9HG, ☎ 0171/409–6060, ℻ 0171/409–6035; DFDS Seaways USA Inc., 6555 NW 9th Ave., Suite 207, Fort Lauderdale, FL 33309, ☎ 800/533–3755, ℻ 305/491–7958; Box 8895, Scandiahamnen, S–402 72 Göteborg, Sweden, ☎ 46/8–650650).

PLYING SCANDINAVIAN WATERS

Connections from Denmark to Norway and Sweden are available through DFDS and the Stena Line. Fjord Line sails along the magnificent west coast of Norway. Connections to the Faroe Islands from Norway and Denmark are available through the Smyril Line. Silja Line offers luxurious cruises to Finland, with depar-

tures from Stockholm to Åbo, Helsingfors, Helsinki and Turku, and a
crossing from Umeå to Vaasa

➤ MAJOR OPERATORS: **DFDS Seaways**
(☞ *above*). **Stena Line** (✉ Trafikham-
nen, DK–9900 Frederikshavn, Den-
mark, ☎ 45/96–20–02–00, FAX 45/96–
20–02–81; Jernbanetorget 2, N–0154
Oslo 1, Norway, ☎ 47/23–17–90–00,
FAX 47/22–41–44–40; Scandinavia AB,
S–405 19 Göteborg, Sweden, ☎ 46/
31–775–0000, FAX 46/31–858595).
Fjord Line (✉ Slottsgatan 1, N–5003
Bergen, Norway, ☎ 47/55–32–37–70,
FAX 47/55–32–38–15). **Smyril Line**
(☞ DFDS Seaways, *above*; or
J. Bronksgoøta 37, Box 370, FR-110
Tórshavn, Faroe Islands, ☎ 298/
15–900, FAX 298/15–707; Bergen,
Norway, ☎ 47/55–32–09–70, FAX 47/
55–96–02–72). **Silja Line** (✉ Kungs-
gatan 2, S–111 43 Stockholm, Swe-
den, ☎ 46/8–22–21–40, FAX 46/8–
667–8681; c/o Scandinavian Seaways,
Parkeston Quay Scand. House, Har-
wich, England, ☎ 44/255–240–240,
FAX 44/255–240–268).

CAR FERRIES

Travel by car in Scandinavia often
necessitates travel by ferry. Some
well-known vehicle and passenger
ferries run between Dragør, Denmark
(just south of Copenhagen), and
Limhamn, Sweden (just south of
Malmö); between Helsingør, Denmark, and Helsingborg, Sweden; and
between Copenhagen and Göteborg,
Sweden. On the Dragør/Limhamn
ferry (ScandLines), taking a car one-
way costs SKr395 (about $60 or
£39). An easy trip runs between
Copenhagen and Göteborg on Stena
Line. The Helsingør/Helsingborg ferry
(ScandLines also) takes only 25
minutes; taking a car along one-way
costs SKr330 (about $50 or £33).
Fares for round-trip are cheaper, and
on weekends the Öresund Runt pass
(for crossing between Dragoør and
Limhamn one way and Helsingborg
and Helsingoør the other way) costs
only SKr495 (about $75 or £49).

➤ MAJOR OPERATORS: **Stena Line**
(Sweden, ☎ 031/75–00–00). **Scand-
Lines** (☞ *above*).

Bus tours can be effective for smaller
regions within Norway, Sweden,
Finland, and Denmark, but all have
excellent train systems, which offer
much greater coverage in less time
than buses. Detailed information on
bus routes is available through local
tourist offices.

C

Always **keep your film, tape, or
computer disks out of the sun.** Carry
an extra supply of batteries, and **be
prepared to turn on your camera,
camcorder, or laptop** to prove to
security personnel that the device is
real. Always **ask for hand inspection
of film,** which becomes clouded after
successive exposure to airport x-ray
machines, and **keep videotapes and
computer disks away from metal
detectors.**

GREAT SHOTS

*Kodak Guide to Shooting Great Travel
Pictures* is available in bookstores or
from Fodor's Travel Publications
(☎ 800/533–6478; $16.50 plus $4
shipping).

➤ PHOTO HELP: **Kodak Information
Center** (☎ 800/242–2424).

CUSTOMS

Before departing, **register your for-
eign-made camera or laptop with U.S.
Customs** (☞ Customs & Duties,
below). If your equipment is U.S.-
made, call the consulate of the country you'll be visiting to find out
whether the device should be registered with local customs upon arrival.

Rates in Stockholm begin at $110 a
day and $210 a week for an economy
car without air conditioning, and
with a manual transmission and
unlimited mileage. Rates in Oslo
begin at $111 a day and $284 a
week. This does not include tax on
car rentals, which is 25% in Sweden,
23% in Norway.

➤ RENTAL AGENCIES: **Avis** (☎ 800/
331–1084, (☎ 800/879–2847 in
Canada). **Budget** (☎ 800/527–0700,
0800/181181 in the U.K.). **Dollar**
(☎ 800/800–4000; 0990/565656 in
the U.K., where it is known as Euro-
dollar). **Hertz** (☎ 800/654–3001,
800/263–0600 in Canada, 0345/
555888 in the U.K.). **National Inter-**

THE GOLD GUIDE / SMART TRAVEL TIPS

Rent (☎ 800/227–3876; 01345/222525 in the U.K., where it is known as Europcar InterRent).

CUT COSTS

To get the best deal, **book through a travel agent who is willing to shop around.**

Also **ask your travel agent about a company's customer-service record.** How has it responded to late plane arrivals and vehicle mishaps? Are there often lines at the rental counter, and, if you're traveling during a holiday period, does a confirmed reservation guarantee you a car?

Be sure to **look into wholesalers,** companies that do not own fleets but rent in bulk from those that do and often offer better rates than traditional car-rental operations. Prices are best during off-peak periods. Rentals booked through wholesalers must be paid for before you leave the United States.

➤ RENTAL WHOLESALERS: **Auto Europe** (☎ 207/842–2000 or 800/223–5555, FAX 800–235–6321). **Europe by Car** (☎ 212/581–3040 or 800/223–1516, FAX 212/246–1458)**DER Travel Services** (✉ 9501 W. Devon Ave., Rosemont, IL 60018, ☎ 800/782–2424, FAX 800/282–7474 for information or 800/860–9944 for brochures). The **Kemwel Group** (☎ 914/835–5555 or 800/678–0678, FAX 914/835–5126).

NEED INSURANCE?

When driving a rented car you are generally responsible for any damage to or loss of the vehicle. Before you rent, **see what coverage you already have** under the terms of your personal auto-insurance policy and credit cards.

Collision policies that car-rental companies sell for European rentals typically do not cover stolen vehicles. Before you buy additional coverage for theft, find out if your credit card or personal auto insurance will cover the loss.

BEWARE SURCHARGES

Before you pick up a car in one city and leave it in another, **ask about drop-off charges or one-way service fees,** which can be substantial. Note, too, that some rental agencies charge extra if you return the car before the time specified on your contract. To avoid a hefty refueling fee, **fill the tank just before you turn in the car,** but be aware that gas stations near the rental outlet may overcharge.

MEET THE REQUIREMENTS

Ask about age requirements: Several countries require drivers to be over 20 years old, but some car-rental companies require that drivers be at least 25. In Scandinavia your own driver's license is acceptable for a limited time; check with the country's tourist board before you go. An International Driver's Permit is a good idea; it's available from the American or Canadian automobile association, or, in the United Kingdom, from the Automobile Association or Royal Automobile Club.

CAR TRAVEL

Excellent, well-marked roads make driving a great way to explore Scandinavia—but beware that gasoline costs about $1 per liter of lead-free gas, roughly four times the typical U.S. price. Ferry costs are steep, and reservations are vital. Tolls on some major roads add to the expense, as do the high fees for city parking; tickets for illegal parking are painfully costly.

Also be aware that there are relatively low legal blood-alcohol limits and tough penalties for driving while intoxicated in Scandinavia. Penalties include suspension of the driver's license and fines or imprisonment and are enforced by random police roadblocks in urban areas on weekends. In addition, an accident involving a driver with an illegal blood-alcohol level usually voids all insurance agreements, so the driver becomes responsible for his own medical bills and damage to the cars.

In a few remote areas, especially in Iceland and northern Norway, Sweden, and Finland, road conditions can be unpredictable, and careful planning is required for safety's sake. It is wise to **use a four-wheel-drive vehicle** and to **travel with at least one other car** in these areas.

Keep your headlights on at all times; this is required by law in most of Scandinavia. Also by Scandinavian law, everyone, even babies, must **wear seat belts.**

➤ AUTO CLUBS: U.S.: **American Auto-mobile Association** (AAA, ☎ 800/564–6222). U.K.: **Automobile Association** (AA, ☎ 0990/500–600), **Royal Automobile Club** (RAC, membership ☎ 0990/722–722; insurance 0345/121–345).

CHILDREN & TRAVEL

CHILDREN IN SCANDINAVIA

In Scandinavia children are to be seen *and* heard and are genuinely welcome in most public places.

Be sure to plan ahead and **involve your youngsters** as you outline your trip. When packing, include things to keep them busy en route. On sightseeing days try to schedule activities of special interest to your children. If you are renting a car don't forget to **arrange for a car seat** when you reserve. Most hotels Scandinavia allow children under a certain age to stay in their parents' room at no extra charge, but others charge them as extra adults; be sure to **ask about the cutoff age for children's discounts.** Many youth hostels offer special facilities (including multiple-bed rooms and separate kitchens) for families with children. Family hostels also provide an excellent opportunity for children to meet youngsters from other countries. Contact Hostelling International–American Youth Hostels (☞ Students, *below*).

DISCOUNTS

Children are entitled to discount tickets (often as much as 50% off) on buses, trains, and ferries throughout Scandinavia, as well as reductions on special City Cards. Children under 12 pay half-price and children under 2 pay 10% on SAS and Linjeflyg round-trips. The only restriction on this discount is that the family travel together and return to the originating city in Scandinavia at least two days later. With the Scanrail Pass (☞ Discount Passes *in* Train Travel, *below*)—good for rail journeys throughout Scandinavia—children under 4 (on lap) travel free; those 4–11 pay half-fare and those 12–25 can get a Scanrail Youth Pass, providing a 25% discount off of the adult fare.

FLYING

As a general rule, infants under two not occupying a seat fly at greatly reduced fares and occasionally for free. If your children are two or older **ask about children's airfares.**

In general the adult baggage allowance applies to children paying half or more of the adult fare. When booking, **ask about carry-on allowances for those traveling with infants.** In general, for babies charged 10% of the adult fare you are allowed one carry-on bag and a collapsible stroller, which may have to be checked; you may be limited to less if the flight is full.

According to the FAA it's a good idea to use safety seats aloft for children weighing less than 40 pounds. Airlines, however, can set their own policies: U.S. carriers allow FAA-approved models but usually require that you buy a ticket, even if your child would otherwise ride free, since the seats must be strapped into regular seats. Airline rules vary as regards their use, so it's important to **check your airline's policy about using safety seats during takeoff and landing.** Safety seats cannot obstruct any of the other passengers in the row, so get an appropriate seat assignment as early as possible.

When making your reservation, **request children's meals or a free-standing bassinet** if you need them; the latter are available only to those seated at the bulkhead, where there's enough legroom. Remember, however, that bulkhead seats may not have their own overhead bins, and there's no storage space in front of you—a major inconvenience.

GROUP TRAVEL

If you're planning to take your kids on a tour, look for companies that specialize in family travel.

➤ FAMILY-FRIENDLY TOUR OPERATORS: **Families Welcome!** (✉ 92 N. Main St., Ashland, OR 97520, ☎ 541/482–6121 or 800/326–0724, ℻ 541/482–0660). **Rascals in Paradise** (✉ 650 5th St., Suite 505, San Francisco, CA 94107, ☎ 415/978–9800 or 800/872–7225, ℻ 415/442–0289).

CONSUMER PROTECTION

Whenever possible, **pay with a major credit card** so you can cancel payment if there's a problem, provided that you can provide documentation. This is a good practice whether you're buying travel arrangements before your trip or shopping at your destination.

If you're doing business with a particular company for the first time, **contact your local Better Business Bureau and the attorney general's offices** in your state and the company's home state, as well. Have any complaints been filed?

Finally, if you're buying a package or tour, always **consider travel insurance** that includes default coverage (☞ Insurance, *below*).

➤ LOCAL BBBs: **Council of Better Business Bureaus** (✉ 4200 Wilson Blvd., Suite 800, Arlington, VA 22203, ☎ 703/276–0100, ℻ 703/525–8277).

CUSTOMS & DUTIES

When shopping, **keep receipts** for all of your purchases. Upon reentering the country, **be ready to show customs officials what you've bought.** If you feel a duty is incorrect, appeal the assessment. If you object to the way your clearance was handled, get the inspector's badge number. In either case, first ask to see a supervisor, then write to the port director at the address listed on your receipt. Send a copy of the receipt and other appropriate documentation. If you still don't get satisfaction you can take your case to customs headquarters in Washington.

ENTERING SCANDINAVIA

Limits on what you can bring in duty-free vary from country to country. **Check with individual country tourist boards for limits on alcohol, cigarettes, and other items.** Also be careful to check before bringing food of any kind into Iceland.

ENTERING THE U.S.

You may bring home $400 worth of foreign goods duty-free if you've been out of the country for at least 48 hours and haven't already used the $400 allowance or any part of it in the past 30 days.

Travelers 21 and older may bring back 1 liter of alcohol duty-free. In addition, regardless of your age, you are allowed 200 cigarettes and 100 non-Cuban cigars. (At press time, a federal rule restricting tobacco access

to persons 18 years and older did not apply to importation.) Antiques, which the U.S. Customs Service defines as objects more than 100 years old, enter duty-free, as do original works of art done entirely by hand, including paintings, drawings, and sculptures.

You may also send packages home duty-free: up to $200 worth of goods for personal use, with a limit of one parcel per addressee per day (and no alcohol or tobacco products or perfume worth more than $5); label the package PERSONAL USE, and attach a list of its contents and their retail value. Do not label the package UNSOLICITED GIFT, or your duty-free exemption will drop to $100. Mailed items do not affect your duty-free allowance on your return.

➤ INFORMATION: **U.S. Customs Service** (Inquiries, ✉ Box 7407, Washington, DC 20044, ☎ 202/927–6724; complaints, Office of Regulations and Rulings, 1301 Constitution Ave. NW, Washington, DC 20229; registration of equipment, ✉ Resource Management, 1301 Constitution Ave. NW, Washington DC, 20229, ☎ 202/927–0540).

ENTERING CANADA

If you've been out of Canada for at least seven days you may bring in C$500 worth of goods duty-free. If you've been away for fewer than seven days but more than 48 hours, the duty-free allowance drops to C$200; if your trip lasts 24–48 hours, the allowance is C$50. You may not pool allowances with family members. Goods claimed under the C$500 exemption may follow you by mail; those claimed under the lesser exemptions must accompany you.

Alcohol and tobacco products may be included in the seven-day and 48-hour exemptions but not in the 24-hour exemption. If you meet the age requirements of the province or territory through which you reenter Canada you may bring in, duty-free, 1.14 liters (40 imperial ounces) of wine or liquor *or* twenty-four 12-ounce cans or bottles of beer or ale. If you are 16 or older you may bring in, duty-free, 200 cigarettes and 50 cigars; these items must accompany you.

You may send an unlimited number of gifts worth up to C$60 each duty-free to Canada. Label the package UNSOLICITED GIFT—VALUE UNDER $60. Alcohol and tobacco are excluded.

➤ INFORMATION: **Revenue Canada** (✉ 2265 St. Laurent Blvd. S, Ottawa, Ontario K1G 4K3, ☎ 613/993–0534, 800/461–9999 in Canada).

ENTERING THE U.K.

If your journey was wholly within European Union (EU) countries you needn't pass through customs when you return to the United Kingdom. If you plan to bring back large quantities of alcohol or tobacco, check on EU limits beforehand.

From countries outside the EU, including Iceland, Norway, and Sweden, you may import, duty-free, 200 cigarettes or 50 cigars; 1 liter of spirits or 2 liters of fortified or sparkling wine or liqueurs; 2 liters of still table wine; 60 milliliters of perfume; 250 milliliters of toilet water; plus £136 worth of other goods, including gifts and souvenirs.

➤ INFORMATION: **HM Customs and Excise** (✉ Dorset House, Stamford St., London SE1 9NG, ☎ 0171/202–4227).

D

DINING

Scandinavia's major cities offer a full range of dining choices, from traditional to international restaurants. Restaurants in smaller towns stick to traditional local fare. Local dishes can be very good, especially in the seafood and game categories, but bear in mind that northern climes beget exceptionally hearty, and heavy, meals. Sausage appears in a thousand forms, likewise potatoes. Some particular northern tastes can seem very different, such as the fondness for pickled and fermented fish—to be sampled carefully at first—and a universal obsession with sweet pastries, ice cream, and chocolate. Other novelties for the visitor might be the use of fruit in main dishes and soups, or sour milk on breakfast cereal, or preserved fish paste as a spread for crackers, or the prevalence of crackers and complete absence of sliced bread. The Swedish *smörgåsbord* and its

Scandinavian cousins are often the traveling diner's best bet, providing you find an authentic sampling. They include fresh fish and vegetables alongside meat and starches, and are also among the lower-priced menu choices.

Restaurant meals are a big-ticket item throughout Scandinavia, but there are ways to keep the cost of eating down. Take full advantage of the large, buffet breakfast usually included in the cost of a hotel room. At lunch, look for the "menu" that offers a set two- or three-course meal for a set price, or limit yourself to a hearty appetizer. At dinner, pay careful attention to the price of wine and drinks, since the high tax on alcohol raises these costs considerably. For more information on affordable eating, *see* Costs *in* Money, *below*.

DISABILITIES & ACCESSIBILITY

ACCESS IN SCANDINAVIA

Facilities for travelers with disabilities in Scandinavia are generally good, and most of the major tourist offices offer special booklets and brochures on travel and accommodations.

LODGING

Best Western offers properties with wheelchair-accessible rooms in Helsinki, Oslo, Stockholm, and just outside Copenhagen. If wheelchair-accessible rooms are not available, ground-floor rooms are provided.

➤ WHEELCHAIR-FRIENDLY CHAIN: **Best Western** (☎ 800/528–1234).

TIPS AND HINTS

When discussing accessibility with an operator or reservationist, **ask hard questions.** Are there any stairs, inside or out? Are there grab bars next to the toilet *and* in the shower/tub? How wide is the doorway to the room? To the bathroom? For the most extensive facilities meeting the latest legal specifications, **opt for newer accommodations,** which are more likely to have been designed with access in mind. Older buildings or ships may offer more limited facilities. Be sure to **discuss your needs before booking.**

COMPLAINTS

If a situation that warrants a complaint arises, call the U.S. Department of Justice Disability Rights Section.

For problems with surface transportation, call the Civil Rights Office at the Department of Transportation.

➤ COMPLAINT INFORMATION: **Disability Rights Section** (✉ U.S. Department of Justice, Box 66738, Washington, DC 20035–6738, ☎ 202/514–0301 or 800/514–0301, FAX 202/307–1198, TTY 202/514–0383 or 800/514–0383). **Aviation Consumer Protection Division** (☞ Air Travel, *above*) for airline-related problems. **Civil Rights Office** (✉ U.S. Department of Transportation, Departmental Office of Civil Rights, S-30, 400 7th St. SW, Room 10215, Washington, DC, 20590, ☎ 202/366–4648).

TRAVEL AGENCIES & TOUR OPERATORS

The Americans with Disabilities Act requires that travel firms serve the needs of all travelers. That said, you should note that some agencies and operators specialize in making travel arrangements for individuals and groups with disabilities.

Access Adventures is run by a former physical-rehabilitation counselor. Accessible Journeys works exclusively with escorted tours for travelers with mobility impairments. The Travel agency Wheels Travel specializes in European cruises and tours. Hinsdale Travel Service benefits from the advice of wheelchair traveler Janice Perkins. Call Wheelchair Journeys for general travel arrangements.

➤ CONTACTS: **Access Adventures** (✉ 206 Chestnut Ridge Rd., Rochester, NY 14624, ☎ 716/889–9096). **Accessible Journeys** (✉ 35 W. Sellers Ave., Ridley Park, PA 19078, ☎ 610/521–0339 or 800/846–4537, FAX 610/521–6959). **Flying Wheels Travel** (✉ 143 W. Bridge St., Box 382, Owatonna, MN 55060, ☎ 507/451–5005 or 800/535–6790, FAX 507/451–1685). **Hinsdale Travel Service** (✉ 201 E. Ogden Ave., Suite 100, Hinsdale, IL 60521, ☎ 630/325–1335). **Wheelchair Journeys** (✉ 16979 Redmond Way, Redmond, WA 98052, ☎ 425/885–2210 or 800/313–4751).

DISCOUNTS & DEALS

Be a smart shopper and **compare all your options before making a choice.** A plane ticket bought with a promotional coupon may not be cheaper than the least expensive fare from a discount ticket agency. For high-price travel purchases, such as packages or tours, keep in mind that what you get is just as important as what you save. Just because something is cheap doesn't mean it's a bargain.

LOOK IN YOUR WALLET

When you use your credit card to make travel purchases you may get free travel-accident insurance, collision-damage insurance, and medical or legal assistance, depending on the card and the bank that issued it. American Express, MasterCard, and Visa provide one or more of these services, so **get a copy of your credit card's travel-benefits policy.** If you are a member of the American Automobile Association (AAA) or an oil-company-sponsored road-assistance plan, always **ask hotel or car-rental reservationists about auto-club discounts.** Some clubs offer additional discounts on tours, cruises, or admission to attractions. And don't forget that auto-club membership entitles you to free maps and trip-planning services.

DIAL FOR DOLLARS

To save money, **look into "1-800" discount reservations services,** which use their buying power to get a better price on hotels, airline tickets, even car rentals. When booking a room, always **call the hotel's local toll-free number** (if one is available) rather than the central reservations number—you'll often get a better price. Always ask about special packages or corporate rates.

When shopping for the best deal on hotels and car rentals **look for guaranteed exchange rates,** which protect you against a falling dollar. With your rate locked in you won't pay more even if the price goes up in the local currency.

➤ AIRLINE TICKETS: ☎ 800/FLY–4–LESS.

➤ HOTEL ROOMS: **Hotels Plus** (☎ 800/235–0909). **International Marketing & Travel Concepts** (IMTC, ☎ 800/790–4682). **Steigenberger Reservation Service** (☎ 800/223–5652). **Travel Interlink** (☎ 800/888–5898).

SAVE ON COMBOS

Packages and guided tours can both save you money, but don't confuse the two (☞ Tour Operators, *below*). When you buy a package your travel remains independent, just as though you had planned and booked the trip yourself. Fly/drive packages, which combine airfare and car rental, are often a good deal.If you **buy a rail/drive pass** you'll save on train tickets and car rentals. All EurailPass and EuroPass holders get a discount on Eurostar fares through the Channel Tunnel. Also check rates for Scanrail Passes (☞ Discount Passes *in* Train Travel, *below*).

JOIN A CLUB?

Many companies sell discounts in the form of travel clubs and coupon books, but these cost money. You must use participating advertisers to get a deal, and only after you recoup the initial membership cost or book price do you begin to save. If you plan to use the club or coupons frequently you may save considerably. Before signing up, find out what discounts you get for free.

➤ DISCOUNT CLUBS: **Entertainment Travel Editions** (✉ 2125 Butterfield Rd., Troy, MI 48084, ☎ 800/445–4137; $23–$48, depending on destination). **Great American Traveler** (✉ Box 27965, Salt Lake City, UT 84127, ☎ 800/548–2812; $49.95 per year). **Moment's Notice Discount Travel Club** (✉ 7301 New Utrecht Ave., Brooklyn, NY 11204, ☎ 718/234–6295; $25 per year, single or family). **Privilege Card International** (✉ 237 E. Front St., Youngstown, OH 44503, ☎ 330/746–5211 or 800/236–9732; $74.95 per year). **Sears's Mature Outlook** (✉ Box 9390, Des Moines, IA 50306, ☎ 800/336–6330; $14.95 per year). **Travelers Advantage** (✉ CUC Travel Service, 3033 S. Parker Rd., Suite 1000, Aurora, CO 80014, ☎ 800/548–1116 or 800/648–4037; $49 per year, single or family). **Worldwide Discount Travel Club** (✉ 1674 Meridian Ave., Miami Beach, FL 33139, ☎ 305/534–2082; $50 per year family, $40 single).

E
ELECTRICITY

To use your U.S.-purchased electric-powered equipment, **bring a converter and adapter.** The electrical current in Scandinavia is 220 volts, 50 cycles alternating current (AC); wall outlets take Continental-type plugs, with two round prongs.

If your appliances are dual-voltage, you'll need only an adapter. Don't use 110-volt outlets, marked FOR SHAVERS ONLY, for high-wattage appliances such as blow-dryers. Most laptops operate equally well on 110 and 220 volts and so require only an adapter.

EMERGENCIES

Ambulance, fire, and police assistance is available 24 hours in Scandinavia.

➤ GENERAL EMERGENCY NUMBER: **Denmark, Finland, Iceland, Norway, Sweden** (☎ 112).

G
GAY & LESBIAN TRAVEL

➤ GAY- AND LESBIAN-FRIENDLY TRAVEL AGENCIES: **Advance Damron** (✉ 1 Greenway Plaza, Suite 800, Houston, TX 77046, ☎ 713/850–1140 or 800/695–0880, FAX 713/888–1010). **Club Travel** (✉ 8739 Santa Monica Blvd., West Hollywood, CA 90069, ☎ 310/358–2200 or 800/429–8747, FAX 310/358–2222). **Islanders/Kennedy Travel** (✉ 183 W. 10th St., New York, NY 10014, ☎ 212/242–3222 or 800/988–1181, FAX 212/929–8530). **Now Voyager** (✉ 4406 18th St., San Francisco, CA 94114, ☎ 415/626–1169 or 800/255–6951, FAX 415/626–8626). **Yellowbrick Road** (✉ 1500 W. Balmoral Ave., Chicago, IL 60640, ☎ 773/561–1800 or 800/642–2488, FAX 773/561–4497). **Skylink Women's Travel** (✉ 3577 Moorland Ave., Santa Rosa, CA 95407, ☎ 707/585–8355 or 800/225–5759, FAX 707/584–5637).

H
HEALTH

MEDICAL PLANS

No one plans to get sick while traveling, but it happens, so **consider signing up with a medical-assistance company.** Members get doctor referrals, emergency evacuation or repatriation, 24-hour telephone hot lines for medical consultation, cash for emergencies, and other personal and legal assistance. Coverage varies by plan, so **review the benefits carefully.**

THE GOLD GUIDE / SMART TRAVEL TIPS

➤ MEDICAL-ASSISTANCE COMPANIES: **International SOS Assistance** (⊠ Box 11568, Philadelphia, PA 19116, ☎ 215/244–1500 or 800/523–8930; ⊠ 1255 University St., Suite 420, Montréal, Québec H3B 3B6, ☎ 514/874–7674 or 800/363–0263; ⊠ 7 Old Lodge Pl., St. Margarets, Twickenham TW1 1RQ, England, ☎ 0181/744–0033). **MEDEX Assistance Corporation** (⊠ Box 5375, Timonium, MD 21094-5375, ☎ 410/453–6300 or 800/537–2029). **Traveler's Emergency Network** (⊠ 3100 Tower Blvd., Suite 1000B, Durham, NC 27707, ☎ 919/490–6055 or 800/275–4836, FAX 919/493–8262). **TravMed** (⊠ Box 5375, Timonium, MD 21094, ☎ 410/453–6380 or 800/732–5309). **Worldwide Assistance Services** (⊠ 1133 15th St. NW, Suite 400, Washington, DC 20005, ☎ 202/331–1609 or 800/821–2828, FAX 202/828–5896).

I

INSURANCE

Travel insurance is the best way to **protect yourself against financial loss.** The most useful policies are trip-cancellation-and-interruption, default, medical, and comprehensive insurance.

Without insurance you will lose all or most of your money if you cancel your trip, regardless of the reason. It's essential that you **buy trip-cancellation-and-interruption insurance,** particularly if your airline ticket, cruise, or package tour is nonrefundable and cannot be changed. When considering how much coverage you need, look for a policy that will cover the cost of your trip plus the nondiscounted price of a one-way airline ticket, should you need to return home early. Also **consider default or bankruptcy insurance,** which protects you against a supplier's failure to deliver.

Medicare generally does not cover health-care costs outside the United States, nor do many privately issued policies. If your own policy does not cover you outside the United States, **consider buying supplemental medical coverage.** Remember that travel health insurance is different from a medical-assistance plan (☞ Health, *above*).

Citizens of the United Kingdom can buy an annual travel-insurance policy valid for most vacations during the year in which it's purchased. If you are pregnant or have a preexisting medical condition, make sure you're covered.

If you have purchased an expensive vacation, particularly one that involves travel abroad, comprehensive insurance is a must. **Look for comprehensive policies that include trip-delay insurance,** which will protect you in the event that weather problems cause you to miss your flight, tour, or cruise. A few insurers sell waivers for preexisting medical conditions. Companies that offer both features include Access America, Carefree Travel, Travel Insured International, and Travel Guard.

Always **buy travel insurance directly from the insurance company;** if you buy it from a travel agency or tour operator that goes out of business you probably will not be covered for the agency or operator's default, a major risk. Before you make any purchase, **review your existing health and home-owner's policies** to find out whether they cover expenses incurred while traveling.

➤ TRAVEL INSURERS: U.S.: **Access America** (⊠ 6600 W. Broad St., Richmond, VA 23230, ☎ 804/285–3300 or 800/284–8300). **Carefree Travel Insurance** (⊠ Box 9366, 100 Garden City Plaza, Garden City, NY 11530, ☎ 516/294–0220 or 800/323–3149). **Near Travel Services** (⊠ Box 1339, Calumet City, IL 60409, ☎ 708/868–6700 or 800/654–6700). **Travel Guard International** (⊠ 1145 Clark St., Stevens Point, WI 54481, ☎ 715/345–0505 or 800/826–1300). **Travel Insured International** (⊠ Box 280568, East Hartford, CT 06128–0568, ☎ 860/528–7663 or 800/243–3174). **Travelex Insurance Services** (⊠ 11717 Burt St., Suite 202, Omaha, NE 68154-1500, ☎ 402/445–8637 or 800/228–9792, FAX 800/867–9531). **Wallach & Company** (⊠ 107 W. Federal St., Box 480, Middleburg, VA 20118, ☎ 540/687–3166 or 800/237–6615). Canada: **Mutual of Omaha** (⊠ Travel Division, 500 University Ave., Toronto, Ontario M5G 1V8, ☎ 416/598–4083, 800/

268–8825 in Canada). U.K.: **Association of British Insurers** (⊠ 51 Gresham St., London EC2V 7HQ, ☎ 0171/600–3333).

L

LANGUAGE

Despite the fact that four of the five Scandinavian tongues are in the Germanic family of languages, it is a myth that someone who speaks German can understand Danish, Icelandic, Swedish, and Norwegian. Fortunately, English is widely spoken in Scandinavia. German is the most common third language. English becomes rarer outside major cities, and it's a good idea to **take along a dictionary or phrase book.** Even here, however, anyone under the age of 50 is likely to have studied English in school.

Danish, Norwegian, and Swedish are similar, and fluent speakers can generally understand each other. A foreigner will most often be struck by the lilting rhythm of spoken Swedish, which takes a bit of getting used to for Danes and Norwegians, who often choose to speak English with Swedes.

Characters special to these three languages are the Danish "ø" and the Swedish "ö," pronounced a bit like a very short "er", similar to the French "eu"; "æ" or "ä," which sounds like the "a" in "ape" but with a glottal stop, or the "a" in "cat," depending on the region, and the "å" (also written "aa"), which sounds like the "o" in "ghost." The important thing about these characters isn't that you pronounce them correctly—foreigners usually can't—but that you know to look for them in the phone book at the very end. Mr. Søren Åstrup, for example, will be found after "Z." Æ or Ä and Ø or Ö follow.

Icelandic, because of its island isolation, is the language closest to what the Vikings spoke 1,000 years ago. Although Norwegian, Danish, and Swedish have clearly evolved away from the roots common to all four languages, Icelandic retains a surprising amount of its ancient heritage, and Icelanders want to keep it that way: A governmental committee in Iceland has the express task of coming up with Icelandic versions of new words such as *computer.* Two characters are unique to Icelandic and Faroese: the "Þ," which is pronounced like the "th" in "thing"; and the "ð," which is pronounced like the "th" in "the."

Finnish is a non-Germanic language more closely related to Hungarian than to the other Scandinavian languages. A visitor isn't likely to recognize anything on the average newspaper's front page. A linguistic cousin to Finnish is still spoken by the Sami (Lapps), who inhabit the northernmost parts of Norway, Sweden, Finland, and Russia.

LODGING

In the larger cities, lodging ranges from first-class business hotels run by SAS, Sheraton, and Scandic to good-quality tourist-class hotels, such as RESO, Best Western, Scandic Budget, and Sweden Hotels, to a wide variety of single-entrepreneur hotels. In the countryside, look for independently run inns and motels. In Denmark they're called *kroer;* in Norway, *fjellstuer* or *pensjonat;* in Finland, *kievari;* and elsewhere, guest houses. Before you leave home, **ask your travel agent about discounts** (☞ Hotels, *below*), including summer hotel checks for Best Western, Scandic, and Inter Nor hotels, a summer Fjord pass in Norway, and enormous year-round rebates at SAS hotels for travelers over 65. All EuroClass (business class) passengers can get discounts of at least 10% at SAS hotels when they book through SAS.

Two things about hotels usually surprise North Americans: the relatively limited dimensions of Scandinavian beds and the generous size of Scandinavian breakfasts. Scandinavian double beds are often about 60 inches wide or slightly less, close in size to the U.S. queen size. King-size beds (72 inches wide) are difficult to find and, if available, require special reservations.

Older hotels may have some rooms described as "double," which in fact have one double bed plus one fold-out sofa big enough for two people. This arrangement is occasionally called a combi-room but is being phased out.

Many older hotels, particularly the country inns and independently run smaller hotels in the cities, do not have private bathrooms. Ask ahead if this is important to you.

Scandinavian breakfasts resemble what many people would call lunch, usually including breads, cheeses, marmalade, hams, lunch meats, eggs, juice, cereal, milk, and coffee. Generally, the farther north you go, the larger the breakfasts become. Breakfast is often included in the price of the hotel, except in Finland and in deluxe establishments elsewhere.

Make reservations whenever possible. Even countryside inns, which usually have space, are sometimes packed with vacationing Europeans.

Ask about high and low seasons when making reservations, since different countries define their tourist seasons differently. Some hotels lower prices during tourist season, whereas others raise them during the same period.

APARTMENT AND VILLA RENTALS

If you want a home base that's roomy enough for a family and comes with cooking facilities, **consider a furnished rental.** These can save you money, however some rentals are luxury properties, economical only when your party is large. Home-exchange directories list rentals (often second homes owned by prospective house swappers), and some services search for a house or apartment for you (even a castle if that's your fancy) and handle the paperwork. Some send an illustrated catalog; others send photographs only of specific properties, sometimes at a charge. Up-front registration fees may apply.

➤ RENTAL AGENTS: **Europa-Let/Tropical Inn-Let** (✉ 92 N. Main St., Ashland, OR 97520, ☎ 541/482–5806 or 800/462–4486, FAX 541/482–0660). **Property Rentals International** (✉ 1008 Mansfield Crossing Rd., Richmond, VA 23236, ☎ 804/378–6054 or 800/220–3332, FAX 804/379–2073).

HOME EXCHANGES

If you would like to exchange your home for someone else's, **join a home-exchange organization,** which will send you its updated listings of available exchanges for a year and will include your own listing in at least one of them. Making the arrangements is up to you. Charges apply: HomeLink International charges $83 per year.

➤ EXCHANGE CLUB: **HomeLink International** (✉ Box 650, Key West, FL 33041, ☎ 305/294–7766 or 800/638–3841, FAX 305/294–1148).

HOTELS

All five Scandinavian countries offer Inn Checks, or prepaid hotel vouchers, for accommodations ranging from first-class hotels to country cottages. These vouchers, which must be purchased from travel agents or from the Scandinavian Tourist Board (☞ Visitor Information, *below*) before departure, are sold individually and in packets for as many nights as needed and offer savings of up to 50%. Most countries also offer summer bargains for foreign tourists. For further information about Scandinavian hotel vouchers, contact the Scandinavian Tourist Board.

M

MONEY

In this book currencies are abbreviated DKr (Danish kroner), FM (Finnish mark), IKr (Icelandic kroner), NKr (Norwegian kroner), and SKr (Swedish kronor). In individual countries you may see prices indicated with Kr only, and you may see exchange rates in banks quoted for DKK, FIM, ISK, NOK, and SEK, respectively. Currency-exchange rates at press time are listed in the country A to Z sections at the end of each chapter, but **since rates fluctuate daily, you should check them at the time of your departure.**

ATMS

Before leaving home, **make sure that your credit cards have been programmed for ATM use in Scandinavia.** Note that Discover is accepted mostly in the United States. Local bank cards often do not work overseas or may access only your checking account; **ask your bank about a MasterCard/Cirrus or Visa debit card,** which works like a bank card but can be used at any ATM displaying a MasterCard/Cirrus or Visa logo. These cards, too, may tap only your checking account; check with your bank about their policy. A list of Plus locations is available at your local bank.

➤ ATM LOCATIONS: **Cirrus** (☎ 800/424–7787).

COSTS

Costs are high in Denmark, Norway, and Sweden, higher still in Finland, and highest in Iceland, where so many things must be imported. Basic sample prices are listed in the country A to Z section at the end of each chapter. Throughout the region, be aware that sales taxes can be very high, but foreigners can get some refunds by shopping at tax-free stores (☞ Taxes, *below*). City cards can save you transportation and entrance fees in many of the larger cities.

You can **reduce the cost of food by planning.** Breakfast is often included in your hotel bill; if not, you may wish to buy fruit, sweet rolls, and a beverage for a picnic breakfast. Electrical devices for hot coffee or tea should be bought abroad, though, to conform to the local current. **Opt for a restaurant lunch instead of dinner,** since the latter tends to be significantly more expensive. Instead of beer or wine, **drink tap water**—liquor can cost four times the price of the same brand in a store—but do specify tap water, as the term "water" can refer to soft drinks and bottled water, which are also expensive. Throughout Scandinavia, the tip is included in the cost of your meal.

In most of Scandinavia, liquor and strong beer (over 3% alcohol) can be purchased only in state-owned shops, at very high prices, during weekday business hours, usually 9:30 to 6. A 70- or 75-centiliter bottle of whiskey in Sweden, for example, can easily cost SKr250 (about $35). Denmark takes a less restrictive approach, with liquor and beer available in the smallest of grocery stores, open weekdays and Saturday morning, but Danish prices, too, are high. (When you visit relatives in Scandinavia, a bottle of liquor or fine wine bought duty-free on the trip over is often a much-appreciated gift.)

CURRENCY EXCHANGE

For the most favorable rates, **change money at banks.** Although fees

charged for ATM transactions may be higher abroad than at home, Cirrus and Plus exchange rates are excellent, because they are based on wholesale rates offered only by major banks. You won't do as well at exchange booths in airports or rail and bus stations, in hotels, in restaurants, or in stores, although you may find their hours more convenient. To avoid lines at airport exchange booths, **get a small amount of local currency before you leave home.**

➤ EXCHANGE SERVICES: **International Currency Express** (☎ 888/842–0880 East Coast, 888/278–6628 West Coast). **Thomas Cook Currency Services** (☎ 800/287–7362).

TRAVELER'S CHECKS

Whether or not to buy traveler's checks depends on where you are headed. **Take cash if your trip includes rural areas** and small towns, traveler's checks to cities. If your checks are lost or stolen, they can usually be replaced within 24 hours. To ensure a speedy refund, buy your checks yourself (don't ask someone else to make the purchase). When making a claim for stolen or lost checks, the person who bought the checks should make the call.

P

PACKING FOR SCANDINAVIA

Bring a folding umbrella and a lightweight raincoat, as it is common for the sky to be clear at 9 AM, rainy at 11 AM, and clear again in time for lunch. **Pack casual clothes,** as Scandinavians tend to dress more casually than their Continental brethren. If you have trouble sleeping when it is light or are sensitive to strong sun, **bring an eye mask and dark sunglasses;** the sun rises as early as 4 AM in some areas, and the far-northern latitude causes it to slant at angles unseen elsewhere on the globe. **Bring bug repellent** if you plan to venture away from the capital cities; large mosquitoes can be a real nuisance on summer evenings in Denmark as well as in the far-northern reaches of Norway and Sweden.

Bring an extra pair of eyeglasses or contact lenses in your carry-on luggage, and if you have a health problem, **pack enough medication** to last

THE GOLD GUIDE / SMART TRAVEL TIPS

the entire trip **or have your doctor write you a prescription using the drug's generic name,** because brand names vary from country to country. It's important that you **don't put prescription drugs or valuables in luggage to be checked**: it might go astray. To avoid problems with customs officials, carry medications in the original packaging. Also, don't forget the addresses of offices that handle refunds of lost traveler's checks.

LUGGAGE

In general, you are entitled to check two bags on flights within the United States and on international flights leaving the United States. A third piece may be brought on board, but it must fit easily under the seat in front of you or in the overhead compartment.

If you are flying between two foreign destinations, note that baggage allowances may be determined not by piece but by weight—generally 88 pounds (40 kilograms) in first class, 66 pounds (30 kilograms) in business class, and 44 pounds (20 kilograms) in economy. If your flight between two cities abroad *connects* with your transatlantic or transpacific flight, the piece method still applies.

Airline liability for baggage is limited to $1,250 per person on flights within the United States. On international flights it amounts to $9.07 per pound or $20 per kilogram for checked baggage (roughly $640 per 70-pound bag) and $400 per passenger for unchecked baggage. Insurance for losses exceeding these amounts can be bought from the airline at check-in for about $10 per $1,000 of coverage; note that this coverage excludes a rather extensive list of items, which is shown on your airline ticket.

Before departure, **itemize your bags' contents** and their worth, and label the bags with your name, address, and phone number. (If you use your home address, cover it so that potential thieves can't see it readily.) Inside each bag, **pack a copy of your itinerary.** At check-in, **make sure that each bag is correctly tagged** with the destination airport's three-letter code. If your bags arrive damaged or fail to arrive at all, file a written report with the airline before leaving the airport.

Once your travel plans are confirmed, **check the expiration date of your passport.** It's also a good idea to **make photocopies of the data page;** leave one copy with someone at home and keep another with you, separated from your passport. If you lose your passport, promptly call the nearest embassy or consulate and the local police; having a copy of the data page can speed replacement.

U.S. CITIZENS

All U.S. citizens, even infants, need only a valid passport to enter any Scandinavian country for stays of up to three months.

➤ INFORMATION: **Passport Agency** (☎ 202/647–0518).

CANADIANS

You need only a valid passport to enter any Scandinavian country for stays of up to three months.

➤ INFORMATION: **Passport Office** (☎ 819/994–3500 or 800/567–6868).

U.K. CITIZENS

Citizens of the United Kingdom need only a valid passport to enter any Scandinavian country for stays of up to three months.

➤ INFORMATION: **London Passport Office** (☎ 0990/21010).

S

To qualify for age-related discounts, **mention your senior-citizen status up front** when booking hotel reservations (not when checking out) and before you're seated in restaurants (not when paying the bill). Note that discounts may be limited to certain menus, days, or hours. When renting a car, **ask about promotional car-rental discounts,** which can be cheaper than senior-citizen rates.

➤ EDUCATIONAL TRAVEL PROGRAMS: Elderhostel (✉ 75 Federal St., 3rd floor, Boston, MA 02110, ☎ 617/426–8056). Interhostel (✉ University of New Hampshire, 6 Garrison Ave., Durham, NH 03824, ☎ 603/862–1147 or 800/733–9753, FAX 603/862–1113).

TRAIN TRAVEL

Travelers over 60 can buy a **SeniorRail Card** for DKr150 (about $27) in Scandinavia. It gives 30% discounts on train travel in 21 European countries for a whole year from purchase.

SHOPPING

Prices in Scandinavia are never low, but quality is high, and specialties are sometimes less expensive here than elsewhere. Swedish crystal, Icelandic sweaters, Danish Lego blocks and furniture, Norwegian furs, and Finnish fabrics—these are just a few of the items to look for. Keep an eye out for sales, called *udsalg* in Danish, *rea* in Swedish, and *ale* in Finnish.

STUDENTS

To save money, **look into deals available through student-oriented travel agencies.** To qualify you'll need a bona fide student ID card. Members of international student groups are also eligible. Call the Council on International Educational Exchange for mail orders only, in the United States. Travel Cuts is a good resource in Canada.

➤ STUDENT IDs AND SERVICES: **Council on International Educational Exchange** (⊠ CIEE, 205 E. 42nd St., 14th floor, New York, NY 10017, ☎ 212/822–2600 or 888/268–6245, ℻ 212/822–2699). **Travel Cuts** (⊠ 187 College St., Toronto, Ontario M5T 1P7, ☎ 416/979–2406 or 800/667–2887).

➤ STUDENT TOURS: **AESU Travel** (⊠ 2 Hamill Rd., Suite 248, Baltimore, MD 21210-1807, ☎ 410/323–4416 or 800/638–7640, ℻ 410/323–4498).

HOSTELS

Membership to Hostelling International is $25 in the U.S., C$26.75 in Canada; and in the U.K., £9.30).

➤ HOSTELLING INFORMATION: **Hostelling International—American Youth Hostels** (AYH, ⊠ 733 15th St. NW, Suite 840, Washington, DC 20005, ☎ 202/783–6161, ℻ 202/783–6171). **Hostelling International—Canada** (⊠ 400-205 Catherine St., Ottawa, Ontario K2P 1C3, ☎ 613/237–7884, ℻ 613/237–7868). **Youth Hostel Association of England and Wales** (⊠ Trevelyan House, 8 St. Stephen's Hill, St. Albans, Hertfordshire AL1 2DY, ☎ 01727/855215 or 01727/845047, ℻ 01727/844126).

T

TAXES

Specific information on V.A.T. (value-added taxes) can be found in the country A to Z section at the end of each chapter.

VALUE-ADDED TAX (V.A.T.)

One way to beat high prices is to **take advantage of tax-free shopping.** Throughout Scandinavia, you can make major purchases free of tax if you have a foreign passport. Ask about tax-free shopping when you make a purchase for $50 (about £32) or more. When your purchases exceed a specified limit (which varies from country to country), you receive a special export receipt. Keep the parcels intact and take them out of the country within 30 days of purchase. When you leave, you can obtain a refund of the V.A.T. (called *moms* all over Scandinavia) in cash from a special office at the airport, or, upon arriving home, you can send your receipts to an office in the country of purchase to receive your refund by mail. Be aware that limits for EU tourists are higher than for those coming from outside the EU. In Sweden, for non-EU tourists, the refund is about 15%; in Finland, 12% to 16% for purchases over FM200; in Norway, 23% for purchases over NKr300; in Denmark, 18% for purchases over DKr300; in Iceland, 15% for purchases over IKr5,000.

TELEPHONES

The country code for Denmark is 45; for Finland, 358; for Iceland, 354; for Norway, 47; and for Sweden, 46.

CALLING HOME

Before you go, **find out the local access codes** for your destinations. AT&T, MCI, and Sprint long-distance services make calling home relatively convenient, but you may find the local access number blocked in many hotel rooms. First ask the hotel operator to connect you. If the hotel operator balks, ask for an international operator, or dial the international operator yourself. One way to improve your odds of getting connected to your long-distance carrier is to travel with more than one company's calling card (a hotel may block Sprint, for example, but not MCI). If all else fails, call your phone company collect in the United States or call from a pay phone in the hotel lobby.

➤ LOCAL ACCESS CODES: **AT&T USADirect** (Denmark ☎ 800/10010, Finland ☎ 9800/10010, Norway ☎ 800/19011, Iceland ☎ 800/9001, Sweden ☎ 020/795611).

MCI Call USA: (Denmark ☎ 800/10022, Finland ☎ 0800/110280, Norway ☎ 800/19912, Iceland ☎ 999/002, Sweden ☎ 020/795922).

Sprint Express: (Denmark ☎ 800/10877, Finland ☎ 9800/10284, Norway ☎ 050/12877 or 800/19877, Iceland ☎ 800/9003, Sweden ☎ 020/799011).

TOUR OPERATORS

Buying a prepackaged tour or independent vacation can make your trip to Scandinavia less expensive and more hassle free. Because everything is prearranged you'll spend less time planning.

Operators that handle several hundred thousand travelers per year can use their purchasing power to give you a good price. Their high volume may also indicate financial stability. But some small companies provide more personalized service; because they tend to specialize, they may also be more knowledgeable about a given area.

A GOOD DEAL?

The more your package or tour includes, the better you can predict the ultimate cost of your vacation. Make sure you know exactly what is covered, and **beware of hidden costs.** Are taxes, tips, and service charges included? Transfers and baggage handling? Entertainment and excursions? These can add up.

If the package or tour you are considering is priced lower than in your wildest dreams, **be skeptical.** Also, **make sure your travel agent knows the accommodations** and other services. Ask about the hotel's location, room size, beds, and whether it has a

pool, room service, or programs for children, if you care about these. Has your agent been there in person or sent others you can contact?

BUYER BEWARE

Each year consumers are stranded or lose their money when tour operators—even very large ones with excellent reputations—go out of business. So **check out the operator.** Find out how long the company has been in business, and ask several agents about its reputation. **Don't book unless the firm has a consumer-protection program.**

Members of the National Tour Association and United States Tour Operators Association are required to set aside funds to cover your payments and travel arrangements in case the company defaults. Nonmembers may carry insurance instead. Look for the details, and for the name of an underwriter with a solid reputation, in the operator's brochure. Note: When it comes to tour operators, **don't trust escrow accounts.** Although the Department of Transportation watches over charter-flight operators, no regulatory body prevents tour operators from raiding the till. You may want to protect yourself by buying travel insurance that includes a tour-operator default provision. For more information, *see* Consumer Protection, *above.*

It's also a good idea to choose a company that participates in the American Society of Travel Agents Tour Operator Program (TOP). This gives you a forum if there are any disputes between you and your tour operator; ASTA will act as mediator.

➤ TOUR-OPERATOR RECOMMENDATIONS: **American Society of Travel Agents** (☞ Travel Agencies, *below*). **National Tour Association** (NTA, ✉ 546 E. Main St., Lexington, KY 40508, ☎ 606/226–4444 or 800/755–8687). **United States Tour Operators Association** (USTOA, ✉ 342 Madison Ave., Suite 1522, New York, NY 10173, ☎ 212/599–6599, ℻ 212/599–6744). **American Society of Travel Agents** (☞ *below*).

USING AN AGENT

Travel agents are excellent resources. In fact, large operators accept bookings made only through travel agents. But it's good idea to **collect brochures from several agencies** because some agents' suggestions may be influenced by relationships with tour and package firms that reward them for volume sales. If you have a special interest, **find an agent with expertise in that area**; ASTA (☞ Travel Agencies, *below*) has a database of specialists worldwide. Do some homework on your own, too: local tourism boards can provide information about lesser-known and small-niche operators, some of which may sell only direct.

SINGLE TRAVELERS

Prices for packages and tours are usually quoted per person, based on two sharing a room. If traveling solo, you may be required to pay the full double-occupancy rate. Some operators eliminate this surcharge if you agree to be matched with a roommate of the same sex, even if one is not found by departure time.

GROUP TOURS

Among companies that sell tours to Scandinavia, the following are nationally known, have a proven reputation, and offer plenty of options. The classifications used below represent different price categories, and you'll probably encounter these terms when talking to a travel agent or tour operator. The key difference is usually in accommodations, which run from budget to better, and better-yet to best.

➤ SUPER-DELUXE: **Abercrombie & Kent** (⊠ 1520 Kensington Rd., Oak Brook, IL 60521-2141, ☎ 630/954–2944 or 800/323–7308, ℻ 630/954–3324). **Travcoa** (⊠ Box 2630, 2350 S.E. Bristol St., Newport Beach, CA 92660, ☎ 714/476–2800 or 800/992–2003, ℻ 714/476–2538).

➤ DELUXE: **Globus** (⊠ 5301 S. Federal Circle, Littleton, CO 80123-2980, ☎ 303/797–2800 or 800/221–0090, ℻ 303/347–2080). **Maupintour** (⊠ 1515 St. Andrews Dr., Lawrence, KS 66047, ☎ 913/843–1211 or 800/255–4266, ℻ 913/843–8351). **Tauck Tours** (⊠ Box 5027, 276 Post Rd. W, Westport, CT 06881-5027, ☎ 203/226–6911 or 800/468–2825, ℻ 203/221–6828).

➤ FIRST-CLASS: **Bennett Tours** (⊠ 270 Madison Ave., New York, NY 10016-0658, ☎ 212/532–5060 or 800/221–2420, ℻ 212/779–8944). **Brandan Tours** (⊠ 15137 Califa St., Van Nuys, CA 91411, ☎ 818/785–9696 or 800/421–8446, ℻ 818/902–9876). **Brekke Tours** (⊠ 802 N. 43rd St., Ste. D, Grand Forks, ND 58203, ☎ 701/772–8999 or 800/437—5302, ℻ 701/780–9352). **Caravan Tours** (⊠ 401 N. Michigan Ave., Chicago, IL 60611, ☎ 312/321–9800 or 800/227–2826, ℻ 312/321–9845). **Finnair** (☎ 800/950–5000). **KITT Holidays** (⊠ 2 Appletree Sq., #150, 8011 34th Ave. S., Minneapolis, MN 55425, ☎ 612/854–8005 or 800/262—8728, ℻ 612/854–6948). **Scantours** (⊠ 1535 6th St., #205, Santa Monica, CA 90401-2533, ☎ 310/451–0911 or 800/223–7226, ℻ 310/395–2013). **Scan Travel Center** (⊠ 66 Edgewood Ave., Larchmont, NY 10538, ☎ 803/671–6758 or 800/759–7226). **Trafalgar Tours** (⊠ 11 E. 26th St., New York, NY 10010, ☎ 212/689–8977 or 800/854–0103, ℻ 800/457–6644).

➤ BUDGET: **Cosmos** (☞ Globus, *above*). **Trafalgar Tours** (☞ *above*).

PACKAGES

Like group tours, independent vacation packages are available from major tour operators and airlines. The companies listed below offer vacation packages in a broad price range.

➤ AIR/HOTEL: **Delta Dream Vacations** (☎ 800/872–7786). **DER Tours** (⊠ 9501 W. Devon St., Rosemont, IL 60018, ☎ 800/782–2424, ℻ 800/282–7474; ℻ 800/860–9944, for brochures). **Icelandair** (☎ 800/757–3876).

➤ FLY/DRIVE: **Delta Dream Vacations** (☞ *above*).

THEME TRIPS

➤ ADVENTURE: **Borton Overseas** (⊠ 1621 E. 79th St., Bloomington, MN 55425, ☎ 612/883–0704 or 800/843–0602, ℻ 612/883–0221). **Scandinavian Special-Interest Network** (⊠ Box 313, Sparta, NJ 07871, ☎ 201/729–8961, ℻ 201/729–6565).

➤ BICYCLING: **Backroads** (⊠ 801 Cedar St., Berkeley, CA 94710-1800, ☎ 510/527–1555 or 800/462–2848,

FAX 510-527–1444). **Euro-Bike Tours** (✉ Box 990, De Kalb, IL 60115, ☎ 800/321–6060, FAX 815/758–8851).

➤ CRUISES: **Bergen Line** (✉ 405 Park Ave., New York, NY 10022, ☎ 800/323–7436, FAX 212/319–1390). **Euro-Cruises** (✉ 303 W. 13th St., New York, NY 10014, ☎ 800/688—3876). **Swan Hellenic/Classical Cruises & Tours** (✉ 132 E. 70th St., New York, NY 10021, ☎ 800/252–7745, FAX 212/774–1545). **Euro-Cruises** (✉ Box 30925, New York, NY 10011, ☎ 212/688–3876).

➤ FISHING: **Scandinavian Special-Interest Network** (☞ *above*).

➤ FOLK ART AND CRAFTS: **Borton Overseas** (☞ *above*). **Scandinavian Special-Interest Network** (☞ *above*).

➤ GENEALOGY: **Brekke Tours** (☞ *above*). **KITT Holidays** (☞ *above*). **Scan Travel Center** (☞ *above*).

➤ HIKING/WALKING: **Above the Clouds Trekking** (✉ Box 398, Worcester, MA 01602, ☎ 508/799–4499 or 800/233–4499, FAX 508/797–4779). **Backroads** (☞ *above*).

➤ HORSEBACK RIDING: **FITS Equestrian** (✉ 685 Lateen Rd., Solvang, CA 93463, ☎ 805/688–9494 or 800/666–3487, FAX 805/688–2943).

➤ LEARNING: **Earthwatch** (✉ Box 9104, 680 Mount Auburn St., Watertown, MA 02272, ☎ 617/926–8200 or 800/776–0188, FAX 617/926–8532).

➤ MUSIC: **Dailey-Thorp Travel** (✉ 330 W. 58th St., #610, New York, NY 10019-1817, ☎ 212/307–1555 or 800/998–4677, FAX 212/974–1420).

TRAIN TRAVEL

To save money, **look into rail passes,** but be aware that if you don't plan to cover many miles, you may come out ahead by buying individual tickets.

DISCOUNT PASSES

Consider a Scanrail Pass, available for travel in Denmark, Sweden, Norway, and Finland for both first- and second-class train travel: you may have five days of unlimited travel in a 15 day period ($222 first-class/$176 second-class); 10 days of unlimited travel in a month ($354/$248); or one month of consecutive day unlimited train travel ($516/$414). With the

Scanrail Pass, you also enjoy travel bonuses, including free or discounted ferry, boat, and bus travel and a Hotel Discount Card that allows 10–30% off rates for select hotels June–August. Passengers 12–25 can **buy Scanrail Youth Passes** ($167 first-class/$132 second-class, five travel days in 15 days; $266/$213 for 10 travel days in a month; $387/$311 for one month of unlimited travel). Those over 55 can **take advantage of the Scanrail 55+ Pass,** which offers the travel bonuses of the Scanrail Pass and discounted travel ($198 first-class/$157 second-class, five days; $315/$253 10 days; $459/$368 one month). Buy Scandrail passes through Rail Europe and travel agents.

For car and train travel, price the Scanrail'n Drive Pass: in 15 days you can get five days of unlimited train travel and three days of car rental (choice of three car categories) with unlimited mileage in Denmark, Finland, Norway, and Sweden. You can purchase extra car rental days and choose from first- or second-class train travel. Rates for two adults (compact car $315 first-class/$275 second-class), are considerably lower (about 25%) than for single adults.

Scandinavia is one of 17 countries in which you can **use EurailPasses,** which provide unlimited first-class rail travel, in all of the participating countries, for the duration of the pass. If you plan to rack up the miles, get a standard pass. These are available for 15 days ($522), 21 days ($678), one month ($838), two months ($1,188), and three months ($1,468). Eurail- and EuroPasses are available through travel agents and Rail Europe.

In addition to standard EurailPasses, **ask about special rail-pass plans.** Among these are the Eurail YouthPass (for those under age 26), the Eurail SaverPass (which gives a discount for two or more people traveling together), a Eurail FlexiPass (which allows a certain number of travel days within a set period), the Euraildrive Pass, and the EuroPass Drive (which combines travel by train and rental car).

Whichever pass you choose, remember that you must **purchase your pass before you leave** for Europe.

Many travelers assume that rail passes guarantee them seats on the trains they wish to ride. Not so. You need to **book seats ahead even if you are using a rail pass**; seat reservations are required on some European trains, particularly high-speed trains, and are a good idea on trains that may be crowded—particularly in summer on popular routes. You will also need a reservation if you purchase sleeping accommodations.

➤ WHERE TO BUY RAIL PASSES: **Rail Europe** (✉ 226–230 Westchester Ave., White Plains, NY 10604, ☎ 914/682–5172 or 800/438–7245; 2087 Dundas East, Suite 105, Mississauga, Ontario L4X 1M2, ☎ 416/602–4195). **DER Tours** (✉ Box 1606, Des Plaines, IL 60017, ☎ 800/782–2424, FAX 800/282–7474). **CIT Tours Corp.** (✉ 342 Madison Ave., Suite 207, New York, NY 10173, ☎ 212/697–2100 or 800/248–8687, or 800/248–7245 in western U.S.).

TRANSPORTATION

Vast distances between cities and towns make air transportation a cost-efficient mode of travel in Scandinavia. SAS is Scandinavia's major air carrier; it also operates domestic lines in Norway, Sweden, and Denmark. SAS offers discount packages for travel among the Scandinavian capitals, as well as reduced domestic fares in the summer.

Trains—comfortable, clean, and fast—are good for covering large distances in Scandinavia. Remember to ask for a smoking or non-smoking seat or compartment. You should inquire with your travel agent about Scanrail Passes for travel within the region.

Another means of getting around Scandinavia's countries is to go by ferry. These huge vessels offer a combination of efficient travel (you sleep aboard and wake up in your destination the next morning) and amenities approaching what you might expect on a cruise ship: luxury dining, gambling, and entertainment. Travelers should beware, however, that the noise level may be high and the crowd is usually very lively.

If you prefer the freedom of planning an itinerary and traveling at your own pace, a rental car is a good, albeit expensive, alternative. Most major car rental companies operate in Scandinavia. Roads are generally good, but allow plenty of time for navigating the region's winding highway network. Scandinavia enforces some of the most strict drinking-and-driving laws in the world—a drunk driver could end up in jail after one offense.

Public transportation in Scandinavia's cities is safe, fast, and inexpensive. Some cities, including the capitals, offer day passes reducing the cost of buses and train travel.

Taxis in Scandinavia are safe, clean, *and* expensive. All taxis should be clearly marked and have a meter inside; unmarked taxis—usually operated illegally by unlicensed drivers—are not recommended. A 10% tip is a friendly gesture, but by no means necessary. Most taxis accept major credit cards and cash.

TRAVEL AGENCIES

A good travel agent puts your needs first. Look for an agency that has been in business at least five years, emphasizes customer service, and has someone on staff who specializes in your destination. In addition, **make sure the agency belongs to the American Society of Travel Agents (ASTA)**. If your travel agency is also acting as your tour operator, *see* Payments *and* Tour Operators, *above*).

➤ LOCAL AGENT REFERRALS: **American Society of Travel Agents** (ASTA, ☎ 800/965–2782 24-hr hot line, FAX 703/684–8319). **Alliance of Canadian Travel Associations** (✉ Suite 201, 1729 Bank St., Ottawa, Ontario K1V 7Z5, ☎ 613/521–0474, FAX 613/521–0805). **Association of British Travel Agents** (✉ 55–57 Newman St., London W1P 4AH, ☎ 0171/637–2444, FAX 0171/637–0713).

TRAVEL GEAR

Travel catalogs specialize in useful items, such as compact alarm clocks and travel irons, that can **save space when packing.** They also offer dual-voltage appliances, currency converters, and foreign-language phrase books.

➤ MAIL-ORDER CATALOGS: **Magellan's** (☎ 800/962–4943, FAX 805/568–5406). **Orvis Travel** (☎ 800/541–

3541, FAX 540/343–7053). Travel-
Smith (☏ 800/950–1600, FAX 800/
950–1656).

U
U.S. GOVERNMENT

The U.S. government can be an excellent source of inexpensive travel
information. When planning your
trip, **find out what government materials are available.**

➤ ADVISORIES: **U.S. Department of
State** (✉ Overseas Citizens Services
Office, Room 4811 N.S., Washington, DC 20520); enclose a self-ad-
dressed, stamped envelope. **Interactive
hot line** (☏ 202/647–5225, FAX 202/
647–3000). **Computer bulletin board**
(☏ 301/946–4400).

➤ PAMPHLETS: **Consumer Information
Center** (✉ Consumer Information
Catalogue, Pueblo, CO 81009,
☏ 719/948–3334 free catalog).

VISITOR INFORMATION

➤ SCANDINAVIAN TOURIST BOARD:
U.S.: (✉ 655 3rd Ave., New York,
New York 10017-5617, ☏ 212/949–
2333, FAX 212/983–5260).

U.K.: Danish Tourist Board (✉ 55
Sloan St., London SW1X 9SY, ☏
071/259–5959, FAX 071/259–5955).
Finnish Tourist Board (✉ 30–35 Pall
Mall, London SW1Y 5LP, ☏ 0171/
839–4048, FAX 0171/321–0696).
Iceland Tourist Information Bureau
(✉ 172 Tottenham Court Rd., London WP1 9LG, ☏ 0171/388–5599,
FAX 0171/387–5711). **Norwegian
Tourist Board** (✉ 5 Lower Regent
St., London SW1Y 4LR, ☏ 0171/
839–6255, FAX 0171/839–6014).
Swedish Travel and Tourism Council
(✉ 73 Welbeck St., London W1M
8AN, ☏ 0171/935–9784, FAX 0171/
935–5853).

W
WHEN TO GO

The Scandinavian tourist season
peaks in June, July, and August,
when daytime temperatures are often
in the 70s (21°C to 26°C) and sometimes rise into the 80s (27°C to
32°C). Detailed temperature charts
are below and in individual country
chapters. In general, the weather is
not overly warm, and a brisk breeze
and brief rainstorms are possible
anytime. Nights can be chilly, even in
summer.

Visit in summer if you want to experience the delightfully long summer
days. In June, the sun rises in Copenhagen at 4 AM and sets at 11 PM and
daylight lasts even longer farther
north, making it possible to continue
your sightseeing into the balmy
evenings. Fall, spring, and even winter are pleasant, despite the area's
reputation for gloom. The days become shorter quickly, but the sun
casts a golden light not seen farther
south.

The Gulf Stream warms Denmark,
the western coast of Norway, and
Iceland, making winters in these
areas similar to those in London.
Even the harbor of Narvik, far to the
north in Norway, remains ice-free
year round. Away from the protection of the Gulf Stream, however,
northern Norway, Sweden, and
Finland experience very cold, clear
weather that attracts skiers; even
Stockholm's harbor, well south in
Sweden but facing the Baltic Sea,
freezes over completely.

CLIMATE

The following are average daily
maximum and minimum temperatures for major Scandinavian cities.

COPENHAGEN

Jan.	36F	2C	May	61F	16C	Sept.	64F	18C
	28	-2		46	8		52	11
Feb.	36F	2C	June	66F	19C	Oct.	54F	12C
	27	-3		52	11		45	7
Mar.	41F	5C	July	72F	22C	Nov.	45F	7C
	30	-1		57	14		37	3
Apr.	52F	11C	Aug.	70F	21C	Dec.	39F	4C
	37	3		57	14		34	1

HELSINKI

Jan.	30F	-1C	May	64F	18C	Sept.	53F	11C
	26	-3		49	9		39	4
Feb.	34F	1C	June	60F	16C	Oct.	46F	8C
	24	-4		48	9		36	2
Mar.	36F	2C	July	68F	20C	Nov.	32F	0C
	26	-3		55	13		26	-3
Apr.	46F	8C	Aug.	64F	18C	Dec.	32F	0C
	32	0		53	12		24	-4

REYKJAVÍK

Jan.	36F	2C	May	50F	10C	Sept.	52F	11C
	28	-2		39	4		43	6
Feb.	37F	3C	June	54F	12C	Oct.	45F	7C
	28	-2		45	7		37	3
Mar.	39F	4C	July	57F	14C	Nov.	39F	4C
	30	-1		48	9		32	0
Apr.	43F	6C	Aug.	57F	14C	Dec.	36F	2C
	34	1		46	8		28	-2

OSLO

Jan.	28F	-2C	May	61F	16C	Sept.	60F	16C
	19	-7		43	6		46	8
Feb.	30F	-1C	June	68F	20C	Oct.	48F	9C
	19	-7		50	10		38	3
Mar.	39F	4C	July	72F	22C	Nov.	38F	3C
	25	-4		55	13		31	-1
Apr.	50F	10C	Aug.	70F	21C	Dec.	32F	0C
	34	1		54	12		25	-4

STOCKHOLM

Jan.	30F	-1C	May	57F	14C	Sept.	59F	15C
	23	-5		43	6		48	9
Feb.	30F	-1C	June	66F	19C	Oct.	48F	9C
	23	-5		52	11		41	5
Mar.	37F	3C	July	72F	22C	Nov.	41F	5C
	25	-4		57	14		34	1
Apr.	46F	8C	Aug.	68F	20C	Dec.	36F	2C
	34	1		55	13		28	-2

➤ FORECASTS: **Weather Channel Connection** (☎ 900/932–8437, 95¢ per minute from a Touch-Tone phone).

1 Destination: Scandinavia

FAIRY TALES AND FJORDS

THE ISLANDS OF STOCKHOLM mirrored in the water, the ships and Little Mermaid of Copenhagen, Oslo and its majestic fjord, the bay and peninsulas of Helsinki, Reykjavík with its busy deep-blue harbor: The capitals of Scandinavia are unthinkable without the water that surrounds and sustains them.

What is true of the capitals is equally true of the countries. Denmark consists of one peninsula and more than 400 islands, half of them inhabited. Finland and Sweden used to dispute which country was really "the land of a thousand lakes." Finland settled it, after counting almost 190,000. An island summer in the archipelago is part of every Stockholmer's childhood memory. The mail packets of Norway's *Hurtigruten* sail north from Bergen along the fjord-indented coast and turn around at Kirkenes on the Russian border, 2,000 km (1,242) later. Iceland is so dependent on the surrounding sea that it has been known to take on the British navy to protect its fishing limits.

Water has never separated the Scandinavian nations. In the early days it was far easier to cross a stretch of water than it was to penetrate dense and trackless forests. It was their mastery of shipbuilding that enabled the Vikings to rule the waves 1,000 years ago. Their ocean-going ships could be beached, and this gave them the advantage of surprise.

Viking exploration and conquests ranged from North America to the Black Sea and from Greenland to Majorca. These voyagers developed the angular Runic alphabet, ideal for carving in stone. In Sweden alone, more than 2,000 runic stones still stand, in memory of Vikings who fell in far-away battles. The Vikings also devised a complex mythology and created literature of such realism and immediacy that even today the Icelandic sagas can be read with admiration and enjoyment.

You might think that, with so much in common, the Scandinavians would keep peace among themselves, but this was not to be. By the 11th century the passion that had inflamed the Vikings was spent, and Christianity defeated the old beliefs. The Swedes departed on a dubious crusade to conquer the Finns and annex their land. The Norwegians, having colonized Iceland, squabbled among themselves and disappeared as a nation for 500 years. By the 16th century, Scandinavia was divided between Denmark and Sweden, bound together by mutual antagonism. The two countries were at war with one another for a total of 134 years, and the conflict was perpetuated by history books written from nationalistic points of view.

What happened in the distant past has acquired the status of myth and deeply influenced the Scandinavians' self-image. Modern history has left more obvious marks. Allegiances and dependencies were reshuffled early in the 19th century as a consequence of the Napoleonic Wars, which transformed the European landscape. Sweden lost Finland, which spent the next 100 years as a czarist province. Norway declared its independence from Denmark but was thrust into a union with Sweden.

Scandinavian cultures thrived throughout these years. Artist Akseli Gallen-Kallela painted the scenes of a mythical past that Jean Sibelius fashioned into tone poems. Norway experienced a cultural renaissance, led by artists such as Edvard Grieg, Henrik Ibsen, and Edvard Munch. From Denmark came philosopher Søren Kierkegaard, writer Hans Christian Andersen, and the composer Carl Nielsen. Sweden produced the painters Anders Zorn and Carl Larsson and dramatist August Strindberg.

Large-scale emigration to the United States (including a million Swedes) peaked during the latter half of the century, only decades before new industries transformed the old farming economy.

In the early years of this century the Norwegians finally became masters in their own house. This could not have happened without strong nationalist sentiment, and it is to the credit of both Norway and Sweden that the divorce was amicable. The Russian revolution brought civil war to Finland, followed by independence, for the first time in that nation's history. Finland was attacked again in 1939, by Stalin's forces, and was eventually defeated but never occupied. Denmark and Norway, attacked by Germany in 1940, were not spared that fate. After the war had ended, Iceland declared its independence from Denmark.

Denmark, Norway, and Iceland are members of NATO. Denmark is also a fully paid member of the European Union. Sweden and Finland also joined the EU in January 1995. Norwegians, however, turned down the government's proposal for EU membership in a referendum in 1994, and did not join with its neighbors.

Scandinavians, like the British, often talk of Europe as though they were not part of it. They see themselves as different. They dream of the *joie de vivre* that they believe all southerners enjoy, but maintain that the moral fiber and know-how of the Scandinavians are superior to anything you find south of the border.

It used to be said that sick-leave levels were so high in Sweden that there were more sick people in a factory than in a hospital. Scandinavians in all five countries have become so used to high levels of social services that the political coloration of the government seems to matter less, as long as the services are delivered. This requirement is not easily squared with the vociferous demand for lower taxes, but compromises are being made. In Sweden, for example, the government and labor unions agreed to make the first day of sick leave an unpaid day, virtually evaporating the absenteeism that led to the old factory–hospital joke.

More than the rest of Europe, Scandinavia has been influenced by the American lifestyle and its ethos of professionalism. This coexists, sometimes precariously, with the "socialism with a human face" that has influenced these societies for the past 50 years or more. Among the measures introduced recently is Sweden's 12-month maternity–paternity leave, which requires fathers to take at least 30 days for themselves—an idea that was decried as madness has done wonders for marriage and fatherhood.

The English language, too, has influenced the Scandinavians, who are not bound by a native language. Iceland was colonized from Norway, but present day Icelandic is

incomprehensible to other Scandinavians. Finnish, like Hungarian, is one of the enigmatic Finno-Ugric languages. Danish, a language rich in glottal stops, is not understood by many Swedes, and Danish TV programs have to be subtitled. Norwegian, in pronunciation and vocabulary halfway between Danish and Swedish, sometimes serves as an intra-Scandinavian mode of communication. But get a group of Scandinavians together and what are they most likely to speak? English.

THERE IS STILL MUCH TRUTH in the myth of the taciturn Scandinavian. A story tells of the two Danes, two Norwegians, and two Swedes who were marooned on a desert island. When a rescue party arrived six months later, they found that the two Danes had started a cooperative and that the two Norwegians had founded a local chapter of the patriotic society Sons of Norway. The two Swedes were waiting to be introduced.

Stereotypes about national characteristics abound among Scandinavians. Danes believe the saving grace of humor will take the sting out of most of life's vicissitudes. The Finns attribute their survival to their *sisu,* or true grit. Icelanders are known as a nation of hard workers, singers, and drinkers, who think there is always a way for things to get fixed. The Norwegians find virtue in being, like Ibsen's Peer Gynt, *sig selv nok,* which means self-reliant in all things. The Swedes, the most introspective of the lot, take pride in their reliability and admit to "Royal Swedish envy" as their principal vice.

The strain of melancholy that runs through the Scandinavian character becomes pronounced in the lonely north. In Finland, the most popular dance—one in which dance halls specialize to the exclusion of all others—is the tango, precisely because it is so sad. But there's no need to look only to Argentine imports: Virtually all Scandinavian folk music, even when rhythms are rapid and gay, is in a minor key.

Perhaps this tendency to melancholia is natural in a region where solitude abounds. In northern Scandinavia the woods close in, pine and spruce mingling with white-trunked birches, with a clearing or a field here and there. Farther north the hegemony of the forest becomes complete, challenged only by the lakes. On a clear night, from an aircraft, the moonlight is reflected in so many lakes that it seems to cut a shining path to the horizon.

But the forest is not as silent and lonely as you might think. Walk along a Scandinavian country road on an evening in early summer, and you will hear the barking of roe deer at your approach and the forlorn hooting of loons from the lakes. You will see stately moose coming out of the woods to graze in the fields. Juniper bushes cast long, eerie shadows, and on a hilltop skeletal pines are silhouetted against a still clear sky. No wonder that in ages past, popular imagination peopled these forests with sprites and trolls and giants.

Having a summer home is not a great luxury in Scandinavia. On Friday afternoons there are traffic jams in Oslo, as the Norwegians escape to their cabins in the mountainous interior. In Stockholm the waterways are clogged with motorboats heading for summer cottages in the archipelago. The Finns and Icelanders, less urbanized than their neighbors, almost always have a village or isolated farmstead they consider their real home.

Modern Scandinavia is largely a secular society, but woods and lakes hold a special mystique. A midnight boat ride on an island-studded lake, with the moon suspended just above the treetops, is very close to a religious experience for the people of the north, as their souls fill with a tremendous wistfulness and a sense of simultaneous sadness and joy.

— Eric Sjogren

Eric Sjogren, a Swedish travel writer based in Brussels, is a frequent contributor to the New York Times *and other publications.*

NEW AND NOTEWORTHY

Denmark

In 1998, Roskilde celebrates its 1,000 year anniversary. Established in 998 by Harald Bluetooth, it served as the country's first capital and center for trade, art, science, and religion. Concerts, performances, and exhibits will run all year, and on June

23, Midsummer Eve will be celebrated with a huge fireworks display over the fjord. On September 5th, a cultural blowout will keep shops, cinemas, museums, and libraries open late into the night. Call the Roskilde Tourist Board for a schedule of events.

The biennial Golden Days in Copenhagen, held September 4–20 in 1998, celebrate the artistic flowering of the city between 1800 and 1850, highlighting the work of luminaries such as author Hans Christian Andersen, philosopher Søren Kierkegaard, sculptor Bertil Thorvaldsen, and painter Kristoffer Eckersberg. Exhibitions, concerts, ballet performances, poetry, literature readings, and walking tours top the list of enlightening events.

The last leg of Denmark's interpretation of the Channel Tunnel, the Storebæltsbro (the Great Belt) rail and automobile link between Fyn and Sjælland, is scheduled for completion in June 1998. Construction of the bridge connecting Copenhagen and Malmö, Sweden, is underway, with completion estimated for the year 2000.

Plans to streamline travel between Copenhagen Airport and the city center are in the works: Cars are expected to make the trip from city center on the new highway in 10 minutes; the newest extension of the city train system will supposedly get you to the airport in an astonishing eight minutes. In addition, by 2005 the Copenhagen Airport will be improved by a cool $1 billion addition, showing off a swank Danish-designed refurbishment: linked international and domestic terminals, a new train terminal with check-in facilities, and an east terminal primarily for SAS and its partner airlines, notably Lufthansa. The total number of gates will increase from 35 to 80.

Finland

Once one of Europe's most expensive countries, Finland has become more financially reasonable and—in spite of a persistent unemployment problem—enjoys close to zero inflation. In fact, food prices have dropped since the nation joined the EU in 1995.

Cross-border travel between Finland and its former Soviet neighbors, Russia and Estonia, continues to grow rapidly in both directions. In particular, the Estonian capital, Tallinn, with its medieval Old Town and bargain shopping, is a popular day-trip destination from Helsinki. A one-way trip there takes an hour and a half by hydrofoil, three and a half by ferry. Finland has strengthened its links with its Baltic neighbors, and Finland's Baltic coast region is emerging, year by year, with its own identity. This will be exemplified in the Biennale Balticum art event in Rauma, on the southwest coast, scheduled for summer 1998 with the theme of change.

Spring '98 will herald the opening of Helsinki's new Nykytaidemusco (Museum of Contemporary Art), marking the unveiling of American architect Stephen Holl's daring new structure. Meanwhile, the Suomen Kansallismuseo (National Museum) is closed for renovation until December 1999—just before Helsinki is honored as the Cultural Capital of Europe in 2000, one of nine European cities to share the honor that year.

In 1998, Finland celebrates the 100th anniversary of the birth of architect Alvar Aalto, who helped put Finnish design on the map. The town of Jyväskylä features the greatest concentration of his buildings and will be a hub of celebration.

Iceland

With the economic decline in Germany, once a reliable source of many visitors to Iceland, Iceland's tourism industry is diversifying targets and intensifying efforts to lure you to Iceland. As part of this, Icelandair will be adding Minneapolis, Minnesota, to its flight schedule in spring '98. Deregulation has occurred in local air travel, and Icelandair domestic is now Air Iceland, having merged with smaller Norlandair. The resulting fierce competition with Íslandsflug airlines has brought a welcome drop in domestic air prices. Competition is indeed stiffening in all aspects of tourism, since the krónur has been unusually strong in relation to other currencies and, alas, there seems to be no leeway for lower taxes.

President Ólafur Ragnar Grímsson has become an ally in promoting cultural heritage as a tourist attraction. He even suggested to President Bill Clinton that the United States and Iceland jointly celebrate the year 2000 as the 1,000th anniversary of Leifur Eiríksson's discovery voyage from Iceland to North America. Iceland-born astronaut Bjarni Tryggvason made his own recent voyage of discovery on the namesake space shuttle, allowing Icelanders a dramatic rekindling of their tradition of exploring new worlds.

No rekindling was needed for one of Iceland's volcanoes, which made headlines by melting a hole through Europe's largest glacier, Vatnajökull, and caused massive flooding. Though only temporary, flood damage to bridges and roads reinforced the need for better paved roads throughout the country—good news both to drivers and the rapidly growing number of visiting bicyclists.

Volcanic aftermath has also driven home the importance of preserving existing flora and continuing reforestation and nature conservation. In addition to the area around Reykjavík's Norræna Húsið (Nordic House), another wetland preserve has been established near the southern village of Eyrarbakki to spare water-bird nesting sites.

Norway

At the end of 1997, Norway's economic boom was in full swing. Despite Norway's Euroskepticism—and some say because of it—the country's economy has never looked better. The rate of unemployment sunk so low in 1997 that companies feared a labor shortage and slowly started enlisting immigrants to do many jobs. The boom is thanks in large part to the discovery, between 1995 and 1997, of at least 20 new oil and gas fields in the Norwegian sector of the North Sea. What the booming economy means for travellers is more museums to visit and better services, since the government tends to invest in tourism and educational projects. Hotels and restaurants remain expensive, but Norway's membership in the European Economic Area helps exert a downward pressure on prices.

At the end of 1996, Norway's longtime Prime Minister, Gro Harlem Brundtland, surprised everyone by quitting her job. Brundtland had been a supporter of joining the EU and saw Norway's 1994 rejection as a major political defeat. The Labor Party's Thorbjorn Jagland replaced Brundtland.

Ever nostalgic, Lillehammer will inaugurate Norway's new Olympic Museum in 1998. A series of life-sized multimedia exhibits will celebrate the history of the

Olympics, starting with the 1896 Athens Games and recapping Lillehammer's own 1994 Winter Games.

North Americans just can't get enough of the fjords, according to the Norwegian Tourist Board. It reported a 20 percent increase in fjord cruise traffic in 1996 and thanked Americans and Canadians for being the third most frequent cruise takers. One of those fjord towns, Alesund, is celebrating its 150th birthday in 1998, with festivities planned througout the year.

Sweden

Scandinavia's largest country, Sweden has always been politically independent and commercially prolific, but despite strong exports, domestically Swedes are still fighting the effects of the worst economic recession to hit the country since the 1930s. The downturn began in the late '80s and shook the very foundations of Sweden's social structure, changing it in a way that not even the country's membership of the EU, which it joined in January 1995, could measurably influence.

But this is good news for you, as the weak kronor means that Sweden has become a relatively inexpensive place to vacation, although hotel and restaurant prices are still relatively higher than those in the United States.

Stockholm will be the 1998 Cultural Capital of Europe, and in the nick of time the Moderna Museet (Museum of Modern Art) has moved back to its newly refurbished home on Skeppsholmen. The yearlong celebrations and the strength of the dollar will make travel to Sweden in 1998 even more appealing.

WHAT'S WHERE

Denmark

The Kingdom of Denmark dapples the Baltic Sea in an archipelago of some 450 islands and the arc of one peninsula. Measuring 43,069 square km (16,628 square mi), with a population of 5 million, it is the geographical link between Scandinavia and Europe.

The island of Sjælland, the largest of the Danish isles, is the most popular tourist destination. Here you'll find Copenhagen, Scandinavia's largest city (population 1.5 million), Denmark's capital, and the seat of the oldest kingdom in the world. If there's such as a thing as a cozy city, this is it: Bicycles spin alongside cars in the narrow streets, and a handful of skyscrapers are tucked away amid cafés, museums, and quaint old homes. To the north of the city are royal castles (including Helsingør's Kronberg of *Hamlet* fame) and ritzy beach towns. To the west, Roskilde holds relics of medieval Denmark. And to the west and south, rural towns and farms edge up to beach communities and fine white beaches, often surrounded by forests.

Fyn (Funen), the smaller of the country's two main islands, is the site of Denmark's third-largest city, Odense, the birthplace of Hans Christian Andersen. It's no wonder this area inspired many fairy tales: 1,120 km (700 mi) of coastline and lush stretches of vegetable and flower gardens are punctuated by manor houses, beech glades, castles, swan ponds, and thatched houses.

Jylland, Denmark's western peninsula, shares its southern border with Germany. At the northern tip lies Skagen, a luminous, dune-covered point, and just below it are Århus and Aalborg, respectively Denmark's second- and fourth-largest cities. The heart of the peninsula, mostly lakeland and beech forests, is dotted with castles and parklands and is home to the famed Legoland. Along the east coast, deep fjords are rimmed by forests. The south holds marshlands, gabled houses, and Ribe, Denmark's oldest town.

Finally, there's the island of Bornholm, 177 km (110 mi) southeast of Sjælland, with a temperate climate that distinguishes it from the rest of Denmark. Bornholm's natural beauty and winsomely rustic towns have earned it the title of Pearl of the Baltic.

Finland

Finland is one of the world's northernmost countries, with its entire Lapland region above the Arctic Circle. It's a country of beautiful scenery and strong, spirited citizens. Sweden and Russia fought over the land for centuries, but the Finns themselves are neither Scandinavian nor Slavic. Helsinki, the capital since 1812, is a meeting ground for eastern and western Europe. Built on peninsulas and islands along the Baltic coast, the city's streets curve around bays, and bridges arch across to nearby islands. Stunning architecture abounds, from 19th-century neoclassical buildings to sleek, modern high-rises. Helsinki is the country's cultural hub and home to one-sixth of the nation's population.

In the southwest lies Turku, the former capital. Founded more than 750 years ago, the city was the main gateway through which cultural influences reached Finland over the centuries. It remains a busy harbor, from which you can sail for the rugged and fascinating autonomous Åland Islands. Encompassing some 6,500 of the more than 30,000 islands that form the magnificent archipelago along Finland's coastline, the Ålands were long the subject of a territorial dispute between Finland and Sweden. The islands are home to many families that fish or run small farms, and the rural settlements form an intriguing contrast with the striking coastal scenery.

Eastern and central Finland are dimpled with nearly 200,000 lakes, most fringed with tiny cabins—Finnish vacation institutions. Amid the many delightful small towns of the Lakelands, the larger Savonlinna is hugged by gigantic Lake Saimaa and is worth a visit for its waterbound scenery and cultural life. Opera, drama, ballet, and instrumental performances fill the month of July at the Savonlinna Opera festival.

Lapland, north of the Arctic Circle, remains unspoiled wilderness. Summer is a time of round-the-clock daylight, whereas the winter landscape is lit only by reflections on the snow. As the area has become more accessible, comfortable hotels and modern amenities have popped up, but nature is the star attraction: reindeer—there are more than 300,000 here—great forests, gin-clear streams, and the midnight sun's reflection on a lake's dark water.

Iceland

Iceland is the westernmost outpost of Europe, 800 km (500 mi) from the nearest European landfall in Scotland, and more than 80% of its 103,000 square km (40,000 mi) remains uninhabited. The capital city of Reykjavík is home to half the island's 250,000 citizens. Set on a fjord, against the backdrop of Mt. Esja,

the city's concrete houses, with their red, blue, and green roofs, create a vibrant tableau. The thriving arts scene here includes theater, ballet, symphonies, museums, and private galleries. An hour's drive from Reykjavík is Þingvellir, a national park and a symbol of the nation's heritage. In AD 930, settler Grímur Geitskór chose it as the meeting site of the Icelandic general congress. In the north, Akureyri, Iceland's second-largest city, offers several museums and the Lystigarðurinn (Arctic Botanical Gardens). The east coast's Hallormsstaður Forestry Reserve offers camping spots in the country's largest forest. Throughout the island, waterfalls and fjords are sites of stunning natural beauty.

Norway

Norway, roughly 400,000 square km (155,000 square mi), is about the same size as California. Approximately 30% of this long, narrow country is covered with clear lakes, lush forests, and rugged mountains. Western Norway, bordered by the Norwegian Sea and the Atlantic Ocean, is the fabled land of the fjords—few places on earth can match the power and splendor of this land. The magnificent Sognefjord, the longest inlet in western Norway, is only one of many fjords found here, including the Hardangerfjord, Geirangerfjord, Lysefjord, and Nordfjord.

Bergen, often hailed as the "Fjord Capital of Norway," is the second-largest city in the country. The cobblestone streets, well-preserved buildings at the Bryggen, and seven mountains that surround the city all add to its storybook charm.

Eastern Norway, bordered by Sweden, and by Finland and Russia to the north, is punctuated by rolling hills, abundant valleys, and fresh lakes—much more subdued than the landscape of the west. Near Gudbrandsdalen (Gudbrands Valley) you'll find Lillehammer, the site of the 1994 Winter Olympics. Almost directly south, rising from the shores of the Oslofjord, is the capital of Norway—Oslo. With a population of about a half million, Oslo is a friendly, manageable city.

If you follow the coast south, you'll come to Kristiansand, one of Sørlandet's (the Southland's) leading cities. Sørlandet is known for its long stretches of unspoiled, uncrowded beach. Stavanger, farther west, is one of the most cosmopolitan cities in

Scandinavia—its oil and gas industry draws people from around the globe.

Halfway between Oslo and Bergen lies Hardangervidda (Hardanger Plateau), Norway's largest national park. At the foot of the plateau is Geilo, one of the country's most popular ski resorts. Almost directly north is the bustling city of Trondheim.

From here, a thin expanse of land stretches up to the Nordkapp (North Cape). Known as the Land of the Midnight Sun (the display of the northern lights in the winter is pretty amazing, too), this region is marked with exquisite landscapes: glaciers, fjords, and rocky coasts. Narvik, a major Arctic port, is the gateway to the Lofoten Islands, where puffins and penguins march about. Even farther north is one of Norway's major universities, Tromsø, the lifeline to settlements and research centers at the North Pole. At the very top of Norway is the county of Finnmark, where many Sami (native Laplanders) live. Access to the area is primarily through Hammerfest, Europe's northernmost city, where the sun is not visible from November 21 to January 21, but is uninterrupted May 17 through July 29.

Sweden

In Sweden, streamlined, ultramodern cities give way to lush forests and timbered farmhouses, and modern western European democracy coexists with strong affection for a monarchy. With 277,970 square km (107,324 square mi) for only 8.6 million residents, almost all have room to live as they choose.

Stockholm, one of Europe's most beautiful capitals, is built on 14 small islands. Bustling, skyscraper-lined boulevards are a short walk from twisting medieval streets in this modern yet pastoral city. South of the city, in Småland province, are isolated villages whose names are bywords when it comes to fine crystal glassware: Kosta, Orrefors, Boda, and Strömbergshyttan. Skåne, the country's southernmost province, is an area of fertile plains, sand beaches, scores of castles and manor houses, thriving farms, medieval churches, and summer resorts.

Sweden's second-largest city, Göteborg, is on the west coast. A Viking port in the 11th century, today the city is home to the Scandinavium indoor arena; Nordstan,

one of Europe's largest indoor shopping malls; and Liseberg, Scandinavia's largest amusement park. A cruise on the Göta Canal provides a picturesque coast-to-coast journey through the Swedish countryside.

Dalarna, the central region of Sweden, is considered the most typically Swedish of all the country's 24 provinces, a place of forests, mountains, and red-painted wooden farmhouses and cottages by the shores of pristine, sun-dappled lakes. The north of Sweden, Norrland, is a place of wide-open spaces. Golden eagles soar above snowcapped crags; huge salmon fight their way up wild, tumbling rivers; rare orchids bloom in Arctic heathland; wild rhododendrons splash the land with color.

GREAT ITINERARIES

Our itineraries suggest ways in which Scandinavian destinations can be combined; note they tend to allow the minimum amount of time needed in various destinations. Elements from different itineraries can be combined to create an itinerary that suits your interests.

Sand, Surf, and Ships, Scandinavia-Style

Scandinavia is defined by water. Glaciers, rivers, and sea tides determine the geography; oceans shape the history and culture. Tiny Denmark, for example, would probably not exist as a country today, except that it sticks up like a cork in the bottleneck entrance to the Baltic Sea, making it strategically important for great shipping and trading countries such as England, which has both attacked and defended the country over trading issues during the past 400 years. What better way, then, to see the land of the Vikings than by water?

Duration
2 weeks

Main Route
3 NIGHTS: DENMARK➤ Fly to Copenhagen. Explore the city and its waterways: Nyhavn's tall ships and myriad

restaurants; Christianshavn, with its encircling moat and canals reflecting colorful old buildings; and the canal-ringed palace of Christiansborg, where you can visit the Danish Parliament and the royal reception rooms. Enjoy the twinkling lights and happy atmosphere of Tivoli from May to September. Take a harbor cruise, passing the Little Mermaid perched on her rock. Sun on the beaches north of town or sail the Øresund—maybe even all the way around Sjælland. You'll love the museum castle of Frederiksborg, set in its lake an hour north of Copenhagen, and the Karen Blixen Museum at Rungstedlund. Continue by air to Stockholm.

6 NIGHTS: SWEDEN➤ Beautiful Stockholm comprises 14 islands surrounded by sparkling water, clean enough for fishing and swimming even in the city center. You can take ferries all around town and out into the enchantingly lovely archipelago, with its 24,000 islands. Don't miss the picturesque Old Town, the new museum for the salvaged 17th-century warship *Vasa,* or Skansen, the world's oldest open-air museum.

From Stockholm, take the train across Sweden to Göteborg, where you can explore the west-coast beaches warmed by the Gulf Stream. Try sea fishing or windsurfing, and visit the 17th-century fortress of Elfsborg, guarding the harbor entrance. Take a ferry to Oslo.

5 NIGHTS: NORWAY➤ In Oslo, visit the Viking Ship and Kon-Tiki museums and the fabulous Frogner sculpture park. The Bergen Railway will carry you across the roof of Norway in 6½ dramatic hours. If you can spare an extra day, stop in Myrdal for a side trip on the Flåm Railway and a short cruise on the beautiful Aurland Fjord before continuing to Bergen. Here you'll enjoy Bryggen, a collection of reconstructed houses dating from the Hansa period in the 14th century, the famous fish market, and funicular. Marvel at the magnificent, ever-changing Norwegian coastline aboard a steamship to Trondheim, from which you can fly to Oslo or Copenhagen, then home.

ALTERNATE NIGHTS: BORNHOLM AND GOTLAND➤ If you already know Copenhagen and Stockholm, consider visiting the beautiful islands of Bornholm (the Danish Pearl of the Baltic) or Sweden's Gotland. Bornholm is graced by lovely scenery and beaches perfect for surfing and sailing; excellent golf courses; one of the largest castle ruins in Scandinavia; and some charming architecture, including the famous round churches from the 12th and 13th centuries. You can reach it by ferry from Copenhagen or from Ystad, in southern Sweden, bringing your car if you like.

Gotland is the largest island in the Baltic, with peaceful little towns and fishing villages, and a picturesque capital, Visby, with a medieval flavor and a well-preserved city wall dating from the 14th and 15th centuries. "Medieval Week" in early August is celebrated with mummers, knights, tournaments, and lots of other special attractions. Ferries sail from Stockholm and several other Swedish ports.

Information
☞ Chapters 2, 5, and 6

Scandinavian Mountains

If you like snow-clad mountains, Scandinavia has plenty of terrain for you: glacier climbing, reindeer and dogsledding, cross-country skiing, and just plain old hiking amid gorgeous surroundings.

Duration
2 weeks

Main Route
5 NIGHTS: NORWAY➤ Fly to Oslo and then on to Bodø or another destination in northern Norway. Some of the country's most striking ranges are the Lofoten and Vesterålen mountains, near Bodø, along with the Lyngen Peninsula in Troms. Begin with a four-day hiking tour or a glacier walk guided by **Den Norske Turistforening** (DNT, Norwegian Mountain Touring Association, ✉ Postboks 1963 Vika, N–0125 Oslo 1, ☎ 22/82–28–00, FAX 22/83–24–78). From Bodø, fly to Narvik; then take the train to Kiruna, Sweden, the largest town in Swedish Lapland.

5 NIGHTS: SWEDEN➤ Welcome to the Arctic Circle, the land of the midnight sun, where the sun stays above the horizon 24 hours during the summer solstice. In Kiruna, join a three-day white water canoeing trip. Take a rest, rent a car, and visit the beaver colonies at Ramsele and the fine collection of Sami art in Jokkmokk. Drive to Gällivare, where the Sami celebrate their annual church festivals. Drive or

take the train to Rovaniemi, Finland, about 323 km (200 mi) from Kiruna, a five- or six-hour drive. Watch out for deer and other animals on the road.

4 NIGHTS: FINLAND➤ Rovaniemi is an end point for the Road of the Four Winds, or, simply, the Arctic Road, which runs 1,000 km (620 mi) north from Helsinki. In summer, look for the salmon-fishing competition, reindeer herding, gold panning, logging, and the Russian Orthodox Skolt Lappish festivals that are held throughout the region. Fly from Rovaniemi to Helsinki and then home.

Information

☞ Chapters 3, 5, and 6

Tracing the Vikings

Traces can still be found of the seafaring warriors who, from the 8th through the 11th century, traded with, settled in, or raided the part of the world that became known as Western Europe, Iceland, Greenland, Labrador, Newfoundland, and Russia. The Vikings' 1,000-year-old remains are scattered throughout Scandinavia and provide a fascinating record of their culture.

Duration

10 days

Main Route

3 NIGHTS: DENMARK➤ Begin in Copenhagen with a visit to the Nationalmuseet, which has many Viking exhibits labeled in English; one discusses how the Vikings could navigate their ships across vast oceans at a time when most people believed the world was flat. Take the hour-long train ride to the Vikingeskibshallen (Viking Ship Museum) in Roskilde, where five ships found in the Roskilde Fjord and dating from around AD 1000 have been restored. At the nearby Lejre Forsøgscenter (Lejre Archaeological Research Center), you can see how the Vikings lived. On the way back, visit Trelleborg in western Sjælland, where you'll find the remains of a staging area for troops led by Knud (Canute), who in 1016 became king of England, Denmark, Norway, and part of Sweden. In May, you can enjoy a colorful Viking pageant in the lovely park at Frederikssund.

Rent a car or take a train and stay overnight in Vejle, on the large peninsula of Jylland; then head for Jelling, where two Viking kings—Gorm the Old and his son, Harald Bluetooth, Knud's great-grandfather—reigned. They left two large burial mounds and two runic stones, dating from around AD 950. In June, attend a performance of the Viking play *The Stoneship* on Fårup Sø.

If you have more time, you can visit many other Viking sites in Denmark: Ribe, Denmark's oldest town and site of a Viking village open-air museum; Hedeby; Høje, where graves are marked by four-ft-tall stones placed in the pattern of a ship; Moesgård museum near Århus; Fyrkat, a 10th-century ring fortress near Hobro; Lindholm; Mammen; Aggersborg; and Viborg. Return to Copenhagen and fly to Oslo, Norway.

3 NIGHTS: NORWAY➤ Go straight to the Vikingskiphuset (Oslo Viking Ship Museum), where you'll see the finest single collection of excavated and preserved Viking ships, once used as burial sepulchres for nobles. Families can entertain the children at VikingLandet, an Oslo amusement park re-creating Viking-era adventures. The next day, in Oslo's Historisk Museum, you'll find beautiful jewelry from the 9th century: gold necklaces, silver ornaments, and "gripping beasts"— whimsical monsters fashioned from amber and other materials. Fly to Stockholm.

4 NIGHTS: SWEDEN➤ In the Historiska Museet you'll find swords, saddlery, and wonderful Viking gold jewelry, including amulets shaped as hammers, the symbol of Thor, the thunder god. At Gamla Uppsala (Old Uppsala), an easy drive north of Stockholm, burial grounds for three 6th-century Viking monarchs remain. In summer take the ferry to the island of Gotland in time for the Folk Sports Olympiad to see games the way they were played in the distant past. One contest, known as *varpa*, is won by tossing a stone nearest a stake. Another, *stångstörtning*, involves the tossing of 16-ft poles. In the Gotland Historiska Museet, you'll find valuables that were buried with the Vikings, including Arabic, Byzantine, German, Bohemian, Hungarian, and Anglo-Saxon coins that reflect the warriors' wanderings. Return to Stockholm and then home.

Information

☞ Chapters 2, 5, and 6

Architecture and Crafts

Scandinavian design—furniture, architecture, and crafts—is world renowned.

Duration

11 days

Main Route

3 NIGHTS: DENMARK➤ Strolling through Copenhagen you'll be amazed by the number of beautiful buildings, punctuated by green copper spires and tinkling fountains. Don't miss the 15th-century Helligånds Kirken (Church of the Holy Ghost) and the Gothic Vor Frelsers Kirken (Church of Our Saviour). Brick Renaissance buildings date from the reign of King Christian IV. The Børsen (Stock Exchange) is surmounted by a spire of twisting dragontails. The exquisite Rosenborg Slot (Rosenborg Castle) in its flowery park houses the crown jewels, royal art, and furniture, including the famous life-size silver lions. From the Rundetårn (Round Tower), Copenhagen's first observatory, you'll see the old town spread out like a map. Enjoy charming Gråbrødretorv and the colorful old buildings reflected in the canals of Nyhavn and Christianshavn. Monumental are Christiansborg Slot, housing the Parliament and royal reception rooms, and Amalienborg, home of the royal family. Examples of modern monumentality are the exciting Tycho Brahe Planetarium and the golden brick mass of Gruntvig Church. An hour north of Copenhagen, visit the museum castles of Frederiksborg in Hillerød and Kronborg (Hamlet's castle) in Helsingør.

Danish applied art is famed for fine design and high quality. In Copenhagen, visit Illum's Bolighus, a mecca for all kinds of home furnishings, and have a gourmet lunch at Paustian, where fine contemporary furniture and accessories are installed in a building by the Danish architect Jørn Utzon (of Sydney Opera House renown). Enjoy the porcelain showrooms of Royal Copenhagen and Bing & Grøndahl. Watch exquisite glass being blown at the Holmegård Glass factory, about an hour south of town. Visit the Georg Jensen Museum and the Kunstindustrimuseet (Museum of Decorative Art), with its Rococo buildings and fine exhibits of European and Asian crafts. His-

torical walking tours in English are held daily and are the best introduction to the city's architecture. Take the overnight train or fly to Stockholm.

2 NIGHTS: SWEDEN➤ Stroll around Stockholm's Gamla Stan (Old Town) for views of the magnificent 700-year-old cathedral and the 608-room Kungliga Slottet (Royal Palace). From the tower of the beautiful modern Stadshuset (City Hall)—with its handmade brickwork and golden mosaics—gaze over Stockholm's 14 islands and glittering, clean waters. Visit the Skansen open-air museum's collection of 150 regional buildings and handicraft shops, ending with dinner, a concert, or outdoor entertainment. The National Museet has a fine collection of Scandinavian applied arts, while the Nordiska Museet documents examples of daily life from the past 500 years. Noteworthy is the Vasa Museet's fabulous warship, recently raised from where it sank on its maiden voyage in 1628. Slightly outside the city, visit the Ulriksdal Slott and park and Millesgården, or Carl Milles Sculpture Garden, in Lidingö. If you can spend an extra day, take a ferry or drive to Gripsholm Slott or Drottningholm, the royal residence. Alternatively, drive to Insjöen to visit Säterglänten, a center for courses in traditional crafts; or take a train to Växjö and see the Småland Museum glass collection of startling Swedish designs in crystal. From Stockholm, take the overnight ferry to Helsinki.

5 NIGHTS: FINLAND➤ The Taideteollisuusmuseo (Museum of Applied Arts) will give you an overview of the development of Finnish architecture and design. See the fine neoclassical Senaatintori (Senate Square) and the Art Nouveau buildings at Eira and Katajanokka, as well as Eliel Saarinen's Helsinki railway station from 1914. Don't miss Finlandiatalo, the concert hall designed by Finland's greatest architect, Alvar Aalto; the Temppeliaukio Kirkko, hollowed out from rock with only its dome showing; or the magnificent sculpture commemorating the composer Jean Sibelius. The Gallen-Kallela Estate is a studio-castle in the National Romantic style built on a rocky peninsula, designed by the artist for his paintings, drawings, sculpture, textiles, and furniture. Check with the University of Industrial Arts in Helsinki, the largest of its kind in Scandinavia, on its current exhibits, often held

in collaboration with Design Forum Finland. Fine china and pottery are displayed at the Arabia Museum and traditional folk handicrafts at the Virkki Museum of Handicrafts. Visit the Artek factory, which features furniture by Alvar Aalto, and the Marimekko and Vuokko textile factories. Rent a car to visit the Suomen Lasimuseo (Finnish Glass Museum), 50 km (31 mi) north of Helsinki in Riihimäki, with permanent exhibits on glassmaking and exhibitions of old Finnish glassware and crystal as well as works by contemporary designers. Stop by the Hvitträsk, a turn-of-the-century studio designed by and for three Finnish architects as a laboratory for their aesthetic principles.

From Helsinki take a ferry to Suomenlinna Island fortress, partly built by Russians, where you will find the Nordic Art Center. Also stop in at the garden city of Käpylä, a residential area built in the 1920s in a unique neoclassical style reminiscent of traditional Finnish wood architecture. If you have time, drive or take a bus along the King's Road, west to Lovisa or east to Turku. This historic road affords spectacular coastal views and is studded with buildings and monuments of interest.

Information

☞ Chapters 2, 3, and 6

FODOR'S CHOICE

Dining

Denmark

★ **Kong Hans, Copenhagen.** Franco-Danish-Asian inspired dishes, from foie gras with raspberry-vinegar sauce to warm oysters with salmon roe, are served in a subterranean space with whitewashed walls and vaulted ceilings. *$$$$*

★ **Restaurant Le St. Jacques, Copenhagen.** Though the chef and owners come from some of the finest restaurants in town, this unassuming little place manages a casual, friendly ambience—and some of the most creative seasonal cuisine around. *$$*

Finland

★ **Alexander Nevski, Helsinki.** Czarist-era dishes are the specialty at this Russian restaurant—try the roast bear in a pot. *$$$$*

★ **Kynsilaukka, Helsinki.** Three young owner-chefs produce tasty cuisine that favors garlic; there's even garlic beer. *$$*

Iceland

★ **Við Tjörnina, Reykjavík.** Some claim the food here is the best in the country. Unusual ingredients are the secret. *$$$*

Norway

★ **Bagatelle, Oslo.** One of the best restaurants in Europe features the Franco-Norwegian cuisine of internationally known owner-chef Eyvind Hellstrøm. *$$$$*

★ **Refsnes Gods, Moss.** Chef Erwin Stocker adds a French touch to traditional Norwegian seafood to create what some call the best fare in Norway. *$$$*

Sweden

★ **Ulriksdals Wärsdhus, Stockholm.** The lunchtime smörgåsbord is renowned at this restaurant in an 1868 country inn. *$$$$*

★ **The Place, Göteborg.** Sample delicious and exotic dishes, from smoked breast of pigeon to beef tartar with caviar. *$$$*

★ **Wedholms Fisk, Stockholm.** Traditional Swedish fare here, especially the fresh fish, is simple but outstanding. *$$$*

★ **Örtagården, Stockholm.** This delightful vegetarian, no-smoking restaurant is above the Östermalmstorg food market. *$*

Lodging

Denmark

★ **D'Angleterre, Copenhagen.** This grande dame has hosted everyone from royalty to rock stars. *$$$$*

★ **Skovshoved, Copenhagen.** Licensed since 1660, this lovely art-filled inn is nestled amid fishing cottages on the harbor, 8 km (5 mi) from the city. *$$$*

★ **Vandrehjem (youth hostels), anywhere in Denmark.** More than 100 excellent youth hostels welcome travelers of all ages. *$*

Finland

★ **Kalastajatorppa, Helsinki.** This hotel slightly out of town has a gorgeous seaside address and superb cuisine. *$$$$*

★ **Lord Hotel, Helsinki.** Fit for a king, this hotel is central and cozy, with a remarkable, romantic Jugendstil exterior and interior. *$$$$*

Iceland

★ **Hótel Borg, Reykjavík.** The art deco rooms and modern inventions—fluffy down comforters among them—in Reykjavík's oldest hotel are the country's finest. *$$$$*

★ **Hótel Holt, Reykjavík.** Luxuriously appointed rooms are a bit small, but the excellent service, gourmet restaurant, and central locale more than compensate. *$$$$*

Norway

★ **Ambassadeur, Oslo.** Hand-picked antiques, china tea sets, and tapestries in the salon only hint at the sweet, individual styles of the rooms with monikers like "Roma" and "Osa." *$$$–$$$$*

★ **Frogner House, Oslo.** Sitting inconspicuously amid rows of other turn-of-the-century townhouses, Frogner is cozily dressed in pastels and abundant lace coverings. *$$$–$$$$*

★ **Clarion Admiral Hotel, Bergen.** Right on the water across the harbor from Bryggen, this former dockside warehouse–cum–geometric Art Nouveau hotel dates from 1906. *$$–$$$*

★ **Kvikne's Hotel, Balestrand.** This huge wooden gingerbread house at the edge of the Sognefjord has been a landmark since 1915. *$$*

Sweden

★ **Berns, Stockholm.** This 132-year-old hotel employs discreet lighting, modern Italian furniture, and swank marble, granite, and wood inlays to create a wonderful art deco atmosphere. *$$$$*

★ **Marina Plaza, Helsingborg.** The use of space, style, and elegance—especially in the lofty lobby atrium—lends a decidedly modern appeal to this lodging. *$$$*

Castles and Churches

Denmark

★ **Christianborg Slot, Copenhagen.** The queen still receives guests in this 12th-century castle.

★ **Kronborg Slot, Helsingør, Sjælland.** William Shakespeare never saw this fantastic castle, but that didn't stop him from using it as the setting for *Hamlet*.

★ **Rosenborg Slot, Copenhagen.** The only castle that is still passed down from monarch to monarch, Rosenborg Slot is home to the crown jewels.

Finland

★ **Temppeliaukion Kirkko, Helsinki.** A copper dome is the only part of this modern church visible from above ground, since the church itself is carved into the rock outcropping.

★ **Uspenskin Katedraali, Helsinki.** Glistening onion domes top this Russian Orthodox cathedral, built in 1868 in the Byzantine-Slavonic style.

Norway

★ **Akershus Slott, Oslo.** Parts of this historic fortress, on the brow of the fjord, date to the 1300s.

Sweden

★ **Drottningholms Slott, Stockholm.** One of the most delightful European palaces embraces all that was best in the art of living practiced by mid-18th-century royalty.

★ **Kalmar Slott, Småland.** The "Key to the Realm" during the Vasa era, this Renaissance palace commands the site of an 800-year-old fortress on the Baltic shore.

★ **Kungliga Slottet, Stockholm.** In this magnificent granite edifice, you can tour the State Apartments, the Royal Armory, and the Treasury, where the crown jewels are kept.

Museums

Denmark

★ **Louisiana, Copenhagen.** A half-hour drive from the city, this world-class modern art collection displays the likes of Warhol and Picasso.

★ **Nationalmuseet, Copenhagen.** Brilliantly restored and regarded as one of the best national museums in Europe, this institution curates exhibits chronicling Danish cultural history.

Finland

★ **Lusto Finnish Forest Museum, Punkaharju.** Every kind of forestry—industrial to artistic—and Finland's close relationship with its most abundant natural resource are examined here.

★ **Ortodoksinen Kirkkomuseo, Kuopio.** Religious art from Karelia's monasteries was brought to Kuopio after World War

II, creating a rare collection of Orthodox art in this small town in the Lakelands.

⭐ **Seurasaaren Ulkomuseo, Helsinki.** Old farmhouses and barns were brought from all over Finland to create this outdoor museum of Finnish rural architecture.

⭐ **Taidekeskus Retretti Punkaharju.** This uniquely designed modern art complex, with a cavern section built into the Punkaharju ridge, is the setting for outdoor summer concerts.

Iceland

⭐ **Árbæjarsafn, Reykjavík.** Tour this outdoor village of 18th- and 19th-century houses, furnished with period reproductions and displaying household utensils and tools.

Norway

⭐ **Munchmuseet, Oslo.** Edvard Munch, who painted *The Scream*, bequeathed thousands of his works to Oslo when he died in 1944.

⭐ **Norsk Folkemuseum, Bygdøy, Oslo.** Some 140 structures from all over the country have been reconstructed on the museum grounds.

Sweden

⭐ **Skansen, Stockholm.** Farmhouses, windmills, barns, and churches are just some of the buildings brought from around the country for preservation at this museum.

⭐ **Vasa Museet, Stockholm.** Visit the *Vasa*, a warship that sank on its maiden voyage in 1628, was raised nearly intact in 1961, and now resides in its own museum.

⭐ **Zorn Museet, Mora.** Many fine paintings by Anders Zorn (1860–1920), Sweden's leading Impressionist painter, are displayed in this museum next to the beautiful house he built in his hometown.

Special Moments

Denmark

Walking through Tivoli at dusk

Watching a bonfire on Skt. Hansaften, the longest day of the year

Finland

Cloudberry-picking in Lapland in August

Iceland

Bobbing among glacial ice floes in Jökulsárlón lagoon

Watching the Northern Lights in December from Þingvellir

Norway

Eating dinner in a Sami tent, with your reindeer parked outside

People-watching along Oslo's Karl Johans Gate during the 17th of May (Constitution Day) celebrations

Admiring the monumental sculptures in Oslo's Vigeland Park

Sweden

Dogsledding in Norrland

Watching a Lucia procession at Christmastime

Sailing in the Stockholm archipelago

FESTIVALS AND SEASONAL EVENTS

Denmark

MAR.➤ The **Ice Sculpture Festival** takes place in Nuuk, Greenland; the **Nuuk Marathon** draws a hardy crowd of runners.

APR.➤ In Greenland, the **Arctic Circle Race** begins in Kangangerlussuaq and ends in Sisimiut.

APR. 16➤ The **Queen's Birthday** is celebrated with the royal guard in full ceremonial dress as the royal family appears before the public on the balcony of Amalienborg.

MAY➤ **Copenhagen Carnival** includes boat parades in Nyhavn and costumed revelers in the streets.

MAY–AUG.➤ **Tivoli** in Copenhagen twinkles with rides, concerts, and entertainment.

MAY–SEPT.➤ **Legoland,** a park constructed of 35 million Lego blocks, is open in Billund, Jylland.

JUNE➤ The **Around Fyn Regatta** starts in Kerteminde. The **Round Zealand Regatta,** one of the largest yachting events in the world, starts and ends in Helsingør. The **Aalborg Jazz Festival** fills the city with four days of indoor and outdoor concerts, many of them free. The **Viking Festival** in Frederikssund includes open-air performances of a Viking play. On **Midsummer's Night,** Danes celebrate the longest day of the year with bonfires and picnics.

JUNE 21➤ **Greenland National Day** celebrates the anniversary of Home Rule.

➤ JUNE–JULY➤ The **Roskilde Festival,** the largest rock concert in northern Europe, attracts dozens of bands and 75,000 fans.

➤ JULY➤ The **Copenhagen Jazz Festival** gathers international and Scandinavian jazz greats for a week of concerts, many of them free.

➤ JULY 4➤ The **Fourth of July** celebration in Rebild Park, near Aalborg, sets off the only American Independence Day festivities outside the United States.

➤ MID-JULY➤ The **Århus Jazz Festival** gathers European and other world-renowned names, with indoor and outdoor concerts.

➤ AUG.➤ Between the 7th and 10th, the **Cutty Sark Tall Ship Race** brings more than 100 ships to the Copenhagen harbor.

➤ MID-AUG.➤ The annual **Copenhagen Water Festival** celebrates the city's ties to the sea with concerts, exhibits, and plenty of outdoor activities.

➤ SEPT.➤ The **Århus Festival,** Denmark's most comprehensive fête, fills the city with concerts, sports, and theater.

➤ NEW YEAR'S EVE➤ Fireworks at the Town Hall Square are set off by local revelers.

Finland

JAN.➤ The **Arctic Rally** gets into gear yearly in Rovaniemi, Lapland.

FEB.➤ **Shrove Tuesday** celebrations throughout Finland include skiing, skating, and tobogganing events; **Finlandia Ski** is a 75-km (47-mi) Hämeenlinna–Lahti ski event. Weather permitting, the **"world's biggest snow castle"** is erected in the small town of Kemi, with concerts and church services held inside the structure.

MAR.➤ The **Tar Skiing Race** in Oulu is the oldest cross-country ski trek (75 km/47 mi) in the country, and the **Oulu Music Festival** is a classical music event, with solo performers and orchestras. The **Porokuninkuusajot Reindeer Races** are run in Inari at the end of the month. The **Lady Day church festival** in Enontekiö includes reindeer racing and lassoing competitions. The **Tampere International Short Film Festival** features some of the best film in its category in Finland's third-largest city.

APR.➤ **Jazz Espoo** features foreign and Finnish performers in this Helsinki suburb; Rovaniemi is host to **Lapland's Ski-Orienteering Days.** The **Tampere Biennale,** scheduled for 1998 and 2000, is a festival of contemporary music.

MAY➤ **Vapunaatto** and **Vappu** (May Day Eve and May Day) celebrations occur nationwide and include picnicking and drinking; **Kainuu Jazz** means four days of listening to native and foreign musicians jamming in Kajaani.

JUNE➤ The **Kuopio Music and Dance Festival** is on stage in Kuopio, while the **Naantali Music Festival** soothes the ears of chamber-music lovers; **Joensuu Festival** stages a wide variety of musical events, from classical to modern, many held on an open-air stage; **Juhannus** (Midsummer Eve and Day) is celebrated nationwide with bonfires and all-night boat cruises. The **Hanko Regatta** is a popular open-sea sailing competition.

Avanti! Summer Sounds fest in Porvoo focuses on baroque and contemporary music. The **Midnight Sun Film Festival** unites established moviemakers and young celluloid hopefuls in Sodankylä, north of the Arctic Circle. The **Big Band Festival** in Imatra near the Russian border is a cheerful lakeside meeting of bands from all over the world. The famed Mariinsky Theater regularly sends its performers to the **Mikkeli Music Festival.**

JULY➤ The **Savonlinna Opera Festival,** on a grand scale and a month long, is a festival of international opera staged at Olavinlinna Castle, Savonlinna. **Pori Jazz,** Finland's premier international jazz festival, is set in Pori. The **Kuhmo Chamber Music Festival** is a week of chamber music in eastern Finland. The **Kaustinen Folk Music Festival** is based in Kaustinen, western Finland.

The **Ruisrock Festival,** held in Turku's Ruissalo Recreational Park, is Finland's oldest and largest rock festival. Finland's tango capital, Seinäjoki in Ostrobothnia, is the venue for the annual **Tango Festival,** where tango kings and queens are selected. The **Lahti Organ Festival** examines every

aspect—not just ecclesiastical—of this versatile instrument. The **Jyväskylä Arts Festival** is one of the Finland's longest-established cultural events, with the country's oldest multiart discussion forum.

AUG.➤ The **Turku Music Festival** has baroque to contemporary performances; the **Tampere International Theater Festival** includes plays staged by Finnish and foreign troupes; the **Helsinki Festival** means two weeks of dance, music, drama, and children's shows in the capital and its environs; the world's top drivers test their skills in Jyväskylä at the **Thousand Lakes Rally** for a grueling three days.

OCT.➤ The **Baltic Herring Festival** is the biggest fishermen's fish market, for one weekend on the quayside in Helsinki.

NOV.➤ **Tampere Jazz,** a modern jazz event, holds court in Tampere; the **Children's Festival** in Helsinki consists of performance art of all kinds; for an entire week children's films from around the world are shown at the **Oulu International Children's Film Festival; Kaamos Jazz** is a jazz fest held in Lapland's winter twilight, at Saariselkä/ Tankavaara, near Ivalo.

DEC.➤ **Independence Day** (December 6) means a parade to the candlelit Senate Square in Helsinki; **Lucia Day** is celebrated in Helsinki on December 13 with a concert at Finlandiatalo; **New Year's celebrations** vary, but the fireworks can be seen every year from Senate Square in Helsinki.

Iceland

JAN. 19–MID-FEBRUARY➤ Traditional Icelandic foods and drinks are served at **Þorri Banquets** around the country.

MAR. 23–31➤ Fjord cruises, jazz concerts, and dances accompany a week of skiing at the **Ski Festival** in Safjörður.

JUNE 1➤ Many coastal towns celebrate **Sjómannadagur** (Seamen's Day); in Reykjavík there are rowing and swimming competitions.

JUNE 17➤ **Iceland National Day** is cause for a nationwide party, with parades and outdoor dancing downtown in Reykjavík, Akureyri, and other towns.

LATE JUNE➤ The **Arctic Open Golf Tournament** is held, in the midnight sun, on the 18-hole golf course at Akureyri.

JUNE–JULY➤ Just south of Reykjavík in Hafnarfjörður, the **International Viking Festival** celebrates the country's Viking heritage with a Viking village, living-history demonstrations, battle enactments, and a Viking-ship sailing competition.

JULY–AUG.➤ The **Skálholt Music Festival,** at the south's Skálholt Cathedral, includes concerts of baroque and contemporary music every weekend.

AUG. 3–5➤ **Bank Holiday Weekend** draws large crowds for outdoor celebrations throughout the country; **Þjóðhátið 1874** (National Festival) is celebrated in Vestmannæyjar (the Westman Islands).

MID-AUG.➤ Icelandic and European musicians give performances during the

Kirkjubæjarklaustur Chamber Music Festival.

AUG.➤ **Reykjavik Marathon** sends world-class distance runners on their annual race around the city.

Norway

JAN.➤ In Tromsø, the **Northern Lights Festival** celebrates the return of daylight with performances by notable Norwegian and international musicians.

FEB.➤ Lillehammer's **Winter Festival** is a cultural affair including music, theater, and art exhibitions. The **Røros Fair** in the town of Røros (designated as Cultural Heritage Landmark by UNESCO) has been an annual tradition since 1854.

FEB. 20–MAR. 2➤ The **Nordic World Ski Championships** in Trondheim is the biggest event celebrating Trondheim's 1,000th-year anniversary.

MAR.➤ Europe's largest dogsledding competition, the **Finnmark Race,** follows old mail routes across Finnmarksvidda. The **Birkebeiner Race** commemorates a centuries-old cross-country ski race from Lillehammer to Rena. At the **Voss Jazz Festival,** European and American jazz and folk artists appear at Voss, a major ski resort in western Norway.

MAR.–APR.➤ The **Karasjok Easter Festival** features a variety of concerts, theater performances, art exhibits, snowmobile rallies, and reindeer races.

MAY 17➤ **Constitution Day** brings out every Norwegian flag and crowds of marchers for parades and celebrations throughout the country.

MAY➤ The **Grete Waitz Race** is a 5-km (3-mi), women-only race in Oslo. The festivities of the annual **Bergen International Festival,** customarily opened by the king, include dance, music, and theater performances.

MAY 30–JUNE 8➤ Trondheim's 1,000-year anniversary is in full swing during the city's **Festival Week.**

JUNE 23➤ **Midsummer Night,** called *Sankt Hans Afton,* is celebrated nationwide with bonfires, fireworks, and outdoor dancing. Meet fellow Norwegian Americans and Norwegians at the annual **Emigration Festival** in Stavanger.

JULY➤ The plays, exhibitions, concerts, and historic walking tours of the **Kristin Festival** pay tribute to *Kristin Lavransdatter,* the novel by Nobel prize–winning author Sigrid Undset; they are held at Jorund Farm, the site of Liv Ullmann's movie based on the same novel. More than 400 jazz musicians participate in the extremely popular **Molde International Jazz Festival.**

JULY 23–26➤ Boats and crews of the **Cutty Sark Regatta** will be in Trondheim.

AUG.➤ You'll find none other than folk music, folk dancing, and folk songs at the **Telemark International Folk Music Festival** in the town of Bø in Telemark. The **Peer Gynt Festival** in Lillehammer brings art exhibits, processions with national costumes, and open-air theater performances of Henrik Ibsen's *Peer Gynt*—as well as Edvard Grieg's music. The **Oslo Chamber Music Festival** draws participants from around the world.

LATE AUG.➤ The **Norwegian Food Festival** awards the Norwegian Championship in cooking, seminars, and lectures.

SEPT.➤ The **Oslo Marathon** stretches 42 km (26 mi) through the streets of Oslo.

DEC. 10➤ The **Nobel peace prize** is awarded—by invitation only—in Oslo.

Sweden

JAN. 13➤ **Knut** signals the end of Christmas festivities and "plundering" of the Christmas tree: Trinkets are removed from the tree, edible ornaments gobbled up, and the tree itself thrown out.

FEB. (FIRST THURS., FRI., AND SAT.)➤ A **market** held in Jokkmokk features both traditional Lapp artifacts and plenty of reindeer. On **Shrove Tuesday** special buns called *semlor*—lightly flavored with cardamom, filled with almond paste and whipped cream—are traditionally placed in a dish of warm milk, topped with cinnamon, and eaten.

MAR. (FIRST SUN.)➤ The **Vasaloppet Ski Race** treks 88 km (55 mi) from Sälen to Mora in Dalarna, and attracts entrants from all over the world.

APR.➤ On Maundy Thursday, small girls dress up as witches and hand out "Easter letters" for small change. *Påskris,* twigs tipped with brightly dyed feathers, decorate homes. On April 30, for the **Feast of Valborg,** bonfires are lit to celebrate the end of winter. The liveliest celebrations involve the students of the university cities of Uppsala, 60 km (37 mi) north of Stockholm, and Lund, 16 km (10 mi) north of Malmö.

MAY 1➢ **Labor Day** marches and rallies are held nationwide.

JUNE 6➢ **National Day** is celebrated, with parades, speeches, and band concerts nationwide.

JUNE➢ **Midsummer's Eve** and **Day** celebrations are held on the Friday evening and Saturday that fall between June 20 and 26. Swedes decorate their homes with flower garlands, raise maypoles, and dance around them to folk music.

AUG.➢ **Stockholm Water Festival** celebrates the city's clean water environment with water-sports performances, a fireworks competition, and many other events all over town. Crayfish are considered a delicacy in Sweden, and the second Wednesday of August marks the **Crayfish premiere,** when friends gather to eat them at outdoor parties.

NOV. 11➢ **St. Martin's Day** is celebrated primarily in the southern province of Skåne. Roast goose is served, accompanied by *svartsoppa,* a bisque made of goose blood and spices.

DEC.➢ For each of the four weeks of **Advent,** leading up to Christmas, a candle is lit in a four-pronged candelabra.

DEC. 10➢ **Nobel Day** sees the presentation of the Nobel prizes by King Carl

XVI Gustaf at a glittering banquet held in the Stockholm City Hall.

DEC. 13➢ On **Santa Lucia Day** young girls are selected to be "Lucias"; they wear candles—today usually electric substitutes—in their hair and sing hymns with their handmaidens and "star boys" at ceremonies around the country.

DEC. 24➢ **Christmas Eve** is the principal day of Christmas celebration. Traditional Christmas dishes include ham, rice porridge, and *lutfisk* (ling that is dried and then boiled).

DEC. 31➢ **New Year's Eve** is the Swedes' occasion to set off an astounding array of fireworks. Every household has its own supply, and otherwise quiet neighborhood streets are full of midnight merrymakers.

2 Denmark

With its highest mountain standing at a mere 442 ft and its most-visited attraction an amusement park, it's no wonder Denmark is so often described as hyggelig—*cozy, warm, and welcoming. A tiny land made up of 450 islands and the arc of one long peninsula, Hans Christian Andersen's home has the fairy tale quality you'd expect: Half-timber villages nestle up to provincial towns, and footsteps—not traffic—mark the tempo.*

THE KINGDOM OF DENMARK dapples the Baltic Sea in an archipelago of some 450 islands and the crescent of one peninsula. Measuring 43,069 square km (17,028 square mi) and with a population of 5 million, it is the geographical link between Scandinavia and Europe. Half-timber villages and tidy agriculture rub shoulders with provincial towns and a handful of cities, where pedestrians set the pace, not traffic. Mothers safely park baby carriages outside bakeries while outdoor cafés fill with cappuccino-sippers, and lanky Danes pedal to work in lanes thick with bicycle traffic. Clearly this is a land where the process of life is the greatest reward.

By Karina Porcelli

While in Denmark, visitors pinch themselves in disbelief and make long lists of resolutions to emulate the natives. The Danes' lifestyle is certainly enviable, not yet the pressure-cooked life of some other Western countries. Long one of the world's most liberal countries, Denmark has a highly developed social-welfare system. Hefty taxes are the subject of grumbles and jokes, but Danes remain proud of their state-funded medical and educational systems and high standard of living. They enjoy monthlong vacations, 7½-hour workdays, and overall security.

Educated, patriotic, and keenly aware of their tiny international stance, most Danes travel extensively and have a balanced perspective of their nation's benefits and shortfalls. As in many other provincial states, egalitarianism is often a constraint for the ambitious. In Denmark, the *Jante* law, which refers to a literary principle penned in the early 20th century by Axel Sandemose, essentially means "Don't think you're anything special"—and works as an insidious cultural barrier to talent and aspiration. On the other hand, free education and state support give refugees, immigrants, and the underprivileged an opportunity to begin new, often prosperous lives.

The history of the little country stretches back 250,000 years, when Jylland was inhabited by nomadic hunters, but it wasn't until AD 500 that a tribe from Sweden, called the Danes, migrated south and christened the land Denmark. The Viking expansion that followed was based on the country's strategic position in the north. Struggles for control of the North Sea with England and western Europe, for the Skagerrak (the strait between Denmark and Norway) with Norway and Sweden, and for the Baltic Sea with Germany, Poland, and Russia ensued. With high-speed ships and fine-tuned warriors, intrepid navies navigated to Europe and Canada, invading and often pillaging, until, under King Knud (Canute) the Great (995–1035), they captured England by 1018.

After the British conquest, Viking supremacy declined as feudal Europe learned to defend itself. Internally, the pagan way of life was threatened by the expansion of Christianity, introduced under Harald Bluetooth, who in AD 980 "baptized" the country, essentially to avoid war with Germany. For the next several hundred years, the country tried to maintain its Baltic power with the influence of the German Hanseatic League. Under the leadership of Valdemar IV (1340–1375), Sweden, Norway, Iceland, Greenland, and the Faroe Islands became a part of Denmark. Sweden broke away by the mid-15th century and battled Denmark for much of the next several hundred years, whereas Norway remained under Danish rule until 1814, Iceland until 1943. Greenland and the Faroe Islands are still self-governing Danish provinces.

Denmark prospered again in the 16th century, thanks to the Sound Dues, a levy charged to ships crossing the Øresund, the slender waterway between Denmark and Sweden. Under King Christian IV, a construction boom crowned the land with what remain architectural gems today,

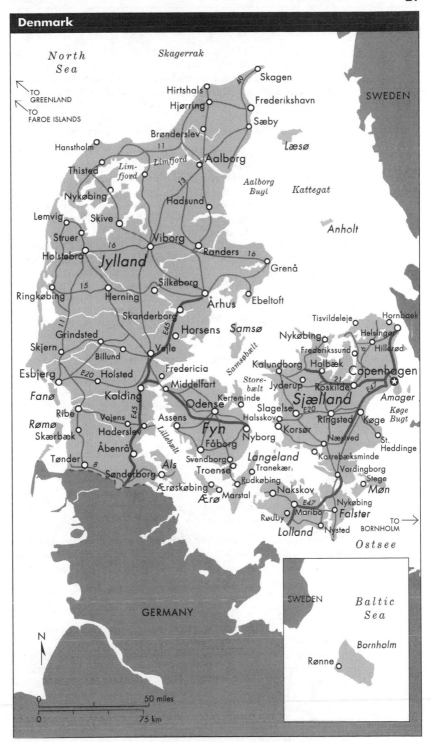

Denmark

North Sea

Skagerrak

TO GREENLAND

TO FAROE ISLANDS

Skagen
Hirtshals
Hjørring
Frederikshavn
Sæby
SWEDEN

Brønderslev
11
Hanstholm
Læsø
Thisted
Lim-fjord
Limfjord
Aalborg
Nykøbing
Hadsund
Aalborg Buyl
Kattegat
13
Lemvig
Skive
Anholt
Struer
Viborg
16
Holstebro
Jylland
Randers
16
Grenå
Ringkøbing
15
Herning
Silkeborg
Skanderborg
Århus
Ebeltoft
Tisvildeleje
Hornbæk
Grindsted
Horsens
Samsø
Nykøbing
Helsingør
Skjern
Vejle
E45
Frederikssund
Hillerød
Billund
Samsøbælt
Kalundborg
Holbæk
Esbjerg
E20
Holsted
Fredericia
Copenhagen
Fanø
Kolding
Middelfart
Store-bælt
Jyderup
Roskilde
21
E47
Odense
Kerteminde
Sjælland
Amager
Ribe
Vojens
E45
Assens
Slagelse
E20
Ringsted
Køge
Køge Bugt
Rømø
Haderslev
Halsskov
Korsør
Skærbæk
Lillebælt
Fyh
Nyborg
Næstved
Åbenrå
Fåborg
Karrebæksminde
St. Heddinge
Tønder
8
Svendborg
Langeland
Vordingborg
Sønderborg
Als
Troense
Tranekær
Stege
Møn
Ærøskøbing
Rudkøbing
Nakskov
Ærø
Marstal
Falster
Nykøbing
Rødby
Maribo
Nysted
E47
Lolland
TO BORNHOLM
Ostsee

N

GERMANY

SWEDEN
Baltic Sea

Bornholm
Rønne

0   50 miles
0   75 km

but his fantasy spires and castles, compounded with the Thirty Years' War in the 17th century, led to state bankruptcy.

By the 18th century, absolute monarchy had given way to representative democracy, and culture flourished. Then—in a fatal mistake—Denmark sided with France and refused to surrender its navy to the English during the Napoleonic Wars. In a less than valiant episode of British history, Lord Nelson turned his famous blind eye to the destruction and bombed Copenhagen to bits. The defeated King Frederik VI handed Norway to Sweden. Denmark's days of glory were over.

Though Denmark was unaligned during World War II, the Nazis invaded in 1940. Against them, the Danes used the only weapons they had: a cold shoulder and massive underground resistance. After the war, Denmark focused inward, refining its welfare system and concentrating on its main industries of agriculture, shipping, and financial and technical services. It is an outspoken member of the European Union (EU), championing environmental responsibility and supporting development in emerging economies. It was one of the only countries to forgive a considerable amount of third-world debt during the World Summit in Copenhagen in 1995. Expensive as it is, Denmark is in many ways less pricey than the rest of Scandinavia.

Copenhagen fidgets with its modern identity as both a Scandinavian–European link and cozy capital. The center of Danish politics, culture, and finance, it copes through balance and a sense of humor with a taste for the absurd. Stroll the streets and you'll pass classic architecture painted in candy colors, businessmen clad in jeans and T-shirts.

Sjælland's surrounding countryside is not to be missed. Less than an hour from Copenhagen, fields and half-timber cottages checker the land. Roskilde, to the east, has a 12th-century cathedral, and in the north, the Kronborg Castle of *Hamlet* fame crowns Helsingør. Beaches, some chic, some deserted, are powdered with fine white sand.

Fyn rightly earned its storybook reputation by making cuteness a local passion. The city of Odense, Hans Christian Andersen's birthplace, is cobbled with crooked old streets and Lilliputian cottages. Jylland's landscape is the most severe, with Ice Age–chiseled fjords and hills, sheepishly called mountains by the Danes. In the cities of Århus and Aalborg, you'll find museums and nightlife rivaling Copenhagen's.

The best way to discover Denmark is to strike up a conversation with an affable and hospitable Dane. *Hyggelig* defies definition but comes close to meaning a cozy and charming hospitality. A summertime beach picnic can be as hyggelig as tea on a cold winter's night. The only requirement is the company of a Dane.

Pleasures and Pastimes

Beaches
In this country of islands, coastline, and water, beaches come in many breeds. In Sjælland, a series of chic strands stretches along Strandvejen—the old beach road—pinned down by a string of lovely old seaside towns; here is where young people go to strut and preen. Fyn's gentle, golden beaches are less a showplace than a quiet getaway for a largely northern European crowd. Windswept Jylland has the country's most expansive and dramatic beaches—at its tip you can even see the line in the waves where the Kattegat meets the Skaggerak Sea.

Biking
Without a doubt, Denmark is one of the best places for biking. More than half of the population pedals along city streets that effectively co-

ordinate public transportation and cycle traffic and along the country paths laced through Jylland and the island of Bornholm.

Boating and Sailing

Well-marked channels and nearby anchorages make sailing and boating easy and popular along the 7,300-km (4,500-mi) coastline. Waters range from the open seas of the Kattegat and the Baltic to Smålandshavet (between Sjælland, Lolland, and Falster) and the calm Limsfjord in Jylland. The country's calm streams are navigable for canoes and kayaks. In Copenhagen, the historic harbors of Christianshavn and Nyhavn and scores of marinas bristling with crisp, white sails are lined with old wooden houseboats, motorboats, yachts, and their colorful crews. And it's not only the well-heeled taking up this pastime: Tousle-haired parents and babes, partying youths, and leathery pensioners tend to their boats and picnics, lending a festive, community spirit to the marinas.

Danish Design

Danish design has earned an international reputation for form and function. The best sales take place after Christmas until February, when you can snatch up glassware, stainless steel, pottery, ceramics, and fur for good prices. Danish antiques and silver are also much cheaper here than in the United States. For major purchases—Bang & Olufsen products, for example—check prices stateside first so you can spot a good price.

Dining

From the hearty meals of Denmark's fishing heritage to the inspired creations of a new generation of chefs, Danish cuisine combines the best of tradition and novelty. Though the country has long looked to the French as a beacon of gastronomy, chefs have proudly returned to the Danish table, emphasizing fresh, local ingredients. Sample fresh fish and seafood from the Baltic, beef and pork from Jylland, and more exotic delicacies, such as reindeer, caribou, seal meat, and whale from Greenland. Denmark's famed dairy products—sweet butter and milk among them—as well as a burgeoning organic foods industry, all contribute to the freshness of the modern Danish kitchen.

Lunchtime is reserved for *smørrebrød.* You'll find the best, most traditional sampling of these open-face sandwiches in modest family-run restaurants that focus on generous portions—though never excessive—and artful presentation. If you fix your gaze on tender mounds of roast beef topped with pickles or baby shrimp marching across a slice of French bread, you are experiencing a slice of authentic Danish culture. Another specialty is *wienerbrød,* a confection far superior to anything billed as "Danish pastry" elsewhere. All Scandinavian countries have versions of the cold table, but Danes claim that theirs, *det store kolde bord,* is the original and the best.

On the liquid refreshment front, slowly the ubiquitous Carlsberg and Tuborg are facing international competition. You can't do better than to stick with the Danish brands, which happily complement the traditional fare better than high-priced wine. If you go for the harder stuff, try the famous *snaps,* the aquavit traditionally savored with cold food.

CATEGORY	COPENHAGEN*	OTHER AREAS*
$$$$	over DKr400	over DKr350
$$$	DKr200–DKr400	DKr200–DKr350
$$	DKr120–DKr200	DKr100–DKr200
$	under DKr120	under DKr100

*per person for a three-course meal, including taxes and service charge and excluding wine

Lodging

Accommodations in Denmark range from spare to resplendent. Luxury hotels in the city or countryside offer rooms of a high standard, and in a manor-house hotel you may find yourself sleeping in a four-poster bed. Even inexpensive hotels are well designed with good materials and good, firm beds—and the country's 100 youth and family hostels and 500-plus campgrounds are among the world's finest. Usually for all of July, conference hotels often lower prices and offer weekend specials.

Farmhouses and *kroer* (old stagecoach inns) offer a terrific alternative to more traditional hotels. Perhaps the best way to see how the Danes live and work, farm stays allow you to share meals with the family and maybe even help with the chores. If you prefer a more independent setup, consider renting a summer home in the countryside.

CATEGORY	COPENHAGEN*	OTHER AREAS*
$$$$	over DKr1,100	over DKr850
$$$	DKr800–DKr1,100	DKr650–DKr850
$$	DKr670–DKr800	DKr450–DKr650
$	under DKr670	under DKr450

Prices are for two people in a double room and include service and taxes and usually breakfast.

Exploring Denmark

Denmark is divided into three regions: the two major islands of Sjælland and Fyn, and the peninsula of Jylland. To the east, Sjælland is Denmark's largest and most populated island, with Copenhagen its focal point. Denmark's second largest island, Fyn, is a pastoral, undulating land dotted with farms and summer-house beach villages, with Odense as its one major town. To the west, the relatively vast Jylland connects Denmark to the European continent; here you'll find the towns of Århus and Aalborg.

Numbers in the text correspond to numbers in the margin and on the maps.

Great Itineraries

IF YOU HAVE 3 DAYS

Take at least two days to explore and enjoy ⊞ **Copenhagen** ①–㊶. The last day, head north of the city, first to **Rungsted** ㊷ to see Karen Blixen's manor-house and the lush garden surrounding it, then to the Louisiana modern art museum in **Humlebæk** ㊸.

IF YOU HAVE 5 DAYS

After two days and nights in ⊞ **Copenhagen** ①–㊶, head north to **Rungsted** ㊷ and **Humlebæk** ㊸; then spend the night in ⊞ **Helsingør** ㊹. The next day, visit the castles of Helsingør and **Hillerød** ㊻, and spend the night in medieval ⊞ **Roskilde** ㊽. Day five, venture southeast to enjoy the dramatic nature and history of **Møn** ㊿ and the villages and beaches of Lolland and Falster. An alternative last-day tour is to head west to Hans Christian Andersen's birthplace of **Odense** ㊼, on Fyn.

IF YOU HAVE 7 DAYS

In a week you can see Copenhagen and environs and explore Fyn and Jylland. Rent a car for the latter—it's the quickest way to make it from the historic cities of ⊞ **Århus** ㊴ and ⊞ **Aalborg** ㊵ to the blond beaches of **Skagen** ㊶, with time left over to meander through a couple of smaller villages. With good planning, you'll be able to fit in a short trip to Greenland or the Faroe Islands.

When to Tour Denmark

Summertime—when the lingering sun of June, July, and August brings out the best in the climate and the Danes—is the best time to visit. In summer, Bornholm tends to stay warmer and sunnier longer than elsewhere; this is also the best time to visit Greenland and the Faroe Islands. The jazz-festival season gets underway in Copenhagen and Aalborg in June and in Århus in July. In July most Danes flee to their summer homes or go abroad.

Winter is dark and rainy, but it's a great time to visit museums, libraries, and the countless atmospheric meeting places in which the Danes take refuge. The weeks preceding Christmas are a prime time to experience Tivoli without the crowds, though everything—save the shops, restaurants, and theater in Danish—will be closed.

COPENHAGEN

Copenhagen—København in Danish—has no glittering skylines, few killer views, and only a handful of meager skyscrapers. Bicycles glide alongside manageable traffic at a pace that's utterly human. The early morning air in the pedestrian streets of the city's core, Strøget, is redolent of freshly baked bread and soap-scrubbed storefronts. If there's such a thing as a cozy city, this is it.

Extremely livable and relatively calm, Copenhagen is not a microcosm of Denmark, but rather a cosmopolitan city with an identity of its own. Denmark's political, cultural, and financial capital is inhabited by 1.5 million Danes, a fifth of the population, as well as a growing immigrant community. Filled with museums, restaurants, cafés, and lively nightlife, it has its greatest resource in its spirited inhabitants. The imaginative, unconventional, and affable Copenhageners exude an egalitarian philosophy that embraces nearly all lifestyles and leanings.

The town was a fishing colony until 1157, when Valdemar the Great gave it to Bishop Absalon, who built a castle on what is now Christianborg. It grew as a center on the Baltic trade route and became known as *købmændenes havn* (merchants' harbor) and eventually København. In the 15th century it became the royal residence and the capital of Norway and Sweden. A hundred years later, Christian IV, a Renaissance king obsessed with fine architecture, began a building boom that crowned the city with towers and castles, many of which still exist. They are almost all that remain of the city's 800-year history; much of Copenhagen was destroyed by two major fires in the 18th century and by Lord Nelson's bombings during the Napoleonic Wars.

Despite a tumultuous history, Copenhagen survives as the liveliest Scandinavian capital. With its backdrop of copper towers and crooked rooftops, the venerable city is humored by playful street musicians and performers, soothed by one of the highest standards of living in the world, and spangled by the thousand lights and gardens of Tivoli.

Exploring Copenhagen

The sites in Copenhagen rarely jump out at you; its elegant spires and tangle of cobbled one-way streets are best sought out on foot, and lingered over. Excellent bus and train systems can come to the rescue of weary legs. It is not divided into single-purpose districts; people work, play, shop, and live throughout the central core of this multilayered, densely-populated capital.

Be it sea or canal, Copenhagen is surrounded by water. A network of bridges and drawbridges connects the two main islands—Sjælland

and Amager—that Copenhagen is built on. The seafaring atmosphere is indelible, especially around Nyhavn and Christianshavn.

You might wonder why so many Copenhagen sites, especially churches, keep such peculiar, and often short, hours. It's a good idea to call and confirm opening times, especially in fall and winter.

Rådhus Pladsen, Christiansborg Slot, and Strøget

In 1728, and again in 1795, fires broke out in central Copenhagen with devastating effect. Disaster struck again in 1801, when Lord Nelson bombed the city—*after* the Danes had surrendered and *after* he was ordered to stop, he feigned ignorance and turned his famed blind eye to the command. These events still shape modern Copenhagen, which was rebuilt with wide, curved-corner streets—making it easier for fire trucks to turn—and large, four-sided apartment buildings centered with courtyards.

Arguably the liveliest area of the city, central Copenhagen is packed with shops, restaurants, businesses, and apartment buildings, as well as the crowning architectural achievements of Christian IV—all of it aswarm with Danes and visitors. Copenhagen's central spine consists of the five consecutive pedestrian strands known as Strøget and the surrounding tangle of roads and courtyards—less than a mile square in total. Across the capital's main harbor is the smaller, 17th-century Christianshavn. In the early 1600s, this area was mostly a series of shallows between land, which were eventually dammed. Today Christianshavn's colorful boats and postcard maritime character make it one of the toniest parts of town.

A GOOD WALK

The city's heart is the Rådhus Pladsen, home to the Baroque-style **Rådhus** ① and its clock tower. On the right side of the square is the landmark **Lurblæserne** ②. Off the square's northeastern corner is Frederiksberggade, the first of the five pedestrian streets that make up **Strøget** ③, Copenhagen's shopping district. Walk past the cafés and trendy boutiques to the double square of Gammeltorv and Nytorv.

Down Rådhusstræde toward Frederiksholms Kanal, the **Nationalmuseet** ④ contains an amazing collection of Viking artifacts. Cross Frederiksholms Kanal to Christiansborg Slotsplads, a small atoll divided by the canal and dominated by the burly **Christiansborg Slot** ⑤. North of the castle is **Thorvaldsen Museum** ⑥, devoted to the works of one of Denmark's most important sculptors, Bertel Thorvaldsen. On the south end of Slotsholmen is the three-story Romanesque-style **Kongelige Bibliotek** ⑦ (closed for renovations through late 1998), edged by carefully tended gardens and tree-lined avenues. Back on the south face of Christiansborg are the **Teatermuseum** ⑧ and the **Kongelige Stald** ⑨.

On the street that bears its name is the **Tøjhusmuseet** ⑩, and a few steps away is the architecturally marvelous **Børsen** ⑪ and the **Holmens Kirken** ⑫. To the east is **Christianshavn,** connected to Slotsholmen by the drawbridge Knippelsbro. Farther north, the former shipyard of Holmen is marked by expansive venues and several departments of the Københavns Universitet.

From nearly anywhere in the area, you can see the green-and-gold spire of **Vor Frelsers Kirken** ⑬. Across the Knippels Torvegade Bridge, under a mile down Børgsgade through Højbroplads, is Amagertorv, one of Strøget's five streets. On the left is **W. Ø. Larsens Tobakmuseet** ⑭, and farther down the street and to the left is the 18th-century **Helligånds Kirken** ⑮. On Strøget's Østergade, the massive spire of **Nikolaj Kirken** ⑯ looks many sizes too large for the tiny cobbled streets below.

The walk itself takes about two hours. Typically, Christiansborg Slot and its ruins and the Nationalmuseet both take at least an hour and a half to see—even more for Viking fans. Expect to spend more than an hour if you want to see a film at the Omnimax Theater at the Tycho Brahe Planetarium. The hundreds of shops along Strøget are enticing, so plan extra shopping and café time—at least as much as your wallet can spare. Note that many sites in this walk are closed Sunday or Monday, and some have odd hours; always call ahead.

SIGHTS TO SEE

⑪ Børsen (Stock Exchange). Believed to be the oldest stock exchange still in use, this masterpiece of fantasy and architecture is topped by a spire of three intertwined dragons' tails—said to have been twisted by its builder, King Christian IV. Built between 1619 and 1640, it was originally used as a sort of medieval mall, filled with shopping stalls. With its steep roofs, tiny windows, and gables, the treasured building is used only for special occasions. ☒ *Christiansborg Slotspl.* ☉ *Not open to the public.*

★ **⑤ Christiansborg Slot** (Christiansborg Castle). Surrounded by canals on three sides, the massive granite castle is where the queen officially receives guests. From 1441 until the fire of 1795, it was used as the royal residence. Even though the first two castles on the site were burned, Christiansborg remains an impressive Baroque compound, even by European standards: there's the **Folketinget** (Parliament House); the **Kongelige Repræsantationlokaler** (Royal Reception Chambers), where you'll be asked to don slippers to protect the floors; and the **Højesteret** (Supreme Court), on the site of the city's first fortress and built by Bishop Absalon in 1167. The guards at the entrance are knowledgeable and friendly; call them first to double-check the complicated opening hours.

While the castle was being rebuilt at the turn of the century, the Nationalmuseet (☞ *below*) excavated the **ruins** beneath it. This dark, subterranean maze contains fascinating models and architectural relics.

Wander around **Højbro Plads** and the delightful row of houses that border the northern edge of Slotsholmen. The quays were long Copenhagen's fish market, but today a lone early-morning fisherwoman hawking fresh fish, marinated herring, and eel is the sole fish monger you'll see carrying on the tradition. ☒ *Christiansborg. Ruins,* ☎ *33/ 92–64–92. Folketinget,* ☎ *33/37–55–00.* ☒ *Ruins DKr15; reception chambers DKr28; Folketinget free.* ☉ *Ruins: May–Sept., daily 9:30– 3:30; Oct.–Apr., Tues., Thurs, and weekends 9:30–3:30. Reception chambers (guided tours only): May and Sept., Tues.–Sun., English tours at 11 and 3; June–Aug., Tues.–Sun., tours at 11, 1, and 3; Oct.–Dec. and Feb.–Apr., Tues., Thurs., and Sun., tours at 11 and 3. Folketinget: May– Sept., Mon.–Sat., tours hourly (except noon) 10–4; Oct.–Apr., Tues., Thurs., and Sat., tours hourly (except noon) 10–4.*

Christianshavn. This tangle of cobbled avenues, antique street lamps, and Left Bank charm makes up one of the oldest neighborhoods in the city. Even the old system of earthworks—the best preserved of Copenhagen's original fortification walls—still exists. In the 17th century, King Christian IV offered what were patches of partially flooded land for free, and with additional tax benefits; in return, takers would have to fill them in and construct sturdy buildings for trade, commerce, housing for the shipbuilding workers, and defense against sea attacks. Gentrified today, the area harbors restaurants, cafés, and boutiques, and its ramparts are edged with green areas and walking paths, making it the perfect neighborhood for an afternoon or evening amble.

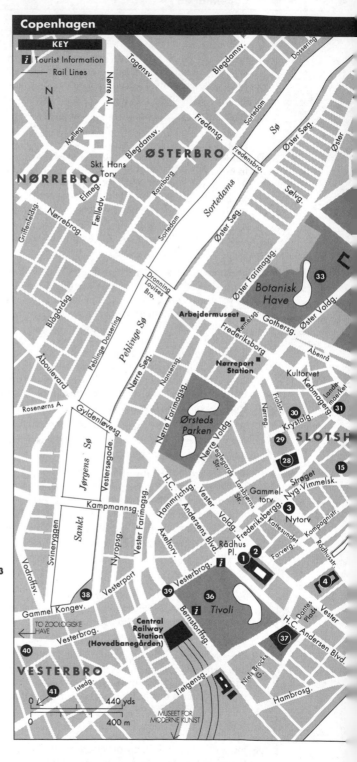

CHRISTIANIA – If you are nostalgic for the '60s counterculture, head to this anarchists' commune on Christianshavn. Founded in 1971, when students occupied army barracks, it is now a peaceful community of nonconformists who run a number of businesses, including a bike shop, bakery, rock club, and communal bathhouse. Wall cartoons preach drugs and peace, but the inhabitants are less fond of cameras—picture-taking is forbidden. ⊠ *Prinsesseg. and Badsmandsstr.*

HOLMEN – Previously isolated (indeed closed) from central Copenhagen, this former shipyard just north of Christianshavn produced ships and ammunition until a few years ago. It was formally opened as the sight of the 1995 United Nations Summit on Human Development and played an important role as a cultural area during Copenhagen's 1996 reign as the Cultural Capital of Europe. Today, among its several cultural venues is the city's biggest performance space, the Torpedo Hall, where torpedoes were actually produced. You'll also find the Danish Art Academy's Architecture School, the National Theater School, the Rhythmic Music Conservatory, and the Danish Film School, which all host special activities.

⑮ Helligånds Kirken (Church of the Holy Ghost). This 18th-century church was founded as an abbey of the Holy Ghost and is still one of the city's oldest places of worship. Its choir contains a font by the sculptor Thorvaldsen, and more modern art is found in the large exhibition room—once a hospital—that faces Strøget. ⊠ *Niels Hemmingseng. 5, Amagertorv section,* ☎ *33/12–95–55.* 🎫 *Free.* ☉ *Weekdays noon–4.*

⑫ Holmens Kirken (Islet's Church). Two of the country's most revered naval heroes are buried here: Niels Juel crushed the Swedish fleet at Køge in 1677. Peder Tordenskjold defeated Charles XII of Sweden during the Great Northern War in the early 18th century. ⊠ *Holmens Kanal,* ☎ *33/13–61–78.* 🎫 *Free.* ☉ *May 15–Sept. 15, weekdays 9–2, Sat. 9–noon; Sept. 16–May 14, Mon.–Sat. 9–noon.*

➐ Kongelige Bibliotek (Royal Library). Closed for renovation until sometime in late 1998, the Royal Library ordinarily houses the country's largest collection of books, newspapers, and manuscripts. Among the more than 2 million volumes are accounts of Viking journeys to America and Greenland and original manuscripts by Hans Christian Andersen and Karen Blixen (a.k.a. Isak Dinesen). If you happen to be in the area anyway and are craving a literary encounter, ramble around the statue of philosopher Søren Kierkegaard (1813–55), formal gardens, and tree-lined avenues surrounding the scholarly building. When it reopens, the library will be expanded with a new, massive granite annex between the current building and the waterfront. ⊠ *Christians Brygge 8,* ☎ *33/93–01–11.* ☉ *Closed until late 1998; call for hrs when reopened.*

🖐 ➒ Kongelige Stald (Royal Stables). Between 9 and noon, time stands still while riders elegantly clad in breeches and jackets exercise the horses. The vehicles, including coaches and carriages, and harnesses on display have been used by the Danish monarchy from 1778 to the present. ⊠ *Christiansborg Ridebane 12,* ☎ *33/40–10–10.* 🎫 *DKr10.* ☉ *May–Oct., Fri.–Sun. 2–4; Nov.–Apr., weekends 2–4.*

➋ Lurblæserne (Lur Blower Column). Topped by two Vikings blowing an ancient trumpet called a *lur,* this column displays a good deal of artistic license—the lur dates from the Bronze Age, 1500 BC, whereas the Vikings lived a mere 1,000 years ago. City tours often start at this important landmark. ⊠ *East side of Rådhus Pl.*

★ 🖐 ➍ Nationalmuseet (National Museum). This brilliantly restored 18th-century royal residence, peaked by massive overhead windows, has housed what is regarded as one of the best national museums in Europe since the 1930s. Extensive collections chronicle Danish cultural history from prehistoric to modern times—included is one of the largest collections of Stone Age tools in the world—and Egyptian, Greek, and Roman antiquities are on display. The children's museum, with a Viking ship, castles from the Middle Ages, and other touchable exhibits, closes one hour before the rest of the museum. ⊠ *Ny Vesterg. 10,* ☎ *33/13–44– 11.* ◫ *DKr30.* ☉ *Tues.–Sun. 10–5.*

⑯ **Nikolaj Kirken** (Nicholas Church). Though the green spire of the imposing church—named for the patron saint of seafarers—appears as old as the surrounding medieval streets, it is actually relatively young. The current building was finished in 1914; the previous structure, which dated from the 13th century, was destroyed by the 1728 fire. Today the church is an art gallery and exhibition center that often shows more experimental work. ⊠ *Nikolaj Pl.,* ☎ *33/93–16–26.* ◫ *Varies according to special exhibitions.* ☉ *Daily noon—5.*

NEED A BREAK?

Café Nikolaj (⊠ Nikolajpl., ☎ 33/93–16–26), inside Nikolaj Kirken, is a reliable, inexpensive café with good Danish pastries and light meals. It's open noon to 3 for lunch and until 5 for cakes and drinks.

---

❶ **Rådhus** (City Hall). Completed in 1905, the mock-Renaissance building dominates **Rådhus Pladsen** (City Hall Square), the hub of Copenhagen's commercial district. Architect Martin Nyrop's creation was popular from the start, perhaps because he envisioned that it should give "gaiety to everyday life and spontaneous pleasure to all . . ."; accordingly, a statue of Copenhagen's 12th-century founder, Bishop Absalon, sits atop the main entrance.

Besides being an important ceremonial meeting place for Danish VIPs, the intricately decorated Rådhus contains the first **World Clock.** The multidialed, superaccurate astronomical timepiece has a 570,000-year calendar and took inventor Jens Olsen 27 years to complete before it was put into action in 1955. If you're feeling energetic, take a guided tour up the 350-ft bell tower for the panoramic, but not particularly inspiring, view.

The modern glass and gray-steel **bus terminal** flanking the square's northwest side has French granite floors, pear-tree-wood shelving, and underground marble bathrooms. The $2.8 million creation proved so architecturally contentious—more for its placement than for its design— that there was serious discussion of moving it.

Look up to see one of the city's most charming bronze sculptures, created by the Danish artist E. Utzon Frank in 1936. Diagonally across Rådhus Pladsen, atop a corner office building you'll see a **neon thermometer** and a **gilded barometer.** On sunny days there's a golden sculpture of a girl on a bicycle; come rain, a girl with an umbrella appears. ⊠ *Rådhus Pl.,* ☎ *33/66–25–82.* ◫ *Tours DKr20, tower DKr10.* ☉ *Weekdays 9:30–3. Tours in English, weekdays at 3, Sat. at 10. Tower tours Mon.–Sat. at noon; additionally June–Sept. at 10 and 2. Call to confirm hrs.*

★ ❸ **Strøget.** Though it is referred to as one street, the city's pedestrian spine, pronounced *Stroy*-et, is actually a series of five streets: Frederiksberggade, Nygade, Vimmelskaftet, Amagertorv, and Østergade. By mid-morning, particularly on Saturday, it is congested with people, baby strollers, and street performers. Past swank and trendy, and sometimes flashy and trashy, boutiques of **Frederiksberggade** is the double square of **Gammeltorv** (Old Square) and **Nytorv** (New Square), in summer often crowded with street vendors selling cheap jewelry

In 1728 and again in 1795, much of Strøget was heavily damaged by fire. When rebuilding, the city fathers straightened and widened the streets. Today, you can still see buildings from this reconstruction period, as well as a few that survived the fires.

In addition to shopping, you'll enjoy Strøget for strolling, as hundreds do. Outside the posh fur and porcelain shops and bustling cafés and restaurants, the sidewalks have a festive street-fair atmosphere.

⑧ Teatermuseum (Theater Museum). After you brush up on theater and ballet history, wander around the boxes, stage, and dressing rooms of the **Royal Court Theater** of 1766, which King Christian VII had built as the first court theater in Scandinavia. ⊠ *Christiansborg Ridebane 18,* ☏ *33/11–51–76.* ▣ *DKr20.* ⊙ *Wed. 2–4, Sun. noon–4.*

⑥ Thorvaldsen Museum. The 19th-century artist Bertel Thorvaldsen (1770–1844) is buried at the center of this museum in a simple, ivy-covered tomb. Greatly influenced by the statues and reliefs of classical antiquity, he is recognized as one of the world's greatest neoclassical artists and completed many commissions all over Europe. The museum, once a coachhouse to Christiansborg, now houses Thorvaldsen's interpretations of classical and mythological figures, and an extensive collection of paintings and drawings by other artists that Thorvaldsen assembled while living—for most of his life—in Rome. The outside frieze by Jørgen Sonne depicts the sculptor's triumphant return to Copenhagen after years abroad. ⊠ *Porthusg. 2, Slotsholmen,* ☏ *33/32–15–32.* ▣ *Free.* ⊙ *Tues.–Sun. 10–5.*

⑩ Tøjhusmuseet (Royal Danish Arsenal Museum). This Renaissance structure—built by King Christian IV and one of central Copenhagen's oldest—contains impressive displays of uniforms, weapons, and armor in an arched hall 600 ft long. ⊠ *Tøjhusg. 3,* ☏ *33/11–60–37.* ▣ *DKr20.* ⊙ *Tues.–Sun. 10–4.*

⑬ Vor Frelsers Kirken (The Church of Our Savior). Dominating the area around Christianshavn is the green-and-gold tower of this church, a Gothic structure built in 1696. Local legend has it that the staircase encircling it was built curling the wrong way around, and that when its architect reached the top and realized what he'd done, he jumped. At press time, a renovation was possible (but not yet scheduled) for 1999 or earlier. ⊠ *Skt. Annæg. 29,* ☏ *31/57–27–98.* ▣ *Tower DKr20.* ⊙ *Mid-Mar.–May and Sept.–Oct., Mon.–Sat. 9–3:30, Sun., 9–1:30 and 3–4:30; June–Aug., Mon.–Sat. 9–4:30, Sun. 1:30–4:30; Nov., Mon.–Sat. 10–2, Sun. 11:30–1:30. Tower closed Dec.–mid-Mar. and during inclement weather.*

⑭ W. Ø. Larsens Tobakmuseet (W. O. Larsens Tobacco Museum). Looking like a storefront window from the outside, the Tobacco Museum in fact has a full-fledged collection of pipes made in every conceivable shape from every possible material. Look for the tiny pipe that's no bigger than an embroidery needle. There are also paintings, drawings, and an amazing collection of smoking implements. ⊠ *Amagertorv 9,* ☏ *33/12–20–50.* ▣ *Free.* ⊙ *Mon.–Thurs., 10–6, Fri. 10–7, Sat. 10–4.*

Around Amalienborg and Sites North

North of Kongens Nytorv, the city becomes a fidgety grid of parks and wider boulevards pointing northwest across the canal toward upscale Østerbro—wreathed by manors commissioned by wealthy merchants and bluebloods. In the mid-1700s, King Frederik V donated parcels of this land to anyone who agreed to build from the work of architect Niels Eigtved, who also designed the Kongelige Teater. The jewel of this crown remains Amalienborg and its Rococo mansions.

A GOOD WALK

At the end of Strøget, **Kongens Nytorv** ⑰ is flanked on its south side by the **Kongelige Teater** ⑱, and backed by **Charlottenborg** ⑲, which contains the Danish Academy of Fine Art (call to see if an exhibition has opened the castle to the public). The street leading southeast from Kongens Nytorv is **Nyhavn** ⑳, a onetime sailors' haunt and now a popular waterfront hub. From the south end of the harbor (north end of Havnegade) depart high-speed craft to Malmö, Sweden; on the other north side, Kvævthusbroen—at the end of Skt. Annæ Plads (☞ *below*)— is the quay for boats to Oslo, Norway, and Bornholm, Denmark.

West of the harbor front is the grand square called Skt. Annæ Plads. Perpendicular to the square is Amaliegade, its wooden colonnade bordering the cobbled square of **Amalienborg** ㉑, the royal residence with a pleasant garden on its harbor side. Steps west from the square is Bredgade, where the Baroque **Marmorkirken** ㉒ flaunts its Norwegian marble structure. Farther north on Bredgade is the Rococo **Kunstindustrimuseet** ㉓. Back on Bredgade (you can also take the more colorful, café-lined Store Kongensgade, just west), turn right onto Esplanaden and you'll see the enormously informative **Frihedsmuseet** ㉔. At the Churchillparken's entrance stands the English church, St. Albans. In the park's center, the **Kastellet** ㉕ serves as a reminder of the city's grim military history. At its eastern perimeter is Langelinie, a waterfront promenade with a view of Denmark's best-known pinup, *Den Lille Havfrue* ㉖. Wending your way back toward Esplanaden and the town center, you'll pass the **Gefion Springvandet** ㉗.

TIMING

This walk amid parks, gardens, canals, and building exteriors should take a full day. If it's nice, linger in the parks, especially along Kastellet and Amalienhaven, and plan on a long lunch at Nyhavn. The Kunstindustrimuseet merits about an hour, more if you plan on perusing the design books in the museum's well-stocked library. The Frihedsmuseet may require more time: its evocative portrait of Danish life during World War II intrigues even the most history-weary teens. Avoid taking this tour Monday, when some sites are closed.

SIGHTS TO SEE

㉑ **Amalienborg** (Amalia's Castle). The four identical Rococo buildings occupying this square have housed the royals since 1784. The Christian VIII palace across from the Queen's residence houses the **Amalienborg Museum,** which displays the second division of the Royal Collection (the first is at Rosenborg Slot, ☞ *below*) and chronicles royal lifestyles between 1863 and 1947. Here you can view the study of King Christian IX (1818–1906) and the drawing room of his wife, Queen Louise. Rooms are packed with family gifts and regal baubles ranging from tacky knickknacks to Fabergé treasures, including a nephrite and ruby table clock, and a small costume collection.

In the square's center is a magnificent equestrian statue of King Frederik V by the French sculptor Jacques François Joseph Saly. It reputedly cost as much as all the buildings combined. Every day at noon, the Royal Guard and band march from Rosenborg Slot through the city for the changing of the guard. At noon on Queen Margrethe's birthday, April 16, crowds of Danes gather to cheer their monarch, who stands and waves from her balcony. On Amalienborg's harbor side are the trees, gardens, and fountains of **Amalienhaven.** ✉ *Amalienborg Castle,* ☎ *33/12–21–86.* ▣ *DKr35.* ☉ *May–mid-Oct., daily 11–4; mid-Oct.–Apr., Tues.–Sun. 11–4.*

⑲ **Charlottenborg** (Charlotte's Castle). This Dutch Baroque–style castle was built by Frederik III's half brother in 1670. Since 1754 the garden-flanked property has housed the faculty and students of the Danish Academy of Fine Art. It is open only during exhibits, usually in winter. ⊠ *Nyhavn 2,* ☎ *33/13–40–22.* 🎟 *DKr20.* ⊘ *Closed to public, except for exhibitions. Exhibition hrs daily 10–5, Wed. until 7.*

㉖ *Den Lille Havfrue (The Little Mermaid).* On the Langelinie promenade, this somewhat overrated 1913 statue commemorates Hans Christian Andersen's lovelorn creation, and is the subject of hundreds of travel posters. Donated to the city by Carl Jacobsen, the son of the founder of Carlsberg Breweries, the innocent waif has also been the subject of some cruel practical jokes, including decapitation and the loss of an arm, but she is currently in one piece. Especially on a sunny Sunday, the Langelinie promenade is thronged with Danes and visitors making their pilgrimage to see the statue.

★ ㉔ **Frihedsmuseet** (Resistance Museum). Evocative, sometimes moving displays commemorate the heroic Danish resistance movement, which saved 7,000 Jews from the Nazis by hiding them and then smuggling them to Sweden. The homemade tank outside was used to spread the news of the Nazi surrender after World War II. ⊠ *Churchillparken,* ☎ *33/13–77–14.* 🎟 *Free.* ⊘ *May–Sept. 15, Tues.–Sat. 10–4, Sun. 10–5; Sept. 16–Apr., Tues.–Sat. 11–3, Sun. 11–4.*

㉗ **Gefion Springvandet** (Gefion Fountain). Not far from *The Little Mermaid,* yet another dramatic myth is illustrated. The goddess Gefion was promised as much of Sweden as she could carve in a night. The story goes that she changed her sons to oxen and created the island of Sjælland. ⊠ *East of Frihedsmuseet.*

㉕ **Kastellet** (Citadel). At Churchill Park's entrance stands the spired English church, **St. Albans.** From there, walk north on the main path and you'll reach the Citadel. The structure's smooth, peaceful walking paths, marina, and greenery belie its fierce past as a city fortification. Built in the aftermath of the Swedish siege of the city on February 10, 1659, the double moats were among the improvements made to the city's defense. The Citadel served as the city's main fortress into the 18th century; in a grim reversal during World War II, the Germans used it as their headquarters during their occupation. ⊠ *Center of Churchill Park.* 🎟 *Free.* ⊘ *Daily 6 AM–sunset.*

⑱ **Kongelige Teater** (Danish Royal Theater). The stoic, pillared and gallery-fronted theater is the country's preeminent venue for music, opera, ballet, and theater. The Danish Royal Ballet, its repertoire ranging from classical to modern works, performs here.

The current building was opened in 1874, though the annex, known as the **Nesting Box,** was not inaugurated until 1931. Statues of Danish poet Adam Oehlenschläger and author Ludvig Holberg—whose works remain the core of Danish theater—flank the facade. Born in Bergen, Norway, in 1684, Holberg came to Denmark as a student and stayed. Often compared to Molière, he wrote 32 of his comedies in a "poetic frenzy" between 1722 and 1728, and, legend has it, he complained of interminable headaches the entire time. He published the works himself, made an enormous fortune, and invested in real estate. Perhaps the theater is taking his cue: an annex designed by Norwegian architect Sverre Fehn is being constructed on the eastern side of the theater. With an estimated budget of roughly $115 million and a completion date of 2001, the pale concrete, marble, and oak structure will transform Tordenskjoldsgade into a covered shopping promenade. ⊠ *Tordenskjoldsg. 3,* ☎ *33/14–10–02.* ⊘ *Not open for tours.*

★ **⑰** **Kongens Nytorv** (King's New Square). A mounted statue of Christian V dominates the square. Crafted in 1688 by the French sculptor Lamoureux, he is conspicuously depicted as a Roman emperor. Every year, at the end of June, graduating high-school students arrive in horse-drawn carriages and dance beneath the furrowed brow of the sober statue.

NEED A
BREAK?
Dozens of restaurants and cafés line Nyhavn. Among the best is **Cap Horn** (✉ Nyhavn 21, ☎ 33/12–85–04) for moderately priced, hearty, light Danish treats served in a cozy, art-filled dining room that looks like a ship's galley. Try the fried plaice, swimming in a sea of parsley butter with boiled potatoes.

㉓ **Kunstindustrimuseet** (Museum of Decorative Art). Originally built in the 18th century as a royal hospital, the fine Rococo-style museum houses a large selection of European and Asian crafts. You'll also find ceramics, silverware, tapestries, and special exhibitions usually focusing on contemporary design. The museum's excellent library is stocked with design books and magazines, and there's also a small café. ✉ *Bredg. 68,* ☎ *33/14–94–52.* ✆ *DKr35 (additional fee for some special exhibits).* ✆ *Permanent collection, Tues.–Sun. 1–4; changing exhibits, Tues.–Sat. 10–4, Sun. 1–4.*

㉒ **Marmorkirken** (Marble Church). Officially the Frederikskirke, the ponderous Baroque sanctuary of precious Norwegian marble was begun in 1749 and lay unfinished from 1770 to 1874 due to budget restraints. It was finally completed and consecrated in 1894. Around the exterior are 16 statues of various religious leaders from Moses to Luther, and below them stand sculptures of outstanding Danish ministers and bishops. The hardy can scale 273 steps to the outdoor balcony. Walk past the exotic gilded onion domes of the **Russiske Ortodoks Kirke** (Russian Orthodox Church). ✉ *Bredg.,* ☎ *33/15–37–63.* ✆ *Free; balcony, DKr20.* ✆ *Mon., Tues., Thurs., Fri. 11–2, Wed 11–6, Sat. 11–4, Sun. noon–4.*

Nyboder. Tour the neat, mustard-colored enclave of Nyboder, a perfectly laid-out compound of flat, long, former sailors' homes built by Christian IV. Like Nyhavn, this salty sailors' area was seedy and boisterous at the beginning of the 1970s, but today has become one of Copenhagen's more fashionable neighborhoods. ✉ *West of Store Kongensg. and east of Rigensg.*

★ **⑳** **Nyhavn** (New Harbor). This harbor-front neighborhood was built 300 years ago to attract traffic and commerce to the city center. Until 1970, the area was a favorite haunt of sailors. Though restaurants, boutiques, and antiques stores now outnumber tattoo parlors, many old buildings have been well preserved and have retained the harbor's authentic 18th-century maritime atmosphere; you can even see a fleet of old-time sailing ships from the quay. Hans Christian Andersen lived at various times in the Nyhavn houses at numbers 18, 20, and 67.

Down Vesterbrogade and Nørrebro

To the southwest of the city are the vibrant working-class and immigrant neighborhoods of Vesterbro, where you'll find a good selection of inexpensive ethnic restaurants and shops. You'll find more cafés, restaurants, clubs, and shops on Nørrebrogade and Skt. Hans Torv.

By the 1880s, many of the buildings that now line Vesterbro and Nørrebro were being hastily thrown up as housing for area laborers. Many of these flats—typically decorated with a row of pedimented windows and a portal entrance—have been renovated through a massive urban renewal program. But to this day, many share hall toilets, have no showers, and are heated only by kerosene ovens.

A GOOD WALK
Take the train from Østerport Station, off of Oslo Plads, to Nørreport Station on Nørrevoldgade and walk down Fiolstræde to **Vor Frue Kirken** ㉘, its very tall copper spire and four shorter ones crowning the area. Backtracking north on Fiolstræde you'll come to the main building of **Københavns Universitet** ㉙; on the corner of Krystalgade is the **Københavns Synagoge** ㉚.

Fiolstræde ends at the Nørreport train station. Perpendicular to Nørrevoldgade is Frederiksborggade, which leads northwest to the neighborhood of Nørrebro; to the south after the Kultorvet, or Coal Square, Frederiksborggade turns into the pedestrian street Købmagergade. From anywhere in the area, you can see the stout **Rundetårn** ㉛: it stands as one of Copenhagen's most beloved landmarks, with an observatory open fall and winter evenings. Straight down from the Rundetårn on Landemærket, Gothersgade gives way to **Rosenborg Slot** ㉜, its Dutch Renaissance design standing out against the vivid green of the well-tended Kongens Have. For a heavier dose of plants and living things, head across Øster Voldgade to the 25-acre **Botanisk Have** ㉝.

Leave the garden's north exit to reach the **Statens Museum for Kunst** ㉞ (closed for reconstruction through late 1998), notable for exceptional Matisse works. An adjacent building houses the **Hirschsprungske Samling** ㉟, with 19th-century Danish art.

Back at the Nørreport station, you can catch a train back to Copenhagen's main station, Hovedbanegården. When you exit on Vesterbrogade, take a right and you'll see the city's best-known attraction, **Tivoli** ㊱. At the southern end of the gardens, on Hans Christian Andersen Boulevard, the neoclassical **Ny Carlsberg Glyptotek** ㊲ contains one of the most impressive collections of antiquities and sculpture in northern Europe. Tucked between Sankt Jørgens Sø, or St. Jørgens Lake, and the main arteries of Vestersøgade and Gammel Kongevej is the **Tycho Brahe Planetarium** ㊳, with an Omnimax Theater.

Continue down Vesterbrogade into **Vesterbro** ㊴, Copenhagen's own Lower East Side of New York. Parallel to the south is **Istedgade,** Copenhagen's half-hearted red-light district.

Farther west down Vesterbrogade is **Københavns Bymuseum** ㊵, its entrance flanked by a miniature model of medieval Copenhagen. Beer enthusiasts and zymurgy fanatics can head south on Enghavevej and take a right on Ny Carlsbergvej for a tour of **Carlsberg Bryggeri** ㊶.

TIMING
All of the sites on this tour are relatively close together and can be seen in one day. Tivoli offers charms throughout the day; visit in the late afternoon, and stay until midnight, when colored electrical bulbs and fireworks illuminate the park. Note that some sites below close Monday or Tuesday; call ahead.

SIGHTS TO SEE
㉝ **Botanisk Have** (Botanical Garden). Trees, flowers, ponds, sculptures, and a spectacular *Palmehuset* (Palm House) of tropical and subtropical plants blanket the garden's 25-plus acres. There's also an observatory and a geological museum. Take time to explore the gardens and watch the pensioners feed the birds. Some have been coming here so long that the birds actually alight on their fingers. ⊠ *Gothersg. 128,* ☎ *35/32–22–40.* ⌷ *Free.* ☉ *Gardens Apr.–mid-Sept., daily 8:30–6; mid-Sept.–Mar., daily 8:30–4. Palm House daily 10–3.*

ARBEJDERMUSEET – The Workers Museum chronicles the working class from 1870 to the present, with evocative life-size "day-in-the-life-of" exhibits, including reconstructions of a city street and tram and an original apartment once belonging to a brewery worker, his wife, and eight children. Changing exhibits focusing on Danish as well as international issues are often excellent. The museum also has a 19th-century-style restaurant serving old-fashioned Danish specialties and a '50s-style coffee shop. ⊠ *Rømersg. 22,* ☎ *33/13–01–52.* ⌑ *DKr25.* ☉ *July–Oct., daily 10–5; Nov.–June, Tues.–Fri., 10–3, weekends 11–4.*

㊶ Carlsberg Bryggeri (Carlsberg Brewery). Four giant Bornholm granite elephants guard the entrance to this world-famous brewery; a tour of the draft horse stalls and **Carlsberg Museum** meets at this gate. At the end, you're rewarded with a few minutes to quaff a beer. ⊠ *Ny Carlsbergvej 140,* ☎ *33/27–13–14.* ☉ *Tours weekdays at 11 and 2 or by arrangement for groups.*

㉟ Hirschsprungske Samling (Hirschsprung Collection). This Danish art collection showcases works from the country's golden age—especially the late-19th-century paintings of the Skagen School. Their luminous works capture the play of light and water so characteristic of the Danish countryside. ⊠ *Stockholmsg. 20,* ☎ *31/42–03–36.* ⌑ *DKr20.* ☉ *Mon. and Thurs.–Sun. 11–4, Wed. 11–9.*

Istedgade. In Copenhagen's half-hearted red-light district, mom-and-pop kiosks and ethnic restaurants stand side by side with seedy porn shops and shady outfits aiming to satisfy all proclivities. Though it is relatively safe, you may want to avoid the area for a late-night stroll. ⊠ *Street south and parallel to Vesterbrogade, west of Tivoli.*

㊵ Københavns Bymuseum (Copenhagen City Museum). For a surprisingly evocative collection detailing Copenhagen's history, head to this 17th-century building in the heart of Vesterbro. Outside is a meticulously maintained model of medieval Copenhagen; inside there is also a memorial room for philosopher Søren Kierkegaard, the father of existentialism. ⊠ *Vesterbrog. 59,* ☎ *31/21–07–72.* ⌑ *Free.* ☉ *May–Sept., Tues.–Sun. 10–4; Oct.–Apr., Tues.–Sun. 1–4.*

㉚ Københavns Synagoge (Copenhagen Synagogue). This synagogue was designed by the contemporary architect Gustav Friedrich Hetsch, who borrowed from the Doric and Egyptian styles in creating the arklike structure. ⊠ *Krystalg. 12.* ☉ *Daily services 4:15.*

㉙ Københavns Universitet (Copenhagen University). Denmark's leading school for higher learning was constructed in the 19th century on the site of the medieval bishops' palace. ⊠ *Nørreg. 10,* ☎ *35/32–26–26.*

The nearby **Sømods Bolcher** (⊠ Nørreg. 36, ☎ 33/12–60–46) is a must for children and candy lovers: its old-fashioned hard candy is pulled and cut by hand.

★ ㊲ Ny Carlsberg Glyptotek (New Carlsberg Museum). Among Copenhagen's most important museums—thanks to its exquisite antiquities and Gauguins and Rodins—the neoclassical New Carlsberg Museum was donated in 1888 by Carl Jacobsen, son of the founder of the Carlsberg Brewery. Surrounding its lush indoor garden, a series of nooks and chambers houses works by Degas and other Impressionists, plus an extensive assemblage of Egyptian, Greek, Roman, and French sculpture, not to mention the best collection of Etruscan art outside Italy and Europe's finest collection of Roman portraits. ⊠ *Dantes Pl. 7,* ☎

33/41–81–41. 🖾 *DKr15, free Wed. and Sun.* ⊙ *May–Aug., Tues.–Sun. 10–4; Sept.–Apr., Tues.–Sat. noon–3, Sun. 10–4.*

★ ㉜ **Rosenborg Slot** (Rosenborg Castle). This Dutch Renaissance castle contains ballrooms, halls, and reception chambers, but for all of its grandeur, there's an intimacy that makes you think the king might return any minute. Thousands of objects are displayed, including beer glasses, gilded clocks, golden swords, family portraits, a pearl-studded saddle, and gem-encrusted tables; an adjacent treasury contains the royal jewels. The castle's setting is equally welcoming: it's smack in the middle of the **Kongens Have** (King's Garden), amid lawns, park benches, and shady walking paths.

King Christian IV built the Rosenborg Castle as a summer residence but loved it so much that he ended up living and dying there. In 1849, when the absolute monarchy was abolished, the royal castles became state property, except for Rosenborg, which is still passed down from monarch to monarch. Once a year, during the fall holiday, the castle stays open until midnight, and visitors are invited to explore its darkened interior with bicycle lights. 🖾 *Øster Voldg. 4A,* ☎ *33/15–32–86.* 🖾 *DKr40.* ⊙ *May–mid-Oct., daily 11–3; mid-Oct.–mid-Dec. and Jan.–Apr., Tues., Fri., and Sun. 11–2.*

★ ㉛ **Rundetårn** (Round Tower). Instead of climbing the stout Round Tower's stairs, visitors scale a smooth, 600-ft spiral ramp on which—legend has it—Peter the Great of Russia rode a horse alongside his wife, Catherine, who took a carriage. From its top, you enjoy a panoramic view of the twisted streets and crooked roofs of Copenhagen. The unusual building was constructed as an observatory in 1642 by Christian IV and is still maintained as the oldest such structure in Europe.

The art gallery features changing exhibits, and occasional concerts are held within its massive stone walls. An observatory and telescope are open to the public evenings mid-October through March, and an astronomer is on hand to answer questions. 🖾 *Købmagerg. 52A,* ☎ *33/93–66–60.* 🖾 *DKr15.* ⊙ *June–Aug., Mon.–Sat. 10–8, Sun. noon–8; Sept.–May, Mon.–Sat. 10–5, Sun. noon–5. Observatory and telescope mid-Oct.–Mar., Tues.–Wed. 7 PM–10 PM.*

㉞ **Statens Museum for Kunst** (National Art Gallery). Works from the golden age to modern Danish art, plus examples of Rubens, Dürer, and the Impressionists, comprise the gallery collection. A sculpture garden filled with classical, modern, and whimsical pieces flanks the building. The museum is closed until sometime in late 1998 for major reconstruction and expansion. 🖾 *Sølvg. 48–50,* ☎ *33/91–21–26.* ⊙ *Closed through late 1998; call for hours when reopened.*

★ ✆ ㊱ **Tivoli.** Copenhagen's best-known attraction, conveniently next to its main train station, attracts an astounding number of visitors: 4 million people from May to September. Tivoli is more sophisticated than a mere funfair; among its attractions are a pantomime theater, open-air stage, elegant restaurants (24 in all), and frequent classical, jazz, and rock concerts. Fantastic flower exhibits color the lush gardens and float on the swan-filled ponds.

On Wednesday and Saturday night, elaborate fireworks are set off, and every day the Tivoli Guard, a youth version of the Queen's Royal Guard, performs. Try to see Tivoli at least once by night, when 100,000 colored lanterns illuminate the Chinese pagoda and the main fountain. The park was established in the 1840s, when Danish architect George Carstensen persuaded a worried King Christian VIII to let him build an amusement park on the edge of the city's fortifications, rationalizing that "when people amuse themselves, they forget politics." Call to double-check prices, which include family discounts at various times during the day. ⊠ *Vesterbrog. 3,* ☎ *33/15–10–01.* 🖭 *Mon.–Sat. 10–1, DKr30; 1–9:30, DKr44; 9:30–midnight, DKr20; Sun. 11–9:30, DKr30; 9:30–midnight, DKr20.* ☉ *Late-Apr.–mid-Sept., daily 10 AM–midnight.*

🖑 ㊳ **Tycho Brahe Planetarium.** This modern, cylindrical planetarium, which appears to be sliced at an angle, features astronomy exhibits. The **Omnimax Theater** takes you on visual odysseys as varied as journeys through space and sea, the stages of the Rolling Stones, or Kuwaiti fires from the Persian Gulf War. These films are not recommended for children under seven. ⊠ *Gammel Kongevej 10,* ☎ *33/12–12–24.* 🖭 *DKr65.* ☉ *Show times vary. Open Mon., Wed., and Fri.–Sun. 10:30–9, Tues. 9:45–9, Thurs. 9:30–9.*

㊴ **Vesterbro.** Copenhagen's equivalent of New York's Lower East Side is populated by immigrants, students, and union workers, it's a great place to find ethnic groceries, discount shops, and cheap international restaurants. ⊠ *At the southern end of Vesterbrogade.*

㉘ **Vor Frue Kirken** (Church of Our Lady). Copenhagen's cathedral since 1924 occupies a site that has drawn worshipers since the 13th century, when Bishop Absalon built a chapel here. Today's church is actually a reconstruction: the original church was destroyed during the Napoleonic Wars. Five towers top the neoclassical structure. Inside you can see Thorvaldsen's marble sculptures depicting Christ and the 12 Apostles, and Moses and David, cast of bronze. ⊠ *Nørreg., Frue Pl.,* ☎ *33/15–10–78.* 🖭 *Free.* ☉ *Apr.–Aug., Mon.–Sat. 8–5, Sun. noon–4; Sept.–Mar., Mon.–Sat. 8–5, Sun. noon–1.*

OFF THE
BEATEN PATH

ZOOLOGISKE HAVE – Kids love the Zoological Gardens, home to more than 2,000 animals. In the small petting zoo and playground live cows, horses, rabbits, goats, and hens. The indoor rain forest is abuzz with butterflies, sloths, alligators, and other tropical creatures. Sea lions, lions, and elephants are fed in the early afternoon. ⊠ *Roskildevej 32,* ☎ *36/30–25–55.* 🖭 *DKr55.* ☉ *June–Aug., daily 9–6; Sept.–Oct. and Apr.–May, daily 9–5; Nov.–Mar., Tues.–Sun. 11–5.*

Dining

In the more than 2,000 restaurants in Copenhagen, traditional Danish fare spans all price categories: you can order a light lunch of traditional smørrebrød, munch alfresco from a street-side *pølser* (sausage) cart, or dine out on Limfjord oysters and local plaice. Even the most upscale restaurants have moderate-price fixed menus. Though few Danish restaurants require reservations, it's best to call ahead to avoid a wait. The city's more affordable ethnic restaurants are concentrated in Vesterbro, Nørrebro, and the side streets off Strøget. And for less-expensive, savory noshes in stylish digs, consider lingering at a café (☞ Cafés *in* Nightlife and the Arts, *below*).

Rådhus Pladsen, Christiansborg Slot, and Strøget

$$$$ ✕ **Gyldne Fortun's Fiskekældere.** Among the city's finest seafood restaurants, this "fish cellar" is brightly decorated with seashell-shaded halogen lamps and aquariums. Across the street from Christiansborg, it is popular with politicians as well as businesspeople. Try the fillets of Scandinavian sole poached in white wine, stuffed with salmon mousseline, glazed with hollandaise, and served with prawns. ⊠ *Ved Stranden 18,* ☎ *33/12–20–11. Reservations essential. AE, DC, MC, V. No lunch weekends.*

Dining
Copenhagen
Corner, **27**
El Meson, **8**
Els, **11**
Flyvefisken, **21**
Gyldne Fortun's
Fiskekældere, **23**
Havfruen, **17**
Ida Davidsen, **7**
Kasmir, **2**
Kommandanten, **10**
Kong Hans, **25**
Krogs, **24**
L'Alsace, **14**
Pakhuskælderen, **26**
Peder Oxe, **13**
Quattro Fontane, **1**
Restaurant Le
St. Jacques, **5**
Riz Raz, **22**
Skt. Gertrudes
Kloster, **6**
Victor, **15**
Wiinblad, **16**

Lodging
Ascot, **19**
Cab–Inn
Scandinavia, **3**
Copenhagen
Admiral, **18**
Copenhagen
Danhostel, **32**
D'Angleterre, **16**
Kong Frederik, **20**
Missionhotellet
Nebo, **30**
Neptun, **12**
Nyhavn 71, **26**
Phoenix, **9**
Plaza, **29**
SAS Scandinavia, **31**
Skovshoved, **4**
Triton, **28**

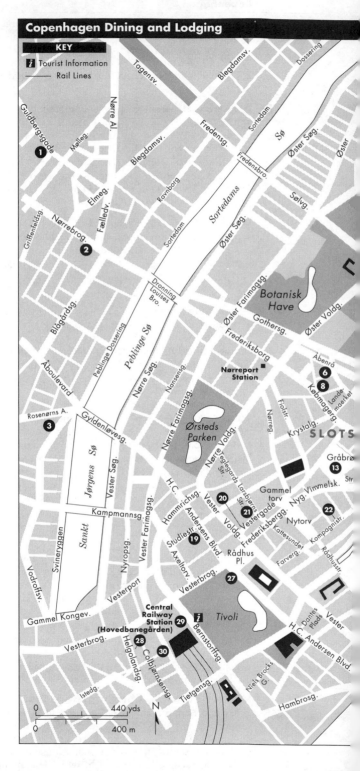

Copenhagen Dining and Lodging

KEY

i Tourist Information
— Rail Lines

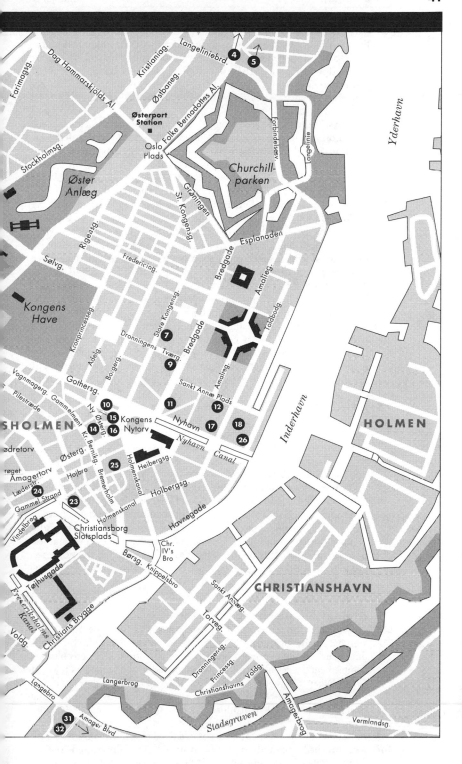

$$$$ ✕ **Kong Hans.** Five centuries ago this was a Nordic vineyard; now it's
★ one of Scandinavia's finest restaurants. Chef Thomas Rode Andersen's
French-Danish-Asian–inspired dishes employ the freshest local ingredients and are served in a mysterious subterranean space with whitewashed walls and vaulted ceilings. Try the foie gras with
raspberry-vinegar sauce or the warm oysters with salmon roe. Jackets
are recommended. ⊠ *Vingårdstr. 6,* ☎ *33/11–68–68. AE, DC, MC,
V. Closed July. No lunch.*

$$$$ ✕ **Krogs.** This elegant canal-front restaurant has developed a loyal clien-
★ tele—both foreign and local. Pale-green walls are simply adorned with
paintings of old Copenhagen to create an understated ambience. The
menu includes such specialties as pan-grilled lobster flavored with
vanilla oil. Jackets are recommended. ⊠ *Gammel Strand 38,* ☎ *33/
15–89–15. Reservations essential. AE, DC, MC, V.*

$$ ✕ **Copenhagen Corner.** Diners here are treated to a superb view of the
Rådhus Pladsen, as well as to terrific smørrebrød, both of which com-
pensate for the often harried staff. Specialties include fried veal with
bouillon gravy and fried potatoes; entrecôte in garlic and bordelaise
sauce paired with creamed potatoes; and a herring plate with three types
of spiced, marinated herring and boiled potatoes. ⊠ *Rådhus Pl.,* ☎
33/91–45–45. AE, DC, MC, V.

$$ ✕ **Peder Oxe.** On a 17th-century square, this lively, countrified bistro
has rustic tables and 15th-century Portuguese tiles. All entrées—among
them grilled steaks and fish and the best fancy burgers in town–come
with an excellent self-service salad bar replete with whole tomatoes,
feta cheese, and fresh greens. Damask-covered tables are set with heavy
cutlery and opened bottles of hearty Pyrénées wine. A clever call-light
for the waitress is above each table. ⊠ *Gråbrødretorv 11,* ☎ *33/11–
00–77. D, MC, V.*

$ ✕ **Flyvefisken.** Silvery stenciled fish swim along blue-and-yellow walls
in this funky Thai eatery. Spicy concoctions include chicken with
cashew nuts, and herring shark in basil sauce. The less-expensive
health-food café in the basement serves excellent food to a steady
stream of students and hipsters. ⊠ *Lars Bjørnstr. 18,* ☎ *33/14–95–
15. DC, MC, V. Closed Sun.*

$ ✕ **Riz Raz.** On a corner off Strøget, this Middle Eastern restaurant hops
★ with young locals, families, couples, and anyone who appreciates good
value and spicy fare. The inexpensive all-you-can-eat buffet is heaped
with lentils, tomatoes, potatoes, olives, hummus, warm pita bread, *kufte*
(Middle Eastern meatballs), yogurt and cucumbers, pickled vegetables,
bean salads, and occasionally pizza. Don't be put off by the hordes—
just join them, either in the restaurant's endless labyrinth of dining rooms
or in the jam-packed summertime patio. ⊠ *Kompagnistr. 20,* ☎ *33/
15–05–75. Reservations essential. DC, MC, V.*

Around Amalienborg and North

$$$ ✕ **Els.** When it opened in 1853, the intimate Els was the place to be
seen before the theater, and the painted Muses on the walls still watch
diners rush to make an eight o'clock curtain. Antique wooden columns
complement the period furniture, which includes tables inlaid with Royal
Copenhagen tile work. Chef Pierre Gravelund changes his nouvelle
French-Danish four-course menu every two weeks, always incorporating
game, fish, and market produce. Jackets are recommended. ⊠ *Store
Strandestr. 3,* ☎ *33/14–13–41. AE, DC, MC, V.*

$$$ ✕ **Kommandanten.** Fancifully decorated by master florist Tage Andersen
★ with brushed iron and copper furniture, down pillows, and foliage-
flanked lights, this is among the city's most chic dinner spots, attracting well-heeled businesspeople and local celebrities—as well as two
Michelin stars. The adventuresome international fare includes rabbit

with bouillon-cooked lentils, herbs, and bacon, and marinated salmon with oysters and parsley. Jackets are recommended. ⊠ *Ny Adelg. 7,* ☎ *33/12–09–90. AE, DC, MC, V. Closed Sun. No lunch Sat.*

$$$ ✕ **L'Alsace.** Set in the cobbled courtyard of Pistolstræde and hung with
★ paintings by Danish surrealist Wilhelm Freddie, this restaurant is peaceful and quiet, attracting such diverse diners as Queen Margrethe, Elton John, and Pope Paul II. The hand-drawn menu lists oysters from Brittany, terrine de foie gras, and *choucrôute à la Strasbourgeoise* (a hearty mélange of cold cabbage, homemade sausage, and pork). Try the superb fresh-fruit tarts and cakes for dessert, and ask to sit in the patio overlooking the courtyard. ⊠ *Ny Øster. 9,* ☎ *33/14–57–43. AE, DC, MC, V. Closed Sun.*

$$$ ✕ **Pakhuskælderen.** Part of the Nyhavn 71 hotel, this intimate restaurant attracts a mix of business and holiday guests. The three- or four course chef's menu may feature a main course of beef fillet in a shallot sauce served with organic potatoes or baked catfish with lobster sauce and saffron rice. The Danish lunch special usually includes a herring starter, followed by a light plate, drink, and dessert. The restaurant's thick white walls and raw timbers lend it a mood of antiquity. ⊠ *Nyhavn 71,* ☎ *33/11–85–85. Reservations essential. AE, DC, MC, V. Closed July. No lunch.*

$$$ ✕ **Wiinblad.** This restaurant doubles as a gallery inspired by the work of contemporary Danish artist Bjørn Wiinblad. Almost everything—tiles, wall partitions, plaques, candlesticks, vases, and even some tables—has been made by the great Dane, and the effect is bright, cheerful, and very elegant. The eatery offers an ample breakfast buffet, lunch, tea, and grilled specialties for dinner. Try the pickled herring with new potatoes and topped with sour cream, or the breast of duck in cranberry cream sauce. It's in the D'Angleterre hotel (☞ Lodging, *below*). ⊠ *D'Angleterre, Kongens Nytorv 34,* ☎ *33/12–80–95. AE, DC, MC, V.*

$$ ✕ **Havfruen.** A life-size wooden mermaid swings from the ceiling in this small, rustic fish restaurant in Nyhavn. Natives love the cozy, maritime-bistro air and come for the daily changing French and Danish menu, heavy on cream sauces, fresh salmon, turbot, and cod. ⊠ *Nyhavn 39,* ☎ *33/11–11–38. DC, MC, V.*

$$ ✕ **Ida Davidsen.** Five generations old, this world-renowned lunch spot is synonymous with smørrebrød. Dimly lit, with worn wooden tables and news clippings of famous visitors, it's usually packed. Creative sandwiches include the H. C. Andersen, with liver pâté, bacon, and tomatoes, and the airplane clipper—steak tartare shaped like a plane and topped with caviar, smoked salmon, and egg yolk. You'll also enjoy a terrific smoked duck that Ida's husband, Adam, smokes himself and serves alongside a horseradish-spiked cabbage salad. ⊠ *Store Kongensg. 70,* ☎ *33/91–36–55. Reservations essential. DC, MC, V. Closed weekends and July. No dinner.*

$$ ✕ **Restaurant Le St. Jacques.** This tiny restaurant barely accommodates
★ a dozen tables, but as soon as the sun shines, diners spill out of its icon filled dining room to sit at tables facing busy Østerbrogade. The chef and owners come from some of the finest restaurants in town, but claim they started this place to slow down the pace and enjoy the company of their customers. The fare changes according to what is available at the market, but expect fabulous concoctions—smoked salmon with crushed eggplant, Canadian scallops with leeks and salmon roe in a beurre blanc sauce, sole with basil sauce and reduced balsamic glaze, and a savory *poussin* (young, small chicken) with sweetbreads scooped into phyllo pastry atop a bed of polenta and lentils. Close tables and chitchat with the owners give this a true café atmosphere. ⊠ *Skt. Jacobs Pl. 1,* ☎ *31/42–77–07. Reservations essential. DC, MC, V.*

$$ ✕ **Victor.** Excellent people-watching and good bistro fare are the calling cards at this French-style corner café. It's best during weekend lunches, when young and old gather for such specialties as rib roast, homemade pâté, and smoked-salmon and cheese platters. Come here for one of the best brunches in town. Be warned, however, that the formal restaurant in the back of the space is quite expensive—order from the front café side for a less expensive meal. ⊠ *Ny Østerg. 8,* ☎ *33/13–36–13. AE, DC, MC, V.*

Down Vesterbrogade and Nørrebro

$$$$ ✕ **Skt. Gertrudes Kloster.** The history of this medieval monastery goes back 700 years, and from the beginning its vaulted stone interiors have welcomed tradesmen and wayfarers. The dining room is bedecked with hundreds of icons, and the only light is provided by 2,000 candles. The French menu is extensive, with such specials as fresh fillet of halibut steamed in oyster sauce and l'Alsace duck breast in a sherry vinaigrette. A jacket and tie are recommended. ⊠ *32 Hauser Pl.,* ☎ *33/14–66–30. Reservations essential. AE, DC, MC, V. No lunch.*

$$ ✕ **El Meson.** At Copenhagen's best Spanish restaurant, you are seated at smoothly worn wooden tables in a dimly lit dining room hung with earthen crockery. The wait staff is knowledgeable and serves generous portions of beef spiced with spearmint, lamb with honey sauce, or paella Valenciano—a mixture of rice, chicken, ham, shrimp, lobster, squid, green beans, and peas—for two. ⊠ *Hausers Pl. 12 (behind Kultorvet),* ☎ *33/11–91–31. AE, DC, MC, V. Closed Sun. No lunch.*

$ ✕ **Kasmir.** This quiet, carpet-shrouded Indian restaurant is a favorite with locals, who come for the unusual vegetarian and fish menu. Specialties include tandoori-baked salmon, a hearty lentil soup, and the basic side dishes—such as *bhajis* (fried vegetables in tomato sauce), *raita* (yogurt and cucumbers), and nan, the thick round bread. ⊠ *Nørrebrog. 35,* ☎ *35/37–54–71. AE, MC, V.*

$ ✕ **Quattro Fontane.** On a corner west of the lakes, one of Copenhagen's best Italian restaurants is a busy, noisy, two-story affair, packed tight with marble-topped tables and a steady flow of young Danes. Served by chatty Italian waiters, the homemade food includes cheese or beef ravioli or cannelloni, linguine with clam sauce, and thick pizza. ⊠ *Guldbergsg. 3,* ☎ *31/39–39–31. No credit cards.*

Lodging

Copenhagen is well served by a wide range of hotels, overall among Europe's most expensive. The hotels around the seedy red-light district of Istedgade—which looks more dangerous than it is—are the least expensive. In summer, reservations are recommended, but should you arrive without one, try the hotel-booking desk in the tourist office. They can give you a same-day, last-minute price (if available) for about DKr200–DKr250 for a single hotel room. This service will also find rooms in private homes, with rates starting at about DKr160 for a single. Young travelers should head for **Huset** (⊠ Rådhusstr. 13, ☎ 33/15–65–18) to get lodging information. Breakfast is included in the room rate and rooms have bath or shower at the following hotels unless otherwise noted.

Rådhus Pladsen, Christiansborg Slot, and Strøget

$$$$ ⊡ **SAS Scandinavia.** Near the airport, this is one of northern Europe's largest hotels and Copenhagen's token skyscraper. An immense lobby, with cool, recessed lighting and streamlined furniture, gives access to the city's first (and only) casino. Guest rooms are large and somewhat institutional but offer every modern convenience, making this a good choice if you prefer convenience over character. Breakfast is not included in the rates. ⊠ *Amager Boulevarden 70, DK–2300 KBH S,* ☎ *33/11–24–23,* FAX *31/57–01–93. 542 rooms, 52 suites. 4 restaurants, bar, room service, indoor pool, health club, casino, concierge, meeting rooms, free parking. AE, DC, MC, V.*

$$$ ⌑ **Kong Frederik.** North of Rådhus Pladsen and a two-minute walk from Strøget, this intimate hotel has the same British style as its sister hotel, the D'Angleterre (☞ *above*). The difference is the sun-drenched Queen's Restaurant, where a hearty morning buffet is served (not included in rates) in addition to lunch and dinner. The rooms are elegant, with Asian vases, mauve carpets, and blue bedspreads. Ask for a top room for tower views. ⊠ *Vester Voldg. 25, DK–1552 KBH V,* ☎ *33/12–59–02,* FAX *33/93–59–01. 110 rooms, 13 suites. Restaurant, bar, room service, meeting rooms, free parking. AE, MC, V.*

$$ ⌑ **Ascot.** This charming downtown hotel's two outstanding features are a wrought-iron staircase and an excellent breakfast buffet. The lobby is classic, with marble and columns, but the guest rooms and apartments are comfy, with modern furniture and bright colors; some have kitchenettes. ⊠ *Studiestr. 61, DK–1554 KBH V,* ☎ *33/12–60–00,* FAX *33/14–60–40. 143 rooms, 30 apartments. Restaurant, bar, exercise room, meeting rooms, free parking. AE, DC, MC, V.*

$ ⌑ **Copenhagen Danhostel.** This simple lodging is 4½ km (3 mi) outside out of town, close to the airport. The hostel is spread over nine interconnecting buildings, all laid out on one floor. International Youth Hostel members—including student backpackers as well as families—use the communal kitchen or buy breakfast and dinner from the restaurant. The hostel is also wheelchair-accessible. Before 5 PM on weekdays, take Bus 46 from the main station directly to the hostel. After 5, from Rådhus Pladsen or the main station, take Bus 10 to Mozartplads, and change to Bus 37. Ask the driver to signal your stop. ⊠ *Vejlands All 200, DK–2300 KBH S,* ☎ *32/52–29–08,* FAX *32/52–27–08. 64 rooms with 2 beds, 80 family rooms with 5 beds, 4 large communal bathrooms. Restaurant. No credit cards.*

Around Amalienborg and North

$$$$ ⌑ **D'Angleterre.** The grande dame of Copenhagen welcomes royalty
★ and rock stars in palatial surroundings: an imposing New Georgian facade leads into an English-style sitting room. Standard guest rooms are furnished in pastels, with overstuffed chairs and modern and antique furniture. The spit-and-polish staff accommodates every wish. Breakfast is not included in the rates. ⊠ *Kongens Nytorv 34, DK–1050 KBH K,* ☎ *33/12–00–95,* FAX *33/12–11–18. 130 rooms, 28 suites. 2 restaurants, bar, room service, indoor pool, nightclub, concierge, meeting rooms, parking (fee). AE, DC, MC, V.*

$$$$ ⌑ **Nyhavn 71.** In a 200-year-old warehouse, this quiet and slightly fraying hotel is a good choice for privacy-seekers. It overlooks the old ships of Nyhavn, and its nautical interiors have been preserved with their original thick plaster walls and exposed brick. The rooms are tiny but cozy, with warm woolen spreads, dark woods, soft leather furniture, and crisscrossing timbers, but at least some of this may be changing as the hotel is renovated throughout the late '90s. The staff promises, however, that the rooms will remain elegantly cozy. Breakfast is not included. ⊠ *Nyhavn 71, DK–1051 KBH K,* ☎ *33/11–85–85,* FAX *33/93–15–85. 82 rooms, 6 suites. Restaurant, bar, room service, concierge, meeting rooms, free parking. AE, DC, MC, V.*

$$$ ⌑ **Neptun.** This elegant, central hotel was bought years ago with the intention of making it the bohemian gathering place of Copenhagen, but proprietress Bente Noyens has also made it practical. The lobby and lounge are light, with slender furnishings and peach tones. Guest rooms have a tasteful modern decor; they vary greatly in size within

the same price category, so specify a larger room when booking. Next door is a regional Danish restaurant. ⊠ *Skt. Annæ Pl. 14–20, DK–1250 KBH K,* ☎ *33/13–89–00,* FAX *33/14–12–50. (In the U.S., call Best Western, 800/528–1234.) 133 rooms, 13 suites. Restaurant, room service, meeting rooms, free parking. AE, DC, MC, V.*

$$$ ⊡ **Phoenix.** This luxury hotel has automatic glass doors, crystal chandeliers, and gilt touches everywhere. The staff is multilingual and adept at accommodating both a business and tourist clientele. The suites and business-class rooms are adorned with faux antiques and 18-carat-gold bathroom fixtures, whereas the standard rooms are very small, measuring barely 9 by 15 ft. It's so convenient to central-city attractions that the hotel gets a certain amount of street noise; light sleepers should ask for rooms above the second floor. ⊠ *Bredg. 37, DK–1260 KBH K,* ☎ *33/95–95–00,* FAX *33/33–98–33. 212 rooms, 7 suites. Restaurant, pub (closed Sun.), meeting room. AE, DC, MC, V.*

$$$ ⊡ **Skovshoved.** This delightful, art-filled inn is 8 km (5 mi) north of
★   town, near a few old fishing cottages beside the yacht harbor. Licensed since 1660, it has retained its provincial charm. Its larger rooms overlook the sea, smaller ones rim the courtyard; all have both modern and antique furnishings. ⊠ *Strandvejen 267, DK–2920 Charlottelund,* ☎ *31/64–00–28,* FAX *31/64–06–72. 20 rooms. Restaurant, bar, meeting room. AE, DC, MC, V.*

$$ ⊡ **Copenhagen Admiral.** A five-minute stroll from Nyhavn, overlooking old Copenhagen and Amalienborg, the monolithic Admiral was once a grain warehouse but now affords travelers no-nonsense accommodations. With massive stone walls—broken by rows of tiny windows—it's one of the less expensive top hotels, cutting frills and prices. Its guest rooms are spare, with jutting beams and modern prints. ⊠ *Toldbodg. 24–28, DK–1253 KBH K,* ☎ *33/11–82–82,* FAX *33/32–55–42. 365 rooms, 52 suites. Restaurant, bar, sauna, nightclub, meeting rooms, free parking. AE, DC, MC, V.*

Down Vesterbrogade and Nørrebro

$$$ ⊡ **Plaza.** With its convenient location and plush homey atmosphere, this hotel attracts the likes of Tina Turner and Keith Richards. Close to Tivoli and the main station, the building opens with a stately lobby and the adjacent Russian restaurant, Alexander Nevski, with perhaps the best vodka selection in town. The older rooms are scattered with antiques; newer ones are furnished in a more modern style. ⊠ *Bernstorffsg. 4, DK–1577 KBH V,* ☎ *33/14–92–62,* FAX *33/93–93–62. 93 rooms, 6 suites. Restaurant, bar, room service, concierge, meeting rooms, parking (fee). AE, DC, MC, V.*

$$ ⊡ **Triton.** Despite seedy surroundings, this streamlined hotel attracts a cosmopolitan clientele thanks to a central location in Vesterbro. The large rooms, in blond wood and warm tones, all include modern bathrooms and state-of-the-art fixtures. The buffet breakfast is exceptionally generous, the staff friendly. There are also family rooms, with a bedroom and a dining-sitting area with a foldout couch. ⊠ *Helgolandsg. 7–11, DK–1653 KBH V,* ☎ *31/31–32–66,* FAX *31/31–69–70. 123 rooms, 2 suites, 4 family rooms. Bar, meeting room. AE, DC, MC, V.*

$ ⊡ **Cab–Inn Scandinavia.** This bright hotel is just west of the lakes and Vesterport Station. Its impeccably maintained rooms are distinctly small, but designed with superefficiency to include ample showers, stowaway and bunk beds, and even electric water kettles. The hotel is popular with business travelers in winter and kroner-pinching backpackers and families in summer. Its sister hotel, the Cab–Inn Copenhagen (☎ *31/21–04–00,* FAX *31/21–74–09) is just around the corner, at Danasvej 32–34. ⊠ *Vodroffsvej 55–57, Frederiksberg C, DK–1900,* ☎ *35/36–*

11–11, FAX 35/36–11–14. 201 rooms. Breakfast room, snack bar, exercise room, meeting rooms. AE, DC, MC, V.

$ 🖭 **Missionhotellet Nebo.** Though it's between the main train station and Istedgade's seediest porn shops, this budget hotel is still prim, comfortable, and well maintained by a friendly staff. Its dormlike guest rooms are furnished with industrial carpeting, polished pine furniture, and gray-stripe duvet covers. Baths, showers, and toilets are at the center of each hallway, and downstairs there's a breakfast restaurant with a tiny courtyard. ✉ *Istedg. 6, DK–1650 KBH V,* ☎ *31/21–12–17,* FAX *31/23–47–74. 96 rooms, 40 with bath. AE, DC, MC, V.*

Nightlife and the Arts

Nightlife

Most nightlife is concentrated in the area in and around Strøget, though there are student and "leftist" cafés and bars in Nørrebro and more upscale spots in Østerbro. Many restaurants, cafés, bars, and clubs stay open after midnight, a few until 5 AM. Copenhagen used to be famous for jazz, but unfortunately that has changed in recent years, with many of the best clubs closing down. However, you'll find nightspots catering to almost all musical tastes, from bop to ballroom music—and for the younger crowd, house, rap, and techno—in trendy clubs soundtracked by local DJs. The area around Nikolaj Kirken has the highest concentration of trendy discos and dance spots.

BARS AND LOUNGES

Peder Oxe's basement (✉ Gråbrødretorv 11, ☎ 33/11–11–93) is casual and young, though nearly impossible to squeeze into on weekends. The **Library,** in the Plaza (✉ 4 Bernstorffsg., ☎ 33/14–92–62), is an elegant spot for a quiet drink. The more than 270-year-old **Hviids Vinstue** (✉ Kongens Nytorv 19, ☎ 33/15–10–64) attracts all kinds, young and old, single and coupled, for a glass of wine or cognac. **Vin & Ølgod** (✉ Skinderg. 45, ☎ 33/13–26–25) draws a diverse crowd for singing, beer drinking, and linking of arms for old-fashioned dancing to corny swing bands.

CAFÉS

Café life appeared in Copenhagen in the '70s and quickly became a compulsory part of its urban existence. The cheapest sit-down eateries in town, where a cappuccino and sandwich often cost less than DKr40, cafés are lively and relaxed at night, the crowd always interesting. **Café Sommersko** (✉ Kronprinsensg. 6, ☎ 33/14–81–89) is the granddaddy, with a surprisingly varied menu (try the delicious french fries with pesto) and an eclectic crowd. **Krasnapolsky** (✉ Vesterg. 10, ☎ 33/32–88–00) packs a young, hip, and painfully well-dressed audience at night, a more mixed group for its quiet afternoons. **Café Dan Turrell** (✉ Skt. Regneg. 3, ☎ 33/14–10–47), another old café, as of late has become terribly chic with good food and candlelight. **Victors Café** (✉ Ny Østerg. 8, ☎ 33/13–36–13) is all brass and dark wood, lovely for a light lunch. At the very chic **Europa** (✉ Amagertorv 1, ☎ 33/14–28–09), people-watching and coffee far surpass the fare. The juncture of Købmagergade and Strøget marks the art nouveau–style **Café Norden** (✉ Østerg. 61, ☎ 33/11–77–91), where substantial portions make up for minimal table space. On Nørrebro's main square, Skt. Hanstorv, the all-in-one rock club-restaurant-café **Rust** (✉ Guldbergsg. 8, ☎ 35/37-72-83) is packed all the time. Hearty, fresh dishes are served inside, and there's grill food outside on the terrace. Come evening, **Sebastopol** (Guldbergsg. 2, ☎ 35/36–30–02) is packed with gussied-up locals; sample the ample weekend brunch.

CASINO

The **Casino Copenhagen** at the SAS Scandinavia (✉ Amager Boulevarden 70, ☎ 33/11–51–15) has American and French roulette, blackjack, baccarat, and slot machines. Admission is DKr80 (you must be 18 years old and show a photo ID), and a dress code (jackets required and no sportswear or jeans) is enforced. The casino is open 2 PM to 4 AM.

DISCOS AND DANCING

Most discos open at 11 PM, have cover charges of about DKr40, and pile on steep drink prices. Among the most enduring clubs is **Woodstock** (✉ Vesterg. 12, ☎ 33/11–20–71), where a mixed audience grooves to '60s music. The very popular English-style **Rosie McGees** (✉ Vesterbrog. 2A, ☎ 33/32–19–23) pub serves up Mexican eats and dancing. At the fashionable **Park Café** (✉ Østerbrog. 79, ☎ 35/26–63–42), there's an old-world café with live music downstairs, a disco upstairs, and a movie theater next door. The lively **Club Absalon** (✉ Frederiksbergg. 38, ☎ 33/16–16–99), popular with folks in uniforms (policemen, soldiers, and nurses among them), has live music on the ground floor and a disco above. **Søpavillionen** (✉ Gyldenløvesg. 24, ☎ 33/15–12–24), between St. Jørgen's and Peblinge lakes, glows white on the outside; within there's pop and disco on Friday and Saturday night for an older crowd. At the **Røde Pimpernel** (✉ Hans Christian Andersen Blvd. 7, ☎ 33/12–20–32), an adult audience gathers for dancing to live orchestras, trios, and old-time music. **Sabor Latino** (✉ Vester Voldg. 85, ☎ 33/11–97–66) is the United Nations of discos, with an international crowd dancing to salsa and other Latin rhythms.

GAY BARS

Women and men pack **Pan Café**'s (✉ Knabrostr. 3, off Strøget, ☎ 33/11–37–84) five floors of coffee-and-cocktail bars; the disco's open Wednesday through Saturday night (DKr40 cover). The **Amigo Bar** (✉ Schønbergsg. 4, ☎ 31/21–49–15) serves light meals and is popular with men of all ages. Much larger is the mammoth **Club Amigo** (✉ Studiestr. 31A, ☎ 33/15–33–32), which includes a indoor pool and sauna, as well as a disco, GeO2. The dark, casual **Cosy Bar** (✉ Studiestr. 24, ☎ 33/12–74–27) is the place to go in the wee hours (it usually stays open until 8 AM). **Sebastian Bar Café** (✉ Hyskenstr. 10, ☎ 33/32–22–79) is relaxed for a drink or coffee, and is among the best cafés in town, with art exhibits upstairs and a bulletin board downstairs.

The small **Central Hjørnen** (✉ Kattesundet 18, ☎ 33/11–85–49) has been around for about 70 years. **Masken** (✉ Studiestr. 33, ☎ 33/91–67–80) is a relaxed bar welcoming both men and women. The cozy lesbian café **Babooshka** (✉ Turesensg. 6, ☎ 33/15–05–36) also welcomes men. **Hotel Windsor** (✉ Frederiksborgg. 40, ☎ 33/11–08–30, FAX 33/11–63–87) is a gay-friendly hotel that doubles as a great breakfast greasy spoon. The men-only **Men's Bar** (✉ Teglgaardstraede 3, ☎ 33/12–73–03) is dark and casual, with a leather and rubber dress code. It's easy to meet mostly men at **Can Can** (✉ Mikkel Bryggesg. 11, ☎ 33/11–50–10), a small place with a friendly bartender.

For more information, call or visit the **Lesbiske og Bøsser Landsforening** (Lesbian and Gay Association, ✉ Teglgaardstr. 13, 1452 KBH K, ☎ 33/13–19–48), which has a library and more than 45 years of experience. Check out *Xpansion*, a supplement of the larger free paper *Pan Bladet,* for listings of nightlife events and clubs.

JAZZ CLUBS

Hard times have thinned Copenhagen's once-thriving jazz scene. Among the clubs still open, most headline local talents, but European and international artists also perform, especially in July, when the Copenhagen

Jazz Festival spills over into the clubs. **La Fontaine** (✉ Kompagnistr. 11, ☎ 33/11–60–98) is Copenhagen's quintessential jazz dive, with sagging curtains, impenetrable smoke, and lounge lizards. **Copenhagen Jazz House** (✉ Niels Hemmingsensg. 10, ☎ 33/15–26–00) is infinitely more up-scale, attracting European and some international names to its chic, modern, bar-like ambience. **Jazzhus Slukefter** (✉ Vesterbrog. 3, ☎ 33/11–11–13) is Tivoli's jazz club, attracting big names.

ROCK CLUBS

Copenhagen has a good selection of rock clubs, most of which cost less than DKr40. Almost all are filled with young, fashionable crowds. They tend to open and go out of business with some frequency, but you can get free entertainment newspapers and flyers advertising gigs at almost any café. **Cafe'en Funk** (✉ Blegdamsvej 2, ☎ 31/35–17–41) plays jazz, rock, and folk. The **Pumpehuset** (✉ Studiestr. 52, ☎ 33/93–19–60) is the place for soul and rock. For good old-fashioned rock and roll, head to **Lades Kælder** (✉ Kattesundet 6, ☎ 33/14–00–67), a local hangout just off Strøget.

The Arts

The most complete English calendar of events is listed in the tourist magazine **Copenhagen This Week,** and includes musical and theatrical events as well as films and exhibitions. Copenhagen's main theater and concert season runs from September through May, and tickets can be obtained either directly from theaters and concert halls or from ticket agencies. **Billetnet** (✉ Main post office, Tietgensg. 37, ☎ 35/28–91–83), a box-office service available at all post offices, has tickets for most major events. The main phone line is impossible to get through to: for information go in person to the post office on Købmagergade, just off Strøget, or check in at any post office. Billetnet's owner, **ARTE** (✉ Hvidkildevej 64, ☎ 38/88–49–00), is another good source for tickets; same-day purchases at the ARTE box office (✉ Near the Nørreport train station, Fiolstr. side, no phone) are half off. Tivoli's **Billetcenter** (✉ Vesterbrog. 3, ☎ 33/15–10–12) issues tickets for its own events.

FILM

Films open in Copenhagen a few months to a year after their U.S. premieres. Nonetheless, the Danes are avid viewers, willing to pay DKr60 per ticket, wait in lines for premieres, and read subtitles. Call the theater for reservations, and pick up tickets (which include a seat number) an hour before the movie. Most theaters have a café. Among the city's alternative venues for second-run films is **Vester Vov Vov** (✉ Absalonsg. 5, ☎ 31/24–42–00) in Vesterbro. The **Grand** (✉ Mikkel Bryggersg. 8, ☎ 33/15–16–11) shows new foreign and artsy films, and is just next door to its sister café.

OPERA, BALLET, AND THEATER

Tickets at the **Kongelige Teater** (Danish Royal Theater, ✉ Tordenskjoldsg. 3, ☎ 33/14–10–02; ☞ Exploring Copenhagen, *above*) are reasonably priced at DKr70–DKr400; the season runs October to May. It is home to the Royal Danish Ballet, one of the premier companies in the world. Not as famous, but also accomplished, are the **Royal Danish Opera** and the **Royal Danish Orchestra**, the latter of which performs in all productions. Plays are exclusively in Danish. For information and reservations, call the theater. Beginning at the end of July, you can order tickets for the next season by writing to the theater (✉ Danish Royal Theater, Attn. Ticket Office, Box 2185, DK–1017 KBH). For English-language theater, call either the professional **London Toast Theater** (☎ 33/33–80–25) or the amateur **Copenhagen Theater Circle** (☎ 31/62–86–20); both troupes perform in various venues.

Outdoor Activities and Sports

Beaches

North of Copenhagen along the old beach road, **Strandvejen,** you'll find a string of lovely old seaside towns and beaches. **Bellevue Beach** (⊠ Across the street from Klampenborg Station) is packed with locals and has cafés, kiosks, and surfboard rentals. **Charlottelund Fort** (⊠ Bus 6 from Rådhuspl.) is a bit more private, but you'll have to pay (about DKr10) to swim off the pier. The beaches along the tony town of **Vedbæk,** 18 km (11 mi) north of Copenhagen, are not very crowded.

Biking

Bike rentals (DKr100–DKr200 deposit and DKr30–DKr60 per day) are available throughout the city, and most roads have bike lanes. Follow all traffic signs and signals; bicycle lights must be used at night. For more information, contact the **Dansk Cyclist Forbund** (Danish Cyclist Federation, ⊠ Rømersg. 7, ☎ 33/32–31–21).

Golf

Some clubs do not accept reservations; call for details. Virtually all clubs in Denmark require your being a member of another club for admittance. Handicap requirements vary widely.

One of Denmark's best courses, often the host of international tournaments, is the 18-hole **Rungsted Golf Klub** (⊠ Vestre Stationsvej 16, ☎ 42/86–34–44). A 30 handicap for all players is required on weekdays; on weekends and holidays there's a 24 handicap for men and a 29 handicap for women. The 18-hole **Københavns Golf Klub** (⊠ Dyrehaven 2, ☎ 39/63–04–83) is said to be Scandinavia's oldest. Greens fees range from DKr180 to DKr240.

Health and Fitness Clubs

A day pass for weights and aerobics at the **Fitness Club** (⊠ Vesterbrog. 2E at Scala, across the street from Tivoli, ☎ 33/32–10–02) is DKr65. **Form og Figur** (Form and Figure) offers one-hour aerobics classes for DKr75 at the SAS Globetrotter Hotel (⊠ Engvej 171, ☎ 31/55–00–70) in Amager, and weights, treadmill, and stationary bikes for DKr75 at the SAS Scandinavia Hotel (⊠ Amager Boulevarden 70, ☎ 31/54–28–88) and Øbro-Hallen (⊠ Ved Idrætsparken 1, ☎ 35/26–79–39).

Horseback Riding

You can ride at the Dyrehavebakken (Deer Forest Hills) in Lyngby at the **Fortunens Ponyudlejning** (⊠ Ved Fortunen 33, ☎ 45/87–60–58). A one-hour session, in which both experienced and inexperienced riders go out with a guide, costs about DKr85.

Running

The 6-km (4-mi) loop around the three lakes just west of city center— St. Jorgens, Peblinge, and Sortedams—is a runner's nirvana. There are also paths at the Rosenborg Have; the Frederiksberg Garden (near Frederiksberg Station, corner of Frederiksberg Allé and Pile Allé); and the Dyrehaven, north of the city near Klampenborg.

Soccer

Danish soccer fans call themselves *Rolegans*—which loosely translates as well-behaved fans—as opposed to hooligans, and idolize the national team's soccer players as superstars. When the rivalry is most intense (especially against Sweden and Norway), fans don face paint, wear head-to-toe red and white, incessantly wave the *Dannebrog* (Danish flag), and have a good time whether or not they win. The biggest stadium in town for national and international games is **Parken** (⊠ Øster Allé 50, ☎ 35/43–31–31). Tickets (DKr120 for slightly obstructed views,

DKr250–DKr300 for unobstructed; local matches are less expensive than international ones) can be bought at any post office.

Swimming

Swimming is very popular here, and pools are crowded but well maintained. Separate bath tickets can also be purchased. Admission to local pools (DKr20–DKr50) includes a locker key, but you'll have to bring your own towel. Most pools are 25 m long. The beautiful **Frederiksberg Svømmehal** (⊠ Helgesvej 29, ☎ 38/14–04–04) still maintains its old Art Deco decor with sculptures and decorative tiles. **Øbro Hallen** (⊠ Ved Idrætsparken 3, ☎ 31/42–30–65) is in the large sports compound north of the center. The pool is lined with sculptures, and there is a 10-m diving tower; massage is also available. In the modern concrete **Vesterbro Svømmehal** (⊠ Angelg. 4, ☎ 31/22–05–00), many enjoy swimming next to the large glass windows. The 50-m **Lyngby Svømmehal** (⊠ Lundoftevej 53, ☎ 45/87–44–56) is one of metropolitan Copenhagen's newest pools, with a separate diving pool.

Tennis

Courts fees for guests are very high, often including court rental (DKr75 per person) and a separate nonmembers' user fee (as high as DKr130). If you must volley, courts are available to guests at some sports centers before 1 PM only. **Københavns Boldklub** (⊠ PeterBangs Vej 147, ☎ 38/71–41–50) is in Frederiksberg, a neighborhood just west of central Copenhagen. **Hellerup Idræts Klub** (⊠ Hartmannsvej 37, ☎ 31/62–14–28) is about 5 km (3 mi) north of town. **Skovshoved Idræts Forening** (⊠ Krørsvej 5A, ☎ 31/64–23–83) is along the old beach road about 10 km (6 mi) north of town.

Shopping

A showcase for world-famous Danish design and craftsmanship, Copenhagen seems to have been designed with shoppers in mind. The best buys are such luxury items as crystal, porcelain, silver, and furs. Look for sales (*tilbud* or *udsalg* in Danish) and check antiques and secondhand shops for classics at cut-rate prices.

Although prices are inflated by a hefty 25% Value-Added Tax (Danes call it MOMS), non–European Union citizens can receive about a 20% refund. For more details and a list of all tax-free shops, ask at the tourist board for a copy of the *Tax-Free Shopping Guide* (☞ Sales-Tax Refunds *in* Denmark A to Z, *below*).

Department Stores

Illum (⊠ Østerg. 52, ☎ 33/14–40–02), not to be confused with Illums Bolighus (☞ Design, *below*), is well stocked, with a lovely rooftop café and excellent basement grocery. **Magasin** (⊠ Kongens Nytorv 13, ☎ 33/11–44–33), Scandinavia's largest, also has a top-quality basement marketplace. **Daells** (⊠ Fiolstr., ☎ 33/12–78–25) is best for basic Danish goods, like wool underwear and frying pans, at relatively reasonable prices.

Shopping Districts, Streets, and Malls

The pedestrian only **Strøget** and adjacent **Købmagergade** are *the* shopping streets, but wander down the smaller streets for lower-priced, offbeat stores. You'll find the most exclusive shops at the end of Strøget, around Kongens Nytorv, and on Ny Adelgade, Grønnegade, and Pistolstræde. **Scala,** the city's glittering café- and boutique-studded mall, is across the street from Tivoli and has a trendy selection of clothing stores. Farther south in the city, on **Vesterbrogade,** you'll find discount stores—especially leather and clothing shops.

Specialty Stores

ANTIQUES

For silver, porcelain, and crystal, the well-stocked shops on **Bredgade** are upscale and expensive. On Strøget, **Royal Copenhagen Porcelain** (⊠ Amagertorv 6, ☎ 33/13–71–81) carries old and new china, porcelain patterns, and figurines, as well as seconds. **Kaabers Antikvariat** (⊠ Skinderg. 34, ☎ 33/15–41–77) is an emporium for old and rare books, prints, and maps. For silver, Christmas plates, or porcelain, head to **H. Danielsens** (⊠ Læderstr. 11, ☎ 33/13–02–74). **Danborg Gold and Silver** (⊠ Holbergsg. 17, ☎ 33/32–93–94) is one of the best places for estate jewelry and silver flatware. For furniture, the dozens of **Ravnsborggade** stores carry traditional pine, oak, and mahogany furniture, and smaller items as lamps and tableware. (Some of them sell tax-free items and can arrange shipping.)

AUDIO EQUIPMENT

For high-tech design and acoustics, **Bang & Olufsen** (⊠ Østerg. 3, ☎ 33/15–04–22) is so renowned that its products are in the permanent design collection of New York's Museum of Modern Art. (Check prices at home first to make sure you are getting a deal.) You'll find B&O and other international names at **Fredgaard** (⊠ Nørre Voldg. 17, ☎ 33/13–82–45), near Nørreport Station.

CLOTHING

At **Jens Sørensen** (⊠ Vester Voldg. 5, ☎ 33/12–26–02) you'll find fine men's and women's clothing and outerwear, and a Burberry collection. **Petitgas Chapeaux** (⊠ Købmagerg. 5, ☎ 33/13–62–70) is a venerable shop for old-fashioned men's hats. The **Company Store** (⊠ Frederiksbergg. 24, ☎ 33/11–35–55) is for trendy, youthful styles, typified by the Danish Matinique label. If you are interested in the newest Danish designs, keep your eyes open for cooperatives and designer-owned stores. Among the most inventive handmade women's clothing shops is **Met Mari** (⊠ Vesterg. 11, ☎ 33/15–87–25). Thick, traditional, patterned, and solid Scandinavian sweaters are available at the **Sweater Market** (⊠ Frederiksbergg. 15, ☎ 33/15–27–73). **Artium** (⊠ Vesterbrog. 1, ☎ 33/12–34–88) offers an array of colorful, Scandinavian-designed sweaters and clothes alongside useful and artful household gifts.

CRYSTAL AND PORCELAIN

Minus the V.A.T., such Danish classics as Holmegaard crystal and Royal Copenhagen porcelain are less expensive than they are back home. Signed art glass is always more expensive, but be on the lookout for seconds as well as secondhand and unsigned pieces. Tucked in a lovely courtyard is the elegant shop **Hinz/Kjær Glasdesign** (⊠ Østerg. 24, ☎ 33/32–83–82), where the work of this American-Danish couple includes bright glasses, bowls, and other functional art. **Chicago** (⊠ Vimmelskaftet 47 on Strøget, ☎ 33/12–30–31) shows off a wide variety of Scandinavian art and functional glass. **Skandinavisk Glas** (⊠ Ny Østerg. 4, ☎ 33/13–80–95) has a large selection of Danish and international glass and a helpful, informative staff.

Holmegaards Glass has a Strøget store (⊠ Østerg. 15, ☎ 33/12–44–77), as well as a factory (☎ 55/54–62–00), 97 km (60 mi) south of Copenhagen near the town of Næstved, that is smaller than the shop in Copenhagen but has a larger selection of seconds, discounted 20% to 50%. (The store on Østergade has a limited selection of seconds.) The **Royal Copenhagen** shop (⊠ Amagertorv 6, ☎ 33/13–71–81) has firsts and seconds. For a look at the goods at their source, try the **Royal Copenhagen Factory** (⊠ Smalleg. 45, ☎ 31/86–48–48).

DESIGN

Part gallery, part department store, **Illums Bolighus** (⊠ Amagertorv 6, ☎ 33/14–19–41) shows off cutting-edge Danish and international design—art glass, porcelain, silverware, carpets, and loads of grown-up toys. **Lysberg, Hansen and Therp** (⊠ Bredg. 3, ☎ 33/14–47–87), one of the most prestigious interior-design firms in Denmark, has sumptuous showrooms done up in traditional and modern styles. **Interieur** (⊠ Gothersg. 91, ☎ 33/13–15–56) displays fresh Danish style and chic kitchenware. Wizard florist **Tage Andersen** (⊠ Ny Adelg. 12, ☎ 33/93–09–13) has a fantasy-infused gallery-shop filled with one-of-a-kind gifts and arrangements; browsers (who generally don't purchase the pricey items) are charged a DKr40 admission.

FUR

Denmark, the world's biggest producer of ranched minks, is the place to go for quality furs. Furs are ranked into four grades: Saga Royal, Saga, Quality 1, and Quality 2. Copenhagen's finest furrier, dealing only in Saga Royal quality, and purveyor to the royal family is **Birger Christensen** (⊠ Østerg. 38, ☎ 33/11–55–55), which presents a new collection yearly from its in-house design team. Expect to spend about 20% less than in the United States for same-quality furs ($5,000–$10,000 for mink, $3,000 for a fur-lined coat). Birger Christensen is also among the preeminent fashion houses in town, carrying Donna Karan, Chanel, Prada, Kenzo, Jil Sander, and Yves Saint Laurent. **A. C. Bang** (⊠ Østerg. 27, ☎ 33/15–17–26) carries less expensive furs, but has an old-world, old-money aura and very high quality. **Otto D. Madsen** (⊠ Vesterbrog. 1, ☎ 33/13–41–10) is not as chichi as some of Copenhagen's furriers, but has less expensive items.

SILVER

Check the silver standard of a piece by its stamp. Three towers and "925S" (which means 925 parts out of 1,000) mark sterling. Two towers are used for silver plate. The "826S" stamp (also denoting sterling, but less pure) was used until the 1920s. Even with shipping charges, you can expect to save 50% versus American prices when buying Danish silver (especially used) at the source. For one of the most recognized names in international silver, visit **Georg Jensen** (⊠ Amagertorv 4, ☎ 33/11–40–80), an elegant, austere shop aglitter with velvet-cushioned sterling. **Peter Krog** (⊠ 4 Bredg., ☎ 33/12–45–55) stocks collectors' items in silver, primarily Georg Jensen place settings, compotes, and jewelry. **Ketti Hartogsohn** (⊠ Palæg. 8, ☎ 33/15–53–98) carries all sorts of silver knickknacks and settings. The **English Silver House** (⊠ Pilestr. 4, ☎ 33/14–83–81) is an emporium of used estate silver. The city's largest (and brightest) silver store is **Sølvkælderen** (⊠ Kompagnistr. 1, ☎ 33/13–36–34), with an endless selection of tea services, place settings, and jewelry.

Street Markets

Check with the tourist board or the tourist magazine *Copenhagen This Week* for flea markets. Bargaining is expected. For a good overview of antiques and junk, visit the flea market at **Israels Plads** (⊠ Near Nørreport Station), open May–October, Saturday 8–2. It is run by more than 100 professional dealers, and prices are steep, but there are loads of classic Danish porcelain, silver, jewelry, and crystal, plus books, prints, postcards, and more. Slightly smaller than the Israels Plads market, and with lower prices and more junk, is the market behind **Frederiksberg Rådhus** (summer Saturday mornings). The junk and flea market that takes place Saturday in summer and stretches from Nørrebros Runddel down the road along the Assistens Kirkegårn (cemetery) claims to be one of the longest in the world.

Copenhagen A to Z

Arriving and Departing

BY CAR

The E–66 highway, via bridges and ferry routes, connects Fredericia (on Jylland) with Middelfart (on Fyn), a distance of 16 km (10 mi), and goes on to Copenhagen, another 180 km (120 mi) east. Farther north, from Århus (in Jylland), you can get direct ferry service to Kalundborg (on Sjælland). From there, Route 23 leads to Roskilde, about 72 km (45 mi) east. Take Route 21 east and follow the signs to Copenhagen, another 40 km (25 mi). Make reservations for the ferry in advance through the Danish State Railways (DSB, ⊠ Hovedbanegården, DK–1570 KBH K, ☎ 33/14–17–01).

BY FERRY

Frequent ferries connect Copenhagen with Sweden, including several daily ships from Malmö, Limhamn, Landskrona, and Helsingborg. There is also a high-speed craft from Malmö.

BY PLANE

Copenhagen Airport, 10 km (6 mi) southeast of downtown in Kastrup, is the gateway to Scandinavia. International and domestic flights are served by **SAS** (☎ 32/33–68–48). Among the other airlines that serve Copenhagen Airport are **British Airways** (☎ 33/14–60–00), **Icelandair** (☎ 33/12–33–88), and **Delta** (☎ 33/11–56–56).

Between the Airport and Downtown: Although the 10-km (6-mi) drive from the airport to downtown is quick and easy, public transportation is also a good option. **SAS coach buses** leave the international arrivals terminal every 15 minutes, from 5:42 AM to 9:45 PM, cost DKr32, and take 25 minutes to reach Copenhagen's main train station on Vesterbrogade. Another SAS coach from Christianborg, on Slotsholmsgade, to the airport runs every 15 minutes between 8:30 AM and noon, and every half-hour from noon to 6 PM. **HT** city buses depart from the international arrivals terminal every 15 minutes, from 4:30 AM (Sunday 5:30) to 11:52 PM, but take a long, circuitous route. Take Bus 250S for the Rådhus Pladsen and transfer. Tickets (one way) cost DKr15.

The 20-minute **taxi** ride downtown costs from DKr75 to DKr120 and up. Lines form at the international arrivals terminal. In the unlikely event there is no taxi available, call ☎ 31/35–35–35.

BY TRAIN

Copenhagen's **Hovedbanegården** (Central Station, ⊠ Vesterbrog.) is the hub of the DSB network and is connected to most major cities in Europe. Intercity trains leave every hour, usually on the hour, from 6 AM to 10 PM for principal towns in Fyn and Jylland. Find out more from **DSB** (☎ 33/14–17–01). You can make reservations at the central station, at most other stations, and through travel agents.

Getting Around

Copenhagen is small, with most sights within its one square-mi center. Wear comfortable shoes and explore it on foot. Or follow the example of the Danes and rent a bike. For those with aching feet, an efficient transit system is available.

BY BICYCLE

Bikes are delightfully well suited to Copenhagen's flat terrain and are popular among Danes as well as visitors. Bike rental costs DKr25–DKr60 a day, with a deposit of DKr100–DKr200. You may also be lucky enough to find a free city bike chained up at bike racks in various spots throughout the city, including Nørreport and Nyhavn. Insert a DKr20 coin, which will be returned to you when you return the bike.

Rentals: Københavns Cycle (✉ Reventlowsg. 11, ☎ 33/33–86–13). **Danwheel-Rent-a-Bike** (✉ Colbjørnsensg. 3, ☎ 31/21–22–27). **Urania Cykler** (✉ Gammel Kongevej 1, ☎ 31/21–80–88).

BY BUS AND TRAIN

The **Copenhagen Card** offers unlimited travel on buses and suburban trains (S-trains), admission to more than 60 museums and sites around Sjælland, and a reduction on the ferry crossing to Sweden. You can buy the card, which costs DKr140 (24 hours), DKr255 (48 hours), or DKr320 (72 hours) and is half-price for children, at tourist offices and hotels and from travel agents.

Trains and buses operate from 5 AM (Sunday 6 AM) to midnight. After that, night buses run every half hour from 1 AM to 4:30 AM from the main bus station at Rådhus Pladsen to most areas of the city and surroundings. Trains and buses operate on the same ticket system and divide Copenhagen and surrounding areas into three zones. Tickets are validated on a time basis: on the basic ticket, which costs DKr10 per hour, you can travel anywhere in the zone in which you started. A discount *klip kort* (clip card), good for 10 rides, costs DKr75 and must be stamped in the automatic ticket machines on buses or at stations. Get zone details for S-trains by their information line (☎ 33/14–17–01). The buses have an automatic answering menu that is barely helpful in Danish. You'll do better by asking a bus driver.

BY CAR

If you are planning on seeing the sites of central Copenhagen, a car is not convenient. Parking spaces are at a premium and, when available, are expensive. A maze of one-way streets, relatively aggressive drivers, and bicycle lanes make it even more complicated. If you are going to drive, choose a small car that's easy to parallel park, bring a lot of small change to feed the meters, and be very aware of the cyclists on your right-hand side: they always have the right-of-way.

BY TAXI

The shiny computer-metered Mercedes and Volvo cabs are not cheap. The base charge is DKr15, plus DKr8–DKr10 per km. A cab is available when it displays the sign FRI (free); it can be hailed or picked up in front of the main train station or at taxi stands, or by calling ☎ 31/35–35–35. Outside of the central city, always call for a cab, as your attempts will be in vain.

Contacts and Resources

CAR RENTALS

All major international car rental agencies are represented in Copenhagen; most are located near the Vesterport Station. Try **Europcar** (✉ Copenhagen Airport, ☎ 32/50 30 90). Also try **Pitzner Auto** (✉ Copenhagen Airport, ☎ 32/50–90–65).

CURRENCY EXCHANGE

Almost all banks (including the Danske Bank at the airport) exchange money. Most hotels cash traveler's checks and exchange major foreign currencies, but they charge a substantial fee and give a lower rate. The exception to the rule—if you travel with cash—are the several locations of **Forex** (including the main train station and close to the Nørreport station). For up to $500, Forex charges only DKr20 for the entire transaction. Keep your receipt and they'll even change it back to dollars for free. For travelers checks, they charge DKr10 per check.

Den Danske Bank exchange is open during and after normal banking hours at the **main railway station,** daily June to August 7 AM–10 PM, and daily September to May, 7 AM–9 PM. **American Express** (✉ Amagertorv 18, ☎ 33/12–23–01) is open weekdays 9–5 and Saturday 9–noon. In Copenhagen center are the four locations of the **Danish Change** (✉ Vesterbrog. 9A; Østerg. 61; Vimmelskaftet 47; Frederiksbergg. 5; ☎ 33/93–04–18), open April to October, daily 10–8, November to March, daily 10–6. **Tivoli** (✉ Vesterbrog. 3, ☎ 33/15–10–01) also exchanges money; it is open May to September, daily noon–11 PM.

You can use **ATM**s to get cash with credit cards; you will find machines in all of Denmark's cities and many larger towns. ATMs typically accept Visa, MasterCard, and Cirrus cards, and Jyske Bank machines accept PLUS cards.

DOCTORS AND DENTISTS

Emergency dentists (✉ 14 Oslo Pl.), near Østerport Station, are available weekdays 8 PM–9:30 PM and weekends and holidays 10 AM–noon. Cash only is the accepted payment.

Look in the phone book under *læge.* After normal business hours, **emergency doctors** (☎ 38/88–60–41) make house calls in the central city. Fees are payable in cash only; night fees are approximately DKr300–DKr400.

EMBASSIES AND CONSULATES

U.S. (✉ Dag Hammarskjölds Allé 24, ☎ 35/55–31–44). **Canada** (✉ Kristen Bernikows G. 1, ☎ 33/12–22–99. **U.K.** (✉ Kastesvej 36–40, ☎ 35/26–46–00).

EMERGENCIES

Police, fire, and **ambulance** (☎ 112). **Auto Rescue/Falck** (☎ 31/14–22–22). **Rigshospitalet** (✉ Blegdamsvej 9, ☎ 35/45–35–45). **Frederiksberg Hospital** (✉ Nordre Fasanvej 57, ☎ 38/34–77–11).

ENGLISH-LANGUAGE BOOKSTORES

Steve's Books and Records (✉ Ved Stranden 10, ☎ 33/11–94–60) stocks new and used English books. **Boghallen** (✉ Rådhus Pl. 37, ☎ 33/11–85–11, ext. 309), the bookstore of the Politiken publishing house, offers a good selection of English-language books. **Arnold Busck** (✉ Kobmagerg. 49, ☎ 33/12–24–53), has an excellent selection, and also textbooks, CDs, and comic books.

GUIDED TOURS

The Copenhagen Tourist Board monitors all tours and has brochures and information. Most tours run through the summer until September. Only the Grand Tour of Copenhagen is year-round. In any case, it's always a good idea to call first to confirm availability. For tour information call **Copenhagen Excursions** (☎ 31/54–06–06).

Biking Tours (Self-Guided): BikeDenmark (✉ Åboulevarden 1, ☎ 35/36–41–00) offers two different self-guided city cycling tours. Choose between the 3- to 4-hour **Copenhagen Tour,** which includes the exteriors of the "musts" of the city, including *The Little Mermaid* and Amalienborg. The second is the 8- to 9-hour **Dragør Tour,** during which you leave the city and bike to the old-fashioned fishing hamlet near Copenhagen. There, you can swim at the beach and explore the ancient heart of the former Dutch colony. The tour package includes maps and a detailed route description. The rental price of the bike, which is available from **Københavns Cycle** (✉ Reventlowsg. 11, ☎ 33/33–86–13) is an additional DKr50 per bike.

Boat Tours: The **Harbor and Canal Tour** (1 hour) leaves from Gammel Strand and the east side of Kongens Nytorv from May to mid-September. Contact Canal Tours (☎ 33/13–31–05) or the tourist board (☞ Visitor Information, *below*). The **City and Harbor Tour** (2½ hours) includes a short bus trip through town and sails from the Fish Market on Holmens Canal through several more waterways, ending near Strøget. Just south of the embarkation point for the City and Harbor Tour, you'll find the equally charming **Netto Boats,** which also offer an hourlong tour for about half the price of their competitors.

Commercial Tours: Tours of the **Carlsberg Bryggeri** (⊠ Ny Carlsbergvej 140, ☎ 33/27–13–14; ☞ Exploring Copenhagen, *above*), which include a look into the draft horse stalls, meet at the Elephant Gate weekdays at 11 and 2. **The Royal Porcelain Factory** (⊠ Smalleg. 45, ☎ 31/86–48–48) conducts tours that end at its shop on weekdays at 9, 10, and 11 from mid-September through April, and weekdays at 9, 10, 11, 1, and 2 from May through mid–September.

Walking Tours: All tours begin at Lurblæserne, in front of the Palace Hotel at the Rådhus Pladsen, and reservations are not necessary. Walking tours begin in front of the Tourist Information Office (⊠ Bernstorffsg. 1, ☎ 33/11-13-25) at 10:30 and 2 daily (call to confirm); the 2-hour tour takes in the exteriors of most of the city's major sights. **The Royal Tour of Copenhagen** (2¾ hours) covers the exhibitions at Christiansborg and Rosenborg, and visits Amalienborg Square. **The Grand Tour of Copenhagen** (2½ hours) includes Tivoli, the New Carlsberg Museum, Christiansborg Castle, Stock Exchange, Danish Royal Theater, Nyhavn, Amalienborg Castle, Gefion Fountain, Grundtvig Church, and Rosenborg Castle. The **City Tour** (1½ hours) is more general, passing the New Carlsberg Museum, Christiansborg Castle, Thorvaldsen's Museum, National Museum, Stock Exchange, Danish Royal Theater, Rosenborg Castle, National Art Gallery, Botanical Gardens, Amalienborg Castle, Gefion Fountain, and *The Little Mermaid.*

LATE-NIGHT PHARMACIES
Steno Apotek (⊠ Vesterbrog. 6C, ☎ 33/14–82–66) is open 24 hours a day. **Sønderbro Apotek** (⊠ Amangerbrog. 158, ☎ 31/58–01–40) is also open around the clock.

TRAVEL AGENCIES
American Express (⊠ Amagertorv 18, ☎ 33/12–23–01). **Carlsen Wagons-Lits** (⊠ Ved Vesterport 6, ☎ 33/14–27–47). **Skibby Rejser** (⊠ Vandkunsten 10, ☎ 33/32–85–00).

For student and budget travel, try **Kilroy Travels Denmark** (⊠ Skinderg. 28, ☎ 33/11–00–44). For charter packages, stick with **Spies** (⊠ Nyropsg. 41, ☎ 33/32–15–00). **Star Tours** (⊠ H. C. Andersens Boulevard 12, ☎ 33/11–50–70 also handles packages.

VISITOR INFORMATION
Danmarks Turistråd (Danish Tourist Board, ⊠ Bernstorffsg. 1, DK–1577 Copenhagen V, ☎ 33/11–13–25) is open May through the first two weeks of September, weekdays 9–8, weekends 9–5; and the rest of September through April, Monday to Saturday 9–5. Youth information in Copenhagen is available at **Use-It** (⊠ Huset, Rådhusstr. 13, ☎ 33/15–65–18).

SIDE TRIPS FROM COPENHAGEN

Eksperimentarium

8 km (6 mi) north of Copenhagen.

In the beachside town of Hellerup is the user-friendly **Experimentarium,** where more than 300 exhibitions are clustered in various Discovery Islands, each exploring a different facet of science, technology, and natural phenomena. A dozen body and hands-on exhibits allow you to take skeleton-revealing bike rides, measure your lung capacity, stir up magnetic goop, play ball on a jet stream, and gyrate to gyroscopes. Once a bottling plant for the Tuborg Brewery, this center organizes one or two special exhibits a year; one past installation had interactive exhibits of the brain. Until mid-April, 1998, the special exhibition will focus on dinosaurs. Take Bus 6 or 650S from Rådhus Plads or the S-train to Hellerup; transfer to bus 21, 23, or 650S. ⊠ *Tuborg Havnevej 7,* ☎ *39/27–33–33.* 🎟 *DKr69; combined admission for a child and parent, DKr98.* ⊘ *Mid-June–mid-Aug., daily 10–5; mid-Aug.–mid-June, Mon. and Wed.–Fri. 9–5, Tues. 9–9, weekends 11–5.*

Dragør

22 km (14 mi) east of Copenhagen (take Bus 30 or 33 from Rådhus Pladsen).

On the island of Amager, less than a half hour from Copenhagen, the quaint fishing town of Dragør (pronounced *drah*-wer) feels far away in distance and time. The town's history is apart from the rest of Copenhagen's because it was settled by Dutch farmers in the 16th century. King Christian II ordered the community to provide fresh produce and flowers for the royal court. Today, neat rows of white, terra-cotta-roofed houses trimmed with wandering ivy, roses, and the occasional waddling goose characterize the still meticulously maintained community. According to local legend, the former town hall's chimney was built with a twist so that meetings couldn't be overheard.

The **Dragør Museum** (⊠ Strandlinien 4, ☎ 32/53–41–06), in one of the oldest houses in town, contains a collection of furniture, costumes, drawings, and model ships. Admission is DKr20; it's open weekends 2–5. A ticket to the Dragør Museum also affords entrance to the nearby **Mølsted Museum** (⊠ Dr. Dichs Pl. 4, ☎ 32/53–41–06), displaying paintings by the famous local artist Christian Mølsted; call ahead for hours. If you're still energetic, swing by the **Amager Museum** (⊠ Hovedg. 4 and 12, ☎ 32/53–93–07), which details the Dutch colony. It's open Tuesday through Sunday noon to 4; admission is DKr20.

Frilandsmuseet

16 km (10 mi) north of Copenhagen.

Just north of Copenhagen is Lyngby, its main draw the Frilandsmuseet, an open-air museum. About 50 farmhouses and cottages representing various periods of Danish history have been painstakingly dismantled, moved, reconstructed, and filled with period furniture and tools. The museum is surrounded by trees and gardens; bring lunch and plan to spend the day. To get here, take the S-train to the Sorgenfri Station, then walk right and follow the signs. ⊠ *Frilandsmuseet, 100 Kongevejen, Lyngby,* ☎ *45/85–02–92.* 🎟 *DKr30.* ⊘ *Easter–Sept., Tues.–Sun. 10–5; Oct., daily 10–4; call to confirm Oct. hrs.*

Museet for Moderne Kunst

20 km (12 mi) south of Copenhagen (take the S-train in the direction of either Hundige, Solrød Strand, or Køge to Ishøj Station, then pick up bus 128 to the museum).

Architect Søren Robert Lund was just 25 when awarded the commission for this forward-looking museum, which he designed in metal and white concrete set against the flat coast south of Copenhagen. The museum, also known as the Arken, opened in March 1996 to great acclaim, both for its architecture and its collection. Unfortunately, it has been plagued with a string of stranger-than-fiction occurrences, including a director with a completely bogus resume and financial difficulties that often leave it depressingly bare of art. Nonetheless, when filled, its massive sculpture room exhibits both modern Danish and international art, as well as experimental works. Dance, theater, film, and multimedia exhibits are additional attractions. ⊠ *Skovvej 42,* ☎ *43/42–02–22.* ⊠ *DKr45.* ⊙ *Tues.–Sun., 10–5.*

SJÆLLAND AND ITS ISLANDS

The goddess Gefion is said to have carved Sjælland (Zealand) from Sweden. If she did, she must have sliced the north deep with a fjord, while she chopped the south to pieces and left the sides bowing west. Though the coasts are deeply serrated, Gefion's myth is more dramatic than the flat, fertile land of rich meadows and beech stands.

Slightly larger than the state of Delaware, Sjælland is the largest of the Danish islands. From Copenhagen, almost any point on it can be reached in an hour and a half, making it the most traveled portion of the country—and it is especially easy to explore thanks to the road network. To the north of the capital, ritzy beach towns line up between Hellerup and Humlebæk. Helsingør's Kronborg, which Shakespeare immortalized in *Hamlet,* and Hillerød's stronghold of Frederiksborg, considered one of the most magnificent Renaissance castles in Europe, also lie to the north. To the west of Copenhagen is Roskilde, medieval Denmark's most important town, with an eclectic cathedral that served as northern Europe's spiritual center 1,000 years ago.

West and south, rural towns and farms edge up to seaside communities and fine white beaches, often encompassed by forests. Beaches with summer cottages, white dunes, and calm waters surround Gilleleje and the neighboring town of Hornbæk. The beach in Tisvildeleje, farther west, is quieter and close to woods. Even more unspoiled are the lilliputian islands around southern Sjælland, virtually unchanged over the past century. Most of Sjælland can be explored in day trips from Copenhagen. The exceptions are the northwestern beaches around the Sejerø Bugt (Sejerø Bay) and those south of Møn, all of which require at least a night's stay and a day's loll.

Biking
Sjælland's flat landscape allows easy biking. Most roads have cycle lanes, and tourist boards stock with maps detailing local routes.

Canoeing
About 15 km (10 mi) north of Copenhagen, especially in the Lynby area, several calm lakes and rivers are perfect for canoeing; the Mølleå (Mølle River) and the Bagsværd, Lyngby, and Furesø (Bagsværd, Lyngby, and Fur lakes). **Frederiksdal Kanoudlejning** (⊠ Nybrovej, Lyngby, ☎ 45/85–67–70) offers hourly and daily rentals and package canoe tours throughout the region.

Fishing
Sjælland's lakes, rivers, and coastline teem with plaice, flounder, cod, and catfish. Buy the DKr100 license, required to fish along Sjælland's coast, at any post office. Elsewhere, check with the local tourist office for license requirements. It is illegal to fish within 1,650 ft of the mouth of a stream.

Shopping
Shopping here can be considerably cheaper than in Copenhagen. Pedestrian streets run through the center of most towns, and flea markets are usually held Saturday morning.

Rungsted

㊷   *21 km (13 mi) north of Copenhagen.*

Between Copenhagen and Helsingør is **Rungstedlund,** the elegant, airy former manor of Baroness Karen Blixen. The author of *Out of Africa* and several accounts of aristocratic Danish life wrote under the pen name Isak Dinesen. The manor house, where she lived as a child and to which she returned in 1931, is open as a museum and displays manuscripts, photographs, and memorabilia documenting her years in Africa and Denmark. Leave time to wander around the gardens. ⊠ *Rungstedlund,* ☎ *42/57–10–57.* ▣ *DKr30 (for combined train and admission tickets, call DSB (☞ Arriving and Departing in Sjælland and Its Islands A to Z, below). ☉ May–Sept., daily 10–5; Oct.–Apr., Wed.–Fri. 1–4, weekends 11–4.*

Dining

\$\$ ✕ **Strandmollekroen.** Stop for a meal at this 200-year-old beachfront
★ inn in Klampenborg as you drive north from Copenhagen to Rungsted. It's burnished with deep-green walls and filled with antiques and hunting trophies, but the best views are of the Øresund from the back dining room. Elegantly served seafood and steaks are the mainstays, and for a bit of everything, try the seafood platter, with lobster, crab claws, and Greenland shrimp. ⊠ *Strandvejen 808,* ☎ *31/63–01–04. AE, DC, MC, V.*

Humlebæk

㊸   *10 km (6 mi) north of Rungsted, 30 km (19 mi) north of Copenhagen.*

★ ☾ This elegant seaside town is home of the must-see **Louisiana,** a modern art museum famed for its stunning location and architecture as much as for its collection. Even if you can't tell a Monet from a Duchamp, you should make the 30-minute trip to see its elegant rambling structure, surrounded by a large park. Housed in a pearly 19th-century villa surrounded by dramatic views of the Øresund waters, the permanent collection includes modern American paintings and Danish paintings from the COBRA (a trend in northern European painting that took its name from its active locations, Copenhagen, Brussels, Amsterdam) and Deconstructionism movements. Be sure to see the haunting collection of Giacomettis backdropped by picture windows overlooking the sound. The children's wing has pyramid-shape chalkboards, kid-proof computers, and weekend activities under the guidance of an artist or museum coordinator. This makes for a good side trip from Copenhagen; walk north from the station about 10 minutes. ⊠ *Gammel Strandvej 13,* ☎ *49/19–07–19.* ▣ *DKr48 (for combined train and admission tickets, call DSB ☞ Arriving and Departing in Sjælland and Its Islands A to Z, below). ☉ Daily 10–5, Wed. until 10.*

Helsingør

㊹   *19 km (12 mi) north of Humlebæk, 47 km (29 mi) north of Copenhagen.*

★ At the northeastern tip of the island is Helsingør, the departure point for ferries to the Swedish town of Helsingborg, and the site of **Kronborg Slot** (Kronborg Castle). William Shakespeare based *Hamlet* on Danish mythology's Amleth, and used this castle as the setting even though he had never seen it. Built in the late 16th century, it's 600 years younger than the Elsinore we imagine from the tragedy. It was built as a Renaissance tollbooth: From its cannon-studded bastions, forces collected Erik of Pomerania's much-hated Sound Dues, a tariff charged

61

Sjælland and Its Islands

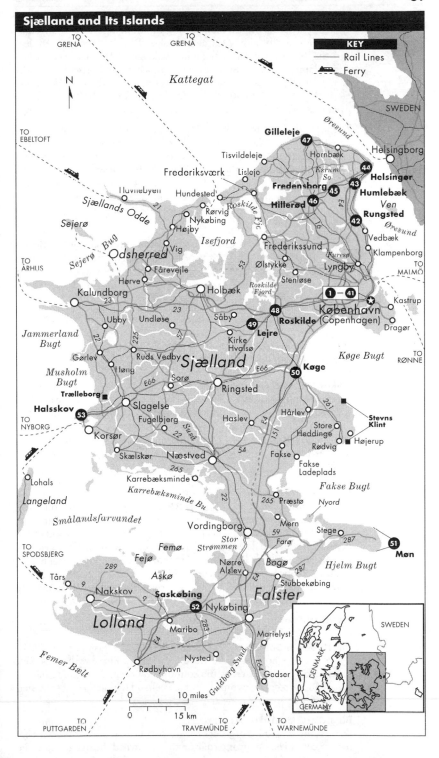

KEY
— Rail Lines
🚢 Ferry

TO GRENÅ · TO GRENÅ · Kattegat · SWEDEN · TO EBELTOFT · Øresund · Gilleleje · 47 · Tisvildeleje · Hornbæk · Helsingborg · Frederiksværk · Lisleje · Esrum Sø · 44 · Helsingør · Fredensborg · 45 · 43 · Humlebæk · Hundested · Hillerød · 46 · Ven · Huvnebyen · Rørvig · Roskilde Fjd · Rungsted · 42 · Sjællands Odde · 21 · Nykøbing · Vedbæk · Sejerø · Højby · Isefjord · Frederikssund · Klampenborg · Sejerø Bug · Vig · Ølstykke · Furesø · Lyngby · TO MALMÖ · TO ÅRHUS · Odsherred · Fåreveile · Stenløse · Kastrup · Hørve · Holbæk · Roskilde Fjord · 1 — 41 · København · Kalundborg · 23 · 23 · Såby · 48 · (Copenhagen) · Ubby · Undløse · Roskilde · Dragør · Jammerland Bugt · 22 · 225 · 49 · Kirke Hvalsø · Lejre · Køge Bugt · TO RØNNE · Gørlev · Ruds Vedby · Sjælland · E66 · Musholm Bugt · Høng · Sorø · Køge · Trælleborg · E66 · Ringsted · 50 · Halsskov · Slagelse · Fugelbjerg · Haslev · Hårlev · Stevns Klint · TO NYBORG · 53 · Korsør · 22 · Suså · 151 · Store Heddinge · Skælskør · Næstved · Rødvig · Højerup · 265 · 54 · Fakse · Lohals · Karrebæksminde · Fakse Ladeplads · Langeland · Karrebæksminde Bu · 22 · Fakse Bugt · Smålandsfarvandet · 265 · Præstø · Nyord · Vordingborg · Mern · Stege · TO SPODSBJERG · Femø · Stor Strømmen · Farø · 59 · 287 · 51 · Fejø · Nørre Alslev · Bogø · 287 · Møn · Tårs · 289 · Askø · Hjelm Bugt · Nakskov · Saskøbing · Stubbekøbing · Falster · Lolland · 52 · Nykøbing · Marielyst · Maribo · 283 · Femer Bælt · Nysted · Guldborg Sund · Rødbyhavn · Gedser · E64 · DENMARK · SWEDEN · GERMANY · 0 — 10 miles · 0 — 15 km · TO PUTTGARDEN · TO TRAVEMÜNDE · TO WARNEMÜNDE to all ships crossing the sliver of water between Denmark and Sweden. Well worth seeing are the 200-ft-long dining hall and the dungeons, where there is a brooding statue of Holger Danske. According to legend, the Viking chief sleeps, but will awaken to defend Denmark when it is in danger. (The largest Danish resistance group during World War II called itself Holger Danske after its fearless forefather.) ⊠ *Helsingør,* ☎ *49/21–30–78.* ⌷ *DKr30.* ☉ *May–Sept., daily 10:30–5; Oct. and Apr., Tues.–Sun. 11–4; Nov.–Mar., Tues.–Sun. 11–3.*

Thanks to the hefty tolls collected by Erik of Pomerania, Helsingør prospered. Stroll past the carefully restored medieval merchants' and ferrymen's houses in the middle of town. On the corner of Stengade and Skt. Annæ Gade near the harbor you'll find **Skt. Olai's Kirke,** the country's largest parish church and worth a peek for its elaborately carved wooden altar. ⊠ *St. Olai G. 51,* ☎ *49/21–00–98 between 9 and noon only.* ⌷ *Free.* ☉ *May 15–Sept. 14, daily noon–3, tours at 2; Sept. 15–May 14, daily noon–2.*

Next door to Skt. Olai's Kirke is the 15th-century **Carmelite Kloster** (Carmelite Convent), one of the best-preserved examples of medieval architecture in Scandinavia. After the Reformation it was used as a hospital, and by 1630 it had become a poorhouse. ⊠ *Skt. Annæ G. 38,* ☎ *49/21–17–74.* ⌷ *DKr10.* ☉ *Tour daily at 2; call ahead.*

If you want to know more about Helsingør, head to the modest **By Museum** (Town Museum), which has exhibits of 19th-century handicrafts, dolls, and a model of the town. ⊠ *Skt. Annæ G. 36,* ☎ *49/21–00–98.* ⌷ *DKr10.* ☉ *Daily noon–4.*

OFF THE
BEATEN PATH

MARIENLYST SLOT – One kilometer (½ mile) north of Helsingør is the Louis XVI–style Marienlyst Castle. Built in 1587, it provided King Frederik II with a garden, as well as a delicate change of scenery from the militant Kronborg. Today the gardens have been replanted, and inside are paintings by north Sjælland artists and a gallery with changing arts and crafts exhibitions. ⊠ *Marienlyst Allé,* ☎ *49/28–37–91.* ⌷ *DKr20.* ☉ *Daily noon–5.*

Dining and Lodging

$$$ ✕▥ **Hotel Hamlet.** A few minutes from the harbor, this overly renovated hotel has lost some of its charm but makes an attempt at character with raw timbers and deep-green walls. The rooms are furnished in rose schemes and dark wood, and all are comfortable, if nondescript. Downstairs, the Ophelia Restaurant serves traditional Danish seafood, steaks, and open-face sandwiches. ⊠ *Bramstrstrædet 5, DK–3000,* ☎ *49/21–28–02,* ℻ *49/26–01–30. 36 rooms. Restaurant, bar, meeting room. AE, DC, MC, V.*

Outdoor Activities and Sports

GOLF

The **Helsingør Golf Klub** (⊠ Gamle Hellebækvej, Helsingør, ☎ 49/21–29–70) has 18 holes on a beautiful, parklike course, with trees and, on clear days, views across the sound to Sweden. A weekday handicap of 36 for men and women, and a weekend handicap of 24 for men and 36 for women, is expected.

Nightlife and the Arts

Some summers, **Kronborg Castle** (☞ *above*) is the site of outdoor performances of *Hamlet* by internationally renowned theater groups. The schedule varies from year to year, so check with the tourist board.

Fredensborg

⑤ *15 km (9 mi) southwest of Helsingør, 33 km (20 mi) northwest of Copenhagen.*

Commanding this town is the **Fredensborg Slot** (Castle of Peace), built by Frederik IV to commemorate the 1720 peace treaty with Sweden. The castle, with a towering domed hall in the center, was originally inspired by French and Italian castles, but 18th-century reconstructions, concealing the original design, instead serve as a review of domestic architecture. The castle became a favorite of Frederik V, who lined the gardens with marble sculptures of ordinary people. It is now the summer residence of the royal family, and interiors are closed except in July. The lovely Baroque Gardens include a series of wide, horizontal waterfalls, called Cascades. The neatly trimmed park around the palace, connecting with Lake Esrum, is lovely for a stroll. ☎ *42/28–00–25.* ☯ *Palace July, daily 1–5; Baroque Gardens, May–Aug., daily 10–9; Sept., daily 10–7; Mar., Apr., and Oct., daily 10–5; Nov.–Feb., daily 10–4.*

Dining and Lodging

$$$$ ✕🏨 **Hotel Store Kro.** Built by King Frederik IV, this magnificent Re-
★ naissance annex to Fredensborg Castle is the archetypal stately inn. Inside it's appointed with European antiques and paintings; outside, glass gazebos and classical statues overlook a lovely garden. The rooms are equally sumptuous, with delicately patterned wallpapers and antiques. The romantic restaurant, specializing in French fare, has a fireplace and a grand piano. ✉ *Slotsg. 6, DK–3480,* ☎ *42/28–00–47,* ⅢⅩ *42/28–45–61. 49 rooms. Restaurant, bar, room service, sauna, meeting rooms. AE, DC, MC, V.*

$$$$ 🏨 **Marienlyst.** This hotel is full of flashy neon, bolts of drapery, and
★ glass. A large casino and endless lounges provide weekend entertainment, but when guests tire of gambling, there's a huge second-floor "Swinging Pool," with a water slide, swim-up bar, and sauna. The rooms are all plush and pastel, with every convenience. ✉ *Nordre Strandvej 2, DK–3000,* ☎ *49/21–40–00,* ⅢⅩ *49/21–49–00. 220 rooms, 11 suites. 2 restaurants, 2 bars, room service, indoor pool, sauna, casino, nightclub, meeting rooms. AE, DC, MC, V.*

Hillerød

⑥ *10 km (6 mi) southwest of Fredensborg, 41 km (26 mi) northwest of Copenhagen.*

Hillerød's **Frederiksborg Slot** was acquired and rebuilt by Frederik II, but the fortress was demolished by his son, king-cum-architect Christian IV, who rebuilt it as one of Scandinavia's most magnificent castles. With three wings and a low entrance portal, the moated Dutch-Renaissance structure covers three islets and is peaked with dozens of gables, spires, and turrets. The two-story marble gallery known as the **Great Hall**, audaciously festooned with drapery, paintings, and reliefs, sits on top of the vaulted chapel, where monarchs were crowned for 200 years. Devastated by a fire in 1859, the castle was reconstructed with the support of the Carlsberg Foundation, and it now includes the National Portrait Gallery. ☎ *42/26–04–39.* 🎟 *DKr30.* ☯ *May–Sept., daily 10–5; Apr. and Oct., daily 10–4, Nov.–Mar., daily 11–3.*

Dining

$ ✕ **Slotsherrenskro.** Under the shadow of the Frederiksborg Castle, this family restaurant bustles in what used to be the castle stables. Antique on the outside, it's bright orange inside, with prints and paintings of royalty and the castle. Popular with visitors to the castle, the Danish menu ranges from quick open-face sandwiches to savory stews, soups, and steaks. ⊠ *Slotherrens Kro,* ☎ *42/26–75–16. DC, MC, V. Nov.– Mar., no dinner Thurs.*

Gilleleje

 25 km (16 mi) north of Hillerød, 55 km (35 mi) northwest of Copenhagen.

Gilleleje is at the very top of Sjælland. Once a small fishing community, it experiences a population explosion every summer, when northern Europeans take to its woods and fine, sandy beaches. It was a favorite getaway of philosopher Søren Kierkegaard, who wrote: "I often stood there and reflected over my past life. The force of the sea and the struggle of the elements made me realize how unimportant I was." The less existential will go for a swim and visit the philosopher's monument on a nearby hill. The old part of town, with its thatched and colorfully painted houses, is good for a walk.

Odsherred

34 km (21 mi) southwest of Gilleleje, 80 km (50 mi) northwest of Copenhagen (via Roskilde).

This hammer-shape peninsula is curved by the Sejerø Bugt (Sejerø Bay) and dotted with hundreds of **burial mounds.** Getting here involves driving to Hundested, then taking the 25-minute ferry ride to Rørvig.

If you are a devotee of ecclesiastical art, make a pilgrimage to explore the frescoes of the Romanesque-Gothic-Renaissance **Højby Kirke** (Højby Church) in the town of Højby, near Nykøbing Sjælland. In the town of Fårevejle is the Gothic **Fårevejle kirke,** with the earl of Bothwell's chapel. **Sjællands Odde** (Zealand's Tongue), the tiny strip of land north of the Sejerø Bay, offers slightly marshy but private beach strands. Inside the bay, the beaches are once again smooth and blond.

Roskilde

 101 km (63 mi) southeast of Odsherred, 32 km (20 mi) west of Copenhagen (on Rte. 156).

Roskilde is Sjælland's second-largest town and one of its oldest, celebrating its 1,000-year anniversary in 1998 (☞ Nightlife and the Arts, *below*). For a weekend in the end of June, it's filled with the rock music of the **Roskilde Festival,** said to be the largest outdoor concert in northern Europe, attracting some 75,000 people.

Roskilde was the royal residence in the 10th century and became the spiritual capital of Denmark and northern Europe in 1170, when Bishop Absalon built the **Roskilde Domkirke** (Roskilde Cathedral) on the site of a church erected 200 years earlier by Harald Bluetooth. Overwhelming the center of town, the current structure took more than 300 years to complete and thus provides a one-stop crash course in Danish architecture. Inside are an ornate Dutch altarpiece and the sarcophagi—ranging from opulent to modest—of 38 Danish monarchs. Predictably, Christian IV is interred in a magnificent chapel with a massive painting of himself in combat and a bronze sculpture by Thorvaldsen. In modest contrast is the newest addition, the simple brick chapel of King Frederik IX, who died in 1972, outside the church. On the interior south wall above the entrance is a 16th-century clock showing St. George charging a dragon, which hisses and howls, echoing throughout the church and causing Peter Døver, "the Deafener," to sound the hour. A squeamish Kirsten Kiemer, "the Chimer," shakes her head in fright but manages to strike the quarters. ⊠ *Domkirkestr. 10,* ☎ *46/ 35–27–00.* ☜ *DKr10.* ⊙ *Hours vary; call ahead.*

Less than a kilometer (½ mi) north of the cathedral, on the fjord, is the modern **Vikingeskibshallen** (Viking Ship Museum), containing five Viking ships sunk in the fjord 1,000 years ago. Submerged to block the passage of enemy ships, they were discovered in 1957. The painstaking recovery involved building a watertight dam and then draining the water from that section of the fjord. The splinters of wreckage were then preserved and reassembled. A deep-sea trader, warship, ferry, merchant ship, and fierce 92½-ft man-of-war attest to the Vikings' sophisticated and aesthetic boat-making skills. ⊠ *Strandengen,* ☎ *46/35–65–55.* ☜ *DKr40.* ⊙ *Apr.–Oct., daily 9–5; Nov.–Mar., daily 10–4.*

Dining and Lodging

$$ ✕ **Club 42.** This popular Danish restaurant spills out into the walking
★ street with a few tables in the summertime, while inside the roof opens over the dining room. The fare is typically Danish, including smørre-brød and spare ribs, simply prepared and served with potato salad. The rest of the menu includes lots of meat and potatoes, as well as fish. ⊠ *Skomagerg. 42,* ☎ *46/35–17–64. DC, MC, V.*

$$ ▥ **Hotel Prindsen.** Central in downtown Roskilde, this convenient hotel, built 100 years ago, is popular with business guests. The elegant dark-wood lobby leads to nondescript rooms that are, nonetheless, homey and comfortable. Downstairs, the restaurant La Bøf serves up grill and fish fare, and next door there's a cozy bar. ⊠ *Alg. 13, DK– 4000,* ☎ *46/35–80–10,* 𝔽𝔸𝕏 *42/35–81–10. 38 rooms. Restaurant, bar, meeting room. AE, DC, MC, V.*

$ ▥ **Roskilde Vandrehjem Hørgården.** In front of a grassy yard, this youth hostel is perfect for families and budget travelers. In a former school-house 2 km (1 mi) east of the Roskilde Domkirke, it looks straight out of third grade, and the rooms, with bunks, look like camp. You can have use of the kitchen. ⊠ *Hørhusene 61, DK–4000,* ☎ *42/35–21– 84,* 𝔽𝔸𝕏 *46/32–66–90. 21 rooms with 4 beds each, 8 showers. No credit cards. Closed Oct.–Apr.*

Nightlife and the Arts

To celebrate the town's 1,000th birthday in 1998, concerts, performances, and exhibits will run all year, and on September 5th, a cultural blowout will keep shops, cinemas, museums, and libraries open late into the night. Call the Roskilde Tourist Board (☞ Visitor Information *in* Sjælland and Its Islands, *below*) for a schedule of events.

The young head to **Gimle** (⊠ Ringstedg. 30, ☎ 46/35–12–13) for live rock on the weekends. At **Bryggerhesten** (⊠ Alg. 15, ☎ 46/35–01– 03), or "The Draft Horse," adults have a late supper and beer in cozy surroundings. During the summer, **Mullerudi** (⊠ Djalma Lunds Gord 7, ☎ 46/37–03–25) is an arty spot with indoor and outdoor seating and live jazz.

Outdoor Activities and Sports

GOLF

Roskilde has an 18-hole **golf course** (⊠ Kongemarken 34, ☎ 46/37– 01–80) with views of the twin-peaked Roskilde Cathedral and an en-circling forest.

Shopping

CRAFTS

Between Roskilde and Holbæk is **Kirke Sonnerup Kunst-håndværk** (Art Handicrafts, ⊠ Englerupvej 62, Såby, ☎ 46/49–25–77), with a good selection of pottery, glass, clothing, and woodwork produced by more than 50 Danish artists.

Lejre

49 *10 km (6 mi) west of Roskilde, 40 km (25 mi) west of Copenhagen.*

The 50-acre **Lejre Forsøgscenter** (Lejre Archaeological Research Center) compound contains a reconstructed village dating from the Iron Age and two 19th-century farmhouses. In summer a handful of hardy Danish families live here and are under the observation of researchers; they go about their daily routine—grinding grain, herding goats—providing a clearer picture of ancient ways of life. In Bodalen (Fire Valley), visitors (especially children) can grind corn, file an ax, and sail in a dugout canoe. ⊠ *Slangæleen,* ☎ *46/48–08–78.* 🎫 *DKr50.* ☉ *May–Sept., daily 10–5.*

Køge

50 *20 km (13 mi) southeast of Lejre, 40 km (25 mi) southwest of Copenhagen.*

The well-preserved medieval town of Køge is known for its historic witch hunts. In the centrally located **Køge Museum,** a 17th-century merchant's house, you will see souvenirs from Hans Christian Andersen, costumes, local artifacts, an executioner's sword, and a 13th-century stone font. The story goes that the font had to be removed from the town church after a crippled woman committed an unsavory act into it, hoping her bizarre behavior would cure her. Also on exhibit are 16th-century silver coins from a buried treasure of more than 2,000 coins found in the courtyard of Langkildes Gård. ⊠ *Nørreg. 4,* ☎ *56/63–42–42.* 🎫 *DKr20.* ☉ *June–Aug., daily 10–5; Sept.–May, weekdays 2–5, weekends 1–5.*

The old part of Køge is filled with 300 half-timber houses, all protected by the National Trust; it's a lovely area for a stroll. At the end of Kirkestræde, the 15th-century **Skt. Nikolai Kirke** (St. Nicholas Church) was once a lighthouse; its floor is covered with more than 100 tombs of Køge VIPs. Carved angels line the church's walls, but most have had their noses struck off—a favorite pastime of drunken Swedish soldiers in the 1700s. ⊠ *Kirkestr.,* ☎ *53/65–13–59.* 🎫 *Free.* ☉ *June–Aug., weekdays 10–4; Sept.–May, weekdays 10–noon. Tower tours late July–mid-Aug., weekdays at 11, noon, and 1.*

If you have time, visit the **Køge Kunst Museet** (Køge Art Museum) for its changing exhibitions and an extensive permanent collection of sketches, sculpture, and other modern Danish art. ⊠ *Nørreg. 29,* ☎ *53/66–24–14.* 🎫 *DKr15. Free with admission ticket from the Køge Museum (☞ above).* ☉ *Tues.–Sun. 11–5.*

En Route   Twenty-four kilometers (15 miles) south of Køge near Rødvig, you should stop at the chalk cliffs called Stevns Klint to see the 13th-century **Højerup Kirke** built above them. As the cliffs eroded, first the cemetery, then the choir toppled into the sea. In recent years the church has been restored and the cliffs below bolstered by masonry to prevent further damage. ⊠ *Højerup Church, Stevns Klint.* 🎫 *DKr5.* ☉ *Apr.–Sept., daily 11–5.*

Møn

51 *85 km (52 mi) south of Stevns Klint, 130 km (81 mi) south of Copenhagen.*

The whole island of Møn is pocked with nearly 100 Neolithic burial mounds, but it is most famous for its dramatic chalk cliffs, the northern **Møns Klint,** three times as large as Stevns Klint (☞ En Route, *above*). Rimmed by a beech forest, the milky-white 75-million-year-old bluffs plunge 400 ft to a small, craggy beach—accessible by a path and more than 500 steps. Wear good walking shoes, and take care; though a park ranger checks the area for loose rocks, the cliffs crumble suddenly. Once there, Danish families usually hunt for blanched fossils of cuttlefish, sea urchins, and other sea life. The cliffs are an important navigational marker for ships, defining south Sjælland's otherwise flat topography.

You can walk to a delightful folly of the 18th century, **Liselund Slot** (not to be confused with a hotel of the same name), 4 km (2½ mi) north of the cliffs. Antoine de la Calmette, the island's sheriff and a royal chamberlain, took his inspiration from Marie Antoinette's *Hameau* (*Hamlet*) at Versailles and built the structure in 1792 for his beloved wife. The thatched palace, complete with English gardens, combines a Norwegian country facade with elegant Pompeian interiors. In this lovely setting, Hans Christian Andersen wrote his fairy tale *The Tinder Box.* The palace has been open to the public since 1938. ☎ 55/81–21–78. ☞ DKr20. ۞ *Tours (Danish and German only) May–Oct., Tues.–Fri. 10:30, 11, 1:30, and 2; weekends also 2, 4, and 4:30.*

Møn's capital, **Stege,** received its town charter in 1268. Take time to explore its medieval churches, including Elmelunde, Keldby, and Fanefjord, all famous for their naive frescoes. Thought to have been completed by a collaborative group of artisans, the whimsical paintings include pedagogic and biblical doodlings.

Lodging

$$ ⊞ **Liselund Ny Slot.** Set in a grand old manor on an isolated estate,
★ this modern hotel offers refined accommodations minus stodginess. The square staircase and painted ceilings have been preserved. The rooms are fresh and simple, with wicker and pastel schemes, half of them overlooking a swan-filled pond and the forest. The downstairs restaurant serves Danish cuisine. ⊠ *Liselund Ny Slot, DK–4791 Børre,* ☎ 55/81–20–81, ☒ 55/81–21–91. *25 rooms, 1 suite. Restaurant, meeting rooms. AE, DC, MC, V.*

Falster

3 km (2 mi) south of Bogø, 24 km (15 mi) south of Møn, 99 km (62 mi) south of Copenhagen.

Accessible by way of the striking Farø Bridge or the parallel Storstrømsbroen (Big Current Bridge) from Vordingborg, Falster is shaped like a tiny South America and has excellent blond beaches to rival those of its tropical twin. Among the best are the southeastern Marielyst and southernmost Gedser. Almost everywhere on the island you'll find cafés, facilities, and water-sports rentals. Falster is also one of the country's major producers of sugar beets.

۞ The **Middelaldercentret** (Center for the Middle Ages), a reconstructed medieval village, invites school classes to dress up in period costumes and experience life a millennium ago. Day guests can participate in activities that change weekly—from cooking to medieval knife-making to animal herding and, on weekends, folk dances and other cultural happenings. ⊠ *Nykøbing Falster,* ☎ 54/86–19–34. ☞ *DKr45.* ۞ *May–mid-Sept., Tues.–Sat., 10–4, Sun. 10–5.*

Dining and Lodging

$$$ ✕ **Czarens Hus.** This stylish old inn dates back more than 200 years, when it was a guest house and supply store for area farmers and merchants. Deep-green walls, gold trim, and chandeliers provide a background for antique furnishings. The specialty of the house is Continental Danish cuisine, which translates as creative beef and fish dishes, often served with cream sauces. Try the *Zar Beuf* (calf tenderloin in a mushroom-and-onion cream sauce). ☒ *Langg. 2, Nykøbing Falster,* ☎ *54/85–28–29. AE, DC, MC, V.*

$$ ✕ **Brasserie Kæller and Køkken.** Done up in bright colors with a modern decor, this central and very popular café-restaurant is touted as one of the best in the area. The menu varies, with basics like steaks, sandwiches, and nachos, as well as the slightly more experimental, including ham with pineapple sauce, grilled ostrich steaks, and beef slices with Gorgonzola. ☒ *Torvet 19, Nykøbing Falster,* ☎ *54/85–82–82. DC, MC, V. Closed Dec. 24–Jan. 2.*

$$ ⌂ **Hotel Falster.** This sleek and efficient hotel accommodates conference guests as well as vacationers with a comfortable and businesslike ambience. Rustic brick walls and Danish antiques mix with sleek Danish-design lamps and sculpture. Rooms are comfortably done with dark wood and modular furniture. ☒ *Skovalleen, Nykøbing Falster, DK–4800,* ☎ *54/85–93–93,* FAX *54/82–21–99. 70 rooms. Restaurant, bar, meeting room. AE, DC, MC, V.*

Outdoor Activities and Sports

GOLF

The 18-hole **Sydsjælland Golf Klub** (☒ Præstolandevej 39, Mogenstrup, ☎ 53/76–15–55) is more than 25 years old, and the park course is lined with a number of small lakes.

Lolland

52 *19 km (12 mi) west of Nykøbing Falster.*

The history of Lolland dates back more than 1,000 years, to a man named Saxe, who sat at the mouth of the fjord and collected a toll. He later cleared the surrounding land and leased it. It became known as Saxtorp and eventually Sakskøbing, the island's capital. Though most people head straight for the beaches, the area has a few sights, including a water tower with a smiling face and an excellent car museum near the central 13th-century **Ålholm Slot** (closed to the public). The **Åholm Automobile Museum** is northern Europe's largest, with more than 200 vehicles. The town is accessible by bridge from Nykøbing Falster. ☒ *Ålholm Parkvej, Nysted,* ☎ *53/87–15–09.* ☜ *DKr60.* ☉ *Sept. and Oct., Thurs. and Sun. 11–4.*

☾ The **Knuthenborg Safari Park,** just 8 km (5 mi) west of Sakskøbing and also on Lolland, has a drive-through range where you can rubberneck at tigers, zebras, rhinoceroses, and giraffes, and pet camels, goats, and ponies. Besides seeing 20 species of animals, children can also play in Miniworld's jungle gym, minitrain, and other rides. ☒ *Knuthenborg Safaripark, DK–4930 Maribo,* ☎ *53/88–80–89.* ☜ *DKr74.* ☉ *May–Sept. 15, daily 9–6.*

Lodging

$$ ⌂ **Lalandia.** This massive water-park hotel has an indoor pool, beachside view, and lots of happy families. On the southern coast of Lolland, about 27 km (16 mi) southwest of Sakskøbing, the modern white apartments, with full kitchen and bath, accommodate up to eight people. There are three family-style restaurants—a steak house, Italian buffet, and pizzeria. ☒ *Rødbyhavn, DK–4970 Rødby,* ☎ *54/60–42–00,* FAX *54/60–41–44. 636 apartments. 3 restaurants, bar, indoor pool, sauna, 9-hole golf course, 5 tennis courts, health club, playground, meeting rooms. AE, DC, MC, V.*

$ ☷ **Hotel Saxkjøbing.** Behind its yellow half-timber facade, this comfortable hotel is short on character and frills, but the rooms are bright, sunny, and modern, if very simply furnished. In town center, the hotel is convenient to everything. Its family-style restaurant serves pizzas, steaks, and salads. ⊠ *Torvet 9, Sakskøbing, DK–4990,* ☎ *54/70–40–39,* ☎ *54/89–53–50. 30 rooms, 20 with bath. Restaurant, bar, meeting room. AE, DC, MC, V.*

En Route Kids adore and flock to **BonBon Land,** in the tiny southern Sjælland town of Holme Olstrup between Rønnede and Næstved. Filled with rides and friendly costumed grown-ups, the park is an old-fashioned playland, with a few eating and drinking establishments thrown in for adults. ☎ *53/76–26–00.* ☷ *DKr95, DKr89 off-season.* ☉ *Early May–mid-June and early Aug.–mid-Sept., daily 10–7; mid-June–early Aug., daily 10–9.*

Halsskov

⓼ *95 km (60 mi) northwest of Falster, 110 km (69 mi) southwest of Copenhagen.*

Europe's second-longest tunnel-bridge, Storebæltsbro—the entire fixed-link length of which will be 18 km (11 mi)—will soon link Halsskov, on west Sjælland, to Nyborg, on east Fyn. Rail traffic traverses the west bridge and tunnel; at press time, auto traffic was scheduled to commence in summer 1998 on the east and west bridge. The **Storebæltsbro Udstillings Center** (Great Belt Exhibition Center), detailing the work, includes videos and models and makes for an informative stop. ⊠ *Halsskov Odde,* ☎ *58/35–01–00.* ☷ *DKr35.* ☉ *May–Sept., daily 10–8; Oct.–Apr., Tues.–Sun. 10–5.*

Outdoor Activities and Sports

CANOEING

Just 15 km (10 mi) east of Slagelse and 30 km (19 mi) east of Halsskov is the Suså (Sus River), where you can arrange hour-, day-, and week-long trips. Call **Susåen Kanoudlejning** regarding canoe rentals (☎ 53/64–61–44).

GOLF

The 18-hole **Korsør Course** (⊠ Ørnumvej 8, Korsør, ☎ 53/57–18–36) is in Korsør, less than 3 km (2 mi) south of Halsskov.

Shopping

In Næstved, 49 km (31 mi) southeast of Halsskov, the **Holmegaards Glassværker** (Glass Workshop, ⊠ Glassværksvej 52, Fensmark, ☎ 55/54–62–00) sells seconds of glasses, lamps, and occasionally art glass, with savings of up to 50% off wholesale costs.

OFF THE BEATEN PATH **TRÆLLEBORG –** Viking enthusiasts will want to head 18 km (11 mi) northeast from Halsskov to Slagelse to see its excavated Viking encampment with a reconstructed army shelter. No longer content to rely on farmer warriors, the Viking hierarchy designed the geometrically exact camp within a circular, moated rampart, thought to be of Asian inspiration. The 16 barracks, of which there is one model, could accommodate 1,300 men. ⊠ Trælleborg Allé, ☎ 53/54–95–06. ☷ DKr35. ☉ Mid-Mar.–Oct., daily 10–5; Nov.–mid-Mar., daily noon–4.

Sjælland and Its Islands A to Z

Arriving and Departing

BY CAR

There are several **DSB** car ferries from Germany. They connect Kiel to Bagenkop, on the island of Langeland (from there, drive north to

Spodsbjerg and take another ferry to Lolland, which is connected to
Falster and Sjælland by bridges); Puttgarden to Rødbyhavn on Lolland;
and Travemünde and Warnemünde to Gedser on Falster. Sjælland is
connected to Fyn, which is connected to Jylland, by bridges and frequent ferries. If you are driving from Sweden, take a car ferry from either Helsingborg to Helsingør or Limhamn to Dragør. Or sail directly
to Copenhagen (☞ Arriving and Departing *in* Copenhagen A to Z,
above). In Denmark, call DSB (☎ 33/14–17–01); in Sweden, call DSB
Sweden (☎ 46/31–80–57–00).

BY PLANE

Copenhagen Airport is Sjælland's only airport (☞ Arriving and Departing *in* Copenhagen A to Z, *above*).

BY TRAIN

Most train routes to Sjælland, whether international or domestic, are
directed to Copenhagen. Routes to north and south Sjælland almost
always require a transfer at Copenhagen's main station. For timetables, call **DSB** (☎ 33/14–17–01).

Getting Around

BY CAR

Highways and country roads throughout Sjælland are excellent, and
traffic—even around Copenhagen—is manageable most of the time.
As elsewhere in Denmark, take care to give right-of-way to the bikes
driving to the right of the traffic.

BY PUBLIC TRANSPORTATION

The **Copenhagen Card,** which affords free train and bus transport, as
well as admission to museums and sites, is valid within the HT-bus and
rail system, which extends north to Helsingør, west to Roskilde, and
south to Køge (☞ Getting Around *in* Copenhagen A to Z, *above*). Every
town in Sjælland has a central train station, usually within walking distance of hotels and sights. (For long distances, buses are not convenient.) The only part of the island not connected to the DSB network
is the sliver of northwestern peninsula known as Sjællands Odde.
Trains leave from Holbæk to Højby, where you can bus to the tip of
the point. For information, call the private railway company **Odsherrede**
(☎ 53/41–00–03). Two vintage trains dating from the 1880s run from
Helsingør and Hillerød to Gilleleje; call for info (☎ 48/30–00–30 or
42/12–00–98).

Contacts and Resources

EMERGENCIES

Police, Fire, or **Ambulance:** (☎ 112).

Hospitals: Helsingør (✉ Esrumvej 145, ☎ 48/29–29–29). **Roskilde** (✉
Roskilde Amtssygehus, Køgevej 7, ☎ 46/32–32–00).

Pharmacies: Helsingør (✉ Axeltorvs, Groskenstr. 2A, ☎ 49/21–12–
23). **Stengades** (✉ Steng. 46, ☎ 49/21–86–00). **Roskilde** (✉ Dom
Apoteket, Alg. 8, ☎ 42/35–40–16). **Svane** (✉ Skomagerg. 12, ☎ 42/
35–83–00).

GUIDED TOURS

Check with the local tourism boards for general sightseeing tours in
the larger towns or for self-guided walking tours. Most tours of Sjælland begin in Copenhagen. For information, call Vikingbus (☎ 31/57–
26–00) or Copenhagen Excursion (☎ 31/54–06–06).

Boat Tour: The turn-of-the-century *Saga Fjord* (☎ 46/35–35–75) gives
tours of the waters of the Roskildefjord from April through September; meals are served on board. Schedules vary; call ahead.

Castle Tours: The **Afternoon Hamlet Tour** (4½ hours) includes Frederiksborg Castle and the exterior of Fredensborg Palace. The 7-hour **Castle Tour of North Zealand** visits Frederiksborg Castle and the outside of Fredensborg Palace, and stops at Kronborg Castle.

Walking Tours: The 6-hour Roskilde **Vikingland Tour** includes the market and cathedral, Christian IV's Chapel, and the Viking Ship Museum.

VISITOR INFORMATION

Helsingør (⊠ Havnepl. 3, ☎ 49/21–13–33). **Hillerød** (⊠ Slotsg. 52, ☎ 42/26–28–52). **Køge** (⊠ Vesterg. 1, ☎ 53/65–58–00). **Lolland** (⊠ Østergårdg. 7, Nykøbing Falster, ☎ 54/85–13–03). **Roskilde** (⊠ Fondens Bro 3, ☎ 42/35–27–00). **Sakskøbing** (⊠ Torveg. 4, ☎ 53/89–56–30 summer; ☎ 53/89–45–72 winter). **Stege** and **Møn** (⊠ Storeg. 2, Stege, ☎ 55/81–44–11).

FYN AND THE CENTRAL ISLANDS

Christened the Garden of Denmark by its most famous son, Hans Christian Andersen, Fyn (Funen) is the smaller of the country's two major islands. A patchwork of vegetable fields and flower gardens, the flat-as-a-board countryside is relieved by beech glades and swan ponds. Manor houses and castles pop up from the countryside like magnificent mirages. Some of northern Europe's best-preserved castles are here: the 12th-century Nyborg Slot, travel pinup Egeskov Slot, and the lavish Valdemars Slot. The fairy-tale cliché often attached to Denmark really does spring from this provincial isle, where the only faint pulse emanates from Odense, its capital. Trimmed with thatched houses and green parks, the city makes the most of the Andersen legacy but surprises with a rich arts community at the Brandts Klædefabrik, a former textile factory turned museum compound.

Towns in Fyn are best explored by car. It's even quick and easy to reach the smaller islands of Langeland and Tåsinge—both are connected to Fyn by bridges. Slightly more isolated is Ærø, where the town of Ærøskøbing, with its painted half-timber houses and winding streets, seems caught in a delightful time warp.

Biking

Flat and smooth, Fyn is perfect for biking. Packages with bike rental, hotel accommodations, and half-board (breakfast and one meal) for the entire region are available from **Hotel Svendborg** (⊠ Centrumpl., 5700 Svendborg, ☎ 62/21–17–00).

Markets

Wednesday and Saturday are market days in towns across Fyn throughout the summer. Often held in the central square, these morning markets offer fresh produce, flowers, and cheeses.

Nightlife and the Arts

Castle concerts are held throughout the summer at Egeskov, Nyborg, and Valdemar castles and the rarely opened Krengenrup manor house near Assens.

Nyborg

 75 km (47 mi) southwest of Copenhagen, including ferry passage across the Great Belt, 30 km (19 mi) southeast of Odense.

Like most visitors, you should begin your tour of Fyn in Nyborg, a 13th-century town that was Denmark's capital during the Middle Ages. The city's major landmark, the moated 12th-century **Nyborg Slot** (Nyborg Castle), was the seat of the Danehof, the Danish parliament

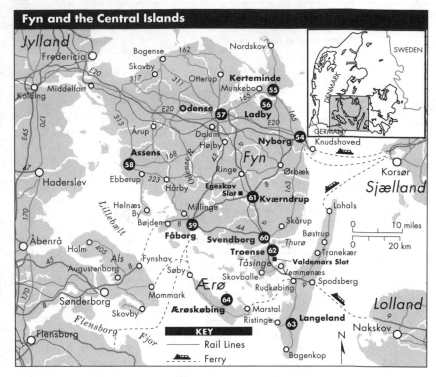

Fyn and the Central Islands

from 1200 to 1413. It was here that King Erik Klipping signed the country's first constitution, the Great Charter, in 1282. In addition to geometric wall murals and an armory collection, the castle houses changing art exhibits. ⊠ *Slotspl.,* ☎ *65/31–02–07.* 🎟 *DKr10.* ☉ *June–Aug., daily 10–5; Mar.–May and Sept.–Oct., Tues.–Sun. 10–3.*

Cross Gammel Torv and walk down the street to the **Nyborg Museum,** housed in a half-timber merchant's house from 1601, for a picture of 17th-century life. Aside from furnished rooms, there's a small brewery. ⊠ *Slotspl. 11,* ☎ *65/31–02–07.* 🎟 *DKr10.* ☉ *June–Aug., daily 10–5; Mar.–May and Sept.–Oct., Tues.–Sun. 10–3.*

Dining and Lodging

\$\$ ✕ **Danehofkroen.** Outside Nyborg Slot, this family-run restaurant does a brisk lunch business, serving traditional Danish meals to tourists who enjoy a view of the castle and its tree-lined moat. The menu is basic meat and potatoes, with such dishes as *flæskesteg* (sliced pork served with the crisp rind). ⊠ *Slotspl.,* ☎ *65/31–02–02. Reservations essential. No credit cards. Closed Mon.*

\$\$\$\$ 🏨 **Hesselet.** A modern brick slab outside, this hotel is a refined Anglo-Asian sanctuary on the inside. Guest rooms have cushy, modern furniture, most with a splendid view of the Storebæltsbro. ⊠ *Christianslundsvej 119, DK–5800 Nyborg,* ☎ *65/31–30–29,* 📠 *65/31–29–58. 43 rooms, 3 suites. Restaurant, bar, room service, indoor pool, sauna, tennis courts, meeting rooms. AE, DC, MC, V.*

Shopping

ANTIQUES

Many of Fyn's manor houses and castles now double as antiques emporiums. The largest is at **Hindemae** (⊠ Near Rte. 315, 12 km/7 mi west of Nyborg, exit 46 or 47 in Ullerslee, ☎ 65/35–22–05). A modest selection of antiques is for sale at **Hønnerup Hougård** (✉ Hougårdsvej 6, Hønnerup, 40 km/25 mi northwest of Nyborg, ☎ 64/49–13–00); take exit 55 to Route 161 toward Middelfart; follow the signs to Hønnerup.

Kerteminde

⑤ *21 km (13 mi) north of Nyborg, 20 km (13 mi) northeast of Odense.*

Kerteminde is an important fishing village and picturesque summer resort. On Langegade, walk past the neat half-timber houses to Møllebakken and the museum of the Danish painter **Johannes Larsen** (1867–1961). Across from a crimson strawberry patch and a 100-year-old windmill, the artist built a large country villa that has been perfectly preserved, right down to the teacups. In front, you'll see a sculpture of a woman by Kai Nielsen. Local legend has it that one night, after a particularly wild party in Copenhagen, its legs were broken off. An ambulance was called, and once it arrived, the enraged driver demanded that the artists pay a fine. A chagrined Larsen paid, and in return kept the wounded sculpture. ✉ *Møllebakken,* ☎ *65/32–37–27.* 🎫 *DKr30.* ☉ *June–Aug., daily 10–5; Mar.–May and Sept.–Oct., Tues.–Sun. 10–4; Nov.–Feb., Tues.–Sun. 11–4.*

Dining

$$ ✕ **Rudolf Mathis.** This busy harborside restaurant is topped by two chimneys venting open grills that broil popular fish dishes. Favorites are catfish with butter, fennel, and Pernod sauce, and grilled turbot in green-pepper-and-lime sauce. ✉ *Dosserengen 13,* ☎ *65/32–32–33. AE, DC, MC, V. Closed Mon. Jan.–Mar. and Sun. Oct. and Dec.*

Shopping

CERAMICS

Just a few miles north of Kerteminde is **Bjørnholt Keramik** (✉ Risingevej 12, Munkebo, ☎ 65/97–40–90), where you can watch ceramics in the making.

Ladby

⑤ *4 km (2½ mi) south of Kerteminde, 16 km (10 mi) east of Odense.*

The village of Ladby is best known as the home of the 1,100-year-old remains of the **Ladbyskibet.** This Viking chieftain's ship burial is complete with hunting dogs and horses for his trip to Valhalla—the afterlife. ✉ *Vikingevej 12,* ☎ *65/32–16–67.* 🎫 *DKr20.* ☉ *Mid-May–mid-Sept., daily 10–6; Mar.–mid-May and mid-Sept.–Oct., daily 10–4; Nov.–Feb., weekends 11–3.*

Odense

⑤ *20 km (12 mi) southwest of Ladby on Route 165, 144 km (90 mi) west of Copenhagen.*

It's no coincidence that Odense, the capital of Fyn and third largest city in Denmark, is reminiscent of a storybook village—much of its charm is built upon the legend of its most famous son, author Hans Christian Andersen. First see the flourishing **Kongens Have** (King's Garden) and 18th-century **Odense Castle,** now a government building. Walking east on Stationsvej to Thomas B. Thriges Gade and Hans Jensensstræde, you'll come to the **Hans Christian Andersen Hus** (Hans Christian Andersen House) amid half-timber houses and cobbled streets. Inside, the storyteller's life is chronicled through his photographs, drawings, letters, and personal belongings. The library has Andersen's works in more than 100 languages, and you can listen to fairy tales on tape. ⊠ *Hans Jensensstr. 37-45,* ☎ *66/13–13–72 ext. 4611.* 🎦 *DKr25.* ⊙ *June–Aug., daily 9–6; Sept.–May, daily 10–4.*

The sleek **Carl Nielsen Museum** creates multimedia exhibits of the life and work of Denmark's most famous composer (1865–1931) and of his wife, the sculptor Anne Marie Carl-Nielsen (yes, that's the way she took his name). ⊠ *Claus-Bergs G. 11,* ☎ *66/13–13–72, ext. 4671.* 🎦 *DKr15.* ⊙ *Daily 10–4.*

Møntergården, Odense's museum of urban history, occupies four 17th-century row houses in a shady, cobbled courtyard. Exhibits range from interiors of the Middle Ages to Denmark's Nazi occupation to an impressive coin collection. ⊠ *Overg. 48–50,* ☎ *66/13–13–72 ext. 4611.* 🎦 *DKr15.* ⊙ *July and Aug., daily 10–5; Sept.–June, Tues.–Sun. 10–5.*

The stately **St. Knuds Kirke,** built from the 13th to the 15th century, is the only purely Gothic cathedral in Denmark. The intricate wooden altar covered with gold leaf was carved by German sculptor Claus Berg. Beneath the sepulchre are the bones of St. (King) Knud, killed during a farmers' uprising in 1086, and his brother. ⊠ *Toward the pedestrian zone of St. Knuds Kirkestræde, in front of Andersen Park.*

In the diminutive **H. C. Andersens Barndomshjem** (H. C. Andersen's Childhood Home), the young boy and his parents lived in a room barely 5 ft by 6 ft. ⊠ *Munkemøllestr. 3–5,* ☎ *66/13–13–72, ext. 4611.* ⊙ *Jun.–Aug., daily 10–4; Sept.–May, daily 11–3.*

Filosofgangen is the embarkation point for the **Odense River Cruises** (☎ *65/95–79–96*). Here you can catch a boat (May–mid-Aug., daily 10, 11, 1, 2, 3, and 5, returning 35 minutes later) downriver to the Fruens Bøge (Lady's Beech Forest) and then walk down Erik Bøghs Sti (Erik Bøgh's Footpath) to **Den Fynske Landsby** (the Fyn Village). Among the country's largest open-air museums, it includes 25 farm buildings and workshops, a vicarage, a water mill, and a theater, which in summer stages adaptations of Andersen's tales. Afterward, cruise back to town center or catch Bus 21 or 22, and walk down the boutique- and café-lined pedestrian street Vestergade (Kongsgade running perpendicular to the town hall), which in summer is abuzz with street performers, musicians, and brass bands. ⊠ *Sejerskovvej 20,* ☎ *66/13–13–72 ext. 4642.* 🎦 *DKr20.* ⊙ *June–Aug., daily 10–7; Apr.–May and Sept.–Oct., daily 10–5; Nov.–Mar., Sun. and holidays 10–4.*

Occupying a former textile factory, the four-story artist compound ★ **Brandts Klædefabrik** now houses the **Museet for Fotokunst** (Museum of Photographic Art), **Danmarks Grafiske Museum** (Danish Graphics Museum), **Dansk Presse Museum** (Danish Press Museum), and **Kunsthallen** (Art Gallery). National and international exhibits vary widely, but the photography museum and the art gallery show especially experimental work. ⊠ *North of the river and parallel to Kongensgade, Brandts Passage 37,* ☎ *66/13–78–97.* 🎦 *Combined ticket DKr40; photography museum DKr20; graphics museum DKr20; press museum DKr20; art gallery DKr25.* ⊙ *July and Aug., daily 10–5; Sept.–June, Tues.–Sun. 10–5.*

OFF THE
BEATEN PATH

HOLLUFGÅRD – This 16th-century manor now houses the city's archaeological department. Although the house itself remains closed, its grounds contain a completely renovated old barn and adjacent buildings showing special exhibits, including the archaeological find of the month and an ecology display. Nearby are a sculpture center, where you can see an artist at work, and a sculpture garden. Take Bus 91 from the railway center on Jernbanegade 10 km (6 mi) south of Odense. ⊠ *Hestehaven*

*201, ☎ 66/14–88–14, ext. 4638 ⌾ DKr25. ☉ Apr.–Oct., Tues.–Sun.
10–5.; Nov.–Apr., Sun. 11–4.*

Dining and Lodging

$$$ ✕ **La Petite Cuisine Française.** This romantic little restaurant, tucked
in the Brandts Passage, can accommodate about 40 guests, all of whom
must make reservations a least a few days in advance. The southern
French specialties change every day according to what can be purchased
fresh at the market. Typical dishes include Asian-inspired marinated
duck breast, grilled skewered salmon or catfish with vegetables, and
white mocha parfait for dessert. Dishes can be combined in three- to
five-course menus. ⌂ *Brandts Passage 13,* ☎ *66/14–11–00. Reservations essential. DC, MC, V.*

$$$ ✕ **Marie Louise.** Near the pedestrian street, this elegant whitewashed
dining room glitters with crystal and silver. The daily French-Danish
menu typically offers such specialties as salmon scallop with bordelaise sauce and grilled veal with lobster-cream sauce. Business and
holiday diners are sometimes treated to gratis extras—such as quail's
egg appetizers or after-dinner drinks. ⌂ *Lottrups Gaard, Vesterg. 70–
72,* ☎ *66/17–92–95. AE, DC, MC, V. Closed Sun. and July.*

$$ ✕ **Den Gamle Kro.** Built within the courtyards of several 17th-century
homes, this popular restaurant has walls of ancient stone sliced by a
sliding glass roof. The French-Danish menu includes fillet of sole
stuffed with salmon mousse and chateaubriand with garlic potatoes,
but there's also inexpensive smørrebrød. ⌂ *Overg. 23,* ☎ *66/12–14–
33. DC, MC, V.*

$$ ✕ **La Provence.** A few minutes from the pedestrian street, this intimate
restaurant with a bright yellow and orange dining room puts a modern twist on Provençal cuisine. Dishes might be venison in blackberry
sauce and tender duck breast cooked in sherry. ⌂ *Dogstr. 31,* ☎ *66/
12–12–96. DC, MC, V.*

$ ✕ **Den Grimme Ælling.** The name of this chain restaurant means the
★ Ugly Duckling, but inside it's simply homey, with pine furnishings and
family-style interiors. It's also extremely popular with tourists and locals alike, thanks to an all-you-can-eat buffet heaped with cold and
warm dishes. ⌂ *Hans Jensensstr. 1,* ☎ *65/91–70–30. DC, MC.*

$ ✕ **Målet.** A lively crowd calls this sports club its neighborhood bar.
After the steaming plates of schnitzel served in a dozen ways, soccer
is the chief delight of the house. ⌂ *Jernbaneg. 17,* ☎ *66/17–82–41.
Reservations not accepted. No credit cards.*

$$$ ⌸ **Grand Hotel.** A century old, with renovated fin-de-siècle charm, this
imposing four-story, brick-front hotel greets guests with old-fashioned
luxury. The original stone floors and chandeliers lead to a wide staircase and upstairs guest rooms that are modern, with plush furnishings
and sleek marble bathrooms. ⌂ *Jernabaneg. 18, DK–5000 Odense C,*
☎ *66/11–71–71,* FAX *66/14–11–71. 134 rooms, 13 suites. Room service, sauna. AE, DC, MC, V.*

$ ⌸ **Hotel Ydes.** Constantly under undisturbing renovation, this well-
kept, bright, and colorful hotel is a good bet for students and budget-
conscious travelers tired of barracks-type accommodations. The plain
hospital-style rooms are spotless and comfortable. ⌂ *Hans Tausensg.
11, DK–5000 Odense C,* ☎ *66/12–11–31. 30 rooms, 24 with bath.
Café. MC, V.*

Nightlife and the Arts

CAFÉS AND BARS

Odense's central Arcade is an entertainment mall, with bars, restaurants, and live music ranging from corny sing-alongs to hard rock. For a quiet evening, stop by **Café Biografen** (⊠ Brandts Passage, ☎ 66/13–16–16) for an espresso or beer, light snack, and the atmosphere of an old movie house. Or settle in to see one of the wide variety of films screened here.

The **Air Pub** (⊠ Kongsg. 41, ☎ 66/14–66–08) is a Danish café that caters to a slightly older crowd—30- and 40-something—with light meals and a small dance floor. **Klos Ands** (⊠ Vineg. 76, ☎ 66/13–56–00) used to be just for grown-ups, but its specialty, malt whiskey, is now drawing a younger crowd, too. At the **All Night Boogie Dance Café** (⊠ Nørreg. 21, ☎ 66/14–00–39), a laid-back crowd grooves to pop, disco, and '60s music.

CASINO

Fyn's sole casino is in the slick glass atrium of the **SAS Hans Christian Andersen Hotel** (⊠ Claus Bergs G. 7, Odense, ☎ 66/14–78–00), where you can gamble at blackjack, roulette, and baccarat.

JAZZ CLUBS

The Cotton Club (⊠ Pantheonsg. 5C, ☎ 66/12–55–25), with its crowd of old-timers and earnest youths, is a venue for traditional jazz. **Dexter's** (⊠ Vinderg. 65, ☎ 66/13–68–88) has all kinds of jazz—from Dixieland to fusion—Thursday to Saturday nights.

THEATER

In summer the thespians of the **Odense Street Theater** parade through the streets, dramatizing the tales of the town's most famous son, Hans Christian Andersen. **Den Fynske Landsby** (☞ *above*) stages regular Andersen plays from mid-July to mid-August.

Outdoor Activities and Sports

GOLF

The **Odense Eventyr Golfklub** (☎ 66/17–11–44) is 4 km (2½ mi) southwest of Odense, and was built in 1993. The 27-hole **Odense Golf Klub** (☎ 65/95–90–00), 6 km (4 mi) southeast of Odense, was built in 1980 and is relatively flat, with some trees and woods. The nine-hole driving range and putting greens in **Blommenlyst** (☎ 65/96–80–08) are 12 km (7 mi) from Odense, west toward Middlefart.

Shopping

Flensted Uromageren Hus (⊠ Ravnsherred 4, ☎ 66/12–70–44), famous for its paper mobiles, is just across from the Hans Christian Andersen Hus. Inside, handmade mobiles range from simple paper hangings to intricate ceramic balloons.

Assens

❸ *38 km (24 mi) southwest of Odense; take Rte. 168, then drive south on the Strandvej (Beach Rd.) off Rte. 323 in the town of Å.*

★ Near the quiet town of Assens is one of the most extraordinary private gardens in Denmark: Tove Sylvest's sprawling **Seven Gardens.** A privately owned botanical United Nations, the gardens represent the flora of seven European countries, including many plants rare to Denmark. ⊠ *Å Strandvej 62, Ebberup,* ☎ *64/74–12–85.* ☐ *DKr40.* ☉ *May–Oct., daily 10–5.*

☕ Children will appreciate a detour 18 km (11 mi) northeast to Fyn's **Terrarium,** where they can examine all kinds of slippery and slithery creatures, including snakes, iguanas, alligators, and the nearly extinct blue frog. ⊠ *Kirkehelle 5, Vissenbjerg,* ☎ *64/47–18–50.* ☐ *DKr40.* ☉ *May–Aug., daily 10–6; Sept.–Apr., daily 10–4.*

Fåborg

59 *30 km (18 mi) south of Odense (via Rte. 43).*

The surrounding beaches of this lovely 12th-century town are invaded by sun-seeking Germans and Danes in summer. Four times a day you can hear the dulcet chiming of a carillon, the island's largest. In town center is the controversial *Ymerbrønden* sculpture by Kai Nielsen, depicting a naked man drinking from an emaciated cow while it licks a baby. The 18th-century **Den Gamle Gård** (Old Merchant's House), of 1725, chronicles the local history of Fåborg through furnished interiors and exhibits of glass and textiles. ⊠ *Holkeg. 1,* ☎ *62/61–33–38.* ☞ *DKr20.* ⊙ *Mid-May–Sept., daily 10:30–4:30.*

The **Fåborg Museum for Fynsk Malerkunst** (Fyn Painting Museum) has a good collection of turn-of-the-century paintings and sculpture by the Fyn Painters, a school of artists whose work captures the dusky light of the Scandinavian sun. ⊠ *Grønneg. 75,* ☎ *62/61–06–45.* ☞ *DKr25.* ⊙ *June–Aug., daily 10–5; Apr.–May and Sept.–Oct., daily 10–4; Nov.–Mar., daily 11–3.*

Dining and Lodging

$ ✕ **Vester Skerninge Kro.** Midway between Fåborg and Svendborg, this traditional inn is cluttered and comfortable. Pine tables are polished from years of serving hot stews and homemade *mediste pølse* (mild grilled sausage) and *æggkage* (fluffy omelet made with cream, smoked bacon, chives, and tomatoes). ⊠ *Krovej 9, Vester Skerninge,* ☎ *62/24–10–04. No credit cards. Closed Tues.*

$$$$ ✕🛏 **Falsled Kro.** Once a smuggler's hideaway, the 500-year-old Fal-
★ sled Kro is now one of Denmark's most elegant inns. A favorite among well-heeled Europeans, it has appointed its cottages sumptuously with European antiques and stone fireplaces. The restaurant combines French and Danish cuisines, using ingredients from its garden and markets in Lyon. ⊠ *Assensvej 513, DK–5642 Millinge,* ☎ *62/68–11–11,* 𝖥𝖠𝖷 *62/68–11–62. 14 rooms, 3 apartments. Restaurant, room service, 3-hole golf course, horseback riding, boating. AE, DC, MC, V. Closed Jan. and Feb.*

$$$$ ✕🛏 **Steensgaard Herregårdspension.** A long avenue of beeches leads to this 700-year-old moated manor house, 7 km (4½ mi) northwest of Fåborg. The rooms are elegant, with antiques, four-poster beds, and yards of silk damask. The fine restaurant serves wild game from the manor's own reserve. ⊠ *Steensgaard 4, DK–5642 Millinge,* ☎ *62/61–94–90,* 𝖥𝖠𝖷 *62/61–78–61. 15 rooms, 13 with bath. Restaurant, tennis court, horseback riding. AE, DC, MC, V. Closed Jan.*

Svendborg

60 *25 km (15½ mi) east of Fåborg (via Rte. 44 east), 44 km (28 mi) south of Odense.*

Svendborg is Fyn's second-largest town, and one of the country's most important—not to mention happy—cruise harbors. It celebrates its eight-century-old maritime traditions every July, when old Danish wooden ships congregate in the harbor for the circular Fyn *rundt,* or regatta. Play your cards right, and you might hitch aboard and shuttle between towns. Contact the tourist board or any agreeable captain. With many charter-boat options and good marinas, Svendborg is an excellent base from which to explore the hundreds of islands of the South Fyn archipelago.

In Svendborg center is Torvet—the town's market square. To the left on Fruestræde is the black-and-yellow **Anne Hvides Gård,** the oldest secular structure in Svendborg and one of the four branches of **Svendborgs Omegns Museum** (Svendborg County Museum). This evocative exhibit includes 18th- and 19th-century interiors and glass and silver collections. ⊠ *Fruestr. 3,* ☎ *62/21–02–61.* ⊞ *DKr15.* ☉ *Late May–mid-June, daily 10–4; mid-June–late Oct., daily 10–5.*

Bagergade (Baker's Street) is lined with some of Svendborg's oldest half-timber houses. At the corner of Grubbemøllevej and Svinget is the **Viebæltegård,** the headquarters of the Svendborg County Museum, a former poorhouse. You can wander through dining halls, washrooms, and the "tipsy clink," where, as recently as 1974, inebriated citizens were left to sober up. ⊠ *Grubbemøllevej 13,* ☎ *62/21–02–61.* ⊞ *DKr20. Combined admission to Anne Hvides and Svendborgs Omegns museums DKr30.* ☉ *May–mid-June, daily 10–4; mid-June–Oct., daily 10–5; Nov., Dec., Mar., and Apr., daily 1–4; Jan. and Feb., weekdays 1–4.*

Dining and Lodging

$ ✗ **Ærø.** A dim hodgepodge of ship parts and nautical doodads, this restaurant looks like it's always been there, just as is. It's peopled by brusque waitresses and serious local trenchermen who exchange orders from a menu that is staunchly old-fashioned, featuring *frikadeller* (fried meatballs), fried *rødspætte* (plaice) with hollandaise sauce, and dozens of smørrebrød options. ⊠ *Brøg. 1 ved, Ærøfærgen,* ☎ *62/21–07–60. DC, MC, V. Closed Sun.*

$$ ⊞ **Margrethesminde.** The Fyn equivalent of a bed-and-breakfast, this manor house is 16 km (10 mi) west of Svendborg. Owners Marlene Philip and Henrik Nielsen furnished the sunny house with bright colors and modern furnishings, and serve their guests a generous breakfast, ranging from Danish pastries or dark bread and cheese to bacon and eggs. Two of the six rooms are singles. ⊠ *Fåborgvej 154, DK–5762 Vester Skerninge,* ☎ *62/24–10–44,* ℻ *62/24–10–62. 6 rooms, 1 with bath. Bicycles. MC.*

Nightlife and the Arts

A diverse crowd congregates at **Bortløbne Banje** (⊠ Klosterpl. 7, ☎ 62/22–31–21) to hear live rock and blues. **Chess** (⊠ Vesterg. 7, ☎ 62/22–17–16) is popular with a young crowd that comes for the live bands. **Crazy Daizy** (⊠ Frederiksg. 6, ☎ 62/21–67–60) attracts a casual, over-21 crowd to dance to oldies and rock on Saturday nights, and a younger crowd on Fridays. The restaurant **Orangi** (⊠ Jessens Mole, ☎ 62/22–82–92), an old sailing ship moored in the harbor, hires live jazz in summer.

Kværndrup

🄕 *15 km (9 mi) north of Svendborg, 28 km (18 mi) south of Odense.*

★   Over this town presides the moated Renaissance **Egeskov Slot,** one of the best-preserved island-castles in Europe. Peaked with copper spires and surrounded by Renaissance, Baroque, English, and peasant gardens, the castle has an antique-vehicle museum and the world's largest maze, designed by the Danish scientist-turned-poet Piet Hein. The castle is still a private home, though visitors can see a few of the rooms, including the great hall, the hunting room, and the Riborg Room, where the daughter of the house was locked up from 1599 to 1604 after giving birth to a son out of wedlock. ⊠ *Kværndrup,* ☎ *62/27–10–16.* ⊞ *Castle and museum DKr100.* ☉ *Castle May–June and Aug.–Sept., daily 10–5; July, daily 10–8. Museum June and Aug., daily 9–6; July, daily 9–8; May and Sept., daily 10–5.*

Troense

⑥ *3 km (2 mi) south of Svendborg (via the Svendborg Sound Bridge), 43 km (27 mi) south of Odense.*

Tåsinge island is known for its local 19th-century drama involving Elvira Madigan (recall the movie?) and her married Swedish lover, Sixten Sparre. Preferring heavenly union to earthly separation, they shot themselves and are now buried in the island's central Landet churchyard. Brides throw their bouquets on the lovers' grave.

★ Troense is Tåsinge's main town, and one of the country's best-preserved maritime villages, with half-timber buildings opening through hand-carved doors. South of town is **Valdemars Slot** (Valdemars Castle), dating from 1610, one of Denmark's oldest privately owned castles. You can wander through almost all the sumptuously furnished rooms, libraries, and the candle-lit church. There's also an X-rated 19th-century cigar box not to be missed. ⊠ *Slotsalleen 100, Troense,* ☎ *62/22–61–06 or 62/22–50–04.* ⛟ *DKr45.* ☉ *June–Aug., daily 10–6; May and Sept.–Oct., daily 10–5.*

Dining

$$$$ ✕ **Restaurant Valdemars Slot.** Beneath the castle, this domed restaurant is ankle-deep in pink carpet and aglow with candlelight. Fresh French and German ingredients and wild game from the castle's preserve are the menu staples. Venison with cream sauce and duck breast *à l'orange* are typical of the French-inspired cuisine. A less expensive annex, Den Grå Dame, serves traditional Danish food. The third eatery, Æblehaven, serves inexpensive sausages and upscale fast-food. ⊠ *Slotsalleen 100, Troense,* ☎ *62/22–59–00. AE, DC. Closed Mon.*

Shopping

For delicate hand-blown glass, visit **Glasmagerne** (⊠ Vemmenæsvej 10, Tåsinge, ☎ 62/54–14–94).

Langeland

⑥ *16 km (10 mi) southeast of Troense, 64 km (40 mi) southwest of Odense.*

Reached by a causeway bridge from Tåsinge and also by a one-hour ferry ride from Fåborg, Langeland is the largest island of the southern archipelago, rich in relics, with smooth, tawny beaches. Bird-watching is excellent on the southern half of the island, where migratory flocks roost before setting off on their cross-Baltic journey. To the south are Ristinge and Bagenkop, two towns with good beaches; at Bagenkop you can catch the ferry to Kiel, Germany.

Outdoor Activities and Sports

FISHING

Langeland has particularly rich waters for fishing, with cod, salmon, flounder, and gar. For package tours, contact **Ole Dehn** (⊠ Sønderg. 22, Lohals, DK–5953 Tranekær, ☎ 62/55–17–00).

Ærøskøbing

★ ⑥ *30 km (19 mi) south of Svendborg, 74 km (46 mi) south of Odense, plus a one-hour ferry ride, either from Svendborg or Langeland.*

The island of Ærø, where country roads wend through fertile fields, is aptly called the Jewel of the Archipelago. About 27 km (16 mi) southeast of Søby on the island's north coast, the storybook town of Ærøskøbing is the port for ferries from Fåborg. Established as a market town in the 13th century, it did not flourish until it became a sailing center during the 1700s. At night when the street lights illuminate the cobbled streets, it is as though time has stood still.

Ferries provide the only access to Ærø. The ferry from Svendborg to Ærøskøbing takes 1 hour, 15 minutes. In addition, there's a one-hour ferry from Fåborg to Søby, a town on the northwest end of the island; and a shorter one from Rudkøbing—on the island of Langeland—to Marstal, on the eastern end of Ærø.

Down the main central road in Ærøskøbing, take a left onto Smegade to visit one of Denmark's most arresting shrines to obsession. History is recorded in miniature at the **Flaskeskibssamlingen** (Bottle Ship Collection), thanks to a former ship's cook known as Peter Bottle, who painstakingly built nearly 2,000 bottle ships in his day. The combination of his life's work and the enthusiastic letters he received from fans and disciples around the world make for a surprisingly moving collection. ⊠ *Smeg. 22, Ærøskøbing,* ☎ *62/52–29–51.* ⊞ *DKr20.* ۞ *May–Oct., daily 10–5; Nov.–Apr., Tues.–Thurs. 1–3, Sat., 10–2, Sun. 10–1.*

Lodging

$$ ⛶ **Ærøhus.** A half-timber building with a steep red roof, the Ærøhus looks like a rustic cottage on the outside, an old, but overly renovated, aunt's house on the inside. Hanging pots and slanted walls characterize the public areas, and pine furniture and cheerful duvets keep the guest rooms simple and bright. The garden's five cottages have small terraces. ⊠ *Vesterg. 38, DK–5970,* ☎ *62/52–10–03,* ⛶ *62/52–21–23. 30 rooms, 17 with bath; 5 cottages. Restaurant. AE, V.*

Fyn and the Central Islands A to Z

Arriving and Departing

BY CAR AND FERRY

From Copenhagen, take the E20 west to Halsskov, near Korsør, and drive aboard the Great Belt ferry, which costs about DKr300 per car, with up to five passengers and a reservation. For ferry reservations, call **DSB** (☎ 33/14–17–01). The ferry departs daily every 40 minutes. You'll arrive in Knudshoved, near Nyborg, which is a half hour from either Odense or Svendborg. Passage on the Great Belt Bridge costs DKr200.

BY PLANE

Odense Airport (☎ 65/95–50–72), 11 km (7 mi) north of Odense, is served by Mærsk Air (☎ 65/95–53–55) and Muk Air (☎ 65/95–50–20 or 98/19–03–88), which make eight daily flights between Copenhagen and Odense. The 25-minute hop costs about DKr1,300. You can make reservations with the airlines themselves or through SAS (☎ 32/32–00–00).

Between the Airport and Downtown: Metered **airport taxis** charge about DKr140 for the 15-minute drive downtown. A **Mærsk Airbus** meets each flight and stops at the Grand Hotel, Hans Christian Andersen Hotel, and the main railway station. The fare is about DKr60.

BY TRAIN

Trains from Copenhagen's main station depart for the three-hour trip to Odense's train station hourly, every day. Stations in both towns are central, close to hotels and sites. The one-way fare is about DKr150. A reservation costs an additional DKr30 (☎ 33/14–17–01).

Getting Around

BY BICYCLE

With their level terrain and short distances, Fyn and the Central Islands are perfect for cycling. You can rent bikes at **Cykel Biksen** (⊠ Nederg.

14–16, Odense, ☎ 66/12–40–98). **Fåborg Sportshandel** (✉ Havneg. 40, Fåborg, ☎ 62/61–28–22) also lets bikes.

BY BUS AND TRAIN

Large towns are served by intercity trains. The Nyborg–Odense–Middelfart and the Odense–Svendborg routes are among the two most important. The other public transportation option is by bus. Timetables are posted at all bus stops and central stations. Passengers buy tickets on board and pay according to the distance traveled (☎ 66/11–71–11). For central Odense, the **Odense Eventyrpas** (Adventure Pass), available at the tourism office, affords admission to sites and museums and free city bus and train transport. The cost for a two-day pass is DKr90; for a one-day pass, DKr50.

BY CAR

The highways of Fyn are excellent, and small roads meander beautifully on two lanes through the countryside. Traffic is light, except during the height of summer in highly populated beach areas.

Contacts and Resources

EMERGENCIES

Police, fire, or **ambulance** (☎ 112). **Odense Hospital,** (✉ J. B. Winsløws Vej, ☎ 66/11–33–33). **Doctor** (☎ 65/90–60–10 between 4 PM and 7 AM). **Other Emergencies** (Falck, ☎ 66/11–22–22). **Ørnen Apoteket** (✉ Vesterg. 80, Odense, ☎ 66/12–29–70).

GUIDED TOURS

Few towns offer organized tours, but check the local tourist offices for step-by-step walking brochures.

Hans Christian Andersen Tours: Full-day tours to Odense depart from Copenhagen's Rådhus Pladsen mid-May–mid-September, Sunday at 8:30 AM, and cost DKr480. (Six of 11 hours are spent in transit.) Call ☎ 31/54–06–06 for reservations.

Walking Tours: The two-hour Odense tour departs from the tourist office during July and early August at 11 AM every Tuesday, Wednesday, and Thursday. It includes the exteriors of the Hans Christian Andersen sites and the cathedral.

VISITOR INFORMATION

Odense (✉ City Hall, ☎ 66/12–75–20). **Kerteminde** (✉ Strandg. 1, ☎ 65/32–11–21). **South Fyn Tourist Board** (✉ Centrumpl., Svendborg, ☎ 62/21–09–80). **Nyborg** (✉ Torvet 9, ☎ 65/31–02–80). **Ærøskøbing** (✉ Torvet, ☎ 62/52–13–00).

JYLLAND

Jylland (Jutland), Denmark's western peninsula, is the only part of the country naturally connected to mainland Europe; its southern boundary is the frontier with Germany. In contrast to the smooth, postcard-perfect land of Fyn and Sjælland, this Ice Age–chiseled peninsula is bisected at the north by the craggy Limfjord and spiked below by the Danish "mountains." Himmelbjerget, the zenith of this modest range, peaks at 438 ft. Farther south, the Yding Skovhøj plateau rises 568 ft—modest hills just about anywhere else.

Hunters first inhabited Denmark, in southern Jylland, some 250,000 years ago. You can see flint tools and artifacts from this period locked away in museums, but the land holds more stirring relics from a later epoch: after 1,000 years, Viking burial mounds and stones still swell the land, some in protected areas, others lying in farmers' fields, tended by grazing sheep.

The windswept landscapes filmed in *Babette's Feast,* the movie version of the Karen Blixen (Isak Dinesen) novel, trace the west coast northward to Skagen, a luminous, dune-covered point (geographically similar to the Outer Banks of North Carolina). To the west, facing Fyn, Jylland is cut by deep fjords rimmed with forests. The center is dotted with castles, parklands, and the famed Legoland. Ribe, Denmark's oldest town, lies to the south and west; Århus and Aalborg, respectively Denmark's second- and fourth-largest cities, face east and have nightlife and sights to rival Copenhagen's.

Nearly three times the size of the rest of Denmark, with long distances between towns, the peninsula of Jylland can easily take at least several days, even weeks, to explore. If you are pressed for time, concentrate on a single tour or a couple of cities. Delightful as they are, the islands are suitable only for those with plenty of time, as many require an overnight stay. The following tour focuses on chunks of the peninsula and is organized as you would explore them with a car.

Canoeing

Canoe rentals (about DKr200 per day) are available in the lake district, Limfjord, and almost all lakes and rivers. One- to three-day package tours are available throughout the region, with either camping or hostel accommodations. For more information, contact the local tourist boards.

Fishing

The lake district is a great place for fishing and angling. License requirements vary and package tours are also available; contact any local tourist office for details.

Kolding

65 *71 km (44 mi) northwest of Odense (via the Little Belt Bridge), 190 km (119 mi) west of Copenhagen.*

The well-preserved **Koldinghus,** a massive stonework structure that was once fortress, then a royal residence in the Middle Ages, is today a historical museum. In the winter of 1808, during the Napoleonic Wars, Spanish soldiers set fire to most of it while trying to stay warm. ⊠ *Rådhusstr.,* ☎ *75/50–15–00, ext. 5400.* 🎫 *DKr40.* ⊙ *Daily 10–5.*

Dining and Lodging

$$$ ✕🏨 **Hotel Koldingfjord.** This impressive neoclassical hotel has mahogany
★   floors and pyramid skylights. It's five minutes from town and faces the Kolding Fjord and 50 acres of countryside. The rooms vary in size (with 39 in a separate annex), but all have mahogany beds and bright prints. There's also an excellent French-Danish restaurant. ⊠ *Fjordvej 154, DK–6000 Strandhuse,* ☎ *75/51–00–00,* 🆁 *75/51–00–51. 115 rooms, 8 suites. Restaurant, bar, indoor pool, sauna, 2 tennis courts, health club. AE, DC, MC, V.*

Ribe

★ 66 *60 km (36 mi) southwest of Kolding, 150 km (103 mi) southwest of Århus.*

In the southeastern corner of Jylland, the country's oldest town is well worth the detour for its medieval center preserved by the Danish National Trust. From May to mid-September, a night watchman circles the town, recalling its history and singing traditional songs. If you who want to accompany him, gather at the main square at 10 PM.

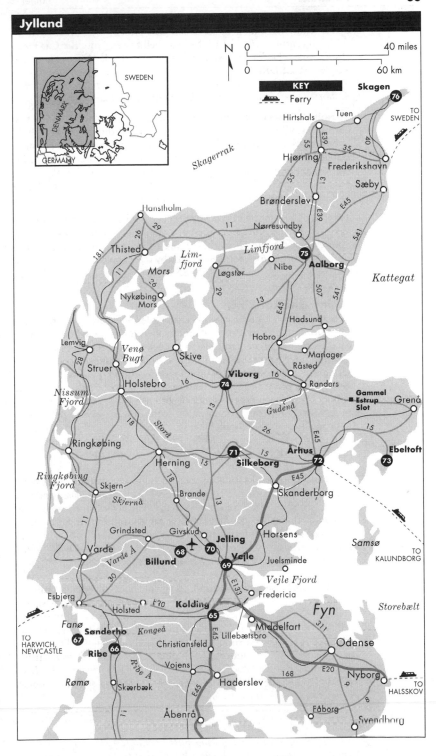

The **Ribe Domkirke** (Cathedral) stands on the site of one of Denmark's earliest churches, built around AD 860. The present structure dates from the 12th century, with a 14th-century bell tower. Note the Cat Head Door, said to be for the exclusive use of the devil. ⊠ *Torvet,* ☎ *75/ 42–06–19.* ☞ *DKr5.* ⊘ *May and Sept., Mon.–Sat. 10–5, Sun. noon– 5; June–Aug., Mon.–Sat. 10–6, Sun. noon–6; Oct.–Apr., Mon.–Sat. 11– 3, Sun. noon–3. Call first to confirm hours.*

The **Ribes Vikinger** (Museum for the Viking Period and the Middle Ages) chronicles Viking history with conventional exhibits of household goods, tools, and clothing. There's a multimedia room, with an interactive computer screen where you can search for more Viking information in the form of text, pictures, and videos. ⊠ *Odinspl.,* ☎ *75/ 42–22–22.* ☞ *DKr40.* ⊘ *June–Aug., daily 10–5; Apr.–May and Sept.– Oct., daily 10–4; Nov.–Mar., Tues.–Sun. 10–4.*

Take Bus 52 from the railway station across the street from the Ribes Vikinger 2 km south, and you'll arrive at the **Viking Center,** an outdoor exhibit detailing how the Vikings lived day-to-day, with demonstrations about homes, food, and crafts by real people. ⊠ *Lustrupsholm, Lustrupvej 4,* ☎ *75/41–16–11.* ☞ *DKr30.* ⊘ *Mid-May–mid-Sept., Tues.–Sun. 11–4.*

Dining and Lodging

$ ✕ **Sælhunden.** This 300-year-old canal-side "Male Seal" tavern barely fits a dozen tables, but its cozy atmosphere draws wayfarers and locals. The only seal mementos left are a few skins and pictures, but you can still order a "seal's special" of cold shrimp, sautéed potatoes, and scrambled eggs or—an old Danish favorite—fat strips of bacon served with cream gravy and boiled potatoes, only served Wednesday in the winter. Console yourself in summer with *rød grød med fløde* (red porridge with cream); the pronunciation of the dessert—which defies phonetic spelling—is so difficult Danes get a kick out of making foreigners pronounce it. ⊠ *Skibbroen 13,* ☎ *75/42–09–46. Reservations not accepted. DC, MC, V. Sept.–June, closed for dinner after 8:45.*

$$$ ✕🏠 **Hotel Dagmar.** In Ribe's quaint center, this cozy half-timber hotel
★ encapsulates the charm of the 16th century—with stained-glass windows, sloping wooden floors, and carved chairs. The lavish rooms are all appointed with antique canopy beds, fat armchairs, and chaise longues. The fine French restaurant serves such specialties as fillet of salmon in sorrel cream sauce. ⊠ *Torvet 1, DK–6760,* ☎ *75/42–00–33,* 📠 *75/42– 36–52. 48 rooms. Restaurant, bar, meeting rooms. AE, DC, MC, V.*

$ 🏠 **Ribe Family and Youth Hostel.** In town center, this plain, redbrick hostelry is run by helpful wardens Jens Philipsen and Gudrun Rishede. Six- and four-bed family rooms are arranged in clusters of two, each with its own private bath and toilet in a small hallway. There are also eight newish four-bed rooms with completely private facilities. They are functional and childproof, with pine bunks and industrial carpeting. A kitchen is available for use. ⊠ *Ribehallen, Skt. Pedersg. 16, DK– 6760,* ☎ *75/42–06–20,* 📠 *75/42–42–88. 152 beds in 34 family rooms. Cafeteria. No credit cards. Closed Dec. and Jan.*

Sønderho

🟢 *30 km (19 mi) northwest of Ribe, plus 12-min ferry from Esbjerg, 153 km (96 mi) southwest of Århus, plus 12-min ferry from Esbjerg.*

During the 19th century, the tiny island of **Fanø** had an enormous shipbuilding industry and a fleet second only to Copenhagen's. The shipping industry deteriorated, but the proud maritime heritage remains.

From Fanø's ferry port in Nordby, take a bus south to Sønderho. Along the tiny winding lanes are thatched cottages decorated with ships' relics, figureheads, painted doors, and brass lanterns. You may even see people wearing the traditional costumes, especially on *Sønderhodag,* a town festival held on the third Sunday in July.

Dining and Lodging

$$ ✗ 🏨 **Sønderho Kro.** Just 13 km (8 mi) from Fanø's main town of
★ Nordby, this 270-year-old thatched inn is one of Jylland's finest, its charm preserved with a beamed foyer, painted doors, and timbered ceilings. Rooms are jazzed up with four-poster beds, elegant tapestries, and gauzy curtains. The French-Danish restaurant serves excellent seafood on its old tables. ✉ *Kropl. 11, DK–6720, Sønderho,* ☎ *75/16–40–09, 6 rooms, 2 suites. Restaurant. AE, DC, MC, V. Closed Feb. and weekdays Nov.–Jan.*

Billund

68 *101 km (63 mi) southwest of Århus.*

★ ☕ Billund's only claim to fame is **Legoland,** an amusement park in which everything is constructed from 35 million plastic Lego bricks. Among its incredible structures are scaled-down versions of cities and villages, working harbors and airports, a Statue of Liberty, statue of Sitting Bull, Mount Rushmore, safari park, and Pirate Land. Grown-ups might marvel at toys from pre-Lego days, the most exquisite of which is Titania's Palace, a sumptuous dollhouse built in 1907 by Sir Neville Wilkinson for his daughter. The Lego empire is expanding: the company's goal is to open one park globally every three years, but Danes maintain that theirs, the original, will always be the best. ✉ *Billund,* ☎ *75/33–13–33.* 🎫 *DKr110.* ☉ *Apr.–Sept., daily 10–8.*

Vejle

69 *40 km (25 mi) east of Billund, 73 km (46 mi) southwest of Århus.*

On the east coast, Vejle is beautifully positioned on a fjord, amid forest-clad hills. You can hear the time of day chiming on the old **Dominican monastery clock**; the clock remains, but the monastery long ago gave way to the town's imposing 19th-century city hall.

In town center, at Kirke Torvet, is **Skt. Nikolai Kirke** (St. Nicholas Church). In the left arm of the cross-shape church, lying in a glass Empire-style coffin, is the body of a bog woman found preserved in a peat marsh in 1835; she dates to 500 BC. The church walls contain the skulls of 23 thieves executed in the 17th century. ✉ *Kirke Torvet,* ☎ *75/82–41–39.* ☉ *May–Sept., weekdays 9–5, Sat. 9–noon, Sun. 9–11:30.*

Lodging

$$$$ 🏨 **Munkebjerg Hotel.** Seven kilometers (4½ miles) southeast of town, surrounded by a thick beech forest and majestic views of the Vejle Fjord, this elegant hotel attracts guests who prefer privacy. Beyond the rustic lobby, rooms furnished in blond pine and soft green overlook the forest. There are also two top-notch French-Danish restaurants and a swank casino. ✉ *Munkebjergvej 125, DK–7100,* ☎ *75/72–35–00,* FAX *75/72–08–86. 145 rooms, 2 suites. 2 restaurants, room service, indoor pool, sauna, tennis court, health club, casino, meeting rooms, helipad. AE, DC, MC, V.*

Nightlife

The casino at the **Munkebjerg Hotel** (☞ *above*) has blackjack, roulette, baccarat, and slot machines.

Jelling

⑦⓪ *10 km (6 mi) northwest of Vejle (via Rte. 18), 83 km (52 mi) south-west of Århus.*

In Jelling, two 10th-century burial mounds mark the seat of King Gorm and his wife, Thyra. Between the mounds are two **Runestener** (runic stones), one of which is Denmark's certificate of baptism, showing the oldest known figure of Christ in Scandinavia. The inscription explains that the stone was erected by Gorm's son, King Harald Bluetooth, who brought Christianity to the Danes in AD 960.

The most scenic way to get to Jelling is via the **vintage steam train** that runs from Vejle every Sunday in July and the first Sunday in August. Call the Jelling tourist office for schedules.

Silkeborg

⑦① *60 km (38 mi) north of Jelling, 43 km (27 mi) west of Århus.*

At the banks of the River Gudenå begins Jylland's lake district. Stretching from Silkeborg in the west to Skanderborg in the east, this area contains some of Denmark's loveliest scenery and most of its meager mountains, including the 438-ft **Himmelbjerget,** at Julsø (Lake Jul). You can climb the narrow paths through the heather and trees to the top, where an 80-ft tower stands sentinel, placed there on Constitution Day in 1875 in memory of King Frederik VII.

The best way to explore the lake district is by water, as the Gudenå winds its way some 160 km (100 mi) through lakes and wooded hillsides down to the sea. Take one of the excursion boats or the world's last coal-fired paddle steamer, **Hjejlen,** which departs in summer from Silkeborg Harbor. Since 1861 it has paddled its way through narrow stretches of fjord, where the treetops meet overhead, to the foot of the Himmelbjerget. ⊠ *Havnen, Silkeborg,* ☎ *86/82–07–66 (reservations).* ⌑ *DKr76 round-trip.* ⊙ *Mid-June–early Aug., Sun. 10 and 1:45.*

★ Silkeborg's main attractions are housed in the **Kulturhistoriske Museum** (Museum of Cultural History): the 2,200-year-old Tollund Man and Elling Girl, two bog people preserved by natural ingredients in the soil and water. Discovered in 1950, the Tollund Man remains the best-preserved human face from the Iron Age. He was killed by strangulation—the noose remains around his neck—with a day's worth of stubble that can still be seen on his hauntingly serene face. ⊠ *Hovedgådsvej,* ☎ *86/82–15–78.* ⌑ *DKr20.* ⊙ *Apr. 15–Oct. 23, daily 10–5; Oct. 24–Apr. 14, Wed. and weekends noon–4.*

Dining

$$ ✕ **Spisehuset Christian VIII.** Cut off from Silkeborg's center by a highway, this tiny crooked building seems transported from another time. Inside it's elegant and busy, with an international group of diners occupying the dozen cramped tables. The inventive menu includes tournedos of guinea fowl with mushrooms, and fish specialties such as poached turbot with scallops and spring onions. ⊠ *Christian VIII Vej 54,* ☎ *86/82–25–62. AE, DC, MC, V. Closed Sun.*

Århus

⑦② *40 km (24 mi) east of Silkeborg.*

Århus is Denmark's second-largest city, and, with its funky arts and college community, one of its most pleasant. The town is liveliest during the 10-day **Århus Festival** in September, which combines everything from concerts, theater, and exhibitions to beer tents and sports. In addition, the **Århus International Jazz Festival** in early or mid-July bills international and local greats. In July, the **Viking Moot** draws aficionados to the beach below the Museum of Prehistory at Moesgård. Activities and exhibits include market booths, ancient defense techniques, and rides on Viking ships.

A good starting point is the **Rådhus,** probably the most unusual city hall in Denmark. Built in 1941 by noted architects Arne Jacobsen and Erik Møller, the pale Norwegian-marble block building is controversial but cuts a startling figure when illuminated in the evening. ⊠ *Park Allé,* ☎ *86/12–16–00.* ⛁ *City hall DKr10, tower DKr5.* ⊙ *Guided tours in Danish only mid-June–early Sept., weekdays at 11; tower tours weekdays at noon and 4.*

★ Don't miss the town's open-air museum, known as **Gamle By** (Old Town). Its 70 half-timber houses, mill, and millstream were carefully moved from locations throughout Jylland and meticulously re-created, inside and out. ⊠ *Viborgvej,* ☎ *86/12–31–88.* ⛁ *DKr50.* ⊙ *June–Aug., daily 9–6; May and Sept., daily 9–5; Jan.–Mar. and Nov., daily 11–3; Apr., Oct., and Dec., daily 10–4. Grounds always open.*

In a 250-acre forest south of Århus is the **Moesgård Forhistorisk Museum** (Prehistoric Museum), with exhibits on ethnography and archaeology, including the famed Grauballe Man, a 2,000-year-old corpse so well bog-preserved that scientists could determine his last meal. Also, take the Forhistoriskvej (Prehistoric Trail) through the forest, which leads past Stone- and Bronze-Age displays to reconstructed houses from Viking times. ⊠ *Moesgård Allé,* ☎ *86/27–24–33.* ⛁ *DKr30.* ⊙ *Apr.–Sept., daily 10–5; Oct.–Mar., Tues.–Sun. 10–4.*

☾ If you are visiting Århus with children, visit its provincial **Tivoli,** with rides, music, and lovely gardens. ⊠ *Skovbrynet,* ☎ *86/14–73–00.* ⛁ *DKr30.* ⊙ *Mid-Apr.–May, daily 1–9; May–mid-June, daily 1–10; mid-June–mid-Aug., daily 1–11.*

Be sure to ask at the tourist office about the **Århus Pass,** which affords free passage on buses, free or discounted admission to museums and sites, and tours. A two-day pass is DKr110, and a seven-day is DKr155.

Dining and Lodging

$ ✗ **Rio Grande.** Full of the standard-issue blankets, straw hats, and bright colors ubiquitous in Mexican restaurants the world over, Rio Grande is a favorite with youngsters, families, and even businesspeople. Heaping plates of tacos, enchiladas, and chili are a good value—and tasty, too. ⊠ *Vesterg. 39,* ☎ *86/19–06–96. AE, MC, V.*

$$$ 🏨 **Royal Hotel.** In operation since 1838, Århus's grand hotel has welcomed such greats as Arthur Rubinstein and Marian Anderson. Well-heeled guests are welcomed into a stately lobby appointed with Chesterfield sofas, modern paintings, and a winding staircase. Plush rooms vary in style and decor, but all have rich drapery, velour and brocade furniture, and marble bathrooms. ⊠ *Store Torv 4, DK–8100 Århus C,* ☎ *86/12–00–11,* FAX *86/76–04–04. 105 rooms, 7 suites. Restaurant, bar, sauna, casino, business services. AE, DC, MC, V.*

$ 🏨 **Youth Hostel Pavilionen.** As in all Danish youth and family hostels, the rooms here are clean, bright, and functional. The secluded setting in the woods near the fjord is downright beautiful. Unfortunately, the hostel can get a bit noisy. You can have use of the kitchen. ⊠ *Marienlunsdvej 10, DK–8100,* ☎ *86/16–72–98,* FAX *86/10–55–60. 32 rooms, 11 with private shower, 4 shared showers and toilets. Cafeteria (breakfast only). AE, MC, V. Closed mid-Dec.–mid-Jan.*

Nightlife and the Arts

There's no better time to visit Århus than during the 10-day **Århus Festival Week** in September, when jazz, classical, and rock concerts are nonstop, in addition to drama, theater, and dance.

BARS, LOUNGES, AND DISCOS

The **Café Mozart** (⊠ Vesterport 10, ☎ 86/18–55–63) plays classical music and serves homemade organic Middle Eastern and other ethnic specialties, including what it claims as the world's biggest pita bread. The **Hotel Marselis** (⊠ Strandvejen 25, ☎ 86/14–44–11) attracts a varied crowd to its two venues: the **Beach Club** with danceable rock and disco and the more elegant **Nautilas** piano bar for an older crowd. **Blitz** (⊠ Klosterg. 34, ☎ 86/19–10–99) is one of the more trendy and alternative spots in Århus, cranking out techno-pop tunes.

CASINO

The **Royal Hotel** (⊠ Store Torv 4, ☎ 86/12–00–11) is the city's casino with blackjack, roulette, baccarat, and slot machines.

JAZZ CLUBS

For jazz, head to **Bent J's** (⊠ Nørre Allé 66, ☎ 86/12–04–92), a small club with free-admission jam sessions three times a week and occasional big-name concerts. **Glazz Huset** (⊠ Åboulevarden 35, ☎ 86/12–13–12) is Århus's big jazz club, attracting some international stars.

Ebeltoft

73 *45 km (28 mi) east of Århus.*

Drive northeast to the tip of what Danes call Jylland's nose, Ebeltoft, a town of crooked streets, sloping row houses, and local crafts shops. Danish efficiency is showcased beside the ferry, at the **Vindmølleparken,** one of the largest windmill parks in the world, where 16 wind-powered mills on a curved spit of land generate electricity for 600 families. ⊠ *Færgehaven,* ☎ *86/34–12–44.* ⊡ *Free.* ☉ *Daily.*

You can't miss the *Frigate Jylland,* dry-docked on the town's main harbor. The renovation of the three-masted tall ship was financed by Danish shipping magnate Mærsk McKinney Møller, and it's a testament to Denmark's seafaring days of yore: Wander through to examine the bridge, gun deck, galley, captain's room, and perhaps most impressive of all, the 10½-ton pure copper and pewter screw, and view the voluptuous Pomeranian pine figurehead. ⊠ *Strandvejen 4,* ☎ *86/34–10–99.* ⊡ *DKr40.* ☉ *Daily 10–5.*

Also on the Ebeltoft harbor is the small, light, and airy **Glasmuseum.** The setting is perfect for the collection, ranging from mysterious symbol-imbedded monoliths of Swedish glass sage Bertil Vallien to the luminous gold pavilions of Japanese artist Kyohei Fujita. Once a customs and excise house, the museum has a glass workshop where international students come to study. Functional pieces, art, and books are sold at the shop. ⊠ *Strandvejen 8,* ☎ *86/34–17–99.* ⊡ *DKr40.* ☉ *Mid-May–mid-Sept., daily 10–5; mid-Sept.–mid-May, daily 1–4.*

Viborg

74 *60 km (36 mi) west of Randers, 66 km (41 mi) northwest of Århus.*

Viborg dates to at least the 8th century, when it was a trading post and a place of pagan sacrifice. Later it became a center of Christianity, with monasteries and an episcopal residence. The 1,000-year-old **Hærvejen,** the old military road that starts near here, was once Denmark's most important connection with the outside world—though today it lives on as a bicycle path. Legend has it that in the 11th century, King Canute set out from Viborg to conquer England; he succeeded, of course, and ruled from 1016 to 1035. Today you can buy reproductions of a silver coin minted by the king, embossed with the inscription "Knud, Englands Kong" (Canute, King of England).

Built in 1130, Viborg's **Domkirke** (Cathedral) was once the largest granite church in the world. Today only the crypt remains of the original building, restored and reopened in 1876. The dazzling early 20th-century biblical frescoes are by Danish painter Joakim Skovgard. ⊠ *Mogensg.,* ☎ *86/62–10–60.* 🎫 *Free.* ⊙ *June–Aug., Mon.–Sat. 10–4, Sun. noon–5; Sept. and Apr.–May, Mon.–Sat. 11–4, Sun. noon–4; Oct.–Mar., Mon.–Sat. 11–3, Sun. noon–3.*

Aalborg

🅱 *80 km (50 mi) northeast of Viborg, 112 km (70 mi) north of Århus.*

The gentle waters of the Limfjord sever Jylland completely. Clamped to its narrowest point is Aalborg, Denmark's fourth-largest community. The town celebrated its 1,300th birthday with a year of festivities in 1992—once and for all cementing the town's party reputation. The gateway between north and south Jylland, the city is a charming combination of new and old: twisting lanes filled with medieval houses and, nearby, broad modern boulevards.

★ The local favorite site is the magnificent 17th-century **Jens Bang Stenhus** (Jens Bang's Stone House), built by a wealthy merchant. Chagrined he was never made a town council member, the cantankerous Bang avenged himself by caricaturing his political enemies in gargoyles all over the building and then adding his own face, its tongue sticking out at town hall. The five-story building dating from 1624 has a vaulted stone beer-and-wine cellar, one of the most atmospheric in the country (☞ Nightlife and the Arts, *below*). ⊠ *Østerä 9.*

The Baroque **Budolfi Kirke** (Budolfi Cathedral) is dedicated to the English saint Botolph. The church, originally made of wood, has been rebuilt several times in its 800-year history and is now made of stone. It includes a copy of the original tower of the Rådhus in Copenhagen, which was taken down about a century ago. The money for the construction was donated to the church by a generous local merchant and his sister, both of whom, locals say, had no other family on which to lavish their wealth. ⊠ *Gammel Torv.*

Next to Budolfi Kirke is the 15th-century **Helligandsklosteret** (Monastery of the Holy Ghost). One of Denmark's best-preserved monasteries—and perhaps the only one that admitted both nuns and monks—it is now a home for the elderly; unfortunately, it is generally not open to the public. During World War II the monastery was the meeting place for the Churchill Club, a group of Aalborg schoolboys who became world-famous for their sabotage of the Nazis, even after the enemy thought they were locked up. ⊠ *C. W. Obels Plads, Gammel Torv,* ☎ *98/12–02–05.*

In the center of the old town is **Jomfru Ane Gade,** named, as the story goes, for an aristocratic maiden accused of being a witch, then beheaded. Now the street's fame is second only to that of Copenhagen's Strøget. Despite the flashing neon and booming music of about 30 discos, bars, clubs, and eateries, the street attracts a thick stream of mixed pedestrian traffic and appeals to all ages.

The only Fourth of July celebrations outside the United States annually blast off in nearby **Rebild Park,** a salute to the United States for welcoming some 300,000 Danish immigrants. The tradition dates back to 1912.

Just north of Aalborg at Nørresundby (still considered a part of greater Aalborg) is **Lindholm Høje,** a Viking and Iron Age burial ground where stones placed in the shape of a ship enclose many of the site's 682 graves and sheep often outnumber tourists. At its entrance there's a museum that chronicles Viking civilization and recent excavations. ⊠ *Hvorupvej,* ☎ *98/17–55–22.* 🏛 *Museum DKr20; burial-ground free.* ☉ *Easter–mid-Oct., daily 10–5; mid-Oct–Easter, daily 10–4.*

Dining and Lodging

$$ ✕ **Dufy.** Light and bright on an old cobbled street, this is one of the most popular eateries in town. Downstairs, it has a French-style bistro ambience, with marble-topped tables, engraved mirrors, and windows overlooking Jomfru Ane Gade. The upstairs is more elegant and quieter. The French menu includes lobster-and-cognac soup for two, sliced roast duck with Waldorf salad, and beef fillet. ⊠ *Jomfru Ane G. 8,* ☎ *98/16–34–44. AE, DC, MC, V.*

$$ ✕ **Spisehuset Knive og Gaffel.** In a 400-year-old building parallel to
★ Jumfru Ane Gade, this busy restaurant is crammed with oak tables, crazy slanting floors, and candlelight; the year-round courtyard is a veritable greenhouse. Young waitresses negotiate the mayhem to deliver inch-thick steaks, the house specialty. ⊠ *Maren Turisg. 10,* ☎ *98/16–69–72. DC, MC, V. Closed Sun.*

$ ✕ **Duus Vinkælder.** Most people come to this cellar—part alchemist's
★ dungeon, part neighborhood bar—for a drink, but you can also get a light bite. In summer enjoy smørrebrød, in winter sup on grilled specialties like frikadeller and *biksemad* (a meat-and-potato hash), and the restaurant's special liver pâté. ⊠ *Østerä 9,* ☎ *98/12–50–56. DC, V. Closed Sun.*

$$$$ 🏨 **Helnan Phønix.** In a central and sumptuous old mansion, this hotel is popular with international and business guests. The rooms are luxuriously furnished with plump chairs and polished, dark-wood furniture; in some the original raw beams are still intact. The Brigadier serves excellent French and Danish food. ⊠ *Vesterbro 77, DK–9000,* ☎ *98/12–00–11,* 📠 *98/16–31–66. 185 rooms, 3 suites. Restaurant, bar, café, room service, sauna, meeting room. AE, DC, MC, V.*

Nightlife and the Arts

BEER-WINE CELLAR

Duus Vinkælder (☞ *above*) is extremely popular, one of the most classic beer and wine cellars in all of Denmark.

CASINO

The city's sole casino is at the **Limsfjordshotellet** (⊠ Ved Stranden 14–16, ☎ 98/16–43–33) with blackjack and more.

MUSIC AND DISCOS

Aalborg doesn't have a regular jazz club, but local musicians get together at least once a week for **jam sessions.** Ask the tourist board for details. If you're there in the fall or winter, head to the harborside **Kompasset** (⊠ Vesterbådehavn, ☎ 98/13–75–00), where live jazz is paired with a Saturday-afternoon lunch buffet. **Gaslight** (⊠ Jomfrue Ane G. 23, ☎ 98/10–17–50) plays rock and grinding dance music to a young crowd. **Rendez-Vous** (⊠ Jomfrue Ane G. 5, ☎ 98/16–88–80) has an upstairs dance floor packed with 18- to 25-year-olds dancing to standard disco. **Ambassadeur** (⊠ Vesterbro 76, ☎ 98/12–62–22), with four dance restaurants and live music, is popular with a mature audience.

Skagen

⑦ *88 km (55 mi) northeast of Aalborg, 212 km (132 mi) north of Århus.*

At the windswept northern tip of Jylland is Skagen (pronounced *skane*), a very popular summer beach area for well-heeled Danes, where, historically, the long beaches and luminous light have inspired painters and writers alike. The 19th-century Danish artist Holger Drachmann (1846–1908) and his friends, including the well-known P. S. Kroyer, founded the Skagen School of painting, which captured the special quality of northern light; you can see their efforts on display in the **Skagen Museum.** ✉ *Brøndumsvej 4,* ☎ *98/44–64–44.* 🎟 *DKr40.* ☉ *June–Aug., daily 10–6; May and Sept., daily 10–5; Apr. and Oct., Tues.– Sun. 11–4; Nov.–Mar., Wed.–Fri. 1–4, Sat. 11–4, Sun. 11–3.*

Danes say that in Skagen you can stand with one foot on the Kattegat, the strait between Sweden and eastern Jylland, the other in the Skagerrak, the strait between western Denmark and Norway. The point is so thrashed by storms and clashing waters that the 18th-century **Tilsandede Kirke** (Sand-Buried Church), 2 km (1 mi) south of town, is completely covered by dunes.

Even more famed than the Buried Church is the west coast's dramatic ★ **Råbjerg Mile,** a protected migrating dune that moves about 33 ft a year and is accessible on foot from the Kandestederne.

Dining and Lodging

$$$ ✕🏠 **Brøndums Hotel.** A few minutes from the beach, this 150-year-
★ old gabled inn is furnished with antiques and Skagen School paintings. The very basic 21 guest rooms in the main building are beginning to show their age; their old-fashioned decor includes wicker chairs, Oriental rugs, and pine four-poster beds. The 25 annex rooms are more modern. The fine French-Danish restaurant, where the Skagen School often gathered, has a lavish cold table. ✉ *Anchersvej 3, DK–9990,* ☎ *98/44–15–55,* 🆁🆇 *98/45–15–20. 46 rooms, 12 with bath. Restaurant, meeting rooms. AE, DC, MC, V.*

Jylland A to Z

Arriving and Departing

BY CAR AND FERRY

More than 25 ferry routes connect the peninsula to the rest of Denmark (including the Faroe Islands), as well as England, Norway, and Sweden, with additional connections to Kiel and Puttgarden, Germany, the Baltics, Poland, and Russia. Most travelers however, drive north from Germany, or arrive from the islands of Sjælland or Fyn. Ferry prices can get steep, and vary according to how many are traveling and the size of the vehicle. For most ferries, you can get information and make reservations by calling **FDM,** the Danish automobile association (☎ 35/43–02–00).

From Copenhagen or elsewhere on Sjælland, you can drive the 110 km (69 mi) across the island, then cross the Storebæltsbro aboard either the Halsskov–Knudshoved (1 hour) or the Korsør–Nyborg (1 hour, 15 minutes) ferry. You then drive the 85 km (53 mi) across Fyn and cross from Middelfart to Fredericia, Jylland over the Lillebæltsbro (Little Belt Bridge). More choices abound here, since two bridges link Middelfart to Fredericia. The older, lower bridge (2 km/1¼ mi) follows Route 161, whereas the newer suspension bridge (1 km/½ mi) on E20 is faster. For direct Sjælland to Jylland passage, you can take the ferry between Sjællands Odde and Ebeltoft (1 hour, 40 minutes), or a car-ferry hydrofoil (1 hour, 25 minutes) between Århus and Kalundborg. The conventional

DSB ferry (3¼ hours) is larger and slower, but more akin to a cruise ship. Also from Kalundborg, you can sail to Juelsminde (3 hours), 74 km (46 mi) south of Århus. Keep in mind that once the Great Belt train and auto links between Sjælland and Fyn are completed, many of the connections between Jylland and the rest of Denmark will be shortened by an hour. For ferry schedules, call **DSB** (☎ 33/14–17–01).

Ferries from Hundested, Sjælland, to Grena in east Jylland take 2½ hours; those from Kalundborg to Århus take three hours. For information, call **DSB** (☎ 33/14–17–01). Other major routes include those of **Scandinavian Seaways** (Esbjerg, ☎ 79/17–79–17; Copenhagen, ☎ 33/42–33–42), which links England's Harwich and Newcastle to Esbjerg in the southwest. There are ferries from Göteborg (3¼ hours), on Sweden's west coast and Oslo, Norway (10 hours), to Frederikshavn in the northeast. Call **Stena Line** (☎ 96/20–02–00) for both.

BY PLANE

Billund Airport, 2 km (1¼ mi) southwest of downtown, receives flights from London, Stockholm, Brussels, Amsterdam, and Frankfurt on **Mærsk Air** (☎ 75/33–28–44) and on the Norwegian carrier **Braathens** (☎ 75/35–44–00 Billund Airport, ☎ 47/67–58–60–00 Oslo Fornebu Airport) from Oslo. **Sunair** (☎ 75/33–16–11) serves Billund, Århus, Oslo, Stockholm, and Göteborg. Several domestic airports, including Aalborg, Århus, and Esbjerg, are served by Mærsk and **SAS** (75/16–03–33), both of which have good connections to Copenhagen. **Cimber Air** (☎ 74/42–22–77) links Sønderborg, just north of the German border with Copenhagen.

BY TRAIN

DSB (☎ 33/14–17–01) makes hourly runs between Copenhagen and Fredericia. The 3½-hour trip includes train passage aboard the ferry, which crosses the Store Bælt between Korsør, on west Sjælland, and Nyborg, on east Fyn.

Getting Around

At the Århus tourist office check out the **Århus Pass,** which affords free bus travel, free or discounted admission to museums and sites, and tours.

BY BICYCLE

Jylland has scores of bike paths, and many auto routes also have cycle lanes. Keep in mind that distances are much longer here than elsewhere in the country, and that even these humble hills are a challenge for children and novice cyclists. Consider prearranged package holidays, which range from island day trips to eight-day excursions. Among the offices that can help with bike tips are the tourist boards in Viborg, Silkeborg, and Vejen (☞ Visitor Information, *below*), or the **County of North Jylland** tourist office (✉ Niels Bohrsvej, Box 8300, DK-9220 Aalborg, ☎ 96/35–10–00).

Bike rentals are available in most towns from the tourism board, which can also supply maps and brochures. In the west, the **Vestkyst-stien** (west-coast path) goes from Skagen in the north to Bulbjerg in the south. In the east, the **Vendsyssel-stien** (winding path) goes from Frederikshavn to the mouth of the Limfjord. The **Stkyst-stien** (east-coast path) follows and leads to the south of the Limfjord. In the south, much of the 1,000-year-old **Hærvejen** (Old Military Road) has been converted into a network of picturesque cycling lanes. It's signposted for all 240 km (145 mi) through the center of Jylland, from Padborg in the south to Viborg in the north.

Intercity buses are punctual but slower than trains. Passengers can buy tickets on the bus and pay according to destination. For schedules and fares, call **DSB** (☎ 86/12–67–03) weekdays. For intercity travel, schedules are posted at all bus stops and fares are usually under DKr10.

BY CAR
Although train and bus connections are excellent, sites and towns in Jylland are widely dispersed, and the peninsula is best explored by car. Whether you decide to take speedy, modern highways or winding old roads, traffic is virtually nonexistent.

BY TRAIN
For long trips, the **DSB** (☎ 86/13 17 00) trains are fast and efficient, with superb views of the countryside. Smaller towns do not have innercity trains, so you'll have to switch to buses once you arrive.

Contacts and Resources

EMERGENCIES
Ambulance, fire, or **police** (☎ 112).

Doctor: Aalborg (☎ 98/13–62–11). **Århus** (☎ 86/20–10–22).

Pharmacies: Aalborg (✉ Budolfi Apotek, corner of Vesterbro and Algade, ☎ 98/12–06–77). **Århus** (✉ Løve Apoteket, Store Torv 5, ☎ 86/12–00–22).

GUIDED TOURS
Guided tours are few and far between, but check with the local tourism offices for tips and reservations. Some carry brochures that describe walking tours.

Legoland Tours: Between mid-June and mid-August, the tour departs from Copenhagen at 7:30 AM on Thursday (call ☎ 31/57–26–00 to reserve) and Saturday (call ☎ 31/54–06–06 to reserve), and costs DKr350. The trip takes about 13 hours, with four hours spent at the park; you'll also have to pay admission into the park.

Walking Tours: The **Århus Round the City** tour (2½ hours) begins at the tourist office and includes Den Gamle By, the Domkirke, concert hall, university, and harbor. **Aalborg's City Tour** (two hours) departs from Adelgade and includes most of the town museums, the Budolfi Cathedral, Monastery of the Holy Ghost, Town Hall, the Jens Bang Stone House, and Jomfru Ane Gade.

VISITOR INFORMATION
County of North Jylland tourist office (✉ Niels Bohrsvej, Box 8300, DK–9220 Aalborg, ☎ 96/35–10–00).

Aalborg (✉ Østerå 8, ☎ 98/12–60–22). **Århus** (✉ Rådhuset, ☎ 86/12–16–00). **Billund** (✉ c/o Legoland A/S, Åstvej, ☎ 75/33–19–26). **Jelling** (✉ Gormsg. 4, ☎ 75/87–13–01). **Randers** (✉ Erik Menveds Pl. 1, ☎ 86/42–44–77). **Ribe** (✉ Torvet 3–5, ☎ 75/42–15–00). **Silkeborg** (✉ Godthåbsvej 4, ☎ 86/82–19–11). **Vejen** (✉ Sønderg., ☎ 75/36–26–96). **Vejle** (✉ Den Smiatske Gård, Sønderg. 14, ☎ 75/82–19–55). **Viborg** (✉ Nytorv 5, ☎ 86/61–16–66).

BORNHOLM

Called the Pearl of the Baltic for its natural beauty and winsomely rustic towns, Bornholm, 177 km (110 mi) southeast of Sjælland, is geographically unlike the rest of Denmark. A temperate climate has made this 588-square-km (436-square-mi) jumble of granite bluffs, clay soil, and rift valleys an extravagance of nature. Rich plantations of fir bristle beside wide dunes and vast heather fields; lush gardens teem with fig, cherry, chestnut, mulberry, and blue-blooming Chinese Emperor trees; and meadows sprout 12 varieties of orchids. Denmark's third-largest forest, the Almindingen, crowns the center; the southern tip is ringed with some of Europe's whitest beaches.

During the Iron and Bronze ages, Bornholm was inhabited by seafaring and farming cultures that peppered the land with burial dolmens and engravings. From the Middle Ages to the 18th century, the Danes battled the Swedes for ownership of the island, protecting it with strongholds and fortified churches, many of which still loom over the landscape.

Today Bornholmers continue to draw their livelihood from the land and sea—and increasingly from tourism. Chalk-white chimneys rise above the rooftops, harbors are abob with painted fishing boats, and in spring and summer fields blaze with amber mustard and grain.

Certainly, few people come to Bornholm to stay indoors. Long, silky beaches, rolling hills, and troll-inspiring forests make this a summer haven for walking, hiking, and swimming—particularly for families, many of whom take their summer vacations by packing provisions and children onto a pair of bikes, and winding throughout the island.

Bornholm is famous throughout Scandinavia for its craftspeople, especially glassblowers and ceramicists, whose work is often pricier in Copenhagen and Stockholm. In the center of each town (especially Gudhjem and Svaneke), you'll find crafts shops and *værksteder* (workshops). When you're on the road, watch for *keramik* (ceramics) signs, which direct you to artists selling from home.

Fishing

Cod, salmon, and herring fishing are excellent in season, though better from a boat than from shore. Licenses cost DKr25 per day, DKr75 per week, and DKr100 per year. Contact the tourist board for details and information on charter trips. Among the handful of charter companies is **Peter Prüssing** (✉ Gudhjem, ☎ 56/48–54–63), who arranges three-day trips from either Gudhjem and Snogebæk between July and September.

Hiking

In contrast to the rest of Denmark, Bornholm is hilly and rugged. Marked trails crisscross the island, including three 4-km (2½-mi) hikes through the Almindingen Forest and several more through its Ekkodalon (Echo Valley). The northern coastline is beautiful but a rocky and more strenuous walk. Ask for a map, routes, and tips from any tourism office. The *Bornholm Green Guide,* available in shops and tourism offices, offers suggestions for walking and hiking tours.

Swimming

Beach worshipers thrive in Bornholm. The swimming and sunning are best south, between Pedersker and Snogebæk, where the dunes are tall and the beaches wide. As elsewhere in Denmark, topless bathing is common and nude bathing is tolerated.

Rønne

77 *190 km (120 mi) southeast of Copenhagen (7 hrs by ferry).*

Borhholm's capital, port, and largest town is Rønne, a good starting point for exploring northward or eastward. East of Nørrekås Harbor on Laksegade, you'll find an enchanting area of rose-clad 17th- and 18th-century houses, among them the tile-roof **Erichsens Gård** (farm). The home

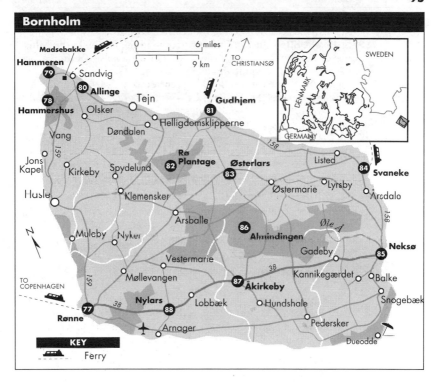

Bornholm

KEY

Ferry

of the wealthy Erichsen family, whose daughter married the Danish poet Holger Drachmann, it is preserved with paintings by Danish artist Kristian Zahrtmann, period furnishings, and a lovely garden. ⊠ *Lakseg. 7,* ☎ *56/95–87–35.* ⊡ *DKr25.* ⊙ *June–Aug., Tues.–Sat. 10–5.*

Near Store Torv, the main square, is the **Bornholm Museum,** which features local geologic and archaeological exhibits in addition to more than 4,500 pieces of ceramics and glass. The museum also displays 25 18th-century *Bornholmure* (Bornholm Clocks), as characteristic of the island as smoked herring. In 1744, a Dutch ship was wrecked on Bornholm, and the English grandfather clocks it carried became the models for the island's clocks. ⊠ *Skt. Mortensg. 29,* ☎ *56/95–07–35.* ⊡ *DKr25.* ⊙ *May–Oct., Tues.–Sat. 10–5; Nov.–Apr., Tues., Thurs., and Sat. 1–4.*

Dining and Lodging

$$ ✕ **Rådhuskroen.** With exposed timbers, comfortable armchairs, and close-set tables, this restaurant provides a softly lit change from Rønne's busy streets. The menu has changed in recent years to highlight substantial beef dishes like pepper steak with wine and cream sauce, but you can still get a couple of local fish specialities—like poached Baltic salmon or grilled filet of sole, both served with lobster sauce. ⊠ *Nørreg. 2,* ☎ *56/95–00–69. AE, DC, MC, V.*

$$$ ⌂ **Fredensborg.** The island's standard for luxury is set at this hotel, situated on a curve of forest near a small beach. The glass-and-tile lobby is spare and sunny, the staff pleasant and eager. The dozen ample apartments have full kitchens, and guest rooms are done in pastel schemes, with modern furniture and balconies overlooking the sea. The rustic restaurant, De Fem Ståuerne, serves traditional French-Danish food. ⊠ *Strandvejen 116, DK–3700,* ☎ *56/95–44–44,* 𝖥𝖠𝖷 *56/95–03–*

14. 60 rooms, 12 apartments. Restaurant, bar, room service, hot tub, sauna, tennis court, meeting rooms. AE, DC, MC, V.

$$$ 🏨 **Hotel Griffen.** Just off a busy street and the Rønne harbor, this is one of Bornholm's largest and most modern hotels. It's three stories tall, with plenty of windows and views of the sea on one side and Rønne on the other. The rooms, done in deep-brown tones, have every modern convenience. ⊠ Kredsen 1, DK–3700, ☎ 56/95–51–11, FAX 56/95–52–97. 140 rooms, 2 suites. Restaurant, bar, room service, indoor pool, sauna, dance club, meeting rooms. AE, DC, MC, V.

$ ⛺ **Galløkken Camping.** This site is just a short walk from the Rønne center, near an old military museum. The grounds are open, but trees surround the perimeter. There are good shower and cooking facilities. ⊠ Strandvejen 4, DK–3700 Rønne, ☎ 56/95–23–20.

Nightlife and the Arts

Bornholm's nightlife is limited to a handful of discos and clubs in Rønne, which open and close frequently as tastes change. An old stand-by however, is **Vise Vesth Huset** (⊠ Brøddeg. 24, ☎ 56/48–50–80), popular for light meals and live folk music.

Outdoor Activities and Sports

GOLF

The **Bornholm Golf Club** near Rønne (☎ 56/95–68–54) is an 18-hole park course in a natural setting with plenty of wildlife and fauna—the brochure even boasts that you can enjoy nightingales and wild orchids along the course. There's also a restaurant and pro shop.

Shopping

CLOCKS

A Bornholmure is a type of grandfather clock handmade on the island. Antique versions cost from DKr10,000 to DKr80,000 and more. The clocks often have round faces but can be rectangular as well and are completely hand-painted. On the hour, the modern clocks sound the hour with music—which ranges from Mozart and Verdi to Sondheim and Andrew Lloyd Webber. New reproductions modeled from museum originals are custom-made by **Bornholmerure** (⊠ Torneværksvej 26, Rønne, ☎ 56/95–31–08). A handmade custom clock costs, on the average, DKr37,000.

CLOTHING

You can pick up unusual gifts and one-of-a-kind clothing made of hand-printed textiles at **Bente Hammer** (⊠ Nyker Hovedg. 32, Rønne, ☎ 56/96–33–35).

MARKET

There is a large **vegetable and fruit market** on Wednesday and Saturday mornings in Store Torv, the main square in Rønne.

En Route   Fourteen kilometers (8½ miles) north of Rønne is the bluff known as **Jons Kapel.** A medieval legend has it that a monk, Brother Jon, lived in a cave and used these treacherous sea cliffs as a pulpit for his impassioned sermons. Wear rubber-sole hiking boots to climb the stairs that lead to the pulpit, where the agile friar stood atop the dramatic 72-ft-high cliffs that loom over the crashing waves.

Hammershus

★ 78   8 km (5 mi) north of Jons Kapel, 30 km (19 mi) north of Rønne.

The ruins of the fortress of Hammershus constitute northern Europe's largest stronghold. The hulking fortress was begun in 1255 by the archbishop of Lund (Sweden), and became the object of centuries of struggle between Denmark and Sweden. In 1658 Danes under Jens Kofoed killed its Swedish governor, and the castle was given back to Denmark. Used until 1743, it became a ruin when it was quarried for stone to fortify Christiansø and that island's buildings. The government finally intervened in 1822, and the site is now a mass of snaggletoothed walls and towers atop a grassy knoll. During restoration work in 1967, 22 gold German guilders were found. Occasionally, concerts and other performances are held at the ruins. 🖃 *Free.*

Nightlife and the Arts

They don't happen nearly enough, but check with the local tourism office (☞ Bornholm A to Z, *below*) to see if any special events are planned at or near Hammershus: the ruins add a spectacular dimension to classical music and the performing arts.

Hammeren

⑦⑨ *5 km (3 mi) north of Hammershus, 36 km (23 mi) north of Rønne.*

Despite constant Baltic winds, rare plants and trees grow on the warm, granite-scattered Hammeren (the Hammer), including radiant anemones. The knuckle of land jutting from the island's northern tip is nearly separated from the island by a deep rift valley and the Hammer Sø (Hammer Lake). Look across the water south of the tip to the stone formation known as the Camel Heads.

En Route A little more than 3 km (2 mi) southeast of Hammeren, **Madsebakke** is the largest collection of Bronze Age rock carvings in Denmark. They are presumed to be ceremonial carvings, which ancient fishermen and farmers hoped would bring good weather and bountiful crops. The most interesting of them depicts 11 ships, including one with what's called a sun wheel.

Allinge

⑧⓪ *3 km (2 mi) east of Madsebakke, 21 km (13 mi) north of Rønne.*

In Allinge and its twin town Sandvig, you'll find centuries-old neighborhoods and, particularly in Allinge, half-timber houses and herring smokehouses sprouting tall chimneys. Just south is a wood that the islanders call the **Trolleskoven** (Troll Forest). Legend says trolls live in the woods, and when they "brew" fog, they escape the heat in the kitchen and go out looking for trouble. The most mischievous is the littlest troll, Krølle Bølle.

Lodging

$$ ☆ 🏠 **Strandhotellet.** Romantic old world charm is the draw at this venerable hotel. On a corner across from the harbor, it has a white arched entry into a stone-and-whitewashed lobby. The rooms are furnished in plain beech furniture with woolen covers and pastel colors. ⊠ *Strandpromenaden 7, Sandvig, DK–3770,* ☎ *56/48–03–14,* FAX *56/48–02–09. 50 rooms, 1 suite. Restaurant, bar, sauna, steam room, health club. AE, DC, MC, V. Closed mid-Oct.–mid-Apr.*

$ 🏕 **Sandvig Familie Camping.** This site is pleasantly close to the beach, so that most of its sites enjoy a view of the water. The large kitchen and bathing facilities were renovated a few years ago. ⊠ *Sandlinien 5, DK–3770 Allinge,* ☎ *56/48–04–47 or 56/48–00–01.*

Shopping

Kampeløkken (⊠ Havneg. 45, Allinge, ☎ 56/48–17–66) gallery shop stocks the work of 24 potters and four glassblowers.

En Route Eight kilometers (5 miles) southeast of Allinge along the coastal path, you'll come upon the grottoes and granite cliffs of the **Helligdom-sklipperne** (Cliffs of Sanctuary), which contain a well-known rock formation best seen from the boats that ply the nearby waters in summer. In the Middle Ages, people used to visit these waters, believing that they had holy, healing powers—hence the name.

Just southeast of the Helligdomsklipperne, a pastoral coastal path leads to the tiny, preserved **Døndalen Forest.** Its fertile soil bears a surprising array of Mediterranean vegetation, including fig and cherry trees. During rainy periods look for a waterfall at the bottom of the dale.

Gudhjem

★ ⑧ *18 km (11 mi) east of Allinge, 33 km (21 mi) northeast of Rønne.*

Especially at the height of summer, Gudhjem (God's Home) is perhaps the most tourist-packed town on Bornholm—and the reason is obvious. Tiny half-timber houses and gift shops with lace curtains and clay roofs line steep stone streets that loop around the harbor. The island's first smokehouses still produce alder-smoked golden herring.

★ ☺ Walk down Brøddegade, which turns into Melstedvej; here you'll find the **Landsbrugs Museum** (Agricultural Museum) and Mestedgaard, a working farm with cows, horses, sheep, pigs, geese, and wandering kittens. The farm includes the well-kept house and garden of a 19th-century farm family. Notice the surprisingly bright colors used on the interior of the house, and leave time to visit the old shops, where you can buy locally produced woolen sweaters, wooden spoons, and even homemade mustard. ⊠ *Melstedvej 25,* ☎ *56/48–55–98.* ▨ *DKr25.* ☺ *Mid-May–mid-Oct., Tues.–Sun. 10–5.*

OFF THE   **BORNHOLM KUNST MUSEUM –** Follow the main road, Hellidomsvej, out
BEATEN PATH of town in the direction of Allinge/Sandvig, and you'll come to Bornholm's art museum, an excellent example of the Danes' ability to integrate art, architecture, and natural surroundings. Built by the architectural firm of Fogh and Følner, the white-painted brick, granite, and sandstone building is centered by a thin stream of "holy" trickling water that exits the building and leads the visitor to a walkway and overlook above the Helligdomsklipperne (☞ *above*). Throughout, the walls of the museum are punched out by picture windows overlooking nearby grazing cows and the crashing Baltic: a natural accompaniment to the art. Most of the works are by Bornholmers, including a body of Modernist work by Olaf Høst, Karl Esaksen, and Olaf Rude, who recognized a particular ability in Bornholm's sea-surrounded light to bring out the poignancy in abstract scenes of local life. The museum also displays some sculpture and glass, as well as a survey of more historical paintings. Check out the restaurant and shop. ⊠ *Hellidomsvej 95,* ☎ *56/48–43–86.* ▨ *DKr30.* ☺ *May–mid-Oct., Tues.–Sun. 10–5; mid-Oct.–Apr., Tues., Thurs., Sun. 1–5.*

Lodging

$ ▥ **Skt. Jørgens Gård Vandrehjem.** In a half-timber 100-year-old former manor house, this hostel in the middle of Gudhjem offers single-to eight-bed rooms with standard Danish hostel style: pine bunks and industrial carpeting. There are six kitchens available for use. ⊠ *Gudhjem Vandrehjem, DK–3760,* ☎ *56/48–50–35,* ▣ *56/48–56–35. 52 rooms, 26 with bath. Restaurant. No credit cards.*

Shopping

Baltic Sea Glass (⊠ Melstedvej 47, Gudhjem, ☎ 56/48–56–41), on the main road just on the outskirts of town, offers high-quality, bright, and imaginative decanters, glasses, candlesticks, and one-of-a-kind pieces, including an old-fashioned contraption to catch flies. In town, see the delicate porcelain bowls of **Per Rehfeldt** (⊠ Kastenievej 8, ☎ 56/48–54–13). Unique, hand-thrown ceramic work is available from and by **Julia Manitius** (⊠ Holkavej 12, ☎ 56/48–55–99).

OFF THE BEATEN PATH

CHRISTIANSØ – A 45-minute boat ride northeast from Gudhjem will bring you to the historic island of Christiansø. Though it was originally a bastion, the Storetårn (Big Tower) and Lilletårn (Little Tower) are all that remain of the fort, built in 1684 and dismantled in 1855. The barracks, street, and gardens, for which the earth was transported in boats, have hardly changed since that time. They remain under the jurisdiction of the defense ministry, making this a tiny tax-free haven for its 100 inhabitants. Nearby, the rocky, uninhabited island of Græsholmen is an inaccessible bird sanctuary—the only place in Denmark where the razorbill and guillemot breed.

Rø Plantage

⑧ *6 km (4 mi) southwest of Gudhjem, 24 km (15 mi) northeast of Rønne.*

Rø Plantation is a new but dense forest that serves as a quiet foil to the hubbub of Gudhjem. A century ago it was a heather-covered grazing area, but after stone dikes were erected to keep the cattle out, spruce, pine, larch, and birch were cultivated. The cool refuge now consists largely of saplings and new growth—the result of devastating storms in the late '50s and '60s.

Outdoor Activities and Sports

GOLF

Rø Golfbane (⊠ Spellingevej 3, ☎ 56/48–40–50) has won various European and Scandinavian awards for its natural beauty—and challenges. Its 18 holes are set close to the coastal cliffs, and enjoys views of the sea. It has a pro shop and restaurant.

Østerlars

⑧ *5 km (3 mi) southeast of Rø Plantage, 22 km (14 mi) northeast of Rønne.*

The standout attraction here is the **Østerlars Kirke.** The largest of the island's four round churches, it was built in about 1150; extensions, including the buttresses, were added later. Constructed from boulders and slabs of limestone, the whitewashed church was part spiritual sanctuary, part fortification, affording protection from enemy armies and pirates. Inside is the island's only painted tympanum, with a faded image of a cross and decorative foliage. Several Gothic wall paintings including depictions of the Annunciation and Nativity—have survived from the 1300s. ⊠ *Gudhjemsvej 28,* ☎ *56/49–82–64.* ⌨ *DKr4.* ☺ *Apr.–mid-Oct., Mon.–Sat. 9–5.*

Svaneke

⑧ *21 km (13 mi) east of Østerlars, 49 km (31 mi) northeast of Rønne.*

The coastal town of Svaneke, Denmark's easternmost settlement, is an enchanting hamlet of 17th- and 18th-century houses, winding cobbled streets, and a harbor sliced from the rocky earth. Once a fishing village, it is now immaculately preserved and home to a thriving artists' community.

Dining and Lodging

$$ XⒽ **Siemsens Gaard.** Built in a 270-year-old merchant house, this U-shape hotel with a gravel-courtyard café overlooks the harbor. The inside is cushy, with Chesterfield sofas below severe black-and-white prints and antiques. The rooms differ, but all are done up in stripped pine and soft colors. The bright, modern restaurant serves French-Danish food, with a menu of 125 options—from club sandwiches to smoked Baltic salmon to smørrebrød. ⊠ *Havnebryggen 9, DK–3740,* ☎ *56/49–61–49,* ℻ *56/49–61–03. 50 rooms. Restaurant, café, sauna, health club. AE, DC, MC, V.*

$$ Ⓗ **Hotel Østersøen.** Across from the harbor, this hotel has a provin-
★ cial facade and a Key West courtyard with palm trees and a pool. Industrial carpets and century-old beams line the modern lobby, and the stark apartments (rented by the week) are appointed with leather sofas, swanky teak dinette sets, and streamlined furniture. The hotel is well suited for families and couples traveling in pairs. ⊠ *Havnebryggen 5, DK–3740,* ☎ *56/49–60–20,* ℻ *56/49–72–79. 21 apartments. Pool, business services. AE, DC.*

Shopping

Stroll through the ateliers and boutiques in the central Glastorvet in Svaneke. Among them is the studio of **Pernille Bülow** (⊠ Glastorvet, Brænderigængget 8, ☎ 56/49–66–72), one of Denmark's most famous glassblowers. Her work is sold in Copenhagen's best design shops. Even if you buy directly from her studio, don't expect bargains—though you may be lucky to find seconds—but do expect colorful, experimental work. **Askepot** (⊠ Postg. 5, Svaneke, ☎ 53/99–70–42), whose name means Cinderella, sells handmade leather hats, jackets, shoes, bags, belts, and wallets.

Neksø

85 *9 km (5½ mi) south of Svaneke, 48 km (30 mi) northeast of Rønne.*

Neksø (or Nexø) bustles with visitors and locals who shop and live around its busy harbor, lined with fishing boats from throughout the Baltics and Eastern Europe. It might seem like a typical 17th-century town, but it was rebuilt almost completely after World War II, when the Russians bombed it to dislodge stubborn German troops who refused to surrender—three days after the rest of Denmark had been liberated. The Russians lingered on the island until April 1946.

Wander down to the harbor to find, in a mustard-yellow building, the **Neksø Museum** with its fine collection of fishing and local history exhibits. The museum also houses photographs and memorabilia of Danish author Martin Andersen Hansen (1909–55), who changed his last name to Nexø after his beloved town. A complicated and vehement socialist, he wrote, among other works, *Pelle the Conqueror,* set in Bornholm at the turn of the century, when Swedish immigrants were exploited by Danish landowners. The story was turned into an Academy Award–winning film. ⊠ *Havnen,* ☎ *56/49–25–56.* 🎫 *DKr10.* ⊘ *May–Oct., Tues.–Sun. 10–4.*

Outdoor Activities and Sports

GOLF

The 18-hole **Nexø Golf Club** (☎ 56/48–89–87) is close to the island's best sandy, rock-free beaches.

WINDSURFING

The best windsurfing beaches are on the southern sandy coast, where the winds are strong and the beaches sandy (the shores are rockier north of Neksø). **Windsurfing ved Balke Strand** (☎ 56/95–00–77), 4 km (2½ mi) south of Neksø, offers classes and board rentals.

Shopping

For exquisite **woodwork** see Bernard Romain (⊠ Rønnevej 54, Neksø, ☎ 56/48–86–66).

Almindingen

⑧⑥ *23 km (14 mi) west of Neksø, 27 km (17 mi) northeast of Rønne.*

The lush Almindingen, Denmark's third-largest forest, is filled with ponds, lakes, evergreens, well-marked trails, and blooms with lily of the valley in spring. Within it, the oak-lined **Ekkodalen** (Echo Valley)—where children love to hear their shouts resound—is networked with trails leading to smooth rock faces that soar 72 ft high. At the northern edge, near the road to Østermarie, stood one of Bornholm's most famous sights until 1995: seven evergreens growing from a single trunk. The tree fell that year, but pass by, and you might see the remains of its curious trunk.

Outdoor Activities and Sports

HIKING

Check with the tourist board for a map delineating three 4-km (2½-mi) hikes through the Almindingen Forest and several more through its Echo Valley. The *Bornholm Green Guide,* available in shops and tourism offices, offers walking and hiking routes.

Åkirkeby

⑧⑦ *5 km (3 mi) south of Almindingen, 24 km (15 mi) east of Rønne.*

Åkirkeby is the oldest town on the island, with a municipal charter from 1346. The town's church, the **Åkirke,** is Bornholm's oldest and largest, dating from the mid-13th century. Though it is not a round church, both walls and tower were well suited for defense. The altarpiece and pulpit are Dutch Renaissance from about 1600, but the carved sandstone font is as old as the church itself. ⊠ *Torvet,* ☎ *56/ 97–41–03.* ▣ *DKr5.* ☉ *Mon.–Sat. 10–4.*

Nylars

⑧⑧ *8 km (5 mi) west of Åkirkeby, 9 km (6 mi) east of Rønne.*

Like the Østerlars church, the round **Nylars Kirke** dates from 1150. The chalk paintings from the Old Testament on its central pillar are the oldest on the island, possibly dating from 1250. Even older are the runic stones on the church's porch. Both are of Viking origin. ⊠ *Kirkevej,* ☎ *56/97–20–13.* ▣ *Suggested donation DKr3.* ☉ *Mid-May–mid-Sept., Mon.–Sat. 9–5.*

Bornholm A to Z

Arriving and Departing

BY BUS

A *Gråhund* (Greyhound) No. 866 bus from Copenhagen's main station travels to Dragør, boards a ferry to Limhamn, and then continues to Ystad, where it connects with a ferry to Rønne. Buses depart twice daily, once in the morning and again in late afternoon. Call **Bornholm Bussen** (☎ 44/68–44–00).

BY CAR FERRY AND HYDROFOIL

The *Bornholmstrafikken* car ferry from Copenhagen's Kvæsthusbro Harbor (near Nyhavn) departs at 11:30 PM year-round and from June through July daily (except Wednesday) at 8:30 AM. The trip takes seven hours. To avoid delays, make reservations. Comfortable sleeping bunks in a massive hall are also available for an extra cost.

The Nordbornholms Turistbureau (North Bornholm Tourist Board, ☎ 56/48–00-01) is the agent for a summer ferry that links Neu Mukran (3½ hours) and Sassnitz (3½ hours) on the island of Rügen in Germany. **Bornholmstrafikken** (☎ 56/95–18–66), a competing company, offers passage aboard the ferry to Neu Mukran (3½ hours), just 5 km (3 mi) from Sassnitz. Prices vary according to the number of people traveling and the size of the vehicle. There is also a boat between Świnoujście, Poland and Rønne (seven hours); call **Polferries** (☎ 48/97–32–1614–0) in Poland. A hydrofoil from Nyhavn goes to Malmö, Sweden, where it connects with a bus to Ystad and a ferry to Rønne. The four-hour voyage runs twice daily, usually in the morning and again in the late afternoon. Call **Flyve Bådene** (☎ 33/12–80–88).

BY PLANE
The **airport** is 5 km (3 mi) south of Rønne at the island's southwestern tip. **Mærsk Air** (☎ 56/95–11–11) makes several daily flights only from Copenhagen. **Lufthansa** (☎ 33/37–73–33) flies from Berlin and Hamburg; **Eurowings** (☎ 49/231–924–5306) from Dortmund and Osnabrück.

Getting Around
BY BICYCLE
Biking is eminently feasible and pleasant on Bornholm, thanks to a network of more than 200 km (125 mi) of cycle roads, including an old railway converted to a cross-island path. Rentals of sturdy two-speeds and tandems are available for about DKr50 a day at more than 20 different establishments all over the island—near the ferry, at the airport, and in Allinge, Gudhjem, Hasle, Pedersker (near Åkirkeby), Rønne, Svaneke, and most other towns. Try Bornholms Cykleudlejning (✉ Nordre Kystevej 5, ☎ 56/95–13–59) or Cykel-Centret (✉ Sønderg. 7, ☎ 56/95–06–04), both in Rønne.

BY BUS
Though bus service is certainly not as frequent as in major cities, there are regular connections between towns. Schedules are posted at all stations, and you can usually pick one up on board. The fare is DKr8 per zone, or you can buy a klip kort (punch ticket) of 10 klips for DKr64. A 24-hour bus pass costs DKr100. Children 5–11 pay half-price.

BY CAR
There are excellent roads on the island, but be alert for cyclists and occasional leisurely paced cows.

Contacts and Resources
EMERGENCIES
Ambulance, accident, or **fire** (☎ 112). **Bornholm's Central Hospital** (✉ Sygehusvej, Rønne, ☎ 56/95–11–65). **Rønne Apotek** (Rønne Pharmacy, ✉ Store Torveg. 12, Rønne, ☎ 56/95–01–30).

GUIDED TOURS
Aerial Tours: An aerial tour in a Cessna or Piper plane (20–45 min) covers either the entire coast or the northern tip. Call **Klippefly** (☎ 56/95–35–73 or 56/48–42–01).

BAT Tours: The **BAT** (Bornholm Municipality Traffic Company, ☎ 56/95–21–21) offers some inventive summer tours. All are offered Tuesday through Friday, from mid-July until early August. All begin at the red bus terminal at Snellemark 30 in Rønne at 10 AM and cost DKr100. (You can also buy a 24-hour bus card for DKr100, or a five- or seven-day card for DKr350, good for both the regional buses and the tours.) Tour prices do not include some DKr5–DKr10 admissions or lunch at a herring smokehouse. The five-hour Kunst og håndværk (Arts and Crafts) tour includes stops at glass, pottery, textile, and silver studios. In summer, different studios are visited each day. The Grønne Bus (Green Bus) visits sights that illustrate the ways in which the island's exquisite flora and fauna are being preserved. Bondegårdsbussen (Farm Bus) visits chicken, cow, and pig farms, as well as a "free-range" pig farm, to show the differences in practice and attitude between conventional and progressive farming. The Veteranbus (Veteran Bus), a circa World War II Bedford, connects some of Bornholm's oldest industries, including a clockmaker, water mill, and Denmark's last windmill used for making flour.

Boat Tours: From mid-June to mid-September, boats to the Helligdomsklipperne (Sanctuary Cliffs) leave Gudhjem at 10:30, 1:30, and 2:30, with extra sailings mid-June to mid-August. Call **Thor Båd** (☎ 56/48–51–65). Boats to Christiansø depart from Svaneke at 10 AM daily year-round; May to September daily at 10:20 from Gudhjem, and at 1 from Allinge; between mid-June and August, an additional boat leaves Gudhjem weekdays at 9:40 and 12:15. Call **Christiansø Farten** (☎ 56/48–51–76) for additional information.

Sightseeing Tours: The **Bornholmrund** (Round Bornholm) bus tour (8½ hours), beginning at 9:30 Tuesday and Thursday, includes Rønne, Hammershus, Allinge, Gudhjem, Østerlars Church, Svaneke, Nexø, Balka, Åkirkeby, and the Almindingen Forest. To make reservations, call the Bornholm tourist board (☞ *below*).

VISITOR INFORMATION

Nordbornholms Turistbureau (North Bornholm Tourist Board, ☎ 56/ 48–00–01). **Bornholm** (✉ Nordre Kystvej 3, Rønne, ☎ 56/95–95–00).

Allinge (✉ Kirkeg. 4, ☎ 56/48–00–01). **Åkirkeby** (✉ Torvet 2, ☎ 56/ 97–45–20). **Gudhjem** (✉ Åbog. 9, ☎ 56/48–52–10. **Hasle** (✉ Havneg. 1, ☎ 56/96–44–81). **Nexø,** (✉ Åsen 4, ☎ 56/49–32–00). **Svaneke** (✉ Storeg. 24, ☎ 56/49–63–50).

GREENLAND

When Eric the Red discovered Greenland (Kalaallit Nunaat in Greenlandic, Grønland in Danish) a thousand years ago, his Norsemen thought they had reached the edge of the world. After it, there was only *Ginnungagap,* the endless abyss.

Greenland still commands awe from the growing number of visitors who venture off the usual Scandinavian path to explore the world's largest island. Measuring more than 1.3 million square km (840,000 square mi), it's larger than Italy, France, Great Britain, unified Germany, and Spain combined. The coastal regions are sparsely populated with about 7,500 Danes and 48,000 Inuit—the indigenous people, whose roots can be traced to the native inhabitants of Canada's Arctic, and further back to the people of Alaska. More than 80% of the land is eternally frozen beneath an ice cap that, at its deepest, reaches a thickness of 3 km (2 mi). If it melted, sea levels around the world would rise nearly 20 ft.

The number of tourists is growing at a enormous rate, from just 3,000 in 1993 to 16,000 in 1996. But relatively speaking, with these few tourists (almost all on package tours), Greenland remains one of the world's least developed regions. By its nature, the region is far more difficult to explore than dwarfed mother Denmark. Travel is possible only by helicopter or coastal boat, since there are few roads and no railroads. However, the southern and western towns—trimmed with building-block red-and-green houses and well-used harbors—have adequate hotels, airfields and helicopter pads, and some summertime ferry service. Man-made luxuries are few, but the rewards of nature are savagely beautiful. Below the Arctic Circle, the draws include Norse ruins, Ice Age–gouged mountains, and jagged fjords. Farther north, dogsleds whip over icy plains, and ferries glide past icebergs as big as city blocks.

Greenland's first inhabitants probably arrived some 4,000 years ago from what is today Canada. Various Inuit peoples continued to migrate to and roam across the island, but current Greenlanders are descendants of a particular Canadian Inuit culture that arrived around AD 1000. Greenland's recorded history began at about the same time, in AD 982, when Eric and his Norse settlers claimed the land, but after 400 years of colonization they mysteriously disappeared. During this period Denmark and Norway were joined under the Danish crown, a union that muddled ownership of Greenland until 1933, when the International High Court awarded Denmark complete sovereignty. (Until 1997, this dual heritage lead every town to have both a Greenlandic and a Danish name; today only the Greenlandic names are used on modern maps.) Geographically isolated and increasingly politically independent, Greenlanders are intent on redefining their ethnic identity in a modern world. They refer to themselves as Inuit, in solidarity with native peoples of Canada, Alaska, and the former Soviet Union, and speak their own language in addition to Danish.

In 1978 Denmark granted Greenland home rule, vesting its tiny Landsting (parliament) in the capital Nuuk/Godthåb with power over internal affairs. Though Denmark continues to devolve power, it still administers foreign policy and provides financial aid to an economy based on fishing, animal husbandry, construction, and tourism.

Since most travelers follow preset routes, towns and sites are arranged south to north in geographic order and not necessarily in the order they would be visited. Perhaps only one major museum or site is noted per village, but there is much more to see in Greenland's changeable nature. Venture along the wooden stairs and boardwalks that connect most private homes and provide inner-village walking paths. Cruise beneath the expanse of an iceberg and listen to it moan. Rise at 3 AM to take a stroll through the sunshine. There is no private property in Greenland—nature is free for all to enjoy, and in Greenlandic fashion, it is best savored slowly. Those who love this island do not move through it at a clip: it's more gratifying to let it move you.

Fishing
Visitors can buy fishing licenses (DKr200) from the local police, major hotels, and tourism offices. Call the local tourist board for details.

Hiking
Hiking in Greenland is unlimited. Keep in mind, however, that it's wiser to join an organized hike with an experienced guide than to attempt a solo expedition, since it's not uncommon for rescue crews to have to go out in search of lost hikers. Organized excursions are available in Nuuk/Godthåb and Narsarsuak for about DKr150 for a half day, DKr300 for a full day. The tourist offices of Qaqortoq/Julianehåb and Sisimiut/Holsteinsborg arrange hikes on request and charge according to the number of participants. For the most popular hiking areas in Greenland, new topographic maps at 1:50,000 are available. In these areas, experienced hikers can find their way without a guide. To cross the polar ice cap or to enter Greenland's national parkland—which is

the size of Great Britain and France combined—you must obtain a license. Contact the **Danish Polar Center** (⊠ Strandg. 100H, DK–1401 KBH K, ☎ 32/88–01–00, FAX 32/88–01–01).

Narsarsuaq

⑧⑨ *4 hrs, 50 min northwest of Copenhagen by plane.*

Narsarsuaq, meaning Great Plain in English, aptly describes the wide, smooth land harboring one of Greenland's largest civilian airports. The town is accessible from Copenhagen, Reykjavík, and Kangerlussuaq only by plane, and from Nuuk/Godthåb by plane and boat—though boats are booked months in advance.

Not far from the edge of town, visitors can take a 10-km (6-mi) boat ride from the Narsarsuaq harbor to an area where icebergs have broken off from a nearby glacier. There they are invited to collect glacial ice for the cocktails served on board.

Also near Narsarsuaq is the point locals call **Hospitalsdalen** (Hospital Valley), a controversial area named for an alleged American hospital where Korean War wounded were said to have been hidden away so as not to weaken morale back home. Though most history books deny the story, many locals swear it's true.

Qaqortoq/Julianehåb

⑨⓪ *6 hrs south of Narsarsuaq by ferry.*

With a population of 3,600, this is the largest town in southern Greenland and one of the loveliest. In the town square you'll see the island's only fountain, surrounded by half-timber and brightly colored houses. Though the oldest building in town is the cooper shop, which dates from 1797, the most interesting is the smithy, from 1871, which now houses the **Julianehåb Museum.** Inside are handmade hunting tools, kayaks, Inuit clothing, and a furnished sod house you can enter. A traditional dwelling, it remained cozy and warm even during the harsh winter. ⊠ *Free.* ⊙ *Weekdays 11–4.*

Lodging

$$ ⌶ **Hotel Qaqortoq.** Built in 1987, this hotel is among the more modern on the huge island. Its glass-and-white facade atop a hill overlooks the surrounding fjord and the picturesque town center. Rooms are simple but comfortable, all with private bath, TV, and phone. ⊠ *Box 155, DK–3920,* ☎ *299/3–82–82,* FAX *299/3–72–34. 21 rooms. Restaurant, bar, billiards. DC, MC, V.*

OFF THE BEATEN PATH **HVALSEY CHURCH** – A nice half-day excursion from Qaqortoq is the 14½-km (9-mi) sailboat ride to the well-preserved Hvalsey Church ruins, site of a well-attended Norse wedding in 1408—the community's last recorded activity before it mysteriously disappeared. As the church is close to a rocky beach, the hardy can opt for a frigid dip.

Qassiarsuk

⑨① *30 min northwest of Narsarsuaq by boat.*

The main focus of the tiny village of Qassiarsuk is sheep breeding. Though there are few modern facilities in town, the **Norse ruins** are fascinating and include, for example, the Brattahlíð—1,000-year-old ruins of Eric the Red's farm.

Greenland

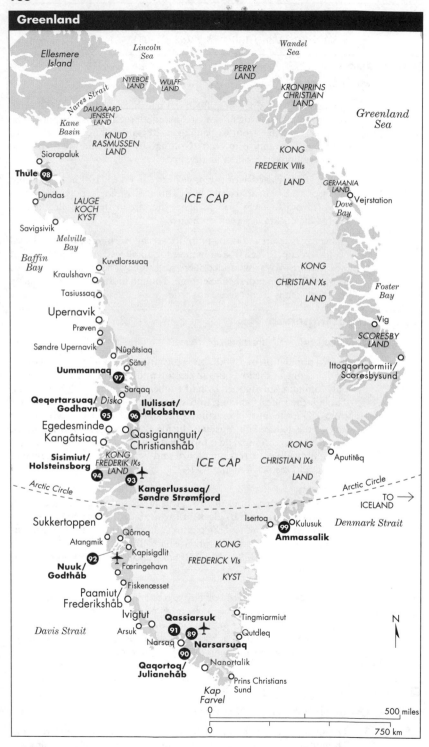

Ellesmere
Island

Lincoln
Sea

Wandel
Sea

PERRY
LAND

NYEBOE
LAND

WULFF
LAND

KRONPRINS
CHRISTIAN
LAND

Greenland
Sea

Nares Strait

DAUGAARD-
JENSEN
LAND

Kane
Basin

KNUD
RASMUSSEN
LAND

KONG
FREDERIK VIIIs
LAND

GERMANIA
LAND

Siorapaluk

Thule **98**

Dundas

LAUGE
KOCH
KYST

ICE CAP

Vejrstation

Dove
Bay

Savigsivik

Melville
Bay

Baffin
Bay

Kuvdlorssuaq

KONG

CHRISTIAN Xs

LAND

Foster
Bay

Kraulshavn

Tasiussaq

Upernavik

Prøven

Søndre Upernavik

Nûgâtsiaq

Sätut

Vig

SCORESBY
LAND

Uummannaq **97**

Sarqaq

Qeqertarsuaq/
Godhavn **95**

Disko

Ilulissat/
Jakobshavn **96**

Ittoqqortoormiit/
Scoresbysund

Egedesminde
Kangâtsiaq

Qasigiannguit/
Christianshåb

KONG

CHRISTIAN IXs

LAND

Aputitêq

Sisimiut/
Holsteinsborg **94**

KONG
FREDERIK IXs
LAND **93**

ICE CAP

Arctic Circle

Kangerlussuaq/
Søndre Strømfjord

Arctic Circle

TO
ICELAND

Sukkertoppen

Qôrnoq

Atangmik

Kapisigdlit

Isertoq

Kulusuk

Ammassalik **99**

Denmark Strait

KONG

FREDERICK VIs

KYST

Nuuk/
Godthåb **92**

Færingehavn

Fiskenæsset

Paamiut/
Frederikshåb

Ivigtut

Arsuk

Qassiarsuk **91**

Narsaq **89**

Tingmiarmiut

Qutdleq

Narsarsuaq

Davis Strait

Qaqortoq/
Julianehåb **90**

Nanortalik

Prins Christians
Sund

Kap
Farvel

N

0   500 miles

0   750 km

The remains of **Tjodhilde Kirke** are especially intriguing: this was touted as the first Christian church on the North American continent (Greenland is geographically considered part of North America and politically thought to be part of Europe). It was from this point that Eric the Red's son, Leif Ericsson, began the expedition in AD 1000 that took him to Vinland, somewhere on the coast of North America. The first Greenlandic Ting (outdoor parliament), fashioned after those in Iceland, was also held here at about the same time.

Nuuk/Godthåb

⑨ *1 hr, 25 min northwest of Narsarsuaq by small plane (15 hrs by ferry),7 hrs east of Ottawa by plane.*

Nuuk/Godthåb, the capital of Greenland, is beautifully situated on a peninsula between two fjords. It was founded in 1728 by the Norwegian missionary Hans Egede; his harborside home is now the private residence of the island's home-rule premier.

The city's newest landmark is **Katvaq,** the Greenland Cultural Center in town center. A triangular-shape construction fronted by a wavy wall—inspired by the Aurora Borealis—contains spaces for concerts, exhibitions, theater, conventions, and cinema, as well as a café. Its residents include the Greenland Art School, Nordic Institute on Greenland, and the Groenlandica Collection, a modern lending library with what is thought to be the largest collection of literature on the Arctic regions. ⊠ *Skibshavnsvej,* ☎ *299/2–33–00.* ⌨ *Free.* ☉ *Weekdays, 10–9:30, weekends 1:30–9:30.*

The centrally located **Landsmuseet** (National Museum) has a good permanent display of kayaks, costumes, and hunting weapons, an art exhibit, and the five 15th-century mummies of Qilakitsoq, one of Greenland's archaeological treasures. Among the most striking are a woman and child so well preserved that even their 500-year-old clothes are in pristine condition. ⊠ *Hans Egede Vej 8,* ☎ *299/2–26–11.* ⌨ *Free.* ☉ *Tues.–Sun. 1–4.*

Dining and Lodging

$$$$ ✕⊞ **Hotel Hans Egede.** This hotel is the largest in Greenland. The rooms are plain and functional but have such extras as minibars, TVs, VCRs, and phones. The sixth-floor Sky Top Restaurant, known for its lovely view of the fjords and its inventive nouveau Greenlandic menu, prepares local fish employing French methods. ⊠ *Box 289, DK–3900,* ☎ *299/2–42–22,* ℻ *299/2–44–87. 108 rooms. Restaurant, pub, dance club, meeting rooms. DC, MC, V.*

Kangerlussuaq/Søndre Strømfjord

⑨ *1 hr northeast of Nuuk/Godthåb by plane, 4 hrs, 20 min northwest of Copenhagen by plane.*

Kangerlussuaq/Søndre Strømfjord is at the head of one of the longest and deepest fjords in the world. The airport, Greenland's most vital, lies just 25 km (15½ mi) from the ice cap. Until World War II, nobody lived here permanently, but Greenlanders came in the spring to hunt reindeer. During the war, the U.S. Air Force chose its dry, stable climate for an air base, called Blue West Eight. The military moved out in the fall of 1992, selling all the facilities to the local government for the sum of $1.

Sisimiut/Holsteinsborg

94 *40 min west of Kangerlussuaq/Søndre Strømfjord by helicopter.*

On the Davis Strait, this hilltop town is full of Danish-style wooden houses—a local luxury, as all wood is imported. A favorite area for dogsledging, during which you are pulled by a team of rabid wolf-dogs; they are harnessed in a fan shape rather than a straight line, so if one falls through the ice, you won't all plummet to an icy death. It is also the southernmost boundary for walrus hunting; the walrus, though extremely rare, is a popular game animal because of its valuable tusks. The Greenlandic name Sisimiut means Burrow People.

Qeqertarsuaq/Godhavn

95 *1 hr, 20 min west of Illulissat by helicopter (8 hrs, 30 min by coastal boat; reserve far in advance).*

In the Disko Bugt (Bay) is the island of Qeqertarsuaq/Disko, where the main town is Qeqertarsuaq/Godhavn. Until 1950 this was the capital of northern Greenland; Nuuk/Godthåb served as the southern capital. The task was divided because it was too difficult to rule the entire island from one town. Accessible by helicopter and ship, Godhavn is often booked to capacity by European tourists; they come for the organized dogsledging trips, as this is the only area in Greenland with summertime dogsledging.

Ilulissat/Jakobshavn

96 *45 min north of Kangerlussuaq/Søndre Strømfjord by plane.*

In the center of Disko Bay is Ilulissat/Jakobshavn, 300 km (185 mi) north of the Arctic Circle. At the tip of its fjord is the Northern Hemisphere's most productive glacier, calving 20 million tons of floes each day—equivalent, according to the Greenland tourist board, to the amount of water New York City uses in a year. For a humbling experience, take one of the helicopter tours encircling the glacier. A violent landscape of floating ice giants and dazzling panoramas, it's been inhabited by the Inuit for as long as 4,000 years. The town was founded in 1741 by a Danish merchant, Jakob Severin. Today the largest industry is shrimping, though in the winter dogsledgers fish for halibut along the fjord.

Visit the **Knud Rasmussens Fødehjem** (boyhood home of Knud Rasmussen); this Danish-Greenlandic explorer (1879–1933) initiated the seven Thule expeditions, which enhanced the knowledge of Arctic geography and Inuit culture. At the museum you can follow his explorations through photographs, equipment, and clothing. ▣ *DKr20.* ☉ *Daily 10–4.*

Dining and Lodging

$$$ ✕▥ **Hotel Arctic.** This modern hotel, divided into two low-lying red buildings, is in the mountains on the edge of town, and provides views of the ice fjord and the mountains. Rooms are simple, with bathroom, phone, radio, and TV. The main dining room has panoramic views of the iceberg-filled harbor and serves fine beef and fish dishes. ▧ *Box 1501, DK–3952,* ☎ *299/4–41–53,* ℻ *299/4–39–24. 40 rooms. Restaurant, sauna, billiards, meeting rooms. AE, DC, MC.*

$$$ ✕▥ **Hotel Hvide Falk.** The compact rooms in this central, moderate-size, two-story building are furnished with TVs and small desks, and have magnificent views of the icebergs and the Disko Mountains. The restaurant, which specializes in seafood—especially herring, cod, and salmon—looks out over the bay and its looming icebergs. The director of the hotel, Lars Rasmussen, is explorer Knud Rasmussen's grandson. ✉ *Box 20, DK–3952,* ☎ *299/4–33–43,* FAX *299/4–35–08. 27 rooms. Restaurant. DC.*

Uummannaq

⑨⑦ *55 min north of Ilulissat/Jakobshavn by helicopter.*

The inhabitants of the town of Uummannaq, on the island of the same name, maintain Greenlandic traditions in step with modern European life. Ranging from hunters to linguists, they are as apt to drive dogsleds as they are four-wheel drives. The town lies beneath the magnificent hues and double humps of the granite Uummannaq Mountain, 3,855 ft high. Because the village is also perched on uneven stone cliffs, housing largely consists of brightly painted, freestanding cottages rather than the ugly Danish barracks that line some of the larger towns.

The **Uummannaq Museum** will give you a good overview of life on the island, with photographs and costumes of local hunters and displays on the now-defunct mines of the area. Exhibits also detail the doomed 1930 expedition of German explorer Alfred Wegener, and there is also a bit on the Qilakitsoq mummies (☞ Nuuk/Godthåb, *above*), found in a nearby cave in 1977. ✉ *Uummannaq Museum,* ☎ *299/4–81–04.* ▦ *Free.* ☉ *Weekdays 8–4.*

The **Uummannaq Church,** dating from 1937, is the only stone church in Greenland and is made from local granite. Next door to it are three sod huts, typical Inuit dwellings until just a couple of decades ago.

Though there is plenty of **dogsledging** north of the Arctic Circle, the trips that set forth from Uummannaq are the most authentic, as local hunters drive; they are also the most gentle, since the terrain here is especially smooth. Visitors sit comfortably in heavy, fur-lined sleighs that tear across the frozen fjord in the hands of experienced Inuit drivers. Trips can be arranged at the Hotel Uummannaq and range from a few hours to several days of racing through the terrifying beauty of the landscape and sleeping in the shadows of towering icebergs.

Dining and Lodging

$$ ✕▦ **Uummannaq Hotel.** This natty harborside hotel and brand-new extension offer bright, compact rooms with white, Danish-designed furniture. The fine restaurant serves local specialties, including polar bear, caribou, seal, and plenty of fish. ✉ *Box 202, DK–3961,* ☎ *299/4–85– 18,* FAX *299/4–82–62. 22 rooms, 10 in a nearby annex. Restaurant, bar. AE, MC, V.*

Thule

⑨⑧ *2 hrs, 40 min north of Uummannaq by passenger-cargo plane, 1 hr, 45 min north of Kangerlussuaq/Søndre Strømfjord by plane.*

The northern reaches of Greenland are sparsely populated, with few hotels. The American air base at Thule, used for monitoring the Northern Hemisphere, is difficult to visit, but check with the Danish Ministry of Foreign Affairs in Copenhagen (✉ ☎ 33/92–00–00) or the Royal Danish Embassy in Washington, DC (✉ 3200 Whitehaven St. NW 20008-3683, ☎ 202/234–4300, FAX 202/328–1470).

Ammassalik

⑨⑨ *2 hrs west of Reykjavík by plane, connecting via helicopter from Kulusuk.*

Much of the east coast is empty. The most accessible towns are Ammassalik and Kulusuk, a tiny village slightly farther northeast. Both towns welcome most of Greenland's visitors, day-trippers from Iceland. Though tours, arranged through Icelandair, are usually short—often just day trips—they are very well organized, offering an accurate (and relatively affordable) peek at Greenlandic culture and the natural splendor of the Arctic.

Lodging

$$ ⌂ **Hotel Angmagssalik.** Perched on a mountain, with a lovely view of the town and harbor, this hotel is decorated with a simple wood interior, both in the guest rooms and common areas. ⌂ *Box 117, DK–3900,* ☎ *299/1–82–93,* ℻ *299/1–83–93. 30 rooms, 18 with shower. Restaurant, bar. AE, DC, MC, V.*

Greenland A to Z

Arriving and Departing

BY PLANE AND HELICOPTER

The main airport in Greenland is **Kangerlussuaq/Søndre Strømfjord.** International flights also arrive less frequently into **Narsarsuaq** for those who are destined for south Greenland. **Kulusuk** is the main airport for the east coast. **Nuuk** and **Ilulissat** also serve as domestic airports.

Helicopters and small planes connect small towns. Because of Greenland's highly variable weather, delays are frequent. As with all arrangements in Greenland, confirm all flights, connections, and details with your local travel agent or airline representative before you leave home.

The most common points of departure for Greenland are Denmark and Iceland. If you're going by way of **Iceland,** Icelandair (☎ 354/505–0300) has flights from New York, Baltimore, Fort Lauderdale, and Orlando to Keflavík, Iceland, daily in summer, and **Greenlandair** (Grønlands-fly in Danish) makes three flights a week between Keflavík and Narsar-suaq in summer and winter. It's more expensive to go by way of **Copenhagen** with **SAS** (☎ 32/33–68–48), which flies seven times a week in summer to Kangerlussuaq/Søndre Strømfjord. Connections are also available through **Canada,** where you can catch an early morning flight from Ottowa to Frobisher Bay on Baffin Island, then cross the Davis Strait to Kangerlussuaq/Søndre Strømfjord on **Firstair** (☎ 613/839–8840).

Getting Around

BY BOAT

The most beautiful passage between towns is by water. Every town has a harbor, where private boats can be hired for connections or excursions. Some cruise and coastal boats, as well as the privately-owned *Disko,* which plies the waters of the west coast, and the M/S *Ioffe,* which sails around the east and south coasts, make frequent stops. You can only reserve through a travel agency. Boat voyages, including luxury cruises, are also available from Canada's Frobisher Bay, Norway's Svalbard (archipelago), and Iceland. Contact **KNI Service** (⌂ Box 608, DK–3900 Nuuk, ☎ 299/2–52–11, ℻ 2–32–11) or Greenland Travel in Copenhagen (☎ 33/13–10–11).

BY PLANE AND HELICOPTER

Greenlandair is the only airline licensed for domestic flights on the island. Its modest fleet of helicopters and small planes is booked year-round, so make reservations well in advance.

Contacts and Resources

EMERGENCIES

Every community has its own fire, ambulance, and police numbers and dentist and doctor, all of which you may reach through your hotel. The best way to handle emergencies is to avoid danger in the first place. Don't take risks, ask for advice, and give your travel agent and hotel your itinerary so that they can reach you in case of emergencies—or if you don't show up when you're due.

Hospital: Sana Dronning Ingrids Hospital (✉ DK–3900 Nuuk, ☎ 299/2–11–01).

GUIDED TOURS

On-the-spot excursions are available in most towns and range from about DKr250 for a half-day to DKr600 for a full day, more for dogsledging, boat, and helicopter trips. Because transportation and accommodations are limited, have all details of your trip—connections, accommodations, sightseeing, and meals—arranged by an experienced travel agent, tour organizer, or airline. (It's also helpful to bring a copy of your tour contract and all confirmations.)

Tour packages range from one- to four-day east-coast excursions from Reykjavík by Icelandair to monthlong excursions, which can include sailing, hiking, hunting, dogsledging (February to May), whale safaris, and iceberg-watching.

United States: Bennett of Scandinavia (✉ 270 Madison Ave., New York, NY 10016, ☎ 800/221–2420). **Eurocruises** (✉ 303 W. 13th St., New York, NY 10014, ☎ 800/688–3876). **Icelandair** (✉ Symphony Woods, 5950 Symphony Woods Rd., Columbia, MD 21044, ☎ 800/223–5500). **Quark Expeditions** (✉ 980 Post Rd., Darien, CT 06820, ☎ 203/656–0499). **Scanam** (✉ 933 Hwy. 23, Pompton Plains, NJ 07444, ☎ 800/545–2204). **Scantours Inc.** (✉ 1535 6th St., Suite 209, Santa Monica, CA 90401, ☎ 800/223–7226). **Travcoa** (✉ 4000 McArthur Blvd. E, Suite 650, Newport Beach, CA 92660, ☎ 714/476–2800).

Canada: Marine Expeditions Inc. (✉ 30 Hazelton Ave., Toronto, Ontario M5R 2E2, ☎ 416/964-9069). **Pedersen World Tours** (✉ 15 Wertheim Ct., Suite 402, Richmond Hill, Ontario L4B 3H7, ☎ 416/882–5470).

In Denmark, contact **Arctic Adventure** (✉ Reventlowsg. 30, DK–1651 KBH V, ☎ 33/25–32–21). **Greenland Travel** (☞ Visitor Information, *below*) also operates out of Denmark.

LATE-NIGHT PHARMACIES

If you are taking medication, bring enough to last throughout your visit. In emergencies, the local hospital can fill prescriptions.

VISITOR INFORMATION

There is a tourism office in almost every town, but brochures, maps, and specific information may be limited. Call ahead for an exact street address (a 299 access code must be dialed before all phone numbers when calling from outside Greenland).

Ammassalik (✉ Box 120, DK–3913 Ammassalik, ☎ 299/1–82–77, FAX 299/1–80–77). **Ilulissat/Jakobshavn** (✉ Box 272, DK–3952 Ilulissat, ☎ 299/4–43–22, FAX 299/4–39–33). **Kangerlussuaq/Søndre Strømfjord** (✉ Box 49, DK–3910, Kangerlussuaq, ☎ 299/1–10–98, FAX 299/1–14–98). **Nuuk/Godthåb** (✉ Box 199, DK–3900 Nuuk, ☎ 299/2–27–00, FAX 299/2–27–10). **Nielsen Travel** (✉ Box 183, DK–3920 Qaqortoq, ☎ 299/3–89–13, FAX 299/3–89–87). **Qasigiannguit/Christianshåb** (✉ Hotel Igdlo, Box 160, DK–3951 Qasigiannguit, ☎ 299/4 50 81, FAX 299/4–55–24). **Qeqertarsuaq/Godhavn** (✉ Box 113, DK–3953 Qeqertarsuaq, ☎ 299/4–71–96, FAX 299/4–71–98). **Sisimiut/Holsteinsborg** (✉ Box 65, DK–3911 Sisimiut, ☎ 299/1–48–48, FAX 299/1–56–22). **Uummannaq** (✉ c/o Hotel Uummannaq, Box 202, DK–3961 Uummannaq, ☎ 299/4–85–18, FAX 299/4–82–62).

In Copenhagen, **Greenland Travel** (✉ Gammel Mønt 12, ☎ 33/13–10–11) has a helpful and knowledgeable staff. **Greenland Tourism** (✉ Pilestr. 52, ☎ 33/13–69–75) is another reliable Copenhagen-based operation.

THE FAROE ISLANDS

The 18 Faroe Islands (Føroyar in Faroese; Færøerne in Danish) lift up out of the North Atlantic in an extended knuckle of a volcanic archipelago. All but one are inhabited, by 43,700 people and 70,000 sheep. The native Faroese live by fishing, fish farming, and shepherding, and carefully maintain their refreshingly civilized pace of life.

Situated 300 km (188 mi) northwest of Scotland, 430 km (270 mi) southeast of Iceland, and 1,300 km (812 mi) northwest of Denmark, the fjord-chiseled islands support little vegetation besides a bristle of short grasses and moss. The climate is oceanic: humid, changeable, and stormy, with surprisingly mild temperatures—52°F in the summer, and 40°F in the winter—and a heavy annual rainfall of 63 inches.

Of their 1,399 square km (540 square mi), only 6% is fertile, the rest rough pasture—an Eden for 70 breeding and 120 migratory species of birds, among them thousands of gannets, auks, and puffins. Beneath azure skies and rugged, mossy mountains, villages of colorful thatched houses cling to hillsides while large trawlers and small fishing boats stream in and out of their harbors. Religious and proud, the Faroese have built churches in nearly every settlement.

Catholic monks from Ireland were the first to settle the islands, but they died out and were replaced by Norwegian Vikings, who settled the land about AD 800. It was here that the *Løgting* (parliament) met for the first time in AD 900 in Tórshavn—where it still meets. Under the Danish crown, the islands have had a home-rule government since 1948, with their own flag and language. The roots of the Faroese language are in Old West Norse. Most people speak English, but a Danish dictionary can be helpful to the visitor, as Danish is the second language.

It's difficult for visitors to understand the isolation or the practical relationship the Faroese have with the natural world. Dubious outsiders, for example, accuse locals of cruelty during the traditional pilot-whale harvests. An essential foodstuff, the sea mammals are killed in limited numbers to reduce the islands' dependence on imported meat. The profit factor is eliminated: whale meat is not sold—it's given away to the townspeople in equal portions on a per capita basis. The hunt is also an important social bond involving both the young and the old.

In 1993 the islands plunged into a severe depression, with unemployment, formerly an unknown phenomenon, surging from less than 3% to more than 20%. Toward the end of 1996, however, unemployment was pushed back down to 8% as the numbers of cod surrounding the islands mysteriously tripled (scientists and biologists are at a loss to explain why). Tourism is also a part of this brighter picture, and is increasing at a rate of 10% to 15% yearly. Though there appears an upward trend, there is also some fear: large international oil companies believe there is oil in the region. If they strike it rich, the islands could get out of their financial difficulties and return the DKr4 billion they currently owe Denmark. But many people fear that the black gold will irrevocably change the face of their islands.

Tórshavn on the island of Streymoy makes for a good touring base; spend one night in Klaksvík on the island of Borðoy. The very efficient bus and connecting boat service is the best way to travel between towns (☞ The Faroe Islands A to Z, *below*).

Tórshavn

1,343 km (839 mi) northeast of Copenhagen, 2 hrs, 15 min by plane.

Most visitors who arrive on the Faroe Islands by plane begin their explorations on the largest and most traveled island of Streymoy, which, though carved by sheer cliffs and waterfalls, has good roads and tunnels. On the northern end of the island are bird sanctuaries and a NATO base. On its southeastern flank is one of the world's tiniest capitals, Tórshavn, named for the Viking god Thor. Centrally located among the islands, Tórshavn has a population of 16,000. A Viking parliament was founded here in about AD 1000, but it did not have any real legislative power until 1948. St. Olav's Day, July 29, is named for the Norwegian king who brought Christianity to the islands. Celebrations include rowing competitions and group dances in the form of a chain—a sort of North Atlantic ring dance.

The rugged **Tinganes** is a small peninsula between the east and west bays that was the site of both the old trading post and the meetings of the local parliament (*tinganes* means "assembly place"). Here you can see some of the town's oldest buildings, dating from the 17th and 18th centuries, and some old warehouses, which today house the government offices. At the end of the docks is **Skansin,** a fort built in 1580 by Magnus Heinason to protect the town against pirate attacks. After many reconstructions, it reached its present shape in 1790 and was used as the Faroe headquarters of the British Navy during World War II. Two guns from that period remain.

Down from the Tinganes is Old Main Street, lined with small 19th-century houses and crossed by twisting streets. You'll come to the slate **Havnar Kirkja** (Tórshavn's Church), rebuilt many times in its 200-year history. Inside is a model of a ship salvaged from an 18th-century wreck, the ship's bell, and an altarpiece dating from 1647.

There are very few trees on the islands. **Tórshavn Park,** a walk up Hoyviksvegur, used to be the pride of the town—it was a rare cultivated oasis of green trees in a land where storms and strong winds flatten tall vegetation. Planted around the turn of the century, the park thrived until 1988, when a storm virtually destroyed it.

Standing atop a hill, **Kongaminnið** (King's Memorial) commands a good view of the old town. The basalt obelisk commemorates the visit of King Christian IX in 1874. ⊠ *Norðrari Ringvegur, just off R. C. Effersøes Gøta.*

At the northern tip of Tórshavn is the modern **Norðurlandahúsið** (Nordic Culture House), built in 1983. It hosts an international jazz festival in mid-August and theater and concerts throughout the year. ⊠ *Norðrari Ringvegur,* ☎ *298/17900.* ☉ *Call for event schedules.*

Dining and Lodging

$$$ ✕🏨 **Hotel Föroyar.** Five minutes from Tórshavn center, this hotel has a view of the Old Town. The rooms all have TVs, refrigerators, and phones, and there's a good restaurant with island specialties. ⊠ *Oyggjarvegur, FR–110,* ☎ *298/17500,* ☒ *298/16019. 216 beds. Restaurant. AE, DC, MC.*

$$$ ✕🏨 **Hotel Hafnia.** Close to the pedestrian streets of town, this modern business hotel offers a good buffet and big-city ambience. The rooms vary in size, but all are comfortably appointed with TVs, telephones, desks, and private showers. The restaurant serves Faroese seafood, in-

The Faroe Islands

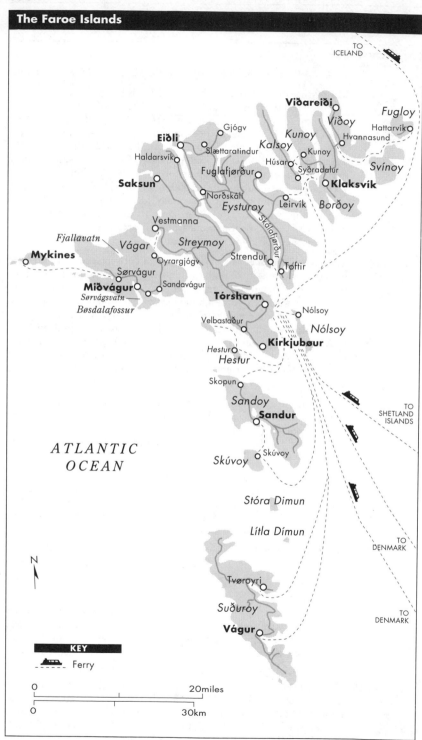

TO
ICELAND

Viðareiði

Viðoy

Fugloy

Hattarvík

Gjógv

Kunoy

Eiði

Slættaratindur

Kalsoy

Hvannasund

Haldarsvík

Húsar

Kunoy

Svínoy

Fuglafjørður

Syðradalur

Saksun

Klaksvik

Norðskáli

Eysturoy

Leirvík

Borðoy

Vestmanna

Skálafjørður

Fjallavatn

Vágar

Streymoy

Mykines

Oyrargjógv

Strendur

Tóftir

Sørvágur

Miðvágur

Sandavágur

Tórshavn

Sørvágsvatn

Nólsoy

Bøsdalafossur

Velbastaður

Nólsoy

Hestur

Kirkjubøur

Hestur

Skopun

Sandoy

ATLANTIC
OCEAN

Sandur

TO
SHETLAND
ISLANDS

Skúvoy

Skúvoy

Stóra Dímun

Lítla Dímun

TO
DENMARK

N

Tvøroyri

Suðuroy

TO
DENMARK

Vágur

KEY

Ferry

0

20miles

0

30km

cluding local cod and flounder. ⊠ *Áarvegur 4, FR–110,* ☎ *298/11270,* FAX *298/15250. 76 beds. Restaurant. AE, DC, MC.*

$$ 🏠 **Skansin Guesthouse.** Hard times have forced owner Frantz Restorff to close part of his guest house, but the rest of it, where he and his wife live, remains open to guests, who will experience typical Faroese hospitality within the modesty and personality of this private home. Filled with their belongings—a watercolor of a family-owned island, family photos, a collection of old records—the house is familiar and cozy. The Restorffs serve a generous breakfast (included in the room rate) and offer expert advice and assistance in planning activities. Guests have use of the kitchen. ⊠ *Jekaragøta 8, Box 57, FR–110 Tórshavn,* ☎ *298/ 12242,* FAX *298/10657. 22 beds. No credit cards.*

$$ 🏠 **Youth Hostel Tórshavn.** Open as a hotel from July to September, this summer-only hotel is a school during the winter. ⊠ *Vesturgøta 15, FR– 1100,* ☎ *2998/18900,* FAX *298/15707. 100 beds. AE, DC, MC. Closed Oct.–June.*

$ 🏠 **Tórshavnar Sjómansheim.** In the middle of Tórshavn, this modest hotel caters to those who need only a bed to be happy. Rooms are clean and basic, with dark hand-me-down furniture. The restaurant serves one special of the day, ranging from beef stew to—if there is a catch— whale. ⊠ *Tórsgøta 4, FR–1100,* ☎ *298/13515,* FAX *298/13286. 55 beds. Restaurant. No credit cards.*

OFF THE
BEATEN PATH

BOAT TRIP FROM VESTMANNA – You can take a bus from Tórshavn to Vestmanna (40 km/25 mi north of Tórshavn), where a boat takes you through narrow channels from which you can see sheep grazing atop sheer cliffs. In the spring the sheep are hoisted up the 2,310 ft with ropes, and in the fall they are caught and brought back down—apparently this process makes them taste better. Double-check the bus schedule before you leave to avoid geting stranded. Contact Aldan Tourist Information in Tórshavn (☞ The Faroe Islands A to Z, *below*).

Kirkjubøur

13 km (8 mi) south of Tórshavn.

From Tórshavn, a bus takes you to the outskirts of Kirkjubøur, from which you will have to walk a mile—through fields grazed by ponies and sheep—to the tiny town populated by 60 (ask the tourist office in Tórshavn for detailed directions). The townsfolk live in black houses with red window frames and green grass roofs perched on hillsides around the tiny, often fog-shrouded harbor. At the southern tip of the island, the town was the Faroes' spiritual and cultural center from 1269 to 1308.

A particularly ambitious priest, Bishop Erland, built a cathedral in the town in the 13th century—there is some controversy over whether or not it was ever completed—and the ruins of the Gothic **Magnus Cathedral** still stand. Inside the church is a large stone tablet engraved with an image of Christ on the cross, flanked by the Virgin Mary and Mary Magdalene, and an inscription to St. Magnus and St. Thorlak. During restoration work in 1905, the tablet was removed to reveal well-preserved relics of the saints. In 1538, after the Reformation, the episcopal see was dissolved and with it the town's power.

Just next door to the Magnus Cathedral is the restored **St. Olav's Church,** which dates from 1111 and is now the only church from that time still in use. Most of its sculptures have been removed to Copenhagen, leaving little to see, but there's a hole in the north wall that once allowed lepers standing outside to watch the mass and receive the Eucharist. The altarpiece is the work of the most famous painter of the islands, Sámal Mikines.

Near the church is a farmhouse, the **Roykstovan.** Legend has it that the lumber for the building came drifting to the town, neatly numbered and bundled, from the Sogne Fjord in Norway. Inside are the traditional Faroese one-main-room living quarters and a dozen other rooms. It's been in the same family for the last 16 generations, and it is here that foreign dignitaries are welcomed to the town.

Saksun

30 km (18 mi) northwest of Tórshavn.

Among the fjords slicing the northern end of Streymoy is the tiny town of Saksun, one of the most popular excursions on the island. Set around a pastoral lake in the midst of a deep valley are scattered sod-roof houses with lovely views. The town also swarms with great skuas, large brown seabirds prone to low dives. As you unwittingly near their nests, you will certainly notice their cantankerous presence.

Eiði

52 km (32 mi) northwest of Tórshavn.

The island of Eysturoy, just east of Streymoy, is connected to the latter by bridge and buses. The center of activity is the town of Eiði, which lies to the northwest in a spectacular landscape. Looking northwest, you can see two 250-ft cliffs, a part of local mythology: one night an Icelandic giant and his wife came to carry the islands to Iceland, but she dropped them, giving the islands their cracked geography. Once the sun rose, the giants were petrified and transformed into the bluffs.

Due east of Eiði is the islands' highest point, the 2,910-ft **Slættaratindur** mountain. On the shores of the southern **Skálafjørður,** the longest fjord in the archipelago, the majority of the island's 10,500 people live.

Lodging

$$ 🏨 **Hotel Eiði.** Perched on a hilltop in a village near the sea, about an hour by bus from Tórshavn, this slightly dated hotel is small and clean, with TVs and refrigerators in all rooms. ⊠ *FR–470 Eiði,* ☎ *298/ 23456,* 📠 *298/23200. 28 beds. Restaurant. DC, MC, V.*

$ 🏨 **Gjáargarður.** This youth hostel, built in traditional Faroese style, has a prime position on the north end of the island, near the ocean and the mountains. ⊠ *FR–476 Eiði,* ☎ *298/23171,* 📠 *298/23505. 100 beds. No credit cards.*

Klaksvík

35 km (22 mi) northeast of Tórshavn.

The island of Borðoy is accessible by boat from eastern Eysturoy. On its southwest coast, nearly divided by two fjords, Klaksvík is the Faroes' second-largest town and most important fishing harbor; its fleet of sophisticated boats harvests cod, haddock, herring, and other fish. Within this scattering of islands, Borðoy, Viðoy, and Kunoy are connected by causeways. The other three islands, Fugloy, Svinoy, and Kalsoy, are accessible by passenger boat or helicopter.

Within Klaksvík, the baptismal font in the **Christianskirkjan** (Christian's Church) is a piece of carved granite thought to have been used in pagan rituals in Denmark 4,000 years ago. Suspended from the church roof is a 24-ft boat used by a former vicar to visit nearby towns; the boat—

common in Danish churches—is a symbol that God is watching over the village fishermen.

Lodging

$$ ⊞ **Klaksvíkar Sjómansheim.** Sheep graze on the front lawn of this big, white hotel; the back overlooks the colorful harbor. The staff is cheery and helpful, and rooms—request one with a harbor view—offer no-frills comfort; showers and toilets are in the hallways, but sinks are in the rooms. The restaurant serves generous portions of the homemade special of the day. ⊠ *Vikavegur 39, FR–700 Klaksvík,* ☎ *298/55333. 34 rooms. No credit cards.*

$ ⊞ **Youth Hostel and Guest House Ibuð.** This youth and family hostel, the only one on the northern islands, is in a former hotel, built in 1945. It is near a ferry slip and surrounded by hiking trails. ⊠ *Garðavegur 31, FR–700 Klaksvík,* ☎ *298/55403 or 298/57555. 28 youth hostel beds, 8 guest house beds. No credit cards.*

Viðareiði

18 km (11 mi) north of Klaksvík.

The island of Viðoy is among the wildest and most beautiful of the islands, with mountains of 2,800 ft and sheer cliffs plunging into extremely rough, unnavigable waters. Amazingly, 600 people live here, many in the town of Viðareiði. Cape Enniberg, at its northernmost tip, reaches 2,460 ft; it's the world's highest cape rising directly from the sea. From the town of Viðareiði you can take a boat tour (call Tora Tourist Travel; ☞ The Faroe Islands A to Z, *below*) to see many seabirds nesting on cliff walls, including kittiwakes and puffins—endearing little black-and-white birds with enormous orange beaks. The Faroese have a remarkable relationship with the puffins, harvesting them by the thousands for food and yet not endangering their numbers.

Lodging

$ ⊞ **Hotel Norð.** In a small town of 300 inhabitants on the northern end of the island, this simple business hotel has beautiful surroundings and great bird-watching. ⊠ *FR–750 Viðareiði,* ☎ *298/51061,* ℻ *298/ 51144. 20 beds. No credit cards. Closed Oct.–May.*

Miðvágur

18 km (11 mi) west of Tórshavn.

Vágar, the third-largest island, takes its name from its fjords, and it is cut by three of them, as well as by the Fjallavatn and Sørvágsvatn lakes, the last of which is fed by the Bøsdalafossur, a 100-ft waterfall. The main town here is Miðvágur, an excellent perch for auk- and gannet-watching.

Lodging

$$ ⊞ **Hotel Vágar.** A standard small hotel, this one is modern. ⊠ *FR–380 Sørvágur,* ☎ *298/32955,* ℻ *298/32310. 50 beds. Restaurant. AE, DC, MC.*

Mykines

48 km (30 mi) west of Miðvágar (1 hr, 15 min by boat, 15 min by helicopter).

It's rough sailing to the tiny atoll of Mykines and only manageable when weather permits. In the town of the same name, population 15, the few dwellings are roofed with sod. The town was sited here to be close to the **Mykineshólmur,** an islet swarming with thousands of puffins, which

are harvested for food. You can get here by traversing the island northward on foot about 2 km (1¼ mi) from the boat landing in Søvágur.

Sandur

25 km (16 mi) south of Tórshavn, 16 km (10 mi) south of Klaksvík.

Sandoy, the fifth-largest island, lies to the south. Relatively fertile, it's
named for the sandy white beaches of the town of Sandur, on its bay.
Sheep graze on green hills, and the lakes north and west of town swell
with auks, purple sandpipers, and great skuas. This is great walking
or biking country; bike rentals are available in town.

Vágur

64 km (40 mi) south of Tórshavn.

The southernmost island, Suðuroy, is milder than the others, with cultivated green fields at its center and mountains along the coast. Ferries
from Tórshavn dock either in Vágur or the quieter village of Tvøroyri.

Lodging

$$ ☷ **Hotel Tvøroyri.** In the middle of town, this old hotel has simple, clean
rooms and minimal service. ⊠ *FR–800 Tvøroyri,* ☎ *298/71171,* 𝖥𝖠𝖷
298/72171. 21 beds. AE.

$ ☷ **Hotel Bakkin.** This plain lodging is usually booked by fishermen and
local workers. ⊠ *FR–900 Vágur,* ☎ *298/73961. 18 beds. No credit
cards.*

The Faroe Islands A to Z

Arriving and Departing
BY FERRY
There is frequent ferry service to all islands, with the most remote areas
served by helicopter as well. Once a week in summer there are car fer-
ries from Esbjerg (33 hours) to Tórshavn. Call **DFDS** (☎ 33/11–22–
55). Year-round ferries depart from Hirtshals, Jylland on Friday and
arrive in Tórshavn on Monday (48 hours), and there are regular con-
nections to and from Aberdeen. Call **Faroeship** (☎ 39/29–26–88) for
more information.

BY PLANE
SL Visitor Cards are sold at airports (☞ Getting Around, *below*). De-
lays due to heavy fog are common. **From Copenhagen** there are daily
connections to the western island of Vágar that take about two hours.
From there, count another 2½ hours to get to Tórshavn by bus and
ferry. For reservations on either **Danair** or **Atlantic Airways,** call SAS
(☎ 32/32–68–68) in Copenhagen or Flogfelag Føroya (☎ 298/32755)
in the Faroe Islands. **Mærsk Air** (☎ 32/31–45–45 in Copenhagen; ☎
298/11025 in Tórshavn) flies year-round between Copenhagen and Bil-
lund, on Jylland, and the Faroe Islands, with other connections avail-
able from Amsterdam, Brussels, Frankfurt, London, Paris, and
Stockholm. Two weekly flights are also available from **Reykjavík** (☎
912–5100) on **Icelandair,** which also flies once a week, in the summer,
from Glasgow to the Faroes and on to Iceland.

Getting Around
BY BUS, FERRY, AND HELICOPTER
The main islands are connected by regular ferries; smaller ones are linked
by mailboat and helicopter. The **SL Visitor Card** is a good value for ex-
ploring the islands; it affords free passage on all SL (the local trans-
portation company) buses and ferries. Be sure to buy the card at the
airport (or from your travel agent) to pay for the trip to Tórshavn. It

costs DKr385 for four days, DKr600 for seven days, DKr900 for 14 days; it's half-price for children under 13, free for those under 7 years old. For ferries, call **Strandfaraskip Landsins** (☎ 298/14550, ⊠ /298/16000) in Tórshavn. **Helicopter Service** (☎ 298/33410) is available in Vagar. In towns, and between islands that are connected by bridges, there is regular bus service. For schedules and reservations, call **Bygdaleiðir** (☎ 298/14550) in Tórshavn.

BY CAR

Driving laws are the same as in Denmark. Car rentals are available in Tórshavn and at Vagar Airport. A network of two-lane asphalt roads has been built between towns, using tunnels and bridges. The roads are best on the nine main islands. Speed limits are 50 kph (30 mph) in urban areas, 80 kph (50 mph) outside. Once outside towns, beware of untethered animals.

Contacts and Resources

EMERGENCIES

Ambulance, fire, police (☎ 000).

Pharmacy: Tórshavn (⊠ by SMS shopping center, ☎ 298/11100). **Klaksvík** (⊠ Klaksvíksvegur, ☎ 298/55055. **Tvøroyri Pharmacy** (☎ 298/71076).

GUIDED TOURS

In addition to the local tours offered by many hotels, two main tour operators on the islands, **Kunningarstovan** (⊠ Vaglid, Tórshavn, ☎ 298/15788) and **Tora Tourist Travel** (⊠ N. Finsensgøta, Tórshavn, ☎ 298/15505), offer angling, city, and bird-watching tours.

Bird-Watching–Cave Tours: Tora Tourist Travel runs tours to Vestmanna Birdcliffs Tour (six hours), which includes a look at bird colonies and nearby caves.

Boat–Fishing Tours: Tours of Nolsoy and Hestur (Kunningarstovan) leave from Tórshavn harbor and include coastal sailing through the Kapilsund strait and along Hestur's west coast to see puffins and other seabirds. The three-hour trips are aboard the 50-year-old wooden schooner *Nordlys* (*Northern Light*), and guests may even get a chance to do some fishing.

Sightseeing Tours: Tora Tourist Travel organizes a tour to Gjógv, the northernmost village on Eysturoy (five hours), including a view of mountains and a local village.

VISITOR INFORMATION

The helpful brochure *Around the Faroe Islands*, is published by the tourist board. In Copenhagen, call the **Faroese Government Office** (⊠ Højbropl. 7, ☎ 33/14–08–66). The **Danish Tourist Board** (branches in Denmark and abroad) can also supply information.

Klaksvik Tourist Information (⊠ N. Palsgøta, FR–700 Klaksvík, ☎ 298/56939). **Aldan Tourist Information** (⊠ Reyngøta 17, FR–100 Tórshavn, ☎ 298/19391).

DENMARK A TO Z

Arriving and Departing

By Boat

FROM THE UNITED KINGDOM

Scandinavian Seaways Ferries (DFDS, ⊠ Scandinavia House, Parkeston Quay, Harwich, Essex CO12 4QG, England, ☎ 01255/24–02–

40; in Denmark, ☎ 33/11–22–55) sail from Harwich to Esbjerg (20 hours) on Jylland's west coast and from Newcastle to Esbjerg (21 hours). Schedules in both summer and winter are very irregular. There are many discounts, including 20% for senior citizens and the disabled, and 50% for children between the ages of 4 and 16. For car ferry information, *see* By Car, *below.*

By Bus

Not particularly comfortable or fast, bus travel is inexpensive. **Eurolines** (✉ 52 Grosvenor Gardens SWI London, ☎ 0158/240–4511; Copenhagen office, ✉ Reventlowsg. 8, DK–1651, ☎ 33/25–95–11) travels from London's Victoria Station on Saturday at 2:30 PM, crossing the North Sea on the Dover-Calais ferry, and arrives in Copenhagen 22 hours later.

By Car

The only part of Denmark that is connected to the European continent is Jylland, via the E45 highway from Germany. The E20 highway then leads to Middelfart on Fyn and east to Knudshoved. From there a ferry crosses to Korsør on Sjælland and E20 leads east to Copenhagen.

Another option is to take the two-hour car ferry from Århus directly to Kalundborg in western Sjælland. From there, Route 23 leads to Copenhagen. Make reservations for the ferry in advance through the **Scanlines** (☎ 33/15–15–15). (*Note:* During the busy summer months, passengers without reservations for their vehicles can wait hours.)

The **Storebæltsbro Bridge,** connecting Fyn and Sjælland via the E20 highway, has greatly reduced the travel time between the islands. The **Storebæltsbro railway link** has also cut train travel time sharply.

By Plane

Copenhagen Airport, the hub of Scandinavian air travel, is 10 km (6 mi) from the capital's center.

From New York, flights to Copenhagen take 7 hours, 40 minutes. From Chicago they take 8 hours, 15 minutes. From Seattle the flight time is 9 hours, 30 minutes.

Scandinavian Airlines System (SAS, ☎ 800/221–2350), the main carrier, makes nonstop flights from Chicago, Newark, and Seattle. **British Airways** (☎ 800/247–9297) offers connecting flights via London from Atlanta, Boston, Chicago, Dallas, Detroit, Los Angeles, Miami, New York, Orlando, Philadelphia, Pittsburgh, San Francisco, Seattle, and Washington, D.C. **Icelandair** (☎ 800/223–5500) makes connecting flights via Reykjavík from Baltimore, Fort Lauderdale, New York, and Orlando. **Delta** (☎ 800/221–1212) has direct service from Atlanta and New York, connecting to 217 cities in North America.

From London to Copenhagen the flight takes 1 hour, 55 minutes.

British Airways (✉ 156 Regent St., London W1, ☎ 0181/897–4000) flies nonstop from Heathrow, Gatwick, Birmingham, and Manchester. **SAS Scandinavian Airlines** (✉ SAS House, 52–53 Conduit St., London W1R 0AY, ☎ 0171/734–6777) flies nonstop from Heathrow, Manchester, and Glasgow and also from London to Århus. **Aer Lingus** (✉ 67 Deans Gate, Manchester, ☎ 0161/832–5771) flies direct from Dublin. **Mærsk Air** (✉ Terminal House, 52 Grosvenor Gardens, London, SW1, ☎ 0171/333-0066) flies nonstop from Gatwick to Billund and Copenhagen.

By Train

Trains within Europe are well connected to Denmark, with Copenhagen serving as the main hub; however, it's often little cheaper than flying, especially if you make your arrangements from the United States. Scanrail Passes offer discounts on train, ferry, and car transportation in Denmark, Finland, Sweden, and Norway (☞ *below*). EurailPasses, purchased only in the United States, are accepted by the Danish State Railways and on some ferries operated by DSB (☞ *below*).

FROM THE UNITED KINGDOM

From London, the crossing takes 23 hours, including ferry. **British Rail European Travel Center** (⊠ Victoria Station, London, ☎ 0171/834–2345). **Eurotrain** (⊠ 52 Grosvenor Gardens, London SW1, ☎ 0171/730–3402). **Wasteels** (⊠ 121 Wilton Rd., London SW1, ☎ 0171/834–7066).

DISCOUNT PASSES

The **ScanRail** pass, which affords unlimited train travel throughout Denmark, Finland, Norway, and Sweden and restricted ferry passage in and beyond Scandinavia, comes in various denominations: 5 days of travel within 15 days ($222 first class, $176 second class); 10 days within a month ($354 first class, $284 second class); or 1 month ($516 first class, $414 second class). For info on the ScanRail'n Drive Pass, *see* Train Travel *in* the Gold Guide). In the United States, call Rail Europe (☎ 800/848–7245) or **DER** (☎ 800/782–2424). You may want to wait to buy the pass until you get to Scandinavia; unlike the EurailPass, which is cheaper in the United States, the ScanRail Pass is cheaper in Scandinavia. Double-check prices before you leave home. No matter where you get it though, various discounts are offered to holders of the pass by hotel chains and other organizations; ask DER, Rail Europe, or your travel agent for details.

Getting Around

By Bicycle

Biking is a way of life in Denmark, with more people biking to work than driving. Biking vacations in Denmark are popular, as they are easy for all ages due to the flat landscape.

By Boat

Once upon a time, ferries were an indispensable mode of transport in and around the many islands of Denmark. This is changing as more people drive or take trains over new bridges spanning the waters. However, ferries are still a good way to explore Scandinavia, especially of you have a rail pass.

DISCOUNT PASSES

The ScanRail Pass, for travel anywhere within Scandinavia (Denmark, Sweden, Norway, and Finland), and the Interail and EurailPasses are valid on some ferry crossings. Call the **DSB** Travel Office (☎ 33/14–17–01 or 42/52–92–22) for information.

By Bus

Traveling by bus or train is easy because **DSB** (☎ 33/14–17–01 or 42/52–92–22) and a few private companies cover the country with a dense network of services, supplemented by buses in remote areas. Bus tickets are usually sold on buses. Children under five travel free, and those between five and 12 travel for half-price. Ask about discounts for senior citizens and groups of three or more.

By Car

Roads here are good and largely traffic-free (except for the manageable traffic around Copenhagen); you can reach most islands by toll bridges.

EMERGENCY ASSISTANCE

Before leaving home, consult your insurance company. Members of organizations affiliated with Alliance International de Tourisme (AIT) can get technical and legal advice from the **Danish Motoring Organization** (FDM, ✉ Firskovvej 32, 2800 Lyngby, ☎ 45/93–08–00), open 10–4 weekdays. All highways have emergency phones, and you can call the rental company for help. If you cannot drive your car to a garage for repairs, the rescue corps **Falck** (☎ 33/14–22–22) can help anywhere, anytime. In most cases they do charge for assistance.

GASOLINE

Gasoline costs about DKr6 per liter.

PARKING

You can usually park on the right-hand side of the road, though not on main roads and highways. Signs reading PARKERING/STANDSNING FOR-BUNDT mean no parking or stopping, though you are allowed a three-minute grace period for loading and unloading. In town, parking disks are used where there are no automatic ticket-vending machines. Get disks from gas stations, post offices, police stations, or tourist offices, and set them to show your time of arrival. For most downtown parking, you must buy a ticket from an automatic vending machine and display it on the dash. Parking costs about DKr10 or more per hour.

RENTAL AGENCIES

Major international **car rental** agencies are represented throughout Denmark. In Copenhagen, most car-rental agencies are located near the Vesterport Station.

Europcar (✉ Copenhagen Airport, ☎ 32/50–30–90). **Pitzner Auto** (✉ Copenhagen Airport, ☎ 32/50–90–65).

RULES OF THE ROAD

To drive in Denmark you need a valid driver's license, and if you're using your own car, it must have a certificate of registration and national plates. A triangular hazard-warning sign is compulsory in every car and is provided with rentals. No matter where you sit in a car, you must wear a seat belt, and cars must have low beams on at all times. Motorcyclists must wear helmets and use low-beam lights as well.

Drive on the right and give way to traffic—*especially to bicyclists*—on the right. A red-and-white YIELD sign or a line of white triangles across the road means you must yield to traffic on the road you are entering. Do not turn right on red unless there is a green arrow indicating that this is allowed. Speed limits are 50 kph (30 mph) in built-up areas; 100 kph (60 mph) on highways; and 80 kph (50 mph) on other roads. If you are towing a trailer, you must not exceed 70 kph (40 mph). Speeding and, especially, drinking and driving are treated severely, even if no damage is caused. Americans and other foreign tourists must pay fines on the spot.

By Plane

Copenhagen Airport is the hub of all domestic routes. Most other airports are located in areas that serve several cities. Flight times within the country are all less than one hour. Denmark's major carriers are **SAS** (☎ 32/32–68–68), **Danair** (☎ 31/51–50–55), and **Mærsk Air** (☎ 32/45–35–35).

DISCOUNT PASSES

Intra-Scandinavian travel is usually expensive. If you want to economize, look into the **Visit Scandinavia Fare.** One coupon costs about $85; six are about $510, for unlimited air travel in Denmark, Sweden, Norway, and also between Sweden and Finland. It is sold only in the

United States and only to non-Scandinavians. Coupons can be used year-round for a maximum of three months and must be purchased in conjunction with transatlantic flights.

By Train

DSB and a few private companies cover the country with a dense network of services, supplemented by buses in remote areas. Hourly intercity trains connect the main towns in Jylland and Fyn with Copenhagen and Sjælland, using high-speed diesels, called IC-3, on the most important stretches. All these trains make one-hour ferry crossings of the Great Belt. You can reserve seats on intercity trains, and you *must* have a reservation if you plan to cross the Great Belt. Buy tickets at stations.

DISCOUNT PASSES

The ScanRail Pass and the Interail and Eurailpasses are also valid on all DSB trains. Call the **DSB** Travel Office (☎ 33/14–17–01 or 42/52–92–22) for additional information.

Contacts and Resources

Customs

If you are 21 or older, have purchased goods in a country that is a member of the European Union (EU), and pay that country's value-added tax (V.A.T.) on those goods, you may import duty-free 1½ liters of liquor; 300 cigarettes or 150 cigarillos or 75 cigars or 400 grams of tobacco. If you are entering Denmark from a non-EU country or if you have purchased your goods on a ferryboat or in an airport not taxed in the EU, you must pay Danish taxes on any amount of alcoholic beverages greater than 1 liter of liquor or 2 liters of strong wine, plus 2 liters of table wine. For tobacco, the limit is 200 cigarettes or 100 cigarillos or 50 cigars or 250 grams of tobacco. You are also allowed 50 grams of perfume. Other articles (including beer) are allowed up to a maximum of DKr1,350.

Embassies

U.S. (⊠ Dag Hammarskjölds Allé 24, DK-2100 Copenhagen Ø, ☎ 35/55–31–44). **Canada** (⊠ Kristen Bernikowsg. 1, DK-1105 Copenhagen K, ☎ 33/12–22–99. **U.K.** (⊠ Kastesvej 36–40, DK-2100 Copenhagen Ø, ☎ 35/26–46–00).

Emergencies

The general emergency number throughout Denmark is ☎ 112.

Guided Tours

Call the Danish Tourist Board, as well as **Copenhagen Excursions** (☎ 31/54–06–06). ☞ Outdoor Activities and Sports, *below.*

Language

Most Danes, except those in rural areas, speak English well. Bring a phrase book if you plan to visit the countryside or the small islands.

Lodging

CAMPING

If you plan to camp in one of the 500-plus approved campsites, you'll need an International Camping Carnet or Danish Camping Pass (available at any campsite and valid for one year). Call **Campingrådet** (⊠ Hessegløg. 16, DK-2100 Copenhagen Ø, ☎ 39/27–88–44) for info.

FARM VACATIONS

There's a minimum stay of three nights for most farm stays. Bed-and-breakfast costs DKr150; half-board, around DKr245. Lunch and dinner can often be purchased for DKr25 to DKr35, and full board can be arranged. Contact **Ferie på Landet** (Holiday in the Country, ✉ Ceresvej 2, DK 8410 Rønde, Jylland, ☎ 70/10–41–90) for details.

HOTELS

Make your reservations well in advance, especially in resort areas near the coasts. Many places offer summer reductions to compensate for the slowdown in business travel and conferences.

Many Danes prefer a shower to a bath, so if you particularly want a bath, ask for it, but be prepared to pay more. Taxes are usually included in prices, but check when making a reservation. As time goes on, it appears that an increasing number of hotels are eliminating breakfast from their room rates; even if it is not included, breakfast is usually well worth its price.

The very friendly staff at the **hotel booking desk** (☎ 33/12–28–80) in the main tourist office (✉ Bernstorffsg. 1, DK–1577 Copenhagen V, ☎ 33/11–13–25) can help find rooms in hotels, hostels, and private homes, or even at campsites. Prices range from budget upward. Prebooking in private homes and hotels must be done two months in advance, but last-minute (as in same-day) hotel rooms can also be found and will save you 50% off the normal price.

INNS

Contact **Dansk Kroferie** (✉ Vejlevej 16, DK–8700 Horsens, ☎ 75/64–87–00) to order a free catalog of B&B inns, but choose carefully: the organization includes some chain hotels that would be hard-pressed to demonstrate a modicum of inn-related charm. The price of an inn covers one overnight stay in a room with bath, breakfast included. Note that some establishments tack an additional DKr125 surcharge onto the price of a double. You can save money by investing in **Inn Checks,** valid at 84 inns. Each check costs DKr585 per couple. **Family checks** (DKr665–DKr745) are also available.

RENTALS

A simple house with room for four will cost from DKr2,500 per week and up. Contact **DanCenter** (✉ Falkoner Allé 7, DK–2000 Frederiksberg, ☎ 31/19–09–00).

YOUTH AND FAMILY HOSTELS

If you have a Hosteling International–American Youth Hostels card (obtainable before you leave home, ☎ 202/783–6161 in Washington, D.C.), the average cost is DKr70 to DKr85 per person. Without the card, there's a surcharge of DKr25. The hostels fill up quickly in summer, so make your reservations early. Most hostels are particularly sympathetic to students and will usually find them at least a place on the floor. Bring your own linens or sleep sheet, though these can usually be rented at the hostel. Sleeping bags are not allowed. Contact **Danhostel Danmarks Vandrehjem** (✉ Vesterbrog. 39, DK–1620, Copenhagen V, ☎ 31/31–36–12, FAX 31/31–36–26). It charges for information, but you can get a free brochure, *Camping/Youth and Family Hostels,* from the Danish Tourist Board.

Mail

POSTAL RATES

Airmail letters and postcards to the United States cost DKr5.25 for 20 grams. Letters and postcards to the United Kingdom and EU countries cost DKr4. You can buy stamps at post offices or from shops selling postcards.

RECEIVING MAIL

You can arrange to have your mail sent general delivery, marked *poste restante,* to any post office, hotel, or inn. The address for the main post office in Copenhagen is Tietgensgade 37, DK–1704 KBH. If you do not have an address, **American Express** (✉ Amagertorv 18, DK–1461 KBH K, ☎ 33/12–23–01) will also receive and hold cardholders' mail.

Money and Expenses

CREDIT CARDS

Most major credit cards are accepted in Denmark, American Express less frequently than others. Traveler's checks can be exchanged in banks and at many hotels, restaurants, and shops.

CURRENCY

The monetary unit in Denmark is the krone (DKr), divided into 100 øre. At press time (summer 1997), the krone stood at 6.5 to the dollar, 10.5 to the pound sterling, and 4.65 to the Canadian dollar. New 50, 100, 200, 500 and 1,000 kroner notes, featuring Great Danes like authoress Karen Blixen and physicist Niels Bohr, are to be issued in the years up to the millennium, as the old notes are phased out.

SALES-TAX REFUNDS

All hotel, restaurant, and departure taxes and V.A.T. (what the Danes call *moms*) are automatically included in prices. V.A.T. is 25%; non-EU citizens can obtain an 18% refund. The more than 1,500 shops that participate in the tax-free scheme have a white TAX FREE sticker on their windows. Purchases must be at least DKr300 per store and must be sealed and unused in Denmark. At the shop, you'll be asked to fill out a form and show your passport. The form can then be turned in at any airport or ferry customs desk, where you can choose cash or charge-card credit. Keep all your receipts and tags; occasionally, customs authorities do ask to see purchases, so pack them where they will be accessible.

SAMPLE PRICES

Denmark's economy is stable, and inflation remains reasonably low. Although lower than Norway's and Sweden's, the Danish cost of living is nonetheless high, especially for cigarettes and alcohol. Prices are highest in Copenhagen, lower elsewhere in the country. Some sample prices: cup of coffee, DKr14–DKr20; bottle of beer, DKr15–DKr30; soda, DKr10–DKr15; ham sandwich, DKr25–DKr40; 1-mi taxi ride, DKr35–DKr50, depending on traffic.

TIPPING

The egalitarian Danes do not expect to be tipped. Service is included in bills for hotels, bars, and restaurants. Taxi drivers round up the fare to the next krone but expect no tip. The exception is hotel porters, who receive about DKr5 per bag.

Opening and Closing Times

BANKS

Banks in Copenhagen are open weekdays 9:30 to 4 and Thursdays until 6. Several *bureaux de change,* including the ones at Copenhagen's central station and airport, stay open until 10 PM. Outside Copenhagen, banking hours vary.

MUSEUMS

A number of Copenhagen's museums hold confounding hours, so always call first to confirm. As a rule, however, most museums are open 10 to 3 or 11 to 4 and are closed on Monday. In winter, opening hours are shorter, and some museums close for the season. Check the local papers or ask at tourist offices for current schedules.

SHOPS

Though many Danish stores are expanding their hours, sometimes even staying open on Sundays, most shops still keep the traditional hours:

weekdays 10 to 5:30, until 7 on Thursday and Friday, until 1 or 2 on Saturday—though the larger department stores stay open until 5. Everything except bakeries, kiosks, flower shops, and a handful of grocers are closed on Sunday, and most bakeries take Monday off. The first and last Saturday of the month are Long Saturdays, when even the smaller shops, especially in large cities, stay open until 4 or 5. Grocery stores stay open until 8 PM on weekdays, and kiosks until much later.

Outdoor Activities and Sports

BIKING

Bicycles can be sent as baggage between most train stations and can also be carried onto most trains and ferries; contact **DSB** (☎ 33/14–17–01) for information. All cabs must be able to take bikes and are equipped with racks (they add a modest fee).

Most towns have rentals, but check with local tourism offices for referrals. For more information, contact the **Danish Cyclist Federation** (✉ Rømersg. 7, DK–1362 KBH K, ☎ 33/32–31–21). The Danish Tourist Board also publishes bicycle maps and brochures.

Copenhagen-based **BikeDenmark** (✉ Åboulevarden 1, ☎ 35/36–41–00) combines the flexibility of individual tours with the security of an organized outing. Choose from seven preplanned 5- to 10-day tours, which include bikes, maps, two fine meals per day, hotel accommodations, and hotel-to-hotel baggage transfers.

Many United States tour companies can arrange booking. **Borton Oversees** (✉ 5516 Lyndale Ave. S, Minneapolis, MN 55419, ☎ 800/843–0602). **Nordique Tours** (✉ 5250 W. Century Blvd., Suite 626, Los Angeles, CA 90045, ☎ 800/995–7997). **Scanam World Tours** (✉ 933 Rte. 23, Pompton Plains, NJ 07444, ☎ 800/545–2204). **Gerhard's Bicycle Odysseys** (✉ Box 757, Portland Oregon, 97207, ☎ 503/223-2402).

FISHING AND ANGLING

Licenses are required for fishing along the coasts; requirements vary from one area to another for fishing in lakes, streams, and the ocean. Licenses generally cost around DKr100 and can be purchased from any post office. Remember—it is illegal to fish within 1,650 ft of the mouth of a stream.

Telephones

Telephone exchanges throughout Denmark were changed over the past couple of years. If you hear a recorded message or three loud beeps, chances are the number you are trying to reach has been changed. **KTAS** information (☎ 118) can always find current numbers.

COUNTRY CODE

The country code for Denmark is 45.

DIRECTORY ASSISTANCE AND OPERATOR INFORMATION

Most operators speak English. For national directory assistance, dial ☎ 118; for an international operator, dial ☎ 113; for a directory-assisted international call, dial ☎ 115.

INTERNATIONAL CALLS

Dial ☎ 00, then the country code (1 for the United States and Canada, 44 for Great Britain), the area code, and the number. It's very expensive to telephone or fax from hotels, although the regional phone companies offer a discount after 7:30 PM. It's more economical to make calls from either the Copenhagen main rail station or the airports.

You can reach U.S. operators by dialing local access codes: **AT&T USA Direct** (☎ 800/10010), **MCI Call USA** (☎ 800/10022), **Sprint Express** (☎ 800/10877).

Phones accept 1-, 5-, 10-, and 20-kroner coins. Pick up the receiver, dial the number, always including the area code, and wait until the party answers; then deposit the coins. You have roughly a minute per krone, so you can make another call on the same payment if your time has not run out. When it does, you will hear a beep and your call will be disconnected unless you deposit another coin. Dial the eight-digit number for calls anywhere within the country. For calls to the Faroe Islands (☎ 298) and Greenland (☎ 299), dial ☎ 00, then the three-digit code, then the five-digit number.

Visitor Information

Danish Tourist Board (✉ 655 3rd Ave., New York, NY 10017, ☎ 212/ 949–2333; ✉ 55 Sloane St., London SW1 X9SY, ☎ 0171/259–5959).

Danmarks Turistråd (✉ Danish Tourist Board, Bernstorffsg. 1, DK– 1577 Copenhagen V, ☎ 33/11–13–25).

3 Finland

*Nature dictates life in this Nordic land,
where winter brings perpetual
darkness, and summer, perpetual light.
Gin-clear streams run through vast
forests lit by the midnight sun, and
reindeer roam free. Even the arts mimic
nature: Witness the soaring monuments
of Alvar Aalto, evocative of Finland's
expansive forests—and the music of
Jean Sibelius, which can swing from a
somber nocturne to a joyful crescendo,
like a streak of sunlight in the woods.*

Updated by
Tim Bird

IF YOU LIKE MAJESTIC OPEN SPACES, combined with civilized living, Finland is for you. The music of Jean Sibelius, Finland's most famous son, tells you what to expect from this Nordic landscape. Both can swing from the somber andante of midwinter darkness to the tremolo of sunlight slanting through pine and birch, or from the crescendo of a blazing sunset to the pianissimo of the next day's dawn. The architecture of Alvar Aalto and the Saarinens, Eliel and son Eero, visible in many U.S. cities, also bespeaks the Finnish affinity with nature, with soaring spaces evocative of Finland's moss-floored forests. Eliel and his family moved to the United States in 1923 and became American citizens—but it was to a lonely Finnish seashore that Saarinen had his ashes returned.

Until 1917, Finland was under the domination of its nearest neighbors, Sweden and Russia, who fought over it for centuries. After more than 600 years under the Swedish crown and 100 under the Russian czars, the country inevitably bears many traces of the two cultures, including a small (6%) but influential Swedish-speaking population and a scattering of Russian Orthodox churches.

But the Finns themselves are neither Scandinavian nor Slavic. They are descended from wandering tribes who probably came from west of Russia's Ural Mountains and settled on the swampy shores of the Gulf of Finland before the Christian era. The Finnish tongue belongs to the Finno-Ugric language group; it is related to Estonian and, very distantly, Hungarian.

There is a tough, resilient quality to the Finn. Finland is one of the very few countries that shared a border with the Soviet Union in 1939 and retained their independence. Indeed, no country has fought the Soviets to a standstill as the Finns did in the grueling 105-day Winter War of 1939–40. This resilience stems from the turbulence of the country's past and from the people's determination to work the land and survive the long, brutal winters. The Finn lives in a constant state of confrontation—against the weather and the land. Finns are stubborn, patriotic, and self-sufficient, yet not aggressively nationalistic. On the contrary, rather than boasting of past battles, Finns are proud of finding ways to live in peace with their neighbors. They are trying to cling to their country's independence and their personal freedom even as they make a cautious but active start to their membership in the European Union (EU), which they joined in January of 1995. Finland has one of the highest per-capita Internet connection rates in the world, and technology there is surprisingly advanced for such a small country. Nokia Telecommunications is the most conspicuous commercial manifestation of this; the company's mobile telephones are becoming almost as common in Finland as wristwatches.

The average Finn volunteers little information, but that's a result of reserve, not indifference. Make the first approach and you may have a friend for life. Finns like their silent spaces, though, and won't appreciate backslapping familiarity—least of all in the sauna, still regarded by many as a spiritual as well as a cleansing experience.

Pleasures and Pastimes

Boating

Finns love all kinds of boating, and there are good facilities for guests' boats in most ports. Southwest Finland is a sailor's paradise, and the town marinas will welcome you and provide a full range of services.

Finland

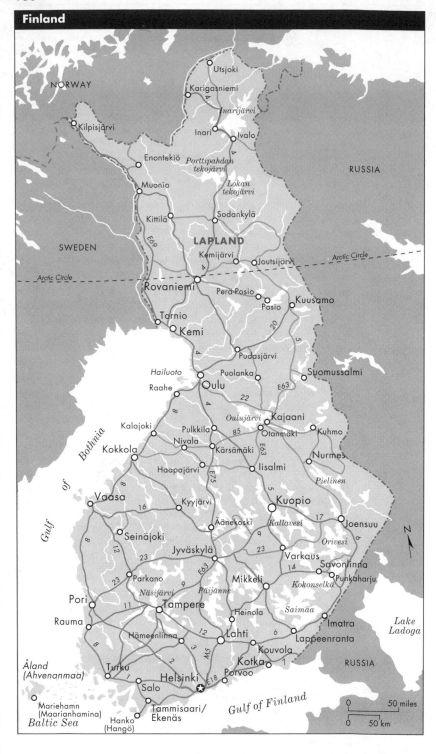

Hanko, the southernmost town in Finland, has the country's largest marina.

Cafés

That more coffee is consumed per capita in Finland than in any other country is evidenced by the staggering number of cafés throughout the country. Particularly in Helsinki, patrons of cafés downtown and around the waterfront spill outside onto the streets. In addition to coffee, Finnish cafés serve a variety of baked goods: *munkki* (doughnuts), *pulla* (sweet bread), and other confections are consumed with vigor by both young and old.

Dining

Finnish food accents freshness rather than variety, although recent years have seen more and more innovation with restaurant cuisine. Ironically, the hardest meal to find is the authentic Finnish meal—pulled from forest, lake, and sea. It is far easier to find pizza, upon which Finns pile many toppings.

However, search and you will find stunning game—pheasant, reindeer, hare, and grouse—accompanied by wild-berry compotes and exotic mushroom sauces. The chanterelle grows wild in Finland, as do dozens of other edible mushrooms, the tasty morel among them. Fish wears many hats in Finland, and is especially savored smoked. Come July 21, crayfish season kicks in.

Other specialties are *poronkäristys* (reindeer casserole), *lihapullat* (meatballs in sauce), *uunijuusto* (light, crispy baked cheese), and *hiilillä paistetut silakat* (charcoal-grilled Baltic herring). *Voileipäpöytä*, the Finnish cousin to *smörgåsbord*, is a cold table served at breakfast or lunch.

Local yogurt and dairy products are extremely good, and the Finns' baked goods are renowned. *Mämmi*, a dessert made of wheat flour, malt, and orange zest and served with cream and sugar, is a treat during Easter. More filling are *karjalan piirakka*, thin, oval wheat-bread pirogi filled with rice or mashed potatoes and served warm with a mixture of egg and butter.

Prices of alcohol in Finland are steep, but beer-lovers should not miss the well-made Finnish brews. Jacket and tie are required in most of the restaurants in the $$$$ category.

CATEGORY	HELSINKI*	OTHER AREAS*
$$$$	over FM 200	over FM 170
$$$	FM 150–FM 200	FM 140–FM 170
$$	FM 80–FM 150	FM 80–FM 140
$	under FM 80	under FM 80

Prices are per person for a three-course meal including tax and service charge, excluding wine.

Fishing

The fish-rich waters of the Baltic archipelago and innumerable inland lakes and streams assure you will never run out of fishing opportunities. The waters of the Ålands are especially rich with pike, whitefish, salmon, and perch, and ice fishing makes this a year-round sport.

Lodging

Every class of lodging exists in Finland, from five-star urban hotels to rustic cabins on lake shores and in the forest. Cleanliness and modern comforts are standard. Expect private baths in rooms unless otherwise noted.

The price categories below are based on weekday rates. Greater discounts are available on weekends and in summer months, especially between midsummer and July 31, when prices are usually 30% to 50% lower.

CATEGORY	HELSINKI*	OTHER AREAS*
$$$$	over FM 900	over FM 700
$$$	FM 600–FM 900	FM 550–FM 700
$$	FM 400–FM 600	FM 400–FM 550
$	under FM 400	under FM 400

All prices are for a standard double room, including service charge and taxes. Prices almost always include a generous breakfast

Saunas

An authentic Finnish sauna is an obligatory experience, and not hard to find: there are 1.4 million saunas in this country of 5 million people. The traditional Finnish sauna—which involves relaxing on wooden benches, occasionally pouring water onto hot coals and swatting your neighbor's back with birch branches—is an integral part of cabin life. In the cities, almost every hotel has at least one sauna. Public swimming pools are also equipped with saunas that can be used at no extra charge. For information, call the Finnish Sauna Society (☎ 09/678–677).

Shopping

Like some of its Nordic counterparts, Finland is known for its design. Helsinki has the widest selection of goods—from Arabia ceramics to Iittala glass to Marimekko clothing and textiles—and the highest prices. Furs, called *turkki* in Finnish, are a good buy. You might also want to take home some of the delicious smoked or marinated fish—available vacuum-packed at Helsinki Airport.

Wilderness Expeditions

Opportunities to explore the forests and moors, rapids and waterfalls, mountains and gorges of Lapland abound. Intrepid explorers can probe the deepest areas of the national forests on skis or by snowmobile, take a photo safari to capture the unrivaled landscape, canoe down the clear rivers filled with salmon and trout, forage for mushrooms in the forest, or pick cloudberries and lingonberries in the bogs.

Exploring Finland

Finland's capital, Helsinki, commands the southern coast and shelters more than one-tenth of the country's population. Towns were first settled in the southwest, where the culture of the South Coast and the Åland Islands has a decidedly Swedish influence. Northern Finland—Finnish Lapland—straddles the Arctic Circle and is populated by few. Finland's central region is dominated by the Lakelands, the country's vacation belt.

Numbers in the text correspond to numbers in the margin and on the maps.

Great Itineraries

Keep in mind that Finland is a large country, and though train service between towns is quite good, some trips can take an entire day. To make the most of your time, take advantage of Finnair's efficient domestic air service between Helsinki and destinations farther afield, such as Savonlinna and Rovaniemi.

IF YOU HAVE 2 DAYS

You'll have plenty of time to take in all the sites of 🏛 **Helsinki** ①–㊲, but not enough to venture outside the capital city area. Since Helsinki is fairly small and its major attractions are within walking distance of one another, in one day you can see the architectural highlights and at least one important museums. On the second day, you might take a harbor tour and visit the island fortress **Suomenlinna** ㉗, or take a side trip to **Espoo, Porvoo,** or **Vantaa,** or to the **Gallen-Kallela Estate** in Tarvaspää. The museum in the former studio home of the architects Saarinen, Gesellius, and Lindgren at **Hvitträsk** is another must.

IF YOU HAVE 5 DAYS

After spending one or two nights in 🏨 **Helsinki** ①–㊲, head to the destination of your choice: 🏨 **Lapland,** the 🏨 **Southwestern Coast and the Åland Islands,** or the 🏨 **Lakelands.** Another option is to spend four nights in Helsinki, venturing out for easy, fun day trips to nearby towns: the cultural center **Turku** ㊶; **Tampere** ㊽, with its amusement park; and the castle town **Hämeenlinna** ㊾ are all less than two hours away by train.

IF YOU HAVE 10 DAYS

Ten days allows the tireless traveler time to explore much of Finland. If your goal is to see all of the regions, one option is to spend your first night in 🏨 **Helsinki** ①–㊲, then take a train to 🏨 **Turku** ㊶, on the southwest coast, the following day. Using Turku as a base, take a side trip to see the fancy homes and beaches of **Hanko** ㊵, the historic wooden town of **Rauma** ㊷, or the medieval pilgrimage village, **Naantali** ㊸. From Turku you can fly to 🏨 **Rovaniemi** ㊿, the gateway to Finnish Lapland. From Rovaniemi, go as deep into the Lapland wilderness as you desire. Take a train or a plane back down south to 🏨 **Savonlinna** ㊺ in eastern Finland, home of Finland's greatest castle. Take a scenic boat ride through the heart of Finland from Savonlinna to 🏨 **Kuopio** ㊼, site of the Ortodoksinen Kirkkomuseo and within reach of the New Valamon Luostari. From Kuopio, you can fly back to Helsinki.

When to Tour Finland

Finland's tourist season commences in June, when the growing daylight hours herald the opening of summer restaurants and outdoor museums, and the start of boat tours and cruises. Summer is by far the best time to visit Helsinki, the Lakelands, and the Southwestern Coast and Ålands, which come out of hibernation to enjoy the long, bright, but not overly hot, summer days. A special draw in the Lakelands is the Savonlinna Opera Festival, held in late July or early August.

Finland can also be exhilarating on clear, brisk winter days. For a real treat, visit Lapland—home of Santa Claus—in December. Operating on a different schedule altogether, the tourist season in the north focuses on winter events, when the snow is deep and the Northern Lights bright. Summer weather in Lapland offers a different repertoire to the traveler, when the snow and ice of the north give way to flowing rivers and greenery.

HELSINKI

A city of the sea, Helsinki was built along a series of odd-shape peninsulas and islands jutting into the Baltic coast along the Gulf of Finland. Streets and avenues curve around bays, bridges reach to nearby islands, and ferries ply among offshore islands.

Having grown dramatically since World War II, Helsinki now absorbs about one-sixth of total Finns and covers a total of 1122 square km (433 square mi) and 315 islands. Most sites, hotels, and restaurants cluster on one peninsula, forming a compact central hub. The greater Helsinki metropolitan area, which includes the suburbs of Espoo and

Vantaa, each with city status, has a total population not far short of a million.

Helsinki is a relatively young city compared with other European capitals. In the 16th century, King Gustav Vasa of Sweden decided to woo trade from the Estonian city of Tallinn and thus challenge the Hanseatic League's monopoly on Baltic trade. Accordingly, he commanded the people of four Finnish towns to pack up their belongings and relocate at the rapids on the River Vantaa. The new town, founded on June 12, 1550, was named Helsinki.

For three centuries, Helsinki (Helsingfors in Swedish) had its ups and downs as a trading town. Turku, to the west, remained Finland's capital and intellectual center. Ironically, Helsinki's fortunes improved when Finland fell under Russian rule as an autonomous grand duchy. Czar Alexander I wanted Finland's political center closer to Russia and, in 1812, selected Helsinki as the new capital. Shortly afterward, Turku suffered a disastrous fire, forcing the university to move to Helsinki. Helsinki's future was secure.

Just before the czar's proclamation, a fire destroyed many of Helsinki's traditional wooden structures, precipitating the construction of new buildings suitable for a nation's capital. The German-born architect Carl Ludvig Engel was commissioned to rebuild the city, and as a result, Helsinki has some of the purest neoclassical architecture in the world. Add to this foundation the influence of Stockholm and St. Petersburg with the local inspiration of 20th-century Finnish design, and the result is a European capital city that is as architecturally eye-catching as it is distinct from other Scandinavian capitals. The attentive observer is bound to discover endless delightful details—a grimacing gargoyle; a foursome of males supporting the weight of a balcony on their shoulders; a building painted in striking colors, with contrasting flowers in the windows.

Exploring Helsinki

The city center is densely packed and easily explored on foot, the main tourist sites grouped in several clusters; nearby islands are easily accessible by ferry. Just west of Katajanokka, Senaatintori and its Tuomiokirkko mark the beginning of the city center, which extends westward along Aleksanterinkatu.

Museums and Markets

The orange tents of the Kauppatori market brighten even the coldest snowy winter months with fresh flowers, fish, crafts, and produce. In warm weather, the bazaar fills with shoppers and browsers who stop for the ubiquitous coffee and munkki, the seaborne traffic in Eteläsatama, or South Harbor, a backdrop. From here you can take the local ferry service to Korkeasaari Island, home of the zoo, or take a walk through the neighborhoods of Helsinki, encompassing the harbor, city center shopping district, tree-lined Bulevardi, and the indoor Hietalahden Tori, another marketplace.

A GOOD WALK

Begin your walk at the indoor redbrick market hall, **Vanha Kauppahalli** ①, along the South Harbor. From here you can see the orange tents of the outdoor market, the **Kauppatori** ②. If you are with kids and want to take a jaunt, Helsinki's zoo, **Korkeasaari Elaintarha** ③, is accessible by metro or daily ferry from the South Harbor, just east of the market.

Helsinki's oldest public monument, the **Obeliski Keisarinnan kivi,** stands in Kauppatori along Pohjoisesplanadi. The series of beautiful old buildings along Pohjoisesplanadi includes the pale-blue **Kaupung-intalo** ④ and, at the easternmost end of the street, the well-guarded **Presidentinlinna** ⑤. Walk back west along Pohjoisesplanadi and cross the street to the square with the **Havis Amanda** ⑥ statue and fountain. You can stop at the City Tourist Office at Pohjoisesplanadi 19. The Esplanadi is the sprawling area to your left.

A few yards west of the City Tourist Office, you'll see the Art Nouveau **Jugendsali** ⑦. After walking past the Arabian ceramics and the Marimekko clothing stores, you'll see the elephantine Gröngvistin Talo, or Grönqvist's block, on your left across the park: designed by architect Theodor Höijer and built in 1903, this was Scandinavia's largest apartment building in its day. On your right as you pass an ornate block under restoration is the site of the luxurious Kämp Hotel, renowned in Scandinavia at the end of the last century; it's due to reopen in 1998. Before hitting Mannerheimintie, you'll pass Akateeminen Kirjakauppa and Stockmann's, respectively Finland's largest bookstore and department store (☞ Shopping, *below*). The bookstore was designed by Alvar Aalto, Finland's most famous architect.

At the intersection of Pohjoisesplanadi and Mannerheimintie, the distinctive round **Svenska Teatern** ⑧ is sure to catch your eye. Turn left on Mannerheimintie, cross the street, and take a right onto broad, tree-shaded Bulevardi, passing Vanha Kirkkopuisto, or Old Church Park, usually called Ruttopuisto, or Plague Park, for the 18th-century plague victims buried there. Continue southwest on Bulevardi until you reach the **Sinebrychoffin Taidemuseo** ⑨, a former mansion surrounded by a beautiful park. The **Hietalahden Tori** ⑩ is just across the street and slightly southeast of the museum, with an indoor food market and a flea market outside.

TIMING
It will take about 45 minutes to walk this route from Kauppatori to Hietalahden Tori, stops not included. Head out early if you want to see both markets in action, as they close around 2 PM. In summer, the Kauppatori by the South Harbor, reopens at 3:30 PM, when the fruit and berry vendors do a brisk trade and local crafts stalls set up shop. Note that the Sinebrychoffin Taidemuseo is closed on Tuesday. For a side trip to the zoo, the ferry to Korkeasaari Island takes less than a half hour, but allow time to wait for the ferry coming and going.

SIGHTS TO SEE

❻ **Havis Amanda.** This fountain's brass centerpiece, a young woman perched on rocks surrounded by dolphins, was commissioned by the city fathers to embody Helsinki. Sculptor Ville Vallgren completed her in 1908 using a Parisian girl as his model. Partying university students annually crown the Havis Amanda with their white caps on the eve of Vappu, the May 1 holiday. ⊠ *Eteläespl. and Eteläranta.*

❿ **Hietalahden Tori** (Hietalahti Market). The brick market hall is crammed with vendors selling fish, flowers, produce, and meat. A simultaneous outdoor flea market has tables piled with the detritus of countless Helsinki attics and cellars. Shoppers can stop amid the action for coffee, doughnuts, and meat pies. This market is especially popular with Helsinki's Russian community. ⊠ *Bulevardi and Hietalahdenk.* ☉ *Mon.–Sat. 7–2; mid-May–Aug., also weekdays 3–8.*

❼ **Jugendsali.** Originally designed as a bank in 1906, this now serves as a cultural information office and a temporary exhibition hall for Finnish photography. ⊠ *Pohjoisespl. 19,* ☎ *09/169–2277.* ☉ *Weekdays 9–6, Sun. noon–4.*

136

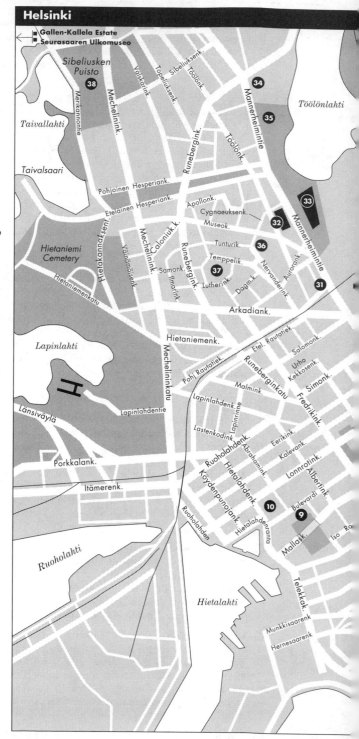

Helsinki

Gallen-Kallela Estate
Seurasaaren Ulkomuseo

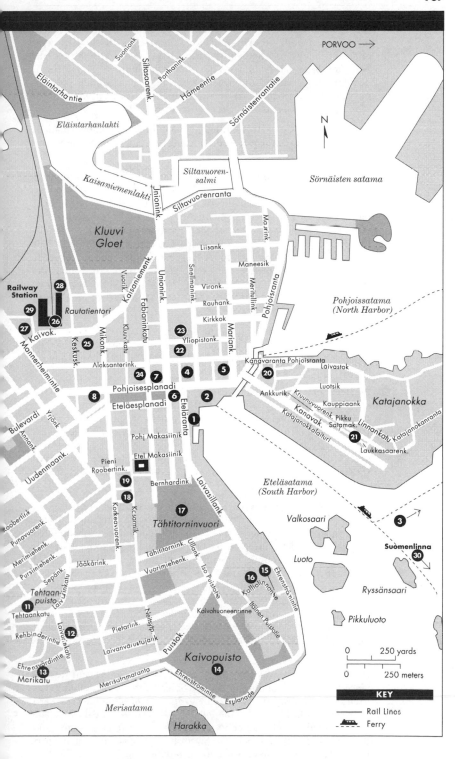

PORVOO →

Eläintarhantie

Eläintarhanlahti

Suomonk.

Siltasaarenk.

Porthanink.

Hämeentie

Sörnäistenrantatie

Kaisaniemenlahti

Siltavuoren-
salmi

Siltavuorenranta

Sörnäisten satama

Jnionink.

N

*Kluuvi
Gloet*

Liisank.

Mariink.

Maneesik.

Snellmanink.

Vironk.

Rauhank.

Meritullink.

Pohjoisranta

*Pohjoissatama
(North Harbor)*

Railway
Station

28

29

26

27

Kaivok.

Rautatientori

Keskusk.

Kaisaniemenk.

Vuorik.

Fabianinkatu

Unionink.

Kluuv'katu

Mikonk.

Kirkkok.

Yliopistonk.

Mariank.

23

25

22

Aleksanterink.

24

7

Pohjoisesplanadi

8

Eteläesplanadi

6

Eteläranta

4

5

1

2

Kanavaranta Pohjoisranta

20

Ankkurik.

Kruunuvuorenk.

Kauppiaank.

Kanavak.

Katajanokkalaituri

Pikku
Satamak.

Laivastok.

Luotsik.

Linnankatu

Katajanokanranta

Katajanokka

21

Laukkasaarenk.

Mannerheimintie

Bulevardi

Vironk.

Annank.

Uudenmaank.

Roobertink.

Pieni
Roobertink.

Etel Makasiinik

Bernhardink.

Pohj Makasiinik

19

18

Korkeavuorenk.

17

Tähtitorninvuori

Laivasillank.

*Eteläsatama
(South Harbor)*

Valkosaari

3

Punavuorenk.

Merimiehenk.

Pursimiehenk.

Sepänk.

Jääkärink.

Tähtitornink.

Ullank.

Vuorimiehenk.

Iso Puistotie

16

15

Kalliolinnantie

Ehrenströmintie

Luoto

Suomenlinna

30

Ryssänsaari

Tehtaan-
puisto

11

Tehtaankatu

Laivurinkatu

Pietarink.

Neitsytp.

Iloinen Puistotie

Kaivohuoneenrinne

Pikkuluoto

Rehbinderintie

12

Laivurinkatu

Laivanvarustujank.

Puistok.

Kaivopuisto

0   250 yards

Ehrensvärdintie

13

Merikatu

Merisatamaranta

Ehrenströmintie

Esplanade

14

0   250 meters

Merisatama

Harakka

KEY

— Rail Lines

🚂 Ferry

➋ **Kauppatori** (Market Square). At this Helsinki institution open year-round, wooden stands with orange and gold awnings bustle in the mornings when everyone—tourists and locals alike—comes to shop, browse, or sit and enjoy coffee and conversation. You can buy a freshly caught perch for the evening's dinner, a bouquet of bright flowers for a friend, or a fur pelt or hat. In summer the fruit and vegetable stalls are supplemented by an evening arts-and-crafts market. ⊠ *Eteläranta and Pohjoisespl.* ⊙ *Mon.–Sat. 7–2 (June–Aug. also 3:30–8).*

➍ **Kaupungintalo** (City Hall). The light blue building on Pohjoisesplanadi (North Esplanade), the political center of Finland, is the home of city government offices. ⊠ *Pohjoisespl. 1,* ☎ *09/169–3757.*

🐣 ➌ **Korkeasaari Elaintarha** (Helsinki Zoo). Snow leopards and reindeer enjoy the cold climate at one of the world's most northern zoos. The zoo is entirely within the limits of this small island, but the winding paths make the zoo seem much larger than it actually is. Kids love the outdoor play equipment. The ferry departs approximately every 30 minutes from Eteläsatama (South Harbor). The trip takes less than a half hour; arrival and departure times are posted at the harbor. Alternatively, you can take the metro to the Kulosaari stop, cross under the tracks, and follow the signs 20 minutes to the zoo. ⊠ *Korkeasaari island,* ☎ *09/19981.* 🎫 *FM 20.* ⊙ *Mar.–Apr., daily 10–6; May–Sept., daily 10–8; Oct.–Feb., daily 10–4.*

Obeliski Keisarinnan kivi (Czarina's Stone). This obelisk with a double-headed golden eagle, the symbol of Imperial Russia, was erected in 1835, toppled during the Russian Revolution in 1917, and fully restored in 1972. ⊠ *Kauppatori along Pohjoisespl.*

➎ **Presidentinlinna** (President's Palace). The long history of this edifice mirrors the history of Finland itself: originally built as a private residence for a German businessman, it was redesigned in 1843 as a palace for the czars; then it served as the official residence of Finland's presidents from 1919 to 1993. Today it houses President Martti Ahtisaari's offices and is the venue for official receptions. The best part of the house is said to be its hall of mirrors, but the uniformed guards won't let you in. ⊠ *Pohjoisespl. 1,* ☎ *09/641–200.*

➒ **Sinebrychoffin Taidemuseo** (Sinebrychoff Museum of Foreign Art). The wealthy Russian Sinebrychoffs owned a brewing company and lived in this splendid yellow-and-white 1840 neo-Renaissance mansion filled with wildly opulent furniture. The family's home and foreign art collection are now a public museum; you'll find a staid collection of Dutch and Swedish 17th- and 18th-century portraits, a lively collection of landscapes, miniatures, and porcelain, and the mansion's original decorative furniture. In summer, outdoor concerts are occasionally held in the once-private **Sinebrychoffin Park.** ⊠ *Bulevardi 40,* ☎ *09/1733–6360.* 🎫 *FM 10; FM 25 for special exhibitions.* ⊙ *Mon., Thurs., and Fri. 9–5; Wed. 9–9; weekends 11–5.*

➑ **Svenska Teatern** (Swedish Theater). Dating from 1827, the first wooden theater on this site was considered too vulnerable to fire and was replaced by a stone building in 1866. Ironically, the stone building was itself nearly destroyed by a fire. In 1936, a team of architects—Eero Saarinen and Jarl Eklundhe among them—renovated the theater. The whitewashed round theater today displays an attractive shape and dignified simplicity of design. The Swedish Theater's own company performs plays in Swedish year-round. ⊠ *Pohjoisespl. 2,* ☎ *09/170–238.* ⊙ *Box office daily noon–performance time.*

NEED A
BREAK? The **Aalto Café** (⊠ Pohjoisespl. 39, ☎ 09/121–446) on the Academic
Bookstore's mezzanine is pleasant for lunch or a snack.

❶ Vanha Kauppahalli (Old Market Hall). From piles of colorful fish roe
to marinated Greek olives, the old brick market hall on the waterfront
is a treasury of delicacies. The vendors set up permanent stalls with
decorative carved woodwork. ⊠ *Eteläranta, along the South Harbor.*
☉ *Weekdays 8–5, Sat. 8–2.*

Residential and Seaside Helsinki

Bordered by the sea, the south side of Helsinki is resplendent with elegant 20th-century residences and parks with winding paths. The waterfront Kaivopuisto leads into the upscale embassy neighborhood.

A GOOD WALK

Begin at the sharp-spired **Mikael Agricolan Kirkko** ⑪ in the small park,
Tehtaanpuisto. Cross Tehtaankatu and walk south down Laivurinkatu
past Eiran Sairaala, or Eira Hospital, with its witch-hat towers and triangular garret windows. Continue south on Laivurinkatu, passing the
Art Nouveau **Villa Johanna** ⑫ on your left. An open view of the Baltic
will be just ahead. At the end of the street, turn right on Merikatu. After
passing the beautiful **Villa Ensi** ⑬, you'll arrive at the eternal flame of
the Merenkulkijoiden Muistomerkki, or Seafarers' Torch, commissioned by the city as a tribute to Finnish sailors and a symbol of hope
for their safe return.

Turn east to walk along Merisatamaranta, the seaside promenade.
Out at sea is a handful of the thousands of islands that make up the
Gulf of Finland Archipelago. Turn away from the water and walk
north on Iso Puistotie to the shady **Kaivopuisto** ⑭ bordered by opulent estates and embassies; plan on spending half an hour wandering
along its pleasant paths. From the park, follow the eastward loop of
Kalliolinnantie through the embassy district to the **Mannerheim
Museo** ⑮. On the same street, is the tiny **Cygnaeuksen Galleria** ⑯. Follow Itäinen Puistotie north to Tehtaankatu 1, where you'll see the enormous fenced-in Russian Embassy complex; then walk up Ullankatu to
the park **Tähtitorninvuori** ⑰. For those seriously interested in architecture,
the **Suomen Rakennustaiteen Museo** ⑱ is just west of the observatory;
follow any of the small streets that go west, and turn right on
Kasarmikatu. Just north is the **Taideteollisuusmuseo** ⑲.

TIMING

It takes a little more than one hour to walk this route, not counting
time to relax in the parks and see art collections. Although the Seafarers' Torch is best seen at night, you might choose to make the walk
during the day to take in the subtle beauty of the elegant residences in
the area. Note some of the sites below are closed Monday and Tuesday; Monday–Friday the Mannerheim Museo requires an appointment;
the Mikael Agricolan Kirkko is only open for Sunday service.

SIGHTS TO SEE

❻ Cygnaeuksen Galleria (Cygnaeus Gallery). This diminutive gallery, in
a cottage with a tower overlooking the harbor, is the perfect setting
for works by various Finnish painters, sculptors, and folk artists. This
was once the summer home of Fredrik Cygnaeus (1807–81), a poet
and historian who generously left his cottage and all the art inside to
the Finnish public. ⊠ *Kalliolinn. 8,* ☎ *09/656–928.* 💷 *FM 10.* ☉ *Thurs.–
Sun. 11–4, Wed. 11–7.*

Gulf of Finland Archipelago. In winter Finns walk across the frozen sea
to the nearby islands with dogs and even baby buggies. On the land
side, the facades of the Eira and Kaivopuisto districts' grandest build-

ings form a parade of architectural splendor. One tradition that remains, even in this upscale neighborhood, is rug-washing in the sea—an incredibly arduous task. You may be astounded to see people leave their rugs to dry in the sea air without fear of theft. ⊠ *South of Merisatamaranta.*

⑭ **Kaivopuisto** (Well Park). This large, shady, path-filled park was once the site of a popular spa that drew people from St. Petersburg, Tallinn, and all of Scandinavia until its popularity faded during the Crimean War. All the spa structures were eventually destroyed except one, the **Kaivohuone,** now a popular bar-restaurant (☞ Nightlife and the Arts, *below*). Across from the entrance of Kaivohuone, take Kaivohuoneenrinne through the park past a grand Empire-style villa built by Albert Edelfelt, father of the famous Finnish painter who bore the same name. Built in 1839, it is the oldest preserved villa in the park. ⊠ *South of Puistok. on water.*

⑮ **Mannerheim Museo** (Mannerheim Museum). Marshal Karl Gustaf Mannerheim (1867–1951) was a complex character sporting a varied resume: he served as a high-level official in the Russian czar's guard, was a trained anthropologist who explored Asia, and is revered as a great general who fought for Finland's freedom and later became the new country's president. The Mannerheim Museo is set in the great Finnish military leader's well-preserved family home and exhibits his letters and personal effects. European furniture, Asian art, and military medals and weaponry are on display. ⊠ *Kalliolinnantie 14,* ☎ *09/ 635–443.* ▣ *FM 30 includes guided tour.* ☉ *Fri.–Sun., 11–4; Mon.– Thurs. by appointment.*

⑯ **Mikael Agricolan Kirkko** (Mikael Agricola Church). Built in 1935 by Lars Sonck, this church is named for the Finnish religious reformer considered the father of written Finnish. Mikael Agricola (circa 1510–57) wrote the first Finnish children's speller, the *Abckiria* (published around 1543), and translated the New Testament into Finnish (published in 1548). The church's sharp spire and tall brick steeple are visible amid **Tehtaanpuisto,** a small neighboring park. The inside of the church is quite bare, and no visitors are allowed except during Sunday services. ⊠ *Tehtaank. 23A,* ☎ *09/633–654. Services Sun. from 10 AM; check outside for additional times.*

⑱ **Suomen Rakennustaiteen Museo** (Museum of Finnish Architecture). Stop by to pick up a list of Helsinki buildings designed by Alvar Aalto, the most famous being Finlandiatalo in Töölö (☞ Side Trips from Helsinki, *below*). The permanent exhibits of this museum are far from comprehensive, and specialists will want to visit the extensive library and bookstore. ⊠ *Kasarmik. 24,* ☎ *09/661–918.* ▣ *FM 20.* ☉ *Tues. and Thurs.–Sun. 10–4, Wed. 10–7.*

⑰ **Tähtitorninvuori** (Observatory Tower Hill). Named for the astronomical observatory within its borders, this park has sculptures, winding walkways, and a great view of the South Harbor. The observatory belongs to the astronomy department of Helsinki University and is closed to the public. ⊠ *West of Laivasillank. and South Harbor.*

⑲ **Taideteollisuusmuseo** (Museum of Applied Arts). The best of Finnish design can be seen here in displays of furnishings, jewelry, ceramics, and more, plus temporary exhibits of international design. At press time, the museum was scheduled to move at the end of 1997 from its temporary space on Laivurinkatu 3 to here, its traditional site. ⊠ *Korkeavourenk. 23,* ☎ *09/622–0540.* ▣ *FM 20.* ☉ *June–Aug., daily 11– 5; Sept.–May, Tues. and Thurs.–Sun. 11–5, Wed. 11–8.*

Café Ursula (✉ Ehrenström. 3, ☎ 09/652–817) by the sea with views across to Suomenlinna, is a favorite among locals for coffee, ice cream, pastries, and light lunches.

🔞 **Villa Ensi.** This pale ocher Art Nouveau villa, now a private apartment building, was designed by Selim A. Lindqvist and named after his daughter, Ensi. The two bronze statues in front—*Au Revoir* and *La Joie de la Maternité* by J. Sören-Ring—date from 1910. ✉ *Merik. 23.* ⊘ *Closed to the public.*

⑫ **Villa Johanna.** Although this stunning Art Nouveau villa (circa 1906) is now privately owned by the Post Office Bank of Finland, which uses the villa for corporate dinners and events, it's still worth a look from the outside. Look for the carved roaring serpent above the front door ✉ *Laivurink. 25.* ⊘ *Closed to the public.*

Katajanokka and Senaatintori

Katajanokka is separated from the mainland by a canal and begins just east of Kauppatori. A charming residential quarter as well as a cargo and passenger-ship port, this area is home to one of the city's main landmarks, the dazzling Russian Orthodox Uspenskin Katedraali, the biggest cathedral in western Europe. Not far from Katajanokka is the elegant Lutheran Cathedral that dominates Senaatintori. The Valtion Taidemuseo is also nearby.

A GOOD WALK

The first sight on Katajanokka is the onion-domed **Uspenskin Katedraali** ⑳ on Kanavakatu. From the cathedral, walk down Kanavakatu, turn left on Ankkurikatu, and then right on Laukkasaarenkatu, where a sign will point out the **Wanha Satama** ㉑, a cleverly converted complex of brick warehouses now sheltering an exhibition center and restaurants. From there, head back southwest a short distance to the seafront and cross one of the two short bridges back over to Kauppatori.

From Kauppatori, take any street north to **Senaatintori** ㉒. The north side of the square is dominated by the **Tuomiokirkko** ㉓; the Valtionneuvosto, or Council of State, and the main building of Helsingin Yliopisto, or Helsinki University, flank the east and west sides, respectively. The main university library is just north of the main building on Unioninkatu. At the south end of the square, old merchants' homes are currently occupied by stores, restaurants, and the Kiseleff Bazaar Hall (☞ Shopping, *below*).

Walk one block west to Fabianinkatu; just south is **Pörssitalo** ㉔, on the west side of the street. Head back north on Fabianinkatu 1½ blocks; then turn left on Yliopistonkatu. You'll run into the side of the **Valtion Taidemuseo** ㉕, the Finnish National Gallery at the Ateneum; to enter the museum, turn right on Mikonkatu and then immediately left on Kaivokatu. Just west on Kaivokatu are the **Rautatieasema** ㉖ and **Mannerheimin Patsas** ㉗, standing sentinel over Mannerheimintie. **Suomen Kansallisteatteri** ㉘, at the north side of the square Rautatientori, stages Finnish theater. At press time (summer 1998), the **Nykytaiteenmuseo** ㉙ was scheduled to move into its new premises next to the main post office.

TIMING

Allow 45 minutes to an hour to walk this route. Be sure to check the opening hours of both cathedrals before you leave; both close on religious holidays, and the Uspenskin Katedraali is always closed Monday, and also Saturday off-season. The Pörssitalo closes weekends and the Valtion Taidemuseo closes Monday; plan accordingly.

SIGHTS TO SEE

㉗ Mannerheimin Patsas (Statue of Marshal Karl Gustaf Mannerheim). The equestrian gazes down Mannerheimintie, the major thoroughfare named in his honor. ⊠ *Mannerheim., in front of the main post office, west of the station.*

㉙ Nykytaiteenmuseo (Museum of Contemporary Art). This collection of national and contemporary art from the 1960s to the present was, at press time, scheduled to open in this new venue in spring 1998. The new digs are specially designed in this long-awaited new building, adjacent to the main post office. ⊠ *Mannerheim. Call the tourist office for further details.*

㉔ Pörssitalo (Stock Exchange). Although the trading is fully automated, the beautiful interior of the Stock Exchange, with its bullet-shaped chandeliers, is worth seeing. The Pörssitalo was designed by Lars Sonck and built in 1911. ⊠ *Fabianink. 14,* ☎ *09/676–621.* ☉ *Weekdays 8–5.*

㉖ Rautatieasema (train station). This outdoor square and the adjoining train station are the city's bustling commuter hub. The station's huge granite figures are by Emil Wikström; the solid building they adorn was designed by Eliel Saarinen, one of the founders of the early 20th-century National Romantic style. ⊠ *Kaivok., Rautatientori,* ☎ *09/7071.*

★ **㉒ Senaatintori** (Senate Square). You've hit the heart of neoclassical Helsinki. The harmony of the three buildings flanking Senaatintori exemplifies one of the purest styles of European architecture, as envisioned and designed by German architect Carl Ludvig Engel. On the square's west side is one of the main buildings of **Helsingin Yliopisto** (Helsinki University), and up the hill is the university library. On the east side is the pale yellow **Valtionneuvosto** (Council of State), completed in 1822 and once the seat of the Autonomous Grand Duchy of Finland's Imperial Senate. At the lower end of the square, stores and restaurants now occupy former merchants' homes. ⊠ *Bounded by Aleksanterink. to the south and Yliopistonk. to the north.*

㉘ Suomen Kansallisteatteri (National Theater). Productions in the three theaters inside are in Finnish. In front you'll see the statue of writer Aleksis Kivi. ⊠ *North side of Rautatientori,* ☎ *09/173–311.*

㉓ Tuomiokirkko (Lutheran Cathedral of Finland). The steep steps and green domes of the church dominate Senaatintori. Completed in 1852, it is the work of famous architect Carl Ludvig Engel, who also designed parts of Tallinn and St. Petersburg. Wander through the tasteful blue-gray interior, with its white moldings and the statues of German reformers Martin Luther and Philipp Melancthon, as well as the famous Finnish bishop Mikael Agricola. Concerts are frequently held inside the church. The crypt at the rear is the site of frequent historic and architectural exhibitions and bazaars. ⊠ *Yliopistonk. 7.* ☉ *May–Sept., weekdays 9–7, Sat. 9–6, Sun. noon–6; Oct.–Apr., weekdays 10–4, Sat. 10–6, Sun. noon–6.*

NEED A BREAK?
Café Engel (⊠ Aleksanterink. 15, ☎ 09/652–776), named for the architect Carl Ludvig Engel, serves coffee and berry cheesecake right on Senaatintori.

★ **㉒⁰ Uspenskin Katedraali** (Uspenski Cathedral). Perched atop a small rocky cliff over the North Harbor in Katajanokka is the main cathedral of the Russian Orthodox religion in Finland. Its brilliant gold onion domes are its hallmark, but its imposing redbrick edifice, decorated by 19th-century Russian artists, is no less distinctive. The cathedral was built and dedicated in 1868 in the Byzantine-Slavonic style and remains the biggest Orthodox church in Scandinavia. ✉ *Kanavak. 1,* ☎ *09/ 634–267.* ⊙ *May–Sept., Tues. 9:30–6, Wed.–Fri. 9:30–4, Sat. 9–noon, Sun. noon–3; Oct.–Apr., Tues. and Thurs. 9–2, Wed. and Fri. noon– 6, Sun. noon–2.*

NEED A
BREAK?

On the north flank of Katajanokka, near the end of Katajanokan Pohjois-ranta, you'll see the **Katajanokan Casino** (✉ Laivastok. 1, ☎ 09/622–2772). It was built in 1911 as a warehouse, later became a naval offi-cers' casino, and today is a seaside restaurant. Set on its own head-land, the casino has a summer terrace from which you can gaze across the North Harbor to the Kruunuhaka district while sipping a cold beer.

㉕ Valtion Taidemuseo (Finnish National Gallery). This fine collection of traditional Finnish art reposes in the splendid neoclassical **Ateneum**. The gallery features major European works, but the outstanding at-traction is the Finnish art, particularly the works of Akseli Gallen-Kallela, inspired by the national epic *Kalevala* (☞ Side Trips from Helsinki, *below*). The rustic portraits by Albert Edelfelt are enchanting, and many contemporary Finnish artists are well represented. ✉ *Kaivok. 2–4,* ☎ *09/173–361.* 🎫 *FM 20.* ⊙ *Tues. and Fri. 9–6, Wed. and Thurs. 9–8, weekends 11–5.*

OFF THE
BEATEN PATH

LINNANMÄKI – Helsinki's amusement park to to the north of the city can be reached by Trams 3B and 3T from in front of the railway station. ✉ *Tivolikuja 1,* ☎ *09/773–99.* 🎫 *FM 15.* ⊙ *Late Apr.–mid-May, week-end hrs vary; May–mid-June, weekdays 4–10, Sat. 1–10, Sun. 1–9; mid-June–mid-Aug., daily 1–10; mid-Aug.–first wk in Sept., days and hrs vary.*

㉑ Wanha Satama (Old Harbor). Despite its old-brick-warehouse ap-pearance, this is actually a small shopping center with several food stores, restaurants, and cafés. There's even an exhibition hall in the left-hand (north) wing. The "W" in Wanha is pronounced "V." ✉ *Kanavak. and Pikku Satamak.*

Suomenlinna

㉚ A former island fortress now taken over by resident artists, Suomen-linna (Finland's Castle) is a quirky, perennially popular collection of museums, parks, and gardens. In 1748 the Finnish army helped build the impregnable fortress, long referred to as the Gibraltar of the North; since then it has expanded into a series of interlinked islands. Al-though Suomenlinna has never been taken by assault, its occupants sur-rendered once to the Russians in 1809 and came under fire from British ships in 1855 during the Crimean War. Today Suomenlinna makes a lovely excursion from Helsinki, particularly in early summer when the island is engulfed in a mauve-and-purple mist of lilacs, introduced from Versailles by the Finnish architect Ehrensvärd.

There are no street names on the island, so get a map for about FM 7 from the Helsinki City Tourist Office before you go or buy one at the Tourist Information kiosk on the island. From June 1 to August 31, guided English-language tours leave from the information kiosk daily at 12:30 and 2:30. The general information number is ☎ 09/668–341; to book a group tour, call ☎ 09/668–154.

A GOOD WALK
Suomenlinna is easily reached by public ferry (FM 9) or round-trip pri-vate boat tour (FM 20), both of which leave from Helsinki's Kaup-patori. Although its fortification occupied six islands, its main attractions are now concentrated on two, Susisaari and Kustaanmiekka. When you

land at Suomenlinna, go through the archway and proceed uphill to the **Suomenlinna Kirkko,** the local church-lighthouse. Walk past the church and the pastel-colored private wooden homes to the **Ehrensvärd Museo,** a historical museum. The Tourist Information kiosk is nearby, alongside Tykistölahti Bay; it is open May 5–August, daily 10–5. Walk along the eastern coast of Susisaari until you reach the submarine **Vesikko.** From there, walk south and cross over to Kustaanmiekka, where you can visit the **Rannikkotykistömuseo** and learn everything you ever wanted to know about arms and artillery.

TIMING

The ferry ride from South Harbor to Suomenlinna takes about a half hour. Plan to spend an afternoon on the islands; you'll need about four hours to explore the fortress and museums. Note that days open and hours of sites are limited off-season.

SIGHTS TO SEE

Ehrensvärd Museo (Ehrensvärd Museum). Augustin Ehrensvärd directed the fortification of the islands of Suomenlinna from 1748 until 1772, the year of his death. This historical museum named for the military architect exhibits a model-ship collection and officers' quarters dating from the 18th century. Ehrensvärd's tomb is also here. ⊠ *Susisaari, Suomenlinna,* ☎ *09/668–154.* ☞ *FM 10.* ☉ *May 8–Sept., daily 10– 5; Oct.–Nov., weekends 11–4:30; Jan.–May 7, weekends 11–5.*

Rannikkotykistömuseo (Coastal Guard Artillery Museum). Arms from World Wars I and II are on display in a vaulted arsenal. ⊠ *Kustaanmiekka, Suomenlinna,* ☎ *09/161–5295.* ☞ *FM 10.* ☉ *May 8–Aug., daily 10–5; Sept., daily 11–5.*

Suomenlinna Kirkko (Suomenlinna Church). This dual-function church-lighthouse was built in 1854 as an Orthodox church and has since become Lutheran. ☉ *Open for services only.*

Vesikko. Jump aboard this submarine, built in Turku in 1931–33 and served in World War II. ☞ *FM 10.* ☉ *May 13–Sept., daily 11–4.*

Töölö

Most of Helsinki's major cultural buildings—the opera house, concert hall, and national museum—are within a short distance of each other around the perimeter of the inlet from the sea called Töölönlahti. The inlet itself is lovely in all seasons, and the walking and biking paths are well trodden by locals. The winding streets just east of Mannerheimintie enfold the Temppeliaukio Kirkko (Temple Square Church), whose unexceptional facade covers its amazing cavernous interior. Also nearby, the Sibelius park cuts a large swath out of the neighborhood and borders the sea.

A GOOD WALK

Begin in the lakeside area of Mannerheimintie by the equestrian statue of Gustaf Mannerheim, directly behind the main post office and next to the new location for the Museum of Contemporary Art. Walk northwest on Mannerheimintie, passing the red granite **Eduskuntatalo** ㉛ on your way to the **Suomen Kansallismuseo** ㉜, Finland's national museum, on the left. If the building looks familiar to you, it probably is; its spired outline was the backdrop for televised reports on the 1990 U.S.–Soviet summit, and again for the Clinton–Yeltsin meeting in March 1997. When you leave the museum, cross Mannerheimintie to the Helsingin Kaupungin Museo, or Helsinki City Museum, then follow the road a short distance north to the **Finlandiatalo** ㉝, the Alvar Aalto–designed concert and congress hall. Behind the hall lies the inlet bay of Töölönlahti. If you walk along the well-used paths that follow the contour of the lake, you'll soon come to the **Suomen Kansallisooppera** ㉞, Helsinki's opera house. From here, you can take the lengthy walk to the Seurasaaran Ulkomuseo.

From the opera house, walk southeast on Mannerheimintie until you see the white tower of the **Olympiastadion** ㉟ on your left. Return to Mannerheimintie, crossing over to Cygnaeuksenkatu; take a left on Nervanderinkatu, where you'll reach the **Helsingin Taidehalli** ㊱, with its fine collection of Finnish art. Go a few steps farther and take the small street directly across from the art hall to the modern **Temppeliaukio Kirkko** ㊲, a church carved into rock outcrops. If you still have energy, cross Runeberginkatu and walk west on Samonkatu until you reach Mechelininkatu. Walk a ways north on Mechelininkatu, and **Sibeliusken Puisto** ㊳ will appear on your left. Here you'll find the reason you came: the magnificent Sibelius-Monumentti.

TIMING

Allow 45 minutes to follow this tour as far as the Temppeliaukio Kirkko, adding half an hour for each museum if you decide to venture inside; from the church, it's a 20-minute walk to the Sibelius Puisto. Be sure to check the Temppeliaukio Kirkko's hours, which are slightly erratic. Note the Suomen Kansallismuseo closes its doors Monday.

SIGHTS TO SEE

㉛ **Eduskuntatalo** (Parliament House). The imposing, colonnaded, red granite Eduskuntatalo stands near Mannerheim's statue on Mannerheimintie. The legislature has one of the world's highest proportions of women. ⊠ *Mannerheim. 30,* ☎ *09/4321.* ⊙ *Open for meetings.*

㉝ **Finlandiatalo** (Finlandia Hall). This white, winged concert hall was one of Alvar Aalto's last creations. It's especially impressive on foggy days or at night. If you can't make it to a concert here, try to take a guided tour. ⊠ *Karamzinink. 4,* ☎ *09/40241.* ⊡ *Tickets FM 40–FM 80.* ⊙ *Concerts usually held Wed. and Thurs. nights.*

㊱ **Helsingin Taidehalli** (Helsinki Art Hall). Here you'll see the best of contemporary Finnish art, including painting, sculpture, architecture, and industrial art and design. ⊠ *Nervanderink. 3,* ☎ *09/4542–0616.* ⊡ *FM 20, can vary according to exhibition.* ⊙ *June–July, weekdays 11–5, Sun. noon–4; Aug.–May, Tues.–Sat. 11–6, Sun. noon–5.*

㉟ **Olympiastadion** (Olympic Stadium). At this stadium built for the 1952 Games, take a lift to the top of the tower for sprawling city views. ⊠ *East of Mannerheim.*

㊳ **Sibeliusken Puisto.** The Sibelius-Monumentti (Sibelius Monument) itself is worth the walk to this lakeside park. What could be a better tribute to Finland's great composer than this soaring silver sculpture of organ pipes? ⊠ *West of Mechelinink.*

㉜ **Suomen Kansallismuseo** (National Museum). Exhibits take you from Finnish prehistory through medieval church art to contemporary Sami culture. Decorating the vaulted ceiling are Akseli Gallen-Kallela's vibrant frescoed illustrations of the *Kalevala,* Finland's national epic. Temporary exhibits usually focus on different cultures from around the world. A charming turn-of-the-century–style café on the first floor serves homemade pastries and freshly brewed coffee. ⊠ *Mannerheim. 34,* ☎ *09/405–0470.* ⊡ *FM 15.* ⊙ *June–Aug., Tues. 11–8, Wed.–Sun. 11–5; Sept.–May, Tues. 11–8, Wed.–Sun. 11–4.*

㉞ **Suomen Kansallisooppera** (Finnish National Opera). Grand gilded operas, classical ballets, and booming concerts all take place in Helsinki's splendid opera house, a striking example of modern Scandinavian architecture that opened its doors in 1993. All events at the Opera House draw crowds, so buy your tickets early. ⊠ *Helsingink. 58, box office* ☎ *09/4030–2211, tours 09/4030–2350.* ⊟ *FM 25 tours.* ☉ *Guided tours by appointment only.*

OFF THE BEATEN PATH

SEURASAAREN ULKOMUSEO – On an island about 3 km (2 mi) northwest of city center, the Seurasaari Outdoor Museum was founded in 1909 to preserve rural Finnish architecture. The old farmhouses and barns that were brought to Seurasaari come from all over Finland. Many are rough-hewn log buildings dating from the 17th century, of primary inspiration to the late 19th-century architects of the national revivalist movement in Finland. All exhibits are marked by signposts along the trails; be sure not to miss the church boat and the gabled church. Seurasaari Island is connected to land by a pedestrian bridge and is a restful place for walking throughout the year, with its forest trails and ocean views. You can walk there in about 40 minutes from the opera house; follow Mannerheimintie northeast, then turn left onto Linnankoskenkatu and follow signs along the coast. Alternatively, take Bus 24 from city center, in front of the Swedish Theater at the west end of Pohjoisesplanadi. Plan on spending at least three hours exploring and getting to the museum. ⊠ *Seurasaari,* ☎ *09/484–712 or 09/484–562.* ⊟ *Museum FM 10.* ☉ *June–Aug., Thurs.–Tues. 11–5, Wed. 11–7; Sept.–May, daily 11–5.*

TAMMINIEMI – The grand house overlooking Seurasaari from the mainland is Tamminiemi, where the late Finnish president Urho Kekkonen lived from 1956 to 1986. Originally known as Villa Nissen, Tamminiemi was built in 1904. Inside are the scores of gifts presented to Finland's longest-serving president by leaders from around the world. His study is the most fascinating room, with its gift from the United States of a cupboard full of *National Geographic* maps of the world. To assure an English-speaking guide, call ahead. When you've seen the house, stop for pastries and Russian-style tea at **Tamminiemintien Kahvila** (⊠ Tamminiem. 8, ☎ 09/481–003) or the nearby **Café Angelica** (⊠ Tamminiemientie 3, ☎ 09/481–003). To get here, follow directions to Seurasaarem Ilkomuseo (☞ *above*); it's on the mainland before the footbridge. ⊠ *Seurasaarentie 15,* ☎ *09/480–684.* ⊟ *FM 15.* ☉ *Entry by guided tour only; large groups call ahead; Sept.–June, Tues.–Sun. 11–5, Thurs. until 7; July–Aug., daily 11–5, Thurs. until 7.*

★ ③⑦ **Temppeliaukio Kirkko** (Temple Square Church). Topped with a copper dome, the church looks like a half-buried spaceship from the outside. In truth, it's really a modern Lutheran church carved into the rock outcrops below. The sun shines in from above, illuminating the stunning interior with its birch pews, modern pipe organ, and cavernous walls. Ecumenical and Lutheran services in various languages are held throughout the week. ⊠ *Lutherink. 3,* ☎ *09/494–698.* ☉ *Daily 11– 8; closed Tues. 1–2 and during concerts and services.*

Dining

Helsinki is home to some of Finland's best eating establishments. Although the Russian restaurants are the star attraction, try to seek out Finnish specialties such as game—pheasant, reindeer, hare, and grouse—accompanied by wild-berry compotes and exotic mushroom sauces.

Most restaurants close on major national holidays—only a few hotel restaurants stay open for Christmas. Many of the more expensive establishments close on weekends.

Around Kauppatori and Katajanokka

$$$$ ✕ **Alexander Nevski.** Helsinki is reputed to have the best Russian restau-
★ rants in the Nordic region, and the Nevski is foremost among them.
It sets high standards in the preparation of czarist-era dishes, with an
emphasis on game. Try the breast of willow grouse baked in a clay pot,
traditional roe-filled blintzes, or borscht. Among the more extraordinary offerings is roast bear in a pot, which must be ordered in advance.
Set at the edge of the harbor and marketplace, Nevski has all the trap-
pings you'd expect to find in a czar's dining hall—heavy draperies, glis-
tening samovars, potted palms, and crisp linen tablecloths. ☒ *Pohjoisespl.
17,* ☎ *09/639–610. AE, DC, MC, V.*

$$$$ ✕ **Amadeus.** The elegant decor in this old town house between Senaat-
★ intori and the South Harbor matches the czarist architecture of the neighborhood. The game, reindeer, and mushroom dishes have made it a
favorite of Helsinki gourmets. The two dining rooms are tinted in soft
browns and pinks. As an appetizer, try the slightly salted salmon with
vegetable tartare, and as a main course, one of the many game dishes.
☒ *Sofiank. 4,* ☎ *09/626–676. AE, DC, MC, V. Closed Sun.*

$$$$ ✕ **Havis Amanda.** Across the street from the Havis Amanda statue,
its namesake restaurant specializes in seafood dishes. Several different
fixed menus are available for both lunch and dinner. Try the flamed
cloudberry crepes with ice cream for dessert. ☒ *Unionink. 23,* ☎ *09/
666–882. AE, DC, MC, V. Closed Sun.*

$$$$ ✕ **Restaurant Palace.** This outstanding hotel restaurant has a magnificent
view of the South Harbor. Chef Markus Maulavirta's specialty is
French and Finnish fare, including such creations as jellied roe of ven-
dance (a type of whitefish) with sour cream-dill sauce, or reindeer fillet and tongue with rowanberry sauce. ☒ *Eteläranta 10, Palace Hotel,*
☎ *09/134–561. AE, DC, MC, V. Closed weekends. No lunch July.*

$$$$ ✕ **Savoy.** With its airy, Alvar Aalto–designed, functionalist dining
room overlooking the Esplanade Gardens, the Savoy is a frequent
choice for business lunches and was also Finnish statesman Marshal
Karl Gustaf Mannerheim's favorite; he is rumored to have introduced
the *Vorschmack* (minced lamb and anchovies) recipe. Savoy's menu includes the ubiquitous reindeer fillet served with cumin potatoes, as well
as such old-fashioned Finnish home-cooked dishes as meatballs, grilled
herring, and *läski soosi* (fried fatty pork in brown sauce). ☒ *Eteläespl. 14,* ☎ *09/176–571.*

$$$ ✕ **Bellevue.** The spare lines of Bellevue belie its real age—it has been
around since 1917, serving imaginative dishes inspired by Russian
cuisine of yore and Finnish country fare. In a room with pale table linens,
wood-and-plush seats, and tremendous modern paintings, you can
sample the innovative meat dishes and blinis for which the Bellevue is
famous. As an appetizer, try the salted cucumbers topped with sour
cream and honey, or *shashlik*—lamb fillet served with mushroom rice.
The plush interior of this elegant town house has many shining
samovars, but only some of them are functional; each table has lighted
candles. Appropriately, the restaurant is tucked behind the Uspenski
Cathedral. ☒ *Rahapajank. 3,* ☎ *09/179–560. AE, DC, MC, V. No lunch
weekends and in July.*

$$$ ✕ **Sipuli.** Sipuli stands at the foot of the Russian Orthodox Uspenski
Cathedral and gets its name—meaning onion—from the church's
golden onionlike cupolas. In this warehouse building dating from the
19th century, the redbrick walls and dark-wood panels are enhanced
by a skylight with a spectacular view of the cathedral. For starters try
the escargots in sherry and Gorgonzola sauce, and for the main course
the smoked fillet of pike perch with salmon mousse and gravy sauce,
or noisettes of reindeer topped with game sauce. ☒ *Kanavaranta 3,*
☎ *09/179–900. AE, DC, MC, V. Closed weekends. No lunch.*

148

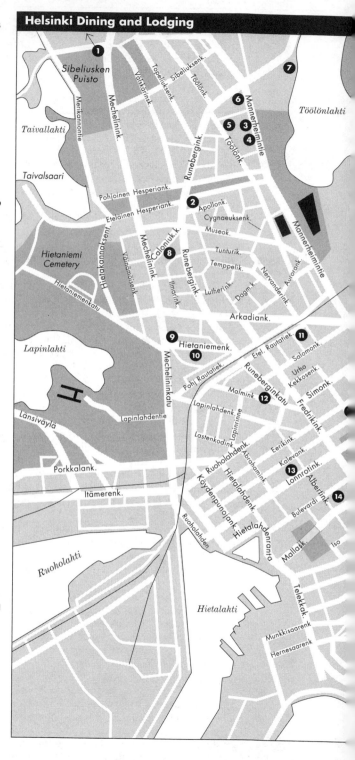

Helsinki Dining and Lodging

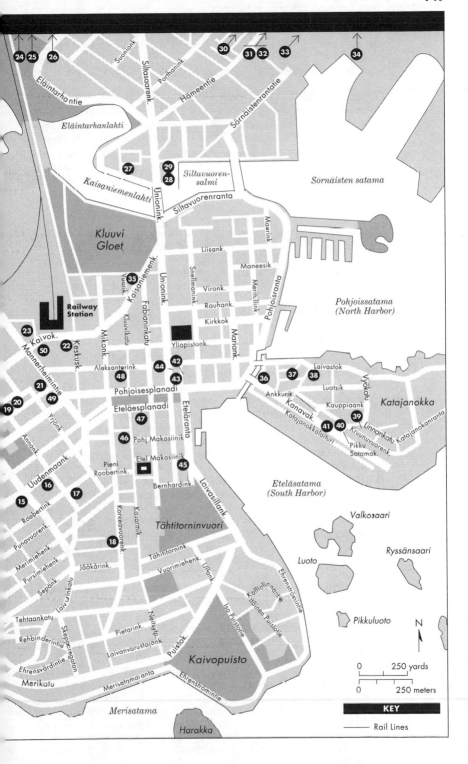

Eläintarhantie

Suolionk.

Siltasaarenk.

Porthaninl.

Hämeentie

Sörnäistenrantalie

Eläintarhanlahti

Sörnäisten satama

Kaisaniemenlahti

Siltavuoren-salmi

Unionink.

Siltavuorenranta

Kluuvi
Gloet

Maurink.

Liisank.

Maneesik.

Merikillink.

Pohjoisranta

Pohjoissatama
(North Harbor)

Kaisaniemenk.

Vuorik.

Unionink.

Fabianinkatu

Snellmanink.

Vironk.

Rauhank.

Kirkkok.

Railway
Station

Kluvikatu

Mikonk.

Keskusk.

Yliopistonk.

Mariank.

Kaivok.

Mannerheimintie

Aleksanterink.

Pohjoisesplanadi

Eteläesplanadi

Eteläranta

Laivastok.

Luotsik.

Vyökatu

Ankkurik.

Kanavak.

Kauppiaank.

Katajanokka

Linnankatu

Katajanokankatu

Katajanokkalaituri

Kruunuvuorenk.

Pikku
Satamak.

Yrjönk.

Annank.

Uudenmaank.

Pohj Makasiink.

Etel Makasiink.

Pieni
Roobertink.

Bernhardink.

Laivasillank.

Tähtitorninvuori

Eteläsatama
(South Harbor)

Valkosaari

Ryssänsaari

Luoto

Roobertink.

Punavuorenk.

Merimiehenk.

Pursimiehenk.

Korkeavuorenk.

Kasarmk.

Tähtitornink.

Vuorimiehenk.

Ullank.

Ehrenströmintie

Kalliolinnantie

Itäinen Puistotie

Pikkuluoto

Sepank.

Jääkärink.

Laiv rinkatu

Tehtaankatu

Skepparegatan

Pietarink.

Neitsyp.

Puistok.

Läntinen Puistotie

N

Rehbinderintie

Laivanvarustajank.

Kaivopuisto

Ehrensvärdintie

Merisalmiranta

Ehrenströmintie

Merikatu

0   250 yards

0   250 meters

Merisatama

Harakka

\$\$ ✕ **Café Raffaello.** In the heart of Helsinki's Wall Street, this cozy Italian restaurant with redbrick walls, parquet floors, and decorative frescoes is reputed for friendly service, reasonable prices, and tasty pasta, salad, and meat dishes; try the grilled Cajun beefsteak with garlic potatoes or the minted chicken breast with rice. ⊠ *Aleksanterink. 46,* ☎ *09/653–930. AE, DC, MC, V.*

\$\$ ✕ **Omenapuu.** Generous windows overlook the downtown bustle at this restaurant on the second floor of a large office building in the heart of a busy shopping district. The fare is Finnish and international; periodic theme weeks feature various assortments of game, vegetables, and fish. Live piano music adds to the pleasant atmosphere in the mirrored, red-carpeted room. Take the outside elevator in front of the shopping mall up to the second floor. ⊠ *Keskusk. 6, 2nd floor,* ☎ *09/630– 205. AE, DC, MC, V.*

\$\$ ✕ **Wellamo.** Unbeatable for cheerful atmosphere, intimacy, and local flavor, this well-kept secret is tucked away in the shadows of the masterpieces of Katajanokka, not far from the icebreaker quay. Prices are reasonable for a simple but hearty menu; don't miss the fried Baltic herring entrée, and the quirky dessert of fried Camembert. Spontaneous piano recitals and small art shows hung in the interior add to the warmth. Be sure to reserve in advance; insiders fill it up quickly. ⊠ *Vyök. 9,* ☎ *09/663–139. AE, DC, MC, V. Closed Mon.*

\$ ✕ **Pikku Satama.** This casual eatery in Katajanokka's Wanha Satama serves a variety of food—pizza, baked potatoes with various toppings, and hot dishes—in an informal but impressive setting. ⊠ *Pikku Satamak. 3,* ☎ *09/174–093. AE, DC, MC, V. Closed Sun.*

West of Mannerheimintie

\$\$\$ ✕ **Kosmos.** Just a short walk from Stockmann's, this cozy restaurant has become a lunchtime favorite among businesspeople working nearby. Come evening, it's given over to artists and journalists. Its high ceilings and understated decor give it a Scandinavian atmosphere of simplicity and efficiency. Among the specialties are sweetbreads with a sauce of curry, cream, and port, and mutton chops stuffed with ground veal and olives and served with garlic potatoes. ⊠ *Kalevank. 3,* ☎ *09/607– 603. AE, DC, MC, V. Closed weekends.*

\$\$\$ ✕ **Ravintola Torni.** The Finnish-based cuisine at this recently renovated gourmet establishment—the main restaurant of the central Torni Hotel (☞ Lodging, *below*)—varies during special theme weeks. Favorite spins on Finn mainstays include roasted perch and fried whitefish with cheese potatoes. The decor has reverted to the 1930s style of the original building. ⊠ *Kalevank. 5, Hotel Torni,* ☎ *09/131–131. AE, DC, MC, V. Closed weekends.*

\$\$\$ ✕ **Villa Thai.** Near Helsinki's shopping district, this restaurant offers authentic Thai food in traditional surroundings. The staff dress in Thai silks, and diners can chose between Western and Thai-style seating. The prawn curry with coconut milk and pineapple is a house specialty. Live music in the evenings adds extra ambience. ⊠ *Bulevardi 28,* ☎ *09/680–2778. AE, DC, MC, V.*

\$\$ ✕ **Kynsilaukka.** This rustic, comfortable restaurant is one of Helsinki's
★ most imaginative. Dominated by garlic—there's even garlic beer—the food is fresh and beautifully presented, often served by the three young owner-chefs themselves. The seafood bouillabaisse is superb, as are the cold marinated reindeer, garlic cream soup, and lamb pot. For dessert, try the pancakes with cloudberry sauce. All portions are served in two sizes. The set lunch menu is a good buy. ⊠ *Fredrikink. 22,* ☎ *09/651– 939. AE, DC, MC, V.*

$$ ✕ **Maxill.** Helsinki's café boom and an increasing demand for continental-style bars have inspired this hybrid, serving the absolute best omelet in town. It's frequented by the young, trendy clientele ubiquitous on this lively street just south of city center. *Korkeavuorenk. 4, 09/638–873. AE, DC, MC, V.*

$ ✕ **China.** One of the city's oldest Chinese restaurants, this place specializes in Cantonese fare. Apart from an extensive variety of beef, pork, and chicken dishes, there's an unusual pike perch with sweet-and-sour sauce. The Peking duck is recommended but must be ordered two days in advance. ✉ *Annank. 25,* ☎ *09/640–258. AE, DC, MC, V.*

$ ✕ **Ravintola Mechelin.** Helsinki's catering school operates this brasserie-style restaurant decorated in pine. In summer the emphasis is on Finnish food, particularly salmon and reindeer. Low prices and a good location—just west of Mannerheimintie—make it a favorite. ✉ *Perhonk. 11,* ☎ *09/4056–2118. AE, DC, MC, V.*

North of City Center

$$$$ ✕ **Pamir.** On the second floor of the Strand Inter-Continental Hotel
★ (☞ Lodging, *below*), this intimate restaurant may not offer terrific views of the adjacent waterfront, but good service and fine fare make up for it. Pamir's accent is on Finnish game and fish dishes. Renowned chef Pertti Lipäinen prepares superb reindeer liver, smoked fillet of reindeer, stuffed hare, fillet of duck, and rainbow trout. ✉ *John Stenbergin ranta 4,* ☎ *09/39351. AE, DC, MC, V. Closed weekends. No lunch.*

Töölö

$$$$ ✕ **Galateia.** The white grand piano and paintings of languid mermaids lend a classy, serene ambience to Helsinki's best seafood restaurant. From the top floor of the Inter-Continental Helsinki (☞ Lodging, *below*), Galateia offers a nocturnal panorama that takes in the city lights and an illuminated Finlandia Hall reflected in Töölö Bay. Fresh Continental-style seafood is served, along with caviar and roe specialties. If you are in Helsinki during the crayfish season, this is one of the best places to sample it. Attentive and knowledgeable waiters open an impressive selection of appropriate wines. ✉ *Mannerheim. 46, Inter-Continental Hotel,* ☎ *09/405–5900 or 09/40551. AE, DC, MC, V. Closed weekends. No lunch.*

$$$$ ✕ **Töölönranta.** Rebuilt near the site of an old city favorite destroyed by fire, the new Töölönranta has gone upscale. It packs in plenty of opera-goers, since it's right behind the National Opera House overlooking the bay. An innovative water-cooled wok on display in the wide-open kitchen turns out stir-fried specials. Other favorites include arctic char, wild duck, and lamb dishes. In summer, when the patio catches the evening sun, this a superb place to savor a beer. ✉ *Töölönlahdenranta,* ☎ *09/499–571. AE, MC, V.*

$$$ ✕ **Elite.** A little ways from town center, but a welcome oasis after excursions to the Temppeliaukio Kirkko and the Sibelius monument, Elite's simple art deco interior and spacious layout are popular with artists and writers. Traditional Finnish dishes to sample are fried Baltic herring, salmon soup with rye bread, and select game. The outdoor seating in summer is a favorite with all walks of life. ✉ *Etelä Hesperiank. 22,* ☎ *09/495–542. AE, DC, MC.*

$$$ ✕ **Kuu.** If you thrive on getting to the true character of a city and enjoy local color, try looking in simple, friendly restaurants such as Kuu, literally Moon. The menu combines Finnish specialties with imaginative international fare. The restaurant prides itself on its wine list and holds monthly wine evenings. It's especially convenient for nights at the opera. ✉ *Töölönk. 27,* ☎ *09/2709–0973. AE, DC, MC, V.*

$$$ ✕ **Lyon.** As you would expect, French cuisine is the specialty in this award-winning eatery across Mannerheimintie from the opera. Lyon is small and unpretentious, but consistent in high quality and service—as tasted in the savory cream of in-season mushroom soup and fillet of perch in chardonnay sauce. It's a perfect stop for a bite before or after the opera. ⊠ *Mannerheim. 56,* ☎ *09/408–131. AE, DC, MC, V.*

$$$ ✕ **Troikka.** The Troikka takes you back to czarist times in decor—samovars, icons, portraits of Russian writers—and music, and offers exceptionally good Russian food and friendly service. Try the *zhakuska,* an assortment of Russian appetizers including such delicacies as Baltic herring, homemade poultry pâté, wild mushrooms, and marinated garlic. Other Troikka specialties include Siberian *pelmens* (small meat pastries), beef Stroganoff, and cutlet Kiev. ⊠ *Caloniuksenk. 3,* ☎ *09/445–229. AE, DC, MC, V. Closed Sun. and weekends in July.*

Lodging

Helsinki's top hotels are notoriously expensive, have small standard-size rooms, and most cater to the business traveler. The standards of cleanliness are high, and the level of service usually corresponds to the price. Rates are almost always less expensive on weekends and usually include a generous breakfast. Many hotels in Helsinki close for the weeks before and after Christmas and Easter, and in midsummer.

Around Kauppatori and Katajanokka

$$$$ 🏨 **Sokos Hotel Vaakuna.** The quirky 1950s architecture and interior design of the Vaakuna dates back to the 1952 Helsinki Olympics; the hotel has undergone an extensive overhaul but has retained its simple style; rooms are spacious. The rooftop terrace restaurants are traditionally the haunts of parliament members. The hotel is at the top of the Sokos department store, opposite the train station. ⊠ *Asemaaukio 2, 00100,* ☎ *09/131–181,* 𝖥𝖠𝖷 *09/1311–8234. 262 rooms, 12 suites. 2 restaurants, brasserie, sauna, nightclub, meeting rooms. AE, DC, MC, V.*

$$$ 🏨 **Cumulus Seurahuone.** Built in 1914, this Viennese-style town house hotel has a loyal clientele won over by ageless charm and cosmopolitan atmosphere. A patina of well-worn elegance pervades all areas, from the grand main stairway and the chandeliered Art Nouveau café to the ornate, skylit Socis pub. Specify your preference: the traditionally furnished rooms in the old section are brass-bed, high-ceiling, chandelier, and teak-cabinet affairs; rooms in the new area have sleek, modern appointments mixed with Victorian antiques. More spacious "superior" rooms are more expensive. The lobby and public area are among the busiest in town, being across from the train station. ⊠ *Kaivok. 12, 00100,* ☎ *09/69141,* 𝖥𝖠𝖷 *09/691–4010. 118 rooms, 5 suites. Restaurant, bar, café, pub, sauna, nightclub. AE, DC, MC, V.*

$$$ 🏨 **Grand Marina.** Housed inside an early 19th-century customs warehouse in the plush Katajanokka, the Grand Marina has one of the best convention centers in Finland, accommodating up to 1,500 people. Its good location, friendly service, ample modern facilities, and reasonable prices have made this hotel a favorite among tourists. Ask for a room with a view of South Harbor. ⊠ *Katajanokanlaituri 7, 00160,* ☎ *09/16661,* 𝖥𝖠𝖷 *09/664–764. 462 rooms. 5 restaurants, bar, pub, saunas. AE, DC, MC, V.*

$$$ 🏨 **Rivoli Jardin.** This central town house is just two short blocks off
★ the Esplanade Gardens, with small rooms overlooking a quiet courtyard. Standard doubles have twin beds, though queen-size beds are also available. The hotel is small and places emphasis on personal service. Breakfast—included in the room rate—is served at the hotel's Winter Garden, next to the lobby bar. ⊠ *Kasarmik. 40, 00130,* ☎ *09/177–*

880, FAX 09/656–988. 53 rooms, 1 suite. Restaurant, bar, sauna. AE, DC, MC, V.

$$ ⊞ **Hotel Pilotti.** In a quiet suburban setting within a five-minutes drive of the airport, the Pilotti is also about 5 km (3 mi) from Heureka, the Finnish Science Center. Built in 1989, it is modern inside and out; each compact room has a large, round porthole-style window. ⊠ *Veromäentie 1, 01510 Vantaa,* ☎ *09/870–2100,* FAX *09/870–2109. 112 rooms, 4 suites. Restaurant, pub, sauna, meeting rooms. AE, DC, MC, V.*

$ ⊞ **Skatta.** Set in the quiet Katajanokka neighborhood, this modest hotel began as a home for sailors at the turn of the century and was converted into a hotel in 1960. The brownish-red rooms offer good views of the South Harbor. ⊠ *Linnank. 3, 00160,* ☎ *09/659–233,* FAX *09/ 631–352. 23 rooms with shower and kitchenette. Sauna, exercise room. AE, DC, MC, V.*

West of Mannerheimintie

$$$$ ⊞ **Lord Hotel.** On a quiet side street, this small luxury hotel distinguishes
★   itself with a rare combination of character, consistency, and service. The front section is a handsome 1903 stone castle with wood-beamed, medieval-style restaurants, lounges, conference rooms, a cavernous banquet hall, and more. A walkway across an inner court brings you to the modern building housing the guest rooms. Each of the rooms exhibits fine attention to detail: fine desks with good lighting; comfortable contemporary-style furnishings in soothing pastel blue and gray tones; and ample storage space. Ask for discounts on weekends and in summer. ⊠ *Lönnrotink. 29, 00180,* ☎ *09/615–815,* FAX *09/680–1315. 48 rooms, 1 suite. 2 restaurants, bar, breakfast room, hot tubs (17 rooms), sauna, meeting rooms, free parking. AE, DC, MC, V.*

$$$$ ⊞ **Radisson SAS Hotel Helsinki.** Opened in the summer of 1991, this hotel was conceived and built to serve the business traveler. It's set in a residential section of the central city, right on the metro line. Two floors are made up of Royal SAS Club rooms, including several suites and conference areas. The decor varies with the rooms; some are elegant Scandinavian (light colors and wood), others are Asian (warm colors and silk bedcovers), and some are Italian (modern with primary colors). If you want more space and privacy, try the art deco–style business-class rooms on the top floor. The Johan Ludvig restaurant specializes in grilled meats; Ströget is cheaper and offers pasta, salads, and hamburgers. There's a SAS check in counter and service center in the lobby. ⊠ *Runebergink. 2, 00100,* ☎ *09/69580,* FAX *09/6958–7100. 260 rooms, 7 suites. 2 restaurants, bar, room service, sauna, health club, meeting rooms. AE, DC, MC, V.*

$$$$ ⊞ **Ramada Presidentti.** In the heart of Helsinki, this hotel is spacious, quiet, and has well-lighted rooms, with a wide range of facilities. Its main restaurant, Four Seasons, serves tasty buffet meals. Finland's first international casino was inaugurated here in 1991. ⊠ *Eteläinen Rautatiek. 4, 00100,* ☎ *09/6911,* FAX *09/694–7886. 495 rooms. 2 restaurants, 2 coffee shops, no-smoking rooms, indoor pool, massage, sauna, casino, nightclub, meeting rooms. AE, DC, MC, V.*

$$$$ ⊞ **Sokos Hotel Marski.** Thoroughly renovated and reopened in spring 1997, the Marski is favored for its absolutely central spot, on the main Mannerheimintie artery and dead opposite Stockmann's. The suites are the last word in modern luxury, and all rooms are soundproofed, shutting out the traffic. The restaurant Marskin Kellari makes somewhat grounded claims to serve up the best French cuisine in Helsinki; Mulligan's Irish Bar is a weekend hot-spot for live music and the young, beautiful set. *Mannerheim. 10, 00100,* ☎ *09/68061,* FAX *06/680– 6255. 236 rooms, 6 suites. Restaurant, 2 bars, sauna, meeting rooms. AE, DC, MC, V.*

$$$$ ⊡ **Torni.** The original part of this hotel was built in 1903, and its towers and internal details still reflect some of the more fanciful touches of Helsinki's Jugendstil period, although a new functionalist-style section was added in 1931. The original section has striking views of Helsinki from the higher floors, not least the Atelier Bar with some of the best views of Helsinki. Old-section rooms on the courtyard are best; some have high ceilings with original carved-wood details and wooden writing desks; many also have little alcoves and other pleasing design oddities. A conference room at the top of the tower has art exhibitions that change monthly. ✉ *Yrjönk. 26, 00100,* ☎ *09/131–131,* ℻ *09/131–1361. 154 rooms with bath or shower, 9 suites. 2 restaurants, 3 bars, room service, sauna, meeting rooms. AE, DC, MC, V.*

$$ ⊡ **Anna.** Pleasantly situated in a central, residential neighborhood, the Anna is in a seven-story apartment building dating from the 1930s. Room fittings are modern, with light, comfortable furniture. The room price includes a buffet breakfast. ✉ *Annank. 1, 00120,* ☎ *09/616–621,* ℻ *09/602–664. 60 rooms, 1 suite. Brasserie, no-smoking floor, sauna. AE, DC, MC, V.*

$$ ⊡ **Marttahotelli.** This convenient establishment is small and cozy, with simply decorated, fresh, white rooms. The hotel was fully renovated in 1989. ✉ *Uudenmaank. 24, 00120,* ☎ *09/646–211,* ℻ *09/680–1266. 40 rooms with shower, 5 with bath. Sauna. AE, DC, MC, V. Closed midsummer.*

$ ⊡ **Hostel Academica.** Fully renovated in 1992, this summer hotel is made up of what are, during the rest of the year, university students' apartments. Each floor has a small lounge; the rooms are sturdy, modern, and have their own small kitchens. Family rooms and extra beds are also available, and there are special family rates. Guests can eat reduced-price meals at the nearby Perho restaurant. The central location is good for shopping and transport. ✉ *Hietaniemenk. 14, 00100,* ☎ *09/402–0206,* ℻ *09/441–201. 115 rooms. Pool, sauna, tennis court, coin laundry. AE, DC, MC, V. Closed Sept.–May.*

$ ⊡ **Vantaa Hostel.** As hostels go, this is one of the cleanest and brightest you'll ever find. It was built in 1980 and enlarged in 1989; the old wing is cheaper than the rooms in the new extension. ✉ *Valkoisenlähteentie 52, 01300 Vantaa,* ☎ *09/839–3310,* ℻ *09/839–4366. 30 rooms, 6 rooms with shared bath and shower.*

North of City Center

$$$$ ⊡ **Holiday Inn Helsinki, Congress Center.** As its name suggests, this new hotel as of spring 1997 has the Helsinki Fair and Congress Center on its doorstep; it caters mainly to visitors to events. Transport to city center, 3 km (2 mi) away, is by local train (the Pasila station is a three-minute walk away) or by tram. A shuttle bus to the airport is handy. Select rooms are for the allergy-sensitive, and some cater to people with disabilities. There's even a ballroom for 2,000. ✉ *Messuaukio 1, 00520,* ☎ *09/150–900,* ℻ *09/150–901. 239 rooms (34 executive), 6 suites. Brasserie, bar, sauna, meeting rooms. AE, DC, V.*

$$$$ ⊡ **Palace.** Built for the 1952 Olympic games, this small hotel is on the 9th and 10th floors of a waterfront commercial building, affording splendid views of the South Harbor. Its faithful clientele—largely British, American, and Swedish—appreciates the personal service that comes with its small size, daily afternoon tea included. The decor is nondescript, except for the wood paneling and plush carpet, and amenities in the guest rooms are few. The hotel's restaurants, especially the Palace Gourmet, are among Helsinki's best. ✉ *Eteläranta 10, 00130,* ☎ *09/134–561,* ℻ *09/654–786. 50 rooms, 14 junior suites, 2 suites. 2 restaurants, bar, café, room service, sauna. AE, DC, MC, V.*

$$$$ ⚃ **Strand Inter-Continental.** From the tastefully furnished rooftop
★ saunas and the large, crisply decorated rooms to the bathrooms with
heated floors and the car-wash service in the basement garage, this hotel
pampers you for a price. The hotel's distinctive use of granite and Finnish
marble in the central lobby is accentuated by a soaring atrium. Choose
from a lobby bar and two restaurants—the superb Pamir (☞ Dining,
above) or the Atrium Plaza for light meals. Though it's in a working-
class neighborhood, it's central and the waterfront vistas are a pleasure. An entire floor is reserved for nonsmokers, and five of the eight
suites have panoramic views of the sea. ✉ *John Stenbergin ranta 4,
00530,* ☎ *09/39351,* 𝖥𝖠𝖷 *09/393–5255. 200 rooms, 10 suites. 2 restaurants, bar, room service, indoor pool, saunas. AE, DC, MC, V.*

$$$ ⚃ **Airport Hotel Rantasipi.** This fully equipped, modern accommoda-
★ tion satisfies Helsinki's need for an airport hotel that meets the high-
est international standards. Convenient for layovers, the hotel borders
the airport commercial zone and has the best conference facilities near
the airport. A standard room includes a large sofa and usually a king-
size bed and has such soft touches as paisley bedspreads and wicker
furniture; all rooms are soundproof and air-conditioned. ✉ *Robert Hu-
bert. 4, 01510 Vantaa,* ☎ *09/87051,* 𝖥𝖠𝖷 *09/822–846. 300 rooms, 4
suites. 2 restaurants, piano bar, minibars, no-smoking rooms, indoor
pool, convention center. AE, DC, MC, V.*

$$$ ⚃ **Gateway Hotel.** The Gateway is in the heart of the International
Terminal at Helsinki-Vantaa Airport. It's ideal for early morning re-
grouping or quick overnights before connecting flights amid clean, modern design typical of new Finnish hotels. Some rooms are "air-side,"
for transit passengers who have no need or wish to leave the airport.
Personal computer connections are available and there's a 24-hour breakfast service. ✉ *Helsinki-Vantaa Airport, 01530 Vantaa,* ☎ *09/818–
3606,* 𝖥𝖠𝖷 *09/818–3609. 35 rooms. Sauna, meeting rooms. AE, DC,
MC, V.*

$$ ⚃ **Anton.** The furnishings in this hotel's rooms are much like those you'd
find in a typical Finnish home: simple, clean lines; a plethora of wood
tones; and duvets in bright, primary colors. In a traditional Helsinki
working-class neighborhood and near the center and Kauppatori, the
Anton is also conveniently close to the airport bus stop and the
Hakaniemi metro stop. ✉ *Paasivuorenk. 1, 00530,* ☎ *09/750–311,*
𝖥𝖠𝖷 *09/701–4527. 32 rooms, 3 suites. AE, DC, MC, V.*

$$ ⚃ **Arthur.** Owned by the Helsinki YMCA, the Arthur is centrally located,
unpretentious, and comfortable. ✉ *Vuorik. 19, 00100,* ☎ *09/173–441,*
𝖥𝖠𝖷 *09/626–880. 143 rooms. Restaurant, sauna. AE, DC, MC, V.*

$$ ⚃ **Aurora.** Built in 1970 and since renovated, this redbrick hotel has
small modern rooms decorated in pale blues, greens, and peach; larger
rooms have brown wood paneling. A 10-minute bus ride from the city
center, it's also just across from the Linnanmäki Amusement Park and
has therefore become a favorite of families. ✉ *Helsingink. 50, 00530,*
☎ *09/770–100,* 𝖥𝖠𝖷 *09/7701–0200. 70 rooms. Restaurant, pool, sauna,
spa, squash. AE, DC, MC, V.*

$$ ⚃ **Merihotelli.** Next to Hakaniemi Market Square, Merihotelli is only
a 10-minute walk from the heart of Helsinki. The smallish guest rooms
are done in shades of pale blue, and the ambience is serene. All rooms
have showers. ✉ *John Stenbergin ranta 6, 00530,* ☎ *09/69121,* 𝖥𝖠𝖷 *09/
691–2214. 87 rooms. Café, bar. AE, DC, MC, V.*

$$ ⚃ **Olympia.** There's a fine ambience in the public areas of this hotel,
with their stone floors, wood-paneled walls, and sturdy furniture. By
contrast, the rooms are light, with white walls and blue-green textiles
and upholstery. The hotel dates from 1962. ✉ *Läntinen Brahenk. 2,
00510,* ☎ *09/69151,* 𝖥𝖠𝖷 *09/691–5219. 98 rooms, 1 suite. 2 restaurants,
no-smoking rooms, sauna, nightclub. AE, DC, MC, V.*

$ ⊞ **Finn Apartments.** On a side street north of Hakaniemi Square, 10 minutes by tram from the city center, this apartment hotel offers clean, reasonably priced rooms. One option for guests, many of whom are businesspeople, is a private studio apartment with kitchenette and bathroom; an even less expensive choice is an unpretentious, light-colored economy room. The cheapest rooms must be shared with another guest. ⊠ *Franzenink. 26, 00530,* ☎ *09/773–1661,* FAX *09/701–6889. 100 rooms. Café, sauna, coin laundry. AE, DC, MC, V.*

$ ⊞ **Omapohja.** Dating from 1906, this inn, which occupies a mint-green Jugendstil building, used to be a base for actors performing at the state theater next door. Rooms are cozily old-fashioned, with wood-paneled walls and handwoven bedspreads; they also have tremendous windows. ⊠ *Itäinen Teatterikuja 3, 00100,* ☎ *09/666–211. 15 rooms, 3 with shower. MC, V.*

Töölö

$$$$ ⊞ **Inter-Continental Helsinki.** One of the most popular hotels in Helsinki,
★   this local institution is modern and central, and particularly popular with American business travelers. Decor in the rather small rooms is pleasant—oatmeal and light green carpets, subtle floral-print bedspreads and curtains. Services for business travelers are excellent, including a business center and 30 hotel rooms equipped with fax machines. Galateia offers good seafood and a wonderful view. ⊠ *Mannerheim. 46, 00260,* ☎ *09/40551,* FAX *09/405–5255. 552 rooms, 12 suites. 2 restaurants, bar, café, no-smoking rooms, room service, indoor pool, beauty salon, sauna, business services, meeting rooms. AE, DC, MC, V.*

$$$$ ⊞ **Kalastajatorppa.** In the plush western Munkkiniemi neighborhood,
★   this hotel has catered to the likes of Ronald Reagan and George Bush. A 15- to 25-minute taxi ride from city center, the hotel has also been a favorite of international artists seeking anonymity. The best rooms are in the seaside annex, but all are large and airy, done in fresh pastel colors with clear pine and birchwood paneling. Rooms in the main building may be equipped with bath and terrace or with showers only; prices vary accordingly. ⊠ *Kalastajatorpantie 1, 00330,* ☎ *09/458– 152 or 09/45811,* FAX *09/458–1683. 235 rooms, 8 suites. 2 restaurants, 2 bars, no-smoking rooms, 2 indoor pools, sauna, beach, nightclub, meeting rooms. AE, DC, MC, V.*

$$$$ ⊞ **Sokos Hotel Hesperia.** Close to the city center, the Hesperia is modern with a Finnish flair. The marble-floored lobby's convenient semicircle of service booths includes a hairdresser and barbershop, car-rental service, and gift shop. The relatively spacious contemporary rooms are well equipped but unmemorable, except for those with king-size beds— a rarity in Helsinki hotels. Some rooms overlook Töölö Bay and Mannerheimintie; back rooms face a quieter street. ⊠ *Mannerheim. 50, 00260,* ☎ *09/43101,* FAX *09/431–0995. 383 rooms, 4 suites. Restaurant, bar, café, minibars, no-smoking rooms, room service, indoor pool, beauty salon, sauna, health club, helipad. AE, DC, MC, V.*

Nightlife and the Arts

Nightlife

Helsinki nightlife has perked up considerably in recent years, and your choice extends from a variety of noisy bars and late-night clubs to more intimate cafés. The relatively small size of the central area makes it possible to hit several places in one night, but after around 9 on weekends expect lines at the popular hangouts. Cover charges, when requested, are on average FM 15–FM 50.

The Helsinki City Tourist Office has a *Clubs and Music Bars* listing of music nights and cover charges for various venues.

BARS AND LOUNGES

Kappeli (✉ Eteläespl. 1, ☎ 09/179–242) was the first Finnish restaurant to brew its own beer. Its leaded windows offer an excellent view of the Havis Amanda statue. The **Socis Pub** (✉ Kaivok. 12, ☎ 09/691–4004) at the Seurahuone has a turn-of-the-century European ambience. **Baker's Family** (✉ Kalevank. 2, ☎ 09/605–607) is a popular central café, with a lively nightclub upstairs. **Raffaello** (✉ Aleksanterink. 46, ☎ 09/653–930) attracts a young crowd of professionals from the Helsinki financial district. For a taste of Hibernia, visit one of Helsinki's most popular pubs, **O'Malley's** (✉ Hotel Torni, Yrjönk. 28, ☎ 09/131–131). The Irish theme is spreading like the gift of the gab in Helsinki, and one bar following suit is **Molly Malone's** (✉ Kaisaniemenk. 1C, ☎ 09/171–272). **Richard O'Donaghues** (✉ Richardink. 4, ☎ 09/7002–4460) is informal and intimate, prone to spontaneous music gigs on weekends. On weekends the young and beautiful crowd the large, cavernous cellar **Mulligan's** (✉ Hotel Marski, ☎ 09/68061).

Cosmopolitan beer culture is catching on in Helsinki. The welcoming, atmospheric **William K** pubs (✉ Annank. 3, ☎ 09/680–2562; ✉ Mannerheim. 72, ☎ 09/409–484) are pioneering this trend, with extraordinary varieties of brews from all over the world, especially central and eastern Europe. **Vanha Ylioppilastalo** (✉ Mannerheim. 3, ☎ 09/1311–4224) has an impressive range of beers and attracts students with live music, usually on weekends—blues, folk, and jazz. **Cantina West** (✉ Kasarmik. 23, ☎ 09/622–0900) is a lively spot for enjoying imported country, country-rock, and Tex-Mex food and music.

CASINOS

Casino Ray (✉ Eteläinen Rautatie 4, ☎ 09/694–2900), open since 1991, offers roulette, blackjack, and slot machines on the third floor of the Ramada Presidentti Hotel.

GAY AND LESBIAN BARS

For up-to-date details of the gay scene, contact the gay switchboard, **SETA** (Wed.–Fri. and Sun. 6–9 PM, ☎ 09/135–8305). **H20** (✉ Eerikink. 14, ☎ 09/608–826) is a popular gay bar. On the same street is the **Stonewall** (✉ Eerikink. 3, ☎ 09/694–4043) bar and club. **Don't Tell Mama** (✉ Annank. 32, ☎ 09/694–1122) is for men only. Just around the corner is the intimate **Cafe Escale** (✉ Kansakouluk. 1, ☎ 09/693–1533). **New Faces** (✉ Lönnrotink. 29, ☎ 09/719–257) is a lesbian nightspot. **Lost and Found** (✉ Annank. 6, ☎ 09/680–1701) is a bar as well as full-scale restaurant.

JAZZ CLUBS

Helsinki's most popular jazz club, **Storyville** (✉ Museok. 8, ☎ 09/408–007), offers live jazz and dancing every night. More serious jazz buffs may head for **The Cotton Club** (✉ Pohjoisespl. 2, ☎ 09/634–865), combining a fine restaurant with jazz evenings, often featuring international name acts. Advance bookings are advisable at both.

NIGHTCLUBS

The **Hesperia Hotel Nightclub** (✉ Mannerheim. 50, ☎ 09/43101), Helsinki's largest and most famous club, occasionally hosts big-name acts. **Tenth Floor** (✉ Hotel Vaakuna, Asemaaukio 2, ☎ 09/131–181) is currently the city's main hot spot——and consequently the one with the longest lines, unless you make a reservation or arrive early. For a night of dancing, head downtown to **Fennia** (✉ Mikonk. 17, ☎ 09/621–7170). **Kaivohuone** (✉ Kaivohuone Kaivopuisto, ☎ 09/177–

881) is an old spa structure in beautiful Kaivopuisto; its dance floor is often packed weekends.

On weekends, late night at **Botnia Club** (✉ Museok. 10, ☎ 09/446–940) is an extraordinary cocktail of elegant tango in the main hall and frenetic disco on the top floor. The university-owned **Tavastia Club** (✉ Urho Kekkosenk. 4–6, ☎ 09/694–3066) is one of the best rock clubs for top Finnish talent and some solid imports.

The Arts

For a list of events, pick up *Helsinki This Week*, available in hotels and tourist offices. For tickets, contact **Lippupalvelu** (✉ Mannerheim. 5, in the Bio-Bio cinema arcade, ☎ 09/9700–4700 or 09/664–466). **Tiketti** (✉ Yrjönk. 29C, ☎ 09/9700–4204) is the other main ticket agency.

In summer, plays and music are performed at many outdoor theaters, including Keskuspuisto, Suomenlinna, Mustikkamaa, and the Seurasaari Islands, and also at the Rowing Stadium. **The Helsinki Festival,** a performance and visual-arts celebration set in venues around the city, including a specially erected tent near the City Theater, is held yearly in August. The Festival includes the unique **Night of the Arts,** a late summer event during which much of the population takes to the streets to watch street performances, while galleries and cinemas are open late and free of charge. For festival info, call ☎ 09/135–4522.

Another important aspect of Helsinki's cultural and artistic life is the **Kaapeli Tehdas** (Cable Factory, ✉ Tallbergink. 1, ☎ 09/4763–8300). This huge converted industrial building houses a restaurant, the Cable Gallery, which doubles as a vast theater and various small but worthy museums, including the **Suomen Valokuvataiteen Museo** (Photographic Museum of Finland). The complex also houses radio stations and artists' studios. It's a short bus or metro ride (Ruoholahti station) away to west of the center.

CONCERTS

Finlandiatalo (Finlandia Hall, ✉ Karamzinink. 4, ☎ 09/40241), the home of the Helsinki Philharmonic, hosts many visiting world-class orchestras. Finland has produced many fine conductors, and because many of them are based abroad—Esa-Pekka Salonen, Jukka-Pekka Saraste, and Paavo Berglund, for example—their homecomings are lavishly fêted. Concerts are generally held from September through May on Wednesday and Thursday evenings. The splendid **Suomen Kansallisooppera** (Finnish National Opera, ✉ Helsingink. 58, ☎ 09/4030–2211), is in a waterside park by Töölönlahti. Original Finnish opera is often performed here, in addition to international favorites. The rock-hewn **Temppeliaukio Kirkko** (✉ Lutherink. 3, ☎ 09/494–698) is a favorite venue for choral and chamber music. The **Sibelius Academy** (✉ Pohjois Rautatiek. 9, ☎ 09/405–441) hosts frequent performances, usually by students.

FILM

There are about 50 cinemas in Helsinki. Foreign films have Finnish and Swedish subtitles. You'll find movie listings in most daily papers and also posted at the kiosk near the eastern entrance of the main train station. Most cinemas have assigned seats, and tickets cost FM 35–FM 45. Afternoon shows may be cheaper; there are discounts on blocks of tickets should you be a celluloid junkie.

THEATER

Though the recession has forced the state to cut back on its generous financing, private support of the arts continues to be strong—especially for the theaters, the best-known of which are the **National Theater,**

City Theater, Swedish Theater, and Lilla Teatern. However, unless you are fluent in Finnish or Swedish, you'll have a difficult time understanding the performances. Check *Helsinki This Week* for a listing of the latest performances.

Outdoor Activities and Sports

Biking

Helsinki and environs make for excellent biking through a decent network of trails, many traversing the downtown area and running through parks, forests, and fields. The free area sporting map ("Ulkoilukartta") gives details of all trails; pick up a copy at the tourist office. Daily rentals, including mountain bikes, are available from **Green Bike** (⊠ Mannerheim. 13, 00100 Helsinki, ☎ 050/550–1020).

Golf

For full information on golf in Helsinki and outskirts, contact the **Finnish Golf Union** (⊠ Radiok. 20, 00240 Helsinki, ☎ 09/348–121). There are 9- and 18-hole and par-3 (FM 60–FM 70) courses in Helsinki and surroundings, with greens fees from FM 160 to FM 250.

Swimming

The best beaches in Helsinki are Pihlajasaari, Mustikkamaa, and Uunisaari. The beach at **Hietaniemi** is especially popular with young people. Among Helsinki's indoor pools and saunas, the oldest and one of the most famous is **Yrjönkatu Uimahalli** (⊠ Yrjönk. 21B, ☎ 09/60981), where swimming is in the nude.

Tennis

There are some six tennis centers and 31 clubs in Helsinki. It's best to bring your own equipment, although rentals are available. For specifics, contact the **Finnish Tennis Association** (⊠ Myllypuro Tennis Center, Varikkotie 4, 00900 Helsinki, ☎ 09/338–122).

Shopping

Helsinki's shopping facilities are constantly improving. Although many international stores are still absent, there are several malls and shopping districts where you can shop thoroughly and in comfort. Stores are generally open weekdays 9–6 and Saturday 9–1. A new government bill permits Sunday shopping during June, July, August, and December. The Forum and Stockmann's are open weekdays 9–8, Saturday 9–6, and Sunday 12–6. An ever-expanding network of pedestrian tunnels connects the Forum, Stockmann's, and the train-station tunnel.

Kiosks remain open late and on weekends; they sell such basics as milk, juice, camera film, and tissues. Stores in Asematunneli, the train-station tunnel, are open weekdays 10–10 and weekends noon–10.

Department Stores

Stockmann's (⊠ Aleksanterink. 52, ☎ 09/1211) is Helsinki's premier department store. **Aleksi 13** (⊠ Aleksanterink. 13, ☎ 09/131–441) is less expensive than Stockmann's. Newly renovated and reopened 1950s showpiece landmark near the train station, **Sokos** (⊠ Mannerheim. 9, ☎ 09/125–61) is also well stocked.

Shopping Districts

Pohjoisesplanadi, on the north side of the Esplanade, packs in most of Helsinki's trademark design stores and a wide array of other goods. The southern part of **Senaatintori** has a host of souvenir and crafts stores, with several antiques shops and secondhand bookstores on the adjoining streets. Next to Senaatintori is the **Kiseleff Bazaar Hall,** an attractive shopping gallery.

You'll find many smaller boutiques in the streets **west of Manner-heimintie,** Fredrikinkatu and Annankatu, for example. There is one pedestrian shopping street a few blocks south of the Esplanade, on **Iso Roobertinkatu;** stores here are conventional, but the atmosphere is more relaxed than around Mannerheimintie and the Esplanade.

Shopping Malls

All of Helsinki's shopping malls have a good mix of stores plus several cafés and restaurants. **Forum** (⊠ Mannerheim. 20) is a large shopping complex. **Kaivopiha** (⊠ Kaivok. 10) is across from the train station. **Kluuvi** (⊠ Aleksanterink. 9–Kluuvik. 5) is a major mall. The large **Itäkeskus** shopping complex in east Helsinki, claimed to be the biggest indoor mall in Scandinavia, can be reached by metro.

Specialty Stores

ANTIQUES

Many shops sell china, furniture, and art. Cut glass and old farm furniture are other popular products; the latter is harder to find. The **Kruunuhaka** area north of Senaatintori is the best bet for antiques. Try **Antik Oskar** (⊠ Rauhank. 7, ☎ 09/135–7410), **Antiikkiliike Karl Fredrik** (⊠ Mariank. 13, ☎ 09/630–014), **Punavuoren Antiikki** (⊠ Mariank. 14, ☎ 09/662–682), and **Atlas Antiques** (⊠ Rauhank. 8, ☎ 09/628–186), if you are interested in coins, banknotes, medals, and silver. Also try the **Punavuori district,** between Eerikinkatu and Tehtaankatu; many shops here also sell secondhand books (there's usually a small selection in English).

CERAMICS AND ACCESSORIES

Firms like **Pentik** (⊠ Pohjoisespl. 27C, ☎ 09/625–558), **Hackman Shop Arabia** (⊠ Pohjoisespl. 25, ☎ 09/170–055), and **Aarikka** (⊠ Pohjoisespl. 25–27, ☎ 09/652–277) sell ceramics, leather, accessories, wooden toys, and jewelry. The **Arabia factory** (⊠ Hämeentie 135), at the end of the Tram 6 line, exhibits older designs, and has its own shop where slightly flawed items are sold at a discount.

CLOTHING

Bright, modern, unusual clothes for men, women, and children in quality fabrics are sold at **Marimekko** (⊠ Pohjoisespl. 31, ☎ 09/177–944; Eteläespl. 14, ☎ 09/170–724). The **Forum shopping mall** (⊠ Mannerheim. 20, ☎ 09/694–1498), on the Esplanade, also has clothes; though the products are costly, they're worth a look even if you don't plan to spend.

JEWELRY

Kaunis Koru (⊠ Aleksanterink. 28, ☎ 09/626–850) produces avant-garde silver and gold designs. **Lapponia Jewelry** (⊠ Mäkelänk. 60A, ☎ 09/146–4600) creates innovative styles. **Kalevala Koru** (⊠ Unionink. 25, ☎ 09/171–520) bases its designs on traditional motifs dating back as far as the Iron Age.

SAUNA SUPPLIES

For genuine Finnish sauna supplies like wooden buckets, bath brushes, and birch-scented soap, visit the **Sauna Shop** in the Kiseleff Bazaar (⊠ Aleksanterink. 28) or the fourth floor of Stockmann's (⊠ Aleksanterink. 52, ☎ 09/1211).

Street Markets

Helsinki's main street markets specialize in food, but all have some clothing (new and used) and household products. **Hakaniemi** (⊠ North of town center, off Unionink.) has everything from Eastern spices to used clothing; it's open Monday–Thursday 8–5, Friday 8–6, and Saturday 8–3. **Kauppatori** sells some furs in addition to its standard products. Hours are Monday–Saturday 7–2; in summer they reopen from 3:30 to 8. Almost adjacent to Kauppatori is the **Old Market Hall,** open weekdays 8–5 and Saturday 8–2, where you can browse and shop for anything from flowers to vegetables, meat, and fish. **Hietalahden Tori,** at Bulevardi and Hietalahdenkatu, is open every day but Sunday. At the outdoor flea market you can get an ever-changing assortment of used items; the indoor market is brimming with food, flowers, fish, and more.

Helsinki A to Z

Arriving and Departing

BY PLANE

All domestic and international flights to Helsinki use **Helsinki-Vantaa International Airport,** 20 km (14 mi) north of city center. Helsinki is served by most major European airlines, as well as several East European carriers. North American service is available with **Finnair** (⊠ City Terminal, Asemaaukio 3, ☎ 09/818–800) in cooperation with **Delta** (⊠ Salomonk. 17B, ☎ 09/612–2020). European airlines include **SAS** (⊠ Keskusk. 7A, ☎ 09/228–021), **Lufthansa** (⊠ Yrjönk. 29A, ☎ 09/348–110), **SwissAir** (⊠ Mikonk. 7, ☎ 09/175–300), **British Airways** (⊠ Aleksanterink. 21A, ☎ 09/650–677), and **Air France** (⊠ Pohjoisespl. 27C, ☎ 09/625–862).

Between the Airport and Downtown: A local **Bus 615** runs three to four times an hour between the airport and the main railway station. The fare is FM 15, and the trip takes about 40 minutes. Local **Bus 614** runs three times a day between the airport and the main bus station; the trip takes approximately 40 minutes, the fare FM 15. **Finnair** buses carry travelers to and from the railway station (Finnair's City Terminal) two to four times an hour, with a stop at the Inter-Continental Helsinki. Stops requested along the route from the airport to the city are also made. Travel time from the Inter-Continental to the airport is about 30 minutes, 35 minutes from the main railway station; the fare is FM 24.

A limousine ride into central Helsinki will cost about FM 600; contact **International Limousine System** (⊠ Alkutic 32H, 00660, ☎ 09/744–577 or 049/421–801).

There is a taxi stop at the arrivals building. A cab ride into central Helsinki will cost between FM 100 and FM 140. Driving time is 20 to 35 minutes, depending on the time of day. Check to see if your hotel has a shuttle service, although this is not common here. **Airport Taxi Service** (☎ 09/2200–2500) costs FM 60, FM 90 for two passengers, and FM 110 for three, and operates shuttles between the city and the airport. You must reserve two hours before flight departure; for flights departing before 7 AM, call before 8 PM.

Getting Around

Helsinki center is compact and best explored on foot. The City Tourist Office provides a free Helsinki route map detailing all public transportation. The *Helsinki Kortti* (**Helsinki Card**) allows unlimited travel on city public transportation, free entry to many museums, a free sightseeing tour, and a variety of other discounts. It's available for one, two, or three days (FM 105, FM 135, FM 165) and can be bought at most hotels or at the City Tourist Office.

BY BOAT

All boat tours depart from Kauppatori. The easiest way to choose one is to go to the square in the morning and read the information boards describing the tours. Most tours run in the summer only. You can go as far afield as Porvoo (☞ Side Trips from Helsinki, *below*) or take a short jaunt to the Helsinki Zoo on Korkeasaari.

A ferry to the Suomenlinna fortress island runs about twice an hour, depending on the time of day, and costs FM 9. Ten-trip tickets issued for city public tranport can be used on the ferry, too. From June to August, private water buses run from Kauppatori to Suomenlinna; call 06/633–800 for information and schedules.

BY BUS, METRO, AND TRAM

The bus and tram networks are compact but extensive, and service is frequent, from around 5:25 AM to 11:20 PM, Monday through Saturday, with infrequent service on Sunday. Be sure to pick up a route map at the tourist office—many stops do not have them. Fares are the same for buses and trams. You must validate a one-trip ticket (*Kertalippu,* FM 9) by punching it in the machine, and a 10-trip ticket (*Kymmenen matkan lippu,* FM 75) yourself; buy them at R-Kiosks. Single-trip tram tickets (FM 7, no transfer; FM 9, one transfer allowed) are available on board. The main bus station in downtown Helsinki is **Linja-autoasema** (✉ Simonk. 3, ☎ 09/682–701; 0100–111 local info).

BY CAR

Ring Roads One and Three are the two major highways that circle the city. Mannerheimintie and Hämeentie are the major trunk roads out of Helsinki. Mannerheimintie feeds into Highway E79, which travels west and takes you to the Ring Roads. Hämeentie leads you to Highway E4 as well as Roads 4 and 7. From either route, you will find directions for Road 137 to the airport. For specific route information, contact the **Automobile and Touring Club of Finland** (✉ Autoliitto ry, Hämeentie 105 A, PL 35, 00550 Helsinki, ☎ 09/774–761) or the City Tourist Office.

BY TAXI

There are numerous taxi stands; central stands are at Rautatientori at the station, the main bus station, Linja-autoasema, and in the Esplanade. Taxis can also be flagged, but this can be difficult, as many are on radio call and are often on their way to stands, where late-night lines may be very long. An average taxi ride in Helsinki costs under FM 40; a taxi from the airport costs FM 145.

BY TRAIN

Helsinki's suburbs and most of the rest of southern, western, and central Finland are well served by trains. Travel on trains within the Helsinki city limits costs the same as all public transport, FM 9 or less if you use the 10-trip tickets (☞ *above*). A 10-trip **Helsinki Area Ticket,** or *Seutulippu,* for FM 125 also provides a small discount for travel back and forth to adjacent areas such as Espoo and Vantaa.

Contacts and Resources

DOCTORS AND DENTISTS

Dial ☎ 09/10023 for doctor referrals. **Töölö Dental Care Center** (✉ Runebergink. 47 A, ☎ 09/431–4500) is open weekdays 8–3.

EMBASSIES

U.S. (✉ Itäinen Puistotie 14A, 00140 Helsinki, ☎ 09/171–931). **Canada** (✉ Pohjoisespl. 25B, 00100 Helsinki, ☎ 09/171–141). **U.K.** (✉ Itäinen Puistotie 17, 00140 Helsinki, ☎ 09/2286–5100).

EMERGENCIES

The general emergency number is ☎ 112; call it for any emergency situation. Coins are not needed to make this call on pay phones.

Police. ☎ 112.

Ambulance. ☎ 112. Specify whether the situation seems life-threatening so medical attendants can prepare for immediate treatment in the ambulance.

Hospital. Töölön Sairaala (✉ Töölönk. 40, ☎ 09/471–7358) is central, about 2 km (1 mi) from city center, with a 24-hour emergency room and first-aid service.

ENGLISH-LANGUAGE BOOKSTORES

Akateeminen Kirjakauppa (Academic Bookstore, ✉ Pohjoisespl. 39, ☎ 09/12141) is the largest English-language bookstore; it's also the most expensive. Like the Academic Bookstore, **Suomalainen Kirjakauppa** (The Finnish Bookstore, ✉ Aleksanterink. 23, ☎ 09/651–855) sells English-language books, newspapers, and magazines. English-language newspapers are also on sale at the **kiosks** in the main train station.

GUIDED TOURS

Orientation Tours: Bus tours are a good way to get oriented in Helsinki. A 1½-hour bus tour of central Helsinki sites comes free with the Helsinki Card (☞ Getting Around, *above*); otherwise the cost is FM 70. The tour leaves from Railway Square (✉ Asemaaukio, west side) daily at 11 AM and 1:30 PM May–September, Sunday at 11 AM October–April. It also departs from Olympia Terminal (✉ Eteläsatama, or South Harbor) daily at 9:45 AM May–September and from the Havis Amanda (✉ Kauppatori) daily at 10:30 AM, 12:30 PM, and 2:30 PM May–September. For more information, contact **Suomen Turistiauto** (☎ 09/477–4750).

A year-round two-hour tour leaves from the Olympic Harbor daily at 9:30 AM. The cost is FM 90 for adults and FM 45 for children under 12, not including lunch. For more information, call **Ageba Travel** (☞ Travel Agencies, *below*). From April through October, Ageba also has a daily 2½-hour tour at 11 AM from the Olympic Harbor costing FM 100, excluding lunch.

The Helsinki City Tourist Office distributes a pamphlet called *Helsinki Sightseeing: 3T,* which describes points of interest along the 3T tram's downtown route. The tram ride provides a good orientation to the city for the price of a regular fare (FM 7). You can get on board in front of the railway station on Kaivokatu for the 60-minute round-trip.

Personal Guides: Helsingin Matkailuyhdistys (Helsinki Tourist Association; ☞ Visitor Information, *below*) is a guide booking center that will arrange personal tour guides.

Walking Tours: The City Tourist Office has an excellent brochure, *See Helsinki on Foot,* with six walks covering most points of interest.

LATE-NIGHT PHARMACIES

Yliopiston Apteekki (✉ Mannerheim. 5, ☎ 09/4178–0101) is open daily 24 hours.

OPENING AND CLOSING TIMES

Banks are open weekdays 9 or 9:15 to 4 or 5. Many offices and embassies close at 3 PM June–August. Stores are open weekdays 9–6 and Saturday 9–1 or 2 and are closed on Sunday. Big stores in the town center will now be open Sunday, June–August, December, and five other Sundays throughout the year from noon to 7. Some stores in malls stay open until 8 PM on weekdays and until 4 on Saturday. In the Asematunneli (train station tunnel), stores are open weekdays 10–10 and weekends noon–10.

TRAVEL AGENCY
Try **Ageba Travel** (⊠ Pohjoisranta 4, ☎ 09/6150–1588) for tour (or sightseeing) information.

VISITOR INFORMATION
The **Helsinki City Tourist Office** (⊠ Pohjoisespl. 19, 00100 Helsinki, ☎ 09/169–3757) is open May–September, weekdays 8:30–6, weekends 10–3; October–April, weekdays 8:30–4. **Helsingin Matkailuyhdistys** (Helsinki Tourist Association, ⊠ Lönnrotink. 7, 00120, ☎ 09/645–225).

The **Finnish Tourist Board's Information Office** (⊠ Eteläespl. 4, 00130 Helsinki, ☎ 09/4030–1211 or 09/4030–1300), covering all of Finland, is open June–August, weekdays 8:30–5, Saturdays 10–2; September–May, weekdays 8:30–4. **Suomen Matkatoimisto** (Finland Travel Bureau, ⊠ Kaivok. 10 A, PL 319, 00100 Helsinki, ☎ 09/18261) is the country's main travel agency.

SIDE TRIPS FROM HELSINKI

Helsinki's outskirts are full of attractions, most of them no more than a half-hour bus or train ride from the city center. From the idyllic former home of Finland's national artist to the utopian garden city of Tapiola in Espoo, options abound.

Gallen-Kallela Estate

10 km (6 mi) northwest of Helsinki.

Set at the edge of the sea and surrounded by towering, wind-bent pines, the turreted brick-and-stucco Gallen-Kallela Estate was the self-designed studio and home of the Finnish Romantic painter Akseli Gallen-Kallela. Gallen-Kallela (1865–1931) lived in the mansion on and off from its completion in 1913 until his death. Inside, the open rooms of the painter's former work spaces make the perfect exhibition hall for his paintings. Also displayed are some of his posters and sketches of the ceiling murals he made for the Paris Art Exhibition at the turn of the century. A café is on the grounds. To get to the estate, take Tram 4 from in front of the Sokos department store on Mannerheimintie. From the Munkkiniemi stop transfer to Bus 33, or walk the 2 km (1 mi) through the woods. ⊠ *Gallen-Kallelantie 27, Tarvaspää,* ☎ *09/513–388.* 🖭 *FM 35.* ☉ *Mid-May–Aug., Mon.–Thurs. 10–8, Fri.–Sun. 10–5; Sept.–mid-May, Tues.–Sat. 10–4, Sun. 10–5.*

Espoo

20 km (13 mi) west of Helsinki.

Tapiola, an architectural showpiece in its day, is one of the Helsinki suburbs that make up Espoo. Designed by top Helsinki artists of the 1950s—Ervi, Blomstedt, and Rewell among them—the urban landscape of alternating high and low residential buildings, fountains, gardens, and swimming pools blends into the natural surroundings. Guides and sightseeing tours for architecture enthusiasts and professionals are available from the **Espoo Visitor and Convention Bureau** (⊠ Keskustorni, 13th floor, 02100 Espoo, ☎ 09/460–311). The Helsinki Area Ticket (☞ Helsinki A to Z, *above*) provides discount fares to Espoo.

Hvitträsk

40 km (25 mi) west of Helsinki.

On the northwest edge of the Espoo area is Hvitträsk, the studio home of architects Herman Gesellius, Armas Lindgren, and Eliel Saarinen.

In an idyllic position at the top of a wooded slope, the property dates back to the turn of the century, and is now converted into a charming museum. The whimsical main house reveals the national Art Nouveau style, with its rustic detail and paintings by Akseli Gallen-Kallela; Saarinen lived here, and his grave is nearby. A café and restaurant are set up in one of the architects' houses. Hvitträsk can be reached in 45 minutes by Bus 166 from Helsinki's main bus station, Linja-autosema. ☎ 09/221–9230. ⊠ FM 20. ⊙ Museum June–Aug., weekdays 10–7, weekends 10–6; Sept.–May, daily 11–5.

Ainola

50 km (31 mi) north of Helsinki.

The former home of Finland's most famous son, composer Jean Sibelius, takes its name from his wife, Aino. From late spring through summer, the intimate wooden house set in secluded woodland is open to the public as a museum. Buses leave from platforms 9, 11, and 12 at Helsinki's Linja-autoasema bus station, or you can take a local train first to the town of Järvenpää; Ainola is 2 km (1 mi) farther by bus or taxi. ⊠ 04400 Järvenpää, ☎ 09/287–322. ⊙ June–Aug., Tues.–Sun. 11–7; May and Sept., Wed.–Sun. 11–7.

Porvoo

50 km (31 mi) east of Helsinki.

Porvoo is a living record of the past, with its old stone streets and painted wooden houses lining the riverbank. Artisan boutiques around the old Town Hall Square invite exploration. Take a stroll into the Old Quarter to see the multicolored wooden houses. Visit the 15th-century stone-and-wood cathedral, **Porvoon Tuomiokirkko,** where the diet of the first duchy of Finland was held in the 1800s. The **Walter Runebergin Veistoskokoelma** (Walter Runeberg Sculpture Collection, ⊠ Aleksanterink. 3–5, ☎ 019/582–186) is a lovely sculpture collection. The **Porvoo Museo** (⊠ Välik. 11, ☎ 019/580–589) captures the region's social and cultural history through exhibits on daily life and household objects. Next door to the Porvoo Museo, the **Edelfelt-Vallgren Museo** (⊠ Välik. 11, ☎ 019/580–589) exhibits Edelfelt's art.

Near Porvoo in Haikko, you can visit the **Albert Edelfeltin Atelje,** the painter's studio of Albert Edelfelt. Also near Porvoo is the **Savilinna Taide-ja Käsityökeskus** (Savilinna Arts and Handicrafts Center, ⊠ Suomenkyläntie 32, ☎ 019/583–483), a ceramics workshop where you can watch ceramics artists at work, participate in classes, view art exhibits, and visit the gift shop and café. Contact the **Porvoo City Tourist Office** (⊠ Rauhank. 20, 06100 Porvoo, ☎ 019/580–145) for details about all local sights. A branch at old Town Hall Square is open June–August 15.

Part of the fun of visiting Porvoo is the journey to get there. Occasionally in summer, a **steam train** runs from Helsinki to Porvoo, a truly delightful alternative for those with time to spare; contact the Porvoo City Tourist Office for details. Far more regular than the steam train is the boat service. Mid-June–mid-August daily cruises depart from Helsinki's South Harbor: the **J. L. Runeberg** takes 3½ hours, the **Queen** 2½ hours each way. Average round-trip cost is FM 135. You will be taken westward through dozens of islands before landing at Porvoo, which is small enough to be covered on foot. Contact **Porvoon Sataman Info** (Porvoo Harbor Information, ☎ 019/584–727). There are also bus and road connections.

Vantaa

20 km (13 mi) north of Helsinki.

Though not remarkable, Vantaa—the municipality just north of Helsinki proper and the home of the international airport—has a few notable attractions. A welcome surplus of open green space and trails for biking, hiking, and running create an oasis for outdoor enthusiasts. Don't miss the 15th-century **Helsingin Pitajan Kirkko** (Parish Church).

Consider using Vantaa is home base if your trip to Helsinki coincides with a convention and you can't find accommodations there: The airport is within the city's municipal boundaries and easily reached by public transport; you can use the Helsinki Area Ticket (☞ Helsinki A to Z, *above*) in Vantaa.

The **Heureka Suomalainen Tiedekeskus** (Heureka Finnish Science Center) has interactive exhibits on topics as diverse as energy, language, and papermaking. There is also a cafeteria, a park, and a planetarium with taped commentary in English. ☒ *Tiedepuisto 1, Tikkurila, Vantaa,* ☎ *09/85799.* ☞ *FM 75.* ☉ *Daily 10–6, Thurs. until 8.*

Also in Vantaa are the peaceful **Viherpaja, Japanese, and Cactus gardens.** ☒ *Meiramitie 1,* ☎ *09/822–628.* ☞ *Japanese Garden FM 5, other gardens free.* ☉ *June–Aug., weekdays 8–7, weekends 9–5; Sept.–May, weekdays 8–6, weekends 9–2.*

The **Suomen Ilmailumuseo** (Finnish Aviation Museum) has 50 military and civilian aircraft on display. ☒ *Tietotie 3,* ☎ *09/821–870.* ☞ *FM 20.* ☉ *Daily noon–6.*

Contact the **Vantaa Tourist Office** (☒ Unikkotie 2, Tikkurila, 01300 Vantaa, ☎ 09/839–3134) for more information.

SOUTHWESTERN COAST AND THE ÅLAND ISLANDS

If you harbor a weakness for islands you'll be thrilled to see their magical world stretching along Finland's coastline. There, in the Gulf of Finland and the Baltic, more than 30,000 islands form a magnificent archipelago. The rugged and fascinating Åland Islands group lies westward from Turku, forming an autonomous province of its own. Turku, the former capital, was the main gateway through which cultural influences reached Finland over the centuries.

A trip to Turku via Hanko and Tammisaari will give you a taste of Finland at its most historic and scenic. Many of Finland's oldest towns lie in this southwest region of the country, having been chartered by Swedish kings—hence the predominance of the Swedish language here.

The southwest is a region of flat, often mist-soaked rural farmlands, and villages peppered with traditional wooden houses. At other times pastoral and quiet, the region's cultural life comes alive in summer.

It's easy to explore this region by rail, bus, or car, then to hop on a ferry bound for the Ålands, halfway between Finland and Sweden. Drive along the southern coast toward Turku, the regional capital, stopping at the charming coastal towns along the way. Or take a train from Helsinki to Turku, catching buses from Turku to other parts of the region.

Snappertuna

39 *124 km (77 mi) southeast of Turku, 75 km (47 mi) southwest of Helsinki.*

Southwestern Coast and Åland Islands

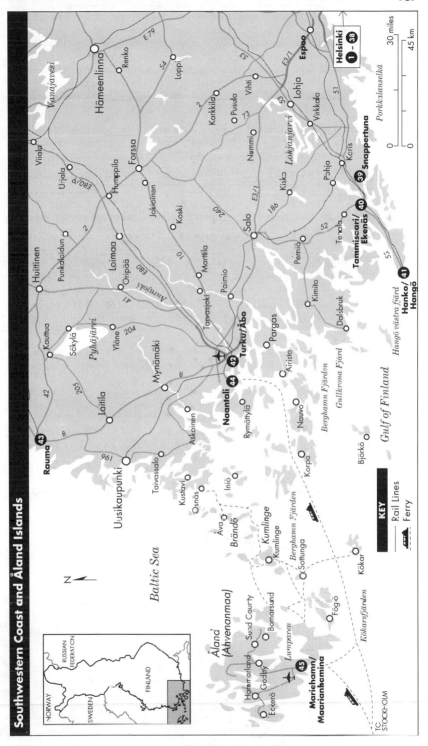

KEY
- —— Rail Lines
- --- Ferry

Baltic Sea

Gulf of Finland

Åland (Ahvenanmaa)

Mariehamn/ Maarianhamina

Hanko/ Hangö

Tammiscari/ Ekenäs

Snappertuna

Helsinki
1 – 38

Espoo

Rauma

Turku/Åbo

Naantali

Snappertuna is a small farming town with a proud hilltop church, a charming homestead museum, and the handsome restored ruin of **Raaseporin Linna** (Raseborg Castle), set in a small dale. The castle is believed to date from the 12th century. One 16th-century siege left the castle damaged, but restorations have given it a new face. In summer, concerts, dramas, and old-time market fairs are staged here. ☎ 019/234–015. 🚩 FM 5. *Guided tours arranged by the local tourist office* ☎ 019/278–6540. ☉ *May–Aug., daily 10–8.*

En Route En route to Tammisaari, you'll want to take the kids to the amusement
☾ park in Karjaa, where **Lystiland** (Amusement Land) includes a minia-
ture train tour on an enchanted forest path. ⊠ *Vanha Turuntie,* ☎ 019/236–450. 🚩 FM 30. ☉ *June–mid-Aug., daily noon–7.*

Tammisaari

㊵ *16 km (10 mi) west of Snappertuna, 109 km (68 mi) southeast of Turku.*

Tammisaari (or Ekenäs) has a colorful Old Quarter, 18th- and 19th-century buildings, and a lively marina. The scenery is dazzling in summer, when the sun glints off the water and marine traffic is at its peak. The **Tammisaaren Museo** (Tammisaari Museum) is the provincial museum of western Uusimaa, providing a taste of the region's culture and history. ⊠ *Kustaa Vaasank. 13,* ☎ 019/263–3161. 🚩 FM 10. ☉ *May 20–July, Tues.–Sun. 11–4; Aug.–May 19, Tues.–Thurs.* 6 PM–8 PM.

Dining and Lodging

$$ ✕🏨 **Ekenäs Stadshotell and Restaurant.** This modern, airy hotel is right in the heart of Tammisaari, amid fine lawns and gardens and near the sea and Old Quarter. The rooms, each with its own balcony, have wide picture windows and comfortable modern furnishings, all in pale and neutral colors. The restaurant offers Continental food and Swedish-Finnish seafood specialties prepared by a veteran chef. ⊠ *Pohjoinen Rantak. 1, 10600 Tammisaari,* ☎ 019/241–3131, 🄵🄰🄷 019/246–1550. *16 rooms, 2 suites. Restaurant, 3 bars, pub, room service, indoor pool, nightclub. AE, DC, MC, V.*

Nightlife and the Arts

The **Scandinavian Guitar Festival** comes to Tammisaari in August.

Outdoor Activities and Sports

BOATING
A variety of boats can be rented from the local tourist office.

TENNIS
There are public tennis courts on Tammisaari. Contact the local tourist office for details.

Hanko

㊶ *37 km (23 mi) southwest of Tammisaari, 141 km (88 mi) southeast of Turku.*

In the coastal town of Hanko (Hangö), you'll find long stretches of sandy beach—about 30 km, or 19 mi of it—some sandy and some with sea-smoothed boulders. Sailing abounds here, thanks to Finland's largest guest harbor. A sampling of the largest and most fanciful private homes in Finland dot the seacoast, their porches edged with gingerbread iron detail and woodwork, and crazy towers sprouting from their roofs. Favorite pastimes here are beachside strolls, bike rides along well-kept paths, and, best of all, long walks along the main avenue past the great wooden houses with their wraparound porches.

This customs port has a rich history. Fortified in the 18th century, Hanko defenses were destroyed by the Russians in 1854, during the Crimean War. Later it became a popular spa town for Russians, then the port from which more than 300,000 Finns emigrated to North America between 1880 and 1930.

🕰 Through the telescope of **Vesitorni** (Hanko's Watch Tower), you can follow the comings and goings of the town's marine traffic and get a grand view of some of the very small islands sprinkled around the peninsula's edges. ⊠ *Vartiovuori,* ☎ *019/280–3411.* ☞ *FM 5.* ☉ *May 15–June 11 and Aug. 13–Aug. 27, daily 11–3; June 12–Aug. 12, daily 11–7.*

Lodging

$ 🏕 **Camping Silversand.** There are various facilities at this large campground near the water, including eight-person cabins and full hookups for trailers, as well as trailers and tents for rent. ⊠ *Hopeahietikko, 10960 Hanko,* ☎ *019/248–5500 (off-season, 09/716–422),* FAX *019/713–713. Cafeteria, store, cooking facilities, sauna, showers, bathrooms.* ☉ *Closed Aug.–Apr.*

Outdoor Activities and Sports

BOATING

A variety of boats can be rented at the guest harbor Info-Point in Hanko, or through the local tourist office (☞ Visitor Information *in* Southwestern Coast and Åland Islands A to Z, *below*). Young people and families race in and attend the annual **Hanko Regatta,** setting sail during a weekend at the end of June or beginning of July.

TENNIS

For information about Hanko's public tennis courts, contact the local tourist office.

Turku

🅰 *140 km (87 mi) northwest of Hanko, 166 km (103 mi) west of Helsinki.*

Founded at the beginning of the 13th century, Turku is the nation's oldest and fifth largest city and was the original capital of newborn Finland. Its early importance in the history of Finland has earned Turku the title of "the cradle of Finnish culture." Turku has a long history as a commercial and intellectual center (the city's name means trading post); once the site of the first Finnish university, it has two major universities, the Finnish University of Turku and the Swedish-speaking Åo Akademi. Turku is home to more than 160,000 people and a year-round harbor.

The 700-year-old **Turun Tuomiokirkko** (Turku Cathedral) remains the seat of the archbishop of Finland. Although partially gutted by fire in 1827, the cathedral has been completely restored. In the choir are R. W. Ekman's frescoes portraying Bishop Henry (an Englishman) baptizing the then-heathen Finns and Mikael Agricola offering the Finnish translation of the New Testament to Gustav Vasa of Sweden. The cathedral also houses a museum, which displays medieval church vestments, silver chalices, and wooden sculptures. ⊠ *Turun Tuomiokirkko,* ☎ *02/251–0651.* ☞ *Free.* ☉ *Mid-Apr.–mid-Sept., daily 9–8; mid-Sept.–mid-Apr., daily 9–7.*

Where the Aura flows into the sea stands **Turun Linna** (Turku Castle), one of the city's most important historical monuments. The oldest part of the fortress was built at the end of the 13th century, and the newer part dates from the 16th century. The castle was damaged by bombing in 1941, and its restoration was completed in 1961. Many of its seemingly infinite rooms hold rather incongruous exhibits: next to a display on medieval life (featuring a dead rat to illustrate the Black Death) is a roomful of 1920s flapper costumes. The vaulted chambers themselves give you a sense of the domestic lives of the Swedish royals. A good gift shop and a pleasant café are on the castle grounds. ⊠ *Linnank. 80,* ☎ *02/262–0300.* ➕ *FM 20.* ☉ *Apr. 16–Sept. 15, daily 10–6; mid-Sept.–mid-Apr., Mon. 2–7, Tues.–Sun. 10–3.*

The **Luostarinmäki Handicrafts Museum** is an authentic collection of wooden houses and buildings containing shops and workshops where traditional crafts are demonstrated and sold. ⊠ *Vartiovuorenk. 4,* ☎ *02/262–0350.* ➕ *FM 20.* ☉ *mid-Apr.–mid-Sept., daily 10–6; mid-Sept.–mid-Apr., Tues.–Sun 10–3.*

The **Aboa Vetus/Ars Nova** museum displays a unique combination of history and art. Begun as a straightforward extension of the Villa von Rettig collection, the museum's concept changed when workers discovered archeological remains, which were excavated and incorporated into the museum. Modern art in the old villa includes works by Herbin and Ernst, as well as *The Swordsman* by Picasso. The preserved excavations in the Aboa Vetus section date to the 15th century. ⊠ *Itäinen Rantak. 4–6,* ☎ *02/250–0552.* ➕ *FM 50 combined ticket for villa and excavations, FM 35 each.* ☉ *May–Aug., daily 10–7; Sept.–Apr., Tues.–Sun. 11–7.*

The **Turun Taidemuseo** (Turku Art Museum) holds some of Finland's most famous paintings, including Akseli Gallen-Kallela's oft-reproduced *Defense of the Sampo* (1896). In addition to his works, there's a broad selection of turn-of-the-century Finnish art and modern multimedia works. ⊠ *Aurak. 26, Puolanpuisto,* ☎ *02/233–0954.* ➕ *FM 30 or more, depending on current exhibits.* ☉ *Apr.–Sept., Tues., Fri., and Sat. 10–4, Wed. and Thurs. 10–7, Sun. 11–6; Oct.–Mar., Tues.–Sat. 10–4, Sun. 11–6.*

Dining and Lodging

$$$ ✕ **Calamare.** In the heart of the city at the Hotel Marina Palace, this restaurant has maintained a high standard for its fish and meat dishes. Try the Delicacy Plate, a tasty dish with Baltic herring, roe in mustard sauce, shrimp, fillet of beef, egg, and marinated mushrooms. Calamare has impressive views of the Auajoki River and a Mediterranean atmosphere with Roman-style statues and palm trees. ⊠ *Linnank. 32,* ☎ *02/336–2126. AE, DC, MC, V.*

$$$ ✕ **Julia.** French country fare is the specialty in this informal and cozy restaurant, where you can enjoy a tasty meal by the warmth of a fireplace. ⊠ *Eerikink. 4,* ☎ *02/336–3251. AE, DC, MC, V. Closed Sun.*

$$ ✕ **Suomalainen Pohja.** Next to the attractive Turku Art Museum and a stone's throw from the market square, this restaurant has large windows offering a splendid view of an adjacent park. Seafood, poultry, and game dishes have earned a good reputation here. Try the fillet of reindeer with sautéed potatoes or the cold smoked rainbow trout with asparagus. ⊠ *Aurak. 24,* ☎ *02/251–2000. AE, DC, MC, V. Closed weekends.*

$$$$ 🏨 **Park Hotel.** Built in 1904 in the Art Nouveau style for a British executive who ran the local shipyard, the castlelike Park Hotel is one of Finland's most unusual lodgings. Rooms have high ceilings and are filled with antique furniture. It's in the heart of Turku, just two blocks from the main market square. ⊠ *Rauhank. 1, 20100 Turku,* ☎ *02/251–9666,* ℻ *02/251–9696. 21 rooms. Restaurant, minibars, sauna. AE, DC, MC, V.*

$$$$ 🏨 **Sokos Hotel Hamburger Börs.** One of Turku's best-known and finest hotels, the Hamburger has well-appointed rooms with TV and

modern amenities. There's even a jazz club. The German-style tavern is great for drinks; the main restaurant serves Continental cuisine and Finnish specialties like fillet of reindeer with bacon. ⊠ *Kauppiask. 6, 20100 Turku,* ☎ *02/337–301,* FAX *02/251–8051. 248 rooms, 2 suites. 2 restaurants, bar, café, nightclub. AE, DC, MC, V.*

Nightlife and the Arts

A lively artistic community thrives in Turku, and like most Finnish towns, it comes into its own in the summer. It is most active in July during the **Ruisrock Festival,** which draws international acts to the seaside park 5 km (3 mi) west of the city. August's **Turku Music Festival** features baroque and contemporary performances. The highlight of the festival is the well-attended, outdoor **Down by the Laituri,** with stages set up along the city waterfront.

Outdoor Activities and Sports

TENNIS

For details on Turku's public tennis courts, contact the local tourist office (☞ Visitor Information, *below*).

Rauma

⑬ *92 km (57 mi) northwest of Turku, 238 km (148 mi) northwest of Helsinki.*

The third-oldest city in Finland, Rauma is renowned for its old wooden houses painted in original, distinctive 18th- and 19th-century colors. The colors are so extraordinary, in fact, that no house can be repainted until the Old Rauma Association approves the color. UNESCO has designated Rauma's Gamla (Old Town) a World Heritage Site. It's also widely known for its tradition of lace making and its annual **Lace Week,** held every year at the end of July. The Biennale Balticum art event— with a theme of change—is scheduled for summer 1998. You can take a bus to Rauma from Turku in 1½ hours. For information and bus schedules, contact the local tourist office (☞ Visitor Information, *below*).

Naantali

⑭ *17 km (10½ mi) west of Turku.*

Built around a convent of the Order of Saint Birgitta in the 15th century, the coastal village of Naantali is an aging medieval town, former pilgrimage destination, artists' colony, and modern resort all rolled into one. Many of its buildings date from the 17th century, following a massive rebuilding after the Great Fire of 1628. You'll also see a number of 18th- and 19th-century buildings, which form the basis of the Old Town—a settlement by the water's edge. These shingled wooden buildings were originally built as private residences, and many remain so, although a few now house small galleries.

Naantali's extremely narrow cobblestone lanes gave rise to a very odd law. During periods when economic conditions were poor, Naantalians earned their keep by knitting socks and exporting them by the tens of thousands. Men, women, and children all knitted so feverishly that the town council forbade groups of more than six from meeting in narrow lanes with their knitting—and causing road obstructions.

A major attraction in the village is **Kultaranta,** the summer residence for Finland's presidents, with its more than 3,500 rosebushes. Guided tours can be arranged through the Naantali tourist board year-round. ⊠ *Luonnonmaasaari.* ☻ *Tour hrs vary, call the local tourist office (☞ Visitor Information, below).*

The convent **Naantalin Luostarikirkko** (Naantali's Vallis Gratiae) was founded in 1443 and completed in 1462. It housed both monks and nuns, and operated under the aegis of the Catholic church until it was dissolved by the Reformation in the 16th century. Buildings fell into disrepair, then were restored from 1963 to 1965. The church is all that remains of the convent. ⊠ *Nunnak., Naantali,* ☎ *02/850–109.* 🎫 *Free for nonguided visits. For group tours, call local tourist office.* ☉ *May– Aug., daily; Sept.–Apr., Sun. afternoon (call for hours).*

Near Naantali's marina, a footbridge leads to **Kailo Island,** in summer abuzz with theater, beach, sports, picnic facilities, and a snack bar. 🦢 **Moomin World** theme park brings to life all the famous characters of the beloved children's stories written by the Finnish woman Tove Jansson. The stories emphasize family, respect for the environment, and new adventures. ⊠ *Kailo Island, PL 48, 21101 Naantali,* ☎ *02/436–5100.* 🎫 *FM 75 (includes boat trip to Viski Island).* ☉ *mid-June–mid-Aug., daily 10–8.*

Dining and Lodging

$$ ✕ **Tavastin Kilta.** This summer restaurant has a view of the boat harbor. Broiled steaks and fish, plus some vegetarian dishes, are served in an Old World bishop's dining room, a nautical bar, or a tapas bar decorated in 19th-century style—choose your fancy. Lemon pastries are a dessert specialty. ⊠ *Mannerheimink. 1,* ☎ *02/435–1066. AE, DC, MC, V.*

$$–$$$$ 🏨 **Naantali Kylpylä Spa.** The emphasis here is on pampering, with foot massages, shiatsu physical therapy, mud packs, spa-water, and algae baths. Activities include gymnastics and a special seven-day fasting program offered twice a year under medical supervision. All kinds of health packages can be arranged, including health-rehabilitation programs. It is set on a peninsula in a grandiose building that replaced the original spa on the site. ⊠ *Matkailijantie 2, 21100,* ☎ *02/44550,* 🖷 *02/445–5621. 229 rooms. 2 pools, beauty salon, massage, Turkish bath. AE, DC, MC, V.*

Nightlife and the Arts

The **Naantali Music Festival** offers chamber music at the beginning of June (☞ *Festivals and Seasonal Events in* Chapter 1).

Outdoor Activities and Sports

SWIMMING

Naantali has several bathing areas. Contact the local tourist board (☞ Visitor Information, *below*).

Shopping

In Naantali you'll find the workshop of a famous Finnish contemporary jewelry designer, **Karl Laine** (⊠ Mannerheimink. 10B, ☎ 02/435– 4431). His use of brass and gold and his combinations of starkly geometric and richly clustered metals, sometimes studded with tiny precious stones, are singular in their creativeness.

Mariehamn and the Åland Islands

㊺   *155 km (93 mi) west of Turku.*

The Ålands are composed of more than 6,500 small rocky islands and skerries, inhabited in large part by families that fish or run small farms. Virtually all the locals are Swedish speaking and very proud of their largely autonomous status. Their connection with the sea is indelible, their seafaring traditions revered.

Nearly half the population lives in the tiny capital of Mariehamn (Maarianhamina), the hub of Åland life and the main port, on the main island of Åland. Some of the greatest grain ships sailing the seas were built by the Gustav Eriksson family in Mariehamn.

The **Museifartyget Pommern** (*Pommern* Museum Ship), in Mariehamn West Harbor at town center, is one of the last existing grain ships in the world. Once owned by the sailing fleet of the Mariehamn shipping magnate Gustaf Erikson, the ship carried wheat between Australia and England from 1923 to 1939. ☎ *018/531–421.* ◻ *FM 15.* ◔ *May–June and Aug., daily 9–5; July, daily 9–7; Sept.–Oct., daily 10–4.*

In prehistoric times the islands were, relatively speaking, heavily populated, as is shown by traces of no fewer than 10,000 ancient settlements, graves, and strongholds. A visit to **Sund County** will take you back to the earliest days of life on the islands, with its remains from prehistoric times and the Middle Ages. **Kastelholm** is a medieval castle built by the Swedes to strengthen their presence on Åland. ◻ *Kastelholm,* ☎ *018/43812.* ◻ *FM 20.* ◔ *Guided tours May–June and Aug.–Sept., daily 10–5, July daily 9:30–8.*

Jan Karlsgården Friluftsmuseum (Jan Karl Garden Outdoor Museum) is a very popular open-air museum, with buildings and sheds from the 18th century that portray farming life on the island 200 years ago. ◻ *Kastelholm,* ☎ *018/43812.* ◻ *FM 10.* ◔ *May–June and Aug.–Sept., daily 9:30–5; July, daily 9:30–8.*

About 8 km (5 mi) from the village of Kastelholm in Sund are the scattered ruins of **Bomarsund Fort,** a huge naval fortress built by the Russians in the early 19th century and only half finished when it was destroyed by Anglo-French forces during the Crimean War.

Spend a few days in the outdoors, staying in **Hammarland,** north of Mariehamn near Eckerö. This makes a perfect getaway in the Ålands, with snug, wooden cabins in the timeless style of Finnish summer cottages, including the genuine wood-fired Finnish sauna.

Dining and Lodging

$$–$$$ ✕▥ **Arkipelag.** In the heart of Mariehamn, the bayside Arkipelag Hotel is known for its fine marina and lively disco-bar. Rooms are modern and comfortable, with huge picture windows, and the restaurants, set in long, wood-paneled rooms with wide windows overlooking an ocean inlet, serve fresh Åland seafood. Try the crayfish when it's in season. In the terrace restaurant, the fresh shrimp sandwiches with dill mayonnaise are a treat. ◻ *Strandgatan 31, 22100 Mariehamn,* ☎ *018/ 24020,* 𝔽𝔸𝕏 *018/24384. 78 rooms, 8 suites. 2 restaurants, bar, indoor-outdoor pool, sauna, casino, nightclub, meeting rooms. DC, MC, V.*

$$ ▥ **Björklidens Stugby.** The cabins are small, but the draw here is really the outdoors. Enjoy the free rowboats, grassy lawns, and trees with swings. It is 25 km (16 mi) north of Mariehamn. You can use the outdoor grills and washing machines. ◻ *22240 Hammarland,* ☎ *018/ 37800,* 𝔽𝔸𝕏 *018/37801. 15 cabins. Beach, fishing, playground. No credit cards. Closed late Nov.–Mar.*

Outdoor Activities and Sports

BIKING

Most towns have bikes for rent from about FM 35 per day (FM 150 per week). The fine scenery and the terrain, alternately dead flat and gently rolling, make for ideal cycling. The roads are not busy once you leave the highway. **Suomen Retkeilymajajärjestö** (Finnish Youth Hostel Association, ◻ Yrjönk. 38B, 00100 Helsinki, ☎ 09/694–0377) has bicycle trips varying in length from four days to two weeks (with overnight stops at hostels if you wish). For Åland bicycle routes and tour packages, contact **Ålandsresor Ab** (✉ PB 62, 22101 Mariehamn, ☏ 018/28040). Another velo-friendly outfit is **Viking Line** (✉ Storagatan 2, 22100 Mariehamn, ☏ 018/26011).

BOATING

These are marvelous sailing waters for experienced mariners. A variety of boats can be rented through the local tourist office (☞ Visitor Information, *below*).

FISHING

Many fishing packages are available in the Ålands. Try **Ålandsresor** (✉ Torggatan 2, 22100 Mariehamn, ☏ 018/28040). **Viking Line** (✉ Storagatan 2, 22100 Mariehamn, ☏ 018/26011) also offers packages for anglers.

TENNIS

Mariehamn and Hammarland have public tennis courts. Contact the local tourist offices for details.

Southwestern Coast and the Åland Islands A to Z

Arriving and Departing

BY BUS

Good bus service connects the capital to the southwest from Helsinki's long-distance bus station, just west of the train station off Mannerheimintie. Contact **Matkahuolto** (✉ Simonk. 3, 00200 Helsinki, ☏ 09/682–701) for information.

BY CAR

The Helsinki–Turku trip is 166 km (103 mi) on Route E3; signs on E3 will tell you where to turn off for the south-coast towns of Tammisaari and Hanko. Most of southwestern Finland is well served by public transport, so a car is not necessary.

BY FERRY

Åland is most cheaply reached by boat from Turku and Naantali. Call **Silja Line** in Turku (☏ 02/652–6244), Mariehamn (☏ 018/16711), Tampere (☏ 03/216–2000), or Helsinki (☏ 09/180–4422). Or call **Viking Line** in Turku (☏ 02/63311), Mariehamn (☏ 018/26011), Tampere (☏ 03/249–0111), or Helsinki (☏ 09/12351). Tickets can also be purchased at the harbor.

BY PLANE

The region's airports are at **Mariehamn** and **Turku.** Both have connections to Helsinki and Stockholm, with service by Finnair (☏ 018/21423).

BY TRAIN

Trains leave Helsinki for Turku several times a day. For most smaller towns, you must stop at stations along the Helsinki–Turku route and change to a local bus. Bus fares are usually a bit cheaper than train fares.

Contacts and Resources

EMERGENCIES

The nationwide emergency number is ☏ **112;** it can be used to call police and ambulance services. A major medical center in the region is the **Turun Yliopistollinen Keskussairaala** (University of Turku Central Hospital, ✉ Kiinamyllynk. 4–8, Turku, ☏ 02/261–1611). For a dentist, call the **Turun Hammaslääkärikeskus** (Turku Dental Center, ✉ Hämeenk. 2, Turku, ☏ 02/233–3778).

Ageba Special Travel Service (⊠ Pohjoisranta 4, Helsinki, ☎ 09/6150–1588) arranges a variety of tours in the region.

Churches and Manor House Tour: The 100-km (62-mi) Seven Churches tour from Turku takes in the area's major medieval churches and a country manor house. It lasts about seven hours and is arranged (for groups of 25 or more only) through **Varsinais-Suomen Matkailuyhdistys** (⊠ Läntinen Rantak. 13, 20100 Turku, ☎ 02/251–7333).

Boat Tours: The Tammisaari tourist office offers a variety of boat tours run by **Archipelago Tours.** You board a restaurant boat and visit the national park; costs range from FM 70 to FM 100 per person depending on the length of the cruise. You can take a three-hour steamship cruise between Turku and Naantali, enjoying a smörgåsbord lunch or gourmet dinner while drifting around the archipelago (FM 65–FM 95); contact the Naantali tourist office or the **Steamship Company s/s Ukkopekka** (⊠ Linnank. 38, 20100 Turku, ☎ 02/233–0123).

Åland (⊠ Storagatan 11, 22100 Mariehamn, ☎ 018/24000). **Hanko** (⊠ Bulevardi 10, 10900, ☎ 019/220–3411). **Naantali** (⊠ Kaivotori 2, 21100, ☎ 02/435–0850). **Tammisaari** (Ekenäs, ⊠ Raatihuoneentori, 10600, ☎ 019/263–2100). **Turku** (⊠ Aurak. 4, 20100, ☎ 02/233–6366).

THE LAKELANDS

According to recent counts, nearly 200,000 lakes dimple Finland's gentle topography. Almost every lake, big or small, is fringed with tiny cabins. The lake cabin is a Finnish institution, and until the recent advent of cheap package tours abroad, nearly every Finnish family vacationed in the same way—in its cabin on a lake.

In general, the larger towns of this region are much less appealing than the smaller lake locales. But Savonlinna stands out among the towns, not only for its stunning, waterbound views—it is hugged by gigantic Lake Saimaa—but for its cultural life. The monthlong Savonlinna Opera Festival in July is one of Finland's—and Europe's—greatest. The quality of the opera, ballet, drama, and instrumental performance here during the annual festival weeks is world-class. Most events are staged at the 14th-century Olavinlinna Castle, splendidly positioned just offshore. To the west, the smaller Hämeenlinna has its own lakeside castle. There are small medieval churches scattered through the Lakelands, the most famous of which is the stone church in Hattula, its interior a gallery of medieval painted scenes.

For centuries the lakeland region was a much-contested buffer zone between the warring empires of Sweden and Russia. After visiting the people of the Lakelands, you should have a basic understanding of the Finnish word *sisu* (guts), a quality that has kept Finns independent.

Savonlinna is the best-placed town in the Lakelands and can make a convenient base from which to begin exploring the region. Savonlinna, Tampere, and Hämeenlinna are only short train rides from Helsinki; all three make good daylong excursions from the capital city. The Land of a Thousand Lakes is also the perfect setting for a long or short boat cruise. Travel from one town to the next by boat, enjoy a lake cruise with dinner, or simply take a relaxing sightseeing cruise.

Canoeing

The Finlandia Canoe Relay takes place in mid-June. Stretching over a grueling seven days, the 400- to 500-km (250- to 310-mi) relay is a real test of endurance. For information on where the race will kick off, contact the Finnish Canoe Association.

Outdoor Produce Markets

Traditional outdoor markets are held throughout the region, usually on Saturdays. Most sell produce, and you'll find the wild mushrooms and berries that are so abundant in this region. The various preserves—jams, compotes, and sauces included—are all delicacies and make good gifts; Finns slather them on thin pancakes. In the autumn you'll find slightly larger markets when towns have their September fairs. These vestiges of harvest festivals are now mostly excuses to hold fun fairs and sip coffee and gobble up doughnuts.

Shopping

Many Lakelands towns have textile workshops or factories, called *Tekstiilitehdas* or *Tekstiilimyymälä,* featuring woven wall hangings and rya rugs (*ryijy* in Finnish). The Lakelands region is the birthplace of famous Finnish glassware, and you'll find the Iittala Glass Center just outside of Hämeenlinna. The soil here yields a rich clay, and ceramics works selling dishes and pottery are ubiquitous.

Windsurfing

There are numerous windsurfing centers on the shores of Lakes Saimaa and Paijanne. For details, contact the Finnish Windsurfing Association (☞ Sports *in* Finland A to Z, *below*).

Savonlinna

46 *335 km (208 mi) northeast of Helsinki.*

One of the larger Lakelands towns, Savonlinna is best known for having the finest castle in all of Finland. The town takes advantage of this stunning attraction by holding major events, such as the annual opera festival, in the castle courtyard. The islands that make up Savonlinna center are linked by bridges. First, stop in at the tourist office for information; then cross the bridge east to the open-air market that flourishes alongside the main passenger quay. From here you can catch the boat to Kuopio and Lappeenranta. In days when waterborne traffic was the major form of transportation, Savonlinna was the central hub of the passenger fleet serving Saimaa, the largest lake system in Europe. Now the lake traffic is dominated by cruise and sightseeing boats, but the quayside still bustles with arrivals and departures every summer morning and evening.

A 10-minute stroll from the quay to the southeast brings you to Savonlinna's most famous site, the castle **Olavinlinna.** First built in 1475 to protect Finland's eastern border, the castle retains its medieval character and is one of Scandinavia's best-preserved historic monuments. Still surrounded by water that once bolstered its defensive strength, the fortress rises majestically out of the lake. Every July the **Savonlinna Opera Festival** (☎ 015/514–700 or 015/21866) is held in the castle's courtyard, offering a spellbinding combination of music and setting. You will need to make reservations well in advance for both tickets and hotel rooms, as Savonlinna becomes a mecca for music lovers. Contact the Savonlinna Tourist Service (☞ Visitor Information, *below*) for a current festival schedule and ticket information. The festival also includes arts and crafts exhibits around town. ✉ *Olavinlinna,* ☎ *015/531–164.* 🎫 *FM 20 includes guided tour on the hr.* ☉ *June–Aug., daily 10–5; Sept.–May, daily 10–3.*

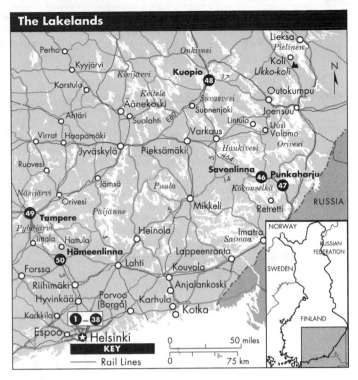

The Lakelands

Near Olavinlinna, the 19th-century steam schooners **SS Salama, SS Mikko,** and **SS Savonlinna** house an excellent museum on the history of lake traffic, including the fascinating floating timber trains still a common sight on Saimaa today. ⊠ *FM 15.* ⊙ *Aug.–June, Tues.–Sun. 11–5; July, Tues.–Sun. 10–8.*

OFF THE
BEATEN PATH

VISULAHDEN MATKAILUKESKUS – In Mikkeli, 5 km (3 mi) from Savonlinna, the Visulahti Tourist Center includes a waxworks, an old car museum, and an amusement park.

Dining and Lodging

$$$ ✕ **Rauhalinna.** This romantic turn-of-the-century timber villa was built by a general in the Imperial Russian Army. From town it's 16 km (10 mi) by road, 40 minutes by boat. Both food and atmosphere are Old Russian, but some Finnish specialties are also available. Popular dishes include fish *solyanka* (rainbow trout soup) and fried pork chops with a sour cream sauce, fried onions, pickled cucumbers, and sweet peppers. ⊠ *Lehtiniemi,* ☎ *015/523–119, for special bookings in winter* ☎ *015/57500. Reservations essential during festival season. AE, DC, MC, V. Closed Aug. 17–June 3.*

$$ ✕ **Majakka.** Founded in 1969, Majakka is central and has an intimate atmosphere with booths, two aquariums, and plenty of plants. Some tables offer nice views of the adjacent park and the Haukivesi Lake harbor. Try the pepper steak topped with a pepper-and-cream sauce. ⊠ *Satamak 11,* ☎ *015/21456. Reservations essential during festival season. AE, DC, MC, V.*

$$ ✕ **Paviljonki.** Just 1 km (½ mi) from the city center is Paviljonki, the restaurant of the Savonlinna restaurant school. The menu is short but sweet; try the noisettes of wild boar with an apple cognac sauce and potato blinis. The restaurant closes early (8 PM) and has a lunch buffet. ⊠ *Rajalahdenk. 4,* ☎ *015/574–9303. DC, MC, V.*

$$ ✕ **Ravintola Hopeasalmi.** Right on the market square is a 100-year-old steamboat that has been converted into a restaurant and bar. The restaurant specializes in generous portions of local fish; the *muikku* (whitefish) is fried with rye, salt, and pepper and served with mashed potatoes. ⊠ *Kauppatori,* ☎ *015/21701. DC, MC, V. Closed mid-Sept.–Apr.*

$$ ✕ **Snellman.** This small, 1920s-style mansion is in the town center. Meals are served against a quiet background of classical music. Among the specialties of the house are cold-salted salmon and steak with morel sauce. ⊠ *Olavink. 31,* ☎ *015/273–104. AE, DC, MC, V.*

$$$–$$$$ 🛏 **Seurahuone.** This old town house is near the market and passenger harbor. A new extension opened in 1989 to accommodate the growing number of tourists that visit in summer. Rooms are small but modern; be sure to ask for one that overlooks the picturesque harbor. ⊠ *Kauppatori 4–6, 57130,* ☎ *015/5731,* FAX *015/273–918. 84 rooms. 6 restaurants, bar, sauna, dance club, nightclub. AE, DC, MC, V.*

$$$ 🛏 **Casino Spa.** A 1960s relic, the Casino Spa has a restful lakeside location on an island linked to the town by a pedestrian bridge. Rooms are basic, with brown cork floors, white walls, and simple furnishings; all except one have a balcony. ⊠ *Kylpylaitoksentie, Kasinonsaari, 57130,* ☎ *015/73950,* FAX *015/272–524. 80 rooms. Restaurant, pool, sauna, spa, boating. AE, DC, MC, V.*

$–$$ 🛏 **Vuorilinna Holiday Hotel.** The simple white rooms of this modern student dorm become hotel rooms in summer. Guests may use the facilities, including the restaurant, of the nearby Casino Spa hotel (☞ *above*). Rooms share showers, toilets, and kitchenettes. ⊠ *Kasinonsaari, 57130,* ☎ *015/73950,* FAX *015/272–524. 225 rooms without bath. AE, DC, MC, V. Closed Sept.–May.*

$ 🛏 **Family Hotel Hospits.** In the heart of Savonlinna overlooking Saimaa Lake, this YMCA hotel has small, unpretentious rooms. ⊠ *Linnank. 20, 57130,* ☎ *015/515–661,* FAX *015/515–120. 22 rooms. Breakfast room, sauna. AE, DC, MC, V.*

Outdoor Activities and Sports

BOATING

Saimaa Sailing Oy (⊠ Valtak. 37 B 18, 53100 Lappeenranta, ☎ 05/411–8560) is the biggest boat-rental firm in the Lakeland region. Sailboats and motorboats can be rented on a daily or weekly basis. The base is the handsome, historic coastal town of Lappeenranta, 155 km (96 mi) southeast of Savonlinna.

OFF THE
BEATEN PATH

OLD MINE OF OUTUKUMPU – This child-friendly complex 187 km (116 mi) north of Savonlinna consists of an amusement park, mining museum, and mineral exhibition. ⊠ *Kiisuk. 6,* ☎ *013/554–795.*

Punkaharju

47 *35 km (22 mi) east of Savonlinna.*

Rising out of the water and separating the Puruvesi and Pihlajavesi lakes, the 8-km (5-mi) ridge of Punkaharju is a geographic wonder that predates the Ice Age. At times the pine-covered rocks narrow to only 25 ft, yet the ridge still manages to accommodate a road and train tracks.

★ Just south of Punkaharju is the **Taidekeskus Retretti** (Retretti Art Center). One of the most popular excursions from Savonlinna, Retretti is accessible via a two-hour boat ride or a 30-minute, 29-km (18-mi) bus trip. It consists of a modern art complex of unique design and includes a new cavern section built into the Punkaharju ridge. It's also a magnificent setting for concerts in summer and the site of more than 40 different indoor and outdoor scheduled summertime activities. ☎ *015/644–253* ▨ *FM 65.* ⊘ *May 23–Aug., daily 10–5; exhibitions daily 10–6.*

★ Combine your trip to Retretti with a visit to the nearby **Lusto Finnish Forest Museum.** Every kind of forestry—from the industrial to the artistic—and every aspect of Finland's close relationship with its most abundant natural resource are examined here in imaginative and absorbing displays. ⊠ *Lustontie 1, 58450 Punkaharju.* ☎ *015/345–100.* ▨ *FM 35.* ⊘ *May–Sept., daily 10–6; Oct.–Apr., Tues.–Sun. 10–5.*

Dining and Lodging

$$ ✕▥ **Punkaharju Valtion Hotelli.** Near Retretti, the Punkaharju National Hotel was constructed as a gamekeeper's lodge for Czar Nicholas I in 1845. Enlarged and restored, it is now a restful spot for a meal or an overnight visit. The manor house with small rooms is decorated in the old Finnish country style. The restaurant serves simple local dishes such as fried vendace, the tiny, tasty fish abundant in the lakes. It's a half-hour drive from Savonlinna. ⊠ *Punkaharju 2, 58450,* ☎ *015/644–251,* FAX *015/441–784. 24 rooms. Restaurant, sauna, 2 tennis courts, beach. DC, MC, V.*

Kuopio

⓽ *220 km (137 mi) northwest of Punkaharju, 185 km (115 mi) northwest of Savonlinna.*

You'll get a deeper understanding of the meaning of Finland's proximity to Russia and the East in Kuopio, with its Russian Orthodox monastery and museum. The boat from Savonlinna arrives at Kuopio's passenger harbor, where a small evening market holds forth daily from 3 to 10.

Kuopio's tourist office is close to the **Tori** (marketplace). Coined *maailman napa*—the belly-button of the world—Kuopio's market square should be one of your first stops, for it is one of the most colorful outdoor markets in Finland. ⊘ *Apr.–Sept., weekdays 7–5, Sat. 7–2; Oct.–Mar., weekdays 7–2.*

★ The **Ortodoksinen Kirkkomuseo** (Orthodox Church Museum) possesses one of the most interesting and unusual collections of its kind. When Karelia (the eastern province of Finland) was ceded to the Soviet Union after World War II, religious art was taken out of the monasteries and brought to Kuopio. The collection is eclectic and, of its type, one of the rarest in the world. ⊠ *Karjalank. 1, Kuopio,* ☎ *017/287–2244.* ▨ *FM 15.* ⊘ *May–Aug., Tues.–Sun. 10–4; Sept.–Apr., weekdays noon–3, weekends noon–5.*

Visitors fascinated by the treasures in the museum will want to visit the Orthodox convent of Lintula and the **Valamon Luostari** (Valamo Monastery). As a major center for Russian Orthodox religious and cultural life in Finland, the monastery hosts daily services. Precious 18th-century icons and sacred objects are housed in the main church and in the icon conservation center. The Orthodox library is the most extensive in Finland and is open to visitors. A café-restaurant is on the grounds, and very modest hotel and hostel accommodations are available at the monastery. ⊠ *Uusi Valamo,* ☎ *017/570–111, hotel reservations 017/570–1501.* ▨ *Guided tours FM 20.* ⊘ *Mar.–Sept., daily 7 AM–9 PM; Oct.–Feb., daily 8 AM–9 PM.*

The **Lintulan Luostari** (Lintula Convent) can be reached by boat from Valamo, or you can visit both the convent and the monastery by boat on scenic day excursions from Kuopio. Tickets are available from the Kuopio Tourist Service (☞ *Visitor Information, below*). ☎ *Tours FM 210, cruises FM 240. ☉ Convent June 13–Aug., bus tours June–Aug., Sat. at 10 AM, boat cruises June 25–Aug., Tues.–Sun.*

Three kilometers (2 mi) northwest of Kuopio, the slender **Puijon Näkö-torni** (Puijo Tower) is best visited at sunset, when the lakes shimmer with reflected light. It has two observation decks and is crowned by a revolving restaurant with marvelous views. ☎ *017/209–560.* ☎ *Summer FM 15, Oct.–Apr. free.* ☉ *May 2–Sept., daily 11–11; Oct.–Apr., daily 11–10.*

Dining and Lodging

$$ ✕ **Musta Lammas.** Near the passenger harbor, Musta Lammas is in the basement of a brewery founded in 1862. It has been attractively adapted from its beer-cellar days, retaining the original redbrick walls and beer barrels. The specialty here is the smoked muikku with sour cream and mashed potatoes. ⊠ *Satamak. 4,* ☎ *017/262–3494. AE, DC, MC, V. Closed Sun. No lunch.*

$$ ✕ **Sampo Vapaasatama.** In the town center, Sampo was founded in 1931, and its Scandinavian furniture dates from the 1950s. High ceilings and large chandeliers impart an elegant look. Try the muikku smoked, fried, grilled, or in a stew with pork, potatoes, and onions. ⊠ *Kauppak. 13,* ☎ *017/261–4677. AE, DC, MC, V.*

$$$ ⊞ **Arctia Hotel Kuopio.** The Arctia is the newest and most modern of the local hotels. Rooms are spacious by European standards, with large beds and generous towels. It's on the lakefront and also close to the town. ⊠ *Satamak. 1, 70100,* ☎ *017/195–111,* ☏ *017/195–170. 141 rooms. Pool, sauna, hot tub, boating. AE, DC, MC, V.*

$$ ⊞ **Hotel Spa Rauhalahti.** About 5 km (3 mi) from town center, Rauha-lahti is set near the lakeshore and has no-frills rooms and cabins. A number of amenities cater to sports lovers and families. The hotel has three restaurants, including the tavern-style Vanha Apteekkari—a local favorite. ⊠ *Katiskaniementie 8, 70700,* ☎ *017/473–111,* ☏ *017/ 473–470. 106 rooms, 13 apartments, 20 hostel rooms. Pool, hot tub, sauna, spa, tennis court, exercise room, squash, horseback riding, boating. AE, DC, MC, V.*

$$ ⊞ **Iso-Valkeinen Hotel.** On the lakeshore only 5 km (3 mi) from town center, this hotel has large, quiet rooms in six one-story buildings. Several rooms have balconies with views of the nearby lake. ⊠ *Päiväranta, 70420,* ☎ *017/539–6100,* ☏ *017/539–6555. 100 rooms with shower. 2 restaurants, pool, sauna, miniature golf, tennis court, beach, boating, fishing, nightclub. AE, DC, MC, V.*

Outdoor Activities and Sports

GOLF

Karelia Golf (⊠ 80780 Kontioniemi, ☎ 013/732–411) is one of Finland's best 18-hole golf courses.

Tampere

④⑨ *293 km (182 mi) southwest of Kuopio, 174 km (108 mi) northwest of Helsinki.*

The country's third-largest city, Tampere is an industrial center with a difference. From about the year 1000, this was a base from which traders and hunters set out on their expeditions to northern Finland; it was not until 1779 that a Swedish king, Gustav III, founded the city itself. In 1828 a Scotsman named James Finlayson came to the infant city and established a factory for spinning cotton. This was the beginning of "big business" in Finland. The Finlayson firm is today one of the country's major industrial enterprises.

Artful siting is the secret of this factory town. An isthmus little more than a half mile wide at its narrowest point separates the lakes Näsijärvi and Pyhäjärvi, and at one spot the **Tammerkoski Rapids** provide an outlet for the waters of one to cascade through to the other. Called the Mother of Tampere, these rapids once provided the electrical power on which the town's livelihood depended. Their natural beauty has been preserved in spite of the factories on either bank, and the well-designed public buildings grouped around them enhance their general effect.

The old workers' wooden-housing area of **Pispala,** clustered around the steep slopes of the **Pyynikki Ridge,** is one of the most picturesque urban districts in Finland. The old **observation tower** at the top of the ridge offers marvelous views across both lake systems to the north and south. The café at the foot of the tower serves excellent fresh doughnuts.

Adding to Tampere's natural beauty is the **Hämeensilta Bridge** in the heart of town, with its four statues by the well-known Finnish sculptor Wäinö Aaltonen. Close to the bridge, near the high-rise Sokos Hotel Ilves, are some old factory buildings that have been restored as shops and boutiques. At Verkatehtaankatu 2, the city **tourist office** offers helpful service and sells a 24-hour Tourist Ticket (FM 25), which allows unlimited travel on city transportation.

A 1½-km (1-mi) walk west, then north from the heart of Tampere brings you to the **Särkänniemen Huvikeskus** (Särkänniemi Recreation Center), a major recreation complex for both children and adults. Its many attractions include an amusement park, a children's zoo, a planetarium, and a well-planned aquarium with a separate dolphinarium. Within Särkänniemi, the **Sara Hildénin Taidemuseo** (Sara Hildén Art Museum) is a striking example of Finnish architecture, with the works of modern Finnish and international artists, including Chagall, Klee, Miró, and Picasso. Särkänniemi's profile is punctuated by the 550-ft **Näsinneulan Näkötorni** (Näsinneula Observatory Tower), Finland's tallest observation tower and the dominant feature of the Tampere skyline. The top of the tower holds an observatory and a revolving restaurant. The views are magnificent, commanding the lake, forest, and town—the contrast between the industrial maze of Tampere at your feet and the serenity of the lakes stretching out to meet the horizon is unforgettable. ⊠ *Särkänniemi,* ☎ *03/248–8111, museum* ☎ *03/214–3134.* ☒ *Museum FM 15, observatory tower FM 12, Särkänniemen Passport (dolphinarium and 3 other attractions, excluding amusement park rides) FM 75.* ☉ *Museum daily 11–6; children's zoo May–Aug., daily 10–6 or 8; tower June–Aug., daily 10–10; Sept.–May, daily 10–4; other attractions May–Aug., daily 10–10.*

While in western Tampere, be sure to visit one of the city's best museums, the **Amurin Työläiskorttelimuseo** (Amuri Museum of Workers' Housing). Its 30-plus wooden houses, sauna, bakery, and haberdashery date from the 1880s to the 1970s and are so well done that you half expect the original inhabitants to return at any minute. ⊠ *Makasininkb 12,* ☎ *03/219–6690.* ☒ *FM 15.* ☉ *Mid May–mid-Sept., Tues.–Sat. 9–5, Sun. 11–5.*

It was in Tampere that Lenin and Stalin first met, and this fateful occasion is commemorated with displays of photos and mementos in the **Lenin Museo** (Lenin Museum). ⊠ *Hämeenpuisto 28, 3rd floor,* ☎ *03/212–7313.* ☒ *FM 15.* ☉ *Weekdays 9–5, weekends 11–4.*

At the foot of the Pyynikki ridge is the **Pyynikin Kesäteatteri** (Pyynikki Summer Theater, ⊠ Pyynikin Kesäteatteri, ☎ 03/216–0300), with an outdoor revolving auditorium that can be moved, even with a full load of spectators, to face any one of the sets. It's open June 25–Aug. 17. On the east side of town is the modern **Kalevan Kirkko** (Kaleva Church). What may appear from the outside to be a grain elevator is in fact, as seen from the interior, a soaring monument to space and light. ⊙ *May–Aug., daily 10–5; Sept.–Apr., daily 11–3.*

Most buildings in Tampere, including the cathedral, are comparatively modern. The **Tuomiokirkko** (Cathedral) was built in 1907 and houses some of the best-known masterpieces of Finnish art, including Magnus Encknell's fresco *The Resurrection* and Hugo Simberg's *Wounded Angel* and *Garden of Death.* ⊙ *May–Aug., daily 10–6; Sept.–Apr., daily 11–3.*

OFF THE
BEATEN PATH

HAIHARAN NUKKE-JA PUKUMUSEO – Only 3 km (2 mi) southwest of the city center, the Haihara Doll and Costume Museum exhibits thousands of dolls from all over the world dating from the 12th to the 20th centuries. Costumes are mainly Finnish from the 19th century. ⊠ *Hatanpää kartano, Hatanpäänpuistokuja 1,* ☎ *03/222–6261.* ⊡ *FM 30.* ⊙ *Mar.– Apr., Wed.–Sun. noon–5; May–Sept., Tues.—Sat. noon–5.*

Dining and Lodging

$$$ ✗ **Laterna.** This place shares the same ownership as Tiiliholvi, but specializes more in Slav-style dishes. ⊠ *Puutarhak. 11,* ☎ *03/272–0241. AE, DC, MC, V.*

$$$ ✗ **Tiiliholvi.** This former bank vault has been turned into a romantic cellar restaurant with Jugendstil furniture, redbrick walls, and stained-glass decorations. Try the willow grouse Stroganoff or sour-cream mutton with hash potatoes. The chocolate cake is a good choice for dessert. ⊠ *Kauppak. 10,* ☎ *03/272–0231. AE, DC, MC, V.*

$$ ✗ **Astor.** The most recent appearance on the Tampere scene has a moderately priced brasserie section and a more expensive restaurant. Parquet floors, soft yellow and red walls, and candlelight lend a touch of elegance. Try the reindeer fillet with cranberry sauce or the willow grouse. ⊠ *Aleksis Kivenk. 26,* ☎ *03/213–3522. Reservations essential. DC, MC, V.*

$$ ✗ **Bodega Salud.** The Salud has a well-earned reputation for Spanish specialties, though it also offers such unconventional dishes as grilled alligator and stewed kangaroo. The decor is unconventional, too, with stuffed animals—birds, turtles, bulls' heads, and cow pelts. ⊠ *Otavalank. 10,* ☎ *03/223–5996. AE, DC, MC, V.*

$$ ✗ **Silakka.** The name of this restaurant translates into the main gastronomic theme: Baltic herring. The buffet—a must—offers four cold and three warm Baltic herring dishes, salmon soup, and six salads. Other specialties include flambéed salmon topped with a cream chanterelle sauce and fried perch with a cream morel sauce. On the second floor of the Koskikeskus shopping mall, Silakka has a casual, unpretentious atmosphere. ⊠ *Hatanpään valtatie 1, Koskikeskus,* ☎ *03/214–9740. DC, MC, V.*

$$ ⊡ **Cumulus Koskikatu.** This central hotel overlooks the tamed rapids of Tammerkoski. Rooms are fresh and modern; for an extra FM 40 you can enjoy a view of the rapids. The Finnair terminal is in the same building. ⊠ *Koskik. 5, 33100,* ☎ *03/242–4399,* 𝙵𝙰𝚇 *03/242–4111. 227 rooms. Restaurant, bar, pool, sauna, nightclub. AE, DC, MC, V.*

$$ ⊡ **Sokos Hotel Ilves.** Soaring above a newly gentrified area of old warehouses near city center, this 18-story hotel is Tampere's tallest build-

ing. All rooms above the sixth floor have spectacular views of the city and Pyhäjärvi and Näsijärvi lakes. ⊠ *Hatanpään valtatie 1, 33100,* ☎ *03/262–6262,* FAX *03/262–6263. 336 rooms. 4 restaurants, no-smoking rooms, pool, hot tub, sauna, exercise room, nightclub. AE, DC, MC, V.*

$ 🏠 **Domus Summer Hotel.** About 3 km (2 mi) from town center, in the Kaleva district, this hotel is a student dormitory that rents rooms during the summer. All rooms are equipped with refrigerators and hot plates; a room with a shower costs an extra FM 50. This is a good option for cost-conscious families. ⊠ *Pellervonk. 9, 33540,* ☎ *03/255–0000,* FAX *03/317–1200. 147 rooms, 80 with shower. Pool, sauna, dance club. MC, V. Closed Sept.–May.*

Nightlife and the Arts

Tampere has a lively pub and beer bar scene. Try the in-house brew at **Plevna** (⊠ Itäinenk. 8, ☎ 03/223–0111), timing your visit to coincide with a performance by the German-style brass band. The English-style **Salhojenkadun Pub** (⊠ Salhojenk. 29, ☎ 03/255–3376) is an old favorite. The converted post office is now the family-run **Wanha Posti** (⊠ Hämeenk. 13; ☎ 03/223–3007), lauded for its own brews and other local brands. The Irish theme makes its inevitable appearance at **Pik-ilinna** (⊠ Ilmarink. 9, ☎ 03/261–7885).

OFF THE BEATEN PATH	**RUNOILIJAN TIE –** One of the most popular excursions from Tampere is the Poet's Way boat tour along Lake Näsijärvi. The boat passes through the agricultural parish of Ruovesi, where J. L. Runeberg, Finland's national poet, used to live. Shortly before the boat docks at Virrat, you'll pass through the straits of Visuvesi, where many artists and writers spend their summers. ⊠ *Finnish Silverline and Poet's Way, Verkatehtaank. 2, 33100 Tampere,* ☎ *03/212–4804.* ⊞ *FM 333 round-trip by boat; FM 222 one-way; FM 240 out by boat, return by bus.* ☉ *June–Aug. 17, Tues., Thurs., and Fri.*
	ÄHTÄRI – Not far north of Virrat is Ähtäri, where Finland's first wildlife park has been established in a beautiful setting, with a holiday village, good hotel, and recreation facilities.

Hämeenlinna

🔟 *78 km (49 mi) southeast of Tampere, 98 km (61 mi) north of Helsinki (via Hwy. 12).*

The big castle and small museums of Hämeenlinna make this town a good place for a day trip. It's also a good point from which to visit nearby gems such as the **Iittalan Lasikeskus** (Iittala Glass Center). The magnificent glass is produced by top designers, and the seconds in the factory shop are bargains you won't find elsewhere. ⊠ *14500 Iittala,* ☎ *03/535–6230.* ⊞ *FM 10, FM 7 in winter.* ☉ *Museum May–Aug., daily 10–6; Sept.–Apr., weekdays 10–5, weekends 10–6. Factory shop May–Aug., daily 10–8; Sept.–Apr., daily 10–6.*

Hämeenlinna's secondary school has educated many famous Finns, among them composer Jean Sibelius (1865–1957). The only surviving timber house in the town center is the **Sibeliuksen syntymäkoti** (Sibelius birthplace), a modest dwelling built in 1834. The museum staff will play your favorite Sibelius CD as you tour the rooms, one of which contains the harmonium Sibelius played as a child. ⊠ *Hallitusk. 11.* ⊞ *FM 10.* ☉ *May–Aug., daily 10–4; Sept.–Apr., daily noon–4.*

Swedish crusaders began construction on **Hämeen Linna** (Häme Castle) in the 13th century to strengthen and defend the Swedish position in the region. What began as a fortified camp evolved over the centuries into a large castle of stone and brick. In modern times, the castle, one of Finland's oldest, has served as a granary and a prison, and it is now restored and open to the public for tours and exhibitions. The castle sits on the lakeshore, 1 km (½ mi) north of Hämeenlinna's town center. Tours in English take place every hour in the summer and are available every hour in winter by appointment only. ⊠ *Kustaa III:n k. 6,* ☎ *03/675–6820.* ⊴ *FM 15 includes guided tour.* ⊙ *May–mid-Aug., daily 10–6; Aug.–mid-Apr., daily 10–4.*

OFF THE
BEATEN PATH

HATTULAN KIRKO – Six kilometers (3½ miles) north of Hämeenlinna is Hattula, whose Church of the Holy Cross is the most famous of Finland's medieval churches. Its interior is a fresco gallery of biblical scenes whose vicious little devils and soulful saints are as vivid and devious as when they were first painted around 1510. ⊠ *Hattula,* ☎ *03/672–3383 during opening hrs; 03/637–2477 all other times.* ⊴ *FM 15.* ⊙ *Mid-May–mid-Aug., daily 11–5; open at other times by appointment.*

Dining and Lodging

$$ ✕ **Huviretki.** In the heart of the city at the Cumulus Hotel is Huviretki, the city's most popular restaurant. Specialties include "vineyard lamb," a fillet of lamb with garlic potatoes, zucchini, mushrooms, tomatoes, and garlic cloves; salmon and crayfish with a Gouda cheese sauce; and pepper steak with a cream-pepper sauce and french fries. There's a wide range of salads and meat dishes. ⊠ *Cumulus Hotel, Raathuneenk. 16–18,* ☎ *03/64881. AE, DC, MC, V.*

$$ ✕ **Piiparkakkutalo.** In a renovated old-timber building, Piiparkakkutalo specializes in meat dishes; try the chateaubriand with cream cognac sauce and blue-cheese potatoes. ⊠ *Kirkkorinne 2,* ☎ *03/612–1606. AE, DC, MC, V.*

$$$ 🏨 **Rantasipi Aulanko.** One of Finland's top hotels sits on the lakeshore
★   in a beautifully landscaped park 6½ km (4 mi) from town. All rooms have wall-to-wall carpeting and overlook the golf course, park, or lake. ⊠ *13210 Hämeenlinna,* ☎ *03/658–801,* 𝔽𝔸𝕏 *03/658–1922. 245 rooms. Restaurant, indoor pool, massage, sauna, 18-hole golf course, tennis court, horseback riding, boating, nightclub. AE, DC, MC, V.*

Outdoor Activities and Sports

GOLF

Hotel Vaakuna (⊠ Possentie 7, 13200 Hämeenlinna, ☎ 03/5831) has an 18-hole lakeside golf course.

SKIING

The **Finlandia Ski Race Office** (⊠ Urheilukeskus, 15110 Lahti, ☎ 03/734–9811) has details on events. In February the **Hämeenlinna–Lahti Finlandia Race** gets underway. The March **Salpausselkä Ski Games** and jumping events are also in Lahti.

En Route   If you're driving between Helsinki and Hämeenlinna along Highway 12, around Riihimäki you'll see signs for the **Suomen Lasimuseo** (Finnish Glass Museum). Follow them! It's an outstanding display of the history of glass from early Egyptian times to the present, beautifully arranged in an old glass factory. ⊠ *Tehtaank. 21, Riihimäki,* ☎ *019/741–494.* ⊴ *FM 15.* ⊙ *Apr.–Sept., daily 10–6; Oct.–Dec. and Feb.–Mar., Tues.–Sun. 10–6.*

Lakelands A to Z

Arriving and Departing

BY BUS

Buses are the best form of public transport into the region, with frequent connections to lake destinations from most major towns. It is a six-hour ride from Helsinki to Savonlinna.

BY CAR

The region is vast, so the route you choose will depend on your destination. You can drive inland or follow the coast to the eastern lake region from the capital. A drive to Kuopio could take you either through Tampere to Jyväskyla or to the east, close to the border with Russia. Consult the **Finnish Automobile Association** (⊠ Hämeentie 105A, Helsinki 55, ☎ 09/774–761) or tourist boards for route advice.

BY PLANE

Airports in the Lakelands are at **Tampere, Mikkeli, Jyväskylä, Varkaus, Lappeenranta, Savonlinna, Kuopio,** and **Joensuu.** Flight time to the Savonlinna area from Helsinki is 40 minutes. All airports are served by Finnair's domestic service.

BY TRAIN

Trains run from Helsinki to Lahti, Mikkeli, Imatra, Lappeenranta, Joensuu, and Jyväskylä. There is sleeping-car service to Joensuu and Kuopio and, in summer only, to Savonlinna. The trip from Helsinki to Savonlinna takes 5½ hours.

Getting Around

BY CAR

The Joensuu–Kuopio–Lahti–Tampere road belt will transport you quickly from one major point to the next, but if you are going to be taking a lake vacation you will usually finish your journey on small roads. The last stretch to the *mökki* (cabin) may be unpaved. You will need a detailed map to find most mökkis, which tend to be tucked away in well-hidden spots.

Contacts and Resources

EMERGENCIES

The nationwide emergency number is ☎ **112;** it can be used to call police and ambulance services. A major hospital is **Tampere Keskussairaala** (Tampere Central Hospital; ⊠ Teiskontie 35, Tampere, ☎ 03/247–5111). For dental care, call **Hammaslääkäri Päivystys** (☎ 049/625–555), weekdays 9–8, weekends 11–3.

GUIDED TOURS

Canoe Trips: Avid canoeists should contact the Finnish Canoe Association (☞ Finland A to Z, *below*). Almost all of its 67 clubs arrange guided tours; canoes are rented at about FM 100 per day. **Lintusalon Melontakeskus** (⊠ 52200 Puumala, ☎ 015/468–8759) arranges numerous lakeland canoe tours. **Ikaalinen Tourist Service** (⊠ Valtak. 7, 39500, ☎ 03/450–1221) runs white-water trips and canoe safaris in the region. **Lieksan Matkailu Oy** (⊠ Pielisentie 7, 81700 Lieksa, ☎ 013/520–2400) is another river-trip outfitter. **Mike's Canoe and Paddling Service** (⊠ Mikan Kanotti-ja Melontapalvelu and Haukank. 27, 50190 Mikkeli, ☎ 049/840–362) designs tailor-made canoe tours.

Cruises: There are dozens of boat-tour companies operating in the Lakelands; contact the Finnish Tourist Board or local tourist offices in the region for a complete list as well as details of routes. Also try **Western Lakeland Silverline and Poets' Way Tour** (⊠ Verkatehtaank. 2, 33100 Tampere, ☎ 03/124–803). **Western Lakeland and Lake Päijänne Tour**

(✉ Lake Päijänne Cruises, Pellonpää, 40820 Haapaniemi, ☎ 014/618–885 or 014/263–447) is another outfitter. Also try **Saimaa Lakeland** (✉ Roll Cruises of Finland Ltd., Matkustajasatama, Kauppak. 1, 70100 Kuopio, ☎ 017/262–6744).

Sightseeing Tours: A program of **Friendly Finland Tours,** available trough travel agencies in Finland and abroad, offers escorted packages that include stops in the Lakelands. The three-day "Saimaa Lake Tour" and the seven-day "Scenic Tour" both start in Helsinki. Brochures are available from the **Finland Travel Bureau** in Helsinki (☎ 09/18261).

SAILING SCHOOL

Many sailing schools, such as **Naviconsult Sailing** (✉ 06830 Kullonkylä, ☎ 049/840–312 or 019/22532), operate in the lakes region, with courses for sailors of all levels. The **Finnish Yachting Association** (✉ Radiok. 20, Helsinki, ☎ 09/417–6911) is a good resource for info.

VISITOR INFORMATION

Heinola (✉ Torik. 8, 18100, ☎ 03/715–8444). **Hämeenlinna** (✉ Sibeliuksenk. 5A, 13100, ☎ 03/621–2388). **Imatra** (✉ Liikekeskus Mansikkapaikka, PL 22, 55121, ☎ 05/681–2500). **Joensuu/North Karelia** (✉ Koskik. 1, 80100, ☎ 013/267–5300). **Jyväskylä** (✉ Asemak. 6, 40100, ☎ 014/624–903/904). **Kuopio** (✉ Haapaniemenk. 17, 70110, ☎ 017/182–584). **Lahti** (✉ Torik. 3B, PL 175, 15111, ☎ 03/814–4568). **Lappeenranta** (✉ Linja-autoasema, PL 113, 53101, ☎ 05/616–2600). **Mikkeli** (✉ Hallitusk. 3A, 50100, ☎ 015/151–444). **Savonlinna** (✉ Puistok. 1, 57100, ☎ 015/273–492). **Tampere** (✉ Verkatehtaank. 2, PL 87, 33100, ☎ 03/212–6652).

LAPLAND

Lapland is often called Europe's last wilderness, a region of endless forests, fells, and great silences. Settlers in Finnish Lapland walked gently and left the landscape almost unspoiled. Now easily accessible by plane, train, or bus, this Arctic outpost offers comfortable hotels and modern amenities, yet you won't have to go very far to find yourself in an almost primordial setting.

The oldest traces of human habitation in Finland have been found in Lapland, and hordes of Danish, English, and even Arabian coins indicate the existence of trade activities many centuries ago. Only about 4,500 Sami (natives of Lapland) still live here; the remainder of the province's population of 200,000 is Finnish. Until the 1930s, Lapland was still largely unexploited, and any trip to the region was an expedition. Lapland's isolation ended when the Canadian-owned Petsamo Nickel Company completed the great road connecting Rovaniemi with the Arctic Sea, now known as the Arctic Highway. Building activities increased along this route, the land was turned and sown, and a few hotels were built to cater to an increasing number of visitors.

The Sami population makes up a small minority in the northern regions of Finland, Norway, Sweden, and Russia. Though modern influences have changed many aspects of their traditional way of life, the inquisitive and respectful visitor will discover a thriving Sami culture. Sami crafts make use of natural resources, reflected in skilled woodwork, bonework, and items made of reindeer pelts. The Lady Day church festival in Enontekiö in March is particularly colorful, attended by many Sami in their most brilliant dress and usually featuring reindeer racing or lassoing competitions.

Summer in Lapland has the blessing of round-the-clock daylight, and beautiful weather typically accompanies the nightless days. In early fall the colors are so fabulous that the Finns have a special word for it: *ruskaa*. If you can take the intense but dry cold, winter in Lapland is full of fascinating experiences, from the Northern Lights to reindeer roundups. Depending on how far north of the Arctic Circle you travel, the sun might not rise for several weeks around midwinter. But it is never pitch-black; light reflects from the invisible sun below the horizon even during midday, and there is luminosity from the ever-present snow.

But Finns cherish the outdoors no matter what the light. Here it is the wilderness that's the draw. For although the cities have fine facilities and cultural events, it is the lonely moors with the occasional profile of a reindeer herd crossing, the gin-clear forest streams, and the bright trail of the midnight sun reflected on a lake's blackest waters that leave the most indelible impressions.

While you're here sample such local foods as cloudberries, lingonberries, fresh salmon, and reindeer, served smoked and sautéed, in meatballs and steaks. Restaurants serve hearty soups, crusty rye bread, delicious baked Lappish cheese, and dark brewed coffee in wooden cups with meals—you won't leave hungry.

Crafts

You'll find unique souvenirs in Lapland, and you may learn to love the traditional Lapp crafts, both functional and attractive. Keep an eye out for the camping knives with beautifully carved bone or wooden handles, colorful weaving and embroidered mittens and gloves, felt shoes, and birch-bark baskets and rucksacks.

Summer Sports

In summer, canoeing opportunities are unlimited, ranging from canoe trips on Lake Inari to forays over the rapids of the Ivalojoki River. Summer golf takes on such unusual guises as midnight-sun golf and Green Zone Tornio-Haparanda Golf—you'll play nine holes in Finland and the other nine in Sweden (Meri-Lapin Golfklubi, ☎ 016/431–711).

Winter Sports

Winter sports reign here, from the quirky ice golfing to the traditional cross-country skiing. Vuokatti, Ylläs, Saariselkä, and Kiilopää are Lapland's leading downhill and cross-country ski centers. Try the **Levi resort** in western Lapland (⊠ Levin Matkailu, 99100 Kittilä, ☎ 016/643–466), **Pyhätunturi** in southern Lapland (⊠ Hotelli Pyhätunturi, 98530 Pyhätunturi, ☎ 016/812–081), **Saariselkä** in eastern Lapland (⊠ Pohjois-Lapin Matkaialu, 99800 Ivalo, ☎ 016/662–521), and **Ruka** (⊠ Rukakeskus, 93620 Rukatunturi, ☎ 08/868–1231), on the eastern border just below Lapland.

Rovaniemi

⑤ *832 km (516 mi) north of Helsinki.*

The best place to start your tour of Lapland is Rovaniemi, where the Ounas and Kemi rivers meet almost on the Arctic Circle. Often called the Gateway to Lapland, Rovaniemi is in fact the administrative hub and communications center of the province.

If you're expecting an Arctic shantytown, you're in for a surprise. After Rovaniemi was all but razed by the retreating German army in 1944, Alvar Aalto directed the rebuilding and devised an unusual street layout: from the air, the layout mimics the shape of reindeer antlers! During rebuilding, the population rose from 8,000 to more than 34,000—so be prepared for a contemporary city, university town, and cultural center on the edge of the wilderness.

Lapland

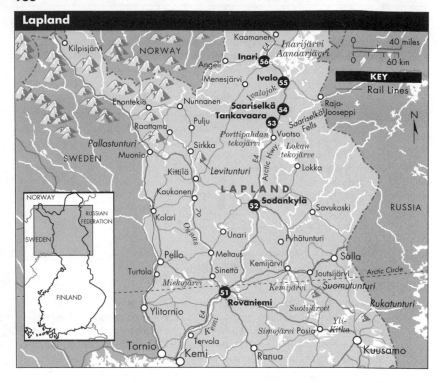

One of the town's architectural wonders is **Lappia-Talo** (Lappia House), the Aalto-designed concert and congress center that houses the world's northernmost professional theater. ⊠ *Hallitusk. 11,* ☎ *016/322–2944.*

One of the best ways to tune in to the culture of Finland's far north is to visit the **Arktikum** (Arctic Research Center). The Arktikum houses the Museum of the Province of Lapland, whose riveting exhibit on Sami life tells the full story of their survival. ⊠ *Pohjoisranta 4,* ☎ *016/317–840.* ⊒ *FM 45.* ☉ *May–Aug., daily 10–6; Sept.–Apr., Tues.–Sun. 10–6.*

Rovaniemi's real claim to fame is that Santa Claus lives in its suburbs at **Joulupukin Pajakylä** (Santa Claus Village). Lapps in native dress and reindeer hauling sleighs enhance its feeling of authenticity. (This is likely to be the only place where your children will be able to pet a reindeer— the ones you'll see in the wild are shy.) Here gifts can be bought in midsummer for shipping at any time of year, and postcards can be mailed from the special Arctic Circle post office. There's also a complete souvenir shopping complex, plus the impressive mountains of mail that pour in from children all over the world. Yes, he answers every letter! The village is closed when he is abroad, on December 25. ⊠ *Santa Claus Village, 96930 Arctic Circle,* ☎ 𝖥𝖠𝖷 *016/356–2096, Santa's Post Office* ☎ *016/356–2157.* ⊒ *Free.* ☉ *June–Aug., daily 8–8; Sept.–Nov. and Jan.–May, daily 10–5; Dec., daily 9–7.*

Dining and Lodging

$$ ✕ **Fransmanni.** This restaurant, with a nice view of the Kemijoki River, specializes in different types of international, Finnish, and Lapp casserole dishes. Try the pepper-beef casserole with its tasty cream sauce. Service is friendly. ⊠ *Vaakuna Hotel, Koskik. 4,* ☎ *016/332–211. AE, DC, MC, V.*

$$ ✕ **Ounasvaaran Pirtit.** This is one of Rovaniemi's best restaurants, focusing on traditional Finnish and Lapp food. Try the sautéed salmon with cream and boiled potatoes or sautéed reindeer with mashed potatoes. If possible, call ahead to order. ✉ *Antinmukka 4,* ☎ *016/369–056. Reservations essential. AE, DC, MC, V.*

$$ ✕▥ **Sky Hotel Ounasvaara.** On a hilltop 3 km (2 mi) from the town, Sky Hotel is the top choice in Rovaniemi for views, hiking, and skiing, both slalom and cross-country—especially for those with a car. Some rooms have bathtubs—a rarity—and many have saunas (47 rooms). Especially large rooms with kitchenettes are available for families. At Panorama dine on barbecued whitefish, reindeer casserole, fried snow grouse, and desserts such as Lapland cheese with Arctic cloudberries and lingonberry parfait. ✉ *96400 Rovaniemi,* ☎ *016/335–3311,* 𝔽𝔸𝕏 *016/318–789. 69 rooms. Restaurant, sauna, hiking, cross-country skiing, downhill skiing. AE, DC, MC, V.*

$$$ ▥ **Hotelli Lapponia.** Opened in 1992, this modern hotel is in the heart of Rovaniemi. Light blue, gray, and brown color schemes decorate the rooms, some of which have individual saunas (9 rooms) or hot tubs (8 rooms). ✉ *Koskik. 23, 96200,* ☎ *016/33661,* 𝔽𝔸𝕏 *016/313–770. 167 rooms. 5 restaurants, bar, pub, no-smoking rooms, nightclub. AE, DC, MC, V.*

$$–$$$ ▥ **Hotel Pohjanhovi.** Stretched along the shore of the Kemijoki River, this hotel combines modern amenities with quick access to the moors. Rooms are large, with low ceilings and big windows. The decor varies from white-walled rooms with autumn-toned upholstery and wood trim to black walls with light upholstery—for those who have trouble sleeping during the days of the midnight sun. ✉ *Pohjanpuistikko 2, 96200,* ☎ *016/33711,* 𝔽𝔸𝕏 *016/313–997. 216 rooms, 4 suites. Restaurant, bar, café, sauna, squash, boating, fishing, casino, meeting rooms. AE, DC, MC, V.*

$$ ▥ **Hotel Rudolf.** Set in the center of Rovaniemi, the Rudolf has bright, homey rooms with parquet floors and soft, subtle lighting; the furniture is modern. The restaurant caters to groups and is nothing extraordinary. The short menu lists such basics as onion steak with fried potatoes and reindeer pepper steak with creamed potatoes. ✉ *Koskik. 41, 96100,* ☎ *016/342–3222,* 𝔽𝔸𝕏 *106/342–3226. 41 rooms. Restaurant, indoor pool, sauna, meeting room. AE, DC, MC, V.*

$$ ▥ **Sokos Hotel Vaakuna.** Open since January 1992, the Vaakuna is a recent addition to the hotel scene in Rovaniemi. The lobby has comfortable armchairs and marble floors; rooms are small and painted in pastel shades. There are two restaurants: Fransmanni (☞ *above*) and Rosso, which turns out Italian pastas and pizzas. ✉ *Koskik. 4, 96200 Rovaniemi,* ☎ *016/332–211,* 𝔽𝔸𝕏 *016/332–2199. 159 rooms. 2 restaurants, pub, sauna, exercise room, nightclub. AE, DC, MC, V.*

$–$$ ▥ **Hotelli Oppipoika.** Attached to one of Finland's premier hotelier and restaurateur schools, this hotel promises good service and fine cuisine. Modern rooms have pressed birch paneling and are well lit. ✉ *Korkalonk. 33, 96200 Rovaniemi,* ☎ *016/338–8111,* 𝔽𝔸𝕏 *016/346–969. 40 rooms. Restaurant, no-smoking rooms, indoor pool, sauna, exercise room, meeting room. AE, DC, MC, V.*

Outdoor Activities and Sports

HIKING

Karttakeskus (✉ *Hallitusk. 1–3C, 96100 Rovaniemi,* ☎ *016/329–4111*) provides maps of marked trails in Lapland.

OFF THE   **SALLA REINDEER FARM** – In winter, visitors of all ages can obtain a rein-
BEATEN PATH   deer driver's license and feed the animals at this farm 150 km (93 mi)
                 east of Rovaniemi. ⊠ *PL 7, 98901 Salla*, ☎ *016/37771*. ☜ *License
                 FM 30*.

Sodankylä and the Moors

52 *130 km (81 mi) north of Rovaniemi (via Rte. 4 or 5), 960 km (595
mi) north of Helsinki.*

The Sodankylä region is one of the oldest Sami settlements, and today
it is one of the most densely populated areas of Finnish Lapland. In
the town of Sodankylä is a Northern Lights Observatory (for professionals only) and an ancient wooden church.

Lapland is dominated by great moorlike expanses. The modern tourist
center of **Luosto**, 25 km (16 mi) south of Sodankylä, is in the heart of
the moor district of southern Lapland—an area of superb hiking,
mountain cycling, orienteering, and skiing. If you don't have a car, a
daily bus makes the 60-km (37-mi) trip from Kemijärvi to Luosto. Kemi-
jarvi is 87 km (54 mi) north of Rovaniemi and can be reached via local
train.

Lodging

$$ ☷ **Arctia Hotel Luosto.** Amid the plains southeast of Sodankylä, this
small-scale hotel is modern and comfortable. It is built in a unique *kelo*
(dead wood) timber style. Each cabin has a fireplace, sauna, and kitch-
enette. ⊠ *Luostotunturi, 99550 Aska*, ☎ *016/624–400*, ℻ *016/624–
410. 54 cabins, 5 rooms. Restaurant, sauna, boating, cross-country ski-
ing, snowmobiling. AE, DC, MC, V.*

Tankavaara

53 *105 km (65 mi) north of Sodankylä, 130 km (81 mi) north of Luosto,
225 km (140 mi) north of Rovaniemi.*

The town of Tankavaara is the most accessible and the best-developed
☺ of several gold-panning areas. The **Kultamuseo** (Gold Museum) tells the
century-old story of Lapland's hardy fortune seekers. Real prospectors
will show you how to pan for gold dust and tiny nuggets from the silt
of an icy stream. ⊠ *Kultakylä, 99695 Tankavaara*, ☎ *016/626–158.* ☜
Summer FM 55 (includes gold panning), winter FM 25. ☉ *June–mid-
Aug., daily 9–6; mid-Aug.–Oct., daily 9–5; Nov.–May, daily 10–4.*

Dining and Lodging

$$ ✕ **Wanha Waskoolimies.** In the tradition of the old gold prospectors,
this rustic restaurant consists of three rooms hewn from logs. Daily
specials such as Fish in the Gold Pan and Prospector's Beef will give
you a taste of simple but high-quality Lapland fare. The restaurant has
received the Lappi à la Carte gourmet citation. ⊠ *Tankavaaran Kul-
takylän*, ☎ *016/626–158. DC, V.*

$ ☷ **Hotel Korundi.** In a quiet setting just off the Arctic Highway, this
hotel has cozy, contemporary rooms for two to five people, most with
a fireplace. You can try your luck at panning for gold here. The restaurant is in a separate building. ⊠ *99695 Tankavaara*, ☎ *016/626–158*,
℻ *016/626–261. 8 rooms. Restaurant, sauna, hiking, bicycles, cross-
country skiing. AE, DC, MC, V.*

Saariselkä

54 *40 km (25 mi) north of Tankavaara, 135 km (84 mi) north of Sodankylä, 265 km (165 mi) north of Rovaniemi.*

You could hike and ski for days in this area without seeing another soul. Saariselkä has a variety of accommodations and makes a central base from which to set off on a trip into the true wilderness. Marked trails traverse forests and moors, where little has changed since the last Ice Age. More than 1,282 square km (560 square mi) of this magnificent area has been named the **Uhrokekkosen Kansallispüisto** (Urho Kekkonen National Park). The park guide center is at Tankavaara.

Lodging

$$$–$$$$ **Riekonlinna.** The pinewood and blue-textile decor of this contemporary Lappish hotel goes well with its natural setting. All of the modern rooms have a balcony. It has a meeting center and a multisport complex, and it is only 30 minutes from Ivalo Airport. The restaurant serves fresh local specialties, including reindeer, salmon, and snow grouse. The hotel's location provides excellent cross-country and downhill skiing possibilities; snowmobiling and reindeer safaris are also offered. ✉ *Lutontie, Saariselkä, 99839,* ☎ *016/668–601,* FAX *016/668–602. 124 rooms, 2 suites. Restaurant, 2 pools, massage, sauna, 2 tennis courts, squash, boating. AE, DC, MC, V.*

$–$$$$ **Saariselkä Spa.** New as of 1990, this hotel is known for its luxurious spa center. The glass-domed swimming area is crammed with foliage, fountains, water slides, wave machines, and a hot tub. The solarium, saunas, and Turkish baths are adjacent. The guest rooms' decor includes pressed blond and dark wood, slate blue carpet, and bedspreads in muted blues, purples, and pinks. Moderately priced cabin accommodations are also available. Note that the breakfast and spa facilities are included in prices. Children seven to 14 stay at half-price; children under seven stay free. The bus stops at the hotel. ✉ *99830 Saariselkä,* ☎ *016/6828,* FAX *016/682–328. 36 cabins, 37 rooms. Restaurant, miniature golf (Sept.–May), tennis court, badminton, exercise room, paddle tennis, squash, volleyball, meeting rooms. AE, DC, MC, V.*

$$$ **Hotelli Riekonkieppi.** The piney comfort of the rooms and the quietude of the setting make this a good Lapland base. Eight wood buildings with 12 to 16 rooms each make it especially popular with families. The restaurant has a cozy fireplace, pine furniture, and a small exhibition of Sami jewelry. Its regional and Continental menu is strong on reindeer and fish. ✉ *Raitopolku 2, 9983 Saariselkä,* ☎ *016/668–601,* FAX *016/668–602. 104 rooms. Restaurant, 2 pools, sauna, squash. AE, DC, MC, V. Closed May.*

Outdoor Activities and Sports

SWIMMING

Lapland's waters are exceptionally clean and good for swimming. Many hotels have pools, and **Saariselkä Spa** at Saariselkä features an indoor water world.

Ivalo

55 *40 km (25 mi) north of Saariselkä, 193 km (116 mi) north of Rovaniemi.*

The village of Ivalo is the main center for northern Lapland. With its first-class hotel, airport, and many modern amenities, it offers little to the tourist in search of a wilderness experience, but the huge island-studded expanses of **Inarijärvi** (Lake Inari), north of Ivalo, offer virtually limitless boating, fishing, hiking, and hunting opportunities.

Outdoor Activities and Sports

♻ **Tunturikeskus Kiilopää** (⊠ 99800 Ivalo, ☎ 016/667–101) has a mul-
tiactivity center for children, including snow-castle building, centrifuge
sledding, ski tracks, and reindeer and dogsled trips; there are summer
activities, too.

BOATING

A seven-hour trip up the Lemmenjoki River from Ivalo can be arranged
by **Lemmenjoen Lomamajat** (⊠ Lemmenjoki, ☎ 016/57135).

Lodging

$–$$$$ 🏨 **Tunturikeskus Kiilopää.** This "Fell Center" is in the midst of a hik-
ers' and cross-country skiers' paradise in the Urho Kekkonen National
Park district, 45 km (28 mi) south of Ivalo Airport. Accommodations
are in beautifully crafted log cabins, apartments, or individual hotel
rooms, all made of wood and stone. Apartments have picture windows
and fireplaces. The casual restaurant serves reindeer and other game
entrées. ⊠ 99800 Ivalo, ☎ 016/667–101, ℻ 016/667–121. 8 cabins,
8 apartments, 34 rooms, 9 youth hostel rooms. Restaurant, no-smok-
ing rooms, cross-country skiing, ski shop. AE, DC, MC, V.

$$ 🏨 **Ivalo.** Modern and well equipped for business travelers and families, this hotel is 1 km (½ mi) from Ivalo, right on the Ivalojoki River.
The lobby has marble floors, the lounge a brick fireplace. The rooms
are spacious and modern, with burlap woven wallpaper, oatmeal carpets, and lots of blond birchwood trimming; ask for one by the river.
The restaurant offers local and continental fare, as well as delicious
"Lappi à la Carte" meals. ⊠ Ivalontie 34, 99800 Ivalo, ☎ 016/688–
111, ℻ 016/661–905. 94 rooms. 2 restaurants, pool, sauna, boating,
recreation room, baby-sitting. AE, DC, MC, V.

$ 🏨 **Kultahippu.** In the heart of Ivalo, along the Ivalojoki River, Kultahippu
claims to have the northernmost nightclub in Finland. Guest rooms are
cozy, with simple birchwood furnishing; larger rooms with sauna are
available for families. The restaurant serves traditional Lapp meals à
la carte. ⊠ Petsamontie 1, 99800 Ivalo, ☎ 016/661–825, ℻ 016/662–
510. 30 rooms. Restaurant, hot tub, sauna, beach. AE, DC, MC, V.

Inari

56 40 km (24 mi) northwest of Ivalo, 333 km (207 mi) north of Rovaniemi.

It is a stunning drive northwest from Ivalo along the lakeshore to
Inari, home of the *Sámi Parlamenta* (Sami Parliament). The **Saame-
laismuseo** (Sami Museum), on the village outskirts, covers all facets
of Sami culture. ⊠ Inari, ☎ 016/671–014. ▦ FM 20. ☺ June–Aug.
10, daily 8–10; Aug. 11–31, daily 8–8; Sept. 1–20, weekdays 9–3:30.
Call ahead for winter hrs (☎ 016/51014).

OFF THE   **INARIN POROFARMI** – Racing reindeer are trained at this working rein-
BEATEN PATH   deer farm 14 km (9 mi) southeast of Inari. You can drive a reindeer sled
                 or be pulled on skis by the magical beasts. ⊠ Kaksamajärvi, Inari, ☎
                 016/673–912.

Dining and Lodging

$$ ✕🏨 **Inari Kultahovi.** This cozy inn is on the wooded banks of the swiftly
flowing Juutuajoki Rapids. The no-frills double rooms are small, with
handwoven rugs and birchwood furniture. In summer you'll need a reser-
vation to get a table at Kultahovi's restaurant; the specialties are
salmon and reindeer, but try the tasty whitefish caught from nearby
Lake Inari. ⊠ 99870 Inari, ☎ 016/671–221, ℻ 016/671–250. 29 rooms.
Restaurant, saunas. DC, MC, V.

Outdoor Activities and Sports

Lapptreks (✉ 99870 Inari, ☎ 016/58567) offers a combined canoeing, hiking, and gold-panning trip. For more tour ideas, *see* Guided Tours, *below.*

Lapland A to Z

Arriving and Departing

The best base for exploring is Rovaniemi, which connects with Helsinki and the south by road, rail, and air links; there is even a car-train from Helsinki.

BY BUS

Bus service into the region revolves around Rovaniemi; from there you can switch to local buses.

BY CAR

If you are driving north, follow Arctic Highway No. 4 (national highway) to Kuopio–Oulu–Rovaniemi, or go via the west coast to Oulu, then to Rovaniemi. From Rovaniemi, the national highway continues straight up to Lake Inari via Ivalo. Roads are generally good, but some in the extreme north may be rough.

BY PLANE

The airports serving Lapland are at **Enontekiö, Ivalo, Kemi, Kittilä, Kuusamo, Oulu, Rovaniemi,** and **Sodankylä.** Finnair serves all these airports with flights from Helsinki, though not all flights are nonstop. You can also fly to the north from most of southwestern Finland's larger cities and from the lakes region.

BY TRAIN

Train service will get you to Rovaniemi and Kemijärvi. From there you must make connections with other forms of transport.

Getting Around

BY BUS

Buses leave five times daily from Rovaniemi to Inari (five hours) and five times a day to Ivalo (four hours).

BY CAR

The Arctic Highway will take you north from Rovaniemi at the Arctic Circle to Inari, just below the 69th parallel. If you'd rather not rent a car, however, all but the most remote towns are accessible by bus, train, or plane.

BY PLANE

There is service every day but Sunday between Rovaniemi and Ivalo. You can also fly between Oulu or Rovaniemi to Ivalo, Enontekiö, Kemi, and Sodankylä, all on Finnair domestic services. Finnair also has daily flights directly from Helsinki to Kuusamo. There are seasonal schedules.

BY TAXI

You can take countryside taxis to your final destination; taxi stands are at most bus stations. Fares range from FM 50 for a few km to FM 700 for 100 km. Taxi drivers invariably use their meters, and specially negotiated fares—even for long distances—are unusual.

Contacts and Resources

EMERGENCIES

The nationwide emergency number is ☎ **112;** it can be used for police and ambulance services. Lapland's leading hospital is **Lapin Keskussairaala** (Lapland Central Hospital, ✉ Ounasrinteentie 22, Rovaniemi, ☎ 016/3281). Dentists can be reached at **Hammashoitola Viisaudenhammas** (✉ Koskik. 9 B, Rovaniemi, ☎ 016/347–620).

Guided tours in towns are arranged through city tourist offices. Tours
to Lapland can be purchased through **Area Travel** (⊠ Mikonk. 2,
00100 Helsinki, ☎ 09/818–383).

A great variety of specialty tours cater to both general and special interests, from white-water rafting to nature-photography tours. The national tourist board's *Lappi à la Carte* booklet suggests gourmet trails
through the north. **Lapptreks** (⊠ 99870 Inari, ☎ 016/58567) arranges
reindeer, canoe, and snowmobile safaris; ski treks; and fishing trips.

Adventure Tours: Finland Travel Bureau (⊠ Kaivok. 10A, 00100
Helsinki, ☎ 09/18261) offers a winter Polar Safari Adventure Tour (four
days, three nights).

Arctic Circle Tour: From Rovaniemi, the tourist board has a 2½-hour
evening Arctic Circle tour.

Biking Safaris: For independent travelers, the **Finnish Youth Hostel Association** (⊠ Yrjönk. 38B, 00100 Helsinki, ☎ 09/694–0377, FAX 09/
693–1349) can suggest various itineraries, including cycling "safaris"
through Lapland. The association will also recommend accommodations in various hostels, cabins, and campgrounds.

Fly-Fishing, Fishing, and Canoe Trips: Lapland Travel Ltd. (⊠ Koskik.
1, 96100 Rovaniemi, ☎ 016/346–052) offers fly-fishing and combined canoe-and-fishing trips.

Sami Tours: From Inari, Feelings Unlimited runs two-hour Lake Inari
tours that leave from the Sami Museum and visit a Sami stone altar
and burial island. Make reservations through **Raimo Mustkangas** (⊠
Inari, July–Sept., ☎ 016/671–352; Rovaniemi, year-round, ☎ 049/
396–841).

Santa Claus Tour: Finnair also arranges the Santa Claus Flight to
Rovaniemi (one day, one night); call the Finnair Tours Desk (☞ *below*).

Ski Trips and Safaris: Finnair arranges many tours from Helsinki, including ski trips for three or seven days; the Arctic Safari to Lapland
(one day, one night); the Husky Safari (three days, two nights). Reservations and itinerary details are available from **Finnair Tours Desk** (☎
09/818–8690, FAX 09/818–8655).

Ivalo (⊠ Ivalontie 12, 99800, ☎ 016/662–521). **Kemijärvi** (⊠ Ku-
umaniemenk. 2 A, 98100, ☎ 016/813–777). **Kuusamo** (⊠ Torangin-
taival 2, 93600, ☎ 08/850–2910). **Oulu** (⊠ Torik. 10, 90100, ☎ 08/
314–1294). **Rovaniemi** (⊠ Koskik. 1, 96200, ☎ 016/346–270).
Saariselkä (⊠ Saariselkätie, PL 22, 99831, ☎ 016/668–122). **Salla** (⊠
PL 59, 98901 Salla, ☎ 016/832–141). **Sodankylä** (⊠ Sodankylä
Matkailu Oy, Jäämerentie 9, 99600, ☎ 016/613–474).

FINLAND A TO Z

Arriving and Departing

By Boat

DFDS Scandinavian Seaways (⊠ Scandinavia House, Parkeston Quay,
Harwich, Essex, ☎ 1255/240–234) sails from Harwich to Göteborg,
Sweden, with overland (bus or train) transfer to Stockholm; from
there, Silja and Viking Line ships cross to the Finnish Åland Islands,

Turku, and Helsinki. Traveling time is about two days (☞ Getting Around by Ferry, *below*).

By Bus

You can travel by bus between Finland and Norway, Sweden, or Russia; contact **Matkahuolto** (✉ Linja-autoasema, Simonk. 3, 00200 Helsinki, ☎ 09/682–701).

By Plane

FROM NORTH AMERICA

Flying time from New York to Helsinki is about 8 hours, 9 hours for the return trip.

All international flights arrive at **Helsinki-Vantaa International Airport,** 20 km (12 mi) north of city center. For 24-hour arrival and departure information, call ☎ 9600/8100. **Finnair** (☎ 800/950–5000) offers domestic and international flights, with daily direct service from New York. **Delta** (☎ 800/241–4141) works with Finnair on its direct service from New York. **British Airways** (☎ 800/247–9297), **Lufthansa** (☎ 800/645–3880), and **Scandinavian Airlines System** (SAS, ☎ 800/221–2350) also fly to Helsinki.

FROM THE UNITED KINGDOM

Flying time from London to Helsinki is 2 hours, 45 minutes.

Finnair (✉ 14 Clifford St., London W1X 1RD, ☎ 0171/629–4349), **British Airways** (✉ Speedbird House, Heathrow Airport, London TW6 2JA, ☎ 0181/759–5511, 0345/222111 reservations), and some charter companies fly from London to Helsinki. Ask the Finnish Tourist Board for names of companies specializing in travel packages to Finland.

By Train

Passenger trains leave Helsinki twice daily for St. Petersburg (8 hours) and once daily on an overnighter to Moscow (15 hours). Travel to Russia requires a visa. To get to northern Sweden or Norway, you must combine train–bus or train–boat travel.

Getting Around

By Bicycle

Finland is a wonderful place for biking, with its easy terrain, light traffic, and wide network of bicycle paths. You can get bike-route maps for most major cities. In Helsinki, cycling is a great way to see the main peninsula as well as some of the surrounding islands, linked by bridges. Rentals average FM 40–FM 60 per day. **Suomen Retkeilymajajärjestö** (Finnish Youth Hostel Association, ✉ Yrjönk. 38B, 00100 Helsinki, ☎ 09/694–0377, FAX 09/693–1349) offers a free brochure with information on long-distance cycling trips and hostels. Bicycle rentals are available from **Green Bike** (✉ Mannerheim. 13, 00100 Helsinki, ☎ 050/550–1020).

By Boat

Finland is one of the world's major shipbuilding nations, and the ferries that cruise the Baltic to the Finnish Åland Islands and Sweden seem more like luxury liners. The boat operators make so much money selling duty-free alcohol, perfume, and chocolate that they spare no expense on facilities, which include saunas, children's playrooms, casinos, a host of bars and cafés, and often superb restaurants.

All classes of sleeping accommodations are available on board the journeys from Stockholm to Turku (about 11 hours) and from Stockholm to Helsinki (about 15 hours). Other connections are Vaasa–Sundsvall and Umeå (Sweden), Kokkola–Skellefteå (Sweden), Helsinki–Travemünde (Germany), and Helsinki–Tallinn (Estonia).

In Helsinki, the **Silja** (✉ Mannerheim. 2, ☎ 9800/74552) terminal for ships arriving from Stockholm is at Olympialaituri (Olympic Harbor), on the west side of the South Harbor. The **Viking Line** (✉ Mannerheim. 12, ☎ 09/123–577) terminal for ships arriving from Stockholm is at Katajanokkanlaituri (Katajanokka Harbor), on the east side of the South Harbor. Both Silja and Viking have downtown agencies where brochures, information, and tickets are available.

By Bus

The Finnish bus network, **Matkahuolto** (✉ Linja-autoasema, Simonk. 3, 00200 Helsinki, ☎ 09/682–701), is extensive and the fares reasonable. Full-time students can purchase a discount card for FM 30 that translates into a 50% discount on longer trips. Senior citizens will get good discounts with the **65 Card** for FM 32; it's available at Matkahuolto offices. Adults in groups of three or more are entitled to a 25% discount. A **Coach Holiday Ticket** (FM 340) is good for up to 1,000 km (621 mi) of travel for two weeks.

By Car

Driving is pleasant on Finland's relatively uncongested roads.

EMERGENCY ASSISTANCE

Foreigners involved in road accidents should immediately notify the **Finnish Motor Insurers' Bureau** (✉ Liikennevakuutuskeskus, Bulevardi 28, 00120 Helsinki, ☎ 09/680–401) as well as the police.

GASOLINE

At press time gasoline cost FM 5.54 per liter.

ROAD CONDITIONS

Late autumn and spring are the most hazardous times to drive. Roads are often icy in autumn (*kelivaroitus* is the slippery road warning), and the spring thaw can make for *kelirikko* (heaves). The **Automobile Touring Club of Finland** (✉ Autoliitto ry, Hämeentie 105 A, 00550 Helsinki, ☎ 09/774–761) has a wealth of information, including where to rent studded tires, which are mandatory—except for foreign-registered cars—from December through February.

RULES OF THE ROAD

Driving is on the right-hand side of the road. You must always use low-beam headlights outside built-up areas. Seat belts are compulsory for everyone. You must yield to cars coming from the right at most intersections where roads are of equal size. There are strict drinking-and-driving laws.

Speed limits range from 40 to 80 and sometimes 100 kph (25 to 50 and sometimes 62 mph), depending on road size and proximity to settled areas.

RENTAL AGENCIES

Car rental in Finland is not cheap, but a group rental might make it worthwhile. Be on the lookout for weekend and summer discounts. It is cheaper to rent directly from the United States before coming to Finland. Some Finnish service stations also offer car rentals at reduced rates.

Avis (✉ Pohjoinen Rautatiek. 17, Helsinki, ☎ 09/441–155; airport office, ☎ 09/822–833 or 9800/2828). **Budget** (✉ Hotel Inter-Continental, 09/497–477; airport office, ☎ 09/870–1606 or 9800/2535). **Hertz** (✉ Mannerheim. 44, ☎ 09/446–910; airport office, ☎ 09/821–052 or 9800/2012). **Europcar Interrent** (✉ John Stenbergin ranta 6, ☎ 09/758–3354; airport office, ☎ 09/826–677 or 9800/2154).

RENTAL RATES

Regular daily rates range from FM 300 to FM 550, with per km surcharges from FM 2 to FM 7. Car rentals are normally 30% cheaper on weekends. Insurance is sold by the rental agencies.

By Plane

Finnair runs an extensive domestic service. Domestic flights are relatively cheap, and as some planes have a set number of discount seats allotted, it's best to reserve early. Finnair's Finnish Holiday Tickets provide 10 one-way coupons good for 30 days of travel within Finland. At press time, the price for these coupons was about FM 2,500. For information, contact **Finnair** (⊠ Helsinki-Vantaa Airport, Tietotie 11, 01530 Vantaa, ☎ 09/818–800).

By Taxi

Taxis travel everywhere in Finland. The meter starts at FM 30, with surcharges at certain times and on certain days. In cities people generally go to one of the numerous taxi stands and take the first available taxi. You can hail a cab, but most are on radio call. The main phone number for taxi service in the Helsinki area is ☎ 700–700. Many taxi drivers take credit cards. Tipping is unnecessary; if you want to leave something, round up to the nearest FM 5–FM 10. A receipt is a *kuitti*.

By Train

The Finnish State Railways, or VR (☎ 09/100–127), serve southern Finland well, but connections in the central and northern sections are scarcer and are supplemented by buses. Helsinki is the main junction, with Riihimäki to the north a major hub. You can get as far north as Rovaniemi and Kemijärvi by rail, but to penetrate farther into Lapland, you'll need to rely on buses, domestic flights, or local taxis.

First- and second-class seats are available on all express trains. Children ages 6–16 travel half-fare, and there is a 20% reduction when three or more people travel together. You must make a seat reservation on special fast trains (FM 15–FM 70). For FM 50, senior citizens (over 65) can buy a special pass entitling them to 50% discounts on train fares. For a supplement you can take one of the new, fast Pendolino trains that have started up on the Helsinki–Turku line, cutting travel time on the route by half an hour. Car and passenger trains leave daily for northern Finland.

Inquiries on train travel can be made to the Finnish State Railways at the main railroad station in Helsinki or to the **Information Service** (⊠ Vilhonk. 13, PL 488, 00101 Helsinki, ☎ 09/010–0121).

DISCOUNT PASSES

The **Finnrail Pass** gives unlimited first- or second-class travel within a set time; the 3 day pass costs FM 505 (FM 760 for first-class), the 5-day pass FM 685 (FM 1,030), and the 10-day pass FM 945 (FM 1,420). Children pay half-fare. Passes can be bought in the United States and Canada by calling **Rail Europe** (☎ 800/438–7245); in the United Kingdom from **Norvista** (☎ 0171/409–7334); and from the **Finnish State Railways,** or VR (☎ 09/100127).

The **ScanRail Pass** comes in various denominations: five days of travel within 15 days ($222 first class, $176 second class); 10 days within a month ($354 first class, $284 second class); or one month ($516 first class, $414 second class). For information on the ScanRail'n Drive Pass, *see* Train Travel *in* the Gold Guide. The **Eurailpass** is good for train travel throughout all of Europe. In the United States, call **Rail Europe** (☎ 800/848–7245) or **DER** (☎ 800/782–2424).

Contacts and Resources

Customs

Spirits containing over 60% alcohol by volume may not be brought into Finland. Visitors ages 18–20 may not bring in spirits. Visitors to Finland may import goods for their own use from another European Union (EU) country duty-free, with the exception of tobacco and alcohol. Visitors older than 21 may bring in 1 liter of spirits (more than 22% alcohol by volume) or 3 liters of aperitifs or sparkling wines, plus 5 liters of table wine and 15 liters of beer. If the items were purchased in a duty-free shop at an airport or harbor, or on board an airplane or ship, visitors older than 21 may bring in 1 liter of spirits, 2 liters of aperitifs or sparkling wines, 2 liters of table wine, and 15 liters of beer.

Dining

Finnish food focuses on the fresh rather than diverse, although restaurant chefs today are making strides toward innovation. While there, treat yourself to a traditional Finnish meal of succulent game—pheasant, reindeer, hare, and grouse—paired with wild-berry compotes and exotic mushroom sauces.

Embassies

U.S. (⊠ Itäinen Puistotie 14A, 00140 Helsinki, ☎ 09/171–931). **Canada** (⊠ Pohjoisespl. 25B, 00100 Helsinki, ☎ 09/171–141). **U.K.** (⊠ Itäinen Puistotie 17, 00140 Helsinki, ☎ 09/2286–5100.

Emergencies

The nationwide emergency number is ☎ 112.

Guided Tours

The **Finland Travel Bureau** (⊠ Kaivok. 10A, Box 319, 00101 Helsinki, ☎ 09/18261, FAX 09/622–1524) specializes in all kinds of travel arrangements, including special-interest tours throughout Finland, as well as Scandinavia, Russia, and the Baltic Republics.

Language

Finnish, the principal language, is a Finno-Ugric tongue related to Estonian with distant links to Hungarian. The country's second official language is Swedish, although only about 6% of the population speaks it. In the south, most towns have Finnish and Swedish names; if the Swedish name is listed first, it indicates more Swedish than Finnish speakers live in that area. The third language is Sami, the language of the Laplanders. English is spoken in most cities and resorts.

Late-Night Pharmacies

Late-night pharmacies are found only in large towns. Look under *Aptekki* in the phone book; listings include pharmacy hours.

Lodging

Lomarengas (⊠ Malminkaari 23C, 00700 Helsinki, ☎ 09/3516–1321; Eteläespl. 4, 00130 Helsinki, 09/170–611) has lists of reasonably priced bed-and-breakfasts, holiday cottages, farm accommodations, and car-rental services available in Finland. It also arranges stays at a range of facilities, including mökki holidays.

CAMPING

Finland's wealth of open space promises prime camping territory. If you camp outside authorized areas and in a settled area, you must get the landowner's permission, and you cannot camp closer than 300 ft to anyone's house. Finncamping Cheque (FM 70) is a coupon system for campers. For more information, and to find out about the National Camping Card, contact the **Finnish Travel Association** (⊠ Camping Department, Mikonk. 25, PL 776, 00101 Helsinki, ☎ 09/170–868). The annually updated list of campsites, including classifications and English-language summary, is sold at large bookstores and R-kiosks. A free brochure listing 200 campsites in Finland is available from city tourist offices.

FARM VACATIONS
Suomen 4H-liitto (✉ Abrahamink. 7, 00180 Helsinki, ☎ 09/642–233) arranges farm vacations.

HOTELS
The **Hotel Booking Center** (✉ Rautatieasema, 00100, ☎ 09/171–133) in Helsinki, at the railway station, will make reservations only in Helsinki and surroundings for FM 12 (telephone reservations are free). **Suomen Hotellivaraukset** (✉ Nervanderink. 5 D 40, 00100 Helsinki, ☎ 09/499–155) will make reservations anywhere in Finland at no cost. **Best Western Hotels Finland** (✉ Merimiehenk. 29 A, 00150 Helsinki, ☎ 09/655–855) is a reliable national hotel chain. **Arctia Hotel Partners** (✉ Ankkurik. 1, 00160 Helsinki, ☎ 09/696–901) is another national hotel chain.

SUMMER DORMITORIES
During the summer season (June–August) many university residence halls in Finland open their doors to visitors. Prices (usually from FM 173 per night in Helsinki and FM 124 elsewhere in Finland) are much lower than those in ordinary hotels, and meals are generally available. Ask the Finnish Tourist Board or the Finnish Youth Hostel Association (✉ Yrjönk. 38B, 00100 Helsinki, ☎ 09/694–0377) for its brochure on budget accommodations.

Mail
Post offices are open weekdays 9–5; stamps, express mail, registered mail, and insured mail service are available. There is no Saturday delivery.

POSTAL RATES
Airmail letters and postcards to destinations outside Europe cost FM 3.40; letters and postcards to other Scandinavian countries, the Baltics, and within Finland, FM 2.40; to the rest of Europe, FM 3.20.

RECEIVING MAIL
You may receive letters care of *poste restante* anywhere in Finland; the *poste restante* address in the capital is Mannerheimintie 11F, 00100 Helsinki, at the side of the rail station. It is open weekdays 8 AM–9 PM, Saturday 9–6, and Sunday 11–9. You can also post mail 24 hours a day at Finland Post's Express Service (✉ Läkkisepäntie 11, 00620 Helsinki, ☎ 9800/70784), 8–5.

Money and Expenses
CURRENCY
The unit of currency is the Finnmark (FM), also abbreviated as FIM and FMK. The Finnmark is divided into 100 *penniä* (pennies) in denominations of 10- and 50-penniä and 5- and 10-mark coins. Bills begin with the FM 20 note and progress to FM 50, 100, 500, and 1,000. At press time the exchange rate was around FM 5.24 to the U.S. dollar, FM 8.51 to the pound sterling, and FM 3.81 to the Canadian dollar.

EXCHANGING MONEY
There are exchange bureaus in all bank branches; some post offices, which also function as banks (Postipankki); major hotels; the Forex booths at the train station and in Esplanadi; and at Helsinki-Vantaa Airport. Some large harbor terminals also have exchange bureaus, and international ferries have exchange desks. The Forex offices give the best rates and charge no commission.

PREPAID CASH CARDS

Finland is making advancements in the use of "smart" prepaid electronic cash cards that process even the smallest of anonymous cash transactions, made at designated public pay phones, vending machines, and McDonald's—of all places. Disposable prepaid cards can be purchased at kiosks. Reloadable purse cards, available to customers of major Finnish banks in early 1997, will eventually be integrated with existing ATM and debit cards; service will initially be available in major cities, including Helsinki and Tampere.

SALES-TAX REFUNDS

There is a 22% sales tax on most consumer goods. Nonresidents can recover 12% to 16% by going through the "tax-free for tourists" procedure: when you ask for your tax rebate—and be sure to ask for it at the point of purchase—you'll get a tax-free voucher and your goods in a sealed bag. Present the voucher and unopened bag at tax-free cashiers when leaving Finland or when departing the EU. These are located at most major airports, on board most long-distance ferries, and at major overland crossings into Norway and Russia. Refunds are available only in Finnish marks. For a high fee, the tax refund can also be sent to your home country.

SAMPLE PRICES

The devaluations of its currency in November 1991 and September 1992 brought Finland's notoriously high prices down to more reasonable levels. Some sample prices: cup of coffee, FM 7; soda, FM 10–FM 13; Continental breakfast in hotel, FM 32–FM 75; bottle of beer, FM 15–FM 20; 1-mi taxi ride, around FM 30.

TIPPING

Tipping is not the norm in Finland, but it is not unheard of, so use your own discretion. Finns normally do not tip cab drivers, but if they do they round up to the nearest FM 5. Give FM 5 to train or hotel porters. Coat-check fees are usually posted, and tips above this amount are not expected. For all other services, no tip or FM 5 is acceptable.

Outdoor Activities and Sports

For general information, contact the **Finnish Sports Association** (✉ Radiok. 20, 00240 Helsinki, ☎ 09/1581), the umbrella organization for the many specific sports associations.

BIKING

Route maps are available from local tourist offices and from the Finnish Youth Hostel Association. Pick up a copy of *Finland for Cyclists,* an informative booklet available at the Finnish Tourist Board.

BOATING

Contact the **Finnish Yachting Association** (✉ Radiok. 20, 00240, Helsinki, ☎ 09/348–121). Also try the **Finnish Motorboating Association** (✉ Radiok. 20, 00240 Helsinki, ☎ 09/158–2561).

CANOEING

Contact the **Finnish Canoe Association** (✉ Olympic Stadium, 00250 Helsinki, ☎ 09/494–965).

FISHING

A fishing license (FM 30–FM 200) can be obtained from any post office and is valid for one year. In addition to this general fishing license, a regional fishing permit must also be obtained. The **Finnish Forest and Parks Service** (✉ Vernissäk. 4, 01300 Vantaa, ☎ 09/857–841) will provide a brochure listing 100 fishing spots and guidance, too. Pick up a copy of *Finland for Anglers,* an informative booklet available at the Finnish Tourist Board.

GOLF

Contact the **Finnish Golf Union** (⊠ Radiok. 20, 00240 Helsinki, ☎ 09/ 158–2244).

HIKING

Pick up the informative *Finland for Hikers* booklet at the Finnish Tourist Board. If you want to hike on state-owned land in eastern and northern Finland, write to the **Finnish Forest and Parks Service** (⊠ Vernissäk. 4, 01300 Vantaa, ☎ 09/857–841). For organized hiking tours for families with children, as well as beginners, contact **Suomen Latu** (Finnish Ski Track Association, ⊠ Fabianink. 7, 00130 Helsinki, ☎ 09/170–8101). Maps of marked trails throughout Finland can be ordered through **Karttakeskus Pasila** (⊠ Opastinsilta 12, 00520 Helsinki, ☎ 09/154–521).

ORIENTEERING

Contact the **Finnish Orienteering Association** (⊠ Radiok. 20, 00240 Helsinki, ☎ 09/348–121).

SAILING

Some of Finland's most popular inland sailing races are the Hanko Regatta, the Helsinki Regatta, the Rauma Sea Race, and the Päijänne Regatta. Contact the **Finnish Yachting Association** (☞ *above*) for details.

SKIING

Contact **Suomen Latu** (Finnish Ski Track Association, ⊠ Fabianink. 7, 00130 Helsinki, ☎ 09/170–8101) for information about ski centers and resorts nationwide. Finnair offers fly–ski packages to the north.

WATERSKIING

Contact the **Finnish Water-Ski Association** (⊠ Op. 2, 20200 Harjevalta, ☎ 02/740–600).

WINDSURFING

Contact the **Finnish Windsurfing Association** (⊠ c/o the Finnish Yachting Association, Radiok. 20, Helsinki, ☎ 09/348–121).

Telephones

COUNTRY CODE

The country code for Finland is 358.

DIRECTORY ASSISTANCE AND OPERATOR INFORMATION

For an operator in the United States, dial ☎ 9800/10010; in Canada, dial ☎ 9800/10011; and in the United Kingdom, dial 9800/10440. Other important numbers are as follows: ☎ 112 general emergency; ☎ 10040 news in English; ☎ 100–151 wake-up call; ☎ 118 information in Helsinki and elsewhere in Finland; ☎ 020–208 international information.

INTERNATIONAL CALLS

You can call overseas at the post and telegraph office. In Helsinki, at Mannerheimintie 11B, the "Lennätin" section is open weekdays 9–9, Saturdays 10–4. The *Finland Direct* pamphlet tells you how to reach an operator in your own country for collect or credit-card calls. Use any booth that has a green light, and pay the cashier when you finish. You can also ask for a clerk to arrange a collect call; when it is ready, the clerk will direct you to a booth. The local access code for **AT&T USA-Direct** calls is ☎ 9800/10010. The **MCI Call USA** access code is ☎ 0800/110280. For **Sprint Express** dial ☎ 9800/10284.

The front of the phone book has overseas calling directions and rates. You must begin all direct overseas calls with 990, or 999, or 994, or 00, plus country code (1 for the United States/Canada, 44 for Great

Britain). Finnish operators can be reached by dialing ☎ 020–208 for overseas information or for placing collect calls.

Finland is gradually moving to the phone-card system, and some phones only accept the *Tele Kortti,* available at post offices, R-kiosks, and some grocery stores in increments of FM 30, 50, 100, and 150. Public phones charge FM 2 and take coins of up to FM 5. Kiosks often have phones. Airport and hotel phones take credit cards. Ringing tones vary but are distinguishable from busy signals, which are always rapid. Most pay telephones have picture instructions illustrating how they operate.

Remember that if you are dialing out of the immediate area you must dial 0 first; drop the 0 when calling Finland from abroad.

Travel Agencies
Suomen Matkatoimisto (Finland Travel Bureau, ✉ Kaivok. 10 A, PL 319, 00100 Helsinki, ☎ 09/18261) is the country's main travel agency.

The Finland Travel Bureau's affiliate in the United Kingdom is **Norvista** (✉ 227 Regent Street, W1R 8PD London, ☎ 0171/409–7334). **Finnway Inc.** (✉ 228 E. 45th St., 14th Floor, New York, NY 10017, ☎ 212/818–1198) is the United States' affiliate of the Finland Travel Bureau.

Visitor Information
Finnish Tourist Board (✉ Suomen Matkailun edistämiskeskus, Eteläespl. 4, PL 625, 00101 Helsinki, ☎ 09/417–6911; ✉ 655 3rd Ave., New York, NY 10017, ☎ 212/949–2333; ✉ 1900 Avenue of the Stars, Suite 1070, Los Angeles, CA 90067, ☎ 310/277–5226; ✉ 66–68 Haymarket, London SW1Y 4RF, ☎ 0171/839–4048).

Weather
The tourist summer season runs from mid-June to mid-August, marked by long hours of sunlight and cool nights. Generally speaking, the spring and summer seasons begin a month earlier in the south of Finland than they do in the far north. Though many establishments and sights close or drastically reduce hours off-season, the advantages to off-season travel are many: avoiding the mosquitoes, especially fearsome in the north; spectacular fall foliage; and cross-country skiing. Spring is brief but magical: the snow melts, the ice breaks up, and nature explodes into life almost overnight.

CLIMATE
You can expect warm (not hot) days in Helsinki from mid-May, and in Lapland from mid-June. The midnight sun can be seen from May to July, depending on the region. For a period in midwinter, the northern lights almost make up for the fact that the sun does not rise at all. Even in Helsinki, summer nights are brief and never really dark, whereas in midwinter daylight lasts only a few hours.

4 Iceland

*On the highway from Keflavík
International Airport into Iceland's
capital, Reykjavík, the traveler is met
by an eerie moonscape under a
mystical sub-Arctic sky. The low
terrain is barely covered by its thin
scalp of luminescent green moss. Here
and there columns of steam rise from
hot spots in the lava fields. Although
trees are few and far between, an
occasional scrawny shrub clings to a
rock outcropping. The very air smells
different—clean and crisp—and it's so
clear you can see for miles.*

WELCOME TO ICELAND, one of the most dramatic natural spectacles on this planet. It is a land of dazzling white glaciers and black sands, blue
Updated by
Michael J.
Kissane
hot springs, rugged lava fields, and green, green valleys. This North Atlantic island offers insight into the ferocious powers of nature, ranging from the still-warm lava from the 1973 Vestmannæyjar (Westman Islands) and the 1991 Mt. Hekla volcanic eruptions to the chilling splendor of the Vatnajökull Glacier. The country is mostly barren, with hardly a tree to be seen, but its few birches, wildflowers, and delicate vegetation are all the more lovely in contrast. Contrary to the country's forbidding name, the climate is surprisingly mild.

So far north—part of the country touches the Arctic Circle—Iceland has the usual Scandinavian long hours of darkness in winter. Maybe this is why Icelanders are such good chess players (Iceland played host to the memorable Fischer–Spassky match of 1972). Such long nights may also explain why, per capita, more books are written, printed, bought, and read in Iceland than anywhere else in the world. No surprise the birth rate is unusually high for Europe, too!

Another reason for Iceland's near-universal literacy might be its long tradition of participatory democracy, dating from AD 930, when the first parliament met at Þingvellir. Today it's a modern Nordic—most would find the term "Scandinavian" too limited—society with a well-developed social welfare system. Women have a unique measure of equality: they keep their surname on marriage. Children are given a surname created from their father's first name, so that Magnús, son of Svein, becomes Magnús Sveinsson; Guðrún, daughter of Pétur, becomes Guðrún Pétursdóttir. Guðrún keeps her maiden name even after she marries, as naturally enough she remains her father's daughter rather than becoming her father-in-law's son. Her children will take a patronymic from their father's first name. Perhaps there is no connection, but it is interesting to note that in 1980 Iceland also voted in as president the first woman head of state to take office in a democratic election anywhere in the world, Vigdís Finnbogadóttir. After four 4-year terms in office, she did not seek reelection in 1996, and a new president, Ólafur Ragnar Grímsson, was chosen.

Iceland was settled by Vikings, with some Celtic elements, more than a thousand years ago (the first Norse settlers arrived in AD 874, but there is some evidence that Irish monks landed even earlier). Icelanders today speak a language remarkably similar to the ancient Viking tongue in which the sagas were recorded in the 13th century. The Norse settlers brought to the island sturdy horses, robust cattle, and Celtic slaves. Perhaps Irish tales of the supernatural inspired Iceland's traditional lore of the *huldufólk,* or hidden people, said to reside in splendor in rocks, crags, caves, and lava tubes. Look for a sharp, inexplicable bend in the road with a rock beside it, and the chances are you'll be peeping into an elf's private residence.

Iceland is the westernmost outpost of Europe, 800 km (500 mi) from the nearest European landfall, Scotland, and nearly 1,600 km (1,000 mi) from Copenhagen, the country's administrative capital during Danish rule from 1380 to 1918. Where the warm southern Gulf Stream confronts the icy Arctic currents from the north you'll find Iceland, straddling the mid-Atlantic ridge at the merger of the North American and European tectonic plates. Volcanic activity slowly forces the plates to separate, which continues to form the island. On average, a volcanic eruption has occurred every five years in the past few centuries. And

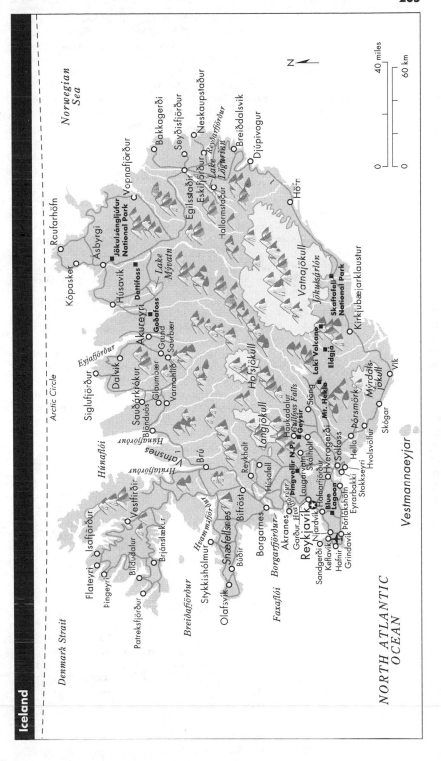

40 miles

60 km

Norwegian Sea

Denmark Strait

Arctic Circle

Raufarhöfn

Kópasket

Húsavík **Dettifoss**

Ásbyrgi

Jökulsárgljúfur National Park

Lake Mývatn

Akureyri **Goðafoss**

Grund Saurbær

Varmahlíð

Glaumbær

Dalvík

Eyjafjörður

Siglufjörður

Sauðárkrókur

Blönduós

Húnaflói

Hrútafjörður

Vatnsnes

Brú

Reykholt

Búðardalur

Stykkishólmur

Olafsvík

Breiðafjörður

Snæfellsnes

Búðir

Bifröst

Hvammsfjörður

Borgarnes

Borgarfjörður

Faxaflói

Akranes

Garður Hlíð

Þingvellir N.P.

Laugarvatn

Langjökull

Haukadalur

Geysir *Gullfoss Falls*

Stöng

Mt. Hekla

Skálholt

Hveragerði Selfoss

Hella

Þórsmörk

Mýrdals- jökull

Vík

Skógar

Hvolsvöllur

Stokkseyri

Eyrarbakki

Þorlákshöfn

Blue Lagoon

Hafnarfjörður

Reykjavík

Sandgerði Njarðvík

Keflavík

Grindavík

Vestmannaeyjar

NORTH ATLANTIC OCEAN

Patreksfjörður

Þingeyri

Flateyri

Bíldudalur

Ísafjörður

Vestfirðir

Brjánslækur

Hvalfjörður

Húsafell

Hraunfjörður

Hofsjökull

Laki Volcano

Eldgjá

Kirkjubæjarklaustur

Skaftafell National Park

Jökulsárlón

Vatnajökull

Höfn

Djúpivogur

Breiðdalsvík

Neskaupstaður

Seyðisfjörður

Reyðarfjörður

Eskifjörður

Egilsstaðir

Lake Lögurinn

Hallormstaður

Bakkagerði

Vopnafjörður

Vopnafjörður

Hrútafjörður

Hvítá

Mt. Hekla's no slacker, dramatically erupting under Vatnajökull in the fall of 1996 on the heels of a 1991 blast. Yet no one need wait for an eruption to be reminded of the fiery forces' presence, because they also heat the hot springs and geysers that gurgle, bubble, and spout in many parts of the country. The springs, in turn, provide hot water for public swimming pools and heating for most homes and buildings, helping to keep the air smog-free. Furthermore, hydropower generated by harnessing the country's many waterfalls is another main energy source, so pollution from fossil fuels is at a minimum.

More than 80% of the island's 103,000 square km (40,000 square mi) remains uninhabited. Ice caps cover 11% of the country, more than 50% is barren, 6% consists of lakes and rivers, and less than 2% of the land in Iceland is cultivated. Surrounded by the sea, the Icelanders have become great fishermen, and fish remains the cornerstone of the Icelandic economy. Seafood exports pay for the imported foodstuffs and other goods, all of which could not be produced economically in such a small society (population 267,000). Because of importation needs and high value-added taxes on most goods and services, prices tend toward the steep side in Iceland. Hotels and restaurants are pricey, but with a little digging you can always find a number of inexpensive alternatives.

Start your visit in the capital, Reykjavík, before venturing out into the countryside, where rainbow-arched waterfalls cleave mountains with great spiked ridges and snowcapped peaks. Climb mountains, ford rivers, watch birds, catch trout or salmon, even tend sheep and cattle at a typical Icelandic farm. Most visitors flock here in the warmest months of June, July, and August, but a growing number come in winter for the promise of skiing, snowmobiling, and snow-trekking vehicle tours. The frigid ocean prohibits swimming year-round, but hot springs and naturally heated pools dimple the landscape. Icelanders from all walks of life—cabinet ministers on down—congregate for a soak or a swim any time of year.

Pleasures and Pastimes

Bird-Watching

Even in settled areas bird-watchers are likely to find a fascinating assortment of species, among them the golden plover, a harbinger of spring; arctic terns, streamlined circumpolar migrators; and the colorful broad bills, tuxedo plumage, and expressive eyes of the puffin. Of several birds of prey, two earn special status because of their rarity: the regal gyrfalcon, the emblem for Iceland's Independent Party, and the majestic white-tailed eagle, whose grayish head and white tail are strikingly similar to the bald eagle.

A summer walk along Reykjavík's Tjörnin Lake might be accompanied duck species, swans, gulls, and the ever-present terns. Puffins can be spotted closest to Reykjavík at Lundey (Puffin Island, where else?). If you are a serious bird-watcher, by all means make a summer visit to Lake Mývatn, where you will find Europe's largest variety of ducks and water birds, from barrow's goldeneye to the riotous harlequin duck. Grebes, mergansers, phalaropes, and even ever-elusive snipes further reward the sharp-eyed visitor.

Dining

Chefs in Iceland are marrying elements of classic French cuisine and the best in traditional Scandinavian cooking. And more and more of them are dreaming up innovative dishes employing exotic ingredients, imported and available year-round.

The distinctly wild taste of Icelandic lamb its cultivated by allowing the animals to roam free amid the grasslands of the interior and feed on highland herbs. Iceland also produces traditional *hangikjöt* (smoked lamb) and a more lightly flavored alternative, London lamb. Game such as duck and reindeer shows up on fancier restaurant menus. And you have not eaten in Iceland until you've tried the seafood: lobster, ocean perch, turbot, *tindabikkja* (starry ray), salmon, and trout pulled from clear mountain rivers. Herring is pickled and also marinated in wine, garlic, and other spices. Salmon is cut fresh from ample fillets, smoked with aromatic woods, or cured with dill to create gravlax.

Like other Scandinavian countries, Iceland is renowned for its ales and spirits, the most famous being *brennivín*, an 80-proof liquor similar to aquavit. Icelandic vodkas, such as *Elduris* and *Icy*, are also of high quality.

CATEGORY	COST*
$$$$	over IKr3,500
$$$	IKr2,500–IKr3,500
$$	IKr1,500–IKr2,500
$	under IKr1,500

Prices are per person for a three-course meal, including tax and service charge, and excluding wine.

Fishing

The countryside abounds with rivers and lakes where you can catch salmon (April–mid-October), sea and brown trout (early June–September), and char. Permits can be bought at the closest farmstead, and sometimes at nearby gas stations and tackle shops. Fees range from a couple of hundred krónas to up to several thousand per day. Guides and accommodations are provided at most rivers and lakes.

Fishing at the most popular (and expensive) rivers, usually those stocked with salmon, must be booked in most cases at least a year in advance, and you will pay the equivalent of $800–$2,000 per fishing rod per day. Usually there is no catch limit, and only a certain number of fishermen are allowed on each section, or "beat."

Hiking

Much of Iceland's terrain, especially the highlands, offers breathtaking scenery and unparalleled solitude for hikers. Panoramas of vast, surreal volcanic mountains crowned by glaciers await every turn. Wide vistas punctuated by steamy hot-spring plumes and pierced by pristine streams and waterfalls are a photographer's dream. In late summer, you might find wild blueberries, crowberries, or bramble berries—a special bonus for your efforts.

Horseback Riding

The Icelandic horse is a purebred descendant of its ancestors from the Viking age, small but strong, exceptionally surefooted, intelligent, and easy to handle. This horse has a particularly interesting stepping style called the *tölt*, or "running walk," which yields an extraordinarily smooth ride. This gait is actually so smooth that a popular demonstration has the rider carrying a tray of drinks at full speed without spilling a drop! Horse lovers from around the world come to try these amazing five-speed steeds for themselves. A number of firms offer a variety of tours, from short one-day trips to 12-day treks for more experienced riders.

Lodging

Hotels in Reykjavík and larger towns usually offer standard amenities: hair dryer, trouser press, telephone, and satellite TV. Unless otherwise noted, assume rooms listed have bath or shower. Breakfast is usually included in the hotel price, but inquire to be certain.

Many travelers find simple guest houses adequate, whereas others prefer a bed-and-breakfast in a private home. Icelandic farm holidays are growing in popularity, even among Icelanders. On about 110 properties—half of them working farms—you can come in close contact with the country, its people, and magnificent natural surroundings (☞ Lodging *in* Iceland A to Z, *below*). Accommodations vary widely: you might stay in a separate cottage, in a bed in the farmhouse, or in a sleeping bag in an outbuilding. Some farms have cooking facilities, others serve full meals if requested. Make reservations well in advance.

CATEGORY	COST*
$$$$	over IKr12,000
$$$	IKr9,000–IKr12,000
$$	IKr6,000–IKr9,000
$	under IKr6,000

Prices are for a standard double room with bath and breakfast.

Shopping

The classic gift to bring home is the Icelandic sweater, hand-knit in traditional designs, no two alike. The natural lanolin in the thick, soft Icelandic yarn lightly mats its fibers for extra protection from cold and damp. A good sweater costs about IKr6,500 to IKr8,000.

You may want to pick up a small jar of Icelandic lumpfish caviar or some *harðfiskur* (dried fish), best eaten in small bits (and some say with a clothespin on the nose).

For upwards of IKr1,000 you can bring home silver replicas of Viking brooches, rings, necklaces, and religious symbols, such as the *Þórshamar* (Thor's hammer), runic letters, and pagan magical letters. A number of silversmiths also design beautiful modern jewelry with Icelandic stones—agate, jasper, and black obsidian.

Skiing

About 90 ski lifts whisk people up Iceland's mountains. Skiing season begins in January, when the days gradually become longer, and usually lasts through April. From late winter through summer you can ascend even higher on Jeep tours. The larger resorts offer both alpine and cross-country skiing trails. If you are less experienced on the slopes, you may take comfort in the fact that there's a scarcity of trees.

Snowmobiling

People aged 18 to 80 glide across Iceland's amazing white wonderland, within two hours of Reykjavík. Unlike elsewhere, this glacial grandeur occurs at just over 3,000 ft, so only the scenery and the rush leave you breathless, not the altitude. Supervised tours run from late winter through summer and include snowmobile instruction, mandatory helmets, and snowsuits.

Swimming

Almost every sizable community in Iceland has at least one public outdoor swimming pool, usually of fresh water that has been slightly chlorinated. Most are heated by thermal springs and enjoyed year-round. Groups of adults from all walks of life routinely start their day swimming laps, socializing, and soaking in a hot pot. Swimming is a required course in school and the nation's most popular sport. During the long days of summer pools are open until 9:30 PM.

Exploring Iceland

Iceland almost defies division into separate regions, thanks to its inlets and bays, thorough lacework of rivers, and complex coastline of fjords, all crowned by an unpopulated highland of glaciers and barrens. To divide the country into four compass directions is to oversimplify, but since the Icelandic national emblem depicts four legendary symbols—one for each corner of the country—the number is not totally arbitrary.

Reykjavík is the logical starting point for any visit to Iceland. The west is an expansive section of rugged fjords and lush valleys, starting just north of Reykjavík and extending all the way up to the extreme northwest. The north is a region of long, sometimes broad valleys and fingerlike peninsulas reaching toward the Arctic Circle. The east has fertile farmlands, the country's largest forest, and its share of smaller fjords. Iceland's south stretches from the lowest eastern fjords, essentially all the way west to the capital's outskirts. It encompasses rich piedmont farmland and wide, sandy coastal and glacial plains. Powerful rivers carved with impressive waterfalls drain the area. Here you'll find the national parks of Skaftafell and Þingvellir, as well as the nation's highest peak, Hvannadalshnúkur.

Great Itineraries

With only a few days on your hands, you can experience a fair number of Iceland's major attractions. You can take organized day-trips from Reykjavík (☞ Guided Tours *in* Reykjavík A to Z, *below*) or explore the surrounding area yourself with a rental car. Ask travel agents or tour operators about special offers within Iceland that allow you to fly one way and take a bus the other. Theoretically, you can drive the Ring Road—the most scenic route, which skirts the entire Iceland coast—in two days, but that pace qualifies as rally-race driving, and you won't see much. You should plan to travel the Ring Road in a week, enjoying roadside sightseeing and relaxing in the tranquil environment along the way. Side jaunts add significant time, as secondary roads are often not paved. When traveling outside Reykjavík, always allow plenty of time to make it back for departing flights.

IF YOU HAVE 4 DAYS

Start by taking a leisurely tour of 🖼 **Reykjavík** ①–㉓. The mix of the old and new in the capital's midtown is seen in the 19th-century **Alþingishús** and the **Ráðhús,** less than a decade old. Colorful rooftops abound, and ornate gingerbread can be spotted on the well-kept older buildings. A family favorite is the pool at **Laugardal Park,** where you'll find a **botanical garden** and **farm animal zoo.** Those who prefer a wider, less urban scope should opt for the **Golden Circle** approach on their first day, and take in spectacular **Gullfoss** waterfall, the **Geysir** hot springs area, and **Þingvellir National Park.**

On day two, check the weather report. Depending on conditions, you could take a flight for a day in the 🖼 **Westman Islands** and see how the islanders have turned the 1973 eruption of **Heimaey** to their advantage. A cruise around the island takes you to bird cliffs, and you may even spot seals or whales. On the third day, spend a leisurely morning in Heimaey, and head back to Reykjavík to take in any missed sights.

If it's sunny in the west on your second day, another alternative is to head north to the **Snæfellsnes peninsula.** The 9:30 AM *Akraborg* ferry takes you and your vehicle across to Akranes for a leisurely start. Look for dolphins arcing along the way and comical puffins splashing clear of the ship. Driving north to 🖼 **Borgarnes** and west out on the peninsula takes you to 🖼 **Búðir** for lunch and a stroll on the beach. Start to circle the mystic mountain whose profile changes by the minute, peek in at the small harbor of **Arnarstapa,** and on the peninsula's north, go from **Ólafsvík** on to 🖼 **Stykkishólmur.** If there's time, a cruise among the islets of **Breiðifjörður** will give both a visual and gourmet taste of the life at sea, as fresh shellfish is taken aboard for sampling.

On the third day, depart Stykkishólmur and cross the Snæfellsnes arm, going south from here to close the loop. Don't worry about making the last ferry at 5 PM from Akranes, because the drive around **Hvalfjörður,** or Whale Fjord, back to the capital takes you through beautiful country on a good, paved road. On day four, be otherwise packed for your flight home, and stop at the surreal **Blue Lagoon,** not far from **Grindavík,** for a late morning–early afternoon dip that will leave you refreshed and only 20 minutes from the airport for an afternoon flight connection.

IF YOU HAVE 6 DAYS

Complete the first three days of the four-day tour above, and on the morning of day four fly northeast to ☷ **Akureyri.** With a rental car visit the numerous historical houses here, such as **Matthíasarhús, Nonnahús, Laxdalshús,** and **Davíðshús.** After lunch, take some time at the **Lystigarðurinn.** Next drive east to the Lake Mývatn area, taking in **Goðafoss** and maybe even **Dettifoss** along the way. Spend a good part of day five in ☷ **Mývatn,** visiting **Dimmuborgir** lava formations, **Námaskarð** sulfur springs, and the shoreline birding areas. Return to Akureyri and stay the fifth night, possibly taking in a trio of fascinating churches at **Saubær, Grund,** and **Möðruvellir.** On day six, leave the north on a morning flight back to Reykjavík, and if time permits, duck in for a quick dip in the **Blue Lagoon.**

IF YOU HAVE 10 DAYS

Having first made reservations for you and your vehicle on the car ferry *Baldur* for day two (☞ Arriving and Departing *in* West and the Western Fjords A to Z, *below*), follow the Snæfellsnes peninsula itinerary from the four-day tour above as far as ☷ **Stykkishólmur** and spend the first night there, perhaps taking an evening cruise of the **Breiðarfjörður Islands.** On day two take the *Baldur* ferry to Brjánslækur, where you disembark and take a rather rough gravel road for nearly two hours west toward the village of ☷ **Patreksfjörður** and the incredible bird cliffs at **Látrabjarg.** Overnight in Patreksfjörður and return back along the rugged Barðarstönd coast toward the inland area of **Hrútafjörður,** staying in ☷ **Brú,** ☷ **Glaumbær,** or ☷ **Sauðákrókur** for night three.

Day four starts with the **Vatnsnes Circle,** where the peculiar, huge **Hvítserkur** stands offshore. Back on Route 1, turn north at **Varmahlíð** and visit the major classic farmstead **Glaumbæ,** and go through **Sauðárkrókur** to the ancient cathedral at **Hólar.** Once back on the Ring Road, end the day in ☷ **Akureyri.**

After exploring Akureyri on the morning of day six, head east past **Goðafoss** and **Dettifoss** to the aviary crossroads at **Lake Mývatn.** By all means spend at least one night in ☷ **Mývatn,** and on day seven visit the false craters, the eerie shapes at Dimmuborgir, and the bubbling sulfur muds of **Námaskarð.** Spend the night near the lake in ☷ **Reykjahlíð.** Head three hours east to ☷ **Egilsstaðir** for the eighth night. A nice outing from here is to the large forestry station at Hallormstaðir.

Rest well in Egilsstaðir, because day nine is a long haul around the entire southeast corner of Iceland. You'll see the southeastern fjords, the south end of Europe's largest glacier **Vatnajökull,** the town of **Höfn,** glacier lagoons, and **Skaftafell National Park.** The Ring Road takes you over wide lava flows and broad sandy plains to the town of ☷ **Vík.** The sea arch of **Dyrhólaey,** with its beautiful black beach, is just east of town. Overnight in Vík and depart early the next morning, about 9 AM, for **Reykjavík** ①–㉓. Along the way you'll pass the stunning waterfalls of **Skogarfoss** and **Seljalandsfoss,** beneath the glacier Eyjafjallajökull. If you have an afternoon departure from Keflavík on this same day, you'll have to be satisfied with a Ring Road glimpse of **Mt. Hekla** to the north of **Hella.** If you have time for a quick jaunt, after seeing **Selfoss** you will come to **Hveragerði,** where you can climb up the plateau along the home stretch to the capital area.

When to Tour Iceland

Don't let its name fool you—Iceland is a year-round destination. If you want to go fishing, ride Icelandic horses, or be enchanted by the midnight sun, May through August is the time to visit. Unruly fall is beyond prediction: it can be a crisp time of berry picking and beautiful colors on the heaths, or of challenging gales, when you'll want to join a friend for a cup of coffee in a cozy café. Fall and winter bring a surprising assortment of cultural performances, both modern and classic. Nature provides its share of drama with the spellbinding Northern Lights, seen most often on cold, clear nights. First-time viewers are sure to be mesmerized by the magical iridescence of huge clouds and curtains of yellow-green to magenta, arching as if alive across the evening sky.

REYKJAVÍK

Sprawling Reykjavík, the nation's nerve center and government seat, is home to almost half of the island's population. On a bay overlooked by proud Mt. Esja, with its ever-changing hues, Reykjavík presents a colorful sight, its concrete houses painted in light colors and topped by vibrant red, blue, and green roofs. In contrast to the almost treeless countryside, Reykjavík has many tall, native birches, rowans, and willows, as well as imported pines and spruces.

Reykjavík's name comes from the Icelandic words for smoke, *reykur,* and bay, *vík.* In AD 874, Norseman Ingólfur Arnarson saw Iceland rising out of the misty sea and came ashore at a bay eerily shrouded with plumes of steam from nearby hot springs. Today most of the houses in Reykjavík are heated by near-boiling water from the hot springs. Natural heating avoids air pollution, so that even though Reykjavík's name literally means Smoky Bay, there's no smoke around. You may notice, however, that the hot water brings a slight sulfur smell to the bathroom.

Prices are easily on a par with other major European cities. As of summer 1997, the Þjóðminjasafn (National Museum) established a special IKr300 ticket, good for admission to the National Museum, Sjóminjasafn Íslands in Hafnarfjörður, and the Nesstofusafn in Seltjarnarnes.

Numbers in the text correspond to numbers in the margin and on the Reykjavík map.

Exploring Reykjavík

Any part of town can be reached by city bus, but take a walk around to get an idea of the present and past. In the Old Town, classic wooden buildings rub shoulders with modern timber and concrete structures.

Old Town

A GOOD WALK

What better guiding presence on a tour of historic Reykjavík than the man who started it all, one of the first settlers of Iceland and Reykjavík's founder, Ingólfur Arnarson. Overlooking the old city center and harbor is a grassy knoll known as Arnarhóll, topped by the **Ingólfur Arnarson statue** ①. From here there's a fine panorama of Reykjavík.

212

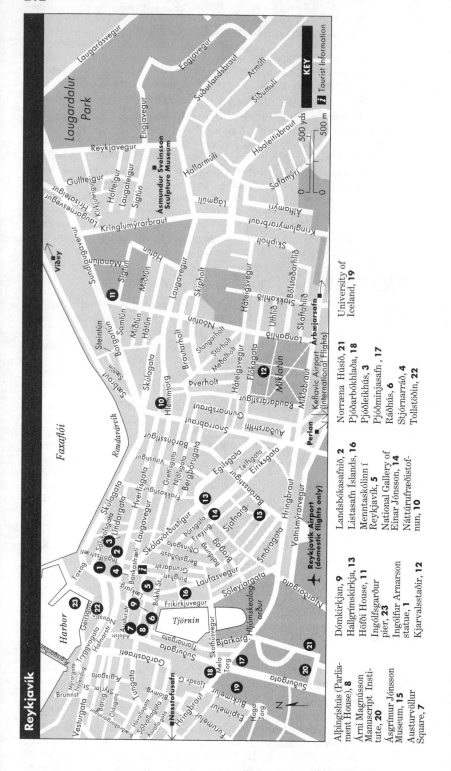

Reykjavík

KEY

i Tourist Information

500 yds
500 m

Laugardalur Park

Ásmundur Sveinsson Sculpture Museum

Faxaflói

Harbor

Tjörnin

Reykjavík Airport (domestic flights only)

Keflavic Airport (International Flights)

Perlan

Árbæjarsafn

Nesstofusafn

N

Alþingishús (Parliament House), **8**
Árni Magnússon Institute, **20**
Ásgrímur Jónsson Museum, **15**
Austurvöllur Square, **7**

Dómkirkjan, **9**
Hallgrímskirkja, **13**
Höfði House, **11**
Ingólfsgarður pier, **23**
Ingólfur Arnarson statue, **1**
Kjarvalsstaðir, **12**

Landsbókasafnið, **2**
Listasafn Íslands, **16**
Menntaskólinn í Reykjavík, **5**
National Gallery of Einar Jónsson, **14**
Náttúrufræðistofnun, **10**

Norræna Húsið, **21**
Þjóðarbókhlaða, **18**
Þjóðleikhús, **3**
Þjóðminjasafn, **17**
Ráðhús, **6**
Stjórnarráð, **4**
Tollstöðin, **22**

University of Iceland, **19**

Behind him on his left, on Hverfisgata, is the classic white, now defunct **Landsbókasafnið** ②, its crests paying tribute to giants of Icelandic literature. Next to it is the black basalt **Þjóðleikhús** ③, its interior also reflecting the natural influence of polygonal lava columns. Walk back down from these buildings to Lækjargata, just left of Hverfisgata, to the **Stjórnarráð** ④, which contains the offices of the prime minister. Across Bankastræti, continuing along the hill above Lækjargata and the oversize pavement chessboard on the same side, stands the historic mid-19th-century Bernhöftstorfa—a row of distinct two-story wooden houses, two of which are now restaurants. The building across Amtmannsstígur and closer to the lake is **Menntaskólinn í Reykjavík** ⑤.

Go south on Lækjargata to the corner of the Tjörnin Lake. Lækjargata, as the name "Brook Street" suggests, once connected the lake and the shore. Today it is the busy main artery linking city center with main roads out to residential parts of town. Overlooking Tjörnin Lake from its northwest corner is the modern **Ráðhús** ⑥, on the corner of Vonarstræti and Tjarnargata.

Sometimes referred to as the heart of the city, Austurvöllur, the area between Tjörnin Lake and the harbor, was the first area developed in Reykjavík. From the lake, follow Templarasund a little more than a block north to **Austurvöllur Square** ⑦, dominated by a statue of Jón Sigurðsson (1811–79), who led Iceland's fight for independence from Denmark. Sigurðsson looks approvingly at the 19th-century **Alþingishús** ⑧, on Kirkjustræti. Next to the Parliament is the **Dómkirkjan** ⑨, on the corner of Templarasund and Kirkjustræti. From the square toward the harbor runs Pósthússtræti, taking its name from the main post office, the large red building on the corner of **Austurstræti**. Lækjartorg plaza is less than a minute away, and here you can end your tour at a nearby café. If you still have some time left, the bus terminus at Lækjargata a couple of blocks east is a good place to depart for the Perlan or the Árbæjarsafn, a re-created Icelandic village. Or, you can take a bus ride to Nesstofusafn, a museum chronicling medical history in Iceland in Seltjarnarnes, on the city's outskirts. However, if you don't want to leave the city proper, you can take a detour to the **Náttúrufræðistofnun** ⑩ and the **Höfði House** ⑪. The museum is near the bus station at Hlemmur, and the Höfði House is just a little farther on, about a 15-minute walk northeast from the museum. Farther east is the Laugardalur Park and the Ásmundur Sveinsson Sculpture Museum.

SIGHTS TO SEE

★ ⑧ **Alþingishús** (Parliament House). Built in 1880–81, this structure is one of Iceland's oldest stone buildings. Iceland's Alþing Parliament held its first session in AD 930 and therefore is the oldest continually functional representative parliament in the world. From October through May you can view the parliament proceedings from the visitors' gallery here. Depending on the urgency of the agenda, any number of Iceland's 63 parliament members, representing a spectrum of five political parties, may be present. Rarely are the current 11 ministers, who oversee 15 ministries, all gathered together. ⊠ *Austurvöllur Sq.,* ☎ *563–0631.*

Austurstræti. Sometimes closed to cars, this street starts at the junction of Lækjargata and Bankastræti (Bankastræti actually becomes Austurstræti). On those select weekends when the street is closed, an impromptu market with vendors selling anything from sweaters to foods and souvenirs gets underway.

OFF THE
BEATEN PATH

PERLAN – On the top of Öskjuhlíð, the hill overlooking Reykjavík Airport, Perlan, or the Pearl, was built in 1991 as a monument to Iceland's invaluable geothermal water supplies. Art exhibits, musical performances, and a fountain spurting water like a geyser are among the spectacles. Above the six vast tanks holding up to 800,000 cubic ft of hot water, the panoramic viewing platform offers telescopes and multilingual recorded commentaries, plus a coffee bar and an ice-cream parlor. The crowning glory is a revolving restaurant (☞ Dining, *below*) under the glass dome; it's pricey, but the view is second to none. ⊠ *Öskjuhlíð Hill,* ☎ *562–0200.* ⊙ *Daily 11:30–10.*

ÁRBÆJARSAFN – At the Open-Air Municipal Museum, 18th- and 19th-century houses furnished in old-fashioned style display authentic household utensils and tools for cottage industries. On summer weekends the museum hums with a variety of educational events. You'll see demonstrations of old-fashioned farm activities and taste piping-hot *lummur* (chewy pancakes) baked in a peat-fired farmhouse stove. Take Bus 10 from Hlemmur station (or Bus 100 from Austurstræti) 20 minutes to the museum. ⊠ *Ártúnsblettur,* ☎ *577–1111.* ▦ *IKr300.* ⊙ *June–Aug., Tues.–Sun. 10–6.*

❼ Austurvöllur Square. East Field is a peculiar name for a west central square. The reason: it's just east of the presumed spot where first settler Ingólfur Arnarson built his farm, today near the corner of Aðalstræti.

OFF THE   **NESSTOFUSAFN –** What was originally the home of the nation's first chief
BEATEN PATH doctor, Bjarni Pálsson, houses the Nesstofa Medical History Museum. A fine collection of instruments and exhibits explains the tough battle for public health services during the last two centuries. When the house was built back in 1763, it was one of the few stone structures in Iceland. Bus 3 takes you to Seltjarnarnes, a community on Reykjavík's west boundary, within a couple of short blocks from the museum. ⊠ *IS-170 Seltjarnarnes,* ☎ *561–1016,* ℻ *561–1095.* ▦ *IKr300.* ⊙ *May 15–Sept. 14, Tues., Thurs., and weekends 12–4; also open for groups by appointment.*

★ ❾ Dómkirkjan (Lutheran Cathedral). A place of worship has existed on this site since AD 1200. The small, charming church, built 1788–96, represents the state religion, Lutheranism. It was here that sovereignty and independence were first blessed and endorsed by the church. It's also where Iceland's national anthem, actually a hymn, was first sung in 1874. Since 1845, members and cabinet ministers of every Alþing parliament session have gathered here for a service. Among the treasured items displayed is a baptismal font carved and given by the famous 19th-century master sculptor Bertel Thorvaldsen, who was half Icelandic. ⊠ *Austurvöllur Sq.,* ☎ *551–2113.* ⊙ *Mon., Tues., Thurs., Fri. 9–5; Wed. 10–5, unless in use for services.*

⓫ Höfði House. Standing solitary, unadorned, and defiantly open to the sea on Borgartún is this historic building. Some say this is where the Cold War began to thaw when Mikhail Gorbachev and Ronald Reagan met at the Reykjavík Summit of 1986. The massive, impressive Höfði was built in 1909 as a residence for the French consul. Subsequent owners included the eccentric writer Einar Benediktsson and the British consul during the early part of World War II. Winston Churchill once stayed here in wartime. Apparently, he wasn't bothered at the time, but the British consuls were repeatedly haunted by a ghostly presence, which was consistent with legend, and moved out. Eventually, the British sold the house and it became city property. It now serves as a venue for special city business and is decorated with some of the city's art holdings. ⊠ *Near junction of Borgartún and Nótún.*

❶ Ingólfur Arnarson statue. If you look beyond Ingólfur, who faces you from his knoll, you'll see the city's architectural mélange: 18th-century stone houses, 19th-century small wooden houses, office blocks from the '30s and '40s, and to the north, the black, futuristic Seðlabanki (Central Bank). Take any of the crosstown buses that stop at Lækjartorg plaza. ✉ *Arnarhóll Hill.*

OFF THE
BEATEN PATH

LAUGARDALUR PARK – Besides a large swimming pool, this recreational area, has picnic and barbecuing facilities, as well as the Húsdýraga-rðurinn (Farm Animal Park), home to goats, cows, horses, seals, and fish. The Fjölskyldugarðurinn (Family Park) has a variety of rides and games, such as "crazy bikes"—a driving school complete with miniature traffic lights—and a scale model of a Viking ship. The Grassagarður (Botanical Garden) has an extensive outdoor collection of native and exotic plants. Coffee and baked items are sold in summer at the cozy conservatory. Take Bus 2 or 5 east; in summer a Museum Bus runs hourly from Lækjatorg Plaza to numerous cultural sites, including the park ✉ *East of city center, bounded by Sundlaugarvegur to the north and Keykjavegur to the west.* 🕿 *Free. Farmyard Animal Zoo:* ☎ *553–7700.* 🕿 *IKr300.* ☉ *June–Aug., daily 10–7; Sept.–May, Mon.–Tues. and Thurs.–Fri. 1–5, weekends 10–6. Botanical Garden:* ☎ *553–8870,* FAX *568–1278.* 🕿 *Free.*

ÁSMUNDUR SVEINSSON SCULPTURE MUSEUM – Some originals by this sculptor, depicting ordinary working people, myths, and folktale episodes, are exhibited in the museum's gallery and studio and in the surrounding garden. It's on the southwest edge of Laugardalur Park, opposite the traffic circle at its entrance. ✉ *v/Sigtún (5-min ride from Hlemmur station on Bus 5),* ☎ *553–2155.* ☉ *June–Sept., daily 10–4; Oct.–May, daily 1–4.*

Lækjartorg (Brook Square). Now a focal point in Reykjavík's otherwise rambling city center, this square opens onto **Austurstræti,** a semipedestrian shopping street. A brook used to drain Tjörnin Lake into the sea (hence the street's name). ✉ *At junction of Bankastræti and Lækjargata.*

❷ Landsbókasafnið (Old National Library). Crests on the facade of this impressive building name significant Icelandic literary figures. Erected between 1906 and 1908, the building is now closed and the book collection has been moved to the new **Þjóðarbókhlaðan,** at the University of Iceland. ✉ *The first building on Hverfisgata at old midtown.*

Laugavegur. This has traditionally been the city's main shopping street, although it now meets stiff competition from the Kringlan Mall (☞ Shopping, *below*) uptown.

❺ Menntaskólinn í Reykjavík (Reykjavík Grammar School). Many graduates from the country's oldest educational institution, established in 1846, have gone on to dominate political and social life in Iceland. Former president Vigdís Finnbogadóttir and numerous cabinet ministers, including Iceland's current prime minister, Davíð Oddsson, are graduates, as were classmates film producer Hrafn Gunnlaugson and well-known author Þórarinn Eldjarn. ✉ *Corner of Amtmannsstígur and Lækjargata.*

❿ Náttúrufræðistofnun (Museum of Natural History). One of the last great auks on display and several exhibits that focus on Icelandic natural history share space in the main terminus of the city's bus system. It's small as museums go. ✉ *Hverfisgata 116,* ☎ *562–9822.* 🕿 *Free.* ☉ *Tues., Thurs., and weekends 1:30–4.*

★ ❸ **Þjóðleikhús** (National Theater). Construction on this black basalt edifice designed by architect Guðjón Samúelsson was started in 1928, but interrupted during the Depression for lack of funds. British troops occupied it during World War II, before it opened in 1950. The concrete interior ceiling—an amazing architectural accomplishment in its day—mimics polygonal basalt columns occuring in Icelandic nature. From fall to spring diverse cultural events are given here; the biennial Reykjavík Arts Festival is the solo act every other summer. Theatrical works are usually performed in Icelandic, but musicals and operettas are sometimes given in original languages. ⊠ *Hverfisgata 19,* ☎ *551–1200.*

❻ **Ráðhús** (City Hall). Modern architecture and nature converge at this building overlooking **Tjörnin Lake.** The architects deliberately planted moss on the northwest and east stone walls to further emphasize the scheme. Inside is a tourist information desk and a coffee bar. A three-dimensional model of Iceland is usually on display in the gallery, which often hosts various temporary exhibitions. The natural pond attracts birds—and bird-lovers—year-round and is also popular among ice-skaters in winter. ⊠ *Bounded by Fríkirkjuvegi, Vonarstræti, and Tjarnargata,* ☎ *563–2000.* ◷ *Weekdays 8:20–4:15; coffee shop, weekdays 11–6, weekends 12–6.*

❹ **Stjórnarráð** (Government House). This low white building, constructed in the 18th century as a prison, today houses the office of the prime minister. ⊠ *At Lækjatorg Plaza.*

Museums and the University

Art lovers will be busy in what is still called Reykjavík's "eastern" quarter (even though it is now geographically in the west and center, as the city expands to the east). This tour will give you a good look at some of Iceland's finest paintings and sculpture collections.

A GOOD WALK

Start at **Kjarvalsstaðir** ⑫, reached by Buses 1, 111, and 114 from downtown. From here, set your sights on the 210-ft, stair-stepped gray-stone tower of **Hallgrímskirkja** ⑬, about a 10-minute walk from the art museum. From Flókagata, take a left at Snorrabraut and then a right onto Egilsgata. The church tower offers the city's highest vantage point, with a fantastic panoramic view of the city. Exit the church and spend some time at the **National Gallery of Einar Jónsson** ⑭, which faces the church across Eiríksgata at the corner with Njarðargata. The monumental works here explore a wide range of religious and mythical subjects. Walk four short blocks down Njarðargata and take a left on Bergsstaðstræti to the **Ásgrímur Jónsson Museum** ⑮ to see how a well-loved neo-Impressionist painter responded to national inspiration.

Back on Njarðargata go downhill toward the park to Sóleyjargata, where you will turn right and walk along Tjörnin Lake. As you pass the music tower and a bridge dividing the lake, Sóleyjargata becomes Fríkirkjuvegur. At this intersection you'll see Bertel Thorvaldsen's rendering of *Adonis,* guarding the corner of the grounds of the ornate Reykjavík Youth and Recreational Council, across Njarðargata from the new president's offices.

Next to the Youth and Recreational Council are the **Listasafn Íslands** ⑯. Exit past the pleasant, corrugated-iron-covered Fríkirkja; follow Fríkirkjuvegur over the bridge on Skothúvegur, which divides the lake. At the end of Skothúvegur, you will pass the old Reykjavík cemetery on your right and a traffic circle on your left.

On the south side is the gray concrete **Þjóðminjasafn** ⑰, the National Library, where you'll see Viking artifacts, national costumes, weaving, and more. Just north is the red **Þjóðarbókhlaða** ⑱, new in 1994. You're now on the campus of the **University of Iceland** ⑲, founded in 1911. Walking out of the National Library's main entrance side you'll see the Félagsstofnun Stúdenta, the Student Union, with an excellent international bookshop. Continue south along a tree-lined walk to the main university building.

Head south, directly in front of the main building, above the crescent, and along the tree-lined walk. Once past the Lögberg Law Building you will see Oddi, the Social Sciences Building, on your left; some of the University Art Collection is displayed on Oddi's second and third floors.

The Árnargarður Humanities Building is to your right; on its ground floor is the **Árni Magnússon Manuscript Institute** ⑳, a must-see for all visitors interested in the sagas or ancient literature. End your tour with a snack at the **Norræna Húsið** ㉑ cultural center on the east edge of campus.

SIGHTS TO SEE

⑳ **Árni Magnússon Manuscript Institute.** Here you'll see priceless original vellum manuscripts of many of the sagas. These are kept under carefully controlled conditions on the ground floor of the Árnagarður Humanities Building. ⊠ *Suðurgata.* ☎ *552–5540.* ☜ *Free.* ☼ *Mid-June–Aug., Mon.–Sat. 2–4; other times by appointment.*

⑮ **Ásgrímur Jónsson Museum.** Except for rotating exhibits of the artist's extraordinary works in oils and watercolors, Ásgrímur Jónsson's house is left as it was when he died at the age of 82 in 1958. ⊠ *Bergstaðastræti 74,* ☎ *551–3644.* ☜ *Free.* ☼ *June–Aug., Tues.–Sun. 1:30–4; Sept.–Nov. and Feb.–May, weekends 1:30–4.*

⑬ **Hallgrímskirkja** (Hallgrimur's Church). Completed in 1986 after more than 40 years of construction, the church is named for the 17th-century hymn writer Hallgrímur Pétursson, and has a stylized concrete facade recalling both organ pipes and the distinctive columnar basalt formations you can see around Iceland. Depending on timing, you may luck into hearing a performance or practice on the church's huge pipe organ. In front of Hallgrímskirkja is a **statue of Leifur Eiríksson,** the Icelander who discovered America 500 years before Columbus did. (Leif's father was Eric the Red, who discovered Greenland.) The statue, by American sculptor Alexander Stirling Calder, was presented to Iceland by the United States in 1930 to mark the millennium of the Alþing parliament. ⊠ *At the top of Skólavörðurstígur,* ☎ *551–0745.* ☜ *Tower IKr200.* ☼ *May–Sept., daily 9–6; Oct.–Apr., daily 10–6.*

⑫ **Kjarvalsstaðir** (Reykjavík Municipal Art Museum). This municipal art museum is named for Jóhannes Kjarval, the nation's best-known painter, and displays the artist's lava landscapes, portraits, and images of mystical beings. It also shows works by Icelandic contemporary artists and great masters, as well as visiting art collections. ⊠ *Flókagata,* ☎ *552–6131.* ☜ *IKr300.* ☼ *Daily 10–6.*

⑯ **Listasafn Íslands** (National Gallery). Originally built as an icehouse, this was Reykjavík's hottest nightspot in the '60s. So hot, in fact, that it was gutted by fire in 1971. Now it has been adapted and extended as a temple to art. You'll find an impressive 20th-century Icelandic art collection, including old masters Kjarval and Gunnlaugur Scheving, as well as examples of 19th-century Danish art. In addition, the gallery stages international exhibitions, often from Nordic or Baltic countries, or from international collections of Icelandic paintings. The coffee shop with a view of the lake makes for a pleasant stop. ⊠ *Fríkirkjuvegur 7,* ☎ *562–1000.* ☜ *IKr200.* ☼ *Jan.–late Dec., Tues.–Sun. noon–6.*

⑭ National Gallery of Einar Jónsson. Cubic and fortresslike, this building was once the home and studio of Iceland's leading early 20th-century sculptor. His monumental works found inside and in the sculpture garden explore profound symbolic and mystical subjects. The figure of Christ in Hallgrímskirkja is by Jónsson, and several of his unmistakable statues can be found around Reykjavík. ⊠ *Njarðargata,* ☎ *551–3797.* 🎫 *IKr200.* ۞ *June–Sept. 15, Tues.–Sun. 1:30–4; mid-Sept.–Nov. and Feb.–May; 1:30–4 weekends only; closed Dec.–Jan.*

㉑ Norræna Húsið (Nordic House). Designed by Finnish architect Alvar Aalto, this blue-and-white Scandinavian cultural center hosts exhibitions, lectures, and concerts, and has a coffee shop. A university noontime chamber concert series and other recitals are often held upstairs. On Sunday afternoon free children's film matinees are screened. Much of the nearby terrain is being returned to its former marshy condition to entice wetland birds that used to nest here. ⊠ *At the corner of Sturlugata and Sæmundurgata,* ☎ *551–7030.* ۞ *Daily 2–7.*

NEED A
BREAK?   Looking for more than food for thought? The **Nordic House** (☞ *above*) cafeteria offers a tempting selection of sandwiches and cakes. Its bright atmosphere is a favorite haunt of the university intelligentsia.

⑲ University of Iceland. On the large crescent-shape lawn in front of the main university building is a **statue of Sæmundur Fróði,** a symbol of the value of book learning. Legend has it that after studying abroad, Sæmundur made a pact with the devil to get himself home, promising his soul if he arrived without getting wet. The devil changed into a seal to carry him home. Just as they arrived, Sæmundur hit the seal on the head with his Psalter, got his coattails wet, and escaped with his soul. ⊠ *Across from Hringbraut Street and diagonally southwest from the park lake.*

⑱ Þjóðarbókhlaða (National and University Library). Clad in red aluminum, this structure is hard to miss. It houses the tome collection from the now-closed Landsbókasafnið (Old National Library). ⊠ *Arngrímsgata, on the corner of Suðurgata and Hringbrautand,* ☎ *563–5600.* ۞ *Weekdays 9–7, Sat. 10–5.*

⑰ Þjóðminjasafn (National Museum). Viking treasures and artifacts, silver work, wood carvings, and some unusual whalebone carvings are on display here, as well as maritime objects, historical textiles, jewelry, and crafts. The coffee shop offers refreshment. ⊠ *Suðurgata 41,* ☎ *552–8888.* 🎫 *IKr200.* ۞ *Mid-May–mid-Sept., Tues.–Sun. 11–5; mid-Sept.–mid-May, Tues., Thurs., and weekends noon–5.*

Harborfront

A GOOD WALK

Reykjavík's harborfront is an easy three-block stroll north from Lækjargata Plaza to the harbor. Amble along the pier at Ægisgarður, which branches north off Geirsgata, to see the freighters and colorful fishing and pleasure boats of all sizes as they come and go.

Walking a quick two blocks inland as you return toward Lækjargata Plaza brings you to the **Tollstöðin** ㉒. A walk around to the inland side on Tryggvagata reveals Iceland's largest mosaic mural, a harbor scene by Gerður Helgadóttir.

Looping back to the waterfront and curving southwest brings you to **Ingólfsgarður pier** ㉓, closest to Lækjatorg Plaza. Here you may spot Iceland's Coast Guard vessels docked for service. If you continue walking east along the shoreline, you'll pass the green, dual-pointed *Partnership* sculpture, a gift to Iceland from a former U.S. ambassador and his wife. Even more dramatic, a few hundred yards farther along the shore, is *Sólfar,* a stunning modern tribute to Viking seafarers who first sailed into this harbor 1,100 years ago. It points proudly offshore toward Mt. Esja. The design for this brilliant stainless-steel sculpture won first prize in an art competition in conjunction with Reykjavík's bicentennial.

In good weather take a boat from the Klettahöfn/Maríhöfn section of the Sundahöfn Pier east of town to the verdant nearby island of Viðey: don't miss *Áfangar,* Richard Serra's landscape art arrangement of basalt pillars on the island's northern side.

SIGHTS TO SEE

㉓ **Ingólfsgarður pier.** A berth for Coast Guard vessels, this pier has a distinctive yellow beacon pylon at its end. A handful of ships, which tenaciously stood up to the British Navy during the cod wars, still vigorously enforce offshore fishing limits. The Coast Guard is the closest thing Iceland has to a national military. In 1996 a full-size replica of a Viking ship (the Gokstad ship) was christened the *Íslendingur (Icelander).* The port authorities set up an exhibition marquee in summer and arrange cruises (☎ 551–5800 information) on Wednesday. ⊠ *Just off Faxagata.*

㉒ **Tollstöðin** (Customs House). A bureaucratic necessity, especially for an island nation, the Customs House is decorated with an impressive mural. ⊠ *Tryggvagata 19.*

OFF THE
BEATEN PATH

VIÐEY – This unspoiled island in Kollafjörður is great for a walk and a picnic. If you're a bird-watcher, definitely make the trip—it's a paradise for nesting birds. Here you can also see a little church and the 18th-century governor's residence, Viðey House, which once hosted aviator Charles Lindbergh during a stopover flight in his heyday; now it's an upscale restaurant. The island is accessible only by ferry from its own pier. *Take Buses 4, 8, and 9 to the nearby Sundahöfn freight harbor. Ferries:* ☎ *568–1085 or 562–1632.*

Dining

The dining scene in Reykjavík is diversifying of late: traditional Icelandic restaurants now face competition from Asian, Italian, Mexican, Indian, Lebanese, and vegetarian restaurants.

Old Town

$$$ ✕ **Astro.** By day, Astro is a café. Weeknights you'll find a restaurant that serves up savory Mediterranean- and Asian-influenced dishes. Come weekend nights, the story is altogether different—the place pulses with life as a dance spot, attracting some of Reykjavík's glitterati in an atmosphere described more as a "party house" than a nightclub. ⊠ *Austurstræti 22,* ☎ *552–9222. MC, V.*

$$$ ✕ **Pasta Basta.** This small restaurant has four seating options: an area with intimate booths on the lower level; a small, bright conservatory at ground level; an open-air, canvas-covered patio; and in good weather, under the large silver rowan tree, which they managed to spare when the place was converted. Crayons are provided for creative and otherwise fidgety kids. The fare is mostly Italian with a Mediterranean flair. You may also want to visit the **La Dolce Vita** bar upstairs. ⊠ *Klapparstíg 38,* ☎ *561–3131. MC, V. No lunch on winter weekends.*

$$$ ✕ **Við Tjörnina.** Enter through a classic wooden doorway and go up a
★ flight of stairs and back in time in this early-20th-century house with a hand-carved bar and chairs, embroidered tablecloths, and crocheted drapes. This is one of the best places in Iceland for delicious, innova-

tive seafood. The owner, epicure Rúnar Marvinsson, runs the kitchen himself, turning out imaginative dishes like tindabikkja with grapes, capers, and Pernod. The lunchtime dish of the day can be a bargain. ⊠ *Templarasund 3,* ☎ *551–8666. AE, MC, V.*

$$ ✕ **Hornið.** This welcoming bistro is light and airy, with lots of natural wood, potted plants, and cast-iron bistro tables. The emphasis is on pizzas and pasta, but there's also a selection of meat and fish dishes. Try the lamb pepper steak with garlicky mushrooms or the seafood soup, a favorite for lunch. A variety of delicious cakes can be enjoyed with the obligatory espresso at any time of day. ⊠ *Hafnarstræti 15,* ☎ *551–3340. AE, DC, MC, V.*

$$ ✕ **Humarhúsið.** This is another good restaurant in Bernhöftstorfa district. The house specialty is lobster, as the name in Icelandic implies. Try it in salad, soup, or as one of the many main courses. ⊠ *Amtmannsstíg 1,* ☎ *561–3303. AE, MC, V.*

$$ ✕ **Lækjabrekka.** Locals and visitors alike frequent this established eatery for its excellent food at reasonable prices. On weekends, live background music escapes from a tight corner of this charming, classic restaurant convenient to midtown. ⊠ *Bankastræti 2,* ☎ *551–4430. AE, MC, V.*

$ ✕ **Bæjarins beztu.** The most famous fast-food eatery in Iceland may easily escape you. Facing the harbor, set in a parking lot at the corner of Tryggvagata and Pósthússtræti, this tiny hut is home of the original Icelandic hot dog; one person serves about a thousand hot dogs a day from the window. Ask for *ayn-ah-mud-lou* (pronounced quickly in monotone with stress on "mud"), which will get you "one with everything": mustard, tomato sauce, *rémoulade* (mayonnaise with finely chopped pickles), and chopped raw and fried onions. ⊠ *Tryggvagata and Pósthússtræti, no phone. No credit cards.*

Museums and the University and Beyond

$$$$ ✕ **Gallery Restaurant.** Icelandic art covers the walls of this restaurant in the Hótel Holt (☞ Lodging, *below*); the cocktail lounge and bar feature drawings by Jóhannes Kjarval. Within walking distance of downtown, it has long been in the forefront of Icelandic restaurants, with impeccable service and mouthwatering wild game and seafood dishes. Favorites include gravlax and reindeer. The wine list and whiskey selection are famed for their breadth—and price. ⊠ *Hótel Holt, Bergstaðastræti 37,* ☎ *552–5700. AE, DC, MC, V.*

$$$$ ✕ **Grillið.** Near the university campus atop the Saga Hotel, this quiet, cozy restaurant has a spectacular view of the capital and the surrounding hinterlands. Specialties include glazed scallops in blue-cheese sauce and crisp-broiled duck Bigarade. ⊠ *Hagatorg Circle,* ☎ *552–5033. AE, DC, MC, V. No lunch.*

$$$$ ✕ **Perlan.** This rotating restaurant, atop Reykjavík's hot-water distribution tanks on Öskjuhlíð Hill, is the city's trendiest, with the most spectacular views in town (one revolution takes about two hours). The international menu emphasizes fresh, quality Icelandic ingredients, such as succulent lamb and seafood. Seafood dishes, prepared with the freshest fish available, change daily. ⊠ *Öskjuhlíð Hill,* ☎ *562–0203. AE, DC, MC, V. No lunch.*

$$$ ✕ **Óðinsvé.** Just east of downtown, this cozy restaurant is on the first floor of the Óðinsvé Hotel. Decorated in pastel colors, half the dining area is under a glassed-in porch. The chefs prepare Scandinavian-French dishes that focus on seafood. The fish chowder is a favorite. Try the grilled lamb or butter-fried trout with almonds and shrimp for the main course; the best dessert is hot apple strudel. ⊠ *Óðinstorg,* ☎ *552–5090. AE, DC, MC, V.*

$$ ✕ **Carpe Diem.** Attached to Hotel Lind, this restaurant is sparsely decorated with mechanical paraphernalia in a pleasantly peculiar way. Lunch

dishes include huge sandwiches or pasta with soup. Dinner entrées are equally hearty. ⊠ *Rauðarárstíg 18,* ☎ *552–4555. AE, MC, V.*

$$ ✕ **Potturinn og pannan.** Here you'll get bang for your buck with meal prices that include soup, bread, and coffee. Tiled floors, copper light fixtures, and tables with benches create a simple yet pleasant setting. Of the excellent meat and fish dishes served here, try the marinated lamb with green-pepper sauce. A play corner and kid's menu appease young diners. It's only a 10- to 15-minute walk from the uptown hotels. You may have to wait at lunch and dinner. ⊠ *Brautarholt 22 (entered from Nóatún),* ☎ *551–1690. Reservations not accepted. AE, DC, MC, V.*

$$ ✕ **Þrir Frakkar Hjá Úlfari.** At this restaurant in an unassuming white building you'll enjoy meals in cozy booths and tables or in a small, bright annex. Tasty seafood dishes include succulent whale, butter-fried trout, and ever-evolving chef's specials. ⊠ *Baldursgata 14, on the corner of Baldursgata and Nönnugata,* ☎ *552–3939. AE, DC, MC, V.*

Harborfront

$$$$ ✕ **Jónatan Livingston Mávur.** In fine gourmet tradition, everything
★ here is lovingly prepared by the chef, so don't be in any hurry. Start with one of the sublime appetizers, such as three kinds of caviar. The lamb entrée nearly melts in your mouth. Inventive sorbet desserts— rhubarb, mango, and sorrel, to name a few—are just part of this restaurant's magic. ⊠ *Tryggvagata 4–6,* ☎ *551–5520. MC, V.*

Cafés

Icelanders challenge the Finns for the record for per capita caffeine consumption. So it should come as no surprise that coffee bars have now replaced clothing boutiques as the most common enterprise in town. All cafés listed are in the Old Town or on Laugavegur.

Kaffi Reykjavík (⊠ Vesturgata 2, ☎ 562–5530) is in a picturesque 19th-century wooden building, with a veranda where you can sit outside if it's sunny. **Fógetinn** (⊠ Aðalstræti 10, ☎ 551–6323) is intimate, with low ceilings. At artsy **Cafe Solon Islandus** (⊠ Bankastræti 7a, ☎ 551–2666) you can see some modern art, eat a snack, and people-watch. **Kaffi List** (⊠ Klappastíg 26, ☎ 562–5059) is another trendy hangout, serving tapas. The new **Kaffi Pucini** (⊠ Vítastíg 10A, ☎ 552–3388) is a tiny two-level retreat off Laugavegur, with freshly ground flavored coffees. The man who started the Icelandic coffee revolution runs **Te og Kaffibúðin** (⊠ Laugavegi 27, ☎ 552–6260). **Tíu Dropar** (⊠ Laugavegur 27, ☎ 551–9380) coffeehouse serves a tantalizing selection of homemade goodies.

Lodging

Lodgings range from modern, first-class Scandinavian-style hotels to inexpensive guest houses and bed-and-breakfasts offering basic amenities at relatively low prices (contact the Tourist Information Center for a register). Ask if your hotel offers complimentary admission tickets to the closest swimming pool. The **Reykjavík Youth Hostel** (⊠ Sundlaugavegur 34, ☎ 553–8110, ℻ 588–9201) has 108 beds for around IKr1,250 (not including breakfast) per night.

Old Town and East

$$$$ ⌷ **Grand Hotel Reykjavík.** This hotel—a renovated Holiday Inn—has good-size rooms by European standards. Perks include free entry to Laugardalur Park and its pool, plus a morning shuttle bus to town. ⊠ *Sigtún 38, IS-101,* ☎ *568–9000,* ℻ *568–0675. 100 rooms, 3 suites. Restaurant, bar, lobby lounge, convention center. AE, DC, MC, V.*

$$$$ **⌨ Hótel Borg.** Some rooms in Reykjavík's oldest hotel, built in the Art
★ Deco era of 1930, may not seem too spacious, but they are otherwise
elegant. You can expect good old-fashioned quality combined with modern comforts. All rooms have fluffy down comforters, tasteful prints
(some antique), satellite TVs, VCRs, and CD players, plus fax service
on request. The hotel is in the heart of the city, overlooking Austurvöllur and close to Parliament House. Breakfast is great, with homebaked breads, cheeses, cold cuts, fruit, and more. ⌧ *Pósthússtræti 11,
IS-101,* ☎ *551–1440,* ⅏X *551–1420. 32 rooms, 5 suites. Restaurant,
bar. AE, DC, MC, V.*

$$$$ **⌨ Hótel Esja.** Renovated in 1997, this hotel puts a strong emphasis on
health facilities and pampering its guests. The new Planet Pulse on the
second floor features a wide variety of exercise facilities—spinning bikes
and treadmills—and spa-like therapies. ⌧ *Suðurlandsbruat 2, IS-101,*
☎ *505–0950,* ⅏X *505–0955. 160 rooms, 12 suites. Restaurant, bar,
massage, sauna, spa, steam room, health club. AE, DC, MC, V.*

$$$$ **⌨ Hotel Reykjavík.** Built in 1993, this hotel within a few blocks of Reykjavík's Kjarvalsstaðir Municipal Art Museum and the Hlemmur bus
station is operated by the same management as the Grand Hotel (☞
above). The hotel has two good restaurants, the Korean Café Kim and
a steak house. ⌧ *Rauðarárstígur 39, IS-101,* ☎ *562–6250,* ⅏X *562–
6350. 53 rooms, 7 suites. 2 restaurants. AE, DC, MC, V.*

Museums and the University and Beyond

$$$$ **⌨ Hótel Holt.** Excellent service and a gourmet restaurant make this qui-
★ etly elegant hotel a favorite among business travelers. Though the
rooms are small by modern standards, many are decorated with works
by leading Icelandic artists. It's in a pleasant neighborhood close to town
center. ⌧ *Bergstaðastræti 37, IS-101,* ☎ *552–5700,* ⅏X *562–3025. 42
rooms, 12 suites. Restaurant, bar, lobby lounge, meeting room. AE,
DC, MC, V.*

$$$$ **⌨ Hótel Loftleiðir.** The advantage of this rather remote hotel is nearby
Öskjuhlíð Hill, where you can take pleasant walks and stroll up to Perlan for ice cream. Rooms are decorated in modern Scandinavian style,
with pine furniture and pastel fabrics. Take bus route 1. ⌧ *Reykjavík
Airport, IS-101,* ☎ *505–0900,* ⅏X *505–0905. 220 rooms, 1 apartment
suite. Restaurant, bar, pool, sauna, convention center, travel services.
AE, DC, MC, V.*

$$$$ **⌨ Hótel Saga.** Just off the university campus, this hotel is a 15-minute
walk from most museums, shops, and restaurants. All rooms are above
the fourth floor and have spectacular views. ⌧ *Hagatorg, IS-107,* ☎
552–9900, ⅏X *562–3980. 216 rooms, 8 suites. Restaurant, 6 bars, grill,
no-smoking rooms, sauna, health club, nightclub, meeting rooms,
travel services. AE, DC, MC, V.*

$$$ **⌨ Hótel Ísland.** This chunky postmodern silver-and-blue hotel is close
to the Laugardalur Park and recreation area. The light and airy rooms
are done in floral prints of peach-and-brown pastels, with dark wood
and smooth, curved shapes. ⌧ *Ármúli 9, IS-101,* ☎ *568–8999,* ⅏X *568–
9957. 119 rooms, 3 suites. Restaurant, bar, kitchenettes (5 rooms only),
nightclub. AE, DC, MC, V.*

$$$ **⌨ Hótel Lind.** This quietly unpretentious hotel is uptown, a block
south of the Hlemmur bus station. Rooms in shades of red and blue
have a fresh feel. The clientele is largely Icelanders from the country
attending conferences or cultural events in Reykjavík. ⌧ *Rauðarárstígur
18, IS-105,* ☎ *562–3350,* ⅏X *562–3351. 44 rooms. Restaurant, bar,
meeting rooms. AE, DC, MC, V.*

$$$ **⌨ Hotel Óðinsvé.** This family-run hotel is an interesting combination
of three different buildings sharing a calm corner in an older part of
town. No two rooms are alike, but all are cheery and efficient, some

with nice views over colorful rooftops. Repeat customers prefer its intimacy and convenience to Old Town. ⊠ *Óðinstorg, IS-101,* ☎ *552–5090,* FAX *552–9613. 40 rooms. Restaurant. AE, DC, MC, V.*

$$ 🏨 **City Hotel.** This small hotel, renovated in 1997, stands on a quiet, central residential street. Rooms are done in light colors, with furnishings of pale wood. ⊠ *Ránargata 4a, IS-101,* ☎ *511–1155,* FAX *552–9040. 31 rooms. Restaurant. AE, DC, MC, V.*

$$ 🏨 **Hotel Leifur Eiríksson.** Right across the street from the hilltop church of Hallgrímskirkja, this plain but pleasant hotel is within a short walk of most of Reykjavík's major attractions. Rooms are decorated in floral prints; some have balconies. ⊠ *Skólavörðustígur 45, IS-107,* ☎ *562–0800,* FAX *562–0804. 29 rooms. Restaurant, bar. AE, DC, MC, V.*

$ 🏨 **Garður.** This is a student residence, open as a hotel only in summer when students flee. Basic, modernized rooms are quite adequate and ideal for travelers on a tight budget. Convenient to the National Museum, downtown, and other attractions. Shared bath and shower are on each floor. ⊠ *Hringbraut, IS-107 (bookings through Hótel Örk,* ☎ *483–4700,* FAX *483–4775). 44 rooms without bath. AE, DC, MC, V.*

$ 🏨 **Smárar Guest House.** This guest house near the main bus terminal provides spartan but clean accommodations. Rooms have washbasins and access to a fully equipped kitchen. ⊠ *Snorrabraut 61, IS-105,* ☎ *562–3330,* FAX *551–8945. 15 rooms without bath. AE, DC, MC, V.*

Nightlife and the Arts

You can find a wide variety of cultural goings-on—especially in the visual arts—in Reykjavík for most of the year. The performing arts scene tends to quiet down somewhat in summer, except on even-numbered years when the Reykjavík Arts Festival happens in June. Past events have brought performers ranging from Luciano Pavarotti to David Bowie. Consult the bimonthly *Around Reykjavík* and the biweekly *What's on in Reykjavík,* both at hotels.

Nightlife

Nightlife in Reykjavík essentially means two types of establishments: pubs and nightclubs with dancing with live music. Nightspots usually enforce some basic dress rules, so men should wear a jacket and tie and women should avoid wearing jeans.

The fashionable place to see and be seen is **Café Solon Islandus** (⊠ Bankastræti 7a, ☎ 551–2666), where live music—everything from blues to classical—goes on into the wee hours on weekends. The latest arrival on the Reykjavík social scene is **Kaffi Reykjavik,** a spacious coffee bar-pub-restaurant (☞ *Cafés, above*). **Hótel Ísland** (⊠ Ármúli 9, ☎ 568–7111), the largest restaurant and dance hall in Iceland, swallows more than a thousand guests at a time and offers nightclub shows and reviews.

The Arts

FILM

The eight movie houses around the capital have up to six screens each and usually show recent English-language films with Icelandic subtitles. In summer, recent Icelandic films are screened with English subtitles for tourists. For listings, see the daily newspaper *Morgunblaðið.* The **Háskólabíó** (University Cinema, ☎ 552–2140) is on Hagatorg Circle, near the university.

FOLKLORE

Traditional folklore in English, based on the Icelandic sagas and folktales, is offered in summer by the **Light Nights** (⊠ Tjarnargata 12, opposite City Hall) actors' show and sometimes at other venues. Another group performs in English daily at 4 PM in summer at the **Kaffileikhús** (⊠ Hlaðvarpinn, Vesturgata 3, ☎ 551–9055).

MUSIC

Visiting musicians play everything from classical to jazz, opera to rock. The **Icelandic Opera** (☎ 551–1475), a resident company, performs in winter at its home on Ingólfsstræti. The **Nordic House** (☎ 551–7030), **Sigurjón Ólafsson Sculpture Museum** (☎ 553–2906), **Gerðuberg Cultural Center** (☎ 557–9166), and the churches **Langholtskirkja** (☎ 553–5750) and **Hallgrímskirkja** (☎ 551–0745) are popular venues for classical concerts. The **Iceland Symphony Orchestra** (☎ 562–2255) plays regularly during the winter, usually alternate Thursday and Saturday evenings, at the University Cinemas.

THEATER

In winter, the **National Theater** (⊠ Hverfisgata, ☎ 551–1200) and **City Theater** (⊠ Listabraut, ☎ 568–0680) stage plays by Icelandic writers, such as Nobel Prize winner Halldór Laxness, as well as works by such diverse dramatists as Henrik Ibsen, Tennessee Williams, and Rodgers and Hammerstein.

Outdoor Activities and Sports

Fishing

In Reykjavík, contact the **Angling Club of Reykjavík** (⊠ Háaleitisbraut 68, ☎ 568–6050). Also try the **Federation of Icelandic River Owners** (⊠ Bolholt 6, ☎ 553–1510). For tackle in Reykjavík, head to **Veiðihúsið** (⊠ Nóatún 17, ☎ 561–4085). **Vesturröst** (⊠ Laugavegur 178, ☎ 551–6770) also sells tackle.

Golf

At the southern tip of Seltjarnarnes, the westernmost part of the Reykjavík area, **Golfklúbbur Ness** (⊠ Suðurnes, ☎ 561–1930) has a well-kept nine-hole course with a great view in all directions. **Golfklúbbur Reykjavíkur** (⊠ Grafarholti, ☎ 568–2215) is the granddaddy of them all, a challenging 18-hole course just east of Reykjavík.

Handball

Team handball, a national obsession and a big crowd-puller, is *the* winter sport in Iceland. For fast, furious, and exciting matches between Iceland's leading teams, as well as thrilling confrontations with some of the world's best handball nations, contact the **Handball Federation** (☎ 568–5422).

Horseback Riding

Two stables in the Reykjavík area rent horses by the hour or by the day. **Laxnes Horse Farm** (⊠ Mosfellsdalur, ☎ 566–6179, or 562–1011 at Reykjavík Excursions) offers three-hour riding tours for IKr3,000, including guides and transportation to and from Reykjavík. **Icelandic Riding Tours** (⊠ Bæjarhraun 2, Hafnarfjörður, ☎ 565–3044) offers two- to seven-hour rides for IKr2,000–IKr7,000, which also includes guides and transportation from Reykjavík hotels.

Ice Skating

The artificial skating rink in Laugardalur Park, adjacent to the Botanical Gardens and Farmyard Animal Zoo, rents ice skates and is open October–April. If temperatures have been below freezing long enough, and winds are relatively still, then Tjörnin Lake is often groomed, and sometimes even floodlit at night for skaters of all ages.

Running

In the crisp, clean air of the Reykjavík area, running is a pleasure on the wide sidewalks and in the parks. Favorite routes are around Tjörnin

Lake, in Laugardalur Park, Miklatún Park, and Öskjuhlíð. For distance runners, there is the **Reykjavík Marathon** in August.

Skiing

In wintertime, try the downhill and cross-country skiing at the **Bláfjöll** (☎ 561–8400), outside Reykjavík. You can also ski at **Skálafell** (☎ 566–6095), also outside Reykjavík. Both have ski lifts, are within a 30-minute drive of the capital, and can be reached by Bifreiðastöð Íslands (BSÍ; ☞ Getting Around *in* Iceland A to Z, *below*).

Soccer

In summer catch an Icelandic soccer match, revved up by thousands of fans. A number of Icelandic soccer players are with professional soccer teams in Europe, but most come home to participate in international matches. The most important matches are played at **Laugardalsvöllur Stadium** (☎ 553–3527; take Bus 2 or 5 going east). Buy tickets at the box office just before the game, or inquire at downtown bookstores for advance sales.

Swimming

There are 11 swimming pools in the greater Reykjavík area, some with saunas. Rules of hygiene are strictly enforced—you must shower thoroughly, without a swimsuit, before entering the pool. There is a popular pool in **Vesturbær** at Hofsvallagata (take Bus 4). The pool at **Laugardalur Park** (Bus 2 or 5 going east) is also a favorite summer spot. Both are open weekdays 7 AM–9:30 PM, weekends 8–7:30. A locker and access to the swimming pool cost IKr150; you can rent towels and swimsuits. Use of the sauna is extra. *Note:* Swimming pools are one of the few places in Iceland where you should be on your guard against petty theft. If you are wearing snazzy running shoes, lock them up in a locker.

Shopping

Mall

The **Kringlan Mall** is on the east side of town at the intersection of Miklabraut and Kringlumýrarbraut; take Bus 3 or 6 from Lækjartorg, or Bus 8 or 9 from Hlemmur bus station.

Shopping Streets

The main shopping streets downtown are on and around **Austurstræti, Aðalstræti, Hafnarstræti Bankastræti, Laugavegur,** and **Skólavörðustígur.**

Specialty Stores

ART GALLERIES

You'll find crafts workshops and galleries all around town. **Gallery Borg** (✉ Adalstræti 6, ☎ 552–4215 or 552–4211) displays the latest works by contemporary Icelandic artists. **Gallery Fold** (✉ Laugavegur 118d, entrance from Raudarárstíur, ☎ 551–0400) has a large selection of prints, drawings, paintings, and sculpture by contemporary Icelandic artists, as well as some older Icelandic art. **Listhús** (✉ Engjateigur 17–19), opposite Hotel Esja, is a complex of art stores and ateliers where you will find Icelandic arts and crafts. **Snegla** (✉ Grettisgata 7, ☎ 562–0426) is operated by a group of accomplished women artists who work in many different medias.

COINS AND STAMPS

Hjá Magna (✉ Laugavegur 15, ☎ 552–3011) offers a wide selection. Due to the limited size of the issues involved, a number of Icelandic stamps and coins are considered valuable items. **Postphil** (✉ Ármúli 25, Box 8445, 128 Reykjavík; take Bus 11 from Hlemmur station), Reykjavík's main post office, has a special philatelic service with subscription schemes for new issues.

CRAFTS

Lava ceramics, sheepskin rugs, and Viking-inspired jewelry are also popular souvenirs. An amble along Skólavörðustígur from Laugavegur to Hallgrímskirkja church takes you past many tempting woolen, jewelry, and crafts shops. **Álafoss** (⊠ Posthússtræti 13, ☎ 551–3404) sells primarily woolens but also stocks other souvenirs. **Hornstofan Handverkshús Arts and Crafts** (⊠ Laufásvegi 2, IS-101 Reykjavík, ☎ 551–7800), closed Thursday, is a summer showroom, working studio, and store run cooperatively by the Icelandic Handicrafts Association. **Handprjónasambandið** (⊠ Skólavörð 19, ☎ 552–1890), the Handknitting Association, has its own outlet, selling, of course, only hand-knit items. **Islandia** (⊠ Kringlan Mall, ☎ 568–9960) offers a range of woolens, giftware, and souvenirs.

Íslenskur Heimilisiðnaður (⊠ Hafnarstræti 3, ☎ 551–1785), the Icelandic Handcrafts Center, offers knitted and woven woolen goods, as well as materials and kits if you want to try knitting or tapestry for yourself, and handmade gifts of glass, pottery, and precious metals. **Rammagerðin** (⊠ Hafnarstræti 19, ☎ 551–1122; ⊠ Hotel Loftleiðir, ☎ 552–5460; ⊠ Hotel Esja, ☎ 568–1124) stocks a large variety of hand- and machine-knitted woolen goods.

Street Markets

In summertime **Lækjartorg** sometimes fills with the stands of outdoor merchants offering anything from woolens, records, and books to vegetables, fruit, and bread. During the weekend (and an occasional weekday), the lively and colorful **Kolaport** flea market (☎ 562–5030) is open in an old ground-floor warehouse by the harborside (look for the big banner).

Reykjavík A to Z

Arriving and Departing

BY PLANE

Keflavík Airport (☎ 425–0600, 50 km/31 mi southwest of Reykjavík), hosts all international flights. For reservations and information in Reykjavík, contact **Icelandair** (☎ 505–0300) or **SAS** (☎ 562–2211). **Reykjavík Airport** (☎ 569–4100) is the central hub of domestic air travel in Iceland. For reservations and information, contact **Icelandair** (☎ 505–0300) and **Íslandsflug** (☎ 561–6060).

Between the Airport and Downtown. The **Reykjavík FlyBus** (☎ 562–1011) leaves Keflavík (from directly outside the terminal building) and arrives in Reykjavík at the Hótel Loftleiðir at Reykjavík Airport. From there you can take a taxi or municipal bus to your destination. Fly-Buses are scheduled in connection with each flight arrival and departure. For departures catch the FlyBus at the Saga, Esja, and Loftleiðir hotels and the Grand Hotel Reykjavík. The FlyBus also leaves the youth hostel in Laugardalur at 5 AM daily June–August. The fare is IKr600 per person. The ride takes 40–50 minutes.

From Reykjavík Airport, the municipal (SVR) Bus 5 leaves from the Icelandair terminal on the western side of the airport. Other airlines operate from the east terminal (behind the Loftleiðir Hotel), which is served by Bus 1. A **taxi** from the Keflavík Airport to Reykjavík is a little faster than the FlyBus and will cost IKr4,500; if you share it with others, you can split the cost. From Reykjavík Airport a taxi to your hotel will cost around IKr600; there are direct phones to taxi companies in the arrivals hall. Taxi companies include **Aðalstöðin** (☎ 421–1515 or 425–2525) and **Ökuleiðir** (☎ 421–4141).

Getting Around

The best way to see Reykjavík is on foot. Many of the interesting sights are in the city center, within easy walking distance of one another. There is no subway system.

BY BUS

The municipal bus system, **SVR** (☎ 551–2700), is extensive, cheap, and reliable. Buses run from 7 AM to midnight or 1 AM. On most routes, buses run every 20 minutes during the day and every half hour evenings and weekends. Bus stops are marked by signposts with an SVR or AV on top or by a bus shelter with a posted list of routes to outlying communities in the greater Reykjavík area. Route booklets are available at the main terminals of Lækjatorg, Hlemmur, Mjódd, and Ártún. The flat fare within Reykjavík is IKr120, payable to the driver in exact change on boarding. You can buy strips of tickets at a lower price from the drivers or at the main terminals. The fare allows you to travel any distance in town; if you have to change buses, ask for *skiptimiða* (*skiff-tee-mee-tha*), a transfer ticket that you give the second bus driver. The SVR system connects with **AV,** the bus system in the Kópavogur (bus routes numbered in the 60s), Garðabær (routes numbered 50s), and Hafnarfjörður (routes numbered in the 40s, and buses 140 and 141) municipalities south of Reykjavík. Buses marked with the AV logo (which actually looks more like a stylized, slanting "N") travel circuits about once an hour. From Reykjavík, the fare to these communities is IKr130. If you plan an extended stay in the Reykjavík area, it may be worthwhile to buy a monthly season ticket, the **Green Card,** valid on all SVR and AV routes. A recent innovation in the bus system is a summertime **Museum Bus,** which makes four hourly cycles daily, departing Lækjatorg Plaza and making 16 stops at cultural sites. A ticket costs IKr300 and is good for unlimited travel for three days. Also, a **Tourist Card,** available from the Tourist Information Center (☞ Visitor Information, *below*), will entitle you to unlimited bus travel in the city.

BY CAR

The excellent bus system and quick and inexpensive taxis make automobiles unnecessary for getting around town, doubly so considering how expensive car rentals and gasoline are. **Gas stations** are usually open 7:30 AM–11 PM. Most have self-service pumps that accept IKr500 and IKr1,000 notes. **Car-rental agencies** in Reykjavík include **Hertz/Iceland** (☎ 505–0600, FAX 505–0650), **Geysir** (☎ 568–8888, FAX 581–3102), **Avis** (☎ 562–4433, FAX 562–3590), and **Europcar** (☎ 568–6915). **Gamla bílaleigan** (☎ 588–4010, FAX 551–4014) rents slightly older cars at lower prices.

For information on road conditions and the availability of gas off the beaten track, call **Vegagerð Ríkisins** (Public Roads Administration, ☎ 563–1500).

BY TAXI

Most cabs are newer, fully equipped passenger sedans, including a fleet of Mercedes. They have small TAXI signs on top and can be hailed anywhere on the street; the LAUS sign indicates that the cab is available. There are taxi stands in a few locations around the city, but it is common to order a taxi by phone. Normally you will have to wait only a few minutes. Some taxis accept major credit cards, but you must state that you want to pay with a credit card when requesting the taxi. Fares are regulated by meter; rides around Reykjavík run between IKr500 and IKr800. There is no tipping. **Taxi companies** to call are BSR (☎ 561–0000), **Bæjarleiðir** (☎ 553–3500), or **Hreyfill** (☎ 588–5522).

Contacts and Resources

CAR RENTALS

Avis (☎ 425–0760) operates offices in the Leifur Eiríksson Terminal at Keflavík Airport. **Hertz/Icelandair** (☎ 505–0600) is also at Keflavík Airport.

CURRENCY EXCHANGE

The Change Group (✉ Bankastræti 2, ☎ 552–3735).

DOCTORS AND DENTISTS

Six health centers with officially appointed family doctors receive patients on short notice 8–5 weekdays. Call the **Reykjavík Health Center** (☎ 552–2400) or look under *Heilsugæslustöð* in the phone book. At other times, call **Læknavakt** (Duty Doctors, ☎ 552–1230). You can also get medical help by calling ☎ 551–8888.

Call ☎ 568–1041 for assistance with dental emergencies.

EMBASSIES

U.S. (✉ Laufásvegur 21, IS-101, ☎ 562–9100). **Canada** (✉ Suður-landsbraut 10, IS-101, ☎ 568–0820). **U.K.** (✉ Laufásvegur 31, IS-108, ☎ 550–5100).

EMERGENCIES

The emergency ward at **Sjúkrahús Reykjavíkur city hospital** (☎ 569–6600) is open 24 hours a day. In all of Iceland, dial ☎ 112 for emergency assistance.

ENGLISH-LANGUAGE BOOKSTORES

Eymundsson-Penninn (✉ Austurstræti 18, ☎ 551–1130; also opposite Hlemmur bus station and at the Kringlan Mall) carries some English-language books, newspapers, and magazines, but some may be several days old. **Mál og menning** (✉ Laugavegur 18, ☎ 552–4240; ✉ Síðumúli 7–9, ☎ 568–8577), the largest bookstores in the city, have an extensive foreign section; the Laugavegur store has added a congenial coffee bar. **Bóksala stúdenta** (Students Union Building, ✉ Hringbraut, next to Gamli Garður on the university campus, ☎ 561–5961) stocks English-language books.

GUIDED TOURS

The **Association of Travel Guides** (✉ Suðurlandsbraut 30, IS-108 Reyk-javík, ☎ 588–8670) can provide qualified guides who work in a variety of languages and have different specialties.

Bird-Watching Tours: Ferjuleiðir (✉ Skipholt 25, IS-105 Reykjavík, ☎ 562–8000, ℻ 562–2725) runs short excursions on the boat *Ms. Árnes.*

Sightseeing Tours: Kynnisferðir's (Reykjavík Excursions, ✉ Loftleiðir Hotel, ☎ 562–1011; Bankastræti 2, ☎ 562–4422, adjacent to the Tourist Information Center) daily 2½-hour "Reykjavík City Sightseeing" tour covers museums and art galleries, shopping centers, and the like.

LATE-NIGHT PHARMACIES

Reykjavík pharmacies take turns staying open around the clock. Signs indicating which establishment has the night watch (*næturvakt*) are posted in all pharmacies, and details are also published in newspapers. For information, call ☎ 551–8888.

OPENING AND CLOSING TIMES

Most of the capital closes down early on weekdays, and most places are closed Sunday. **Post offices** are open weekdays 8:30–4:30. The main post office at Ármúli 25 and the post office in the Kringlan Mall stay open until 6 on weekdays, and the post office at the BSÍ bus terminal is also open 9–1 on Saturday. **Museums** and **galleries** are generally open Tuesday–Saturday 11–4 and Sunday 2–6, and usually closed Monday. **Shops** are open weekdays 9–6. A growing number of stores, especially food stores, open on Saturday and Sunday with shorter hours. Many smaller food stores are open daily until 10 or 11 PM. Bakeries, souvenir shops, florists, and kiosks are open daily.

TRAVEL AGENCIES

Úrval-Útsýn Travel (⊠ Lágmúli 4, IS-108 Reykjavík, ☎ 569–9300, FAX 568–5033). **Samvinn Travel** (⊠ Austurstræti 12, IS-101 Reykjavík ☎ 569–1010, FAX 552–7796).

VISITOR INFORMATION

The Reykjavík **Tourist Information Center** (⊠ Bankastræti 2, IS-101, ☎ 562–3045, FAX 562–4749), a few feet up the street from Lækjartorg Square, is open June–August weekdays 8:30–6, Saturday 8:30–2, and Sunday 10–2; September–May it's open weekdays 9–5, Saturday 10–2. The **Icelandic Tourist Board**'s headquarters (Gimli, ⊠ Lækjargata 3, IS-101, ☎ 552–7488, FAX 562–4749) next door is open June–August, weekdays 8–4; September–May, 9–5.

SIDE TRIPS FROM REYKJAVÍK

Hafnarfjörður

10 km (6 mi) south of Reykjavík. Take AV (metro area) Bus 140 or 141 from Lækjatorg Plaza or Hlemmur station.

"Harbor fjord" was home to an important commercial port centuries before Reykjavík, and today there's still healthy competition between the two. Iceland's biennial **International Viking Festival**, last held in 1997, is held here. Residents are not ashamed of their role as the butt of Icelanders' own odd ethnic humor, but they are serious about their respect for hidden folk said to live in local lava formations. The Tourist Information Center (⊠ Vesturgata 8) will give you a map of the town's sites and possible elfin homes. Next to the Tourist Information Center is a **Sjóminjasafn Íslands** (Maritime Museum) and a **folk museum.** Just off the harbor is the red-roofed **Hafnarborg Art Center.**

Dining

$$ ✕ **A. Hansen.** In a classic building, this restaurant serves up a nice atmosphere and tasty nouvelle cuisine. If you'd rather enjoy wine without worrying about driving or transportation, you can order a package with dinner and round-trip stretch limousine service. ⊠ *Vesturgötu 4, Hafnarfjörður,* ☎ 565–1130. AE, MC, V.

$$ ✕ **Fjörukráin Restaurant.** Immerse yourself in everything Viking— from architecture to menu to service. Excellent seafood and meat dishes are served for those leery of the traditional chow. ⊠ *Strandgötu 55, Hafnarfjörður,* ☎ 565–1213. AE, MC, V.

$ ✕ **Nönnukot.** This diminutive, homey, old-fashioned coffee spot barely seats 12 at a handful of tables, and is Iceland's only totally no-smoking coffee house. Soup (served in a bowl of home-baked bread), waffles, and carrot cake are all delicious. Take the 20-step walk up a small hill from Strandgötu. It closes at 6. ⊠ *Mjósund 2, Hafnarfjörður,* ☎ 565–2808. *Closed Mon.* MC, V.

$ ✕ **Súfistinn.** At this modern coffee joint, you can choose from an excellent selection of coffees, teas, and liqueurs—to blend if you fancy. A variety of à la carte dishes and desserts round out the meal. ⊠ *Strandgötu 9, Hafnarfjörður,* ☎ 565–3740. AE, MC, V.

Outdoor Activities and Sports

BIKING

Biking tours are offered by **Blue Biking** (⊠ Booking at Vesturgata 8, IS-220 Hafnarfjörður, ☎ 565–2915).

GOLF

Golfing can be done at the 18-hole **Hvaleyrarvöllur course** (⊠ South of Hafnarfjörður, ☎ 565–3080).

HORSEBACK RIDING

You can rent horses at **Íshestar** (⊠ Bæjarhraun 2, IS-220 Hafnarfjörður, ☎ 565–3044).

SWIMMING

The town has two pools: the older one is indoors (⊠ Herjólfsgata 10, ☎ 555–0088) and the newer one is outdoors with a water slide (⊠ Hringbraut 77, ☎ 565–3080).

Reykjanes Peninsula

This boot-shaped region south of Reykjavík is most often seen just superficially en route to or from the international airport. But closer examination reveals more to it than the Blue Lagoon (☞ *below*) or the modest landscape you see from a bus window. **Reykjanesbæ** (a bureaucratic union of the communities of **Keflavík, Njarðvík,** and **Hafnir**), **Grindavík, Garður,** and **Sandgerði** are busy fishing communities, each with their own character.

At **Garður** you'll find not one, but two lighthouses and a shoreline where you can spot birds and seals. Offshore dolphins and whales sometimes reward keen-eyed visitors, and in good weather Snæfellsnes peninsula can be seen gleaming on the horizon. **Hafnir,** at the arch of the peninsular foot, has a local aquarium containing most of Iceland's fish species. The neighbor to the north, **Sandgerði,** is site of a new **Nature Center** (☞ Outdoor Activities and Sports, *below*), which in addition to having fine indoor exhibits, offers organized outdoor activities like bird- and whale-watching and beachcombing. Also near Sandgerði is the church, **Hvalaneskirkja,** where Iceland's most famous hymnist, Hallgrímur Pétursson (1614–74), was once pastor. Most of his Passion Hymns were composed here.

Good-sized **Grindavík** is close to the bird cliffs **Krísuvíkurberg,** the unharnessed geothermal area **Krísuvík,** as well as the noted Blue Lagoon. In 1532 a fierce battle ensued in Grindavík when a group of Icelanders, Danes, and Hanseatic merchants drove English merchants away. A century later, Barbary pirates ransacked the village. **Keflavík** (pronounced *Kep*-lah-veek) is a large community also with a centuries-old history of trade. Testifying to this are the many trails originally used by fishermen and traders that run through the Reykjanes area. Some of these are still marked by ancient rock cairns.

The newly established **Reykjanes Way Trail** (☞ Outdoor Activities and Sports, *below*) is a seven-part, 130-km (81-mi) trek through the region. It takes hikers past fascinating geologic formations, including features from a wide variety of volcanic activity, like conical eruptions and fissure flows. The highest part of the area is the normally submarine tectonic seam, the **Reykjanes Ridge,** where the North American and Eurasian plates meet. Locals mean it when they say a visit to Reykjanes expands your horizons, as these plates continue to drift apart.

Lodging

$$$$ 🏨 **Flug Airport Hótel.** This is perfect if you don't want to get up at the crack of dawn to get from Reykjavík to meet a morning departure from

Keflavík. Modern rooms have all the latest amenities. ⊠ *Hafnagata 57, IS-230 Keflavík,* ☏ *421–5222. 39 rooms, 3 suites. Restaurant, bar. MC, V.*

$$$$ ☷ **Hótel Keflavík.** One of several year-round Rainbow Hotels in Iceland, this property is convenient to the airport and well situated in Keflavík. It has wheelchair access and conference facilities. ⊠ *Vatnesvegur 12, IS-230 Keflavík,* ☏ *421–4377,* FAX *421–5590. 32 rooms. Restaurant, bar, minibars, no-smoking rooms, meeting rooms. MC, V.*

$ ☷ **Youth Hostel Þórustig.** Like most hostels, this place offers little extras, but it's clean. ⊠ *Þórustígur 1, IS-260 Njarðvík,* ☏ *421–5662,* FAX *421–5316. 60 beds. No credit cards.*

$ ☷ **Youth Hostel Strönd.** This no-nonsense hostel is a good bet for budget travelers. ⊠ *Njarðvíkurbraut 48–50, IS-260 Innri Njarðvík,* ☏ FAX *421–6211. 28 beds. No credit cards.*

Outdoor Activities and Sports

The Nature Center (⊠ Garðvegur 1, IS-245 Sandgerði, ☏ 423–7551) organizes bird- and whale-watching and beachcombing.

GOLF

Suðurnes Golf Club (⊠ Hólmsvöllur, Leira, near Keflavík, ☏ 421–4100). **Grindavík Golf Club** (⊠ Húsatóftur, ☏ 426–8720). **Sandgerði Golf Club** (⊠ Vallarhús, ☏ 423–7802).

HIKING

On the 130-km (81-mi) **Reykjanes Way Trail** (information ☏ 564–1788) system, you can take a seven-day self-guided hike with some 20-km (13-mi) days; it's challenging for beginners, but by no means insurmountable. It begins at the Reykjanesviti Lighthouse on the extreme southwestern tip of the peninsula and ends near Þingvellir National Park.

HORSEBACK RIDING

Call **Blue Lagoon Riding Tours** (⊠ IS-240 Grindavík, ☏ 426–8303.)

SWIMMING

Blue Lagoon (☞ *below*). **Keflavík Pool** (⊠ Sunnubraut, IS-230 Keflavík, ☏ 421–1500). **Njarðvík Pool** (⊠ Grundarvegur, IS-260 Njarðvk, ☏ 421–2744). **Garður Pool** (⊠ Garðbraut, IS 250 Garður, ☏ 422–7300). **Sandgerði Pool** (⊠ IS-245 Sandgerði, ☏ 423–7736).

WHALE-WATCHING AND DOLPHIN TOURS

Eldey Travel (☏ 421–3361, 421–5575, and 896–5598).

Blue Lagoon

★ *15 km (10 mi) from Keflavík Airport and 50 km (31 mi) from Reykjavík (turn off toward the village of Grindavík). Buses run from the BSÍ bus terminal in Reykjavík to the Blue Lagoon twice daily and three times a day in July and August.*

You can visit this eerie man-made wonder—with foglike clouds looming above and large power plant stacks as a backdrop—for a unique swimming experience. Superheated water is pumped up from 2 km (1¼ mi) beneath the earth's surface to power the nearby geothermal energy plant. The run-off water collects in the lava to form a warm, salty, mineral-rich lagoon. There are separate areas for therapeutic and recreational use. If you've forgotten your bathing suit, you can rent one here. ⊠ *Bláalónið, Svartsengi power plant,* ☏ *426–8800.* ☐ *IKr350.*

GOLDEN CIRCLE

If you make only one foray outside Reykjavík, take this popular trip to the lakes, waterfalls, and hot springs just inland from the capital. You'll begin at Þingvellir, the ancient seat of the world's first parliament; then you'll see the original Geysir hot spring (hence the term *geyser*); and then on to the famed Gullfoss, the "Golden Waterfall."

Þingvellir

About 50 km (30 mi) northeast of Reykjavík. Take Ring Road about 9 km (6 mi) just past the town of Mossfellsbær; turn right on Rte. 36.

After an hour-long drive from Reykjavík along Route 36 across the Mosfellsheiði heath, the broad lava plain of Þingvellir suddenly opens in front of you. This has been the nation's most hallowed place since AD 930, when the settler Grímur Geitskór chose it as the site for the world's oldest parliament, the Icelandic Alþingi (General Assembly). In July of each year delegates from all over the country camped at Þingvellir for two weeks, meeting to pass laws and render judicial sentences. Iceland remained a sovereign nation-state, ruled solely by the people without a personal sovereign or central government, until 1262 when it came under the Norwegian crown; even then, the Alþingi continued to meet at Þingvellir until 1798, when it was dissolved by Iceland's Danish rulers.

In AD 1000 the Alþingi decided that Iceland should become a Christian country, but the old heathen gods continued to be worshiped in private. These Viking gods remain part of everyday English: Týr (as in Tuesday), Óðinn (as in Wednesday), Þór (Thursday), and the goddess Frigg (Friday).

Þingvellir National Park, at the northern end of Þingvallavatn—Iceland's largest lake—remains a potent symbol of the Icelandic heritage. Many national celebrations are held here. Besides its historic interest, Þingvellir holds a special appeal for naturalists: it is the geologic meeting point of two continents. At Almannagjá, on the west side of the plain, is the easternmost edge of the American tectonic plate, otherwise submerged in the Atlantic Ocean. Over on the plain's east side, at the Heiðargjá Gorge, you are at the westernmost edge of the Eurasian plate. In the 9,000 years since the Þingvellir lava field was formed, the tectonic plates have moved 231 ft apart. And they are still moving, at a rate of about a half an inch a year.

You can drive straight to the central plain once you enter the park, or walk there after turning right along the short road at the sign for **Almannagjá** (Everyman's Gorge). At the rim, there is a fabulous view from the orientation marker.

A path down into Almannagjá from the top of the gorge overlooking Þingvellir leads straight to the high rock wall of **Lögberg** (Law Rock), where the person chosen as guardian of the laws would recite them from memory. At the far end of the gorge is the **Öxarárfoss** (Öxará Waterfall). Beautiful, peaceful picnic spots are just beyond it. Just below the waterfall in a deep stretch of the river lies the forbidding **Drekkingarhylur** pool, where it is said unfaithful wives were drowned.

Across the plain from Lögberg stand the church and **Þingvallabær,** the gabled manor house of Þingvellir, where the government of Iceland often hosts visiting heads of state. The **Nikulásargjá Gorge,** reached by a footbridge, is better know these days as **Peningagjá** (Money Gorge) because it's customary to fling a coin into the gorge's icy-cold water and make a wish. Don't even dream about climbing down to wade here—it might look shallow, but it's more than 30 ft deep!

Dining and Lodging

$$ ✕⊞ **Valhöll.** This small, comfortable, first-class hotel near the lake has rooms decorated in pastel colors and floral-print furnishings. The restaurant serves fresh trout from Þingvellir Lake, smoked or broiled, and delicious *pönnukökur* (crepes filled with whipped cream and jam). ⊠ *Þingvellir National Park,* ☎ *482–2622,* ℻ *482–3622. 30 rooms. Restaurant. MC, V. Closed Oct.–Apr.*

Outdoor Activities and Sports

BOATING

At Þingvellir you can rent boats for rowing on Þingvallavatn; the rental facility is on the lake by the Valhöll Hotel. Take extraordinary safety precautions: the shoreline drops off precipitously and the water is ice-cold.

FISHING

Trout and char are plentiful in Þingvallavatn. Obtain fishing permits at the Valhöll Hotel at Þingvellir.

HORSEBACK RIDING

A number of stables offer guided trail rides in this area. Call the **Laxnes Pony Farm** (☎ 566–6179) on Route 36 to Þingvellir.

En Route Follow Route 36 for 7 km (4½ mi) east of the Þingvellir plain to Route 365, which climbs 16 km (10 mi) across the moor. If you keep a close lookout, halfway along this road to the left under a high bluff is the large opening of a shallow cave in which a handful of people lived in the early 20th century.

Laugarvatn

About 20 km (12 mi) east of Þingvellir along Rtes. 36 and 365.

True to its name, Laugarvatn, or Warm Springs Lake, is warm enough for bathing. Its water is naturally heated by hot springs at the northern end of the lake. A cluster of buildings houses a school in winter and hotels in summer. Drive around them to a bathhouse at the lake's edge where you can rent towels and take showers year-round. The entrance fee also covers a natural steam bath in an adjoining hut, where you actually sit atop a hissing hot spring.

Lodging

$ ⊞ **Edda Hússtjórnarskóli.** This comfortable hotel-restaurant is right on the lake. ⊠ *IS-840 Laugarvatn,* ☎ *486–1154. 27 rooms. Restaurant, bar. MC, V. Closed Sept.–mid-June.*

$ ⊞ **Edda Menntaskóli.** This neighbor of the Edda Húsmæðraskóli (☞ *above*) is also lakeside, although accommodations are a little less plush. ⊠ *IS-840 Laugarvatn,* ☎ *486–1118. 88 rooms, some with shared bath. Restaurant, bar. MC, V. Closed Sept.–mid-June.*

Outdoor Activities and Sports

BOATING

Rowboats and sailboards can be rented on Laugarvatn Lake. At **Svínavatn** (⊠ Grímsnes, ☎ 486–4437) you can rent jet skis.

HORSEBACK RIDING

Contact **Íshestar** (Icelandic Riding Tours, ☎ 486–1169) at Miðdalur near Laugarvatn.

Haukadalur

From Laugarvatn on Rte. 37 (or from Lake Laugarvatn take the short spur, Rte. 364, southwest to Rte. 37) continue on Rte. 37 northeast for 25 km (16 mi) to the junction with Rte. 35. Take Rte. 35 not quite 10 km (6 mi) northeast until you see Hótel Geysir.

The Geysir geothermal field in Haukadalur, home of the Geysir and Strokkur geysers, is one of Iceland's classic tourist spots.

The famous **Geysir** hot spring used to gush a column of scalding water 130–200 ft into the air, but the old geyser has now gone into retirement. **Strokkur** is a more reliable performer, having been drilled open in 1964 after a quiet period of 70 years; it spouts up boiling water as high as 100 ft at five-minute intervals. In the same area there are small boreholes from which steam rises, as well as beautiful pools of blue water. Don't crowd Strokkur, and always be careful when approaching hot springs or mud baths—the ground may be treacherous, suddenly giving way beneath you.

Dining and Lodging

$ ✕🛏 **Hótel Geysir.** Next to the famous Geysir and Strokkur springs, this hotel is done in an exuberant Viking style, with replica medieval carved decorations, such as dragon heads, galore. As hotel rooms go, these are small and basic with shared bath, but there's a large restaurant. The menu includes various Icelandic specialties, such as salmon, rye bread baked in the heat of geothermal springs, and *skyr* (a delicious yogurtlike food made from skim milk) with cream. ✉ *Haukadalur, IS-801,* ☎ *486–8915,* ℻ *486–8715. 15 rooms without bath. Restaurant, bar, pool. MC, V. Closed Sept.–May.*

Gullfoss

About 6 km (4 mi) east of Geysir along Rte. 35.

Measuring 105 ft high, thundering Gullfoss (Golden Falls) is a double cascade in the Hvítá River, turning at right angles in mid-drop. Gullfoss enters a dramatic chasm, which nonetheless has its gentle sides. On the western bank of the river—where the steep walls begin to slant more—is a beautiful hidden spot a short, steep climb from the road. Called **Pjaxi,** from the Latin *pax* (meaning "peace"), this nook of grassy knolls, natural springs, clear streams, and birch trees is ideal for a picnic.

Outdoor Activities and Sports

HORSEBACK RIDING

Horses can be hired for rides at **Brattholt** farm (☎ 486–8941), adjacent to Gullfoss.

WHITE-WATER RAFTING

Take a one-hour journey down the churning glacial Hvítá River below Gullfoss Falls, waterproof clothing and life jackets provided. Call **Hvítárferðir** (✉ Háagerði 41, IS-108 Reykjavík, ☎ 568–2504).

Skálholt

From Gullfoss, follow the southbound Rte. 35 for 36 km (22 mi); turn left onto Rte. 31 and go another 3½ km (2 mi) to the right-hand turnoff.

The seat of the southern bishopric, Skálholt was the main center of learning and religion in Iceland until the 18th century. On the way back from the Gullfoss falls to Reykjavík, stop at **Skálholt Cathedral.** This ancient sanctuary was established in 1056, soon after Iceland converted to Christianity. A stone near the entry drive is believed to be where the last Catholic bishop, Jón Arason, and his son (celibacy was difficult to enforce so far from Rome) lost their heads when the Lutheran faith was ultimately enforced in 1550. The wonderfully simple building, consecrated in 1963, is the 11th church to be built on this site. Beneath it lies an ancient crypt.

The **modern memorial church** at Skálholt houses historic relics and contemporary pieces. Works by two of Iceland's most important modern artists adorn the cathedral: a unique mosaic altarpiece by Nína Tryggvadóttir and stained glass windows by Gerður Helgadóttir. Each summer the cathedral hosts the **Skálholt Music Festival,** which brings together musicians from Iceland and abroad who perform baroque music on original instruments.

En Route   The return route from Skálholt to Reykjavík rolls through one of the most prosperous agricultural regions in Iceland. Drive 10 km (6 mi) from the cathedral along Route 31 and turn right to go south on Route 30; after 21 km (13 mi), Route 30 ends at the Ring Road. Take a right onto Route 1 and head 73 km (44 mi) west to; if you have time, stop halfway in Hveragerði.

Hveragerði

40 km (25 mi) southeast of Reykjavík.

Hveragerði is home to a horticultural school, a large number of greenhouses heated by hot springs, and a fine swimming pool. The state's greenhouse research facility, where flowers and crops are grown with natural steam in large hot houses, is up the hill from the town's center. One of the country's most unabashed tourist spots, **Eden** awaits with an exotic display of tropical plants, souvenir items, and a snack bar. The rather garish, large roadside building of fiberglass panels, discreetly set back from the Ring Road, is all that's left of a failed amusement park.

Dining and Lodging

$$$ ✕▥ **Hótel Örk.** This white-concrete, blue-roofed hotel is a couple of blocks away from Hveragerði's attractions. Rooms and public spaces have mahogany furniture, original Icelandic art, and plenty of potted plants. Specialties at the ground-floor restaurant might be lobster soup with a touch of champagne, leg of lamb roasted with Icelandic herbs, or fresh ocean fish from the nearby town of Þorlákshöfn. ⊠ *Breiðamörk 1,* ☎ *483–4700,* 𝖥𝖠𝖷 *483–4775. 81 rooms. Restaurant, outdoor pool, sauna, spa, 9-hole golf course, tennis court. AE, MC, V.*

$ ▥ **Ból.** This youth hostel in Hveragerði, open May–August, has 26 beds. ⊠ *Hveramörk 14, IS-810 Hveragerði,* ☎ *483–4198 or 483–4588. 26 beds. No credit cards. Closed Sept.–Apr.*

Outdoor Activities and Sports

SWIMMING
The region has numerous swimming pools, located wherever there is plenty of natural hot water. Contact the swimming pool in Hveragerði at ☎ 483–4113.

Golden Circle A to Z

Arriving and Departing

BY BUS
It is possible to explore this area by BSÍ bus, but you must allow plenty of time and perhaps stay overnight en route. **BSÍ Travel** (☎ 552–2300) serves Þingvellir twice daily (June–mid-Sept.) and Gullfoss and Geysir twice daily (June 15–Aug.).

BY CAR
This circuit should take seven or eight hours by car, allowing time for stops at the various sights. At the farthest point, Gullfoss, you'll only be 125 km (78 mi) from Reykjavík, and most of the drive is along paved main roads.

Contacts and Resources

EMERGENCIES
In Hveragerði the **police** can be reached at ☎ 483–1154. Dial ☎ 112 for emergency assistance anywhere in Iceland.

GUIDED TOURS
Kynnisferðir (Reykjavík Excursions, ☎ 562–1011 or 568–8922) offers an eight-hour guided Golden Circle tour May–September, daily at 9 AM, and October–April, daily except Tuesday and Thursday.

VISITOR INFORMATION
General information is available in Reykjavík at the **Tourist Information Center** or the **Icelandic Tourist Board** (☞ Visitor Information *in* Reykjavík A to Z, *above*). Hveragerði: **South Coast Travel Service and Information Center** (✉ Breiðumörk 10, ☎ 483–4280).

THE WEST AND THE VESTFIRÐIR

If you imagine the map of Iceland as the shape of a beast, two rugged western peninsulas—Snæfellsnes and Vestfirðir (Western Fjords)— would make up the jaws of a peculiar dragonlike head, opening wide around the huge bay of Breiðafjörður. The North Atlantic, just off this coast, is one of the country's prime fishing grounds. Busy fishing villages abound in the Vestfirðir, but there are also tall mountains, remote cliffs thick with seabirds, and deep fjords carved out of basaltic rock. Inland in the extreme northwest corner, abandoned farmsteads and vestiges of ancient habitation speak of isolation and the forces of nature.

In the southern reaches, just north of the town of Borgarnes, the Ring Road northbound bends to the northeast, giving the traveler a choice of routes. You can follow Route 54, which branches northwest, leading along the southern reaches of the Snæfellsnes Peninsula, which is crowned by the majestic Snæfellsjökull (Snæfells Glacier). Or you can choose to follow the Ring Road to the east. Here you'll enter a world rich in natural beauty and steeped in the history of the sagas. You should plan to give the east and west options a day each.

Borgarnes

The starting point for this regional tour is 116 km (72 mi) north of Reykjavík along the Ring Road. The Reykjavík–Akranes ferry is a convenient shortcut.

Borgarnes is the only coastal town of any size that does *not* rely on fishing for its livelihood; you're more likely to see industrial buildings than fishing fleets. If you're coming from the south, take the new bridge—barely a decade old—which shortens the Ring Road approach to town. You no longer need to drive around Borgarfjörður.

Dining and Lodging

$$ ✕🏨 **Hótel Borgarnes.** The newer rooms in this large hotel are bright with neutral-colored interiors. A number of south-facing rooms overlook the fjord with views to nearby mountains. No-smoking rooms are available and an elevator makes upper level access convenient. ✉ *Egilsgata 14–16, IS-310 Borgarnes,* ☎ *437–1119,* ‖FAX‖ *437–1443. 75 rooms. Restaurant, bar, cafeteria. AE, DC, MC, V.*

$ 🛏 **Kleppjárnsreykir.** This youth hostel has 14 beds. ✉ *Runnar, Blómaskálinn, Kleppjárnsreykir, IS-311 Borgarnes,* ☎ *435–1262 or 435–1185,* FAX *435–1437. 14 beds. No credit cards.*

Outdoor Activities and Sports

HORSEBACK RIDING

To rent horses for exploring the Borgarfjörður area, call **Jafnaskarð** farm (☎ 435–0028 or 437–7033). Also try the **Varmaland Summer Hotel** (☎ 435–1303).

SWIMMING

You can take a refreshing dip at the pool in Borgarnes (✉ Skallagrímsgata, ☎ 437–0027).

En Route   To explore the area inland from Borgarfjörður, drive northeast from Borgarnes on the Ring Road 11 km (7 mi) to Route 53 leading east. Turn right onto Route 53 and cross the one-lane bridge over the cloudy glacial Hvítá River. Take the first left turn onto Route 52 and in 10 minutes you'll arrive at the **Laxfoss** (Salmon Falls) on the Grímsá River, where salmon leap the rapids in summer. Continue across the Grímsá north on Route 50 a little more than 10 km (6 mi) to the **Kleppjárnsreykir** horticultural center, with its many greenhouses heated by thermal water from the region's hot springs.

Reykholt

Head northeast on Rte. 50 past Kleppjárnsreykir about 1 km (½ mi); turn east onto Rte. 518 and follow 8 km (5 mi).

Reykholt is the home of scholar-historian Snorri Sturluson (1178–1241). Author of the prose work *Edda,* a textbook of poetics, and the *Heimskringla,* a history of Norway's kings, Sturluson was also a wealthy chieftain and political schemer. He was murdered in Reykholt in 1241 on the orders of the Norwegian king. A hot bathing pool believed to date from Snorri's time can be seen here; the underground passage once led from Snorri's homestead to the pool. The institute for Old Norse study, named for Snorri Sturluson, is an area secondary school.

Dining and Lodging

$ ✕🛏 **Edda Hotel.** This functional, modern building is a secondary school in winter and a hotel in summer. ✉ *Reykholt,* ☎ *435–1260. 48 rooms. Restaurant, bar. MC, V. Closed Sept.–mid-June.*

En Route   Continue for about 30 minutes on Route 518 to the colorful **Hraunfossar** (Lava Falls). A multitude of natural springs under a birch-covered lava field above the Hvítá River creates a waterfall hundreds of feet wide, seemingly appearing out of nowhere across the bank from you. A little farther up the Hvítá, a 10-minute walk from Hraunfossar, is the **Barnafossar** (Children's Falls), which has carved out strange figures from the rock. Tradition says that two children lost their lives when a natural stone bridge over the churning maelstrom gave way. Today a trusty footbridge gives safe access to the opposite bank.

Húsafell Park is about 4 km (2½ mi) up the Route 518 eastward. This somewhat sheltered wooded area is a popular summer camping site, with birch trees, swimming pool, and chalets. A gasoline station is here and a restaurant serves visitors June–August.

Bifröst

From Húsafell, return west past Reykholt along Routes 518 and 523 some 50 km (30 mi) to the Ring Road; go north about 13 km (8 mi) to Bifröst.

About 1½ km (1 mi) north of Bifröst just off the Ring Road is the **Grábrók** volcanic cone, which you can easily scale for a panoramic view. Grábrók's lava field, covered with moss, grass, and birches, has many quiet spots for a picnic. Eight kilometers (5 miles) north is the distinctive pyramid-shape **Mt. Baula,** a pastel-colored rhyolite mountain. In the 19th century, Icelanders delighted in telling gullible foreign travelers fantastic stories of the beautiful green meadows and forests populated by dwarfs shepherding herds of fat sheep at Baula's summit.

Lodging

$$ 🏨 **Hótel Bifröst.** Low white school buildings with red roofs house this summer hotel beside the Ring Road in Borgarfjörður. ✉ *Hreðavatn,* ☎ *435–0000 or 435–0005,* 🅵🅰🆇 *435–0020. 26 rooms, 8 with bath. Restaurant, bar, horseback riding. MC, V.*

Snæfellsnes Peninsula

The southern shore of this peninsula begins about 40 km (25 mi) northwest of Borgarnes; if you're heading south from Bifröst, it's about 30 km (18 mi) to the turnoff onto the peninsula from the Ring Road.

Begin the journey north from the crossroads with Route 54. As you drive farther west on the peninsula, you'll pass through the Staðarsveit district, with its beautiful mountain range. Many small lakes abound with water flowers, and there are myriad sparkling springs. At **Lýsuhóll,** a few minutes north of Route 54, you can bathe in the warm water of a naturally carbonated swimming pool. About 10 km (6 mi) farther west is the **Búðahraun** lava field, composed of rough, slaggy lava. Its surface makes walking difficult, but it's more hospitable to vegetation than are most other Icelandic landscapes; flowers, shrubs, herbs, and berries grow abundantly here.

Búðir

102 km (61 mi) northwest of Borganes.

This tiny shoreline establishment on the Snæfellsnes Peninsula has ancient origins as an inlet mooring for fishermen in the days of sails and rowing. If you look carefully, you may find centuries-old relics of the fishermen's shelters. An unpretentious church from 1850—a successor to the first chapel on this site in 1703—has retained its original visage. The lava surrounding this site fosters unique flora, including a rare subspecies of the buttercup, called Goldilocks, or *Ranunculus auricomus islandicus* among scholars. The area is protected as a registered nature preserve.

Dining and Lodging

$$ ✕🏨 **Hótel Búðir.** Under the magical Snæfellsjökull and close to a beach of black lava and golden sand, this rustic hotel has an excellent restaurant. ✉ *Staðarsveit, IS-355 Snæfellsnes,* ☎ *435–6700,* 🅵🅰🆇 *435–6701. 26 rooms without bath, 4 with bath. Restaurant, horseback riding. MC, V. Closed Oct.–Apr.*

En Route From Búðir, take a left turn onto coastal Route 574 for a 61-km (36-mi) drive circling the tip of the peninsula clockwise. On your right you'll see the majestic Snæfells Glacier, **Snæfellsjökull,** which, like that on Fujiyama in Japan, caps a volcano. The glacier did a cameo in Jules Verne's novel *Journey to the Center of the Earth* as the spot where the explorers enter the depths of the world.

The coastal drive will take you past many small, beautiful villages. One such is **Arnarstapi,** where the roof of a shore cave has fallen in, leaving a high arch for cliff birds to loop through to and from their nests.

Hellnar—with its sea-level cave, Baðstofa, that radiates blue at high tide—is also quaint. About an hour's walk from the road at the western tip of the peninsula lie the **Svörtuloft Cliffs,** where multitudes of seabirds take refuge in nesting season.

Ólafsvík

Either 61 km (36 mi) clockwise around the peninsula on Rte. 574 or 14 km (7 mi) across the Fróðárheiði cutoff from Búðir.

Commerce has taken place in this small village under the north shoulder of Snæfellsjökull since 1687.

Outdoor Activities and Sports
HIKING AND SNOWMOBILING
From here you can hike to the top of the glacier or arrange snowmobile tours through the **Tourist Information Center** (☎ 436–1543).

SWIMMING
The local Ólafsvík **pool** (✉ Ennisbraut 9, ☎ 436–1199) is open to the public.

Stykkishólmur

67 km (42 mi) east of Ólafsvík.

Stykkishólmur is an active fishing and port community on the peninsula's north coast with a well-sheltered natural harbor. A pair of classic timber houses from the 1800s give a clue to the distinguished past, when many of the now-abandoned islets of Breiðafjörður were settled. One, from 1828, bears the name of Árni Thorlacius, an early merchant who established the nation's oldest weather station in 1845. The large hospital near the water was built in 1936 by the Order of the Franciscans and has been staffed since by its sisters.

A ferry sails twice daily from here to the rugged, sparsely populated islands of the Breiðafjörður. The island **Flatey,** where the ferry stops over on the way to the Western Fjords, is worth a visit. The now sleepy vacation village was an important commerce and learning hub in the 19th century; many delightful old houses still stand today, and the bird life is remarkable.

Dining and Lodging
$$ ✕🏨 **Hótel Stykkishólmur.** This hotel makes a convenient jumping-off point for excursions to the islands of Breiðafjörður and for the ferry to the Western Fjords. The restaurant serves good seafood specialties, plus lamb, pork, and pasta dishes and pizza and hamburgers. ✉ *Vatnási, IS-340 Stykkishólmur,* ☎ *438–1330,* ⅎ⅍ *438–1579. 33 rooms. Restaurant, 9-hole golf course. DC, MC, V.*

$$ 🏨 **Hótel Eyjaferðir.** Some rooms in this comfortable, utilitarian, and quiet family-run hotel have shared bath. ✉ *Aðalgata 8, IS-340 Stykkishólmur* ☎ *438–1450. 14 rooms, some with bath. MC, V.*
$ 🏨 **Youth Hostel.** There are 50 beds here. ✉ *Höfðagata 1, IS-340 Stykkishólmur,* ☎ *438–1095,* ⅎ⅍ *438–1579. 50 beds. No credit cards.*

Outdoor Activities and Sports
SWIMMING
For information about the pool in Stykkishólmur, call ☎ 438–1272.

Ísafjörður

From Stykkishólmur, follow Rte. 57 70 km (50 mi) to Rte. 60. Alternatively, from the Ring Road, pick up Rte. 60 about 10 km (6 mi) past

Bifröst and drive 35 km (27 mi) to the intersection with Rte. 57. From there it's a long drive north—about 340 km (211 mi).

The uncrowned capital of the Western Fjords, Ísafjörður is one of the most important fishing towns in Iceland, and it also hosts a renowned Easter week ski meet. This is a convenient jumping-off point for tours to **Hornstrandir,** the splendidly peaceful and desolate land north of the 66th parallel inhabited by millions of seabirds. Geologically the oldest part of Iceland, Vestfirðir offers spectacular views of mountains, fjords, and sheer cliffs. Anglers come here for trout fishing in the rivers and lakes, and hikers and mountaineers explore this unspoiled region with the help of guides. The northernmost cliffs of **Hornbjarg** and **Hælavíkurbjarg** are home to large bird colonies.

Dining and Lodging

$$ ✕⌂ **Hótel Ísafjörður.** This is a good, family hotel in the heart of town. No two rooms are alike, but all have old-fashioned furnishings and floral fabrics. The restaurant serves tasty seafood dishes, including grilled scallops in pesto sauce. Sightseeing tours and boat trips are offered in summer. ⊠ *Silfurtorgi 2, IS-400,* ☏ *456–4111,* 𝖥𝖠𝖷 *456–4767. 32 rooms. Restaurant. AE, MC, V.*

Outdoor Activities and Sports

BIKING

Bikes can be rented from the **Hotel Ísafjörður** (☏ 456–4111).

SWIMMING

Head to the local Ísafjörður **pool** (⊠ Austurvegur 9, ☏ 456–3200).

Patreksfjörður

190 km (114 mi) southwest of Ísafjörður, or 345 km (207 mi) northwest of Borgarnes. From Borgarnes take the Ring Road north; follow Rte. 60 north to Vatnsfjörður, then take Rte. 62 west. A less arduous approach is to take the ferry from Stykkishólmur. After a brief stop at the isle of Flatey, the ferry stops at Brjánslækur. From here it's 54 km (32 mi) to Patreksfjörður.

One of the Western Fjords' many curious fishing villages, this one is named for the patron saint of Ireland. Houses here seem to crowd every available flat spot, right up to the sea. The harbor, built in 1946, was formed by deepening and opening a brackish lake to the sea.

The region's largest bird colony—with millions of residents—is at Látrabjarg, 60 km (36 mi) from Patreksfjörður. The immense vertical cliff, more than 650 ft high, runs along the south shore of the Western Fjords. In years past, egg collectors dangled over the edges to gather eggs, which were an essential source of protein. This is Iceland's westernmost tip, and the waters offshore are treacherous to sailors. The skill of egg collectors proved heroic in 1947 in what has to qualify as one of maritime history's most incredible rescues: With mind-boggling agility, local Icelanders rappelled down the treacherous cliff and shot a lifeline out to the stranded trawler *Dhoon*. Then, using a single-seat harness, all 12 crew members of the ship were hauled ashore and up to safety on the top of the cliff—in the near-total darkness of December, no less.

Lodging

⌂ **Youth Hostel.** Open year-round, this hostel has eight beds. ⊠ *Afahús, Aðalstræti 65, IS-450 Patreksfjörður,* ☏ *456–1280 or 456–1275. 8 beds.*

The West and the Vestfirðir A to Z

Arriving and Departing

BY BOAT

The **Akranes** car ferry, *Akraborg* (☎ 551–6050), sails three or four times daily between Reykjavík and Akranes year-round. In summer the *Baldur* car ferry (☎ 438–1120 or 456–2020) links **Stykkishólmur,** on the Snæfellsnes Peninsula, with **Brjánslækur,** on the southern coast of the Western Fjords, calling at Flatey Island. *Baldur* leaves Stykkishólmur at 10 AM and 4:30 PM in summer. From Ísafjörður, you can travel by the **Fagranes** ferry (☎ 456–3155 or 456–4655) around the Western Fjords.

BY BUS

BSÍ Travel (Reykjavík Airport, ☎ 552–2300) runs frequent daily service to most towns in the region. It's a two-hour trip to Borgarnes, four hours to Stykkishólmur. Bus travel is not the most convenient way to visit the Western Fjords; service to Ísafjörður runs a couple of days a week in summer only, and it's a 12-hour trip.

BY CAR

From Reykjavík and the north, you reach the west via the Ring Road (Rte. 1). Route 54 branches off to the Snæfellsnes Peninsula; Routes 60 and 68 branch off to the Western Fjords. Those renting cars to drive to the Western Fjords are advised NOT to select the smallest sized cars, as roads can be rough, requiring good ground clearance underneath.

BY PLANE

Air travel is the best way to visit the Western Fjords. You can fly to Ísafjörður on **Air Iceland** (Flugfélag Íslands, Ísafjörður ☎ 456–3000, Reykjavík ☎ 570–3030), the domestic division of Icelandair.

Contacts and Resources

EMERGENCIES

Police: Borgarnes (☎ 437–1166). **Ísafjörður** (☎ 456–4222). **Stykkishólmur** (☎ 488–1008). Dial ☎ 112 for emergency assistance anywhere in Iceland.

GUIDED TOURS

Boat Tours: Eyjaferðir (✉ Egilshús, IS-340 Stykkishólmur, ☎ 438–1450) has boat tours among the countless islets of **Breiðafjörður,** departing daily from Stykkishólmur.

Sightseeing Tours: The **Iceland Tourist Bureau** (☞ Visitor Information *in* Iceland A to Z, *below*) operates a 12-hour day trip from Reykjavík to the **Western Fjords,** with a flight to Ísafjörður and then sightseeing by bus. The tour departs daily June–August. **Vesturferðir** (✉ Torfnes, IS-400 Ísafjörður, ☎ 456–5111, FAX 456–4767) runs tours around the Western Fjords.

One-day sightseeing tours of the **Western Fjords** run in the summers from **Ísafjörður** (☎ 456–3155 or 456–4655). Sightseeing tours of Breiðafjörður, with its innumerable islands and varied bird life, operate from Stykkishólmur; contact **Eyjaferðir** (☎ 438–1450).

Snowmobiling Tours: Take a snowmobile to the top of the Snæfellsjökull in a group of 6, minimum, from **Snjófell** (✉ IS-311 Arnarstapi, ☎ 435–6783, FAX 435–6795) at Arnarstapi for IKr3,800 per person. **West Tours** (✉ Box 37, IS-400 Ísafjörður, ☎ 456–5111) gives hiking and mountaineering trips to the inhabitable parts of **Strandasýsla.**

VISITOR INFORMATION

Akranes (✉ Skólabraut 31, IS-300 Akranes, ☎ 431–3327, FAX 431–4327). **Borgarnes** (✉ Borgarbraut 59, IS-310 Borgarnes, ☎ 437–1529, FAX 437–1529). **Ísafjörður** (✉ Box 277, IS-400 Ísafjörður; office

⊠ Hafnarstræti 8, ☎ 456–5121, ⦿ 456–5122). **Ólafsvík** (⊠ Gamla Pakkhúsið, IS-355 Ólafsvík, ☎ 436–1543).

THE NORTH

From the Hrútafjörður (Rams' Fjord), which gouges deeply into the western end of the coast, to Vopnafjörður in the east, Iceland's north is a land created by the interplay of fire and ice. Inland, you can find the largest lava fields on earth, some with plants and mosses, others barren. Yet valleys sheltered by the mountains are lush with vegetation and rich in color, and the deeply indented coast offers magnificent views north toward the Arctic, especially spectacular under the summer's midnight sun.

A commercial and cultural center, Akureyri is Iceland's fourth-largest town. From there it's a pleasant drive to Lake Mývatn, where birdwatchers can spot vast numbers of waterfowl and hikers can explore weird lava formations. It's unusually mild around Mývatn, making it a pleasant outdoor destination.

Brú

27 km (16 mi) west of Hvammstangi, the nearest town to the Ring Road.

If you're driving the full Ring Road route, you'll enter the north at Brú, snuggled at the inland end of the long Hrútafjörður. It is a tiny settlement, bordering on two regional districts where a post and telegraph station was established in 1950. A local **folk museum** offers a glimpse into the area's past.

Dining and Lodging

$$ ✕🏠 **Staðarskáli í Hrútafirði.** Just east of Brú, this neat, clean accommodation offers good cooking (try the grilled lamb) and reasonable prices. ⊠ *Hrútarfirði, IS-500 Staðarhreppur,* ☎ *451–1150,* ⦿ *451–1107. 36 rooms, 18 with shower. Restaurant, meeting rooms.*

$ ✕🏠 **Edda Hotel.** The restaurant at this summer hotel is open all day. ⊠ *Reykjum, IS-500 Brú,* ☎ *451–0004. 50 rooms. Restaurant, bar, pool, meeting rooms. AE, DC, MC, V. Closed Sept.–mid-June.*

$ 🏠 **Youth Hostel.** There are 30 beds here. ⊠ *Sæberg Reykir, Hrútafjörður, IS-500 Brú,* ☎ *451–0015,* ⦿ *451–0034. 30 beds. No credit cards.*

Outdoor Activities and Sports

BIKING

Rent bikes at **Staðarskáli** (⊠ Hrútafjörður, ☎ 451–1150).

OFF THE
BEATEN PATH

HÚNAFLÓI – The name, Polar Bear Cub Bay, is believed to be based on legend, for you'll catch nary a glimpse of a bear or daredevil bather. From Staðarskáli, follow the Ring Road east. You will be taking what locals call the Vatnsnes Circle around the namesake peninsula. The loop itself totals about 83 km (50 mi) along Routes 72 and 711. As you get farther out on the peninsula's west side, keep a lookout for seals and shore birds, maybe even spouting whales. Eventually the road becomes Route 711, and you turn around the tip of the peninsula and head south. As you near the mainland, look to the east for Hvíserkur, a bizarre dinosaur-shape rock formation offshore. It is as if an escapee from the Jurassic era became petrified as it drank from the sea.

Blönduós

85 km (53 mi) east of Brú and 145 km (91 mi) west of Akureyri on the Ring Road.

The largest town on the west end of the north coast is nestled beneath gently rolling hills at the mouth of the glacially chalky Blandá River. Though unsightly shrimp and shellfish processing plants and small industrial businesses mark the landscape here, from Blönduós it is an easy drive to neighboring picturesque valleys.

About 19 km (12 mi) south, across the Vatnsdalsá River, is the turnoff heading 6 km (4 mi) north to **Þingeyrarkirja** (Þingeyri's Church). The humble stony exterior belies an exquisite blue-domed interior, replete with carvings and beautiful religious ornamentation. To get in, contact the sexton at the farm Steinnes; look for the sign on the right-hand side of the approach road labeled KIRKJUVÖRÐUR—it's about 3 km (2 mi) after you turn north.

Dining and Lodging

$$ ✕🏠 **Sveitasetrið, Blönduós.** This small hotel in the old center of town is a stone's throw from the seashore. Of course, fresh trout and salmon are specialties at the hotel's large restaurant. ⊠ *Aðalgata 6, IS-540 Blönduós,* ☎ *452–4126,* 𝖥𝖠𝖷 *452–4989. 18 rooms, 11 with shower. Restaurant. AE, MC, V.*

Varmahlið

136 km (82 mi) east of Brú and 94 km (56 mi) west of Akureyri at the crossroads of the Ring Road and Rte. 75 north to Sauðárkrókur. If you're coming from Rte. 711, Rte. 75 meets the Ring Road again, and here you should turn left and head east toward Blönduós and Varmahlið.

The inland village of Varmahlið its own local abundant geothermal heating sources. In addition to a bank, hotel, general store, and gas station, a small natural history museum is here.

South of town you'll come to **Víðimýri.** Here you can visit the restored turf-roofed **Víðimýrarkirkja** church, built in 1834 and still serving the local parishioners to this day. The late president of Iceland, Kristján Eldjarn—a world authority of Nordic antiquities—once called it one of the most sublimely built and beautiful remnants of Icelandic architecture.

Glaumbær

Returning north, cross the Ring Road and head north on Rte. 75 about 10 km (6 mi) north of Varmahlíð.

The **Glaumbær Folk Museum,** occupying a turf-roofed farmhouse, offers a glimpse of 18th- and 19th-century living conditions in rural Iceland. In the 11th century, Glaumbær was the home of Guðríður Þorbjarnardottir and Þorfinnur Karlsefni, two of the Icelanders who attempted to settle in America after it was discovered by Leifur Eiríksson. Their son, Snorri, was probably the first European to be born in the New World. ☎ *453–6173.* 🎟 *IKr120.* ☉ *June–Aug., daily 10–noon and 1–7.*

Dining and Lodging

$$ ✕🏠 **Hótel Varmahlið.** This nice hotel is in the namesake crossroads community. Some rooms here have access for people with disabilities. The staff can arrange golfing, fishing, or horseback riding for visitors. ⊠ *Varmahlíð, IS-560,* ☎ *453–8170 or 453–8190,* 𝖥𝖠𝖷 *453 8870. 38 rooms, 15 with shower. Restaurant. MC, V.*

Sauðárkrókur

17 km (11 mi) north on Rte. 75 from Glaumbær.

In summer, boat trips from the large coastal town of Sauðárkrókur to Drangey and the Málmey Islands offer striking views of the fjord and bird cliffs. On the eastern side of Skagafjörður, off Route 75, is the 18th-century stone cathedral at **Hólar,** which contains beautiful and price-less religious artifacts.

Lodging

$$ ⊞ **Hótel Áning.** This good-size hotel has a restaurant. Hiking, horse-back riding, and boat tours can be arranged from here. ⊠ *Sæmundarhlíð, IS-550,* ☎ *453–6717 or 453-5940,* 🖷 *453–6087. 65 rooms. Restaurant, meeting rooms. MC, V.*

Akureyri

95 km (57 mi) east along the Ring Road from the junction with Rte. 75 south of Sauðárkrókur.

Though not as cosmopolitan as Reykjavík, Akureyri—called the Cap-ital of the North—is a lively city. A century ago, the farmers in the pros-perous agricultural area surrounding Akureyri established KEA, a cooperative enterprise to combat the Danish businesses dominating the area's economic life. Today KEA still runs most of the stores and in-dustries in Akureyri.

Hemmed by the 64-km-long (40-mi-long) Eyjafjörður, Akureyri is sheltered from the ocean winds and embraced by mountains on three sides. Late 19th-century wooden houses impart a sense of history, and the twin spires of a modern Lutheran church—rising on a green hill near the waterfront—provide a focal point. The church is named for Akureyri native Matthías Jochumsson, the poet who wrote Iceland's national anthem in 1874.

From the church it's a short walk from the town center on Eyrar-landsvegur to the **Lystigarðurinn** (Arctic Botanical Gardens), planted with more than 400 species of Icelandic flora, including rare Arctic and foreign plants. **Matthíasarhús** (⊠ Eyrarlandsvegur 3), the house where Jochumsson once lived, is now a museum, open daily 2–4. Two other museums honor Icelandic writers: **Davíðshús** (⊠ Bjarkastígur 6), the home of poet Davíð Stefánsson, open weekdays 3–5, and **Nonnahús** (⊠ Aðalstræti 54b), the boyhood home of children's writer and Jesuit priest Jón Sveinsson, open daily 2–4:30.

The **Náttúrugripasafnið** (Natural History Museum) displays specimens of all the bird species that nest in Iceland. ⊠ *Hafnarstræti 81, IS-600 Akureyri,* ☎ *462–2983.* 🖼 *IKr100.* ☾ *June and mid-Aug.–mid-Sept., Sun.–Fri. 1–4; July–mid-Aug., Sun.–Fri. 10–5; mid-Sept.–June, Sun. 1–3.*

The **Minjasafnið** (Folk Museum) has a large collection of local relics and works of art, old farm tools, and fishing equipment. ⊠ *Aðalgata 58, IS-600 Akureyri,* ☎ *462–4162.* 🖼 *IKr150.* ☾ *Daily 1:30–5.*

Dating from the 18th century, the beautifully restored **Laxdalshús** (Laxdal House) is the oldest house in Akureyri. A Lutheran priest now resides here. You can explore the grounds and see the interior if staff is present. ⊠ *Hafnarstræti 11, IS-600 Akureyri,* ☎ *462–6680.*

In June and July, make a point of taking an evening drive north from Akureyri along Route 82. The midnight sun creates breathtaking views along the coast of **Eyjafjörður.** Better still, take a cruise on the fjord: a ferry plies to and from the island of **Hrísey,** home of Galloway cattle in the waters of Eyjafjörður, and out to **Grímsey Island,** 40 km (25 mi) offshore and straddling the Arctic Circle. Contact **Nonni Travel** (⊠ Brekkugata 3, IS-600 Akureyri, ☎ 461–1841).

The **Arctic Open Golf Tournament** is held each year at Akureyri—the most northerly 18-hole course in the world—around the longest day of the year (in the midnight sun, needless to say). For details, contact the Akureyri Golf Club (☎ 462–2974) or the Iceland Tourist Bureau (☞ Visitor Information *in* Iceland A to Z, *below*).

To the south of Akureyri is the pyramid-shape rhyolite mountain **Súlur.** Beyond it is **Kerling,** the highest peak in Eyjafjörður.

Dining and Lodging

$$$$ ✕ **Fiðlarinn.** The view is fabulous from this rooftop restaurant and bar overlooking Akureyri Harbor and Eyjafjörður. Danish haute cuisine is featured; try the lobster tails in champagne-cream sauce or roasted reindeer with game sauce and apple salad. ⌧ *Skipagata 14, IS-600 Akureyri,* ☎ 462–7100. AE, DC, MC, V.

$$$ ✕ **Höfðaberg.** Part of the KEA Hotel (☞ *below*), this fine restaurant has modern Scandinavian decor. Savory Icelandic specialties include the steamed halibut in white-wine sauce and the mustard-glazed lamb with Icelandic mountain herbs. ⌧ *Hafnarstræti 87–89, IS-600 Akureyri,* ☎ 462–2200. AE, DC, MC, V.

$$$ ✕▦ **Hótel KEA.** Mauve-and-maroon hues and dark-wood trim characterize this hotel, on a par with many of the capital's hotels. You'll find the Höfðaberg restaurant and popular weekend dancing here. ⌧ *Hafnarstræti 87–89, IS-600 Akureyri,* ☎ 462–2200, ℻ 461–2285. *71 rooms, 1 suite. Restaurant, bar, lobby lounge, cafeteria, meeting rooms. AE, DC, MC, V.*

$$$ ▦ **Hótel Norðurland.** All rooms here have floral prints, Danish modern furniture, and satellite TV. On the ground floor is the separately run Pizza 67 restaurant. ⌧ *Geislagata 7, IS-600 Akureyri,* ☎ 462–2600, ℻ 462–7962. *28 rooms, 18 with bath. Restaurant, bar, minibars. AE, DC, MC, V.*

$ ▦ **Youth Hostel.** There are 32 beds here. ⌧ *Stórholt 1, IS-600 Akureyri,* ☎ 462–3657. *32 beds. No credit cards.*

Outdoor Activities and Sports

GOLF

Enjoy golf at the world's northernmost 18-hole course at Jaðar, on the outskirts of Akureyri. For information on the **Arctic Open Golf Tournament** (☞ *above*), contact the Akureyri Golf Club (☎ 462–2974) or the Iceland Tourist Bureau (☞ Visitor Information *in* Iceland A to Z, *below*). There are also golf courses in **Ólafsfjörður** and **Sauðárkrókur.**

HIKING

Úrval-Útsýn (⌧ Ráðhústorg 3, IS-600 Akureyri, ☎ 462–5000) runs mountain hiking tours from Akureyri. **Nonni Travel** (⌧ Brekkugata 3, IS-600 Akureyri, ☎ 462–7922) provides similar tours. Also contact **Ferðafélag Akureyrar** (Touring Club of Akureyri; ⌧ Strandgata 23, IS-600 Akureyri, ☎ 462–2720).

HORSEBACK RIDING

In Akureyri, contact **Pólarhestar** (⌧ Grýtubakki 11, IS-600 Akureyri, ☎ 463–3179).

SWIMMING

Akureyri has an excellent open-air **pool** (⌧ Þingvallastræti 13, IS-600 Akureyri, ☎ 462–3260).

Shopping

As Iceland's fourth-largest city, Akureyri offers better shopping than most other towns outside Reykjavík. Woolens, ceramics, and other gift items are available at **París** (✉ Hafnarstræti 96, IS-600 Akureyri, ☎ 462–7744). The **Folda** factory shop (✉ Gleráreyrar, IS-600 Akureyri, ☎ 462–1900) offers woolens and sheepskin rugs at discount prices.

OFF THE   **SIGLUFJÖRÐUR –** In the mid-1960s this town was prosperous due to the
BEATEN PATH   area's abundance of herring, the silver of the sea. When the Klondike
era ended with the collapse of the herring stock in 1968, the fleet turned to other fish types and Siglufjörður settled down. Today, however, the herring era has been reborn with the recovery of the herring stock. Demonstrations on the pier show just how little time it takes to dress and salt herring and fill the barrels. The Herring Adventure, held the first weekend in August, turns the harbor into a festival of living history, followed by merrymaking with music and dancing. If you miss the action, there is the Síldarminnjasafn (Herring Years Memorabilia Museum), on Snorragata, with herring exhibits, pictures, and paraphernalia—including wooden barrel lids with various "brandings." Drive 192 km (115 mi) north of Akureyri on Route 82, and then follow Route 76.

Grund

15 km (9 mi) south along Rte. 821 from Akureyri.

Grund is an ancient farmstead, once home to some of the clansmen of the bloody Sturlungar feuds of the 13th century. Don't miss the attractive turn-of-the-century **church,** which, since 1978, has been on the historical registry. This impressive edifice was built in 1905 entirely at the personal expense of Magnú Sigurðsson, a farmer at Grund. It breaks tradition from the east–west orientation of most churches and is instead built on a north–south line. Behind the altar in its north end is a painting of the resurrection, dating from the 19th century.

Saurbær

13 km (8 mi) south on Rte. 821 from Grund.

Here you'll find a church built in the 1850s from wood and turf, typical of Icelandic dwellings through the centuries. Be prepared for, well, sheepish looks from locals if you ask what the name Saurbær means.

En Route   From the Saurbær pullout, turn left back onto Route 821. After about 1½ km (1 mi), take a right over the Eyjafjarðará River to Route 829, which runs north parallel to Route 821. Within a few hundred yards you'll reach the historic **Möðruvellir farm.** The church at Möðruvellir has an English alabaster altarpiece dating from the 15th century. From here it is 25 km (16 mi) north to the Ring Road.

If you drive east from Akureyri on the Ring Road, passing farms left and right, you'll soon cross the **Vaðlaheiði** (Marsh Heath). You'll then enter the **Fnjóskadalur** (Tree-Stump Valley), formed by glaciers only a few thousand years ago. Go several hundred feet past Route 833, which leads south into the western part of the valley, and turn right onto the next road to the **Vaglaskógur** (Log Forest), one of the largest forests in this relatively treeless country. Its tallest birches reach some 40 ft.

Goðafoss

From the Saurbær pullout, turn left back onto Rte. 821 and travel 28 km (17 mi) north to the Ring Road. Proceed east about 22 km (13 mi). Directly from Akureyri, Goðafoss is about 50 km (30 mi) east.

The name Goðafoss—Waterfall of the Gods—derives from a historic event in AD 1000 when Þorgeir Ljósvetningagoði, ordered by the Icelandic Parliament to choose between paganism and Christianity, threw his pagan icons into the waterfall. Just before you reach Goðafoss, in the Skjálfandi River, you'll pass the **Ljósavatn church** where Þorgeir lived a millennium ago. Although the farm is long gone, you can visit the church, which houses, among other relics, some interesting runic stones newly unearthed. There are plans for a new church and memorial to be built here before the year 2000, the millennial anniversary of Iceland's conversion to Christianity.

Mývatn

About 100 km (62 mi) along the Ring Road east of Akureyri.

Spend at least a day exploring this superbly natural area influenced by active geology; a recent fissure eruption occurred here in 1984. The area's "false craters" were formed when hot lava of ancient eruptions ran over marshland, causing steam jets to spout up, forming small cones. **Lake Mývatn** is an aqueous gem amid mountains and lava fields. Fed by cold springs in the lake bottom and warm springs in the northeastern corner, the shallow lake—42 square km (15 square mi) in area yet only 3 to 13 ft deep—teems with fish, birds, and insects, including the swarming midges for which the lake is named.

Waterfowl migrate long distances to breed at Mývatn, where the duck population numbers up to 150,000 in summer. Indeed, the lake has Europe's greatest variety of nesting ducks, including some—the harlequin duck and barrow's goldeneye—found nowhere else in Europe. Dozens of other kinds of waders, upland birds, and birds of prey also nest here. Be sure to stay on established trails and pathways, as nests can be anywhere. Summer visitors should bring head nets to protect against the huge midge swarms essential in the bird food chain.

Turning off the Ring Road at Route 848, you'll pass **Skútustaðir,** a village on the lake's southern shore. Proceed along the eastern shore to the 1,300-ft-high **Hverfjall** ash cone, several hundred feet from the road. Many paths lead to the top. The outer walls of this volcanic crater are steep, but the ascent is easy. The walk around the top of the crater is about 4,300 ft. Southwest of Hverfjall is the **Dimmuborgir** (Dark Castles) lava field, a labyrinth of tall formations where you can choose between short and longer signposted routes through the eerie landscape. Among its mysterious arches, gates, and caves, the best-known is the **Kirkja** (Church), resembling a Gothic chapel (it's marked by a sign, lest you miss it). Don't wander off the paths, as Dimmuborgir is a highly sensitive environment.

Proceeding a few kilometers south from Mývatn on the Ring Road, you'll pass a factory that processes diatomite—tiny skeletons of algae—sucked from the bottom of the lake, where they have been deposited through the centuries. Diatomite is used in filters and is an important local export. The diatomite factory at Mývatn is highly controversial; conservationists fear that it may endanger the ecosystem of the lake, yet it provides welcome employment for some of the local population. Research is now under way, and the plant could be closed down within a few years.

Dining and Lodging

$$$ ✕🏨 **Hotel Reynihlíð.** This popular hotel has pastel-colored rooms and a helpful general information service for tourists. The restaurant serves entrées such as fresh trout from the lake, and rhubarb pie for dessert. 🖂 *Reykjahlíð, IS 660, Mývatnssveit,* ☎ *464–4170,* FAX *464–4371. 41 rooms. Restaurant, bar, horseback riding, bicycles. AE, DC, MC, V.*

$$ ⌂ **Hotel Reykjahlíð.** This small, family-run hotel has a prime lakeside location with great views. ✉ *Reykjahlíð, IS-660 Mývatnssveit,* ☎ *464–4142,* FAX *464–4336. 9 rooms. AE, MC, V.*

$ ⌂ **Youth Hostel.** This hostel near Mývatn has 50 beds. ✉ *Bárðardalur, IS-645 Fosshóll,* ☎ *464–3108,* FAX *464–3318. 50 beds. No credit cards.*

Outdoor Activities and Sports

BIKING

The **Hótel Reynihlíð** (✉ IS-660 Mývatnssveit, ☎ 464–4170) in Mývatn rents bicycles for exploring the area around the lake.

BOATING

At Mývatn, **Eldá Travel** (✉ Reykjahlíð, IS-660, Mývatnssveit, ☎ 464–4220) rents boats on Lake Mývatn.

FISHING

Angling permits can be obtained from **Hotel Reynihlíð** (✉ IS-660 Mývatnssveit, ☎ 464–4170). For fly fishing June–August on the famous Laxá River, contact **Eldá Travel** (✉ Reykjahlíð, IS-660 Mývatnssveit, ☎ 464–4220).

HORSEBACK RIDING

The **Hotel Reynihlíð** (✉ IS-660 Myývatnssveit, ☎ 464–4170) in Mývatn offers pony treks around the lake. Near Hrútafjörður, **Arinbjörn Jóhannsson** (☎ 451–2938) in Brekkulækur also organizes horseback rides.

En Route   In the **Námaskarð Mountain Ridge,** on the eastern side of the Ring Road, are bubbling mud and purple sulfur, boiling like a witch's cauldron in the strange red and yellow valleys. Hike around this fascinating area, but remember to step carefully. Though the sulfurous vapors may smell like rotten eggs, the brimstone fumes are generally harmless.

Húsavík

From Akureyri, drive east 46 km (29 mi) to the north junction of Rte. 85 and take it 45 km (28 mi) north to Húsavík. Or it's a straight shot 46 km (29 mi) from Lake Mývatn, first on Rte. 87 as it branches northwest off the Ring Road, then 8 km (5 mi) north on Rte. 85

Hússavík is a charming port on the north coast with a bustling harbor and a timber church dating from 1907. Handy to a nearby winter ski area, it is also a good base for summer hiking. Whale watchers have had amazing success on tours aboard a restored oaken boat (☞ Guided Tours *in* the North A to Z, *below*).

Dining and Lodging

$$$ ✕⌂ **Hotel Húsavík.** Popular with skiers, this solid hotel has a good restaurant serving seafood, including delicious smoked salmon pâté and several halibut and trout entrées. ✉ *Ketilsbraut 22, IS-640 Húsavík,* ☎ *464–1220,* FAX *464–2161. 34 rooms. Restaurant, bar, cafeteria. AE, DC, MC, V.*

En Route   From Húsavik take Route 85 north and east for 61 km (38 mi) first, along the coast to Tjörnes, ending up inland at the lush nature reserve of Ásbyrgi.

Ásbyrgi

The forest of Ásbyrgi, or Shelter of the Gods, is surrounded by steep cliffs on all sides except the north, making it a peaceful shelter from the wind. Legend says this horseshoe-shape canyon was formed by the giant hoof of Sleipnir, the eight-legged horse of Óðinn.

Contiguous with Ásbyrgi is the wild and magnificent **Jökulsárgljúfur National Park,** the rugged canyon of the glacial Jökulsá River. At the southernmost point of the park, on Route 864, see Europe's most powerful waterfall, **Dettifoss,** where 212 tons of water cascade each second over a 145-ft drop. Farther inland at **Kverkfjöll,** hot springs rise at the edge of the **Vatnajökull,** creating spectacular ice caves. Tours operate from Húsavík (☞ Guided Tours *in* the North A to Z, *below*).

The North A to Z

Arriving and Departing

BY BUS

BSÍ Travel (☎ 552–2300) runs daily bus service from Reykjavík to the north. It's 4½ hours to Blönduós and 6½ hours to Akureyri. Bus service from Akureyri takes less than 1½ hours to Húsavík and two hours to Mývatn.

The **Akureyri Bus Company** (✉ Gránufélagsgata 4, IS-600 Akureyri, ☎ 462–3510; at bus terminal, ☎ 462–4442) operates scheduled trips around the region, including a tour by bus and ferry to Hrísey Island and to Grímsey Island on the Arctic Circle.

BY CAR

It's a 432-km (268-mi) drive from Reykjavík to Akureyri along the Ring Road (Rte. 1), a full day of driving. Branch off on Route 75 to Sauðárkrókur, or on Route 85 to Húsavík.

BY PLANE

Air Iceland (Flugfélag Íslands, Akureyri ☎ 460–7000, Reykjavík 570–3030) sends flights from Reykjavík to Akureyri, Sauðárkrókur, and Húsavík. The flight to Akureyri takes about an hour. Air Iceland also flies from Akureyri to Grímsey, Húsavík, Kópasker, Ólafsfjörður, Raufarhöfn, Siglufjörður, Þórshöfn, and Vopnafjörður. The **Mýflug** air charter company (☎ 464–4107, FAX 464–4341) flies daily June–August direct from Reykjavík to Mývatn. In Reykjavík, this service is handled by **Íslandsflug** (☎ 561–6060).

Contacts and Resources

EMERGENCIES

Police: Akureyri (☎ 462–3222). Dial ☎ 112 for emergency assistance anywhere in Iceland.

GUIDED TOURS

Sightseeing Tours: The **Iceland Tourist Bureau** (☎ 461–1434) operates a 12-hour day trip from Reykjavík to Akureyri and **Lake Mývatn;** you take a plane to Akureyri and then a bus to Mývatn. The tour departs daily June through mid-September. **Úrval-Útsýn** (✉ Ráðhústorg 3, IS-600 Akureyri, ☎ 462–5000) runs tours from Akureyri to Mývatn, historic sites, and the islands off the north coast. **Nonni Travel** (✉ Brekkugata 3, IS-600 Akureyri, ☎ 461–1841, FAX 461–1843) provides the same service.

Whale-Watching Tours: Norður Sigling (✉ Laugarbrekka 21, IS-640 Húsavík, ☎ 464–1741) conducts whale-watching tours on a classic oak ship. Tours of **Dettifoss, Kverkfjöll,** and **Vatnajökull** are operated from Húsavík; contact **BSH** (✉ Garðabraut 7, Box 115, Húsavík, ☎ 464–2200, FAX 464–2201).

VISITOR INFORMATION

Akureyri (✉ Coach Terminal, Hafnarstræti 82, IS-600 Akureyri, ☎ 462–7733). **Húsavík** (Húsavík Travel, ✉ Stórigarður 7, IS-640 Húsavík, ☎ 464–2100).

THE EAST

In 1974, when the final bridge across the treacherous glacial rivers and shifting sands south of the Vatnajökull was completed, the eastern side of the island finally became accessible from Reykjavík. The journey by car is still long, but as you approach the area from the south you can watch ice floes gliding toward the sea while great predatory skuas swoop across black volcanic beaches.

The east coast has a number of busy fishing towns and villages, each seemingly with its own private fjord. Farming thrives in the major valleys, which enjoy almost continental summers. The Ring Road ties the inland hub Egilsstaðir to the southeastern coastal villages, and secondary roads make outlying communities accessible.

Egilsstaðir

273 km (164 mi) southeast of Akureyri, 700 km (420 mi) northeast of Reykjavík.

This major eastern commercial hub straddles the Ring Road and lies at the northeastern end of the long, narrow **Lake Lögurinn,** the legendary home to a wormlike serpent that guards a treasure chest. New in 1996, the museum **Minjasafn Austurlands** (East Iceland Heritage Museum, ⊠ Laufskógum 1, IS-700, ☎ 471–1412) displays fascinating artifacts found in the area. The most dramatic is a Viking chieftain's grave site and its lavish relics, believed to be nearly 1,000 years old.

★ One of Iceland's most accessible paradises, **Hallormsstaður Forestry Reserve** contains the country's largest forest; more than 40 varieties of trees grow here, mostly aspen, spruce, birch, and larch. It's an easy 25-km (15-mi) drive from town along the lake's southern shore, first on the Ring Road and then onto Route 931. The Atlavík campground is on the lake south of Hallormsstaðaskógur.

In the highlands west of Lögurinn you may be able to spot Icelandic reindeer. Though not indigenous to the island (they were originally brought from Norway in the 18th century), the reindeer have thrived to the point that they have damaged tree saplings and farm growth, so controlled hunting is permitted. Game managers allow the sale of licenses to hunt some 600 animals annually.

OFF THE   **EIÐAR –** Open-air drama and music performances are scheduled weekly
BEATEN PATH   in summer here, just north of Egilsstaðir on the Borgarfjörður Road. Performances are in Icelandic, but English summaries are available, and you don't have to understand the language to learn folk dances. Contact Philip Vogler (⊠ Dalskógar 12, IS-700 Egilsstaðir, ☎ 471–1673) for information.

Lodging

$$ 🏨 **Foss Hotel Hallormsstaður.** New in 1998, this Foss chain hotel is set in the harmony of one of Iceland's largest forests. It's open all year; in summer less-expensive rooms without bath or TV are available. ⊠ IS-707 Hallormsstaður, ☎ 562–3350, ℻ 471–2197. *36 rooms, 17 rooms without bath (summer only). Restaurant. AE, MC, V.*

$$ 🏨 **Hótel Edda Egilsstaðir.** This brand-new hotel is one in the growing number of nice year-round Edda hotels. In a valley with views of the nearby countryside, it's convenient to Egilsstaðir's shopping center and pool. ⊠ IS-701 Egilsstaðir. *Contact tourist board for info:* ☎ 562–3300, ℻ 562–5895. *36 rooms. Restaurant, bar, meeting rooms. AE, MC, V.*

$ 🏠 **Youth Hostel.** This hostel, open May through September, has 23 beds. ✉ *Tunguhreppur, IS-701 Egilsstaðir,* ☎ *471–3010,* FAX *471–3009. 23 beds. No credit cards. Closed Oct.–Apr.*

Outdoor Activities and Sports

BIKING

Bikes can be rented at the **campsite** (☎ 471–2320) in Egilsstaðir.

SWIMMING

There is a swimming **pool** (☎ 471–1467) in Egilsstaðir.

Seyðisfjörður

25 km (16 mi) east of Egilsstaðir.

When visiting this quaint seaside village today—with its Norwegian-style wooded houses and 18th-century buildings—you may find it hard to imagine the tall sailing frigates of yesteryear crowding the fjord. Seyðisfjörður was, in the 19th century, one of Iceland's major trade ports. The ships plying the fjord nowadays include the *Norröna* ferry, in summer dispatching tourists and their vehicles from Europe.

Dining and Lodging

$$ ✕🏠 **Hótel Snæfell.** Red carpets and beige furnishings decorate this old, wooden house turned hotel. The restaurant, with glass walls overlooking the dramatic fjord, serves up tasty fare; special entrées include tindabikkja and, for dessert, chocolate cake. ✉ *Austurvegur 3, IS-710 Seyðisfjörður,* ☎ *472–1460,* FAX *472–1570. 9 rooms. Restaurant, bar, horseback riding, fishing. AE, MC, V.*

$ 🏠 **Youth Hostel.** There are 28 beds here. ✉ *Ránargata 9, IS-710 Seyðisfjörður,* ☎ *472–1410,* FAX *472–1486. 28 beds. No credit cards.*

Bakkagerði

71 km (44 mi) northeast of Egilsstaðir; take Rte. 94.

Bakkagerði is by Borgarfjörður (not to be confused with its larger namesake in the west). The Borgarfjörður Road, though bumpy, is entirely safe, but don't be in a hurry. Savor the swooping descent from the Vatnsskarð mountain pass and the spectacular coast road along Njarðvíkurskriður. In a land of stunning mountain scenery, Borgarfjörður (east) is a natural masterpiece, where the changing tones in the landscape have to be seen to be believed. The painter Jóhannes Kjarval lived here, and as can be seen in his paintings, the countryside made a deep impression on him.

Lodging

$ 🏠 **Youth Hostel.** Open May through September, this hostel has 17 beds. ✉ *Hreppsskrifstofan, IS-685 Bakkafjörður,* ☎ *473–1686,* FAX *473–1668. 17 beds. No credit cards. Closed Oct.–Apr.*

Neskaupstaður

71 km (43 mi) east of Egilsstaðir, driving south along Rte. 92, curving east through Eskifjörður; travel north over Iceland's highest pass, completing a U-shape path on Rte. 92.

In a tranquil position under rugged mountainsides, the east coast's largest town thrived during the '60s herring boom. The settlement started as a trading center in 1882; fishing and minor industrial concerns are the mainstays today. The natural history museum, **Náttúrugripasafnið í Neskaupstað,** is the main attraction.

Lodging

$$ ☷ **Hótel Egilsbúð.** One of the town's major accommodations also provides space for those with sleeping bags. In winter, only five rooms are available. ✉ *Egilsbraut 1, IS-740 Neskaupstaðir,* ☎ *477–1321,* ⓕ *477–1322. 21 rooms. AE, MC, V.*

Outdoor Activities and Sports

FISHING

Angling permits for the Norðfjarðurá are available at **Tröllanaust** (✉ Melgata 11, IS-740 Neskaupstaðir, ☎ 477–1444).

SEA CRUISES

Cruises on the Norðfjörður with sea angling as an option are available by calling ☎ 477–1321 or 853–1718.

SWIMMING

The Neskaupstaður **pool** (✉ Miðstræti 15, IS-740 Neskaupstaðir, ☎ 477–1243) is open to the public.

Eskifjörður

48 km (30 mi) southeast of Egilsstaðir; either backtrack 23 km (14 mi) from Neskaustaður on Rte. 92 over the breathtaking 2,300-ft pass at Oddskarð, or go 48 km (29 mi) from Egilsstaðir.

This charming fishing village has a fish-freezing plant with murals by Iceland's Catalan artist Baltazar. Eskifjörður is on the beautiful Hólmanes Cape, noted for a wide variety of flora and bird life; its southern part is now a protected area. The town's stunning landmark mountain—Hólmatindur at 230 ft—unfortunately shades the town from the sun from late September to April. If you have time, you may want to check out the East Iceland Maritime Museum.

Lodging

$ ☷ **Hotel Askja.** This cozy, old-fashioned year-round hotel offers rooms with a shared bathroom. ✉ *Hólvegur 4, IS-735 Eskifjörður,* ☎ *476–1261. 7 rooms. Restaurant, bar. AE, MC, V.*

$ ☷ **Hótel Buðareyri.** The accommodations at this hotel are simple, including shared bath. ✉ *IS-730 Reyðarfjörður,* ☎ *474–1378. 6 rooms without bath. Restaurant, bar. AE, MC, V.*

$ ☷ **Youth Hostel.** There are 25 beds here. ✉ *Búðargata 4, IS-730 Reyðarfjörður,* ☎ *474–1447,* ⓕ *474–1454. 25 beds. No credit cards.*

Outdoor Activities and Sports

FISHING

Angling permits for the river Eskifjarðará are available by calling the town council at ☎ 476–1170.

SWIMMING

You can swim in Eskifjörður's local **pool** (✉ Lambeyrarbraut 14, IS-735 Eskifjörður, ☎ 476–1238).

En Route   If you drive south along Route 93 from Eskifjörður, you'll skirt **Reyðarfjörður,** the largest of the eastern fjords, 30 km (18 mi) long and 7 km (4½ mi) wide. The sheltered harbor made the namesake town an important commerce center. This was true even more so after Reyðarfjörður was linked to the Fagridalur Valley road in the early 1900s. Iceland's only **museum of World War II memorabilia** (☎ 474–1245) is found here, where some troops were stationed during the war. It's open afternoons only, June through August.

Breiðdalsvík

83 km (50 mi) south of Egilsstaðir along the Ring Road or, more circuitously, about 74 km (45 mi) along Rte. 96 from Reyðarfjörður.

Trade in this tiny village of a few hundred kindred souls dates from 1883. Hugging the shore on its own small inlet, the hamlet is gradually growing thanks to the development of a harbor deep enough for most ships.

Dining and Lodging

$ ✕🍴 **Hótel Bláfell.** This small hotel has a rustic yet cozy-looking exterior; the interior is bright, and there's an award-winning restaurant with a menu emphasizing seafood and lamb. In summer, the hotel offers chalets in the nearby countryside. Fishing permits are available for the area. ✉ *Sólvellir 14, IS-760 Breiðdalsvík,* ☎ *475-6770,* FAX *475-6668. 15 rooms, 7 with bath. Restaurant, bar. AE, MC, V.*

Djúpivogur

144 km (87 mi) south of Egilsstaðir on the Ring Road.

A fishing village has existed on this site since about 1600, and some of the oldest buildings in town date from the days of Danish merchant control from 1788 to 1920. The nearby basaltic **Búlandstindur** mountain, rising to 6,130 ft, is legendary as a force of mystical energy, perhaps because of its pyramidal shape.

Dining and Lodging

$ ✕🍴 **Hótel Framtíð.** This small, wood-frame hotel is right by the harbor. In the dining room, home-style food is served in a friendly atmosphere. Try the wolffish cooked in honey with apple and curry, pan-fried redfish with mushrooms and brandy sauce, or roast puffin from nearby Papey Island. For dessert there's homemade ice cream with fruit and caramel sauce. Rooms have shared bath. There is camping with a laundry facility available nearby. ✉ *Vogalandi 4, IS-765 Djúpivogur,* ☎ *478-8887,* FAX *478-8187. 22 rooms without bath. Restaurant, bar, sauna, bicycles. AE, MC, V.*

$ 🏠 **Youth Hostel.** Open May through September, this hostel has 20 beds. ✉ *Berunes, Berufjörður, IS-765 Djúpivogur,* ☎ *478-8988,* FAX *478-8988. 20 beds. No credit cards. Closed Oct.–Apr.*

En Route To continue along the Ring Road, drive south from Egilsstaðir 150 km (93 mi) to the rugged stretch of coast indented by the inlets of **Álftafjörður** (Swan Fjord) and **Hamarsfjörður.** Surrounded by majestic mountains, these shallow waters host myriad swans, ducks, and other birds that migrate here from Europe in the spring and summer.

Höfn

103 km (62 mi) south of Djúpivogur on the Ring Road.

Höfn is slowly being closed off from the ocean by silt washed down by glacial rivers into the fjord. Spread out on a low-lying headland at the mouth of the fjord, Höfn offers a fine view of the awesome **Vatnajökull.** This monstrous glacier not only is Iceland's largest but is equal in size to all the glaciers on the European mainland put together. From Höfn you can arrange tours of the glacier.

OFF THE BEATEN PATH **JÖKULSÁRLÓN –** At the Glacial River Lagoon, about 50 km (31 mi) west of Höfn, you can see large chunks of the glacier tumble and float around in a spectacular ice show. Boat trips on the lagoon are operated throughout the summer; for details call Fjölnir Torfason (☎ 478–1065). Light meals and refreshments are available at a small coffeehouse at the lagoon. On the **Breiðamerkur sands** west of the lagoon is the largest North Atlantic colony of skua, large predatory seabirds that unhesitatingly dive bomb intruders in the nesting season.

Dining and Lodging

$$$ ✕🏠 **Hótel Höfn.** This modern hotel is clean and comfortable. There's a separate annex, Ásgarður, with an additional 30 rooms, each with bath. You can grab a bite at the fast-food-style restaurant, or opt for the more formal restaurant for specialties such as lobster and reindeer and the nightly seafood buffet. Doubles and singles are available. ⊠ *Víkurbraut IS-780, Höfn, Hornafjörður,* ☎ *478–1240,* ℻ *478–1996. 40 rooms, 8 without bath. 2 restaurants, bar. AE, MC, V.*

$ 🏠 **Youth Hostel.** This hostel, open May through September, has 27 beds. ⊠ *Nýibær, Hafnarbraut 8, IS-780 Höfn,* ☎ *478–1736. 27 beds. No credit cards. Closed Oct.–Apr.*

$ 🏠 **Youth Hostel.** Open May through September, this hostel near Höfn has 45 beds. ⊠ *Stafafell, Lón, IS-781 Höfn,* ☎ *478–1717,* ℻ *478–1785. 45 beds. No credit cards. Closed Oct.–Apr.*

Outdoor Activities and Sports

SWIMMING

The Höfn swimming **pool** (⊠ Hafnarbraut, IS-780 Hornafjörður, ☎ 478–1157) is open to the public.

WHALE-WATCHING

Whale-watching trips are available from Höfn by calling the **campsite** (☎ 478–1701).

The East A to Z

Arriving and Departing

BY BOAT

The **Norröna** car ferry from Norway or Denmark via the Faroe Islands arrives in Seyðisfjörður. Contact **Norröna Travel** (⊠ Laugavegur 3, IS-101 Reykjavík, ☎ 562–6362, ℻ 552–9450) or **Austfar** (⊠ IS-710 Seyðisfjörður, ☎ 472–1111, ℻ 472–1105).

BY BUS

The east is so far from Reykjavík that bus travel is recommended only if you are making the entire Ring Road circuit. From Akureyri the six-hour trip to Egilsstaðir runs daily in summer, three times a week the rest of the year. From Egilsstaðir there's frequent service around the region; it takes about five hours to get to Höfn. Call **Austurleið Coaches** (☎ 577–1717) for information.

BY CAR

The region is accessible by car on the Ring Road (Highway 1). The drive from Reykjavík, along the south coast, to Egilsstaðir is about 700 km (434 mi), from Akureyri 273 km (170 mi).

BY PLANE

Air Iceland (Flugfélag Íslands, Egilsstaðir ☎ 471–1210, Reykjavík, ☎ 570–3030) operates scheduled flights from Reykjavík to Egilsstaðir. **East-air** (☎ 471–1122) provides the same service. From there, connections are to Bakkafjörður, Borgarfjörður, Breiðdalsvík, Fáskrúðsfjörður, Hornafjörður, Norðfjörður, and Vopnafjörður. **Íslandsflug** (☎ 561–6060) flies to Neskaupstaður and Egilsstaðir.

Contacts and Resources

EMERGENCIES

Police: Egilsstaðir (☎ 471–1223). **Eskifjörður** (☎ 476–1106). **Breiðdalsvik** (☎ 475–1280). **Bakkageröi** (☎ 473–1400). **Neskaupstaður** (☎ 477–1332). **Seyðisfjörður** (☎ 472–1334). **Djúpivogur** (☎ 475–1280). **Höfn** (☎ 478–1282). Also, you can dial ☎ 112 for emergency assistance anywhere in Iceland.

GUIDED TOURS

Boat Tours: The **Iceland Tourist Bureau** (☞ Visitor Information *in* Iceland A to Z, *below*) operates a day trip from Reykjavík to **Höfn** by plane, with a snowmobile tour of the Vatnajökull and a boat tour on the Jökulsárlón Glacier Lagoon. The tour runs daily mid-June–August. **Fjarðaferðir** of Neskaupstaður (☎ 477–1321, FAX 477–1322) offers sea trips of **Norðfjörður** and neighboring Mjóifjörður.

Glacier Tours: Glacier tours of **Vatnajökull** are operated from many different locations: from Eskifjörður by **Tanni** (☎ 476–1399, FAX 476–1599) and from Höfn by **Jöklaferðir** (☎ 478–1000, FAX 478–1901). Also see Nøran Jökuls/Tanni Travel *and* Glacier Tours, *below.*

Sightseeing Tours: Sightseeing cruises of the fjords (with or without fishing along the way) operate from various coastal villages. **Nøran Jökuls/Tanni Travel** (☎ 471–1673 or 471–1399, FAX 872–1473), based in Egilsstaðir, specializes in great day trips at reasonable prices, including an English-speaking guide or driver-guide. They cover **waterfalls, forests, historic sites,** and majestic **Snæfellsnes.** Talk to Philip, a transplanted Texan who is tri-lingual.

Snowmobiling Tours: Glacier Tours (✉ Box 66, IS-780 Hornafjörður, ☎ 478–1000, FAX 478–1901) offers a 9-hour bus tour from **Höfn** in Hornafjörður; the tour includes a snowmobile or Sno-Cat ride and a visit to a glacier lagoon. The trip costs IKr9,200 per person or IKr23,900 as a day trip with flight from Reykjavík.

Whale-Watching Tours: All day whale-watching trips from **Höfn** (☎ 478–1701, FAX 478–1901)—including hot lunch, morning and afternoon coffee, and sea angling—are available for groups of 15 or more at IKr10,000 per person.

VISITOR INFORMATION

Egilsstaðir (Tourist Information Office is at the campsite, ✉ IS-700 Egilsstaðir, ☎ 471–2320). **Seyðisfjörður** (Austfar Travel Agency, ✉ Fjarðargata 8, IS-710 Seyðisfjörður, ☎ 472–1111). **Höfn** (Tourist Information Center is at the campsite, ✉ IS-780 Höfn, ☎ 478–1701).

THE SOUTH

The power of volcanoes is all too evident on this final leg of the Ring Road tour. At Kirkjubæjarklaustur you can still see scars of the great Laki eruption of 1783. At Ström you can visit excavated ruins of a farmstead buried in 1104 by the eruption of Mt. Hekla, known throughout medieval Europe as the abode of the damned—and still mightily active. Off the coast, the Vestmannæyjar (Westman Islands) are still being melded by volcanic activity, and a 1973 eruption almost wiped out all habitation. Other natural wonders include Skaftafell National Park and Þórsmörk (Thor's Wood), a popular nature reserve.

Following-up on a fiery 1991 eruption, Hekla exploded in fierce glory again in 1996, this time under Vatnajökull. Clues before the eruption gave the media and geologists time to observe this rare type of eruption. A gigantic hole was melted through several hundred feet of the glacier; as a result powerful flooding destroyed a minor bridge and took out many sections of the long bridge over the river Skeiðará. This temporary disconnection of the Ring Road has been mended and the aftermath of the flood is a spectacular plain decorated with colossal, ever-changing ice sculptures. They resemble giant, rough diamonds when the sun shines through them.

Skaftafell National Park

50 km (31 mi) west of Jökulsárlón.

Bordering on Vatnajökull is Skaftafell National Park, the largest of Iceland's three national reserves. Glaciers branching off Vatnajökull shelter Skaftafell from winds, creating a verdant oasis. In the park, you can walk for days on beautiful trails through a rare combination of green forest, clear water, waterfalls, sands, mountains, and glaciers. Farther up is the highest mountain in Iceland, **Hvannadalshnúkur,** reaching 6,950 ft. The famous **Svartifoss** (Black Falls) tumbles over a cliff whose sides resemble the pipes of a great organ. Do not miss **Sel,** a restored gabled farmhouse high up on the slope. Guided walks in the national park are organized daily.

Lodging

$ ☷ **Hótel Skaftafell.** Few hotels in Iceland can match this one's setting—near breathtaking Skaftafell National Park. The Saturday buffet dinner in summer is a bargain feast at the restaurant. A travel shop, gas station, and campsite are also on the property. There are rooms for sleeping bags with shared bath, but kitchen facilities are a plus. ⊠ *Skaftafell, IS-785 Fagurhólsmýri,* ☎ *478–1945,* FAX *478–1846. 33 rooms. Restaurant. AE, MC, V.*

Outdoor Activities and Sports

HAY RIDES AND BIRD-WATCHING

For a more sedate adventure, you can enjoy a hay wagon ride across a tidal flat to nearby Ingólfshöfði for bird-watching (⊠ Hofsnes, IS-785 Fagurhólsmýri, ☎ 478–1682).

MOUNTAIN CLIMBING

Öræfaferðir (⊠ 785 Fafurhólsmýri, Hofsnes-Öræfi, IS-785 Fagurhólsmýri, ☎ 478–1682), a father-son outfit, puts together tours ranging from introductory ice climbing to assaults on the summit of Iceland's highest mountain to bird-watching.

SIGHTSEEING FLIGHTS

Jórvik Aviation (⊠ Box 5308, IS-125 Reykjavík, ☎ 562–5101) runs spectacular sightseeing flights that bring you face to face with the majesty of the Skaftafell National Park; they leave from Reykjavík or the southern airfield near the turnoff to the national park.

Kirkjubæjarklaustur

272 km (163 mi) east of Reykjavík along the Ring Road.

Aptly named Kirkjubæjarklaustur—or church farmstead cloister—was once the site of a medieval convent. Two waterfalls and the three-day August chamber music festival are among local attractions; contact the Community Center (☞ Visitor Information *in* the South A to Z, *below*). North of here is the **Laki Volcano,** with more than 100 craters dotting the landscape. The great lava field was created by this volcano in a single eruption in 1783–84. The worst in Iceland's history, it wiped out about 70% of the country's livestock and a fifth of the population. Jón Steingrímsson, then the priest at Kirkjubæjarklaustur, is said to have stopped the advance of the lava by prayer. To get to Laki, take the high-

We'll give you a $20 tip for driving.

See the real Europe with Hertz.

It's time to see Europe from a new perspective. From behind the wheel of a Hertz car. And we'd like to save you $20 on your prepaid Affordable Europe Weekly Rental. Our low rates are guaranteed in U.S. dollars and English is spoken at all of our European locations. Computerized driving directions are available at many locations, and Free Unlimited Mileage and 24-Hour Emergency Roadside Assistance are standard in our European packages. For complete details call 1-800-654-3001. Mention PC #95384 So, discover Europe with Hertz.

Offer is valid at participating airport locations in Europe from Jan.1 – Dec.15,1998, on Economy through Full size cars. Reservations must be made at least 8 hours prior to departure. $20 will be deducted at time of booking. Standard rental qualifications, significant restrictions and blackout periods apply

Hertz europe

Pick up the phone.

Pick up the miles.

MCI Calling Card

415 555 1234 2244
J.D. SMITH

WORLDPHONE

Use your MCI Card® to make an international call from virtually anywhere in the world and earn frequent flyer miles on one of seven major airlines.

Enroll in an MCI Airline Partner Program today. In the U.S., call **1-800-FLY-FREE.** Overseas, call MCI collect at **1-916-567-5151.**

1. To use your MCI Card, just dial the WorldPhone access number of the country you're calling from. (For a complete listing of codes, visit www.mci.com.)
2. Dial or give the operator your MCI Card number.
3. Dial or give the number you're calling.

# Austria (CC) ♦	022-903-012		# Netherlands (CC) ♦	0800-022-91-22
# Belarus (CC)			# Norway (CC) ♦	800-19912
From Brest, Vitebsk, Grodno, Minsk	8-800-103		# Poland (CC) ÷	00-800-111-21-22
From Gomel and Mogilev regions	8-10-800-103		# Portugal (CC) ÷	05-017-1234
# Belgium (CC) ♦	0800-10012		Romania (CC) ÷	01-800-1800
# Bulgaria	00800-0001		# Russia (CC) ÷ ♦	
# Croatia (CC) ★	99-385-0112		To call using ROSTELCOM ■	747-3322
# Czech Republic (CC) ♦	00-42-000112		For a Russian-speaking operator	747-3320
# Denmark (CC) ♦	8001-0022		To call using SOVINTEL ■	960-2222
# Finland (CC) ♦	08001-102-80		# San Marino (CC) ♦	172-1022
# France (CC) ♦	0-800-99-0019		# Slovak Republic (CC)	00-421-00112
# Germany (CC)	0130-0012		# Slovenia	080-8808
# Greece (CC) ♦	00-800-1211		# Spain (CC)	900-99-0014
# Hungary (CC) ♦	00▼800-01411		# Sweden (CC) ♦	020-795-922
# Iceland (CC) ♦	800-9002		# Switzerland (CC) ♦	0800-89-0222
# Ireland (CC)	1-800-55-1001		# Turkey (CC) ♦	00-8001-1177
# Italy (CC) ♦	172-1022		# Ukraine (CC) ÷	8▼10-013
# Kazakhstan (CC)	8-800-131-4321		# United Kingdom (CC)	
# Liechtenstein (CC) ♦	0800-89-0222		To call using BT ■	0800-89-0222
# Luxembourg	0800-0112		To call using MERCURY ■	0500-89-0222
# Monaco (CC) ♦	800-90-019		# Vatican City (CC)	172-1022

Is this a great time, or what? :-)

land road leading north. About 30 km (19 mi) east of Kirkjubæjarklaustur on the Ring Road, don't miss the little chapel at **Núpsstaður**, one of a handful of extant turf churches. This well-preserved building has remained almost unchanged since the 17th century.

Lodging

$ ⛉ **Edda Hotel.** One of the few year-round Edda Hotels, this facility is in a modern building. Sleeping-bag accommodations are available. ✉ *IS-880 Kirkjubæjarklaustur*, ☎ 487–4799, 𝔉𝔄𝔛 *487–1996. 73 rooms, 57 with shower. Restaurant, pool. AE, MC, V.*

Outdoor Activities and Sports

BOATING

Boats can be rented for a cruise on Lake Hæðargarðsvatn near Kirkjubæjarklaustur; call 487–4723.

HIKING

Hannes Jónsson (✉ Hvoll, IS-880 Kirkjubæjarklaustur, ☎ 487–4785 or 853–4133), a driver-guide, knows Núpsstaðarskógur like the back of his hand, and takes visitors on the slopes of the Eystrafjall Mountain. Highlighting the nine-hour trip are large twin falls: the clear Núpsárfoss and the glacially milky Hvítárfoss. A good bit of hiking is well rewarded; pack a good lunch and wear hiking shoes.

En Route   Travel west from Kirkjubæjarklaustur 25 km (15 mi) on Route 1, turn right onto Route 208, and continue for 20 km (12 mi) on the mountain road Route F22 to **Eldgjá**, a 32-km-long (20-mi-long) volcanic rift. Historic records suggest that it erupted in AD 934 with a ferocity similar to that of the Laki eruption.

Vík

80 km (48 mi) west of Kirkjubæjarklaustur.

Proceeding west along the Ring Road from Kirkjubæjarklaustur, you'll cross the Mýrdalssandur Desert and arrive at the coastal village of Vík, with its vast population of Arctic terns. Twelve kilometers (7 miles) past Vík, turn left toward the ocean to reach the southernmost point of the country, the **Dyrhólaey Promontory,** with its lighthouse. The ocean has worn the black basalt rock here into the shape of an arch, 394 ft high; ships can sail through it in calm weather. This headland is also a bird sanctuary, so expect it to be closed during the nesting period in early summer.

Lodging

$ ⛉ **Hótel Vík.** Open year-round, this hotel has 20 rooms, some with private bath. ✉ *Klettsvegur, IS-871 Vík,* ☎ *487–1480 or 487–1230,* 𝔉𝔄𝔛 *487–1418. 20 rooms, 21 rooms. MC, V.*

$ ⛉ **Youth Hostel.** There are 25 beds at this hostel, open May through mid-September. ✉ *Reynisbrekka Mýdalur, IS-870 Vík,* ☎ *487–1106,* 𝔉𝔄𝔛 *487–1303. 25 beds. No credit cards. Closed mid-Sept.–Apr.*

Outdoor Activities and Sports

BIKING

Bikes can be rented at the **Ársalir Guesthouse** (✉ Austuvegur 7, Vík, ☎ 487–1400).

SEA TRIPS

From Vík, sea trips are made by amphibious vehicle: there is no harbor, so the vehicles simply drive from the sandy beach into the sea. You can go angling, whale-watching, or sightseeing to nearby Dyrhólæy. Contact **Adventure Tours** (☎ 487–1334).

SNOWMOBILING

Snowmobiling is possible in summer on the Mýrdalsjökull Glacier overlooking Vík through **Snjósleðaferðir** (⊠ Dugguvogur 10, IS-104 Reykjavík, ☎ 568–2310).

Shopping

In the small town of Vík, there are **factory outlets** selling woolen goods: **Katla** (⊠ Víkurbraut 16, ☎ 487–1170) and **Víkurprjón** (⊠ Smiðjuvegur 15, ☎ 487–1250).

Skógar

32 km (19 mi) west of Vík.

The tiny settlement of Skógar is home a **folk museum,** one of Iceland's best. Old houses are preserved in their original state, and there is a vast collection of household items from the surrounding area. Among the mementos of this region's past is one of the tiny, frail boats in which local fishermen once navigated the treacherous coast. ☎ 487–8845. ◔ *May–mid-September, daily 9–noon and 1–6, or by appointment.*

Lodging

$ 🖫 **Edda Hotel.** Close to Skógafoss (☞ *below*), this hotel also has views of the sea and the mountains and glaciers. The downside is shared baths for all. It has a restaurant that serves a supper buffet. Sleeping-bag accommodations are available. ⊠ *Skógum, IS-861 Hvollsvöllur* ☎ *487–8870,* 🆋 *562–5895. 34 rooms without bath. Restaurant. AE, MC, V. Closed Sept.–mid-June.*

En Route   Several hundred feet west of Skógar, just off the Ring Road is the impressive **Skógafoss,** a waterfall that's more than 197 ft high. If you drive 30 km (19 mi) farther west along the Ring Road from Skógar, follow the turnoff to **Seljalandsfoss,** another waterfall on the right. This graceful ribbonlike waterfall drops from an overhanging lava cliff and looks as if it belongs in Hawaii. If you step carefully, you can walk behind it, but be prepared to get wet.

Þórsmörk

30 km (19 mi) north of Skógar along the Ring Road.

You'll come to the powerful **Markarfljót River.** Route 249 on its east bank leads 15 km (9 mi) east across some treacherous streams into the Þórsmörk nature reserve, a popular vacation area bounded on its eastern and southern sides by the Eyjafjalla and Mýrdals glaciers. This route is passable only to four-wheel-drive vehicles, preferably traveling in groups. Þórsmörk, nestled in a valley surrounded by mountain peaks, enjoys exceptionally calm and often sunny weather, making it a veritable haven of birch trees and other Icelandic flora.

The road on the west bank of the Markarfljót leads 10 km (6 mi) north into saga country, to **Hlíðarendi,** the farm where Gunnar Hámundarson lived and died. He was one of the heroes of *Njál's Saga,* the single greatest classic work of Icelandic saga literature, written around the 12th century. Exiled by the Alþing parliament for murdering Þorgeir Oddkelsson, he refused to leave "these beautiful slopes."

In the lowlands to the southwest of the Markarfljót (turn off the Ring Road toward shore, and then onto Route 252 and drive 20 km/12 mi) to another famous place from *Njál's Saga,* **Bergþórshvoll.** This is where Njál's enemies surrounded his farmhouse and burned it to the ground, killing all but one. Kári, Njál's son-in-law, survived from beneath a collapsed roof under cover of smoke from the burning house.

Outdoor Activities and Sports
HIKING

There are many excellent trekking routes such as a day's trip over the **Fimmvörðuháls Mountain Pass** down to Skógar (bring a compass). Adventurers can take a three-day hike into the interior to visit **Landmannalaugar,** where hot and cold springs punctuate a landscape rich in pastel, yellow, brown, and red rhyolite hills carved by glacial rivers.

Hvolsvöllur

54 km (33 mi) west of Skógar along the Ring Road, and 39 km (24 mi) from Þórsmörk Preserve.

This small community is a relatively recent establishment, settled in 1932. Hvolsvöllur is now a busy service center for the fertile farm country surrounding it. A major meat-processing operation has moved here from the capital, infusing new vigor into the area. Hvolsvöllur is a good base if you are interested in *Njál's Saga* or the glacial scenery.

Lodging

$$ ⊞ **Hótel Hvolsvöllur.** This hotel in Hvolsvöllur offers basic rooms. ⊠ *Hlíðarvegur 7, IS-861 Hvollsvöllur,* ☎ *487–8187,* 𝔽𝔸𝕏 *487–8391. 28 rooms. Restaurant, bar. AE, MC, V.*

$ ⊞ **Youth Hostel.** There are 15 beds at this hostel which is open mid-April through mid-October. ⊠ *Fljótsdalur, Fljótshlíð, IS-861 Hvolsvöllur,* ☎ *487–8498. 15 beds. No credit cards. Closed mid-Oct.–mid-Apr.*

Outdoor Activities and Sports
HIKING

Both main Icelandic touring clubs, **Ferðafélag Íslands** (⊠ Mörkin 6, IS-108 Reykjavík, ☎ 568–2533) and **Útivist** (⊠ Hallveigarstígur 1, IS-101 Reykjavík, ☎ 551–4606) maintain large cabins with sleeping-bag accommodations in Þórsmörk; many long-distance hikes are organized from there.

Hella

12 km (7 mi) west of Hvolsvöllur on the Ring Road and 51 km (31 mi) west of Þórsmörk; 93 km (58 mi) traveling west to Reykjavík.

About 10 km (6 mi) west of Hella, turn right onto Route 26 and drive 40 km (25 mi) or so until you see, on your right, the tallest peak in the region. **Hekla** is also an active volcano, rightfully infamous since the Middle Ages as it has erupted 20 times in recorded history. In the Middle Ages, Hekla was known throughout Western Europe as the abode of the damned. Some 25 km (16 mi) farther, Route 26 intersects Route 32; turn left and go 15 km (9 mi) to the right turn for **Stöng,** an ancient settlement on the west bank of the Þjórsá River, Iceland's longest. The original farm here dates back almost 900 years; it was buried in 1104 when Hekla erupted, but you can visit the excavated ruins. A complete replica has been built, using the same materials the settlers used, south of Stöng at Búrfell on Route 32.

Lodging

$ ⊞ **Youth Hostel.** This hostel has 50 beds. ⊠ *Leirubakki (near Selfoss) Landssveit, IS-851 Hella,* ☎ *487–6591,* 𝔽𝔸𝕏 *487–6591. 50 beds. No credit cards.*

Selfoss

36 km (22 mi) west of Hella on the Ring Road.

This bustling town on the shores of the turbulent Ölfusá River is the largest in southern Iceland. Selfoss came into being in the 1930s and is a major agricultural community with the country's largest and oldest intact cream and butter plant. Guided tours of the plant and other sites—including Þuríðurbúð in Stokkseyri, where a rugged woman ran a fishing operation herself for 25 years in the 1800s—are given (☞ Guided Tours *in* the South A to Z, *below*).

Lodging

$$ 🏨 **Hótel Selfoss.** This quality hotel in Selfoss has an excellent restaurant and bar. ✉ *Eyarvegur 7, IS-800 Selfoss,* ☎ *482–2500,* FAX *482–2524. 28 rooms. Restaurant, bar. AE, MC, V.*

Outdoor Activities and Sports

BIKING

Bikes can be rented at **Vallholt 21** (✉ Selfoss, ☎ 482–2714).

GOLF

The **Svarfhólsvöllur** course (☎ 482–2417), in Selfoss, is on the banks of the Ölfusá River.

SWIMMING

There is a swimming pool in Selfoss (✉ Bankavegur, IS-800 Selfoss, ☎ 482–1227).

Shopping

The **Vöryhús KA** (✉ Ring Road, IS-800 Selfoss, ☎ 482–1000) is the area's largest supermarket, and the department store has a wide selection of goods.

En Route   At Hveragerði, take a left turn onto Route 38 and drive 20 km (12 mi) to **Þorlákshöfn**—the gateway to Vestmannæyjar, the Westman Islands, and one of three interesting coastal villages.

Eyrarbakka

12 km (7 mi) southwest of Selfoss along Rte. 34.

This now-close-knit village right on the shore of the North Atlantic was the largest community in the south less than a century ago. A few buildings remaining from the era have been restored. One, an older gentry house, is the pleasant **Árnes Folk Museum** (✉ Húsið, ☎ 483–1504), with interesting exhibits. It's surrounding turf walls were the most effective means of shelter from stiff onshore breezes. Another attraction is the **Eyrarbakki Maritime Museum** (✉ Túngata 10, ☎ 483–1165). Nearby tidal marshes are a bird-watcher's wonderland.

Dining

$ ✕ **Kaffi Lefolü.** Don't let the fancy name discourage you from this local eatery, which serves pizzas and seafood dishes in a quaint atmosphere. Artwork by local artists usually decorates the interior walls of this classic structure only a few steps from the shore. ✉ *Búðarstígur, IS-800 Eyrarbakki,* ☎ *483–1113. AE, MC, V.*

Stokkseyri

14 km (8 mi) southwest of Selfoss; take Rte. 34 and Rte. 33.

Third in a trio of neighboring shoreline villages, Stokkseyri lacks a good harbor, but fishing is nonetheless important to this tiny community. On the beach you can look for water birds and imagine how it must have been when Þuríður Einarsdóttir ran her fishing operation out of a sod-covered base some 150 years ago.

Outdoor Activities and Sports

KAYAKING

Suðurströnd runs tours by self-paddled kayaks through the area's calm marshes, canals, and offshore skerries. This is a quiet and a tranquil way to get closer to waterfowl in their own territory. Book through Green Ice Travel of Selfoss (☞ Guided Tours *in* the South A to Z, *below*).

Vestmannæyjar

3¼-hours south from Þorlákshöfn on the passenger-car ferry Herjól-fur; *1 hr by plane.*

Hjörleifur, sworn brother of Reykjavík settler Ingólfur Arnarson, settled in Heimay (the only inhabited island of the Westman archipelago) with five Irish slaves—called Westmen. The slaves soon after murdered their master and fled to the offshore islands. Ingólfur avenged his brother by driving most of the slaves off the cliffs of the islands and killing them. This tiny cluster of 15 islands off the south coast was named in honor of the Irish slaves—the Westmen.

The Vestmannæyjar (Westman Islands) were formed by volcanic eruptions only 5,000 to 10,000 years ago, and there is still much volcanic activity here. **Surtsey,** the latest addition, was formed in November 1963 with an eruption that lasted 3½ years. It is now totally restricted from human visitation and influence as a research area for biologic succession. In 1973 a five-month-long eruption on **Heimaey** wiped out part of the town of the Westman Islands. The island's entire population of about 5,000 was forced to flee in fishing boats, with only a few hours' notice. A few years later, however, the people of the Westman islands had removed tons of black lava dust and cinder from their streets and rebuilt all that was ruined. The lava, still hot, is used for heat by the resourceful islanders.

The main industry here is fishing, but another occupation—nowadays more a sport than a job—is more unusual: egg hunting. Enthusiasts dangle from ropes over the sheer black volcanic cliffs to collect eggs from the nests of seabirds. The islands are rich in birds, especially puffins, which number to about a million and are used for food.

Heimaey has one of Iceland's best natural history museums, **Náttúru-gripasafn Vestmannaeyja,** with an aquarium containing peculiar creatures of the deep. On the first weekend of August, islanders celebrate the 1874 grant of Icelandic sovereignty with a huge festival in the town on Heimaey. The population moves into a tent city in the **Herjólfsdalur** (Herjolf's Valley), a short distance west of town, for an extended weekend of bonfires, dance, and song.

Lodging

$$ ☷ **Hotel Bræðraborg.** Like most places on the island, this hotel is not far from the harbor. Island excursions can be arranged for guests. ✉ *Herjólfsgata 4, IS-900 Vestmannæyjar,* ☎ *481–1515,* FAX *481-2922. 30 rooms, some with bath. MC, V.*

$ ☷ **Youth Hostel.** Open May through mid-September, this hostel has 35 beds. ✉ *Faxastígur 38, IS-900 Vestmannæyjar,* ☎ *481–2915,* FAX *481–1497. 35 beds. No credit cards. Closed mid-Sept.–Apr.*

🔥 **Herjólfsdalur.** Camping is possible here, except when locals take over the spot on the first weekend in August for their holiday. ✉ *Dalvegur,* ☎ *481–1471. Closed Sept.–May.*

Outdoor Activities and Sports

GOLF

An 18-hole **golf course** (✉ Hamarsvegur, IS-900 Vestmannæyjar, ☎ 481–2363) is on Heimaey.

SIGHTSEEING CRUISES AND FLIGHTS

Sightseeing cruises run around the Westman Islands, offering views of dramatic sea caves and neighboring islands. Sightseeing flights over Surtsey and the rest of the Westman Islands can be arranged from Reykjavík or from Heimaey (☞ Guided Tours *in* the South A to Z, *below*).

SWIMMING

Swim at the sports center on Illugagata (☎ 481–2401 or 481–2402).

The South A to Z

Arriving and Departing

BY BUS

BSÍ has daily service from Reykjavík, stopping in Hella, Hvolsvöllur, Selfoss, Vík, and Þorlakshöfn. The journey to Vík takes less than four hours; to Þorlakshöfn or Selfoss, one hour.

BY CAR

Kirkjubæjarklaustur is 272 km (169 mi) east of Reykjavík on the Ring Road. West from Höfn, it is 201 km (125 mi) to Kirkjubæjarklaustur.

BY FERRY

The passenger and car ferry **Herjólfur** (☎ 481–2800 or 483–3413) sails daily to Vestmannæyjar from Þorlákshöfn. There are immediate bus connections to Reykjavík from the Westman Islands ferry at Þorlákshöfn; the trip takes about 90 minutes.

BY PLANE

Air Iceland (Flugfélag Íslands, Vestmannæyjar ☎ 481–3300, Reykjavík ☎ 570–3030) flies daily from Reykjavík Airport to the Westman Islands. **Íslandsflug** (☎ 561–6060) offers the same service. Flight time is about 30 minutes.

Contacts and Resources

EMERGENCIES

Police: Kirkjubæjarklaustur (☎ 487–4694). **Hvolsvöllur** (☎ 487–8434). **Selfoss** (☎ 482–1154). **Vestmannæyjar** (Westman Islands, ☎ 481–1666). **Vík** (☎ 487–1176). Dial ☎ 112 for emergency assistance anywhere in Iceland.

GUIDED TOURS

Hiking Tours: Hannes Jónsson (✉ Hvoll, IS-880 Kirkjubæjarklaustur, ☎ 487–4785 or 853-4133, 📠 487–4890) runs driving-hiking tours of **Núpsstaðarskógur** and **Eystrafjall**.

Kayaking Tours: Self-paddled kayak tours of the area around Stokkseyrirun are run by **Suðurströnd**; book through Green Ice Travel of Selfoss (☞ *below*). **Green Ice Travel** (✉ Eyravegi 1, IS-800 Selfoss, ☎ 482–3444, 📠 482–3443) operates 17 different and fascinating historic tours from Selfoss.

Sea Trips (Fishing, Whale-Watching): For sea trips from Vík by amphibious vehicle, offering angling, whale-watching, or sightseeing to nearby **Dyrhólæy**, contact **Adventure Tours** (☎ 487–1334, 📠 487–1330).

Sightseeing Tours: The **Iceland Tourist Bureau** (☞ Visitor Information *in* Iceland A to Z, *below*) operates a 10-hour day trip from Reykjavík to the **Westman Islands** by plane, running daily all year. Arrangements can also be made for a three-hour sightseeing flight over Heimaey.

The enthusiastic Páll Helgasson from **Westman Islands Travel Service** (✉ Herjólfsgötu 4, IS-900 Vestmannæyjar, ☎ 481–2922, FAX 481–2007) offers informative, reasonably priced sightseeing trips by boat and bus in the **Westman Islands;** if you call ahead, he will meet you at the airport. **Austurleið** bus company (✉ Austurvegi 1, IS-861 Hvolsvöllur, ☎ 487–8197) operates tours to **Þórsmörk, Skaftafell,** the **Eastern Fjords,** and the interior.

VISITOR INFORMATION

Kirkjubæjarklaustur (Community Center, ✉ Klausturvegur 10, IS-880 Kirkjubæjarklaustur, ☎ 487–4620). **Vík** (campsite, ✉ Vík, ☎ 487–1345; Víkurskáli, ☎ 487–1230). **Selfoss** (Tryggvaskáli, ✉ Fossnesti, IS 800 Selfoss, next to bridge over Ölfusá River, ☎ 482–1704, FAX 482–3599).

ICELAND A TO Z

Arriving and Departing

By Boat

It is possible to sail to Iceland on the car-and-passenger ferry **Norröna,** operated by **Smyril Line** (✉ Box 370, 3800 Tórshavn, Faroe Islands, ☎ 1/5900, FAX 1/5707; Engelgarden, Nye Bryggen, N-5023 Bergen, Norway, ☎ 5/32–09–70, FAX 5/96–02–72; Norröna Travel, Laugavegur 3, IS-101 Reykjavík, Iceland, ☎ 562–6362, FAX 552–9450).

The **Norröna** plies among the Faroes, Esbjerg in Denmark, Bergen in Norway, and Seyðisfjörður on the east coast of Iceland. Depending on your point of departure and your destination, the trip may involve a stopover of some days in the Faroes. Special offers for accommodations may be available through Smyril Line, and special fly-cruise arrangements are available through Smyril Line and Icelandair. You can also sail between Iceland and Europe by freight vessel. **Eimskip,** Iceland's largest shipping company, offers limited passenger accommodations (plus the option of taking your own car along) on container vessels. You can sail from Immingham (England), Hamburg (Germany), Antwerp (Belgium), or Rotterdam (Netherlands) to Reykjavík. For information and bookings call **Úrval-Útsýn Travel** (✉ Lágmúli 4, IS-108 Reykjavík, ☎ 569–9300).

By Plane

All international flights originate from and arrive at **Keflavík Airport** (☎ 425–0600) 50 km (30 mi) south of Reykjavík. On arrival you may spot some military aircraft, for Keflavík is also a NATO military installation, manned by the U.S. Navy.

FROM NORTH AMERICA

Icelandair (✉ 610 5th Ave., New York, NY 10020, ☎ 800/223–5500) operates regular direct flights—which take 5½ hours—daily from New York City's JFK airport; service from Baltimore flies daily; service from Orlando runs twice a week in winter, once a week in summer; weekly flights operate out of Fort Lauderdale. Flights leave from Boston four times a week; from Halifax, Nova Scotia, planes fly twice weekly.

FROM SCANDINAVIA

Icelandair (Copenhagen ☎ 45/33–12–33–88; Stockholm ☎ 46/8–31–02–40; Oslo ☎ 47/67–53–21–35; and Helsinki ☎ 358/0–693–1588) and **SAS** (Copenhagen ☎ 45/70–10–20–00; Stockholm ☎ 46/020–727–555); Oslo ☎ 47/22–17–41–60; Helsinki ☎ 358/09–22–8021) both operate between mainland Scandinavia and Iceland. Previously in competition, the two airlines now coordinate services.

Icelandair (✉ 172 Tottenham Court Road, 3rd fl., London W1P 9LG, ☎ 0171/388–5599) flies daily from London's Heathrow Airport to Keflavík Airport. There are two flights a week from Glasgow, and once a week Icelandair flies from Glasgow via the Faroe Islands to Iceland. The flight from London takes three hours.

Getting Around

Don't be fooled into thinking all site names on some maps are settlements where services can be had. Many of these sites (Icelanders call them "Örnefni") are landmarks or farmsites, possibly even abandoned. They may have historic significance, but are disappointingly lacking service stations or food stores.

By Boat

There is daily scheduled ferry service year-round between Reykjavík and Akranes on the ferry **Akraborg** (☎ 551–6050). Ferries run daily between Þorlákshöfn and the Westman Islands on the ferry **Herjólfur** (☎ 483–3413, FAX 551–2991). The **Baldur** car ferry (☎ 438–1120 or 456–2020, FAX 438–1093) sails twice daily in summer from Stykkishólmur, on the Snæfellsnes Peninsula, across Breiðafjörður Bay to Brjánslækur.

By Bus

An extensive network of buses serves most parts of Iceland. Services are intermittent in the winter season, and some routes are operated only in summer. Fares range from IKr1,000 for a round-trip to Þingvellir to IKr6,500 for a round-trip to Akureyri. The bus network is operated from **Bifreiðastöð Íslands** (BSÍ, ✉ Vatnsmýrarvegur 10, IS-101, ☎ 552–2300, FAX 552–9973); its terminal is located on the northern rim of Reykjavík Airport.

Holders of BSÍ Passport tickets are entitled to various discounts, for instance at campsites, Edda hotels, ferries, and mountain bikes (those rented from BSÍ).

If you want to explore the island extensively, it's a good idea to buy the **Omnibus Passport,** which covers travel on all scheduled bus routes with unlimited stopovers. The **Full Circle Passport** is valid for a circular trip on the Ring Road mid-July to mid-September; you can take as long as you like to complete the journey but you have to keep heading in the same direction on the circuit (detours into the interior must be paid for separately). The **Air/Bus Rover** ticket offered by Air Iceland (Flugfélag Íslands) and BSÍ allows you to fly one-way to any domestic Air Iceland destination and travel by bus back, so you can save some time and still have a chance to explore the countryside.

By Car

The **Ring Road,** which generally hugs the coastline, runs for 1,400 km (900 mi) around Iceland. Although 80% of the road is paved, a long stretch across the Möðrudalsöræfi highlands in the east is still gravel. Much of Iceland's **secondary road system** is unpaved. Take great care on these roads, as driving on loose gravel surface takes some getting used to and is not for the timid motorist. Also, be careful of livestock that may stray onto roadways; do not expect to travel fast.

Caution pays off when driving in Iceland's **interior,** too. The terrain can be treacherous, and many roads can be traversed only in four-wheel-drive vehicles; always drive in the company of at least one other car. Unbridged rivers, which must be forded, constitute a real hazard and should never be crossed without the advice of an experienced Iceland highland driver. Most mountain roads are closed by snow in winter and do not open again until mid-June or early July, when the road surface has dried out after the spring thaw. Before driving any distance in rural Iceland, be sure to pick up the brochure *Driving in Iceland* from any Tourist Information Center. This offers informative tips and advice about driving the country's back roads.

EMERGENCY ASSISTANCE

The general emergency number, available 24 hours throughout Iceland, is ☎ 112.

GASOLINE

Gas prices are high, IKr67 to IKr75 per liter depending on octane rating. Service stations are spaced no more than half a day's drive apart, on both main roads and side roads. Service stations in the Reykjavík area are open Monday through Saturday 7:30 AM–8 PM; opening hours outside Reykjavík vary, but gas stations are often open until 11:30 PM. For information on the availability of gas off the beaten track, call Vegagerð Ríkisins (**Public Roads Administration,** ✉ Borgartún 5–7, Reykjavík, ☎ 563–1500).

MAPS

It is essential to have a good map when traveling in rural Iceland (☞ Outdoor Activities and Sports *in* Contacts and Resources, *below*).

RENTAL AGENCIES

Avis (☎ 425–0760) operates offices in the Leifur Eiríksson Terminal at Keflavík Airport. **Hertz/Icelandair** (☎ 505–0600) is also at Keflavík Airport. A very competitive newcomer in car rental is **Hasso Car Rental** (✉ Hringbraut 62, IS-220 Hafnarfjörður, ☎ 555–3340, ☎ 555–3330. **Greiði hf. Car Rental** (✉ Dalshraun 9, IS-220 Hafnarfjörður, ☎ 565–3800, ☎ 565–4220) is another option.

RENTAL RATES

Renting a car in Iceland is expensive; it may well be worth arranging a car in advance through your travel agent, who may be able to offer a better deal. A typical price for a compact car is around IKr6,000 per day, with 100 km (62 mi) free, plus IKr31 per km. A four-wheel-drive vehicle for rougher roads will cost about IKr12,000 per day, with 100 km (62 mi) included, plus IKr60 per km. These prices do not include collision damage waiver or gas. There are many car-rental agencies in Iceland, so it is worth shopping around for the best buy. If you plan to explore the interior, make sure you rent a four-wheel-drive vehicle.

ROAD CONDITIONS

For information on road conditions, call **Vegagerð Ríkisins** (Public Roads Administration, ✉ Borgartún 5–7, Reykjavík, ☎ 563–1500).

RULES OF THE ROAD

Traffic outside Reykjavík is generally light, but roads have only one lane going in each direction, so stay within the speed limit: 70 kph (42 mph) on the open road, 50 kph (30 mph) in urban areas. Drivers are required by law to use headlights at all times. Seat belts are required for the driver and all passengers.

By Plane

Because so much of Iceland's central region is uninhabited, domestic air transport has been well developed to link the coastal towns. It isn't particularly cheap—round-trip fares range from IKr8,200 to IKr15,600—but there are various discounts available. The longest domestic flight takes just over an hour.

In summer, **Air Iceland** (Flugfélag Íslands, ☎ 570–3030) schedules daily or frequent flights from Reykjavík to most of the large towns, such as Akureyri, Egilsstaðir, Húsavík, Höfn, Ísafjörður, and Vestmannæyjar. Air Iceland provides bus connections between airports outside Reykjavík and nearby towns and villages.

Íslandsflug (☎ 561–6060) flies daily from Reykjavík to Vestmannæyjar, Egilsstaðir, and Bíldudalur and also flies regularly to Flateyri, Siglufjörður, Neskaupstaður, Hólmavík, and Gjögur. Air Iceland (Flugfélag Íslands, ☎ 570–3030) serves the north from Akureyri. **East-air** (☎ 471–1122) serves the east with charters out of Egilsstaðir. **APEX tickets** are available on domestic flights if booked two days in advance. These offer savings of 50% on the full airfare.

DISCOUNT PASSES
The **Fly As You Please Holiday Ticket** is valid for unlimited travel on all Iceland Air (Flugfélag Íslands) domestic routes for 12 days. It's sold exclusively in advance to Icelandair international passengers. The **Four-Sector Air Iceland Pass** is valid for a month and can be used on any four sectors flown by Icelandair and it's domestic line, Air Iceland (Flugfélag Íslands); this pass must also be booked before arrival in Iceland. Several other types of air passes, covering different combinations of sectors, are also available. The **Mini-Air Iceland Pass** is valid on two sectors.

Contacts and Resources

Customs
Tourists can bring in 6 liters of beer or 1 liter of wine containing up to 21% alcohol, 1 liter of liquor with up to 47% alcohol, and 200 cigarettes.

Dining
Restaurants are small and diverse. You can expect superb seafood and lamb, and the fresh fish is not to be missed—surely some of the best you'll ever have. Besides native cuisine, ethnic eateries range from Asian, Lebanese, and Indian, to French and Italian. Pizzas, hamburgers, and a tasty local version of the hot dog, with fried onions, are widely available. Most restaurants—even the two McDonald's in Reykjavík—accept major credit cards.

More than 50 restaurants around the country participate in a **tourist-menu** scheme: a meal of soup or starter, fish or meat dish, and coffee costs IKr900–IKr1,000 for lunch or IKr1,100–IKr1,700 for dinner, with discounts for children (children under five eat free). Participating restaurants display a TOURIST MENU sticker in their windows. A leaflet listing all participating restaurants is available free from the **Icelandic Hotel and Restaurant Association** (✉ Hafnarstræti 20, IS-101 Reykjavík, ☎ 552–7410 or 562–1410, FAX 552–7478). *Dining and Wining,* available free from the association, covers restaurants all over the country.

Embassies
U.S. (✉ Laufásvegur 21, IS-101 Reykjavík, ☎ 562–9100). **Canada** (✉ Suðurlandsbraut 10, IS-101 Reykjavík, ☎ 568–0820). **U.K.** (✉ Laufásvegur 31, IS-108 Reykjavík, ☎ 550–5100).

Emergencies
Dial ☎ 112 in an emergency; it is a nationwide number.

Guided Tours
Inclusive guided tours are offered by a number of travel agencies in Iceland, the largest of which follow. **Samvinn Travel** (✉ Austurstræti 12, IS-101 Reykjavík, ☎ 569–1010, FAX 569–1095). **Úrval-Útsýn Travel** (✉ Lágmúli 4, IS-108 Reykjavík, ☎ 569–9300, FAX 567–0202). **Iceland Tourist Bureau** (☞ Visitor Information, *below*). **Guðmundur Jónasson Travel** (✉ Boragrtún 34, IS-105 Reykjavík, ☎ 511–1515, FAX 511–1511).

Kynnisferðir (Reykjavík Excursions; office, ✉ Vesturvör 6, IS-200 Kópavogur; sales desks, ✉ Hótels Loftleiðir ☎ 562–1011 and Esja ☎ 568–8922, and at Bankastræti 2 ☎ 562–4422). Most operators offer a range of tours by bus; some itineraries include air travel. Many agencies also combine Icelandic vacations with Greenland tours.

For the fit and active, hiking, biking, or horseback-riding tours are also available. In these cases, accommodations will usually be in tents, guesthouses, or mountain huts. Guided hiking tours of the interior are organized by **Ferðafélag Íslands** (Touring Club of Iceland, ✉ Mörkin 6, IS-108 Reykjavík, ☎ 568–2533, FAX 568–2535). A variety of smaller travel agencies also offer tours, some of them quite specialized. **Landnáma ehf** (✉ Vesturgata 5, IS-101 Reykjavík, ☎ 511–3050, FAX 511–3051) is Iceland's first agency specializing in ecotourism, offering enlightening trips of differing durations on themes of history, water, farming, geology, and more. The **Icelandic Tourist Board** (☞ Visitor Information, *below*) also has information on other agencies. For specific Guided Tours information, *see* specific sections above.

Language
The official language is Icelandic, a highly inflected Germanic tongue brought to the country by the early Viking settlers. Since it has only slightly changed over the centuries, modern Icelanders can read the ancient manuscripts of the sagas without difficulty. English and Danish are widely spoken and understood; many Icelanders also speak other Scandinavian languages or German, and some speak French.

The Icelandic alphabet contains two unique letters—Þ, pronounced like the *th* in thin, and ð, pronounced like the *th* in leather.

Lodging
CAMPING
Organized campgrounds are available throughout the country. Some are on private property, others are owned and operated by local communities, and still others are in protected areas supervised by the Nature Conservation Council. For a comprehensive listing of campgrounds, write or call the **Association of Leisure Site Owners** (c/o Tourist Information Center; ☞ Visitor Information, *below*). On the road, look for signs reading TJALDSTÆÐI BÖNNUÐ (camping prohibited) or TJALDSTÆÐI (camping allowed), or a simple tent symbol. Most campgrounds charge about IKr200 per person per night, plus IKr200 for the tent. Campsites in national parks are more expensive.

It is forbidden to use scrubwood for fuel; bring paraffin or gas stoves for cooking. Camping equipment can be rented in Reykjavík at **Tjaldaleigan Rent-a-Tent** (☎ 551–3072).

FARM HOLIDAYS
Write to **Icelandic Farm Holidays** (✉ Bændahöllinni við Hagatorg, IS-107 Reykjavík, ☎ 562–3640, FAX 551–9200) for a booklet describing all farms and their facilities. A double room without breakfast costs IKr1,950–IKr2,950 per night; sleeping-bag accommodations without breakfast costs IKr800–IKr1,250 per night. **Summer cottages** can be rented by the week; a six-bed cottage costs IKr32,500–IKr39,000 during peak season.

HOTELS AND GUEST HOUSES
The **Icelandic Hotel and Restaurant Association** (☞ Dining, *above*) publishes a brochure each year with details of hotels and guest houses throughout the country. In addition to the **Edda** summer hotels (☞ Summer Hotels, *below*), are three other local hotel "chains," the year-round **Rainbow** hotels (☎ 562–0160, FAX 562–0150), the **Foss** hotels (✉

Hótel Lind, Rauðarástígur, Reykjavík ☎ 562–3350), and the **Lykil** (Key) hotels (✉ Hótel Örk, Breiðamörk 1, Reykjavík, ☎ 483–4700), which also includes a university dormitory. The **Gist-Ís** organization (☎ 564–3090, FAX 564–3091) publishes a brochure on budget accommodations. In summer, hotels and even youth hostels may be fully booked, so make reservations well in advance.

MOUNTAIN HUTS

You can also stay at any of more than 30 mountain huts throughout the country and owned by the **Touring Club of Iceland** (☞ Group Tours, *above*). In summer it is necessary to book space in these in advance. Depending on location, huts accommodate from 12 to 120 and are rated in two categories: **A-class** huts have running water and gas for cooking during summers, in addition to bunk beds and mattresses; **B-class** huts are basic shelters with bunk beds and mattresses.

Rental fees are discounted to Touring Club Members. A-class huts are IKr1,150 per person per night for nonmembers, IKr750 for members; B-class huts are IKr800 per person per night for nonmembers, IKr550 for members.

SUMMER HOTELS

In summer, 18 boarding schools around the country open up as **Edda** hotels, offering both accommodations with made-up beds and more basic sleeping-bag facilities. A double room costs IKr4,550, a single IKr3,400. You can sleep on a mattress in your own sleeping bag for IKr850 to IKr1,350 per night depending on facilities. Most Edda hotels have restaurants offering good home-style cooking. Three Edda hotels are open year-round: at Flúðir, toward the interior; in Kirkjubæjarklaustur, somewhat inland in the central south; and the brand-new facility at Egilsstaðir, in the east. For information and bookings, contact the **Iceland Tourist Bureau** (☞ Visitor Information, *below*).

STUDIO APARTMENTS AND SUMMER HOUSES

A new option in accommodations in Reykjavík is studio apartments, near the Tjörnin Lake and The National Gallery of Iceland, offered by **Skýlir ehf** (✉ Skálholtstígur 2A, ☎ 511–2266, 562–5622, FAX 562–9165). Renting a summer house or cottage is a pleasant, economical alternative for those seeking more independence. **Icelandic Farm Holidays** (☞ Farm Holidays, *above*) has a listing of places around the country, and as their name implies, many are in farm settings, though separate structures. In the south, a number of cottages are available from **Icelandic Summer Houses** (✉ Austurvegi 22, IS-800 Selfoss, ☎ 482–1666, FAX 482–2807). In other regions contact the local Tourist Information Center.

YOUTH HOSTELS

At Iceland's 31 youth hostels, accommodations are predictably inexpensive: about IKr1,250 per night, or IKr1,000 for members of the Youth Hostel Association. You get a bed, access to a kitchen and toilet, pillow, and blanket. Breakfast costs about IKr500. Some hostels are crowded during the summer, so call ahead. Hostels outside Reykjavík permit you to use your own sleeping bag. For information, write to **Farfugladeild Reykjavíkur** (✉ Sundlaugavegi 34, IS-105 Reykjavík, ☎ 553–8110, FAX 567–9201).

Mail

POSTAL RATES

Within Europe, postcards need IKr30 postage, airmail letters IKr35. Letter and postcard postage to the United States is IKr65.

RECEIVING MAIL

Mail to Iceland from northern Europe and Scandinavia usually takes two to three days; other services are slower. All post offices have fax machines.

Money and Expenses

CURRENCY

The unit of currency in Iceland is the króna (IKr). Icelandic notes come in denominations of IKr 500, 1,000, 2,000, and 5,000. Coins are IKr1, 5, 10, 50, and 100. The króna is divided into 100 *aurar,* which are as good as worthless. At press time (summer 1997) the exchange rate of the króna hovered around IKr70 to the U.S. dollar, IKr114 to the pound sterling, and IKr50 to the Canadian dollar.

EXCHANGING MONEY

Don't bother trying to exchange currency before you depart, because Icelandic money is usually unavailable at foreign banks. Also, it is unlikely that Icelandic money will be exchangeable back home, so exchange any last krónas at the departure terminal in Keflavík Airport.

SALES-TAX REFUNDS

A 24.5% *virðisaukaskattur* (value-added tax, or V.A.T.), commonly called VSK, applies to most goods and services. Usually the V.A.T. is included in a price; if not, that fact must be stated explicitly. Foreign visitors can claim a partial refund on the V.A.T., which accounts for 19.68% of the purchase price of most goods and services. Fifteen percent of the purchase price for goods is refunded, providing you buy a minimum of IKr5,000 at one time. Souvenir stores issue "tax-free checks" that allow foreign visitors to collect the V.A.T. rebates directly in the duty-free store when departing from Keflavík Airport. To qualify, keep your purchases in tax-free packages (except woolens), and show them to customs officers at the departure gate along with a passport and the tax-free check. If you depart the country from somewhere other than Keflavík, have customs authorities stamp your tax-free check, then mail the stamped check within three months to Iceland Tax-Free Shopping (⊠ Box 1200, 235 Keflavík, Iceland). You will be reimbursed in U.S. dollars at the current exchange rate.

SAMPLE PRICES

Iceland is an expensive destination. Surprisingly, some luxury items are actually cheaper than in other large international cities.

Cup of coffee, IKr150; imported German beer or Icelandic brew, IKr600; can of soda, IKr150; film, IKr1,100 for 36 exposures; short taxi ride within Reykjavík, IKr600.

TIPPING

Tipping is not conventional in Iceland and may even be frowned upon. Service charges of 15% to 20% are included in some prices.

National Holidays

January 1; April 8–12 (Easter); April 23 (first day of summer); May 1 (Labor Day); May 21 (Ascension); May 31 to June 1 (Pentecost); June 7 (Seamen's Day); June 17 (National Day); August 3 (public holiday); December 24–26; December 31.

Opening and Closing Times

BANKS

All banks in Iceland are open weekdays 9:15–4. A few branches in major towns are also open Thursday 5–6.

POST OFFICES

Post offices in most towns are open weekdays only from 8:30 or 9 to 4:30 or 5.

STORES

Outside Reykjavík it is generally possible to find food stores that remain open seven days a week.

Outdoor Activities and Sports

FISHING

The Icelandic Fishing Guide and a special fishing voucher book available from **Icelandic Farm Holidays** (☞ Farm Holidays, *above*) can be used in 50 river and lake locations around the country. Fishing-rod rental can often be arranged at some of these spots. If you wish to bring your own fishing tackle, it must be disinfected either at home (certificate needed) or by customs at Keflavík Airport.

Sea angling is becoming a popular leisure sport in Iceland. Fishing cruises can be organized from many of the country's fishing towns and villages. Several weekend deep-sea fishing competitions are held each year; a few follow: A competition is held at Whitsun in **Vestmannæyjar** (contact Elínborg Bernódusdóttir, ☎ 481–1279 or 481–1118). In June, one is held in **Reykjavík** (contact Birkir Þór Guðmundsson, ☎ 553–0734). One in July is at **Ísafjörður** (contact Kolbrún Halldórsdóttir, ☎ 456–3069). In August, anglers head to **Akureyri** (contact Júlíus Snorrason, ☎ 462–1173). For further information, contact the **Tourist Information Center** (☞ Visitor Information, *below*).

GOLF

There are about 50 golf courses in Iceland. Most are primitive nine-hole courses, but there are six good 18-hole courses. The **Arctic Open,** played at the Akuryeri Golf course during the midnight sun in June, is one of the world's most unusual tournaments. **Greens fees** range from IKr800 for par-three courses to IKr2,600 for 18-hole minimums. For information on golfing opportunities in Iceland, contact the **Golf Association** (☎ 568–6686, ℻ 568–6086).

HANDBALL

During Icelandic winters, team handball is a national obsession with a huge following; contact the **Handball Federation** (☎ 568–5422).

HIKING

Many organized tours from Reykjavík and other towns include some days of hiking. Contact **Ferðafélag Íslands** (Touring Club of Iceland, ✉ Mörkin 6, IS-108 Reykjavík, ☎ 568–2533, ℻ 568–2535). Also contact **Útivist** (Touring Club Útivist, ✉ Hallveigarstígur 1, IS-101 Reykjavík, ☎ 551–4606, ℻ 561–4606). For serious exploring or hiking, you can obtain good up-to-date maps from **Landmælingar Íslands** (Icelandic Geodetic Survey Map Store, ✉ Laugavegi 178, second level, IS-105 Reykjavík, ☎ 533–4010).

Be aware of the considerable dangers of hiking alone. Hiking trails can be rather rugged, marked with short pegs or less. Lava can be treacherous, with razor-sharp edges that can cut through clothes and skin. Footing can be tricky, as moss layers often hide uneven terrain. Do not stray too close to hot springs and sulfur springs, as the ground surrounding them may suddenly give way, leaving you standing in boiling water or mud. When hiking across country, follow paths made by sheep if footpaths are not available. Don't rely on the sun for orientation, because in summers at this latitude it seems never to set, and technically it's not due west. When admiring the delicate flora, soft mosses, and lichen, remember that in preserves and national parks it is illegal to pick flowers or take rock samples. Remember that at sub-Arctic latitudes, it takes centuries for even the most common flowers to become established on this terrain. Dress in layers, with a windproof outer shell, and have sturdy broken-in hiking shoes. When you are camping, tents should be firmly anchored against possible winds. Don't venture into remote areas unless you have researched the territory in advance and have a detailed map. Finally, always let someone know of your hiking plans. Avoid hiking alone.

HORSEBACK RIDING

Many equestrian events are held around the country during the summer months, from local races and contests to major regional championships. Contact **Landssamband Hestamannafélaga** (Equestrian Federation, ✉ Bændahöllin, Hagatorg, IS-101 Reykjavík, ☎ 552–9899) for details of upcoming horse events. There is even the international association FEIF for those in 20 countries who own or admire the Icelandic horse. And an English version of the magazine *Eiðfaxi* is published five times a year for fanciers of the Icelandic horse.

SKIING

In summer, the **Kerlingarfjöll Ski School** west of the Hofsjökull Glacier runs five- to six-day courses; you can also get lift tickets without taking lessons, and there are accommodations and food at the school. Contact **Úrval-Útsýn Travel Agency** (✉ Lagmúli 4, IS-108 Reykjavík, ☎ 569–9300).

SNOWMOBILING

A company with varied glacier destinations is **ADD-ICE** (☎ 588–5555, FAX 588–5554). One popular excursion visits the glacial tongue, Sólheimarjökull, part of the larger Mýrdalsjökull glacier in the south. Contact **Snjósleðaferðir** (✉ Dugguvogi 10, IS-104 Reykjavík, ☎ 568–2310, FAX 581–3102). *See also* Guided Tours, *in* Iceland A to Z *and* specific sections.

SUPPLIES

Should you need outdoor or camping gear, touring maps, or spares for broken or lost equipment, you may well find what you need in Reykjavík at **Skátabúðin** (The Scout's Store, ✉ Snorrabraut 60, IS-101 Reykjavík, ☎ 561–2045, 562–4145, FAX 562–4122). Also try **Seglagerðin Ægir** (✉ Eyraslóð 7, IS-101 Reykjavík, ☎ 511–2201, FAX 511–2211). Detailed maps at assorted scales showing trails and regional sites are available from the **Icelandic Geodetic Survey Map Store** (✉ Laugavegi 178, second level, IS-105 Reykjavík, ☎ 533–4010, FAX 533–4011). If you prefer to rent a tent, your best bet is **Tjaldaleigjan** (✉ right across from Umferðamiðstöð Bus Terminal, ☎ 551–9800, FAX 511–2211.)

SWIMMING

Almost every sizable community in Iceland has at least one public outdoor swimming pool. Since most are generally heated by thermal springs, they can be enjoyed year-round. Inquire at the tourist office or a local hotel for the nearest pool; *also see* specific sections, *above*.

Packing

It may seem odd to suggest a bathing suit as the first item to pack for visiting a country named Iceland, but the wonderful pools and hot spring baths are a joy to experience. Layering is the secret to comfort in Iceland, so bring a waterproof, wind-tight jacket or shell, regardless of season. In winter, bring a good, heavy coat. Durable, broken-in walking or hiking boots with good ankle support are needed for hiking (forget tennis shoes for this), and a telescoping walking staff might also prove handy. If you'll be going to the highlands to ski or snowmobile, be sure to bring good gloves. Likewise sunscreen and sunglasses are a must to protect against the low, lingering sun of spring and fall, which can be a real bother to drivers. Sweaters are useful—perhaps why Icelanders are so good at making them. Sports enthusiasts note that all fishing tackle, riding tack, and garments should be certified sterile by a veterinarian or doctor unless it is obviously new and unused. If not, gear will be cleaned at your expense upon arrival, or impounded.

Telephones

Iceland's telephone system is, electronically speaking, an entirely digital network, which greatly facilitates computer transmissions.

COUNTRY CODE

Iceland's country code is 354.

DIRECTORY ASSISTANCE AND OPERATOR INFORMATION

For long-distance calls within Iceland, dial ☎ 02 for the operator or ☎ 03 for directory assistance. Dial ☎ 09 for an overseas operator, and ☎ 08 for overseas directory assistance.

INTERNATIONAL CALLS

You can dial direct, starting with 00 then following with the country code and local number. An international calling card is a convenient mode of payment. Avoid charging overseas calls to your hotel bills, as the surcharge can double the cost of the call.

You can dial local access codes to reach U.S. operators: **AT&T USADirect** (☎ 800/9001), **MCI Call USA** (☎ 999/002), **Sprint Express** (☎ 800/9003).

LOCAL CALLS

Names are listed alphabetically in the telephone book by first name as a result of the patronymic system (men add -*son* to their father's first name, women add -*dóttir*). Jobs or professions are often listed together with names and addresses.

Pay phones are usually indoors in post offices, hotels, or at transportation terminals. They accept IKr5-, IKr10-, or IKr50-coins, which are placed in the slot before dialing. The dial tone is continuous. A 10-minute call between regions costs between IKr50 and IKr75. Card phones are becoming more common: 100-unit phone cards (IKr500) can be purchased at all post offices and some other outlets.

Travel Agencies

Samvinn Travel (✉ Austurstræti 12, IS-101, ☎ 569–1010, 569–1070, FAX 569–1095, 552–7796. **Úrval–Útsýn Travel** (✉ Lágmúli 4, IS-108, ☎ 569–9300, FAX 588–0202).

Visitor Information

Icelandic Tourist Board (✉ 655 3rd Ave., New York, NY 10017, ☎ 212/949–2333, FAX 212/983–5260; ✉ Gimli, Lækjargata 3, IS-101 Reykjavík, ☎ 552–7488, FAX 562–4749). **Iceland Tourist Bureau** (✉ Skógarhlíð 18, IS-101 Reykjavík, ☎ 562–3300, FAX 562–5895). In the United Kingdom, contact **Icelandair** (✉ 172 Tottenham Court Road, 3rd floor, London W1P 9LG, ☎ 0171/388–5599, FAX 0171/387–5711).

Weather

The best time to visit is from May to mid-November. From June through July, the sun barely sets. In December the sun shines for only three hours a day, but on clear, cold evenings any time from September to March you may see the Northern Lights dancing among the stars. Weather in Iceland is unpredictable: In June, July, and August, sunny days alternate with spells of rain showers, crisp breezes, and driving winds. Winter temperatures fluctuate wildly—it can be as high as 50°F (10°C) or as low as −14°F (−10°C).

CLIMATE

Iceland enjoys a temperate ocean climate with cool summers and relatively mild winters. The climate in the north is stable and continental, the south fickle and maritime.

5 Norway

Carved by snow-topped mountains and serrated by Gulf Stream–warmed fjords, Norway has an abundance of magnificent views. No matter how or where you approach, if you fly above the clean ivory mountains of Tromsø in the winter, or tear by in a heart-stopping train north of Voss in the spring, getting there is often as eye-popping as arriving.

Updated by
Shelley Pannill
and Marius
Meland

JUST NORTH OF LILLEHAMMER lives a Norwegian family on the banks of Mjøsa Lake. Every year they pack their bags and drive to their holiday retreat, where they bask in the warmth of the long, northern sun for four full weeks—then they pack up and drive the 300 ft back home again.

Although most Norwegians vacation a bit farther from home, their sentiments—attachment to, pride in, and reverence for their great outdoors—remain the same as the feelings of those who only journey across the street. Whether in the verdant dales of the interior, the brooding mountains of the north, or the carved fjords and archipelagoes of the coast, their ubiquitous *hytter* (cabins or cottages) dot even the most violent landscapes. It's a question of perspective: to a Norwegian, it's not a matter of whether to enjoy the land, but how to enjoy it at this very moment.

In any kind of weather, blasting or balmy, inordinate numbers are out of doors, to fish, bike, ski, hike, and, intentionally or not, strike the pose many foreigners regard as larger-than-life Norwegian: ruddy-faced, athletic, reindeer-sweatered. And all—from cherubic children to decorous senior citizens—are bundled up for just one more swoosh down the slopes, one more walk through the forest.

Although Norway is a modern, highly industrialized nation, vast areas of the country (up to 95%) remain forested or fallow, and Norwegians intend to keep them that way—in part by making it extremely difficult for foreigners, who may feel differently about the land, to purchase property.

When discussing the size of their country, Norwegians like to say that if Oslo remained fixed and the northern part of the country were swung south, it would reach all the way to Rome. Perched at the very top of the globe, this northern land is long and rangy, 2,750 km (1,705 mi) in length, with only 4 million people scattered over it—making it the least densely populated land in Europe except for Iceland.

Thanks to the Gulf Stream, the coastal regions enjoy a moderate, temperate climate in winter, keeping the country green, whereas the interior has a more typical northern climate. Of course, throughout the land, winter temperatures can dip far below zero, but that doesn't thwart the activities of the Norwegians. As one North Caper put it, "We don't have good weather or bad weather, only a lot of weather."

Norwegians are justifiably proud of their native land and of their ability to survive the elements and foreign invasions. The first people to appear on the land were reindeer hunters and fisherfolk who were migrating north, following the path of the retreating ice. By the Bronze Age, settlements began to appear, and, as rock carvings show (and modern school children are proud to announce), the first Norwegians began to ski—purely as a form of locomotion—some 4,000 years ago.

The Viking Age has perhaps left the most indelible mark on the country. The Vikings' travels and conquests took them to Iceland, England, Ireland (they founded Dublin in the 840s), and North America. Though they were famed as plunderers, their craftsmanship and fearlessness are revered by modern Norwegians, who place ancient Viking ships in museums, cast copies of thousand-year-old silver designs into jewelry, and adventure across the seas in sailboats to prove the abilities of their forefathers.

Norway

North Cape

TO
SVALBARD

Vardø

Vadsø

Hammerfest

Kirkenes

*ATLANTIC
OCEAN*

Alta

Karasjok

Kautokeino

Tromsø

*Norwegian
Sea*

Harstad

VESTERÅLEN

Svolvær   Narvik

FINLAND

LOFOTEN

Vestfjorden

Bodø   Fauske

Polarsirkelsenteret

Arctic   Circle

Mo i Rana

Sandnessjøen   Mosjøen

Brønnøysund

SWEDEN

Gulf of Bothnia

Rørvik

Namsos

Steinkjer

Trondheim   Meråker

Kristiansund   Støren

Molde   Oppdal   Røros

Ålesund   Andalsnes   Tynset

Geiranger   Dombås

Nordfjord   Lom   Otta   Koppang

Florø   *Jostedalsbreen*   *Gudbrandsdalen*   *Østerdalen*

Rena

Sognefjorden   Lillehammer

Voss   Geilo   Gol   *Lake*   Hamar
Mjøsa

Bergen   Hønefoss   Eidsvoll

Hardangerfjorden   Drammen   Oslo   *Baltic Sea*

Kongsberg   Fredrikstad

Haugesund   Dalen   Larvik   Halden

Oslofjord

Stavanger   Vallø   Porsgrunn

Sandnes   Evje   Arendal

Grimstad   *Skagerrak*

Mandal   Kristiansand   *Kattegat*

N

0   200 miles

0   300 km

Harald I, better known as Harald the Fairhaired, swore he would not cut his hair until he united Norway, and in the 9th century he succeeded in doing both. But a millennium passed between that great era and Norwegian independence. Between the Middle Ages and 1905, Norway remained under the rule of either Denmark or Sweden, even after the constitution was written in 1814.

The 19th century saw the establishment of the Norwegian identity and a blossoming of culture. This romantic period produced some of the nation's most famous individuals, among them composer Edvard Grieg, dramatist Henrik Ibsen, expressionist painter Edvard Munch, polar explorer Roald Amundsen, and explorer-humanitarian Fridtjof Nansen. Vestiges of nationalist lyricism spangle the buildings of the era with Viking dragonheads and scrollwork, all of which symbolize the rebirth of the Viking spirit.

Faithful to their democratic nature, Norwegians held a referendum to choose a king in 1905, when independence from Sweden became reality. Prince Carl of Denmark became King Haakon VII. His baby's name was changed from Alexander to Olav, and he, and later his son, presided over the kingdom for more than 85 years. When King Olav V died in January 1991, the normally reserved Norwegians stood in line for hours to write in the condolence book at the Royal Palace. Rather than simply sign their names, they wrote personal letters of devotion to the man they called the "people's king." Thousands set candles in the snow outside the palace, transforming the winter darkness into a cathedral of ice and flame.

Harald V, Olav's son, is now king, with continuity assured by his own young-adult son, Crown Prince Haakon. Norwegians continue to salute the royal family with flag-waving and parades on May 17, Constitution Day, a spirited holiday of independence that transforms Oslo's main boulevard, Karl Johans Gate, into a massive street party as people of all ages, many in national costume, make a beeline to the palace.

During both world wars, Norway tried to maintain neutrality. World War I brought not only casualties and a considerable loss to the country's merchant fleet but also financial gain through the repurchase of major companies, sovereignty over Svalbard (the islands near the North Pole), and the reaffirmation of Norway's prominence in international shipping. At the onset of World War II, Norway once again proclaimed neutrality and appeared more concerned with Allied mine-laying on the west coast than with national security. A country of mostly fisherfolk, lumber workers, and farmers, it was just beginning to realize its industrial potential when the Nazis invaded. Five years of German occupation and a burn-and-retreat strategy in the north finally left the nation ravaged. True to form, however, the people who had been evacuated returned to the embers of the north to rebuild their homes and villages.

In 1968 oil was discovered in the North Sea, and Norway was transformed from a fishing and shipping outpost to a highly developed industrial nation. Though still committed to a far-reaching social system, Norway developed in the next 20 years into a wealthy country, with a per capita income and standard of living among the world's highest, as well as long life expectancy.

Stand on a street corner with a map, and a curious Norwegian will show you the way. Visit a neighborhood, and within moments you'll be the talk of the town. As a native of Bergen quipped, "Next to skiing, gossip is a national sport." With one foot in modern, liberal Scandinavia and the other in the provincial and often self-righteous countryside, Norway, unlike its Nordic siblings, is clinging steadfastly to its separate and distinct identity within Europe. Famous for its social restrictiveness—smoking is frowned on, liquor may not be served before 3 PM (and never on Sunday), and violence, even among cartoon characters, is closely monitored—Norway is determined to repel outside interference, so much so that a national referendum in November 1994 chose to reject membership in the European Union. Thanks to Norway's oil supply—which has resulted in a major economic boom—no tragic repercussions to its isolation have occurred, and none are expected to before the end of the millennium.

Pleasures and Pastimes

Beaches
Many Norwegians enjoy beaches in the summer, but low water temperatures, from 14°C to 18°C (57°F to 65°F), are enough to deter all but the most hardy visitors from getting into the water. The beaches around Mandal in the south and Jaeren's Ogna, Brusand, and Bore, closer to Stavanger, are the country's best, with fine white sand. However, all along the Oslo Fjord are good beaches too. The western fjords are warmer and calmer than the open beaches of the south—although they have rock, and not sand, beaches—and inland freshwater lakes are chillier still than Gulf Stream–warmed fjords. Topless bathing is common, and there are nude beaches all along the coast.

Dining
Eating is a cultural element of Norwegian society. The Norwegians pride themselves on gracious entertaining and lavish dinner parties using their finest silver and glassware. Dining out in Norway is expensive, so many weekend nights are spent at the houses of friends and relatives enjoying long, candlelit dinners with lively conversation and oftentimes countless glasses of wine. (The BYOB—Bring Your Own Bottle—policy is common in Norway because alcohol prices are so high.) Recently, as Norwegians spend more time in the office and less time at home, eating at restaurants has become more popular, especially in cities like Oslo and Stavanger. In these larger areas, the dining scene is thriving. Until lately, fine restaurants were invariably French, and fine food usually meant meat. Now, in addition to the old reliable restaurants that serve traditional Norwegian dishes, you'll find spots that serve everything from tapas to Thai cuisine.

Norwegians are beginning to feel competition from foreign foods and are taking greater pride in their native cuisine. Today seafood and game have replaced beef and veal. Fish, from common cod and skate to the noble salmon, have a prominent place in the new Norwegian kitchen, and local capelin roe, golden caviar, is served instead of the imported variety. Norwegian lamb, full of flavor, is now in the spotlight, and game, from birds to moose, is prepared with sauces made from the wild berries that are part of their diet.

Desserts, too, often feature fruit and berries. Norwegian strawberries and raspberries ripen in the long, early summer days and are sweeter and more intense than those grown farther south. Red and black currants are also used. Two berries native to Norway are *tyttebær* (lingonberries), which taste similar to cranberries but are much smaller, and *multer* (cloudberries), which look like orange raspberries but have an indescribable taste. These wild berries grow above the tree line and are a real delicacy. Multer are often served as *multekrem* (in whipped cream) as a dessert, whereas tyttebær preserves often accompany traditional meat dishes.

For centuries, Norwegians regarded food as fuel, and their dining habits still bear traces of this. *Frokost* (breakfast) is a fairly big meal, usually with a selection of crusty bread, jams, herring, cold meat, and cheese. *Geitost* (a sweet, caramel-flavored whey cheese made wholly or in part from goats' milk) and Norvegia (a Norwegian Gouda-type cheese) are on virtually every table. They are eaten in thin slices, cut with a cheese plane or slicer, a Norwegian invention, on buttered wheat or rye bread.

Lunsj (lunch) is simple and usually consists of *smørbrød* (open-faced sandwiches). Most businesses have only a 30-minute lunch break, so unless there's a company cafeteria, most people bring their lunch from home. Big lunchtime buffet tables, *koldtbord,* where one can sample most of Norway's special dishes all at once, are primarily for special occasions and visitors.

Middag (dinner), the only hot meal of the day, is early—from 1 to 4 in the country, 3 to 7 in the city—so many cafeterias serving home-style food close by 6 or 7 in the evening. In Oslo it's possible to get dinner as late as midnight at certain dining establishments, especially in summertime. You'll probably find that most restaurants in Oslo usually stop serving dinner around 10 PM.

Traditional, home-style Norwegian food is stick-to-the-ribs fare, served in generous portions and blanketed with gravy. One of the most popular meals is *kjøttkaker* (meat cakes), which resemble small Salisbury steaks, served with boiled potatoes, stewed cabbage, and brown gravy. Almost as popular are *medisterkaker* (mild pork sausage patties), served with brown gravy and caraway-seasoned sauerkraut, and *reinsdyrkaker* (reindeer meatballs), served with cream sauce and lingonberry jam. Other typical meat dishes include *fårikål,* a great-tasting lamb and cabbage stew, and *steik* (roast meat), always served well done. Fish dishes include poached *torsk* (cod) or *laks* (salmon), served with a creamy sauce called Sandefjord butter; *seibiff,* fried pollack and onions; and *fiskegrateng,* something between a fish soufflé and a casserole, usually served with carrot slaw.

Norway is known for several eccentric, often pungent fish dishes, but these are not representative—both *rakørret* and *raklaks* (fermented trout and salmon) and *lutefisk* (dried cod soaked in lye and then boiled) are acquired tastes, even for natives. These dishes are often served at holidays, accompanied by the national drink, *akevitt* (sometimes spelled aquavit), a schnapps-like liquor that is made from potatoes and caraway seeds.

Traditional desserts include *karamellpudding* (crème caramel) and *rømmegrøt* (sour-cream porridge served with cinnamon sugar) and a glass of *saft* (raspberry juice). Rømmegrøt—a typical farm dish—tastes very much like warm cheesecake batter. It's often served with *fenalår* (dried leg of mutton) and *lefsekling,* a thin tortilla-like pancake made with sour cream and potatoes, buttered and coated with sugar. Christmastime brings with it a delectable array of light, sweet, and buttery pastries. The *bløtkake* (layered cream cake with custard, fruit, and marzipan) is a favorite for Christmas and special occasions but can be purchased in bakeries year-round.

CATEGORY	COST*
$$$$	over NKr450
$$$	NKr300–NKr450
$$	NKr150–NKr300
$	under NKr150

*per person for a three-course meal, including tax and 12½% service charge

Fishing

Whether it's fly-fishing in western rivers or deep-sea fishing off the northern coast, Norway has all kinds of angling possibilities.

Hiking

Seemingly, one of the most common expressions in the Norwegian language is *gå på tur,* or go for a walk. Every city has surrounding trails where Norwegians usually spend a good part of their weekends hiking and strolling. Many of the trails have cabins where hikers can rest, eat, and even spend the night. Den Norske Turistforening (☞ Biking *in* Norway A to Z., *below*) and affiliated organizations administer cabins and tourist facilities in the central and northern mountainous areas of the country and will arrange group hikes.

Lodging

Norway is a land of hard beds and hearty breakfasts. Hotel standards are high, and even the simplest youth hostels provide good mattresses with fluffy down comforters and clean showers or baths. Breakfast, usually served buffet style, is almost always included in the room price at hotels, whereas hostels often charge extra for the morning meal.

Norway has several hotel chains. SAS, which is a division of the airline, has a number of luxury hotels designed for the business traveler. Many are above the Arctic Circle and are the "only game in town." Rica and Reso hotels, also luxury chains, have expanded extensively in the past few years. Best Western, Rainbow, and Choice Hotels International are moderate chains, found in most major towns. The most interesting and distinctive hotel chain is Home Hotels (Swedish owned), which has successfully converted existing historic buildings into modern functional establishments in the middle price range. All Home Hotels provide an evening meal, free beer, and other amenities designed to appeal to the single, usually business, traveler. As far as value for money is concerned, they are Norway's best buy. The Farmer's Association operates simple hotels in most towns and cities. These reasonably priced accommodations usually have "-heimen" as part of the name, such as Bondeheimen in Oslo. The same organization also runs cafeterias serving traditional Norwegian food, usually called Kaffistova. All of these hotels and restaurants are alcohol-free.

At times it seems as though the SAS and Rica hotel chains are the only ones in northern Norway, and often that is true. These are always top-rate, usually the most expensive hotels in town, with the best restaurant and the most extensive facilities. Rustic cabins and campsites are also available everywhere, as well as some independent hotels.

In the Lofoten and Vesterålen islands, *rorbuer,* fishing cottages that have been converted into lodgings or modern versions of these simple dwellings, are the most popular form of accommodation. These rustic quayside cabins, with minikitchens, bunk beds, living rooms, and showers, are reasonably priced, and they give a unique experience of the region. *Sjøhus* (sea houses) are larger, usually two- or three-storied buildings similar to rorbuer.

Norway has 90 youth hostels, but in an effort to appeal to vacationers of all ages, the name has been changed to *vandrerhjem* (travelers' home). Norwegian hostels are among the best in the world, squeaky clean and with excellent facilities. Rooms sleep from two to six, and many have private showers. You don't have to be a member, but members get reductions, so it's worth joining. Membership can be arranged at any vandrerhjem, or you can buy a coupon book good for seven nights, which includes the membership fee. Linens are usually rented per night, so it's a good idea to bring your own—if you haven't, you can buy a *lakenpose* (sheet sleeping bag) at specialty stores, or one at the vandrerhjem (☞ Lodging *in* Norway A to Z, *below*).

Norway has more than 900 inspected and classified campsites, many with showers, bathrooms, and hookups for electricity. Most also have cabins or chalets to rent by the night or longer.

CATEGORY	MAJOR CITIES*	OTHER AREAS*
$$$$	over NKr1,300	over NKr1,000
$$$	NKr1,000–NKr1,300	NKr850–NKr1,000
$$	NKr800–NKr1,000	NKr650–NKr850
$	under NKr800	under NKr650

All prices are for a standard double room, including service and 23% VAT.

Orienteering

One of Norway's most popular mass-participation sports is based on running or hiking over territory with a map and compass to find control points marked on a map. Special cards can be purchased at sports shops to be punched at control points found during a season. It's an enjoyable, inexpensive family sport.

Shopping

Almost no one leaves Norway without buying a hand-knit sweater. Although the prices for these sweaters may seem high, the quality is outstanding. The classic knitting designs, with snowflakes and reindeer, are still bestsellers and can be bought at most *Husfliden* (homecraft) outlets and specialty stores, whereas more modern sweaters, made of combinations of brightly colored yarns, can be purchased from yarn shops.

Given the Norwegians' affection for the outdoors, an abundance of high-quality sportsgear and outerwear is available. Good buys include Helly-Hansen rain gear, insulated boots, and the *supertrøye,* a gossamer-thin, insulated undershirt.

Handicraft lovers will marvel at Norway's goods. You'll find handmade pewter and wrought-iron candlesticks, hand-dipped candles, handblown glass, and hand-turned wood bowls, spoons, and platters made of birch roots, decorated with rosemaling (intricate painted or carved floral folk-art designs). Although your visit may be in June, this is a great place to stock up on your Christmas goods. All Husfliden stores and many gift shops sell Christmas ornaments handmade from straw and wood shavings. *Juleduk* (Christmas tablecloths) with typical Norwegian themes are for sale year-round at embroidery shops. Other, more offbeat, items include *ostehøvler* (cheese slicers) and *kransekake-former,* graduated forms for making almond ring cakes. If you're looking for Norwegian recipes, you may want to seek out Arne Brimi's cookbook—*A Taste of Norwegian Nature.* It's sold in most bookstores.

Silver is a good buy in Norway, especially with the value-added tax refund (☞ Taxes *in* Norway A to Z, *below*). Norwegian silver companies produce a wide range of patterns. Although the price of Norwegian silver is competitive, at 830 parts to 1,000 (compared with the standard 925 parts in sterling), it's not as pure as English or American silver. However, some will argue that it's stronger.

Unfortunately, Norwegian rustic antiques may not be exported. Even the simplest corner shelf or dish rack valued at $50 is considered a national treasure if it is known to be more than 100 years old. However, you'll find that there are some really good replicas of old Norwegian farm furniture available.

Skiing

The ski is Norway's contribution to the world of sports. In 1994 the Winter Olympics were held in Lillehammer, which, along with other Norwegian resorts, regularly hosts World Cup competitions and world skiing championships. In addition to downhill and cross-country, the 100-year-old Telemark style is enjoying a revival across the country. It involves a characteristic deep-knee bend in the turns and traditional garb, including heavy boots attached to the skis only at the toe. Cross-country skiing is a great way to see Norway's nature; it requires only basic equipment, and rentals are readily available. Most every city has lit trails for evening skiing. Norway's skiing season lasts from November to Easter. But winter's not the only time for skiing in Norway—you may want to try summer skiing on a glacier.

Exploring Norway

Norway is long and narrow, bordered by Sweden to the east, and jagged coastline to the west. The west coast is carved by deep, dramatic fjords, and small coastal villages dot the shores in between. Bergen, the country's second largest city, is touted as the capital of the West Coast.

Norway's official capital, Oslo, is in the east, only a few hours from the Swedish border. The coast, from Oslo around the southern tip of the country up to Stavanger, is filled with wide beaches and seaside communities. North of here, in Norway's central interior, the country is blanketed with mountains that sculpt the landscape, creating dramatic valleys and plateaus. Moving north, the land becomes wild and untouched. Outside the north's two main cities, Trondheim and Tromsø, the land seems to stretch for miles, which it actually does—into the Arctic Circle and up to the Russian border. We describe each of these regions in its own section below.

Numbers in the text correspond to numbers in the margin and on the maps.

Great Itineraries

What sets Norway apart from other European countries is not so much its cultural tradition or its internationally renowned museums as its spectacular natural beauty. What other world capital has subway service to the forest, or lakes and hiking trails within city limits as Oslo does? Although it takes only a few days to briefly explore Oslo and its environs, a full week or more would allow for more leisurely explorations of Norway's stunning countryside, including its fjords, plateaus, mountains, and valleys.

IF YOU HAVE 5 DAYS

Oslo, Norway's capital, makes a good starting point since most flights to Norway arrive here. Spend your first two days exploring ⊞ **Oslo** ①–㉗. Take it easy the first day and explore the downtown area—meander on Karl Johans Gate, see Akershus Castle and the Kvadraturen, and walk through Vigelands (Frogner) Park. On day two, head out to Bygdøy and visit the area's museums—the Folkemuseum is a must. On the third day, depart for Bergen by train. This six-hour trip across Norway's interior allows you to see some of the country's spectacular scenery, including **Hardangervidda.** When you get to ⊞ **Bergen** ㉞–㊾, check into your hotel and head to Bryggen for dinner. Here along Bergen's wharf you'll see some of the city's oldest and best-preserved buildings. Spend your fourth day exploring Bergen. If you have time, head out to Troldhaugen, which was composer Edvard Grieg's house for 22 years; it's a half-day trip from Bergen's center. Spend your last night in Bergen, and on the fifth day, fly back to Oslo.

Spend your first four days following the tour above. On your fifth day, take the day trip **Norway in a Nutshell** (☞ Guided Tours *in* Bergen A to Z, *below*), which is a bus-train-boat tour that takes you through some of western fjord country. Spend your fifth night in Bergen, and on your sixth day, fly to ▨ **Tromsø** ⑦⑧, which is north of the Arctic Circle. Spend the rest of the day touring Tromsø. Overnight here, and on your seventh day, rent a car and head for ▨ **Alta** ⑦⑨. If you arrive early enough, visit the Alta Museum. Spend the night in Alta, and on the eighth day, continue your voyage, driving farther on to ▨ **Hammerfest** ⑧⓪, the world's northernmost town. Overnight in Hammerfest, and the next day, take an excursion up the treeless tundra of the **Nordkapp** ⑧② (North Cape). Return to Hammerfest, and on your last day, fly back to Oslo via Alta.

When to Tour Norway

To experience the endless days of the Midnight Sun, the best time to visit Norway is mid-May to late July. Hotels, museums, and sights are open and transportation is beefed up. If you decide to travel in May, try to be in Norway on the 17th, or *Syttende Mai,* Norway's Constitution Day, when flag-waving Norwegians bedecked in national costumes, or *bunader,* fill the streets.

Autumn weather is quite unpredictable. The days can be cool and crisp, or wet and bone-chillingly cold. However, the Gulf Stream, which flows along the Norwegian coast, keeps the weather surprisingly mild for such a high latitude.

Norway in winter is a wonderland of snow-covered mountains glowing under the northern lights, and few tourists are around to get in your way (although many tourist sights are closed). The days may seem perpetually dark, and November through February can seem especially dreary. If it's skiing you're interested in, plan your trip for March or April, as there's usually still plenty of snow left. Take note that during Eastertime, many Norwegians head for the mountains, so it's hard to get accommodations, and cities are virtually shut down—even grocery stores close.

OSLO

Although it is one of the world's largest capital cities in area, Oslo has only 480,000 inhabitants. Nevertheless, in recent years the city has taken off: shops are open later, cafés and restaurants are crowded at all hours, and theaters play to full houses every night of the week.

Even without nightlife, Oslo has a lot to offer—parks, water, trees, hiking and skiing trails (2,600 km/1,600 mi in greater Oslo), and above all, spectacular views. Starting at the docks opposite City Hall, right at the edge of the Oslo Fjord, the city sprawls up the sides of the mountains that surround it, providing panoramic vistas from almost any vantage point but no definable downtown skyline. A building spree in the late 1980s and early '90s has added a number of modern towers, particularly in the area around the Central Railway Station, which clash painfully with the neoclassical architecture in the rest of the city.

Oslo has been Norway's center of commerce for about 500 years, and most major Norwegian companies are based in the capital. The sea has always been Norway's lifeline to the rest of the world: the Oslo Fjord teems with activity, from summer sailors and shrimpers to merchant ships and passenger ferries heading for Denmark and Germany.

Oslo is an old city, dating from the mid-11th century. The city has actually burned down 14 times since its creation, and was all but destroyed by a fire in 1624, when it was redesigned and renamed Christiania by Denmark's royal builder, King Christian IV. During the mid-19th century, and under the influence of the Swedish king, Karl Johan, who ruled the newly united Kingdom of Norway and Sweden, the grand axis—named after himself—was constructed. A definite product of the European city planning trends, Karl Johans Gate has been at the center of city life ever since. An act of Parliament finally changed the city's name back to Oslo, its original Viking name, in 1925.

Exploring Oslo

Karl Johans Gate, starting at Oslo Sentralstasjon (Oslo Central Station, also called Oslo S Station) and ending at the Royal Palace, forms the backbone of downtown Oslo. Many of Oslo's museums and historic buildings lie between the parallel streets of Grensen and Rådhusgata. Just north of the center of town is a historic area with a medieval church and old buildings. West of downtown is Frogner, the residential area closest to town, with embassies, fine restaurants, antiques shops, galleries, and the Vigeland sculpture park. Farther west is the Bygdøy Peninsula, with five interesting museums and a castle. Northwest of town is Holmenkollen, with beautiful houses, a famous ski jump, and a restaurant. On the east side, where many new immigrants live, are the Munch Museum and the botanical gardens.

Downtown: The Royal Palace to City Hall

Although the city is huge (454 square km/175 square mi), downtown Oslo is compact, with shops, museums, historic sights, restaurants, and clubs concentrated in a small, walkable center—brightly illuminated at night.

A GOOD WALK

Oslo's main promenade, Karl Johans Gate, runs from **Slottet** ① through town. Walk down the incline, and to your left you will see three yellow buildings of the old **Universitet** ②—today they are used only by the law school. Murals painted by Edvard Munch decorate the interior walls of these buildings. Around the corner from the university on Universitetsgata is the **Nasjonalgalleriet** ③, which contains hundreds of Norwegian, Scandinavian, and European works, including Munch's famous painting *The Scream*. Back-to-back with the National Gallery, across a parking lot, is a big cream-brick Art Nouveau–style building housing the **Historisk Museum** ④, whose collection of Viking artifacts is impressive. Continue along Frederiksgate to the university and cross Karl Johans Gate to the **Nationalteatret** ⑤ and Studenterlunden Park. This impressive building is not only the national theater, but a popular meeting place—many buses stop out front, and the T-bane (subway) is right beside it.

Walk past the Lille Grensen shopping area and once again cross Karl Johans Gate to see **Stortinget** ⑥, the Norwegian Parliament. Then go back to Stortingsgata. From here, turn left on Universitetsgata, and walk through a cul-de-sac–type area toward the water to reach the redbrick **Rådhuset** ⑦, a familiar landmark with its two block towers, dedicated during Oslo's 900th-year jubilee celebrations in 1950. After visiting Rådhuset, end your tour with an øl (beer) or mineral water at one of the many outdoor cafés at Aker Brygge (☞ Dining, *below*).

TIMING

The walk alone should take no more than two hours, even if you take time to wander around in Royal Palace park. If you happen to be at

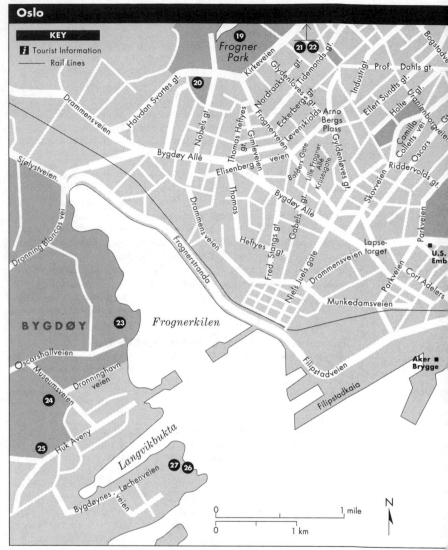

Oslo

KEY

i Tourist Information
—— Rail Lines

Frogner Park

Akershus Slott og Festning, **11**
Astrup Fearnley Museet for Moderne Kunst, **10**
Fram-Museet, **26**
Gamle Aker Kirke, **14**
Gamlebyen, **16**
Historisk Museum, **4**
Holmenkollbakken, **22**
Kon-Tiki Museum, **27**
Kunstindustri-museet, **15**
Munchmuseet, **13**

Museet for Samtidskunst, **9**
Nasjonalgalleriet, **3**
Nationalteatret, **5**
Norges Hjemmefront Museum, **12**
Norsk Folkemuseum, **24**
Oscarshall Slott, **23**
Oslo Domkirke, **8**
Oslo Ladegård, **18**
Rådhuset, **7**
St. Halvards Kirke, **17**

Slottet, **1**
Stortinget, **6**
Tryvannstårnet, **21**
Universitet, **2**
Vigelandsparken, **19**
Vigelandsmuseet, **20**
Vikingskiphuset, **25**

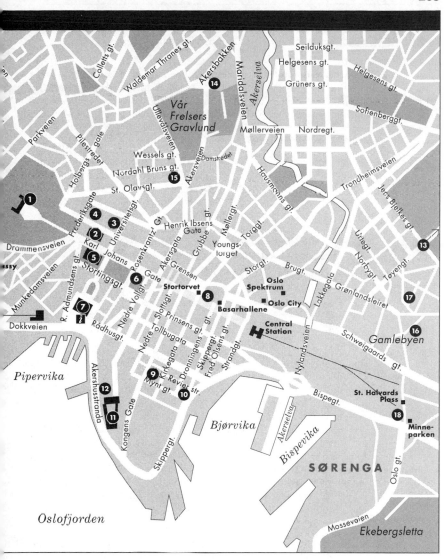

Seilduksgt.

Helgesens gt.

Grüners gt.

Helgesens gt.

Colletts gt.

Waldemar Thranes gt.

Akersbakken

Maridalsveien

Akerselva

14

Vår
Frelsers
Gravlund

Sofienberggt.

Møllerveien

Nordregt.

Parkveien

Ullevålsveien

Pilestredet

Holbergs gate

Wessels gt.

Nordahl Bruns gt.

15

St. Olavsgt.

Damstredet

Akersveien

Hausmanns gt.

Trondheimsveien

Jens Bjelkes gt.

1

Frederiks gate

Universitetsgt.

Henrik Ibsens
Gate

Grubbe

gt.

Møllergt.

Torggt.

Uttelgt.

Norbygt.

Tøyengt.

13

Drammensveien

4

3

2

Karl Johans

Rosenkrantz' Gt.

Akersgata

Aker Grensen

Youngs-
torget

Storgt.

Brugt.

ssy

5

Gate

Storgt.

**Oslo
Spektrum**

Løkkegata

Grønlandsleiret

17

Munkedamsveien

R. Admundsens gt.

Stortingsgt.

6

Stortorvet

8

Oslo City

Gamlebyen

16

Nedre Vollgt.

Slottsgt.

Prinsens gt.

Basarhallene

**Central
Station**

Schweigaards gt.

7

i

Rådhusgt.

Tollbugata

Skippergt.

Nylandsveien

Dokkveien

Nedre Slottsgt.

Kirkegata

Dronningens gt.

Fred Olsens gt.

Strandgt.

**St. Halvards
Plass**

Bispegt.

Pipervika

9

Revier str.

18

**Minne-
parken**

Akershusstranda

12

10

Mynt gt.

Bjørvika

Akselva

Bispevika

Oslo gt.

11

Kongens Gate

SØRENGA

Skippergt.

Oslofjorden

Mossevaien

Ekebergsletta

the Royal Palace midday, you might catch the changing of the guard, which happens every day at 1:30. When you are planning your tour, take note that many museums are closed on Mondays.

SIGHTS TO SEE

❹ Historisk Museum (Historical Museum). Intricately carved *stav kirke* (wood church) portals and other Viking and medieval artifacts are on display here. There's an exhibition about the Arctic, as well as Asian and African ethnographic exhibits. ✉ *Frederiksgt. 2,* ☎ *22/85–99–12.* ▦ *Free.* ☉ *Mid-May–mid-Sept., Tues.–Sun. 11–3; late Sept.–early May, Tues.–Sun. noon–3.*

❸ Nasjonalgalleriet (The National Gallery). Many Scandinavian impressionists, who have recently been discovered by the rest of the world, are represented here in Norway's official art museum. Some impressive fjord and moonlight scenes by Norwegian artists such as Christian Krogh and J.C. Dahl fill the walls of the 19th- and early 20th-century Norwegian rooms. The gallery also has an extensive Munch collection. ✉ *Universitetsgt. 13,* ☎ *22/20–04–04.* ▦ *Free.* ☉ *Mon., Wed., Fri., and Sat. 10–6; Thurs. 10–8; Sun. 11–4.*

❺ Nationalteatret (National Theater). In front of this neoclassical theater, built in 1899, are statues of Norway's great playwrights, Bjørnstjerne Bjørnson (who wrote the words to the national anthem and won a Nobel Prize for his plays) and Henrik Ibsen, author of *A Doll's House, Hedda Gabler,* and *The Wild Duck.* Most performances are in Norwegian, so you may just want to take a guided tour of the interior. Call for details. ✉ *Stortingsgt. 15,* ☎ *22/41–27–10.*

★ **❼ Rådhuset** (City Hall). The redbrick exterior of Oslo's City Hall may seem dull compared with the marble-floored interior, whose murals and frescoes are bursting with color. Many sculptures outside, as well as murals inside, reflect the artistic climate in Norway in the 1930s—socialist modernism in its highest form. Much of the adornment depicts not only daily life but also Viking gods and Norwegian literary figures. This may be the only City Hall in the world with a sculpture of a prostitute; it's on the east side of the building facing the fjord. The Nobel Peace Prize has been handed out in the Main Hall since 1990. ✉ *Rådhuspl.,* ☎ *22/86–16–00.* ▦ *NKr 15.* ☉ *May–Aug., Mon.–Sat. 9–5, Sun. noon–5; Sept.–Apr., Mon.–Sat. 9–3:30, Sun. noon–5. Guided tours year-round, weekdays 10, noon, and 2.*

★ **❶ Slottet** (The Royal Palace). The neoclassical palace, completed in 1848, is closed to visitors, but the garden is open to the public. An equestrian statue of Karl Johan, king of Sweden and Norway from 1818 to 1844, stands in the square in front of the palace.

❻ Stortinget (The Norwegian Parliament). Built in the middle of the 19th century, this classic building is perched on the top of a small hill. At night, the steps here become a great spot for people-watching. When Parliament is in session, the public gallery is open to curious onlookers. ✉ *Karl Johans Gt. 22,* ☎ *22/31–30–50.* ▦ *Free.* ☉ *Guided tours on weekdays in July and Aug.; tours Sat. only Sept.–June.*

❷ Universitetet (The University). The great hall of the center building is decorated with murals by Edvard Munch, such as *The Sun,* whose penetrating rays over a fjord give a whole new meaning to the notion of daylight. It was the site of the Nobel Peace Prize award ceremony until 1989. The hall still receives other notable visitors, such as Salman Rushdie, who showed up almost unannounced in 1995. ✉ *Aulaen, Karl Johans Gt. 47,* ☎ *22/85–97–11* ▦ *Free.* ☉ *July, weekdays 10:45–2.*

Kvadraturen and Akershus Castle

The Kvadraturen is the oldest part of Oslo still standing. In 1624, after the town of Oslo burned down for the 14th time, King Christian IV renamed the city Christiania and moved it from the area that is today south of Oslo S Station, called Gamlebyen (☞ *below*), and rebuilt it adjacent to the Akershus fortress. The king decreed that houses were to be built in stone or brick instead of wood—in order to prevent future fires. He also built a stone wall around the newly rebuilt city to protect it from his enemies, the Swedes.

A GOOD WALK

The Kvadraturen area, which includes Akershus Slott, is bound on the east side of the fortress by Skippergata and on the north side by Karl Johans Gate between Oslo Domkirke and Stortorvet. The boundary follows Øvre Vollgata around to the other side of the fortress. Kvadraturen translates roughly as "square township," which refers to the area's geometrically ordered streets. Be aware that the streets around Skippergata and Myntgata are known as a mini–red-light district, so you may see some unsavory characters. The area, however, is not dangerous, especially if you go during daylight.

Start at Stortorvet, Oslo's main square. On the right of the square is **Oslo Domkirke** ⑧, completed in 1697. Take a look inside—artists have been contributing to the cathedral's richly decorated interior since the 18th century. Behind the cathedral is a semicircular arcade called Kirkeristen, or **Basarhallene,** housing many artisans' small shops.

From the cathedral, follow Kirkegata left past Karl Johan to the **Museet for Samtidskunst** ⑨, which is housed in the 1902 Bank of Norway building. Take some time to view the museum's contemporary works, especially the ones by Norwegian artists. From the museum, take the side street Revierstredet to Dronningensgate, where you'll come across a building that does not seem to fit in with its 17th-century neighbors. Designed and built in the early 1990s, this brick and steel office building houses the **Astrup Fearnley Museet for Moderne Kunst** ⑩. This stop is a must for modern-art lovers.

Take Dronningensgate back to Rådhusgata and turn left. As you go up the street, notice the 17th-century building at 11 Rådhusgata. It houses the celebrated restaurant Statholdergården (☞ Dining, *below*). This was the home of the "statholder," the official representative from Copenhagen when Norway was under Danish rule.

Continue on Rådhusgata until you reach the corner of Nedre Slottsgate. The yellow building you see was the old city hall; now it's the 141-year-old Gamle Rådhus (☞ Dining, *below*) restaurant. This structure, first built in 1641, has also served as a courthouse, prison, and wine cellar. It became a restaurant in 1856. The revered dining spot closed down in 1996 after an unexplained fire, but the management hopes to reopen it sometime in the next few years. Diagonally across Rådhusgata in the two 17th-century buildings are an art gallery and an artsy café. The building that houses Kafé Celcius was one of the first buildings erected in Christian IV's town. The building has had many functions, starting as a schoolhouse and eventually serving as a military hospital and the living quarters of a mayor.

Turn left on Akersgata and walk alongside the grassy hill to the entrance of **Akershus Slott og Festning** ⑪, the central element of Christian IV's Kvadraturen. It's a slight climb, but the views from the top are worth it. The castle became the German headquarters during the occupation of Norway in World War II, and many members of the Resistance were executed on the castle grounds. Their memorial has been erected at the site, across the bridge at the harbor end of the castle precinct. In a building next to the castle, at the top of the hill, is the **Norges Hjemmefront Museum** ⑫.

Walk back to Rådhusgata to see another interesting building, **Skogbrand Insurance** (Rådhusgt. 23B). Architects Jan Digerud and Jon Lundberg have won awards for their innovative 1985 vertical addition to this 1917 building. Once you have your fill of history and architecture, you can get in touch with something a bit more corporeal at the Emanuel Vigeland Museum, which displays artistic erotica created by the brother of the celebrated sculptor Gustav Vigeland. To get here, turn right on any of the streets along Rådhusgata back to Karl Johans and take the T-bane (T-bane is short for *tunnelbane,* which is an underground railway, or subway) line 1 from Nationalteatret station direction Frognerseteren and get off at Slemdal.

TIMING

The walk alone should take at least three hours. Combined with museum visits and breaks, the itinerary could take up more than half a day. Akershus Festning will take at least half an hour. Many museums are closed Mondays. Astrup Fearnley is open afternoons only; and the Teatermuseet is open only a few days a week—plan your tour accordingly. Try to do this tour during daylight hours, catching late-afternoon sun from atop the Akershus grounds. Also note that the T-bane ride to the Emanuel Vigeland Museet in Slemdal takes about 15 minutes and that the museum is open only a few hours on Sunday afternoons.

SIGHTS TO SEE

⑪ **Akershus Slott og Festning** (Akershus Castle and Fortress). The oldest part of the castle was built around 1300 and includes an "escape-proof" room built four centuries later for a thief named Ole Pedersen Høyland. In fact he broke out of this cell, robbed the Bank of Norway, was caught, and brought back to jail. With no possibility of a second escape, he killed himself here. Today some of the building is used for state occasions, but a few rooms, including the chapel, are open to the public. ⊠ *Akershus Slott, Festningspl.,* ☎ *22/41–25–21.* ▣ *Grounds and concerts free; castle NKr20.* ⊙ *Grounds daily 6 AM–9 PM; concerts, mid-May–mid-Oct., Sun. at 2; castle May–mid-Sept., Mon.–Sat. 10–4. Guided tours May–Sept., Mon.–Sat. 11, 1, and 3; Sun. 1 and 3.*

⑩ **Astrup Fearnley Museet for Moderne Kunst** (Astrup Fearnley Museum for Modern Art). Shiny marble floors and white and gray walls (whose colors may change with the exhibitions) provide a neutral and elegant background for a series of fascinating and often disturbing works. Several works by the German artist Anselm Kiefer are part of the museum's permanent collection. Spacious exhibition rooms lead to a glassed-in sculpture garden with Niki de St. Phalle's sparrow and several other oversize 20th-century figures. ⊠ *Dronningens Gt. 4,* ☎ *22/93–60–60.* ▣ *NKr30.* ⊙ *Tues., Wed., and Fri.–Sun. noon–4; Thurs. noon–7. Guided tours weekends at 1.*

OFF THE
BEATEN PATH

EMANUEL VIGELANDS MUSEET – Although he never gained the fame of his brother Gustav, the creator of Vigeland Park, the younger Emanuel is an artist of some notoriety. His alternately saucy, natural, and downright erotic frescoes make even the sexually liberated Norwegians blush. To get here, take T-bane line 1 in the direction of Frognerseteren and get off at Slemdal, one of Oslo's hillside residential neighborhoods. ⊠ *Grimelundsvn. 8,* ☎ *22/14–93–42.* ▣ *Free.* ⊙ *Sun. noon–3.*

⑨ **Museet for Samtidskunst** (The Museum of Contemporary Art). The building, a good example of Norwegian Art Nouveau architecture,

In case you want to see the world.

At American Express, we're here to make your journey a smooth one. So we have over 1,700 travel service locations in over 120 countries ready to help. What else would you expect from the world's largest travel agency?

do more

AMERICAN
EXPRESS

http://www.americanexpress.com/travel

Travel

In case you want to be welcomed there.

We're here to see that you're always welcomed at establishments everywhere. That's why millions of people carry the American Express® Card – for peace of mind, confidence, and security, around the world or just around the corner.

do more

Cards

In case you're running low.

We're here to help with more than 118,000 Express Cash locations around the world. In order to enroll, just call American Express before you start your vacation.

do more

Express Cash

And just in case.

We're here with American Express® Travelers Cheques and Cheques *for Two*® They're the safest way to carry money on your vacation and the surest way to get a refund, practically anywhere, anytime.

Another way we help you...

do more

Travelers
Cheques

houses a fine collection of international and Norwegian contemporary works in small rooms. ⊠ *Bankpl. 4,* ☎ *22/33–58–20.* ☎ *Free.* ⊙ *Tues.–Wed., Fri. 10–5, Thurs. 10–8, Sat. 11–4, Sun. 11–5. Guided tours by appointment only.*

⑫ **Norges Hjemmefront Museum** (Norwegian Resistance Museum). Winding hallways take you through a series of audiovisual displays documenting events that took place during the German occupation (1940–45). ⊠ *Norges Hjemmefrontmuseum, Akershus Festning,* ☎ *23/09–31–38.* ☎ *NKr20.* ⊙ *Mid-Apr.–mid-June and Sept., Mon.–Sat. 10–4, Sun. 11–4; mid-June–Aug., Mon.–Sat. 10–5, Sun. 11–5; Oct.–mid-Apr., Mon.–Sat. 10–3, Sun. 11–4.*

❽ **Oslo Domkirke** (Oslo Cathedral). In the 19th century, the fire department operated a fire lookout point from the bell tower here, which you can visit today. This dark brown brick structure has been Oslo's main church since the 17th century. Inside is an intricately carved Baroque pulpit and a five-story organ. Built in 1697, the church underwent extensive renovations before reopening in the summer of 1997 to celebrate its 300th anniversary. ⊠ *Stortorvet 1,* ☎ *22/41–27–93.* ☎ *Free.* ⊙ *June–Aug., weekdays 10–3, Sat. 10–1; Sept.–May, weekdays 10–3.*

NEED A BREAK?	**Pascal** (⊠ Tollbugt. 11, ☎ 22/42–11–19), a Parisian patisserie inside an old-fashioned Norwegian *konditori* (café), serves enormous croissants and pastries with French coffee. Look for the little angels baking bread—they're painted on the ceiling.

East, North, and South of Downtown: Munch Museum, Damstredet, and Gamlebyen

The Munch Museum is east of the city center in Tøyen, an area in which Edvard Munch spent many of his years in Oslo. The Tøyen district has a much different feel than Oslo's cushy west side—it's simpler and more industrial. West of Tøyen, just north of the city center, is the quiet, old-fashioned district of Damstredet, its quaint streets lined with artisans' shops. If you're a die-hard history buff, you'll probably enjoy the last half of this tour through Gamlebyen. However, if this is your first time in Oslo and you have a limited amount of time, you may want to end your tour at the Kunstindustrimuseet. Gamlebyen, south of the city center, is somewhat off the beaten track, and although the area is interesting, some of the ruins are barely discernible.

A GOOD WALK

Start by taking any T-bane from the city center to Tøyen, where **Munchmuseet** ⑬ sits on a hill near the **Botanisk Hage,** a quiet oasis of plants and flowers. Munch's family lived in a house in the neighborhood during part of his life. After visiting the museum, head back toward the city center. Take the T-bane toward Sentrum and get off at Stortinget.

Head down Karl Johans Gate and take a right onto Akersgata. Follow it past the offices of **Aftenposten,** Norway's leading daily paper, which display the day's headlines in the window. As you head up the hill, you will see a huge rotund building, **Deichmanske Bibliotek,** the city's library. When you reach St. Olavs Church, veer gently to the right on Akersveien. You may want to take a detour down **Damstredet** when you come to it—it's one of the city's oldest streets. Afterward, continue back along Akersveien. **Vår Frelsers Gravlund** (Our Savior's Graveyard), where you can seek out the gravestones of many famous Norwegians who are buried here, including Ibsen and Munch, will be on your left. At the graveyard's northeastern corner is **Gamle Aker Kirke** ⑭, the city's only remaining medieval church.

On the other side of the cemetery, follow Ullevålsveien down the hill to the corner of St. Olavs Gate and Akersgata, where you'll find the **Kunstindustrimuseet** ⑮. The museum has a superb furniture collection.

If history and archaeology interest you, visit **Gamlebyen** ⑯, the old town, on the south side of Oslo S Station. South of here on Oslo Gate is St. Halvards Plass. During the 13th century, the area near St. Halvards Plass was the city's ecclesiastical center. Still intact are the foundations of **St. Halvards Kirke** ⑰, dating from the early 12th century. Some other ruins, including Korskirke and Olavs Kloster, lie in **Minneparken.** Nearby on Bispegata is **Oslo Ladegård** ⑱, a restored Baroque-style mansion that sits on the site and foundations of a 13th-century Bishop's Palace. Government construction of the Gardemoebanen (commuter railway) to the new Oslo Airport at Gardemoen has inspired many archaeologists and city historians to mobilize in an effort to preserve the ruins area.

The oldest traces of human habitation in Oslo are the 5,000-year-old carvings on the runic stones near **Ekebergsletta Park.** They are across the road from the park on Karlsborgveien and are marked by a sign reading FORTIDSMINNE. To reach the park, walk south on Oslo Gate until it becomes Mosseveien. The park will be on your right. Here is a good spot to rest your feet and end your tour.

TIMING
The Munchmuseet will take up most of the morning, especially if you take a guided tour. Don't plan your tour for a Monday because the Munchmuseet and Kunstindustrimuseet are closed. The second half of the tour, from Gamlebyen to Ekebergsletta, is a perfect way to spend a summer Sunday afternoon. Things are quiet, and locals tend to stroll around this area when the weather is nice.

SIGHTS TO SEE

⑭ **Gamle Aker Kirke** (Old Aker Church). Oslo's medieval stone basilica has undergone many changes since it was constructed around 1100. ☒ *Akersvn. 26,* ☎ *22/69–35–82.* ☒ *Free.* ☉ *Mon.–Sat. noon–2, Sun. 9–1.*

⑯ **Gamlebyen** (The Old City). This area contains the last remains of medieval Oslo. Because of repeated fires, Christian IV moved Oslo from this site (after the fire of 1624) to a safer area near Akershus Festning (Akershus Fort). Today it's the largest homogeneous archaeological site found in any capital city in Scandinavia. To get here, go back to Stortorvet and take *trikk* (as the Norwegians fondly call the streetcars) 18, marked "Ljabru," from Stortorvet to St. Halvards Plass (you can also take trikk 19 from Nationalteatret). Contact Oslo Byantikvar (☎ 22/20–85–80) for information on guided tours of the area, or for a self-guided tour ask the Norway Information Center where you can get a copy of *Guide to Gamlebyen* by Morten Krogstad and Erik Schia.

⑮ **Kunstindustrimuseet** (Museum of Applied Art). Clothes worthy of any fairy tale, including Queen Maud's jewel-encrusted coronation gown from 1904, are displayed here in the museum's Royal Norwegian Costume Gallery. Extensive collections of industrial designs and arts and crafts include more than 35,000 objects. ☒ *St. Olavs Gt. 1,* ☎ *22/20–35–78.* ☒ *NKr25.* ☉ *Tues.–Fri. 11–3, weekends noon–4.*

Minneparken. Oslo was founded by Harald Hårdråde ("Hard Ruler") in 1048, and the earliest settlements were near what is now Bispegata, a few blocks behind Oslo S Station. Ruins are all that are left of the city's former spiritual center: the **Korskirke** (Cross Church, ☒ Egedes Gate 2), a small stone church dating from the end of the 13th century;

and **Olavs Kloster** (Olav's Cloister, ⊠ St. Halvards Plass 3), built around 1240 by Dominican monks (⊠ Entrance at Oslo Gt. and Bispegt). Call the Oslo Bymuseum (☎ 22/42–06–45) for guided tours.

★ ⑬ **Munchmuseet** (Munch Museum). Edvard Munch, one of Scandinavia's leading artists, bequeathed an enormous collection of his work (about 1,100 paintings, 4,500 drawings, and 18,000 graphic works) to the city when he died in 1944. It languished in warehouses for nearly 20 years, until the city built a museum to house it in 1963. For much of his life Munch was a troubled man, and his major works, dating from the 1890s, with such titles as *The Scream* and *Vampire,* reveal his angst, but he was not without humor. His extraordinary talent as a graphic artist emerges in the print room, with its displays of lithograph stones and woodblocks. ⊠ *Tøyengt. 53,* ☎ *22/67–37–74.* ☞ *NKr40.* ☉ *June–mid-Sept., daily 10–6; mid-Sept.–May, Tues.–Sat. 10–4, Thurs. and Sun. 10–6.*

⑱ **Oslo Ladegård.** The original building, a 13th-century Bispegård (Bishop's Palace), burned down in the 1624 fire, but its old vaulted cellar was not destroyed. The building was restored and rebuilt in 1725; it now belongs to the city council and contains scale models of 16th- to 18th-century Oslo. ⊠ *St. Halvards Pl., Oslogt. 13,* ☎ *22/19–44–68.* ☞ *NKr20.* ☉ *May–Sept.; guided tours on Wed. at 6, Sun. at 1.*

⑰ **St. Halvards Kirke** (St. Halvard's Church). This medieval church, named for the patron saint of Oslo, remained the city's cathedral until 1660. St. Halvard became the city's patron saint when his murdered body was found floating in the Drammensfjord, despite the presence of a heavy stone around his neck. He had been trying to save a pregnant woman from three violent pursuers when they caught and murdered him along with her. ⊠ *Minneparken, entrance at Oslogt. and Bispegt.*

Frogner, Majorsturen, and Holmenkollen

One of the city's most stylish neighborhoods, Frogner combines old-world Scandinavian elegance with contemporary European chic. Most of the pastel-and-white buildings in the area were constructed in the early years of this century. Many have interesting wrought-iron work and sculptural detail. Terribly hip boutiques and galleries coexist with embassies and ambassadors' residences on the streets near and around Bygdøy Allé. Holmenkollen, the hill past Frogner Park, features miles of ski trails—and more beautiful homes of the affluent.

A GOOD WALK

Catch the No. 12 "Majorstuen" trikk from Nationalteatret on the Drammensveien side of the Royal Palace. You can also take the No. 15 from Aker Brygge.

Opposite the southwest end of the palace grounds is the triangular **U.S. Embassy,** designed by Finnish-American architect Eero Saarinen and built in 1959. Look to the right at the corner of Drammensveien and Parkveien for a glimpse of the venerable **Nobel Institute.** Since 1905 these stately yellow buildings have been the secluded setting where the five-member Nobel Committee decides who will win the Nobel Peace Prize. The 15,000-volume library is open to the public.

Stay on the trikk and ride to Frogner Park or walk the seven short blocks. To walk, follow Balders Gate to Arno Bergs Plass, with its central fountain. Turn left on Gyldenløves Gate until you reach Kirkeveien. Turn right past the Dutch Embassy, and cross the street at the light. Frogner Park, also called Vigelandspark interchangeably, is just ahead.

Walk through the front gates of the park and toward the monolith ahead: you are entering **Vigelandsparken** ⑲. There's nothing anywhere else in the world quite like this stunning sculpture garden designed by one of Norway's greatest artists; who is, ironically, virtually unknown to the rest of the world. Across from the park, you can study the method to his madness at **Vigelandsmuseet** ⑳.

After you leave the park, continue on Kirkeveien to the Majorstuen underground station. Here you have two options: you can take a walk down Bogstadveien, look at the shops, and explore the Majorstuen area and then take the Holmenkollen line of the T-bane to Frognerseteren; or you can skip the stroll down Bogstadveien and head right up to Holmenkollen. The train ride up the mountain passes some stunning scenery. If you have brought your children, you may want to make a detour at the first T-bane stop, Frøen, and visit the **Barnekunstmuseet.**

Continue on the T-bane to the end of the line. This is Frognerseteren—where city dwellers disappear to on winter weekends. The view of the city here is spectacular. The **Tryvannstårnet** ㉑ has an even better panoramic view of Oslo. Downhill is **Holmenkollbakken** ㉒, where Norway's most intrepid skiers prove themselves every February during the Holmenkollen Ski Festival.

TIMING

This is a good tour for Monday, since the museums mentioned are open, unlike most others in Oslo. You will need a whole day for both neighborhoods since there is some travel time involved. The trikk ride from the city center to Frogner Park is about 15 minutes; the T-bane to Frognerseteren is about 20. You're no longer in the compact city center, so distances between sights are greater. The walk from Frognerseteren is about 15 minutes and is indicated with signposts. Try to save Holmenkollen with its magnificent views for a clear day. Summer hours for museums and lookout points are extended because the days are so long. In the spring, though, go before the sun starts to set.

If you want to see Norwegians younger than two years old on skis, a winter Sunday in Frognerseteren is your best bet. Frogner Park has some skiers and sledders, and families flock to Holmenkollen for Sunday ski school.

SIGHTS TO SEE

Barnekunstmuseet (Children's Art Museum). The museum was the brainchild of Rafael Goldin, a Russian immigrant who has collected children's drawings from more than 150 countries. ⊠ *Lille Frøensvn. 4,* ☎ *22/46–85–73.* ☞ *NKr30.* ☼ *Mid-June–mid-Aug., Tues.–Thurs. and Sun. 11–4; mid-Aug.–mid-Dec. and late Jan.–mid-June, Tues.–Thurs. 9:30–2, Sun. 11–4.*

★ ㉒ **Holmenkollbakken** (Holmenkollen Ski Museum and Ski Jump). Oslo's ski jump holds a special place in the hearts of Norwegians, who contend they invented the sport. The 1892 jump was rebuilt for the 1952 Winter Olympics and is still used for international competitions. At the base of the jump, turn right, past the statue of the late King Olav V on skis, to enter the museum. It displays equipment from the Fritjof Nansen and Roald Amundsen polar voyages and a model of a ski maker's workshop, in addition to a collection of skis, the oldest dating from pre-Viking times. You can also climb (or ride the elevator) to the top of the jump tower. ⊠ *Kongevn. 5,* ☎ *22/92–32–64.* ☞ *NKr50.* ☼ *July–Aug., daily 9 AM–10 PM; June, daily 9–8; Apr.–May and Sept., daily 10–5; Oct.–Mar., daily 10–4.*

㉑ Tryvannstårnet (Tryvann's Tower). The view from Oslo's TV tower encompasses 36,000 square ft of hills, forests, cities, and several bodies of water. You can see as far as the Swedish border to the east and nearly as far as Moss to the south. ✉ *Voksenkollen,* ☎ *22/14–67–11.* 🎫 *NKr30.* ☉ *May and Sept., daily 10–5; June, daily 10–8; July, daily 9 AM–10 PM; Aug., daily 9–8; Oct.–Apr., daily 10–4*

㉒ Vigelandsmuseet. This small museum displays many of the plaster models for the Vigeland Park sculptures, the artist's woodcuts and drawings, and mementos of his life. ✉ *Nobelsgt. 32,* ☎ *22/44–11–36.* 🎫 *NKr20.* ☉ *May–Sept., Tues.–Sat. 10–6, Sun. noon–7; Oct.–Apr., Tues.–Sat. noon–4, Sun. noon–6.*

★ **㉓ Vigelandsparken** (Frogner Park). This park, formally called Frogner Park, contains more than 50 copper statues by sculptor Gustav Vigeland, hence the moniker Vigelandspark. Vigeland began his career as a wood-carver, and his talent was quickly appreciated and supported by the townspeople of Oslo. In 1921 they provided him with a free house and studio, in exchange for which he began to chip away at his life's work, which he would ultimately donate to the city. He worked through World War II and the German occupation, and after the war the work was unveiled to the combined enchantment and horror of the townsfolk. Included was the 470-ton monolith that is now the highlight of the park, as well as hundreds of writhing, fighting, and loving sculptures representing the varied forms and stages of human life. The figures are nude, but they're more monumental than erotic—bullet-headed, muscular men and healthy, solid women with flowing hair. Look for the park's most beloved sculpture—an enraged baby boy stamping his foot and scrunching his face in fury. Known as *Sinnataggen* (The Really Angry One), this ball of rage has been filmed, parodied, painted red, and even stolen from the park.

The grassy grounds of Vigelandspark are a living part of the city—people walk dogs on the green and bathe chubby babies in the fountains, and they jog, ski, and sunbathe throughout. The park complex also includes the City Museum, a swimming pool (☞ Outdoor Activities and Sports, *below*) an ice rink and skating muscum (☎ 22/43–49–20), several playgrounds, and an outdoor restaurant, Herregårdskroen, where you can have anything from a buffet lunch to a three-course dinner. ✉ *Middlethunsgt.* 🎫 *Park entrance free.*

Bygdøy

Oslo's most important historic sights are concentrated on Bygdøy Peninsula, as are several beaches, jogging paths, and the royal family's summer residence.

A GOOD WALK

The most pleasant way to get to Bygdøy, from May to September, is to catch a ferry from the Rådhuset. Times vary, so check with Nortra (☞ Visitor Information *in* Oslo A to Z, *below*) for schedules. Another alternative is to take Bus 30, marked "Bygdøy," from Stortingsgata at Nationalteatret along Drammensveien to Bygdøy Allé, a wide avenue lined with chestnut trees. The bus passes Frogner Church and several embassies on its way to Olav Kyrres Plass, where it turns left, and soon left again, onto the peninsula. If you see some horses on the left, they come from the king's stables (the dark red building with the monogram); the royal family's current summer residence, actually just a big white frame house, is on the right. Get off at the next stop, Norsk Folkemuseum. The pink castle nestled in the trees is **Oscarshall Slott** ㉓, once a royal summer palace.

Next is the **Norsk Folkemuseum** ㉔, which consists of some 150 structures from all over the country that have been reconstructed on site. Around the corner to the right is the **Vikingskiphuset** ㉕, one of Norway's most famous attractions, which houses some of the best-preserved remains of the Viking era found yet.

Follow signs on the road to the **Fram-Museet** ㉖, an A-frame structure in the shape of a traditional Viking boathouse, which houses the famed *Fram* polar ship as well as artifacts from various expeditions. Across the parking lot from the Fram-Museet is the older **Kon-Tiki Museum** ㉗ with Thor Heyerdahl's famous raft, along with the papyrus boat *Ra II*. You can get a ferry back to the City Hall docks from the dock in front of the Fram-Museet. Before heading back to Oslo, you may want to have a snack at **Lanternen Kro,** which overlooks the entire harbor.

If your kids are squirming to break out of the museum circuit, entertain the thought of a trip to **VikingLandet,** an attraction park that stages the more peaceful aspects of the Vikings' existence, from farming to burial mounds. You can combine the excursion with a trip to Tusen-Fryd, an amusement park next door.

TIMING

Block out a day for Bygdøy. You could spend at least half a day at the Folkemuseum alone. Note that the museums on Bygdøy tend to be open daily but close earlier than their counterparts that close Mondays.

The HMK trip to VikingLandet is an afternoon trip, so count on spending half a day. It takes between 10 and 20 minutes to reach the park from downtown Oslo by bus. If you decide to go on your own from Oslo S Station, you might want to spend the whole day playing in both parks.

SIGHTS TO SEE

★ ㉖ **Fram-Museet.** The *Fram* polar ship takes up almost every inch of this museum, which was constructed around it. Matter-of-fact displays of life on board ship vividly depict the history of polar exploration. The *Fram* was constructed in 1892 by Scottish-Norwegian shipbuilder Colin Archer. Fridtjof Nansen led the first *Fram* expedition, across the ice surrounding the North Pole; the ship's most famous voyage took Roald Amundsen to Antarctica, the first leg of his successful expedition to the South Pole in 1911. ⊠ *Bygdøynes,* ☎ *22/43–83–70.* ☜ *NKr20.* ☉ *June–Aug., daily 9–6:45; May and Sept., daily 10–4:45; Mar.–Apr. and Oct.–Nov., weekdays 11–2:45, weekends 11–3:45; Dec.–Feb., weekends 11–3:45.*

★ ㉗ **Kon-Tiki Museum.** The museum celebrates Norway's most famous 20th-century explorer. Thor Heyerdahl continued the Norwegian tradition of exploration in his 1947 voyage from Peru to Polynesia on the *Kon-Tiki,* a balsa raft, to confirm his theory that the first Polynesians originally came from Peru. The *Kon-Tiki,* now showing its age, is suspended on a plastic sea. The *Ra II* sailed from Morocco to the Caribbean in 1970. ⊠ *Bygdøynesvn. 36,* ☎ *22/43–80–50.* ☜ *NKr 25.* ☉ *Apr.–May and Sept., daily 10:30–5; June–Aug., daily 9:30–5:45; Oct.–Mar., daily 10:30–4.*

★ ㉔ **Norsk Folkemuseum** (Norway's Folk Museum). You'll get a bird's-eye view of the entire country with imaginative exhibitions, 153 authentic houses, and tour guides in traditional garb. The **Gol Stavkirke** (Gol Stave Church), constructed around 1200, is one of the most important buildings here. In summer and on weekends year-round, guides in the buildings demonstrate various home crafts, such as weaving tapestries, sewing national costumes, and baking flatbread. Indoor collections in the main building include toys, dolls and dollhouses, a Sami (Lapp) collection, national costumes, and Ibsen's actual study. On one side of this museum is a reconstructed 19th-century village, with shops and houses. The museum puts on a summer calendar of special events, including daily activities from folk dancing to concerts. ✉ *Museumsvn. 10,* ☎ *22/12–37–00.* 🎫 *NKr 50.* ⏲ *May and Sept. daily 10–5; June–Aug., daily 9–6; Oct.–Apr., weekdays 11–3, Sun. 11–4.*

23 **Oscarshall Slott.** This eccentric neo-Gothic palace, built in 1852 for King Oscar I, served as a site for picnics and other summer pursuits. It now houses Norwegian art, including works by Tidemand and Gude. ✉ *Oscarshallvn.,* ☎ *22/43–77–49.* 🎫 *NKr15.* ⏲ *Mid-May–mid-Sept., Tues., Thurs., and Sun. noon–4.*

VikingLandet. Norway's first and only theme park on the Viking Age takes you back 1,000 years to experience daily life as a Viking. You encounter Viking warriors and nobles throughout the park, which is built on the idea of an early Viking community's farms and market places. You can combine the trip with a visit to **Norgesparken Tusenfryd,** Oslo's amusement park. There are carnival rides, such as a merry-go-round, a Ferris wheel, and a roller coaster with a loop, and a water slide. There's a separate entrance fee, but both parks are under the same management. HMK provides an afternoon bus excursion from Norway Information Center (☞ Guided Tours *in* Oslo A to Z, *below*). There's also a free shuttle bus that departs from the south side of Oslo S Station. ✉ *Both parks: Vinterbro,* ☎ *64/94–63–63.* 🎫 *Combined ticket NKr180.* ⏲ *May and late Aug.–Sept., weekends noon–6; early June, weekdays 10:30–3; mid-June–late Aug., daily noon–6.*

★ 25 **Vikingskiphuset.** Norway's claim to fame centers on its incorrigible Viking explorers, and this museum celebrates their fascinating culture. The building resembles a cathedral on the outside, and inside the feeling of reverence is very real. It's hard to believe that the three ships on display, all found buried along the Oslo Fjord, are nearly 1,200 years old. Viking elites wanted to make sure their dead were well equipped for life after death, so they buried them in long ships with all the necessities, which sometimes included a servant. The discoverers of the *Oseberg* even found wood, leather, and woolen textiles intact. Burial ships often reflected the social status of the person buried. The richly carved *Oseberg,* thought to have been the burial chamber for Queen Åse, is the most decorative, whereas the *Gokstad* is a functional longboat, devoid of ornament. Items found with the ships, including tools, household goods, and a tapestry, are also on view. ✉ *Huk Aveny 35,* ☎ *22/43–83–79.* 🎫 *NKr30.* ⏲ *May–Aug., daily 9–6; Sept., daily 11–5; Apr. and Oct., daily 11–4; Nov.–Mar., daily 11–3.*

Dining

Food was once an afterthought in Oslo, but not anymore. The city's chefs are winning contests worldwide. Norwegian cuisine, based on products from the country's pristine waters and lush farmland, is now firmly in the culinary spotlight. Menus change daily, weekly, or according to the season in many of Oslo's finer restaurants.

In Oslo, bad food is expensive and good food doesn't necessarily cost more—it's just a matter of knowing where to go. If you visit Oslo in summer, head for Aker Brygge, the wharf turned shopping area. Hundreds of café goers vie for the sun and the view at the fjord-side outdoor tables. Most restaurants here offer a summer menu that is considerably less expensive than the regular one. Aker Brygge is also a good place to buy shrimp, an activity that heralds the coming of summer for many locals. If you don't want to buy them fresh off the boat, order them at one of the floating restaurants. Generally they come on a baguette or in a big bowl with mayonnaise on the side.

A good place to get a meal that won't cost more than your hotel room is the food court at Paléet Shopping Center, which is open daily 10–8. A bit pricier, and a lot snazzier than the fast-food bonanzas of most American malls, this food court has a variety of stands with international fare, ranging from Danish and Greek to American.

Many of the less expensive restaurants listed below are simply cafés, bars, and even sometimes discotheques. These types of establishments are becoming increasingly popular as restaurants as Oslo's twentysomething generation decides it likes to eat out. (Because of high prices, eating out is a huge luxury for most Norwegians.) Meals at these cheaper spots invariably include pasta dishes, shellfish, pizzas, and salads rather than lobsters and lamb chops. For a more exhaustive list of Oslo cafés, pick up a copy of *Café Guiden*, a glossy publication describing more than 100 spots in detail. It is available in most bars and cafés. ☞ Cafés *in* Nightlife and the Arts, *below*.

Downtown: Royal Palace to the Parliament

$$$$ ✕ **D'Artagnan.** Diplomas, certificates, and prizes from all over the world
★ line the walls of this downtown *restaurant gastronomique*. Owner Freddie Nielsen, one of Norway's most celebrated restaurateurs, received both his education and inspiration in France, but do not expect nouvelle cuisine here. Only the famished should embark upon the seven-course Grand Menu. The saffron-poached pike with asparagus is a good way to start a meal, and the boned fillet of salmon with dill lobster-cream sauce is delectable. The veal is so tender you can cut it with your fork. The dessert cart is loaded with jars of fruit preserved in liqueurs, which are served with sorbets and ice creams. ☒ *Øvre Slottsgt. 16,* ☎ *22/41–50–62. AE, DC, MC, V. Closed Sun. and mid-July–mid-Aug. No lunch Jan.–Aug.*

$$$ ✕ **Babette's Gjestehus.** Chef Ortwin Kulmus and his friendly staff make their guests feel welcome at this tiny restaurant hidden in the shopping arcade by City Hall. Bright blue walls, starched white tablecloths, and lace curtains against paned windows contribute to the rustic, homey feel. The food is Scandinavian with a French twist. Try the garlic-marinated rack of lamb in rosemary sauce or pan-fried breast of duck with creamed spring cabbage. Dishes vary according to season but are always well prepared. ☒ *Rådhuspassasjen, Roald Amundsensgt. 6,* ☎ *22/41–64–64. Reservations essential. AE, DC, MC, V. Closed Sun. No lunch.*

$$$ ✕ **Theatercafeen.** This Oslo institution, on the ground floor of the Hotel
★ Continental, is *the* place to see and be seen. Built in 1900, the last Viennese-style café in northern Europe retains its Art Nouveau character. The menu is small and jumbled, with starters and main dishes interspersed; the only hint of the serving size is the price column. Pastry chef Robert Bruun's *konfektkake* (a rich chocolate cake) and apple tart served with homemade ice cream are reasons enough to visit. ☒ *Stortingsgt. 24–26,* ☎ *22/82–40–50. AE, DC, MC, V.*

$$ ✕ **Dinner.** Though its name is not the best for a restaurant specializ-
★ ing in Szechuan-style cuisine, this is the place for Chinese food. Don't bother with the other Chinese restaurants. ☒ *Stortingsgt. 22,* ☎ *22/42–68–90. AE, DC, MC, V. No lunch.*

$$ ✕ **A Touch of France.** Just downstairs from D'Artagnan (☞ *above*), Freddie Nielsen's clean, inviting wine bistro is straight out of Paris. The French ambience is further accented by the waiters' long, white aprons, the Art Nouveau decor, old French posters, and closely packed tables. The tempting menu includes a steaming hot bouillabaisse. ⊠ *Øvre Slottsgt. 16,* ☎ *22/42–56–97. AE, DC, MC, V.*

$ ✕ **Brasserie 45.** Overlooking the fountain on Karl Johans Gate, this brasserie serves a solid meal in an elegant Scandinavian setting, complete with candlelight, red walls, and shiny wooden floors. The idea is simple: 45 dishes for 45 kroner each. There are both meat and fish dishes, often garnished with a tasty Brasserie 45 sauce (a tomato sweet-and-sour sauce) and potatoes or pasta. The portions are small, but a three-course meal at NKr135 is still a bargain in Oslo. ⊠ *Karl Johans Gt. 45 (upstairs),* ☎ *22/41–34–00. AE, DC, MC, V.*

$ ✕ **Café Sjakk Matt.** This popular spot between Vika and Karl Johan is one of the many bars that serve food as well—although they've made it a specialty. However, you do have to order at the bar. A variety of pita sandwiches and melts, ratatouille, quiche, and the house specialty, lasagna, are some of what's on the menu. Hot dishes usually come with salad and nutty Norwegian bread. The place has a modern Scandinavian feel: dozens of candles, potted plants, and shiny floors. ⊠ *Haakon VII's Gt. 5,* ☎ *22/83–41–56. AE, DC, MC, V.*

$ ✕ **Den Grimme Ælling.** Dane Bjarne Hvid Pedersen's smørbrød are the best buy in town: lots of meat, fish, or cheese on a small piece of bread. This popular Copenhagen restaurant in the food court at Paleet also has daily dinner specials, such as homemade *hakkebøf* (Danish Salisbury steak) with gravy, onions, and potatoes. ⊠ *Paleet, Karl Johans Gt. 41B,* ☎ *22/42–47–83. No credit cards.*

$ ✕ **Kaffistova.** Norwegian country cooking is served, cafeteria style, at this downtown restaurant. Everyday specials include soup and a selection of entrées, including a vegetarian dish. Kjøttkaker (meat cakes) served with creamed cabbage is a Norwegian staple, and the steamed salmon with Sandefjord butter is as good here as in places where it costs three times as much. Low-alcohol beer is the strongest drink served. ⊠ *Rosenkrantz' Gt. 8,* ☎ *22/42–99–74. AE, DC, MC, V.*

$ ✕ **Vegeta.** Next to the Nationalteatret bus and trikk station, this no-smoking restaurant is a popular spot for hot and cold vegetarian meals and salads. The all-you-can-eat specials offer top value. ⊠ *Munkedamsvn. 3B,* ☎ *22/83–40–20. AE, DC, MC, V.*

Kvadraturen and Aker Brygge

$$$$ ✕ **Statholdergaarden.** Award-winning chef Bent Stiansen is currently the shining star of Norwegian haute cuisine. As a result, it is hard to get a table here—especially around Christmastime—so plan early. The four-course gastronomic menu changes daily. You can also order directly from the à la carte menu. Try one of the imaginative appetizers, such as smoked duck breast with fried goat cheese and pine nut salad. Specialties include salmon mousse and other fish delicacies. This restaurant, in a building that dates back to 1640, is in the heart of Oslo's oldest standing neighborhood. ⊠ *Rådhusgt. 11,* ☎ *22/41–88–00. Reservations essential. Jacket and tie. AE, DC, MC, V. Closed Sun. and 3 wks in July.*

$$$ ✕ **Engebret Café.** This somber, old-fashioned restaurant at Bankplassen was a haunt for bohemian literati at the turn of the century. Today it draws tourists, especially in summer, for casual fare and drinks at the outdoor café. The more formal dinner menu includes traditional Norwegian staples, such as reindeer and salmon. Food critics give these two dishes rave reviews year after year. This is a good spot for refreshment after visiting the Contemporary Art Museum; try to get an outdoor table and listen to the museum's fountain trickle away in the distance. ⊠ *Bankplassen 1,* ☎ *22/33–66–94. AE, DC, MC, V.*

Oslo Dining and Lodging

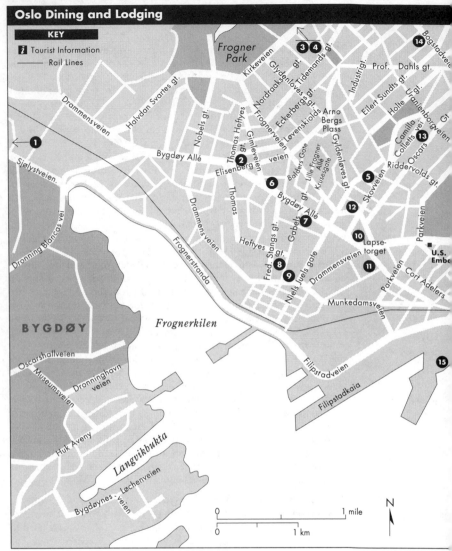

KEY

ℹ️ Tourist Information

—— Rail Lines

Dining

A Touch of France, **31**

Babette's
Gjestehus, **19**

Bagatelle, **10**

Brasserie 45, **25**

Café Sjakk Matt, **16**

Clodion Art Café, **2**

Coco Chalet, **34**

D'Artagnan, **31**

De Fem Stuer, **3**

Den Grimme
Ælling, **26**

Det Gamle
Raadhus, **35**

Dinner, **18**

Dionysos Taverna, **40**

Engebret Café, **37**

Feinschmecker, **6**

Frognerseteren, **4**

Hos Thea, **9**

Kaffistova, **32**

Kastanjen, **7**

Klosteret, **41**

Lofoten
Fiskrestaurant, **15**

Markveien Mat og
Vinhus, **42**

Maud's, **17**

Palace Grill, **11**

Restaurant
Le Canard, **5**

Statholdergaarden, **36**

Theatercafeen, **20**

Vegeta, **23**

Lodging

Ambassadeur, **13**

Bristol, **28**

Frogner House, **12**

Gabelshus, **8**

Grand Hotel, **33**

Haraldsheim, **43**

Holmenkollen Park
Hotel Rica, **3**

Hotell
Bondeheimen, **32**

Hotel Continental, **20**

Hotel Karl Johan, **27**

Munch, **30**

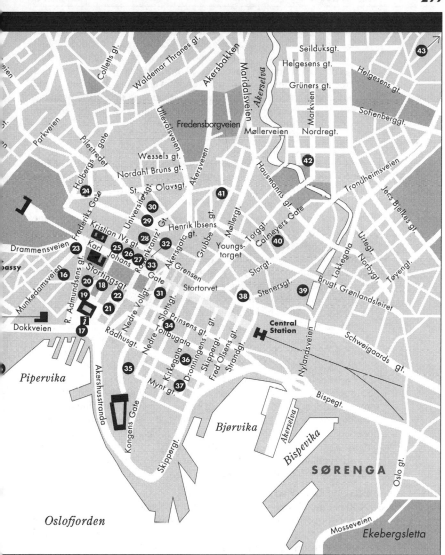

Radisson SAS
Park Royal, **1**

Radisson SAS Plaza
Hotel Oslo, **39**

Radisson SAS
Scandinavia Hotel, **24**

Rainbow Cecil, **22**

Rainbow
Gyldenløve, **14**

Rainbow Hotel
Stefan, **29**

Rica Victoria, **21**

Royal Christiania, **38**

$$–$$$ ✕ **Lofoten Fiskerestaurant.** With all windows overlooking the water
at Aker Brygge, this is Oslo's quintessential fish restaurant. All types
of fish, from salmon to cod to monkfish, are served fresh and cooked
in a variety of sauces, from house bouillabaisse to classic wine or saf-
fron sauce. The clientele is well-heeled, and the elegant wood-paneled
interior brings to mind a vintage Scandinavian cruise ship. Try to get
an outdoor table in summer: you take advantage of a cheaper menu
as well as late-evening sunlight on the fjord. Service can be slow on
busy evenings, but it's definitely worth the wait. ⊠ *Stranden 75, Aker
Brygge,* ☎ *22/83–08–08. AE, DC, MC, V.*

$$ ✕ **Det Gamle Raadhus.** This restaurant in the former city hall is fa-
mous for its lutefisk, a Scandinavian specialty made from dried fish
that has been soaked in lye and then poached. However, the menu here
does allow ample choice for the less daring. This is Oslo's oldest
restaurant—it celebrated its 350th birthday in 1991. Unfortunately the
restaurant suffered extensive fire damage in 1996, but at press time
was scheduled to reopen in late 1997. Call 22/41–44–41 to be certain.
⊠ *Nedre Slottsgt. 1,* ☎ *22/42–01–07. AE, DC, MC, V. Closed Sun.*

$$ ✕ **Maud's.** In the same building as the Norway Information Center,
this restaurant would logically attract tourists. However, it seems to
attract more locals. The regional Norwegian dishes are so traditional
that they seem exotic to some Norwegian city folk who left the nest
long ago. Specialties include potato dumplings and myriad fish and meat
dishes served with none other than potatoes boiled to perfection.
Lunch plates and open-faced sandwiches are reasonably priced, as are
the "everyday meals," served from 1 to 7. ⊠ *Vestbaneplassen. 1,* ☎
22/83–72–28. AE, DC, MC, V. Closed Sun.

$ ✕ **Coco Chalet.** Best known for its homemade cakes and pies, Coco Chalet
is moving into the world of affordable haute cuisine. The Asian-inspired
menu features a delectable chicken breast with vegetables julienne. The
dining room of this restaurant in Oslo's oldest neighborhood feels
somewhat like a haunted mansion: white tablecloths bedeck the tables
at all hours of the day, spooky candelabras sit on the mantle, and the
mostly female staff wears black uniforms with white aprons and col-
lars. ⊠ *Øvre Slottsgt. 8,* ☎ *22/33–32–66. AE, DC, MC, V.*

East of Downtown

$$$ ✕ **Klosteret.** This popular east-side eatery's name means "the cloisters."
Its not-so-medieval dining room is downstairs in a spacious cellar with
a rounded brick ceiling. Wacky iron candelabras sprouting from red
walls like thorny branches and stark steel-backed chairs are somehow
in perfect harmony with the gold-bedecked saints and Christ childs that
adorn the walls. The handwoven menus are sheathed in monastic
hymnal pages and offer a variety of meat and fish, as well as a daily
vegetarian dish. Main courses are often served atop a bed of sautéed
leafy greens, which makes for an innovative presentation as well as a
refreshing change from traditional Norwegian *kinakål*, a white lettuce-
cabbage usually substituted for greens. Take a taxi. ⊠ *Fredensborgvn.
13,* ☎ *22/20–66–90. AE, DC, MC, V. Closed Sun. and 3–4 wks in July.*

$$$ ✕ **Markveien Mat og Vinhus.** This artsy food and wine house in the
heart of the Grunerløkka district serves fresh French-inspired cuisine.
The atmosphere is relaxed and the clientele is bohemian. Paintings cover
the yellow walls, and the tables are black and somber. As most touristy
spots in Oslo lie in the *Vest* (west), a trip to the *Øst* (east) will give you
a chance to see how the other side lives. ⊠ *Torvbakkgt. 12 (entrance
on Markvn. 57),* ☎ *22/37–22–97. AE, DC, MC, V. Closed Sun.*

$$ ✕ **Dionysos Taverna.** Nicola Murati gives his guests a warm welcome
★   in this unpretentious little Greek restaurant. The hors d'oeuvre plat-
ter, which includes stuffed grape leaves, meatballs, feta cheese, toma-

toes, and cucumbers, is a meal in itself. The souvlaki and moussaka are authentically prepared, as are the more unusual casserole dishes. A bouzouki duo provides live music on Thursday, Friday, and Saturday. ⊠ *Calmeyersgt. 11,* ☎ *22/60–78–64. AE, MC, V. No lunch.*

Frogner and Majorstuen

$$$$ ✕ **Bagatelle.** One of Oslo's best restaurants is a short walk from
★ downtown. Paintings by contemporary Norwegian artists accent the otherwise subdued interior, but the food is the true show here. Internationally known chef-owner Eyvind Hellstrøm's cuisine is modern Norwegian with French overtones. His grilled scallops with a saffron-parsley sauce and the marinated salmon tartare with an herbed crème fraîche are extraordinary. Bagatelle has a wine cellar to match its food. ⊠ *Bygdøy Allé 3,* ☎ *22/44–63–97. Jacket and tie. AE, DC, MC, V. Closed Sun. No lunch.*

$$$$ ✕ **Feinschmecker.** The name is German, but the food is modern Scandinavian. The atmosphere is friendly and intimate, with green rattan chairs, yellow tablecloths, and floral draperies. Owners Lars Erik Underthun, one of Oslo's foremost chefs, and Bengt Wilson, one of Scandinavia's leading food photographers, make sure the food looks as good as it tastes. The roast rack of lamb with crunchy fried sweetbreads on tagliatelle and the chocolate-caramel teardrop with passion-fruit sauce are two choices on the menu, which makes for fascinating reading. ⊠ *Balchensgt. 5,* ☎ *22/44–17–77. Reservations essential. AE, DC, MC, V. Closed Sun. and last 3 wks of July. No lunch.*

$$$ ✕ **Hos Thea.** An old-fashioned–looking gem with blue-and-beige decor,
★ this restaurant has only 36 seats. It's at the beginning of Embassy Row, a short distance from downtown. Owner Sergio Barcilon, originally from Spain, is one of the pioneers of the new Scandinavian cooking. The small menu offers four or five choices in each category, but every dish is superbly prepared, from the venison in a sauce of mixed berries to the sherbets and fruitcake. Noise and smoke levels can be high late in the evening. ⊠ *Gabelsgt. 11, entrance on Drammensvn.,* ☎ *22/44–68–74. Reservations essential. AE, DC, MC, V. No lunch.*

$$$ ✕ **Palace Grill.** This tiny dining spot across from the Royal Palace has won its way into the ranks of the hip on the Oslo restaurant scene. You can sip a beer in the adjoining cowboy rock-and-roll bar while you wait for one of about eight tables. Don't let the "grill" part confuse you: it may be relaxed, but it's far from fast food. The Norwegian ingredients of the French-inspired menu, which is written on a hanging chalkboard, change daily. If you've had your fill of reindeer in Norway, you can still take a glimpse at the exotic sauces. Try the chicken leg with eggplant and sweet green shallot sauce if it's on the menu. ⊠ *Solligt. 2 (just off Dramensveien),* ☎ *22/56–14–02. Reservations not accepted. AE, DC, MC, V. Closed Sun. and 1 month in summer.*

$$$ ✕ **Restaurant Le Canard.** Undoubtedly one of Oslo's plushest locales, this oasis in Frogner is brimming with eclectic antiques, Oriental rugs, chandeliers, and Baroque paintings. It is housed in a looming brick mansion with spires and wrought iron decorations that was built at the turn of the century. The main dining room is spread throughout the first floor's rooms and color-coded salons; upstairs is reserved for private parties. In summer you can dine on the lawn in the garden. The specialty is, of course, duck, from beef with duck-liver in Madeira sauce to sautéed breast of duck with horseradish and cognac sauce. The wine cellar holds more than 2,000 bottles. ⊠ *Pres. Harbitzgt. 4,* ☎ *22/43–40–28. AE, DC, MC, V. Closed Sun. No lunch in winter.*

$$ ✕ **Kastanjen.** This casual Frogner bistro, named after the chestnut trees
★ that line the street, is the kind every neighborhood needs. The style of food is new traditional—modern interpretations of classic Norwegian

dishes. Be sure to check out the warmly lit downstairs lounge for before or after-dinner drinks. ✉ *Bygdøy Allé 18,* ☎ *22/43–44–67. AE, DC, MC, V. Closed Sun. and 2 wks in July.*

$ ✕ **Clodion Art Café.** A bright blue facade and cartoons of the suns, stars, and moon adorn the entrance to this trendy Frogner café. Meals here are light but always tasty: try the spicy shrimp brochette with rice for a nice change from usual café fare. Go for aesthetic reasons instead, and your hunger for creativity will be sated. Not an inch of the place is left unpainted, and the curvy, colorful couches will make you want to stay all day. ✉ *Bygdøy Allé 63, entrance on Thomas Heftyes Gt.,* ☎ *22/44–97–26. AE, DC, MC, V, DC.*

Holmenkollen

$$$$ ✕ **De Fem Stuer.** Near the famous Holmenkollen ski jump, in the his-
★ toric Holmenkollen Park Hotel, this restaurant has first-rate views and food. Chef Frank Halvorsen's modern Norwegian dishes have strong classic roots. Well worth trying is the three-course "A Taste of Norway" meal. ✉ *Holmenkollen Park Hotel, Kongevn. 26,* ☎ *22/92–27–34. Jacket and tie. AE, DC, MC, V.*

$$ ✕ **Frognerseteren.** Just above the Holmenkollen ski jump, this restaurant, specializing in fish and venison, looks down on the entire city. Be sure not to miss the house specialty—scrumptious apple cake. The upstairs room has the same view as the more expensive panoramic veranda, and there is also an outdoor café. Take the Holmenkollbanen to the end station and then follow the signs downhill to the restaurant. ✉ *Hollmenkollvn. 200,* ☎ *22/14–05–50. DC, MC, V.*

Lodging

Most hotels are centrally located, a short walk from Karl Johans Gate, and often between the Royal Palace and the central railway station. The newest hotels are in the area around Oslo S Station, at the bottom end of Karl Johan. For a quiet stay, choose a hotel in Frogner, the elegant residential neighborhood just minutes from downtown.

Oslo usually has enough hotel rooms to go around, but it's always a good idea to reserve a room at least for the first night of your stay, especially if you will be arriving late. Otherwise, the hotel accommodations office at Oslo S Station (☞ Visitor Information *in* Oslo A to Z, *below*) is open from 8 AM to 11 PM and can book you in anything from a luxury hotel to a room in a private home for a fee of NKr20. Usually there are last-minute discount rooms.

Lodging in the capital is expensive. Prices for downtown accommodations are high, even for bed-and-breakfasts, although just about all hotels have weekend, holiday, and summer rates (25% to 50% reductions). Taxes and service charges, unless otherwise noted, are included. Breakfast is usually included also, but be sure to ask before booking your room.

You can cut your lodging costs considerably—and get more for your money than with summer or weekend rates—by buying an Oslo Package in advance. This combines an Oslo Card (☞ Getting Around *in* Oslo A to Z, *below*) with discounted room rates at almost all of Oslo's better hotels. Contact local agents of the Scandinavian Tourist Board for more information and reservations. In the United States or Canada, call **Scanam World Tours** (☎ 201/835–7070, ℻ 201/835–3030); in Australia, the **Mansions Travel Service** (☎ 61/7–229–5631, ℻ 61/7–221–9731); in the United Kingdom, **Scantours UK** (☎ 0171/839–2927, ℻ 0171/839–4327).

If you want to rent an apartment, contact **B&B Oslo Apartments** (⊠ Stasjonsvn. 13, Blommenholm, 1300 Sandvika, ☎ 67/54–06–80, FAX 67/54–09–70), which is open weekdays 8:30–4. Most are in Bærum, 15 minutes from downtown Oslo, and about 20 are in Skøyen, a grassy suburban area, closer to both the airport and the center. All are no more than a 10-minute walk from public transport.

Downtown: Royal Palace to the Parliament

$$$$ 🏨 **Grand Hotel.** Right in the center of town on Karl Johans Gate, the
★ Grand has been Oslo's premier hotel since it opened in 1874. Ibsen used to start his mornings with a brisk walk followed by a stiff drink at the Grand Café in the company of journalists. Munch was also a regular guest, and since his time the Grand has hosted many famous people and all recipients of the Nobel Peace Prize. Many Norwegians check in on Constitution Day, May 17, in order to have a room overlooking the parades. The lobby only hints at the style and flair of the rooms. Even standard rooms are large, looking more like guest quarters in an elegant house than hotel rooms. Those in the newer wing are smaller, cheaper, and not as nice. The hotel's restaurant, Julius Fritzner, is considered one of Oslo's most elegant dining establishments. ⊠ *Karl Johans Gt. 31, 0159,* ☎ *22/42–93–90,* FAX *22/42–12–25. 287 rooms, 50 suites. 3 restaurants, 3 bars, indoor pool, sauna, health club, meeting rooms. AE, DC, MC, V.*

$$$$ 🏨 **Hotel Continental.** An elegant turn-of-the-century facade has put the
★ Continental on Norway's historic-preservation list. Its location—across from Nationalteatret and next door to a high concentration of cafés, clubs, and cinemas—is perfect for both vacationers and business travelers. The Brockmann family, owners since 1900, have succeeded in combining the rich elegance of the Old World with modern living. Munch graphics from the family's own collection adorn the walls. Antique furniture and shiny white porcelain fixtures add a distinctive touch to the rooms. Theatercafeen (☞ Dining, *above*) is a landmark, and the newest addition, Lipp, a restaurant-café-bar-nightclub, is among Oslo's "in" places. Dagligstuen (The Sitting Room) is a wonderful place in which to start or end the evening with an appetizer or nightcap. ⊠ *Stortingsgt. 24–26, 0161,* ☎ *22/82–40–00,* FAX *22/42–96–89. 154 rooms, 23 suites. 3 restaurants, 2 bars. AE, DC, MC, V.*

$$$$ 🏨 **Radisson SAS Scandinavia Hotel.** Oslo's established business hotel, built in 1974, has some competition but can still hold its own: there's a business-class airline check-in in the lobby, and the lower-level shopping arcade has stylish clothing and leather-goods shops. The simple, elegant rooms come in four different styles: art deco, Italian, Asian, and predictably, for a hotel run by an airline, high-tech "business class." The SAS is across the street from the palace grounds; downtown is a few blocks downhill. ⊠ *Holbergs Gt. 30, 0166,* ☎ *22/11–30–00,* FAX *22/11–30–17. 496 rooms, 3 large suites. 2 restaurants, 2 bars, pool, health club, nightclub, dance club, business services. AE, DC, MC, V.*

$$$ 🏨 **Bristol.** The Bristol caters to people who want a dignified hotel in the center of town. The immense lobby lounge was decorated in the 1920s with an intricate Moorish theme and feels more like Fez than Scandinavia. Nevertheless, it is a tribute to style, and the piano bar is one of Oslo's best. The rooms do not necessarily reflect the lobby's lushness: small and comfortable, they have all the amenities of modern Scandinavia and are simply decorated with Scandinavian or Regency-style furniture. ⊠ *Kristian IV's Gt. 7, 0164,* ☎ *22/82–60–00,* FAX *22/82–60–01. 141 rooms, 4 suites. 2 restaurants, 2 bars, nightclub, convention center. AE, DC, MC, V.*

$$$ ⚏ **Hotel Karl Johan.** The hundred-year-old Karl Johan, once known as the Nobel, is elegant: one look at the wrought-iron railing and stained-glass windows that line the circular staircase will make you feel you're in 19th-century Paris. The lobby's hardwood floors are shiny and covered with Oriental rugs and velvety navy carpet; fabrics are gold and navy striped; and Old English caricatures hang on the off-white walls. Every room has a different Norwegian treasure, but the feel is sophisticated, not rustic. Its location, next door to the Grand, couldn't be better, and the hotel claims to have a set of regulars who prefer it to its overshadowing neighbor. If you're sensitive to noise, ask for a room away from Rosenkrantz' Gate, where bar hoppers and night-clubbers boogie until the wee hours. ⊠ *Karl Johans Gt. 33 , 0162,* ☎ *22/42–74–80,* ⅎ⅍ *22/42–05–19. 74 rooms, 12 suites. Restaurant, bar. AE, DC, MC, V.*

$$$ ⚏ **Rainbow Hotel Stefan.** This hotel makes every aspect of a stay here a positive experience, from hot drinks for late arrivals to breakfast tables complete with juice boxes and plastic bags for packing a lunch (request this service in advance). The top-floor lounge has books and magazines in English. The Stefan's kitchen is famous for creating the best buffet lunch in town. ⊠ *Rosenkrantz' Gt. 1, 0159,* ☎ *22/42–92–50,* ⅎ⅍ *22/33–70–22. 138 rooms. Restaurant, library, meeting rooms. AE, DC, MC, V.*

$$$ ⚏ **Rica Victoria.** This modern business hotel occupies one of the city center's taller buildings, giving some top-floor rooms glimpses of Oslo's rooftops. The rooms, built around a center atrium, are elegant and very stylish, furnished with Biedermeier reproductions, brass lamps, and paisley-print textiles in bold reds and dark blues. Rooms with windows on the atrium may be claustrophobic for some but colorful and fun for others. ⊠ *Rosenkrantz' Gt. 13, 0160,* ☎ *22/42–99–40,* ⅎ⅍ *22/41–06–44. 199 rooms, 5 suites. Restaurant, bar. AE, DC, MC, V.*

$$ ⚏ **Hotell Bondeheimen.** Founded in 1913 for country folk visiting the city, Bondeheimen, which means "farmers' home," still gives discounts to members of Norwegian agricultural associations. The interior is simple, furnished with all the makings of a contemporary Norwegian country home. Cube-shape cushioned chairs, sofas, and solid tables are made of pine, and fabrics and carpets are dyed in farmers' colors: green, blue, yellow, and red. Modern Norwegian graphics hang on the walls, and bathrooms have rustic swigs of hay on the walls. The lobby has a small library of books on Norway, even some in English. Bondeheimen is affiliated with the country kitchen Kaffistova (☞ Dining, *above*). It is a good choice for families, but if you are looking for quiet, ask for a room in back. ⊠ *Rosenkrantz' Gt. 8 (entrance on Kristian IV's Gate), 0159,* ☎ *22/42–95–30,* ⅎ⅍ *22/41–94–37. 76 rooms. Cafeteria, sauna, library, meeting rooms. AE, DC, MC, V.*

$$ ⚏ **Rainbow Cecil.** This modern hotel, one block from Parliament, is down the road from several other, more expensive hotels and is closer to the main drag than most. The second floor opens onto a plant-filled atrium, the hotel's activity center. In the morning it's a breakfast room, but in the afternoon it becomes a lounge, serving coffee, juice, and fresh fruit, with newspapers available in many languages. Many rooms face the atrium for the sake of peace and quiet, but others have a view of the Stortinget and its many passers-by (where you'll get a better feel for the city). The hotel provides umbrellas for rainy days and claims to have the best air-conditioning in the city for those rare—but beloved—summer heat waves. ⊠ *Stortingsgt. 8, 0130,* ☎ *22/42–70–00,* ⅎ⅍ *22/42–26–70. 112 rooms, 2 suites. AE, DC, MC, V.*

East of Downtown

$ **Haraldsheim.** Oslo's hilltop youth hostel is one of Europe's largest. Most of the rooms have four beds, and those in the new wing have showers. Bring your own sheets or rent them there. It is 6 km (almost 3 mi) from the city center—take trikk 10 or 11 (marked "Kjelsås") to Sinsen. Nonmembers of the International Youth Hostel organization and those older than 25 years pay a surcharge. ✉ *Haraldsheimvn. 4, 0409,* ☎ *22/15–50–43,* FAX *22/22–10–25. 264 beds. V.*

$ **Munch.** This modern B&B, about a 10-minute walk from Karl Johans Gate, is unpretentious, well run, clean, and functional. The decent-size rooms are painted in pastels or blue with floral curtains. The lobby, with Chinese rugs and leather couches, contrasts with the rest of the hotel. ✉ *Munchsgt. 5, 0165,* ☎ *22/42–42–75,* FAX *22/20–64–69. 180 rooms. Breakfast room. AE, DC, MC, V.*

Frogner, Majorstuen, and Holmenkollen

$$$$ **Holmenkollen Park Hotel Rica.** The magnificent 1894 building in the national romantic style commands an unequaled panorama of the city in a quiet and natural setting. It is worth a visit even if you don't lodge there, perhaps for a meal at its legendary restaurant, De Fem Stuer (☞ Dining, *above*). The rather ordinary guest rooms are in a newer structure behind it. The ice-covered snowflake sculpture in the lobby is appropriate for a hotel that's a stone's throw from the Holmenkollen ski jump. Ski and walking trails are just outside. ✉ *Kongevn. 26, 0390,* ☎ *22/92–20–00,* FAX *22/14–61–92. 221 rooms. 2 restaurants, bar, pool, sauna, cross-country skiing, nightclub, convention center. AE, DC, MC, V.*

$$$–$$$$ **Ambassadeur.** Hidden behind a pale pink facade with wrought-iron
★   balconies in a stylish residential area near the Royal Palace, the Ambassadeur is a 15-minute walk from both downtown and Frogner Park. Originally built in 1889 as an apartment hotel, it still has a turn-of-the-century feel. The owner has hand-picked antiques, china tea sets, and tapestries for the small downstairs salon. The rooms are individually furnished according to themes. "Roma" rooms have canopy beds draped in pale taffeta and maps of old Rome on the walls. "Peer Gynt" rooms have Scandinavian landscape paintings and a Norwegian farmhouse feel. If it's a special occasion, request the pricey "Osa" suite. The painted wooden furniture, carved canopy bed, and exquisite printed fabrics could easily be on display at the Norwegian Folk Museum. The hotel's small, professional staff doesn't bother with titles because everyone does whatever task presents itself, from laundering a shirt on short notice to delivering room service. ✉ *Camilla Colletts vei 15, 0258,* ☎ *22/44–18–35,* FAX *22/44–47–91. 41 rooms, 8 suites. Bar, indoor pool, sauna, meeting room. AE, DC, MC, V.*

$$$–$$$$ **Frogner House.** This elegant hotel opened in 1992 and receives mainly business clients, but welcomes independently traveling tourists looking for a quiet stay. The five-story red-brick and stone building went up in 1890 as an apartment house and now sits inconspicuously amid rows of other turn-of-the-century townhouses. Dressed in pastels and abundant lace coverings, the rooms are spacious and insulated. Some have balconies, and many have views of the boutique-lined residential streets. ✉ *Skovveien 8, 0257,* ☎ *22/56 00–56,* FAX *22/56–05–00. 60 rooms, 8 suites. Meeting room. AE, DC, MC, V.*

$$ **Gabelshus.** With only a discreet sign above the door, this ivy-covered brick house in a posh residential area is one of Oslo's most personal hotels. It's been owned by the same family for almost 50 years. The lounges are filled with antiques, some in the national romantic style, but the rooms are plain. It's a short walk to several of Oslo's best restaurants and a short trikk ride to the center of town. The Ritz Hotel, across the parking lot, is owned by the same family and takes the overflow.

✉ *Gabels Gt. 16, 0272,* ☎ *22/55–22–60,* FAX *22/44–27–30. 50 rooms (plus 42 rooms in Ritz). Restaurant. AE, DC, MC, V.*

$ 🏨 **Rainbow Gyldenløve.** Nestled among the many shops and cafés on Bogstadveien, this hotel is one of the city's most reasonable. It is within walking distance of Vigeland Park, and the trikk stops just outside the door. 🏨 *Bogstadvn. 20, 0355,* ☎ *22/60–10–90,* FAX *22/60–33–90. 169 rooms. Coffee shop. AE, DC, MC, V.*

Near Fornebu Airport and Oslo S Station

$$$$ 🏨 **Radisson SAS Plaza Hotel Oslo.** Northern Europe's largest hotel is a three-minute walk from Karl Johans Gate and just across from Oslo's central train station. A snazzy 33-story skyscraper in a city that has few, Oslo Plaza has become a part of the city's skyline. It is favored by business travelers, who tend toward the pricier deluxe suites in the tower, where the views of Oslo are worth the price. Below the 27th floor, the standard rooms are decorated in red and blue tones and have ample marble baths. ✉ *Sonja Henies Pl. 3, 0134,* ☎ *22/17–10–00,* FAX *22/17–73–00. 653 rooms, 20 suites. 2 restaurants, bar, indoor pool, health club, convention center. AE, DC, MC, V.*

$$$$ 🏨 **Royal Christiania.** It started out as bare-bones housing for 1952
★   Olympians. The original plain exterior has been retained, but inside it's a whole new luxury hotel, built around a central seven-story atrium. The emphasis here is on discreet comfort—the large rooms are decorated with soft-colored love seats and armchairs. ✉ *Biskop Gunnerus' Gt. 3, 0106,* ☎ *22/42–94–10,* FAX *22/42–46–22. 451 rooms, 73 suites. 2 restaurants, 2 bars, indoor pool, health club, nightclub, convention center. AE, DC, MC, V.*

$$$ 🏨 **Radisson SAS Park Royal.** Oslo Fornebu Airport's only hotel is somewhat anonymous, with long, narrow corridors and standard American-style hotel rooms. There are excellent business facilities, including a business-class airline check-in, and the airport bus stops right outside. ✉ *Fornebuparken, Box 185, 1324 Lysaker,* ☎ *67/12–02–20,* FAX *67/12–00–11. 254 rooms, 14 suites. Restaurant, bar, tennis court, health club, business services. AE, DC, MC, V.*

Nightlife and the Arts

Nightlife

For the past few years Oslo has strived to be the nightlife capital of Scandinavia, although local government factions have talked about toughening laws on noise pollution and drinking. At any time of the day or night, people are out on Karl Johan, and many clubs and restaurants in the central area stay open until the wee hours. Still, strict zoning laws have prohibited the sale of anything harder than "light" beer after 2:30 AM, which means many nightclubs close their doors earlier than one would expect.

Night-lifers can pick up a copy of the free monthly paper *Natt og Dag* at almost any café, bar, or hip-looking shop. It lists rock, pop, and jazz venues and contains an "øl barometer," listing the city's cheapest and most expensive places for a beer—a necessary column in a city where a draft, on average, costs NKr33. The listings are in Norwegian, but some ads are in English.

Many bars and nightclubs in Oslo have a minimum age, which will often give you a sense of who goes there. A minimum age of 18 will generally draw high schoolers, whereas 24 will draw young professionals.

BARS AND LOUNGES

Barbeint (✉ *Drammensvn. 20,* ☎ *22/44–59–47*) is an ultrahip spot where students, media folk, and local celebrities from the fashionable Frogner district convene on their way in from or out on the town. Avant-garde art adorns the walls, and the loud, cutting-edge music ranges from funk-metal and rock to rap. The trendiest twentysomethings imbibe the night away at **Beach Club** (⊠ Aker Brygge, ☎ 22/83–83–82), a kitschy American hamburger joint with life-size stuffed fish on the walls and diner-style tables and booths. If you're more partial to lounging than drinking, try the English-style bar at the **Bristol Hotel** (⊠ Kristian IV's Gt. 7, ☎ 22/41–58–40). **Børsen Online Café** (⊠ Nedre Vollgt. 19, enter on Stortingsgt., ☎ 22/33–08–00) caters to the cyber crowd and the upwardly mobile. The former can surf the net on one of several monitors that overlook a starry-skied dance floor, while the latter speculate on beer prices, which fluctuate according to supply and demand. For variety, get an outdoor table at **Lorry** (⊠ Parkvn. 12, ☎ 22/69–69–04), just over from the Royal Palace. Filled with a cast of grizzled old artists, the place advertises 204 brews, but don't be surprised if not all of them are in stock. For the serious beer connoisseur, **Oslo Mikrobryggeriet** (⊠ Bogstadvn. 6, ☎ 22/56–97–76) brews eight varieties of beer, including the increasingly popular Oslo Pils, on the premises. **Studenten Bryggeri** (⊠ Karl Johans Gt. 45, ☎ 22/42–56–80), another microbrewery, is often packed with students and loud music as well.

CAFÉS

Many cafés are open for cappuccino and quiet conversation practically around the clock, and they're the cheapest eateries as well (☞ Dining, *above*). The **Broker Café** (⊠ Bogstadvn. 27, ☎ 22/69–36–47) in Majorstuen has great pasta and salads and old, cushiony sofas on which to drink or dine. **Café Bacchus** (⊠ Dronningensgt. 27, ☎ 22/42–45–49), in the old railroad offices by Oslo Domkirke, is tiny but serves a mean brownie. Background music is classical during the day, jazz into the night. **Clodion Art Café** (☞ Dining, *above*) is one of Oslo's hippest spots for coffee. Downtown, **Nichol & Son** (⊠ Olavs Gt. 1, ☎ 22/83–19–60), a must for Jack Nicholson fans, is an amiable spot to relax with a newspaper. In the trendy area around Frogner and Homansbyen, try **Onkel Oswald** (⊠ Hegdehaugsvn. 34, ☎ 22/69–05–35) for a burger or sandwich. The Spanish-inspired **Tapas** (⊠ Hegdehaugsvn. 22, ☎ 22/60–38–28) serves bowls of café au lait in the morning and aperitif-size chunks of potatoes, chorizo, and cheese later on.

GAY BARS

For information about gay and lesbian activities in Oslo, you can read *Blikk*, the gay newsletter, or call **LLH** (Landsforening for Lesbisk of Homofil Frigjøring, ☎ 22/36–19–48), the nationwide gay and lesbian liberation association. The main gay bar in town is the all-new **Club Castro** (⊠ Kristian IV's Gt. 7, ☎ 22/41–51–08), which caters to a young, energetic crowd. **Andy Capp Pub** (⊠ Fr. Nansens Pl. 4, ☎ 22/41–41–65) draws an older crowd of mostly men, and it reeks of old smoke. **Den Sorte Enke** (The Black Widow, ⊠ Karl Johans Gt. 10, ☎ 22/33–23–01), Oslo's self-designated "gay-house," attracts a crowd of mainly younger men to dance the night away. **London Bar og Pub** (⊠ C.J. Hambros Pl. 5, ☎ 22/41–41–26) is packed on weekends with an over-30 crowd. **Potpurriet** (⊠ Øvre Vollgt. 13, ☎ 22/41–14–40) organizes well-attended women's dance nights on the last Friday of each month.

JAZZ CLUBS

Norwegians love jazz. Every August, the **Oslo Jazz Festival** (⊠ Tollbugt. 28, ☎ 22/42–91–20) brings in major international artists and attracts big crowds. Festivities commence with a Dixie-style parade, but all types of jazz are present and explained in free leaflets and newsletters everywhere. **Herr Nilsen** (⊠ C.J. Hambros Pl. 5, ☎ 22/33–

54–05) features some of Norway's most celebrated jazz artists in a Manhattanesque setting. There is live music three days a week and a jazz café on Saturday afternoons. **Oslo Jazzhus** (⌧ Stockholmsgt. 12, ☎ 22/38–59–63) is in an out-of-the-way location and is open only Thursday through Saturday, but the music is worth the journey. **Stortorvets Gjæstgiveri**(⌧ Grensen 1, ☎ 22/42–88–63) often presents New Orleans–style and ragtime bands and is known for its swinging dance nights.

NIGHTCLUBS

Most dance clubs open late, and the beat doesn't really start until around midnight. There's usually a minimum age, and the cover charge is around NKr50. Oslo's beautiful people congregate at the elegant **Barock** (⌧ Universitetsgt. 26, ☎ 22/42–44–20). **Cosmopolite** (⌧ Industrigt. 36, ☎ 22/69–16–63) has a big dance floor and music from all over the world, especially Latin America. **Kristiania** (⌧ Kristian IV's Gt. 12, ☎ 22/42–56–60), another hot spot, has a live jazz club, a disco, and a bar filling up its three art-bedecked floors. **Lipp** (⌧ Olav V's Gt. 2, ☎ 22/41–44–00) is extremely popular as a restaurant, nightclub, and bar. Most of the big hotels have discos that appeal to the over-30 crowd. **Smuget** (⌧ Rosenkrantz Gt. 22, ☎ 22/42–52–62) is an institution: live rock and blues every night except Sunday bring crowds who then flock to the in-house discotheque. Thursday is student disco night at **Snorre-Kompagniet** (⌧ Rosenkrantz' Gt. 11, ☎ 22/33–52–60), where the hip-hopping clientele is often still teenaged.

ROCK CLUBS

At Oslo's numerous rock clubs, the cover charges are low, the crowds young and boisterous, and the music loud. If your taste leans toward reggae and calypso, try the **Afro International Night Club** (⌧ Brennerivn. 5, ☎ 22/36–07–53), which has frequent Caribbean evenings. **Blue Monk** (⌧ St. Olavs Gt. 23, ☎ 22/20–22–90) has live music on Wednesdays, Fridays, and Saturdays—and the beer is surprisingly cheap. In the basement you'll find the boisterous Sub Pub, which airs punk and '80s classics. **Rockefeller** (⌧ Torggt. 16, ☎ 22/20–32–32) presents a good mix of musical styles, from avant-garde to salsa. **Sentrum Scene** (⌧ Arbeidersamfunnets Pl. 2, ☎ 22/20–60–40) claims to be Scandinavia's largest live-music venue. It certainly attracts big names, such as Lenny Kravitz and the Neville Brothers.

The Arts

The monthly tourist information brochure *What's on in Oslo* lists cultural events in Norwegian, as does *Aftenposten,* Oslo's (and Norway's) leading newspaper, in its evening "Oslo Puls" section. The Wednesday edition of *Dagbladet,* Oslo's daily liberal tabloid, also gives an exhaustive preview of the week's events. Tickets to virtually all performances in Norway, from classical or rock concerts to hockey games, can be purchased at any post office. You can also call **Billet Service** (☎ 810–33–133) and pick up tickets at the post office later.

ART

Art galleries are cropping up all over town as a generation of young artists comes of age. Although much official Norwegian art is folk art, some of the newer artists take a more postmodern approach to their craft. Pick up a copy of *Listen,* a brochure that lists all current exhibitions.

FILM

All films are shown in the original language with subtitles, except for some children's films, which are dubbed. You can buy tickets to any film showing at the box office of any of Oslo's cinemas, and you can reserve tickets by calling any cinema and leaving your phone number. Tickets cost NKr50 and are discounted some days in summer. If you like alternative and classic films, try **Cinemateket** (⊠ Dronningensgt. 16, ☎ 22/47–45–00), the city's only independent cinema.

MUSIC

The **Norwegian Philharmonic Orchestra,** under the direction of Mariss Janssons, is among Europe's leading ensembles. Its house, **Konserthuset** (⊠ Munkedamsvn. 14, ☎ 22/83–32–00), was built in 1977 in marble, metal, and rosewood. In the summer, folkloric dances are staged here twice a week. **Den Norske Opera** (⊠ Storgt. 23, ☎ 22/42–94–75 for information; 22/42–77–24 to order tickets between 10 and 6) and the ballet perform at Youngstorvet. The breathtaking **Gamle Logen** (⊠ Grev Wedels Pl. 2, ☎ 22/33–54–70), Norway's oldest concert hall, often sponsors classical music series, especially piano music.

For a thoroughly Norwegian cultural experience, check out the **Norwegian Masters** (☎ 22/43–34–70), who play character monologues from Ibsen's *Peer Gynt* against a backdrop of Munch paintings and to the music of the beloved Grieg, who originally wrote music to accompany the Norwegian fable. The performance takes place in English, and its venue changes from year to year.

THEATER

Nationalteatret (⊠ Stortingsgt. 15, ☎ 22/41–27–10) performances are in Norwegian: bring along a copy of the play in translation, and you're all set. The biennial Ibsen festival, which features plays by the great dramatist in both Norwegian and English, is set for summer 1998 and 2000. **Det Norske Teater** (⊠ Kristian IV's Gt. 8, ☎ 22/42–43–44) is a showcase for pieces in Nynorsk (☞ Languages *in* Contacts and Resources *in* Norway A to Z, *below*) and guest artists from abroad.

Outdoor Activities and Sports

Surrounding Oslo's compact center is a variety of lovely and unspoiled landscapes, including forests, farmland, and, of course, the fjord. Just 15 minutes north of the city center by tram is the **Oslomarka,** where locals ski in winter and hike in summer. The area is dotted with 27 small hytter, which are often available free of charge for backpackers on foot or on ski. These can be reserved through the **Norske Turistforening** (⊠ Stortingsgt. 28, ☎ 22/82–28–00), which has maps of the *marka* (fields and land), surrounding Oslo as well. The **Oslo Archipelago** is also a favorite with sunbathing urbanites, who hop ferries to their favorite isles.

Aerobics

If you need a fitness fix, you can visit one of the many health studios around the city. Most have a "klippekort" system, which means you buy 10 hours' worth of fitness and they "klip," or punch, your card with each entry. The ever-popular **Trim Tram** (⊠ Stranden 55, Aker Brygge, ☎ 22/83–66–50) offers myriad low- and high-intensity aerobics and step classes at reasonable rates. **Friskis & Svettis** (⊠ Munkedamsvn. 17–18, ☎ 22/83–25–40) holds free aerobics classes on the green in Frogner Park. From mid-May to mid-August you can watch or join the hundreds of health-conscious Osloites huffing and puffing and rolling in the dirt. Call for times and intensity levels.

Beaches

Beaches are scattered throughout the archipelago and sun-loving Scandinavians pack every patch of sand during the long summer days to make up for lack of light in winter. The most popular beach is Paradisbukta at Huk (on the Bygdøy peninsula), which devotes one portion of the beach to nude bathers and the other to "clothed." To get there, follow signs along Huk Aveny from the Folk- and Viking Ship museums. You can also take Bus 30A, marked "Bygdøy," to its final stop.

Biking

Oslo is a bike-friendly city. There are many marked paths in and around town meant for bicycles and pedestrians, and cyclists are allowed to use sidewalks. (Note, however, that cars do not have to stop for bicycles the way they do for pedestrians at crosswalks.) One great ride starts at Aker Brygge and takes you along the harbor to the Bygdøy peninsula, where you can visit the museums or cut across the fields next to the royal family's summer house. Ask locals how to get to Huk, the peninsula's popular beach (☞ Beaches, *above*).

Den Rustne Eike (The Rusty Spoke, ✉ Vestbanepl. 2, ☎ 22/83–72–31), just a few doors down from the Norway Information Center, rents bikes and equipment, including helmets. The store also offers five different sightseeing tours and has maps of the area for those braving it on their own. If you feel like roughing the terrain of the Holmenkollen marka (woods), you can rent mountain bikes from **Tomm Murstad Skiservice** (✉ Tryvannsvn. 2, ☎ 22/14–41–24) in the summer. Just take T-bane 1 to Frognerseteren and get off at the Voksenkollen station. **Syklistenes Landsforening** (National Organization of Cyclists, ✉ Stortingsgt. 23C, ☎ 22/41–50–80) sells books and maps for cycling holidays in Norway and abroad and gives friendly, free advice.

Fishing

A national fishing license (NKr90, available in post offices) and a local fee (NKr100 from local sports shops) are required to fish in the Oslo Fjord and the surrounding lakes. You can also fish throughout the Nordmarka woods area in a canoe rented from Tomm Murstad (☞ Biking, *above*). Ice fishing is popular in winter, but you'll have a hard time finding an ice drill—truly, you may want to bring one from home.

Golf

Oslo's international-level golf course, **Oslo Golfklubb** (✉ Bogstad, 0740 Oslo 7, ☎ 22/50–44–02) is private, and heavily booked, but will admit members of other golf clubs (weekdays before 2 PM and weekends after 2 PM) if space is available. Visitors must have a handicap certificate of 20 or lower for men, 28 or lower for women. Fees range from NKr275 to NKr325.

Hiking and Running

Head for the woods surrounding Oslo, the marka, for jogging or walking; there are thousands of kilometers of trails, hundreds of them lit. Frogner Park has many paths, and you can jog or hike along the Aker River, but a few unsavory types may be about late at night or early in the morning. Or you can take the Sognsvann trikk to the end of the line and walk or jog along the Sognsvann stream. For walks or jogs closer to town, explore the stately residential area around Drammensveien west of the Royal Palace, which has paths leading to Bygdøy. The Norske Turistforening (☞ *above*) has many maps of trails around Oslo and can recommend individual routes.

Grete Waitz and Ingrid Kristiansen have put Norway on the marathon runners' map in recent years. The first national marathon championships were held in Norway in 1897, and the Oslo Marathon always attracts a large following. **Norges Friidretts Forbund** (✉ Karl Johans Gt. 2, 0104 Oslo, ☎ 22/42–03–03) has information about local clubs and competitions.

Skiing

The **Skiforeningen** (✉ Kongevn. 5, 0390 Oslo 3, ☎ 22/92–32–00) provides national snow-condition reports and can provide tips on the multitude of cross-country trails. They also offer cross-country classes for young children (3- to 7-year-olds), downhill for older children (7-

to 12-year-olds), and both, in addition to Telemark-style and racing techniques, for adults.

Among the floodlit trails in the Oslomarka are the **Bogstad** (3½ km/ 2 mi), marked for the disabled and blind, the **Lillomarka** (about 25 km/15½ mi), and the **Østmarken** (33 km/20½ mi).

For downhill, which usually lasts from mid-December to March, there are 15 local city slopes as well as organized trips to several outside slopes, including **Norefjell** (☎ 32/14–94–00), 100 km (66 mi) north of the city, are also available.

You can rent both downhill and cross-country skis from **Tomm Murstad Skiservice** (✉ Tryvannsvn. 2, ☎ 22/14–41–24) at the Tryvann T-bane station. This is a good starting point for skiing; although there are but few downhill slopes in this area, a plethora of cross-country trails for every level of competence exist.

Swimming

Tøyenbadet (✉ Helgesensgt. 90, ☎ 22/67–18–87) and **Frogner Park** (☎ 22/08–22–50) have large outdoor swimming pools that are open from mid-May through late August, depending on the weather (weekdays 7–7:30, weekends 10–5:30). Tøyenbadet also has an indoor pool that's open year-round. All pools cost NKr37. Pools are free with the Oslo Card (☞ Getting Around, *below*).

Shopping

Oslo is the best place for buying anything Norwegian. Prices of handmade articles, such as knitwear, are controlled, making comparison shopping unnecessary. Otherwise shops have both sales and specials—look for the words *salg* and *tilbud*. Sales of seasonal merchandise, combined with the value-added tax refund, can save you more than half the original price. Norwegians do like au courant skiwear, so there are plenty of bargains in last season's winter sportswear.

Stores are generally open from 9 to 5 during the week, but they often close by 3 on Saturdays. Shopping malls and department stores are open later, until 8 during the week and 6 on weekends. Shops also stay open late Thursdays as well as on the first Saturday of the month, known as *super lørdag* (super Saturday) to enthusiastic shoppers. Only during the holiday season are stores open Sunday.

Several shopping districts stand out. From the city center, you can wander up the tree-lined Bygdøy Allé and poke around the fashionable **Frogner** area, which is brimming with modern and antique furniture stores, interior design shops, gourmet food shops, art galleries, haute couture, and a solid majority of Oslo's beautiful people. Stores of every ilk are crammed into the downtown area around **Karl Johans Gate,** where many shoppers flock. The concentration of department stores is especially high in this part of town. **Majorstuen** starts at the T-bane station with the same name and proceeds down Bogstadveien to the Royal Palace. Once you're off the main shopping street, a tiny smattering of independent shops and galleries cater to needs as obscure as your next safari hunt. **Vikaterrassen,** near Aker Brygge (☞ *below*), is a pleasant shopping street with small, exclusive stores. Its glass and concrete facade sits directly underneath a more magnificent building that houses Norway's Ministry of Foreign Affairs.

Department Stores

Christiania GlasMagasin (✉ Stortorvet 9, ☎ 22/90–89–00) is an amalgamation of shops under one roof rather than a true department store, but it has a much more extensive selection of merchandise than most department stores in town. The best buys are glass and porcelain. Christmas decorations reflecting Norway's rural heritage are easily packed. There is also a wide selection of pewter ware. **Steen & Strøm** (⊠ Kongens Gt. 23, ☎ 22/00–40–01), one of Oslo's first department stores, sells the usual: cosmetics, clothing, books, accessories. It also has a well-stocked outdoors floor.

Shopping Centers

Aker Brygge, Norway's first major shopping center, is right on the water across from the Tourist Information Office at Vestbanen. Shops are open until 8 most days, and some even on Sundays. **Oslo City** (⊠ Stenersgt. 1E, ☎ 22/17–09–92), at the other end of downtown, with access to the street from Oslo S Station, is the largest indoor mall, but the shops are run-of-the-mill, and the food is mostly fast. The elegant **Paleet** (⊠ Karl Johans Gt. 39–41, between Universitetsgt. and Rosenkrantz' Gt., ☎ 22/41–70–86) opens up into a grand atrium lined with supports of various shades of black and gray marble. There's a good bookstore and some high-end clothing shops on the main floor; the basement houses a food court.

Specialty Stores

ANTIQUES

Norwegian rustic antiques cannot be taken out of the country, but just about anything else can with no problem. The Frogner district is dotted with antiques shops, especially Skovveien and Thomas Heftyes Gate between Bygdøy Allé and Frogner Plass. Deeper in the heart of the Majorstua district, Industrigate is famous for its good selection of shops. **Blomqvist Kunsthandel** (⊠ Tordenskiolds Gt. 5, ☎ 22/41–26–31) has a good selection of small items and paintings, with auctions six times a year. The rare volumes at **Damms Antiqvariat** (⊠ Tollbugt. 25, ☎ 22/41–04–02) will catch the eye of any antiquarian book buff, with books in English as well as Norwegian, which could be harder to find back home. **Esaias Solberg** (⊠ Dronningens Gt. 27, ☎ 22/42–41–08), behind Oslo Cathedral, has exceptional small antiques. **Kaare Berntsen** (⊠ Universitetsgt. 12, ☎ 22/20–34–29) sells paintings, furniture, and small items, all very exclusive and priced accordingly. **Marsjandisen** (⊠ Paléet, ☎ 22/42–71–68), nestled in the slickest of shopping centers, carries "merchandise" ranging from discontinued Hadeland glasses to letter openers and authentic war-era postcards, pins, and buttons. **West Sølv og Mynt** (⊠ Niels Juels Gt. 27, ☎ 22/55–75–83) has the largest selection of silver, both old and antique, in town.

BOOKS

Bjørn Ringstrøms Antikvariat (⊠ Ullevålsvn. 1, ☎ 22/20–78–05), across the street from the Museum of Applied Art, has a wide selection of used books and records. **Erik Qvist** (⊠ Drammensvn. 16, ☎ 22/44–52–69), across from the Royal Palace, has an extensive English-language selection. **Pocketboka** (⊠ Ole Vigs Gt. 25, ☎ 22/69–00–18) at Majorstuen sells used paperbacks. **Tanum Libris** (⊠ Karl Johans Gt. 37–41, ☎ 22/41–11–00) has scores of English-language books, ranging from travel guides to contemporary fiction.

EMBROIDERY

Randi Mangen (⊠ Jacob Aalls Gt. 17, ☎ 22/60–50–59), near Majorstuen, sells only embroidery. **Husfliden** (☞ Handicrafts, *below*) sells embroidery kits, including do-it-yourself *bunader* (national costumes); traditional yarn shops also sell embroidery.

FOOD

Buy a smoked salmon or trout for a special treat. Most grocery stores sell vacuum-packed fish. **W. Køltzow** (⊠ Stranden 3, ☎ 22/83–00–70), at Aker Brygge, can pack fish for export.

FUR

Look for the Saga label for the best-quality farmed Arctic fox and mink. Other popular skins include Persian lamb, beaver, and mink. **Hansson** (⊠ Kirkevn. 54, ☎ 22/69–64–20), near Majorstuen, has an excellent selection of furs. **Studio H. Olesen** (⊠ Karl Johans Gt. 31, enter at Rosenkrantz' Gt., ☎ 22/33–37–50) has the most exclusive designs.

FURNITURE

Norway is well known for both rustic furniture and orthopedic yet well-designed chairs. **Tannum** (⊠ Stortingsgt. 28, ☎ 22/83–42–95) is a good starting point. Drammensveien and Bygdøy Allé have a wide selection of interior-design stores.

GLASS, CERAMICS, AND PEWTER

Abelson Brukskunst (⊠ Skovvn. 27, ☎ 22/55–55–94), behind the Royal Palace, is crammed with the best modern designs. The shops at **Basarhallene** behind the cathedral also sell glass and ceramics. If there's no time to visit a glass factory (☞ Side Trips, *below*), department stores are the best option: **Christiania GlasMagasin** (⊠ Stortorvet 9, ☎ 22/90–89–00) stocks both European and Norwegian glass designs. **Lie Antikk & Kunsthandverk** (⊠ Hegdehaugsveien 27, ☎ 22/60–98–61) is a tiny shop at the bottom of Hegdehaugsveien that sells colorful wine glasses and claims to have the city's best collection of blown glass. **Norway Designs** (⊠ Stortingsgt. 28, ☎ 22/83–11–00) specializes in glass crafted by Norwegian and Scandinavian folk artists.

HANDICRAFTS

Basarhallene, the arcade behind the cathedral, is also worth a browse for handicrafts made in Norway. **Format Kunsthandverk** (⊠ Vestbanepl. 1, ☎ 22/83–73–12) has beautiful, yet pricey, individual pieces (but you can buy a postcard to show your friends back home). **Heimen Husflid AS** (⊠ Rosenkrantz' Gt. 8, ☎ 22/41–40–50, enter at Kristian IV's Gt.) has small souvenir items and a specialized department for Norwegian national costumes. **Husfliden** (⊠ Møllergt. 4, ☎ 22/42–10–75), one of the finest stores with handmade goods in the country, has an even larger selection, including pewter, ceramics, knits, handwoven textiles, furniture, handmade felt boots and slippers, hand-sewn loafers, sweaters, national costumes, wrought-iron accessories, Christmas ornaments, and wooden kitchen accessories—all made in Norway.

JEWELRY

Gold and precious stones are no bargain, but silver and enamel jewelry, along with reproductions of Viking pieces, are. Some silver pieces are made with Norwegian stones, particularly pink thulite. **David-Andersen** (⊠ Karl Johans Gt. 20, ☎ 22/41–69–55; Oslo City, ☎ 22/17–09–34) is Norway's best-known goldsmith, with stunning silver and gold designs. **ExpoArte** (⊠ Drammensvn. 40, ☎ 22/55–93–90), also a gallery, specializes in custom pieces and displays work of avant-garde Scandinavian jewelers. **Heyerdahl** (⊠ Roald Amundsensgt. 6, ☎ 22/41–59–18), near City Hall, is a good, dependable jeweler.

KNITWEAR AND CLOTHING

Norway is famous for its handmade, multicolored ski sweaters, and even mass-produced (machine-knit) models are of top quality. The prices are regulated, so buy what you like when you see it. **Husfliden** (☞ Handicrafts, *above*) stocks handmade sweaters in the traditional style. **Maurtua** (⊠ Fr. Nansens Pl. 9, ☎ 22/41–31–64), near City Hall, has a huge selection of sweaters and blanket coats. **Oslo Sweater Shop** (⊠ SAS Scandinavia Hotel, Tullinsgt. 5, ☎ 22/11–29–22) has one of the city's widest selections. **Rein og Rose** (⊠ Ruseløkkvn. 3, ☎ 22/83–21–39), in the Vikaterassen strip, has extremely friendly salespeople and a good selection of knitwear, yarn, and textiles. **Siril** (⊠ Rosenkrantz' Gt. 23, ☎ 22/41–

01–80), near City Hall, is a small shop with attentive staff. **William Schmidt** (⊠ Karl Johans Gt. 41, ☎ 22/42–02–88), founded in 1853, is Oslo's oldest shop specializing in sweaters and souvenirs.

SPORTSWEAR

Look for the ever-popular Helly-Hansen brand. The company makes everything from insulated underwear to rainwear, snow gear, and great insulated mittens. **Sportshuset** (⊠ Ullevålsvn. 11, ☎ 22/20–11–21; ⊠ Frognervn. 9C, ☎ 22/55–29–57) has the best prices. **Gresvig** (⊠ Storgt. 20, ☎ 22/17–39–80) is a little more expensive but has a good selection. **Sigmund Ruud** (⊠ Kirkevn. 57, ☎ 22/69–43–90) also has a comprehensive stock of quality sportswear.

WATCHES

For some reason, Swiss watches are much cheaper in Norway than in many other countries. **Bjerke** (⊠ Karl Johans Gt. 31, ☎ 22/42–20–44; Prinsensgt. 21, ☎ 22/42–60–50) has a large selection.

Street Markets

Although some discerning locals wonder where it procures its wares, the best flea market is on Saturday at **Vestkanttorvet,** near Frogner Park at Amaldus Nilsens Plass at the intersection of Professor Dahlsgate and Eckerberg Gate. Check the local paper for weekend garage sales, or *loppemarkeder,* held in schools.

Oslo A to Z

Arriving and Departing

BY BOAT

Several ferry lines connect Oslo with the United Kingdom, Denmark, Sweden, and Germany. **Color Line** (☎ 22/22–94–44–00) sails to Kiel, Germany, and to Hirtshals, Denmark; **DFDS Scandinavian Seaways** (☎ 22/41–90–90) to Copenhagen via Helsingborg, Sweden; and **Stena Line** (☎ 23/17–90–00) to Frederikshavn, Denmark.

BY BUS

The main bus station, **Bussterminalen** (☎ 23/00–24–00), is under Galleri Oslo, across from the Oslo S Station. You can buy local bus tickets at the terminal or on the bus. Tickets for long-distance routes on **Nor-Way Bussekspress** (☎ 22/17–52–90, FAX 22/17–59–22) can be purchased here or at travel agencies. For local traffic information, call **Trafikanten** (☎ 22/17–70–30 or 177).

BY CAR

Route E18 connects Oslo with Göteborg, Sweden (by ferry between Sandefjord and Strömstad, Sweden); Copenhagen, Denmark (by ferry between Kristiansand and Hirtshals, Denmark); and Stockholm directly overland. The land route from Oslo to Göteborg is the E6. All streets and roads leading into Oslo have toll booths a certain distance from the city center, forming an "electronic ring." The toll is NKr12 and was implemented to reduce pollution downtown. If you have the correct amount in change, drive through one of the lanes marked "Mynt." If you don't, or if you need a receipt, use the "Manuell" lane.

BY PLANE

Oslo Fornebu Airport (☎ 67/59–33–40), 20 minutes southwest of the city, will remain Oslo's main international and domestic airport until late 1998. It is a relatively small airport, but walks between international arrivals, baggage claim, and passport control can seem long.

SAS (☎ 810/03–300) is the main carrier, with both international and domestic flights. The main domestic carriers are **Braathens SAFE** (☎ 67/59–70–00) and **Widerøe** (☎ 67/11–14–60).

Other major airlines serving Fornebu include **British Airways** (☎ 22/82–20–00), **Air France** (☎ 22/83–56–30), **Delta Air Lines** (☎ 22/41–56–00), **Finnair** (☎ 67/53–11–97), **Icelandair** (☎ 22/83–35–70), **KLM** (☎ 67/58–38–00), and **Lufthansa** (☎ 22/83–65–65).

Gardermoen Airport (☎ 63/97–84–77), 50 km (30 mi) north of Oslo, is slated to become Oslo's main airport by October 1998. At press time, Gardermoen was served mostly by charter airlines.

Between the Airport and Downtown: Oslo Fornebu Airport is a 15- to 20-minute ride from the center of Oslo at off-peak hours. At rush hour (7:30–9 AM from the airport and 3:30–5 PM to the airport), the trip can take more than twice as long. None of the downtown hotels provide free shuttle service, although some outside the city do. The trip to Gardermoen Airport from the city center takes 19 minutes by express train; there are six trains scheduled per hour. By taxi the trip takes about 40 minutes but is extremely expensive, upwards of $100.

Flybussen (☎ 67/59–62–20; NKr40; *to Oslo* weekdays and Sun. 7:30 AM–11:30 PM, Sat. 7:30 AM–11:00 PM; *to Fornebu* weekdays, 6 AM–9:40 PM, Sat. 6 AM–7:40 PM, Sun. 6 AM–9:50 PM) departs from its terminal under Galleri Oslo shopping center every 10–15 minutes and reaches Fornebu approximately 20 minutes later. Another bus departs from the SAS Scandinavia Hotel. Between the two buses, there are stops at the central train station as well as at Stortinget, Nationaltheatret, and near Aker Brygge. There is also a bus that departs Galleri Oslo for Gardermoen daily; the trip takes about 40 minutes. Call for specific departure times.

Another alternative is Suburban Bus 31, marked "Snarøya," which stops outside the Arrivals terminal. On the trip into town it stops on the main road opposite the entrance to the airport. You can catch this bus at both the central railway station, Jernbanetorget, or at Nationaltheatret. The cost is Nkr21.

There is a taxi line to the right of the Arrivals exit. The fare to town is about NKr130. All taxi reservations should be made through the **Oslo Taxi Central** (☎ 22/38–80–90; dial 1 for direct reservation) no less than 20 minutes before pickup time.

BY TRAIN

Long-distance trains arrive at and leave from **Oslo S Station** (☎ 22/17–14–00), whereas most suburban commuter trains use **Nationaltheatret** or **Oslo S.** Commuter cars reserved for monthly pass holders are marked with a large black "M" on a yellow circle. Trains marked "C," or InterCity, offer such upgraded services as breakfast and "office cars" with phones and power outlets, for an added fee.

Getting Around

Most public transportation starts running by 5:30 AM, with the last run just after midnight. On weekends there is night service on certain routes. Tickets on all public transportation within Oslo cost NKr18 with a one-hour transfer, whereas tickets that cross communal boundaries have different rates. It pays to buy a pass or a multiple-travel card, which includes transfers. A one-day "Tourist Ticket" pass costs NKr40, and a seven-day pass costs NKr130. A "Flexikort," purchased at post offices, tourist information offices, T-banc stations, and on some routes, is good for 8 trips with free transfer within one hour and costs NKr105. Oslo Sporveier operates most modes of transport in the city, including tram, bus, underground, train, and boat. **Trafikanten** (✉ Jernbanetorget, ☎ 22/17–70–30 or 177), the information office for public transportation, is open weekdays 7 AM–11 PM, weekends 8 AM–11 PM.

The **Oslo Card** offers unlimited travel on all public transport in greater Oslo as well as free admission to museums, sightseeing attractions, and the race track, as well as discounts at various stores and cinemas (May–July). A one-day Oslo Card costs NKr130, a two-day card NKr200, and a three-day card NKr240. It can be purchased at tourist information offices, hotels, and central post offices. The Oslo Package, available through the same office, combines a four-day Oslo Card with a discount on accommodations (☞ Lodging, *above*).

BY BUS

About 20 bus lines, including six night buses on weekends, serve the city. Most stop at Jernbanetorget opposite Oslo S Station. Tickets can be purchased from the driver.

BY CAR

If you plan to do any amount of driving in Oslo, buy a copy of the *Stor Oslo* map, available at bookstores and gasoline stations. It may be a small city, but one-way streets and few exit ramps on the expressway make it very easy to get lost.

Oslo Card holders can park for free in city-run street spots or at reduced rates in lots run by the city (P-lots), but pay careful attention to time limits and be sure to ask at the information office exactly where the card is valid. Parking is very difficult in the city—many places have one-hour limits and can cost up to NKr17 per hour. Instead of individual parking meters in P-lots, you'll find one machine that dispenses validated parking tickets to display in your car windshield. Travelers with disabilities with valid parking permits from their home country are allowed to park free and with no time limit in spaces reserved for those with disabilities.

BY FERRY

A ferry to Hovedøya and other islands in the harbor basin leaves from Vippetangen, behind Akershus Castle (take Bus 29 from Jernbanetorget or walk along the harbor from Aker Brygge). These are great spots for picnics and short hikes. From April through September, ferries run between Rådhusbrygge 3, in front of City Hall, and Bygdøy, the western peninsula, where many of Oslo's major museums are located. There is also ferry service from Aker Brygge to popular summer beach towns along the fjord's coast, including Drøbak (☞ East of the Oslo Fjord, *below*).

BY STREETCAR/TRIKK

Eight trikk lines serve the city. All stop at Jernbanetorget opposite Oslo S Station. Tickets can be purchased from the driver.

BY SUBWAY/T-BANE

Oslo has seven T-bane lines, which converge at Stortinget station. The four eastern lines all stop at Tøyen before branching off, whereas the four western lines run through Majorstuen before emerging above ground for the rest of their routes to the northwestern suburbs. Tickets can be purchased at the stations. Get a free map, "Sporveiens hovedkart," of Oslo's extensive public transportation system at post offices, Trafikanten, and most centrally located stations. It is undoubtedly the best public transport map of Oslo for tourists.

BY TAXI

All city taxis are connected with the central dispatching office (☎ 22/38–80–90), which can take up to 30 minutes to send one during peak hours. Cabs can be ordered from 20 minutes to 24 hours in advance. (If you leave a cab waiting after you've sent for one, there is an additional fee added to your fare.) Special transport, including vans and cabs equipped for people with disabilities, can be ordered (☎ 22/38–80–90; then dial 1 for direct reservations, 2 for advance reservations, 3 for information, and 4 if you have special needs). Taxi stands are located all over town, usually alongside Narvesen kiosks, and are listed in the telephone directory under "Taxi" or "Drosjer."

It is possible to hail a cab on the street, but cabs are not allowed to pick up passengers within 100 yards of a stand. It is not unheard of to wait for more than an hour at a taxi stand in the wee hours of the morning, after everyone has left the bars. A cab with its roof light on is available. Rates start at NKr18 for hailed or rank cabs, NKr55 for ordered taxis, depending on the time of day.

Contacts and Resources

CURRENCY EXCHANGE

After normal banking hours, money can be changed at a few places. The bank at **Oslo S Station** is open June–September, daily 8 AM–11 PM; October–May, weekdays 8 AM–7:30 PM, Saturday 10–5. The bank at **Oslo Fornebu Airport** is open weekdays 6:30 AM–9 PM, Saturday 7–5, Sunday 7 AM–8 PM. All post offices exchange money. **Oslo Central Post Office** (⊠ Dronningensgt. 15) is open weekdays 8–6, Saturday 9–3.

DOCTORS AND DENTISTS

Doctors: Norway's largest private clinic, **Volvat Medisinske Senter** (⊠ Borgenvn. 2A, ☎ 22/95–75–00) is near the Borgen or Majorstuen T-bane stations, not far from Frogner Park. It is open weekdays from 8 AM to 10 PM, weekends 10 to 10. **Oslo Akutten** (⊠ N. Vollgt. 8, ☎ 22/41–24–40) is an emergency clinic downtown, near Stortinget. **Centrum Legesenter** (⊠ Fritjof Nansens Pl., ☎ 22/41–41–20) is a small, friendly clinic across from City Hall.

Dentists: For emergencies only, **Oslo Kommunale Tannlegevakt** (⊠ Kolstadgt. 18, ☎ 22/67–30–00) at Tøyen Senter is open evenings and weekends. **Oslo Private Tannlegevakt** (⊠ Hansteens Gt. 3, ☎ 22/44–46–36), near the American Embassy, is a private clinic open seven days a week.

EMBASSIES

U.S. (⊠ Drammensvn. 18, ☎ 22/44–85–50). **Canada** (⊠ Oscars Gt. 20, ☎ 22/46–69–55). **U.K.** (⊠ Thomas Heftyes Gt. 8, ☎ 22/55–24–00).

EMERGENCIES

Police: ☎ 112 or 22/66–90–50. **Fire:** ☎ 110 or 22/11–44–55. **Ambulance:** ☎ 113 or 22/11–70–80. **Car Rescue:** ☎ 22/23–20–85. **Emergency Rooms: Oslo Legevakt** (⊠ Storgt. 40, ☎ 22/11–70–70), the city's public and thus less expensive, but slower, hospital, is near the Oslo S Station and is open 24 hours. **Volvat Medisinske Senter** (⊠ Borgenvn. 2A, ☎ 22/95–75–00) operates an emergency clinic from 8 AM to 10 PM during the week, 10 to 10 on weekends.

GUIDED TOURS

Tickets for all tours are available from Tourist Information at Vestbanen (☞ Visitor Information, *below*) and at the Oslo S Station. Tickets for bus tours can be purchased on the buses. All tours, except HMK's Oslo Highlights tour (☞ *below*), operate during summer only.

Dogsled Tours: For a fast and exciting experience, tour the marka by dogsled. Both lunch and evening tours are available. Contact **Norske Sledehundturer** (⊠ Einar Kristen Aas, 1514 Moss, ☎ 69/27–56–40, FAX 69/27–37–86).

Forest Tours: Tourist Information at Vestbanen can arrange four- to eight-hour motor safaris through the forests surrounding Oslo (☎ 22/83–00–30).

Orientation: HMK Sightseeing (⊠ Hegdehaugsvn. 4, ☎ 22/20–82–06) offers several bus tours in and around Oslo. Tours leave from the Norway Information Center at Vestbanen; combination boat-bus tours depart from Rådhusbrygge 3, the wharf in front of City Hall. **Båtservice Sightseeing** (⊠ Rådhusbryggen 3, ☎ 22/20–07–15) has a bus tour, five cruises, and one combination tour.

Personal Guides: Tourist Information at Vestbanen can provide an authorized city guide for your own private tour. **OsloTaxi** (⊠ Trondheimsvn. 100, ☎ 22/38–80–70) also gives private tours.

Sailing: Norway Yacht Charter (⊠ H. Heyerdahls Gt. 1, ☎ 22/42–64–98) arranges sailing or yacht tours and dinner cruises for groups of five people to 600.

Sleigh Rides: Vangen Skistue (⊠ Laila and Jon Hamre, Fjell, 1404 Siggerud, ☎ 64/86–54–81) will arrange an old-fashioned sleigh ride through Oslomarka, the wooded area surrounding the city. In summertime, they switch from sleighs to carriages.

Street Train: Starting at noon and continuing at 45-minute intervals until 10 PM, the Oslo Train, which looks like a chain of dune buggies, leaves Aker Brygge for a 30-minute ride around the town center. The train runs daily in summer. Ask at the Norway Information Center (☞ Visitor Information, *below*) for departure times.

Walking: Organized walking tours are listed in *What's on in Oslo,* available from Tourist Information and at most hotels.

LATE-NIGHT PHARMACIES

Jernbanetorgets Apotek (⊠ Jernbanetorget 4B, ☎ 22/41–24–82), across from Oslo S Station, is open 24 hours. **Sfinxen Apotek** (⊠ Bogstadvn. 51, ☎ 22/46–34–44), near Frogner Park, is open weekdays from 8:30 AM to 9 PM, Saturdays from 8:30 AM to 8 PM, and Sundays from 5 PM to 8 PM.

TRAVEL AGENCIES

Winge Reisebureau (⊠ Karl Johans Gt. 33/35, ☎ 22/00–45–90) is the agent for American Express—here you can cash travelers' checks. An **American Express** office is near the Rådhuset (⊠ Fritjof Nansens pl. 6, ☎ 22/98–37–35). **Bennett Reisebureau** (⊠ Linstowsgt. 6, ☎ 22/69–71–00) is a business travel agency. **Kilroy Travels Norway** (⊠ Universitetssenteret, Blindern, ☎ 22/85–32–40; or Nedre Slottsgt. 23, ☎ 22/42–01–20) distributes ISIC cards for students and GO cards for people younger than 25.

VISITOR INFORMATION

The main tourist office, the **Norway Information Center** (☎ 22/83–00–50 from outside Norway; or the local number, ☎ 82/06–01–00, which is a toll call), is in the old Vestbanen railway station. The hours are as follows: spring and fall 9–6; summer 9–8; winter 9–4. The office at the main railway station, **Sentralstasjonen** (⊠ Jernbanetorget, no phone) is open daily 8 AM–11 PM; during winter the office takes a break from 3 PM to 4:30 PM. Look for the big, round blue-and-green signs marked with a white I. Information about the rest of the country can be obtained from **NORTRA** (⊠ Nortravel Marketing, Postboks 2893, Solli, 0230 Oslo, ☎ 22/92–52–00, ℻ 22/56–05–05).

SIDE TRIPS FROM OSLO

Henie-Onstad Kunstsenter and Bærums Verk

1 The **Henie-Onstad Kunstsenter** (Henie-Onstad Art Center) is just a short journey from Oslo, about 12 km (7 mi) southwest of the city on E18. This modern art center resulted from a union between Norway's famous skater Sonja Henie and Norwegian shipping magnate Niels Onstad. Henie had a shrewd head for money and marriage, and her third, to Onstad, resulted in the Center. They put together a fine collection of early 20th-century art, with important works by Leger, Munch, Picasso, Bonnard, and Matisse. Henie died in 1969, but she still skates her way through many a late-night movie. The three-time Olympic gold-medal winner was the first to realize the potential of the ice show, and her technical assistant, Frank Zamboni, has been immortalized in skating rinks around the world by the ice-finishing machine he developed just for her, the Zamboni. Buses 151, 152, and 251 from Oslo S Station stop near the entrance to the Henie-Onstad Center grounds. ⊠ *1311 Høvikodden,* ☎ *67/54–30–50.* ⊟ *NKr50.* ☉ *Mon. 9–5, Tues.–Fri. 9–9, weekends 11–9.*

One of Oslo's fashionable suburbs, Bærum is about 20 minutes from the city. The area is mostly residential, but along the banks of the Lomma **2** River you'll find charming **Bærums Verk.** In the 1960s, the owners of the Bærums Verk iron foundry fixed up their old industrial town and made it into a historical site. Created in the 17th century after iron ore was discovered in the region, the ironworks of Bærum quickly became the country's primary iron source. Anna Krefting, a woman who ran the works during the 18th century, believed that workers who spent their days and nights in the foundry should live there as well and be protected by it. The ironworks of Bærum thus became a village in its own right.

As you explore the beautifully restored village, you'll first notice the cramped wooden cottages lining **Verksgata** where the workers once lived. Notice that the doors are in the back of the buildings; this was in case a fire from the works spread through the main street. Crafts makers now lease space in the former living quarters. Here you can purchase wares from a doll maker, a glass blower, a carpenter, a chocolatier, and an embroiderer.

Cross the Lomma River to the entrance of the **Ovnmuseet** (Stove Museum), which displays centuries-old cast-iron stoves in the basement of the iron foundry's enormous smelter. Bærums Verk stoves were exported for centuries and still serve as antique fireplaces in many Oslo homes and service establishments. From Oslo, follow E16 in the direction of Hønefoss. Veer north on Route 168, following signs to Bærums Verk Senteret until you reach the tourist information office. ⊠ *Verksgt. 8B, Boks 39, 1353 Bærum,* ☎ *67/13–00–18 (information office).* ☉ *Verksgata weekdays 10–6, Sat. 10–3; some shops open Sun. Stove Museum weekends noon–3. Other times on request.*

NEED A   Stop in at **Pannekake Huset** (The Pancake House, ⊠ Verksgt. 9, ☎ 67/
BREAK?   15–07–02) for sweet or salty Dutch-style crepes and a cherry beer or
             hot chocolate. It's open Tuesday–Sunday noon to 8.

Dining

$$$ ✕ **Værtshuset Bærums Verk.** Norway's oldest standing restaurant,
★   this spot is a must on any itinerary that includes the neighboring iron
       works. The inn opened in 1640 and was a frequented stop on the

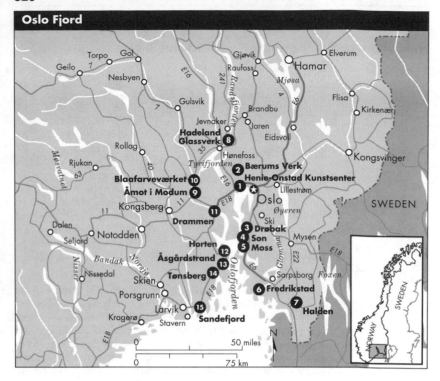

Oslo Fjord

"King's" road from Oslo to Bergen. Restored in 1987, it is now one of Norway's finest restaurants. Low ceilings, pastel-painted wooden floors, shiny pewter tableware, and the tick-tock of a grandfather clock in the dining room all create the impression that you are walking into 19th-century Scandinavia. Each room has a charm of its own, from the quiet, oblong Doctor's Room to the rustic kitchen with a blazing fire. Perhaps the most innovative menu of the year, which lasts only three days in March, is one modeled after the famous meal served in the film *Babette's Feast,* complete with a faux turtle soup (it is illegal to hunt turtles in Norway), blinis, and quail. ⊠ *Vertshusvn. 10, Brums Verk,* ☎ *67/80–02–0. AE, DC, MC, V. No lunch.*

EAST OF THE OSLO FJORD

If you've got a weakness for the water and things maritime, getting out of Oslo to the more savage fjord beaches might be a good idea. The eastern side of the Oslo Fjord is summer-vacation country for many Norwegians, who retreat to cabins on the water during July. The towns have developed facilities to cater to them and brag that they inhabit the "sunny" side of the fjord.

Many towns along the fjord offer history and culture as well as a place to bathe. Viking ruins and inscriptions, fortified towns, and bohemian 19th-century artists' colonies provide just a glimpse into the region's rich past.

Some of the towns mentioned can easily be visited as day trips from Oslo. Roads can be winding, though, so you might want to devote several days to exploring the area. Note that ferries shuttle cars and people back and forth between the archipelago islands and either side of

SCANDINAVIA BY TRAIN

The best way to experience the sights Scandinavia has to offer is by train.

With a *Scanrail Pass* choose unlimited rail travel throughout Denmark, Finland, Norway and Sweden for as many days as you need. Individual country rail passes are also available.

And with a *Scanrail 'n Drive,* you can take advantage of the benefits of both rail *and* car to get even more out of your Scandinavian vacation.

For information or reservations call your travel agent or Rail Europe:

1-800-4-EURAIL(US)

1-800-361-RAIL(CAN)

Your one source for European travel!

Speakeasy.

Fodor's and Living Language® bring you the most useful, up-to-date language course for travelers. Phrasebook/dictionary, two cassettes, booklet.

www.fodors.com/

the fjord, so it is possible to combine this tour with the West of the Oslo Fjord (☞ *below*) and make a complete circle without backtracking.

Drøbak

❸ *35 km (21 mi) south of Oslo.*

Mention the summer resort town of Drøbak to many Norwegians, and strangely enough, they'll start talking about Father Christmas. Although there is some question as to where the *Julenisse* (literally, "Christmas elf") came from, Norwegians claim—at least his adopted home—is here in Drøbak.

Norwegian legend says that Julenisse is one of many elves who live in the woods and have magical powers. This Julenisse, who has established his own post office, **Julenissens Posthuset** in Drøbak, responds to nearly 30,000 letters a year from children all over the world, the majority of which come from Japan. ⊠ *Julenissen, 1440 Drøbak.*

The inviting **Tregaardens Julehus** (Christmas House) dominates the town's central square. Just around the corner from the post office, this 1876 house was once a mission for seafarers unable to reach Oslo because the fjord was frozen over. Now it sells Christmas wares and gifts such as wooden dolls and mice made of cloth—all handmade by Eva Johansen, the store's creator and owner. Spin-offs of this ever-so-authentic Christmas shop include Drøbak's gift of a fir tree to the cities of Berlin and Osaka. ⊠ *1440 Drøbak,* ☎ *64/93–41–78.*

NEED A BREAK? Back on the main square, stop in **Det Gamle Bageri Ost & Vinstue** (The Old Bakery Wine and Cheese Room, ☎ 64/93–21–05) for some home-brewed smoky-tasting *Rauchbier,* a German specialty. Originally a bakery, this tiny pub serves wine with cheese and fruit plates on heavy wood-slab tables by the central oven.

Lodging

$–$$ 🏨 **Reenskaug Hotel.** The Norwegian author Knut Hamsun frequented this hotel and wrote a book here at the turn of the century. Back then, it was just a wooden house on a dirt road. The 100-year-old hotel's whitewashed exterior complements the quaintness of the town's main road. Inside, the rooms are rather small and nondescript, but they are nonetheless clean. Reasonable summer prices make it worth your while to stay the night in Drøbak. ⊠ *Storgt. 32, 1440 Drøbak,* ☎ *64/93–33–60,* 𝔽𝔸𝕏 *64/93–36–66. 29 rooms. Restaurant, bar, nightclub, meeting rooms. AE, MC, V.*

Son

❹ *25 km (15 mi) south of Drøbak.*

You can swim, sail, or sun on the banks of Son (pronounced *soon*), just south of Drøbak. An old fishing and boating village, this resort town has traditionally attracted artists and writers. Artists still flock here, as do city folk in summer. With them comes a rash of activity, which loungers on the immense boulders by the water can hear in the distance.

In the summer season, you can count on **Klubben Soon** (☎ 64/95–70–42) for a good mix of disco, jazz, concerts and stand-up comedy.

Moss

⑤   *10 km (6 mi) south of Son.*

Although the area has been inhabited since Viking times, Moss gained borough status in the 18th century and is one of the area's main commercial and shipping centers. This industrial town is also home to the manufacturers of Helly-Hansen sportswear, which is becoming ever-so-popular in the United States—you'll find it in sporting goods stores from Duluth, Minnesota, to New York City.

OFF THE   **GALLERI F15 –** A 5-km (3-mi) ride outside Moss, on the island of Jeløy, is
BEATEN PATH   an art center set in an old farm. Exhibits displayed here range from photography to Scandinavian crafts, or just stroll the beautiful grounds. ✉ *Alby Gård,* ☎ *69/27–10–33.* ✑ *NKr20.* ☉ *June–Sept., Tues.–Sun. 11–7; Oct.–May, Tues.–Sat. 11–5, Sun. 11–7.*

Dining and Lodging

$$$ ✕⊤ **Refsnes Gods.** Refsnes has one of Norway's best kitchens and a
★   wine cellar with some of the oldest bottles of Madeira in the country. Chef Erwin Stocker utilizes the fjords' resources and adds a French touch to traditional Norwegian seafood. The main building dates from 1770, when it was a family estate, but it did not become a hotel until 1938. In the back is a long, tree-lined promenade extending to the shores of the Oslo Fjord. The blue-and-beige rooms are airy and pretty. ✉ *Box 236, 1502 Moss,* ☎ *69/27–04–11,* ☒ *69/27–25–42. 61 rooms. Restaurant, pool, sauna, beach, boating, meeting rooms. AE, DC, MC, V.*

Fredrikstad

⑥   *34 km (20 mi) south of Moss.*

Norway's oldest fortified city, Fredrikstad lies peacefully at the mouth of the Glomma, the country's longest river. Its bastions and moat date from the 1600s. The **Gamlebyen** (Old Town) has been preserved and has museums, art galleries, cafés, artisans' workshops, antiques shops, and old bookstores.

The **Fredrikstad Museum** documents the town's history. ☎ *69/30–68–75.* ✑ *NKr20.* ☉ *May–Sept., weekdays 11–5, Sun. noon–5.*

Just east of the Fredrikstad town center is **Kongsten Festning** (Kongsten Fort), which mounted 200 cannons and could muster 2,000 men at the peak of its glory in the 16th century. ☎ *69/32–05–32.* ✑ *Free.* ☉ *May–Sept., 24 hrs. Call for guided tour.*

Halden

⑦   *30 km (18 mi) south of Fredrikstad.*

Halden is practically at the Swedish border, a good enough reason to fortify the town. Norwegians and Swedes had ongoing border disputes, and the most famous skirmish at Fredriksten fortress resulted in the death of King Karl XII in 1718. Few people realize that slavery existed in Scandinavia, but until 1845 there were up to 200 slaves at Fredriksten, mostly workers incarcerated and sentenced to a lifetime of hard labor for trivial offenses.

Fredriksten Festning (✉ Fredriksten Fort, ☎ 69/17–35–00), built on a French star-shaped plan in the late 17th century, is perched on the city's highest point. Inside the fort itself is **Fredriksten Kro,** a good, old-fashioned pub with outdoor seating. ☎ *69/17–52–32.* ✑ *NKr25.* ☉ *Mid-May–mid-Sept., Mon.–Sat. 10–5, Sun. 10–6.*

East of the Oslo Fjord A to Z

Arriving and Departing

BY BOAT

A ferry links Drøbak, on the east side of the fjord, with Hurum, on the west side just north of Horten. Contact Drøbak Turistinformasjon (☞ *below*) for schedule information.

BY BUS

Bus 541 from Oslo's City Hall to Drøbak affords great glimpses of the fjord (and its bathers). The trip takes an hour, and buses depart roughly every half hour during the week, with reduced service weekends. Bus 117 links Halden and Fredrikstad eight times a day during the week, with reduced service Saturdays. Contact **Nor-Way Bussekspress** (☎ 22/17–52–90) for schedules.

BY CAR

Follow Route E18 southeast from Oslo to Route E6. Follow signs to Drøbak and Son. Continue through Moss, following signs to Halden, farther south on E6. The route then takes you north to Sarpsborg, where you can turn left to Fredrikstad.

BY TRAIN

Trains for Halden leave from Oslo S Station and take two hours to make the 136-km (85-mi) trip, with stops in Moss, Fredrikstad, and Sarpsborg.

Contacts and Resources

VISITOR INFORMATION

Drøbak (Drøbak Turistinformasjon, ☎ 64/93–50–87). **Fredrikstad** (Fredrikstad Turistkontor, ✉ Turistsentret vøstre Brohode and ✉ 1632 Gamle Fredrikstad, ☎ 69/32–03–30 or 69/32–10–60). **Halden** (Halden Turist Kontor, ✉ Storgt. 6, Box 167, 1751 Halden, ☎ 69/17–48–40). **Moss** (Moss Turistkontor, ✉ Fleischersgt. 17, 1531 Moss, ☎ 69/25–32–95). **Son** (Son Kystkultursenter, ✉ 1555 Son, ☎ 64/95–89–20).

WEST OF THE OSLO FJORD

Towns lining the western side of the fjord are more industrial on the whole than their neighbors on the eastern side. Still, the western towns have traditionally been some of Norway's oldest and wealthiest, their fortunes derived from whaling and lumbering. Although these activities no longer dominate, their influence is seen in the monuments and in the wood architecture. The area northwest of Oslo draws many visitors to its green, hilly countryside. These once industrial towns are now catering more and more to tourists.

Jevnaker

Follow E16 toward Hønefoss, then follow Rte. 241 to Jevnaker, which is about 70 km (42 mi) northwest of Oslo; it's about a 2-hr drive.

A day trip to Jevnaker combines a drive along the Tyrifjord, where you can see some of the best fjord views in eastern Norway, with a visit to a glass factory that has been in operation since 1762. At **Hadeland Glassverk** you can watch artisans blowing glass, or, if you get there early enough, you can blow your own. Both practical table crystal and one-of-a-kind art glass are produced here, and you can buy (first quality and seconds) at the gift shop. The museum and gallery have a collection of 15,000 items, with about 800 on display. Bus 171, marked "Hønefoss," leaves from the university on Karl Johans Gate at seven minutes after the hour. Change in Hønefoss for the Jevnaker bus (it has no number). ✉ *Rte. 241, Postboks 85, 5320 Jevnaker,* ☎ *61/31–05–55.* ⊙ *June–Aug., Mon.–Sat. 9–6, Sun. 11–6; Sept.–May, weekdays 9–4, Sat. 10–3, Sun. noon–5.*

Åmot i Modum

❾ *Take Rte. 35 south, along the Tyrifjord. If you are coming from the E18, take Rte. 11 west to Hokksund, and Rte. 35 to Åmot. Then turn onto Rte. 287 to Sigdal. 70 km (45 mi) from Oslo.*

The small village of Åmot is famous for its cobalt mines. The blue mineral was used to make dyes for the world's glass and porcelain industries. The **Blaafarveværket** (Cobalt Works) was founded in 1773 to extract cobalt from the Modum mines. Today the complex is a museum and a national park. A permanent collection displays old cobalt-blue glass and porcelain. For children there's a petting farm, and there's a restaurant that serves Norwegian country fare. Up the hill from the art complex is Haugfossen, the highest waterfall in eastern Norway. Outdoor concerts are held on the grounds throughout the summer. The bus to Modum leaves from the university on Karl Johans Gate at 9:45 AM on Tuesday, Thursday, and Saturday. ✉ *Rte. 507, 3370 Morud,* ☎ *32/78–49–00.* ✉ *Special exhibitions NKr50; cobalt works free. Guided tours in English.* ⊙ *Late May–Sept., daily 10–6.*

Drammen

⓫ *40 km (25 mi) from Oslo; 45 km (27 mi) south of Åmot i Modum.*

Drammen, a timber town and port for 500 years, is an industrial city of 50,000 on the Simoa River at its outlet to a fjord. It was the main harbor for silver exported from the Kongsberg mines. Today cars are imported into Norway through Drammen.

The **Spiralen** (Spiral), Drammen's main attraction, is a corkscrew road tunnel that makes six complete turns before emerging about 600 ft above, on Skansen Ridge. The entrance is behind the hospital by way of a well-marked road. ✉ *NKr10 parking fee.*

Drammens Museum, a small county museum, is on the grounds of Marienlyst Manor, which dates from 1750. Glass from the Nøstetangen factory, which was in operation between 1741 and 1777, and a collection of rustic painted pieces are on display here. Its newer addition looks like a small temple set in the manor garden. ✉ *Konnerudgt. 7,* ☎ *32/83–89–48.* ✉ *NKr30.* ⊙ *May–Oct., Tues.–Sat. 11–3, Sun. 11–5; Nov.–Apr., Tues.–Sun. 11–3.*

Dining and Lodging

$$ ✕ **Spiraltoppen Café.** At the top of Bragernes Hill, this café offers excellent views and generous portions of Norwegian food. Try the meatballs with stewed cabbage or the open-face sandwiches. ✉ *Bragernesåsen, Drammen,* ☎ *32/83–78–15. Reservations not accepted. AE, DC, MC, V.*

$$ 🏨 **Rica Park.** As with all Rica hotels, the atmosphere is relaxed and the rooms are comfortable. The nightclub at this hotel is popular with the over-30 crowd. ✉ *Gamle Kirkepl. 3, 3019 Drammen,* ☎ *32/83–82–80,* FAX *32/89–32–07. 95 rooms. 2 restaurants, 2 bars, nightclub. AE, DC, MC, V.*

Horton

⑫ *30 km (17 mi) south of Drammen.*

Off the main route south, the coastal village of Horten has some distinctive museums. The town was once an important naval station and still retains the officers' candidates school.

The **Marinemuseet** (Royal Norwegian Navy Museum), built in 1853 as a munitions warehouse, displays relics from the nation's naval history. Outside is the world's first torpedo boat, from 1872, plus some one-person submarines from World War II. ⊠ *Karl Johans Vern,* ☎ *33/04–20–81.* ☞ *Free.* ☉ *May–Oct., weekdays 10–4, weekends noon–4; Nov.–Apr., weekdays 10–3, Sun. noon–4.*

The **Redningsselskapels Museum** (Museum of the Sea Rescue Association) traces the history of ship-rescue operations. The organization has rescued more than 320,000 people since it was founded more than 100 years ago. ⊠ *Strandpromenaden 8, near Horten Tourist Office,* ☎ *33/04–70–66.* ☞ *NKr10.* ☉ *May.–Oct., Fri.–Sun. noon–4.*

The **Preus Fotomuseum** houses one of the world's largest photographic collections. Exhibits include a turn-of-the-century photographer's studio and a tiny camera that was strapped to a pigeon for early aerial photography. ⊠ *Langgt. 82,* ☎ *33/04–27–37.* ☞ *NKr30.* ☉ *May–Aug., daily 10–4; Sept.–Apr., daily 10:30–2.*

Just beyond Horten, between the road and the sea, lies a Viking grave site, **Borrehaugene,** with five earth and two stone mounds and the 12th-century Borre church.

Åsgårdstrand

⑬ *10 km (6 mi) south of Horten.*

The coastal town of Åsgårdstrand was known as an artists' colony for outdoor painting at the turn of the century. Edvard Munch painted *Girls on the Bridge* here and earned a reputation as a ladies' man. Munch spent seven summers at **Munchs lille hus** (little house), now a museum. ⊠ *Munchsgt.,* ☎ *33/03–17–08 (Horten Tourist Office).* ☞ *NKr10.* ☉ *May, Sept., weekends 1–7; Jun.–Aug., Tues.–Sun. 11–7.*

En Route Travel south from Åsgårdstrand toward Tønsberg and you'll pass **Slagen,** the site where the Oseberg Viking ship, dating from around AD 800, was found. (It's now on display at Vikingskiphuset in Oslo.) Look for the mound where it was buried as you pass Slagen's church.

Tønsberg

⑭ *11 km (6½ mi) south of Åsgårdstrand.*

According to the sagas, Tønsberg is Norway's oldest settlement, founded in 871. The town's fortunes took a turn for the worse after the Reformation, and the city did not recover until shipping and whaling brought it into prominence in the 18th century. Little remains of Tønsberg's early structures, although the ruins at **Slottsfjellet** (Castle Hill), by the train station, include parts of the city wall, the remains of a church from around 1150, and a 13th-century brick citadel, the Tønsberghus. Other medieval remains are below the cathedral and near Storgata 17.

The **Vestfold Fylkesmuseum** (County Museum), north of the railroad station, houses a small Viking ship, several whale skeletons, and some inventions. There's an open-air section, too. ⊠ *Farmannsvn. 30,* ☎ *33/31–29–19.* ☞ *NKr20.* ☉ *Mid May–mid-Sept., Mon.–Sat. 10–5, Sun. noon–5; mid-Sept.–mid-May, weekdays 10–2.*

Sandefjord

⑮ *125 km (78 mi) south of Oslo; 25 km (15 mi) south of Tønsberg.*

Once the whaling capital of the world and possibly Norway's wealth-iest city at the turn of the century, Sandefjord celebrated its 150th birth-day in 1995. Now the whales are gone and all that remains of that trade is a monument to it. Thanks to shipping and other industries, how-ever, the city is still rich and draws many illustrious Norwegians to its beaches, such as film actress Liv Ullmann, who has a cottage here.

Kommandør Christensens Hvalfangstmuseum (Commander Chris-tensen's Whaling Museum) traces the development of the industry from small primitive boats to huge floating factories. An especially ar-resting display chronicles whaling in the Antarctic. ⊠ *Museumsgt. 39,* ☎ *33/46–32–51.* 🖼 *NKr20.* ⊙ *May–Sept., daily 11–5; Oct.–Apr., daily 11–3.*

Dining and Lodging

$$–$$$ ✕ **Ludl's Gourmet Odd Ivar Solvold.** The Austrian chef, Ludl, shows
★   Norwegians that there's more in the sea than cod and salmon. Ludl is a champion of the local cuisine, and specials may include ocean cat-fish, stuffed sole, a fish roulade, and lobster. Ludl's desserts are equally good, especially the cloudberry marzipan basket. ⊠ *Rådhusgt. 7, Sandefjord,* ☎ *33/46–27–41. AE, DC, MC, V.*

$$–$$$$ 🏨 **Rica Park Hotel.** It *looks* formal for a hotel built right on the water in a resort town, but there's no dress code. The decor is 1960s style, but surprisingly, it doesn't seem passé. Ask for one of the newer rooms. ⊠ *Strandpromenaden 9, 3200 Sandefjord,* ☎ *33/46–55–50,* 🗚 *33/46–79–00. 174 rooms, 8 suites. 2 restaurants, bar, indoor pool, health club, nightclub, convention center. AE, DC, MC, V.*

$–$$$ 🏨 **Comfort Home Hotel Atlantic.** The Atlantic Home was built in 1914, when Sandefjord was a whaling center. The history of whaling is traced in exhibits in glass cases and in pictures throughout the hotel. There's no restaurant, but the hotel provides *aftens,* a supper consisting of bread and cold cuts, plus hot soup and light beer, as part of the room rate. A coffeemaker and waffle iron are at your disposal at all times. ⊠ *Jern-banealleen 33, 3201 Sandefjord,* ☎ *33/46–80–00,* 🗚 *33/46–80–20. 72 rooms. Lobby lounge, sauna. AE, DC, MC, V.*

West of the Oslo Fjord A to Z

Arriving and Departing

BY BOAT

The most luxurious and scenic way to see the region is by boat: there are guest marinas at just about every port.

BY BUS

Because train service to towns south of Drammen is infrequent, bus travel is the best alternative to cars. Check with **Nor-Way Bussekspress** (☎ 22/17–52–90) for schedules.

BY CAR

Route E18 south from Oslo follows the coast to the towns of this region.

BY TRAIN

Take a suburban train from Nationaltheatret or trains from Oslo S Sta-tion to reach Horten, Tønsberg, and Sandefjord.

Contacts and Resources

VISITOR INFORMATION

Blaafarveværket (☎ 32/78–49–00). **Drammen** (Drammen Kommunale Turistinformasjonskontor, ✉ Bragernes Torg 6, 3008 Drammen, ☎ 32/80–62–10). **Hadeland** (☎ 61/31–10–00). **Horten and Åsgårdstrand** (Horten Turist Kontor, ✉ Tollbugt. 1a, 3187 Horten, ☎ 33/03–17–08). **Sandefjord** (Sandefjord Reiselivsforening, ✉ Torvet, 3201 Sandfjord, ☎ 33/46–05–90). **Tønsberg** (Tønsberg og Omland Reiselivslag, ✉ Nedre Langgt. 36 B, 3110 Tønsberg, ☎ 33/31–02–20).

TELEMARK AND THE SETESDAL VALLEY

Telemark, the interior region of southern Norway, lies in the shadow of the famed beaches and fjords of the coast but doesn't lack majestic scenery. A land of wide-open vistas and deep forests, it's veined with swift-flowing streams and scattered with peaceful lakes—a natural setting so powerful and silent that a few generations ago, trolls were the only reasonable explanation for what lurked in, or for that matter plodded through, the shadows. These legendary creatures, serious Norwegians explain, boast several heads and a couple of noses (used to stir their porridge, of course) and can grow to the size of a village. Fortunately for humans, however, they turn to stone in sunlight.

Telemark was the birthplace of downhill skiing as well as the birthplace of many ancestors to Norwegian-Americans, for the poor farmers of the region were among the first to emigrate to the United States during the 19th century.

The quiet Setesdal Valley stretches north–south next to Telemark and sits atop rich mineral resources. The region is rich with history and is well-known for its colorful traditional costume and the intricate silver jewelry that decorates it.

Kongsberg

🔟 *84 km (52 mi) southwest of Oslo.*

Kongsberg, with 20,000 people today, was Norway's silver town for more than 300 years. It was here that silver was discovered in its purest form. King Christian IV saw the town's natural potential when he noticed that a cow's horn had rubbed moss off a stone to expose silver. Thereupon, the Danish builder-king began construction of the town. Thus, Norway's first industrial town rose to prominence. The mines are now closed, but the Royal Mint is still going strong.

The **Norsk Bergverksmuseum** (Norwegian Mining Museum), in the old smelting works, documents the development of silver mining and exhibits pure silver, gold, emeralds, and rubies from other Norwegian mines. The **Royal Mint Museum,** in the same building, is a treasure trove for coin collectors, with a nearly complete assemblage of Norwegian coins. Children can pan for silver during summer. The **Kongsberg Ski Museum,** also part of the mining complex, houses exhibits of ancient skis and 23 Olympic and World Championship medals won by Kongsberg skiers. ✉ *Hyttegt. 3,* ☎ *32/73–32–60.* 🎟 *NKr40.* ☉ *Mid-May–late May and mid-Aug.–late Aug., daily 10–4; June–mid-Aug., weekdays 10–6, weekends 10–4; Sept., daily noon–4; Oct.–mid-May, Sun. noon–4. Otherwise, by appointment.*

OFF THE BEATEN PATH
SØLVGRUVENE – In Saggrenda, about 8 km (5 mi) outside Kongsberg toward Notodden, you can visit silver mines. Guided mine tours include a 2½-km (1½-mi) ride on the mine train into Kongensgruve (the King's

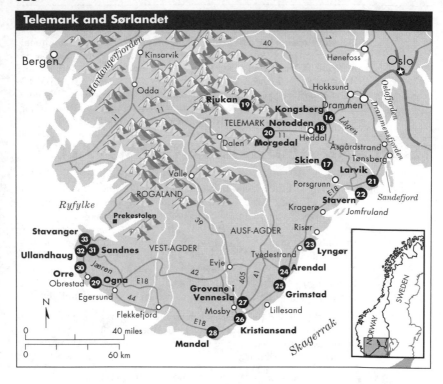

mine) and a ride on the first personnel elevator. The temperature in the mine is about 6°C (43°F) and the tour takes about one hour and 20 minutes, so dress accordingly. ☎ *32/73–32–60.* 🖻 *NKr50.* ☉ *Tours mid-May–June and mid-Aug.–late Aug., daily at 11, 12:30, 2; July–mid-Aug., daily at 11, 12:30, 2, 3:30; Sept.–mid-May, Sun. at 2.*

Kongsberg Kirke (Kongsberg Church), finished in 1761, was built during the heyday of the silver mines, with an impressive gilded Baroque altar, organ, and pulpit all on one wall. It seats 3,000. The royal box and the galleries separated the gentry and mine owners from the workers. Organ concerts are given Wednesdays at 6 in summer. ☎ *32/73–19–02.* 🖻 *NKr20.* ☉ *Mid-May–Aug., weekdays 10–4, Sat. 10–1; Sept.–mid-May, Tues.–Fri. 10–2. Sun. services at 11 with tours afterward until 1:30. Call to confirm times.*

The Arts

Every June jazz fans descend on Kongsberg for its annual **jazz festival.** Contact the tourist office (☞ *below*) for information.

Dining and Lodging

$$ ✕ **Gamle Kongsberg Kro.** This café next to the waterfall at Nybrofossen offers hearty Norwegian dishes at moderate prices. There's a miniature golf course nearby. ⊠ *Thornesvn. 4,* ☎ *32/73–16–33,* 🖷 *32/73–26–03. DC, MC, V.*

$–$$ 🏨 **Quality Grand Hotel.** A statue of Kongsberg's favorite son, Olympic ski jumper Birger Ruud, stands in the park in front of this modern, centrally located hotel. ⊠ *Kristian Augustsgt. 2, 3600,* ☎ *32/73–20–29,* 🖷 *32/73–41–29. 97 rooms, 2 suites. 2 restaurants, 2 bars, indoor pool, exercise room, nightclub, meeting rooms. AE, DC, MC, V.*

Skien

⑰ *88 km (55 mi) south of Kongsberg on Rtes. 32 and 36.*

Best known as the birthplace of playwright Henrik Ibsen, Skien, with a population of 50,000, is the capital of the Telemark region. Ibsen's home town celebrates its favorite son every August with the **Ibsen-Kultur-festival** (✉ Skien Tourist Office, Box 192, 3701 Skien, ☎ 35/58-19–10), which includes concerts as well as drama.

The **Fylkesmuseet** (County Museum), a manor house from 1780, has a collection of Ibsen memorabilia, including his study and bedroom and the "blue salon" from his Oslo flat (other interiors are at the Norsk Folkemuseum in Oslo). Also on display is Telemark-style folk art, including rosemaling and wood carving. ✉ *Øvregt. 41,* ☎ *35/52–35–94.* 🎫 *NKr20.* ☉ *Garden mid-May–Aug., daily 10–8; museum mid-May–Aug., daily 10–6; Sept., Sun. 10–6.*

Venstøp looks just as it did when the Ibsen family lived here from 1835 to 1843. The attic was the inspiration for *The Wild Duck*. This house, part of Skien's County Museum, is 5 km (3 mi) northwest of the city. ☎ *35/52–35–94.* 🎫 *NKr20.* ☉ *Mid-May–Aug., daily 10–6; Sept., Sun. 10–6.*

Dining and Lodging

$$ ✕ **Boden Spiseri.** Boden serves excellent French-influenced Norwegian-style food, such as medallions of reindeer. For dessert, *Gjoegler Boden*—ice cream with rum, raisins, and a touch of ginger—is a delight. ✉ *Landbrygga 5,* ☎ *35/52–61–70. AE, DC, MC, V. No lunch.*

$–$$ 🏨 **Rainbow Høyers Hotell.** The old-fashioned quality of the exterior, with cornices and pedimented windows, is reflected in the Høyers's lobby, which is an incongruous mixture of old and new. The rooms are modern and light, thanks to the big windows. 🏨 *Kongensgt. 6, 3700,* ☎ *35/52–05–40,* 📠 *35/52–26–08. 69 rooms, 1 suite. Restaurant, bar, meeting rooms. AE, DC, MC, V.*

Notodden

⑱ *68 km (42 mi) northwest of Skien and 35 km (20 mi) west of Kongsberg.*

Notodden today is not much more than a small industrial town (although it's well-known for its blues fest). It is believed that the area must have been a prosperous one in the Middle Ages, though, because of the size of the town's stavkirke—85 ft high and 65 ft long.

Heddal Stave Church is Norway's largest. The church dates from the middle of the 12th century and has exceptional stylized animal ornamentation, along with grotesque human heads, on the portals. ☎ *35/02–08–40.* 🎫 *NKr15.* ☉ *Mid-May–June and late Aug.–mid-Sept., Mon.–Sat. 10–5; late June–late Aug., Mon.–Sat. 9–7. Sunday service at 12:30 PM mid-May–mid-Sept.*

Notodden is famous for its **summer blues festival** in August, which lasts four days and brings in Norwegian and American acts such as the Robert Cray Band. Some acts require reserved tickets, which can be done in advance at any post office in Norway (or call ☎ 75/15–75–16 from outside Norway). For more information contact Notodden tourist information (☞ Telemark and the Setesdal Valley A to Z, *below*).

En Route Route 37 northwest from Notodden to Rjukan passes the 6,200-ft **Gaustatoppen,** a looming, snow-streaked table of rock popular with hikers.

Rjukan

⑲ *96 km (59 mi) from Notodden.*

The town of Rjukan may not ring a bell, but mention "heavy water," and anyone who lived through World War II or saw the film *The Heroes of Telemark* with Kirk Douglas knows about the sabotage of the heavy water factory there, which thwarted German efforts to develop an atomic bomb. Rjukan's history actually began in the decade between 1907 and 1916, when the population grew from a few hundred to 10,000 because of a different kind of water, hydroelectric power. Norsk Hydro, one of Norway's largest industries, which uses hydroelectric power to manufacture chemicals and fertilizer, was started here.

Heavy water (used in nuclear reactors as a moderator) was produced as a by-product in the manufacture of fertilizer at Vemork, 6 km (4 mi) west of Rjukan along Route 37, where a museum, **Industriarbeidermuseet Vemork,** has been built. Exhibits document both the development of hydroelectric power and the World War II events. Every year on the first Saturday in July, the work of the saboteurs is commemorated, but their 8-km (5-mi) path, starting at Rjukan Fjellstue (mountain lodge) and finishing at the museum, is marked and can be followed at any time. ☎ *35/09–51–53.* ▣ *NKr50.* ☉ *May–mid-Aug., daily 10–6; mid-Aug.–Sept., weekdays 10–4, weekends 11–6; Oct. and March–Apr., Sat. 11–4.*

Rjukan is the site of northern Europe's first cable car, **Krossobanen,** built in 1928 by Hydro to transport people to the top of the mountain. ▣ *NKr20.* ☉ *Mid-Apr.–mid-Sept. Times vary; call Rjukan tourist information for details,* ☎ *35/09–15–11.*

Lodging

$$ 🏨 **Euro Park Hotell.** This small hotel with a traditional family atmosphere is in the center of town. The rooms are decorated in light colors. The restaurant, with the curious name Ammonia, offers a wide selection. ✉ *Sam Eydes Gt. 67, 3660,* ☎ *35/09–02–88,* ℻ *35/09–05–25. 39 rooms. Restaurant, bar, pub, nightclub. AE, DC, MC, V.*

$$ 🏨 **Gaustablikk Høyfjellshotell.** Built at the foot of Gaustatoppen near Rjukan, this modern timber hotel is a popular ski resort, with nine downhill slopes and 80 km (50 mi) of cross-country trails. In summer, these marked trails are perfect for walks and hikes. ✉ *3660,* ☎ *35/09–14–22,* ℻ *35/09–19–75. 83 rooms, 14 suites. Restaurant, bar, indoor pool, sauna, exercise room. AE, DC, MC, V.*

Morgedal

⑳ *77 km (46 mi) southwest of Rjukan via Åmot.*

In the heart of Telemark is Morgedal, the birthplace of modern skiing, thanks to a persistent Sondre Nordheim, who in the 19th century perfected his skis and bindings and practiced jumping from his roof. His innovations included bindings that close behind the heel and skis that narrow in the middle to facilitate turning. In 1868, after revamping his skis and bindings, he took off for a 185-km (115-mi) trek to Oslo just to prove it could be done. A hundred years ago, skiers used one long pole, held diagonally, much like high-wire artists. Eventually the use of two short poles became widespread, although purists feel that the one-pole version is the "authentic" way to ski. Nordheim's traditional Telemark skiing is now the rage in Norway, though the revival was begun in the United States.

The **Norsk Skieventyr** (Norwegian Skiing Adventure) in Morgedal guides you through the history of the winter sport with life-size exhibits of typical ski cottages and authentic skis and costumes. Displays include the inside of Norway's original and last ski-wax factory where specialists melted a variety of secret ingredients, including cheese, to make uphill and downhill slides smoother. The sport of yore meets its match on the last leg of the exhibit where a multiscreen-panoramic video shows modern-day footage of the don't-try-this-at-home sort. Teenagers in techno-gear and professional ski-trekkers in Telemark-style sweaters zoom around the snow to traditional fiddle music. ⊠ *On Rte. 11 between Brunkeberg and Høydalsmo,* ☎ *35/05–42–50.* ☑ *NKr50.* ☉ *May–mid-June and mid-Aug.–mid-Sept., daily 11–5; mid-June–mid-Aug., daily 9–7; late Sept.–Apr., weekends 11–5.*

Dalen

The Dalen area is the place to hike, bike, and be outdoors. From Skien you can take boat tours on the Telemark waterways, a combination of canals and natural lakes between Skien and either Dalen or Notodden (☞ Notodden, *above*). The trip to Dalen takes you through Ulefoss, where you can leave the boat and visit the neoclassical **Ulefoss Manor** (⊠ Hovedgård, ☎ 35/94–56–10), which dates from 1807. It's open weekdays June through September from 2 PM to 4 PM and Sunday from noon to 3. The historic **Dalen Hotel** (☞ *below*) is worth a peek, whether or not you stay there. A number of royal families have stayed there, and locals are said to think ghosts haunt its creaky wooden walls. *For trips to Dalen, call Telemarkreiser,* ☎ *35/53–03–00; for Notodden, contact Telemarksbåtene,* ⊠ *3812 Akkerhaugen,* ☎ *35/95–82–11,* ℻ *35/ 95–82–96.*

Dining and Lodging

$$$ ✕▥ **Viking Dalen Hotel.** At the end of the Telemark Canals stands this opulent, Victorian "Swiss-style" hotel, complete with dragonhead carvings, stained-glass windows, and a balcony overlooking the stunning entrance hall. Rooms are relatively small and furnished with plain Norwegian antiques. All meals are provided on request. ⊠ *3880 Dalen,* ☎ *35/07–70–00,* ℻ *35/07–70–11. 38 rooms. Breakfast room, lobby lounges, meeting rooms. AE, V. Closed Christmas–Easter.*

$–$$ ▥ **Telemarkstunet Natadal Uppigård.** This cluster of 18th-century farmhouses with grass roofs provides an authentic alternative to a hotel stay. Set on a steep mountainside about an hour's drive from Dalen, the cabins could be on display in Oslo's Folkemuseum. Activities here are plentiful, including horseback riding, pond swimming, and strawberry picking—all the Norwegian favorites. A stay in these rustic accommodations is comparable to camping: breakfast, linens, and housekeeping cost extra. The cabins come with kitchenettes but not always individual bathrooms. ⊠ *3841 Flatdal,* ☎ *35/05–23–00,* ℻ *35/05–20–30. 3 cabins with room for 21 people; four individual rooms in main house. No credit cards.*

Valle

The Setesdal road, Rte. 39, follows the Otra River downstream and then runs alongside the Byglandsfjord; Valle is 56 km (35 mi) southeast of Dalen.

Near Valle sits **Sylvartun,** a clump of grass-roofed cottages that house a local silversmith's workshop, a jewelry shop, and an art gallery. It's also a cultural center that hosts concerts, displays local crafts, and holds summertime "Setesdal Evenings" at which professional musicians and folk dancers perform while a traditional Norwegian dinner is served.

✉ *Rte. 39, Nomeland (near Valle),* ☎ *37/93–63–06.* ☺ *Silversmith's shop: May–Oct., Mon.–Sat. 10–6, Sun. 11–6. Folk dances: summer only. Call for opening hours and program schedules.*

OFF THE   **SETESDAL MINERAL PARK** – About 97 km (57 mi) from Valle, just south of
BEATEN PATH   Evje on Route 39, is an interesting park where rock formations from
               Norway and elsewhere are displayed inside a dark mountain. ✉ *4660
               Evje,* ☎ *37/19–85-33.* ✇ *NKr60.* ☺ *Late June–late Aug., daily 10–6.*

Telemark and the Setesdal Valley A to Z

Arriving and Departing

BY BUS

The many bus lines that serve the region are coordinated through **Nor-Way Bussekspress** in Oslo (✉ Bussterminalen, Galleri Oslo, ☎ 22/17–52–90, FAX 22/17–59–22).

BY CAR

On Route E18 from Oslo, the drive southwest to Kongsberg takes a little more than an hour. If you arrive by way of the Kristiansand ferry, the drive up Route 37 to Evje will take about an hour as well.

BY TRAIN

The train from Oslo S Station to Kongsberg takes 1 hour and 25 minutes; bus connections to Telemark are available.

Getting Around

BY BUS

Buses in the region rarely run more than twice a day, so get a comprehensive schedule from the tourist office or Nor-Way Bussekspress (☞ Oslo A to Z, *above*) and plan ahead.

BY CAR

Roads in the southern part of the interior region are open and flat, but others are still curvy and mountainous. Route 11 passes through Heddal and Morgedal, and connects with 37, which goes north to Rjukan and south toward Dalen. Route 11 also connects with 37, the main Setesdal road, which goes through Evje and Valle all the way to Kristiansand.

BY TRAIN

The only train service in the southern part of the region is the Oslo–Stavanger line (via Kristiansand).

Contacts and Resources

VISITOR INFORMATION

Kongsberg (✉ Storgt. 35, ☎ 32/73–50–00). **Notodden** (✉ Storgt. 39, ☎ 35/01–20–22). **Rjukan** (✉ Torget 2, ☎ 35/09–15–11). **Skien** (✉ Reiselivets Hus, N. Hjellegt. 18, ☎ 35/95–00–61). **Setesdal** (☎ 4660 Evje, tel. 37/93–14–00).

SØRLANDET: ALONG THE COAST

Sørlandet, or southern Norway, is a land of wide beaches toasted by the greatest number of sunny days in Norway, waters warmed by the Gulf Stream, and long, fertile tracts of flatland. Not a people to pass up a minute of sunshine, the Norwegians have sprinkled the south with their hytter and made it their number one domestic holiday spot. Nonetheless, even at the height of summer, you can sail to a quiet skerry or take a solitary walk through the forest.

Southern Norway is an outdoor paradise, with a mild summer climate and terrain varying from coastal flatland to inland mountains and forests. There's plenty of fish in the rivers and lakes, as well as along the coast. The region is particularly well suited to canoeing, kayaking, rafting, and hiking. Beavers, deer, foxes, and forest birds inhabit the area, so bring binoculars if you'd like to see them more closely.

The coast bordering the Skagerak, the arm of the North Sea separating Norway and Denmark, is lined with small communities stretching from Oslo as far as Lindesnes, which is at the southernmost tip. Sørlandet towns are often called "pearls on a string," and in the dusk of a summer evening, reflections of the white-painted houses on the water have a silvery translucence.

The two chief cities of Norway's south, Kristiansand on the east coast and Stavanger on the west coast, differ sharply. Kristiansand is a resort town, scenic and relaxed, whereas Stavanger, once a fishing center, is now the hub of the oil industry and Norway's most cosmopolitan city. Stavanger has many more good restaurants than other cities of comparable size, thanks to the influx of both foreigners and money. More than 100 restaurants, bars, and cafés offer everything from Thai, Chinese, and Indian to Italian, French, and, of course, Norwegian cooking. Try the restored warehouse area in the harbor for some of the best restaurants.

Between Kristiansand and Stavanger is the coastal plain of Jæren, dotted with prehistoric burial sites and the setting for the works of some of the country's foremost painters.

Larvik

㉑ *128 km (79 mi) from Oslo, 19 km (12 mi) south of Sandefjord.*

Larvik is the last of the big whaling towns. It's still a port, but now the traffic is made up of passengers to Fredrikshavn, Denmark.

Kong Haakons Kilde (King Haakon's Spring), also called Farris Kilde (Farris Spring), is Norway's only natural source of mineral water. A spa was built here in 1880, but people now drink the water rather than bathe in it. The spring is near the ferry quays. ⊠ *Fjellvn, 3256,* ☎ *33/18–20–00.* ⊑ *Free.* ☉ *Late June–mid-Aug., weekdays.*

The noble Gyldenløve family once owned the large estate, **Herregården,** which dates back to 1677. Inside, the furnishings are masterful examples of trompe l'oeil: Scandinavian nobility had to make do with furniture painted to look like marble rather than the real thing. ⊠ *Herregaardssletta 1, 3257,* ☎ *33/13–04–04.* ⊑ *NKr25.* ☉ *Late May–late Aug., daily noon–5; early Sept.–late May, Sun. noon–5.*

The **Maritime Museum** is in Larvik's former customs house and chronicles the town's seafaring history. There's heavy coverage of Thor Heyerdahl's voyages, with models of *Kon-Tiki* and *Ra II.* ⊑ ☉ *Charges and opening times vary; check with the tourist office.*

OFF THE BEATEN PATH **PORSGRUNN PORSELÆNFABRIK ASA** – About 27 km (17 mi) west of Larvik in Porsgrunn is a porcelain factory where you can take a tour and purchase factory seconds. ⊠ *Porselensgt. 12,* ☎ *35/55–00–40.* ⊑ *NKr10.* ☉ *Late May–Aug., tours weekdays at 10, 11, and 1.*

Dining and Lodging

$$ ✕ 🖩 **Grand.** The rooms are spotless and the service attentive in this large hotel overlooking the fjord. The restaurant is a good spot to sample the local fish soup and smoked-meat platters—especially at lunch. ⊠

Storgt. 38–40, 3256, ☎ *33/18–78–00,* ⓕ𝔸𝕏 *33/18–70–45. 97 rooms. Restaurant, bar, pub, dance club, nightclub. AE, DC, MC, V.*

Stavern

㉒ *8 km (5 mi) south of Larvik.*

A popular sailing center today, Stavern was Norway's main naval station between 1750 and 1850, then called Fredriksvern, named for King Fredrik V.

A fine example of Scandinavian Rococo architecture, **Stavern Church** was built in 1756. Its pews were designed so their backs could be folded down to make beds in case the church had to be used as a field hospital in time of war. ✉ *On the water east of town,* ☎ *33/19–99–75.* ☉ *Guided tours by appointment.*

En Route From Stavern to Lyngør, you'll pass through Kragerø, a picturesque town with its own small archipelago. Theodor Kittelsen (1857–1914), famous for his drawings of trolls and illustrations of Norwegian fairy tales, lived in Kragerø, and his birthplace is now a museum. The next pearl on the string after Kragerø is Risør, which is just off E18 on the coast. On the first weekend in August the town holds a festival that fills the harbor with beautiful antique boats.

Lyngør

㉓ *18 km (11 mi) south of Risør. To get to Lyngør, follow E18 to the sign for Sørlandsporten (Gateway to the South). Turn off just after the sign and drive 26 km (16 mi) to Lyngørfjorden Marina (☎ 37/16–68–00), where you can take a five-minute watertaxi ride for NKr80.*

Hardly changed since the days of sailing ships, Lyngør is idyllic and carless, lined with rows of white-painted houses bearing window boxes filled with pink and red flowers. This island community, on four tiny rocky islands off the coast, is considered by some to be Europe's best-preserved village. In winter the population is 110, but every summer thousands descend on the village. You'll find white houses all along the south coast, a tradition that began more than 100 years ago, when Dutch sailors traded white paint for wood. Until that time, only red paint was available in Norway.

NEED A
BREAK?
In a historic late-19th-century white house with blue trim, **Den Blå Lanterne** (☎ 37/16–64–80) is Lyngør's only restaurant. Although it's pricey, you can eat as much of the famous fish soup as you like at this well-regarded restaurant—and there's often live music. It's open May through September.

Arendal

㉔ *33 km (20½ mi) from Lyngør on E18.*

Picturesque Arendal has more of the tidy white houses that are common to the area. In Tyholmen, the old town, you'll see many of these, as well as some brightly colored well-preserved wooden houses. This is a good town for strolling around. For a more formal tour, ask about the summer walking tours at the tourist office.

OFF THE
BEATEN PATH
MERDØGAARD MUSEUM – On the island of Merdøy, a 30-minute boat ride from Arendal's Langbrygga (long wharf), is an early 18th-century sea captain's home, now a museum. ☎ 37/08–52–43. ▣ NKr10. ☉ *Late June–mid-Aug., daily 11–5. Guided tours on the hr until 4.*

Dining and Lodging

$$ ✕ **Madam Reiersen.** This authentic restaurant on the waterfront serves good food in an informal atmosphere. ✉ *Nedre Tyholmsvn. 3, 4800,* ☎ *37/02–19–00. AE, DC, MC, V.*

$$ ⊞ **Clarion Tyholmen Hotel.** This maritime hotel, built in 1988, is in Tyholmen, with the sea at close quarters and a magnificent view of the fjord. The open-air restaurant is great in summer. ✉ *Teaterpl. 2, 4800* ☎ *37/02–68–00,* 𝔽𝔸𝕏 *37/02–68–01. 60 rooms. 2 restaurants, bar, sauna. AE, DC, MC, V.*

Grimstad

㉕ *15 km (9.2 mi) south of Arendal.*

Grimstad's glory was in the days of sailing ships—about the same time the 15-year-old Henrik Ibsen worked as an apprentice at the local apothecary shop. Grimstad Apotek is now a part of **Ibsenhuset** (the Ibsen House) and has been preserved with its 1837 interior intact. Ibsen wrote his first play, *Catlina,* here. ✉ *Henrik Ibsensgt. 14, 4890,* ☎ *37/04–46–53.* ▣ *NKr25.* ☉ *Mid-May–mid-Sept., Mon.–Sat. 11–5, Sun. 1–5.*

Kristiansand

㉖ *55 km (34.1 mi) south of Grimstad on E18.*

Kristiansand, with 68,000 inhabitants, is one of Sørlandet's most prosperous cities and the domestic summer-vacation capital of Norway. According to legend, in 1641 King Christian IV marked the four corners of Kristiansand with his walking stick, and within that framework the grid of wide streets was drawn. The center of town, called the **Kvadrat,** still retains the grid, even after numerous fires.

Kristiansand's **Fisketorvet** (fish market) is near the south corner of the town's grid, right on the sea. **Christiansholm Festning** (fortress) is on a promontory opposite Festningsgata. Completed in 1672, the circular building with 15-ft-thick walls has played more a decorative than a defensive role; it was used once, in 1807, to defend the city against British invasion. Now it contains art exhibits.

The Gothic Revival **cathedral** from 1885 is the third-largest church in Norway. It often hosts summertime concerts in addition to an annual weeklong International Church Music Festival in mid-May (☎ 38/02–13–11 for information) that includes organ, chamber, and gospel music. ✉ *Kirkegt., 4610,* ☎ *38/02–11–88.* ▣ *Free.* ☉ *June–Aug., daily 9–2.*

A wealthy merchant-shipowner built **Gimle Gård** (Gimle Manor) around 1800 in the Empire style. It displays furnishings from that period, paintings, silver, and hand-blocked wallpaper. To get there from the city center, head north across the Otra River on Bus 22 or drive to Route E18 and cross the bridge over the Otra to Parkveien. Turn left onto Ryttergangen and drive to Gimleveien, where you'll turn right. ✉ *Gimlevn. 23, 4630,* ☎ *38/09–02–28.* ▣ *NKr20.* ☉ *July–Aug., Tues.–Sat. noon–4, Sun. noon–6.*

The runestone in the cemetery of **Oddernes Kirke** (Oddernes Church) tells that Øyvind, godson of Saint Olav, built this church in 1040 on property he inherited from his father. One of the oldest churches in Norway, it is dedicated to Saint Olav. ✉ *Oddernesvn, 6430,* ☎ *38/09–01–87 or 38/09–03–60.* ▣ *Free.* ☉ *May–Aug., Sun.–Fri. 9–2.*

At **Kristiansand Kanonmuseum** (Cannon Museum) you can see the cannon that the German occupying force rigged during World War II. With a 38-centimeter caliber, the cannon was said to be capable of shooting a projectile halfway to Denmark. ⊠ *Møvik,* ☎ *38/08-50-90.* ▩ *NKr40.* ☉ *May–mid-June and Sept., Thurs.–Sun. 11–6; late-June–Aug., daily 11–6.*

You'll see dwellings and workshops on a reconstructed city street at **Vest-Agder Fylkesmuseum** (County Museum). Here you can visit two *tun*—farm buildings traditionally set in clusters around a common area, which suited the extended families. The museum is 4 km (3 mi) east of Kristiansand on Route E18. ⊠ *Kongsgård, 4631,* ☎ *38/09–02–28.* ▩ *NKr20.* ☉ *Mid-June–mid-Aug., Mon.–Sat. 10–6; late May–mid-June and mid-Aug.–mid-Sept., Sun. noon–6; mid-Sept.–mid-May, Sun. noon–5; or by appointment.*

A favorite with hikers and strolling nannies, **Ravnedalen** (Raven Valley) is a lush park that's filled with flowers in springtime. Wear comfortable shoes and you can hike the narrow, winding paths up the hills and climb 200 steps up to a 304-ft lookout. ⊠ *Northwest of town.*

Ⓒ One of Norway's most popular attractions, **Kristiansand Dyrepark** is actually five separate parks, including a water park (bring bathing suits and towels), a forested park, an entertainment park, a fairy-tale park, and a zoo, which contains an enclosure for Scandinavian wolves and Europe's (possibly the world's) largest breeding ground for Bactrian camels. The fairy-tale park, **Kardemomme By** (Cardamom Town), is named for a book by Norwegian illustrator and writer Thorbjørn Egner. His story comes alive here in a precisely replicated village, with actors playing townsfolk, shopkeepers, pirates, and a delightful trio of robbers. Families who are hooked can even stay overnight in one of the village's cozy apartments or nearby cottages (reserve at least a year in advance). The park is 11 km (6 mi) east of town. ⊠ *Kristiansand Dyrepark, 4609 Kardemomme By,* ☎ *38/04–97–00.* ▩ *NKr170 includes admission to all parks and rides.* ☉ *Mid-May–mid-June, weekdays 9–4, weekends 10–6; late June–mid-Aug., daily 10–6; late Aug.–mid-Sept., weekdays 10–4, weekends 10–6; late Sept.–early May, weekdays 10–3, weekends 10–4.*

Dining and Lodging

$$–$$$ ✕ **Sjøhuset.** Built in 1892 as a salt warehouse, this white-trimmed red building has since become a restaurant. The specialty is seafood, appropriately, and the monkfish with Newburg sauce on green fettuccine is colorful and delicious. ⊠ *Østre Strandgt. 12, 4610,* ☎ *38/02–62–60. AE, DC, MC, V.*

$$ ✕ **Restaurant Bakgården.** At this small and intimate restaurant the menu varies from day to day, but the seafood platter and lamb tenderloin are standard. The staff is especially attentive. ⊠ *Tollbodgt. 5, 4611,* ☎ *38/02–79–55. AE, DC, MC, V. No lunch.*

$ ✕ **Mållaget Kafeteria.** At this cafeteria everything is homemade (except for the gelatin dessert). That includes such dishes as meatballs, brisket of beef with onion sauce, and trout in sour-cream sauce. It's the best deal in town, but it closes right around 6 PM, the time most people think about eating dinner. ⊠ *Gyldenløves Gt. 11, 4611,* ☎ *38/02–22–93. No credit cards.*

$$–$$$ ▥ **Clarion Ernst Park Hotel.** The rooms are decorated with chintz bedspreads and drapes and practical furniture. The corner rooms have a tower nook at one end. On Saturday the atrium restaurant is the local spot for a civilized tea and lovely cakes. ⊠ *Rådhusgt. 2, 4611,* ☎ *38/02–14–00,* ℻ *38/02–03–07. 112 rooms, 4 suites. Restaurant, 3 bars, nightclub, meeting rooms. AE, DC, MC, V.*

$$ ⊡ **Rainbow Hotel Norge.** This quiet, family hotel in the heart of town has an entrance more modern than that of the Ernst Park, but upstairs the difference is negligible. Here the rooms are furnished in bright colors and dark woods. Get up for breakfast to taste the homemade breads and rolls. ⊠ *Dronningens Gt. 5, 4610,* ☎ *38/02–00–00,* FAX *38/ 02–35–30. 114 rooms. Restaurant, library, meeting rooms. AE, DC, MC, V.*

Outdoor Activities and Sports

BIKING

Kristiansand has 70 km (43 mi) of bike trails around the city. The tourist office (☞ Visitor Information *in* Sørlandet A to Z, *below*) can recommend routes and rentals.

FISHING

Just north of Kristiansand there is excellent trout, perch, and eel fishing at Lillesand's **Vestre Grimevann** lake. You can get a permit at any sports store or at the tourist office (☞ Visitor Information *in* Sørlandet A to Z, *below*).

HIKING

In addition to the gardens and steep hills of **Ravnedalen** (☞ *above*), the **Baneheia Forest,** just a 15-minute walk north from the city center, is full of evergreens, small lakes, and paths that are ideal for a lazy walk or a challenging run.

WATER SPORTS

Kuholmen Marina (⊠ Roligheden Camping, ☎ 38/09–67–22) rents boats, water skis, and water scooters. **Anker Dykkersenter** (⊠ Randesundsgt. 2, Kuholmen, ☎ 38/09–79–09) rents scuba equipment. **Kristiansand Diving Club** (⊠ Myrbakken 3, ☎ 38/01–03–32 between 6 PM and 9 PM) has information on local diving.

Combining history and sailing, the magnificent full-rig, square-sail school ship **Sørlandet** (⊠ Gravene 2, 4610 Kristiansand, ☎ 38/02–98–90), built in 1927, takes on passengers for two weeks, usually stopping for several days in a northern European port. The price is about NKr7,000.

Grovane i Vennesla

㉗ *20 km (13 mi) north of Kristiansand. Follow Rte. 39 from Kristiansand to Mosby, veer right onto 405, and continue to Grovane.*

At Grovane i Vennesla you will find the **Setesdalsbanen** (Setesdal Railway), a 4¾-km-long (3-mi-long) stretch of narrow-gauge track on which a steam locomotive from 1894 and carriages from the early 1900s run. ⊠ *Vennesla Stasjon, 4700,* ☎ *38/15–55–08.* ☒ *NKr50.* ☺ *Mid-June–late June and Aug., Sun. at 11:30; July, Tue.–Fri. at 6 and weekends at 11:30 and 2.*

Mandal

㉘ *42 km (28 mi) southwest from Kristiansand and 82 km (51 mi) from Evje.*

Mandal is Norway's most southerly town, famous for its historic core of well-preserved wooden houses and its beautiful long beach, Sjøsanden.

Mandal Kirke, built in 1821, is Norway's largest Empire-style wooden church. ☎ *38/26–35–77.* ☺ *Tues.–Fri. 11–2.*

Lindesnes Fyr, Norway's oldest lighthouse, was built on the southernmost point of the country. The old coal-fired light dates from 1822.

☎ 38/25–88–51. ☺ *Mid-May–mid-Sept., 8 AM–10 PM; rest of yr, open during daylight hours.*

En Route The road from Mandal climbs and weaves its way through steep, wooded valleys and then descends toward the sea. Here you'll find the small town of Flekkefjord, which is known for its **Hollenderbyen** (Dutch Town), a historic district with small, white-painted houses lining narrow, winding streets. From Flekkefjord you can take Route E18, which heads inland here, to Stavanger. It is more rewarding, however, to go on the coast road—Route 44. Follow the coast road 40 km (25 mi) past the fishing port of Egersund to Ogna.

Ogna

㉙ *93 km (57 mi) from Flekkefjord on Rte. 42.*

Ogna is known for the stretch of sandy beach that inspired so many Norwegian artists, among them Kitty Kjelland.

Hå Gamle Prestegaard (Old Parsonage), built in the 1780s, is now a cultural center for the area. ☎ *NKr20. ☺ May–mid-Sept., weekdays 11–7, Sat. noon–5, Sun. noon–7; late Sept.–Apr., Sat. noon–5, Sun. noon–7.*

Whichever road you choose to continue on out of Ogna, they both head northward along the rich agricultural coastal plain of the **Jæren district.** Flat and stony, it is the largest expanse of level terrain in this mountainous country. The mild climate and the absence of good harbors mean that the population here turned to agriculture, and the miles of stone walls are a testament to their labor.

Ancient monuments in Jæren are still visible, notably the **Hå gravesite** below the Hå parsonage near the Obrestad light. It consists of about 60 mounds, including two star-shaped and one boat-shaped, dating from around AD 500, all marked with stones. Take coastal Route 44.

Outdoor Activities and Sports

BIRD-WATCHING

The **Jærstrendene** in Jæren, from Randabergvika in the north to Ogna in the south, is a protected national park—and a good area for spotting puffins, cormorants, and black guillemots, as well as such waders as dunlins, little stints, and ringed plovers. Some areas of the park are closed to visitors, and it is forbidden to pick flowers or, for that matter, to disturb anything.

FISHING

Three of the 10 best fishing rivers in Norway, the **Ognaelva, Håelva,** and **Figgjo,** are in Jæren, just south of Stavanger. Fishing licenses, sold in grocery stores and gas stations, are required at all of them.

Orre

㉚ *North on Rte. 507 26 km (16 mi) from Ogna.*

Orre is the site of a medieval stone church. It also has one of the few preserved Viking graveyards, dating from the Bronze Age and Iron Age. Near Orre pond, slightly inland, is a bird-watching station.

Dining

$$ ✕ **Time Station.** This eatery (in fact the only one in Bryne) is next to the town's train station. Bryne is just up the road from Orre off Highway 507 and about a 40-minute train ride from Stavanger. Though the meat dishes are tasty, the house specialty is the seafood platter, with salmon, monkfish, ocean catfish, mussels, and ocean crayfish in a beurre blanc sauce. For dessert, try the *krumkake*, a cookie baked on an iron, wafer thin, shaped into a cone, and filled with blackberry cream. ⊠ *Storgt. 346, 4340 Bryne,* ☏ *51/48–22–56. Reservations essential. AE, DC, MC, V. Closed Sun. No lunch weekdays.*

Sandnes

🗓 *25 km (16 mi) south of Stavanger, 52 km (32 mi) north of Orre.*

⏱ In Sandnes is **Havana Badeland,** Norway's largest indoor aquapark for kids and adults, complete with a 300-ft water slide, whirlpool baths, saunas, a Turkish steambath, and massage parlors. ⊠ *Hanaveien 17, 4300 Sandnes,* ☏ *51/62–92–00.* 🎟 *NKr95.* ۞ *Mid-June–mid-Aug., daily 10–8; late Aug.–early June, Tues., Thurs. 1–8, Wed., Fri., Sat. 10–9.*

Ullandhaug

🗓 *15 km (9 mi) west of Sandnes.*

Take your imagination further back in time at Ullandhaug, a reconstruction of an Iron Age farm. Three houses have been built around a central garden, and guides wearing period clothing demonstrate the daily activities of 1,500 years ago. ⊠ *Grannesvn.,* ☏ *51/55–76–56.* 🎟 *NKr20.* ۞ *Mid-June–Aug., daily noon–5; early May–mid-June and early Sept., Sun. noon–4.*

You can see the place where what we know as Norway was founded by traveling 1½ km (1 mi) east on Grannesveien Ullandhaug to the **Harfsfjord.** In 872, in the Battle of Harfsfjord, Harald Hårfagre (Harald the Fair-Haired), the warrior king from the eastern country of Vestfold, finally succeeded in quelling the resistance of local chieftains in Rogaland and was promptly declared king of all Norway. A memorial in the shape of three giant swords plunged halfway into the earth marks the spot.

OFF THE
BEATEN PATH

UTSTEIN KLOSTER – Originally the palace of Norway's first king, Harald Hårfagre, and later the residence of King Magnus VI, Utstein was used as a monastery from 1265 to 1537, when it reverted to the royal family. One of the best-preserved medieval monuments in Norway, the monastery opened to the public in 1965 and is today used to host classical and jazz concerts on Sunday afternoons during the summer.

After the concert, try the *Får i kål* (mutton, potatoes, and cabbage boiled in a peppery juice) at **Utstein Kloster Vertshus,** approximately 2 km (1 mi) from the monastery along the water's edge. To get to Utstein: buses depart from Stavanger at 12:15, returning from the monastery at 4:05, weekdays. It's about a half-hour drive from Stavanger. By car, travel north on coastal highway 1, through the world's second-longest undersea car tunnel. There is a toll of NKr75, plus NKr25 per passenger for the tunnel passage. ⊠ *4156 Mosterøy,* ☏ *51/72–01–00.* 🎟 *NKr20.* ۞ *May–mid-Sept., Tues.–Sat. 1–4, Sun. noon–5.*

Stavanger

🗓 *5 km (3 mi) east of Ullandhaug, 198 km (123 mi) from Kristiansand, 6 hrs from Bergen by car and ferry.*

Stavanger has always prospered from the riches of the sea. During the 19th century, huge harvests of brisling and herring established it as the sardine capital of the world. A resident is still called a Siddis, from S(tavanger) plus *iddis*, which means "sardine label," and the city's symbol, fittingly enough, is the key of a sardine can.

During the past two and a half decades, a different product from the sea has been Stavanger's lifeblood—oil. Since its discovery in the late 1960s, North Sea oil has transformed both the economy and the lifestyle of the city. In the early days of drilling, expertise was imported from abroad, chiefly from the United States. Although Norwegians have now taken over most of the projects, foreigners constitute almost a tenth of the inhabitants, making Stavanger the country's most international city. Though the population hovers around 142,000, the city has all the agreeable bustle of one many times its size. However, the city's charm still remains—in the heart of **Old Stavanger** you can wind down narrow cobblestone streets past small, white houses and craft shops with many-paned windows and terra-cotta roof tiles.

Stavanger Domkirke (cathedral), a large, well-preserved medieval church, is in the city center next to Breiavatnet, a small pond. Construction was begun in 1125 by Bishop Reinald of Winchester, who was probably assisted by English craftsmen. Largely destroyed by fire in 1272, the church was rebuilt to include a Gothic chancel. The result: its once elegant lines are now festooned with macabre death symbols and airborne putti. Next to the cathedral is **Kongsgård,** formerly a residence of bishops and kings but now a school and not open to visitors. ⌨ *Free.* ☉ *Mid-May–mid-Sept., Mon.–Sat. 9–6; mid-Sept.–mid-May, Mon.–Sat. 9–2, Sun. 1–6.*

Breidablikk manor house has been perfectly preserved since the '60s and feels as if the owner has only momentarily slipped away. An outstanding example of what the Norwegians call "Swiss-style" architecture, this house was built by a Norwegian shipping magnate. In spite of its foreign label, the house is uniquely Norwegian, inspired by national romanticism. ✉ *Eiganesvn. 40A, 4009,* ☎ *51/52–60–35.* ⌨ *NKr30. Also includes admission to Ledaal, Norsk Hermetikkmuseum, and Sjøfartsmuseet.* ☉ *Mid-June–mid-Aug., daily 11–4; mid-Aug.–mid-June, Sun. 11–4.*

Ledaal, the royal family's Stavanger residence, is a stately house built by the Kielland family in 1799. The second-floor library is dedicated to the writer Alexander Kielland, a social critic and satirist. ✉ *Eiganesvn. 45, 4009,* ☎ *51/52–06–18.* ⌨ *NKr30. Also includes admission to Breidablikk, Norsk Hermetikkmuseum, and Sjøfartsmuseet.* ☉ *Mid-June–mid-Aug., daily 11–4; mid-Aug.–mid-June, Sun. 11–4.*

☾ This fascinating, albeit obscure, museum, the **Norsk Hermetikkmuseum** (Canning Museum), is housed in a former canning factory. Exhibits document the processing of brisling and sardines—the city's most important industry for nearly 100 years, thanks greatly to savvy turn-of-the-century packaging (naturally, the inventor of the sardine-can key was from Stavanger). ✉ *Øvre Strandgt. 88A, 4005,* ☎ *51/53–49–89.* ⌨ *NKr30. Also includes admission to Ledaal, Breidablikk, and Sjøfartsmuseet.* ☉ *Mid-June–mid-Aug., daily 11–4; early June and late Aug., Tues.–Fri. 11–3, Sun. 11–4; Sept.–May, Sun. 11–4.*

Along Strandkaien, warehouses face the wharf; the shops, offices, and apartments face the street on the other side. Housed in the only two shipping merchants' houses that remain completely intact is the **Sjøfartsmuseet** (Maritime Museum). Inside, the house is just as it was a century ago, complete with office furniture, files, and posters, while the apartments show the standard of living for the mercantile class at that time. Although signs are only in Norwegian, an English-language guidebook and guided tours outside normal opening hours are available. ✉ *Nedre Strandgt. 17–19, 4005,* ☎ *51/52–59–11.* ⌨ *NKr30. Also includes admission to Ledaal, Breidablikk, and Norsk Her-*

metikkmuseum. ⊙ *Mid-June–mid-Aug., daily 11–4; early June and late Aug., Sun. 11–4.*

You can easily spot the spiky **Valbergtårnet** (⊠ Valberget 4, ☎ 51/89–55–01) from any spot on the quay. Built on the highest point of the old city, this tower was a firewatch. Today it is a crafts center, which may not interest you, but it's still worth a visit for the view.

If you are of Norwegian stock you can trace your roots at **Det Norske Utvandresenteret** (Norwegian Emigration Center). Bring along any information you have, especially where your ancestors came from in Norway and when they left the country. The center is on the fourth floor of the brick *Ligningskontoret* (Tax Office) building a few minutes' walk from the harbor. You can make arrangements via fax to have the center do research for you, but the wait for this service is long. If you're in the area in early summer, call for information on the "emigration festival" that the center organizes each June. ⊠ *Bergjelandsgt. 30, 4012 Stavanger,* ☎ *51/50–12–74,* FAX *51/50–12–90.* 🖼 *Free, but each written request costs NKr180.* ⊙ *Weekdays 9–3, Sat. 9–1.*

Rogaland Kunstmuseum houses the country's largest collection of works by Lars Hertervig, a Romantic painter who is considered one of the country's greatest artists. Other exhibits include Norwegian art from the early 19th century to the present. The museum is near Mosvannet (Moss Lake), which is just off highway E18 at the northern end of downtown. ⊠ *Tjensvoll 6, 4021 Mosvannsparken,* ☎ *51/53–09–00.* 🖼 *NKr30.* ⊙ *Tues.–Fri. 10–2, Sat. 11–2, Sun. 11–5.*

🔆 **Kongeparken Amusement Park** has a 281-ft-long figure of Gulliver and a lifelike dinosaur exhibit as its main attractions, and plenty of rides. ⊠ *4330 Ålgård,* ☎ *51/61–71–11.* 🖼 *NKr110.* ⊙ *Mid-May–mid-June, weekends 10–6; mid-June–mid-Aug., daily 10–7; mid-Aug.–Sept., weekends 10–7.*

OFF THE BEATEN PATH

PREKESTOLEN – Pulpit Rock, a huge cube with a vertical drop of 2,000 ft, is not a good destination if you suffer from vertigo but is great for a heart-stopping view. The clifflike rock sits on the banks of the finger-shaped Lysefjord. You can join a tour to get there (☞ Guided Tours, *below*), or you can do it on your own from June 16 to August 25 by taking the ferry from Fiskepiren across Hildefjorden to Tau. (It takes about 40 minutes from Stavanger.) In summer, a bus runs regularly from the ferry to the parking lot at the Pulpit Rock Lodge. It takes 1½ to 2 hours to walk from the lodge to the rock—the well-marked trail crosses some uneven terrain, so good walking shoes or boots are vital. Food and lodging are near the trail.

LYSEFJORDSENTERET – Lysefjord Center, whose shape mimics the mountains, takes visitors through a multimedia simulation of how a trickling brook created this sliver of a fjord. A ferry to the bottom side of Pulpit Rock will drop off passengers midway (for more information, call Clipper Fjord Sightseeing, ☎ 51/89–52–70). Note that at press time the center's future opening times were uncertain, but the center will always gladly open for visitors with an appointment, so be sure to call ahead. ⊠ Oanes 4110 Forsand, ☎ 51/70–31–23. 🖼 NKr50. ⊙ May, daily 11–6; June–Aug., daily 10–8; Sept.–Apr., Sun. 11–6.

Dining and Lodging

$$$$ ★ **X Jans Mat & Vinhus.** The cellar setting is rustic, with old stone walls and robust sideboards providing a nice counterpoint to the refined menu. Saddle of Rogaland county lamb is boned and rolled around a thyme-flavored stuffing, and the fillet is topped with a crunchy mustard crust.

For dessert, try the nougat parfait dusted with cocoa. ⊠ *Breitorget 4, 4006,* ☎ *51/89–47–73. Reservations essential. Jacket and tie. AE, DC, MC, V. No lunch. Closed Sun.*

$$$ ✕ **Sjøhuset Skagen.** Just a few doors down from N.B. Sørensen's (☞ *below*), this spot is similar in decor, but with a greater variety of food. Try the crêpes stuffed with roe of chapelin, onion, and sour cream, and the marinated salmon, Norwegian style, with potatoes in a dill-and-cream sauce. The Brie served with cloudberries marinated in whiskey is excellent. ⊠ *Skagen 16, 4006,* ☎ *51/89–51–80. AE, DC, MC, V.*

$$$ ✕ **Straen Fiskerestaurant.** Right on the quay with two old-fashioned dining rooms, Straen is considered by many the city's best fish restaurant. The three-course meal of the day is always the best value. A rock club, a rock café, and a pub are on the premises. ⊠ *Nedre Strandgt. 15, 4005,* ☎ *51/84–37–00 or 51/52–61–00. AE, DC, MC, V. No lunch. Closed Sun.*

$$ ✕ **City Bistro.** Choose from reindeer medallions with rowanberry jelly, deer fillet with lingonberries and pears, or halibut poached in cream with saffron, garnished with shrimp, crayfish, and mussels at this bistro, where you'll dine at massive oak tables in a turn-of-the-century house. ⊠ *Madlavn. 18–20, 4008,* ☎ *51/53–95–70. Reservations essential. AE, DC, MC, V. No lunch.*

$$ ✕ **Harry Pepper.** This trendy Mexican restaurant has a popular bar. The color schemes are fun, bright, and gaudy, as are the displays of tacky souvenirs. ⊠ *Øvre Holmegt. 15, 4006,* ☎ *51/89–39–93. AE, DC, V.*

$–$$ ✕ **N.B. Sørensen's Dampskibsexpedition.** In a restored warehouse dec-
★ orated with nautical ropes, rustic barrels, and gaslights, this bar and restaurant is right on the quay. The food is nouvelle Norwegian. Try the marinated shrimp appetizer and the baked monkfish. The dish of the day, as well as the red house wine, which is always waiting for customers in an N.B. Sørensen's bottle on each table, is one of the better deals in Stavanger. ⊠ *Skagen 26, 4006,* ☎ *51/89–12–70. AE, DC, MC, V.*

$ ✕ **Café Sting.** Right at the foot of the Valbergtårnet, it's a restaurant–gallery–concert hall–meeting place day and night. All food is made in-house and is better than most other inexpensive fare in Norway. There's a skillet dish with crisp fried potatoes and bacon, flavored with leek, and topped with melted cheese and sour cream; and a meat loaf with mashed potatoes and sprinkled with cheese. The chocolate and almond cakes are served with delicious hot chocolate. ⊠ *Valberget. 3, 4006,* ☎ *51/89–38–78. AE, DC, MC, V.*

$$$–$$$$ 🏨 **Radisson Atlantic Hotel.** The largest hotel in Stavanger, the Atlantic overlooks Breiavatnet pond in the heart of downtown. The feel is that of an international luxury hotel with several restaurants and the most popular nightclubs in town, but with little local flair. Rooms, which come in four different standards, are immaculate with heavy quilts, thick carpets, and cushy stuffed chairs. 🏨 *Olav V's Gt. 3, 4005 Stavanger,* ☎ *51/52–75–20,* ℻ *51/53–48–69. 351 rooms, 5 suites. Restaurant, bar, café, pub, dance club, nightclub, meeting rooms. AE, DC, MC, V.*

$$–$$$ 🏨 **Skagen Brygge.** Housed in three rehabilitated old sea houses, almost all rooms are different here, from modern to old-fashioned maritime, with exposed beams and brick and wood walls; many have harbor views. The hotel has an arrangement with 14 restaurants in the area—they make the reservations and the tab ends up on your hotel bill. 🏨 *Skagenkaien 30, 4006,* ☎ *51/89–41–00,* ℻ *51/89–58–83. 106 rooms. Bar, sauna, Turkish bath, health club, convention center. AE, DC, MC, V.*

$–$$$ ⊞ **Victoria Hotel.** Stavanger's oldest hotel was built at the turn of the century and still retains a clubby, Victorian style, with elegant carved beds and leather sofas. Rooms on the front overlook the harbor. Ask about a discount at the Trimoteket health club, just behind the hotel. ⊞ *Skansegt. 1, 4006 Stavanger,* ☎ *51/89–60–00,* FAX *51/89–54–10. 107 rooms, 3 suites. Restaurant, bar, breakfast room, meeting room. AE, DC, MC, V.*

$–$$ ⊞ **Grand Hotel.** This place on the edge of the town center doesn't aim to be fancy; rooms are comfortable and bright, done in light pastels and white. In summer the rates drop significantly. ⊞ *Klubbgt. 3, Boks 80, 4012,* ☎ *51/53–30–20,* FAX *51/56–19–42. 92 rooms. Bar, breakfast room. AE, DC, MC, V.*

Nightlife and the Arts

NIGHTLIFE

In summer people are out at all hours, and sidewalk restaurants stay open until the sun comes up. Start a sunny evening at **Hansen Hjørnet**'s outdoor restaurant and bar (⊠ Skagenkn. 18, ☎ 51/89–52–80). Walk along **Skagenkaien** and **Strandkaien** for a choice of pubs and nightclubs. Among media junkies the place for a beer and a bit of CNN is the **Newsman** (⊠ Skagen 14, ☎ 51/53–57–09). **Taket Nattklubb** (⊠ Nedre Strandgt. 15, ☎ 51/84–37–00) is for the mid-20s and above crowd, whereas **Berlin** (⊠ Lars Hertervigs Gt. 5, ☎ 51/52–40–40) brings in youngish martini drinkers.

THE ARTS

Stavanger Konserthus (⊠ Concert Hall, Bjergsted, ☎ 51/56–17–16) features local artists and hosts free summertime foyer concerts. Built on an island in the archipelago in the Middle Ages, today **Utstein Kloster** (☞ *above*) is used for its superior acoustics and hosts classical and jazz concerts from June to August.

Outdoor Activities and Sports

BIKING

If you want to cycle around town, you can rent a bike at **Sykkelhuset** (⊠ Løkkevn. 33, ☎ 51/53–99–10). From Stavanger you can take your bike onto the ferry that departs for Finnøy. Spend the day or longer: weeklong cottage rentals are available from **Finnøy Fjordsenter** (⊠ 4160, Judaberg, ☎ 51/71–26–46, FAX 51/54–17–62). For more information about cottages in the archipelago and maps, contact the Stavanger Tourist Board (☞ Visitor Information *in* Sørlandet A to Z, *below*). The Ministry of the Environment can also provide information; call its **Bike Project** (⊠ Sandnes Turistinformasjon, Langgt. 8, 4300 Sandnes, ☎ 51/62–52–40).

FISHING

North of Stavanger is the longest salmon river in western Norway, the **Suldalslågen,** made popular 100 years ago by a Scottish aristocrat who built a fishing lodge there. **Lindum** still has cabins and camping facilities, as well as a dining room. Contact the **Lakseslottet Lindum** (⊠ N–4240 Suldalsosen, ☎ 52/79–91–61). The main salmon season is July through September. On the island of **Kvitsøy,** in the archipelago just west of Stavanger, you can rent an apartment, complete with fish-smoking and -freezing facilities, and arrange to use a small sail- or motorboat. Contact **Kvitsøy Maritime Senter** (⊠ Box 35, 4090 Kvitsøy, ☎ 51/73–51–88).

GOLF

The **Stavanger Golfklubb** (⊠ Longebakken 45, 4042 Hafrsfjord, ☎ 51/55–54–31) offers a lush, 18-hole, international-championship course and equipment rental.

HIKING

Stavanger Turistforening (✉ Postboks 239, 4001 Stavanger, ☎ 51/52–75–66) can plan a hike through the area, particularly in the rolling **Setesdalsheiene** and the thousands of islands and skerries of the **Ryfylke Archipelago.** The tourist board oversees 33 cabins for members (you can join on the spot) for overnighting along the way. Also in the Ryfylke area is a hike up **Kjerag,** a sheet of granite mountain that soars 3,555 ft, at the Lysefjord, near Forsand—ideal for thrill seekers.

SKIING

Skiing in **Sirdal,** 2½ hours from Stavanger, is good from January to April. Special ski buses leave Stavanger on the weekends at 8:30 AM during the season. Especially recommended is **Sinnes** for its non–hair-raising cross-country terrain. Downhill skiing is available at **Alsheia** on the same bus route. Contact **SOT Reiser** (✉ Treskeveien 5, 4040 Hafrsfjord, Stavanger, ☎ 51/59–90–66) for transportation information.

WATER SPORTS

Diving is excellent all along the coast—although Norwegian law requires all foreigners to dive with a Norwegian as a way of ensuring that wrecks are left undisturbed. Contact **Dive In** (✉ Madlaveien 5, Stavanger, ☎ 51/52–99–00), which rents equipment.

Shopping

Figgjo Ceramics (✉ Rte. E18, 4333 Figgjo, ☎ 51/68–35–00; 51/68–35–70 after 3:30) is outside town; the factory's beginnings in World War II are documented in an adjoining museum. A seconds shop has discounts of about 50%. **Skjæveland Strikkevarefabrikk** (✉ 4330 Ålgård, ☎ 51/61–85–06) has a huge selection of sweaters at discount prices.

Sørlandet A to Z

Arriving and Departing

BY BOAT

Color Line (✉ Strandkaien, Stavanger, ☎ 51/52–45–45) has four ships weekly on the Stavanger–Newcastle route. High-speed boats to Bergen are operated by **Flaggruten** (☎ 51/89–50–90). There is also a car ferry from Hirtshals, in northern Denmark, that takes about four hours to make the crossing. Another connects Larvik to Frederikshavn, on Denmark's west coast. In Denmark contact **DSB** (☎ 33/14–17–01); in Norway contact **Color Line** (☎ 51/52–45–45, 38/07–88–88 in Kristiansand) or **DFDS Seaways** (☎ 22/41–90–90).

BY BUS

Aust-Agder Trafikkselskap (☎ 37/02–65–00), based in Arendal, has one departure daily in each direction for the 5½- to six-hour journey between Oslo and Kristiansand.

Sørlandsruta (☎ 38/02–43–80), based in Mandal, has two departures in each direction for the 4½-hour trip from Kristiansand (Strandgt. 33) to Stavanger.

For information about both long-distance and local bus services in **Stavanger,** call ☎ 51/56–71–71; the bus terminal is outside the train station. In **Kristiansand,** call ☎ 38/02–43–80.

BY CAR

From Oslo, it is 329 km (203 mi) to Kristiansand and 574 km (352 mi) to Stavanger. Route E18 parallels the coastline but stays slightly inland on the eastern side of the country and farther inland in the western part. Although seldom wider than two lanes, it is easy driving because it is so flat.

BY PLANE

Kristiansand: Kjevik Airport, 16 km (10 mi) outside town, is served by **Braathens SAFE** (☎ 38/00–80–00), with nonstop flights from Oslo, Bergen, and Stavanger, and **SAS** (☎ 81/00–33–00), with nonstop flights to Copenhagen. **MUK Air** serves Aalborg, Denmark; **Agder Fly** serves Göteborg, Sweden, and Billund, Denmark. Tickets on the last two can be booked with Braathens or SAS.

The **airport bus** departs from the Braathens SAFE office (⊠ Vestre Strandgate ☎ 94/67–22–42) approximately one hour before every departure and proceeds, via downtown hotels, directly to Kjevik. Tickets cost NKr40.

Stavanger: Sola Airport is 14 km (9 mi) from downtown. **Braathens SAFE** (☎ 51/51–10–00) has nonstop flights from Oslo, Kristiansand, Bergen, Trondheim, and Newcastle. **SAS** (☎ 81/00–33–00) has nonstop flights from Bergen, Oslo, Copenhagen, Aberdeen, Göteborg, London, and Newcastle. **KLM** (☎ 51/64–81–20) and **British Airways** (☎ 80/03–00–77) have nonstop flights to Stavanger from Billund and London, respectively. **Air UK** (☎ 51/65–26–30) flies nonstop from London.

The **Flybussen** (airport bus) leaves the airport every 15 minutes. It stops at hotels and outside the railroad station in Stavanger. Tickets cost NKr35.

BY TRAIN

The **Sørlandsbanen** leaves Oslo S Station four times daily for the approximately five-hour journey to Kristiansand and three times daily for the 8½- to nine-hour journey to Stavanger. Two more trains travel the 3½-hour Kristiansand–Stavanger route. Kristiansand's train station is at Vestre Strandgata (☎ 38/07–75–30). For information on trains from Stavanger, call ☎ 51/56–96–00.

Getting Around

BY BUS

Bus connections in Sørlandet are infrequent; the tourist office can provide a comprehensive schedule. Tickets on Stavanger's excellent bus network cost NKr14.

BY CAR

Sørlandet is flat, so it's easy driving throughout. The area around the Kulturhus in the Stavanger city center is closed to car traffic, and one-way traffic is the norm in the rest of the downtown area. Parking is available in numerous marked lots and is free with the **Stavanger Card** (☞ *below*).

BY TAXI

All **Kristiansand** taxis are connected with a central dispatching office (☎ 38/03–27–00), as are **Stavanger** taxis (☎ 51/88–41–00). Journeys within Stavanger are charged by the taxi meter, otherwise by the kilometer. The initial charge is NKr24 (NKr36 at night), with NKr13 per kilometer during the day and NKr15 at night.

SIGHTSEEING PASSES

Stavanger: The **Stavanger Card,** sold at hotels, post offices, and Stavanger Tourist Information, gives discounts of up to 50% on sightseeing tours, regional and long-distance, buses, car rentals, and other services and attractions. Parking, local buses, and museum admissions are free with the Stavanger Card, which costs NKr110, NKr190, or NKr240 for one, two, or three days, respectively. For more information call the Stavanger tourist office (☎ 51/85–92–00).

Contacts and Resources

DOCTORS AND DENTISTS

Doctors: In Kristiansand, **Kvadraturen Legesenter** (⊠ Vestre Strandgt. 32, 4611, ☎ 38/02–66–11) is open 8–4. **Dentists:** In Kristiansand, **Skoletannklinikken** (⊠ Festningsgt. 40, ☎ 38/02–19–71) is open 7–3.

EMERGENCIES

Police: ☎ 112. **Fire:** ☎ 111. **Ambulance:** ☎ 113. **Car Rescue:** in Kristiansand, ☎ 38/12–47–00; in Stavanger, ☎ 51/58–29–00.

Hospital Emergency Rooms: In Kristiansand, **Røde Kors** (Red Cross) **Legevakt** (Egsvei, ☎ 38/02–52–20) is open weekdays 4 PM–8 AM and weekends 24 hours. In Stavanger, call **Rogaland Sentralsykehus** (☎ 51/51–80–00).

GUIDED TOURS

Kristiansand: Tours of Kristiansand run summer only. The **City Train** (⊠ Rådhusgt. 11, 4611, ☎ 38/03–05–24) is a 15-minute tour of the center. The M/S *Maarten* (⊠ Pier 6 by Fiskebrygga, ☎ 38/12–13–14) offers two-hour tours of the eastern archipelago and a three-hour tour of the western archipelago early June–late August.

Stavanger: A two-hour bus tour leaves from the marina at **Vågen** daily at 1 between June and August. **Rødne Clipperkontoret** (⊠ Skagenkaien 18, 4006, ☎ 51/89–52–70) offers three different tours. **Rogaland Trafikkselskap** (☎ 51/56–71–71 or 51/52–26–00) does the same, in either high-speed boats or ferries.

LATE-NIGHT PHARMACIES

Elefantapoteket (⊠ Gyldenløvesgt. 13, 4611, Kristiansand, ☎ 38/02–20–12) is open weekdays 8:30–8, Saturday 8:30–6, Sunday 3–6. **Løveapoteket** (⊠ Olav V's Gt. 11, 4005, Stavanger, ☎ 51/52–06–07) is open daily 8 AM–11 PM.

VISITOR INFORMATION

Arendal (SørlandsInfo, ⊠ Arendal Næringsråd, Friholmsgt. 1, 4800, ☎ 37/02–21–93). **Kristiansand** (⊠ Dronningensgt. 2, Box 592, 4601, ☎ 38/12–13–14, FAX 38/02–52–55). **Larvik** (⊠ Storgt. 48, 3250, ☎ 33/13–01–00). **Mandal** (Mandal og Lindesnes Turistkontor, ⊠ Bryggegt., 4500, ☎ 38/27–83–00). **Stavanger** (Stavanger Kulturhus, ⊠ Sølvberget, ☎ 51/85–92–00).

BERGEN

People from Bergen like to say they do not come from Norway but from Bergen. Enfolded at the crook of seven mountains and fish-boned by seven fjords, Bergen does seem far from the rest of Norway.

Hanseatic merchants from northern Germany settled in Bergen during the 14th century and made it one of their four major overseas trading centers. The surviving Hanseatic buildings on Bryggen (the quay) are neatly topped with triangular cookie-cutter roofs and scrupulously painted red, blue, yellow, and green. A monument in themselves (they are on the UNESCO World Heritage List), they now house boutiques, restaurants, and museums. In the evening, when the harborside is illuminated, these modest buildings, together with the stocky Rosenkrantz Tower and the yachts lining the pier, are reflected in the water—and provide one of the loveliest cityscapes in northern Europe.

During the Hanseatic period, this active port was Norway's capital and largest city. Boats from northern Norway brought dried fish to Bergen to be shipped abroad by the Dutch, English, Scottish, and German merchants who had settled here. By the time the Hansa lost power, the city had an ample supply of wealthy local merchants and shipowners to replace them. For years Bergen was the capital of shipping, and until well into the 19th century, it remained the country's major city.

Culturally Bergen has also had its luminaries, including dramatist Ludvig Holberg, Scandinavia's answer to Molière—whom the Danes claim as their own. Bergensers know better. Norway's musical geniuses Ole Bull and Edvard Grieg also came from the city of the seven hills. Once you've visited Troldhaugen, Grieg's "Hill of Trolls," you'll understand his inspiration. In fact, the city of Bergen has been picked as the European Union's "European Center of Culture" for the year 2000.

About 219,000 people live in the greater metropolitan area now, compared with nearly 500,000 in Oslo. Even though the balance of power has shifted to the capital, Bergen remains a strong commercial force, thanks to shipping and oil, and is a cultural center, with an international music and arts festival every spring. Although it's true that an umbrella and slicker are necessary in this town, the raindrops—actually 219 days per year of them—never obstruct the lovely views.

Exploring Bergen

The heartbeat of Bergen is at Torgalmenningen, the main pedestrian street that runs from the city's central square to the Fisketorget, which sits on the harbor and faces *Bryggen* (the wharf). From here, the rest of the city spreads up the sides of the seven mountains that surround Bergen, with some sights concentrated near the university or a small lake called Lille Lungegårdsvann. Fløyen, the mountain to the east of the harbor, is the most accessible for day-trippers. Before you begin your walking tour, you can take the funicular up to the top of it for a particularly fabulous overview of the city. Bergen is a very walkable city—especially when the sun's shining. If the weather's nice, you may want to take a couple of hours and just wander the streets, exploring the narrow cobblestone alleyways, charming wood houses, and quaint cafés.

Historic Bergen: Bryggen to Fløyen

A GOOD WALK

Start your tour in the center of town at Torget, also called **Fisketorget** ㉞ or the Fish Market, where fisherman and farmers deal their goods. Next, walk over to **Bryggen** ㉟, the wharf on the northeast side of Bergen's harbor. The gabled wood warehouses lining the docks mark the site of the city's original settlement. Take time to walk the narrow passageways between buildings; shops and galleries are hidden among the wooden facades. Follow the pier to the **Hanseatisk Museum** ㊱ at Finnegården and have a look inside. Afterward, continue your walk down the wharf, past the historic buildings to the end of the Holmen promontory and to **Bergenhus Festning** ㊲ (Bergenhus Fort), which dates from the 13th century; the nearby **Rosenkrantztårnet** is a 16th-century tower residence. After you've spent some time out here, retrace your steps back to the Radisson SAS Hotel. Beside the hotel is **Bryggens Museum** ㊳, which houses some magnificent archaeological finds. Just behind the museum is the 12th-century church called **Mariakirken** ㊴. Around the back of the church up the small hill is Øvregaten, a street that's the back boundary of Bryggen. Walk down Øvregaten four blocks to **Fløybanen** ㊵, the funicular that runs up and down Fløyen, one of the city's most popular hiking mountains. Don't miss a trip to the top, whether you hike or take the funicular—the view is like no other. At the base of the funicular is Lille Øvregaten. On this street, and in the area of crooked streets and hodgepodge architecture nearby, you'll find most of Bergen's antiques shops. On your left, at the in-

Bergen

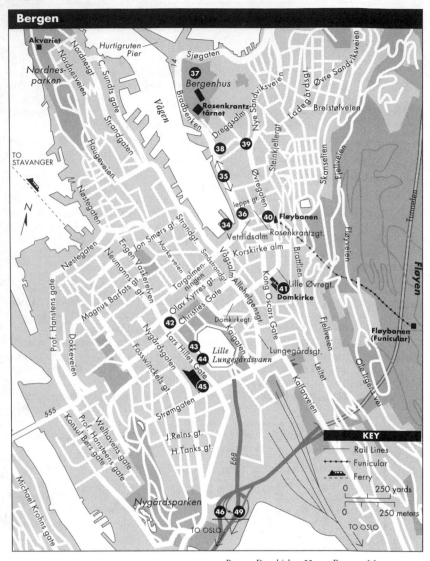

KEY

— Rail Lines
···· Funicular
--- Ferry

0 ——— 250 yards
0 ——— 250 meters

Bergen Domkirke, **41**
Bergenhus Festning, **37**
Bryggen, **35**
Bryggens Museum, **38**
Fantoft Stavkirke, **48**
Fisketorget, **34**
Fløybanen, **40**
Grieghallen, **45**
Hanseatisk Museum, **36**
Lysøen, **47**
Mariakirken, **39**

Rasmus Meyers Samlinger, **44**
Stenersens Samling, **43**
Troldhaugen, **46**
Ulriken Mountain, **49**
Vestlandske Kunstindustri-museum, **42**

How not to watch TV

DAVID GRIMES

SARASOTA, Fla.

WARNING! The following news item should not be read by children, teenagers, adults, people in nursing homes, the unborn or people recently deceased. In fact, if I were you, I'd just turn immediately to *Family Circus.* Thank you.

News item: A Moscow woman set fire to her ex-husband's penis as he sat naked watching television and drinking vodka, police said.

"I don't know what I did to deserve this," blubbered the ex-husband, who presumably now understands why exes shouldn't continue living together.

I certainly don't know what he did to deserve that, either, though I am not the kind of person who makes a habit of sitting around naked watching television and drinking vodka. I'm more of a gin man, myself.

The Reuters news account was exasperatingly stingy with details about this dreadful incident, so, as usual, we'll just have to piece it together (so to speak) ourselves.

My guess is that the man was sitting naked because he had just ordered his ex-wife to do his laundry. Wives, at least the ones of my association, do not react well when you order them to do your laundry, or anything else for that matter. No man who has been married more than 10 minutes would do such a thing because he would be inviting a harangue about his laziness, general incompetence and that his wife does all the chores around the house, up to and including re-shingling the roof.

Any man who orders his ex-wife to do his laundry is asking for serious trouble, though I think we can all agree that the Moscow woman's reaction took things a little too far.

Also, no one wants to sit in a chair that has just been vacated by a naked man, especially if the man is excessively hairy and the chair has leather upholstery. (This is neither here nor there, but I am so modest that I shower in my pajamas, which seems to suit all concerned.)

The story also mentions that the man was watching television while drinking vodka. I'm not familiar with Russian TV fare, but if it's anything like ours, you can't abide it without a stiff drink in your hands. Still, one has to wonder if it was the program the man was watching that caused the woman to snap and reach for the matches and lighter fluid.

I don't think this would ever be a problem for my wife and me because our marriage is made stronger by our mutual loathing of certain things that appear on TV, especially commercials. The one that currently has us reaching for the cinder blocks and paperweights is the public-service announcement where one little girl tells the other little girl what a disgusting pig she is. This, apparently, is meant to discourage girls from sending hateful e-mails to one another and start playing nice. Which would be fine, I suppose, if the message weren't pounded into our ears and eyeballs on an average of 10 times an hour. It's so bad that I've pretty much come to the conclusion that the ugly little girl deserves all she gets because she doesn't have the gumption to slug her tormentor in the kisser.

At least that's the way we solved that kind of problem when I was a kid, and look what a great generation we turned out to be.

David Grimes is a columnist for the Herald-Tribune in Sarasota, Fla.

Records

Continued from Page A1

with express provisions of the statute."

In particular, the ACLU highlights the five "striking and disturbing" incidents over a two-month period that it says demonstrated a "widespread nonchalance" for the public records law.

The report details the following instances in which officials withheld public records from The Providence Journal:

■ The state Department of Environmental Management denied The Journal's request for information on the boat registration for the vessel involved in a July accident on the Barrington River that killed teenager Patrick Murphy.

The DEM refused the request on the basis that the information is part of an investigation, but the law provides for such records to remain public, the ACLU notes.

The DEM and the Barrington Police Department also refused to fully release arrest reports in the matter. Ryan Greenberg, a classmate of Murphy's, has been charged with a felony count of reckless operation, death resulting, as well as underage alcohol possession and refusing to submit to a chemical breath test.

"This Barrington tragedy, unfortunately, supplies a textbook case, in more than one respect, of the low respect with which [the public records law] is held by some agencies," the ACLU study says.

those documents."

A DEM spokeswoman, in a statement yesterday, said, "DEM determined that disclosure of all the information requested would have negatively impacted this important investigation at that time."

■ Providence officials refused to provide The Journal with a copy of a settlement the city had reached with two former Providence police officers who were fired from their jobs and accused of cheating on a police exam.

The law says that all legal settlements against government agencies are public records.

■ The Warwick Police Department initially refused to release convicted killer Alfred "Freddie" Bishop's arrest report on a new murder charge, saying the investigation was ongoing.

The Warwick police chief, Col. Stephen M. McCartney, said yesterday, "I most certainly did recognize that I owed The Providence Journal a public document delineating the circumstances of the arrest of Mr. Bishop."

He said the ACLU report "grossly exaggerated the situation."

McCartney said he thought Bishop's arrest affidavit would be read aloud in open court, but when that didn't happen, he spoke with the attorney general's office and a Journal reporter and lawyer to resolve the matter. The police eventually provided the report.

"Contrary to what the ACLU asserts, I was not trying to be

said.

■ The lease a l for "Mino prise" stat application public me

Additio the state a Provider provide hi his date of obtain a port. Whe was aske barracks.

Govern man, Jeff is only pc

"The A liberately sands and and piece the state to report and every the over cases, re cords are far greate by law. In also waiv bor fees

The AC compreh public re

■ Req ports, in tives, be as possil three bu quest.

■ Req tify tha open-rec been tra quireme

■ Inc $5,000 f

tersection with Kong Oscars Gate is **Bergen Domkirke** ㉑ (Bergen Cathedral). Last, head back to Torgalmenningen in the center of town for a late afternoon snack at one of the square's cafés.

TIMING

This tour will take a good portion of a day. Be sure to get to the Fisketorget early in the morning, as many days it may close as early as 1 or 2. Also, try to plan your trip up Fløyen for a sunny day. Although it may be tough, as Bergen is renowned for rain, you may want to wait a day or two to see if the skies clear up.

SIGHTS TO SEE

OFF THE
BEATEN PATH

AKVARIET – Penguins—several kinds, one of which has a platinum feather "hairdo," strangely appropriate in this land of blonds—seem to be the main attraction at the aquarium. There are also several seals and 50 tanks with a wide variety of fish. Try to catch the movie on Bergen, which is presented on a 360° "supervideograph" screen; it's directed by one of Norway's most beloved animators, Ivo Caprino. The aquarium is on Nordnes Peninsula, a 15-minute walk from the fish market, or take Bus 4. ⊠ *Nordnesparken,* ☎ *55/23–85–53.* ⌦ *NKr50.* ⊙ *May–Sept, daily 9–8; Oct.–Apr., daily 10–6. Feeding times: 11, 2, and 6 in summer; noon and 4 in winter.*

㉑ **Bergen Domkirke** (Bergen Cathedral). This building is constructed in a profusion of styles. The oldest parts, the choir and lower portion of the tower, date from the 13th century. ⊠ *Kong Oscars gt. and Domkirkegt.,* ☎ *55/31–04–70.* ⊙ *Weekdays 11–2 in summer only.*

㊲ **Bergenhus Festning** (Bergenhus Fortress). The buildings here date from the mid-13th century. **Håkonshallen,** a royal ceremonial hall erected during the reign of Håkon Håkonsson between 1247 and 1261, was badly damaged by the explosion of a German ammunition ship in 1944 but was restored by 1961. The nearby **Rosenkrantztårnet** (Rosenkrantz Tower), also damaged in the same explosion, has been extensively restored as well. The Danish governor of Bergenhus, Erik Rosenkrantz, built this tower in the 1560s as an official residence and fortification. It is furnished in a formal, austere style. ⊠ *Bergenhus,* ☎ *55/31–60–67.* ⌦ *NKr15.* ⊙ *Mid-May–mid-Sept., daily 10–4; mid-Sept.–mid-May, daily noon–3, also Thurs. 3–6. Guided tours every hr. Closed during Bergen International Music Festival.*

㉟ **Bryggen** (The Docks, Wharf, or Quays). A trip to Bergen is not complete until you visit Bryggen. One of the most charming walkways in Europe (especially on a sunny day—this town is known for rain, just ask any Bergenser), this row of 14th-century painted wooden buildings facing the harbor was built by Hansa merchants. The buildings, which are on the UNESCO World Heritage List, are mostly reconstructions, with the oldest dating from 1702. Several fires, the latest in 1955, destroyed the original structures.

㊳ **Bryggens Museum.** Artifacts found during excavations on Bryggen, including 12th-century buildings constructed on site from the original foundations, are on display here. The collection provides a good picture of daily life before and during the heyday of the Hansa, down to a two-seater outhouse. ⊠ *Bryggen, 5020,* ☎ *55/31–67–10.* ⌦ *NKr20.* ⊙ *May–Aug., daily 10–5; Sept.–Apr., weekdays 11–3, Sat. noon–3, Sun. noon–4.*

㉞ **Fisketorget** (Fish Market). At the turn of the century, views of this active and pungent square, with fishermen in Wellington boots and mackintoshes and women in long aprons, were popular postcard subjects. Times haven't changed; the marketplace remains just as picturesque—bring your camera. ☉ *Mon.–Wed. and Fri. 7–4, Thurs. 7–7, Sat. 7–3.*

NEED A
BREAK? For an inexpensive snack, try one of the open-face salmon sandwiches sold at the Fish Market. In summer, an array of beautiful, juicy berries is usually available at the adjacent fruit stands. The Norwegian *jordbær* (strawberries) are sure to be some of the best you'll ever have—smaller, but much more flavorful than most American varieties.

④⓪ Fløybanen (Fløyen Funicular). The most astonishing view of Bergen is from the top of **Fløyen,** the most popular of the city's seven mountains. A funicular (a cable car that runs on tracks on the ground) takes you to a lookout point 1,050 ft above the sea. Several marked trails lead from Fløyen into the surrounding wooded area, or you can walk back to town on Fjellveien, which is a common Sunday activity for many locals. ▨ *NKr30; one-way tickets are half-price.* ☉ *Rides every half hour 7:30 AM–11 PM, Sat. from 8 AM, Sun. from 9 AM. It runs until midnight May–Sept.*

③⑥ Hanseatisk Museum (Hanseatic Museum). One of the best-preserved buildings in Bergen, it was the office and home of an affluent German merchant. The apprentices lived upstairs, in boxed-in beds with windows cut into the wall so the tiny cells could be made up from the hall. Although claustrophobic, they retained body heat, practical in these unheated buildings. The 16th-century interior here will give you a feel for the life of a Hanseatic merchant. ✉ *Bryggen,* ☎ *55/31–41–89.* ▨ *NKr35; off-season NKr20.* ☉ *June–Aug., daily 9–5; Sept.–May, daily 11–2. Ticket is also valid for entrance to Schøtstuene, Hanseatic Assembly Rooms.*

③⑨ Mariakirken (St. Mary's Church). It began as a Romanesque church in the 12th-century but gained a Gothic choir, richly decorated portals, and a splendid Baroque pulpit, much of it added by the Hanseatic merchants who owned it during the 15th and 16th centuries. Organ recitals are held Tuesday and Thursday mid-June through late August. ✉ *Dreggen, 5020,* ☎ *55/31–59–60.* ▨ *NKr10 in summer.* ☉ *Mid-May–early Sept., weekdays 11–4; early Sept.–mid-May, Tues.–Fri. noon–1:30.*

Rasmus Meyers Allé and Grieghallen

A GOOD WALK

From Torgalmenningen, walk to Nordahl Bruns Gate and turn left for the **Vestlandske Kunstindustrimuseum** ㊷, the West Norway Museum of Applied Art. After viewing some of the museum's elaborately crafted works, exit the museum and head for Christies Gate. Follow it along the park and turn left on Rasmus Meyers Allé, which runs along the small lake, Lille Lungegårdsvann, to reach **Stenersens Samling** ㊸, an art museum that has some very impressive holdings, with works by Kandinsky and Klee. Just beyond Stenersens is **Rasmus Meyers Samlinger** ㊹, another museum with equally exciting works, including a large Munch collection. Behind these museums on Lars Hills Gate is **Grieghallen** ㊺, Bergen's famous music hall. Although the building's architecture is interesting from street level, try to get a peek of it from the top of Fløyen, where the shape may remind you of a grand piano.

TIMING

All of the museums on this tour are quite small and very near to each other, so you probably won't need more than half a day to complete this tour.

⑮ Grieghallen. Home of the Bergen Philharmonic Orchestra and stage for the annual International Music Festival, this music hall is a conspicuous slab of glass and concrete, but the acoustics are marvelous. Built in 1978, the hall was named for the city's famous son, composer Edvard Grieg (1843–1907). ⊠ *Lars Hills Gt. 3A,* ☎ *55/21–61–50.*

⑭ Rasmus Meyers Samlinger. Meyer, a businessman who lived from 1858 to 1916, assembled a superb art collection, with many names that are famous today but were unknown when he acquired them. Here you'll see the best Munch paintings outside Oslo, as well as major works by Scandinavian impressionists. The gallery hosts summertime Grieg concerts. ⊠ *Rasmus Meyers Allé 7,* ☎ *55/56–80–00.* ⊡ *NKr35.* ◷ *Mid-May–mid-Sept., Tues., Wed., Fri. 10–3, Thurs. noon–7, Sat. 11–4, Sun. noon–5; late Sept.–early May, Tues.–Sun. noon–3.*

⑬ Stenersens Samling. This is an extremely impressive collection of modern art for a town the size of Bergen. Modern artists represented at this museum include Max Ernst, Paul Klee, Vassily Kandinsky, Pablo Picasso, and Joan Miró, as well as—guess who—Edvard Munch. There is also a large focus here on Norwegian art since the mid-18th century. ⊠ *Rasmus Meyers Allé 3,* ☎ *55/56–80–00.* ⊡ *NKr35.* ◷ *Mid-May–mid-Sept., Tues., Wed., Fri. 10–3, Thurs. noon–7, Sat. 11–4, Sun. noon–5; mid-Sept.–mid-May, Tues.–Sun. noon–3.*

⑫ Vestlandske Kunstindustrimuseum (West Norway Museum of Applied Art). Seventeenth- and 18th-century Bergen silversmiths were renowned throughout Scandinavia for their heavy, elaborate Baroque designs. Tankards embossed with flower motifs or inlaid with coins form a rich display. ⊠ *Permanenten, Nordahl Bruns Gt. 9,* ☎ *55/32–51–08.* ⊡ *NKr20.* ◷ *Mid-May–mid-Sept., Tues.–Sun. 11–4; mid-Sept.–mid-May, Tues.–Sat. noon–3, Thurs. noon–6, Sun. noon–4* PM.

Troldhaugen, Fantoft, Lysøen, and Ulriken

If you get your fill of Bergen's city life, you can head out to the countryside to four of the area's interesting, but low-key attractions. Follow Route 1 (Nesttun/Voss) out of town about 5 km (3 mi) to **Troldhaugen** ⑯, the villa where Edvard Grieg spent 22 years of his life. After you've spent some time wandering the grounds of Troldhaugen, head out to **Lysøen** ⑰, the Victorian dream castle of Norwegian violinist Ole Bull. Getting here is a 30-minute trek by car and ferry, but it's well worth the effort. From Troldhaugen, get back on Route 1 or Route 586 to Fana, over Fanafjell to Sørestraumen. Follow signs to Buena Kai. From here, take the ferry over to Lysøen. After visiting Lysøen, on your way back to Bergen, you can see the **Fantoft Stavkirke** ⑱, which unfortunately was badly damaged in a fire in 1992 but has been completely rebuilt. Lastly, end your day with a hike up **Ulriken Mountain** ⑲, the tallest of Bergen's seven mountains. If you're too worn out from your day of sightseeing, but still want take in the view from the top, you can always take the Ulriken cable car.

Driving time (or bus time) will consume much of your day on this tour. However, the landscape is beautiful, so visiting these sights is a pleasant way to explore Bergen's environs with some direction. You can enjoy the day at a leisurely pace, but note closing times below. Try to take your tour on a Monday or Friday so you can end your day with a "Music on the Mountain" concert at Ulriken.

★ ⊛ **Fantoft Stavkirke** (Fantoft Stave Church). Originally built in the early 12th century in Sognefjord, this ancient wooden stave church was later moved to its present site. Stave churches are unique to Norway, representing a sort of first step, spiritually and architecturally, into Christianity, without complete relinquishment of pagan beliefs. They also parallel Viking ships, as they are built of strips of wood laid edge to edge rather than in log-cabin style. (The church was badly damaged by an arsonous fire in 1992 but has been completey rebuilt.) From *sentral bystasjonen* (the main bus station next to the railway station), take any bus leaving from Platform 19, 20, or 21. ⊠ *Paradis*, ☎ *55/28–07–10.* ▣ *NKr 30.* ⊙ *Mid-May–mid-Sept., daily 10:30–1:30 and 2–5:30; for other times, please call.*

⊛ **Lysøen.** Ole Bull, not as well known as some of Norway's other cultural luminaries, was a virtuoso violinist and patron of visionary dimension. In 1850, after failing to establish a "New Norwegian Theater" in America, he founded the National Theater in Norway. He then chose the young, unknown playwright Henrik Ibsen to write full-time for the theater and later encouraged and promoted another neophyte—15-year-old Edvard Grieg.

Built in 1873, this villa, complete with an onion dome, gingerbread gables, curved staircase, and cutwork trim just about everywhere, has to be seen to be believed. Inside, the music room is a frenzy of filigree carving, fretwork, braided and twisted columns, and gables with intricate openwork in the supports, all done in knotty pine. Bull's descendants donated the house to the national preservation trust in 1973. The entrance fee includes a guided tour of the villa.

The ferry, *Ole Bull,* leaves from Buena Kai on the hour Monday–Saturday noon–3 and Sunday 11–4; the last ferry leaves Lysøen Monday–Saturday at 4, Sunday at 5; return fare is NKr30. By bus, take the "Lysefjordruta" bus from Gate 20 at the main bus station to Buena Kai. From here take the *Ole Bull* ferry. Return bus fare is NKr68. ☎ *56/30–90–77.* ▣ *NKr25.* ⊙ *Mid-May–late Aug., Mon.–Sat. noon–4, Sun. 11–5; Sept., Sun. noon–4.*

⊛ **Troldhaugen** (Troll Hill). Composer Edvard Grieg began his musical career under the tutelage of his mother, then went on to study music in Leipzig and Denmark, where he met his future wife, Nina, a Danish soprano. Even in his early compositions, his own unusual chord progressions fused with elements of Norwegian folk music. Norway and its landscape were always an inspiration to Grieg, and nowhere is this more in evidence than at his villa by Nordåsvannet, where he and his wife, Nina, lived for 22 years beginning in about 1885. An enchanting white clapboard house with restrained green gingerbread trim, it served as a salon and gathering place for many Scandinavian artists and it's brimming with paintings, prints, and other memorabilia. On Grieg's desk you'll see a small red troll—which, it is said, he religiously bade good night before he went to sleep. The house also contains his Steinway piano, which is still used for special concerts. Behind the grounds, at the edge of the fjord, you'll find a sheer rock face that was blasted open to provide a burial place for the couple. **Troldsalen** (Troll Hall), with seating for 200 people, is used for concerts. Catch a bus from Platform 19, 20, or 21 at the bus station, and get off at Hopsbroen, turn right, walk 200 yards, turn left on Troldhaugsveien, and follow the signs for 20 minutes. ☎ *55/91–17–91.* ▣ *NKr40.* ⊙ *Mid-Apr.–Sept., daily 9–6; Oct.–Nov. and Apr., weekdays, 10–2, Sat. noon–4, Sun. 10–4; Feb.–Mar., weekdays 10–2, Sun. 10–4.*

49 Ulriken Mountain. Admire summer sunsets from the highest of the seven Bergen mountains—Ulriken—while enjoying free "Music on the Mountain" concerts Mondays and Fridays at 7, May through September. The Ulriken cable car will transport you up the mountain. You can catch the cable car near Haukeland hospital. It's best reached near the Montana Youth Hostel (Buses 2 or 4). ⊠ *Ulriken 1, 5009 Bergen,* ☎ *55/ 29–31–60.* ☜ *NKr50.* ☉ *The cable car operates 9–9 in summer, 9– sunset in winter.*

Dining

Among the most characteristic of Bergen dishes is a fresh, perfectly poached whole salmon, served with new potatoes and parsley-butter sauce. To try another typical Bergen repast, without the typical bill, stroll among the stalls at Fisketorvet, where you can munch bagfuls of pink shrimp, heart-shaped fish cakes, and round buns topped with salmon. Top it off with another local specialty, a *skillingsbolle,* a big cinnamon roll, sometimes with a custard center but most authentic without.

$$$$ ✕ **Kafé Kristall.** This small, intimate restaurant is one of the most
★ fashionable in town. The chef here combines his own eclectic contemporary style with traditional Norwegian ingredients. ⊠ *Kong Oscars Gt. 16,* ☎ *55/32–10–84. AE, DC, MC, V. Closed Sun. No lunch.*

$$$$ ✕ **Lucullus.** Although the decor seems a bit out of kilter—modern art matched with lace doilies and boardroom chairs—the food in this restaurant is always good. This is a good place to splurge on the four-course meal that's offered. ⊠ *Hotel Neptun, Walckendorfsgt. 8,* ☎ *55/ 90–10–00. Jacket and tie. AE, DC, MC, V. Closed Sun. No lunch.*

$$$–$$$$ ✕ **Finnegaardstuene.** This classic Norwegian restaurant near Bryggen
★ has four small rooms that make for a snug, intimate atmosphere. Some of the timber interior dates from the 18th century. The seven-course menu emphasizes seafood, although the venison and reindeer are excellent. Traditional Norwegian desserts such as cloudberries and cream are irresistible. ⊠ *Rosenkrantzgt. 6,* ☎ *55/31–36–20. AE, DC, MC, V. Closed Sun.*

$$$ ✕ **To Kokker.** The name means "two cooks," and that's what there are.
★ Ranked among Bergen's best restaurants by many, this spot is on Bryggen, in a 300-year-old building complete with crooked floors and slanted moldings. Try the roasted reindeer or the marinated salmon. Desserts use local fruit. ⊠ *Enhjørningsgården,* ☎ *55/32–28–16. Reservations essential. AE, DC, MC, V. Closed Sun. No lunch.*

$$ ✕ **Bryggeloftet & Stuene.** It's always full, upstairs and down. The menu's the same in both places, but only the first floor is authentically old. Poached halibut served with boiled potatoes and cucumber salad, a traditional favorite, is the specialty, but there's also sautéed ocean catfish with mushrooms and shrimp, and grilled lamb fillet. ⊠ *Bryggen 11,* ☎ *55/31–06–30. AE, DC, MC, V.*

$$ ✕ **Munkestuen.** With its five tables and red-and-white-check table-
★ cloths, this mom-and-pop place looks more Italian than Norwegian, but locals regard it as a hometown legend—make reservations as soon as you get into town, if not before (they can be booked up to four weeks in advance). Try the monkfish with hollandaise sauce or the fillet of roe deer with morels. ⊠ *Klostergt. 12,* ☎ *55/90–21–49. Reservations essential. AE, DC, MC, V. Closed weekends and 3 wks in July. No lunch.*

$ ✕ **Baker Brun.** This Bergen institution, now in several locations, is great
★ for a quick bite. Try skillingsbolle or *skolebrød,* a sweet roll with custard and coconut icing—both are scrumptious. For something less sweet, this bakery serves fresh-baked wheat rolls with Norwegian *hvit ost* (white cheese) and cucumber. ⊠ *Zachariasbryggen,* ☎ *55/31–51– 08; Søstergården, Bryggen,* ☎ *55/31–65–12. No credit cards.*

$ ✕ **Børs Café.** What began as a beer hall in 1894 is now more of a pub, with hearty homemade food at reasonable prices. The corned beef with potato dumplings is served only on Thursday and Friday; meat cakes with stewed peas, fried flounder, and the usual open-face sandwiches are always on the menu. ⊠ *Strandkaien 12,* ☎ *55/32–47–19. No credit cards.*

$ ✕ **Kjøbmandsstuen** and **Augustus.** You can't beat these two cafeterias under the same management for lunch or for cake and coffee in the afternoon. Vegetarians will be impressed by the number of salads and quiches, in addition to pâté and open-faced sandwiches. ⊠ *Kjø-mandsstuen: C. Sundtsgt. 24,* ☎ *55/30–40–00. Augustus: Galleriet,* ☎ *55/32–35–25. AE, DC, MC, V.*

$ ✕ **Pasta Sentralen.** If you're looking for good cheap eats, this place will give you bang for your buck. You can't beat the 45-kroner daily special, which includes a generous main course, bread, and soda. More than 40 types of delicious homemade pasta are served here, as are piz-zas and other Italian dishes. ⊠ *Vestre Strømkaien 6 (near Lars Hilles Gate),* ☎ *55/96–00–37. No credit cards.*

Lodging

From June 20 through August 10, special summer double-room rates are available in 21 Bergen hotels; rooms can be reserved only 48 hours in advance. In the winter, weekend specials are often a fraction of the weekday rates, which are geared toward business travelers. The tourist office (☎ 55/32–14–80) will assist in finding accommodations in ho-tels, guest houses, or private houses.

$$–$$$ 🏨 **Clarion Admiral Hotel.** This dockside warehouse from 1906, right
★   on the water across Vågen from Bryggen, was converted into a hotel in 1987. The building is geometric Art Nouveau, and although the small rooms are ordinary, the larger rooms overlooking the harbor have some of the best nighttime views in town. The harborside restaurant, Emily, has a small but good buffet table. ⊠ *C. Sundts Gt. 9, 5004,* ☎ *55/23–64–00,* FAX *55/23–64–64. 152 rooms, 3 suites. Restaurant, bar. AE, DC, MC, V.*

$$–$$$ 🏨 **Radisson SAS Hotel Norge.** Other hotels come and go, but the Norge stays. It's an established luxury hotel in the center of town, right by the park. The architecture is standard modern, with large rooms that blend contemporary Scandinavian comfort with traditional warmth. The warm, thick *dyner* (featherbed-like comforters) are so comfy, it's hard to get out of bed in the mornings. ⊠ *Ole Bulls Pl. 4, 5012,* ☎ *55/21–01–00,* FAX *55/21–02–99. 347 rooms, 14 suites. 2 restaurants, 2 bars, indoor pool, health club, nightclub, meeting rooms. AE, DC, MC, V.*

$$–$$$ 🏨 **Radisson SAS Royal Hotel.** This popular Bergen hotel opened in 1982 behind the famous buildings at Bryggen on the site of old warehouses. Ravaged by nine fires since 1170, the warehouses have been rebuilt each time in the same style, which SAS has incorporated into the ar-chitecture of the hotel. The rooms are small but pleasant. ⊠ *Bryggen, 5003,* ☎ *55/54–30–00,* FAX *55/32–48–08. 273 rooms, 7 suites. 2 restau-rants, bar, pub, indoor pool, sauna, health club, dance club, conven-tion center. AE, DC, MC, V.*

$–$$ 🏨 **Augustin Hotel.** This small but comfortable hotel in the center of town has been restored to its original late–Art Nouveau character. ⊠ *C. Sundts Gt. 22–24, 5004,* ☎ *55/23–00–25,* FAX *55/30–40–10. 83 rooms. Meeting rooms. AE, DC, MC, V.*

$–$$ 🏨 **Romantik Hotel Park Pension.** Near the university, this small fam-ily-run hotel is in a well-kept Victorian building. Both the public rooms and the guest rooms are furnished with antiques. It's a 10-minute walk from downtown. Don't oversleep and miss the simple and delicious Norwegian breakfast—fresh bread, jams, cheeses, and cereal—included in the price. ⊠ *Harald Hårfagres Gt. 35, 5000,* ☎ *55/32–09–60,* FAX *55/31–03–34. 21 rooms. Breakfast room. AE, DC, MC, V.*

$–$$ ⊞ **Tulip Inn Bryggen Orion.** Facing the harbor in the center of town, the Orion is within walking distance of many of Bergen's most famous sights, including Bryggen and Rosenkrantztårnet. The rooms are decorated in warm, sunny colors. The open fireplace at the bar is cozy in the winter. ⊠ *Bradbenken 3,* ☎ *55/31–80–80,* FAX *55/32–94–14. 229 rooms. Restaurant, bar, nightclub. AE, DC, MC, V.*

$ ⊞ **Fantoft Sommerhotell.** This student dorm, 6 km (3½ mi) from downtown, becomes a hotel from May 20 to August 20. Family rooms are available. Accommodation is simple but adequate. Take Bus 18, 19, or 20 to Fantoft. ⊠ *5036 Fantoft,* ☎ *55/27–60–00,* FAX *55/27–60–30. 72 rooms. Restaurant. AE, DC, MC, V.*

Nightlife and the Arts

Nightlife

BARS AND CLUBS

Most nightlife centers on the harbor area. **Zachariasbryggen** is a restaurant and entertainment complex right on the water. **Engelen** (the Angel) at the SAS Royal Hotel attracts a mixed weekend crowd when it blasts hip-hop, funk, and rock. The **Hotel Norge** piano bar and disco are more low-key, with an older crowd. **Dickens** (⊠ 8–10 Ole Bulls Pl., ☎ 55/90–07–60), across from the Hotel Norge, is a relaxed meeting place for an afternoon or evening drink. Right next to Dickens is **Losjehagen** (☎ 55/90–08–20), an outdoor patio especially popular in summer. **Wesselstuen,** also on Ole Bull Plads (☎ 55/90–08–20) is a cozy place where you'll find students and the local intelligentsia. **Café Opera** (⊠ 24 Engen, ☎ 55/23–03–15) is a sumptuous place to go for a drink or a coffee. It's great for people-watching and whiling away the time. **Banco Rotto** (⊠ Vågsalmenningen 16, ☎ 55/32–75–20), in a 19th-century bank building, is one of Bergen's most popular watering holes, for young and old alike. The café here—one of the fanciest in town—serves delicious desserts. The three-story **Rick's Café & Salonger** (⊠ Veiten 3, ☎ 55/23–03–11) has a disco, an Irish pub, and Bergen's longest bar; the decor is straight out of the film *Casablanca.*

Bergen has an active gay community with clubs and planned events. Call **Landsforeningen for Lesbisk og Homofil Frigjøring** (National Association for Lesbian and Gay Liberation, ⊠ Nygårdsgt. 2A, ☎ 55/31–21–39) Wednesday 7–9 to ask about events in the city. **Café Finken** (⊠ Nygårdsgt. 2A, ☎ 55/31–21–39) is open daily until 1 AM.

LIVE MUSIC

Bergensers love jazz, and the **Bergen Jazz Festival** (⊠ Georgernes Verft 3, 5011 Bergen, ☎ 55/32–09–76) is held here during the third week of August. **Bergen Jazz Forum** (same address) is *the* place, both in winter and summer, when there are nightly jazz concerts. For rock, **Hulen** (the Cave) (⊠ Olav Ryesvei 47, ☎ 55/32–32–87) has live music on weekends.

The Arts

Bergen is known for its **Festspillene** (International Music Festival), held each year during the last week of May and the beginning of June. It features famous names in classical music, jazz, ballet, the arts, and theater. Tickets are available from the Festival Office at Grieghallen (⊠ Lars Hilles Gt. 3, 5015, ☎ 55/21–61–00).

During the summer, twice a week, the **Bjørgvin folk dance group** performs a one-hour program of traditional dances and music from rural

Norway at Bryggens Museum. Tickets are sold at the tourist office and at the door. ⊠ *Bryggen,* ☎ *55/31–67–10.* ⊡ *NKr70. Performances June–Aug., Tues. and Thurs. at 8:30.*

A more extensive program, **Fana Folklore** is an evening of folklore, with traditional wedding food, dances, and folk music, plus a concert, at the 800-year-old Fana Church. The event has been going on for more than 40 years. ⊠ *A/S Kunst (Art Association) Torgalmenning 9,* ☎ *55/ 91–52–40;* ⊠ *Fana Folklore, 5047 Fana,* ☎ *55/91–52–40.* ⊡ *NKr200 (includes dinner).* ⊙ *June–Aug., Mon., Tues., Thurs., and Fri. at 7* PM *(for groups 6:45* PM*). Return trip back to the city center by 10:30* PM.

Concerts are held at **Troldhaugen,** home of composer Edvard Grieg (☞ Exploring, *above*), all summer. Tickets are sold at the tourist office or at the door. Performances are given late June–August, Wednesday and Sunday at 7:30, Saturday at 2, and September–October, Sunday at 2.

Outdoor Activities and Sports

Below is a sampling of activities for the Bergen area, but outdoors lovers should be aware that the city is within easy reach of the Hardangervidda, the country's great plateau, which offers limitless outdoor possibilities (☞ Hardangervidda *in* Central Norway, *below*).

Fishing
The **Bergen Angling Association** (⊠ Fosswinckelsgt. 37, ☎ 55/32–11–64) provides information on permits; it's closed in July. Among the many charters in the area, the *Fiskestrilen* (☎ 56/33-75–00 or 56/33–87–40) offers evening fishing tours from Glesvaer on the island of Sotra, about an hour's drive from Bergen, where you can catch coal fish, cod, mackerel, or haddock. On the sail home, they'll cook part of the catch.

Hiking
Take the funicular up **Fløyen** (☞ Exploring, *above*), and minutes later you'll be in the midst of a forest. For a simple map of the mountain, ask at the tourist office for the cartoon "Gledeskartet" map, which outlines 1½- to 5-km (1- to 3-mi) hikes. **Ulriken Mountain** (☞ Exploring, *above*) is popular with walkers. Maps of the many walking tours around Bergen are available from bookstores and from **Bergens Turlag** (touring club, ⊠ Tverrgata 2–4, 5017 Bergen, ☎ 55/32–22–30), which arranges hikes and maintains cabins for hikers.

In the archipelago west of Bergen, there are many hiking options, ranging from the simple path between Morland and Fjell to the more rugged mountain climb at Haganes. For details, contact the **Sund Tourist Office** (⊠ 5382 Skogsvåg, ☎ 56/33–75–00).

Yachting
The **Bergen Yachting Club** (☎ 55/22–65–45) has its harbor at Hjellestad, about a half-hour bus ride from the city bus station. If you want to do more than ogle the boats, however, the 100-year-old Hardanger yacht *Mathilde* (⊠ Stiftinga Hardangerjakt, 5600 Kaldestad, ☎ 56/55–22–77), with the world's largest authentic yacht rigging, does both one- and several-day trips, as well as coastal safaris.

Shopping

Shopping Centers
Sundt City (⊠ Torgalmenningen 14, ☎ 55/31–80–20) is the closest you'll get to a traditional department store in Norway, with everything from fashion to interior furnishings. However, you'll find better value for your kroner if you shop around for souvenirs and sweaters. **Kløverhuset** (⊠ Strandkaien 10, ☎ 55/21–37–90), between Strandgaten and

the fish market, has 40 shops under one roof. You'll find outlets for
the ever-so-popular Dale knitwear, souvenirs, leathers, and fur. **Galleriet,** on Torgalmenningen, is the best of the downtown shopping malls.
Here you will find **Christiana Glasmagasin** and more exclusive small
shops along with all the chains, like **Hennes & Mauritz** and **Lindex.**
Bystasjonen, a small shopping center by the bus terminal, is conveniently
located for last-minute items.

Specialty Stores
ANTIQUES
There are many antiques shops on **Øvregaten,** especially around Fløybanen. **Cecilie Antikk** (⊠ Kong Oscarsgt. 32, ☎ 55/96–17–53) deals primarily in antique Norwegian glass, ceramics, and old and rare books.

GLASS, CERAMICS, PEWTER
Viking Design (⊠ Torgalmenning 1, ☎ 55/31–05–20) specializes in
pewter—you'll find that some pieces can be picked up quite reasonably. **Tilbords, Bergens Glasmagasin** (⊠ Olav Kyrresgt. 9, ☎ 55/31–
69–67) claims to have the town's largest selection of glass and china,
both Scandinavian and European designs. **Prydkunst-Hjertholm** (⊠ Olav
Kyrresgt. 7, ☎ 55/31–70–27) is the ideal shop for gifts; most everything is of Scandinavian design. You'll find pottery and glassware of
the highest quality—much of it from local artisans.

HANDICRAFTS
Husfliden (⊠ Vågsalmenning 3, ☎ 55/31–78–70) caters to all your handicrafts needs, including a department for Norwegian national costumes. This is one of the best places to pick up handmade Norwegian
goods, especially handwoven textiles and hand-carved wood items. **Berle**
(⊠ Bryggen 5, ☎ 55/31–73–00) has a huge selection of traditional
knitwear and other souvenir items—don't miss the troll cave. Downstairs is an interior design shop with Scandinavian furniture. There's
also an automatic foreign-money exchange machine.

JEWELRY
Theodor Olsens Eftf (⊠ Ole Bulls Pl. 7, ☎ 55/55–14–80) stocks silver
jewelry of distinctive Norwegian and Scandinavian design.

Bergen A to Z
Arriving and Departing
BY BOAT
Boats have always been Bergen's lifeline to the world. **Color Line** (⊠
Skuteviksboder 1–2, 5023, ☎ 55/54–86–60) ferries serve Newcastle.
Others connect with the Shetland and Faroe islands, Denmark, Scot-
land, and Iceland. All dock at Skoltegrunnskaien.

Express boats between Bergen and Stavanger run three times daily on
weekdays, twice daily on weekends, for the four-hour trip. All arrive
and depart from Strandkai Terminalen (☎ 55/23–87–80).

The *Hurtigruten* (⊠ Coastal Express, Veiten 2B, 5012, ☎ 55/23–07–
90) departs daily from Frielenes Quay, Dock H, for the 11-day round-
trip to Kirkenes in the far north.

BY BUS
The summer-only bus from Oslo to Bergen, **Geiteryggekspressen** (literally, "Goat-Back Express," referring to the tunnel through Geiteryggen
Mountain, which looks like a goat's back, between Hol and Aurland)
leaves the Nor-Way bus terminal (⊠ Galleri Oslo, ☎ 22/17–52–90) at
8 AM and arrives in Bergen 12½ hours later. Buses also connect Bergen
with Trondheim and Ålesund. Western Norway is served by several bus
companies, which use the station at Strømgaten 8 (☎ 177).

Bergen is 485 km (300 mi) from Oslo. Route 7 is good almost as far as Eidfjord at the eastern edge of the Hardangerfjord, but then it deteriorates considerably. The ferry along the way, crossing the Hardanger Fjord from Brimnes to Bruravik, runs continually 5 AM to midnight and takes 10 minutes. At Granvin, 12 km (7 mi) farther north, Route 7 joins Route E68, which is an alternative route from Oslo, crossing the Sognefjorden from Refsnes to Gudvangen. From Granvin to Bergen, Route E68 hugs the fjord part of the way, making for spectacular scenery.

Driving from Stavanger to Bergen involves from two to four ferries and a long journey packed with stunning scenery. The Stavanger tourist information office can help plan the trip and reserve ferry space.

Flesland Airport is 20 km (12 mi) south of Bergen. **SAS** (☎ 81/00–33–00) and **Braathens SAFE** (☎ 55/23–55-23) are the main domestic carriers. **British Airways** (serviced by Braathens SAFE) and **Lufthansa** (☎ 55/99–82–30) also serve Flesland.

Between the Airport and Downtown: Flesland is a 30-minute bus ride from the center of Bergen at off-peak hours. The **Flybussen** (Airport Bus) departs three times per hour (less frequently on weekends) from the SAS Royal Hotel via Braathens SAFE's office at the Hotel Norge and from the bus station. Tickets cost NKr35.

Driving from Flesland to Bergen is simple, and the road is well marked. Bergen has an electronic toll ring surrounding it, so any vehicle entering the city weekdays between 6 AM and 10 PM has to pay NKr5. There is no toll in the other direction.

A taxi stand is outside the Arrivals exit. The trip into the city costs about NKr200.

Bergensbanen has five departures daily, plus an additional one on Sunday, in both directions on the Oslo–Bergen route; it is widely acknowledged as one of the most beautiful train rides in the world. Trains leave from Oslo S Station for the 7½- to 8½-hour journey. For information about trains out of Bergen, call ☎ 55/96–60–50.

Getting Around

The best way to see the small center of Bergen is on foot. Most sights are within walking distance of the marketplace.

Tourist tickets for 48 hours of unlimited travel within the town boundaries cost NKr70, payable on the yellow city buses. All buses serving the Bergen region depart from the central bus station at Strømgaten 8 (☎ 177). Buses between the main post office (Småstrandgt. and Olav Kyrres Gt.) and the railway station are free.

Downtown Bergen is enclosed by an inner ring road. The area within is divided into three zones, which are separated by ONE WAY and DO NOT ENTER signs. To get from one zone to another, return to the ring road and drive to an entry point into the desired zone. It's best to leave your car at a parking garage (the Birkebeiner Senter is on Rosenkrantz Gate, and there is a parking lot near the train station) and walk. You pay a NKr5 toll every time you drive into the city—but driving out is free.

Taxi ranks are located in strategic places downtown. All taxis are connected to the central dispatching office (☎ 55/99–70–00) and can be booked in advance (☎ 55/99–70–10).

The 24-hour **Bergen Card,** which costs NKr120 (NKr190 for 48 hours), gives free admission to most museums and attractions, and rebates of 25% to 50% off sightseeing, rental cars, and transportation to and from Bergen. It is available at the tourist office and in most hotels.

Contacts and Resources

The dental emergency center at Lars Hilles Gate 30 (☎ 55/32–11–20) is open daily 10–11 AM and 7–9 PM.

Emergency Rooms: The outpatient center at Lars Hilles Gate 30 (☎ 55/32–11–20), near Grieghallen, is open 24 hours.

Bergen is the guided-tour capital of Norway because it is the starting point for most fjord tours. Tickets for all tours are available from the tourist office.

Fjord Tours: Bergen is the much-acclaimed "Gateway to the Fjords," with dozens of fjord-tour possibilities. The following is only meant as a sampling; check with the tourist office (☞ *below*) for additional recommendations. The ambitious all-day **"Norway-in-a-Nutshell"** bus-train-boat tour (you can book through the tourist office) goes through Voss, Flåm, Myrdal, and Gudvangen—truly a breathtaking trip—and is the best way to see a lot in a short amount of time.

Traveling by boat is an advantage because the contrasts between the fjords and mountains are greatest at water level, and the boats are comfortable and stable (the water is practically still), so seasickness is rare. Stops are frequent, and all sights are explained. **Fjord Sightseeing** (☎ 55/31–43–20) offers a four-hour local fjord tour. **Fylkesbaatane** (County Boats) **i Sogn og Fjordane** (☎ 55/32–40–15) has several combination tours. Tickets are sold at the tourist office (☞ *below*) and at the quay.

Orientation Tours: Bergen Guided Tours (☎ 55/59–32–00 or 55/96–55–00) offers three city tours departing from Hotel Norge, including one to Edvard Grieg's home and the Fantoft Stave Church. The excellent **Bryggen Guiding** (1½ hours, June–Aug., ☎ 55/31–67–10) offers a historic tour of the buildings at Bryggen, as well as entrance to Bryggens Museum, the Hanseatic Museum, and Schøtstuene after the tour, conducted by knowledgeable guides. **Bergens-Expressen** (☎ 55/18–10–19), a "train on tires," leaves from Torgalmenningen for a one-hour ride around the center of town, summer only.

Apoteket Nordstjernen (☎ 55/31–68–84), by the bus station, is open daily from 7:30 AM to midnight, Sundays from 8:30 AM.

Exchanging Money: Outside normal banking hours, the Tourist Information Office on Bryggen can change money. Post offices exchange money and are open Monday through Wednesday and Friday 8 to 5, Thursday 8 to 6, and Saturday 9 to 2.

Most shops are open Monday–Wednesday and Friday 9–5. On Thursday, as well as Friday for some shops, the hours are 9–7. On Saturday shops are open 9–3. The shopping centers are open weekdays 9–8 and Saturdays 9–6.

The **Tourist Information Office** (☎ 55/32–14–80) at Bryggen has brochures and maps and can arrange for accommodations and sightseeing. There is also a currency exchange.

CENTRAL NORWAY: THE HALLINGDAL VALLEY TO HARDANGERFJORD

Norway's interior between Oslo and Bergen is a land of superlatives—the tallest peaks, the biggest national park, and the highest mountain plateau in Europe. There are several varied national parks in this region, and the southern part of Norway's interior, around Hardangervidda, has one of the most popular. It's prime vacation land for wilderness-sports lovers, with fishing, canoeing, rafting, hiking, and horseback riding over the plateau in the summer, and skiing, particularly on the slopes of Geilo, in winter.

Hallingdal Valley

120 km (74½ mi) from Oslo; 92 km (57 mi) from Drammen to Nesbyen.

Route 7 from Drammen winds through the historic Hallingdal Valley, which is lined with small farming communities and ski resorts. Hallingdal is known for its many well-preserved wooden log buildings. **Nesbyen,** a small town in the heart of the valley, has a folk museum as well as many campsites and a youth hostel.

En Route   About 21 km (13 mi) from Nesbyen you'll come across the small community of **Gol.** This town is popular with campers in summer and skiers in winter who throng the mountains to the north and east of Gol during ski season.

Hemsedal

50 *35 km (21½ mi) from Gol.*

Spring, summer, winter, or fall, the valley of Hemsedal, and its surrounding area, is a great destination. Clear streams, blue lakes, and striking mountains provide plenty of outdoor activities; hikers and skiers (both alpine and cross-country) will find hundreds of miles of trails. In fact, here in Hemsedal, Norwegian World Cup skiers often practice in the top local ski center (☞ Skiing, *below*).

Outdoor Activities and Sports
SKIING
Hemsedal Skisenter (☎ 32/05–53–00) has 34 km (21 mi) of alpine slopes, 175 km (108 mi of cross-country trails), and 17 ski lifts. The **Vinterlandkortet ski pass** is accepted at all 71 ski slopes in Geilo, Hemsedal, Gol, and Ål and is available at ski centers and tourist offices.

Torpo

51 *52 km (32 mi) from Hemsedal.*

Driving from Gol to Geilo, you'll pass through the tiny town of Torpo, known for its church, presumably the oldest building in Hallingdal. **Torpo stave church** is believed to have been built in the late 12th century. Its colorful painted ceiling is decorated with scenes from the life of Saint Margaret. It's open June through August, daily 9:30–5:30.

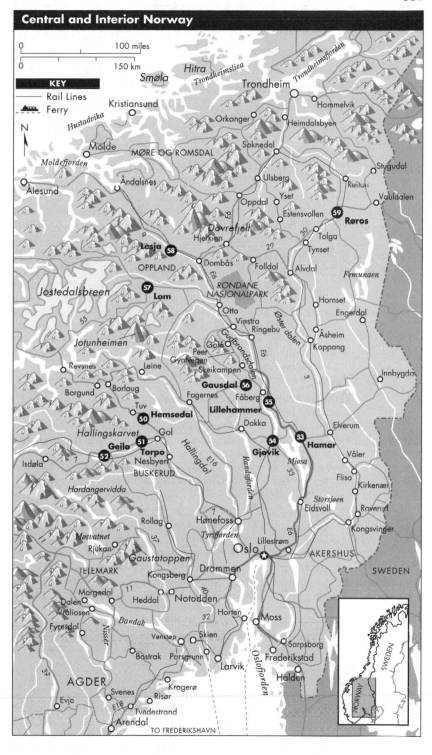

Central and Interior Norway

0   100 miles
0   150 km

KEY
——— Rail Lines
▄▄▄ Ferry

N

Smøla   Hitra   Trondheimsfjorden

Trondheimslica

Trondheim

Hommelvik

Kristiansund

Orkanger   Heimdalsbyen

Hustadvika

Molde   MØRE OG ROMSDAL   Soknedal

Moldefjorden

Stugudal

Ålesund   Åndalsnes   Ulsberg   Reilun

Oppdal   Yset   Vauldalen

Estensvollen   **59**   **Røros**

Dovrefjell

Hjerkinn   Tolga

Lesja   **58**   Dombås   Folldal   Tynset

OPPLAND   Alvdal   Femunaen

Jostedalsbreen   **57**   **Lom**   RONDANE NASJONALPARK   Hornset

Engerdal

Otta

Jotunheimen   Vinstra   Åsheim

Ringebu   Koppang

Revsnes   Peer   Golå

Gynfvegen   Leine   Skeikampen   Innbygda

Borgund   Borlaug   **Gausdal**   **56**

Fagernes   Fåberg   **55**

Tuv   **Lillehammer**

50   **Hemsedal**

Hallingskarvet   Gol   Dokka   Elverum

Geilo   **51**   **54**   **53**   **Hamar**

52   **Torpo**   **Gjøvik**   Våler

Isdøla   Nesbyen   Mjøsa   Flisa

BUSKERUD   Kirkenær

Hardangervidda   Hallingdal   Randsfjorden

Rollag   Storsjøen   Røverud

Møsvatnet   Hønefoss   Eidsvoll   Kongsvinger

Rjukan   Tyrifjorden

Gaustatoppen   Lillestrøm

TELEMARK   Kongsberg   Oslo   AKERSHUS

Drammen   SWEDEN

Morgedal   Heddal   Notodden

Dalen   Horten   Moss

Vråliosen

Fyresdal   Bandak   Skien   Sarpsborg

Venstøp   Nisser

Båstrak   Porsgrunn   Frederikstad

Larvik   Halden

AGDER   Oslofjorden

Evje   Svenes   Risør

Kragerø

Tvedestrand

Arendal

TO FREDERIKSHAVN

NORWAY   SWEDEN

Geilo

⑤② *35 km (21 mi) west of Torpo; 251 km (155½ mi) from Oslo; 256 km (159 mi) from Bergen.*

Geilo, population 3,500, is dead-center between Bergen and Oslo. The country's most popular winter resort, it often draws more than a million visitors a year from throughout northern Europe and Scandinavia to its alpine slopes and cross-country trails; many people ski directly from their hotels and cabins. Recently Geilo has become a popular summer destination, with fishing, boating, hiking, and riding—although, admittedly, it still looks like a winter resort minus the snow. Plan ahead if you want to visit at Easter, when Norwegians flock there for a final ski weekend.

On the first Saturday in August, the **Holsdagen** festival presents folk music and a traditional wedding ceremony in the **Hol Stave Church** and **Hol Folkemuseum** (⊠ Hol Kommune, Kulturkontoret, 3576 Hol, ☎ 32/08–81–40).

Dining and Lodging

$$$ ✕⊞ **Dr. Holms Hotell.** Truly a place to see and be seen (which means ★ it can be quite a scene), Holms Hotell is among Norway's top resort hotels. Chef Jim Weiss has made the gourmet restaurant (not to be confused with the dining room) worth a special trip. Don't miss the game sausages, which are full of flavor, and the butterscotch pudding with crunchy topping—it's sensational. An après-ski stop at the bar-lounge is a must. ⊠ *3580 Geilo,* ☎ *32/09–06–22,* FAX *32/09–16–20. 124 rooms. Restaurant, 3 bars, 2 indoor pools, hot tub, sauna, exercise room, meeting rooms. AE, DC, MC, V.*

Outdoor Activities and Sports

RAFTING AND CANOEING
In Geilo they've combined rafting and canoeing with skiing, outfitting rubber rafts with a wood rudder and taking off down the slopes for a bracing, if peculiar, swoosh. Contact the tourist board for details. **Flaate Opplevelser** (☎ 61/23–50–00) and **Norwegian Wildlife and Rafting** (☎ 61/23–87–27) also have trips in the Sjoa and Dagali areas.

SKIING
Just to the north, between Bergen and Oslo, is **Geilo Skiheiser** (☎ 32/09–03–33) with 24 km (15 mi) of alpine slopes, 130 km (81 mi) of cross-country trails, 18 lifts, and also a ski-board tunnel. Among the area's other four ski centers, **Vestlia** (☎ 32/09–01–88), west of the Ustedalsfjord, is a good choice for families, as children can play under the guidance of the Troll Klub while their parents ski; **Halstensgård** (☎ 32/09–10–20) and **Slaatta** (☎ 32/09–17–10) have a range of alpine and cross-country trails; and **Havsdalsenteret** (☎ 32/09–17–77) attracts a young crowd to its long alpine slopes. One ski pass gives access to all lifts in all five centers for NKr185. The **Vinterlandkortet ski pass** is accepted at all 71 ski slopes in Geilo, Hemsedal, Uvdal, and Ål and is available at ski centers and tourist offices.

Shopping
Brusletto & Co. (☎ 32/09–02–00), in central Geilo, is a purveyor of high-quality hunting knives with silver-inlaid handles made from burnished metal, walnut, and rosewood. Norwegian men wear these knives, used for hunting and hiking, on their belts—something akin to jewelry.

Hardangervidda

90 km (56 mi) from Geilo to Eidfjord; Rte. 7 is the main road that crosses Hardangervidda.

Geilo is the gateway to Hardangervidda, Europe's largest mountain plateau and Norway's biggest national park—10,000 square km (3,861 square mi) of unique scenery, with the largest herd of wild reindeer in Europe, lakes and streams teeming with trout and char, and home to many birds and animals on the endangered list. It also has rich and varied flora, about 450 different species. Flat in the east and at its center, the plateau is more mountainous in the west. Touring the plateau, either on horseback or on foot, you can find a trail for any level of proficiency, and along the trails, the Norwegian Touring Association (DNT) has built cabins.

About an hour's drive north of Geilo is Hardangervidda's highest peak, **Hardangerjøkulen** (Hardanger Glacier), at 6,200 ft above sea level. Near Hardangerjøkulen you can take a guided hike to the archaeological digs of 8,000-year-old Stone Age settlements. Contact the Geilo Tourist Office (☎ 32/09–13–00).

At the base of the plateau is the innermost arm of the **Hardangerfjord.** Although it's not as dramatic as some of the other fjords, it is pastoral, with royal-blue water and lush apple orchards.

En Route The western settlement of Finse (on the Bergen railroad), about 34 km (21 mi) from Geilo is one of the most frigid places in southern Norway, with snow on the ground as late as August. Here polar explorers Nansen and Scott tested their equipment and the snow scenes in the *Star Wars* movies were filmed. It, too, is a good starting point for tours of Hardangervidda.

If you'd like to try summer skiing, contact the **Finse Skisenter** (3590 Finse, ☎ 56/52–67–44).

Central Norway A to Z

Arriving and Departing

BY TRAIN

This region is served by the Oslo–Bergen line, which is as much an attraction as a means of transportation.

Contacts and Resources

VISITOR INFORMATION

The main tourist offices of the region are in **Geilo** (☎ 32/09–13–00); **Gol** (☎ 32/07–51–15); and **Nesbyen** (☎ 32/07–01–70).

INTERIOR NORWAY: LILLEHAMMER TO RØROS

Northward in Norway's inner midsection, the land turns to rolling hills and leafy forests, and the principal town, Lillehammer, attracts skiers from around the world to its slopes and trails; in 1994 it hosted the Winter Olympics. As you travel north, you'll enter Gubrandsdalen (*dal* means valley), one of the longest and most beautiful valleys in the country. Gudbrandsdalen extends from Lake Mjøsa, north of Oslo, diagonally across the country to Åndalsnes. At the base of the lake is Eidsvoll, where Norway's constitution was signed on May 17, 1814. Most visitors come to the region for the beautiful scenery and outdoor activities; tourism has increased substantially in this area since the 1994 Winter Olympics.

At the northern end of the region is the copper-mining town of Røros—which is on UNESCO's World Heritage List—a bucolic little town that's changed little for the past 100 years. The tourist board aptly calls the triangle between Oppland and Hedmark counties, south to Lillehammer, Troll Park. In a reminiscent tribute to the much celebrated 1994 games, this area is also billed as the "Olympic" part of Norway. The otherworldly quality of oblique northern light against wildflower-covered hills has inspired centuries of folk tales as well as artists from Wagner to Ibsen, who was awarded a government grant to scour the land for these very stories. Even today, locals claim he applied for the grant just to have the opportunity to hike the hills.

Hamar

🚳 *134 km (83 mi) from Oslo; 66 km (41 mi) from Eidsvoll.*

During the Middle Ages, Hamar was the seat of a bishopric. Four Romanesque arches, which are part of the cathedral wall, remain the symbol of the city today. Ruins of the town's 13th-century monastery now form the backbone of a glassed-in exhibition of regional artifacts that date back to the Iron Age but also include more recent findings. Also on the grounds of the **Hedmarksmuseet and Domkirkeodden** (Hedemark Museum and Cathedral) sit 50 or so idyllic grass-roofed houses from the region, and a local favorite, the proliferating herb garden. ✉ *2301 Hamar,* ☎ *62/53–11–66.* ✁ *NKr30.* ◷ *Late-May–mid-June and mid-Aug.–Sept., daily 10–4; mid-June–mid-Aug., daily 10–6.*

Hamar got a new lease on life in 1994 when the **Hamar Olympiahall** played host to the speed-skating and figure-skating events of the Lillehammer Winter Olympics. Now used for local exhibitions and conferences, the hall takes the shape of an upside-down Viking ship. Looking out on the town's nature reserve, the hall was built according to the highest environmental and construction standards. Its special laminated wood is so dense that no fire could burn it down. Contact Hamar Olympiahall (✉ Åkersvika, 2300 Hamar, ☎ 62/51–02–25) for details on tours and sports facilities.

One of Europe's first railway museums, the **Jernbanemuseet** documents how Norway's railways developed, with life-sized locomotives on narrow-gauge tracks outside and train memorabilia inside. Tertittoget, NSB's last steam locomotive, gives rides from mid-May to mid-August. ✉ *Strandvn. 132,* ☎ *62/51–31–60.* ✁ *NKr30.* ◷ *June and Aug., daily 10–4; July, daily 10–6.*

The world's oldest paddleboat, the 140-year-old D/S *Skibladner*, also called the "White Swan of the Mjøsa," departs from Hamar, connecting the towns along the lake. The steamer stops daily at Hamar and creeps up to Lillehammer three days a week. The other days it stops at Eidsvoll. Many Norwegian emigrants to North America took the paddler's route from Lillehammer to Eidsvoll to connect with an Oslo-bound train. Be sure to ask for a schedule from the tourist information or the *Skibladner* office. A traditional dinner, consisting of poached salmon and potatoes, with strawberries and cream for dessert, is available for an extra fee. ✉ *Parkgt. 2., 2300 Hamar,* ☎ *62/52–70–85.* ◷ *Mid-June–mid-Aug. The Skibladner is available for charter late May–late Sept.*

NEED A
BREAK?   **Sea Side Mat & Vin Hus** (☎ 62/52–62–10) sits on the dock near where the *Skibladner* calls; the brass fixtures and lakeside view will surely put you in a maritime mood. The simple fare includes sandwiches, salads, and omelets.

Gjøvik

🚵 *45 km (30 mi) from Hamar.*

The *Skibladner* stops several times a week at this quiet, hillside town, which claims to be home to the world's largest underground auditorium. So if you get a chance, check out the **Gjøvik Olympiske Fjellhall** (Olympic Mountain Hall), buried 400 ft below the midtown mountain. ☎ 61/13–82–00.

<table>
<tr><td>OFF THE
BEATEN PATH</td><td>

GILE GÅRD – Farmhouses dot the rolling green countryside along this side of the Mjøsa. Some of them serve as lodgings, and others are just picturesque stops along the way. The Gile family has owned the Gile Farm since the 18th century, although the land has been used as farmland for some 5,000 years. In summer, a variety of uncommon flowers sprout atop the many Viking burial mounds that lie untouched around the house. Call in advance for a schedule of events at the farmhouse. ⊠ *2850 Lena (off Rte. 33),* ☎ *61/16–03–73.* ☼ *Tues. Call for more information.*
</td></tr>
</table>

Lillehammer

⑤ *40 km (25 mi) from Gjøvik, 60 km (37 mi) from Hamar.*

The winter-sports center of Lillehammer has 23,000 inhabitants. In preparation for the 1994 Winter Olympics, this small town built a ski-jumping arena, an ice-hockey hall, a cross-country skiing stadium, and a bobsled and luge track, in addition to other venues and accommodations. However, far-sighted planning kept expansion surprisingly minimal, ensuring that the town was not left in a state of Olympic obsolescence. After the games, which proved hugely successful, many of the structures built to house the foreign media were turned over to the regional college, and one-third of the athletes' quarters were transported to Tromsø to be used as housing.

Kulturhuset Banken, a magnificent, century-old bank building, is the main locale for cultural events. It is decorated with both contemporary and turn-of-the-century art. Don't miss the murals on the ceiling of the ceremonial hall. ⊠ *Kirkegt. 41,* ☎ *61/26–68–10.* ☼ *Tours for groups by appointment only.*

The **Olympiaparken** (Olympic Park) includes the Lysgårdsbakkene ski-jumping arena, where the Winter Olympics' opening and closing ceremonies were held. From the tower you can see the entire town. Also in the park are **Håkons Hall,** used for ice hockey, and the **Birkebeineren Stadion** (ski stadium), which holds cross-country and biathlon events. ⊠ *Elvegaten 19,* ☎ *61/26–07–00.* ▣ *Free, but admission fee charged at individual facilities.*

Norges Olympiske Museum (Olympic Museum), new in June 1998, focuses on the major Olympic sports achievements of Norwegian and other European sports teams. The architects of Maihaugen's "We Won the Land" (☞ *below*) have also created the exhibits here; you'll see many similarities—mannequins, antique sports equipment, video footage, and sound and light effects. ⊠ *Håkons Hall, Olympic Park.* ☎ *61/25–21–00.* ▣ *NKr50.* ☼ *June–Sept., daily 10–6; Oct.–May, Tues.–Sun. 11–4.*

The winter-sports facilities provide amusement all year-round in Lillehammer. You can try the **Downhill and Bobsled simulator** between Håkons Hall and Kristins Hall in the Olympic Park. It's a five-minute ride that replicates the sensations of being on a bobsled. ▣ *NKr25.* ☼ *Jan.–late June, daily 11–4; late June–mid-Aug., daily 10–7; late Aug., daily 11–4.*

Those older than the age of 12 can try the **Bobsled on Wheels**—it's the real thing with wheels instead of blades—at the Lillehammer Bobsled and Luge Stadion. Speeds of 100 km (60 mi) per hour are reached, so you'll get a distinct impression of what the sport is all about. ☎ 94/ 37–43–19. ⌨ *Arena NKr 15.* ۞ *Daily 8–8.* ⌨ *Wheeled bobsled NKr125.* ۞ *Late May–early June and mid-Aug.–mid-Sept., daily noon– 5; June–mid-Aug., daily 11–7.*

A highlight of Lillehammer's ski year is the **Birkebeineren cross-country ski race,** which commemorates the trek of two warriors whose legs were wrapped in birchbark (hence *birkebeiner*—birch legs), which was customary for people who couldn't afford wool or leather leggings. They raced across the mountains from Lillehammer to Østerdalen in 1205, carrying the 18-month-old prince Håkon Håkonsson away from his enemies. The race attracts 8,000 entrants annually. Cartoon figures of Viking children representing Håkon on skis and his aunt Kristin (on ice skates) were the official mascots for the Olympic games.

★ ۞ Lillehammer claims fame as a cultural center as well. Sigrid Undset, who won the Nobel Prize in literature in 1928, lived in the town for 30 years. It is also the site of **Maihaugen,** Norway's oldest (and, according to some, Scandinavia's largest) open-air museum, founded in 1887. The massive collection was begun by Anders Sandvik, an itinerant dentist who accepted folksy odds and ends—and eventually entire buildings—from the people of Gudbransdalen in exchange for repairing their teeth. Eventually Sandvik turned the collection over to the city of Lillehammer, which provided land for the museum.

Maihaugen's permanent indoors exhibit, **"We Won the Land,"** will leave you slack-jawed. Completed in 1993, this inventive meander chronicles Norway's history, starting in 10,000 BC when life was somewhere inside a mere drop of melting ice. After walking past life-sized, blue-hued dolls representing periods from the Black Death and 400 years of Danish rule, you will arrive in the 20th century to unsettling visions of the postwar West: a mannequin-junkie sits crumpled in a city stairwell and a lonely old lady tosses feed to the pigeons. Sound effects, period music (including the Rolling Stones), and realistic smells bring each room eerily to life. ⌧ *Maihaugvn 1,* ☎ *61/28–89–00.* ⌨ *NKr60.* ۞ *June–Aug., daily 9–7; May and Sept., daily 10–5; Oct.–Apr., Tues.– Sun. 11–4. Ticket includes guided tour.*

One of the most important art collections in Norway is housed at the **Lillehammer Kunstmuseum** (Lillehammer Art Museum). In addition to Munch pieces, the gallery has one of the largest collections of works from the national romantic period. ⌧ *Stortorgt. 2,* ☎ *61/26–94–44.* ⌨ *NKr30.* ۞ *June–Aug., Mon.–Thurs. 11–4, Fri.–Sun., 11–8; Sept.– May, Tues.–Sun. 11–4; call for hrs of guided tours.*

OFF THE BEATEN PATH **HUNDERFOSSEN PARK –** This amusement park takes pride in displaying the world's biggest troll, who sits atop a fairy-tale cave where carved-boulder trolls hold up the ceilings, and scenes from troll tales are depicted. There's a petting zoo for small children, plenty of rides, plus an energy center, with Epcot-like exhibits about oil and gas, and a five-screen theater. The park is 13 km (8 mi) north of Lillehammer. ⌧ *2638 Fåberg,* ☎ *61/27– 72–22.* ⌨ *NKr135.* ۞ *Early June–mid-Aug., daily 10–8.*

Dining and Lodging

When the world came to Lillehammer in 1994, not everyone could stay in downtown hotels. A delightful alternative is a farm stay, which many VIPs took advantage of during the Olympics. Many farms lie in the vicinity around Lillehammer, with a good number on the other side of Lake Mjøsa. For more information and a photo-packed brochure, call **Country Holidays in Troll Park** (⌧ Olympia Utvikling, ☎ 61/28– 99–70).

$$–$$$ ✕ **Lundegården Brasserie & Bar.** A piece of the Continent in the middle of Storgata, this restaurant is a haven where guests can enjoy a light snack in the bar area or a full meal. The menu offers such dishes as baked salmon with pepper-cream sauce and seasonal vegetables. The rattan furnishings in the bar and the starched white tablecloths in the dining room make for a pleasant interior. ✉ *Storgt. 108A,* ☎ *61/26–90–22. Reservations essential. AE, DC, MC, V. No lunch.*

$$–$$$ ✕ **Nikkers Spiseri.** The staff is service-minded at this classic Norwegian restaurant, which serves cakes, sandwiches, and hot dishes. Lunch specials and à la carte evening meals are offered. ✉ *Elvegt. 18,* ☎ *61/27–05–56. AE, DC, MC, V.*

$$–$$$ ▣ **Comfort Home Hotel Hammer.** This 1990s hotel is named after the original Hammer farm, which first opened its doors to guests in 1665. The rooms are decorated in shades of green with oak furniture, both modern and rustic. Waffles, coffee, light beer, and an evening meal are included in the price. ✉ *Storgt. 108, 2600,* ☎ *61/26–35–00,* 𝔽𝔸𝕏 *61/26–37–30. 71 rooms. Lobby lounge, sauna, meeting rooms. AE, DC, MC, V.*

$$–$$$ ▣ **Mølla Hotell.** A converted mill houses one of Lillehammer's newer hotels. The intimate reception area on the ground floor gives the feeling of a private home. The top-floor bar—called Toppen—has a good view of Mjøsa, the town, and the ski-jump arena. Downstairs is a cheaper eatery called Egon. ✉ *Elvegt. 12,* ☎ *61/26–92–94,* 𝔽𝔸𝕏 *61/26–92–95. 58 rooms. Bar, sauna, exercise room. AE, DC, MC, V.*

$$–$$$ ▣ **Rica Victoria Hotel.** This classic, centrally located hotel has small, relaxing rooms, some of which look out on the main street and the outdoor café it owns, Terassen. **Victoria Stuene,** the hotel's restaurant, is among Norway's best. ✉ *Storgt. 84b, 2600,* ☎ *61/25–00–49,* 𝔽𝔸𝕏 *61/25–24–74. 121 rooms. Lobby lounge, 2 restaurants, outdoor café, nightclub, meeting rooms, conference center. AE, DC, MC, V.*

$$ ▣ **Gjestehuset Ersgaard.** Dating from the 1500s, originally called Eiriksgård (Eirik's Farm), today this white manor house has all modern facilities but retains its homey atmosphere. The surroundings are beautiful, including views of Lillehammer and Lake Mjøsa, which can be enjoyed from the large terrace. ✉ *Nordseterun. 201 (at the Olympic Park),* ☎ *61/25–06–84,* 𝔽𝔸𝕏 *61/25–06–84. 30 rooms, 20 with bath. AE, DC, MC, V.*

$–$$ ▣ **Birkebeineren Hotel, Motell & Apartments.** Rooms are functional in these central accommodations. ✉ *Olympiaparken,* ☎ *61/26–47–00,* 𝔽𝔸𝕏 *61/26–47–50. 52 hotel rooms, 35 motel rooms, 40 apartments. Dining room, sauna. AE, DC, MC, V.*

$–$$ ▣ **Breiseth Hotell.** This friendly hotel is right beside the railroad station and within walking distance of shops and businesses. The Døla heimen Kafe serves hearty Norwegian meals. ✉ *Jernbanegt. 1–5,* ☎ *61/26–95–00,* 𝔽𝔸𝕏 *61/26–95–05. 89 rooms. Bar, brasserie, sauna. AE, DC, MC, V.*

Outdoor Activities and Sports

FISHING

Within the Troll Park, the **Gudbrandsdalåen** is touted as one of the best-stocked rivers in the country, and the size of Mjøsa trout (locals claim 25 pounds) is legendary. For seasons, permits (you'll need both a national and a local license), and tips, call local tourist boards (☞ Visitor Information *in* Interior A to Z, *below*).

RAFTING AND CANOEING

The **Sjoa River,** close to Lillehammer, offers some of the most challenging rapids in the country. Contact **Heidal Rafting** (☎ 61/23–60–37).

Lillehammer, the 1994 Winter Olympics town, is a major skiing center (20 km of alpine, 400 km of cross-country trails; 7 ski lifts). However, downtown Lillehammer is a good half-hour drive from most ski areas. If you want to ski right out the door of your hotel, call the tourist office to book a hotel by the slopes. Within the Lillehammer area, there are five ski centers: **Hafjell** (☎ 61/27–70–78), 10 km (6 mi) north, is an Olympic venue with moderately steep slopes; **Kvitfjell** (☎ 61/28–21–05), 50 km (31 mi) north, another Olympic site, has some of the most difficult slopes in the world; **Skei** and **Peer Gynt** (☞ *Skiing in* Gausdal, *below*), 30 km (19 mi) north and 80 km (50 mi) northwest, respectively; and **Galdhøpiggen Sommerskisenter** (☞ Skiing *in* Lom, *below*), 135 km (84 mi) northwest of Lillehammer. One ski-lift ticket, called a **Troll Pass** (☒ NKr175), is good for admission to all the lifts at all five sites.

Gausdal

56 *18 km (11 mi) northwest of Lillehammer.*

The composer of Norway's national anthem and the 1903 Nobel Prize winner in literature, Bjørnstjerne Bjørnson lived at **Aulestad,** in Gausdal, from 1875 until he died in 1910. After his wife, Karoline, died in 1934, their house was opened as a museum. ☒ *2620 Follebu,* ☎ *61/22–03–26.* ☒ *NKr30.* ☼ *Late May–Sept., daily 10–3:30.*

At Gausdal, just north of Lillehammer, you can turn onto the scenic, well-marked **Peer Gynt Vegen** (Peer Gynt Road), named for the real-life person behind Ibsen's character. A feisty fellow, given to tall tales, he is said to have spun yarns about his communing with trolls and riding reindeer backward. As you travel along the rolling hills sprinkled with old farmhouses and rich with views of the mountains of Rondane, Dovrefjell, and Jotunheimen, the road is only slightly narrower and just 3 km (2 mi) longer than the main route. It passes two major resorts, **Skeikampen/Gausdal** and **Golå/Wadahl,** before rejoining E6 at Vinstra. Between Vinstra and Harpefoss, at the Sødorp Church, you can visit Peer Gynt's stone grave and what is said to be his old farm. Although you can walk the grounds, the 15th-century farm is privately owned.

En Route The E6 highway passes through **Vinstra,** the village of Peer Gynt, where, around mid-August every year, the Peer Gynt Festival celebrates the character and his lore. The road continues along the great valley of the River Lågen, birthplace of *Gudbrandsdalsost,* a sweet brown goat cheese. From this road you'll see lovely, rolling views of red farmhouses and lush green fields stretching from the valley to the mountainsides.

Dining and Lodging

$$$ ✕☑ **Golå Høyfjellshotell og Hytter.** Tucked away in Peer Gynt terri-
★   tory north of Vinstra, this peaceful hotel is furnished in Norwegian country style. The restaurant has a simple menu of fresh local fish and game, which is elegantly prepared. ☒ *2646 Golå,* ☎ *61/29–81–09,* ☒ *61/29–85–40. 42 rooms. Restaurant, pool, downhill skiing, children's programs, meeting rooms. AE, DC, MC, V.*

Outdoor Activities and Sports

You can pick up maps and the information-packed **"Peer Gynt"** pamphlet at the tourism office in Vinstra; then hike anywhere along the 50-km (31-mi) circular route, passing Peer's farm, cottages, and monument. Overnighting in cabins or hotels is particularly popular on the

Peer Gynt Trail, where you can walk to each of the **Peer Gynt hotels.** (✉ Box 115, N–2647 Hundorp, ☎ 61/29–66–66, ℻ 61/29–66–88).

SKIING

Skei (☎ 61/22–85–55), near Gausdal, has both cross-country and alpine trails. **Peer Gynt** (☎ 61/29–85–28) has respectable downhill but is stronger as a cross-country venue. One ski-lift ticket, called a **Troll Pass** (💳 NKr175), is good for admission to lifts at five sites in the area (☞ Skiing *in* Lillehammer, *above*).

Lom

⑤⑦ *At Otta, Rte. 15 turns off for the 62-km (38-mi) drive to Lom.*

Lom, in the middle of Jotunheimen national park, is a picturesque, rustic town, with log-cabin architecture, a stave church from 1170, and plenty of decorative rosemaling.

Lom Stavkirke (Lom Stave Church), a mixture of old and new construction, is on the main road. The interior, including the pulpit, a large collection of paintings, pews, windows, and the gallery, is Baroque. ☎ 61/21–12–86. 💳 NKr20. ⊙ *June–Aug., daily 9–9.*

Dining and Lodging

$–$$ ✕🏠 **Fossheim Turisthotell.** Arne Brimi's cooking has made this hotel
★ famous. He's a self-taught champion of the local cuisine and now a household name in Norway; his dishes are based on nature's kitchen, with liberal use of game, wild mushrooms, and berries. Anything with reindeer is a treat in his hands, and his thin, crisp wafers with cloudberry parfait make a lovely dessert. ✉ 2686, ☎ 61/21–10–05, ℻ 61/21–15–10. 54 rooms. Restaurant, bar. AE, DC, MC, V.

$$ 🏠 **Vågå Hotel.** About halfway between Otta and Lom on Route 15, this homey, no-frills hotel lies in the lovely mountain village that hosts a number of hang-gliding competitions every summer. It's a good place to park for the night if you're skiing, hiking, or rafting the next day. ✉ 2680 Vågåmo, ☎ 61/23–70–71, ℻ 61/23–75–25. 60 rooms. Restaurant, bar, indoor pool, meeting rooms. AE, D, MC, V.

$ 🏠 **Elveseter Hotell.** There are many reasons to overnight at this unusually original hotel, including a swimming pool in a barn dating from 1579. About 24 km (15 mi) from Lom in Bøverdalen, this family-owned hotel feels like a museum: every room has a history, and doors and some walls have been painted by local artists. The public rooms are filled with museum-quality paintings and antiques. ✉ 2687 Bøverdalen, ☎ 61/21–20–00, ℻ 61/25–48–74. 100 rooms. 2 restaurants, bar, indoor pool, meeting rooms. AE, MC, V. Closed mid-Sept.–May.

Outdoor Activities and Sports

DOGSLEDDING

In Jotunheimen, Magnar Aasheim and Kari Steinaug (✉ Sjoa Rafting, ☎ 61/23–98–50) have one of the biggest kennels in Norway, with more than 30 dogs. You can travel as a sled-bound observer or control your own team of four to six dogs, most of which are ridiculously friendly Siberian and Alaskan huskies.

HIKING

In summer you can hike single-file (for safety purposes, in case of calving or cracks) on the ice and explore ice caves on the **Galdhøpiggen** glacier. Call Lom Fjellføring (☎ 61/21–21–42) or the tourist board (☞ *below*). For hikers with sturdy legs, there's a path along a mountain ridge overlooking Gjende lake that makes for a good day-long hike (it's a favorite with Norwegians). A boat will drop you at the path's starting point and you'll end up atop **Bessegen** in Jotunheimen. For information, call Våa Tourist Office (☞ *below*).

NATIONAL PARKS

In this region you'll find **Ormtjernkampen,** a virgin spruce forest, and **Jotunheimen,** a rougher area spiked with glaciers, as well as Norway's highest peak, the **Galdhøpiggen.**

SKIING

To the east of the Gudbrandsdalen is the **Troll-løype** (Troll Trail), 250 km of country trails that vein across a vast plateau that's bumped with mountains, including the Dovrefjells to the north. For information, contact the Otta Tourist Office (⊠ 2670 Otta, ☎ 61/23–02–44). **Beitostølen** (9 km [5 mi] of downhill slopes, 150 km [93 mi] of cross-country trails; 7 ski lifts), on the southern slopes of the Jotunheim range, has everything from torchlit night skiing to hang gliding. **Galdhøpiggen Sommerskisenter** (⊠ 2686 Bøverdalen, ☎ 61/21–21–42 or 61/21–17–50) sits on a glacier, which makes it great for summer skiing.

Lesja

58   *159 km (99 mi) from Lom.*

As you follow Route E6 towards Lesja, the broad, fertile valleys and snow-capped mountains of the Upper Gudbrandsdal provide staggering scenery for the drive. The area around Lesja is trout-fishing country; Lesjaskogvatnet, the lake, has a mouth at either end, so the current changes in the middle. The landscape becomes more dramatic with every mile as jagged rocks loom up from the river, leaving the tiny settlement of **Marstein** without sun for five months of the year.

OFF THE
BEATEN PATH

JORUNDGÅRD MIDDELALDER SENTER – Anyone who read Sigrid Undset's 1928 Nobel prize-winning trilogy, *Kristin Lavransdatter,* will remember that the tale's heroine grew up on a medieval farm of the same name. In 1996, the film actress Liv Ullmann directed a film based on the book a few feet away from where the story was said to have taken place. The authentic medieval farm she built now serves as Jorundgård Medieval Center, a historical and cultural museum. ⊠ Sel, ☎ 61/23-37-00 or 61/23-02-44. 🎫 NKr40, guided tours every ½ hr. ☉ June–mid-Sept., daily 10-6.

Outdoor Activities and Sports

GUIDED TOURS

From 1932 to 1953, musk ox were transported from Greenland to the Dovrefjell, where about 60 still roam—bring binoculars to see them. For information on safari-like tours, call the Dombås Tourist Office (☎ 61/24–14–44).

NATIONAL PARKS

The scrubby, flat, and wide **Rondane** to the southeast of Lesja, and **Dovrefjell,** peaked to the north, have some of the country's steepest mountains and are home to wild musk ox, reindeer, and birds.

Røros

59   *317 km (197 mi) from Lesja; 157 km (97 mi) from Trondheim.*

At the northern end of the Østerdal, the long valley to the east of Gudbrandsdalen, lies Røros. For more than 300 years practically everyone who lived in this one-company town was connected with the copper mines. Notice there are two main axes: one leading to the church, the other to the company. Since many of the early settlers were German engineers, Røros resembles more closely a crowded German *dorf* (hamlet or village) than it does a more spread-out Norwegian farm village. The last mine in the region closed in 1986, but the town has survived thanks to other industries, including tourism, especially after it was placed on UNESCO's World Heritage List.

Røros's main attraction is the **Old Town,** with its 250-year-old workers' cottages, slag dumps, and managers' houses, one of which is now City Hall. Descendants of the man who discovered the first copper ore in Røros still live in the oldest of the nearly 100 protected buildings. The tourist office has 75-minute guided tours of this part of town, starting at the information office and ending at the church. ☎ *NKr40.* ☉ *Tours early June and late Aug.–mid-Sept., Mon.–Sat. at 11; late June–mid-Aug., Mon.–Sat. at 10, noon, 1, 2, and 3, Sun. at 3; mid-Sept.–May, Sat. at 11.*

The **Røroskirke** (Røros Church), which rises above all the other buildings in the town, is an eight-sided stone structure from 1784 (the mines' symbol is on the tower). It can seat 1,600, quite surprising in a town with a population of only 3,500 today. The pulpit looms above the center of the altar, and seats encircle the top perimeter. Two hundred years ago wealthy locals paid for the privilege of sitting there. ☎ *72/41–00–00.* ☎ *NKr15.* ☉ *Early June and late Aug.–mid-Sept., weekdays 2–4, Sat. noon–2; mid-June–late Aug., Mon.–Sat. 10–5, Sun. 2–4; Oct.–May, Sat. noon–2.*

OFF THE
BEATEN PATH

OLAVSGRUVA – The guided tour of Olaf's Mine, a former copper mine outside town and now a museum, takes visitors into the depths of the earth, complete with sound-and-light effects. Remember to bring warm clothing and good shoes, as the temperature below ground is about 5°C (41°F) year-round. ☒ *Rte. 31,* ☎ *72/41–44–50.* ☎ *NKr45, guided tours early June and late Aug.–Sept., Mon.–Sat. at 1 and 3, Sun. at noon; late June–mid-Aug., daily at 10:30, noon, 1:30, 3, 4:30, and 6 (with entertainment program); Oct.–May, Sat. at 3.*

The **Rørosmuseet** (Røros Museum), in an old smelting plant, documents the history of the mines, with working models in one-tenth scale demonstrating the methods used in mining. ☎ *72/41–05–00.* ☎ *NKr45.*

Dining and Lodging

If you want to explore the green, pastured mountains just south of Røros, more than a dozen farm houses take overnight visitors. Some are hytter, but others, such as the **Vingelsgaard Gjestgiveri** (☎ 62/49–45–43), have entire wings devoted to guest rooms. Call **Vingeln Turistinformasjon** (☎ 62/49–46–65) for more information.

$$–$$$ ✕🍽 **Best Western Bergstadens Hotel.** The lobby here can be very inviting, especially when there's a fire in the stone fireplace. The main draw is the dining room: chef Lars Winther sticks to local traditions and products—fish from mountain streams and berries from the nearby forest. ☒ *Oslovn. 2, 7460,* ☎ *72/41–11–11,* FAX *72/41–01–55. 73 rooms, 2 suites. 2 restaurants, 2 bars, pool, sauna, nightclub, meeting rooms. AE, DC, MC, V.*

Outdoor Activities and Sports

SKIING

At the northern end of the Gubransdalen region, west of Røros, is **Oppdal** (45 km of alpine pistes, 186 km of cross-country trails; 10 ski lifts), a World Cup venue. Like most other areas, it has lighted trails and snow-making equipment.

Shopping

There are so many craftsmen in downtown Røros that the tourist office will arrange a tour of their workshops for those interested. In the mountains south of Røros, Aashilde Westgaard sells a smattering of antiques and junk from her farmhouse-boutique, **Skraphandlerbua** (⊠ 2542 Vingeln, ☎ 62/49–45–40). If you're planning to explore the area, ask the tourist bureau in Røros (☞ *below*) for directions to this odd and wonderful shop.

Interior Norway A to Z

Arriving and Departing

BY CAR

The wide, two-lane Route E6 north from Oslo passes through Hamar and Lillehammer. Route 3 follows Østerdalen (the eastern valley) from Oslo. Route 30 at Tynset leads to Røros and E6 on to Trondheim, 156 km (97 mi) farther north.

BY TRAIN

There are good train connections between Oslo and the major interior towns to the north. The region is served by the Oslo–Trondheim line and two other lines.

Getting Around

BY CAR

Roads in the north become increasingly hilly and twisty as the terrain roughens into the central mountains. The northern end of the region is threaded by E16, E6, and Routes 51 and 3. Don't speed: high-tech markers at the roadside, particularly prevalent in the area of Vinstra and Otta, are actually cameras. Exceed the speed limit and you'll receive a ticket in the mail.

Contacts and Resources

VISITOR INFORMATION

Gjøvik (⊠ Jernbanegt. 2, ☎ 61/17–16–88). **Golå** (⊠ Fjell og Fjord Ferie, DBC–Senteret, ☎ 32/07–45–44). **Hamar** (⊠ Vikingskipet, Olympia Hall, ☎ 62/51–02–17 or 62/51–02–25). **Lillehammer** (⊠ Lilletorget, ☎ 61/25–92–99). **Lom** (☎ 61/21–12–86). **Øyer** (☎ 61/27–70–00). **Røros** (⊠ Peder Hiortsgt. 2, ☎ 72/41–00–00). **Vågåmo** (⊠ Brennvegen 1, 2680, ☎ 61/'23–78–80).

THE WEST COAST: FJORD COUNTRY

This fjord-riddled coast, from south of Bergen to Kristiansund, is stippled with islands and grooved with deep barren valleys, with most of the fertile land edging the water. The farther north you travel, the more rugged and wild the landscape. The motionless Sognefjord is the longest inlet, snaking 190 km (110 mi) inland. It is 4,000 ft deep—a depth that often makes it appear black. Some of its sections are so narrow, with rock walls looming on either side, that they look as if they've been sliced from the mountains.

At the top of Sogn og Fjordane county is a succession of fjords referred to as Nordfjord, with Jostedalsbreen, mainland Europe's largest glacier, to the south. Sunnfjord is the coastal area between Nordfjord and Sognefjord, with Florø, the county seat, on an island close to Norway's westernmost point.

In the county of Møre og Romsdal, you'll see mountains that are treeless moonscapes of gray rock and stone cliffs that hang out over the water far below. Geirangerfjord is the most spectacular fjord, with a road zigzagging all the way down from the mountaintops to the water beside a famous waterfall.

There is more to the central region than fidgety coasts and peaks. In fact, tourists have been visiting central fjord country ever since the English "discovered" the area some 150 years ago in their search for the ultimate salmon. One of these tourists was Germany's Kaiser Wilhelm, who spent every summer except one, from 1890 to 1913, in Molde and helped rebuild Ålesund into one of the most fantastic fits of architectural invention in Scandinavia.

The best way to see the fjord country is to make an almost circular tour—from Oslo to Åndalsnes, out to the coastal towns of Ålesund, Molde, and Kristiansund, then over Trollstigveien to Geiranger, by ferry to Hellesylt, down to Stryn, around Loen and Olden and through the subglacial tunnel to Fjærland, and by ferry to Balestrand, connecting with another ferry down to Flåm, where the railroad connects with Myrdal on the Bergen line (*see* Fjord Tours *in* Bergen A to Z, *above*). Then the trip can either continue on to Bergen or back to Oslo.

While traveling, keep in mind that outside of some roadside snack bars and simple cafeterias, restaurants are few in fjord country. The majority of visitors dine at the hotels, where food is generally abundant and simple. Most feature a cold table at either lunch or dinner.

Åndalsnes

⑥⓪ *495 km (307 mi) from Bergen, 354 km (219 mi) from Trondheim.*

★ Åndalsnes, an industrial town of 3,000 people, has at least three things going for it: as the last stop on the railroad, it is a gateway to fjord country; Trollstigveien (Trolls' Path); and Trollveggen (Trolls' Wall).

From **Horgheimseidet,** which used to have a gingerbread hotel for elegant tourists—often European royalty—you can view **Trollveggen,** the highest sheer rock wall in Europe (3,300 ft). However, the hotel has been a private home for the past 50 years, and the tourists have been replaced by expert rock climbers from around the world.

Trollstigveien, one of Europe's most fantastic roads, starts in Åndalsnes. This road took 100 men 20 summers (from 1916 to 1936) to build, in a constant fight against rock and water. Trollstigveien and Ørneveien (at the Geiranger end) zigzag over the mountains separating two fjords. They're open only during the summer, but there's enough snow for skiing well into July. Trollstigveien has 11 giant hairpin turns, each one blasted from solid rock. Halfway up, the spray from **Stigfoss** (Path Falls) blows across the bridge.

Lodging

$$ ☎ **Grand Hotel Bellevue.** The cheery rooms have bright carpeting and old prints of the fjord decorating the walls. Most rooms have a view of either the mountains or the fjord. ⊠ *Åndalsgt. 5, 6300,* ☎ *71/22-10-11,* ℻ *71/22-60-38. 86 rooms. Restaurant, bar, meeting rooms. DC, MC, V.*

Ålesund

⑥① *240 km (150 mi) west of Åndalsnes.*

★ On three islands and between two bright blue fjords is Ålesund, home to 36,000 inhabitants and one of Norway's largest harbors for exporting dried and fresh fish. Nearly 800 buildings in the center of town were destroyed by fire in 1904, said to have been started by a tipped oil lamp. In the rush to shelter the 10,000 homeless victims, Kaiser Wilhelm II,

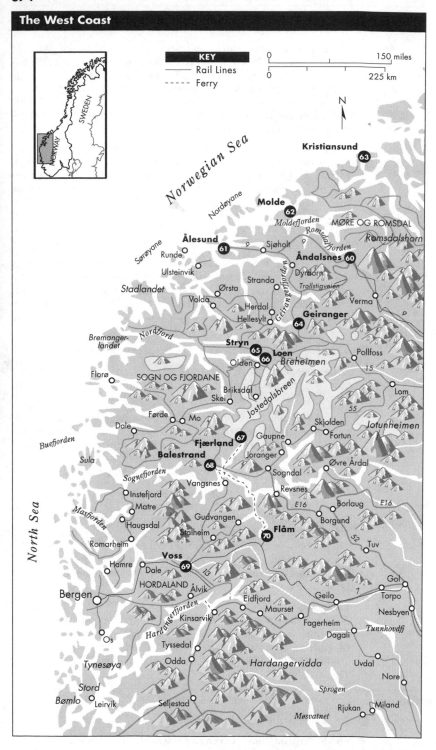

KEY
— Rail Lines
- - - - Ferry

0 — 150 miles
0 — 225 km

N

Norwegian Sea

Kristiansund 63

Nordøyane

Molde 62

Moldefjorden MØRE OG ROMSDAL

Romsdalsfjorden *Romsdalshorn*

Sjøholt 9

Sørøyane **Ålesund** 61 9

Runde **Åndalsnes** 60

Ulsteinvik Stranda Dyrdorn

Trollstigveien Verma

Stadlandet Ørsta

Volda Herdal

Hellesylt **Geiranger** 64

Geirangerfjorden

Bremanger-landet *Nordfjord* **Stryn** 65

Olden **Loen** 66 *Brèheimen* Pollfoss

Florø SOGN OG FJORDANE *Jostedalsbreen* Lom

Briksdal 15

Skei Skjolden *Jotunheimen*

Førde Mo Fortun 55

Dale Gaupne

Fjærland 67

B700fjorden Joranger Øvre Årdal

Balestrand 68 Sogndal

Sula Vangsnes Revsnes

Sognefjorden E16 Borlaug E16

Instefjord Borgund

Matre Gudvangen 52

Haugsdal Stalheim **Flåm** 70 Tuv

Romarheim **Voss** 69

Hamre Dale 13 Gol

HORDALAND Geilo Torpo

Bergen Ålvik 7 Nesbyen

Eidfjord Maurset

Os Kinsarvik Fagerheim *Tunnhovdfj*

North Sea *Hardangerfjorden* Dagali

Tyssedal

Tynesøya Odda *Hardangervidda* Uvdal

Stord Nore

Bømlo Leirvik *Sprogen*

Seljestad Rjukan Miland

Møsvatnet

who often vacationed there, led a mercurial rebuilding that married the German Art Nouveau with Viking roots—much of it carried out by an army of young, foreign-educated architects who threw in their own rabid flourishes. Delightfully, little has changed—except that many of the buildings are now painted in pastel colors, a practice thought too eccentric at the time. Winding streets are crammed with warehouses topped with turrets, spires, gables, dragonheads, and curlicues, all in a delirious spirit that's best seen while wandering behind the local dock to Kongensgate, the walking street. To get the most of what you see, try to join one of the tourist office's walking tours; they also put out an excellent descriptive brochure called "On Foot in Ålesund."

To learn more about what they call Jugendstil architecture, visit the exhaustive **Aalesunds Museum,** whose photographs, drawings, and models of the town before and after the fire will make you appreciate the disaster even more. ⊠ *R. Rønnebergsgt. 16,* ☎ *70/12–31–70.* ☑ *NKr 20.* ☺ *Mid-June–mid-Aug., weekdays 11–4, Sat. 11–3, Sun. noon–3; mid-Aug.–mid-June, Mon.–Sat. 11–3, Sun. noon–3.*

You can drive or take a bus (☎ 70/12–41–70) up nearby Aksla Mountain to a vantage point, **Kniven** (the knife), for a splendid view of the city—which absolutely glitters at night.

If you're traveling by car, you should consider a trip to the islands of **Giske.** A clump of round-topped, temperate islands off the Atlantic coast, they are each newly accessible by tunnel. If you go as far as Godøy in the summertime, stop at the **Alnes Lighthouse** (☎ 70/18–50–90), where owners Eva and Randi Alnes sell local handicrafts and cook delicious homemade fish soup, served with a croissant.

OFF THE BEATEN PATH

RUNDE – Norway's southernmost major bird rock, Runde, is near Ålesund. It's one of the largest in Europe and a breeding ground for some 130 species, including puffins, gannets, and shags. The island is otherwise known for the "Runde Hoard," 1,300 kilograms (2,860 pounds) of silver and gold coins retrieved from a Dutch ship that sank in 1725. A catamaran leaves from Skateflua quay for the 25-minute trip to Hareid, where it connects with a bus for the 50-km (31-mi) trip to Runde. A path leads from the bus stop to the nature reserve. It is also possible to sail around the rock on the yacht *Charming Ruth,* which leaves from Ulsteinvik at 11 on Wednesday and Sunday. Call the Runde tourist office (☞ Visitor Information *in* the West Coast A to Z, *below*) for more information.

Dining and Lodging

$$ ✗ **Fjellstua.** This mountaintop restaurant has tremendous views over the surrounding peaks, islands, and fjords. There are several different eating establishments here, but the main restaurant serves a variety of dishes and homemade desserts. ⊠ *Top of Aksla mountain,* ☎ *70/12–65–82. AE, DC, MC, V. Closed mid-Dec.–Feb.*

$$ ✗ **Gullix.** The decor is a bit much, with stone walls, plants hanging from the ceiling, musical instruments, and even the odd old-fashioned record player, but you can't fault the food, which ranges from sautéed monkfish garnished with shrimp, mussels, and crayfish to grilled, marinated filet mignon of lamb. ⊠ *Rådstugt. 5B,* ☎ *70/12–05–48. AE, DC, MC, V.*

$$ ✗ **Sjøbua.** Pick your own lobster from the large tank at one of Norway's most renowned restaurants. The mixed fish and shellfish platter is the most popular dish on the menu. The lobster soup is excellent, too, but leave room for the raspberry ice cream with nougat sauce. ⊠ *Brunholmgt. 1,* ☎ *70/12–71–00. AE, DC, MC, V. Closed Sun.*

$ ✗ **Brosundet Cafe.** This coffee shop in Hotel Atlantica has its own bak-
★ ery, so there are always homemade bread and rolls. You can order anything from bløtkake or the ever-so-popular *nøttekake* (nut cake) to pepper
steak. ⊠ *R. Rønnebergsgt. 4,* ☎ *70/12–91–00. Reservations not accepted. AE, DC, MC, V.*

$$–$$$ ⌸ **Rainbow Hotel Atlantica.** Reproduction Van Gogh prints hang on
the brightly colored walls of this hotel's cheery guest rooms. A view
of the fjord will cost you more, but potted plants and the classic blue-,
green-, and yellow-upholstered wood furniture give the rooms a homey
feel. ⊠ *R. Rønnebergsgt. 4, 6004,* ☎ *70/12–91–00,* ⑆ *70/12–62–52.
52 rooms. Restaurant, café. AE, DC, MC, V.*

$$ ⌸ **Comfort Home Hotel Bryggen.** This hotel, with stone walls and
glassed-in atria, is housed in a converted turn-of-the-century fish ware-
house. Strewn with wooden oars, life vests, and fishing tools, the lobby
gives a glimpse on the importance of fishing to Ålesund. A light evening
buffet is included in the room price, and waffles and coffee are always
available. Fishing equipment is available; although Bryggen is on the
water, anglers are advised to go farther afield for a better catch. ⊠
Apotekergt. 1–3, 6021, ☎ *70/12–64–00,* ⑆ *70/12–11–80. 85 rooms.
Sauna, Turkish bath, fishing, meeting rooms. AE, DC, MC, V.*

$$ ⌸ **Quality Scandinavie Hotel.** The impressive building with towers and
★ arches dates from 1905, whereas most rooms are modern and beauti-
fully decorated in shades of blue, peach, and green with reproduction
Biedermeier furniture (be sure to ask for a renovated room). Some decorative textiles pay a token tribute to Art Nouveau. ⊠ *Løvenvoldgt.
8, 6002,* ☎ *70/12–31–31,* ⑆ *70/13–23–70. 65 rooms. Restaurant, bar,
pizzeria, meeting rooms. AE, DC, MC, V.*

$$ ⌸ **Scandic Hotel.** This large, postmodern building complex stands
next to the Exhibition Hall. Its interior design has a maritime theme.
The rooms are spacious. ⊠ *Molovn. 6, 6004,* ☎ *70/12–81–00,* ⑆ *70/
12–92–10. 117 rooms, 6 suites. Restaurant, bar, indoor pool, sauna.
AE, DC, MC, V.*

Molde

㊷ *69 km (43 mi) north of Ålesund on Route 668.*

During World War II the German air force suspected that King Haakon
VII was staying in a red house here and bombed every red house in
town. These days, Molde is a modern town, after being almost entirely
rebuilt. The best time to come is during the town's annual jazz festi-
val in late July. Big names from around the world gather for a huge
jam session. Tickets for the fest, where acts like Bob Dylan, Dizzy Gilles-
pie, Miles Davis, and Al Jarreau have performed in the past, can be
purchased at all post offices in Norway.

If you like to walk, take the footpath that leads uphill to the charm-
ing **Romsdalsmuseet** (Romsdal Open-Air Museum). The path begins
on Storgata near the Alexandra Hotel at the King's Birch Tree, named
after the place where the king and crown prince were sheltered dur-
ing the war. On the way to the museum, stop at Reknes Park for a view
of the 222 mountain peaks on the other side of the Romdalsfjord. Cos-
tumed tour guides will lead you through the open air museum's 40 grass-
roofed farm houses and churches dating back to the 14th century. ⊠
Museumsvn. 14, ☎ *71/25–25–34.* ☉ *Early June and late Aug., Mon.–
Sat. 10–2, Sun. noon–3; mid-June–mid-Aug., Mon.–Sat. 10–6, Sun.
noon–6.*

Dining and Lodging

$$–$$$ ✕🏨 **First Hotel Alexandra Molde.** Named after Britain's Princess
★ Alexandra of Wales, who stayed here in the 1880s, this hotel drew royal
visitors from cruise ships as well as Norwegian literary men, such as
Ibsen and Bjørnson. Spisestuen, the restaurant of this premier hotel,
is worth a special trip. Kåre Monsås prepares such dishes as pepper-
marinated veal fillet. The rooms, many of which overlook the water,
are nondescript, with dark-brown wood furniture and textiles in shades
of blue. ⊠ *Storgt. 1–7, 6400,* ☎ *71/25–11–33,* 𝖥𝖠𝖷 *71/21–66–35. 150
rooms, 11 suites. 2 restaurants, bar, sauna, indoor pool, exercise room,
meeting rooms. AE, DC, MC, V.*

Kristiansund

🖎 *68 km (42 mi) north of Molde on Route 64.*

This town was spared the destruction of its historic harbor, Vågen, during World War II. Many buildings in Kristiansund—which celebrated
its 250th birthday in 1992—are well preserved, including **Woldbrygga,**
a cooper's (barrel maker's) workshop from 1875 to 1965, with its original equipment still operational. ⊠ *Dalevn. 17,* ☎ *71/67–15–78.* 🖎
NKr25. ◷ *Tues.–Fri. 10–2, Sun. noon–3.*

For many years, Kristiansund derived its identity from its unique process of drying cod: on cliffs by the ocean. Called "klippfish," the dried
cod then got shipped all over the world for consumption—especially
to Portugal, where it became the main ingredient in the Portuguese dish
bacalao. Housed in an 18th-century warehouse, **Milnbrygge,** the Norwegian Klippfish Museum, pays tribute to the process and the history
of the klippfish industry—fishy smells and all. ⊠ *Kristiansund Harbor,* ☎ *71/58–63–80 tourist information.* 🖎 *Nkr 25.* ◷ *Mid-June–mid-
Aug, Mon.–Sat. noon–5, Sun. 1–4.*

Dining and Lodging

$$–$$$ ✕ **Smia Fiskerestaurant.** Dishes like fishballs and whale peppersteak
are available here, but the decidedly Mediterranean-tasting dish—bacalao—is strangely part of local culture. Built inside an 18th-century
red smithy, the place is decorated with hanging fishnets, Spanish wine
bottles, and vintage klippfish tins. ⊠ *Fosnagt. 30B,* ☎ *71/67–11–70.
AE, DC, MC, V.*

$$–$$$ 🏨 **Hotel Fosna Atlantica.** Ask for a room with a harbor view in this wa-
terfront hotel. It's not as snazzy as the Rica down the street, but it has
more character, with an outdoor café, a mahogany-interiored British-
style pub, and a white marble lobby. Rooms vary widely in size. ⊠ *Hauggt.
16, 6501,* ☎ *71/67–40–11,* 𝖥𝖠𝖷 *71/67–76–59. 50 rooms. Outdoor café,
piano bar, pub, nightclub, meeting rooms. AE, DC, MC, V.*

Geiranger

🖎 *85 km (52½ mi) southwest of Åndalsnes, 413 km (256 mi) from
Bergen.*

★ Geiranger is the ultimate fjord, Norway at its most dramatic, with the
finest sightseeing in the wildest nature compressed into a relatively small
area. The mountains lining the Geiranger Fjord tower 6,600 ft above
sea level. The most scenic route to Geiranger is the two-hour drive along
Route 63 over Trollstigveien from Åndalsnes (☞ *above*). Once you are
there, the Ørneveien (Eagles' Road) down to Geiranger, completed in
1952 with 11 hairpin turns, leads directly to the fjord.

The 16-km-long (10-mi-long), 960-ft-deep Geirangerfjord's best-known
attractions are its waterfalls—the Seven Sisters, the Bridal Veil, and the

Suitor—and the abandoned farms at **Skageflå** and **Knivsflå,** which are visible (and accessible) only by boat (☞ Guided Tours, *below*). Perhaps the inhabitants left because provisions had to be carried from the boats straight up to Skageflå—a backbreaking 800 ft.

Lodging

$$$ 🏨 **Union Hotel.** This family-owned hotel is more than 100 years old. The old building was torn down, but the present hotel is a tribute to the old style. It is modern and comfortable, with lots of windows facing the view, and light-colored furniture in the rooms, which are relatively large. ⊠ *6216,* ☎ *70/26–30–00,* ㎰ *70/26–31–61. 155 rooms, 13 suites. Restaurant, bar, indoor pool, steam room, nightclub. AE, DC, MC, V.*

$ 🏨 **Grande Fjord Hotell.** Idyllically set at the edge of the fjord, this small hotel complex has more charm than the big hotels in the area. The rooms are simple and comfy. ⊠ *6216,* ☎ *70/26–30–90,* ㎰ *70/26–31–77. 48 rooms, 18 cabins. Restaurant, bar, boating, fishing. MC, V.*

Stryn

65 *If you continue on to Stryn from Geiranger, take the ferry across the Geiranger Fjord to Hellesylt, a 75-minute ride. It's about 50 km (30 mi) from Hellesylt to Stryn on Rte. 60.*

Stryn, Loen, and Olden, at the eastern end of Nordfjord, were among the first tourist destinations in the region more than 100 years ago. Stryn is famous for its salmon river and summer ski center—**Stryn Sommerskisenter** (⊠ 6880 Stryn, ☎ 57/87–19–95).

OFF THE   **BRIKSDALSBREEN** – This is the most accessible arm of the Jostedal
BEATEN PATH   glacier. Drive along the mountain road or take a bus (from Olden, Loen, or Stryn) to Briksdal. From here, the glacier is a 45-minute walk from the end of the road, or you can ride there with pony and trap, as tourists did 100 years ago. Local guides lead tours (☞ Guided Tours, *below*) over the safe parts of the glacier. These perennial ice masses are more treacherous than they look, for there's always the danger of calving (breaking off), and deep crevasses are not always visible.

Lodging

$$$ 🏨 **Kong Oscar's Hall.** Mike and Møyfrid Walston have brought back to life a derelict but magnificent hotel from the heyday of the dragon style, 1896, complete with a tower with dragonheads on the eaves. The Great Hall gives new meaning to the word *great,* and the number of royal guests, both present and past, is impressive. ⊠ *6880,* ☎ ㎰ *57/ 87–19–53. 5 suites. Restaurant. No credit cards. Closed Sept.–Apr.*

Shopping

Strynefjell Draktverkstad (⊠ 6890 Oppstryn, ☎ 57/87–72–20) specializes in stylish knickers, trousers, and skirts made of heavy wool. It's a 10-minute drive east of Stryn on Route 15.

Loen

66 *10 km (6 mi) southeast of Stryn.*

Loen and Olden are starting points for expeditions to branches of Europe's largest glacier, Jostedalsbreen. Hovering over the entire inner Nordfjord and Sognefjord regions, this glacier covers 800 square km (309 square mi). In geological time, this 5,000-year-old glacier is relatively young. The ice is in constant motion, crawling as much as 2 km (1¼ mi) a day in certain places.

OFF THE
BEATEN PATH **KJENNDALSBREEN FJELLSTOVE** – It's possible to visit the Kjenndal arm of the glacier on the *M/B Kjendal,* which departs from Sande, near Loen. It sails down the 14-km (9-mi) arm of the lake under mountains covered by protruding glacier arms and past Ramnefjell (Ramne Mountain), scarred by rock slides, to Kjenndalsbreen Fjellstove. A bus runs between the Alexandra lodge (☞ *below*) and the glacier.

Dining and Lodging

$$$ ✕▨ **Alexandra.** The building that houses Alexandra looks more like
★ a huge white hospital than a hotel. English and German tourists stayed here over 100 years ago. Even though the original dragon-style building exists only in pictures in the lobby, it is still the most luxurious hotel around. The facilities are first-rate, but the food, prepared by chef Wenche Loen, is the best part—the trout is outstanding. ⊠ *6878 Loen* ☎ *57/87–50–00,* FAX *57/87–77–70. 193 rooms. 2 restaurants, bar, indoor pool, tennis courts, exercise room, boating, nightclub, convention center. AE, DC, MC, V.*

Fjærland

67 *From Olden it's 62 km (37 mi) of easy, though not particularly inspiring, terrain to Skei, at the base of Lake Jølster, where the road goes under the glacier for more than 6 km (4 mi) of the journey to Fjærland.*

Fjærland, until 1986, was without road connections altogether. In 1991 the **Norsk Bremuseum** (Norwegian Glacier Museum) opened just north of Fjærland. It has a huge screen on which a film about glacier trekking plays and a fiberglass glacial maze, complete with special effects courtesy of the *Star Wars* movies' set designer. ☎ *57/69–32–88.* ▨ *NKr60.* ☉ *June–Aug., daily 9–7; Apr.–May and Sept.–Oct., daily 10–4.*

OFF THE
BEATEN PATH **ASTRUPTUNET** – Halfway across the southern shore of Lake Jølster (about a 10-minute detour from the road to Fjærland) is Astruptunet, the farm of artist Nicolai Astrup (1880–1928). The best of his primitive, mystical paintings sell in the $500,000 range, ranking him among the most popular Norwegian artists. His home and studio are in a cluster of small turf-roofed buildings on a steep hill overlooking the lake. ☎ *57/72–67–82 or 57/72–81–05.* ▨ *NKr50.* ☉ *July, daily 10–8; late May–June and Aug.–early Sept., Tues.–Sun. 10–5.*

Dining and Lodging

$$–$$$ ✕▨ **Hotel Mundal.** This small, old-fashioned yellow-and-white gingerbread hotel opened in 1891. All rooms are individually and simply decorated. The dining room looks rather dreary, but the food is good. ⊠ *5855,* ☎ *57/69–31–01,* FAX *57/69–31–79. 35 rooms. Restaurant, bar, meeting rooms. DC, V. Closed mid-Sept.–mid-May.*

Shopping
Audhild Vikens Vevstove (⊠ Skei, ☎ 57/72–81–25) specializes in the handicrafts, particularly woven textiles.

Balestrand

68 *30 km (18½ mi) up the fjord by ferry, 204 km (126 mi) by car to Fjærland.*

Fjærland is now connected to Sogndal by tunnel (up until 1997 it was only accessible by ferry). Balestrand is on the southern bank of **Sognefjord,** one of the longest and deepest fjords in the world, snaking 200 km (136 mi) into the heart of the country. Along its wide banks are some of Norway's best fruit farms, with fertile soil and lush vegetation (the fruit blossoms in May are spectacular). Ferries are the lifeline of the region.

Lodging

$$ ⊞ **Kvikne's Hotel.** This huge, wooden gingerbread house at the edge of
★ the Sognefjord has been a landmark since 1913. It is fjord country's most elaborate old hotel, with rows of open porches and balustrades. The rooms in the old section have personality, but the view is the best part. This spot also has good swimming, hiking, rowing, and fishing possibilities. ⊠ *5850, Balholm,* ☎ *57/69–11–01,* 𝔽𝔸𝕏 *57/69–15–02. 190 rooms. Restaurant, exercise room, fishing, nightclub. AE, DC, MC, V.*

Voss

69 *80 km (50 mi) south of Vangsnes.*

Voss is the birthplace of American football hero Knut Rockne and a good place to stay the night, either in the town itself or 36 km (23 mi) away at Stalheim. The road to Stalheim, an old resort, has 13 hairpin turns in one 1½-km (1-mi) stretch of road that can be almost dizzying—it's 1,800 ft straight down—but well worth the trip for the view. Voss is connected with Oslo and Bergen by train and by roads (some sections are narrow and steep).

Lodging

$$$–$$$$ ⊞ **Stalheim Hotel.** A large, rectangular building, much like other Norwegian resort hotels, the grand Stalheim has been painted dark red and blends into the scenery better than most other hotels. It has an extensive collection of Norwegian antiques and even its own open-air museum, with 30 houses. The view from the large stone terrace is stunning. ⊠ *5715 Voss,* ☎ *56/52–01–22,* 𝔽𝔸𝕏 *56/52–00–56. 127 rooms, 3 suites. 2 restaurants, bar, fishing. AE, DC, MC, V.*

$$ ⊞ **Fleischers Hotel.** The modern addition along the front detracts from the turreted and gabled charm of this old hotel. Inside, the old style has been well maintained, particularly in the restaurant. The rooms in the old section are pleasantly old-fashioned; in the rebuilt section (1993) they are modern and inviting. There is also a children's playroom. The motel section has apartments as well. ⊠ *Evangervegen 13, 5700,* ☎ *56/51–11–55,* 𝔽𝔸𝕏 *56/51–22–89. 90 rooms, 30 apartments. Restaurant, bar, indoor pool, hot tub, sauna, tennis court, nightclub. AE, DC, MC, V.*

Outdoor Activities and Sports

HIKING
Walks and hikes are especially rewarding in this region, with spectacular mountain and water views everywhere. Be prepared for abrupt weather changes in spring and fall. Voss is a starting point for mountain hikes in Slølsheimen, Vikafjell, and the surrounding mountains. Contact the Voss Tourist Board (☞ *below*) for tips.

RAFTING
For rafting in Dagali or Voss, contact **Dagali-Voss Rafting** (⊠ Dagali Hotel, ☎ 32/09–38–20) for information on organized trips.

SKIING
Voss (40 km of alpine slopes; 1 cable car, 8 ski lifts; 8 illuminated and 2 marked cross-country trails) is an important alpine skiing center in Norway, although it doesn't have the attractions or traditions of some of its resort neighbors to the east. The area includes several schools and interconnecting lifts that will get you from run to run. Call the Voss Tourist Board (☞ *below*) for details.

passengers for points not served by the train. The 124-km (76-mi) trip to Ålesund takes close to two hours.

Getting Around

BY BOAT

In addition to regular ferries to nearby islands, boats connect Ålesund with other points along the coast. Excursions by boat are available through the tourist office.

BY BUS

Bus routes are extensive. The tourist office has information about do-it-yourself tours by bus to the outlying districts. Three local bus companies serve Ålesund; all buses depart from the terminal on Kaiser Wilhelms Gate.

BY CAR

Ferries are a way of life in western Norway, but they are seldom big enough or don't run often enough during the summer, causing built-in delays. Considerable hassle can be eliminated by reserving ahead, as cars with reservations board first. Call the tourist office of the area where you will be traveling for ferry information (☞ Visitor Information, *below*).

Contacts and Resources

EMERGENCIES

Hospital Emergency Rooms/Doctors/Dentists: ☎ 70/12–33–48. **Car Rescue:** ☎ 70/14–18–33.

GUIDED TOURS

Cruises: The M/S *Geirangerfjord* (☎ 70/26–30–07) offers 90-minute guided minicruises on the Geirangerfjord. Tickets are sold at the dock in Geiranger. ✉ NKr67. ☉ June–Aug. *Tours at 10, noon, 2, and 5; late June–mid-Aug., additional tour at 3:30.*

Flying: Firdafly A/S (☎ 57/86–53–88), based in Sandane, has air tours over Jostedalsbreen. Hotel Alexandra in Loen (☞ *above*) arranges group flights.

Glacier: From Easter through September, **Jostedalen Breførlag** (✉ 5828 Gjerde, ☎ 57/68–32–84) offers glacier tours, from an easy 1½-hour family trip on the Nigard branch (equipment is provided) to advanced glacier courses with rock and ice climbing.

Hiking: Aak Fjellsportsenter (☎ 71/22–71–00) in Åndalsnes specializes in walking tours of the area, from rambling in the hills for beginners and hikers to full-fledged rock climbing, along with rafting on the Rauma River. These are the guys who hang out of helicopters to rescue injured climbers, so they know what they're doing.

Orientation: A 1½-hour guided stroll through Ålesund, concentrating mostly on the Art Nouveau buildings, departs from the tourist information center (Rådhuset) Saturday, Tuesday, and Thursday at 1 PM from mid-June to late August. ✉ NKr45.

LATE-NIGHT PHARMACIES

Nordstjernen (✉ Kaiser Wilhelms Gate 22, Ålesund, ☎ 70/12–59–45) is open weekdays from 9 AM to 4:30 PM, Wednesday until 6 PM, and Saturday until 2 PM. Sunday hours are from 6 PM to 8 PM.

VISITOR INFORMATION

Ålesund (✉ Rådhuset, ☎ 70/12–12–02). **Åndalsnes** (✉ Corner Nesgt. and Romsdalsvn., ☎ 71/22–16–22). **Balestrand** (✉ Dockside, ☎ 57/69–12–55). **Flåm** (✉ Railroad station, ☎ 57/63–21–06). **Geiranger** (✉ Dockside, ☎ 70/26–30–99). **Hellesylt** (✉ Dockside, ☎ 70/26–50–52).

Flåm

⑦ *131 km (81 mi) from Voss.*

One of the most scenic train routes in Europe zooms from Myrdal, hig into the mountains and down to the quaint town of Flåm. Flåm's wa terfront is swamped with day-trippers who stream off of the train a noon, have lunch in a cafeteria, and sweep out of town at about 3. Afte they leave, a wonderful stillness descends and Flåm becomes a won derful place to spend the night.

OFF THE
BEATEN PATH

MYRDAL – It's possible to ride a ferry from Balestrand to Flåm, from which you can make Norway's most exciting railway journey to Myrdal. Only 20 km (12 mi) long, it takes 40 minutes to travel 2,850 ft up a steep mountain gorge and 53 minutes to go down, with one stop for photos each way. Don't worry about the brakes. The train has five separate systems, any one of which is able to stop it. A masterpiece of engineering, the line includes 20 tunnels. From Flåm it is also an easy drive back to Oslo on E16 along the Lærdal River, one of Norway's most famous salmon streams and King Harald's favorite.

Lodging

$$ 🚹 **Fretheim Hotell.** With the fjord in front and mountains in back, the setting is perfect. The hotel is anonymous, white, and functional. The inside has comfy lounges and rooms decorated in a Norwegian folk style. ⊠ *5743,* ☎ *57/63–22–00,* 🖷 *57/63–23–03. 56 rooms, 28 with shared bath. 2 restaurants, bar, fishing. AE, MC, V.*

The West Coast A to Z

Arriving and Departing

BY BOAT

The **Hurtigruten** (the coastal steamer) stops at Skansekaia in **Ålesund,** northbound at noon, departing at 3, and stops southbound at midnight, departing at 1. A catamaran runs between Ålesund and Molde at least twice daily.

BY CAR

From Oslo, it is 450 km (295 mi) on Route E6 to Dombås and then Route 9 through Åndalsnes to Ålesund. The well-maintained two-lane road runs inland to Åndalsnes and then follows the coastline out to Ålesund.

The 380-km (235-mi) drive from Bergen to Ålesund covers some of the most breathtaking scenery in the world. Roads are narrow two-lane ventures much of the time; passing is difficult, and in summer traffic can be heavy.

BY PLANE

Ålesund's **Vigra Airport** is 15 km (9 mi) from the center of town. **Braathens SAFE** (☎ 81/00–05–55, Ålesund; ☎ 70/18–32–45, Vigra) has nonstop flights from Oslo, Bergen, Trondheim, and Bodø.

Between the Airport and Downtown: It's a 25-minute ride from Vigra to town with Flybussen. Tickets cost NKr50. Buses are scheduled according to flights—they leave the airport about 10 minutes after all arrivals and leave town about 60 or 70 minutes before each departure.

BY TRAIN

The **Dovrebanen** and **Raumabanen** between Oslo S Station and Åndalsnes via Dombås run three times daily in each direction for the 6½-hour ride. At Åndalsnes, buses wait outside the station to pick up

Lærdal (☎ 57/66–65–09). **Molde** (✉ Storgt 1, ☎ 71/21–92–62). **Sogndal** (☎ 57/67–30–83). **Runde** (☎ 70/08–59–96). **Stryn** (☎ 57/87–23–32). **Ulvik** (✉ Dockside, ☎ 56/52–63–60). **Voss** (☎ 56/51–00–51). **Fjord Norway** (☎ 55/31–93–00) in Bergen is a clearinghouse for information on all of western Norway.

TRONDHEIM TO THE NORTH CAPE

The coast of northern Norway fidgets up from Trondheim, scattering thousands of islands and skerries along the way, until it reaches the northernmost point of Europe. Then it continues even farther, straggling above Sweden and Finland to point a finger of land into Russia.

Long and thin, this area covers an astonishing variety of land- and cityscapes, from bustling Trondheim to elegant Tromsø. Some areas, especially when seen from the deck of the mail boats, seem like endless miles of wilderness marked by an occasional dot—a lonely cabin or a herd of reindeer. Views are often exquisite: glaciers, fjords, rocky coasts, and celestial displays of the midnight sun in summer and northern lights (aurora borealis) in winter.

Nordkapp (North Cape) has a character that changes with the seasons. In summer it teems with visitors and tour buses, and in winter, under several feet of snow, it is bleak, subtle, and astonishingly beautiful. It is accessible then only by squealing Sno-Cat snowmobile, a bracing and thoroughly Norwegian adventure.

Keep in mind while traveling, as in the rest of provincial Norway, that most better restaurants are in hotels. If you visit northern Norway between May and August, try the specialty of *måsegg* and *Mack-øl*, more for curiosity value than for taste. *Måsegg* (seagulls' eggs) are always served hard-boiled and halved in their shells. They're larger than chicken eggs, and they look exotic, with greenish-gray speckled shells and bright orange yolks, but they taste like standard supermarket eggs. *Mack-øl* (similar to pils) is brewed in Tromsø at the world's northernmost brewery.

Trondheim

🕖 *496 km (307½ mi) north of Oslo, 744 km (461 mi) from Bergen.*

Trondheim's original name, Nidaros (still the name of the cathedral), is a composite word referring to the city's location at the mouth of the Nid River. After a savage fire in 1681, the wooden town was rebuilt according to the plan of General Cicignon, a military man from Luxembourg, who also designed Trondheim's fort. The wide streets of the city center are still lined with brightly painted wooden houses and picturesque warehouses.

The Tiffany windows are magnificent at the **Nordenfjeldske Kunstindustrimuseum** (Decorative Arts Museum), which houses one of the finest art collections in Scandinavia. It has superb period rooms from the Renaissance to 1950s Scandinavian modern. ✉ *Munkegt. 5*, ☎ *73/52–13–11.* 🎫 *NKr30.* ☉ *June–late Aug., weekdays 10–5, Sun. noon–5; late Aug.–May, weekdays 10–3, Thurs. until 7, Sun. noon–4.*

Saint Olav, who formulated a Christian religious code for Norway in 1024 while he was king, was killed in battle against local chieftains at Stiklestad. After he was buried, water sprang from his grave and people began to believe that his nails and hair continued to grow beneath the ground. It is here on the grave of Saint Olav that **Nidaros Domkirke** (Nidaros Cathedral) was built. Following a series of other miracles,

Trondheim and the North

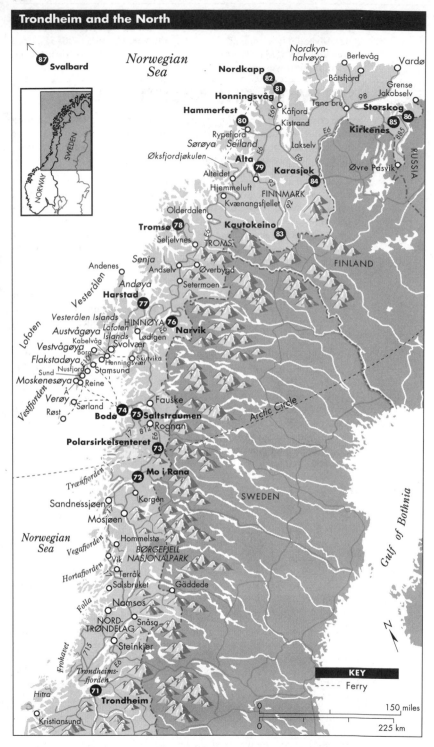

Norwegian Sea

87 Svalbard

SWEDEN

NORWAY

Nordkyn-halvøya
Berlevåg
Vardø

Nordkapp
82
Båtsfjord
81
Honningsvåg
Tana bru
98
Grense Jakobselv
Hammerfest
Kåfjord
E69
Storskog
80
Kistrand
E6
85
86
Rypefjord
Kirkenes
Sørøya *Seiland*
Lakselv
E6
Øksfjordjøkulen
Alta
79
Karasjok
RUSSIA
Alteidet
E6
Øvre Pasvik
Hjemmeluft
93
84
Kvænangsfjellet
FINNMARK
62
Olderdalen
Tromsø 78
Kautokeino
Seljelvnes
83
TROMS
Andenes
Senja
FINLAND
Andselv
Øverbygd
Vesterålen
Andøya
Setermoen
Harstad
77
Lofoten
Vesterålen Islands
HINNØYA 76
Austvågøya
Lofoten Islands
E6
Narvik
Kabelvåg
Lødigen
Vestvågøya
Svolvær
Borg
Flakstadøya
Henningsvær
Skutvika
Sund Nusfjord Stamsund
Moskenesøya Reine
Å
Verøy Sørland
Fauske
Røst
Bodø
74
75 **Saltstraumen**
Bodø
E6
Rognan
17 812
Vestfjorden
Polarsirkelsenteret
73
Arctic Circle
Trænfjorden
72 **Mo i Rana**
Sandnessjøen
Korgen
SWEDEN
Mosjøen
Gulf of Bothnia
Norwegian Sea
Hommelstø
Vegafjorden
BØRGEFJELL NASJONALPARK
Vik
Hortafjorden
Terråk
Salsbruket
Gäddede
Folla
Namsos
NORD-TRØNDELAG
Snåsa
715
Steinkjer
Frohavet
Trondheims-fjorden
E6
Hitra
71
Trondheim
Kristiansund

KEY
- - - - Ferry

0 _____ 150 miles
0 _____ 225 km

the town became a pilgrimage site for the Christians of northern Europe, and Olav was canonized in 1164.

Although construction was begun in 1070, the oldest existing parts of the cathedral date from around 1150. During the Catholic period (circa 1000–1537) it attracted crowds of pilgrims, but after the Reformation its importance declined and fires destroyed much of it. The crown jewels, which visitors can view, are still kept in the cathedral. Guided tours are offered in English mid-June to mid-August, weekdays at 11, 2, and 4. ⊠ *Kongsgårdsgt. 2,* ☎ *73/52–52–33.* ☜ *NKr20. Ticket also permits entry to Erkebispegården (☞ below).* ⊘ *Mid-June–mid-Aug., weekdays 9–6:15, Sat. 9–2, Sun. 1–4; May–mid-June and mid-Aug.–mid-Sept., weekdays 9–3, Sat. 9–2, Sun. 1–4; mid-Sept.–mid-Apr., weekdays noon–2:30, Sat. 11–2, Sun. 1–3.*

Scandinavia's oldest secular building (actually two buildings connected by a gatehouse) is the **Erkebispegården** (Archbishop's Palace). Dating from around 1160, it was the residence of the archbishop until the Reformation. After that, it was a Danish governor's palace and later a military headquarters.

Within the Erkebispegården is the **Forsvarsmuseet** (Army Museum), with displays of uniforms, swords, and daggers. The **Hjemmefrontmuseet** (Resistance Museum), also there, documents the occupation of Norway during World War II through objects and photographs. *Archbishop's Palace:* ☎ *73/50–12–12.* ☜ *NKr20. Ticket also permits entry to cathedral.* ⊘ *June–Aug., weekdays 9–3, Sat. 9–2, Sun. 12:30–3:30. Army and Resistance museums:* ☎ *73/99–59–97.* ☜ *NKr5.* ⊘ *June–Aug., weekdays 10–3; year-round, weekends 11–3.*

Behind the **Biblioteket** (Library, ⊠ Peter Egges Pl. 1) you can see the **remains of St. Olavskirke** (St. Olav's Church). The crypt of another medieval church can be seen inside Trondhjems og Strindens Sparebank (a savings bank at Søndregate 2) during normal banking hours.

Scandinavia's largest wooden building, **Stiftsgården,** was built in 1778 as a private home, the result of a competition between two sisters who were trying to outdo each other with the size of their houses. Today it is the king's official residence in Trondheim. The interior is sparsely furnished. ⊠ *Munkegt. 23,* ☎ *73/52–13–11.* ☜ *NKr30.* ⊘ *June–mid-June, Tues.–Sat. 10–3, Sun. noon–5; mid-June–mid-Aug., Tues.–Sat. 10–5, Sun. noon–5; mid-Aug.–May, open 1 day per month.*

Off Munkegate near the water, you can see an immense variety of seafood at **Ravnkloa Fiskehall** (fish market). The **Sjøfartsmuseet** (Maritime Museum), housed in a former prison, displays galleon figureheads, ship models, a harpoon cannon from a whaling boat, and a large collection of seafaring pictures. ⊠ *Fjordgt. 6A,* ☎ *73/52–89–75.* ☜ *NKr20.* ⊘ *Mon.–Sat. 9–3, Sun. noon–3; closed Sat. in winter.*

Trøndelag Folkemuseum has a collection of rustic buildings from the turn of the century, including a dental office and a lace and ribbon maker's workshop. The museum restaurant is from 1739 and serves traditional Norwegian food. ⊠ *Sverresborg,* ☎ *73/53–14–90.* ☜ *NKr40.* ⊘ *Late May–Aug., daily 11–6, Sept.–Dec., Sun. noon–4.*

OFF THE BEATEN PATH

RINGVE MUSIC MUSEUM – For an unusual museum visit, you can take a half-hour ride to Fagerheim and Ringve Gård, the childhood home of the naval hero Admiral Tordenskiold. Guides (music students) demonstrate the instruments on display and tell about their role in the history of music. Concerts are held regularly. ⊠ *Lade Allé 60,* ☎ *73/92–24–11.* ☜ *NKr50. Guided tours in English late May–June, daily at 11:30 and*

*2:30; July–mid-Aug., daily at 11, 12:30, 2:30, and 4:30; mid-Aug.–
late Aug., daily at 11, 12:30, and 2:30; Sept., daily at noon; Oct.–late
May, Sun. at 1:30. Tour lasts about 75 mins.*

Dining and Lodging

Trondheim is known for several dishes, including *surlaks* (pickled
salmon), marinated in a sweet-and-sour brine with onions and spices
and served with sour cream. A sweet specialty is *tekake* (tea cake), which
looks like a thick-crust pizza topped with a lattice pattern of cinnamon and sugar.

$$$ ✕ **Bryggen.** The furnishings are in bleached wood, with dark-blue and
★ red accessories, and the atmosphere is intimate. The menu features rein-
deer fillet salad with cranberry vinaigrette and herb cream soup with
both freshwater and ocean crayfish for appetizers. ⊠ *Øvre Bakklan-
det 66,* ☏ *73/52–02–30. Reservations essential. AE, DC, MC, V.
Closed Sun. No lunch.*

$$–$$$ ✕ **Havfruen.** "The Mermaid" has a maritime dining room with an open
kitchen at street level. Fish soup is the most popular starter; summer
main dishes include poached halibut. ⊠ *Kjøpmannsgt. 7,* ☏ *73/53–
26–26. AE, DC, MC, V. Closed Sun. No lunch.*

$$ ✕ **Hos Magnus.** The price–value ratio is excellent at this old-fashioned restaurant at Bryggen. The menu ranges from old local-specialty
surlaks to modern dishes such as salmon cured and marinated with aquavit brandy. Lamb roulade stuffed with cheese and mushroom sauce is
on the menu, and there are ample fish and vegetarian choices, too. ⊠
Kjøpmannsgt. 63, ☏ *73/52–41–10. AE, DC, MC, V.*

$$ ✕ **Lian.** In the heights above the city, the views here are spectacular.
The oldest part of the restaurant dates from 1700, but the round sec-
tion, from the 1930s, commands the best view. The food is solid, hon-
est, and hearty, with roast beef, reindeer, smoked pork loin, and the
old standby, *kjøttkaker* (Norwegian meat cakes). ⊠ *Lianvn.,* ☏ *72/
55–90–77. MC, V.*

$$ ✕ **Tavern på Sverresborg.** This big, yellow, wooden former ferry-
★ man's house at the Trøndelag Folkemuseum has been an inn since 1739.
The food is authentic Norwegian, including meat and fish prepared
with old methods—pickled, salted, and dried. Choices include a plate
with four different kinds of herring, roast lamb ribs, trout, meat cakes,
and rømmegrøt. Homemade oatmeal bread and rolls accompany all
dishes. ⊠ *Sverresborg Allé,* ☏ *73/52–09–32. MC, V.*

$ ✕ **De 3 Stuer.** Everything this small bistro chain serves is homemade,
and the daily specials may be fish soufflé, fried fish with sour-cream
sauce, split-pea soup with sausage, boiled beef, and lamb stew, all served
with dessert and coffee. For lunch there's smørbrød, crescent rolls, salads, and cakes. ⊠ *Trondheim Torg,* ☏ *73/52–92–20;* ⊠ *Gågaten
Leuthenhaven,* ☏ *73/52–43–42;* ⊠ *Dronningens Gt. 11,* ☏ *73/52–
63–20. Reservations not accepted. MC, V. Dronningens Gt. closed Sun.*

$$–$$$$ ▦ **Quality Prinsen Hotel.** Rooms in this hotel in the center of the city
are light—monochromatic to the point of being dull. One of the restau-
rants here, Pinocchio, serves a good early dinner. ⊠ *Kongensgt. 30,
7002,* ☏ *73/53–06–50,* FAX *73/53–06–44. 81 rooms, 1 suite. 3 restau-
rants, 3 bars, nightclub. AE, DC, MC, V.*

$$–$$$$ ▦ **Radisson SAS Royal Garden.** The city's showcase hostelry, right on
the river, was built in the same style as the old warehouse buildings
that line the waterfront, but in glass and concrete instead of wood. This
luxury hotel was renovated before the World Championship in Nordic
Skiing in 1997. ⊠ *Kjøpmannsgata 73, 7010,* ☏ *73/52–11–00,* FAX *73/
53–17–66. 297 rooms, 8 suites. 3 restaurants, bar, indoor pool, exercise room. AE, DC, MC, V.*

$$$ ⊞ **Clarion Grand Olav Hotel.** Not too many of the impeccably deco-rated rooms here are similiar—after all, there are 27 different room models. The hotel is part of a complex that contains shops and Olavshallen Concert Hall (home of the Trondheim Philharmonic). ⊠ *Kjøpmannsgt. 48,* ☎ *73/53–53–10,* ℻ *73/53–57–20. 106 rooms. Restaurant, bar, pub, no-smoking rooms, jazz club, meeting rooms. AE, DC, MC, V.*

$$ ⊞ **Ambassadeur.** From the roof terrace of this first-rate modern hotel, you'll see the deep-blue waters of the Trondheimsfjord reflect the dra-matic and irregular coastline. The Ambassadeur is about 300 ft from the market square. Most rooms have fireplaces, and some have bal-conies. ⊠ *Elvegt. 18,* ☎ *73/52–70–50,* ℻ *73/52–70–52. 34 rooms. Bar. AE, DC, MC, V.*

$–$$ ⊞ **Comfort Home Hotel Bakeriet.** The hotel opened in March 1991 in
★ a building built as a bakery in 1863. Few of the rooms look alike, but all are large and stylish in their simplicity, with natural wood furni-ture and beige-and-red-stripe textiles. There's no restaurant, but a hot evening meal is included in the room rate. You can borrow a track suit, and there's free light beer in the lounge by the sauna. ⊠ *Brattørgt. 2, 7011, Trondheim,* ☎ *73/52–52–00,* ℻ *73/50–23–30. 99 rooms. In-room VCRs, sauna. AE, DC, MC, V.*

$–$$ ⊞ **Trondheim.** The building is old on the outside, with a curved cor-ner and wrought-iron balconies, but inside it's new. The rooms are big and light, with what is now considered to be classic Scandinavian bentwood furniture. ⊠ *Kongensgt. 15, 7013,* ☎ *73/50–50–50,* ℻ *73/ 51–60–58. 131 rooms. Bar, meeting room. AE, DC, MC, V.*

Nightlife

Olavskvartalet is the center of much of the city's nightlife, with a disco, a jazz and blues club, and a bar and beer hall in the cellar. **Monte Cristo** (⊠ Prinsensgt. 38–40, ☎ 73/52–18–80) has a restaurant, bar, and disco under the same roof and is popular with the mid-20s and up age group. Students and younger people in search of cheap drinks, music, and danc-ing tend to gravitate toward **Strossa** (⊠ Elgeseter Gt. 1, ☎ 73/89–95–10), which is run by students. **Cafe Remis** (⊠ Kjoepmannsgt. 12, ☎ 73/52–05–52) is the center for gay nightlife in Trondheim.

Outdoor Activities and Sports

FISHING

The **Nidelven** (Nid River) in Trondheim is one of Norway's best salmon and trout rivers. You can fish right in the city, but, as usual, you'll need a license. Contact the tourist office.

SKIING

Bymarka and **Estenstadmarka,** the wooded areas on the periphery of Trondheim, are popular among cross-country skiers. At **Skistua** (ski lodge) in Bymarka, and at **Vassfjellet** south of the city, there are downhill runs.

En Route Nord Trøndelag, as the land above Trondheim is called, is largely agri-cultural. Taken on its own, it's beautiful, with farms, mountains, rock formations, and clear blue water, but compared with the rest of Nor-way, it is subtle, with only an undulating landscape—so many tourists just sleep through it on the night train or fly over it on their way to the North. The first town of any size is Steinkjer, a military base, boot camp for 3,000 Norwegian army recruits every year.

Mo i Rana

🕖 *350 km (218 mi) north of Steinkjer.*

Mo i Rana (the poetic name means Mo on the Ranafjord) is a center for iron and steel production using ore from nearby mines.

Setergrotta is one of almost 200 caves 26 km (16 mi) northwest of Mo i Rana. Setergrotta, with 7,920 ft of charted underground paths, many narrow passages, natural chimneys, and an underground river, is for serious spelunkers. The caves are usually open from mid-June to mid-August; however, times vary with conditions. Check with the tourist office (☎ 75/15–06–22, or 75/15–28–87). ☜ *NKr160 for a two-hour guided tour.*

Grønligrotta, Scandinavia's best-known show cave, even has electric lights. The 20-minute tour goes deep into the limestone cave to the underground river. ☎ 75/16–23–44. ☜ *NKr50.* ⊙ *Mid-June–mid-Aug. Tours daily on the hr 10–7.*

OFF THE
BEATEN PATH

SVARTISEN – Glacier fans can hike on the Svartisen—literally, Black Ice— the second-largest glacier in Norway, covering 375 square km (144 square mi). The glacier is 30 km (19 mi) north of Mo i Rana, about 2½ hours by car south of Bodø. OVDS (☎ 75/52–10–20) offers seven-hour boat tours from Bodø to the ice cap on Saturdays in summer. The easiest way to get to the glacier is from Mo, 32 km (20 mi) by car to Svartisvatn lake. A boat crosses the lake every hour to within 2½ km (1½ mi) of the Østerdal arm of the glacier. If you plan to get to the glacier on your own, you should inquire at the Svartisen Tourist Center (☎ 75/75–00–11) about connecting with a guide. Glacier walking is extremely hazardous and should never be done without a professional guide—even though a glacier may appear fixed and static, it is always changing; there's always the danger of calving and hard-to-spot crevasses.

Polarsirkelsenteret

73 *80 km (50 mi) north of Mo i Rana.*

On a bleak stretch of treeless countryside is the Arctic Circle. The Polarsirkelsenteret (Arctic Circle Center), on E6, presents a multiscreen show about Norway. The post office has a special postmark, and you can get your Arctic Circle Certificate stamped. There's also a cafeteria and gift shop. ☒ *8242 Polarsirkelen,* ☎ *75/16–60–66.* ☜ *NKr40.* ⊙ *May, daily 10–6; June, daily 10–8; July, daily 8–midnight; Aug., daily 10–6 (Apr., Oct. cafeteria only).*

Bodø

74 *174 km (108 mi) north of the Polarsirkelsenteret.*

Bodø, a modern city of about 40,000 just above the Arctic Circle, is best known as the end station of the Nordlandsbanen railroad and the gateway to the Lofoten Islands and the North. The midnight sun is visible from June 2 to July 10. Like many other coastal towns, it began as a small fishing community, but today it is a commercial and administrative center. Like much of northern Norway, the Second World War inevitably touched Bodø. In 1940, the town fell victim to German bombs meant to destroy a British air base.

Bodø is the best base for boat excursions to the coastal bird colonies on the Væren Islands. Bodø is also site of the **Nordland County Museum,** which depicts the life of the Sami and the regional history of the area, particularly its rich fishing heritage. ☒ *Prinsengt. 116,* ☎ *75/52–61–28.* ☜ *NKr 15.* ⊙ *Weekdays 9–3, weekends noon–3.*

Down the road from Bodø's airport and a good 15 minutes from the town's center, the jumbo **Norsk Luftfartssenter** (Norwegian Aviation Center) tells the story of Norwegian aviation with flight simulators and life-size displays of commercial and military planes dating back to 1912.

☎ 75/50–85–50. ▦ NKr 65. ☉ *Early June–mid-Aug., weekdays 10–8, Sat. 10–5; mid-Aug.–early June, Mon., Tues., Thurs., Fri. 10–4, Wed. 10–7, Sat. 11–5, Sun. 11–6.*

Lodging

$$ ▦ **Inter Nor Diplomat Hotel.** This hotel near the harbor is a short walk from the shopping district. The modern rooms are somberly decorated. The restaurant has live entertainment, but the food could be more imaginative. ⊠ *Sjøgt. 23, 8000 Bodø,* ☎ *75/52–70–00,* ₣ₐₓ *75/52–24–60. 109 rooms. 2 restaurants, bar, exercise room, convention center. AE, DC, MC, V.*

$$ ▦ **Norrøna.** This bed-and-breakfast-style establishment is plain yet comfortable and has a prime downtown location. ⊠ *Storgt. 4B,* ☎ *75/52–55–50,* ₣ₐₓ *75/52–33–88. 105 rooms. AE, DC, MC, V.*

$$ ▦ **Radisson SAS Hotel Bodø.** This grandiose hotel pulses with life and has enough services to keep you entertained nearly around the clock. As with all SAS hotels, the rooms have all the amenities, and the service is impeccable. ⊠ *Storgt. 2,* ☎ *75/52–41–00,* ₣ₐₓ *75/52–74–93. 190 rooms. Restaurant, 2 bars, sauna, health club, nightclub. AE, DC, MC, V.*

Saltstraumen

⑦⑤ *33 km (20 mi) southeast of Bodø on Route 80/17.*

Saltstraumen is a 3-km-long (2-mi-long) and 500-ft-wide section of water between the outer fjord, which joins with the sea, and the inner fjord basin. During high tide, the volume of water rushing through the strait and into the basin is so great that whirlpools form. This is the legendary *malstrøm*—and the strongest one in the world. Sometimes as many as four separate whirlpools can be seen, and the noise made by these "cauldrons" can be both loud and eerie. All that rush of water brings enormous quantities of fish, making the malstrøm a popular fishing spot. The nearby **Saltstraumen Opplevelsesenter** (Adventure Center) houses regional artifacts and a multimedia show that recount the scientific and human tales behind the malstrøm. ☎ *75/56–06–55.* ▦ *NKr50.* ☉ *Mid-May–late May and early-Aug.–mid-Aug., daily 11–8; June–July, daily 11–10; mid-Aug.–late Aug. 11–6*

Dining and Lodging

$$$–$$$$ ✕▦ **Saltstraumen Hotel.** This hotel is practically on top of the malstrøm. The restaurant serves delicious steamed halibut in butter sauce. ⊠ *1056* ☎ *75/58–76–85. 28 rooms in hotel, 14 separate bungalows. Restaurant, meeting rooms. AE, DC, MC, V.*

OFF THE
BEATEN PATH

BLODVEIMUSEET – Ninety minutes southeast of Bodø in Rognan, the Bloodstained Road Museum recreates the sinister atmosphere of an icy North Norway Nazi prison camp where Russian, Serb, and Polish prisoners of war were incarcerated. Photographs and documents displayed in a reconstructed wooden prison cabin show the gradual disintegration of men as they built the roads and railway meant to transport weapons from Mosjøen to Kirkenes. The resulting infrastructure is now known as the Bloodstained Road. **Saltdal Bygdetun,** a collection of historic houses, is a few yards away. Call for a guided tour. ☎ *75/69–06–60.* ☉ *June–Aug., weekdays 9–3, Sat. 12–4, Sun. 1–6.*

Narvik

⑦⑥ *336 km (210 mi) north of Saltstraumen.*

Narvik is more easily reached by rail from Stockholm than from most places in Norway, as it is the end station on the *Ofotbanen*, the Norwegian railroad that connects with the Swedish railroad's northern-most line. Narvik was originally established as the ice-free port for exporting Swedish iron ore mined around Kiruna. From mid-June to mid-August, you can take a cable car 2,132 ft above town for a view of the city and Ofotenfjord.

On May 9, 1940, the German army invaded Norway through Narvik, and German occupying forces stayed for more than five years. After the war, Narvik, which had been leveled by the bombing, was rebuilt. The **Krigsminnemuseet** (War Memorial Museum) documents wartime events with artifacts, models, and pictures. ⊠ *Torget,* ☎ *76/94–44–26.* ☑ *NKr25.* ☉ *March–mid June and mid-Aug.–late Sept., daily 11–2; mid-June–mid-Aug., daily 10–10.*

Lodging

$$–$$$ ⊞ **Inter Nor Grand Royal.** It looks like an office building from the outside, but inside it is a top-class hotel, with big, rather formal rooms. ⊠ *Kongensgt. 64, 8500 Narvik,* ☎ *76/94–15–00,* Ⓕ *76/94–55–31. 108 rooms. 2 restaurants, 2 bars, sauna, exercise room, nightclub, convention center. AE, DC, MC, V.*

Lofoten and the Islands of the North

Extending out into the ocean north of Bodø are the Lofoten Islands, a 190-km (118-mi) chain of jagged peaks and mountaintops rising from the bottom of the sea like open jaws. In summer the idyll of farms, fjords, and fishing villages draws caravans of tourists, whereas in winter the coast facing the Arctic Ocean is one of Europe's stormiest. The midnight sun is visible here from May 26 to July 17. If you are lucky enough to be visiting on a clear midnight, drive over to the western side, where the spear-shaped mountains give way to flat, sandy beaches that look oddly fluorescent in the hush of night. The sight is spectacular.

Until about 50 years ago fishing was the only source of income for the area (today tourism helps bolster the still thriving fisheries). Cod and haddock were either dried or salted and sold in other parts of Europe. As many as 6,000 boats with 30,000 fishermen would mobilize between January and March for the Lofotfisket, the world's largest cod-fishing event. During the season they fished in open boats and took shelter during stormy nights in *rorbuer,* simple cabins built right on the water. Today many rorbuer have been converted into lodgings, but Lofotfisket is still an annual tradition. In the summer, crisscrossing wooden racks are densely hung with drying cod while the midnight sun plays on the wooden boats in the harbor.

The best way to visit Lofoten is by car. **Svolvær,** the main town and administrative center for the villages on the islands, is connected with the other islands by express boat and ferry, and by coastal steamer and air to Bodø. It has a thriving summer art colony.

A drive on E10, from Svolvær to the outer tip of Lofoten (130 km [80 mi])—the town with the enigmatic name of **Å**—is an opportunity to see how the islanders really live.

The **Norwegian Fishing Village Museum** (☎ 76/09–14–88) at Å is a spread-out living fishing village with houses, a 19th-century cod-liver-oil factory, and a bread bakery. ☑ *NKr35.* ☉ *June–Aug., daily 10–6; Sept.–May, weekdays 10–4.*

Just south of Svolvær, the hamlet of **Kabelvåg** provides the perfect introduction to the string of islands, their history, and their inhabitants. A cluster of museums less than a mile from the quiet village center sits on the site of an old fishing settlement. Restored fishing cabins displayed at the **Lofotmuseet** (Lofoten Island Museum, ☎ 76/07–82–23) depict the rigorous life of a fishing community on the grassy edge of a fjord inlet. Next door, the **Galleri Espolin** (☎ 76/07–64–05) exhibits the dark, haunting paintings and lithographs of fishermen in stormy weather. Kaare Espolin Johnsen, who died in 1994, was a nationally renowned artist. The **Lofot-Akvariet** (Aquarium, ☎ 76/07–86–65) proves you can't understand a fishing culture without knowing what's in the water. Exhibits include a salmon farm, a seal pond, and a slide show of sea creatures. ✉ *Storvågan.* ☉ *Mid-June–mid-Aug., daily 10–9; mid–late Aug., daily 10–6; Sept.–Apr., weekdays and Sun. 11–3; May–early June, daily 11–3.*

Southwest of Kabelvåg is **Henningsvær.** This enchanting village is home to **Karl Erik Harr Gallery** (☎ 76/07–15–73), which exhibits Lofoten-inspired paintings by acclaimed Norwegian artists, including the gallery's namesake. Upstairs is more on fishing and a reconstructed cod-liver-oil factory.

Viking enthusiasts might want to veer northwest to **Borg,** where archeologists unearthed a long, low chieftain's house—the largest Viking building ever discovered. Now rebuilt exactly as it was, the **Viking Museum Lofotr** houses the 1,000-year-old artifacts discovered there. Tour guides in Viking garb sit around crackling fires and demonstrate the crafts, customs, and cookery of their ancestors. ✉ *Borg i Lofoten.* ☎ *76/08–49–00.* ✑ *NKr70.* ☉ *Late May–mid-June, daily 10–5; mid-June–early Aug., daily 10–7; early Aug.–Sept., daily 10–5.*

Other scenic stops include tucked-away **Nusfjord,** a 19th-century fishing village on an official European Conservation list; **Sund,** with its smithy; and festive **Reine.**

NEED A
BREAK?

The rustic **Gammelbua,** in Reine, serves excellent salmon mousse and chilled Norwegian beer. Locals and tourists flock here to eat, drink, and gossip.

Off the tip of Moskenesøy, the last island with a bridge, is **Moskenesstraumen,** a malstrøm not quite as dramatic as Saltstraumen (☞ *above*) but inspiration to both Jules Verne, who wrote about it in *Journey Beneath the Sea,* and Edgar Allan Poe, who described it in his short story "A Descent into the Maelstrom."

North of the Lofotens are the **Vesterålen Islands,** with more fishing villages and rorbuer, and diverse vegetation. There are fewer tourists in Vesterålen, but more whale sightings. Puffins populate area cliffs, as in the Lofotens. The Coastal Steamer (☞ Arriving and Departing by Boat *in* Trondheim A to Z, *below*) slithers in and around fjords along the coastline of these more subtle islands, such as the steep-cliffed **Trollfjord.** The first arctic cod of the year is caught in Vesterålen.

⑦ East of Vesterålen on Hinnøya, Norway's largest island, is **Harstad,** where the year-round population of 22,000 swells to 42,000 during the annual June cultural festival (the line-up includes concerts, theater, and dance) and its July deep-sea fishing festival.

Dining and Lodging

A word on the fishermen's cabins: although hotels have popped up in some of the bigger fishing villages, rorbu lodging is essential to the Lofoten experience. Rorbuer vary in size and comfort, some date back to the last century and others are new imitations. If you do stay in a rorbu, it is worth your while to bring a few days' worth of food to stick in the refrigerator. Some villages have few cafés, and you may find that the closest thing to a grocery store is a gas station. Unless you have your own linens, remember you'll have to pay extra—usually about NKr100.

$$$ ✕ **Røkenes Gård.** The farm was originally homesteaded in AD 400, and the large white wooden building with an intricately carved portal opened in 1750 as a commercial trading house and inn. The ninth generation of descendants restored it, and it is now a cozy restaurant serving regional specialties, such as marinated reindeer and cloudberry parfait. ⊠ *9400 Harstad,* ☎ *77/01–74–65. Reservations essential. AE, DC, MC, V.*

$$ ✕ **Fiskekrogen.** This quayside restaurant in the fishing village of Henningsvær will prepare your own catch. Chef-owner Otto Asheim's specialties include smoked gravlaks (smoking the dill-marinated salmon gives it extra depth of flavor) and sautéed ocean catfish garnished with mussels and shrimp. ⊠ *8330 Henningsvær,* ☎ *76/07–46–52. Reservations essential. AE, DC, MC, V.*

$$–$$$ ▨ **Grand Nordic.** This hotel is housed in a redbrick Bauhaus-style building; the public rooms are decorated with Norwegian leather furniture from the 1970s. Bedrooms, no bigger than necessary, have darkwood furnishings. The restaurant and conference rooms are lighter and more modern. ⊠ *Strandgt. 9, 9400 Harstad,* ☎ *77/06–21–70,* FAX *77/06–77–30. 82 rooms, 3 suites. Restaurant, bar, nightclub, convention center. AE, DC, MC, V.*

$$–$$$ ▨ **Nyvågar Rorbu og Aktivitetssenter.** This lodging and recreation complex is a 15-minute drive from the Svolvær airport and a five-minute walk from the Storvågan museum complex. Activities are well organized, with fishing-boat tours, eagle safaris, and deep-sea rafting, as well as planned evening entertainment. The cabins, which are not especially authentic (they're new), are spotless. ⊠ *8310 Kabelvåg, Storvågan,* ☎ *76/07–89–00,* FAX *76/07–89–50. 30 rooms. Restaurant, meeting rooms. AE, DC, MC, V.*

$$–$$$ ▨ **Rainbow Vestfjord Hotel.** This simple hotel has spacious rooms and a lovely view of the harbor beyond. It used to be a cod-liver-oil factory. ⊠ *8301 Svolvær,* ☎ *76/07–08–70,* FAX *76/07–08–54. 63 rooms, 3 suites. Restaurant, bar, conference room. AE, DC, MC, V.*

$$–$$$ ▨ **Rica Hotel Svolvær.** One of the rooms in this spruced-up fisherman's inn comes with a hole through which to fish one's dinner. Don't be fooled by the Rica's rorbu look. It's just an elegant hotel on the inside. ⊠ *Lamholmen, 8301 Svolvær,* ☎ *76/07–22–22,* FAX *76/07–20–01. 147 rooms. Restaurant, bar, convention center. AE, DC, MC, V.*

$ ▨ **Henningsvær Rorbuer.** This small group of turn-of-the-century rorbuer, all facing the sea, is just outside the center of Lofoten's most important fishing village. Breakfasts can be ordered from the cafeteria-reception, where there's a fireplace and a TV. Reservations are essential for July. ⊠ *8330 Henningsvær,* ☎ *76/07–46–00,* FAX *76/07–49–10. 16 1- or 2-bedroom rorbuer. Cafeteria, grill, sauna, laundry service. V.*

$ ▨ **Nusfjord Rorbuer.** Families stay at these secluded cabins for weeks at a time. There's plenty to do—hiking, fishing, boating—in the surrounding area, which is crawling with natural life: giant moss-covered boulders seem frozen in motion, and small herds of sheep wander freely along the one-lane highway. For a glimpse at the midnight sun, drive to the other side of the island at Flakstad. Rowboats are included in the price of a rorbu, and you can rent out fishing gear and motor boats. The completely preserved village of Nusfjord with its string of colorful rorbuer is quaint at every turn, starting with the old-fashioned general store. ⊠ *8380 Ramberg,* ☎ *76/09–30–20,* FAX *76/09–33–78. 15 1- or 2-bedroom rorbuer. Restaurant, bar, coin laundry. DC, MC, V.*

$ ⊞ **Reine Rorbuer.** In the heart of Reine, which was named the country's prettiest village by Norwegian travel agents, these authentic fishing cabins are down the hill from Gammelbua (☞ *above*), a local eatery and social spot. The cabins all have typical Norwegian names, like Gro and Liv. The furniture and kitchenware look and feel as old and Norwegian as the cabins. Make reservations early as the cabins tend to get booked early in summer. ⊠ *8390 Reine,* ☎ *76/09–22–22,* FAX *76/09–22–25. 26 1-, 2-, or 3-bedroom rorbuer, most with shower. AE, MC, V.*

$ ⊞ **Wulff-Nilsens Rorbuer.** A five-minute drive from Reine, this tidy cluster of 19th-century rorbuer is an excellent starting point for fishing excursions and mountain walks. Seagulls nest only yards from the cabins, and workers unload fish shipments on the dock below. The rorbuer are rustic but comfortably equipped; they have stoves and refrigerators. Breakfast and light meals are served in the restaurant by request. ⊠ *Hamnøy, 8390 Reine,* ☎ *76/09–23–20,* FAX *76/09–21–54. 14 1-, 2-, or 3-bedroom rorbuer, all with shower. Restaurant, kitchenettes. AE, MC, V.*

Outdoor Activities and Sports

BIRD-WATCHING

There's a constant shrieking hum that emanates from some of North Norway's arctic island cliffs, which virtually pulsate from the thousands of birds perching their sides. From Moskenes, just north of Å (or from Bodø), you can take a ferry to the bird sanctuaries of **Værøy** and **Røst.** Many different types of seabirds inhabit the cliffs, in particular the eider ducks, favorites of the local population, which build small shelters for their nests. Eventually the down collected from these nests ends up in dyner.

WHALE-WATCHING

The stretch of sea that lies north of Lofoten and Vesterålen is perhaps the best place to sight whales, porpoises, and white-beaked dolphins. Whale safari boat tours leave from the tip of Andøy, a salamander-shaped island northwest of Hinnøya. Contact Andøy Nature Center (☎ 76/14–26–11) for more information. Brush up on your knowledge of the sea-faring mammal at the island's **Whale Center** (Destination Lofoten, ☎ 76/07–30–00) before the trip. Farther south from the Vesterålen coastal town of Stø, **Whale Watch A/S** (☎ 76/13–44–99) also scours the sea for sperm, minke, and killer whales. Reservations are necessary for both excursions.

Shopping

Lofoten is a mecca for artists and craftspeople, who come for the spectacular scenery and the ever-changing subtle light; a list of galleries and crafts centers, with all locations marked on a map, is available from tourist offices.

Probably the best-known craftsperson in the region is Tor Vegard Mørkved, better known as **Smeden i Sund** (the blacksmith at Sund, ☎ 76/09–36–29). Watch him make wrought-iron cormorants in many sizes, as well as candlesticks and other gift items. Another fun stop is Åse and Åsvar Tangrand's **Glasshytta and Ceramics Workshop** (☎ 76/09–44–42), near Nusfjord. **Sakrisøy Antiques & Second Hand Store** (☎ 76/09–21–43), which is just outside of Reine (above Dagmar's Museum of Dolls and Toys), sells sundry Lofoten keepsakes.

Tromsø

78 *318 km (197 mi) northeast of Harstad.*

The most important city north of the Arctic Circle, Tromsø looks the way a polar town should—with ice-capped mountain ridges and jagged architecture. The midnight sun shines from May 21 to July 21, and the city's total area—2,558 square km (987 square mi)—is the most expansive in Norway. Still, Tromsø is just about the same size as the country of Luxembourg, but home to only 55,000 people. The city's picturesque center itself sits on a small, hilly island connected to the mountainous mainland by a long-legged, slender bridge with a subtle peak that mimics the craggy surroundings. The 13,000 students at the world's northernmost university are one reason the nightlife here is more lively than in many other northern cities.

Certainly, the **Ishavskatedralen** (Arctic Cathedral) is the city's best-known structure. A looming peak of 11 descending triangles of concrete and glass, it is meant to evoke the shape of a Sami tent and the iciness of a glacier. Inside, an immense jewel-colored stained-glass window by Norwegian artist Viktor Sparre depicts the Second Coming. ☎ 77/63–76–11. ▣ *NKr10.* ⊙ *June–Aug., Mon.–Sat. 10–8, Sun. 1:30–6. Times may vary according to church services.*

☾ The **Tromsø Museum,** part of Tromsø University, offers an extensive survey of local history, lifestyles, and nature, with dioramas on Sami culture, arctic hunting practices, and wildlife. Children can listen to animal sounds over earphones, match animals to tales about them, and play with a nearly life-size dinosaur. An open-air museum is on the same grounds. ⊠ *Universitetet, Lars Thøringsvei 10,* ☎ *77/64–50–00.* ▣ *NKr20.* ⊙ *June–Aug., daily 9–9; Sept.–May, Mon., Tues., Thurs., and Fri. 8:30–3:30, Wed. 7* PM–*10* PM, *Sat. noon–3, Sun. 11–4.*

The **Polarmuseet** (Polar Museum), in an 1830s customs warehouse, documents the history of the polar region, with skis and equipment from Roald Amundsen's expedition to the South Pole and a reconstructed Svalbard hunting station from 1910. ⊠ *Søndre Tollbugt. 11b,* ☎ *77/68–43–73.* ▣ *NKr30.* ⊙ *Mid-May–mid-June, daily 11–6; mid-June–Aug., daily 11–8; Sept.–mid-May, daily 11–3.*

To get a real sense of Tromsø's northerly immensity and peace, take ☾ the **Fjellheisen** (cable car) from behind the cathedral up to the mountains, just a few minutes out of the city center. You'll get a great view of the city from **Storsteinen** (Big Rock), 1,386 ft above sea level. In the late afternoon and on weekends, summer and winter, this is where locals go to ski, picnic, walk their lucky dogs, and admire the view. ☎ *77/63–87–37.* ▣ *NKr 50.* ⊙ *Late Apr.–mid-May, daily 10–5; late May–Sept., daily 10–1* AM *if it's sunny. At other times, call for hours.*

OFF THE BEATEN PATH	**NORDLYSPLANETARIET** – At the Northern Lights Planetarium, 112 projectors guarantee a 360° view of programs, which include a tour through the northern lights, the midnight sun, and geological history, as well as a film and multimedia show about the city. It's just outside town in Breivika. ☎ *77/67–60–00.* ▣ *NKr50.* ⊙ *June–Aug., shows in English weekdays at 12:30 and 4:30, Sat. 4:30; Sept.–May call for show times.*

Dining and Lodging

$$–$$$ ✕ **Brankos.** Branko and Anne Brit Bartolj serve authentic Slovenian dishes here. Try the *pleskavica* (grilled beef with zesty spices and garlic), accompanied by their own imported wines from the former Yugoslavia. The bistro on the ground floor serves an affordable lunch. ⊠ *Storgt. 57,* ☎ *77/68–26–73. Reservations essential. AE, DC, MC, V.*

$$–$$$ ✕ **Compagniet.** An old wooden trading house from 1837 is now a stylish restaurant serving modern Norwegian food. Chef Anders Blomkvist prepares cream of lobster soup with a dash of brandy and escargot in garlic sauce for starters; main dishes include grilled crayfish and reindeer filet in a sauce seasoned with blueberries. ⊠ *Sjøgt. 12,* ☎ *77/65–57–21. Reservations essential. AE, DC, MC, V. No lunch in winter.*

\$\$–\$\$\$ 🏨 **Comfort Home Hotel With.** This hotel on the waterfront's dock area has spacious rooms decorated in shades of gray with occasional colorful accents. The sauna-relaxation room on the top floor has the best view in town. As part of the Home Hotel chain, Hotel With offers alcohol-free beer, a hot meal, and waffles and coffee at all times and at no charge. ⊠ *Sjøgt. 35–37, 9000,* ☎ *77/68–70–00,* ︎FAX *77/68–96–16. 76 rooms. Sauna, Turkish bath, meeting rooms. AE, DC, MC, V.*

\$\$–\$\$\$ 🏨 **Radisson SAS Hotel.** You'll get splendid views over the Tromsø shoreline at this modern hotel, but standard rooms are tiny, and even the costlier "Business Club" rooms aren't big enough for real desks and tables, so modular ones have been attached to the walls. ⊠ *Sjøgt. 7, 9001,* ☎ *77/60–00–00,* ︎FAX *77/66–42–60. 195 rooms with bath, 2 suites. Restaurant, bar, pizzeria, sauna, nightclub. AE, DC, MC, V.*

\$\$–\$\$\$ 🏨 **Rica Ishavshotel.** Tromsø's snazziest hotel sits atop a deck that stretches over the sound toward the Arctic Cathedral, its icicle-like spire mirroring the cathedral's own triangular ridges. Inside, shiny wood furnishings with brass trimmings evoke the maritime life that is inescapable in this North Sea region. A colorful tapestry depicting life in the Arctic city brightens the bustling dining room, where the adjacent bar's piano chimes away. The soft-carpeted rooms are decorated in bold golds, reds, and navy blues, and the bathrooms are shiny and white. Guests represent a mixture of business executives, tourists, and scientific conference attendees. ⊠ *Fr. Langes gt. 2, Box 196, 9001,* ☎ *77/66–64–00,* ︎FAX *77/66–64–44. 180 rooms. 2 restaurants, 2 bars, meeting rooms. AE, DC, MC, V.*

\$\$ 🏨 **Saga.** The central location on a pretty town square and a helpful staff make the Saga a good place to stay. Its restaurant has affordable, hearty meals, and the rooms—though somewhat basic—are quiet. ⊠ *Richard Withs Pl. 2,* ☎ *77/68–11–80,* ︎FAX *77/68–23–80. 66 rooms. Restaurant, cafeteria. AE, DC, MC, V.*

\$–\$\$ 🏨 **Polar Hotell.** This no-frills hotel gives good value for the money in winter, when none of the bigger hotels have special rates. Rooms are small, and the orange-brown color scheme is a bit dated, but it's a pleasant, unassuming place. ⊠ *Grønnegt. 45, 9000,* ☎ *77/68–64–80,* ︎FAX *77/68–91–36. 68 rooms. Restaurant in a separate building across from the hotel, bar, meeting rooms. AE, DC, MC, V.*

Nightlife

Tromsø brags that it has 10 nightclubs, not bad for a city of 50,000 at the top of the world. **Compagniet** (☞ Dining, *above*) has the classiest nightclub; **Charly's** (⊠ Sjøgt. 7) at the SAS Royal Hotel is also popular. **Victoria/Klubb Circus/Amtmannen** (⊠ Amtmann Gt., ☎ 77/68–49–06), a good bar and restaurant complex, has live bands and attracts a younger crowd. **Dampen** (⊠ Kai Gt. 1) is more alternative than any other venue in Tromsø in terms of live music and clientele. The train motif at **Tromsø Jernbanestation** (⊠ Strandgt. 33-35, ☎ 77/61–23–48) suggests that some locals are still crossing their fingers to get a railway. The smoky bar attracts a young crowd who sit in booths akin to train compartments.

Outdoor Activities and Sports

HIKING

In Tromsø there's good hiking in the mountains above the city, reachable by funicular. Other regional possibilities begin anywhere outside the town's limits (usually only a few minutes away).

SKIING

In Tromsø, the mountains, only eight minutes away by funicular, are a great place to ski. Elsewhere, you'll have to ask specifics from the tourist board. Listen to the weather reports and heed warnings. Blizzards come in quickly over the water; the wind alone can knock a sizable person clear off his or her feet.

En Route The drive from Tromsø to Alta is mostly on a coastal road. At one point you'll drive along the **Kvænangsfjellet ridge,** where Kautokeino Sami spend the summer in turf huts—you might see a few of their reindeer along the way. Thirteen kilometers (8 miles) west of Alteidet you'll pass by **Øksfjordjøkelen,** the only glacier in Norway that calves into the sea.

Alta

79 *409 km (253 mi) north of Tromsø, 217 km (134 mi) from the North Cape.*

Alta is a major transportation center into Finnmark, the far north of Norway. Most people come just to spend the night before making the final ascent to the North Cape.

OFF THE   **ALTA MUSEUM –** It's worth a trek to Hjemmeluft, southwest of the city, to
BEATEN PATH   see four groupings of 2,500- to 6,000-year-old prehistoric rock carvings, the largest in northern Europe. The pictographs, featuring ships, reindeer, and even a man with a bow and arrow, were discovered in 1973 and are included on the UNESCO World Heritage List. The rock carvings form part of the Alta Museum. The museum has displays delineating the history of the area from the Stone Age until today, including its destruction in World War II. ☏ *78/43–53–77.* 🎫 *Summer NKr40; winter NKr35.* ☉ *May and Sept. daily 9–6; early-June–mid-June and mid-Aug.–late Aug., daily 8–8; mid-June–mid-Aug., daily 8 am–11 pm; Oct.–Apr., weekdays 9–3, weekends 11–4.*

Lodging

$$$ 🏨 **North Cape Hotel Alta.** This glass-and-white hotel does everything it can to make you forget that you are in a place where it is dark much of the time. Everything is light, from the reflectors on the ceiling of public rooms to the white furniture in the bedrooms. ✉ *Lokkevn. 1, 9500,* ☏ *78/48–27–00,* 🅵🅰🆇 *78/43–58–25. 154 rooms. 2 restaurants, 2 bars, lobby lounge, sauna, nightclub, meeting rooms. AE, DC, MC, V.*

Outdoor Activities and Sports

DOGSLEDDING

Canyon Huskies (☏ 78/43–33–06), in Alta, arranges all kinds of personalized tours, whether you want to stay in a tent or hotel, and whether you want to drive your team or stay in the sled. Like most Norwegian sled dogs, these are very friendly.

Shopping

Manndalen Husflidslag (☏ 77/71–62–73) at Løkvoll in Manndalen, on E6 about 15 km (9 mi) west of Alta, is a center for Coastal Sami weaving on vertical looms. Local weavers sell their rugs and wall hangings along with other regional crafts.

Hammerfest

80 *145 km (90 mi) north of Alta.*

The world's northernmost town is Hammerfest, an important fishing center. At these latitudes the "most northerlies" become numerous, but certainly the lifestyles here are a testament to determination, especially in winter, when night lasts for months. In 1891 Hammerfest decided to brighten the situation and purchased a generator from Thomas Edison. It was the first city in Europe to have electric street lamps.

Hammerfest is home to the **Royal and Ancient Polar Bear Society.** Since the exhibits all depict some aspect of Arctic hunts, don't visit the society if you don't like taxidermic displays. ⊠ *Town Hall Basement.* ☞ *Free.* ☉ *June–Aug., weekdays 8–8, weekends 10–3. Sept.–May, noon–3:30, or by appointment.*

Dining and Lodging

$$–$$$ ✕🏨 **Rica Hotel Hammerfest.** The rooms are functional and small, but the furniture is comfortable. There is also an informal pizza pub and a spacious bar. ⊠ *Sørøygt. 15,* ☎ *78/41–13–33,* ℻ *78/41–13–11. 94 rooms. Restaurant, bar, pizzeria, sauna, convention center. AE, DC, MC, V.*

$$$ 🏨 **Quality Hammerfest Hotel.** Right on the pleasant Rådhusplassen, this guest house has handsome, harborview rooms for tolerable prices in a town where hotels are expensive. The hotel is very accessible for travelers with disabilities. ⊠ *Strandgt. 2–4,* ☎ *78/41–16–22,* ℻ *78/41–21–27. 53 rooms. Restaurant, cafeteria, pub, sauna. AE, DC, MC, V.*

Honningsvåg

⑧ *130 km (80.6 mi) from Hammerfest.*

The last village before the Cape, Honningsvåg was completely destroyed at the end of World War II, when the Germans retreated and burned everything they left behind. Only a single wood church, which still survives, was not left in embers. The **Nordkappmuseet** (North Cape Museum), on the third floor of Nordkapphuset (North Cape House), documents the history of the fishing industry in the region as well as the history of tourism at the North Cape. ⊠ *9750 Honningsvåg,* ☎ *78/47–28–33.* ☞ *NKr20.* ☉ *Mid-June–mid-Aug., Mon.–Sat. 9–8, Sun. 1–8; mid-Aug.–mid-June, weekdays 11–4.*

Lodging

$ 🏨 **Hotel Havly.** This simple hotel is cozy and centrally located, with small, spic-and-span rooms and an ample breakfast buffet. Because this is a seamen's hostel, no alcohol is served. ⊠ *9751 Honningsvåg,* ☎ *78/47–29–66,* ℻ *78/47–30–10. 35 rooms. Cafeteria, meeting rooms. AE, MC, V.*

Outdoor Activities and Sports

BIRD-WATCHING

There are tons of birds in Gjesvær on the east coast of the Honningsvåg. Contact **Ola Thomassen** (☎ 78/47–57–73) for organized outings.

Nordkapp

⑧ *34 km (21 mi) from Honningsvåg.*

On your journey to the Nordkapp (North Cape), you'll see an incredible treeless tundra, with crumbling mountains and sparse dwarf plants. Although this area is notoriously crowded in the summer, with endless lines of tour buses, it's completely different from fall through spring, when the snow is yards deep and the sea is frosty gray. Because the roads are closed in winter, the only access is from the tiny fishing village of Skarsvåg via Sno-Cat, a thump-and-bump ride that's as unforgettable as the beautifully bleak view. For winter information, contact North Cape Travel (☎ 78/47–25–99). Knivsjellodden, slightly west and less dramatic than the North Cape, is actually a hair farther north.

The contrast between this near-barren territory and the **North Cape Hall** is striking. Blasted into the interior of the plateau, the building is housed in a cave and includes a restaurant with incredible views. A tunnel leads past a small chapel to a grotto with a panoramic view of the Arctic Ocean and to the cliff wall itself, passing exhibits that trace the history of the Cape, from Richard Chancellor, an Englishman who drifted around it and named it in 1533, to Oscar II, king of Norway and Sweden, who climbed to the top of the plateau in 1873, and King Chulalongkorn of Siam (now Thailand), who visited the Cape in 1907. Out on the plateau itself, a hollow sculptured globe is illuminated by the midnight sun, which shines from May 11 to August 31. ⊠ 9764 Nordkapp, ☎ 78/47–25–99. Entrance to the hall: ▣ NKr175. ⊙ Mid-Apr.–mid-May and late Sept.–early Oct., daily, 2–5; mid-May–mid-June, daily, noon–1 AM; mid-June–mid-Aug., daily, 10–2 AM; mid-Aug.–early Sept., daily, 10–midnight; early Sept.–mid-Sept., daily, noon–5.

Outdoor Activities and Sports

RAFTING

Deep-sea rafting is a relatively new sport in the area, but one that is as exhilarating as it is beautiful. Among the several tours is a three-hour trip to the North Cape. Call **Nordkapp Safari** (☎ 78/47–27–94).

Trondheim to the North Cape A to Z

Arriving and Departing

BY BOAT

Hurtigruten (the coastal express boat, which calls at 35 ports from Bergen to Kirkenes) stops at Trondheim, southbound at St. Olav's Pier, Quay 16, northbound at Pier 1, Quay 7. Other stops between Trondheim and the North Cape include Bodø, Stamsund (Lofotens), Svolvær, Sortland (Vesterålen), Harstad, Tromsø, Hammerfest, and Honningsvåg. Call ☎ 73/52–55–40 for information on Hurtigruten and local ferries.

BY BUS

Buses run only from Oslo to Otta, where they connect with the train to Trondheim. Buses connect Bergen, Molde, Ålesund, and Røros with Trondheim.

Nor-Way Bussekspress (☎ 22/17–52–90) can help you to put together a bus journey to the North. The Express 2000 travels three times a week between Oslo, Kautokeino, Alta, and Hammerfest. The journey, via Sweden, takes 24, 26, and 29 hours, respectively.

BY CAR

Trondheim is about 500 km (310 mi) from Oslo: seven to eight hours of driving. Speed limits are 80 kph (50 mph) much of the way. There are two alternatives, E6 through Gudbrandsdalen or Route 3 through Østerdalen. Roads are decent for the most part but can become thick with campers during midsummer, sometimes making the going slow. It's 727 km (450 mi) from Trondheim to Bodø on Route E6, which goes all the way to Kirkenes. There's an NKr20 toll on E6 just south of Trondheim for travelers in both directions. Cars entering the downtown area must pay an NKr10 toll (6 AM–10 PM). Anyone who makes it to the **North Cape** sans tour bus will be congratulated with an NKr150 toll.

BY PLANE

Trondheim's **Værnes Airport** is 35 km (22 mi) northeast of the city. **SAS** (☎ 74/84–34–00), **Braathens SAFE** (☎ 73/89–57–00), and **Widerøe** (☎ 73/89–67–00) are the main domestic carriers. **SAS** also has one flight between Trondheim and Copenhagen daily, except Sunday, and daily flights to Stockholm.

With the exception of Harstad, all cities in northern Norway are served by airports less than 5 km (3 mi) from the center of town. Tromsø is a crossroads for air traffic between northern and southern Norway and is served by Braathens SAFE, SAS, and Widerøe. SAS flies to eight destinations in northern Norway, including Bodø, Tromsø, Alta, and Kirkenes. Braathens SAFE flies to five destinations, including Bodø and Tromsø. Widerøe specializes in northern Norway and flies to 19 destinations in the region, including Honningsvåg, the airport closest to the North Cape.

BY TRAIN

The **Dovrebanen** has five departures daily, four on Saturday, in both directions on the Oslo–Trondheim route. Trains leave from Oslo S Station for the seven- to eight-hour journey. Trondheim is the gateway to the North, and two trains run daily in both directions on the 11-hour Trondheim–Bodø route. For information about trains out of Trondheim, call ☎ 73/53–00–10. The **Nordlandsbanen** has two departures daily in each direction on the Bodø–Trondheim route, an 11-hour journey. The **Ofotbanen** has one departure daily in each direction on the Stockholm–Narvik route, a 21-hour journey. In summer, a tourist train travels at 4:30 daily from Narvik to the Swedish border and back.

Getting Around

BY BOAT

Boat is the ideal transportation in Nordland. The **Hurtigruten** stops twice daily (north and southbound) at 20 ports in northern Norway. It is possible to buy tickets between any harbors right on the boats. **OVDS** (Narvik, ☎ 76/92–37–00) ferries and express boats serve many towns in the region. **TFDS, Troms Fylkes Dampskibsselskap** (Tromsø, ☎ 77/64–81–00) operates various boat services in the region around Tromsø.

BY BUS

Most local buses in **Trondheim** stop at the Munkegata/Dronningens Gate intersection. Some routes end at the bus terminal (✉ Skakkes Gt. 40, ☎ 73/82–22–22). Tickets cost NKr12 and allow free transfer between buses (☎ 73/54–71–00) and streetcars (Gråkallbanen, ☎ 72/55–23–55).

North of **Bodø** and **Narvik** (a five-hour bus ride from Bodø), beyond the reach of the railroad, buses go virtually everywhere, but they don't go often. Get a comprehensive bus schedule from a tourist office or travel agent before making plans. Local bus companies include **Harstad Oppland Rutebil** (☎ 77/06–81–70), **Saltens Bilruter** (Bodø, ☎ 75/50–90–00), **Ofotens Bilruter** (Narvik, ☎ 76/92–35–00), **Tromsbuss** (Tromsø, ☎ 77/67–02–33), **Midttuns Busser** (Tromsø, ☎ 77/67–27–87), and **Finnmark Fylkesrederi og Ruteselskap** (FFR, Alta, ☎ 78/43–52–11; Hammerfest, ☎ 78/41–10–00).

BY CAR

The roads aren't a problem in northern Norway—most are quite good, although there are always narrow and winding stretches, especially along fjords. Distances are formidable. Route 17—the *Kystriksvegen* (Coastal Highway) from Namsos to Bodø—is an excellent alternative to E6. Getting to Tromsø and the North Cape involves additional driving on narrower roads off E6. In the northern winter, near-blizzard conditions and icy roads sometimes make it necessary to drive in a convoy. You'll know it when you see it: towns are cut off from traffic at access roads, and vehicles wait until their numbers are large enough to make the crossing safely.

You can also fly the extensive distances and then rent a car for sightseeing within the area, but book a rental car as far in advance as possible. There's no better way to see the Lofoten and Vesterålen islands than by car. Nordkapp (take the plane to Honningsvåg) is another excursion best made by car.

The best way to see the Lofoten Islands is by car since bus service is often limited and there is just so much to see. The main tourist office in Svolvær can point you to local rental agencies, whose rates tend to be quite high. Short distances between neighboring villages are doable by bicycle if you plan to stay in one village for several days.

BY PLANE
Northern Norway has excellent air connections through SAS, Braathens SAFE, and Widerøe (☞ Arriving and Departing by Plane, *above*).

BY TAXI
Taxi stands are located in strategic places in downtown **Trondheim.** All taxis are connected to the central dispatching office (☎ 73/50–50–73). Taxi numbers in other towns include the following: **Harstad** (☎ 77/ 06–20–50), **Narvik** (☎ 76/94–65–00), and **Tromsø** (☎ 77/60–30–00).

Contacts and Resources

GUIDED TOURS
Tromsø: The tourist information office (✉ Storgt. 61/63, 9001, ☎ 77/ 61–00–00) sells tickets for **City Sightseeing** (Dampskipskaia) and **M/F Karlsøy,** an original Arctic vessel that runs a fishing tour in the waters around Tromsø Island.

Trondheim: The Trondheim Tourist Association offers a number of tours. Tickets are sold at the tourist information office or at the start of the tour.

LATE-NIGHT PHARMACIES
Trondheim: St. Olav Vaktapotek (✉ Kjøpmannsgt. 65, ☎ 73/52–66– 66) is open Monday through Saturday 8:30 AM–midnight and Sunday 10 AM–midnight.

Tromsø: Svaneapoteket (✉ Fr. Langes Gt. 9, ☎ 77/68–64–24) is open daily 8:30–4:30 and 6–9.

VISITOR INFORMATION
Alta (✉ Top Of Norway, 9500, ☎ 78/43–54–44). **Bodø** (✉ Sjøgt. 21, 8006, ☎ 75/52–60–00). **Hammerfest** (✉ 9600, ☎ 78/41–21–85). **Harstad** (✉ Torvet 8, 9400, ☎ 77/06–32–35). **Lofoten** (✉ 8301 Svolvær, ☎ 76/07–30–00). **Mo i Rana** (✉ Polarsirkelen Reiselivslag, 8600 Mo, ☎ 75/15–04–21). **Narvik** (✉ Kongensgt. 66, 8500, ☎ 76/94–60–33). **Tromsø** (✉ Storgt. 61/63, 9001, ☎ 77/61–00–00). **Trondheim** (✉ Munkegt. 19, 7000, ☎ 73/92–93–94). **Vesterålen Reiselivslag** (✉ 8400 Sortland, ☎ 76/12–15–55). **Nordkapp** (✉ Nordkapphuset, Honningsvåg, ☎ 78/47–28–94). **Rognan** (Salten Tourist Board, ☎ 75/64–33–03).

SAMILAND TO SVALBARD AND THE FINNISH-RUSSIAN CONNECTION

Everyone has heard of Lapland, but few know its real name, Samiland. The Sami recognize no national boundaries, as their territory stretches from the Kola Peninsula in the Soviet Union through Finland, Sweden, and Norway. These indigenous reindeer herders are a distinct ethnic group, with a language related to Finnish. Although still considered nomadic, they no longer live in tents or huts, except for short periods during the summer, when their animals graze along the coast. They have had to conform to today's lifestyles, but their traditions survive through their language, music (called *joik*), art, and handicrafts. Norwegian Samiland is synonymous with the communities of Kautokeino and colorful Karasjok, capital of the Sami, in Finnmark.

Kautokeino

⠹ *129 km (80 mi) southeast of Alta.*

Kautokeino is the site of the Sami theater and the Nordic Sami Institute, dedicated to the study of Sami culture. It is a center for Sami handicrafts and education, complete with a school of reindeer herding.

Guovdageainnu (Kautokeino in the Sami language) **Gilisillju,** the local museum, documents the way of life of both the nomadic and the resident Sami of that area before World War II, with photographs and artifacts, including costumes, dwellings, and art. ⊠ *9520 Kautokeino,* ☎ *78/48–58–00.* ⎙ *NKr10.* ☉ *Mid-June–mid-Aug., weekdays 9–7, weekends noon–7; mid-Aug.–mid-June, weekdays 9–3.*

The Arts

During Easter, Kautokeino holds its annual **Easter Festival,** including theater, joik (a haunting, ancient form of solo, a cappella song, often in praise of nature), concerts, weddings, and exhibits of traditional crafts. Contact **Top Of Norway** (⊠ 9500 Alta, ☎ 78/43–54–44).

Shopping

Locals say **Juhl's Silver Gallery** (☎ 78/48–61–89) was Finnmark's first silversmith. Also sold are handicrafts and art from around the world.

Karasjok

⠹ *178 km (110 mi) from Kautokeino.*

Karasjok, on the other side of the Finnmark Plateau, is the seat of the 39-member Sami Parliament and capital of Samiland. It has a typical inland climate, with the accompanying temperature extremes. The best time to come is at Easter, when the communities are celebrating the weddings and baptisms of the year and taking part in reindeer races and other colorful festivities. In summer, when many of the Sami go to the coast with their reindeer, the area is not nearly as interesting.

The **Samid Vuorka-Davvirat** (Sami Collections) is a comprehensive museum (indoor and open-air) of Sami culture, with emphasis on the arts, reindeer herding, and the status of women in the Sami community. ⊠ *Museumsgt. 17,* ☎ *78/46–63–05.* ⎙ *NKr25.* ☉ *Mid-June–late Aug., Mon.–Sat. 9–6, Sun. 10–6; late Aug.–Oct., weekdays 9–3, weekends 10–3; Nov.–Mar., weekdays 9–3, weekends noon–3; Apr.–mid-June, weekdays 9–3, weekends 10–3.*

From late fall to early spring you can go **reindeer sledding.** A Sami guide will take you out on a wooden sled tied to a couple of unwieldy reindeer, and you'll clop through the barren, snow-covered scenery of Finnmark. Wide and relatively flat, the colorless winter landscape is veined by inky alder branches and little else. You'll reach a *lavvu,* a traditional Sami tent, and be invited in to share a meal of boiled reindeer, bread, jam, and strong coffee next to an open alder fire. It's an extraordinary experience. Contact Karasjok Opplevelser (☎ 78/46–69–00).

Dining and Lodging

$$$–$$$$ ✕⊡ **North Cape Hotel.** This establishment feels more like a ski chalet
★   than a hotel, with bright rooms, done in warm blues and reds, that are cozy rather than industrial. The lobby is more staid. The hotel's wonderful Sami restaurant, Storgammen, serves traditional fare, including reindeer cooked over open fires. ⊠ *Box 38, 9731 Karasjok,* ☎ *78/46–74–00,* 𝖥𝖠𝖷 *78/46–68–02. 56 rooms. 2 restaurants, bar, saunas, meeting rooms. AE, DC, MC, V.*

Outdoor Activities and Sports

DOGSLEDDING

Sven Engholm, who has won the longest sledge race in Europe, leads tours with his pack dogs. In winter, you can lead your own dog sled, accompany one on skis, or just go along for the ride. In summer, you can hike with the huskies. Contact **Husky Adventure** (☏ 78/46–71–66) for information.

HIKING AND FISHING

In between the Alta and Karasjok areas, the **Finnmarksvidda** has marked trails with overnight possibilities in lodges. Contact the Norske Turistforening (✉ Buks 1963 Vika, 0125 Oslo, ☏ 22/83–25–50) and the Finnmark Travel Association (☏ 78/43–54–44). Finnmark boasts some of Norway's best fishing rivers. For more information, call **Top Of Norway** (☏ 78/43–54–44.)

Shopping

The specialties of the region are Sami crafts, particularly handmade knives. In **Samelandssenteret** (☏ 78/46–71–55) is a large collection of shops featuring northern specialties, including **Knivsmed Strømeng** (☏ 78/46–71–05).

Kirkenes

85   At its very top, Norway hooks over Finland and touches Russia for 122 km (75 mi). The towns in east Finnmark have a more heterogeneous population than those in the rest of the country. A century ago, during hard times in Finland, many industrious Finns settled in this region, and their descendants keep the language alive there.

A good way to visit this part of Norway is to fly to Kirkenes and then explore the region by car. Only Malta was bombed more than Kirkenes during World War II—virtually everything you see in town has been built within the past 45 years.

In winter this entire region, blanketed by snow and cold, is off the beaten track. As the Norwegians say, there is no bad weather, only bad clothes—so bundle up and explore.

During the more than 300 bombings of Kirkenes, its residents sought cover in subterranean tunnels under the town's center. One of them, **Andersgrotta,** is open to the public. ☏ 78/99–25–01. ▧ NKr40. ☉ *Opening hours vary.*

From mid-June to mid-August, the **FFR** (✉ Hammerfest, ☏ 78/41–10–00) operates visa-free day cruises to Murmansk, Russia, on a high-speed catamaran. Booking is required two weeks in advance.

OFF THE   **ST. GEORGS KAPELL** – Forty-five kilometers (28 miles) west of Kirkenes is
BEATEN PATH   the only Russian Orthodox chapel in Norway, where the Orthodox Skolt-Sami had their summer encampment. It's a tiny building, and services are held outside, weather permitting.

Lodging

$$–$$$$ 🏨 **Rica Arctic Hotel.** Do not confuse this hotel with the Rica Hotel Kirkenes, an older establishment, which ends up costing the same during the summer. Rooms here are spacious and pretty, with white-painted furniture and light print textiles. ✉ *Kongensgt. 1–3, 9900,* ☏ *78/99–29–29,* 🖷 *78/99–11–59. 80 rooms. Restaurant, bar, indoor pool, beauty salon, sauna, exercise room, nightclub, convention center. AE, DC, MC, V.*

Storskog

 About 60 km (37 mi) from Kirkenes.

Just east of Kirkenes is Storskog, for many years the only official land crossing of the border between Norway and Russia. The tiny village of **Grense Jakobselv** on the Russian border is where King Oscar II built a chapel right at the border in 1869 as a protest against constant Russian encroachment in the area.

OFF THE
BEATEN PATH

ØVRE PASVIK – The southernmost part of Finnmark, about 118 km (73 mi) south of Kirkens, is Øvre Pasvik national park, a narrow tongue of land tucked between Finland and Russia. This subarctic evergreen forest is the western end of Siberia's taiga and supports many varieties of flora found only here. The area is surprisingly lush, and in good years all the cloudberries make the swamps shine orange.

Svalbard

 640 km (400 mi) north of the North Cape.

The islands of Svalbard, the largest of which is Spitsbergen, have officially been part of Norway only since 1920. They might have remained wilderness, with only the occasional visitor, if coal had not been discovered late in the 19th century. Today both a Norwegian and a Russian coal company have operations there, and there are two Russian coal miners' communities. The islands offer ample opportunities for ski, dogsled, boat, and snowmobile exploring.

Because Svalbard is so far north, it has four months of continual daylight, from April 21 to August 21. Summers can be lush, with hundreds of varieties of wildflowers. The season is so compressed that buds, full-blown flowers, and seed appear simultaneously on the same plant.

The capital, **Longyearbyen,** is 90 minutes by air from Tromsø. Named for an American, John Monroe Longyear, who established a mining operation there in 1906, the "settlement" is home to only about 1,200 Norwegians. Only three species of land mammal besides humans (polar bears, reindeer, and Arctic foxes) and one species of bird (ptarmigan) have adapted to Svalbard winters, but during the summer months, more than 30 species of bird nest on the steep cliffs of the islands, and white whales, seals, and walruses also come for the season. Do heed warnings about polar bears: they can be a real hazard.

Traditionally, only the richest tourists and the most serious scientists traveled to Svalbard. Now the islands have become more accessible. If Hammerfest felt like the edge of Europe, Svalbard feels like the edge of the world. Striations of snow have singed their way across the wild, jagged mountains, splintered down by millennia of arctic conditions. In early summer, antlerless reindeer lounge on the soot-colored tundra. Rumors of hungry polar bears looking to gobble up lonesome travelers tend to precede a trip to the icy island. But adventurous trekkers should not miss the chance to experience this strange, icy wilderness, with its arctic animals and frozen rock formations. Just go with caution, and only travel outside Longyearbyen with an experienced tour guide.

Lodging

$$$–$$$$ **Svalbard Polar Hotel.** Svalbard's only full-service hotel consists of rooms originally built to house the U.S. team sponsor during the Winter Olympics in Lillehammer. An enormous panoramic window in the hotel's dining and bar area provides a view of Mount Hjorthavnfjellet across the waters of the Icefjord. In summer, you can watch the sun

cross from one side of the mountain at dusk to the other at dawn—
many locals do this from the hotel's bar. ⊠ *Box 544, 9170,* ☎ *79/02-
35–00,* F̄AX̄ *79/02–35–00. 67 rooms, 4 suites. Restaurant, 2 bars, sauna.
AE, DC, MC, V.*

The Arts

To get a sense of the frosty place during other times of the year, see the
Kaare Tveter Collection slide presentation. One of Norway's most admired artists, Tveter donated 40 illustrations of Svalbard's pink mountains, black fjords, and charcoal gray skies to the new Galleri Svalbard.
There are more than 60 Arctic region maps, which are centuries old,
that fill an adjacent exhibition room. ⊠ *Galleri Svalbard.* ☎ *79/02-
23–40.* ☉ *Tues.–Thurs, 5–7, Sat. 4–6, Sun. 4–9.*

Samiland to Svalbard A to Z

Arriving and Departing

BY BOAT

Hurtigruten now cruises from Tromsø to Svalbard, dipping down to
the North Cape afterwards. Contact Bergen Line (☞ Norway A to Z,
below).

(☞ Trondheim to the North Cape A to Z, *above*).

Getting Around

(☞ Trondheim to the North Cape A to Z, *above*).

Contacts and Resources

GUIDED TOURS

Contact **Sami Travel A/S** (⊠ Kautokeino, ☎ 78/48–56–00) for adventure
trips to Sami settlements. Because of extreme weather conditions and
the dangers of polar bears, the best way to see Svalbard is through an
organized tour. Longyearbyen's tour operators lead even very small
groups on exploring trips lasting anywhere from a day to several
weeks. **Svalbard Polar Travel** (⊠ 9170 Longyearbyen, ☎ 79/02–19–
71) arranges combination air-sea visits, from five-day minicruises to
12-day trekking expeditions on the rim of the North Pole. **Spitsbergen Travel** (⊠ 9170 Longyearbyen, ☎ 79/02–24–00) offers specialized "exploring" walks and hikes that focus on the plant and animal
life of the region. If you're short on time, the day-long boat trip to Bar-
entsburg provides a snapshot of the surrounding area's icy beauty.

VISITOR INFORMATION

Karasjok (9730 Karasjok, ☎ 78/46–73–60). **Lofoten** (8300 Svolvær,
☎ 76/07–30–00). **Svalbard** (9170 Longyearbyen, ☎ 79/02–23–03).

NORWAY A TO Z

Arriving and Departing

Oslo Fornebu Airport is the gateway to Norway for most visitors. Once
called a "cafeteria with a landing strip," it has been transformed into
a modern airport worthy of a capital city. Fornebu became such a busy
airport that its own air traffic has surpassed its capacity, and therefore
a new airport, Gardermoen, is scheduled to open in 1998. Other international airports include those in Bergen, Kristiansand, Sandefjord,
Stavanger, and Trondheim.

By Boat

FROM THE UNITED KINGDOM

Only one ferry line serves Norway from the United Kingdom, **Color
Line** (⊠ Tyne Commission Quay, North Shields [near Newcastle],

LEN29 6EA, ☎ 091/296–1313; ✉ Skoltegrunnskaien, 5000 Bergen, ☎ 55/32–27–80; or ✉ 405 Park Ave., New York, NY 10022, ☎ 800/ 323–7436), which has three departures a week between Bergen, Stavanger, and Newcastle during the summer season (May 22–Sept. 10) and two during the rest of the year. Crossings take about 22 hours. Monday sailings stop first in Stavanger and arrive in Bergen six hours later, whereas the other trips stop first in Bergen.

By Plane

FROM NORTH AMERICA

A nonstop flight from New York to Oslo takes about 7½ hours.

Scandinavian Airlines (SAS, ☎ 800/221–2350) has daily nonstop flights to Oslo from Newark; daily connections to Oslo via Copenhagen from Chicago, Los Angeles, and Seattle; and twice-weekly connections (also via Copenhagen) from Toronto and Anchorage. **Icelandair** (☎ 800/ 223–5500) flies from New York and Baltimore to Oslo via Reykjavík.

FROM THE UNITED KINGDOM

A nonstop flight from London to Oslo is about 1¾ hours and about 1½ hours to Stavanger.

SAS (☎ 0171/734–4020, FAX 0171/465–0125) flies from Heathrow to Oslo, Stavanger, and Bergen, and from Aberdeen to Stavanger. **Braathens SAFE** (☎ 0191/214–0991) operates flights from Newcastle to Stavanger, Bergen, and Oslo, and from London Gatwick to Oslo. **AirUK** (☎ 0345/ 666–777) has several flights weekly from Aberdeen to Stavanger and Bergen. **British Airways** (☎ 0345/222–111) offers nonstop flights from Heathrow to Bergen, Oslo, and Stavanger. **Aer Lingus** (☎ 0181/899–4747; in Ireland, ☎ 0001/377–777), **Cimber Air** (☎ 0645–737–747), **Business Air** (☎ 01382/66345), **Midtfly** (☎ 01224/723357), and **Icelandair** (☎ 0171/388–5599; or ☎ 0181/745–7051 at Heathrow Airport) all have flights between Great Britain or Ireland and major Scandinavian cities.

By Train

Traveling from Britain to Norway by train is not difficult. The best connection leaves London's Victoria Station (☎ 0171/928–5100) at noon and connects at Dover with a boat to Oostende, Belgium. From Oostende there is a sleeping-car-only connection to Copenhagen that arrives the next morning at 8:25. The train to Oslo leaves at 9:45 AM and arrives at 7:42 PM.

DISCOUNT PASSES

A number of special discounted trips are available, including the **InterRail Pass,** which is available for European residents of all ages, and the **EurailPass,** sold in the United States only.

Getting Around

The southern part of Norway can be considered fairly compact—all major cities are about a day's drive from each other. The distances make themselves felt on the way north, where Norway becomes narrower as it inches up to and beyond the Arctic Circle and hooks over Sweden and Finland to touch Russia. Because distances are so great, it is virtually impossible to visit the entire country from one base.

By Boat

Ferries and passenger ships remain important means of transportation. Along west-coast fjords, car ferries are a way of life. More specialized boat service includes hydrofoil-catamaran trips between Stavanger, Haugesund, and Bergen. There are also fjord cruises out of these cities and others in the north. **Color Line** (✉ Box 1422, Vika 0115, Oslo, ☎ 22/94–44–00, FAX 22/83–07–76) is a major carrier in Norwegian waters.

Norway's most renowned boat trip is **Hurtigruten**, or the *Coastal Steamer,* which departs from Bergen and stops at 36 ports in six days, ending with Kirkenes, near the Russian border, before turning back. Tickets can be purchased for the entire journey or for individual legs. Tickets are available through **Bergen Line travel agents** (✉ 405 Park Ave., New York, NY 10022, ☎ 800/323–7436), or directly from the companies that run the service: **FFR** (✉ 9600 Hammerfest, ☎ 78/41–10–00), **OVDS** (✉ 8501 Narvik, ☎ 76/92–37–00), **Hurtigruten Booking** (✉ Kjøpmannsgt. 52, 7011 Trondheim, ☎ 73/51–51–20, FAX 73/51–51–46), and **TFDS** (✉ 9000 Tromsø, ☎ 77/68–60–88).

By Bus

Every end station of the railroad is supported by a number of bus routes, some of which are operated by NSB, others by local companies. Long-distance buses usually take longer than the railroad, and fares are only slightly lower. Virtually every settlement on the mainland is served by bus, and for anyone with a desire to get off the beaten track, a pay-as-you-go open-ended bus trip is the best way to see Norway.

Most long-distance buses leave from **Bussterminalen** (✉ Galleri Oslo, Schweigaardsgt., 10, ☎ 22/17–01–66), close to Oslo Central Station. **Nor-Way Bussekspress** (✉ Bussterminalen, ☎ 22/17–52–90, FAX 22/17–59–22) has more than 40 different bus services, covering 10,000 km (6,200 mi) and 500 destinations, and can arrange any journey. One of its participating services, **Feriebussen** (✉ Østerdal Billag A/S, 2560 Alvdal, ☎ 62/48–74–00), offers five package tours with English-speaking guides.

By Car

All vehicles registered abroad are required to carry international liability insurance and an international accident report form, which can be obtained from automobile clubs. Collision insurance is recommended. One important rule when driving in Norway: yield to the vehicle approaching from the right.

EMERGENCY ASSISTANCE

Norsk Automobil Forbund (✉ NAF, ☎ 22/34–16–00 for 24-hour service) patrols main roads and has emergency telephones on mountain roads.

GASOLINE

Gas stations are plentiful, and *blyfri bensin* (unleaded gasoline) and diesel fuel are sold virtually everywhere from self-service gas pumps. Those marked *kort* are 24-hour pumps, which take oil-company credit cards or bank cards, either of which is inserted directly into the pump. Gas costs approximately NKr8.50 per liter.

ROAD CONDITIONS

Four-lane highways are the exception and are found only around major cities. Outside of main routes, roads tend to be narrow and sharply twisting, with only token guardrails, and during the summer roads are always crowded. Along the west coast, waits for ferries and passage through tunnels can be significant. Don't expect to cover more than 240 km (150 mi) in a day, especially in fjord country.

Norwegian roads are well marked with directional, distance, and informational signs. Some roads, particularly those over mountains, can close for all or part of the winter. If you drive outside major roads in winter, make sure the car is equipped with studded tires for improved traction. Roads are not salted but are left with a hard-packed layer of snow on top of the asphalt. If you're renting, choose a small car with front-wheel drive. Also bring an ice scraper, snow brush, small shovel, and heavy clothes for emergencies. Although the weather along the coast is sunny, a few hours inland, temperatures may be 15°F colder, and snowfall is the rule rather than the exception.

RULES OF THE ROAD

Driving is on the right. The maximum speed limit is 90 kph (55 mph) on major motorways. On other highways, the limit is 80 kph (50 mph). The speed limit in cities is 50 kph (30 mph), and 30 kph (18 mph) in residential areas.

Dimmed headlights are mandatory at all times, as is the use of seat belts and children's seats (when appropriate) in both front and rear seats. All cars must carry red reflecting warning triangles to be placed a safe distance from a disabled vehicle.

Norway has strict drinking-and-driving laws, and routine roadside checks, especially on Friday and Saturday nights, are common. The legal limit is a blood-alcohol percentage of 0.05%, which corresponds to a glass of wine or a bottle of low-alcohol beer. If you are stopped for a routine check, you may be required to take a breath test. If that result is positive, you must submit to a blood test. No exceptions are made for foreigners, who can lose their licenses on the spot.

Speeding is also punished severely. Most roads are monitored by radar and cameras in gray metal boxes. Signs warning of *Automatisk Trafikkontroll* (Automatic Traffic Monitoring) are posted periodically along appropriate roads. Radar controls are frequent on weekends, especially along major highways. Make sure you double-check all directions and have an up-to-date map before you venture out, because some high way numbers have changed in the past few years, particularly routes beginning with "E." You may come across construction in and around Oslo and other major cities.

By Plane

SAS (☎ 810/03–300) serves most major cities, including Svalbard. **Braathens SAFE** (☎ 67/59–70–00) is the major domestic airline, serving cities throughout the country and along the coast as far north as Tromsø and Svalbard. It also has international routes from Oslo to Billund, Denmark; Malmö, Sweden; and Newcastle, England. **Widerøe** (☎ 67/11–14–60) serves smaller airports (with smaller planes), mostly along the coast, and in northern Norway. **Norsk Air** (☎ 33/46–90–00), a subsidiary of Widerøe, provides similar services in the southern part of the country. **Coast Air** (☎ 52/83–41–10) and **Norlink** (☎ 77/67–57–80), an SAS subsidiary, are commuter systems linking both smaller and larger airports. All flights within Scandinavia are no-smoking, as are all airports in Norway, except in designated areas.

A number of special fares are available within Norway year-round, including air passes, family tickets, weekend excursions, and youth (up to the age of 26) and senior (older than 67) discounts. Youth fares are cheapest when purchased from the automatic ticket machines at the airport on the day of departure. All Norwegian routes have reduced rates from July through the middle of August, and tickets can be purchased on the spot. SAS offers special *"Jackpot"* fares all year within Norway and Scandinavia, as well as reasonable *"Visit Scandinavia"* fares, which must be purchased in the United States in conjunction with, and at the same time as, an SAS flight to Scandinavia

DISCOUNT PASSES

Braathens SAFE sells a **Visit Norway** pass, which includes the Scandinavian BonusPass. It is available at **Passage Tours of Scandinavia** (☎ 800/548–5960) and **Borton Overseas** (☎ 800/843–0602).

By Taxi

Even the smallest villages have some form of taxi service. Towns on the railroad normally have taxi stands just outside the station. All city taxis are connected with a central dispatching office, so there is only one main telephone number, the taxi central. Look in the telephone book under "Taxi" or "Drosje."

By Train

NSB, the Norwegian State Railway System, has five main lines originating from the **Oslo S Station.** Train tickets can be purchased in railway stations or from travel agencies. NSB has its own travel agency in Oslo (⊠ Stortingsgt. 28, ☎ 22/83–88–50). The longest train runs north to Trondheim, then extends onward as far as Fauske and Bodø. The southern line hugs the coast to Stavanger, whereas the western line crosses some famous scenic territory on the way to Bergen. An eastern line to Stockholm links Norway with Sweden, while another southern line through Gothenburg, Sweden, is the main connection with continental Europe. Narvik, north of Bodø, is the last stop on Sweden's Ofot line, the world's northernmost rail system, which runs from Stockholm via Kiruna. It is possible to take a five-hour bus trip between Bodø and Narvik to connect with the other train.

NSB trains are clean, comfortable, and punctual. Most have special compartments for travelers with disabilities and for families with children younger than two years of age. First- and second-class tickets are available. Both seat and sleeper reservations are required on express and overnight trains. Reserve a few days ahead in the summer, during major holidays, and for Friday and Sunday trains.

Discounted fares include family, senior-citizen (including not-yet-senior spouses), and off-peak "mini" fares, which must be purchased a day in advance. NSB gives student discounts only to foreigners studying at Norwegian institutions.

DISCOUNT PASSES

Norway participates in the following rail programs: **EurailPass** (and its flexipass variations), **Eurail Drive, ScanRail Pass, Scanrail 'n Drive, InterRail,** and **Nordturist Card.** A **Norway Rail Pass** is available for one or two weeks of unlimited rail travel within Norway. The ticket is sold in the United States through **ScanAm** (⊠ 933 Hwy. 23, Pomton Plains, NJ 07444, ☎ 800/545–2204). Prices are approximately $190 for one week in second class; $255 for two weeks in second class. First-class rail passes are about 30% higher. Low-season prices are offered October through April. Rail passes do not guarantee that you will get seats on the trains you want to ride, and seat reservations are sometimes required, particularly on express trains. You will also need reservations for overnight sleeping accommodations.

Contacts and Resources

Customs

Residents of non-European countries who are over 18 may import duty-free into Norway 200 cigarettes or 500 grams of other tobacco goods, and souvenirs and gifts to the value of NKr 1,200. Residents of European countries who are over 18 may import 200 cigarettes or 250 grams of tobacco or cigars, a small amount of perfume, and other goods to the value of NKr 1,200. Anyone over 20 may bring in 1 liter of wine and 1 liter of liquor or 2 liters of wine or beer.

Embassies

U.S. (✉ Drammensvn. 18, N-0255 Oslo, ☏ 22–44–85–50). **Canada** (✉ Oscars Gt. 20, N-0352 Oslo, ☏ 22/46–69–55). **U.K.** (✉ Thomas Heftyes Gt. 8, N-0244 Oslo, ☏ 22/55–24–00).

Emergencies

Police: ☏ 112. **Fire:** ☏ 110. **Ambulance:** ☏ 113.

Language

Norwegian has three additional vowels: æ, ø, and å. Æ is pronounced as a short "a." The ø, sometimes printed as *oe*, is the same as ö in German and Swedish, pronounced very much like a short "u." The å is a contraction of the archaic "aa" and sounds like long "o." These three letters appear at the end of alphabetical listings.

There are two officially sanctioned Norwegian languages, Bokmål and Nynorsk. Bokmål is used by 84% of the population and is the main written form of Norwegian, the language of books, as the first half of its name indicates. Nynorsk, which translates as "new Norwegian," is actually a compilation of older dialect forms from rural Norway, which evolved during the national romantic period around the turn of this century. All Norwegians are required to study both languages, and 25% of all state (NRK) television and radio broadcasting is required to be in Nynorsk. Every Norwegian also receives at least seven years of English instruction, starting in the second grade.

The Sami (incorrectly called Lapp) people have their own language, which is distantly related to Finnish.

Lodging

For camping information and a list of sites, contact local tourist offices or the **Norwegian Automobile Federation** (✉ Storgt. 2, 0155, Oslo 1, ☏ 22/34–14–00). For a list of vandrerhjem in Norway, contact **Norske Vandrerhjem** (✉ Dronningensgt. 26, 0154 Oslo, ☏ 22/42–14–10, FAX 22/42–44–76). ☞ Lodging *in* Pleasures and Pastimes, *above*.

Mail

The letter rate for Norway is NKr3.50, NKr4 for the other Nordic countries, NKr4.50 for Europe, and NKr5.50 for outside Europe for a letter weighing up to 20 grams (¾ ounce).

Money and Expenses

CURRENCY

The unit of currency in Norway is the *krone* (plural: *kroner*), which translates as "crown," written officially as NOK. Price tags are seldom marked this way, but instead read "Kr" followed by the amount, such as Kr10. (In this book, the Norwegian krone is abbreviated NKr.) One krone is divided into 100 *øre*, and coins of 10 and 50 øre and 1, 5, 10, and 20 kroner are in circulation, although 10 øre are no longer in production. Bills are issued in denominations of 50, 100, 200, 500, and 1,000 kroner. In summer 1997, the exchange rate was NKr7.12 to U.S.$1, NKr11.6 to £1, and NKr5.17 to C$1. These rates fluctuate, so be sure to check them when planning a trip.

SALES-TAX REFUNDS

Value-added tax, V.A.T. for short but called *moms* all over Scandinavia, is a hefty 23% on all purchases except books; it is included in the prices of goods. All purchases of consumer goods totaling more than NKr300 (approximately $45) for export by nonresidents are eligible for value-added tax refunds.

Shops subscribing to "Norway Tax-Free Shopping" provide customers with vouchers, which they must present together with their purchases on departure to receive an on-the-spot refund of 16.25% of the tax.

Shops that do not subscribe to this program have slightly more detailed forms, which must be presented to the Norwegian Customs Office along with the goods to obtain a refund by mail. This refund is closer to the actual amount of the tax.

It's essential to have both the forms and the goods available for inspection upon departure. Make sure the appropriate stamps are on the voucher or other forms before leaving the country.

SAMPLE PRICES

Cup of coffee, from NKr12 in a cafeteria to NKr25 or more in a restaurant; a 20-pack of cigarettes, NKr50; a half-liter of beer, NKr30–NKr50; the smallest hot dog (with bun plus *lompe*—a flat Norwegian potato bread—mustard, ketchup, and fried onions) at a convenience store, NKr15; cheapest bottle of wine from a government store, NKr60; the same bottle at a restaurant, NKr120–NKr200; urban transit fare in Oslo, NKr15; soft drink, from NKr20 in a cafeteria to NKr35 in a better restaurant; sandwich at a cafeteria, NKr40; 1½-km (1-mi) taxi ride, NKr30–NKr50 depending on time of day.

TIPPING

Tipping is kept to a minimum in Norway because service charges are added to most bills. It is, however, handy to have a supply of NKr5 or 10 coins for less formal service. Tip only in local currency.

Airport and railroad porters (if you can find them) have fixed rates per bag, so they will tell you how much they should be paid. Tips to doormen vary according to the type of bag and the distance carried—NKr5–NKr10 each, with similar tips for porters carrying bags to the room. Room service usually has a service charge included already, so tipping is discretionary.

Round off a taxi fare to the next round digit, or tip anywhere from NKr5 to NKr10, a little more if the driver has been helpful.

All restaurants include a service charge, ranging from 12% to 15%, in the bill. It is customary to add an additional 5% for exceptional service, but it is not obligatory. Maître d's are not tipped, and coat checks have flat rates, ranging from NKr5 to NKr10 per person.

Opening and Closing Times

BANKS

Banks are open weekdays 9 to 4, Thursday until 5. In summer, banks open at 8:15 and close at 3, with a Thursday closing at 5.

POST OFFICES

Most post offices are open weekdays 8 to 5, Saturday 9 to 2. In small towns, post offices are often closed on Saturdays.

SHOPS

Most shops are open 9 or 10 to 5 weekdays, Thursday until 7, Saturday 9 to 2, and are closed Sunday. In some areas, especially in larger cities, stores stay open later on weekdays. Large shopping centers, for example, are usually open until 8 weekdays and 6 on Saturdays. Supermarkets are open until 8 or 10 weekdays and until 6 on Saturdays. During the summer, most shops close weekdays at 4 and at 1 on Saturday.

Outdoor Activities and Sports

Norway is a sports lover's paradise. Close to 100 recreational and competitive sports are recognized in Norway, each with its own national association, 57 of which are affiliated with the **Norges Idrettsforbund** (Norwegian Confederation of Sports, ✉ Hauger Skolevei 1, 1351 Rud, ☎ 67/15–46–00). The tourist board's Norway brochure, which lists sporting- and active-holiday resources and contacts, is a more helpful starting point for visitors.

BIKING

Most cities have marked bike and ski routes and paths. Bicycling on country roads away from traffic is a favorite national pastime, but as most routes are hilly, this demands good physical condition. All cyclists are required to wear protective helmets and use lights at night. You can rent a bike and get local maps through any local tourist board.

Den Norske Turistforening (DNT, ⊠ Box 1963 Vika, 0125 Oslo 1, ☎ 22/82–28–00, FAX 22/83–24–78) provides inexpensive lodging for cyclists planning overnight trips. You can also contact the helpful **Syklistenes Landsforening** (⊠ Maridalsvn. 60, 0458 Oslo 4, ☎ 22/71–92–93) for general information and maps, as well as the latest weather conditions.

BIRD-WATCHING

Northern Norway contains some of northern Europe's largest bird sanctuaries and teems with fantastic numbers of seabirds, even eagles. For organized tours, contact **Borton Overseas** (☎ 800/843–0602) or the Norwegian Tourist Board.

CANOEING

There are plenty of lakes and streams for canoeing in Norway, as well as rental facilities. Contact **Norges Padlerforbund** (⊠ Hauger Skolevei 1, 1351 Bærum, ☎ 67/15–46–00) for a list of rental companies and regional canoeing centers.

DIVING

Diving is very well organized and popular in Norway, especially on the west coast. There are few restrictions regarding sites—special permission is required to dive in a harbor, and diving near army installations is restricted. Contact **Norges Dykkforbund** (⊠ Hauger Skolevei 1, 1351 Baerum, ☎ 67/15–46–00) for a list of diving centers.

FISHING

To fish, you'll have to buy an annual fishing tax card at the post office and a local license from the sporting-goods store nearest the fishing site. Live bait is prohibited, and imported tackle must be disinfected before use.

HANG GLIDING

The mountains and hills of Norway provide excellent take-off spots. However, winds and weather conspire to make conditions unpredictable. For details on local clubs, regulations, and equipment rental, contact **Norsk Aeroklubb** (⊠ Moellesvingen 2, 0854 Oslo, ☎ 22/93–03–00).

RAFTING

Rafting excursions are offered throughout Norway. For more information, contact **Flåteopplevelser** (⊠ Postboks 227, 2051 Jessheim, ☎ 63/97–29–04) or **Norwegian Wildlife and Rafting** (⊠ 2254 Lundersæter, ☎ 62/82–97–24).

SAILING

Contact **Norges Seilforbund** (⊠ Hauger Skolevei 1, 1351 Bærum, ☎ 67/56–85–75) about facilities around the country.

SKIING

The **Skiforeningen** (⊠ Kongevn. 5, 0390 Oslo 3, ☎ 22/92–32–00) provides national snow-condition reports.

SPORTS FOR PEOPLE WITH DISABILITIES

Norway encouraged active participation in sports for people with disabilities long before it became popular elsewhere and has many Special

Olympics medal winners. **Beitostølen Helsesportsenter** (✉ 2953 Beitostølen, ☎ 61/34–12–00) has sports facilities for the blind and other physically challenged people as well as training programs for instructors. Sports offered include skiing, hiking, running, and horseback riding.

Telephones

The telephone system in Norway is modern and efficient; international direct service is available throughout the country. Phone numbers consist of eight digits throughout the country.

Public telephones are of two types. Push-button phones, which accept NKr1, 5, and 10 coins (some accept NKr20 coins), are easy to use: lift the receiver, listen for the dial tone, insert the coins, dial the number, and wait for a connection. The digital screen at the top of the box indicates the amount of money in your "account."

Older rotary telephones sometimes have a grooved slope at the top for NKr1 coins, allowing them to drop into the phone as needed. Place several in the slope, lift the receiver, listen for the dial tone, dial the number, and wait for a connection. When the call is connected, the telephone will emit a series of beeps, allowing coins to drop into the telephone.

Both types of telephones have warning signals (short pips) indicating that the purchased time is almost over.

COUNTRY CODE

The country code for Norway is 47. There are no longer city codes, except in that numbers in each city start with the same two-digit prefix, such as 22 (Oslo) and 55 (Bergen). You have to dial all eight digits whether or not you're in the city. Telephone numbers starting with the prefix 82 cost extra.

DIRECTORY ASSISTANCE AND OPERATOR INFORMATION

Dial 180 for information for Norway and the other Scandinavian countries, 181 for other international telephone numbers.

INTERNATIONAL CALLS

Dial the international access code, 00, then the country code, and number. All telephone books list country code numbers, including the United States and Canada (1), Great Britain (44), and Australia (61). For operator-assisted calls, dial 117 for national calls and 115 for international calls. All international operators speak English.

You can contact U.S. operators from Norway by dialing local access codes: **AT&T USADirect** (☎ 800/19011), **MCI Call USA** (☎ 800/19912), **Sprint Express** (☎ 050/12877 or ☎ 800/12877).

LOCAL CALLS

Local calls cost NKr2 or NKr3 from a pay phone.

LONG-DISTANCE CALLS

All eight digits are required when dialing in Norway, both for local and long-distance calls. Rates vary according to distance and time of day. Toll-free numbers beginning with "800" or "810" are also becoming more common, although this is mostly among large corporations.

Visitor Information

Scandinavian Tourist Board. (✉ 655 3rd Ave., New York, NY 10017, ☎ 212/949–2333, FAX 212/983–5260.)

Norwegian Tourist Board. (✉ 5 Lower Regent St., London SW1Y 4LX, ☎ 0171/839–6255, FAX 0171/839–6014.)

6 Sweden

In the towns and cities of Scandinavia's largest country, contemporary architecture sits side-by-side with dramatic designs of a bygone era. In the south, red-painted wooden farmhouses line the shores of pristine, sun-dappled lakes. Untamed rivers cut through isolated northern moorland, and glacier-topped mountains neighbor vast forests of pine, spruce, and birch.

SWEDEN REQUIRES THE visitor to travel far, in both distance and attitude. Approximately the size of California, Sweden reaches as far north as the Arc-

Updated by
Daniel Cooper

tic fringes of Europe, where glacier-topped mountains and thousands of acres of pine, spruce, and birch forests are broken here and there by wild rivers, countless pristine lakes, and desolate moorland. In the more populated south, roads meander through mile after mile of softly undulating countryside, skirting lakes and passing small villages with their ubiquitous sharp-pointed church spires. Here, the lush forests that dominate Sweden's northern landscape have largely fallen to the plow.

Once the dominant power of the region, Sweden has traditionally looked mostly inward, seeking to find its own, Nordic solutions. During the cold war, it tried with considerable success to steer its famous "Middle Way" between the two superpowers, both economically and politically. Its citizens were in effect subjected to a giant social experiment aimed at creating a perfectly just society, one that adopted the best aspects of both socialism and capitalism.

In the late 1980s, as it slipped into the worst economic recession since the 1930s, Sweden made adjustments that lessened the role of its all-embracing welfare state in the lives of its citizens. Although fragile, the conservative coalition, which defeated the long-incumbent Social Democrats in the fall of 1991, attempted to make further cutbacks in welfare spending as the country faced one of the largest budget deficits in Europe. In a kind of nostalgic backlash, the populace voted the Social Democrats back into power in 1994, hoping to recapture the party's policy of cradle-to-grave protection. The world economy hasn't exactly cooperated, and the country's budget deficit is only now crawling back to parity. An influx of immigrants is reshaping what was once a homogeneous society. As a result, the mostly blond, blue-eyed Swedes may now be more open to the outside world than at any other time in their history. Indeed, another major change was Sweden's decision to join the European Union (EU) as of January 1995, a move that represents a radical break with its traditional independent stance on international issues. So far, the domestic benefits of membership are not tangible, but the country's exporting industries have made considerable gains.

The country possesses stunning natural assets. In the forests, moose, deer, bears, and lynx roam, coexisting with the whine of power saws and the rumble of automatic logging machines as mankind exploits a natural resource that remains the country's economic backbone. Environmental awareness, however, is high. Fish abound in sparkling lakes and tumbling rivers, sea eagles and ospreys soar over myriad pine-clad islands in the archipelagoes off the east and west coasts.

The country is Europe's fourth largest, 482,586 square km (173,731 square mi) in area, and its population of 8.7 million is thinly spread. If, like Greta Garbo—one of its most famous exports—you enjoy being alone, you've come to the right place. A law called *Allemansrätt* guarantees public access to the countryside; NO TRESPASSING signs are seldom seen.

Sweden stretches 1,563 km (977 mi) from the barren Arctic north to the fertile plains of the south. Contrasts abound, but they are neatly tied together by a superbly efficient infrastructure, embracing air, road, and rail. You can catch salmon in the far north and, thanks to the excellent domestic air network, have it cooked by the chef of your luxury hotel in Stockholm later the same day.

Sweden

0 50 miles
0 75 km

Kiruna

*Norwegian
Sea*

E10

Gällivare
Jokkmokk

400

A3

Arjeplog

Tärnaby

E10

Haparanda
Töre

Luleälven

Kalix

E12

Sorsele

Arvidsjaur

Luleå

Storuman

95

Piteå

Lycksele

Skellefteå

342

45

Åsele

Umeälven

92

Umeå

Strömsund

60

E4

Åre

Östersund

Tännäs

E14

Ljungan

Sundsvall

FINLAND

NORWAY

34

*Gulf
of
Bothnia*

Idre

45

Hudiksvall

70

Bollnäs

Mora

Söderhamn

Klardlen

62

Falun
80

Gävle

Borlänge

Avesta

Fagersta

E4

Uppsala

Karlstad

Västerås

E18

Mälaren

Stockholm

Gulf of Finland

E18

Mellerud

Örebro

E20

Strömstad

Vänern

Gotska
Sandön

Uddevalla

Trollhättan

E20

Norrköping

ESTONIA

Göteborg

Vättern

E4

Linköping

*Baltic
Sea*

40

Jönköping

*Gulf of
Riga*

Borås

Nässjö

E22

Visby

Falkenberg

E6/E20

Värnamo

Oskarshamn

Gotland

Halmstad

Växjö

23

Kalmar

Öland

LATVIA

Helsingborg

Karlskrona

Malmö

Kristianstad

DENMARK

LITHUANIA

Trelleborg

Ystad

The seasons contrast savagely: Sweden is usually warm and exceedingly light in the summer, then cold and dark in the winter. The sea may freeze, and in the north, iron railway lines may snap.

Sweden is also an arresting mixture of ancient and modern. The countryside is dotted with runic stones recalling its Viking past: trade beginning in the 8th century eastward to Kiev and as far south as Constantinople and the Mediterranean, expanding to the British Isles in the 9th through 11th centuries, and settling in Normandy in the 10th century. Small timbered farmhouses and maypoles—around which villagers still dance at Midsummer in their traditional costumes—evoke both the pagan early history and the more recent agrarian culture.

Many of the country's cities are sci-fi modern, their shop windows filled with the latest in consumer goods and fashions, but Swedes are reluctant urbanites: their hearts and souls are in the forests and the archipelagoes, and to there they faithfully retreat in the summer and on weekends to take their holidays, pick berries, or just listen to the silence. The skills of the wood-carver, the weaver, the leather worker, and the glassblower are all highly prized. Similarly, Swedish humor is earthy and slapstick. Despite the praise lavished abroad on introspective dramatic artists such as August Strindberg and Ingmar Bergman, it is the simple trouser-dropping farce that will fill Stockholm's theaters, the scatological joke that will get the most laughs.

Again, despite the international musical success of the Swedish rock groups Ace of Base, Roxette, and Abba, the domestic penchant is more often for the good, old-fashioned dance band. Gray-haired men in pastel sweaters playing saxophones are more common on TV than heavy-metal rockers. Strangely, in ultramodern concert halls and discos, it is possible to step back in time to the 1950s, if not the 1940s.

Despite the much-publicized sexual liberation of Swedes, the joys of hearth and home are most prized in what remains in many ways an extremely conservative society. Conformity, not liberty, is the real key to the Swedish character. However, the good of the collective is slowly being replaced by that of the individual as socialism begins to lose its past appeal.

At the same time, Swedes remain devoted royalists and patriots, avidly following the fortunes of King Carl XVI Gustaf, Queen Silvia, and their children in the media, and raising the blue-and-yellow national flag each morning on the flagpoles of their country cottages. Few nations, in fact, make as much of an effort to preserve and defend their natural heritage. It is sometimes difficult in cities such as Stockholm, Göteborg, or Malmö to realize that you are in an urban area. Right in the center of Stockholm, thanks to a cleanup program in the 1970s, you can fish for salmon or go for a swim. In Göteborg's busy harbor, you can sit aboard a ship bound for the archipelago and watch fish jump out of the water; in Malmö hares hop around in the downtown parks. It is this pristine quality of life that can make a visit to Sweden a step out of time, a relaxing break from the modern world.

Pleasures and Pastimes

Beaches
Beaches in Sweden range from wide, sandy strands to steep, rocky shores, from oceanfront to lakefront, from resorts to remote nature preserves. Beaches are wide and sandy on the western side of the country, steep and rocky on the eastern side. The area most favored for the standard sunbathing and wave-frolicking vacation is known as the Swedish Riviera, on the coast south of Göteborg.

Camping

As soon as the winter frost abates, the Swedes migrate en masse to the country, with camping and sports gear in tow. Of the 760 registered campsites nationwide, many offer fishing, boating, or canoeing, and about 200 remain open in winter for skiing and skating. Many campsites also offer accommodations in log cabins at various prices, and some have special facilities for guests with disabilities.

Dining

The nation's standard home-cooked meal is basically peasant fare—sausages, potatoes, and other hearty foods to ward off the winter cold. However, it has also produced the *smörgåsbord*, a generous and artfully arranged buffet featuring both hot and cold dishes. Fish—fresh, smoked, or pickled—is a Swedish specialty; herring and salmon both come in myriad traditional and new preparations.

Husmanskost (home-cooking) recipes are often served in restaurants as a *dagens rätt* (daily special) at lunch. Examples are *pyttipanna* (literally, "bits in the pan"—beef and potato hash topped with a fried egg), *Janssons frestelse* ("Jansson's Temptation"—gratin of potatoes with anchovy), or pea soup with pancakes, a traditional meal on Thursday.

Look for *kräftor* (crayfish), boiled with dill, salt, and sugar, then cooled overnight. Swedes eat them with hot buttered toast, caraway seeds, and schnapps or beer. Autumn heralds an exotic assortment of mushrooms and wild berries. Trout and salmon are common, as are various cuts of elk and reindeer. To the foreign palate, the best of Norrland's culinary specialties is undoubtedly *löjrom*, pinkish caviar from a species of Baltic herring, eaten with chopped onions and sour cream, and the various desserts made from the cloudberries that thrive here.

CATEGORY	COST*
$$$$	over SKr500
$$$	SKr250–SKr500
$$	SKr120–SKr250
$	under SKr120

Prices are per person for a two-course meal, including service charge and tax but not wine.

Fishing

It is not unusual to see a fisherman landing a thrashing salmon from the quayside in central Stockholm. Outside the city limits, the country is laced with streams and lakes full of fish, and there's excellent deep-sea fishing off the Baltic coast.

Lodging

Service in a Swedish hotel, no matter the price category, is always unfailingly courteous and efficient. You'll find that accommodations on the expensive side offer great charm and beauty, but the advantages of location held by less luxurious establishments shouldn't be overlooked. The woodland setting of a camper's *stuga* (small wooden cottage) may be just as desirable and memorable as the gilded antiques of a downtown hotel.

In summer many discounts, special passes, and summer packages are available. Your travel agent or the Swedish Travel and Tourism Council (in New York) will have full details. The Scandic Hotel Summer Check plan enables you to pay for accommodations in advance with checks costing SKr595 each for one night in a double room; with a supplementary PlusCheck, which costs SKr110, you can stay in one of their city-center hotels. Sweden Hotel's Nordic Hotel Pass costs SKr90 and gives discounts of 15% to 50% from June 20 to August 17 and on weekends year-round.

Vandrarhem (youth hostels), also scrupulously clean and well run, are more expensive than elsewhere in Europe. The Swedish Touring Association (STF) has 394 hostels and cabins nationwide, most with four- to six-bed family rooms, around 100 with running hot and cold water. They are open to anyone regardless of age. Prices are about SKr100 per night for members of STF or organizations affiliated with Hostelling International. Nonmembers are charged an additional SKr35 per night. STF publishes an annual hostel handbook.

CATEGORY	COST*
$$$$	over SKr1,400
$$$	SKr1,100–SKr1,400
$$	SKr850–SKr1,100
$	under SKr850

*All prices are for a standard double room, including breakfast and tax.

Sailing

Deep at heart, modern Swedes are still seafaring Vikings. Sweden's cultural dependence on boats runs so deep that a popular gift at Christmas is candles containing creosote, providing the comforting scent of dock and hull for when sailors can't be on their boats—which is most of the year. In summer, thousands of craft jostle among the islands of the archipelago and clog the lakes and rivers. Statistics claim there are more than 250,000 boats in the Stockholm archipelago alone. Boating opportunities for visitors are plentiful, from hourly rentals to chartered cruises in anything from kayaks to motor launches to huge luxury ferry liners.

Tennis

When Björn Borg began to win Wimbledon with almost monotonous regularity, Sweden became a force in world tennis. As such, the country is filled with indoor and outdoor courts, and major competitions, namely the Stockholm Open, take place regularly. One of the most unusual is the annual Donald Duck Cup, in Båstad, for children ages 11 to 15: ever since the young Björn won a Donald Duck trophy, the tournament has attracted thousands of youngsters who hope to imitate his success.

Exploring Sweden

Sweden consists of 24 counties. In the southeast is Stockholm, the capital city. The industrial seaport city of Göteborg and the neighboring west coastal counties of Bohuslän and Halland (the so-called Swedish Riviera) form another region, along with Värmland on the Norwegian border. The southernmost part of Sweden, a lovely mix of farmland, forests, and châteaus, includes Skåne, Småland, Blekinge, Västergötland, Östergötland, and the island of Öland. Dalarna, the country's heartland, is centered on Lake Siljan and the town of Mora; this is where Swedish folklore and traditions are most visible. The northern half of Sweden, called Norrland and including the counties of Lappland and Norrbotten, is a great expanse consisting mostly of mountains and wilderness; here the hardy Sami herd reindeer and hardy tourists come to see the midnight sun.

Numbers in the text correspond to numbers in the margin and on the maps.

Great Itineraries

Sampling all of Sweden's far-flung variety is best suited to a traveler with either no time constraints or an exceedingly generous purse.

However, a few representative stops can make even a short visit worthwhile.

IF YOU HAVE 3 DAYS

Spend two days in the capital city, **Stockholm** ①–㉜; one of these days may be spent on a boat trip in the archipelago or on Lake Mälaren. On the third day either visit **Göteborg** ㊶–(51)—a port town since the Viking era, marked with attractive boulevards, canals, and important museums—by a high-speed train, or fly to **Mora** (83), in the heart of Sweden's folklore country, Dalarna.

IF YOU HAVE 5 DAYS

Start with two days in **Stockholm** ①–㉜; add a third day for a side trip to **Uppsala** ㊳, Sweden's principal university town, along the banks of the Fyris River. On day four, fly to **Mora** (83) and rent a car for a drive around Lake Siljan. On day five, fly to **Göteborg** ㊶–(51).

IF YOU HAVE 10 DAYS

This itinerary can be accomplished using public transportation. Start with three days in **Stockholm** ①–㉜; on day four, take the high-speed train to **Göteborg** ㊶–(51) and stay two nights; on day six, take the train to **Kalmar** (77), with Sweden's best preserved Renaissance castle, via **Växjö** (78). From Kalmar, catch the ferry to **Gotland** ㊲. On day eight, return to Stockholm. Spend day nine either flying to **Mora** (83) or **Kiruna** (86), the northernmost city in Sweden. Return to Stockholm on day ten.

When to Tour Sweden

The official tourist season runs from mid-May through mid-September. This is Sweden's balmiest time of year; summer days are sunny and warm, nights refreshingly cool. (Summer is also mosquito season, especially in the north, but also as far south as Mora.) The colors of autumn fade out as early as September, when the rainy season begins. Winter comes in November and stays through March, and sometimes longer, but winter days can be magnificent when the snow is fresh and the sky is a brilliant Nordic blue. April brings spring, and by the middle of June the whole country goes mad for Midsummer Day.

STOCKHOLM

Positioned where the waters of Lake Mälaren rush into the Baltic, Stockholm is one of Europe's most beautiful capitals. Nearly 1.6 million people now live in the greater Stockholm area, yet it remains a quiet, almost pastoral city.

Built on 14 small islands joined by bridges crossing open bays and narrow channels, Stockholm is a handsome, civilized city filled with parks, squares, and airy boulevards, yet it is also a bustling, modern metropolis. Glass-and-steel skyscrapers abound, but you are never more than a five-minute walk from twisting medieval streets and waterside walkways.

The first written mention of Stockholm dates from 1252, when a powerful regent named Birger Jarl built a fortified castle and township here. King Gustav Vasa took it over in 1523, and King Gustavus Adolphus made it the heart of an empire a century later.

During the Thirty Years' War (1618–48), Sweden gained importance as a Baltic trading state, and Stockholm grew commensurately. But by the beginning of the 18th century, Swedish influence had begun to wane and Stockholm's development had slowed. It did not revive until the Industrial Revolution, when the hub of the city moved north from Gamla Stan.

Nowadays most Stockholmers live in high-rise suburbs that branch out to the pine forests and lakesides around the capital. They are linked by a highly efficient infrastructure of roads, railways, and one of the safest subway systems in the world. Air pollution is minimal, and the city streets are relatively clean and safe.

Exploring Stockholm

Although Stockholm is built on a group of islands adjoining the mainland, the waterways between them are so narrow, and the bridges so smoothly integrated, that the city really does feel more or less continuous. The island of Gamla Stan and its smaller neighbors, Riddarholmen and Helgeandsholmen, lie pretty much at town center. South of Gamla Stan, Södermalm spreads over a wide area, where the many art galleries and bars attract a slightly bohemian crowd. North of Gamla Stan is Norrmalm, the financial and business heart of the city. West of Norrmalm is the island of Kungsholmen, site of Stadshuset, the City Hall, and most of the city government offices. East of Norrmalm is Östermalm, an old residential neighborhood where many of the embassies and consulates are found. Finally, between Östermalm and Södermalm lies the island of Djurgården, once a royal game preserve, now the site of lovely parks and museums such as Skansen, the open-air cultural heritage park.

Modern Stockholm

The area bounded by Stadshuset, Hötorget, Stureplan, and Dramaten is essentially Stockholm's downtown, where the city comes closest to feeling like a bustling metropolis. Shopping, nightlife, business, traffic, dining, festivals—all are at their most intense in this part of town.

A GOOD WALK

Start at the redbrick **Stadshuset** ①, a powerful symbol of Stockholm. Cross the bridge to Klara Mälarstrand and follow the waterfront to Drottninggatan, a pedestrian street that will take you north to the hub of the city, **Sergels Torg** ②. The **Kulturhuset** ③ is in the imposing glass building on the southern side of Sergels Torg. Continuing north on Drottninggatan, you'll come to the market-filled **Hötorget** ④. The intersection of Kungsgatan and Sveavägen, at the corner of Konserthuset, is one of the busiest pedestrian crossroads in town.

Head north up Sveavägen for a brief detour to see the spot where Prime Minister Olof Palme was assassinated in 1986. A plaque has been laid on the right-hand side of the street, just before the intersection with Olof Palmes Gata; his grave is in Adolf Fredrik's Kyrkogård, a few blocks farther on. Continue north along Sveavägen, and turn left up Tegnérgatan to find **Strindbergsmuseet Blå Tornet** ⑤, where playwright August Strindberg lived from 1908 to 1912. Return to Hötorget by way of Drottninggatan.

Next, walk east along Kungsgatan, one of Stockholm's main shopping streets, to Stureplan, where you'll find Sturegallerian, an elegant mall (☞ Shopping, *below*). Head southeast along Birger Jarlsgatan—named for the nobleman generally credited with founding Stockholm around 1252—where there are still more interesting shops and restaurants. When you reach Nybroplan, take a look at the grand **Kungliga Dramatiska Teatern** ⑥.

Heading west up Hamngatan, stop in at **Hallwylska Museet** ⑦ for a tour of the private collection of Countess von Hallwyl's treasures. Continue along Hamngatan to **Kungsträdgården** ⑧, a park since 1562. You'll find many outdoor cafés and restaurants here, and usually public concerts and events in the summer. At the northwest corner of the park you will find Sverigehuset, or Sweden House, the tourist center (☞ Visitor Information *in* Stockholm A to Z, *below*); on the opposite side of Hamngatan is the NK department store (☞ Shopping, *below*).

TIMING
Allow about 4½ hours for the walk, plus an hour each for guided tours of Stadshuset and Hallwylska Museet (September–June, Sunday only). Note the Strindbergsmuseet Blå Tornet is closed Monday.

SIGHTS TO SEE

❼ Hallwylska Museet (Hallwyl Museum). This private turn-of-the-century palace with imposing wood-panel rooms houses a collection of furniture, paintings, and musical instruments in a bewildering mélange of styles assembled by Countess von Hallwyl, who left it to the state on her death. ⊠ *Hamng. 1,* ☎ *08/6661199.* 🖾 *SKr50.* ⊙ *Guided tours only. Tours in English July and Aug., daily at 1; Sept.–June, Sun. at 1.*

❹ Hötorget (Hay Market). Once the city's hay market, this is now a popular gathering place with an excellent outdoor fruit and vegetable market. Also lining the square are the Konserthuset, the PUB department store, and a multiscreen cinema Filmstaden Sergel (☞ Nightlife and the Arts, *below*). ⊠ *Just west of Sveaväg.*

NEED A BREAK?

Stop at **Kungshallen** (⊠ Hötorget opposite Filmstaden Sergel, ☎ 08/218005) and choose from an array of international goodies. Or, get a window table at the **café** inside Filmstaden Sergel.

☾ ❸ Kulturhuset (Culture House). Here you'll find an array of exhibitions for children and adults, plus a library, theater, cyber-café, exhibition center, and restaurant. ⊠ *Sergels Torg 3,* ☎ *08/7000100. Call for details.*

❻ Kungliga Dramatiska Teatern (Royal Dramatic Theater). Locally known as Dramaten, this theater is housed in a grand but appealing building with gilded statuary that looks out over the city harbor. Performances are in Swedish. ⊠ *Nybroplan,* ☎ *08/6670680.*

☾ ❽ Kungsträdgården (King's Garden). This is one of Stockholm's smallest yet most central parks. Once the royal kitchen garden, it now hosts a large number of festivals and happenings each season. There is a playground, an ice-skating rink in winter, and numerous cafés and restaurants. ⊠ *Between Hamng. and the Operan.*

❷ Sergels Torg. This area in Stockholm center was named after Johan Tobias Sergel (1740–1814), one of Sweden's greatest sculptors. The busy junction is dominated by modern, functional buildings and a sunken pedestrian square with subterranean connections to the rest of the neighborhood.

★ **❶ Stadshuset** (City Hall). The architect Ragnar Östberg, one of the founders of the National Romantic movement, completed Stockholm's City Hall in 1923. Headquarters of the city council, the building is functional but ornate: its immense **Blå Hallen** (Blue Hall) is the venue for the Nobel Prize dinner, Stockholm's principal social event. A trip to the top of the 348-ft tower, most of which can be achieved by elevator, is rewarded by a breathtaking panorama of the city and Riddarfjärden. ⊠ *Hantverkarg. 1,* ☎ *08/50829059.* 🖾 *SKr30, tower SKr15.* ⊙ *Guided tours only, daily 10–4:30. Tours in English, June–Aug., daily 10, 11, noon, 2; May and Sept., daily 10, noon, and 2; Oct.–Apr., daily 10 and noon.*

422

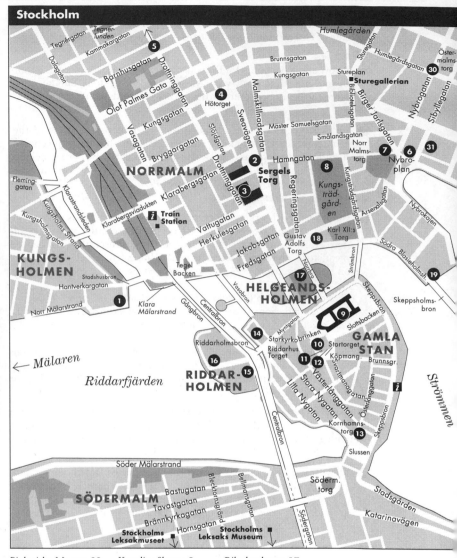

Biologiska Museet, **28**
Gröna Lund
Tivoli, **25**
Hallwylska Museet, **7**
Historiska Museet, **29**
Hötorget, **4**
Järntorget, **13**
Junibacken, **23**
Kaknästornet, **32**
Kulturhuset, **3**
Kungliga Dramatiska
Teatern, **6**

Kungliga Slottet, **9**
Kungsträdgården, **8**
Moderna Museet, **21**
Musik Museet, **31**
National Museet, **19**
Nordiska Museet, **24**
Operan, **18**
Östasiatiska
Museet, **20**
Östermalmstorg, **30**
Riddarholms
Kyrkan, **15**
Riddarhuset, **14**

Riksdagshuset, **17**
Sergels Torg, **2**
Skansen, **26**
Stadshuset, **1**
Stockholms
Fondbörs, **12**
Storkyrkan, **10**
Stortorget, **11**
Strindbergsmuseet Blå
Tornet, **5**
Svea Hovrätt, **16**
Vasa Museet, **22**
Waldemarsudde, **27**

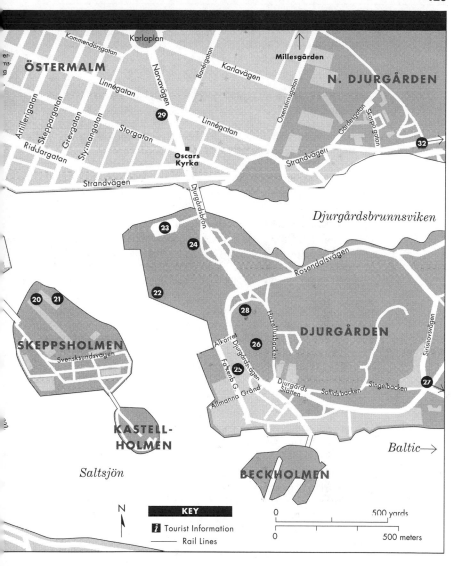

ÖSTERMALM

Kommendörsgatan

Karlaplan

Millesgården

N. DJURGÅRDEN

Artillerigatan
Skepparegatan
Grevgatan
Riddargatan
Styrmansgatan

Linnégatan

Narvavägen

Bantegatan

Karlavägen

Oxenstirnsgatan

Gardesgatan
Storpogatan

Storgatan

29

Linnégatan

32

■
Oscars
Kyrka

Strandvägen

Strandvägen

Djurgårdsbron

Djurgårdsbrunnsviken

23

24

Rosendalsvägen

22

28

DJURGÅRDEN

Sirishovsvägen

20 **21**

SKEPPSHOLMEN

Svensksundsvägen

Alkärret
Djurgårdsvägen
Falkens G.

26

25

Hazeliusbacken

Djurgårds
Slätten

Sofridsbacken

Singelbacken

27

Allmanna Gränd

KASTELL-
HOLMEN

Baltic→

Saltsjön

BECKHOLMEN

N

KEY

i Tourist Information
—— Rail Lines

0   500 yards

0   500 meters

After climbing the Stadshuset tower, relax on the fine grass terraces, which lead down to the bay and overlook Lake Mälaren. Or, have lunch in **Stadshuskällaren** (City Hall Cellar, ☎ 08/6505454), where the annual Nobel Prize banquet is held. You can also head a few blocks down Hantverkargatan to find several good small restaurants.

❺ Strindbergsmuseet Blå Tornet (Strindberg Museum, Blue Tower). Hidden away over a grocery store, this museum is dedicated to Sweden's most important author and dramatist, August Strindberg (1849–1912). This was actually Strindberg's home from 1908 until his death, and the interior has been expertly reconstructed with authentic furnishings and other objects, including one of his pens. It also has a library, printing press, and picture archives, and it is the site of literary, musical, and theatrical events. ⊠ *Drottningg. 85,* ☎ *08/4115354.* ⊠ *SKr30.* ☉ *Tues. 11–7, Wed.–Fri. 11–4, weekends noon–4.*

Gamla Stan and Skeppsholmen

Gamla Stan (Old Town) sits on a cluster of small islands between two of Stockholm's main islands and is the site of the medieval city. Skeppsholmen is the island just east. Narrow, twisting cobbled streets here are lined with superbly preserved old buildings.

A GOOD WALK

Start at the waterfront edge of Kungsträdgården and cross Strömsbron to the **Kungliga Slottet** ⑨, where you can see the changing of the guard at noon every day. Walk up the sloping cobblestone drive called Slottsbacken and bear right past the Obelisk to find the main entrance to the palace. Stockholm's 15th-century Gothic cathedral, **Storkyrkan** ⑩, stands at the top of Slottsbacken, but its entrance is at the other end, on Trångsund.

Following Källargränd from the Obelisk or Trångsund from Storkyrkan, you will reach the small **Stortorget** ⑪, marvelously atmospheric amid magnificent old merchants' houses. The **Stockholms Fondbörs** ⑫ fronts the square.

Walk past Svartmangatan's many ancient buildings, including the Tyska Kyrkan, or German Church, with its magnificent oxidized copper spire and airy interior. Continue along Svartmangatan, take a right on Tyska Stallplan to Prästgatan, and just to your left you'll find Mårten Trotzigs Gränd; this picturesque, lamplit alley stairway leads downhill to **Järntorget** ⑬. From here you can take Västerlånggatan back north across Gamla Stan, checking out the pricey fashion boutiques, galleries, and souvenir shops along the way.

Cut down Storkyrkobrinken to the 17th-century Dutch Baroque **Riddarhuset** ⑭. A short walk takes you over Riddarholmsbron to Riddarholmen—Island of Knights—on which stands **Riddarholms Kyrkan** ⑮. Also on Riddarholmen is the white 17th-century palace that houses the **Svea Hovrätt** ⑯. Returning across Riddarholmsbron, take Myntgatan back toward Kungliga Slottet and turn left at Mynttorget to cross the bridge and pass through the refurbished stone **Riksdagshuset** ⑰ on Helgeandsholmen, Holy Ghost Island. Another short bridge puts you on Drottninggatan; take a right onto Fredsgatan and walk to Gustav Adolfs Torg.

The **Operan** ⑱ occupies the waterfront between Gustav Adolfs Torg and Kungsträdgården. A little farther along on Strömgatan, a host of tour boats dock in front of the stately Grand Hotel. Pass the Grand and visit the **National Museet** ⑲. Cross the footbridge to the idyllic island of Skeppsholmen, where you'll find the **Östasiatiska Museet** ⑳, with a fine collection of Buddhist art. On Skeppsholmen you will also find the **Moderna Museet** ㉑. The adjoining island, Kastellholmen, is a pleasant place for a stroll, especially on a summer evening, with views of the Baltic harbor and Djurgården's lighted parks.

TIMING

Allow three hours for the walk, and double that if you want to tour the various parts of the palace. The National Museet and Östasiatiska Museet will take up to an hour each to view. Note that Kungliga Slottet is closed Monday off-season, and the Stockholms Leksakmuseet, Moderna Museet, National Museet, and Östasiatiska Museet are always closed Monday. The Riddarhuset is open weekdays only; off-season, hit the Riddarholms Kyrkan on a Wednesday or weekend.

SIGHTS TO SEE

⓭ **Järntorget** (Iron Square). Named after its original use as an iron and copper marketplace, this square was also the venue for public executions. ⊠ *Intersection of Västerlångg. and Österlångg.*

OFF THE BEATEN PATH

STOCKHOLMS LEKSAKMUSEET – In Södermalm, Stockholm's Toy Museum has a collection of toys and dolls from all over the world, as well as a children's theater with clowns, magicians, storytellers, and puppet shows. The museum is near the Mariatorget subway station, two stops south of Gamla Stan. ⊠ *Mariatorget 1, Södermalm,* ☎ *08/6416100.* ☞ *SKr30.* ☉ *Tues.–Fri. 10–4, weekends noon–4.*

★ ⑨ **Kungliga Slottet** (Royal Palace). Watch the changing of the guard in the curved terrace entrance of this magnificent granite edifice designed by Nicodemus Tessin and completed in 1760. View the palace's fine furnishings and Gobelin tapestries on a tour of the **Representationsvän** (State Apartments), or survey the crown jewels, which are no longer used in this self-consciously egalitarian country, in the **Skattkammaren** (Treasury). The **Livrustkammaren** (Royal Armory) has an outstanding collection of weaponry, coaches, and royal regalia. Entrances to the Treasury and Armory are on the Slottsbacken side of the palace. ⊠ *Gamla Stan,* ☎ *State Apartments 08/4026130, Treasury 08/4026130, Royal Armory 08/6664475.* ☞ *State Apartments SKr45, Treasury SKr40, Royal Armory SKr55.* ☉ *State Apartments and Treasury, June–Aug., daily 10–4; Sept.–May, Tues.–Sun. noon–3. Armory, May–Aug., daily 11–4; Sept.–May, Tues.–Sun. 11–4.*

㉑ **Moderna Museet** (Museum of Modern Art). Reopened in its original venue on Skeppsholmen, the museum's excellent collection includes works by Picasso, Kandinsky, Dali, Brancusi, and other international artists. You can also view examples of significant Swedish painters and sculptors and an extensive section on photography. ⊠ *Skeppsholmen,* ☎ *08/6664250,* ☞ *SKr50.* ☉ *Tues.–Thurs. noon–7, Fri.–Sun. noon–5.*

⑲ **National Museet** (National Museum). Important old masters—Rembrandt included—and works of many Swedish artists line the walls here. ⊠ *Södra Blasieholmshamnen,* ☎ *08/6664250.* ☞ *SKr50.* ☉ *Wed. and Fri.–Sun. 11–5, Tues. and Thurs. 11–8 (closes some Tues. at 5, mid-May–mid-Oct.).*

⑱ **Operan** (Opera House). Stockholm's Baroque Opera House is almost more famous for its restaurants and bars than for its opera and ballet productions. It has been one of Stockholm's artistic and literary watering holes since the first Operakällaren restaurant (☞ Dining, *below*) opened on the site in 1787. ⊠ *Gustav Adolfs Torg,* ☎ *08/248240.*

⑳ **Östasiatiska Museet** (Museum of Far Eastern Antiquities). Those with an affinity to Asian disciplines will enjoy this fascinating collection of Chinese and Japanese Buddhist sculptures and artifacts. ⊠ *Skepps-*

holmen, ☎ *08/6664250.* ⊠ *SKr50.* ⊙ *Tues. noon–8, Wed.–Sun. noon–5.*

⑮ Riddarholms Kyrkan (Riddarholm Church). Dating from 1270, the Grey Friars monastery is the second-oldest structure in Stockholm and the burial place for Swedish kings for more than four centuries. The most famous figures interred within are King Gustavus Adolphus, hero of the Thirty Years' War, and the warrior King Karl XII, renowned for his daring invasion of Russia, who died in Norway in 1718. The latest of the 17 Swedish kings to be put to rest here was Gustav V, in 1950. The various rulers' sarcophagi, usually embellished with their monograms, are visible in the small chapels given over to the various dynasties. The redbrick structure, distinguished by its delicate iron fretwork spire, is rarely used for services. ⊠ *Riddarholmen,* ☎ *08/ 4026000.* ⊠ *SKr10.* ⊙ *June–Aug., daily noon–4; May and Sept., Wed. and weekends noon–3.*

⑭ Riddarhuset (House of Nobles). Before the abolition of the aristocracy early in the 20th century, the House of Nobles was the gathering place for the First Estate of the realm. Hanging from its walls are 2,325 escutcheons, representing all the former noble families of Sweden. Thanks to the building's excellent acoustic properties, Riddarhuset is often used for concerts. ⊠ *Riddarhustorget,* ☎ *08/7233999.* ⊠ *SKr40.* ⊙ *Weekdays 11:30–12:30.*

⑰ Riksdagshuset (Parliament Building). When in session, the Swedish Parliament meets in this 1905 building. ⊠ *Riksg. 3A,* ☎ *08/7864000.* ⊠ *Free.* ⊙ *Tours in English late June–late Aug., weekdays 2:30 and 2; late Aug.–late June, weekends 1:30. Call ahead for bookings.*

⑫ Stockholms Fondbörs (Stockholm Stock Exchange). The Swedish Academy meets at the Stock Exchange every year to decide the winner of the Nobel Prize for Literature. The Stock Exchange itself is computerized and rather quiet. There are no tours in English, but there is a film about the Stock Exchange in Swedish. ⊠ *Källargränd 2,* ☎ *08/ 6138892.* ⊙ *Group tours by appointment only.*

⑩ Storkyrkan (Great Church). Swedish kings were crowned in the 15th-century Great Church as late as 1907. Today, its main attractions are a dramatic wooden statue of Saint George slaying the dragon, carved by Bernt Notke of Lübeck in 1489, and the *Parhelion,* a painting of Stockholm dating from 1520, the oldest in existence. ⊠ *Trångsund 1,* ☎ *08/7233000.*

⑪ Stortorget (Great Square). Here in 1520, the Danish king Christian II ordered a massacre of Swedish noblemen, paving the way for a national revolt against foreign rule and the founding of Sweden as a sovereign state under King Gustav Vasa, who ruled from 1523 to 1560. One legend holds that if it rains heavily enough on the anniversary of the massacre, the old stones still run red.

NEED A BREAK?   Among the cafés, pubs, and restaurants just south along Västerlång-gatan, stop at the **Grå Munken** (Gray Monk, ⊠ Västerlång. 18, at Stora Gråmunkegränd) for a coffee and pastry.

⑯ Svea Hovrätt (Swedish High Court). The Swedish High Court commands a prime site on the island of Riddarholmen, on a quiet and restful quayside. Sit on the water's edge and watch the boats on Riddarfjärden (Bay of Knights) and, beyond it, Lake Mälaren. From here you can see the lake, the magnificent arches of Västerbron (West Bridge) in the distance, the southern heights, and above all the imposing profile of the City Hall, which appears almost to be floating on the water. At the quay you may see one of the Göta Canal ships. ⊠ *Riddarholmen.* ۞ *Not open to the public.*

Djurgården and Skansen

Djurgården is Stockholm's pleasure island: on it you will find the outdoor museum Skansen, the Gröna Lund amusement park, and the *Vasa*, a 17th-century warship raised from the harbor bed in 1961, as well as other delights.

A GOOD WALK

You can approach Djurgården from the water aboard the small ferries that leave from Slussen at the southern end of Gamla Stan or from Nybrokajen, or New Bridge Quay, in front of the Kungliga Dramatiska Teatern. Alternatively, starting at the theater, stroll down the Strandvägen quayside—taking in the magnificent old sailing ships and the fine views over the harbor—and cross Djurgårdsbron, or Djurgården Bridge, to the island. As you turn immediately to the right, your first port of call should be the **Vasa Museet** ㉓, with a dramatic display of the splendid 17th-century warship. Especially if you have kids in tow, visit the fairy tale house, **Junibacken** ㉓, just off Djurgårdsbron. Return to the main street, Djurgårdsvägen, to find the entrance to the **Nordiska Museet** ㉔, worth a visit for an insight into Swedish folklore.

Continue on Djurgårdsvägen to the amusement park **Gröna Lund Tivoli** ㉕, where Stockholmers of all ages come to play. Beyond the park, cross Djurgårdsvägen to **Skansen** ㉖.

From Skansen, continue following Djurgårdsvägen to Prins Eugens Väg, and follow the signs to the beautiful turn-of-the-century **Waldemarsudde** ㉗. On the way back to Djurgårdsbron, follow the small street called Hazeliusbacken to the charmingly archaic **Biologiska Museet** ㉘ before heading back into town.

TIMING

Allow half a day for this tour, unless you're planning to turn it into a full-day event with lengthy visits to Skansen, Junibacken, and Gröna Land Tivoli. The Vasa Museet warrants two hours, and the Nordiska and Biologiska museums need an hour each. Waldemarsudde requires another half hour. Gröna Lund Tivoli is closed from mid-September to late April. Note the Nordiska Museet closes Monday, and the Biologiska Museet and Waldemarsudde are closed Monday off-season.

SIGHTS TO SEE

㉘ **Biologiska Museet** (Biological Museum). The Biological Museum, in the shadow of Skansen, exhibits real stuffed animals in various simulated environments. ⊠ *Hazeliusporten,* ☎ *08/4428215.* ⌁ *SKr20.* ۞ *Apr.–Sept., daily 10–3; Oct.–Mar., Tues.–Sun. 10–3.*

NEED A BREAK? On Hazeliusbacken, the Cirkus Theater (⊠ Djurgårdsslätten, ☎ 08/6608081) has a lovely terrace café. Or, for terrace dining, head to Hasselbacken Hotel (⊠ Hazeliusbacken 20, ☎ 08/6705000).

☝ ㉕ **Gröna Lund Tivoli.** On a smaller scale than Copenhagen's Tivoli and Göteborg's Liseberg, the amusement park Gröna Lund Tivoli is a clean, well-organized pleasure garden with a wide range of rides, attractions, and restaurants. ⊠ *Allmänna Gränd 9,* ☎ *08/6707600.* ⌁ *SKr40 not including coupons or passes for rides.* ۞ *May.–Aug., daily. Call ahead for prices and hours.*

★ ☝ ㉓ **Junibacken.** In this fairy-tale house, you travel in small carriages through the storybook world of children's book writer Astrid Lindgren, creator of the irrepressible character Pippi Longstocking. Each of Lindgren's tales is explained as various scenes are revealed. It's perfect for children ages 5 and up. ⊠ *Galärvarsv.*, ☎ *08/6600600.* ⊙ *Daily 10–6.*

🖑 ㉔ **Nordiska Museet** (Nordic Museum). In this splendid late-Victorian structure you'll find peasant costumes from every region of the country and exhibits on the Sami (pronounced *sah*-mee)—Lapps, formerly seminomadic reindeer herders who inhabit the far north. Families with children should visit the delightful "village-life" play area on the ground floor. ⊠ *Djurgårdsv. 616,* ☎ *08/6664600.* 🎫 *SKr50.* ⊙ *Tues.–Sun. 11–5.*

★ 🖑 ㉖ **Skansen.** The world's first open-air museum, Skansen was founded in 1891 by philologist and ethnographer Artur Hazelius, who is buried here. He preserved examples of traditional Swedish architecture, including farmhouses, windmills, barns, a working glassblower's hut, and churches, brought from all parts of the country. Not only is Skansen a delightful trip out of time in the center of a modern city, it also provides an easily assimilated insight into the life and culture of Sweden's various regions. In addition, the park has a zoo, carnival area, aquarium, theater, and cafés. ⊠ *Djurgårdsslätten 4951,* ☎ *08/4428000.* 🎫 *May–Aug., SKr45; Sept.–Apr., weekdays SKr30, weekends SKr40. Aquarium SKr45.* ⊙ *May–Aug., daily 9–5; Sept.–Apr., daily 9–4.*

NEED A
BREAK?

For a snack with a view at Skansen, try the **Solliden Restaurant** (☎ 08/6601055) near the front of the park, overlooking the city. The cozy **Bredablick Tower Café** (☎ 08/6634778) is at the back of Skansen, next to the children's circus.

★ ㉒ **Vasa Museet.** The warship *Vasa* sank on its maiden voyage in 1628, was forgotten for three centuries, located in 1956, and raised from the seabed in 1961. Its hull was found to be largely intact, because the Baltic's brackish waters do not support the worms that can eat through ships' timbers. Now largely restored to her former, if brief, glory, the man-of-war resides in a handsome new museum. ⊠ *Galärvarvet, Djurgården,* ☎ *08/6664800.* 🎫 *SKr50.* ⊙ *Thurs.–Tues. 10–5, Wed. 10–8. Jun.–Jul., English tours every hr; Aug.–May, weekdays 12:30 and 2:30, weekends 10:30, 12:30, 2:30, and 4:30.*

㉗ **Waldemarsudde.** This estate, Djurgården's gem, was bequeathed to the Swedish people by Prince Eugen on his death in 1947. It maintains an important collection of Nordic paintings from 1880 to 1940, in addition to the prince's own works. ⊠ *Prins Eugens väg 6,* ☎ *08/6621833.* 🎫 *SKr50.* ⊙ *June–Aug., Wed. and Fri.–Sun. 11–5, Tues. and Thurs. 7 AM–9 PM; Sept.–May, Tues.–Sun. 11–4.*

Östermalm and Kaknästornet

Marked by waterfront rows of Renaissance-era buildings with palatial rooftops and ornamentation, Östermalm is a quieter, more residential section of central Stockholm, its elegant streets lined with museums and fine shopping. On Strandvägen, or Beach Way, the boulevard that follows the harbor's edge from the busy downtown area to the staid diplomatic quarter, you can choose one of the three routes. The waterside walk, with its splendid views of the city harbor, bustles with tour boats and sailboats. The inside walk skirts upscale shops and exclusive restaurants. On the tree-shaded paths down the middle you just might meet the occasional horseback rider, properly attired in helmet, jacket, and high polished boots.

A GOOD WALK

Walk east from the Kungliga Dramatiska Teatern in Nybroplan along Strandvägen. At Djurgårdsbron, stop to admire the ornate little bridge, then turn left up Narvavägen to the **Historiska Museet** ㉙. Cross Narvavägen at Oscars Kyrka, then head up the street to Karlaplan, a pleasant, circular park with a fountain. Go across or around the park to find Karlavägen, a long boulevard lined with small shops and galleries. At Sibyllegatan, turn left and proceed southwest to **Östermalmstorg** ㉚, where you'll find the Saluhall, an excellent indoor food market. Continue down Sibyllegatan to the **Musik Museet** ㉛, installed in the city's oldest industrial building. Then go back to Nybroplan, where you can catch Bus 69 going east to **Kaknästornet** ㉜ for a spectacular view of Stockholm from the tallest tower in Scandinavia.

TIMING

This tour requires a little more than a half day. You'll want to spend around an hour in each of the museums. The bus ride from Nybroplan to Kaknästornet takes about 15 minutes, and the tower merits another half hour. Note the Historiska Museet and Musik Museet are closed Monday, and the Millesgården is closed Monday off-season.

SIGHTS TO SEE

㉙ **Historiska Museet** (Museum of National Antiquities). Viking treasures and the Gold Room are the main draw here, but well-presented changing exhibitions also cover various periods of Swedish history, and an excellent shop sells books and gifts. ⊠ *Narvav. 1317,* ☎ *08/7839400.* ⌨ *SKr55.* ⊙ *Tues.–Sun. 11–5, Thurs. until 8.*

NEED A BREAK?	For a great coffee and a quick snack, the bistro **Cassi** (⊠ Narvav. 30, just off Karlaplan) is just to the right.

OFF THE BEATEN PATH	**MILLESGÅRDEN** – This gallery and sculpture garden north of the city is dedicated to the former owner of the property, the American-Swedish sculptor Carl Milles (1875–1955). On display are Milles's own works as well as his private collection. The setting is exquisite: sculptures top columns on terraces in a magical garden high above the harbor and the city. Millesgården can be easily reached via subway to Ropsten, where you catch the Lidingö train and get off at Herserud, the second stop. The trip takes about 30 minutes. ⊠ *Carl Milles väg 2, Lidingö,* ☎ *08/7315060.* ⌨ *SKr50.* ⊙ *May–Sept., daily 10–5; Oct.–Apr., Tues.–Sun. noon–4.*

㉜ **Kaknästornet** (Kaknäs TV Tower). The 511 ft-high Kaknäs radio and television tower, completed in 1967, is the tallest building in Scandinavia. Surrounded by an impressive array of satellite dishes, it is also used as a linkup station for a number of Swedish satellite TV channels and radio stations. Eat a meal in a restaurant 426 ft above the ground and enjoy panoramic views of the city and the archipelago. ⊠ *Mörkakroken, off Djurgårdsbrunsv.,* ☎ *08/6678030.* ⌨ *SKr20.* ⊙ *May.–Aug., daily 9 AM–10 PM; Sept.–May, daily 10–9.*

㉛ **Musik Museet.** The Music Museum presents a history of music and instruments in its displays. Children are invited to touch and play some of the instruments, and a motion-sensitive "Sound Room" allows visitors to produce musical effects simply by gesturing and moving around. ⊠ *Sibylleg. 2,* ☎ *08/6664530.* ⌨ *SKr30.* ⊙ *Tues.–Sun. 11–4.*

㉚ **Östermalmstorg.** The market square and its neighboring streets represent old, established Stockholm. Saluhall is more like a collection of boutiques than an indoor food market; the fish displays can be especially intriguing. At the other end of the square, **Hedvig Eleonora Kyrka,** a church with characteristically Swedish faux-marble painting throughout its wooden interior, is the site of frequent lunchtime concerts in spring and summer. ⊠ *Nybrov.*

Dining

The Stockholm restaurant scene has evolved of late, with more upscale restaurants offering good value and inexpensive restaurants appearing on the scene. And local chefs are trying their hand at innovation, some making waves in the culinary world: in 1997, Sweden won the Chef of the Year Contest held in Lyon, France. Among Swedish dishes, the best bets are fish, particularly salmon, and the smörgåsbord buffet, which usually offers variety at a good price. Reservations are usually necessary on weekends.

Downtown Stockholm and Beyond

$$$$ ✗ **Operakällaren.** Open since 1787, the haughty grand dame of Stockholm is more a Swedish institution than a great gastronomic experience. Thick Oriental carpeting, shiny polished brass, handsome carved-wood chairs and tables, and a decidedly stuffy atmosphere fill the room. The crystal chandeliers are said to be Sweden's finest, and the high windows on the south side give magnificent views of the Royal Palace. The restaurant is famed for its seasonal smörgåsbord, offered from early June through Christmas. Coveted selections include pickled herring, *rollmops* (rolled herring), reindeer and elk in season, and ice cream with cloudberry sauce. In summer, the veranda opens as the Operabryggan Café, facing Kungsträdgården and the waterfront. ⊠ *Operahuset, Jakobs Torg 2,* ☎ *08/67658010. Reservations essential. Jacket and tie. AE, DC, MC, V. Main dining room closed in July.*

$$$$ ✗ **Ulriksdals Wärdshus.** The lunchtime smörgåsbord is unbeatable at
★   this beautifully situated country inn, built in 1868. The inn is in the park of an 18th-century palace, with a traditional interior overlooking orchards and a peaceful lake. This restaurant is arguably one of the most expensive in Stockholm, but the impeccable service and outstanding cuisine make it worthwhile. ⊠ *Ulriksdals Slottspark, Solna,* ☎ *08/850815. Reservations essential. Jacket required. AE, DC, MC, V. No dinner Sun.*

$$$ ✗ **Edsbacka Krog.** In 1626, Edsbacka, just outside town, became Stockholm's first licensed inn. Its exposed roughhewn beams, plaster walls, and open fireplaces still give it the feel of a country inn for the gentry. The Continental-Swedish cuisine is reliably superb. The owner, Christer Lindström, is an award-winning chef; his tarragon chicken with winter vegetables is worth the occasional long wait. ⊠ *Sollentunav. 220, Sollentuna,* ☎ *08/963300. AE, DC, MC, V. Closed Sun. No lunch Sat., no dinner Mon.*

$$$ ✗ **Fredsgatan 12.** The government crowd files in at lunch, the rest of
★   us come at night. An array of cleverly named fish and meat dishes are well prepared. While enjoying one of the peculiar drinks at the bar, you can get nice view of the kitchen—always a good sign of an unabashed chef. ⊠ *Fredsg. 12,* ☎ *08/248052. AE, DC, MC, V.*

$$$ ✗ **Gåsen.** This is a classic Östermalm restaurant: very classy, cozy, and costly. The Swedish-French menu is excellent, including such dishes as smoked breast of goose with apple chutney, grilled turbot with fresh beet root and spinach, and Arctic raspberry ice cream with blue curaçao sauce. The service is usually impeccable. ⊠ *Karlav. 28,* ☎ *08/6110269. Jacket and tie. AE, DC, MC, V. Closed weekends May–Aug., Sun. Sept.–Apr., and July.*

$$$ ✗ **Greitz.** Home-style Swedish cuisine is served in this classy and comfortable restaurant. Try the *sotare* (grilled Baltic herring with parsley and butter) or perch and salmon roe with sautéed white beets. The decor

is revamped café style, with the once-stained wood paneling around the room painted burgundy red. ⊠ *Vasag. 50,* ☎ *08/234820. AE, DC, MC, V. Closed Sun. and July.*

$$$ ✕ **Stallmästaregården.** A historic old inn with an attractive courtyard and garden, Stallmästaregården is in the Haga Park, just north of Norrtull, about 15 minutes by car or bus from the city center. Fine summer meals are served in the courtyard overlooking the waters of Brunnsviken. Specialties include *anka roti,* charcoal-grilled duck kebab. ⊠ *Norrtull, near Haga,* ☎ *08/6101300. AE, DC, MC, V. Closed Sun.*

$$$ ✕ **Wedholms Fisk.** Noted for its fresh seafood dishes, Wedholms Fisk
★ is appropriately set by a bay in Stockholm center, on Berzelii Park. High ceilings, large windows, and tasteful modern paintings from the owner's personal collection create a spacious, sophisticated atmosphere. The traditional Swedish cuisine, which consists almost exclusively of seafood, is simple but outstanding. Try the poached sole in lobster-and-champagne sauce or the Pilgrim mussels Provençale. ⊠ *Nybrokajen 17,* ☎ *08/6117874. AE, DC, MC, V. Closed Sun. and July.*

$$ ✕ **Calle P.** Palm leaves function as plates at this trendy restaurant, which
★ has an unusual menu of Asian-accented dishes such as spicy wild pig and herb-poached trout on a bed of exotic greens. On the edge of a small park, it provides the younger crowd with plenty of people-watching and hip background music. ⊠ *Berzelli Park,* ☎ *08/6782120. AE, DC, MC, V. Closed Sun.*

$$ ✕ **Rolfs Kök.** Small and modern, Rolfs combines an informal atmosphere with excellent Swedish-French cuisine, serving three meals a day at reasonable prices. The lamb is usually a good bet, as are the stir-fried Asian dishes. ⊠ *Tegnérg. 41,* ☎ *08/101696. AE, DC, MC, V. No lunch weekends.*

$$ ✕ **Saigon Bar.** With time-warp speed you are whisked from Stockholm to an American G.I. bar in Saigon, '70s trappings and all. Unusual dishes include Indonesian-style fish served on sweet and spicy potato hash and lamb cutlets with eggplant and bamboo-shoot gratin. The wok special is always a good bet. ⊠ *Tegnérg. 19–21, from Rdmandsg. T-banan, east along Tegnérg.* ☎ *08/203887. AE, DC, MC, V. No lunch.*

$$ ✕ **Tranan.** A young yuppie crowd frequents Tranan for its bar, which often has live music, and for its unpretentious restaurant. The stark walls and checkered floor are from Tranan's days as a workingman's beer parlor. The chef prepares traditional Swedish cuisine. ⊠ *Karlbergsv. 14,* ☎ *08/300765. AE, DC, MC, V.*

Gamla Stan and Skeppsholmen

$$$$ ✕ **Eriks.** One of the namesake restaurants of the famous chef (in Sweden, at least) Erik Lallerstedt, this restaurant serves traditional Swedish fare of the higher school, with a concentration on meat and fish dishes. Everything is well prepared, delicious, and expensive. For calm, choose the upstairs floor; the ground floor always bustles. You'll be dining among Sweden's rich and famous. ⊠ *Österlångg. 17,* ☎ *08/238500. AE, DC, MC, V.*

$$$$ ✕ **Grands Franska Matsalen.** From this classic French restaurant in the Grand Hotel, you can enjoy an inspiring view of Gamla Stan and the Royal Palace across the inner harbor waters. The menu changes five times a year, but the emphasis is always on Swedish ingredients, used to create such dishes as medallions of deer with shiitake mushrooms in wildberry cream sauce. The lofty measure of opulence here is commensurate with the bill. ⊠ *Grand Hotel, Södra Blasieholmshamnen 8,* ☎ *08/6115214. Reservations essential. Jacket required. AE, DC, MC, V.*

$$$ ✕ **De Fyras Krog.** The name "Inn of the Four Estates" refers to the four social classes originally represented in the Swedish Riksdag—Nobility, Clergy, Burghers, and Peasants. The decor carries out the theme,

Stockholm Dining and Lodging

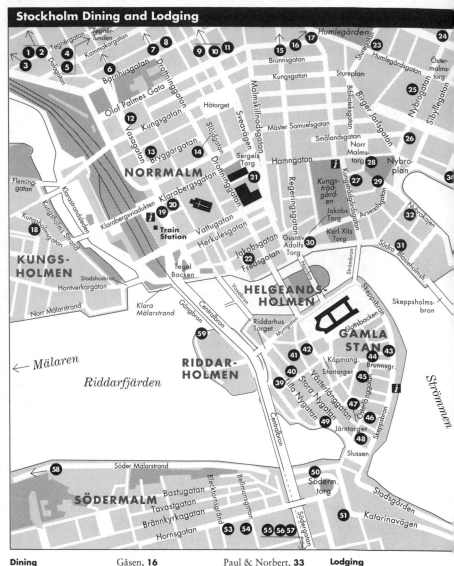

Dining
Calle P, **28**
Cassi, **37**
De Fyras Krog, **48**
Den Gyldene
Freden, **46**
Diana, **44**
Edsbacka Krog, **9**
Eriks, **45**
Eriks Bakficka, **38**
Fredsgatan 12, **22**
Garlic and Shots, **53**

Gåsen, **16**
Grands Franska
Matsalen, **31**
Greitz, **12**
Hannas Krog, **55**
Il Conte, **35**
Källaren Aurora, **39**
Måtten Trotzig, **47**
Nils Emil, **57**
Operakällaren, **30**
Örtagården, **25**

Paul & Norbert, **33**
Rolfs Kök, **5**
Saigon Bar, **11**
Spisen, **54**
Stallmästare-
gården, **7**
Tranan, **1**
Ulriksdals
Wärdshus, **3**
Wedholms Fisk, **29**

Lodging
af Chapman, **60**
Alexandra, **56**
Amaranten, **18**
Anno 1647, **51**
Arcadia, **2**
Bema, **6**
Berns, **27**
Birger Jarl, **15**
Bosön, **36**
Central Hotel, **13**
City, **14**

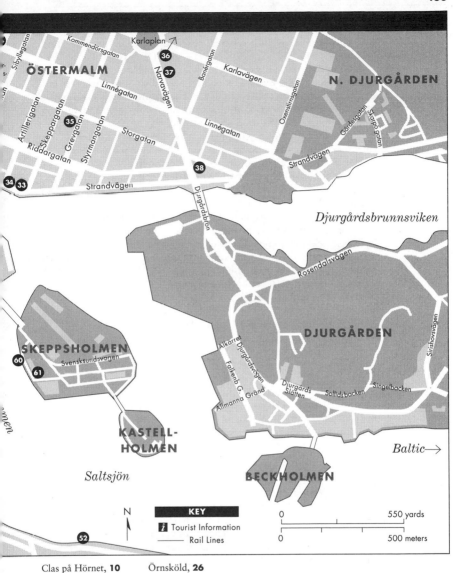

N

with rococo furnishings, church pews, an upper gallery, and a stone-flagged cellar dining room to represent the four lifestyles. De Fyras Krog offers a menu of Swedish regional specialties and an intimate atmosphere. ⊠ *Jårntorgsg. 5,* ☏ *08/241414. AE, DC, MC, V. Closed Sun.*

$$$ ✗ **Den Gyldene Freden.** Sweden's most famous old tavern has been open for business in 1722. Every Thursday, the Swedish Academy meets here in a private room on the second floor. The haunt of bards and barristers, artists and ad people, Freden could probably serve sawdust and still be popular, but the food and staff are worthy of the restaurant's hallowed reputation. The cuisine has a Swedish orientation, but Continental influences are spicing up the menu. Season permitting, try the oven-baked fillets of turbot served with chanterelles and crêpes; the gray hen fried with spruce twigs and dried fruit is another good selection. ⊠ *Österlångg. 51,* ☏ *08/109046. AE, DC, MC, V. Closed Sun. No lunch.*

$$$ ✗ **Källaren Aurora.** Extremely elegant, if a little staid, this Gamla Stan cellar restaurant is set in a beautiful 17th-century house. Its largely foreign clientele enjoys top-quality Swedish and international cuisines served in intimate small rooms. Try charcoal-grilled spiced salmon, veal Parmesan, or orange-basted halibut fillet. ⊠ *Munkbron 11,* ☏ *08/ 219359. AE, DC, MC, V. No lunch.*

$$ ✗ **Cassi.** This downtown restaurant, with an espresso bar dominating the front room, specializes in French bistro cuisine at reasonable prices. ⊠ *Narvav. 30,* ☏ *08/6617461. DC, MC, V. Closed Sat.*

$$ ✗ **Diana.** This atmospheric Gamla Stan cellar dates from the Middle Ages. The menu draws on the best indigenous ingredients from the Swedish forest and shoreline. In summer customers may be predominantly foreign or businesspeople from the provinces. ⊠ *Brunnsgränd 2,* ☏ *08/107310. AE, DC, MC, V. Closed Sun.*

$$ ✗ **Måtten Trotzig.** The nouveau functional dining space is both a dining room and bar. A short menu demonstrates the chef's imagination, blending multicultural accents into interesting twists. The staff is young, the service professional. ⊠ *Västerlångg. 79,* ☏ *08/240231. AE, DC, MC, V.*

Östermalm

$$$$ ✗ **Paul & Norbert.** This quaint, romantic restaurant is rustic but re-
★ fined. It's on the city's most elegant avenue, overlooking one of its most picturesque bays. French-style preparations include indigenous wild game dishes such as reindeer, elk, partridge, and grouse; fish dishes are also a draw. ⊠ *Strandv. 9,* ☏ *08/6638183. Reservations essential. AE, DC, MC, V. Closed weekends.*

$$$ ✗ **Il Conte.** This warm Italian-style restaurant is close to Stockholm's most elegant avenue, Strandvägen. Il Conte offers delicious Italian dishes and wines served by an attentive staff. Tasteful decor creates an alluring, refined atmosphere. ⊠ *Grevg. 9,* ☏ *08/6612628. Reservations essential. AE, DC, MC, V. No lunch.*

$$ ✗ **Eriks Bakficka.** A favorite among locals, Eriks Bakficka is a block from the elegant waterside street Strandvägen, a few steps down from street level. The restaurant serves a wide variety of Swedish dishes, and there's a lower-priced menu in the pub section. The same owner operates Eriks in Gamla Stan (☞ *above*). ⊠ *Frederikshovsg. 4,* ☏ *08/ 6601599. AE, DC, MC, V. Closed weekends in July.*

$ ✗ **Örtagården.** This is a truly delightful vegetarian, no-smoking restau-
★ rant above the Östermalmstorg food market. It offers an attractive buffet of soups, salads, hot dishes, and homemade bread—not to mention the SKr5 bottomless cup of coffee—in a turn-of-the-century atmosphere. ⊠ *Nybrog. 31,* ☏ *08/6621728. AE, MC, V.*

Södermalm
$$$ ✕ **Garlic and Shots.** The menu here can be summed up in one word: garlic—the accent of every dish, save one at lunchtime. Crowds flock for the stuff and for the good prices. Garlic-flavored desserts and 22 kinds of vodka are served. Reservations are advised. ⊠ *Folkungag. 85,* ☎ *08/6408446. AE, DC, MC, V.*

$$$ ✕ **Spisen.** A new menu has given this noteworthy restaurant a welcome lift. Try the poached herring, dipped in garlic oil. Prized lunches and home-baked bread add to the alluring atmosphere. Look for the bar— it's hidden—which offers live jazz each Thursday. ⊠ *Renstiernas Gata 30,* ☎ *08/7022229. AE, DC, MC, V.*

$$ ✕ **Hannas Krog.** What started out as an interesting neighborhood spot has become one of Södermalm's trendiest restaurants. Guests are serenaded at 10 minutes before the hour by a mooing cow that emerges from the cuckoo clock just inside the door. Dishes are tasty and good— ranging from Caribbean shrimp specialties to Provençale lamb dishes— if a bit pricey. The restaurant handles crowds in a relaxed atmosphere with consistent service. ⊠ *Skåneg. 80,* ☎ *08/6438225. Reservations essential. AE, DC, MC, V. No lunch weekends and July.*

$$ ✕ **Nils Emil.** This bustling restaurant in Södermalm is known for a royal
★ following, delicious Swedish cuisine, and generous helpings at reasonable prices; try the *kåldomar* (ground beef wrapped in cabbage) or the Baltic herring. The paintings of personable owner-chef Nils Emil's island birthplace in the Stockholm archipelago are by a well-known Swedish artist, Gustav Rudberg. ⊠ *Folkungag. 122,* ☎ *08/6407209. Reservations essential. Jacket and tie. AE, DC, MC, V. Closed July. No lunch Sat.*

Lodging

In spite of the prohibitively expensive reputation of Stockholm's hotels, great deals can be found during the summer, when prices are substantially lower and numerous discounts are available. More than 50 hotels offer the "Stockholm Package," providing accommodation for one night, breakfast, and the *Stockholmskortet,* or Stockholm Card, which gives free admission to museums and travel on public transport. All rooms in the hotels reviewed are equipped with shower or bath unless otherwise noted. Details are available from travel agents, tourist bureaus, or **Stockholm Information Service** (⊠ Box 7542, S103 93 Stockholm, ☎ 08/7892400, FAX 08/7892450). Also try **Hotellcentralen** (⊠ Central-station, S111 20 Stockholm, ☎ 08/7892425, FAX 08/7918666), where you'll be charged a fee if you call; service is free if you go in person.

Note that you should book lodging far in advance if you plan to travel during the August Stockholm Water Festival.

Downtown Stockholm and Beyond
$$$$ ▥ **Berns.** Successfully distinguishing itself from the rest of the crowd,
★ the 132-year-old Berns opted for an art deco look with the latest renovation. Indirect lighting, modern Italian furniture, and expensive marble, granite, and wood inlays now dominate the decor of the public areas and guest rooms. You can breakfast in the Red Room, immortalized by August Strindberg's novel of the same name: this was one of his haunts. Rates include the use of a nearby fitness center with a pool. ⊠ *Näckströmsg. 8, S111 47,* ☎ *08/7237200, FAX 08/6140700. 65 rooms, 3 suites. Restaurant, bar, no-smoking rooms, meeting room. AE, DC, MC, V.*

$$$$ ▥ **Continental.** In city center across from the train station, the Continental is a reliable hotel that's especially popular with American guests. Rooms are equipped with a minibar, trouser press, and satellite television. An extravagant Scandinavian buffet is served in the Gustavian breakfast rooms. ⊠ *Klara Vattugränd 4, S101 22,* ☎ *08/244020,* 𝔽𝔸𝕏 *08/4113695. 268 rooms. Restaurant, bar, no-smoking rooms, sauna, meeting rooms. AE, DC, MC, V.*

$$$$ ⌶ **Royal Viking (Radisson SAS).** In 1984, what was slated as a convenient storage site only yards from Central Station became the Royal Viking hotel—its best quality, appropriately enough, is convenience, both in location and service. Guest rooms lack nothing except space. They have attractive natural textiles and artwork, sturdy writing desks, separate seating areas, and plush robes in the large bathrooms. Triple-glazed windows and plenty of insulation keep traffic noise to a minimum. The large atrium lobby is spacious, and the split-level lounge is elegant. There is a business-class SAS check-in counter in the lobby. ⊠ *Vasag. 1, S101 24,* ☎ *08/141000 or 800/4488355,* 𝔽𝔸𝕏 *08/108180. 319 rooms. Restaurant, bar, minibars, no-smoking rooms, indoor pool, sauna, convention center. AE, MC, V.*

$$$$ ⌶ **Sergel Plaza.** This stainless-steel-paneled hotel has a welcoming lobby, with cane chairs in a pleasantly skylit seating area. Well-lit rooms are practical but lack the luxury feel the price tag might lead you to expect. The decor is almost disappointing, with run-of-the-mill furnishings and too much gray. It's central, right on the main pedestrian mall, but most windows face only office buildings. ⊠ *Brunkebergstorg 9, S103 27,* ☎ *08/226600,* 𝔽𝔸𝕏 *08/215070. 406 rooms. Restaurant, bar, no-smoking rooms, sauna, shops, convention center. AE, DC, MC, V.*

$$$$ ⌶ **SkyCity Hotel.** This Radisson SAS–run hotel is dead center in the Arlanda Airport's SkyCity complex. With fully air-conditioned rooms, the hotel is equipped and furnished in a variety of tasteful styles. If your room faces the runway, you can watch the planes quietly take off and land. ⊠ *SkyCity, 190 45 Stockholm-Arlanda,* ☎ *08/59077300,* 𝔽𝔸𝕏 *08/ 59378198. 230 rooms. Restaurant, bar, no-smoking rooms, fitness center, conference facilities. AE, DC, MC, V.*

$$$ ⌶ **Amaranten.** A little out of the way on the island of Kungsholmen, this large, modern hotel is, however, just a few minutes' walk from Stockholm's central train station. Rooms are contemporary, with satellite television and complimentary movie channels. Fifty rooms have air-conditioning and soundproofing for an extra charge. Guests can enjoy a brasserie and a piano bar. ⊠ *Kungsholmsg. 31, Box 8054, S104 20,* ☎ *08/6541060,* 𝔽𝔸𝕏 *08/6526248. 410 rooms. Restaurant, piano bar, no-smoking rooms, indoor pool, sauna, meeting rooms. AE, DC, MC, V.*

$$$ ⌶ **Birger Jarl.** A short bus ride from the city center, this contemporary, conservative, thickly carpeted venue attracts business travelers, catered conferences, and tourists requiring unfussy comforts. Breakfast is an extensive buffet just off the lobby, but room service is also available. Rooms are not large but are well furnished and have nice touches, such as heated towel racks in the bathrooms; all double rooms have bathtubs. Four family-style rooms have extra floor space and sofa beds. ⊠ *Tuleg. 8, S104 32,* ☎ *08/151020,* 𝔽𝔸𝕏 *08/6737366. 225 rooms. Coffee shop, no-smoking rooms, sauna, meeting rooms. AE, DC, MC, V.*

$$$ ⌶ **Central Hotel.** Less than 300 yards from the Central Station, this practical hotel was constructed in 1989. Rooms are small and face a pleasant, quiet courtyard; bathrooms have a shower only. ⊠ *Vasag. 38, S101 20,* ☎ *08/220840,* 𝔽𝔸𝕏 *08/247573. 93 rooms. No-smoking rooms, meeting rooms. AE, DC, MC, V.*

$$$ ⌶ **City.** A large, modern-style hotel built in the 1940s and completely renovated in 1984, the City is near the city center and Hötorget market. It is owned by the Salvation Army, so alcohol is not served. Breakfast is served in the atrium restaurant Winter Garden. ⊠ *Slöjdg. 7, S111 81,* ☎ *08/7237200,* 𝔽𝔸𝕏 *08/7237209. 293 rooms with bath. Restaurant, no-smoking rooms, sauna, meeting rooms. AE, DC, MC, V.*

$$$ ⊞ **Clas på Hörnet.** This may be the most exclusive—and smallest—hotel
★ in town, with only 10 rooms in an 18th-century inn converted into a
small hotel in 1982. The rooms, comfortably furnished with period an-
tiques, go quickly. The restaurant is worth visiting even if you don't
spend the night: its old-fashioned dining room is tucked away on the
ground floor of a restored 1739 inn and its Swedish and Continental
menu includes outstanding *strömming* (Baltic herring) and cloudberry
mousse cake. Restaurant reservations are essential, as are a jacket and
tie. ⊠ *Surbrunnsg. 20, S113 48,* ☎ *08/165130, restaurant, 08/165136,*
FAX *08/6125315. 10 rooms. AE, DC, MC, V. Closed July.*

$$$ ⊞ **Lydmar.** Just opposite Hummlegården in the center of Stockholm
lies this modern hotel, a 10-minute walk from the downtown hub of
Sergels Torg. The lobby lounge is alive on weekends with the latest jazz
sounds. ⊠ *Stureg. 10, 114 36,* ☎ *08/223160,* FAX *08/6608067. 61 rooms,*
5 junior suites. AE, DC, MC, V.

$$$ ⊞ **Tegnérlunden.** A quiet city park fronts this modern hotel, a 10-minute
walk from the downtown hub of Sergels Torg, with the shops of
Sveavägen along the way. Although the rooms are small and sparely
furnished, they are clean and well maintained. The lobby is bright with
marble, brass, and greenery, as is the sunny rooftop breakfast room.
⊠ *Tegnérlunden 8, S113 59,* ☎ *08/349780,* FAX *08/327818. 103 rooms.*
Breakfast room, no-smoking rooms, sauna, meeting room. AE, DC,
MC, V.

$$ ⊞ **Arcadia.** On a hilltop near a large waterfront nature preserve, this
converted dormitory is still within 15 minutes of downtown by bus or
subway, or 30 minutes on foot along pleasant shopping streets. Rooms
are furnished in a spare, neutral style, with plenty of natural light. The
adjoining restaurant serves meals on the terrace in summer. Take Bus
43 to Körsbärsvägen. ⊠ *Körsbärsv. 1, 114 89,* ☎ *08/160195,* FAX *08/*
166224. 82 rooms. Restaurant. AE, DC, MC, V.

$$ ⊞ **Stockholm Plaza Hotel.** On one of Stockholm's foremost streets for
shopping and entertainment, this hotel is ideal for the traveler who wants
a central location. The building dates from the turn of the century and
is furnished in an old world, elegant manner with reasonably sized rooms.
⊠ *Birger Jarlsg. 29, 103 95,* ☎ *08/145120,* FAX *08/1034923. 151*
rooms. AE, DC, MC, V.

$ ⊞ **Bema.** This small hotel is reasonably central, on the ground floor
of an apartment block near Tegnérlunden. Room decor is Swedish mod-
ern, with beechwood furniture. One four-bed family room is available.
Breakfast is served in your room. ⊠ *Upplandsg. 13, S111 23,* ☎ *08/*
232675, FAX *08/205338. 12 rooms. AE, DC, MC, V.*

Gamla Stan and Skeppsholmen

$$$$ ⊞ **Grand.** The city's showpiece hotel is an 1874 landmark on the
quayside at Blasieholmen, just across the water from the Royal Palace.
Visiting political dignitaries, Nobel Prize winners, and movie stars
come to enjoy the gracious Old World atmosphere, which extends to
the comfortable, well-furnished rooms. One of the hotel's nicest fea-
tures is a glassed-in veranda overlooking the harbor, where an excel-
lent smörgåsbord buffet is served. Guests have access to the Sturebadet
Health Spa nearby. ⊠ *Södra Blasieholmshamnen 8, Box 16424, S103*
27, ☎ *08/6793500,* FAX *08/6118686. 319 rooms, 20 suites. 2 restau-*
rants, bar, no-smoking rooms, sauna, shops, meeting rooms. AE, DC,
MC, V.

$$$$ ⊞ **Lady Hamilton.** As charming and desirable as its namesake, the Lady
★ Hamilton opened in 1980 as a modern hotel inside a 15th-century build-
ing. Swedish antiques accent the light, natural-toned decor in all the
guest rooms and common areas. Romney's "Bacchae" portrait of Lady
Hamilton hangs in the foyer, where a large, smiling figurehead from

an old ship supports the ceiling. The breakfast room, furnished with captain's chairs, looks out onto the lively cobblestone street, and the subterranean sauna rooms, in whitewashed stone, provide a secluded fireplace and a chance to take a dip in the building's original, medieval well. The honeymoon suite is impeccable. ✉ *Storkyrkobrinken 5, S111 28,* ☎ *08/234680,* FAX *08/4111148. 34 rooms. Bar, breakfast room, no-smoking rooms, sauna, meeting room. AE, DC, MC, V.*

$$$$　⛻ **Lord Nelson.** The owners of the Lady Hamilton and the Victory run this small hotel with a nautical atmosphere right in the middle of Gamla Stan. Space is at a premium—the rooms are little more than cabins—but service is excellent. Noise from traffic in the pedestrian street outside can be a problem during the summer. ✉ *Västerlångg. 22, S111 29,* ☎ *08/232390,* FAX *08/101089. 31 rooms. Café, no-smoking rooms, sauna, meeting room. AE, DC, MC, V.*

$$$$　⛻ **Reisen.** This 17th-century hotel on the waterfront in Gamla Stan has been open since 1819. It has a fine restaurant, grill, tea and coffee service in the library, and what is reputed to be the best piano bar in town. The swimming pool is built under the medieval arches of the foundations. ✉ *Skeppsbron 1214, S111 30,* ☎ *08/223260,* FAX *08/ 201559. 114 rooms. 2 restaurants, bar, no-smoking floor, indoor pool, sauna, meeting rooms. AE, DC, MC, V.*

$$$$　⛻ **Strand (Radisson SAS).** This Old World yellow-brick hotel, built in 1912 for the Stockholm Olympics, has been completely and tastefully modernized. It's on the water right across from the Royal Dramatic Theater. No two of its rooms are the same, but all are furnished with antiques and have such rustic touches as flowers painted on woodwork and furniture. The Piazza restaurant has an outdoor feel to it: Italian cuisine is the specialty, and the wine list is superb. A SAS check-in counter for business-class travelers adjoins the main reception area. ✉ *Nybrokajen 9, Box 163 96, S103 27,* ☎ *08/6787800,* FAX *08/6112436. 148 rooms. Restaurant, no-smoking rooms, sauna, meeting rooms. AE, DC, MC, V.*

$$$$　⛻ **Victory.** Slightly larger than its brother and sister hotels, the Lord Nelson and Lady Hamilton (☞ *above*), this extremely atmospheric Gamla Stan building dates from 1640. Decor is nautical, with items from the HMS *Victory* and Swedish antiques. Each room is named after a 19th-century sea captain. The noted Lejontornet restaurant keeps an extensive wine cellar. ✉ *Lilla Nyg. 5, S111 28,* ☎ *08/143090,* FAX *08/ 202177. 48 rooms. Restaurant, bar, bistro, no-smoking floor, 2 saunas, meeting rooms. AE, DC, MC, V.*

$$$　⛻ **Gamla Stan.** This quiet, cozy hotel is tucked away in one of the Gamla Stan's 17th-century houses. Each of its 51 rooms is uniquely decorated. ✉ *Lilla Nyg. 25,* ☎ *08/244450,* FAX *08/216483. 51 rooms. No-smoking floor, meeting rooms. AE, DC, MC, V.*

$$　⛻ **Mälardrottningen.** One of the more unusual establishments in Stockholm, Mälardrottningen, a Sweden Hotels property, was once Barbara Hutton's yacht. Since 1982, it has been a quaint and pleasant hotel, with a crew as service-conscious as any in Stockholm. Tied up on the freshwater side of Gamla Stan, it is minutes from everything. The small suites are suitably decorated in a navy-blue and maroon nautical theme. Some of the below-deck cabins are a bit stuffy, but in summer you can take your meals out on deck. Its chief assets are novelty and absence of traffic noise. ✉ *Riddarholmen 4, S111 28,* ☎ *08/ 243600 or 800/4488355,* FAX *08/243676. 59 cabins. Restaurant, bar, grill, no-smoking rooms, sauna, meeting rooms. AE, DC, MC, V.*

Östermalm

$$$$　⛻ **Diplomat.** Within easy walking distance of Djurgården, this elegant hotel is less flashy than most in its price range. The building is a turn-of-the-century town house that housed foreign embassies in the 1930s and was converted into a hotel in 1966. Rooms have thick carpeting and high ceilings; those in the front, facing the water, have magnificent views over Stockholm Harbor. Check out the tea room restaurant and second-floor bar. ⊠ *Strandv. 7C, S104 40,* ☎ *08/6635800,* FAX *08/ 7836634. 133 rooms. Restaurant, bar, no-smoking rooms, sauna, meeting room. AE, DC, MC, V.*

$$$ ⊞ **Mornington.** A quiet, modern Best Western hotel that prides itself on a friendly atmosphere, the Mornington is within easy walking distance of Stureplan and downtown shopping areas and particularly handy to Östermalmstorg, with its food hall. Rooms tend to be small; decor is standard Best Western. ⊠ *Nybrog. 53, S102 44,* ☎ *08/6631240,* FAX *08/6622179. 140 rooms. Restaurant, bar, no-smoking rooms, sauna, steam rooms, meeting rooms. AE, DC, MC, V.*

$$ ⊞ **Örnsköld.** Just behind the Royal Dramatic Theater in the heart of
★ the city, this hidden gem has the atmosphere of an old private club, with a brass-and-leather lobby and Victorian-style furniture in the moderately spacious, high-ceilinged rooms. Rooms over the courtyard are quieter, but those facing the street—not a busy one—are sunnier. The hotel is frequented by actors appearing at the Royal Theater. ⊠ *Nybrog. 6, 114 34,* ☎ *08/6670285,* FAX *08/6676991. 30 rooms. AE, MC, V.*

Södermalm

$$$$ ⊞ **Scandic Crown.** Working with what appears to be a dubious location (perched on a tunnel above a six-lane highway), the Scandic Crown has pulled a rabbit out of a hat. The hotel was built in 1988 on special cushions; you know the highway is there, but it intrudes only minimally, mainly in view. The intriguing labyrinth of levels, separate buildings, and corridors is filled with such unique details as a rounded stairway lighted from between the steps. The guest rooms are exquisitely designed and modern, with plenty of stainless steel and polished wood inlay to accent the maroon color scheme. Noteworthy is the Couronne d'Or, a French eatery, and a cellar with wines dating to 1650 where wine tasting is available. The hotel is at Slussen, easily accessible from downtown. ⊠ *Guldgränd 8, S104 65,* ☎ *08/7022500,* FAX *08/6428358. 264 rooms. 2 restaurants, piano bar, no-smoking rooms, indoor pool, beauty salon, sauna, meeting rooms. AE, DC, MC, V.*

$$$ ⊞ **Anno 1647.** Named for the date the building was erected, this
★ small, pleasant, friendly hotel is in Södermalm, three stops on the subway from the city center. Rooms vary in shape, but all have original, well-worn pine floors, with 17th-century-style appointments. There's no elevator in this four-story building. ⊠ *Mariagränd 3, S116 41,* ☎ *08/6440480,* FAX *08/6433700. 42 rooms, 30 with bath. Snack bar. AE, DC, MC, V.*

$$ ⊞ **Alexandra.** Although it is in the Södermalm area, to the south of Gamla Stan, this small, modern hotel is only five minutes by subway from the city center. A new floor was added in 1990. ⊠ *Magnus Ladulåsg. 42, S118 27,* ☎ *08/840320,* FAX *08/7205353. 75 rooms, 6 two-room suites. Breakfast rooms, no-smoking rooms, sauna. AE, DC, MC, V.*

$ ⊞ **Gustav af Klint.** A "hotel ship" moored at Stadsgården quay, near Slussen subway station, the *Gustav af Klint* is divided into two sections-a hotel and a hostel. The hostel section has 18 4-bunk cabins and 10 2-bunk cabins; a 14-bunk dormitory is also available from May through mid-September. The hotel section has 4 single-bunk and 3 two bunk cabins with bedsheets and breakfast included. The hostel rates are SKr120 per person in a 4-bunk room, and SKr140 per person in a 2-bunk room; these do not include bedsheets or breakfast. All guests share common bathrooms and showers. There is a cafeteria and a restaurant, and you can dine on deck in summer. ⊠ *Stadsgårdskajen 153, S116 45,* ☎ *08/6404077,* ℻ *08/6406416. 7 hotel cabins, 28 hostel cabins, 28 dormitory beds. AE, MC, V.*

Youth Hostels

Don't be put off by the "youth" bit: there's actually no age limit. The standards of cleanliness, comfort, and facilities offered are usually extremely high. Hostels listed are on Skeppsholmen and Södermalm.

🖭 *af Chapman.* This circa-1888 sailing ship, permanently moored in Stockholm Harbor just across from the Royal Palace, is a landmark in its own right. Book early—the place is so popular in summer that finding a bed may prove difficult. Breakfast (SKr45) is not included in the room rate; there are no kitchen facilities. ⊠ *Västra Brobänken, Skeppsholmen S111 49,* ☎ *08/6795015,* ℻ *08/6119875. 136 beds, 2- to 6-bed cabins. Café June–Aug. DC, MC, V. Closed Dec. 25–Mar.*

🖭 *Bosön.* Out of the way on the island of Lidingö, this hostel is part of the Bosön Sports Institute, a national training center pleasantly close to the water. You can rent canoes on the grounds and go out for a paddle. Breakfast is included in the room rate. There are laundry facilities and a kitchen for guest use. ⊠ *Bosön, S181 47 Lidingö,* ☎ *08/6056600,* ℻ *08/7671644. 70 beds. Cafeteria, sauna, coin laundry. MC, V.*

🖭 *Långholmen.* This former prison, built in 1724, was converted into a combined hotel and hostel in 1989. The hotel rooms are made available as additional hostel rooms in the summer. Rooms are small and windows are nearly nonexistent—you *are* in a prison—but that hasn't stopped travelers from flocking here. Each room has two to five beds, and all but 10 have bathrooms with shower. The hostel is on the island of Långholmen, which has popular bathing beaches and a Prison Museum. The Inn, next door, serves Swedish home cooking, the Jail Pub offers light snacks, and a garden restaurant operates in the summer. ⊠ *Långholmen, Box 9116, S102 72,* ☎ *08/6680510. 254 beds June–Sept., 26 beds Sept.–May. Cafeteria, restaurant, sauna, beach, coin laundry. AE, DC, MC, V.*

🖭 *Skeppsholmen.* A former craftsman's workshop in a pleasant and quiet part of the island was converted into a hostel for the overflow from the *af Chapman,* an anchor's throw away. Breakfast (SKr45) is not included in the room rate. ⊠ *Skeppsholmen, S111 49,* ☎ *08/ 6795017,* ℻ *08/6117155. 155 beds, 2- to 6-bed rooms. DC, MC, V.*

Camping

You can camp in the Stockholm area for SKr80–SKr130 per night. Try any of the following sites: **Bromma** (⊠ Ängby Camping, S161 55 Bromma, ☎ 08/370420, ℻ 08/378226), **Skärholmen** (⊠ Bredäng Camping, S127 31 Skärholmen, ☎ 08/977071, ℻ 08/7087262), **Sollentuna** (⊠ Rösjöbadens Camping, S191 56 Sollentuna, ☎ 08/962184, ℻ 08/929295).

Nightlife and the Arts

The hubs of Stockholm's nightlife are the streets Birger Jarlsgatan, Stureplan, and the city end of Kungsträdgården. On weekends, discos and bars are often packed with tourists and locals, and you might have to wait in line. Many establishments will post and enforce a minimum age requirement, which could be anywhere from 18 to 30, depending on the clientele they wish to serve.

The tourist guide *Stockholm This Week* is available free of charge at most hotels and tourist centers. The Friday editions of the daily newspapers *Dagens Nyheter* and *Svenska Dagbladet* carry current listings of events, films, restaurants, and museums in Swedish.

The **Stockholm Water Festival** (tel. 08/4595500) is *the* big event in Stockholm. People from all over the world come for the concerts, races, fireworks competition, and general partying between August 8–16.

Stockholm is the 1998 **Cultural Capital of Europe,** hosting events of all kinds—involving the arts, culture, nature—throughout the year. The program features an international dance and ballet series, an art manifestation in Kungsträdgården, guest circus performances, a jubilee exhibit of Orrefors glass at the National Museum, music festival at Ulriksdal's Castle, photographic festival, and theater festival with a whole host of European theaters taking part.

Nightlife

BARS

If you prefer exploring areas not entirely swamped by crowds, you will find a bar-hopping visit to Södermalm rewarding. Start at **Mosebacke Etablissement** (⊠ Mosebacke Torg 3, ☎ 08/6419020), a combined indoor theater and outdoor café with a spectacular view of the city. Wander along Götagatan with its lively bars and head for **Snaps/Rangus Tangus** (⊠ Medborgarplatsen, ☎ 08/6402868), an eatery and cellar bar with live music in a 300-year-old building. A trendy 20-something crowd props up the long bar at **WC** (⊠ Skåneg. 51, ☎ 08/7022963), with ladies' drink specials.

Limerick (⊠ Tegnérg. 10, ☎ 08/6734398) is a favorite Hibernian watering hole. Irish beer enthusiasts rally at **Dubliner** (⊠ Smålandsg. 8, ☎ 08/6797707). **The Tudor Arms** (⊠ Grevg. 31, ☎ 08/6602712) is just as popular as when it opened in the '70s. **Bagpiper's Inn** (⊠ Rörstrandsg. 21, ☎ 08/311855) is another favorite.

CASINOS

Many hotels and bars have a roulette table and sometimes blackjack, operating according to Swedish rules. These are aimed at cutting the amount you can lose. The **Monte Carlo** (☎ 08/4110025), at the corner of Kungsgatan and Sveavägen, offers roulette and blackjack 11:30 AM–5 AM daily; there is food service and a bar, and a disco on weekends. Clientele tends to be on the rough side.

DISCOS AND CABARET

Stockholm's biggest nightclub, **Börsen** (⊠ Jakobsg. 6, ☎ 08/7878500), offers high-quality international cabaret shows. Another popular spot is the **Cabaret Club** (⊠ Barnhusg. 12, ☎ 08/4110608), where reservations are advised.

Café Opera (⊠ Operahuset, ☎ 08/4110026), at the waterfront end of Kungsträgården, is a popular meeting place for young and old alike. It has the longest bar in town, plus dining and roulette, and dancing after midnight; the kitchen offers a night menu until 2:30 AM. **Daily's Bar** (⊠ Kungsträdgården, ☎ 08/215655), a glitzy disco at the other end of Kungsträdgården, near Sweden House, has a restaurant and is open until 3 AM. **King Creole** (⊠ Kungsg. 18, ☎ 08/244700) offers big-band dance music alternating with rock. **Berns' Salonger** (⊠ Berzelii Park, ☎ 08/6140550), an elegant restaurant and bar in a renovated period building with a large balcony facing the Royal Dramatic Theater, turns into a lively disco at night. **Sture Compagniet** (⊠ Stureg. 4, ☎ 08/6117800) is a complex of bars, food service, and dance areas on three levels inside the Sture Gallerian shopping mall. **Penny Lane** (⊠ Birger Jarlsg. 29, ☎ 08/201411) is a soft-disco nightclub specifically for a 30- and 40-something crowd. **Mälarsalen** (⊠ Torkel Knutssonsg. 2, ☎ 08/6581300) caters to the nondrinking jitterbug and fox-trot crowd in Södermalm.

Pronounced "Hus-et," the upscale **Hus 1** (✉ Sveav. 57, ☎ 08/315533) dance club—with a restaurant, café, bookshop, and disco—has mirrored walls, weekend drag shows, and a SKr60 cover charge (SKr40 before 10). A hot spot for gays to hang out is the entrance to the **Kina Teater** (✉ Berzelli Park). **Patricia** (✉ Stadsgården, Berth 25, ☎ 08/7430570) is a floating disco and bar right next to Slussen.

The best and most popular venue is **Fasching** (✉ Kungsg. 63, ☎ 08/216267), where international and local bands play year-round. **Stampen** (✉ Stora Nyg. 5, ☎ 08/205793) is an overpriced, but atmospheric, club in Gamla Stan with traditional jazz nightly. Get there early for a seat. New on the jazz scene is the lobby bar at the **Lydmar Hotel** (✉ Stureg. 10, ☎ 08/223160), where live jazz can be enjoyed on weekends and some weekdays.

Piano bars are part of the Stockholm scene. The **Anglais Bar** at the Hotel Anglais (✉ Humlegårdsg. 23, ☎ 08/6141600) is recommended on weekends. Also try the **Clipper Club** at the Hotel Reisen (✉ Skeppsbron 1214, ☎ 08/223260).

Lido (✉ Hornsg. 92, subway to Zinkensdamm; ☎ 08/6682333) is on Södermalm. Call ahead for reservations. **Krogen Tre Backar** (✉ Tegnérg. 1214, ☎ 08/6734400) can be found just off Sveav̈gen.

The Arts

Stockholm's theater and concert season runs from September through May, so you won't find many big-name artists at the height of the tourist season except during the Stockholm Water Festival in August. For a list of events, pick up the free booklet *Stockholm This Week,* available from hotels and tourist information offices. Contact the Stockholm Information Service for information in 1998 Cultural Capital of Europe happenings. For tickets to theaters and shows try **Biljettdirekt** at Sweden House (☞ Visitor Information *in* Stockholm A to Z, *below*) or any post office.

Free concerts are held in **Kungsträdgården** every summer—for details, contact the tourist office or check *Stockholm This Week.* International orchestras perform at **Konserthuset** (✉ Hötorget 8, ☎ 08/102110), the main concert hall. The **Music at the Palace** series (☎ 08/102247) runs June through August. Off-season, there are weekly concerts by Sweden's Radio Symphony Orchestra at **Berwaldhallen** (Berwald Concert Hall, ✉ Strandv. 69, ☎ 08/7841800).

Stockholm has an abundance of cinemas, all listed in the Yellow Pages under *Biografer.* Current billings are listed in evening papers, normally with Swedish titles; call ahead if you're unsure. Foreign movies are subtitled. Most, if not all, cinemas take reservations over the phone. Popular showings can sell out ahead of time. Most cinemas are part of the SF chain (☎ 08/840500), including the 14-screen **Filmstaden Sergel** (✉ Hötorget, ☎ 08/7896001). The **Grand** (✉ Sveav. 45, ☎ 08/4112400) is said to be the best-quality cinema in town. **Biopalatset** and **Filmstaden Söder** (✉ Medborgarplatsen, ☎ 08/6443100 and 7896060) are on the south side and have many films to choose from.

It is said that Queen Lovisa Ulrika began introducing opera to her subjects in 1755. Since then, Sweden has become an opera center of standing producing such names as Jenny Lind, Jussi Björling, and Birgit Nilsson. **Operan** (The Royal Opera House, ✉ Jakobs Torg 2, ☎ 08/248240), dating from 1898, is now the de facto home of Sweden's operatic tradition. **Folkoperan** (✉ Hornsg. 72, ☎ 08/6160750) is a modern company with its headquarters in Södermalm. Casting traditional presentation and interpretation of the classics to the wind, its productions are refreshingly new.

THEATER

Kungliga Dramatiska Teatern (Royal Dramatic Theater, called Dramaten, ✉ Nybroplan, ☎ 08/6670680) sometimes stages productions of international interest, in Swedish, of course. Productions by the **English Theatre Company** and the **American Drama Group Europe** are occasionally staged at various venues in Stockholm. See newspapers or contact Stockholm Information Service for details.

Outdoor Activities and Sports

Beaches

The best bathing places in central Stockholm are on the island of Långholmen and at Rålambshov at the end of Norr Mälarstrand. Both are grassy or rocky lakeside hideaways. Topless sunbathing is virtually de rigueur.

Biking

Stockholm is laced with bike paths, and bicycles can be taken on the commuter trains (except during peak traveling times) for excursions to the suburbs. Average rental cost is SKr80 a day or SKr400 a week. **Cykelfrämjandet** (✉ Torsg. 31, Box 6027, S102 31, ☎ 08/321680), a local bicyclists' association, publishes an English-language guide to cycling trips. Bikes can be rented from **Cykel & Mopeduthyrning** (✉ Strandv. at Kajplats 24, ☎ 08/6607959). Also try **Skepp & Hoj** (✉ Galärvarvsv. 2, ☎ 08/6605757), pronounced "ship ahoy."

Fitness Centers

Health and fitness is a Swedish obsession. The **Sports Club Stockholm** (✉ City Sports Club, Birger Jarlsg. 6C. ☎ 08/6798310; Atlanta Sports Club, ✉ St. Eriksg. 34, ☎ 08/6506625) chain has four centers in all, with women's and mixed gym facilities for SKr90 a day. For a relatively inexpensive massage, try the **Axelsons Gymnastiska Institut** (✉ Gästrikeg. 1012, ☎ 08/165360). **Friskis & Svettis** (✉ St. Eriksg. 54, 100 28 Stockholm, ☎ 08/6544414) is a local chain of indoor and, in summer, outdoor gyms specializing in aerobics. There are branches all over the Stockholm area. Monday through Thursday at 6 PM, from the end of May into late August, it hosts free sessions in Rålambshovsparken.

Golf

There are numerous golf courses around Stockholm. Contact **Stockholms Golfförbund** (✉ Solkraftsv. 25, 135 70 Stockholm, ☎ 08/7426940) for information. Try **Lidingö Golfklubb** (✉ Kyttingev. 2, Lidingö, ☎ 08/7317900), about a 20-minute drive from the city center. **Ingarö Golfklubb** (✉ Fogelvik, Ingarö, ☎ 08/57028244) is also about 20 minutes away.

Running

Numerous parks with footpaths dot the central city area, among them **Haga Park** (which also has canoe rentals), **Djurgården,** and the wooded **Liljans Skogen.** A very pleasant public path follows the waterfront across from Djurgården, going east from Djurgårdsbron past some of Stockholm's finest old mansions and the wide-open spaces of Ladugårdsgärdet.

Skiing

The **Excursion Shop** in the Sweden House (⊠ Kungsträdgården, Stockholm, ☎ 08/7892415) has information on skiing as well as other sport and leisure activities and will advise on necessary equipment.

Spectator Sports

The ultramodern **Globen** (⊠ Box 10055, S121 27, Globentorget 2, ☎ 08/7251000), at 281 ft the world's tallest spherical building, hosts sports like ice hockey and equestrian events. It has its own subway station. North of the city lies the open-air **Råsunda Stadion** (⊠ Box 1216, Solnav. 51, S171 23 Solna, ☎ 08/7350935), famous as the home of soccer in Stockholm.

Swimming

In town center, **Centralbadet** (⊠ Drottningg. 88, ☎ 08/242403) has an extra-large indoor pool, whirlpool, steambath, and sauna. **Sturebadet** (⊠ Sturegallerian, ☎ 08/54501500) offers aquatic aerobics and a sauna.

Tennis

Former champion Björn Borg once played at **Kungliga Tennishallen** (Royal Tennis Hall, ⊠ Lidingöv. 75, ☎ 08/4591500). **Tennisstadion** (⊠ Fiskartorpsv. 20, ☎ 08/215454) also maintains good courts.

Shopping

If you like to shop till you drop then charge on down to any one of the three main department stores in the central city area. For bargains, peruse the boutiques and galleries in Västerlånggatan, the main street of Gamla Stan, and the crafts and art shops that line the raised sidewalk at the start of Hornsgatan on Södermalm. Drottninggatan, Birger Jarlsgatan, and Hamngatan also offer some of the city's best shopping.

Department Stores and Malls

Sweden's leading department store is **NK** (⊠ Hamng. 1820, across the street from Kungsträdgården, ☎ 08/7628000); the initials, pronounced enn-*koh,* stand for *Nordiska Kompaniet.* Prices are high, as is the quality. Also try **Åhléns** (⊠ Klarabergsg. 50, ☎ 08/6766000). Before becoming a famous actress, Greta Garbo used to work at the **PUB** (⊠ Drottningg. 63 and Hötorget, ☎ 08/7916000), with 42 independent boutiques. Garbo fans should visit the small exhibit on level H2, with an array of photographs beginning with her employee ID card.

Gallerian (⊠ Stureg.) is in the city center. **Sturegallerian** (⊠ Stureplan), the other main shopping mall, is on Stureplan.

Specialty Stores

AUCTION HOUSES

There are three principal local auction houses. Perhaps the finest is **Lilla Bukowski** (⊠ Strandv. 7, ☎ 08/6140800), in its elegant quarters on the waterfront. **Auktions Kompaniet** (⊠ Regeringsg. 47, ☎ 08/235700) is next to NK downtown. **Stockholms Auktionsverk** (⊠ Jakobsg. 10, ☎ 08/4536700) is under the Gallerian shopping center.

BOOKS

Hemlins (⊠ Västerlångg. 6, Gamla Stan, ☎ 08/106180) carries foreign titles and antique books.

CRAFTS

Swedish handicrafts from all over the country are available at **Svensk Hemslöjd** (⊠ Sveav. 44, ☎ 08/232115). Though prices are high at **Svenskt Hantwerk** (⊠ Kungsg. 55, ☎ 08/214726), so is the quality. For elegant home furnishings and timeless fabrics, affluent Stockholmers tend to favor **Svenskt Tenn** (⊠ Strandv. 5A, ☏ 08/6701600), best known for its selection of designer Josef Franck's furniture and fabrics.

GLASS

Nordiska Kristall (⊠ Kungsg. 9, ☏ 08/104372), near Sturegallerian, has a small gallery of one-of-a-kind art glass pieces. **Svenskt Glas** (⊠ Birger Jarlsg. 8, ☏ 08/6797909) is near the Royal Dramatic Theater. The **Crystal Art Center** (⊠ Tegelbacken 4, ☏ 08/217169), near Central Station, has a great selection of smaller glass items. **NK** (☞ *above*) carries a wide, representative line of Swedish glasswork in its Swedish Shop downstairs.

MEN'S CLOTHING

For suits and evening suits for both sale and rental, **Hans Allde** (⊠ Birger Jarlsg. 58, ☏ 08/207191) provides good, old-fashioned service. For shirts, try **La Chemise** (⊠ Smålandsg. 11, ☏ 08/6111494).

WOMEN'S CLOTHING

There are many boutiques on **Biblioteksgatan** and **Västerlånggatan** in Gamla Stan. A shop that specializes in lingerie but carries fashionable clothes as well is **Twilfit** (⊠ Nybrog. 11, ☏ 08/6623817; Gallerian, ☏ 08/216996; and Gamla Brog. 3638, ☏ 08/201954). **Hennes & Mauritz** (⊠ Hamng. 22; Drottningg. 53 and 56; Sergelg. 1 and 22; and Sergels Torg 12; all ☏ 08/7965500) is one of the few Swedish-owned clothing stores to have achieved international success. **Polarn & Pyret** (⊠ Hamng. 10, ☏ 08/4114140; Gallerian, ☏ 08/4112247; Drottningg. 29, ☏ 08/106790) carries high-quality Swedish children's and women's clothing.

Street Markets

Hötorget is the site of a lively market every day. The **Loppmarknaden** flea market (*loppmarknad*) is held in the parking garage of the Skärholmen shopping center, a 20-minute subway ride from downtown. Market hours are weekdays 11–6, Saturday 9–3, and Sunday 10–3, with an entry fee of SKr10 on weekends. Beware of pickpockets. The best streets for bric-a-brac and antiques are **Odengatan** and **Roslagsgatan**; take Odenplan subway station.

Stockholm A to Z

Arriving and Departing

BY BUS

All the major bus and coach services, like Wasatrafik and Swebus, arrive at **Cityterminalen** (City Terminal, ⊠ Klarabergsviadukten 72), next to the central railway station. Reservations to destinations all over Sweden on **Swebus/Vasatrafik** can be made by calling ☏ 020/640640.

BY CAR

You will approach the city by either the **E20** or **E18** highway from the west, or the **E4** from the north or south. The roads are clearly marked and well sanded and plowed during winter. Signs for downtown read CENTRUM.

BY PLANE

Initially opened in 1960 solely for international flights, Stockholm's **Arlanda International Airport** (⊠ 41 km/26 from city center) also contains a domestic terminal. A freeway links the city and airport.

Between the Airport and City Center: Buses leave both the international and domestic terminals every 10 to 15 minutes from 6:30 AM to 11 PM and run to the Cityterminalen at Klarabergsviadukten, next to the central railway station. The trip costs SKr60. For more information, call ☏ 08/6001000.

A **bus-taxi combination package** (☎ 08/6701010) is available. The bus lets you off by the taxi stand at Jarva Krog or Cityterminalen and you present your receipt to the taxi driver, who takes you to your final destination. The cost is SKr160 if your destination is within city limits, SKr220 to anywhere in the Stockholm area.

For **taxis,** the *fast pris* (fixed price) between Arlanda and the city is SKr350. For information and bookings, call ☎ 08/7973700. The best bets for cabs are **Taxi Stockholm** and **Taxi Kurir.** Watch out for unregistered cabs, which charge high rates.

SAS operates a shared **limousine** service to any point in central Stockholm for SKr263 per person; the counter is in the arrivals hall, just past customs. If two or more people travel to the same address together in a limousine, only one is charged the full rate; the others pay SKr140.

BY TRAIN
All trains arrive at Stockholm's **Central Station** (Vasag., ☎ 08/7622000) in downtown Stockholm. From here regular commuter trains serve the suburbs, and an underground walkway leads to the central subway station.

Getting Around
The cheapest way to travel around the city by public transport is to purchase **Stockholmskortet** (Stockholm Card). In addition to unlimited transportation on city subway, bus, and rail services, it offers free admission to more than 60 museums and several sightseeing trips. The card costs SKr185 for 24 hours, SKr350 for two days, and SKr425 for three days and can be purchased from the tourist center at Sweden House on Hamngatan, from the Hotellcentralen accommodations bureau at Central Station, and from the tourist center at Kaknäs Tower.

BY BOAT
Waxholmsbolaget (Waxholm Ferries, ☎ 08/6795830) offers the *Båtluffarkortet* (Inter-Skerries Card), a discount pass for its extensive commuter network of archipelago boats; the price is SKr250 for 16 days of unlimited travel. The **Strömma Canal Company** (☎ 08/233375) operates a fleet of archipelago boats that provide excellent sightseeing tours and excursions.

BY BUS AND SUBWAY
Stockholm has an excellent bus and subway network operated by **SL** (☎ 08/6001000). Tickets for the two networks are interchangeable. The subway system, known as **T-banen** (*Tunnelbanan,* stations marked by a blue-on-white T), is the easiest and fastest way to get around. Servicing over 100 stations and covering more than 96 km (60 mi) of track, trains run frequently between 5 AM and 2 AM. Late-night bus service connects certain stations when trains stop running. The comprehensive bus network serves out-of-town points of interest, such as Waxholm and Gustavsberg.

Maps and timetables for all city transportation networks are available from the SL information desks at Sergels Torg, Central Station, and Slussen.

Bus and subway fares are based on zones, starting at SKr14, good for travel within one zone, such as downtown, for one hour. You pay more if you travel in more than one zone. Single tickets are available at station ticket counters and on buses, but it's cheaper to buy a **SL Tourist Card** from one of the many Pressbyrån newsstands. A coupon is valid for both subway and buses and costs SKr95; it's good for a fixed number of trips (approximately 10) within the greater Stockholm area during an unlimited period of time. If you plan to travel within the greater

Stockholm area extensively during a 24-hour period, you can purchase a one-day pass for SKr60; a 72-hour pass costs SKr120. The 24-hour pass includes transportation on the ferries between Djurgården, Nybroplan, and Slussen. The 72-hour pass also entitles the holder to admission to Skansen, Gröna Lund Tivoli, and Kaknäs Tower. People younger than 18 or older than 65 years pay SKr36 for a one-day pass and SKr72 for a two-day pass.

BY CAR

Driving in Stockholm is often deliberately frustrated by city planners, who impose many restrictions to keep traffic down. Get a good city map, called a **Trafikkarta,** available at most service stations for around SKr75.

BY TAXI

Stockholm's taxi service is efficient but overpriced. If you call a cab, ask the dispatcher to quote you a price, which is usually lower than the meter fare. Reputable cab companies are **Taxi Stockholm** (☎ 08/150000), **Taxi 020** (☎ 020/850400), or **Taxikurir** (☎ 08/300000). **Taxi Stockholm** has an immediate charge of SKr25 whether you hail a cab or order one by telephone. A trip of 10 km (6 mi) should cost about SKr97 between 6 AM and 7 PM, SKr107 at night, and SKr114 on weekends.

Contacts and Resources

CAR RENTALS

Rental cars are readily available in Sweden and are relatively inexpensive. Because of the availability and efficiency of public transport, there is little point in using a car within the city limits. However, if you are traveling elsewhere in Sweden, roads are uncongested and well marked, but gasoline is expensive (SKr8 per liter). All major car-rental firms are represented, including **Avis** (⊠ Ringv. 90, ☎ 08/6449980) and **Hertz** (⊠ Vasag. 2224, ☎ 08/240720).

DOCTORS AND DENTISTS

There is a 24-hour national health-service **emergency number** (☎ 08/6449200). Private care is available via **City Akuten** (☎ 08/4117177). Contact the emergency dental clinic is at **Sankt Erik's Hospital** (☎ 08/6541117, 8 AM–9 PM; ☎ 08/6449200), open 9 PM–8 AM.

EMBASSIES

U.S. (⊠ Strandv. 101, ☎ 08/7835300). **Canada** (⊠ Tegelbacken 4, ☎ 08/4533000). **U.K.** (⊠ Skarpög. 68, ☎ 08/6719000).

EMERGENCIES

Dial ☎ 112 for emergencies—this covers police, fire, ambulance, and medical help, as well as sea and air rescue services.

ENGLISH-LANGUAGE BOOKSTORES

Many bookshops stock English-language books. For newspapers and magazines, try one of the newsstands at the Central Station or the **Press Center** (⊠ Gallerian shopping center, Hamng., ☎ 08/7230191). **Hedengren's** (⊠ Sturegallerian shopping complex, ☎ 08/6115132) has one of the best English-book selections. **Akademibokhandeln** (⊠ Mäster Samuelsg. 32, near the city center, ☎ 08/6136100) is another good bet.

GUIDED TOURS

Boat and Bus Sightseeing Tours: A bus tour in English and Swedish covering all the main points of interest leaves each day at 9:45 AM from the tourist center at Sweden House (⊠ Hamng. 27, Box 7542, S103 93 Stockholm, ☎ 08/7892490); it costs SKr250. Other, more comprehensive tours, taking in museums, Gamla Stan, and City Hall, are also available at the tourist center. **Strömma Kanalbolaget** and **Stockholm Sightseeing** (⊠ Skeppsbron 22, ☎ 08/233375) run a variety of sightseeing tours of Stockholm. Boats leave from the quays outside the Royal Dramatic Theater, Grand Hotel, and City Hall.

Guided Tours: You can hire your own guide from Stockholm Information Service's **Guide Centralen** (⊠ Sweden House, Hamng. 27, Box 7542, S103 93 Stockholm, ☎ 08/7892496, ℻ 08/7892496). In summer, but be sure to book guides well in advance.

Walking Tours: City Sightseeing (☎ 08/4117023 or 08/240470) runs several tours, including the "Romantic Stockholm" tour of the Cathedral and City Hall; the "Royal Stockholm" tour, which features visits to the Royal Palace and the Treasury; and the "Old Town Walkabout," which strolls through Gamla Stan in just over one hour.

LATE-NIGHT PHARMACIES

C. W. Scheele (⊠ Klarabergsg. 64, ☎ 08/4548130) is open around-the-clock.

TRAVEL AGENCIES

For a complete listing, see the Yellow Pages under *Resor-Resebyråer*.

Contact **American Express** (⊠ Birger Jarlsg. 1, ☎ 08/6795200, 020/793211 toll-free). **SJ** (Statens Järnvägar, ⊠ Vasag. 1, ☎ 020/757575), the state railway company, has its main ticket office at Central Station. For air travel, contact **SAS** (⊠ Klarabergsviadukten 72, accessible from Central Station, ☎ 020/727000).

VISITOR INFORMATION

Stockholm Information Service: Sweden House (Sverigehuset, ⊠ Hamng. 27, Box 7542, S103 93 Stockholm, ☎ 08/7892490). **Stockholm Central Station** (⊠ Vasag., ☎ 020/757575). **City Hall** (summer only, ⊠ Hantverkarg. 1, ☎ 08/5082900). **Kaknästornet** (Kaknäs TV Tower, ⊠ Ladugårdsgärdet, ☎ 08/7892435). **Fjäderholmarna** (☎ 08/7180100).

Swedish Travel and Tourism Council (⊠ Box 3030, Kungsg. 36, 103 61 Stockholm, ☎ 08/7255500, ℻ 08/7255531).

SIDE TRIPS FROM STOCKHOLM

Surrounding Stockholm is a latticework of small, historic islands, most of them crowned with castles straight out of a storybook world. Set aside a day for a trip to any of these; half the pleasure of an island outing is a leisurely boat trip to get there. (However, the castles can all be reached by alternative overland routes, if you prefer the bus or train.) Farther afield is the island of Gotland, whose medieval festival, Viking remains, and wilderness reserves will take you back in time. The cathedral town of Uppsala is another popular day trip from Stockholm, its quiet atmosphere providing an enlightening contrast to the mood of the city.

Drottningholm

★ ㉝ *1 km (½ mi) west of Stockholm.*

Occupying an island in Mälaren (Sweden's third-largest lake) some 45
★ minutes from Stockholm's center, **Drottningholms Slott** (Queen's Island Castle) is a miniature Versailles dating from the 17th century. The royal family once used this property only as a summer residence, but, tiring of the Royal Palace back in town, they moved permanently to one wing of Drottningholm in the 1980s. Today it remains one of the most delightful of European palaces, embracing all that was best in the art of living practiced by mid-18th century royalty. The interiors date to the 17th, 18th, and 19th centuries, and most are open to the public. ⊠

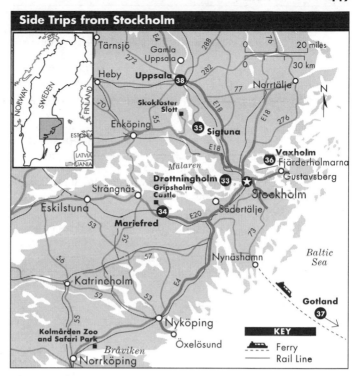

Side Trips from Stockholm

Drottningholm, ☎ 08/4026280. ⓩ SKr40. ⊙ May–Aug., daily 11–4:30; Sept., weekdays 1–3:30, weekends noon–3:30.

The lakeside gardens of Drottningholms Slott are its most beautiful asset, containing **Drottningholms Slottsteater** (Court Theater), the only complete theater to survive from the 18th century anywhere in the world. Built by Queen Lovisa Ulrika in 1766 as a wedding present for her son Gustav III, the theater fell into disuse after his assassination at a masked ball in 1792 (dramatized in Verdi's opera *Un Ballo in Maschera*). In 1922, the theater was rediscovered; there is now a small theater museum here as well. To get performance tickets, book well in advance at the box office; the season runs from late May to early September. A word of caution: the seats are extremely hard—take a cushion. ⊠ *Drottningholm, ☎ 08/7590406, box office 08/6608225. ⓩ SKr40. ⊙ May–Aug., daily noon–4:30; Sept., daily 1–3:30. Guided tours in English at 12:30, 1:30, 2:30, 3:30, and 4:30. Closed for 10 days at beginning of July.*

Arriving and Departing

Boats bound for Drottningholms Slott leave from Klara Mälarstrand, a quay close to City Hall. Call **Strömma Kanalbolaget** (☎ 08/233375) for schedules and fares.

Mariefred

③④ *63 km (39 mi) southwest of Stockholm.*

The most delightful way to experience the true vastness of Mälaren is the trip to Mariefred—an idyllic little town of mostly timber houses—aboard the coal-fired steamer of the same name, built in 1903 and still going strong.

Mariefred's principal attraction is **Gripsholm Slott.** First built in 1540, the castle contains fine Renaissance interiors, a superbly atmospheric theater commissioned in 1781 by the ill-fated Gustav III, and Sweden's royal portrait collection. ☎ *0159/10194.* 🎫 *SKr40.* ⊙ *Guided tours only, May–June and Aug., daily 10–4; July, daily 9–5; Apr. and Sept., Tues.–Sun. 10–3; Oct.–Mar., weekends noon–3.*

The **S.S. Mariefred** departs from Klara Mälarstrand, near Stockholm's City Hall. The journey takes 3½ hours each way, and there is a restaurant on board. You can also travel by narrow-gauge steam railway from Mariefred to a junction on the main line to Stockholm, returning to the capital by ordinary train. Contact the Mariefred Tourist Office for details. ☎ *08/6698850.* 🎫 *SKr160 round-trip.* ⊙ *Departures at 10 AM May, weekends only; mid-June–late Aug., Tues.–Sun. Return trip departs from Mariefred at 4:30.*

Visitor Information
The **Mariefred tourist office** (☎ 0159/29790) is open only in the summer; the rest of the year, call Mälarturism (☎ 0152/29690) for information for all of Lake Mälaren.

Sigtuna

㉟ *48 km (30 mi) northwest of Stockholm.*

An idyllic, picturesque town situated on a northern arm of Lake Mälar, Sigtuna was the principal trading post of the Svea, the tribe that settled Sweden after the last Ice Age; its Viking history is still apparent in the many runic stones preserved all over town. After it was ransacked by Estonian pirates, its merchants founded Stockholm sometime in the 13th century. Little remains of Sigtuna's former glory, beyond parts of the principal church. The town hall dates from the 18th century, the main part of town from the early 1800s, and there are two houses said to date from the 15th century.

About 20 km (12 mi) northeast of Sigtuna and accessible by the same ferry boat is **Skokloster Slott,** an exquisite Baroque castle. Commissioned in 1654 by a celebrated Swedish soldier, Field Marshal Carl Gustav Wrangel, the castle is furnished with the spoils of Wrangel's successful campaigns in Europe in the 17th century. The castle can be reached by boat from Sigtuna. ⊠ *Bålsta,* ☎ *018/386077.* 🎫 *SKr60.* ⊙ *Daily noon–6.*

Arriving and Departing
From June to mid-August Sigtuna can be reached by boat from the quay near City Hall (Strömma Kanalbolaget, ☎ 08/233375); round-trip fare is SKr140. Another option is to take a commuter train from Stockholm's Central Station to Märsta, where you change to Bus 570 or 575.

Vaxholm and the Archipelago

㊱ *32 km (20 mi) northeast of Stockholm.*

Skärgården (the archipelago) is Stockholm's greatest natural asset: more than 25,000 islands and skerries, many uninhabited, spread across an almost tideless sea of clean, clear water. To sail lazily among these islands aboard an old steamboat on a summer's night is a timeless delight.

For the tourist with limited time, one of the simplest ways to get a taste of the archipelago is the one-hour ferry trip to Vaxholm, an extremely pleasant, though sometimes crowded, mainland seaside town of small, red-painted wooden houses. Here, a fortress guarding what was formerly the main sea route into Stockholm now houses a small museum, **Vaxholms Kastell Museum,** showing the defense of Stockholm over the centuries. You have to take a small boat from the town landing, in front of the Tourist Bureau, over to the castle. ☎ *08/54172157.* ⊠ *SKr50, including boat fare.* ⊘ *Mid-May–Aug., daily noon–4. Group admission at other times by arrangement.*

An even quicker trip into the archipelago is the 20-minute ferry ride to **Fjäderholmarna** (the Feather Islands), a group of four secluded islands. After 50 years as a military zone, the islands were opened to the public in the early 1980s. Today they are crammed with arts-and-crafts studios, shops, an aquarium, a small petting farm, a boat museum, a large cafeteria, an ingenious "shipwreck" playground, and even a smoked-fish shop.

For an in-depth tour of the archipelago, seek out the **Blidösund.** A coal-fired steamboat built in 1911 that has remained in almost continuous regular service, it is now run by a small group of enthusiasts who take parties of around 250 on evening music-and-dinner cruises. The *Blidösund* leaves from a berth close to the Royal Palace in Stockholm. ⊠ *Skeppsbron,* ☎ *08/4117113.* ⊠ *SKr120. Departures early May–late Sept., Mon.–Thurs. 7 PM (returns at 10:45).*

Among the finest of the archipelago steamboats is the **Saltsjön,** which leaves from Nybrokajen, close to the Strand Hotel. Tuesday through Thursday evenings you can take a jazz-and-dinner cruise for SKr120; Saturday and Sunday from late June to late August, pay SKr175 to go to Utö, an attractive island known for its bike paths, bakery, and restaurant. In December, there are three daily Julbord cruises, serving a Christmas smörgåsbord. ⊠ *Saltsjön, Strömma Kanalbolaget, Skeppsbron 22,* ☎ *08/233375. Departures July–early Aug. and Dec.*

Dining

$$$ ✗ **Fjäderholmarnas Krog.** A crackling fire on the hearth in the bar area welcomes the sailors who frequent this place. Lacking your own sailboat, you can time your dinner to end before the last ferry returns to the mainland. The food here is self-consciously Swedish: fresh, light, and beautifully presented; the service is professional, and the ambience relaxed. It's a great choice for a quiet, special night out in Stockholm. ⊠ *Fjäderholmarna,* ☎ *08/7183355. AE, DC, MC, V. Closed Oct.–Apr.*

$ ✗ **Gröna Caféet.** A grassy garden terrace and an appealing selection of fresh open sandwiches on hearty brown bread make this small, old-fashioned Vaxholm café a hit. It's on Rådhusgatan, by the town square. ⊠ *Rådhusg. 26,* ☎ *08/54131510. No credit cards.*

Vaxholm and the Archipelago A to Z

ARRIVING AND DEPARTING

Regular ferry services to the archipelago depart from Strömkajen, the quayside in front of the Grand Hotel. Cruises on a variety of boats leave from the harbor in front of the Royal Palace or from Nybrokajen, across the road from the Royal Dramatic Theater. Ferries to the Feather Islands run almost constantly all day long in the summer (April 29–September 17), from Slussen, Strömkajen, and Nybroplan. Contact **Strömma Canal Co.** (☎ 08/233375; Waxholmsbolaget, ☎ 08/6795830; Fjäderholmarna, ☎ 08/7180100).

VISITOR INFORMATION

The **Vaxholms Tyristbyrå** (Vaxholm Tourist Bureau; ⊠ Söderhamnen, 185 83 Vaxholm, ☎ 08/54131480) is in a large kiosk at the bus terminal, adjacent to the marina and ferry landing.

Gotland

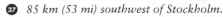 *85 km (53 mi) southwest of Stockholm.*

Gotland is Sweden's main holiday island, a place of wide, sandy beaches and wild cliff formations called *raukar*. Measuring 125 kilometers (78 mi) long and 52 km (32 mi) at its widest point, Gotland is where Swedish sheep-farming has its home. In its charming glades, 35 different varieties of wild orchids thrive, attracting botanists from all over the world.

The first record of people living on Gotland dates from around 5000 BC. By the Roman Iron Age, it had become a leading Baltic trading center. When the German marauders arrived in the 13th century, they built most of its churches and established close trading ties with the Hanseatic League in Lübeck. They were followed by the Danes, and Gotland finally became part of Sweden in 1645.

Gotland's capital, **Visby,** is a delightful, hilly town of about 20,000 people in which medieval houses, ruined fortifications, and churches blend with cobbled lanes of fairy-tale cottages, their facades covered with roses that bloom even in November because the climate is so gentle.

In its heyday Visby was protected by a wall, of which 3 km (2 mi) survive today, along with 44 towers and numerous gateways. It is considered the best-preserved medieval city wall in Europe after that of Carcassonne in southern France. The north gate provides the best vantage point for an overall view of the wall.

Visby's cathedral, **St. Maria Kyrka,** is the only one of the town's 13 medieval churches that is still intact and in use. Near the harbor is the **Gamla Apoteket** (Old Apothecary), a late-medieval four-story merchant's house. ⊠ *Strandg. 28,* ☎ *0498/273184.* ⧉ *Free.* ☉ *Daily 9–5.*

Burmeisterska Huset, the home of the Burmeister, or principal German merchant, offers exhibitions and artisans. Call the tourist office in Visby to arrange for viewing. ⊠ *Strandg. 9, no phone.* ⧉ *Free.*

Fornsalen (the Fornsal Museum) contains examples of medieval artwork, hoards of silver from Viking times, and impressive picture stones that predate the Viking runic stones. ⊠ *Mellang. 19,* ☎ *0498/247010.* ⧉ *SKr30.* ☉ *Mid-May–Sept., daily 11–6; Oct.–mid-May, Tues.–Sun. noon–4.*

The stalactite caves at **Lummelunda,** about 18 km (11 mi) north of Visby on the coastal road, are unique in this part of the world and are worth visiting. A pleasant stop along the way to Lummelunda is the **Krusmyntagården** (☎ 0498/70153), a garden with more than 200 herbs, 8 km (5 mi) north of Visby.

There are approximately 100 old churches on the island that are still in use today, dating from Gotland's great commercial era. **Barlingbo,** from the 13th century, has vault paintings, stained-glass windows, and a remarkable 12th-century font. The exquisite **Dalhem** was constructed in about 1200. **Gothem,** built during the 13th century, has a notable series of paintings of that period. **Grötlingbo** is a 14th-century church with stone sculptures and stained glass (note the 12th-century reliefs on the facade). **Tingstäde** is a mix of six building periods dating from 1169 to 1300. The massive ruins of a Cistercian monastery founded in 1164 are now called the **Roma Kloster Kyrka** (Roma Cloister Church). **Öja,** a medieval church decorated with paintings, houses a famous holy rood from the late 13th century.

Curious rock formations dot the coasts of Gotland, and two **bird sanctuaries, Stora** and **Lilla Karlsö,** stand off the coast south of Visby. The bird population consists mainly of guillemots, which look like penguins. Visits to these sanctuaries are permitted only in the company of a recognized guide. ✉ *Stora Karlsö,* ☎ *0498/241113; Lilla Karlsö,* ☎ *0498/241139.* ⊠ *SKr180 for guided tour of one sanctuary.* ⏲ *May–Aug., daily.*

Dining

$$ ✕ **Gutekällaren.** Despite the name, which means cellar in Swedish, this restaurant is above ground in a building that dates from the 12th century. Mediterranean dishes are the draw. ✉ *Stora Torget 3,* ☎ *0498/210043. DC, MC.*

$$ ✕ **Lindgården.** This atmospheric restaurant specializes in both local dishes and French cuisine. ✉ *Strandg. 26,* ☎ *0498/218700. Reservations essential. AE, DC, MC, V. Closed Sun. No lunch weekends.*

Nightlife and the Arts

Medeltidsveckan (Medieval Week), celebrated in Visby during early August, is a city-wide festival marking the invasion of the prosperous island by the Danish King Valdemar on July 22, 1361. Beginning with Valdemar's grand entrance parade, events include jousting, an open-air market on Strandgatan, and a variety of street-theater performances re-creating the period.

Outdoor Activities and Sports

Bicycles, tents, and camping equipment can be rented from **Gotlands Cykeluthyrning** (✉ Skeppsbron 8, ☎ 0498/214133). **Gotlandsleden** is a 200-km (120-mi) bicycle route around the island; contact the tourist office for details.

Gotland A to Z

ARRIVING AND DEPARTING

Car ferries sail from Nynäshamn, a small port on the Baltic an hour by car or rail from Stockholm; commuter trains leave regularly from Stockholm's Central Station for Nynäshamn. Ferries depart at 11:30 AM year-round. From June through mid-August there's an additional ferry at 12:30 PM. A fast ferry operates from mid-April until mid-September, departing three times a day. The regular ferry takes about five hours; the fast ferry takes 2½ hours. Boats also leave from Oskarshamn, farther down the Swedish coast and closer to Gotland by about an hour. *Gotland City Travel* (✉ Kungsg. 57, ☎ 08/236170 or 08/233180; Nynäshamn, ☎ 08/5206400; Visby, ☎ 0498/247065).

GUIDED TOURS

Sightseeing Tours: Guided tours of the island and Visby, the capital, are available in English by arrangement with the tourist office.

VISITOR INFORMATION

The main tourist office is **Gotlands Turistservice** (☎ 0498/206000, FAX 0498/249059), at Österport in Visby. You can also contact **Gotland City AB** in Stockholm for lodging (☎ 08/233180) or ferry reservations (☎ 08/236170).

Uppsala

⓷ *67 km (41 mi) north of Stockholm.*

Sweden's principal university town vies for that position with Lund in the south of the country. August Strindberg, the nation's leading dramatist, studied here—and by all accounts hated the place. Ingmar Bergman, his modern heir, was born here. It is a historic site where pagan (and extremely gory) Viking ceremonies persisted into the 11th century. Uppsala University, one of the oldest and most highly respected institutions in Europe, was established here in 1477 by Archbishop Jakob Ulfson. As late as the 16th century, nationwide *tings* (early parliaments) were convened here. Today it is a quiet home for about 170,000 people, built along the banks of Fyris River, a pleasant jumble of old buildings dominated by its cathedral, which dates from the early 13th century.

Ideally you should start your visit with a trip to **Gamla Uppsala** (Old Uppsala), 5 km (3 mi) north of the town. Here under three huge mounds lie the graves of the first Swedish kings—Aun, Egil, and Adils—of the 6th-century Ynglinga dynasty. Close by in pagan times was a sacred grove containing a legendary oak from whose branches animal and human sacrifices were hung. By the 10th century, Christianity had eliminated such practices. A small church, which was the seat of Sweden's first archbishop, was built on the site of a former pagan temple. Today the archbishopric is in Uppsala itself, and the church, **Gamla Uppsala Kyrka,** is largely for the benefit of tourists.

To sample a mead brewed from a 14th-century recipe, stop at the **Odinsborg Restaurant** (☎ 018/323525), near the burial mounds of Gamla Uppsala. A small open-air museum in Gamla Uppsala, **Disagården,** features old farm buildings, most of them dating from the 19th century. ▦ *Free.* ☉ *June–Aug., daily 9–5.*

Back in Uppsala, your first visit should be to **Uppsala Domkyrka** (Uppsala Cathedral), whose twin towers—at 362 ft the same height as the length of the nave—dominate the city. Work on the cathedral began in the early 13th century; it was consecrated in 1435 and restored between 1885 and 1893. Still the seat of Sweden's archbishop, the cathedral is also the site of the tomb of Gustav Vasa, the king who established Sweden's independence in the 16th century. Inside is a silver casket containing the bones of Saint Erik, Sweden's patron saint. ▦ *Free.* ☉ *Daily 8–6.*

The **Domkyrka Museet** in the north tower has handicrafts, church vestments, and church vessels on display. ▦ *SKr10.* ☉ *May–Aug., daily 9–5; Sept.–Apr., Sun. 12:30–3.*

Work on **Uppsala Slott** (Uppsala Castle) was started in the 1540s by Gustav Vasa, who intended it to symbolize the dominance of the monarchy over the church. It was completed under Queen Christina nearly a century later. Students gather here every April 30 to celebrate the Feast of Valborg and optimistically greet the arrival of spring. ▦ *Castle SKr40.* ☉ *Guided tours of castle mid-Apr.–Sept., daily at 11 and 2 (additional tours late June–mid-Aug., weekends at 10 and 3).*

In the excavated Uppsala Slott ruins, the **Vasa Vignettes,** scenes from the 16th century, are portrayed with effigies, costumes, light, and sound effects. ▦ *SKr40* ☉ *Mid-Apr.–Aug., daily 11–4; Sept., weekends 10–5.*

One of Uppsala's most famous sons, Carl von Linné, also known as Linnaeus, was a professor of botany at the university during the 1740s and created the Latin nomenclature system for plants and animals. The **Linné Museum** is dedicated to his life and works. ✉ *Svartbäcksg. 27,* ☎ *018/136540.* ▦ *SKr10.* ☉ *Late May and early Sept., weekends noon–4; June–Aug., Tues.–Sun. 1–4.*

The botanical treasures of Linné's old garden have been re-created and are now on view in **Linnéträdgården.** The garden's orangery houses a pleasant cafeteria and is used for concerts and cultural events. ✉ *Svartbäcksg. 27,* ☎ *018/109490.* ▦ *SKr10.* ☉ *May–Aug., daily 9–9; rest of yr, daily 9–7.*

Uppsala Universitetet (Uppsala University, ☎ 018/182500), founded in 1477, is known for its **Carolina Rediviva** (university library), which contains a copy of every book published in Sweden, in addition to a large collection of foreign literature. One of its most interesting exhibits is the *Codex Argentus,* a Bible written in the 6th century.

Completed in 1625, the **Gustavianum,** which served as the university's main building for two centuries, is easy to spot by its remarkable copper cupola, now green with age. The building houses the ancient anatomical theater where lectures on human anatomy and public dissections took place. The Victoria Museum of Egyptian Antiquities and the Museums for Classical and Nordic Archeology are also in the building. ✉ *Akademig. 3,* ☎ *018/182500.* 🖰 *SKr20 (SKr10 to anatomical theater only).* ☉ *June–Aug., daily 11–3. Anatomical Theater also Sept.–May, weekends noon–3.*

Dining

$$$ ✕ **Domtrappkällaren.** In a 14th-century cellar near the cathedral, Domtrappkällaren serves excellent French and Swedish cuisines. Game is the specialty, and the salmon and reindeer are delectable. ✉ *Sankt Eriksgränd 15,* ☎ *018/130955. Reservations essential. AE, DC, MC, V.*

Uppsala A to Z

GUIDED TOURS

Sightseeing Tours: You can explore Uppsala easily by yourself, but English-language guided group tours can be arranged through the tourist office; the guide service number is ☎ 018/274818.

VISITOR INFORMATION

The main **tourist office** (✉ Fyris Torg 8, ☎ 018/117500 or 018/274800) is in town center; in summer, a small tourist information office is also open at Uppsala Castle (☎ 018/554566).

GÖTEBORG

If you arrive in Göteborg (Gothenburg) by car, don't drive straight through the city in your haste to reach your coastal vacation spot; it is well worth spending a day or two exploring this attractive port. A quayside jungle of cranes and warehouses attests to the city's industrial might, yet within a 10-minute walk of the waterfront is an elegant, modern city of broad avenues, green parks, and gardens. This is not to slight the harbor: it comprises 22 km (14 mi) of quays with warehouses and sheds covering more than 1.5 million square ft and spread along both banks of the Göta Älv (river), making Göteborg Scandinavia's largest port. The harbor is also the home of Scandinavia's largest corporation, the automobile manufacturer Volvo (which means "I roll" in Latin), as well as of the roller-bearing manufacturer SKF and the world-renowned Hasselblad camera company.

Historically, Göteborg owes its existence to the sea. Tenth-century Vikings sailed from its shores, and a settlement was founded here in the 11th century. Not until 1621, however, did King Gustav II Adolf grant Göteborg a charter to establish a free-trade port on the model of others already thriving on the Continent. The west-coast harbor would also allow Swedish shipping to avoid Danish tolls exacted for passing through Öresund, the stretch of water separating the two countries. Foreigners were recruited to make these visions real: the Dutch were its builders—hence the canals that thread the city—and many Scotsmen worked and settled here, though they have left little trace.

Today Göteborg resists its second-city status by being a leader in attractions and civic structures: the Scandinavium was until recently Europe's largest indoor arena; the Ullevi Stadium stages some of the Nordic area's most important concerts and sporting events; Nordstan is one of Europe's biggest indoor shopping malls; and Liseberg, Scandinavia's largest amusement park in area, attracts some 2.5 million visitors a year. Over the Göta River is Älvsborgsbron, at 3,060 ft the longest suspension bridge in Sweden, and under a southwestern suburb runs the Gnistäng Tunnel, which at 62 ft claims the odd distinction of being the world's widest tunnel cut through rock for motor vehicles.

Exploring Göteborg

Göteborg is an easy city to explore: most of the major attractions are within walking distance of one another, and the streetcar network is excellent—in summer you can take a sightseeing trip on an open-air streetcar. The heart of Göteborg is Avenyn (the Avenue; actually Kungsportsavenyn, but over the years shortened to simply Avenyn), a 60-ft-wide, tree-lined boulevard that bisects the center of the city in a south–north direction, linking its cultural heart, Götaplatsen, at the southern end, with the main commercial area, now dominated by the modern Nordstan shopping center. Beyond lies the waterfront, busy with all the traffic of the port, as well as some of Göteborg's newer cultural developments.

Cultural Göteborg

A pleasant stroll will take the visitor from Götaplatsen's modern architecture down the Avenyn—the boulevard Kungsportsavenyn lined with elegant shops, cafés, and restaurants—and across both canals to finish at the State Museum building. The street slopes gently up from the canal at Kungsportsplats and ends at Poseidon's fountain in Götaplatsen.

A GOOD WALK

Start your tour in **Götaplatsen** ㊴, a square dominated by a statue of Poseidon; behind him is the **Konstmuseet** ㊵. Stroll downhill past the cafés and restaurants along Avenyn to the intersection with Vasagatan. A short way to the left down Vasagatan, at the junction with Teatergatan, you can visit the **Röhsska Museet** ㊶, the country's only museum of Swedish design.

Continue down Vasagatan to Folkhögskolan, Göteborg Universitet, and, if the weather's good, to the neighboring Vasa Parken, or Vasa Park. Turn right to go north on Viktoriagatan, cross the canal, and then make an immediate left to visit one of the city's most peculiar attractions, **Feske Körkan** ㊷, an archaic spelling of *Fisk Kyrkan,* the Fish Church. It resembles a place of worship but is actually an indoor fish market.

Following this you may feel inspired to visit the city's principal place of worship, **Domkyrkan** ㊸. To get here from Feske Körkan, follow the canal eastward until you come to Västra Hamngatan; then head north about four blocks to the church. Continue northward on Västra Hamngatan to the junction with Norra Hamngatan, where you'll find the **Stadsmuseet** ㊹, housed in the 18th-century Swedish East India Company.

TIMING

Depending on how much time you want to spend in each museum, this walk may take anywhere from a couple of hours to the better part of a day. Note that many sites close Monday off-season.

SIGHTS TO SEE

㊸ **Domkyrkan** (Göteborg Cathedral). The cathedral, in neoclassic yellow brick, dates from 1802; though disappointingly plain from the outside, the interior is impressive. ⊠ *Kungsg. 20,* ☎ *031/130479.* ⊙ *Weekdays 8–5, Sat. 8–3, Sun. 10–3.*

Göteborg

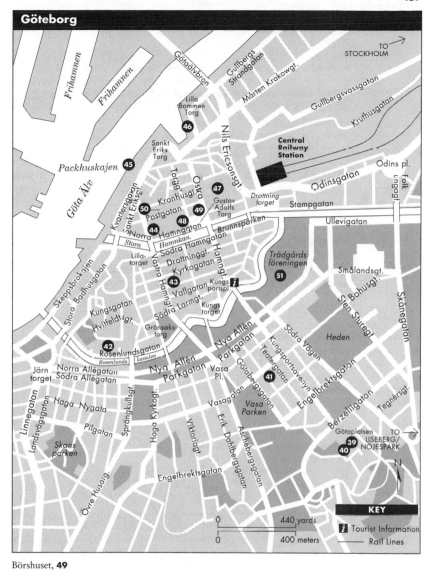

Börshuset, **49**
Domkyrkan, **43**
Feske Körkan, **42**
Götaplatsen, **39**
Konstmuseet, **40**
Kronhuset, **50**
Maritima
Centrum, **46**
Nordstan, **47**
Rådhuset, **48**
Röhsska Museet, **41**
Stadsmuseet, **44**
Utkiken, **45**
Trädgarn, **51**

㊷ Feske Körkan (Fish Church). Built in 1872, this covered fish market gets its nickname for its Gothic-style architectural details. ✉ *Fisktorget-Rosenlundsg.*

OFF THE   **FISKHAMNEN –** An excellent view of **Älvsborgsbron** (Älvsborg Bridge),
BEATEN PATH   the longest suspension bridge in Sweden, is available from Fiskhamnen, the Fish Docks west of Stigbergstorget. Built in 1967, the bridge stretches 3,060 ft across the river and is built high so that ocean liners can pass beneath. The government is considering plans to turn this part of the harbor into a scenic walkway with parks and cafés. Also look toward the sea to the large container harbors, Skarvikshamnen, Skandiahamnen (where boats depart for England), and Torshamnen, which bring most of the cargo and passengers to the city today.

★ **㊴ Götaplatsen** (Göta Place). The cultural center of Göteborg was built in 1923 in celebration of the city's 300th anniversary. In the center is the Swedish-American sculptor Carl Milles' fountain statue of Poseidon choking an enormous shark. Behind the statue of Poseidon stands the Konstmuseet, flanked by the **Konserthuset** (Concert Hall) and the **Stadsteatern** (Municipal Theater), three contemporary buildings in which the city celebrates its important contribution to Swedish cultural life. The **Stadsbiblioteket** (Municipal Library) maintains a collection of more than 550,000 books, many in English.

OFF THE   **LISEBERG NÖJESPARK –** Göteborg proudly claims Scandinavia's largest
BEATEN PATH   amusement park. The city's pride is well earned: Liseberg is one of the best-run, most efficient parks in the world. In addition to a wide selection of carnival rides, Liseberg also has numerous restaurants and theaters, all set amid beautifully tended gardens. It's about a 30-minute walk east from the city center or a 10-minute ride by bus or tram; in summer a vintage open streetcar makes frequent runs to Liseberg from Brunnsparken in the middle of town. ✉ *Örgrytev.,* ☎ *031/400100.* 🎫 *SKr40.* ☉ *Late Apr.–June and late Aug., daily 3–11; July–mid-Aug., daily noon– 11; Sept., Sat. 11–1, Sun. noon–8.*

㊵ Konstmuseet. After an extensive renovation, the Art Museum reopened in January 1996 with a new, more accessible entrance and expanded facilities; one of these is the Hasselblad Center, devoted to progress in the art of photography. The museum continues to display an impressive collection of the works of leading Scandinavian painters and sculptors, encapsulating some of the moody introspection of the artistic community in this part of the world. Among the artists represented are Swedes such as Carl Milles, Johan Tobias Sergel, the Impressionist Anders Zorn, the Victorian idealist Carl Larsson, and Prince Eugen. The 19th- and 20th-century French art collection is the best in Sweden, and there's also a small collection of old masters. ✉ *Götaplatsen, S412 56,* ☎ *031/612980.* 🎫 *SKr35.* ☉ *Weekdays 11–4 (Wed. until 9), weekends 11–5. Closed Mon. Sept.–May.*

㊶ Röhsska Museet (Museum of Arts and Crafts). Fine collections of furniture, books and manuscripts, tapestries, and pottery are on view. ✉ *Vasag. 3739, Box 53178, S400 15,* ☎ *031/613850.* 🎫 *SKr40.* ☉ *Year-round, weekends noon–5; May–mid-June, weekdays noon–4; mid-June–Aug., Mon. and Wed.–Fri. noon–6, Tues. noon–9; Apr. and Sept., Tues. noon–9, Wed.–Fri. noon–4.*

㊹ Stadsmuseet (City Museum). Once the warehouse and auction rooms of the Swedish East India Company, a major trading firm founded in 1731, this palatial structure dates from 1750. Today it contains exhibits on the Swedish west coast, with a focus on Göteborg's nautical and trading past. One interesting exhibit deals with the East India Company and its ship the *Göteborg,* which in 1745, returning from China, sank just outside the city while members of the crew's families watched from shore. ✉ *Norra Hamng. 12, S411 14,* ☎ *031/612770.* 🎫 *SKr40.* ⏲ *Weekdays noon–6, weekends 11–4. Closed Mon. Sept.–Apr.*

NEED A BREAK? In the cellar of Stadsmuseet, the **Ostindiska Huset Krog & Kafé** (☎ 031/135750) re-creates an 18th-century atmosphere. The *dagenslunch,* priced at SKr65, is available from 11:30 to 2.

Commercial Göteborg

Explore Göteborg's portside character, both historic and modern, at the waterfront development near town center, where an array of markets and boutiques may keep you busy for hours.

A GOOD WALK

Begin at the harborside square known as Lilla Bomen, where the **Utkiken** ㊺ offers a bird's-eye view of the city and harbor. The waterfront development here includes the training ship *Viking,* the Opera House, and the **Maritima Centrum** ㊻.

From Lilla Bomen Torg, take the pedestrian bridge across the highway to **Nordstan** ㊼. Leave the mall at the opposite end, which puts you at Brunnsparken, the hub of the city's streetcar network. Turn right and cross the street to Gustav Adolfs Torg, the city's official center, dominated by **Rådhuset** ㊽. On the north side of the square is the **Börshuset** ㊾, built in 1849.

Head north from the square along Östra Hamngatan and turn left onto Postgatan to visit **Kronhuset** ㊿, the city's oldest secular building, dating from 1643. The **Kronhusbodarna** are carefully restored turn-of-the-century shops and handicrafts boutiques that surround the entrance to Kronhuset.

Return to Gustaf Adolfs Torg and follow Östra Hamngatan south across the Stora Hamnkanal to Kungsportsplats, where the Saluhall, or Market Hall, has stood since 1888. A number of pedestrian-only shopping streets branch out through this neighborhood on either side of Östra Hamngatan. Crossing the bridge over Rosenlunds Kanalen from Kungsportsplats brings you onto Kungsportsavenyn and the entrance to **Trädgarn** (51).

TIMING

The walk itself will take about two hours; allow extra time to explore the sites and for shopping. Note that Kronhuset is always closed weekends, and Utkiken is closed weekdays off-season. The Kronhusbodarna is closed Sunday. Trädgarn is closed Monday off-season.

SIGHTS TO SEE

㊾ **Börshuset** (Stock Exchange). Completed in 1849, the former Stock Exchange building houses city administrative offices as well as facilities for large banquets. ✉ *Gustaf Adolfs Torg 5.*

Kronhusbodarna (Historical Shopping Center). Glassblowing and watchmaking are among the handicrafts offered in the adjoining Kronhuset; there is also a nice, old-fashioned café. ✉ *Kronhusg. 1D.* ⏲ *Closed Sun.*

㊿ **Kronhuset** (Crown House). The city's oldest secular building, dating from 1643, was originally the city's armory. In 1660 Sweden's Parliament met here to arrange the succession for King Karl X Gustav, who died suddenly while visiting the city. ✉ *Postg. 68,* ☎ *031/7117377.* 🎫 *SKr30.* ⏲ *Weekends 11–4.*

㊻ Maritima Centrum (Marine Center). Here modern naval vessels, including a destroyer, submarines, lightship, cargo vessel, and various tugboats, provide an insight into Göteborg's historic role as a major port. ✉ *Packhuskajen, S411 04,* ☎ *031/101035 or 031/101290 for English recording.* 🎫 *SKr50.* ☉ *May–June, daily 10–6; July and Aug., daily 10–9; Mar.–Apr. and Sept.–Nov., daily 10–4.*

㊼ Nordstan. Sweden's largest indoor shopping mall—open daily—includes a huge parking garage, 24-hour pharmacy, post office, several restaurants, entertainment for children, the department store Åhlens, and a tourist information kiosk. ✉ *Entrances on Köpmansg., Nils Ericsonsg., Kanaltorgsg., and Östra Hamng.*

㊽ Rådhuset. Though the Town Hall dates from 1672, when it was designed by Nicodemus Tessin Senior, its controversial modern extension by Swedish architect Gunnar Asplund dates from 1937. ✉ *Gustaf Adolfs Torg 1.*

㊿ Trädgarn (Botanic Gardens). Trädgårdsföreningen comprises beautiful open green spaces, a magnificent Rose Garden, Butterfly House, and Palm House. ✉ *Just off Kungsportsavenyn.,* ☎ *031/611911 for Butterfly House.* ☉ *Park 7–8; Palm House 10–4; Butterfly House Oct.–Mar., Tues.–Sun. 10–3; Apr., Tues.–Sun. 10–4; May and Sept., daily 10–4; June–Aug., daily 10–5.*

㊸ Utkiken (Lookout Tower). This red-and-white-striped skyscraper towers 282 ft above the waterfront, offering an unparalleled view of the city and skyscrapers. ✉ *Lilla Bomen.* 🎫 *SKr25.* ☉ *May–Aug., daily 11–7; Oct.–Apr., weekends 11–4.*

OFF THE BEATEN PATH

GASVERKSKAJEN – For an interesting tour of the docks, head east from Lilla Bomen about 1½ km (1 mi) along the riverside to the Gas Works Quay, just off Gullbergsstrandgatan. Today, this is the headquarters of a local boating association, its brightly colored pleasure craft contrasting with the old-fashioned working barges either anchored or being repaired at Ringön, just across the river.

NYA ELFSBORGS FÄSTNING – Boats leave regularly from Lilla Bomen to the Elfsborg Fortress, built in 1670 on a harbor island to protect the city from attack. ✉ *Börjessons, Lilla Bommen, kajskul 205, Box 31084, S400 32,* ☎ *031/800750.* 🎫 *SKr65.* ☉ *6 departures per day early May–Aug., daily; Sept., weekends.*

Viking – This four-masted schooner, built in 1907, was among the last of Sweden's sailing cargo ships. The Hotel and Restaurant School of Göteborg opened a hotel and restaurant inside the ship in February 1995. Visitors are welcome. ✉ *Lilla Bommen,* ☎ *031/635800.* 🎫 *SKr25.*

Dining

You can eat well in Göteborg, but expect to pay dearly for the privilege. Fish dishes are the best bet here. Call ahead to be sure restaurants are open, as many close for a month in summer.

$$$ ✕ **A Hereford Beefstouw.** Probably as close as you come to an American steak house in Sweden, this restaurant has gained popularity in a town dominated by fish restaurants. Diners' beef selections are cooked by chefs at grills in the center of the three dining rooms (one of which is set aside for nonsmokers). The rustic atmosphere is heightened by thick wooden tables, pine floors, and landscape paintings. ✉ *Linnég. 5,* ☎ *031/7750441. AE, DC, MC, V. No lunch weekends or July.*

$$$ ✕ **Åtta Glas.** This casual, lively restaurant in what was formally a barge offers excellent views of the river and of the Kungsportsbron, a bridge spanning the canal in town center. Swedish-style fish and meat dishes are the focus, and a children's menu is available. The second-floor bar gets crowds on weekends. ⊠ *Kungsportsbron 1,* ☎ *031/136015. AE, DC, MC, V.*

$$$ ✕ **The Place.** Possibly Göteborg's finest dining establishment, the Place
★ offers a warm, intimate atmosphere created by terra-cotta ceilings, pastel-yellow walls, and white linen tablecloths. A wide selection of exotic dishes, from smoked breast of pigeon to beef tartare with caviar, are prepared with quality ingredients. This is also the home of one of the best wine cellars in Sweden, with Mouton Rothschild wines dating from 1904. An outdoor terrace is open during summer. ⊠ *Arkivg. 7,* ☎ *031/160333. Reservations essential. AE, DC, MC, V.*

$$$ ✕ **Räkan.** This informal and popular place makes the most of an unusual gimmick: the tables are arranged around a long tank, and if you order shrimp, the house specialty, they arrive at your table in radio-controlled boats you navigate yourself. ⊠ *Lorensbergsg. 16,* ☎ *031/169839. Reservations essential. AE, DC, MC, V. No lunch weekends.*

$$$ ✕ **Sjömagasinet.** Seafood is the obvious specialty at this waterfront restaurant. In a 200-year-old renovated shipping warehouse, the dining room has views of the harbor and suspension bridge. An outdoor terrace opens up in summer. ⊠ *Klippans Kulturreservat,* ☎ *031/246510. Reservations essential. AE, DC, MC, V.*

$$ ✕ **Fiskekrogen.** Its name means Fish Inn, and it has more than 30 fish and seafood dishes to choose from. Lunches are particularly good, and it's just across the canal from the Stadsmuseet. ⊠ *Lilla Torget 1,* ☎ *031/7112184. AE, DC, MC, V. Closed Sun.*

$ ✕ **Amanda Boman.** This little restaurant in one corner of the market hall at Kungsportsplats keeps early hours, so unless you eat an afternoon dinner, plan on lunch instead. The cuisine is primarily Swedish, including fish soup and gravlax (marinated salmon). ⊠ *Saluhallen,* ☎ *031/137676. AE, DC, MC, V. Closed Sun.*

$ ✕ **Gabriel.** A buffet of fresh shellfish and the fish dish of the day draw crowds to this restaurant on a balcony above the fish hall. You can eat lunch and watch all the trading. ⊠ *Feske Körkan,* ☎ *031/139051. AE, DC, MC, V. Closed Sun. and Mon. No dinner.*

Lodging

$$$$ ☷ **Park Avenue (Radisson SAS).** Though a 1991 renovation failed to give this modern luxury hotel the ambience it so sorely lacks, all the facilities are in place, including a SAS check-in counter. The well-equipped rooms are decorated in earth tones and have good views of the city. ⊠ *Kungsportsavenyn 3638, Box 53233, S400 16,* ☎ *031/176520,* FAX *031/169568. 318 rooms. 2 restaurants, bar, 2 no-smoking floors, indoor pool, sauna, meeting room. AE, DC, MC, V.*

$$$$ ☷ **Sheraton Hotel and Towers.** Opened in 1986 across Drottningtorget from the picturesque central train station, the Sheraton Hotel and Towers is Göteborg's most modern and spectacular international-style hotel. The attractive atrium lobby is home to two restaurants: Frascati, which serves international cuisine, and the Atrium piano bar with a lighter menu. Rooms are large and luxurious and decorated in pastels. Guests receive a 20% discount at the well-appointed health club on the premises. ⊠ *Södra Hamng. 5965, S401 24,* ☎ *031/806000,* FAX *031/159888. 344 rooms. Restaurant, piano bar, no-smoking rooms, beauty salon, health club, shops, casino, convention center, travel services. AE, DC, MC, V.*

$$$ ⊡ **Eggers.** Dating from 1859, Best Western's Eggers has more Old
★ World character than any other hotel in the city. It is a minute's walk
from the train station and was probably the last port of call in Sweden
for many emigrants to the United States. Rooms vary in size, and all
are beautifully appointed, often with antiques. Only breakfast is served.
☒ *Drottningtorget, Box 323, S401 25,* ☎ *031/806070,* FAX *031/154243.
65 rooms. No-smoking rooms, meeting rooms. AE, DC, MC, V.*

$$$ ⊡ **Europa.** Large and comfortable, this hotel is part of the Nordstan
★ mall complex, very close to the central train station. ☒ *Köpmansg. 38,
S401 24,* ☎ *031/801280,* FAX *031/154755. 475 rooms, 5 suites. Restaurant, piano bar, no-smoking floors, indoor pool, sauna, conference center, parking. AE, DC, MC, V.*

$$$ ⊡ **Liseberg Heden.** Not far from the famous Liseberg Amusement
Park, Liseberg Heden is a popular family hotel. Rooms are modern and
are done in light colors; most have wood floors, and all have a satellite television, minibar, and large desk. Perks include a sauna and a
gourmet restaurant. ☒ *Sten Stureg., S411 38,* ☎ *031/200280,* FAX *031/
165283. 160 rooms. Restaurant, no-smoking rooms, minibars, sauna,
meeting rooms. AE, DC, MC, V.*

$$$ ⊡ **Opalen.** If you are attending an event at the Scandinavium stadium,
or if you have children and are heading for the Liseberg Amusement
Park, this Reso hotel is ideally located. Rooms are bright and modern.
☒ *Engelbrektsg. 73, Box 5106, S402 23,* ☎ *031/810300,* FAX *031/
187622. 241 rooms. Restaurant, bar, 2 no-smoking floors, sauna. AE,
DC, MC, V.*

$$$ ⊡ **Panorama.** Within reach of all downtown attractions and close to Liseberg, this Best Western hotel nevertheless manages to provide a quiet,
relaxing atmosphere. ☒ *Eklandag. 5153, Box 24037, S400 22,* ☎ *031/
810880,* FAX *031/814237. 339 rooms. Restaurant, no-smoking floors, hot
tub, sauna, nightclub, meeting rooms, free parking. AE, DC, MC, V.*

$$$ ⊡ **Riverton.** Convenient for people arriving in the city by ferry, this
hotel is close to the European terminals and overlooks the harbor. Built
in 1985, it has a glossy marble floor and reflective ceiling in the lobby.
Rooms are decorated with abstract-pattern textiles and whimsical
prints. ☒ *Stora Badhusg. 26, S411 21,* ☎ *031/101200,* FAX *031/130866.
190 rooms. Restaurant, bar, no-smoking rooms, hot tub, sauna, meeting rooms, free parking. AE, DC, MC, V.*

$$$ ⊡ **Royal.** Göteborg's oldest hotel, built in 1852, is small, family owned,
★ and traditional. Rooms, most with new parquet floors, are individually decorated with reproductions of elegant Swedish traditional furniture. It's in the city center a few blocks from the central train station.
☒ *Drottningg. 67, S411 07,* ☎ *031/806100,* FAX *031/156246. 82
rooms. Breakfast room, no-smoking floor. AE, DC, MC, V.*

$$$ ⊡ **Rubinen.** The central location on Avenyn is a plus, but this Reso
hotel can be noisy in summer. ☒ *Kungsportsavenyn 24, Box 53097,
S400 14,* ☎ *031/810800,* FAX *031/167586. 185 rooms. Restaurant, bar,
no-smoking rooms, meeting rooms. AE, DC, MC, V.*

$ ⊡ **Ostkupans Vandrarhem.** Situated in a modern apartment block, this
hostel is 5 km (3 mi) from the train station. Rooms are contemporary,
with Swedish-designed furnishings. Breakfast (SKr40) is not included
in the rates. ☒ *Mejerig. 2, S412 76,* ☎ *031/401050,* FAX *031/401151.
250 beds, 6- to 8-bed apartments. MC, V. Closed Sept.–May.*

$ ⊡ **Partille Vandrarhem.** This hostel is in a pleasant old house 15 km
(9 mi) outside the city, next to a lake for swimming. You can order
meals or prepare them yourself in the guest kitchen. ☒ *Landvetterv.,
Box 214, S433 24, Partille,* ☎ *031/446501,* ☎ FAX *031/446163. 120
beds, 2- to 6-bed rooms. No credit cards.*

Camping

If camping is your bag, then **Uddevalla** (Hafstens Camping, ☎ 0522/
644117), **Göteborg** (Kärralund, ☎ 031/840200, FAX 031/840500), and
Askim (Askim Strand, ☎ 031/286261, FAX 031/681335) have fine sites.

Nightlife and the Arts

Music, Opera, and Theater

Home of the highly acclaimed Göteborg Symphony Orchestra, **Konserthuset** (⊠ Götaplatsen, S412 56, ☎ 031/167000) features a mural
by Sweden's Prince Eugen in the lobby. **Operan** (⊠ Packhuskajen, ☎
031/131300), home of the Göteborg's Opera Company, was completed in 1994 and incorporates a 1,250-seat auditorium with a glassed-
in dining area overlooking the harbor. **Stadsteatern** (⊠ Götaplatsen,
Box 5094, S402 22, ☎ 031/819960 tickets, 031/7786600 information)
has a good reputation in Sweden. The vast majority of its productions
are in Swedish.

Outdoor Activities and Sports

Beaches

There are several excellent local beaches. The two most popular—though
you'll be unlikely to find them crowded—are Näset and Askim.

Fishing

Mackerel fishing is popular here. Among the boats that take expeditions into the archipelago is the **M.S. Daisy** (☎ 031/963018 or 010/
2358017), which leaves from Hjuvik on the Hisingen side of the Göta
River.

Shopping

Department Stores

Try the local branch of **NK** (⊠ Östra Hamng. 42 (☎ 031/107000).
Åhléns (☎ 031/800200) is in the Nordstan mall (☞ *above*).

Specialty Stores

ANTIQUES

Antikhallarna (Antiques Halls, ⊠ Västra Hamng. 6, ☎ 031/7111324)
claims to be the largest of its kind in Scandinavia. You'll find Sweden's
leading auction house, **Bukowskis** (⊠ Kungsportsavenyn 43, ☎ 031/
200360), on Avenyn.

CRAFTS

If you are looking to buy Swedish handicrafts and glassware in a suitably atmospheric setting then visit the various shops in **Kronhusbodarna**.
Excellent examples of local handicrafts can also be bought at **Bohus-
slöjden** (⊠ Kungsportsavenyn 25, ☎ 031/160072).

MEN'S CLOTHING

Ströms (⊠ Kungsg. 2729, ☎ 031/177100) has occupied its street corner location for two generations, offering clothing of high quality and
good taste. The fashions at **Gillblads** (⊠ Kungsg. 44, ☎ 031/108846)
suit a younger, somewhat trendier customer.

WOMEN'S CLOTHING

Gillblads (⊠ Kungsg. 44, ☎ 031/108846) has the most current fashions. **Ströms** (⊠ Kungsg. 2729, ☎ 031/177100) offers clothing of
high quality and mildly conservative style. **Hennes & Mauritz** (⊠
Kungsg. 5557, ☎ 031/7110011) sells clothes roughly comparable to
the standard choices at Sears or Marks & Spencer.

Göteborg A to Z

Arriving and Departing

BY BUS

All buses arrive in the central city area and the principal bus company is **Swebus** (☎ 031/103285).

BY CAR

Göteborg is reached by car either via the E20 or the E4 highway from Stockholm (495 km/307 mi) and the east, or on the E6/E20 coastal highway from the south (Malmö is 290 km/180 mi away). Markings are excellent, and roads are well sanded and plowed in winter.

BY PLANE

Landvetter (☎ 031/941100), is approximately 26 km (16 mi) from the city. Among the airlines operating from the airport are **SAS** (☎ 031/942000 or 020/727000), **British Airways** (☎ 020/781144), **Air France** (☎ 031/941180), and **Lufthansa** (☎ 031/941325 or 020/228800).

Between the Airport and City Center: Landvetter is linked to Göteborg by freeway. Buses leave Landvetter every 15 to 30 minutes and arrive 30 minutes later at Nils Ericsonsplatsen by the central train station, with stops at Lisebergsstationen, Korsvägen, the SAS Park Avenue Hotel, and Kungsportsplatsen; weekend schedules include some nonstop departures. The price of the trip is SKr50. For more information, call **GL** (Göteborg Bus and Tram, ☎ 031/801235).

The **taxi** ride to the city center should cost no more than SKr250. A shared **SAS limousine** for up to four people to the same address costs SKr215 (SAS Limousine Service, ☎ 031/942424).

BY TRAIN

There is regular service from Stockholm, taking a little over 4½ hours, as well as frequent high-speed (X2000) train service, which takes about three hours. All trains arrive at the **central train station** (☎ 031/805000) in Drottningtorget, downtown Göteborg. For schedules, call **SJ** (☎ 031/104445 or 020/757575). Streetcars and buses leave from here for the suburbs, but the hub for all streetcar traffic is a block down Norra Hamngatan, at Brunnsparken.

Getting Around

BY BOAT

Traveling the entire length of the Göta Canal by passenger boat to Stockholm takes between four and six days. For details, contact the **Göta Canal Steamship Company** (✉ Hotellplatsen 2, Box 272, S401 24, Göteborg, ☎ 031/806315; N. Riddarholmshamnen 5, S111 28, Stockholm, ☎ 08/202728). For information about sailing your own boat on the Göta Canal, contact **AB Göta Kanalbolaget** (☎ 0141/53510).

BY BUS AND TRAM

Göteborg has an excellent transit service, called Stadstrafiken; pick up a brochure in English at a TidPunkten office (✉ Drottningtorget, Brunnsparken, Nils Ericsonsplatsen, and Folkungabron, ☎ 031/801235), which explains the various discount passes and procedures.

The best bet for the tourist, however, is the **Göteborg Card,** which covers free use of public transport, various sightseeing trips, and admission to Liseberg and local museums, among other benefits. The card costs SKr125 for one day, SKr225 for two days, and SKr275 for three days; there are lower rates for children younger than 18 years from mid-June to mid-September. You can buy the Göteborg Card as well as regular tram and bus passes at Pressbyrån shops, camping sites, and the tourist information offices.

Avis has offices at the airport (☎ 031/946030) and the central railway station (☎ 031/805780). Also try **Hertz** (✉ Spannmålsg. 16, ☎ 031/803730).

BY TAXI
To order a taxi, call **Taxi Göteborg** (☎ 031/650000); for advance bookings, call ☎ 031/500504.

Contacts and Resources
DOCTORS AND DENTISTS
Dial ☎ 031/7031500 day or night for information on medical services. Emergencies are handled by the **Sahlgrenska Hospital** (☎ 031/601000), **Östrasjukhuset** (☎ 031/374000), and **Mölndalssjukhuset** (☎ 031/861000). There is a private medical service at **City Akuten** weekdays 8–6 (✉ Drottningg. 45, ☎ 031/101010). There is a 24-hour children's emergency service at Östrasjukhuset as well.

The national dental-service emergency number is ☎ 031/807800; the private dental-service emergency number is ☎ 031/800500. Both are available 8 AM–9 PM only; for emergencies after hours, call ☎ 031/7031500.

EMBASSIES AND CONSULATES
U.K. Consulate (✉ Götg. 15, ☎ 031/151327).

EMERGENCIES
Dial ☎ 112.

ENGLISH-LANGUAGE BOOKSTORES
Nearly all bookshops stock English-language books. The broadest selection is at **Eckersteins Akademibokhandeln** (✉ Södra Larmg. 11, ☎ 031/171100).

GUIDED TOURS
Boat and Bus Sightseeing Tours: A 90-minute bus tour and a two-hour combination boat-and-bus tour of the chief points of interest leave from outside the main tourist office at Kungsportsplatsen every day from mid-May through August and on Saturday in April, September, and October. Call the tourist office for schedules.

For a view of the city from the water and an expert commentary on its sights and history in English and German, take one of the **Paddan** sightseeing boats. *Paddan* means "toad" in Swedish, an apt commentary on the vessels' squat appearance. The boats pass under 20 bridges and take in both the canals and part of the Göta River. ✉ *Kungsportsbron,* ☎ *031/133000.* ▣ *SKr70.* ☉ *Late Apr.–late June and mid-Aug.–early Sept., daily 10–5; late June–mid-Aug., daily 10–9; early Sept.–Oct. 1, daily noon–3.*

LATE-NIGHT PHARMACY
Vasen (✉ Götg. 12, ☎ 031/804410), in the Nordstan shopping mall, is open 24 hours.

TRAVEL AGENCIES
See the Yellow Pages under *Resor-Resebyråer.* **Ticket Travel Agency** (✉ Östra Hamng. 35, ☎ 031/176860). **STF** (✉ Drottningtorget 6, Box 305, S401 24, ☎ 031/150930).

VISITOR INFORMATION
The main tourist office is **Göteborg's Turistbyrå** (✉ Kungsportsplatsen 2, S411 10 Göteborg, ☎ 031/100740, FAX 031/132184). There are also offices at the Nordstan shopping center (✉ Nordstadstorget,

S411 05 Göteborg, ☎ 031/150705) and in front of the central train station at Drottningtorget.

A free visitor's guide called *Göteborgarn* is available in English during the summer; you can pick it up at tourist offices, shopping centers, and some restaurants, as well as on the streetcars.

The Friday edition of the principal morning newspaper, *Göteborgs Posten,* includes a weekly supplement called "Aveny"—it's in Swedish but is reasonably easy to decipher.

BOHUSLÄN

The Bohuslän coastal region north of Göteborg, with its indented, rocky coastline, provides a foretaste of Norway's fjords farther north. It was from these rugged shores that the 9th-and 10th-century Vikings sailed southward on their epic voyages. Today small towns and attractive fishing villages nestle among the distinctively rounded granite rocks and the thousands of skerries and islands that form Sweden's western archipelago, best described by Prince Vilhelm, brother of the late King Gustav V, as "an archipelago formed of gneiss and granite and water that eternally stretches foamy arms after life." The ideal way to explore the area is by drifting slowly north of Göteborg, taking full advantage of the uncluttered beaches and small, picturesque fishing villages. Painters and sailors haunt the region in summer.

Kungälv

52 *15 km (9 mi) north of Göteborg.*

Strategically placed at the confluence of the two arms of the Göta River, Kungälv was an important battle grounds in ancient times. Though today it is something of a bedroom suburb for Göteborg, the town still has several ancient sights, including a white wooden church dating from 1679, with an unusual Baroque interior.

For a sense of Kungälv's military past, visit **Bohus Fästning,** now a ruined fortress built by the Norwegians in 1308, where many battles between Swedish, Norwegian, and Danish armies took place. ⊠ *Kungälv.* ☎ *0303/99200.* 🖾 *SKr15.* ☉ *May–June and Aug., daily 10–7; July, daily 10–8; Sept., weekends 11–5.*

Outdoor Activities and Sports
Skärhamn on the island of Tjörn offers excellent **deep-sea fishing,** Mackerel is the prized catch. You can drive over the road bridge from Stenungsund.

Uddevalla

53 *64 km (40 mi) north of Kungälv, 79 km (49 mi) north of Göteborg.*

A former shipbuilding town located at the head of a picturesque fjord, Kungälv is best known in history for a battle in which heavy rains doused musketeers' tinder boxes, effectively ending hostilities.

En Route   Lysekil, off the E6 highway on a promontory at the head of the Gullmarn Fjord, has been one of Sweden's most popular summer resorts since the 19th century. It specializes in boat excursions to neighboring islands and deep-sea fishing trips. The best bathing is at Pinnevik Cove. A little to the north lies the Sotenäs Peninsula and the attractive island of **Smögen,** which can be reached by road bridge. It is renowned locally for its shrimp.

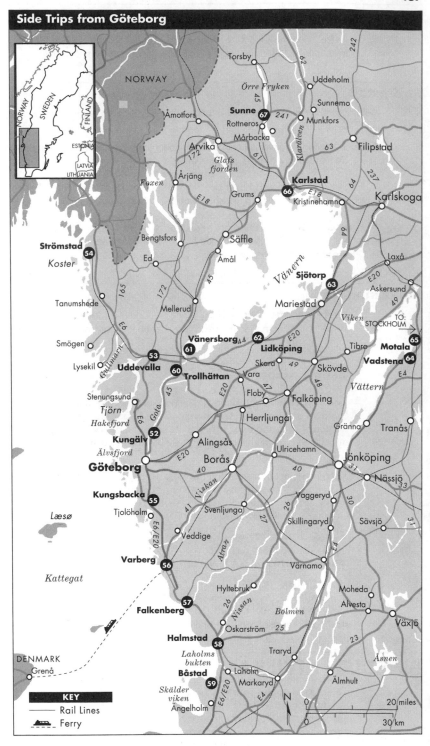

Side Trips from Göteborg

Before the E6 highway reaches Strömstad, stop at **Tanumshede** to see Europe's largest single collection of Bronze Age rock carvings at **Vitlycke**. They cover 673 square ft of rock and depict battles, hunting, and fishing. The carvings are close to the main road and are well marked.

Strömstad

54 *90 km (56 mi) northwest of Uddvalla, 169 km (105 mi) north of Göteborg.*

This popular Swedish resort claims to have more summer sunshine than any other town north of the Alps. Formerly Norwegian, it has been the site of many battles between warring Danes, Norwegians, and Swedes. A short trip over the Norwegian border takes you to Halden, where Sweden's warrior king, Karl XII, died in 1718.

OFF THE   **KOSTER ISLANDS** – There are regular ferry boats from Strömstad to the
BEATEN PATH   Koster Islands, a favorite holiday spot, with uncluttered beaches and trips to catch prawn and lobster.

Bohuslän A to Z

Arriving and Departing

Buses leave from behind the central train station in Göteborg; the main bus lines are **GL** (☏ 031/801235) and **Bohus Trafiken** (☏ 0522/14030). The trip to Strömstad takes between two and three hours.

Getting Around

BY CAR

The best way to explore Bohuslän is by car. The E6 highway runs the length of the coast from Göteborg north to Strömstad, close to the Norwegian border, and for campers there are numerous well-equipped and uncluttered camping sites along the coast's entire length.

BY TRAIN

There is regular service along the coast between all the major towns of Bohuslän. The trip from Göteborg to Strömstad takes about two hours, and there are several trains each day. For schedules, call **SJ** (✉ Göteborg, ☏ 031/103000 or 020/757575).

Visitor Information

REGIONAL TOURIST OFFICE

Göteborg Turistbyrå (☞ Göteborg A to Z, *above*).

LOCAL TOURIST OFFICES

Kungälv (✉ Fästningsholmen, ☏ 0303/99200). **Kungshamn** (✉ Hamng. 6, ☏ 0523/37150). **Öckerö** (✉ Stranden 2, ☏ 031/965080). **Strömstad** (✉ Tullhuset, Norra Hamnen, ☏ 0526/13025). **Uddevalla** (✉ Kampenhof, ☏ 0522/511787).

SWEDISH RIVIERA

The coastal region south of Göteborg, Halland—locally dubbed the Swedish Riviera—is the closest that mainland Sweden comes to having a resort area. Fine beaches abound, and there are plenty of opportunities for many sporting activities. The region stretches down to Båstad in the country's southernmost province, Skåne.

Kungsbacka

55 *25 km (15 mi) south of Göteborg.*

This bedroom suburb of Göteborg holds a market on the first Thursday of every month. A break in a high ridge to the west, the **Fjärås Crack,** offers a fine view of the coast. On the slopes of the ridge are Iron Age and Viking graves.

En Route At **Tjolöholm,** 12 km (7 mi) down the E6/E20 highway from Kungsbacka, you'll encounter Tjolöholms Slott (Tjolöholm Castle), a manor house built by a Scotsman at the beginning of this century in mock English Tudor style. ⊠ *S430 33 Fjärås,* ☏ *0300/44200.* ⚏ *SKr40.* ⊙ *June–Aug., daily 11–4; Apr.–May and Sept., weekends 11–4; Oct., Sun. 11–4.*

Near Tjolöholm is the tiny 18th-century village of **Äskhult,** the site of an open-air museum, the Gamla By. ☏ *0300/42159.* ⚏ *SKr20.* ⊙ *May–Aug., daily 10–6; Sept., weekends 10–6.*

Varberg

⁵⁶ *40 km (25 mi) south of Kungsbacka, 65 km (40 mi) south of Göteborg.*

Varberg is a busy port with connections to Grenå in Denmark. The town boasts some good beaches, but is best known for a suit of medieval clothing preserved in the museum in the 13th-century **Varbergs Fästning** (Varberg Fortress). The suit belonged to a man who was murdered and thrown into a peat bog. The peat preserved his body, and his clothes are the only suit of ordinary medieval clothing in existence. The museum also contains a silver bullet said to be the one that killed Karl XII. ☏ *0340/18520.* ⚏ *SKr20.* ⊙ *Weekdays 10–4, weekends noon–4. Hourly guided tours mid-June–mid-Aug., daily 10–7; May–mid-June and mid-Aug.–Sept., Sun. 10–7.*

Falkenberg

⁵⁷ *29 km (18 mi) south of Varberg, 94 km (58 mi) south of Göteborg.*

With its fine beaches and plentiful salmon in the Ätran River, Falkenberg is one of Sweden's most attractive resorts. Its Gamla Stan (Old Town) is full of narrow, cobblestone streets and quaint old wooden houses.

Shopping
Here you'll find **Törngren's** (⊠ Krukmakareg. 4, ☏ 0346/16920, ☏ 0346/10354 pottery) a pottery shop, probably the oldest still operating in Scandinavia, owned and run by the seventh generation of the founding family. It's open normal business hours, but you might have to call ahead to view pottery.

Halmstad

⁵⁸ *40 km (25 mi) south of Falkenberg, 143 km (89 mi) south of Göteborg.*

With a population of 50,000, including Per Gestle of Roxette, Halmstad is the largest seaside resort on the west coast. The Norreport town gate, all that remains of the town's original fortifications, dates from 1605. The modern Town Hall has interior decorations by the so-called Halmstad Group of painters, formed here in 1929. A 14th-century church in the main square contains fragments of medieval murals and a 17th-century pulpit.

Båstad

⁵⁹ *35 km (22 mi) south of Halmstad, 178 km (111 mi) south of Göteborg.*

In the southernmost province of Skåne, Båstad is regarded by locals to be Sweden's most fashionable resort, where ambassadors and local captains of industry have their summer houses. Aside from this, it is best known for its tennis. In addition to the **Båstad Open,** a Grand Prix tournament in late summer, there is the annual **Donald Duck Cup** in July for children ages 11 to 15; it was the very first trophy won by Björn Borg, who later took the Wimbledon men's singles title an unprecedented five times in a row. Spurred on by Borg and other Swedish champions, such as Stefan Edberg and Mats Wilander, thousands of youngsters take part in the Donald Duck Cup each year. For details, contact the **Svenska Tennisförbundet** (Swedish Tennis Association, ✉ Lidingöv. 75, Stockholm, ☎ 08/6679770).

Norrviken Gardens, 3 km (2 mi) northwest of Båstad, are beautifully laid out in different styles, with a restaurant, shop, and pottery studio. ☎ 0431/69040. 🎫 SKr35. ⊙ Early June–mid-Aug., daily 10–6; late Aug.–May, daily 10:30–5.

Swedish Riviera A to Z

Arriving and Departing

BY BUS
Buses leave from behind Göteborg's central train station.

BY CAR
Simply follow the E6/E20 highway south from Göteborg. It runs parallel to the coast.

BY TRAIN
Regular train services connect the Göteborg central station with all major towns. Contact **SJ** (✉ Göteborg, ☎ 031/103000 or 020/757575).

Visitor Information
Båstad (✉ Stortorget 1, ☎ 0431/75045). **Halmstad** (✉ Lilla Torg, ☎ 035/109345). **Falkenberg** (✉ Stortorget, ☎ 0346/17410). **Halmstad** (✉ Lilla Torg, ☎ 035/109345). **Laholm** (✉ Rådhuset, ☎ 0430/15216 or 0430/15450). **Kungsbacka** (✉ Storg. 41, ☎ 0300/34595). **Varberg** (✉ Brunnsparken, ☎ 0340/88770).

GÖTA CANAL

Stretching 614 km (382 mi) between Stockholm and Göteborg, the Göta Canal is actually a series of interconnected canals, rivers, lakes, and even a stretch of sea. Bishop Hans Brask of Linköping in the 16th century was the first to suggest the idea; in 1718, King Karl XII ordered the canal to be built, but work was abandoned when he was killed in battle the same year. Not until 1810 was the idea again taken up in earnest. The driving force was a Swedish nobleman, Count Baltzar Bogislaus von Platen (1766–1829), and his motive was commercial. Von Platen saw in the canal a way of beating Danish tolls on shipping that passed through the Öresund and of enhancing the importance of Göteborg by linking the port with Stockholm on the east coast. At a time when Swedish fortunes were at a low ebb, the canal was also envisaged as a means of reestablishing faith in the future and boosting national morale.

The building of the canal took 22 years and involved a total of 58,000 men. The linking of the various stretches of water required 87 km (54 mi) of man-made cuts through soil and rock, and the building of 58 locks, 47 bridges, 27 culverts, and 3 dry docks. Unfortunately, the canal never achieved the financial success hoped for by von Platen. By 1857 the Danes had removed shipping tolls, and in the following decade the linking of Göteborg with Stockholm by rail effectively ended the canal's commercial potential. The canal has come into its own as a 20th-century tourist attraction, however.

Drifting lazily down this lovely series of waterways, across the enormous lakes, Vänern and Vättern, through a microcosm of all that is best about Sweden—abundant fresh air; clear, clean water; pristine nature; well-tended farmland—it is difficult to conceive of the canal's industrial origins. A bicycle path runs parallel to the canal, offering another means of touring the country.

En Route   The trip from Göteborg takes you first along the Göta Älv, a wide waterway that 10,000 years ago, when the ice cap melted, was a great fjord. Some 30 minutes into the voyage the boat passes below a rocky escarpment, topped by the remains of **Bohus Fästning** (Bohus Castle), distinguished by two round towers known as Father's Hat and Mother's Bonnet. It dates from the 14th century and was once the mightiest fortress in western Scandinavia, commanding the confluence of the Göta and Nordre rivers. It was strengthened and enlarged in the 16th century and successfully survived 14 sieges. From 1678 onward, the castle began to lose its strategic and military importance and fell into decay, until 1838, when King Karl XIV passed by on a river journey, admired the old fortress, and ordered its preservation.

Just north of Kungälv along the Göta Canal, you'll come to the quiet village of **Lödöse,** once a major trading settlement and a predecessor of Göteborg. From here, the countryside becomes wilder, with pines and oaks clustered thickly on either bank between cliffs of lichen-clad granite.

Trollhättan

(60)   *70 km (43 mi) north of Göteborg.*

In this pleasant industrial town of about 50,000 inhabitants, a spectacular waterfall was rechanneled in 1906 to become Sweden's first hydroelectric plant. In most years, on specific days the waters are allowed to follow their natural course, a fall of 106 ft in six torrents. This sight is well worth seeing. The other main point of interest is the area between what were the falls and the series of locks that allowed the canal to bypass them. Here are disused locks from 1800 and 1844 and a strange Ice Age grotto where members of the Swedish royal family have carved their names since the 18th century. Trollhättan also has a fine, wide marketplace and pleasant waterside parks.

En Route   Soon after leaving Trollhättan, the Göta Canal takes you past Hunneberg and Halleberg, two strange, flat-topped hills, both more than 500 ft high; the woods surrounding them are extraordinarily rich in elk, legend, and Viking burial mounds. It then proceeds through **Karls Grav,** the oldest part of the canal, begun early in the 17th century; its purpose was to bypass the Rommun Falls on the Göta River, which have been harnessed to power a hydroelectric project.

Vänersborg

(61)   *15 km (9 mi) north of Trollhättan, 85 km (53 mi) north of Göteborg.*

Eventually, the canal enters **Vänern,** Sweden's largest and Europe's third largest lake: 3,424 square km (1,322 square mi) of water, 145 km (90 mi) long and 81 km (50 mi) wide at one point.

At the southern tip of the lake is Vänersborg, a town of about 30,000 inhabitants that was founded in the mid-17th century. The church and the governor's residence date from the 18th century, but the rest of the town was destroyed by fire in 1834. Vänersborg is distinguished by its fine lakeside park, the trees of which act as a windbreak for the gusts that sweep in from Vänern.

Lidköping

⑥ *55 km (34 mi) east of Värnersberg, 140 km (87 mi) northeast of Göteborg.*

On an inlet at the southernmost point of Vänern's eastern arm lies the town of Lidköping, which received its charter in 1446 and is said to have the largest town square in Sweden.

OFF THE **LÄCKÖ SLOTT –** Lying 24 km (15 mi) to the north of Lidköping, on an is-
BEATEN PATH land off the point dividing the eastern arm of Vänern from the western, is Läckö Castle, one of Sweden's finest 17th-century Renaissance palaces. Its 250 rooms were once the home of Magnus Gabriel de la Gardie, a great favorite of Queen Christina. Only the Royal Palace in Stockholm is larger. In 1681 Karl XI, to curtail the power of the nobility, confiscated it, and in 1830 all its furnishings were auctioned. Many of them have since been restored to the palace.

En Route On a peninsula to the east of Lidköping, the landscape is dominated by the great hill of **Kinnekulle,** towering 900 ft above the lake. The hill is rich in colorful vegetation and wildlife and was a favorite hike for the botanist Linnaeus.

Sjötorp

⑥ *67 km (42 mi) northeast of Lidköping, 207 km (129 mi) northeast of Göteborg.*

At the lakeside port of Sjötorp, the Göta Canal proper begins: a cut through earth and granite with a series of locks raising the steamer to Lanthöjden, at 304 ft above sea level the highest point on the canal. The boat next enters the narrow, twisting lakes of Viken and Botten-sjön and continues to Forsvik through the canal's oldest lock, built in 1813. It then sails out into **Vättern,** Sweden's second-largest lake, nearly 129 km (80 mi) from north to south and 31 km (19 mi) across at its widest point. Its waters are so clear that in some parts the bottom is visible at a depth of 50 ft. The lake is subject to sudden storms that can whip its normally placid waters into choppy waves.

Vadstena

⑥ *249 km (155 mi) northeast of Göteborg (via Jönköping).*

This little-known historic gem of a town grew up around the monastery founded by Saint Birgitta, or Bridget (1303–73), who wrote in her *Revelations* that she had a vision of Christ in which he revealed the rules of the religious order she went on to establish. These rules seem to have been a precursor for the Swedish ideal of sexual equality, with both nuns and monks sharing a common church. Her order spread rapidly after her death, and at one time there were 80 Bridgetine monasteries in Europe. Little remains of the Vadstena monastery, however; in 1545 King Gustav Vasa ordered its demolition, and its stones were used to build **Vadstena Slott** (Vadstena Castle), the huge fortress dominating the lake. Swedish royalty held court here until 1715. It then fell into decay and was used as a granary. Today it houses part of the National Archives and is also the site of an annual summer opera festival. ☎ *0143/15123.* ▣ *SKr30.* ☉ *Mid-May–June and late Aug., daily noon–4; July–mid-Aug., daily 11–4. Guided tours mid-May–mid-Aug. at 12:30 and 1:30, late Aug. also at 2:30.*

Also worth a visit is **Vadstena Kyrka.** The triptych altarpiece on the south wall features Saint Birgitta presenting her book of revelations to a group of kneeling cardinals. There is also a fine wood carving of the Madonna and Child from 1500.

Lodging

$$ ⛉ **Kungs-Starby Wärdshus.** This functional guest house, reached via Route 50, adjoins a renovated manor house and restaurant, surrounded by a park on the outskirts of town. ⊠ *S592 01 Vadstena,* ☎ *0143/ 75100,* ⊠ *0143/75170. 61 rooms. Restaurant, no-smoking rooms, indoor pool, sauna, meeting rooms. AE, DC, MC, V.*

$$ ⛉ **Vadstena Klosterhotel.** This hotel is housed in Sweden's oldest secular building, parts of which date from the 13th century. Rooms are modern and well appointed, and there are three comfortable lounges. ⊠ *Klosterområdet, off Lasarettsg., S592 30 Vadstena,* ☎ *0143/11530,* ⊠ *0143/13648. 29 rooms. Restaurant, no-smoking rooms, meeting rooms. AE, DC, MC, V.*

Motala

⑥⑤ *13 km (8 mi) north of Vadstena, 262 km (163 mi) northeast of Göteborg.*

Before reaching Stockholm, the canal passes through Motala, where Baltzar von Platen is buried close to the canal. He had envisaged the establishment of four new towns along the waterway, but only Motala fulfilled his dream. He designed the town himself, and his statue is in the main square.

En Route At Borenshult a series of locks take the boat down to **Boren,** a lake in the province of Östergötland. On the southern shore of the next lake, Roxen, lies the city of **Linköping,** capital of the province and home of Saab, the aircraft and automotive company. Once out of the lake, you follow a new stretch of canal past the sleepy town of **Söderköping.** A few miles east, at the hamlet of Mem, the canal's last lock lowers the boat into Slätbaken, a Baltic fjord presided over by the ruins of the ancient **Stegeborg Fortress.** The boat then steams north along the coastline until it enters **Mälaren** through the Södertälje Canal and finally anchors in the capital at Riddarholmen.

Göta Canal A to Z

Arriving and Departing

BY BOAT

For details about cruises along the Göta Canal, *see* Getting Around in Göteborg A to Z, *above.*

BY CAR

From Stockholm, follow E18 west; from Göteborg, take Route 45 north to E18.

BY TRAIN

Call **SJ** (Göteborg, ☎ 054/102160) for information about service.

Visitor Information

REGIONAL TOURIST OFFICES

Uddevalla (Bohusturist, ⊠ Skansg. 3, ☎ 0522/14055). **Skövde** (Västergötlands Turistråd, ⊠ Kyrkog. 11, ☎ 0500/418050).

LOCAL TOURIST OFFICES

Karlsborg (⊠ N. Kanalg. 2, ☎ 0505/17350). **Vadstena** (⊠ Rådhustorget, ☎ 0143/15125).

VÄRMLAND

Close to the Norwegian border on the north shores of Vänern, this province is rich in folklore. It was also the home of Alfred Nobel and the birthplace of other famous Swedes, among them the Nobel Prize–winning novelist Selma Lagerlöf, the poet Gustaf Fröding, former prime minister Tage Erlander, and present-day opera star Håkan Hagegård. Värmland's forested, lake-dotted landscape attracts artists seeking refuge and Swedes on holiday.

Karlstad

66 *255 km (158 mi) northeast of Göteborg.*

Värmland's principal city (population 74,000) is situated on Klaraälven (Klara River) at the point where it empties into Vänern. Founded in 1684, when it was known as Tingvalla, the city was totally rebuilt after a fire in 1865. Its name was later changed to honor King Karl IX—Karlstad, meaning Karl's Town. In **Stortorget,** the main square, there is a statue of Karl IX by the local sculptor Christian Eriksson.

The **Värmlands Museum** has rooms dedicated to both Eriksson and the poet Fröding. ⊠ *Sandgrun, Box 335, S651 08, Karlstad,* ☎ *054/ 211419.* ⊠ *SKr20.* ☉ *Thurs.–Tues. noon–4, Wed. noon–8.*

The **Marieberg Skogspark** (Marieberg Forest Park) is worth visiting. A delight for the whole family, the park has restaurants and an outdoor theater. ☉ *Early June–late Aug., Thurs.–Tues. 11–5, Wed. 11–8; late Aug.–early June, Tues.–Sun. noon–4, Wed. noon–8.*

Karlstad is the site of the **Emigrant Registret** (Emigrant Registry), which maintains detailed records of the Swedes' emigration to America. Visitors of Swedish extraction can trace their ancestors at the center's research facility. ⊠ *Norra Strandg. 4, Box 331, S651 08, Karlstad,* ☎ *054/159272.* ⊠ *Free.* ☉ *May–Sept., daily 8–4; rest of yr, Tues.–Sun. 8–4:30, Mon. 8–7.*

Dining and Lodging

$$$ ✕ **Inn Alstern.** Overlooking Lake Alstern, this elegant restaurant offers Swedish and continental cuisine, with fish dishes as the specialty. Reservations are advised. ⊠ *Morgonv. 4,* ☎ *054/834900. AE, MC, V.*

$$$ ⌷ **Stadshotellet.** On the banks of Klarälven (Klara River), this hotel built in 1870 is steeped in tradition. All of the rooms are decorated differently, some in modern Swedish style, others evoking their original look. You can dine at the gourmet Matsalon or in the more casual atmosphere of the Cafeet Statt. ⊠ *Kungsg. 22, S651 08,* ☎ *054/ 215220,* ⌷ *054/188211. 143 rooms. Restaurant, pub, no-smoking rooms, sauna, nightclub, meeting rooms. AE, DC, MC, V.*

$$ ⌷ **Gösta Berling.** In town center, this small hotel, named for the hero of the Selma Lagerlöf novel, offers nondescript common rooms but inviting, plushly carpeted guest rooms. ⊠ *Drottningg. 1, S652 24,* ☎ *054/ 150190,* ⌷ *054/154826. 66 rooms. No-smoking rooms, sauna, meeting rooms. AE, DC, MC, V.*

En Route   Värmland is, above all, a rural experience. Drive along the **Klaraäl-ven,** through the beautiful Fryken Valley, to Ransater, where author Erik Gustaf Geijer was born in 1783 and where Erlander, the former prime minister, also grew up. The rural idyll ends in **Munkfors,** where some of the best-quality steel in Europe is manufactured.

OFF THE
BEATEN PATH

SUNNEMO AND UDDEHOLM – Ten kilometers (6 miles) north of Munkfors lies the little village of **Sunnemo,** with its beautiful wooden church. At the northern end of Lake Råda, the town of **Uddeholm** is home of the Uddeholm Corporation, which produces iron and steel, forestry products, and chemicals.

Sunne

67   *63 km (39 mi) north of Karlstad, 318 km (198 mi) northeast of Göteborg.*

Straddling the long, narrow Fryken Lake, Sunne is best known as a jumping-off point for Mårbacka, a stone's throw southeast. Here the estate where Nobel Prize winner Selma Lagerlöf was born in 1858 has been kept much as she left it at the time of her death in 1940; it can be seen by guided tour. ⊠ *Östra Ämtervik, S686 26 Sunne,* ☎ *0565/ 31027.* ⌨ *SKr40.* ☉ *Mid-May–June and Aug.–early Sept., daily 10– 5, tours every hr; July, daily 9:30–5, tours every half hr.*

OFF THE
BEATEN PATH

ROTTNEROS HERRGARDS PARK – On the western shore of Fryken Lake, 5 km (3 mi) south of Sunne, you'll find Rottneros Manor, the inspiration for Ekeby, the fictional estate in Lagerlöf's *Gösta Berlings Saga* (*The Tale of Gösta Berling*). The house is privately owned, but visitors are invited to admire its park, with its fine collection of Scandinavian sculpture—including works by Carl Milles, Norwegian artist Gustav Vigeland, and Wäinö Aaltonen of Finland. The entrance fee covers both the sculpture park and the Nils Holgerssons Adventure Park, an elaborate playground for children. ⊠ *S686 02 Rottneros,* ☎ *0565/60295.* ⌨ *SKr50.* ☉ *Mid-May–early June and late Aug., weekdays 10–4, weekends 10–6; rest of June, weekdays 10–5, weekends 10–6; July–Aug., daily 10–6.*

Värmland A to Z

Arriving and Departing

BY CAR

From Stockholm, follow E18 west; from Göteborg, take Route 45 north to E18.

BY TRAIN

There is regular service to Karlstad from Stockholm and Göteborg on **SJ** (Göteborg, ☎ 031/103000 or 020/757575).

Visitor Information

REGIONAL TOURIST OFFICE

Värmlands Turistbyrå (⊠ Tage Erlanderg. 10, Karlstad, ☎ 054/102160).

LOCAL TOURIST OFFICES

Karlstad (Karlstad Conference Center, ☎ 054/149055). **Sunne** (Turistbyrå, ⊠ Mejerig. 2, ☎ 0565/13530).

THE SOUTH AND
THE KINGDOM OF GLASS

Southern Sweden is a world of its own, clearly distinguished from the rest of the country by its geography, culture, and history. Skåne (pronounced *skoh*-neh), the southernmost province, is known as the granary of Sweden. It is a comparatively small province of beautifully fertile plains, sand beaches, thriving farms, medieval churches, and summer resorts. These gently rolling hills and fields are broken every few miles by lovely castles, chronologically and architecturally diverse, that have given this part of Sweden the name Château Country; often they are surrounded by beautiful grounds and moats. A significant number of the estates have remained in the hands of the original families and are still inhabited.

The two other southern provinces, Blekinge and Halland, are also fertile and rolling and edged by seashores. Historically, these three provinces are distinct from the rest of Sweden: they were the last to be incorporated into the country, having been ruled by Denmark until 1658. They retain the influences of the continental culture in their architecture, language, and cuisine, viewing the rest of Sweden—especially Stockholm—with some disdain. Skåne even has its own independence movement, and the dialect here is so akin to Danish that many Swedes from other parts of the country have trouble understanding it.

Småland, to the north, is larger than the other provinces, with a harsh countryside of stone and woods, the so-called Kingdom of Glass. It is an area of small glassblowing firms, such as Kosta Boda and Orrefors, that are world-renowned for the quality of their products. In addition to visiting these works (and perhaps finding some bargains), the traveler forms an insight into a poorer, harsher way of life that led thousands of peasants to emigrate from Småland to the United States in search of a better life. Those who stayed behind developed a reputation for their inventiveness in setting up small industries to circumvent the region's traditional poverty and are also notorious for being extremely careful—if not downright mean—with money.

Your itinerary should follow the coast from the western city of Helsingborg around the southern loop and up the eastern shore, taking a side trip to the Baltic island province of Öland before heading inland to finish at Växjo. The entire route can be followed by train, with the exception of Öland and most of the glassworks in Småland—the Orrefors factory is the only one on the railway line. It's easy to continue your trip in any direction from Växjö, as it lies at a main crossroads for both highways and railway lines.

Helsingborg

68 *221 km (137 mi) south of Göteborg, 186 km (116 mi) southwest of Växjö, 64 km (40 mi) north of Malmö.*

Helsingborg (still sometimes spelled the old way, Hälsingborg), with a population of 108,000, seems to the first-time visitor little more than a nondescript though modern ferry terminal (it has connections to Denmark, Norway, and Germany). Actually, it has a rich history, having first been mentioned in 10th-century sagas and later the site of many battles between the Danes and the Swedes. Together with its twin town, Helsingör (Elsinore in William Shakespeare's *Hamlet*), across the Öresund, it controlled shipping traffic in and out of the Baltic for centuries. Helsingborg was officially incorporated into Sweden in 1658 and totally destroyed in a battle with the Danes in 1710. It was then rebuilt, and Jean-Baptiste Bernadotte, founder of the present Swedish royal dynasty, landed here in 1810.

The Helsingborg **Stadshuset** (Town Hall) has a small museum of exhibits on the city and the region. ⊠ *Södra Storg. 31,* ☎ *042/105963.* ▣ *SKr20.* ☼ *May–Aug., Tues.–Sun. noon–5; Sept.–Apr., Tues.–Sun. noon–4.*

All that remains of Helsingborg's castle is **Kärnan** (the Keep). The surviving center tower, built to provide living quarters and defend the me-

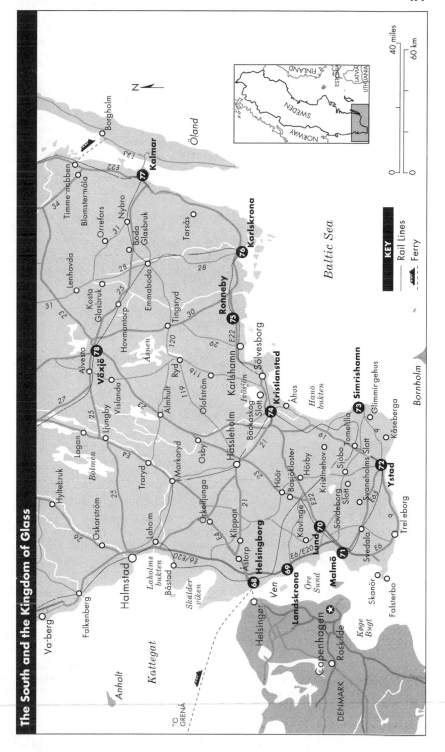

The South and the Kingdom of Glass

dieval castle, is the most remarkable relic of its kind in the north. The interior is divided into several floors, where there is a chapel, kitchen, and other medieval fittings. It stands in a park and offers fine views over the Öresund from the top. ⊠ *Slottshagen,* ☎ *042/105991.* 🎟 *SKr20.* ⊙ *June–Aug., daily 10–7; Apr.–May and Sept., daily 9–4; Oct.–Mar., daily 10–2.*

Sofiero Slott (Sofiero Castle), 5 km (3 mi) outside the town, was, until very recently, a royal summer residence. It opened to the public for the first time in May 1995. Built in 1865 in the Dutch Renaissance style, it has a fine park designed by Crown Princess Margareta. ⊠ *Sofierov. (on the road to Laröd),* ☎ *042/137400.* 🎟 *SKr30.* ⊙ *May–mid-Sept., daily 10–6; guided tours only. Park open year-round.*

Lodging

$$$ 🏨 **Grand Hotel.** One of Sweden's oldest hotels has been completely ren-
★   ovated, maintaining its long-standing reputation for excellence. Antiques and fresh flowers fill the hotel, and the well-equipped guest rooms have cable TV, a hair dryer, minibar, and trouser press. The hotel is conveniently close to the railway station and ferry terminals. The bar offers a good selection of wines at reasonable prices. ⊠ *Stortorget 812, S251 11,* ☎ *042/120170,* 🇫🇦🇽 *042/118833. 117 rooms. Restaurant, bar, no-smoking rooms, sauna, meeting rooms. AE, DC, MC, V.*

$$$ 🏨 **Marina Plaza.** This modern hotel, with its enormous central glass
★   atrium, is right next to the Knutpunkten ferry, rail, and bus terminal. Relaxing and stylish, the Marina Plaza has spacious, elegantly decorated rooms with air conditioning, minibars, trouser presses, and cable TV. ⊠ *Kungstorget 6, S251 11,* ☎ *042/192100,* 🇫🇦🇽 *042/149616. 190 rooms. Restaurant, bar, no-smoking rooms, sauna, conference rooms. AE, DC, MC, V.*

$ 🏨 **Villa Thalassa.** This youth hostel has fine views over Öresund. One large building contains 140 bunks in two-, four-, and six-bunk rooms. There are also 12 cottages near the water, each with two bedrooms (with double bed and bunk bed), bathroom with shower, and kitchen. The SKr40 breakfast is not included. ⊠ *Dag Hammarskjölds väg, S-254 33,* ☎ *042/210384,* 🇫🇦🇽 *042/128792. 140 beds, 4- to 6-bed rooms (in winter 2-bed rooms also available). Meeting rooms. No credit cards.*

Landskrona

⑥⑨ *26 km (16 mi) south of Helsingborg (via E6/E20), 41 km (25 mi) north of Malmö, 204 km (127 mi) southwest of Växjö.*

The 17th-century Dutch-style fortifications of Landskrona are among the best preserved of their kind in Europe. Though it appears to be just another modern town, Landskrona actually dates from 1413, when it received its charter. In 1888, author Selma Lagerlöf worked at Landskrona's elementary school, where she began her novel *Gösta Berlings Saga.*

Landskrona's **Citadellet** (castle) was built under orders of the Danish King Christian III in 1549 and is all that remains of the original town, which was razed in 1747 by decree of the Swedish Parliament to make way for extended fortifications. The new town was then built on land reclaimed from the sea. ⊠ *Slottsg.,* ☎ *0418/16980.* 🎟 *SKr20.* ⊙ *Early June–late Aug., daily 11–4.*

OFF THE   **VEN –** From Landskrona Harbor there are regular 25-minute boat trips to
BEATEN PATH   the island of Ven (🎟 SKr60 round-trip); there are departures every 90 minutes 6 AM–9 PM. The Danish astronomer Tycho Brahe conducted his pioneering research here from 1576 to 1597. The foundations of his Re-

naissance castle, Uranienborg, can be visited, as can Stjärneborg, his reconstructed observatory. The small **Tycho Brahe Museet** is dedicated to Brahe and his work. Landsv., Ven, ☎ *0418/79557.* ▢ *SKr20.* ◷ *May–Sept., daily 10–4:30.*

Outdoor Activities and Sports

Three kilometers (2 miles) north of Landskrona lies the **Borstahusen recreation area** (✉ 261 61 Landskrona, ☎ 0418/10837), with long stretches of beach, a marina, and a holiday village with 74 summer chalets. Ven is ideal for **camping;** check with the local tourist office. There are special paths across Ven for **bicycling;** rentals are available from Bäckviken, the small harbor.

Lund

70 *34 km (21 mi) southeast of Landskrona (via E6/E20 and Route 16), 25 km (15 mi) northeast of Malmö, 183 km (113 mi) southwest of Växjö.*

One of the oldest towns in Europe, Lund was founded in 990. In 1103 Lund became the religious capital of Scandinavia and at one time had 27 churches and eight monasteries—until King Christian III of Denmark ordered most of them razed to use their stones for the construction of Malmöhus Castle in Malmö. Lund lost its importance until 1666, when its university was established. It is now one of Sweden's two chief university towns and one of the nicest of Swedish towns, having managed to preserve its historic character.

Lund's monumental gray stone Romanesque **cathedral** is the oldest in Scandinavia, consecrated in 1145. Its crypt features 23 finely carved pillars, but its main attraction is an astrological clock, *Horologum Mirabile Lundense* (the miraculous Lund clock), dating from 1380 and restored in 1923. It depicts an amazing pageant of knights jousting on horseback, trumpets blowing a medieval fanfare, and the Magi walking in procession past the Virgin and Child as the organ plays *In Dulci Jubilo.* The clock plays at noon and 3 PM on weekdays and at 1 and 3 PM on Sunday.

One block east of the cathedral is the **Botaniska Trädgården** (Botanical Gardens), which contains 7,500 specimens of plants from all over the world—very pleasant on a summer's day. ✉ *Östra Vallg. 20,* ☎ *046/2227320.* ▢ *Free.* ◷ *Gardens daily 6 AM–8 PM, greenhouses noon–3.*

Esaias Tegnér, the Swedish poet, lived from 1813 to 1826 in a little house immediately behind the cathedral. The house has since been turned into the **Tegnér Museet,** providing insight into his life and works. ✉ *Gråbrödersg.,* ☎ *046/691319.* ▢ *SKr10.* ◷ *First Sun. each month noon–3.*

On the southern side of the main square is **Drottens Kyrkoruin** (the Church Ruins of Drotten), an "underground" museum showing life as it was in Lund in the Middle Ages. The foundations of three Catholic churches are here: the first and oldest was built of wood in approximately AD 1000. It was torn down to make room for one of stone built in about 1100; this was replaced by a second stone church built around 1300. ✉ *Kattensund 6,* ☎ *046/141328.* ▢ *SKr10.* ◷ *Tues.–Fri. and Sun. noon–4, Sat. 10–2.*

♨ **Kulturen** (the Museum of Cultural History) is both an outdoor and an indoor museum, including 20 old cottages, farms, and manor houses from southern Sweden plus an excellent collection of ceramics, textiles, weapons, and furniture. ✉ *Karolinsplats,* ☎ *046/350400.* ▢ *SKr30.*

🕐 *May–Sept., Fri.–Wed. 11–5, Thurs. 11–9; rest of yr, Tues.–Sun. noon–4.*

Lodging

$$$ 🏨 **Djingis Khan.** This English colonial–style Best Western hotel is in a quiet part of town. ✉ *Margarethev. 7, S222 40,* ☎ *046/140060,* FAX *046/143626. 55 rooms. No-smoking rooms, hot tub, sauna, exercise room, bicycles, meeting rooms. AE, DC, MC, V. Closed July.*

$$$ 🏨 **Grand.** This elegant red-stone hotel is in the heart of the city, close to the railway station in a pleasant square. Renovated rooms have vintage turn-of-the-century decor and charm. The elegant restaurant offers an alternative vegetarian menu. ✉ *Bantorget 1, S221 04,* ☎ *046/2117010,* FAX *046/147301. 80 rooms. Restaurant, no-smoking rooms, hot tub, meeting rooms. AE, DC, MC, V.*

$$$ 🏨 **Hotel Lundia.** Only 330 ft from the train station, Hotel Lundia is ideal for those who want to be within walking distance of the city center. Built in 1968, the modern, four-story square building has transparent glass walls on the ground floor. Rooms are decorated with Scandinavian fabrics and lithographs. ✉ *Knut den Stores torg 2, Box 1136, S221 04,* ☎ *046/124140,* FAX *046/141995. 97 rooms. Restaurant, no-smoking rooms, nightclub, meeting rooms. AE, DC, MC, V.*

$$ 🏨 **Concordia.** This center-city Sweden Hotel property is in an elegant former home built in 1890. A 1990 renovation gave the rooms a modern and clean, if somewhat colorless, look. ✉ *Stålbrog. 1, S222 24,* ☎ *046/135050,* FAX *046/137422. 49 rooms. No-smoking rooms, sauna, meeting rooms. AE, DC, MC, V.*

$ 🏨 **STF Vandrarhem Tåget.** So named because of its proximity to the train station (*tåget* means "train"), this youth hostel faces a park in central Lund. ✉ *Bjerredsparken, Vävareg. 22, S222 37 Lund,* ☎ *046/142820. 108 beds. No credit cards.*

OFF THE
BEATEN PATH

BOSJÖKLOSTER – About 30 km (19 mi) northeast of Lund via E22 and Route 23, Bosjökloster is an 11th-century, white Gothic castle with lovely grounds on Ringsjön, the second-largest lake in southern Skåne. The castle's original owner donated the estate to the church, which turned it over to the Benedictine order of nuns. They founded a convent school for the daughters of Scandinavian nobility, no longer in existence, and built the convent church with its tower made of sandstone. The 300-acre castle grounds, with a 1,000-year-old oak tree, a network of pathways, a children's park, a rose garden, and an indoor-outdoor restaurant, are ideal for picnics. ✉ *Höör,* ☎ *0413/25048.* 🎟 *SKr40.* 🕐 *Castle grounds May–Oct., daily 8–8, restaurant and exhibition halls May–Sept., Tues.–Sun. 10–6.*

Malmö

71 *25 km (15 mi) southwest of Lund (via E22), 198 km (123 mi) southwest of Växjö.*

Malmö is very different from Lund. Capital of the province of Skåne, with a population of about 250,000, this is Sweden's third-largest city. The city's castle, **Malmöhus,** completed in 1542, was for many years used as a prison (James Bothwell, husband of Mary, Queen of Scots, was one of its notable inmates). Today it houses a variety of museums, including the City Museum, the Museum of Natural History, and the Art Museum with a collection of Nordic art. Across the street you will find the Science and Technology Museum, the Maritime Museum, and a toy museum. ✉ *Malmöhusv.,* ☎ *040/341000.* 🎟 *SKr40.* 🕐 *June–Aug., daily 10–4; Sept.–May, Tues.–Sun. noon–4.*

On the far side of the castle grounds from Malmöhus, **Aq-va-kul** is a water park that offers a wide variety of bathing experiences for children and their parents, from water slides to bubble baths. ⊠ *Regementsg. 24,* ☎ *040/300540.* ⚏ *SKr58 adults.* ☺ *Weekdays 9–9, weekends 9–6; Mon. and Wed. evening adult sessions 7–9:30.*

There's a clutch of tiny red-painted shacks called the **Fiskehodderna** (Fish Shacks), adjoining a dock where the fishing boats come in every morning to unload their catch. The piers, dock, and huts were restored in 1991 and are now a government-protected district. You can buy fresh fish directly from the fishermen Tuesday through Saturday mornings.

In Gamla Staden, the Old Town, look for the **St. Petri Church** on Kalendegatan; dating from the 14th century, it is an impressive example of the Baltic Gothic style, with its distinctive stepped gables. Inside there is a fine Renaissance altar.

Rådhuset (Town Hall), dating from 1546, dominates Stortorget, a huge, cobbled market square in Gamla Staden, and makes an impressive spectacle when illuminated at night. In the center of the square stands an equestrian statue of Karl X, the king who united this part of the country with Sweden in 1658. Off the southeast corner of Stortorget is Lilla Torg, an attractive small cobblestone square surrounded by restored buildings from the 17th and 18th centuries.

The **Museum of Sport** occupies **Baltiska Hallen,** next to Malmö Stadium. It traces the history of sports, including soccer and wrestling, from antiquity to the present. ☎ *040/342688.* ⚏ *Free.* ☺ *Weekdays 8–4.*

Also downtown, the **Rooseum,** in a turn-of-the-century brick building that was once a power plant, is one of Sweden's most outstanding art museums, with exhibitions of contemporary art and a quality selection of Nordic art. ⊠ *Gasverksg. 22,* ☎ *040/121716.* ⚏ *SKr30.* ☺ *Tues.–Sun. 11–5. Guided tours weekends at 2.*

Dining and Lodging

$$$ ✕ **Johan P.** This extremely popular restaurant specializes in seafood and shellfish prepared in Swedish and Continental styles. White walls and crisp white tablecloths give it an elegant air, which contrasts with the generally casual dress of the customers. An outdoor section opens during the summer. ⊠ *Saluhallen, Lilla Torg,* ☎ *040/971818. AE, DC, MC, V. Closed Sun.*

$$$ ✕ **Kockska Krogen Årstiderna.** Marie and Wilhelm Pieplow's former
★ Årstiderna had merged with the Kockska Krogen. The new spot still has a pleasant, intimate atmosphere and serves large portions from a good, medium-price bistro menu and wine list. ⊠ *Stortorget,* ☎ *040/ 230910. AE, DC, MC, V.*

$$ ✕ **Anno 1900.** Here is a curiosity: a charming little restaurant located in a former working-class area of Malmö. It is a popular local luncheon place with a cheerful outdoor garden terrace for summer eating. ⊠ *Norra Bulltoftav. 7,* ☎ *040/184747. Reservations essential. AE, MC, V.*

$$ ✕ **B & B.** It stands for *Butik och Bar* (Bar Shop) because of its location in the market hall in central Malmö. There's always good home cooking, and sometimes even entertainment at the piano. The restaurant is extremely popular with a young crowd on weekday nights. ⊠ *Saluhallen, Lilla Torg,* ☎ *040/127120. AE, DC, MC, V.*

$$ ✕ **Glorias.** This friendly little restaurant usually offers extremely good value. The special menu, *Kvartersmenyn,* is an excellent bet, with a three-course prix fixe for SKr175. Reservations are advised. ⊠ *Foreningsg. 37,* ☎ *040/116816. AE, DC, MC, V.*

$$ ✕ **Valvet.** Centrally located in the St. Jörgen hotel, this restaurant was expanded in 1992. Although the wine list has been deemphasized, the restaurant still offers good Swedish cuisine with a French accent and excels at grilled meats and fish. ⊠ *Stora Nyg. 35,* ☎ *040/77300. AE, DC, MC, V. Closed Sun. and mid-June–mid-Aug.*

$$$$ 🏨 **Mäster Johan Hotel.** The unpretentious exterior of this Best West-
★ ern hotel disguises a plush and meticulously crafted interior. The 1990 top-to-bottom redesign of a 19th-century building, with the focal point an Italianate atrium breakfast room, is unusually personal in tone for a chain hotel. The rooms are impressive, with exposed Dutch brick walls, recessed lighting, oak floors, Oriental carpets, and French cherry-wood furnishings. ⊠ *Mäster Johansg. 13, S211 22,* ☎ *040/71560,* ⅀⅀ *040/127242. 68 rooms. Breakfast room, no-smoking rooms, room service, sauna, meeting rooms. AE, DC, MC, V.*

$$$$ 🏨 **Radisson SAS Hotel.** Only a five-minute walk from the train sta-
tion, this modern luxury hotel has rooms decorated in several styles: Scandinavian, Asian, and Italian. There are even special rooms for guests with pets. Service is impeccable. The restaurant serves Scandinavian and continental cuisine, and there's a cafeteria for quick meals. ⊠ *Österg. 10, S211 25,* ☎ *040/239200,* ⅀⅀ *040/112840. 221 rooms. Restaurant, no-smoking rooms, sauna, exercise room, meeting rooms. AE, DC, MC, V.*

$$$$ 🏨 **Sheraton.** Ultramodern, in steel and glass, the Sheraton is the city's
only skyscraper—at a modest 20 floors. It provides excellent views all the way to Copenhagen on a clear day. Rooms are standard Sheraton style. The hotel is connected to the Triangeln shopping center. ⊠ *Triangeln 2, S200 10,* ☎ *040/74000,* ⅀⅀ *040/232020. 214 rooms. Restaurant, bar, no-smoking rooms, sauna, exercise room, meeting rooms. AE, DC, MC, V.*

$$ 🏨 **Baltzar.** A turn-of-the-century house in central Malmö was converted
★ in 1920 into a small, comfortable hotel. Rooms are modern, with thick carpets. ⊠ *Söderg. 20, S211 34,* ☎ *040/72005,* ⅀⅀ *040/236375. 41 rooms. No-smoking rooms. AE, DC, MC, V.*

$ 🏨 **Prize Hotel.** In a rejuvenated part of Malmö Harbor, this low-over-
head, minimal-service hotel has small but comfortable rooms equipped with satellite TV, telephone, and radio. The large front entrance and lobby atrium are inventively created out of a narrow strip of empty space between two buildings. Though the hotel doesn't add a surcharge to the telephone bill, it also doesn't include the SKr65 breakfast in the room rate: you get exactly what you pay for. ⊠ *Carlsg. 10C, S211 20,* ☎ *040/112511,* ⅀⅀ *040/112310. 109 rooms. Breakfast room. AE, DC, MC, V.*

OFF THE **FALSTERBRO AND SKANÖR –** The idyllic towns of Falsterbo and Skanör
BEATEN PATH are two popular summer resorts located on a tiny peninsula, 32 km (20 mi) away from Mälmö at the country's southwesternmost corner. Fal-sterbo is popular among ornithologists who flock there every fall to watch the spectacular migration of hundreds of raptors.

TORUP SLOTT – Built around 1550 near a beautiful beech forest, Torup Castle is a great example of the classic, square fortified stronghold. From Malmö, drive 10 km (6 mi) southeast on E65, then head north for another 6 km (4 mi) to Torup. ⊠ *Torup.* ⅀ *SKr30.* ☉ *May–June, week-ends 1–4:30. Group tours available at other times through Malmö Turist-byrå,* ☎ *040/341270.*

En Route   One of Skåne's outstanding Renaissance strongholds, **Svaneholms Slott** lies 30 km (19 mi) east of Malmö, on E65. First built in 1530 and rebuilt in 1694, the castle today features a museum occupying four floors with sections depicting the nobility and peasants. On the grounds are a noted restaurant (Gästgiveri, ☎ 0411/40540), walking paths, and a lake for fishing and rowing. ⊠ *Skurup,* ☎ *0411/40012.* ⊡ *SKr30.* ☉ *May–Aug., Tues.–Sun. 11–5; Sept.–mid-Oct., Wed.–Sun. 11–4.*

Ystad

⑫   *64 km (40 mi) southeast of Malmö (via E65), 205 km (127 mi) southwest of Växjö.*

A smuggling center during the Napoleonic Wars, Ystad has preserved its medieval character with winding, narrow streets and hundreds of half-timber houses dating from four or five different centuries. The principal ancient monument is **St. Maria Kyrka,** begun shortly after 1220 as a basilica in the Romanesque style but with later additions.

OFF THE   **SÖVDEBORG SLOTT** – Twenty-one kilometers (13 miles) north of Ystad on
BEATEN PATH Route 13 is Sövdeborg Slott (Sövdeborg Castle). Built in the 16th century and restored in the mid-1840s, the castle, now a private home, consists of three two-story brick buildings and a four-story-high crenellated corner tower. The main attraction is the Stensal (Stone Hall), with its impressive stuccowork ceiling. It's open for tours booked in advance for groups of at least 10. ⊠ *Sjöbo,* ☎ *0416/16012.* ⊡ *SKr50.*

En Route   Eighteen kilometers (11 miles) east of Ystad, on the coastal road off of Route 9, is the charming fishing village of Kåseberga. On the hill behind it stand the impressive **Ales stenar** (Ale's stones), an intriguing 251-ft arrangement of 58 Viking stones in the shape of a ship. The stones are still something of a puzzle to anthropologists.

About 28 km (17 mi) east of Ystad and 10 km (6 mi) southwest of Simrishamn just off Route 9 lies **Glimmingehus** (Glimminge House), Scandinavia's best-preserved medieval stronghold. Built between 1499 and 1505 to defend the region against invaders, the late-Gothic castle was lived in only briefly. The walls are 8 ft thick at the base, tapering to 6½ ft at the top of the 85-ft-high building. On the grounds are a small museum and a theater. There are concerts and lectures throughout the summer and a medieval festival at the end of August. ⊠ *Hammenhög,* ☎ *0414/32089.* ⊡ *SKr40.* ☉ *Apr. and Sept., daily 10–4; May–Aug., daily 9–6; Oct., weekends 11–4.*

Simrishamn

⑬   *41 km (25 mi) northeast of Ystad (via Route 9), 105 km (65 mi) east of Malmö, 190 km (118 mi) southwest of Växjö.*

This bustling fishing village of 25,000 swells to many times that number during the summer. Built in the mid-1100s, the town has cobblestone streets lined with tiny brick houses covered with white stucco. The medieval St. Nicolai's Church, which dominates the town's skyline, was once a landmark for local sailors. Inside are models of sailing ships.

The **Frasses Musik Museum** contains an eclectic collection of music oddities, such as self-playing barrel organs, antique accordions, children's gramophones, and the world's most complete collection of Edison phonographs. ⊠ *Peder Mörksv. 5,* ☎ *0414/14520.* ⊡ *SKr10.* ☉ *Early June–late Aug., Sun. 2–6; July, Sun.–Wed. 2–6.*

En Route If you're in the area between July 1 and August 10, you might want
to stop off at **Kristinehov,** about 8 km (5 mi) west of Brösarp and 35
km (22 mi) north of Simrishamn, via Route 9. A summer wine festival is presented at the castle by a local Swedish wine producer, Åkersson
& Sons (☎ 0417/19700). Known as the pink castle, Kristinehov was
built in 1740 by Countess Christina Piper in the late Caroline style.
Although closed to the public since 1989, the castle is occasionally used
for rock concerts and other summer programs.

Kristianstad

74 *73 km (45 mi) north of Simrishamn (via Routes 9/19 and E22), 95 km
(59 mi) northeast of Malmö (via E22), 126 km (78 mi) southwest of Växjö.*

Kristianstad was founded by Danish King Christian IV in 1614 as a
fortified town to keep the Swedes at bay. Its former ramparts and moats
are today wide, tree-lined boulevards.

About 17 km (11 mi) east of Kristianstad is **Bäckaskog Slott** (Bäckaskog Castle), located on a strip of land between two lakes, just north
of the E22 highway. Originally founded as a monastery by a French
religious order in the 13th century, it was turned into a fortified castle by Danish noblemen during the 16th century and later appropri-
ated by the Swedish government and used as a residence for the cavalry.
The castle was a favorite of the Swedish royalty until 1900. ⊠ *Fjälkinge,*
☎ *044/53250.* 🎫 *SKr30.* ☉ *May 15–Aug. 15, daily 10–6; open off-
season to groups by appointment only.*

Ronneby

75 *86 km (53 mi) east of Kristianstad (via E22), 181 km (112 mi) northeast of Malmö, 86 km (53 mi) southeast of Växjö.*

The spa town of Ronneby has a picturesque waterfall and rapids called
Djupadal, where a river runs through a cleft in the rock just 5 ft wide
but 50 ft deep. There are boat trips on the river each summer.

Karlskrona

76 *111 km (69 mi) east of Kristianstad (via E22), 201 km (125 mi) northeast of Malmö, 107 km (66 mi) southeast of Växjö.*

A small city built on the mainland and five nearby islands, Karlskrona
achieved great notoriety in 1981, when a Soviet submarine ran aground
a short distance from its naval base. The town dates from 1679, when
it was laid out in the Baroque style on the orders of Karl XI. In 1790
it was severely damaged by fire.

The **Admiralitetskyrkan** (Admiralty Church) is Sweden's oldest wooden
church. Two other churches, **Holy Trinity** and **Frederiks,** were designed
by the 17th-century architect Nicodemus Tessin. The **Marinmuseum**
(Naval Museum), dating from 1752, is one of the oldest museums in
Sweden. ⊠ *Admiralitetsslatten,* ☎ *0455/84000.* 🎫 *SKr20.* ☉ *June
and Aug., daily 10–4; July, daily 10–6; Sept.–May, daily noon–4.*

Kalmar

77 *91 km (57 mi) northeast of Karlskrona (via E22), 292 km (181 mi)
northeast of Malmö, 109 km (68 mi) east of Växjö.*

The attractive coastal town of Kalmar, opposite the Baltic island of Öland,
★ is dominated by the imposing **Kalmar Slott,** Sweden's best-preserved
Renaissance castle, part of which dates from the 12th century. The living rooms, chapel, and dungeon can be visited. ⊠ *Slottsv.,* ☎ *0480/*

56450. ✉ SKr60. ⊙ Mid-June–mid-Aug., Mon.–Sat. 10–6, Sun. noon–6; Apr.–mid-June and mid-Aug.–Oct., weekdays 10–4, weekends noon–4; Nov.–Mar., Sun. 1–3.

The **Kalmar Läns Museum** (Kalmar District Museum), with good archaeological and ethnographic collections, contains the remains of the royal ship *Kronan*, which sank in 1676. Consisting primarily of cannons, wood sculptures, and old coins, they were raised from the seabed in 1980. Another exhibit focuses on Jenny Nystrom, a painter famous for popularizing the *tomte*, a rustic Christmas elf. ✉ *Skeppsbrog. 51,* ☎ *0480/15350.* ✉ *SKr40.* ⊙ *Mid-June–mid-Aug., Mon.–Sat. 10–6, Sun. noon–6; rest of yr, weekdays 10–4, Wed. until 8, weekends noon–4.*

Lodging

$$$ ⛭ **Slottshotellet.** Occupying a gracious old house on a quiet street, Slottshotellet faces a waterfront park, a few minutes' walk from both the train station and Kalmar Castle. Guest rooms are charmingly individual, with carved-wood bedsteads, old-fashioned chandeliers, pretty wallpaper, wooden floors, and antique furniture. The bathrooms are spotlessly clean. Only breakfast is served year-round, but in summer, full restaurant service is offered on the terrace. ✉ *Slottsv. 7, S392 33,* ☎ *0480/88260,* 𝔽𝔸𝕏 *0480/88266. 36 rooms. No-smoking rooms, sauna, meeting room. AE, DC, V.*

$$ ⛭ **Stadshotellet.** In city center, Best Western's Stadshotellet is a fairly large hotel with traditional English decor. The main building dates from 1907. Guest rooms are freshly decorated and have hair dryers and radios, among other amenities. There's also a fine restaurant. ✉ *Stortorget 14, S392 32,* ☎ *0480/15180,* 𝔽𝔸𝕏 *0480/15847. 140 rooms. Restaurant, bar, no-smoking rooms, hot tub, sauna, meeting rooms. AE, DC, MC, V.*

Öland

8 km (5 mi) east of Kalmar (via the Ölandsbron bridge).

Linked to the mainland by one of the longest bridges in Europe (6 km/4 mi), Öland is a limestone plateau 139 km (86 mi) long and 37 km (23 mi) at its widest point. First settled some 4,000 years ago, the island is fringed with fine sandy beaches and is dotted with old windmills and such archaeological remains as the massive stone walls of the 6th-century **Gråborg Fortress,** the 5th-century fortified village of **Eketorp,** and the medieval **Borgholm Castle.** In spring and fall, Öland is a way station for hundreds of species of migrating birds.

The royal family has a summer home at **Solliden** on the outskirts of Borgholm, the principal town, 25 km (16 mi) north of the bridge via Route 136.

Lodging

$$ ⛭ **Halltorps Gästgiveri.** This manor house dating from the 17th century has modernized duplex rooms decorated in Swedish landscape tones and an excellent restaurant. Drive north from Ölandsbron, and it's on the left-hand side of the road. ✉ *S387 92 Borgholm,* ☎ *0485/85000,* 𝔽𝔸𝕏 *0485/85001. 35 rooms. Restaurant, no-smoking rooms, 2 saunas, meeting rooms. AE, DC, MC, V.*

OFF THE BEATEN PATH **PATAHOLM AND TIMMERNABBE** – On the mainland coast opposite Öland, along E22, numerous picturesque seaside towns dot the coastline, such as **Pataholm,** with its cobblestone main square, and **Timmernabbe,** which is famous for its caramel factory and from which the Borgholm-bound car ferries depart. Miles of clean, attractive, and easily accessible—if windy—beaches line this strip of the coast.

The Kingdom of Glass

Stretching roughly 109 km (68 mi) between Kalmar and Växjo.

Scattered among the rocky woodlands of Småland province are isolated villages with names synonymous with quality in crystal glassware. In the streets of Kosta, Orrefors, Boda, and Strömbergshyttan, red-painted cottages surround the actual factories, which resemble large barns. The region is the home of 16 major glassworks, and visitors may see glass being blown and crystal being etched by skilled craftspeople. *Hyttsil* evenings are also arranged, a revival of an old tradition in which Baltic herring (*sil*) is cooked in the glass furnaces of the *hytt* (literally "hut," but meaning the works). Most glassworks also have shops selling quality firsts and not-so-perfect seconds at a discount. The larger establishments have restrooms and cafeterias.

Fifteen kilometers (9 mi) north of Route 25 on Route 28 is **Kosta Glasburk,** the oldest works, dating from 1742 and named for its founders, Anders Koskull and Georg Bogislaus Stael von Holstein, two former generals. Faced with a dearth of local talent, they initially imported glassblowers from Bohemia. The Kosta works pioneered the production of crystal (to qualify for that label, glass must contain at least 24% lead oxide). You can see glassblowing off-season (August 18–June 6) between 9–3. To get to Kosta from Kalmar, drive 49 km (30 mi) west on Route 25, then 14 km (9 mi) north on Route 28. ☎ *0478/34500.* ⊙ *Late June–early Aug., weekdays 9–6, Sat. 9–4, Sun. 11–4; early Aug.– late June, weekdays 9–6, Sat. 10–4, Sun. noon–4.*

On Route 31, about 18 km (25 mi) east of Kosta, is **Orrefors,** one of the best known of the glass companies. Orrefors came on the scene late— in 1898—but set particularly high artistic standards. The skilled workers in Orrefors dance a slow, delicate minuet as they carry the pieces of red-hot glass back and forth, passing them on rods from hand to hand, blowing and shaping them. The basic procedures and tools are ancient, and the finished product is the result of unusual teamwork, from designer to craftsman to finisher. One of Orrefors's special attractions is a magnificent display of pieces made during the past century; younger visitors will probably be more interested in the cafeteria and playground. In summer, June 7– August 17, you can watch glassblowing at 9–10 and 11–3. ☎ *0481/34000.* ⊙ *Aug.–May, weekdays 10–6; June and July, weekdays 9–4, Sat. 10–4, Sun. 11–4.*

Boda Glasbruk, part of the Kosta Boda Company, is just off Route 25, 42 km (26 mi) west of Kalmar. ☎ *0481/24030.* ⊙ *Daily 9–4.*

Växjö

⓱ *109 km (68 mi) northwest of Kalmar (via Rte. 25), 198 km (123 mi) northeast of Malmö, 228 km (142 mi) southeast of Göteborg, 446 km (277 mi) southwest of Stockholm.*

Some 10,000 Americans visit this town every year, for it was from this area that their Swedish ancestors set sail in the 19th century. On the second Sunday in August, Växjö celebrates "Minnesota Day": Swedes and Swedish-Americans come together to commemorate their common heritage with American-style square dancing and other festivities. The **Utvandrarnas Hus** (Emigrants' House) in the town center tells the story of the migration, when more than a million Swedes—one quarter of the population—departed for the promised land. The museum exhibits provide a vivid sense of the rigorous journey, and an archive room and research center allow American visitors to trace their ancestry.

⊠ *Museum Park, Box 201, S351 04,* ☎ *0470/20120.* ☞ *Free.* ☉ *June–Aug., weekdays 9–5, Sat. 11–3, Sun. 1–5; Sept.–May, weekdays 9–4.*

The **Småland Museum** has the largest glass collection in northern Europe; it was reopened in summer 1996 after extensive renovation. ⊠ *Södra Jarnvägsg. 2, S351 04,* ☎ *0470/45145.* ☞ *SKr40.* ☉ *Call for hrs.*

<table>
<tr><td>OFF THE
BEATEN PATH</td><td>**KRONOBERGS SLOTT –** About 5 km (3 mi) north of Växjö, this 14th-century castle ruin lies on the edge of the Helgasjön (Holy Lake). The Småland freedom fighter Nils Dacke used the castle as a base for his attacks against the Danish occupiers during the mid-1500s; now it's an idyllic destination. In summer, you can eat waffles from the café under the shade of birch trees or take a lunch or sightseeing cruise around the lake on the toylike *Thor,* Sweden's oldest steamboat. *Castle,* ☎ *0470/45145. Boat tours,* ☎ *0470/63000. Tours offered late June–late Aug.* ☞ *Lunch cruise SKr280, 2½-hr canal trip to Årby SKr120, 1-hr around-the-lake trip SKr85.*</td></tr>
</table>

Lodging

$$$ ☷ **Hotel Statt.** Now a Best Western hotel, this conveniently located, traditional property is popular with tour groups. The building dates from 1853, but the rooms themselves are modern. The hotel has a cozy pub, nightclub, bistro, and café. ⊠ *Kungsg. 6, S-351 04,* ☎ *0470/13400,* 𝔽𝔸𝕏 *0470/44837. 130 rooms. Restaurant, café, pub, no-smoking rooms, sauna, exercise room, meeting rooms. AE, DC, MC, V.*

$ ☷ **Esplanad.** In town center, the Esplanad is a small, family hotel offering basic amenities. ☷ *Norra Esplanaden 21A, S-351 04,* ☎ *0470/22580,* 𝔽𝔸𝕏 *0470/26226. 27 rooms. No-smoking rooms. MC, V.*

The South and the Kingdom of Glass A to Z

Arriving and Departing

BY BOAT

The most common way to get to southern Sweden is by boat. Several regular services run from Copenhagen to Malmö, including hovercraft that make the trip in less than an hour, and a bus-ferry service from Copenhagen Station, which also goes to Lund. There are also regular ferry connections to Denmark, Germany, and Poland from such ports as Malmö, Helsingborg, Landskrona, Trelleborg, and Ystad. **Stena Line** (⊠ Kungsg. 12–14, Stockholm, ☎ 08/141475; ⊠ Danmarksterminalen, Göteborg, ☎ 031/858000) is one of the major Swedish carriers.

Day-trippers can pick up tickets at Malmö Harbor and catch one of the hourly Copenhagen-bound hovercraft operated by the following ferry lines: **Flygbåtarna** (☎ 040/103930), **Pilen** (☎ 040/234411), and **Shopping Linje** (☎ 040/110099). **SFL Skandlines** (☎ 040/362000) runs the only car-ferry service between Dragör, Denmark, and Limhamn, Sweden, a town that adjoins Malmö's southern edge.

BY CAR

Malmö is 620 km (386 mi) from Stockholm. Take the E4 freeway to Helsingborg, then the E6/E20 to Malmö and Lund. From Göteborg, take the E6/E20.

BY PLANE

Malmö's airport, **Sturup** (☎ 040/6131100), is approximately 30 km (19 mi) from Malmö and 25 km (15 mi) from Lund. **SAS** (☎ 040/357200 or 020/727000), **KLM** (☎ 040/500530), and **Malmö Aviation** (☎ 040/502900) serve the airport. SAS offers discounts on trips to Malmö year-round; ask for the "Jackpot" discount package.

Between the Airport and City Center: Buses for Malmö and Lund meet all flights at Sturup Airport. The price of the trip is SKr60 to either destination. For more information on bus schedules, routes, and fares, call ☎ 020/616161 or the airport at ☎ 040/6131100. A **taxi** from the airport to Malmö or Lund costs about SKr250. For SAS **limousine service,** call ☎ 040/500600.

BY TRAIN

There is regular service from Stockholm to Helsingborg, Lund, and Malmö. Each trip takes about 6½ hours, and about 4½ hours by high-speed (X2000) train. All three railway stations are central.

Getting Around

A special 48-hour *Öresund Runt* (Around Öresund) pass is available from the Malmö Tourist Office: at SKr149, the ticket covers a train from Malmö to Helsingborg, a ferry to Helsingør, a train to Copenhagen, and a ferry back to Malmö.

The *Malmökortet* (Malmö Card), entitles the holder to, among other benefits, free admission or discounts to most museums, concert halls, nightclubs, theaters, the Royal Cab company, and many shops and restaurants. A one-day card costs SKr125, two-day card SKr140, and a three-day card SKr155. Cards are available from the tourist office in Malmö.

BY CAR

Roads are well marked and well maintained. Traveling around the coast counterclockwise from Helsingborg, you take the E6/E20 to Landskrona, Malmö, and Lund, then the E6/E22 to Trelleborg; Route 9 follows the south coast from there to Simrishamn and north until just before Kristianstad, where you pick up E22 all the way through Karlshamn, Ronneby, Karlskrona, and up the east coast to Kalmar. From Kalmar, Route 25 goes almost directly west through Växjö to Halmstad, on the west coast between Helsingborg and Göteborg.

BY TRAIN

The major towns of the south are all connected by rail.

Contacts and Resources

CAR RENTALS

If you are coming from Denmark and want to rent a car as soon as you arrive, several rental companies have locations at Malmö Harbor, including **Avis** (☎ 040/77830), **Hertz** (☎ 040/74955), and **Europcar/InterRent** (☎ 040/71640). Hertz car rentals are available for less than SKr600 a day on weekends (less during the summer) if you book a SAS (☎ 040/357200 or 020/727000) flight.

EMERGENCIES

As elsewhere in Sweden, call ☎ 112 for emergencies.

VISITOR INFORMATION

Regional Tourist Offices: Skånes Turistråd (Skåne Tourist Council, ✉ Skifferv. 38, Lund, ☎ 046/124350). **Jönköping** (✉ Västra Storg. 18A, ☎ 036/199570).

Local Tourist Offices: Helsingborg (✉ Knutpunkten terminal, ☎ 042/120310). **Landskrona** (✉ Rådhusg. 3, ☎ 0418/16980; ✉ Landsv. 2, ☎ 0418/72420). **Kalmar** (✉ Larmg. 6, ☎ 0480/15350). **Karlskrona** (✉ Borgnästoreg. 68, ☎ 0455/83490). **Kristianstad** (✉ Stora Torg, ☎ 044/121988). **Lund** (✉ Kyrkog. 11, ☎ 046/355040). **Malmö** (✉ Skeppsbron at the Central Station, ☎ 040/300150). **Ronneby** (✉ Kallingev. 3, ☎ 0457/17650). **Växjö** (✉ Kronobergsg. 8, ☎ 0470/41410). **Ystad** (✉ St. Knuts Torg, ☎ 0411/77681).

DALARNA: THE FOLKLORE DISTRICT

Dalarna is considered to be the most typically Swedish of all the country's 24 provinces, a place of forests, mountains, and red-painted wooden farmhouses and cottages by the shores of pristine, sun-dappled lakes. It is the favorite site for Midsummer Day celebrations, in which Swedes don folk costumes and dance to fiddle and accordion music around maypoles garlanded with wildflowers.

Dalarna played a key role in the history of the nation. It was from here that Gustav Vasa recruited the army that freed the country from Danish domination during the 16th century. The region is also important artistically, both for its tradition of naive religious decoration and for producing two of the nation's best-loved painters, Anders Zorn (1860–1920) and Carl Larsson (1853–1915), and one of its favorite poets, the melancholy, mystical Dan Andersson, who sought inspiration in the remote camps of the old charcoal burners deep in the forest.

As for dining and lodging, do not expect too much in Dalarna. Traditionally, visitors to the area—many from elsewhere in Scandinavia or from Germany—make use either of the region's many well-equipped campsites or of *stugbyar* (small villages of log cabins, with cooking facilities), usually set near lakesides or in forest clearings.

Our itinerary circles Lake Siljan, the largest of the 6,000 lakes in the province and the center of Dalarna's folklore, then crosses east to the coastal town of Gävle. The main points can all be reached by train, except for the southern side of Lake Siljan.

En Route On the route from Stockholm to Dalarna, 158 km (98 mi) from Stockholm and just south of Avesta on Route 70, stands the world's biggest *Dalahäst* (Dala horse), 43 ft tall. The bright orange-red painted monument marks a modern roadside rest stop with a spacious cafeteria and a helpful tourist information center.

Falun

㊳ *224 km (139 mi) northwest of Stockholm (via E18 and Rte. 70).*

Falun is the traditional capital of Dalarna, though in recent years the nondescript railway town of Borlänge has grown in importance. Falun's history has always been very much bound to its copper mine. This has been worked since 1230 by Stora Kopparbergs Bergslags AB (today just *Stora*), which claims to be the oldest limited company in the world. Its greatest period of prosperity was the 17th century, when it financed Sweden's "Age of Greatness," and the country became the dominant Baltic power. In 1650, Stora produced a record 3,067 tons of copper; probably as a result of such rapid extraction, 37 years later its mine shafts caved in. Fortunately, the accident was on Midsummer's Day, when most of the miners were off duty, and as a result no one was killed. Today the major part of the mine is an enormous hole in the ground that has become Falun's principal tourist attraction, with its own museum, **Stora Museum.** ☎ *023/711475.* ☒ *Mine SKr60, museum free with mine tour.* ☉ *Mine May–Aug., daily 10–4:30; Sept.–mid-Nov. and Mar.–Apr., weekends 12:30–4:30; museum May–Aug., daily 10–4:30; Sept.–Apr., daily 12:30–4:30.*

Lodging

$$$ ☒ **Bergmästaren.** This small, cozy hotel in town center is built in tra-
★ ditional Dalarna style and filled with antique furnishings. Some rooms share bathrooms. ☒ *Bergskolegränd 7, S791 26,* ☎ *023/63600,* FAX *023/*

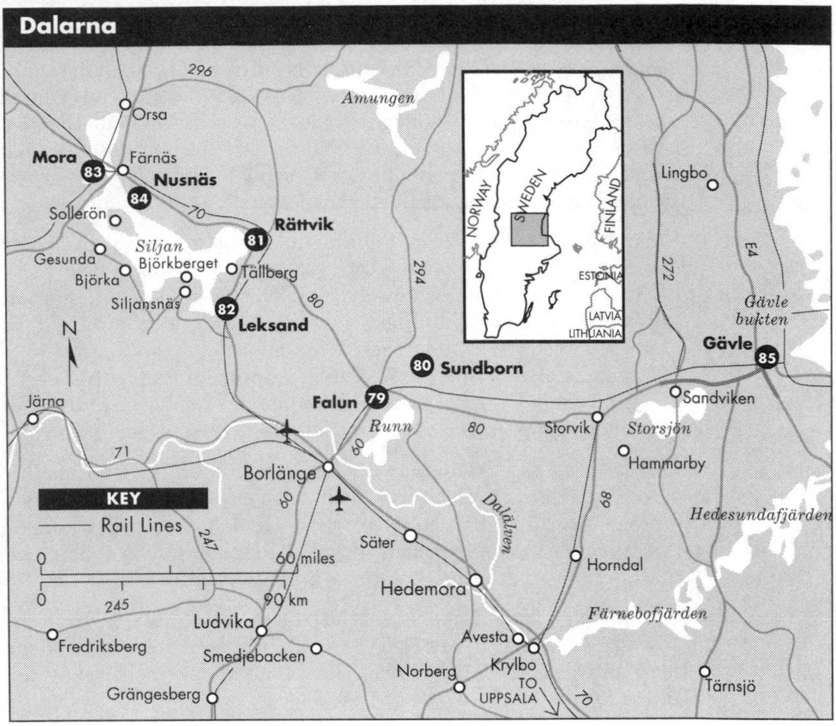

22524. 88 rooms. Restaurant, no-smoking rooms, hot tub, sauna, meeting room. AE, DC, MC, V.

$$$ 🏨 **Grand.** Now part of the First Hotel chain, this conventional, modern hotel is close to town center. The bright rooms are decorated with Chippendale-style furniture, and most have minibars. ✉ *Trotzg. 911, S791 71,* ☎ *023/18700,* FAX *023/14143. 183 rooms. Restaurant, bar, minibars, no-smoking rooms, indoor pool, sauna, exercise room, convention center, parking. AE, DC, MC, V.*

$$$ 🏨 **Scandic.** This ultramodern, Legolike hotel is in the expanded Lugnet sports and recreation center outside Falun, where the 1993 World Skiing Championships took place. The comfortable rooms have good views. ✉ *Svärdsjög. 51, S791 31 Falun,* ☎ *023/22160,* FAX *023/12845. 135 rooms. Restaurant, pub, snack bar, no-smoking rooms, indoor pool, sauna, meeting rooms, parking. AE, DC, MC, V.*

$$ 🏨 **Falun.** Rolf Carlsson runs this small, friendly, but bland-looking hotel just 1,300 ft from the railway station. Twelve rooms have shared baths and are offered at a lower rate. The front desk closes at 9 PM. ✉ *Centrumhuset, Trotzg. 16, S791 30,* ☎ *023/29180,* FAX *023/13006. 27 rooms, 15 with bath. No-smoking rooms, meeting rooms. AE, DC, MC, V.*

$ 🏨 **Birgittagården.** This small hotel, 8 km (5 mi) out of town, is run by the religious order Stiftelsen Dalarnas Birgitta Systrar (the Dalarna Sisters of Birgitta). It's smoke-free and alcohol-free, and set in a fine park. There are no telephones or televisions in the rooms. ✉ *Uddnäsv., S791 46,* ☎ *023/32147,* FAX *023/32471. 25 rooms. No-smoking rooms, meeting rooms. No credit cards.*

Sundborn

80 *10 km (6 mi) northeast of Falun (off Rte. 80).*

In this small village you can visit **Carl Larsson Gården,** the lakeside home of the Swedish artist Carl Larsson. Larsson was an excellent textile designer and draftsman who painted scenes from his family's busy, domestic life. The house itself was creatively painted and decorated by Larsson's wife, Karin, also trained as an artist. Their home's turn-of-the-century fittings and furnishings have been carefully preserved; their great-grandchildren still use the house on occasion. Lines for guided tours can take two hours in summer. ☎ *023/60053 in summer, 023/ 60069 in winter.* ✉ *Guided tours only, SKr60.* ⊙ *May–Sept., daily 10– 5; Oct.–Apr., Tues. 11. Off-season visits by advance reservation.*

Rättvik

㉛ *48 km (30 mi) northwest of Falun (via Rte. 80).*

Surrounded by wooded slopes, Rättvik is a pleasant town of timbered houses on the eastern tip of Lake Siljan. A center for local folklore, the town has several shops that sell handmade articles and produce from the surrounding region.

Every year in June, hundreds of people wearing traditional costumes arrive in longboats to attend Midsummer services at the town's 14th-century church, **Rättvik Kyrka,** which stands on a promontory stretching into the lake. Its interior contains some fine examples of local naive religious art.

The open-air museum **Rättvik Gammalgård** gives the visitor an idea of the peasant lifestyles of bygone days. Tours in English can be arranged through the Rättvik tourist office. ✉ *Free, guided tour SKr20.* ⊙ *Mid-June–mid-Aug., daily 11–6; tours at 1 and 2:30.*

Leksand

㉜ *18 km (11 mi) south of Rättvik (via Rte. 70), 66 km (41 mi) northwest of Falun (via Rättvik).*

Thousands of tourists converge on Leksand in June each year for the Midsummer celebrations; they also come in July for *Himlaspelet (The Play of the Way that Leads to Heaven),* a traditional musical with an all-local cast, staged outdoors near the town's church. It is easy to get seats; ask the local tourist office for details.

Leksand is also an excellent vantage point from which to watch the "church-boat" races on Siljan. These vessels are claimed to be successors to the Viking longboats and were traditionally used to take peasants from outlying regions to church on Sunday. On Midsummer Eve, the longboats, crewed by people in folk costumes, skim the lake.

In the hills around Leksand and elsewhere near Siljan you will find the *fäbodar,* small settlements in the forest where cattle were taken to graze during the summer. Less idyllic memories of bygone days are conjured up by **Käringberget,** a 720-ft-high mountain north of town where alleged witches were burned to death during the 17th century.

En Route From Leksand, drive along the small road toward Mora by the southern shores of Siljan, passing through the small communities of Siljansnäs and Björka before stopping at **Gesunda,** a pleasant little village at the foot of a mountain. A chairlift will take you from there to the top where there are unbeatable views over the lake.

Near Gesunda, **Tomteland** (Santaland) claims to be the home of Santa Claus, or Father Christmas. Toys are for sale at Santa's workshop and kiosks. There are rides in horse-drawn carriages in summer and sleighs in winter. ✉ *Gesundaberget, S792 90, Sollerön,* ☎ *0250/29000.* ✉ *SKr95.* ⊙ *Mid-June–late Aug., daily 10–5; July, daily 10–6; late Nov.– early Jan., call ahead for daily schedule.*

The large island of **Sollerön** is connected to the mainland at Gesunda by a bridge, from which there are fine views of the mountains surrounding Siljan. Several excellent bathing places and an interesting Viking gravesite are also here. The church dates from 1775.

Mora

⟨83⟩ *50 km (31 mi) northwest of Leksand, 83 km (52 mi) northwest of Falun (via Rte. 70).*

To get to this pleasant and relaxed lakeside town of 20,000, you can take Route 70 directly from Rättvik along the northern shore of Lake Silja, or follow the lake's southern shore through Leksand and Gesunda to get a good sense of Dalarna.

Mora is best known as the finishing point for the world's longest cross-country ski race, the *Vasalopp,* which begins 90 km (56 mi) away at Sälen, a ski resort close to the Norwegian border. The race commemorates a fundamental piece of Swedish history: the successful attempt by Gustav Vasa in 1521 to rally local peasants to the cause of ridding Sweden of Danish occupation. Vasa, only 21 years old, had fled the capital and described to the Mora locals in graphic detail a massacre of Swedish noblemen ordered by Danish King Christian in Stockholm's Stortorget. Unfortunately, no one believed him and the dispirited Vasa was forced to abandon his attempts at insurrection and take off on either skis or snowshoes for Norway, where he hoped to evade Christian and go into exile. Just after he left, confirmation reached Mora of the Stockholm bloodbath, and the peasants, already discontented with Danish rule, relented, sending two skiers after Vasa to tell him they would join his cause. The two men caught up with the young nobleman at Sälen. They returned with him to Mora, where an army was recruited. Vasa marched south, defeated the Danes, and became king and the founder of modern Sweden. The commemorative race, held on the first Sunday in March, attracts thousands of competitors from all over the world, including the Swedish king. There is a spectacular mass start at Sälen before the field thins out. The finish is eagerly awaited in Mora, though in recent years the number of spectators has fallen thanks to the fact that the race is now usually televised live. You can get a comfortable glimpse of the race's history in the **Vasaloppsmuseet,** with its collection of past ski gear and photos, news clippings, and a short film. ⊠ *Vasag.,* ☎ *0250/39225.* ✑ *SKr30.* ⊗ *Mid-May–Aug., daily 10–6; Sept.–mid-May, daily 11–5.*

Mora is also known as the home of Anders Zorn (1860–1920), Sweden's leading Impressionist painter, who lived in Stockholm and Paris before returning to his roots here, painting the local scenes for which he is now famous. His former **private residence,** a large, sumptuous house designed with great originality and taste by the painter himself, has retained the same exquisite furnishings, paintings, and decor it had when he lived there with his wife. The garden, also a Zorn creation,
★ is open to the public. Next door, the **Zornmuseet** (Zorn Museum), built 19 years after the painter's death, contains many of his best works. ⊠ *Vasag. 36,* ☎ *0250/16560.* ✑ *Museum SKr30, home SKr30.* ⊗ *Museum mid-May–mid-Sept., Mon.–Sat. 9–5, Sun. 11–5; mid-Sept.–mid-May, Mon.–Sat. 10–5, Sun. 1–5; home (guided tours only) mid-May–mid-Sept., Mon.–Sat. 10–4, Sun. 11–4; mid-Sept.–mid-May, Mon.–Sat. 12:30–4, Sun. 1–4.*

On the south side of town you'll find **Zorns Gammalgård,** a fine collection of old wooden houses from local farms, brought here and donated to Mora by Anders Zorn. One of them was converted in 1995 into the **Textil Kammare,** (Textile Chamber) the first exhibit of Zorn's collection of textiles and period clothing. ⊠ *Yvradsv.,* ☎ *0250/10454 (summer only).* 🎟 *SKr25.* ⊙ *June–Aug., daily 11–5.*

Lodging

$$ 🏨 **Kung Gästa.** This modern, reasonably sized hotel is 2 km (1 mi) from town center and only 330 ft from the Mora train station. ⊠ *Kristeneberg, S792 32,* ☎ *0250/15070,* 🕿 *0250/17078. 47 rooms. Restaurant, no-smoking rooms, indoor pool, sauna, exercise room, meeting rooms. AE, DC, MC, V.*

$$ 🏨 **Mora.** A pleasant little Best Western chain hotel is in town center and 5 km (3 mi) from the airport. Its comfortable rooms are brightly decorated and have minibars and radios. ⊠ *Strandg. 12, S792 01,* ☎ *0250/71750,* 🕿 *0250/18981. 138 rooms. Restaurant, bar, minibars, no-smoking rooms, indoor pool, sauna, meeting rooms. AE, DC, MC, V.*

$$ 🏨 **Siljan.** Part of the Sweden Hotel group, this small, modern hotel affords views over the lake. Rooms are standard, with radio, television, and wall-to-wall carpeting; most are single rooms with sofa beds. ⊠ *Morag. 6, S792 22,* ☎ *0250/13000,* 🕿 *0250/13098. 45 rooms. Restaurant, bar, no-smoking floor, sauna, exercise room, dance club, meeting room. AE, DC, MC, V.*

$ 🏨 **Moraparken.** This modern hotel sits in a park by the banks of the Dala River, not far from town center. ⊠ *Parkgarten 1, S792 25,* ☎ *0250/17800,* 🕿 *0250/18583. 75 rooms. Restaurant, no-smoking rooms, sauna, convention center. AE, DC, MC, V.*

Outdoor Activities and Sports

SKIING

Dalarna's principal ski resort is **Sälen,** starting point for the Vasalopp, about 80 km (50 mi) west of Mora.

Nusnäs

84 *6 km (4 mi) southeast of Mora (via Rte. 70), 28 km (17 mi) northwest of Falun.*

The lakeside village of Nusnäs is where the small, brightly red-painted wooden Dala horses are made. These were originally carved by the peasants of Dalarna as toys for their children, but their popularity rapidly spread with the advent of tourism in the 20th century. Mass production of the little horses started at Nusnäs in 1928. In 1939 they achieved international popularity after being shown at the New York World's Fair, and since then they have become a Swedish symbol—today some of the smaller versions available in Stockholm's tourist shops are, however, made in East Asia. At Nusnäs you can watch the genuine article being made, now with the aid of modern machinery but still painted by hand.

Shopping

Naturally you'll be able to buy some painted horses to take home; the place to visit is **Nils Olsson** (⊠ Edåkerv. 17, ☎ 0250/37200). Shops are open every day except Sunday.

Gävle

85 *176 km (109 mi) east of Mora (via Rtes. 70 and 80), 92 km (57 mi) east of Falun (via Rte. 80).*

The port town of Gävle achieved dubious renown at the time of the Chernobyl nuclear accident in 1986 by briefly becoming the most radioactive place in Europe. A freak storm dumped large amounts of fallout from the Soviet Union on the town. For a while farmers had to burn newly harvested hay and keep their cattle inside. However, the scare soon passed and today one can visit the town in perfect safety. Gävle is worth visiting for a glimpse of its two relatively new museums.

The **Joe Hill Museet** (Joe Hill Museum), dedicated to the Swedish emigrant who went on to become America's first well-known protest singer and union organizer, is in Hill's former home in the oldest section of Gävle. Once a poor, working-class district, this is now the most picturesque and highly sought-after residential part of town, with art studios and crafts workshops nearby. The museum—furnished in the same style as when Hill lived there—contains very few of his possessions but does display his prison letters. The house itself bears witness to the poor conditions that forced so many Swedes to emigrate to the United States (an estimated 850,000 to 1 million between 1840 and 1900). Hill, whose original Swedish name was Joel Hägglund, became a founder of the International Workers of the World and was executed for the murder of a Salt Lake City grocer in 1914, but he maintained his innocence right up to the end. ⊠ *Nedre Bergsg. 28,* ☎ *026/613425.* ◪ *Free.* ☉ *June–Aug., daily 11–3.*

The **Skogsmuseet Silvanum** (Silvanum Forestry Museum) is on the west end of town, by the river. Silvanum, Latin for "The Forest," was inaugurated in 1961; it was the first such museum in the world and is one of the largest. The museum provides an in-depth picture of the forestry industry in Sweden, still the backbone of the country's industrial wealth: trees cover more than 50% of Sweden's surface area, and forest products account for 20% of national exports. Silvanum includes a forest botanical park and an arboretum that contains an example of every tree and bush growing in Sweden. ⊠ *Kungsbäcksv. 32,* ☎ *026/614100.* ◪ *Free.* ☉ *Tues., Thurs.–Fri. 10–4, Wed. 10–9, weekends 1–5.*

Dalarna A to Z

Arriving and Departing

BY BUS
Swebus/Vasatrafik (☎ 020/640640) runs tour buses to the area from Stockholm on weekends.

BY CAR
From Stockholm, take E18 to Enköping and follow Route 70 northwest. From Göteborg, take E20 to Örebro and Route 60 north from there.

BY PLANE
There are 11 flights daily from Stockholm to **Dala Airport** (⊠ 8 km/5 mi from Borlänge, ☎ 0243/55100). **Mora Airport** (⊠ 6 km/4 mi from Mora) is served by **Holmström Air** ☎ 0250/30175), with five flights daily from Stockholm Monday through Friday, fewer on weekends.

Between the Airport and Town: There are half-hourly bus connections on weekdays between Dala Airport and Falun, 26 km (16 mi) away. The 601 bus runs every half hour from Dala Airport to Borlänge; the trip costs SKr15. There are no buses from Mora Airport.

A **taxi** from Dala Airport to Borlänge costs around SKr100, to Falun approximately SKr215. A taxi into Mora from Mora Airport costs SKr90. Order taxis in advance through your travel agent or when you make an airline reservation. Book the **DalaFalun** taxi service by calling ☎ 0243/229290.

BY TRAIN
There is regular daily train service from Stockholm to both Mora and Falun.

Contacts and Resources

CAR RENTALS

Avis has offices in Borlänge (☎ 0243/87080) and Mora (☎ 0250/16711). **Hertz** has offices in Falun (☎ 023/58872) and Mora (☎ 0250/28800). **Europcar/InterRent** has its office in Borlänge (☎ 0243/19050).

DOCTORS AND DENTISTS

Falun Hospital (☎ 023/82000). **Mora Hospital** (☎ 0250/25000). **24-hour medical advisory service** (☎ 023/82900).

EMERGENCIES

For emergencies dial ☎ 112.

GUIDED TOURS

Sightseeing Tours: Call the Falun tourist office for English-speaking guides to Falun and the region around Lake Siljan; guides cost about SKr900.

LATE-NIGHT PHARMACIES

There are no late-night pharmacies in the area, but doctors called to emergencies can supply medication. **Vasen** pharmacy in Falun (⊠ Åsg., ☎ 023/20000) is open until 7 PM weekdays.

VISITOR INFORMATION

Falun (⊠ Stora Torget, ☎ 023/83637). **Leksand** (⊠ Norsg., ☎ 0247/80300). **Ludvika** (⊠ Sporthallen, ☎ 0240/86050). **Mora** (⊠ Ångbåt-skajn, ☎ 0250/26550). **Rättvik** (⊠ Railway Station House, ☎ 0248/70200). **Sälen** (⊠ Sälen Centrum, ☎ 0280/20250).

NORRLAND AND NORBOTTEN

The north of Sweden, Norrland, is a place of wide-open spaces where the silence is almost audible. Golden eagles soar above snowcapped crags; huge salmon fight their way up wild, tumbling rivers; rare orchids bloom in Arctic heathland; and wild rhododendrons splash the land with color.

In the summer the sun shines at midnight above the Arctic Circle. In the winter it hardly shines at all. The weather can change with bewildering speed: a June day can dawn sunny and bright; then the skies may darken and the temperature drop to around zero as a snow squall blows in. Just as suddenly, the sun comes out again and the temperature starts to rise.

Here live the once-nomadic Lapps, or Sami as they prefer to be known. They carefully guard what remains of their identity, while doing their best to inform the public of their culture. Many of the 17,000 Sami who live in Sweden still earn their living herding reindeer, but as open space shrinks, the younger generation is turning in greater numbers toward the allure of the cities. Often the Sami exhibit a sad resignation to the gradual disappearance of their way of life as the modern world makes incursions. This is best expressed in one of their folk poems: "Our memory, the memory of us vanishes/We forget and we are forgotten."

Yet there is a growing struggle, especially among younger Sami, to maintain their identity, and, thanks to their traditional closeness to nature, they are now finding allies in Sweden's Green movement. They refer to the north of Scandinavia as *Sapmi*, their spiritual and physical home, making no allowance for the different countries that now rule it.

Nearly all Swedish Sami now live in ordinary houses, having abandoned the *kåta* (Lapp wigwam), and some even herd their reindeer with helicopters. Efforts are now being made to protect and preserve their language, which is totally unlike Swedish and bears far greater resemblance to Finnish. The language reflects their closeness to nature. The word *goadnil,* for example, means "a quiet part of the river, free of current, near the bank or beside a rock."

Nowadays many Sami depend on the tourist industry for their living, selling their artifacts, such as expertly carved bone-handled knives, wooden cups and bowls, bark bags, silver jewelry, and leather straps embroidered with pewter thread.

The land that the Sami inhabit is vast. Norrland stretches 1,000 km (560 mi) from south to north, making up more than half of Sweden; its size is comparable to that of Great Britain. On the west there are mountain ranges, to the east a wild and rocky coastline, and in between boundless forests and moorland. Its towns are often little more than a group of houses along a street, built around a local industry such as mining, forestry, or hydropower utilities. However, thanks to Sweden's excellent transportation infrastructure, Norrland and the northernmost region of Norbotten are no longer inaccessible and even travelers with limited time can get at least a taste of the area. Its wild spaces are ideal for open-air vacations. Hiking, climbing, canoeing, river rafting, and fishing are all popular in summer, skiing, skating, and dog sledding in winter.

A word of warning: In summer mosquitoes are a constant nuisance, even worse than in other parts of Sweden, so be sure to bring plenty of repellent (you won't find anything effective in Sweden). Fall is perhaps the best season to visit Norrland. Roads are well maintained, but be careful of *gupp* (holes) following thaws. Highways are generally traffic free, but keep an eye out for the occasional reindeer.

Dining and lodging are on the primitive side in this region. Standards of cuisine and service are not nearly as high as prices—but hotels are usually exceptionally clean and staff scrupulously honest. Accommodations are limited, but the various local tourist offices can supply details of bed-and-breakfasts and holiday villages equipped with housekeeping cabins. The area is also rich in campsites—but with the highly unpredictable climate, this may appeal only to the very hardy.

Norbotten is best discovered from a base in Kiruna, in the center of the alpine region that has been described as Europe's last wilderness. You can tour south and west to the mountains and national parks, east and south to Sami villages, and farther south still to Baltic coastal settlements.

Kiruna

86 *1,239 km (710 mi) north of Stockholm.*

About 145 kilometers (90 mi) north of the Arctic Circle, and 1,670 ft above sea level, Kiruna is the most northerly city in Sweden. Although its inhabitants number only around 26,000, Kiruna is one of Sweden's largest cities—it spreads over the equivalent of half the area of Switzerland. Until an Australian community took the claim, Kiruna was often called "the world's biggest city." With 20,000 square km (7,722 square mi) within the municipal limits, Kiruna boasts that it could accommodate the entire world population with 150 square ft of space per person.

Kiruna lies at the eastern end of Lake Luossajärvi, spread over a wide area between two mountains, Luossavaara and Kirunavaara, that are largely composed of iron ore—its raison d'être. Here is the world's largest underground iron mine, with reserves estimated at 500 million tons. Automated mining technology has largely replaced the traditional miner in the Kirunavaara underground mines, which are some 500 km

Norrland and Norbotten

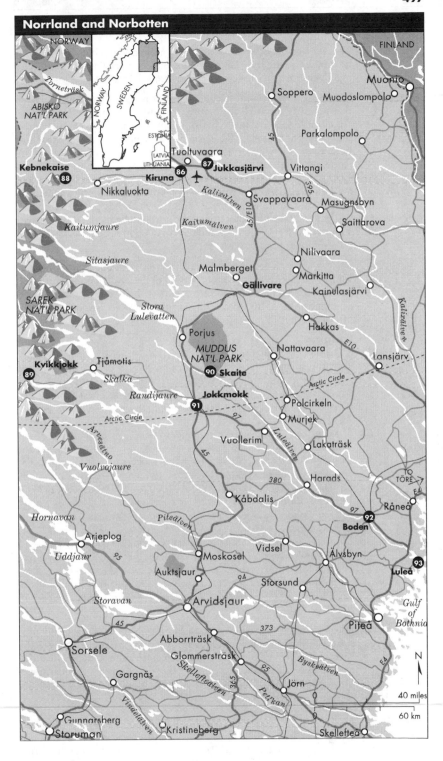

NORWAY

FINLAND

Torneträsk

ABISKO
NAT'L PARK

Soppero

Muodoslompolo

Muonio

Parkalompolo

Tuoltuvaara

Kebnekaise
88

Nikkaluokta

Kalixälven

86 **87** **Jukkasjärvi**

Kiruna

Vittangi

Svappavaara

Masugnsbyn

Kaitumälven

Saittarova

Kaitumjaure

Nilivaara

Sitasjaure

Malmberget

Markitta

Gällivare

Kainulasjärvi

*SAREK
NAT'L PARK*

*Stora
Lulevatten*

Hakkas

Porjus

Nattavaara

Lansjärv

*MUDDUS
NAT'L PARK*

E10

Kvikkjokk
89

Tjåmotis

Skalka

90 **Skaite**

Arctic Circle

Randijaure

Jokkmokk

Polcirkeln

Arctic Circle

91

Murjek

Arrasjåno

97

Luleälven

Vuollerim

Lakaträsk

Vuolvojaure

45

380

Harads

TO
TÖRE

E4

Kåbdalis

Råneå

Hornavan

Piteälven

97

92

Boden

Arjeplog

Vidsel

Älvsbyn

93

Luleå

Uddjaur

95

Moskosel

Auktsjaur

9A

Storsund

*Gulf
of
Bothnia*

Storavan

Arvidsjaur

Piteå

45

373

N

Sorsele

Abborrträsk

Glommersträsk

95

Byskeälven

E4

Gargnäs

Skellefteälven

365

Jörn

40 miles

Vindelälven

Pärlan

60 km

Gunnarsberg

Kristineberg

Skellefteå

Storuman

(280 mi) long. Of the city's 26,000 inhabitants, an estimated fifth are Finnish immigrants who came to work in the mine.

The city was established in 1890 as a mining town, but true prosperity came only with the building of the railway to the Baltic port of Luleå and the northern Norwegian port of Narvik in 1902.

Like most of Norrland, Kiruna is full of remarkable contrasts, from the seemingly pitch-black, months-long winter to the summer, when the sun never sets and it is actually possible to play golf round-the-clock for 50 days at a stretch. Here, too, the ancient Sami culture exists side by side with the high-tech culture of cutting-edge satellite research. In recent years the city has diversified its economy and now supports the Esrange Space Range, about 40 km (24 mi) east, which sends rockets and balloons to probe the upper reaches of the earth's atmosphere, and the Swedish Institute of Space Physics, which has pioneered the investigation of the phenomenon of the northern lights. The city received a boost in 1984 with the opening of Nordkalottvägen, a 170-km-long (106-mi-long) road to Narvik.

One of Kiruna's few buildings of interest is **Kiruna Kyrka** (Kiruna Church), on Gruvvägen, near the center of the city. It was built in 1921, its inspiration a blending of a Sami kåta with a Swedish stave church. The altarpiece is by Prince Eugen (1863–1947), Sweden's painter prince.

Lodging

$$$ ⊞ **Ferrum.** Part of the Reso Hotels chain, this late-1960s-vintage hotel is near the railway station. Rooms have wall-to-wall carpeting and modern, standard furniture. ⊠ *Lars Janssonsg. 15, Box 22, S981 21,* ☎ *0980/18600,* ᡅ *0980/14505. 169 rooms. 2 restaurants, bar, no-smoking rooms, sauna, exercise room, dance club, meeting rooms. AE, DC, MC, V.*

$$ ⊞ **Kebne och Kaisa.** These twin modern hotels—named after the local mountain, Kebnekaise (☞ *below*)—are close to the railway station and the airport bus stop. Rooms are bland but modern and comfortable. The restaurant is one of the best in Kiruna; it's open for breakfast and dinner. ⊠ *Konduktörsg. 3 and 7, S981 34,* ☎ *0980/12380,* ᡅ *0980/82111. 54 rooms. Restaurant, no-smoking rooms, sauna. AE, DC, MC, V.*

$ ⊞ **Fyra Vindar.** Dating from 1903, this small hotel has the advantage of being close to the railway station. ⊠ *Bangårdsv. 9, S981 34,* ☎ *0980/ 12050. 18 rooms. Restaurant, no-smoking rooms. DC, MC, V.*

$ ⊞ **STF Vandrarhem.** Formerly a hospital for the aged, this modernized, 1926 building now serves as a youth hostel. It faces a large park near the railway station. ⊠ *Skytteg. 16A, S981 34,* ☎ *0980/17195 or 0980/ 12784. 35 2- to 5-bed rooms. No credit cards. Closed mid-Aug.–mid-June.*

En Route   Driving south from Kiruna toward Muddus National Park, you'll pass several small former mining villages before coming into the **Kalixälv** (Kalix River) valley, where the countryside becomes more settled, with small farms and fertile meadows replacing the wilder northern landscape.

Jukkasjärvi

87   *16 km (10 mi) east of Kiruna.*

The history of Jukkasjärvi, a Sami village by the shores of the fast-flowing Torneälven (Torne River), dates from 1543 when a market was recorded here. There is a wooden church from the 17th century and a small open-air museum that gives a feeling of Sami life in times gone by.

Here, if you are gastronomically adventuresome you may want to sample one of the most unusual of all Sami delicacies: *kaffeost,* a cup of thick black coffee with small lumps of goat cheese. After the cheese sits in the coffee for a bit, you fish it out with a spoon and consume it, then drink the coffee.

Dining and Lodging

$ ✕⚏ **Jukkasjärvi Wärdshus och Hembygdsgård.** The restaurant spe-
★ cializes in Norrland cuisine—characterized by reindeer, wild berries, mushrooms, dried and smoked meats, salted fish, fermented herring, rich sauces using thick creams—and is the lifework of its manager, Yngve Bergqvist. The manor has one large honeymoon suite with wood floors and antique furniture; there are 45 cabins around it, 30 with bathroom, kitchen, and two bedrooms with bunk beds. Fifteen "camping cabins" are simple shelters that share the use of a common house with toilets, showers, sauna, kitchen, and washing machine. Breakfast is not included. River-rafting and canoeing trips can be arranged. ⊠ *Jukkasjärvi, Marknadsv. 63, S981 91,* ☏ *0980/21190,* 📠 *0980/21406. 1 suite, 45 cabins. Restaurant, sauna, meeting rooms. AE, DC, MC, V.*

$$$ ⚏ **Ice Hotel.** At the peak of winter, tourists are drawn by the annual construction of the world's largest igloo, which opens for business as a hotel from December through April, after which it melts away. Made of snow, ice, and sheet metal, the Ice Hotel offers rooms for 40 guests, who spend the night in specially insulated sleeping bags on top of layers of reindeer skins and spruce boughs. The bar is called In the Rocks, and colored electric lights liven up the solid ice walls. Breakfast is served in the sauna, with a view of the (nonelectric) northern lights. The entire hotel is designated nonsmoking, as it takes only a few puffs to tarnish the snow-white interiors. ⊠ *Marknadsv. 63, S981 91 Jukkasjärvi,* ☏ *0980/21190,* 📠 *0980/21406. 40 beds, 1 suite. Restaurant, bar, sauna, cross-country skiing, snowmobiling, chapel, meeting rooms. AE, DC, MC, V. Closed May–Nov.*

Outdoor Activities and Sports

A challenging local activity is riding the rapids of the Torne River in an inflatable boat. In winter Jukkasjärvi also offers dogsled rides and snowmobile safaris. Call the Gällivare tourist office (☞ Norrland and Norbotten A to Z, *below*).

Kebnekaise

88 *85 km (53 mi) west of Kiruna.*

At 7,000 ft above sea level, Kebnekaise is Sweden's highest mountain, but you'll need to be in good physical shape just to get to it. From Kiruna you travel about 66 km (41 mi) west to the Sami village of Nikkaluokta. (There are two buses a day from Kiruna in the summer.) From Nikkaluokta it is a hike of 19 km (12 mi) to the Fjällstationen (mountain station) at the foot of Kebnekaise, though you can take a boat 5 km (3 mi) across Lake Ladtjojaure. Kebnekaise itself is easy to climb provided there's good weather and you're in shape; mountaineering equipment is not necessary. If you feel up to more walking, the track continues past the Kebnekaise Fjällstationen to become part of what is known as Kungsleden (the King's Path), a 500-km (280-mi) trail through the mountains and Abisko National Park to Riksgränsen on the Norwegian border.

Lodging

$ ⚏ **Kebnekaise Fjällstation.** This rustic, wooden mountain station consists of seven separate buildings. Choose between the main building, with its heavy wood beams, wood floors, and wood bunk beds—five per room—and the newer annex, where more modern rooms each contain two or four beds. All guests share the use of a service house, with toilets, men's and women's showers, and sauna. The facility is 19 km (12 mi) from Nikkaloukta and can be reached by footpath, a combination of boat and hiking, or helicopter. Guided mountain tours are available. ✉ *S981 29 Kiruna,* ☎ *0980/55042,* ℻ *0980/55048; off-season, contact Abisko tourist office (☞ Norrland and Norbotten A to Z, below). 200 beds. Restaurant, bar, sauna. AE, V. Closed mid-Aug.–mid-Mar.*

Outdoor Activities and Sports

All the regional tourist offices can supply details of skiing holidays, but never forget the extreme temperatures and weather conditions. For the really adventuresome, the Kebnekaise mountain station offers combined skiing and climbing weeks at SKr3,795. It also offers weeklong combined dogsledding, skiing, and climbing holidays on the mountains, which vary in price from SKr4,225 to SKr5,395. Because of the extreme cold and the danger involved, be sure to have proper equipment. Consult the **mountain station** (☎ 0980/55000) well in advance for advice.

Kvikkjokk and Sarek National Park

89 *310 km (193 mi) southwest of Kiruna (via Rte. 45).*

Sarek is Sweden's largest high mountain area and was molded by the last Ice Age. The mountains have been sculpted by glaciers, of which there are about 100 in the park. The mountain area totals 487,000 acres, a small portion of which is forest, bogs, and waterways. The remainder is bare mountain. The park has 90 peaks some 6,000 ft above sea level.

The Rapaätno River, which drains the park, runs through the lovely, desolate Rapadalen (Rapa Valley). The area is marked by a surprising variety of landscapes—luxuriant green meadows contrasting with the snowy peaks of the mountains. Elk, bears, wolverines, lynx, ermines, hare, Arctic foxes, red foxes, and mountain lemmings inhabit the terrain. Birdlife includes ptarmigan, willow grouse, teal, wigeon, tufted ducks, bluethroat, and warblers. Golden eagles, rough-legged buzzards, and merlins have also been spotted here.

Visiting Sarek demands a good knowledge of mountains and a familiarity with the outdoors. The park can be dangerous in winter because of avalanches and snowstorms. However, in summer, despite its unpredictable, often inhospitable climate, it attracts large numbers of experienced hikers. At Kvikkjokk, hikers can choose between a trail through the Tarradalen (Tarra Valley), which divides the Sarek from the Padjelanta National Park to the west, or part of the Kungsleden trail, which crosses about 15 km (9 mi) of Sarek's southeastern corner.

Skaite and Muddus National Park

90 *192 km (119 mi) south of Kiruna (via E10 and Rte. 45).*

Established in 1942, Muddus National Park is less mountainous and spectacular than Sarek, its 121,770 acres comprising mainly virgin coniferous forest, some of whose trees may be up to 600 years old. The park's 3,680 acres of water are composed primarily of two huge lakes at the center of the park and the Muddusjåkkå River, which tumbles spectacularly through a gorge with 330-ft-high sheer rock walls and includes a waterfall crashing 140 ft down. The highest point of Muddus is Sör-Stubba mountain, 2,158 ft above sea level. From Skaite, where you enter the park, a series of well-marked trails begins. There are four well-equipped overnight communal rest huts and two tourist cabins. The park shelters bears, elk, lynx, wolverines, moose, ermines, weasels, otters, and many bird species. A popular pastime is picking cloudberries in autumn.

Jokkmokk

⑨ *205 km (127 mi) south of Kiruna (via E10 and Rte. 45).*

Jokkmokk is an important center of Sami culture. Each February it is the scene of the region's largest market, nowadays an odd event featuring everything from stalls selling frozen reindeer meat to Sami handcrafted wooden utensils. If you're an outdoor enthusiast, Jokkmokk makes perhaps the best base in Norrland for you. The village has three campsites and is surrounded by wilderness. The local tourist office (☞ Norrland and Norbotten A to Z, *below*) sells fishing permits, which cost SKr50 for 24 hours, SKr100 for 3 days, SKr150 for 1 week, and SKr300 for the entire year. The office can also supply lists of camping and housekeeping cabins.

Lodging

$$$ **☶ Hotel Jokkmokk.** A modern hotel of this level of luxury seems in-
★ congruous in this remote region but is welcome nevertheless. Rooms are carpeted, and six of them are designated as "Ladies' Rooms," basically all with pastels and florals. The hotel is in town center, but the staff can arrange dogsled rides and helicopter trips to the Sarek and Muddus national parks; there is excellent fishing nearby. ⊠ *Solg. 45, S962 23,* ☎ *0971/55320,* ᖴᴬ᙭ *0971/55625. 75 rooms. Restaurant, no-smoking rooms, indoor pool, sauna, meeting rooms. AE, DC, MC, V.*

$ **☶ Gästis.** This small hotel in central Jokkmokk opened in 1915. Rooms are standard, with television, shower, and either carpeted or vinyl floors. ⊠ *Herrev. 1, S962 31,* ☎ *0971/10012,* ᖴᴬ᙭ *0971/10044. 30 rooms. Restaurant, no-smoking rooms, sauna, meeting rooms. AE, DC, MC, V.*

$ **☶ Jokkmokks Turistcenter.** This complex is in a pleasant forest area, near Luleälven, 3 km (2 mi) from the railway station. Rooms have bunk beds, a small table, and chairs; showers, toilets, and a common cooking area are in the hall. ⊠ *Box 75, S962 22,* ☎ *0971/12370,* ᖴᴬ᙭ *0971/12476. 26 rooms, 84 cabins. 4 pools, sauna, meeting rooms. MC, V.*

Boden

⑨2 *290 km (180 mi) southeast of Kiruna, 130 km (81 mi) southeast of Jokkmokk (on Route 97).*

Boden, the nation's largest garrison town, dates from 1809, when Sweden lost Finland to Russia and feared an invasion of its own territory. The **Garnisonsmuseet** (Garrison Museum), contains exhibits from Swedish military history, with an extensive collection of weapons and uniforms. ⊠ *Garnisonsmuseet, Sveav. 10, Boden,* ☎ *0921/68399.* ᖴᴬ᙭ *Free.* ☉ *Mid-June–late Aug., Tues.–Sat. 11–4, Sun. 1–4.*

Luleå

⑨3 *340 km (211 mi) southeast of Kiruna (via E10 and E4).*

The most northerly major town in Sweden, Luleå is an important port at the top of the Gulf of Bothnia, at the mouth of the Luleälv (Lule River). The town was some 10 km (6 mi) farther inland when it was first granted its charter in 1621, but by 1649 trade had grown so much that it was moved closer to the sea. The development of Kiruna and the iron trade is linked, by means of a railway, with the fortunes of Luleå, where a steelworks was set up in the 1940s. Like its fellow port towns—Piteå, Skellefteå, Umeå, and Sundsvall—farther south, Luleå is a very modern and nondescript city, but it has some reasonable hotels. A beautiful archipelago of hundreds of islands hugs the coastline.

The **Norrbottens Museet** (Norbotten Museum) has one of the best collections of Sami ethnography in the world. ⊠ *Hermelinsparken 2,* ☎ *0920/220355.* ⚌ *Free.* ☉ *Mid-June–mid-Aug., Thurs.–Tues. 10–6, Wed. 10–8.*

Dining and Lodging

$$$ ✕⊡ **Arctic.** Right in town center, the Arctic is known locally for its restaurant, which serves local specialties. The hotel is warm and cozy, with tastefully decorated, rustic rooms. ⊠ *Sandviksg. 80, S972 34,* ☎ *0920/ 10980,* ℻ *0920/60980. 94 rooms. Restaurant, no-smoking rooms, hot tub, sauna, meeting rooms. AE, DC, MC, V.*

$$$$ ⊡ **Luleå Hotel.** As you might expect of a Radisson SAS hotel, this one is large, modern, and central. Each floor is different: the third floor is done in blue tones; the English colonial–style second floor has ceiling fans and dried flowers; and the ground floor is art deco. ⊠ *Storg. 17, S971 28,* ☎ *0920/94000,* ℻ *0920/88222. 216 rooms. Restaurant, no-smoking rooms, indoor pool, sauna, exercise room, nightclub, meeting rooms. AE, DC, MC, V.*

$$$$ ⊡ **Luleå Stads Hotell.** This large, central Best Western hotel has nightly—sometimes boisterous—dancing. Rooms in the building dating back to 1901 are spacious and carpeted, with turn-of-the-century furnishings. ⊠ *Storg. 15, S972 32,* ☎ *0920/67000,* ℻ *0920/67092. 135 rooms, 3 suites. Restaurant, café, no-smoking rooms, sauna, dance club, meeting rooms. AE, DC, MC, V.*

$$$ ⊡ **Scandic.** This hotel on Lake Sjö has an extremely pleasant setting and is 2 km (1 mi) from the railway station. ⊠ *Banv. 3, S973 46,* ☎ *0920/ 228360,* ℻ *0920/69472. 157 rooms. Restaurant, no-smoking rooms, indoor pool, sauna, exercise room, meeting rooms. AE, DC, MC, V.*

$$ ⊡ **Amber.** A particularly fine old building, listed on the historic register, houses this hotel close to the railway station. Rooms are modern, with plush carpeting, minibars, and satellite television. ⊠ *Stationsg. 67, S972 34,* ☎ *0920/10200,* ℻ *0920/87906. 16 rooms. No-smoking rooms. AE, DC, MC, V.*

$$ ⊡ **Aveny.** Rooms are of varying sizes and colors, but all are spotless and fresh. It's close to the railway station. ⊠ *Hermelinsg. 10, S973 46,* ☎ *0920/221820,* ℻ *0920/220122. 24 rooms. No-smoking rooms. AE, DC, MC, V.*

Norrland and Norbotten A to Z

Arriving and Departing

BY PLANE

There are two nonstop SAS flights a day from Stockholm to **Kiruna Airport** (⊠ 5 km/3 mi from Kiruna, ☎ 0980/84810) and three additional flights via Luleå. Check SAS (☎ 020/727000) for specific times.

Between the Airport and Town: In summer, **buses** connect the airport and Kiruna; the fare is about SKr50. A **taxi** from the airport to the center of Kiruna costs about SKr75; book through the airline or call ☎ 0980/12020.

BY TRAIN

The best and cheapest way to get to Kiruna is to take the evening sleeper from Stockholm on Tuesday, Wednesday, or Saturday, when the fare is reduced to SKr595 for a single. The regular one-way price is SKr695 plus SKr90 for the couchette, double for return. You'll arrive at around lunchtime the next day.

Getting Around

Since public transportation is nonexistent in this part of the country, having a car is essential. The few roads are well built and maintained, although spring thaws can present potholes. Keep in mind that habitations are few and far between in this wilderness region.

CAR RENTALS

Kiruna: Avis (⊠ Hotel Ferrum, ☎ 0980/13080). **Hertz** (⊠ Industriv. 5, ☎ 0980/19000). **Europcar/InterRent** (⊠ Växlareg. 20, ☎ 0980/14365).

Contacts and Resources

DOCTORS AND DENTISTS

Kiruna Health Center (⊠ Thuleg. 29, ☎ 0980/73000). Medical advisory service, **Luleå** (☎ 0920/71400). **Jokkmokk Health Center** (⊠ Lappstav. 9, ☎ 0971/44444).

EMERGENCIES

For emergencies dial ☎ 112.

GUIDED TOURS

Local tourist offices have information on guided tours.

Lapland Tours: Same Laüs Resor (⊠ c/o Rental Line I Jokkmokk, Hermelinsg. 20, 962 33, Jokkmokk, ☎ 0971/10606) arranges tours to points of interest in Lappland.

Sami Tours: Call **Swedish Sami Association** (⊠ Brog. 5, S90325, Umeå, ☎ 090/141180).

LATE-NIGHT PHARMACIES

There are no late-night pharmacies in Norbotten, but doctors called to emergencies can dispense medicine. The pharmacy at the Gallerian shopping center in Kiruna (⊠ Föreningsg. 6, ☎ 0980/18775) is open weekdays 9:30–6 and Saturdays 9:30–1.

VISITOR INFORMATION

Regional Tourist Office: Norrbottens Turistråd (⊠ Stationsg. 69, Luleå, ☎ 0920/94070) covers the entire area.

Local Tourist Offices: Abisko (⊠ S980 24 Abisko, ☎ 0980/40200). **Jokkmokk** (⊠ Stortorget 4, ☎ 0971/12140 or 0971/17257). **Kiruna** (⊠ Folkets Hus, ☎ 0980/18880). **Luleå** (⊠ Kulturcentrum Ebeneser, ☎ 0920/293500). **Gällivare** (⊠ Storg. 16, ☎ 0970/16660).

SWEDEN A TO Z

Arriving and Departing

By Car and Boat

You can approach through Denmark, using ferry crossings to Malmö or Helsingborg.

FROM THE UNITED KINGDOM

There are excellent links between Harwich and Göteborg and Newcastle and Göteborg aboard **Scandinavian Seaways** ferries (⊠ Scandinavian Seaways, DFDS Ltd., Scandinavia House, Parkeston Quay, Harwich, Essex, CO12 4QG, England, ☎ 01255/240240).

By Plane

FROM NORTH AMERICA

SAS (☎ 800/221–2350), **American** (☎ 800/433–7300), **TWA** (☎ 800/892–4141) , and other major airlines serve Stockholm's Arlanda International Airport and Göteborg's Landvetter airport.

Stockholm's Arlanda Airport and Göteborg's Landvetter airport are served by **SAS** (☎ 0171/7344020) and **British Airways** (☎ 0181/8974000).

By Train

From London, the **British Rail European Travel Center** (✉ Victoria Station, London, ☎ 0171/8342345) can be helpful in arranging connections to Sweden's SJ (Statens Järnvägar).

Getting Around

By Boat

An excellent way of seeing Sweden is from the many ferry boats that ply the archipelagos and main lakes. In Stockholm, visitors should buy a special *Båtluffarkort* (Inter Skerries Card, SKr250) from **Waxholmsbolaget** (✉ Sodra Blasieholmsh wharf, ☎ 08/6795830). This gives unlimited travel on the archipelago ferry boats for a 16-day period.

Highly popular four-day cruises are available on the Göta Canal, which makes use of rivers, lakes, and, on its last lap, the Baltic Sea. This lovely waterway, which links Göteborg on the west coast with Stockholm on the east, has a total of 65 locks, and you travel on fine old steamers, some of which date almost from the canal's opening in 1832. The oldest and most desirable is the *Juno*, built in 1874. Prices start at SKr5,900 for a bed in a double cabin. For more information, contact the **Göta Canal Steamship Company** (✉ Box 272, S401 24 Göteborg, ☎ 031/806315, FAX 031/158311).

By Bus

There is excellent bus service between all major towns and cities. Consult the Yellow Pages under *Bussresearrangörer* for the telephone numbers of the companies concerned. Recommended are the services offered to different parts of Sweden from Stockholm by **Swebus** (✉ Cityterminalen, Klarabergsviadukten 72).

By Car

Sweden has an excellent highway network of more than 80,000 km (50,000 mi). The fastest routes are those with numbers prefixed with an *E* (for "European"), some of which are the equivalent of American highways or British motorways.

EMERGENCY ASSISTANCE
The **Larmtjänst** organization, run by a confederation of Swedish insurance companies, provides a 24-hour breakdown service. Its phone numbers are listed in the Yellow Pages.

GASOLINE
Sweden has some of the highest gasoline rates in Europe, about SKr8 per liter at press time. Lead-free gasoline is readily available. Gas stations are self-service: pumps marked SEDEL are automatic and accept SKr20 and SKr100 bills; pumps marked KASSA are paid for at the cashier; the KONTO pumps are for customers with Swedish gas credit cards.

MAP
If you plan on extensive road touring, consider buying the *Vägatlas över Sverige*, a detailed road atlas published by the Mötormännens Riksförbund, available at bookstores for around SKr270.

Parking meters and, increasingly, timed ticket machines, operate in larger towns, usually between 8 AM and 6 PM. The fee varies from about SKr6 to SKr35 per hour. Parking garages in urban areas are mostly automated, often with machines that accept credit cards; LEDIGT on a garage sign means space is available.

RENTAL AGENCIES
Major car-rental companies such as **Avis, Hertz, Europcar/InterRent, Bonus, Budget,** and **OK** have facilities in all major towns and cities as well as at airports. It is worth shopping around for special rates. Various service stations also offer car rentals, including **Shell, Statoil, Texaco,** and **Q8.** See the Yellow Pages under *Biluthyrning* for telephone numbers and addresses.

ROAD CONDITIONS
All main and secondary roads are well surfaced, but some minor roads, particularly in the north, are gravel.

RULES OF THE ROAD
Drive on the right, and, no matter where you sit in a car, seat belts are mandatory. You must also have at least low-beam headlights on at all times. Signs indicate five basic speed limits, ranging from 30 kph (19 mph) in school or playground areas to 110 kph (68 mph) on long stretches of *E* roads.

By Plane
All major cities and towns are linked with regular flights by **Scandinavian Airlines System** (**SAS,** ☎ 08/727000 or 08/974175). Most Swedish airports are located a long way from city centers but are served by fast and efficient bus services. SAS also operates a limousine service at leading airports. For more information, contact SAS.

By Train
Statens Järnvägar, or SJ (✉ Central Station, Vasag. 1, ☎ 08/7622000 or 020/757575), the state railway company, has a highly efficient network of comfortable, electric trains. On nearly all long-distance routes there are buffet cars and, on overnight trips, sleeping cars and couchettes in both first and second class. Seat reservations are advisable, and on some trains—indicated with *R, IN,* or *IC* on the timetable—they are compulsory. An extra fee of SKr15 is charged to reserve a seat on a trip of less than 150 km (93 mi); on longer trips there is no extra charge. Reservations can be made right up to departure time (☎ 020/757575). The **high-speed X2000 train** has been introduced on several routes; the Stockholm–Göteborg run takes just under three hours. Travelers younger than 19 years travel at half-fare. Up to two children younger than 12 years may travel free if accompanied by an adult.

DISCOUNT PASSES
For SKr150 you can buy a **Reslustkort,** which gets you 50% reductions on *röda avgångar* ("red," or off-peak, departures).

The **ScanRail Pass** comes in various denominations: five days of travel within 15 days ($222 first class, $176 second class); 10 days within a month ($354 first class, $284 second class); or one month ($516 first class, $414 second class). For information on the ScanRail'n Drive Pass, *see* Train Travel *in* the Gold Guide. In the United States, call **Rail Europe** (☎ 800/848–7245) or **DER** (☎ 800/782–2424).

The **Eurail and InterRail** passes are both valid in Sweden. SJ also organizes reduced-cost package trips in conjunction with local tourist offices. Details are available at any railway station or from SJ.

Contacts and Resources

Customs

Travelers 21 or older entering Sweden from non-EU countries may import duty-free: 1 liter of liquor or 2 liters of fortified wine; 2 liters of wine; 15 liters of beer; 200 cigarettes or 100 cigarillos or 50 cigars or 250 grams of tobacco; 50 grams of perfume; ¼ liter of aftershave; and other goods up to the value of SKr 1,700. Travelers from the United Kingdom or other EU countries may import duty-free: 1 liter of liquor or 3 liters of fortified wine; 5 liters of wine; 15 liters of beer; 300 cigarettes or 150 cigarillos or 75 cigars or 400 grams of tobacco; and other goods, including perfume and aftershave, of any value.

Embassies

U.S. (✉ Strandv. 101, S-11589 Stockholm, ☏ 08/7835300). **Canada** (✉ Tegelbacken 4, Box 16129, S-10323 Stockholm, ☏ 08/4533000). **U.K.** (✉ Skarpög. 68, S-11593 Stockholm, ☏ 08/6719000).

Emergencies

Anywhere in Sweden, dial ☏ 112 for emergency assistance.

Guided Tours

Stockholm Sightseeing (✉ Skeppsbron 22, ☏ 08/233375) runs a variety of sightseeing tours of Stockholm. Contact local tourist offices.

Language

Swedish is closely related to Danish and Norwegian. After "z," the Swedish alphabet has three extra letters, "å," "ä," and "ö," something to bear in mind when using the phone book. Another oddity in the phone book is that *v* and *w* are interchangeable; Wittström, for example, comes before Vittviks, not after. Most Swedes speak English.

Lodging

Sweden offers a variety of accommodation from simple bed-and-breakfasts, camp sites, and hostels to hotels of the highest international standard. Major hotels in larger cities cater mainly to business clientele and can be expensive; weekend rates are more reasonable. Prices are normally on a per-room basis and include all taxes and service charges and usually breakfast. Apart from the more modest inns and the cheapest budget establishments, private baths and showers are standard. Whatever their size, almost all Swedish hotels provide scrupulously clean accommodation and courteous service. Sweden virtually shuts down during the entire month of July, so make your hotel reservations in advance, especially if staying outside the city areas during July and early August.

CAMPING

There are 760 registered campsites nationwide, many close to uncrowded bathing places and with fishing, boating, or canoeing; they may also offer bicycle rentals. Prices range from SKr70 to SKr130 per 24-hour period. Many campsites also offer accommodations in log cabins at various prices, depending on the facilities offered, and some have special facilities for guests with disabilities. Most are open between June and September, but about 200 remain open in winter for skiing and skating enthusiasts. **Sveriges Campingvärdarnas Riksförbund** (Swedish Campsite Owners' Association or SCR, ✉ Box 255, S451 17 Uddevalla, ☎ 0522/39345, FAX 0522/33849), publishes, in English, an abbreviated list of sites; contact the office for a free copy.

CHALET RENTAL

With 250 chalet villages with high standards, Sweden enjoys popularity with its chalet accommodation, often arranged on the spot at tourist offices. Many are organized under the auspices of the **Swedish Touring Association** (STF; ☎ 08/4632200, FAX 08/6781938). **Scandinavian Seaways** (☎ 0171/4096060 and 031/650600) in Göteborg arranges package deals that combine a ferry trip from Britain across the North Sea and a stay in a chalet village.

HOTELS

The official annual guide, *Hotels in Sweden,* published by and available free from the Swedish Travel and Tourism Council (☞ Visitor Information, *below*), gives comprehensive information about hotel facilities and prices. The **Sweden Hotels** group has about 100 independently owned hotels and its own classification scheme—*A, B,* or *C*—based on facilities. **Hotellcentralen** (✉ Central Station, 111 20, ☎ 08/7892425, FAX 08/7918666) is an independent agency that makes advance telephone reservations for any Swedish hotel at no cost. **Countryside Hotels** (✉ Box 69, 830 13 Åre, ☎ 0647/51860, FAX 0647/51920) is comprised of 35 select resort hotels, some of them restored manor houses or centuries-old inns.

Major hotel groups also have their own central reservations services. **Scandic** (☎ 08/6105050). **RESO** (☎ 08/4114040). **Best Western** (☎ 08/330600 or 020/792752). **Sweden Hotels** (☎ 08/7898900). **Radisson SAS** (☎ 020/797592).

Mail

Postcards and letters up to 20 grams can be mailed for SKr7 to destinations within Europe, SKr8 to the United States and the rest of the world.

Money and Expenses

BANK AND CREDIT CARDS

The 1,200 or so blue **Bankomat** cash dispensers nationwide have been adapted to take some foreign cards, including MasterCard, Visa, and bank cards linked to the Cirrus network. For more information, contact Bankomat Centralen (☎ 08/7257240) in Stockholm or your local bank. **American Express** (✉ Birger Jarlsg. 1, ☎ 08/6795200, 020/793211 toll-free) has cash and traveler's check dispensers; there's also an office at Stockholm's Arlanda airport.

CURRENCY

The unit of currency is the krona (plural kronor), which is divided into 100 öre and is written as SKr or SEK. The 10-öre coin was phased out in 1991, leaving only the 50-öre, SKr1, and SKr5 coins. These have been joined by an SKr10 coin. Bank notes are at present SKr20, 50, 100, 500, and 1,000. At press time (summer 1997), the exchange rate was SKr7.83 to the dollar, SKr12.65 to the pound, and SKr5.64 to the Canadian dollar.

EXCHANGING MONEY

Traveler's checks and foreign currency can be exchanged at banks all over Sweden and at post offices displaying the NB EXCHANGE sign.

SALES-TAX REFUNDS

All hotel, restaurant, and departure taxes and V.A.T. (called *moms* all over Scandinavia) are automatically included in prices. V.A.T. is 25%; non-EU residents can obtain a 15% refund on goods of SKr200 or more. To receive your refund at any of the 15,000 stores that participate in the tax-free program, you'll be asked to fill out a form and show your passport. The form can then be turned in at any airport or ferry customs desk. Keep all your receipts and tags; occasionally, customs authorities ask to see your purchases, so pack them where they will be accessible.

SAMPLE PRICES

Cup of coffee, SKr15–SKr20; a beer, SKr30–SKr45; mineral water, SKr10–SKr20; cheese roll, SKr20–SKr40; pepper steak à la carte, SKr120–SKr160; cheeseburger, SKr40; pizza, starting at SKr30.

TIPPING

In addition to the 12% value-added tax, most hotels usually include a service charge of 15%; it is not necessary to tip unless you have received extra services. Similarly, a service charge of 13% is usually included in restaurant bills. It is a custom, however, to leave small change when buying drinks. Taxi drivers and hairdressers expect a tip of about 10%.

Opening and Closing Times

BANKS

Banks are open weekdays 9:30 AM to 3 PM, but some stay open until 5 on most days. The bank at Arlanda International Airport is open every day with extended hours, and the Forex and Valuta Specialisten currency-exchange offices also have extended hours.

MUSEUMS

The opening times for museums vary widely, but most are open from 10 AM to 4 PM weekdays and over the weekend but are closed on Monday. Consult the guide in *På Stan*, the entertainment supplement published in *Dagens Nyheter's* Friday edition, or *Stockholm This Week*.

SHOPS

Shops are generally open weekdays from 9 AM, 9:30 AM, or 10 AM until 6 PM and Saturday from 9 AM to 1 or 4 PM. Most of the large department stores stay open later in the evenings, and some open on Sunday. Several supermarkets open on Sunday, and there are a number of late-night food shops such as the 7-Eleven chain.

Outdoor Activities and Sports

BIKING

Rental costs average around SKr90 per day. Tourist offices and **Svenska Turistförening** (Swedish Touring Association of STF, ⊠ Box 25, S101 20 Stockholm, ☎ 08/4632200, FAX 08/6781938) have information about cycling package holidays that include bike rentals, overnight accommodations, and meals. The bicycling organization, **Cykelfrämjandet** (National Cycle Association, ⊠ Torsg. 31, Box 6027, S102 31 Stockholm, ☎ 08/321680 Mon.–Thurs. 9–noon, FAX 08/310503), publishes a free English-language guide to cycling trips.

BOATING AND SAILING

STF, in cooperation with Telia (Sweden's PTT, or Postal, Telephone, and Telegraph authority), publishes an annual guide in Swedish to all the country's marinas. It is available from **Telia Infomedia** (☎ 08/6341700) or in your nearest Telebutik. **Svenska Kanotförbundet** (Swedish Canoeing Association, ⊠ Skeppsbron 11, 611 35 Nyköping, ☎ 0155/69508) publishes a similar booklet.

GOLFING

Sweden has 365 golf clubs; you can even play by the light of the midnight sun at Boden in the far north. **Svenska Golfförbundet** (Swedish Golfing Association, ⊠ Box 84, S182 11 Danderyd, ☎ 08/6221500,

FAX 08/7558439) publishes an annual guide in Swedish; it costs around SKr100, including postage.

SKIING
There are plenty of downhill and cross-country facilities in Sweden. The best-known resorts are in the country's western mountains: Åre in the north, with 29 lifts; Idre Fjäll, to the south of Åre, offering accommodations for 10,000; and Sälen in the folklore region of Dalarna. You can ski through May at Riksgränsen in the far north.

TENNIS
Contact **Svenska Tennisförbundet** (Swedish Tennis Association, ✉ Lidingöv. 75, Box 27915, S115 94 Stockholm, ☎ 08/6679770, FAX 08/6646606).

Telephones
Post offices do not have telephone facilities, but there are plenty of pay phones, and long-distance calls can be made from special telegraph offices called *Telebutik,* marked TELE.

COUNTRY CODE
Sweden's country code is 46.

DIRECTORY ASSISTANCE AND OPERATOR INFORMATION
For international calls, the operator assistance number is ☎ 0018; directory assistance is ☎ 07977. Within Sweden, dial ☎ 90130 for operator assistance and ☎ 07975 for directory assistance.

INTERNATIONAL CALLS
The foreign dialing code is 009, followed by the country code, then your number. The **AT&T USADirect** access code is ☎ 020/795611. The **MCI call-USA** access code is ☎ 020/795922. The **Sprint Express** access code is ☎ 020/799011.

LOCAL CALLS
A local call costs a minimum of SKr2. For calls outside the locality, dial the area code (see telephone directory). Public phones are of three types: one takes SKr1 and SKr5 coins (newer public phones also accept SKr10 coins); another takes only credit cards; and the last takes only the prepaid **Telefonkort.**

A **Telefonkort** (telephone card), available at Telebutik, Pressbyrån (large blue-and-yellow newsstands), or hospitals, costs SKr35, SKr60, or SKr100. If you're making numerous domestic calls, the card saves money. Many of the pay phones in downtown Stockholm and Göteborg take only these cards, so it's a good idea to carry one.

Visitor Information
Swedish Travel and Tourism Council (✉ 73 Welbeck St., London W15 8AN, ☎ 0171/9359784, FAX 0171/9355853; ✉ 655 3rd Ave., 18th Floor, New York, NY 10017, ☎ 212/9492333, FAX 212/6970835; ✉ Box 3030, Kungsg. 36, 103 61 Stockholm, ☎ 08/7255500, FAX 08/7255531).

Stockholm Information Service at Sweden House (Sverigehuset, ✉ Hamng. 27, Box 7542, S103 93 Stockholm, ☎ 08/7892490).

Weather
The tourist season runs from mid-May through mid-September; however, many attractions close in late August, when the schools reopen at the end of the Swedish vacation season. The weather can be glorious in the spring and fall, and many visitors prefer sightseeing when there are fewer people around.

CLIMATE

Sweden has typically unpredictable north European summer weather, but, as a general rule, it is likely to be warm but not hot from May until September. In Stockholm, the weeks just before and after Midsummer offer almost 24-hour light, whereas in the far north, above the Arctic Circle, the sun doesn't set between the end of May and the middle of July.

7 Portraits of Scandinavia

Scandinavia at a Glance: A Chronology

Books and Videos

SCANDINAVIA AT A GLANCE: A CHRONOLOGY

ca. 12,000 BC The first migrations into Sweden.

ca. 10,000 Stone Age culture develops in Denmark.

ca. 8,000 The earliest settlers reach the coast of Norway.

ca. 7,000 First nomadic settlers come to Finland.

ca. 2,000 Tribes from southern Europe, mostly Germanic peoples, migrate toward Denmark.

ca. 500 Migration of Celts across central Europe impinges on Denmark's trade routes with the Mediterranean world. Trade becomes less economically crucial because of the growing use of abundant iron.

ca. AD 100 Ancestors of present-day Finns move to Finland.

ca. 770 The Viking Age begins. For the next 250 years, Scandinavians set sail on frequent expeditions stretching from the Baltic to the Irish seas, and even to the Mediterranean as far as Sicily, employing superior ships and weapons and efficient military organization.

ca. 800–ca. 1000 Swedes control river trade routes between the Baltic and Black seas; establish Novgorod, Kiev, and other cities.

830 Frankish monk Ansgar makes one of the first attempts to Christianize Sweden and builds the first church in Slesvig, Denmark. Sweden is not successfully Christianized until the end of the 11th century, when the temple at Uppsala, a center for pagan resistance, is destroyed.

ca. 870 The first permanent settlers arrive in Iceland from western Norway.

911 A Scandinavian, Rollo, rules Normandy by treaty with French king.

930 Iceland's parliament, the Alłingi, is founded.

995 King Olaf I Tryggvason introduces Christianity into Norway.

1000 Leif Eriksson visits America. Olaf I sends a mission to Christianize Iceland.

1016–35 Canute (Knud) the Great is king of England, Denmark (1018), and Norway (1028).

1070 Adam of Bremen composes *History of the Archbishops of Hamburg-Bremen*, the first important contemporary source for Danish history.

1169 King Valdemar, who was acknowledged as the single king of Denmark in 1157 and undertook repeated crusades against the Germans, captures Rugen and places it under Danish rule, signifying the beginning of the Danish medieval empire. It culminates in 1219 when Valdemar marches to Estonia and builds a fortress at Ravel. In 1225, Valdemar, after being kidnapped by a German vassal, is forced to give up all his conquests, except for Rugen and Estonia, in exchange for freedom.

1217 Haakon IV becomes king of Norway, beginning its "Golden Age." His many reforms modernize the Norwegian administration; under him, the Norwegian empire reaches its greatest extent when Greenland and Iceland form unions with Norway in 1261.

1248 In Sweden, Erik Eriksson appoints Birger as Jarl, in charge of military affairs and expeditions abroad. Birger improves women's rights, makes laws establishing peace in the home and church, and begins building Stockholm.

1250 Stockholm, Sweden, is officially founded.

1282 At a meeting of the Hof, or Danish Parliament, Danish king Erik Glipping signs a coronation charter that becomes the first written constitution of Denmark.

1319 Sweden and Norway form a union that lasts until 1335.

1349 The Black Death strikes Norway and kills two-thirds of the population.

1370 The Treaty of Stralsund gives the north German trading centers of the Hanseatic League free passage through Danish waters and full control of Danish herring fisheries for 15 years. German power increases throughout Scandinavia.

1397 The Kalmar union is formed as a result of the dynastic ties between Sweden, Denmark, and Norway, the geographical position of the Scandinavian states, and the growing influence of Germans in the Baltic. Erik of Pomerania is crowned king of the Kalmar Union.

1477 University of Uppsala, Sweden's oldest university, is founded.

1479 University of Copenhagen is founded.

1520 Christian II, ruler of the Kalmar Union, executes 82 people who oppose the Scandinavian union, an event known as the "Stockholm bloodbath." Sweden secedes from the Union three years later. Norway remains tied to Denmark and becomes a Danish province in 1536.

1523 Gustav Ericsson founds Swedish Vasa dynasty as King Gustav I Vasa.

1534 Count Christoffer of Oldenburg and his army demand the restoration of Christian II as king of Denmark, initiating civil war between supporters of Christian II and supporters of Prince Christian (later King Christian III).

1611–16 The Kalmar War: Denmark wages war against Sweden in hopes of restoring the Kalmar Union.

1611–60 Gustav II Adolphus reigns in Sweden. Under his rule, Sweden defeats Denmark in the Thirty Years' War and becomes the greatest power in Scandinavia as well as northern and central Europe.

1660 Peace of Copenhagen establishes modern boundaries of Denmark, Sweden, and Norway.

1666 Lund University, Scandinavia's largest university, is founded in Lund, Sweden.

1668 Bank of Sweden, the world's oldest central bank, is founded.

1700–21 Sweden, led by Karl XII, first broadens then loses its position to Russia as northern Europe's greatest power in the Great Northern War.

1754 Royal Danish Academy of Fine Arts is established.

1762 The duke of Gottorp becomes czar of Russia and declares war on Denmark. Catherine, the czar's wife, overrules her husband's war declaration and makes a peaceful settlement.

1763 The first Norwegian newspaper is founded.

ca. 1780 A volcanic eruption causes a famine in Iceland that kills one-fifth of the population.

1801–14 The Napoleonic wars are catastrophic for Denmark economically and politically: the policy of armed neutrality fails, the English destroy the Danish fleet in 1801, Copenhagen is devastated at the bombardment of 1807, and Sweden, after Napoléon's defeat at the Battle of Leipzig, attacks Denmark and forces the Danish surrender of Norway. The Treaty of Kiel, in 1814, calls for a union between Norway and Sweden despite Norway's desire for independence. The Danish monarchy is left with three parts: the Kingdom of Denmark and the duchies of Schleswig and Holstein.

1807 During the Napoleonic wars, Swedish king Gustav III joins the coalition against France and reluctantly accepts war with France and Russia.

1809 Sweden surrenders the Åland Islands and Finland to Russia, Finland becomes a grand duchy of the Russian Empire, and the Instrument of Government, Sweden's constitution, is adopted.

1811 University of Oslo is established.

1818 Sweden takes a Frenchman as king: Karl XIV Johann establishes the Bernadotte dynasty.

1818 National Library of Iceland is founded.

1849 Denmark's absolute monarchy is abolished and replaced by the liberal June Constitution, which establishes freedom of the press, freedom of religion, the right to hold meetings and form associations, and rule by Parliament with two elected chambers as well as the king and his ministers.

ca. 1850 The building of railroads begins in Scandinavia.

1863 National Museum of Iceland is established.

1864 Denmark goes to war against Prussia and Austria; the hostilities end with the Treaty of Vienna, which forces Denmark to surrender the duchies of Schleswig and Holstein to Prussia and Austria.

1874 Iceland adopts a constitution.

1884 A parliamentary system is established in Norway.

1885 The Art Gallery of Iceland is founded.

1887 The Norwegian Labor Party is founded.

1889 The Swedish Social Democratic Party is founded.

1901 Alfred Nobel, the Swedish millionaire chemist and industrialist, initiates the Nobel prizes.

1904 Iceland is granted home rule. The first Icelandic minister takes office. Rule by parliamentary majority is introduced.

1905 Norway's union with Sweden is dissolved.

1914 At the outbreak of World War I, Germany forces Denmark to lay mines in an area of international waters known as the Great Belt. Because the British fleet makes no serious attempts to break through, Denmark is able to maintain neutrality. Norway and Sweden also declare neutrality but are effectively blockaded.

1915 Icelandic women win the right to vote.

1916 Iceland establishes a national organization of trade unions.

1917 Finland declares independence from Russia. Danish writer Henrik Pontoppidan is awarded the Nobel prize for literature.

1918 Iceland becomes a separate state under the Danish crown; only foreign affairs remain under Danish control. Sweden, Denmark, and Norway grant women the right to vote.

1919 A republican constitution is adopted by Finland. Kaarlo Juho Stahlberg is elected president.

1920 Scandinavian countries join the League of Nations.

1929–37 The first social democratic governments take office in Denmark, Sweden, and Finland. During this period, Norway is ruled by a labor government.

ca. 1930 The Great Depression causes unemployment, affecting 40% of the organized industrial workers in Denmark.

1939 Denmark and the other Nordic countries declare neutrality in World War II. Finnish novelist Frans Eemil Sillanpaa wins the Nobel prize for literature.

1939–40 Russia defeats Finland in the Winter War. Russia invades Finland primarily for its larger strategic interests in the area and not because Finland poses a threat.

1940 Germany occupies Norway and Denmark. British forces occupy Iceland until 1941, when U.S. forces replace them.

1941–44 The Continuation War begins when Finland joins Nazi Germany in attacking the Soviet Union. After Russia defeats Finland, an agreement is signed calling for Finnish troops to withdraw to the 1940 boundary lines of Finland and for German troops on Finnish soil to disarm.

1944 The Icelandic Republic, with British and U.S. support, is founded on June 17. Sveinn Björnsson becomes Iceland's first president.

1945 Norway joins the United Nations.

1948 Treaty of Friendship, Cooperation, and Mutual Assistance between Finland and the Soviet Union obligates Finland to defend the U.S.S.R. in the event of an attack through Finnish territory.

1949 Denmark, Norway, and Iceland become members of NATO. Sweden and Finland decline membership.

1952 The Nordic Council, which promotes cooperation among the Nordic parliaments, is founded.

1955 Finland joins the United Nations and the Nordic Council. Halldor Laxness of Iceland receives the Nobel prize for literature.

1970 Finland hosts the Strategic Arms Limitation Talks (SALT).

1972 Sweden, on the basis of its neutral foreign policy, and Norway decline membership in the EU; Denmark becomes a member in 1973. Queen Margarethe II ascends the throne of Denmark.

1975 Sweden's Instrument of Government of 1809 is revised and replaced with a new Instrument of Government. This constitution reduces the voting age to 18 and removes many of the king's powers and responsibilities.

1976 The "cod wars," between Britain and Iceland over the extent of Iceland's fishing waters, end.

1980 Fifty-eight percent of Sweden's voters advocate minimizing the use of nuclear reactors at Sweden's four power plants. Iceland elects as president Vigdis Finnbogadottir, the world's first popularly elected female head of state.

1981 Gro Harlem Brundtland, a member of the Labor party, becomes Norway's first female prime minister.

1982 Poul Schluter becomes Denmark's first Conservative prime minister since 1894.

1983 In Finland, the Greens gain parliamentary representation, making them the first elected environmentalists in the Nordic region.

1985 The Althingi, Iceland's Parliament, unanimously approves a resolution banning the entry of nuclear weapons into the country.

1986 U.S. president Ronald Reagan and Soviet premier Mikhail Gorbachev discuss nuclear disarmament at a summit meeting in Reykjavík, Iceland. Sweden's prime minister, Olof Palme, is assassinated for unknown reasons. Ingvar Carlsson succeeds him.

1988 Due to U.S. pressure, Iceland consents to reducing its quota of whales caught for "scientific purposes." The United States argues that Iceland is acting against a moratorium imposed by the International Whaling Commission.

1989 Tycho Brahe Planetarium opens in Copenhagen; and Denmark becomes the first NATO country to allow women to join front-line military units. Denmark becomes the first country in the world to recognize marriage between citizens of the same sex.

1990 Finland becomes the fourth major route for Jewish emigration from the Soviet Union. Helsinki, Finland, hosts the summit meeting between George Bush and Mikhail Gorbachev.

1991 The Karen Blixen Museum, in Rungstedlund, Denmark, is founded. Norway's King Olav V dies. King Harald V ascends the throne. His wife, Queen Sonja, becomes the first queen since the death of Maud in 1938. Sweden's Social Democrats are voted out of office and the new government launches a privatization policy.

1992 Denmark declines to support the Maastricht Treaty setting up a framework for European economic union. Denmark wins the European Soccer Championships. Sweden's Riksbank (National Bank) raises overnight interest rates to a world record of 500% in an effort to defend the Swedish krona against speculation.

1993 Denmark is the president of the EU for the first half of 1993. In a second referendum, the country votes to support the Maastricht Treaty, as well as its own modified involvement in it. Tivoli celebrates its 150th year, Legoland celebrates its 25th birthday, and the Little Mermaid turns 80. Denmark also commemorates the 50th anniversary of the World War II rescue of Danish Jews, in which they were smuggled into Sweden.

Norway applies for EU membership. Norway's minister of foreign affairs, Thorvald Stoltenberg, is appointed peace negotiator to war-torn Bosnia-Herzegovina. In secret meetings near Oslo, Norwegian negotiators help bring about a historic rapprochement between Israel and the Palestine Liberation Organization.

1994 The XVII Olympic Winter Games are held in Lillehammer, Norway, from February 12 to February 27. Sweden wins the Olympic gold medal for ice hockey, and later makes its biggest soccer achievement, winning the bronze medal in the World Cup. Sweden and Finland accept membership in the EU, while Norway again declines.

1995 The 50th anniversary of the end of World War II in Europe is celebrated, especially in Denmark and Norway, where May 5 marks the end of the German occupation. Finland and Sweden join the EU in January. Finland holds parliamentary elections in March 1995; the government is presided over by Prime Minister Paavo Lipponen, a Social Democrat.

1996 Copenhagen is fêted as the Cultural Capital of Europe. After four 4-year terms in office, Iceland's president Vigdís Finnbogadóttir does not seek reelection; the new appointee is Ólafur Ragnar Grímsson. In its own blaze of glory, Iceland's Mt. Hekla erupts under the glacier Vatnajökull. Norway's longtime prime minister, Gro Harlem Brundtland, announces her resignation; she is succeeded by the Labor Party's Thorbjorn Jagland.

1997 Copenhagen's venerable Carlsberg Brewery, one of the largest supporters of the arts in Denmark, celebrates its 150th anniversary.

1998 Stockholm is the 1998 Cultural Capital of Europe, hosting arts, culture, and nature events throughout the year.

2000 Helsinki will be honored as the Cultural Capital of Europe, one of nine European cities to share the honor this year.

BOOKS AND VIDEOS

Books

A History of the Vikings (Oxford University Press, 1984) recounts the story of the aggressive warriors and explorers who during the Middle Ages influenced a large portion of the world, extending from Constantinople to America. Gwyn Jones's lively account makes learning the history enjoyable.

Excellent reading on Denmark includes: the works of Karen Blixen (Isak Dinesen) set in Denmark; *Pelle the Conqueror* (volumes I and II) by Martin Andersen Nexø (a novel about a young Swedish boy and his father who work on a stone farm in Bornholm under hateful Danish landowners); *Laterna Magica* by William Heinesen (a novel of the Faroe Islands by perhaps Denmark's greatest writer since Karen Blixen); and the satirical trilogy by Hans Scherfig—*Stolen Spring, The Missing Bureaucrat,* and *Idealists.* Wallace Stegner's novel *The Spectator Bird* follows a man's exploration of his Danish heritage. Peter Høeg's acclaimed novel, *Smilla's Sense of Snow,* is a compulsive page-turner that paints a dark and foreboding picture of Copenhagen and the waters around Greenland; the movie version debuted in 1997. Fjord Press (Box 16349, Seattle, WA 98116, ☎ 206/935–7376, FAX 206/938–1991) has one of the most comprehensive selections of Danish fiction in translation of any publisher in the United States.

The Icelandic Sagas, the Nordic countries' most valuable contribution to world literature, have been translated into many languages. They tell of the lives, characters, and exploits of Icelandic heroes during the 10th and 11th centuries in an intricate combination of fantasy and history. The best-known are *Grettir's Saga,* about the outlaw Grettir the Strong; *Laxdæla Saga,* a tragedy spanning four generations in which women play a prominent role; *Egil's Saga,* about the truculent Viking-poet Egill Skallagrímsson; and *Njál's Saga,* generally considered the greatest, about two heroes, one young and brave, the other old and wise. Told in simple language, with emphasis on dialogue, these epic poems are about love and hatred, family feuds and vengeance, loyalty and friendship, and tragic destiny.

In 1936 two young poets, W. H. Auden and Louis MacNeice, summering in Iceland, wrote a miscellany of poetry and prose that were later collected in Auden's *Letters from Iceland.* Full of insights on the country, its people, and its politics, they are an unorthodox and witty introduction to Iceland even 60 years later. Another modern work of at least peripheral interest to those traveling to Iceland is Jules Verne's classic science-fiction novel *Journey to the Center of the Earth,* in which the heroes begin their subterranean adventure with a descent into Iceland's majestic glacier Snæfellsjökull.

More than 50 different volumes on Iceland—including poetry, biographies, travel guides, and picture books in English—can be ordered from *Iceland Review* (Box 8576, IS–128 Reykjavík, Iceland, ☎ 511–5700). The review itself is a quarterly magazine with coverage of tourism and cultural events. It is well worth subscribing to *News from Iceland,* a monthly newspaper published by *Iceland Review,* before your trip.

One of the greatest influences on 20th-century drama is the Norwegian poet and dramatist Henrik Ibsen, best known for his works *A Doll's House* (1879) and *Hedda Gabler* (1890).

In the 20th century, three Norwegian novelists have won the Nobel Prize in Literature: Bjørnstjerne Bjørnson in 1903; Knut Hamsun in 1920 for his novel *Another Growth of the Soil* (Vintage), a story of elemental existence in rural Norway; and Sigrid Undset in 1928 for her masterpiece *Kristin Lavransdatter.* This trilogy, a landmark among historical novels, gives a rich insight into 14th-century Scandinavia.

Jostein Gaarder is one of Norway's modern-day novelists. His book *Sophie's World* (Berkley Publishing, 1997) explores the history of philosophy through a young Norwegian's eyes.

Living in Norway (Abbeville Press, 1993) is a glossy depiction of Norwegian interior design.

One of the easiest and certainly most entertaining ways of finding out about modern Swedish society is to read the Martin Beck detective series of thrillers by Maj Sjöwall and Per Wahlöö, all of which have been translated into English. One of these, *The Terrorists,* was even prophetic, containing a scene in which a Swedish prime minister was shot, a precursor to the murder of Olof Palme in 1986.

Similarly, an entertaining insight into how life was in the bad old days when Sweden was one of the most backward agrarian countries in Europe may be obtained from Vilhelm Moberg's series of novels on poor Swedes who emigrated to America: *The Emigrants, Unto a Good Land,* and *The Last Letter Home.*

The plays of Swedish writer August Strindberg greatly influenced modern European and American drama. Perhaps the most enduringly fascinating of these, *Miss Julie,* mixes the explosive elements of sex and class to stunning effect.

One of the most exhaustive and comprehensive studies in English of the country published in recent years is *Sweden: The Nation's History,* by Franklin D. Scott (University of Minnesota Press). Chris

Mosey's *Cruel Awakening: Sweden and the Killing of Olof Palme* (C. Hurst, London 1991) seeks to provide an overview of the country and its recent history seen through the life and assassination of its best-known politician of recent times and the farcical hunt for his killer.

Films of Interest

Babette's Feast, which won the Oscar for the best foreign film of 1987, was produced in Denmark. Danny Kaye starred in the 1952 film *Hans Christian Andersen.* In fact, his crooning of "Wonderful Copenhagen" became Denmark's official tourism slogan. Disney's *The Little Mermaid* is a great way to get your kids interested in Andersen's fairy tales.

In 1995, Liv Ullmann directed the epic film *Kristin Lavransdatter,* an adaptation of Sigrid Undset's trilogy set in 14th-century Norway.

Of course, Sweden was home to Ingmar Bergman, who produced such classics as *The Virgin Spring* (1959), *Wild Strawberries* (1957), and *Fanny and Alexander* (1982). *The Unknown Soldier* (1955), a novel by Väinö Linna about the Winter War of 1939–40 between Finland and Russia, was adapted for the screen by Edwin Laine, and has become something of a classic.

DANISH VOCABULARY

English	Danish	Pronunciation

Basics

English	Danish	Pronunciation
Yes/no	Ja/nej	yah/nie
Thank you	Tak	tak
You're welcome	Selv tak	**sell** tak
Excuse me (to apologize)	Undskyld	**unsk**-ul
Hello	Hej	hi
Goodbye	Farvel	fa-**vel**
Today	I dag	ee **day**
Tomorrow	I morgen	ee **morn**
Yesterday	I går	ee **gore**
Morning	Morgen	**more**-n
Afternoon	Eftermiddag	**ef-tah**-mid-day
Night	Nat	nat

Numbers

1	een/eet	een/eet
2	to	toe
3	tre	treh
4	fire	fear
5	fem	fem
6	seks	sex
7	syv	syoo
8	otte	**oh**-te
9	ni	nee
10	ti	tee

Days of the Week

Monday	mandag	man-day
Tuesday	tirsdag	**tears**-day
Wednesday	onsdag	**ons**-day
Thursday	torsdag	**trs**-day
Friday	fredag	**free**-day
Saturday	lørdag	**lore**-day
Sunday	søndag	**soo**(n)-day

Useful Phrases

Do you speak English?	Taler du engelsk?	te-ler doo in-galsk
I don't speak Danish.	Jeg taler ikke Dansk.	yi tal-ler **ick** Dansk
I don't understand.	Jeg forstår ikke.	yi fahr-store **ick**
I don't know.	Det ved jeg ikke.	deh **ved** yi ick
I am American/British.	Jeg er amerikansk/britisk.	yi ehr a-mehr-i-**kansk**/bri-**tisk**
I am sick.	Jeg er syg.	yi ehr **syoo**

Please call a doctor.	Kan du ringe til en læge?	can **doo** rin-geh til en lay-eh
Do you have a vacant room?	Har du et værelse?	har **doo** eet va(l)r-sa
How much does it cost?	Hvad koster det?	va cos-ta **deh**
It's too expensive.	Det er for dyrt.	deh ehr **fohr** dyrt
Beautiful	Smukt	smukt
Help!	Hjælp	yelp
Stop!	Stop	stop
How do I get to . . .	Hvordan kommer jeg til . . .	vore-**dan** kom-mer yi til
. . . the train station?	banegarden	**ban** eh-gore-en
. . . the post office?	postkontoret	**post**-kon-toh-raht
. . . the tourist office?	turistkonoret	too-**reest**-kon-tor-et
. . . the hospital?	hospitalet	hos-peet-**tal**-et
Does this bus go to . . . ?	Går denne bus til . . . ?	**goh** den-na boos til
Where is the W.C.?	Hvor er toilettet?	vor **ehr** toi-le(tt)-et
On the left	Til venstre	til **ven**-strah
On the right	Till højre	til **hoy**-ah
Straight ahead	Lige ud	**lee** u(l)

Dining Out

Please bring me . . .	Må jeg få . . .	mo yi foh
menu	menu	me-**nu**
fork	gaffel	gaf-**fel**
knife	kniv	kan-**ew**
spoon	ske	skcc
napkin	serviet	serv-**eet**
bread	brød	brood
butter	smør	smoor
milk	mælk	malk
pepper	peber	**pee**-wer
salt	salt	selt
sugar	sukker	**su**-kar
water/bottled water	vand/Dansk vand	van/dansk van
The check, please.	Må jeg bede om regningen.	mo yi bi(d) om **ri**-ning

FINNISH VOCABULARY

English	Finnish	Pronunciation

Basics

Yes/no	Kyllä/ei	kue-la/ee
Please	Olkaa hyvä	**ol**-kah **hue**-va
Thank you very much.	Kiitoksia paljon	**kee**-tohk-syah **pahl**-yon

You're welcome.	Olkaa hyvä	**ol**-kah **hue**-va
Excuse me. (to get by someone)	Anteeksi suokaa	**ahn**-teek-see **soo**-oh-kah
(to apologize)	Anteeksi	**ahn**-teek-see
Hello	Hyvää päivää terve	**hue**-va **paee**-va **tehr**-veh
Goodbye	Näkemiin	**na**-keh-meen
Today	Tänään	**ta**-naan
Tomorrow	Huomenna	**hoo**-oh-men-nah
Yesterday	Eilen	**ee**-len
Morning	Aamu	**ah**-moo
Afternoon	Iltapäivä	**eel**-tah-**pay**-va
Night	Yö	**eu**-euh

Numbers

1	yksi	uek-see
2	kaksi	**kahk**-see
3	kolme	**kohl**-meh
4	neljä	**nel**-ya
5	viisi	**vee**-see
6	kuusi	**koo**-see
7	seitsemän	**sate**-seh-man
8	kahdeksan	**kah**-dek-sahn
9	yhdeksän	**uef**-dek-san
10	kymmenen	**kue**-meh-nen

Days of the Week

Monday	maanantai	mah-nahn-tie
Tuesday	tiistai	**tees**-tie
Wednesday	keskiviikko	**kes**-kee-veek-koh
Thursday	torstai	**tohrs**-tie
Friday	perjantai	**pehr**-yahn-tie
Saturday	lauantai	**loo**-ahn-tie
Sunday	sunnuntai	**soon**-noon-tie

Useful Phrases

Do you speak English?	Puhutteko englantia?	poo-hoot-teh-koh ehng-lahn-tee-ah
I don't speak . . .	En puhu suomea . . .	ehn **poo**-hoo **soo**-oh-mee-ah
I don't understand.	En ymmärrä.	ehn **eum**-mar-ra
I don't know.	En tiedä.	ehn **tee**-eh-da
I am American/ British.	Minä olen amerikkalainen/ englantilainen.	**mee**-na **oh**-len **ah**-mehr-ee-kah-lie-nehn/**ehn**-glahn-tee-lie-nehn
I am sick.	Olen sairas.	**oh**-len **sigh**-rahs
Please call a doctor.	Haluan kutsua lääkärin.	**hah**-loo-ahn **koot**-soo-ah **lay**-ka-reen
Do you have a vacant room?	Onko teillä vapaata huonetta?	**ohn**-koh **teel**-la **vah**-pah-tah **hoo**-oh-neht-tah?

How much does it cost?	Paljonko tämä maksaa?	**pahl**-yohn-koh **ta**-ma **mahk**-sah
It's too expensive.	Se on liian kallis.	**say** ohn **lee**-ahn **kah**-lees
Beautiful	Kaunis	**kow**-nees
Help!	Auttakaa!	**ow**-tah-kah
Stop!	Seis!/ Pysähtykää!	say(s) **peu**-sa-teu-kay
How do I get to . . .	Voitteko sanoa miten pääsen . . .	**voy**-tay-koh **sah**-noh-ah **mee**-ten **pay**-sen
. . . the train station	asema (. . . pääsen asemalle?)	**ah**-say-mah (**pay**-sen **ah**-say-mah-lay)
. . . the post office?	posti (. . . pääsen postiin?)	**pohs**-tee (**pay**-sen **pohs**-teen)
. . . the tourist office?	matkatoimisto (. . . pääsen matkatoimistoon?)	**maht**-kah-**toy**-mees-toh (**pay**-sen **maht**-kah-**toy**-mees-tohn)
. . . the hospital?	sairaala (. . . pääsen sairaalaan?)	**sigh**-rah-lah (**pay**-sen **sigh**-rah-lahn)
Does this bus go to . . . ?	Kulkeeko tämä bussi n . . . ?	**kool**-kay-koh **ta**-ma **boo**-see-n?
Where is the W.C.?	Missä on W.C.?	**mee**-sa ohn **ves**-sah
On the left	Vasemmalle	**vah**-say-mahl-lay
On the right	Oikealle	**ohy**-kay-ah-lay
Straight ahead	Suoraan eteenpäin	**swoh**-rahn **eh**-tayn-pa-een

Dining Out

Please bring me . . .	Tuokaa minulle . . .	too-oh-kah mee-new
menu	ruokalista	**roo**-oh-kah-lees-tah
fork	haarukka	**hahr**-oo-kah
knife	veitsi	**vayt**-see
spoon	lusikka	**loo**-see-kah
napkin	lautasliina	**low**-tahs-lee-nah
bread	leipä	**lay**-pa
butter	voi	**voh**(ee)
milk	maito	**my**-toh
pepper	pippuri	**pee**-poor-ee
salt	suola	**soo**-oh-lah
sugar	sokeri	**soh**-ker-ee
water/bottled water	vesi/ kivennaisvesi	**veh**-see/**kee**-ven-eyes-veh-see
The check, please.	Lasku, olkaa hyvä/Saanko maksaa	**lahs**-kew, **ohl**-kah **heu**-va/**sahn**-koh **mahk**-sah

ICELANDIC VOCABULARY

English	Icelandic	Pronunciation

Basics

English	Icelandic	Pronunciation
Yes/no	Já/nei	yow/nay
Thank you very much.	Kærar Þakkir takk	**kie**-rahr **thah**-kihr **ta**hkk
You're welcome.	Ekkert að-Þakka	**ehk**-kehrt ath **thah**-ka
Excuse me. (to get by someone)	Afsakið	**ahf**-sah-kith(e)
(to apologize)	Fyrirgefið	**feer**-ee-geh-vith(e)
Hello	Góðan dag	goh-than **dahgh**
Goodbye	Bless	bless
Today	Í dag	ee **dahgh**
Tomorrow	Á morgun	ow **mohr**-gun
Yesterday	Í gær	ee **gah-eer**
Morning	Morgun	**mohr**-gun
Afternoon	Eftirmidagur	**ehf**-teer-mihth-dahg-ur
Night	Nótt	noht

Numbers

1	einn	ehnn
2	tveir	**tveh**-eer
3	Þrír	threer
4	fjórir	**fyohr**-eer
5	fimm	fehm
6	sex	sex
7	sjö	sy-uh
8	átta	**owt**-tah
9	níu	**nee**-uh
10	tíu	**tee**-uh

Days of the Week

Monday	mánudagur	mown-ah-dah-gur
Tuesday	Þriðjudagur	**thrithe**-yoo-dah-gur
Wednesday	miðvikudagur	**meethe**-veek-uh dah-gur
Thursday	fimmtudagur	**feem**-too-dah-gur
Friday	föstudagur	**fuhs**-too-dah-gur
Saturday	laugardagur	**loy**-gahr-dah-gur
Sunday	sunnudagur	**soon**-noo-dah-gur

Useful Phrases

Do you speak English?	Talar Þú ensku?	tah-lahr thoo ehn-skoo
I don't speak Icelandic.	Ég tala ekki islensku.	**yeh** tah-lah **ehk**-keh **ees**-lehn-skoo
I don't understand.	Ég skil ekki.	yeh **skeel ehk**-keh
I don't know.	Ég veit ekki.	yeh **vayt ehk**-keh

I am American/ British.	Ég er ameriskur/ breskur.	yeh ehr **ah**-mehr eeskur/brehs-koor
I am sick.	Ég er veik(ur).	yeh ehr vehk(oor)
Please call a doctor.	Viltu hringja í lækni, takk.	veel-too **hreeng**-yah ee **lahk**-nee **tah**-kk
Do you have a vacant room?	Átt pú laust herbergi?	owt thoo laysht **hehr**-behr-ghee
How much does it cost?	Hvað kostar Það?	kvathe kohs-tahr thathe
It's too expensive.	Það er of dýrt.	thathe ehr ohf deert
Beautiful	Fallegur/t	**fahl**-lehg-oor
Help!	Hjálp!	hyalp
Stop!	Stopp!	stohp
How do I get to . . .	Hvernig kemst ég . . .	**kvehr**-neeg kehmst **yehg**
. . . the post office?	á pósthúsið	ow pohst-hoos-ihthe
. . . the tourist office?	á feramálará	ow **fehr**-tha-mow-lahr-owthe
. . . the hospital?	á spitalan	ow **spee**-tah-lahn
Does this bus go to . . . ?	Fer Þessi vagn . . . ?	fehr **thehs**-see **vakn**
Where is the W.C.?	Hvar er salerni?	kvahr ehr sahl-ehr-nihthe
On the left	Til vinstri	teel **veen**-stree
On the right	Til hægri	teel **hie**-ree
Straight ahead	Beint áfram	baynt **ow**-frahm

Dining Out

Please bring me . . .	Get ég fengið . . .	geht yehg fehn gihthe
menu	matseðil	**maht**-seh-theel
fork	gaffal	**gah**-fahl(t)
knife	hnif	hneef
spoon	skeið	skaythe
napkin	servetta	sehr-**veht**-tah
bread	brauð	braythe
butter	smjor	smyoor
milk	mjólk	myoolk
pepper	pipar	**pay**-pahr
salt	salt	sahlt
sugar	sykur	**say**-koor
water/bottled water	vatn/bergvatn	vahtn/**behrg**-vahtn
The check, please.	takk reikninginn	takk **rehk**-nihn-ghihn

NORWEGIAN VOCABULARY

English	Norwegian	Pronunciation

Basics

English	Norwegian	Pronunciation
Yes/no	Ja/nei	yah/nay
Please	Vær så snill	**vehr** soh snihl
Thank you very much.	Tusen takk.	**tews**-sehn tahk
You're welcome.	Vær så god.	**vehr** soh goo
Excuse me.	Unnskyld.	**ewn**-shewl
Hello	God dag	goo **dahg**
Goodbye	Ha det	**ha** day
Today	I dag	ee **dahg**
Tomorrow	I morgen	ee **moh**-ern
Yesterday	I går	ee **gohr**
Morning	Morgen	**moh**-ern
Afternoon	Ettermiddag	**eh-terr**-mid-dahg
Night	Natt	naht

Numbers

1	en	ehn
2	to	too
3	tre	treh
4	fire	**feer**-eh
5	fem	fehm
6	seks	sehks
7	syv, sju	shew
8	åtte	**oh**-teh
9	ni	nee
10	ti	tee

Days of the Week

Monday	mandag	mahn-dahg
Tuesday	tirsdag	**teesh**-dahg
Wednesday	onsdag	**oonss**-dahg
Thursday	torsdag	**tohsh**-dahg
Friday	fredag	**fray**-dahg
Saturday	lørdag	**loor**-dahg
Sunday	søndag	**suhn**-dahg

Useful Phrases

Do you speak English?	Snakker De engelsk?	snahk-kerr dee ehng-ehlsk
I don't speak Norwegian.	Jeg snakker ikke norsk.	yay **snahk**-kerr **ik**-keh nohrshk
I don't understand.	Jeg forstår ikke.	yay fosh-**tawr** **ik**-keh
I don't know.	Jeg vet ikke.	yay veht **ik**-keh
I am American/British.	Jeg er amerikansk/engelsk.	yay ehr ah-mehr-ee-kahnsk/ehng-ehlsk
I am sick.	Jeg er dårlig.	yay ehr **dohr**-lee

Please call a doctor.	Vær så snill og ring etter en lege.	vehr soh snihl oh ring **eht**-ehr ehn **lay**-geh
Do you have vacant room?	Har du et rom som er ledig?	yay vil **yehr**-neh hah eht room
How much does it cost?	Hva koster det?	vah **koss**-terr deh
It's too expensive.	Det er for dyrt.	deh ehr for **deert**
Beautiful	Vakker	**vah**-kehr
Help!	Hjelp!	yehlp
Stop!	Stopp!	stop
How do I get to . . .	Hvor er , , ,	voor ehr
. . . the train station?	jernbanestasjonen	yehrn-bahn-eh sta-**shoon**-ern
. . . the post office?	posthuset	**pohsst**-hewss
. . . the tourist office?	turistkontoret	tew-**reest**-koon-toor-er
. . . the hospital?	sykehuset	**see**-keh-hoo-seh
Does this bus go to . . . ?	Går denne bussen til . . . ?	gohr **den**-nah boos teel
Where is the W.C.?	Hvor er toalettene?	voor ehr too-ah-**leht**-te-ne
On the left	Til venstre	teel **vehn**-streh
On the right	Til høyre	teel **hooy**-reh
Straight ahead	Rett fram	reht **frahm**

Dining Out

menu	meny	meh-new
fork	gaffel	gahff-erl
knife	kniv	kneev
spoon	skje	shay
napkin	serviett	ssehr-vyeht
bread	brød	brur
butter	smør	smurr
milk	melk	mehlk
pepper	pepper	pehp-per
salt	salt	sahlt
sugar	sukker	sook-kerr
water/bottled water	vann	vahn
The check, please.	Jeg vil gjerne betale.	yay vil **yehr**-neh beh-**tah**-lch

SWEDISH VOCABULARY

English	Swedish	Pronunciation

Basics

Yes/no	Ja/nej	yah/nay
Please	Var snäll; Var vänlig	vahr snehll vahr vehn-leeg

Thank you very much.	Tack så **mee**-keh	tahk soh mycket.
You're welcome.	Var så god.	vahr shoh **goo**
Excuse me. (to get by someone)	Ursäkta.	oor-**shehk**-tah
(to apologize)	Förlåt.	fur-**loht**
Hello	God dag	goo **dahg**
Goodbye	Adjö	ah-**yoo**
Today	I dag	ee **dahg**
Tomorrow	I morgon	ee **mor**-ron
Yesterday	I går	ee **gohr**
Morning	Morgon	**mohr**-on
Afternoon	Eftermiddag	**ehf**-ter-meed-dahg
Night	Natt	naht

Numbers

1	ett	eht
2	två	tvoh
3	tre	tree
4	fyra	fee-rah
5	fem	fem
6	sex	sex
7	sju	shoo
8	åtta	oht-tah
9	nio	nee
10	tio	tee

Days of the Week

Monday	måndag	mohn-dahg
Tuesday	tisdag	tees-dahg
Wednesday	onsdag	ohns-dahg
Thursday	torsdag	tohrs-dahg
Friday	fredag	freh-dahg
Saturday	lördag	luhr-dahg
Sunday	söndag	sohn-dahg

Useful Phrases

Do you speak English?	Talar ni engelska?	tah-lahr nee ehng-ehl-skah
I don't speak Swedish.	Jag talar inte svenska.	yah tah-lahr **een**-teh **sven**-skah
I don't understand.	Jag förstår inte.	yah fuhr-**stohr** **een**-teh
I don't know.	Jag vet inte.	yah **veht een**-teh
I am American/ British.	Jag är amerikan/ engelsman.	yah ay ah-mehr-ee-**kahn**/ **ehng**-ehls-mahn
I am sick.	Jag är sjuk.	yah ay **shyook**
Please call a doctor.	Jag vill skicka efter en läkare.	yah veel **shee**-kah **ehf**-tehr ehn **lay**-kah-reh

Do you have a vacant room?	Har Ni något rum ledigt?	hahr nee noh-goht **room leh**-deekt
How much does it cost?	Vad kostar det?/ Hur mycket kostar det?	vah **kohs**-tahr deh/hor **mee**-keh **kohs**-tahr deh
It's too expensive.	Den är för dyr.	dehn ay foor **deer**
Beautiful	Vacker	**vah**-kehr
Help!	Hjälp	yehlp
Stop!	Stopp!/Stanna!	stop, **stahn**-nah
How do I get to . . .	Kan Ni visa mig vägen till . . .	kahn nee **vee**-sah may **vay**-gehn teel
. . . the train station?	stationen	stah-**shoh**-nehn
. . . the post office?	posten	**pohs**-tehn
. . . the tourist office?	en resebyrå	ehn-**reh**-seh-**bee**-roh
. . . the hospital?	sjukhuset	**shyook**-hoo-seht
Does this bus go to . . . ?	Går den här bussen till . . . ?	gohr dehn hehr **boo**-sehn teel
Where is the W.C.?	Var är toalett?/ toaletten?	vahr ay twah-**leht** twah-**leht**-en
On the left	Till vänster	teel **vehn**-stur
On the right	Till höger	teel **huh**-gur
Straight ahead	Rakt fram	rahkt **frahm**

Dining Out

Please bring me . . .	Var snäll och hämta åt mig . . .	vahr snehl oh hehm-tah oht may
menu	matsedeln	maht-seh-dehln
fork	en gaffel	ehn gahf-fehl
knife	en kniv	ehn kneev
spoon	en sked	ehn shehd
napkin	en servett	ehn sehr-veht
bread	bröd	bruh(d)
butter	smör	smuhr
milk	mjölk	myoolk
pepper	peppar	pehp-pahr
salt	salt	sahlt
sugar	socker	soh-kehr
water	vatten	vaht-n
The check, please.	Får jag be om notan.	fohr yah beh ohm **noh**-tahn

INDEX

Fodor's Travel Publications

Available at bookstores everywhere, or call 1–800–533–6478, 24 hours a day.

Gold Guides
U.S.

Alaska

Arizona

Boston

California

Cape Cod, Martha's Vineyard, Nantucket

The Carolinas & Georgia

Chicago

Colorado

Florida

Hawai'i

Las Vegas, Reno, Tahoe

Los Angeles

Maine, Vermont, New Hampshire

Maui & Lāna'i

Miami & the Keys

New England

New Orleans

New York City

Pacific North Coast

Philadelphia & the Pennsylvania Dutch Country

The Rockies

San Diego

San Francisco

Santa Fe, Taos, Albuquerque

Seattle & Vancouver

The South

U.S. & British Virgin Islands

USA

Virginia & Maryland

Walt Disney World, Universal Studios and Orlando

Washington, D.C.

Foreign

Australia

Austria

The Bahamas

Belize & Guatemala

Bermuda

Canada

Cancún, Cozumel, Yucatán Peninsula

Caribbean

China

Costa Rica

Cuba

The Czech Republic & Slovakia

Eastern & Central Europe

Europe

Florence, Tuscany & Umbria

France

Germany

Great Britain

Greece

Hong Kong

India

Ireland

Israel

Italy

Japan

London

Madrid & Barcelona

Mexico

Montréal & Québec City

Moscow, St. Petersburg, Kiev

The Netherlands, Belgium & Luxembourg

New Zealand

Norway

Nova Scotia, New Brunswick, Prince Edward Island

Paris

Portugal

Provence & the Riviera

Scandinavia

Scotland

Singapore

South Africa

South America

Southeast Asia

Spain

Sweden

Switzerland

Thailand

Toronto

Turkey

Vienna & the Danube Valley

Special-Interest Guides

Adventures to Imagine

Alaska Ports of Call

Ballpark Vacations

Caribbean Ports of Call

The Complete Guide to America's National Parks

Disney Like a Pro

Europe Ports of Call

Family Adventures

Fodor's Gay Guide to the USA

Fodor's How to Pack

Great American Learning Vacations

Great American Sports & Adventure Vacations

Great American Vacations

Great American Vacations for Travelers with Disabilities

Halliday's New Orleans Food Explorer

Healthy Escapes

Kodak Guide to Shooting Great Travel Pictures

National Parks and Seashores of the East

National Parks of the West

Nights to Imagine

Rock & Roll Traveler Great Britain and Ireland

Rock & Roll Traveler USA

Sunday in San Francisco

Walt Disney World for Adults

Weekends in New York

Wendy Perrin's Secrets Every Smart Traveler Should Know

Worldwide Cruises and Ports of Call

WHEREVER YOU TRAVEL, *H*ELP IS NEVER FAR AWAY.

From planning your trip to providing travel assistance along the way, American Express® Travel Service Offices are always there to help you do more.

Scandinavia

American Express TFS/Bureau De Change
Amagertorv 18
Copenhagen, Denmark
45/33/12 23 01

Area Travel Agency Ltd (R)
Paivarinnankatu 1
Helsinki, Finland
358/9/818 383

Area Travel Agency Ltd (R)
Mikonkatu 2
Helsinki, Finland
358/9/818 3500

American Express Foreign Exchange
Karl Johansgatan 33
509 Sentrum
Oslo, Norway
47/22/98 37 20

American Express TFS/Bureau De Change
Fridtjof Nansens Pl 6
509 Sentrum
Oslo, Norway
47/22/98 37 30

American Express Travel Service
Birger Jarlsgatan 1
Stockholm, Sweden
46/8/679 52 00

do more AMERICAN EXPRESS
Travel

http://www.americanexpress.com/travel

**American Express Travel Service Offices are
located throughout Scandinavia.**

173.   Article, "The Problem of Evil," New York, *Publications of the Trinity Educational Corporation*, Spring 1991, 6 lectures (p. 100).

174.   Audio Tapes (5) Lectures, "The Person and Ministry of Jesus Christ," Hitchcock Presbyterian Church, Scarsdale, New York, Spring 1991.

175.   Article, "The Theology of the Burial Office," *The Institute of Theology Publications*, Spring 1991, p. 6ff.

176.   Review of Margaret P. Battin, *Ethics in the Sanctuary: Examining the Practices of Organized Religion, Crosscurrents (Religion and Intellectual Life)*, Winter 1991–1992, pp. 560–564.

177.   Review of William F. May, *The Patient's Ordeal, Second Opinion: Health, Faith, Ethics*, volume 17, No. 3, January 1993, pp. 140–153.

178.   Article, "Major Figures of the Christian Faith," *The Institute of Theology Publications*, New York, February 1993, p. 60ff.

179.   Review of Anita B. Feferman, *Politics, Logic and Love: The Life of Jean van Heijenort, Brandeis Watch*, March 1993 no. 6, pp. 21–22.

180.   Article, "What Ever Happened to Christian Service," *The Christian Century*, March 1993, pp. 20–24.

181.   Article on Henry Mary Warnock, *Encyclopedia of World Biography* (1994 Edition), pp. 374–378.

182.   "The Meaning of Christmas," *Nordstjernan*, December 15, 1994.

183.   Article on Sissela Bok, *Encyclopedia of World Biography* (1995 Edition), pp. 86–90.

184.   Various reviews in *The Bibliography of Philosophy, The Anglican Theological Review, Review of Metaphysics, The Institute of Theology Newsletter*, 1995–2000.

185.   "Major Figures of the Christian Faith," series of 10 lec-
            tures, *Publications of the Trinity Educational Corporation*
            (1997).

186.   Review of "Brava,Wendy Donigen," *The New York
            Times Book Review*, February 9, 1998, pp. 6-7.

187.   *Great Thinkers Seminar*, 10 lectures each year, 1990-
            2004, Lotos Club, various videos.

188.   *Great Ideas in Great Books*, 8 lectures each year, 1998-
            2004, Century Association, various videos.

189.   Videos of lectures:
            The Death of Socrates, 2003
            Dante's World, 2003
            The Message of the Koran, 2004
            God and the Big Bang, 2004
            The Lotos Club

190.   Review of Johanna Fiedler, *Motto Agitato:The Mayhem
            behind the Music at the Metropolitan Opera, The Lotos
            Newsletter*, March 2004.